A PRACTICAL GUIDE TO SOFTWARE LICENSING for Licensees and Licensors

4th Edition

H. WARD CLASSEN

MODEL FORMS AND ANNOTATIONS INCLUDED IN PRINT AND ON CD-ROM

ABA Business Law Section
AMERICAN BAR ASSOCIATION

Cover design by ABA Publishing.

Page layout by Quadrum Solutions.

Printed in the United States of America.

15 14 13 12 5 4 3

Library of Congress Cataloging-in-Publication Data

Classen, H. Ward.
A practical guide to software licensing for licensees and licensors / by H. Ward Classen. — 4th ed.
p. cm.
Rev. ed of: A practical guide to software licensing for licensees and licensors / H. Ward Classen. 3rd ed. c2008.
Includes bibliographical references.
ISBN 978-1-61632-813-9
1. Copyright—Computer programs—United States. 2. Computer software—Law and legislation—United States. 3. Copyright licenses—United States. 4. License agreements—United States. I. Title.
KF3024.C6C56 2011
346.7304'82—dc22

2011004392

Contents

Acknowledgments

A Practical Guide to Software Licensing for Licensees and Licensors is essentially a summary of my practical licensing experiences over the past 25 years. As such, it is difficult to write an acknowledgment when so many people have had a meaningful impact on my career.

Dean Harvey made sure that Chapter 3 correctly reflected the many facets of intellectual property involved in software licensing. Dennis Gallitano taught me quite a bit about negotiations and provided invaluable guidance, especially as to the RFP process described in Chapter 2 and the scope of "use" in international transactions discussed in Chapter 12. Connie Mitchell's thoughts on the issues associated with hosting in Chapter 7 ensured a well-balanced discussion. Hank Jones and Bart Showalter provided invaluable insights to the discussion of open source software in Chapter 8, making sure it was complete and accurate. Amy de La Lama and Brian Hengesbaugh's thoughtful comments on Chapter 10 significantly improved the discussion of data privacy. Michael Moser and Nate Bush provided a wonderful overview of the Foreign Corrupt Practices Act in Chapter 12 while Ranji Srivastava and Abanish Singh provided practical insights on the application of Indian intellectual property law to software licensing. James Sullivan was instrumental in ensuring Chapter 17 accurately reflected the many nuances of bankruptcy law as applied to software licensing. Marie Fogarty's insightful comments made this book much more readable.

Tina Ayiotis, Catie Butt, Cheryl Lardieri, Dan DiGregorio, Bob Feldman, David Gray, Lindsay Naiman and Brett Pynnonen, among others, each took time from their busy schedules to review and comment on prior drafts. Ken Sharp's business insights were invaluable to my efforts to make this book truly a practical guide. Without the encouragement of Eric Goldman of the Business Law Section's Publications Board this book would not have been possible.

Finally, the unending support of Sibley, Keena, and Pierce made a difficult and seemingly endless task very manageable.

September 21, 2010
Ruxton, Maryland

CHAPTER **1**

Introduction

This book examines some of the fundamental issues that both licensors and licensees may confront in the negotiation of a software license and, where appropriate, relevant ancillary issues such as software development, professional services and maintenance and support. It focuses primarily on non-mass-market agreements, as most "retail" or mass-market "off-the-shelf" software is governed by nonnegotiable "shrink-wrap," "browse-wrap" and "click-wrap" licenses. Nonetheless, the principles of software licensing are the same for shrink-wrap, browse-wrap, click-wrap, and custom-developed software. For a brief overview of a few of the significant issues involved in software licensing, see Nimmer & Dodd, *Modern Licensing Law* (Thomson * West 2009); Davidson, *Avoiding Pitfalls and Allocating Risk in Major Software Development and Acquisition Contracts,* 14 COMPUTER LAW. 12 (May 1997); and Boudreau, *An Introduction to Software Licensing,* 20 ACCA DOCKET 54 (No. 9 2002), as well as those resources listed in Chapter 23.

This book does not discuss software transactions with the government, as the laws relating to government contracting are beyond the scope of this treatise. For an overview of intellectual property rights related to government contracting, see Bergman & Aina, *Intellectual Property Rights in Government Contracting,* 156 INTELL. PROP. COUNS. 1 (Dec. 2009).

The structure and context of every software license differs depending on the needs of the parties. While this book discusses some of the most important issues and includes numerous forms, D.C. Toedt III, Esq., in conjunction with the Computer Programs Committee of the Information Division of the Section of Intellectual-Property Law of the American Bar Association, created a model license that—although voluminous—is quite thorough and educational. Toedt's license was created to be a resource but is not a commercially viable form due to its complexity and length. It is included as Form 23.B.6 on the enclosed CD-ROM. For a detailed discussion of this license, see Toedt, *The Model Software License Provisions: Precursor to a Gap-Filling Uniform License Statute,* 18 RUTGERS COMPUTER & TECH. L.J. 521 (1992).

Finally, the nature of software licensing is trending toward vendor hosted delivery models and cloud computing. Vendor hosted applications are commonly referred as Application Service Providers (ASPs). The fundamentals of software licensing transcend alternative delivery models and thus, Chapter 7 discusses several of the most common delivery methods and the principle issues associated with each.

CHAPTER **2**

The Negotiation Process

A. The Traditional Negotiation Process

Traditionally, a customer evaluates various vendor products and narrows the field to one vendor. The customer proceeds to negotiate on an exclusive basis with the selected vendor until an agreement is reached. If an impasse arises, the customer has little recourse but to either accede to the vendor's demands or terminate the negotiations and select a new vendor, which requires a significant amount of duplicative time, effort, and cost.

In this process, a vendor is focused on eliminating its competition to gain significant leverage in the negotiation process. When the customer seeks particular commitments or guarantees, the vendor typically is free to accept or reject the customer's demands without the fear of losing the business. Single vendor negotiations also provide an incentive for the vendor to defer the more contentious issues to the end of the negotiations, a time when the customer is least likely to terminate the negotiations. Further, the vendor can use the threat of time to leverage its position—especially if the customer is under a tight time line to implement the software or system.

The basis for negotiation is usually the vendor's form contract, which naturally favors the vendor. The customer usually accepts the vendor's contract as a starting point because it does not want to expend the time, effort, or cost to create its own single-transaction contract. The vendor often insists on using the vendor's form contract arguing that its expertise in software makes it advantageous for both parties to use its contract in an effort to save time and obtain a comprehensive agreement. While there is nothing wrong with using the vendor's contract as a basis for negotiation, the customer should realize that it is slanted, whether overtly or discreetly, to the vendor's advantage, and further, the types of protections sought by savvy technology buyers are typically not found in the vendor's form.

Regardless of who creates the initial draft, a party should seek to control or at least share responsibilities for the agreement. Many lawyers fail to realize the importance of controlling the draft and the resulting ability to craft the agreement. By controlling the drafting process, a party can provide its interpretation of the agreement while using the language that best represents its interests. There are many ways of stating the same concept. This is especially important for licensees; often when the vendor controls the draft, the vendor's concessions fail to be included in the next draft, or the language is slanted to minimize the vendor's concession. If the vendor insists on controlling the draft, drafting the language of any concession at the negotiating table can minimize its drafting advantage.

See Forms 23.K.1 and 23.K.2 for examples of definitions and clauses that present the same concept but are drafted to benefit a particular party.

B. The Competitive Negotiation Process

1. Overview

Unlike a traditional negotiation discussed above, an increasing number of customers are undertaking a competitive bidding process for software purchases for large systems and negotiating their software licenses as part of the bidding process. While a competitive bidding process can assume different forms, its procurement and negotiation process is different than the traditional software vendor–customer negotiations process.

A competitive bidding process begins when the customer sends a request for information, a request for proposal (RFP), or other qualification document to interested vendors. A competitive bidding process often takes three to four months from initiation through the selection of the winning bidder.

2. Requests for Information ("RFI")

If a customer is unsure of the approach to take in addressing its technology needs, it should submit a Request for Information to interested vendors to solicit their ideas. RFIs usually describe the customer's existing IT infrastructure, the issues it is facing, and what it hopes to gain from the contemplated project. The RFI may include the customer's own ideas on how to address its technology needs.

The RFI should solicit the vendors' ideas and thoughts on how to address the issues, as well as comments on the customer's thought process and plans. Some customers will invite vendors to meet with them to further exchange ideas. This may include having the vendors suggest information and selection criteria to be included in the subsequent Request for Proposal. Utilizing an RFI approach, however, will most likely add four to six weeks to the selection process.

From the customer's perspective, the customer will want the ability to use any ideas exchanged among the parties, regardless of whether the vendor is ultimately selected for the project. From the vendor's perspective, the vendor wants to avoid having the customer use its ideas without retaining the vendor to perform the contemplated service. To protect itself, the vendor may want to either insist on executing a nondisclosure agreement with the customer or submit only very general concepts to the customer. See Form 23.A.7 § 2 for a nondisclosure agreement that expressly permits the customer to disclose/use the information submitted by the vendor in the vendor's RFI/RFP response.

See Form 23.A.1 for a model RFI. Form 23.A.2 is an alternate model RFI and is included on the enclosed CD-ROM.

3. *Requests for Proposal ("RFP")*

Once the customer has received the responses to its RFI and conducted any desired vendor meetings, it should utilize the information obtained from the RFI process to draft the RFP.

In most cases, the RFP sets forth the customer's requirements for the new software or services it intends to purchase. Although it often entails a large effort to capture the customer's technical and functional requirements, the RFP is critical to provide sufficient detail for the vendor to accurately price its response. Ambiguities and missing information increase a vendor's risk and may impact its pricing. Despite their best intentions, individuals who draft RFPs often omit a detailed focus on the buying process itself (i.e., how the customer intends to purchase the system). Important contractual terms such as testing criteria, payment terms, and warranties are usually not identified, or if they are identified, they are not tailored to the specifics of the proposed technology purchase.

The customer should ask direct questions related to the potential vendors' capabilities, which will allow the customer to make an informed decision. It should avoid asking non-critical questions or requesting tangential data solely for the purpose of obtaining all possible information.

In general, customers should request detailed information on the proposed solution/application including its ability to be scaled and to have functionality added. Is it highly/easily configurable? Can the application be provided as a service (ASP, SAAS, hosted)? Is the potential vendor developing new technology that will make the proposed solution obsolete in the near future? How large is the vendor's support organization? Where is it located? What are its hours of operation? What quality assurance standards does the vendor meet?

Historically, many customers have attached their proposed license and services agreement and asked potential vendors (i) to identify any provisions they consider objectionable, state why and provide alternative language, but stated (ii) that doing so will not be interpreted as prohibiting either party from proposing additional contract terms during the negotiation period. Many vendors are hesitant to commit to specific terms during early negotiations and often reply with a "non-response" to allow the vendor maximum flexibility in negotiating the contract, similar to the following:

> Vendor has reviewed the Master License and Services Agreement (MLA) attached to this RFP and believes that at such time as more business details are agreed upon, including with respect to the information to be contained in the various schedules, that the parties will be able to readily come to satisfactory closure on all of the terms contained in the MLA. Vendor reserves the right to comment in greater detail on the MLA terms at such time as is appropriate based on the availability of such details and any down selection of Vendor as may occur.

See Section 23.K.2.GG for more expansive language.

Further, many potential licensees seek to obtain competitive business intelligence on the potential vendor by asking the vendor to disclose previous litigation, representative customers, consistent skill sets, regulatory compliance and potential merger and acquisition activity. Many vendors will not respond with detailed answers and instead prefer to provide a general answer that can be expanded upon during negotiations. See Form 23.A.8 for model RFP questions and vendor responses.

Sophisticated customers purchasing large-scale systems identify in the RFP specific contractual requirements and how the customer intends to conduct the negotiation process. Increasingly, to avoid a "non-response" as discussed in the previous paragraph, customers are breaking their contracts down, paragraph by paragraph, in matrix form and requiring vendors to comment on each section. This approach, once seen only in outsourcing transactions, is becoming more prevalent in software licensing transactions. For instance, the customer would set forth contractual language for its proposed payment terms and require the bidders to state whether they will comply with such language. If the bidder does not accept the customer's language, they must state why they do not accept such language and supply alternative language or a counterproposal. The terms of the RFP prevent the vendor from later changing its position. Potential vendors' responses are submitted in a matrix so they can be easily compared and contrasted. This approach allows customers to evaluate each vendor's technical and functional capabilities, as well as their flexibility and willingness to contract on terms that are acceptable to the customer. See Form 23.A.4 on the enclosed CD-ROM for an example of an RFP Response Matrix.

The customer should carefully consider which vendors it invites to participate in the RFP process. It should include a wide variety of vendors, from its existing vendors to large industry leaders to small, cutting-edge companies. By soliciting a large cross-section of vendors, the customer will hopefully receive a variety of creative responses that in turn will allow it to create the best possible solution for its needs.

Prior to the deadline for submitting vendor responses, the customer should hold a telephonic bidder's conference to discuss any issues that have arisen after the RFP was issued and to allow the vendors to ask any questions they may have. All questions should be asked anonymously. The customer may also request that vendors make a presentation to the customer's project team. After evaluating the first round of responses and "down selecting" several potential vendors, the customer will occasionally solicit a second round of proposals. This may allow the customer to obtain a solution that is more closely tailored to the customer's needs at a more favorable price.

From the time the RFP is submitted to the time several vendors are down selected for negotiations, including bidders' conferences and scoring the vendors' proposals, the process will likely take six to eight weeks.

Many customers are hesitant to walk away from a deal after a long negotiation because they are uncertain they can obtain more advantageous terms with another vendor while potentially delaying an important project. If a customer, however, establishes a competitive negotiation process where there are two or more vendors competing for the business, the leverage shifts in favor of the customer.

By negotiating simultaneously with several vendors, the customer can maximize its leverage and play each vendor against the others. If one vendor makes a concession, the customer can directly or indirectly signal to the second vendor that it is not being competitive on the particular negotiation point, and that if the second vendor will not agree to the point, it will be viewed as a "negative" when the final bids are evaluated. By negotiating simultaneously, the customer has the advantage of negotiating the most favorable terms it can with each vendor and then selecting the best overall deal at the end of the negotiations. Knowing the terms agreed to by the other vendor creates an incentive for each vendor to be flexible in response to the customer's requested terms. Further, large system vendors have sales cycles of six months or longer, creating an incentive not to drop out of the bidding process.

For a very large project, the customer may retain a consultant or technology vendor to draft the RFP. In such situations, the vendor who drafts the RFP should be excluded from responding to the RFP to avoid a conflict of interest (i.e., the vendor could potentially draft the RFP in such a way that it is the only party to meet the selection criteria). If the consultant that is managing the bidding process is allowed to bid, its employees involved in selecting the successful bidder should certify that there was no actual conflict of interest. See Form 23.A.9 for a model certificate.

Many RFPs also include the customer's form license agreement, which the vendor is advised "must be accepted" as the document for licensing/servicing the software system. Including the customer's contract with the RFP and seeking the vendor's comments and any proposed additional terms will reduce the time needed to negotiate a contract after the successful vendor is selected. A prudent customer will negotiate a complete contract prior to selection of the successful vendor—as the customer will lose significant leverage once the successful vendor has been selected.

To ensure fairness in the negotiation process, each vendor should enter into a mutual nondisclosure agreement with the customer so that the customer cannot disclose a vendor's pricing and methodologies to other vendors. Otherwise, a vendor may simply become a means to drive the preferred vendor to the customer's desired terms and price.

Many customers will argue that there is no need to enter into a mutual nondisclosure agreement because only the customer, not the vendor, is disclosing confidential information. The customer usually offers that it will enter into a mutual nondisclosure agreement with the winning bidder once the vendor has been selected. This reasoning is flawed; the vendor's methodology and approach for addressing the issue and its pricing—both of which are proprietary—are the most important types of information to be supplied by the vendor and are the differentiating factors in an RFP process. See Form 23.A.5 for an example of a unilateral nondisclosure agreement used in an RFP process.

See Form 23.A.3 for an example of a model RFP.

In responding to an RFP, a vendor must be careful to accurately answer the questions presented and to clearly indicate those responses by which it does not intend to be bound. Many RFPs provide that if the vendor fails to take issue with a proposed contractual provision, the customer will consider the vendor to be bound by the provision. If the vendor later indicates that it cannot accept that provision, the customer will often eliminate the vendor from consideration. Occasionally, the customer will require the vendor to certify that it will enter into an agreement with the customer if it is selected and require each vendor to submit a performance bond to ensure that it will enter into a contract with the customer.

To avoid these issues, the vendor should include language in its RFP response reserving the right to negotiate the contractual terms in the underlying agreement, especially those that were not included in the customer's proposed agreement. This is especially important if the deliverables have not been definitively determined at the time of the RFP response. Model language the vendor may want to include in its RFP response is as follows:

> Vendor has set forth below its main concerns with the General Terms and Conditions (Section ___ of the RFP), including but not limited to the absence of terms that are standard in contracts for software licensing, such as a limitation of liability and disclaimer of implied warranties. Notwithstanding the exceptions set forth below, Vendor reserves the right to negotiate all contract terms and conditions in the context of the work that is actually awarded. Vendor will work with Customer to resolve successfully any outstanding matters.

4. Procedures and Rules for a Competitive Negotiation

To ensure an orderly and equitable process, the customer should establish clear procedures and rules on how the negotiation process will be conducted. This includes not only the selection criteria but also rules on how information will be disseminated and how prospective vendors may communicate with the customer team. To avoid undue influence and the dissemination of insider information to a preferred vendor, most RFPs require that all communications be in writing through a single point of customer contact. Any violation of this process should result in the vendor's disqualification.

Setting out the rules at the initiation of the process can significantly benefit the customer. More vendors are likely to participate if they believe the process is free of favoritism and undue influence. No vendor wants to expend a significant amount of time and money only to serve as a stalking horse for "pre-selected" vendors. Further, many vendors seek to circumvent the selection process by contacting the customer's friendly executives to have them lobby for the selection of that vendor. The threat of being eliminated from consideration should discourage this behavior, but employees not on the project team should be reminded not to discuss the project either inside or outside of the company. Finally, because the vendors are all receiving the same (limited) information from a single source (which should always offer encouragement), they are incented to remain in the bidding process and offer their best terms and pricing.

It is also important that the customer adhere to its own rules. Vendors can spend millions of dollars in responding to an RFP and engaging in negotiations with a customer. If a customer gains a reputation as an entity that does not treat vendors fairly, it may have difficulty getting the best qualified vendors to participate in future procurements.

See Form 23.A.6 on the enclosed CD-ROM for model procedures and rules for responding to an RFP.

5. *Inclusion of the RFI and RFP Response in the Final Agreement*

Both the vendor and the customer should be wary of incorporating the customer's RFP and the vendor's RFP response into the contract. Often the parties incorporate these documents in the final agreement in an ill-fated attempt to incorporate each party's understanding of the other party's obligations. The customer often wants to include the RFP to hold the vendor to the requirements set forth in the RFP and the standards the customer expects the vendor to meet. Further, the customer may want to include the vendor's RFP response to hold the vendor to any statements (including any sales puffery) set forth in the vendor's RFP response. The vendor often desires to incorporate its RFP response for its own protection, as it will often reject some of the RFP's requirements in its RFP response.

A problem arises, however, when the delivery requirements set forth in the RFP and RFP response differ from each other and from the specifications included in the negotiated contract. Further, disputes often arise in trying to resolve any differences between the RFP and the RFP response and what the parties agreed to. To avoid these potential issues, it is preferable to agree on and attach functional specifications negotiated after the successful bidder has been selected. The importance of accuracy, clarity, and completeness in the specifications cannot be overemphasized. The specifications are the vendor's contractual obligations to the customer. If they do not provide significant detail to hold the vendor to the intended obligations, then the entire negotiation process is undermined. The RFP and RFP response in turn should then be negated by the contract's "integration" or "entire agreement" clause. See Chapter 6.J. The vendor should also resist the customer's demands to represent and warrant that all statements made by the vendor during the RFI and RFP process are true and correct as of the date the parties entered into the license agreement. See Chapter 4.B.1.(a).(ii) for a more detailed discussion.

The courts are unlikely to hold a vendor liable for the typical statements made in the sales process including sales puffery or opinions of future performance. Sales puffery will be viewed in light of the facts of the matter to determine if it exceeds the bounds of fairness. *See I-Conn. Healthcare Solutions, LLC v. Advanced Internet Technologies, Inc.*, 689 S.E.2d 600 (N.C. App. 2010) (Claim of being "The World Leader in Dedicated and Shared Web Hosting" does not constitute fraud in the inducement as sophisticated, knowledgeable purchaser would not make purchasing decision solely based on such statement). To be actionable, such statements must relate to a past or present fact. *American Computer v. Jack Farrell Implet. Co.*, 763 F. Supp. 1473, 1487 (D. Minn. 1991); *Shema Kolainu — Hear Our Voices v. Providersoft, LLC*, 2010 WL 2075921 (E.D.NY. May 21, 2010) (licensor representations regarding software functionality supported claim of fraudulent inducement). Nonetheless, the vendor should make sure to include an integration clause and the customer should make sure to include all statements it has relied on in making its decision in the license agreement. See Chapter 6.N for a more detailed discussion of the importance of integration clauses.

At the conclusion of the RFP process, there is occasionally the temptation to substitute the RFP and RFP response to serve as the Statement of Work. This philosophy often leads to a poor result. The RFP and RFP response usually lack the required detail to deliver a quality product that meets the customer's needs. Further, the parties frequently fail to resolve any inconsistencies between the RFP and RFP response.

Often the customer's RFP will include language similar to the following:

> It is a firm requirement that Vendor's responses to this RFP shall be included either in their entirety or by reference in the final contract.

The vendor's response should be carefully crafted to avoid any commitment that may create ambiguity in the vendor's obligations, the deliverable, or make any commitment that may be superseded by any subsequent negotiations. A model vendor response is as follows:

> Vendor's response to the RFP is a general overview of the ______ System (the "System") and provides general answers to the questions asked. Items in this response to the RFP may be ambiguous and open to differing interpretations because a Requirements Study has not been performed to define Customer's needs. During the Requirements Study, Vendor and Customer will discuss Customer's needs and determine if modifications are needed to completely satisfy Customer's requirements. Although certain functionality may be designated in this response as included in the System, modifications may be required for the System to provide such functionality as required by Customer. Thus, this response is not a specific, technical, or legal document and, therefore, any inconsistencies, questions, uncertainties, or contradictions as to the System shall be controlled by the System's documentation. Further, it is Vendor's intention to be totally responsive to the Request for Proposal ("RFP"). This response is based on the information that you have provided to Vendor concerning your needs. Consequently, while we believe that our response is sound, it cannot constitute express or implied warranties, including, without limitation, the implied warranties of merchantability, fitness, and fitness for a particular purpose. Vendor has reviewed the RFP and it is Vendor's intention that any award resulting there from shall be based on the Software License Agreement and Master Services Agreement to be negotiated between the parties.

If the parties nevertheless decide to include the RFP and/or the RFP response, they should clearly set forth the order of precedence among the various provisions and exhibits of the agreement in the event of a conflict.

For a general overview of the procurement process including RFIs and RFPs, see Gallitano, *The Common Sense Guide to Negotiating Technology Transactions,* National Association of College and University Attorneys, Fall 2005 (November), CLE Workshop available at http://www.nacua.org. (Last viewed September 15, 2010.)

6. *Documenting the Negotiations/Letters of Intent*

As the negotiation process progresses, the parties should carefully document the agreed-upon positions. Some parties prefer to enter into a Letter of Intent (LOI) or Memorandum of Understanding (MOU) to document their positions prior to executing the definitive agreement. Others prefer to negotiate the definitive agreement and not bother with an LOI or MOU under the belief that they are a waste of time that could be applied to the negotiation of the definitive agreement. While either approach may be appropriate depending on the situation, most parties will negotiate only on a definitive agreement. For those parties that prefer to enter into an LOI or MOU, they should ensure that the LOI/MOU contains language similar to that provided below to ensure neither party is bound until all terms of the master/final agreement have been agreed upon. It is exactly because LOI/MOUs are non-binding that most parties do not feel the need to enter into such agreements.

To protect its interests, the licensor should insert language to the following effect.

THIS DOCUMENT IS NOT INTENDED TO BIND [LICENSOR] OR ANY OF ITS AFFILIATES

> There shall be no agreement between the parties relating to this document unless and until the parties have executed and delivered definitive agreement(s) containing the agreement of the parties. Nothing herein is intended to, or does, bind either party and is not intended to waive, nor does it waive, any rights, remedies and/or defenses of Licensor or any of its affiliates, whether legal and/or equitable, under any existing agreement, all of which are expressly reserved.

It cannot be emphasized enough that it be clear that there is no agreement until the definitive contract has been signed. A number of courts have found the existence of a contract in the absence of a signed writing. *See, e.g., Latiivafter Liquidating Trust v. Clear Channel Communications,* 345 Fed. Appx. 46 (6th Cir. 2009) (jury found existence of an "agreement" despite lack of signed document.)

If the successful bidder is going to commence work while the parties are negotiating the license agreement, the vendor may want to enter into an interim agreement to document its ownership of any intellectual property it creates prior to the execution of the agreement. This is important if the vendor wants to protect itself in the event the parties are unable to reach agreement on the definitive agreement and the customer later seeks to utilize the intellectual property the vendor developed. The parties should be careful to avoid acting in such a manner as to give rise to an oral agreement. To the extent the parties perform in accordance with an unsigned license agreement, a court may find the existence of a binding oral agreement. *See In re Golden Books Family Entertainment, Inc.*, 269 B.R. 300 (D. Del. 2001) (license drafts were "binding oral agreements . . . demonstrated by parties course of conduct.")

In *Turner Broadcasting System, Inc. v. McDavid,* 693 S.E.2d 873 (Ga. App. 2010), the parties entered into a letter of intent for the purchase and sale of two sports franchises that provided "neither party nor any of [their] affiliates [would] be bound ... unless and until such party (or affiliate) has executed the Definitive Agreements" and that "[n]o such binding agreement shall exist or arise unless and until the parties have negotiated, executed and delivered to each other Definitive Agreements." *Id.* at 879. The letter of intent expired and the parties continued to negotiate. McDavid brought suit after Turner later sold the franchises to a third party. The Georgia Court of Appeals found the existence of an oral contract concluding that the statement contained within the letter of intent that neither party would be bound until the execution of a definitive agreement expired with the letter of intent. *Id.* at 881. Thus, the parties' oral agreement was sufficient to bind both parties despite the contemplation of a subsequent written agreement.

7. Concerns for Lawyers

Lawyers representing the customer in a dual negotiation process must be careful to abide by the ABA Model Rules of Professional Conduct. Rule 4.1 (Truthfulness in Statements to Others) provides that a lawyer cannot knowingly "make a false statement of material fact or law to a third person." Formal opinion 06-432 (Apr. 12, 2006). A lawyer must be careful not to represent that another party has accepted a provision when in fact it has not done so. Rule 4.1 differentiates "puffery" from "lying" recognizing that puffery is part of any sales process but forbidding any outright misstatements of the truth.

8. Metadata

Metadata refers to the data contained within a document. Often Metadata is revealed or hidden through common commands such as "track data." It has been defined as "information which a computer generates to identify relevant facts about a saved file." Himmelrich, *Metadata: Data About Data*, 43 MD. B. J. 34, 35 (May/June 2010). In its most common form, metadata provides information as to the author of the document, when it was created, who reviewed and commented on the document and the subsequent revisions made to it.

A party can avoid inadvertently disclosing metadata by sending all files in a pdf format or accepting all changes in a document and resaving it prior to sending the document to another party.

There is a dichotomy among the states as to how to treat metadata. Alabama, Arizona, Florida and New York have adopted the position that a lawyer should not try to obtain information from metadata if he or she knows the sending party did not intend for the receiving party to review it. New York Bar Association Committee on Professional Ethics Opinion 749. The ABA and Maryland are in the minority having adopted a different position in that they do not prohibit a receiving party from accessing metadata. Maryland State Bar Association Committee on Ethics, Ethics Docket 2007-09; ABA Standing Committee on Ethics and Professional Responsibility, Formal Opinion 06-422. The District of Columbia prohibits mining metadata if the receiving lawyer has actual knowledge that the metadata was sent inadvertently. District of Columbia Bar Legal Ethics Committee Opinion 341. Pennsylvania leaves it to the individual lawyer to determine the appropriateness of mining metadata.

For a detailed discussion of metadata, see Coyle, *"Metadata" Mining Vexes Lawyers, Bars*, NAT'L. L. J., Feb. 18, 2008 at 1; Himmelrich, *Metadata: Data About Data*, 43 MD. B. J. 34 (May/June 2010).

C. Successful Procurement

Regardless of which approach a customer adopts, the customer should seek to incorporate a number of best practices in its procurement process.

To ensure a successful negotiation, the customer needs to have a clear understanding of its business goals. Key stakeholders in the organization should be consulted both to establish the goals and to obtain buy-in on the procurement. The "user" representative should be open-minded and not wedded to the customer's legacy system. These goals should drive the content of the RFP and the evaluation criteria. For example, if the purpose of the RFP is to acquire a new system to reduce costs, care should be taken not to include technical and functional "requirements" that greatly exceed current operations and that will require increased pricing on the part of the vendor.

It is also important that the customer and vendor assemble a well-rounded team to participate in the negotiations. In addition to an attorney and business sponsor, the team should include members of the information technology, finance, and procurement departments. In some instances, especially in large IT outsourcing transactions and large systems integration projects, it may be appropriate for the customer to retain an independent, third party consultant. Utilizing a comprehensive team will help achieve a productive, livable agreement that ensures the customer's goals will be reached. In addition, a broad based team will likely assure corporate-wide support and avoid "second guessing" if problems arise.

Once the desired number of vendors has been "down selected," the customer should ask to review the vendors' error logs for the system the customer is seeking to license. Error logs are maintained by all vendors to track product defects and errors and subsequent corrections. By examining a vendor's error logs, the customer can ascertain the extent of any problems with the vendor's system and hopefully avoid selecting the wrong vendor.

Even after the customer has identified a preferred vendor, it should inform the preferred vendor that the customer is also negotiating with its second-choice vendor, which should motivate the preferred vendor to negotiate a mutually beneficial agreement with the customer.

During the negotiations, the customer should make sure it understands the vendor's pricing. If the customer is purchasing a license through an ASP model, it should clearly understand what part of the price is attributable to the software license and what part is attributable to the accompanying services. By bifurcating the pricing, the customer will better be able to compare prices and will hopefully be able to better understand the nature of the services that will be provided.

See Willret and Keller, *10 Questions to Ask Before Software License Transactions*, 27 ACC Docket 39 (Sept. 2009); Bodreau, *The Insider's Guide to Technology Procurement*, 23 ACC Docket 29 (July/August 2005).

CHAPTER **3**

Licensing Software

A. Overview

1. The Concept of Licensing

A license can be thought of as the permission of the owner of property to use that property. A more precise understanding, however, can be gained by using the old law school example of comparing property ownership to a bundle of sticks. The owner of the property possesses all of the sticks, which can be separated, subdivided by time and place, transferred outright or licensed, and licensed exclusively or nonexclusively. If the owner grants a license, the property owner is giving some of the sticks from the owner's bundle to the licensee. Thus, to understand software licensing it is necessary to understand the sticks, or intellectual property rights, contained in the software owner's bundle.

2. Intellectual Property Rights Applicable to Software

Software is a unique technology, in that it comprises rights that are protectable under copyright law, patent law, and trade secret law. These multiple protections arise because software can be both a work of authorship as well as a business process. Set forth below is a brief overview of the three primary types of intellectual property rights provided for under U.S. law that are applicable to software.

(a) Patents

Patents are granted on "any new and useful process, machine, manufacture, or composition of matter, or any new and useful improvement thereof." 35 U.S.C. § 101. A patent is an exclusive right to practice an invention granted by the government. Anyone else who practices the invention without a license from the patent holder is infringing the patent. 35 U.S.C. § 121.

In return for granting a patent, the government requires the inventor to disclose the invention to the public in full, clear, and exact terms. 35 U.S.C. § 112. While the inventor has the exclusive right to practice the invention, anyone can examine the patent and understand the invention.

For years, software was not believed to be patentable subject matter. *See, e.g., Gottchalk v. Benson,* 405 U.S. 915 (1972) (reversing judgment of the Court of Customs and Patent Appeals on claims to "the processing of data by program and more particularly to the programmed conversion of numerical information" on the basis that the programs were not patentable subject matter). This belief changed in 1998, when the Federal Circuit issued its opinion in *State Street Bank & Trust Co. v. Signature Financial Group, Inc.,* 149 F.3d 1368 (Fed. Cir. 1998). In *State Street,* the district court granted summary judgment invalidating a patent governing a data processing system, relying in part on the "business method" exception to patentable subject matter. *Id.* at 1375. The theory behind the "business method" exception was that merely doing business did not qualify as patentable subject matter. *Id.* The Federal Circuit reversed the district court's decision that a data processing system did not qualify as patentable subject matter and it eliminated the business method exception, opening the floodgates on software patents.

The ability to obtain a software patent is again facing uncertainty in light of the Federal Circuit's ruling in *In re Bilski,* 545 F.3d 943 (Fed. Cir. 2008), which held that a process or method is patentable only if it is tied to a particular machine or transforms a particular article into another state or item.

In the United States, the term of a patent depends upon when it was filed. For patents issued before June 8, 1995, and patent applications that were pending on that date, the patent term is the longer of either 17 years from the issue date or 20 years from the earliest claimed filing date, the longer term applying. 35 U.S.C. § 154. For applications filed on or after June 8, 1995, the patent term is 20 years from the earliest claimed filing date. *Id.* Generally, a patent holder may not enforce a patent license beyond the term of the patent. *Brulotte v. Thys Co.,* 379 U.S. 29 (1964). Thus, theoretically, a software licensor could have difficulty enforcing a license to its patented software after the expiration of the patent term. Pragmatically, however, a licensor can also protect its software via copyright. Recently, the patentability of software has come under increasing scrutiny. At least one commentator believes the Supreme Court is poised to rollback several previous decisions involving software patents. Scarsi, *Shifting Landscape of Software Protection,* NAT. L. J., Jan. 21, 2008, at S1, S9.

For an overview of the history of patenting software, see *The History of Software Patents,* http://www.bitlaw.com/software-patent/history.html (last viewed September 15, 2010).

(b) Trade Secrets

Trade secrets are another form of intellectual property that can be used to protect software. Trade secrets are protected under the relevant state trade secret laws, almost all of which are derived from the Uniform Trade Secret Act (UTSA), which has been adopted in 46 states and the District of Columbia. *See, e.g.,* California: CAL. CIV. CODE § 3426 *et. seq.;* Maryland: MD. CODE ANN., COMM. LAW § 11–1201 *et. seq.;* Pennsylvania: 18 PA. C.S. § 3930. Only Massachusetts, New Jersey, New York, North Carolina, and Texas have not adopted the Uniform Trade Secret Act, although New York and New Jersey are considering its adoption.

Under the UTSA, a trade secret is information, including a formula, pattern, compilation, program device, method, technique, or process, that: (1) derives independent economic value, actual or potential, from not being generally known to, and not being readily ascertainable by proper means by other persons who can obtain economic value from its disclosure or use, and (2) is the subject of efforts that are reasonable under the circumstances to maintain its secrecy. As set forth above, the scope of trade secrets overlaps patents but is also potentially applicable to information that does not meet the standard of patentability. Thus, trade secret protection is potentially broader than that available under patent law. However, a program that is solely functional in nature, i.e., the program's function is readily available or ascertainable, is not protectable under the UTSA.

The UTSA defines "misappropriation" to mean the (1) acquisition of a trade secret by a person who knows or has reason to know the trade secret was acquired by improper means, or (2) disclosure or use of a trade secret without express or implied consent by a person who improperly acquired knowledge of the trade secret or, who at the time of disclosure or use, knew or had reason to know that the trade secret had been improperly acquired, and there was an obligation to maintain its confidentiality. UTSA § 1(2); *see, e.g.*, MD. CODE ANN. COM. LAW § 11-201(c).

For a further discussion of the UTSA, see Chapter 14.B.3.

A fundamental distinction between patent protection and trade secret protection is the requirement that the owner of a trade secret use reasonable efforts to maintain the secrecy of information. This is in sharp contrast to the duty of disclosure and enablement under patent law. Thus, a licensor seeking to protect software should include confidentiality provisions in the license agreement. Special care should be taken to protect the confidentiality of source code. See Chapter 14 for a detailed discussion of the issues involved in confidentiality provisions.

Trade secret protection offers several advantages over other types of protection for intellectual property law, principally the perpetual protection offered for trade secrets (for example, the formula for Coke) and initially the minimal cost to obtain such protection. These benefits are often outweighed by the fluid nature of such protection and the immediate loss of trade secret status even in the event of an inadvertent disclosure. The disclosure of the protected information in a patent or copyright application will also cause a loss of protection. *See BondPro Corp. v. Siemens Power Generation, Inc.*, 463 F.3d 702 (7th Cir 2006). Further, a competitor who is able to reproduce a trade secret without use of illegal means is free to do so. In short, trade secrets generally retain their value so long as they remain secret.

State trade secret laws offer broader protection than copyright laws because the trade secret laws apply to concepts and information, which are both excluded from protection under federal copyright law. *See 17* U.S.C. § 102(b). Information eligible for protection includes computer code, *Trandes Corp. v. Guy F. Atkinson Co.*, 996 F.2d 655, 663 (4th Cir.), *cert. denied*, 510 U.S. 965 (1993); *University Computing Co. v. Lykes-Youngstown Corp.*, 504 F.2d 518 (5th Cir.), *reh'g denied*, 505 F.2d 1304 (5th Cir. 1974); *Integrated Cash Management Servs., Inc. v. Digital Transactions, Inc.*, 732 F. Supp. 370 (S.D.N.Y. 1989), *aff'd*, 920 F.2d 171 (2d Cir. 1990); program architecture, *Trandes*, 996 F.2d at 661; *Computer Assocs. Int'l, Inc. v. Bryan*, 784 F. Supp. 982

(E.D.N.Y. 1992); information content including order, structure, and sequence, *Q-Co. Indus., Inc. v. Hoffman,* 625 F. Supp. 608, 617 (S.D.N.Y 1985); and algorithms, *Vermont Microsystems, Inc. v. Autodesk, Inc.,* 88 F.3d 142 (2d Cir. 1996); *Micro Consulting, Inc. v. Zubeldia,* 813 F. Supp. 1514, 1534 (W.D. Okla. 1990), *aff'd without opinion,* 959 F.2d 245 (10th Cir. 1992). Mathematical algorithms are also protectable under patent law, *Arrhythmia Research Technology v. Corazonix Corp.,* 958 F.2d 1053 (Fed. Cir.) *reh'g denied,* 1992 U.S. App. LEXIS 9888 (Fed. Cir. 1992); *In re Iwashi,* 888 F.2d. 1370 (Fed. Cir. 1989).

Courts are divided as to the application of trade secret protection for customer lists. See *Morlife, Inc. v. Perry,* 56 Cal. App. 4th 1514 (Cal. App. 1997) (file of customer business cards maintained by sales manager are trade secrets); *Fireworks Spectacular, Inc. v. Premier Pyrotechnics, Inc.,* 147 F. Supp.2d 1057 (D Kan. 2001) (customer lists constitute trade secrets, applying Kansas law), and *In re American Preferred Prescription, Inc.,* 186 B.R. 350 (Bankr. E. D. N. Y. 1995) (client list is trade secret). See also *DeGiorgio v. Megabyte Int'l., Inc.,* 468 S.E.2d 367 (Ga. 1996) (only tangible customer lists are subject to protection as a trade secret), and *Ed Nowogroski Insurance v. Rucker,* 944 P.2d 1093 (Wash. 1997) (memorized client list constitutes trade secret), but see *Vigoro Indus. v. Cleveland Chem. of Ark.,* 866 F. Supp. 1150 (E. D. Ark. 1994) (customer lists alone not considered a trade secret), and *WMW Machinery Company, Inc. v. Koerber A.G.,* 658 N.Y.S.2d 385 (App. Div. 1997) (customer lists are not trade secrets where lists are readily ascertainable from sources outside employee's business). Further, at least one court has held that the execution of a nondisclosure agreement by an employee does not in and of itself create trade secret status for the employer's customer lists. *Equifax Servs., Inc. v. Examination Management Servs., Inc.,* 453 S.E.2d 488 (Ga. App. 1994). For a further discussion, see *Intellectual Property Issues in the Employment Setting,* 119 Intell. Prop. Couns. 1, 4 (Nov. 2006).

A majority of courts have held that claims based on state trade secret laws are not preempted by federal copyright law (§ 301 of Federal Copyright Act). *Dun & Bradstreet Software Services, Inc. v. Grace Consulting, Inc.,* 307 F.3d 197 (3d Cir. 2002); *Nat'l Car Rental Sys., Inc. v. Computer Assocs. Intl., Inc.,* 991 F.2d 426 (8th Cir. 1993); *Bishop v. Wick,* 1998 WL 166652, 11 U.S.P.Q.2d 1360 (N. D. Ill. 1988); *Brignoli v. Balch, Hardy and Scheinman,* 645 F. Supp. 1201 (S.D.N.Y. 1986), but see *Computer Associates International v. Atari,* 775 F. Supp. 544 (E.D.N.Y. 1991); *Enhanced Computer Solutions, Inc. v. Rose,* 927 F. Supp. 738 (S.D.N.Y. 1996); *Benjamin Capital Investors v. Cossey,* 867 P.2d 1388 (Or. Ct. App. 1994). See also *Lennon v. Seaman,* 63 F. Supp.2d 428, 437 (S.D.N.Y. 1999), which discusses in detail the dichotomy among the different courts. At the same time, two commentators have suggested that trade secret laws may be the only method of protection for the ideas incorporated in the functionality of mass distributed commercial software. Johnston & Grogan, *Trade Secret Protection for Mass Distributed Software,* 11 Computer Law, 1 (Nov. 1994).

Matters of public knowledge, general knowledge of an industry, routine or small skill and knowledge readily ascertainable, and differences in procedures or methodology are not considered to be trade secrets. *Anaconda Co. v. Metric Tool & Die Co.,* 485 F. Supp. 410, 421–22 (E.D. Pa. 1996). Furthermore, any skill or experience learned during the course of employee's employment is not considered to be a trade secret. *Rigging Int'l Maintenance Co. v. Gwin,* 128 Cal. App. 3d 594 (1981); *American Red Cross v. Palm Beach Blood Bank, Inc.,* 143 F.3d 1407 (11th Cir. 1998) (employer may not preclude former employees from utilizing contacts and expertise gained during employment), but see *Air Products and Chemicals, Inc. v. Johnson,* 442 A.2d 1114 (Pa. Super. 1982) (details of research and development, projected capital spending, and marketing plans are trade secrets); *Den-Tal-Ez, Inc. v. Siemens Capital Corp.,* 566 A.2d 1214 (Pa. Super. 1989) (detailed units costs, profit margin date, and pricing methods are trade secrets).

An owner of trade secrets is entitled to receive injunctive relief and damages for the misappropriation of its trade secrets. UTSA § 3. Such damages include the actual loss caused by the misappropriation and any unjust enrichment arising as a result of the misappropriation that is not taken into account in computing any actual loss. UTSA § 3; *see, e.g.,* Md. Code Ann. Com. Law § 11-1203. A court may also award attorney's fees if willful and malicious misappropriation exists. UTSA § 4(iii); *see, e.g.,* Md. Code Ann. Com. Law § 11-1204.

Section 7 of the UTSA provides that except for contractual remedies, whether or not based upon the misappropriation of a trade secret or other civil remedies that are not based upon the misappropriation of a trade secret, the UTSA "displaces conflicting tort, restitutionary and other laws . . . providing civil remedies for misappropriation of a trade secret." *See, e.g., Auto Channel, Inc. v. Speedvision Network, LLC,* 144 F. Supp. 2d 784 (W.D. Ky. 2001) (Kentucky Uniform Trade Secrets Act replaces all conflicting civil state law regarding misappropriation of trade secrets, except for those relating to contractual remedies); *Boeing Co. v. Sierracin Corp.,* 738 P.2d 665 (Wash. 1987) (UTSA merely displaces conflicting tort, restitutionary, and other law regarding civil liability for misappropriation and does not displace claims for breach of contractual and confidential relationship).

Given the differences in state trade secret laws, the choice of governing law is very important. For example, South Carolina has enacted legislation providing that written agreements not to disclose trade secrets will be enforced without limitation on duration or geographic scope when the employee knows or has reason to know of the trade secret's existence, S.C. Code Ann. § 39-8-30(d) (Law Co-op. 1997), while the Wisconsin Court of Appeals in an unpublished decision declined to enforce a nondisclosure provision in an agreement because it was unlimited as to time and overly broad. *Williams v. Northern Technical Services, Inc.,* 568 N.W.2d 784 (Wis. App. 1997).

For a general overview of trade secret issues, see Rodgers & Marrs, *Trade Secrets and Corporate Espionage: Protecting Your Company's Crown Jewels,* 22 ACC Docket 60–78 (April 2004); O'Brien, *Trade Secret Reclamation: An Equitable Approach in a Relative World,* 21 J. Computer & Information Law 227 (2003); Peterson, *Trade Secrets in an Information Age,* 32 Hous. L. Rev. 385 (1995); Dodd, *Rights in Information: Conversion and Misappropriation Causes of Action in Intellectual Property Cases,* 32 Hous. L. Rev. 459 (1995); Gross, *What Is Computer "Trade Secret" Under State Law,* 53 A.L.R 4th 1046 (1987); Gulbis, *Disclosure or Use of Computer Application Software as Misappropriation of Trade Secret,* 30 A.L.R 4th 1250 (1984); Pooley, Trade Secrets, Law Journal Press (1997).

For a discussion of trade secret laws as they apply to employees, see Chapter 14, Sections A.3 and B.

(c) Copyrights

Copyright law protects "works of authorship fixed in any tangible medium of expression, now known or later developed, from which they can be perceived, reproduced, or otherwise communicated, either directly or with the aid of a machine or device." 17 U.S.C. § 102. Copyright protection, however, does not "extend to any idea, procedure, process, system, method of operation, concept, principle, or discovery, regardless of the form in which it is described, explained, illustrated, or embodied in such work." *Id.*

Thus, copyright only protects the expression, not the underlying ideas or concepts. Software is a work of authorship that is fixed in a tangible medium of expression. As such, it is entitled to protection under copyright law. Copyright protection does not extend, however, to the processes that software performs or the ideas that it implements. Instead, only the expression itself is protected. This is a fundamental distinction between the protection offered by copyright law and that potentially offered by patent and trade secret law. In a nutshell, copyright law prevents anyone from copying source code without the owner's permission, but it does not prevent third parties from independently writing software that performs the same functions as the copyright software.

In general, for a work created after January 1, 1978, a copyright endures for a period equal to the life of the author and for 70 years after the author's death. For works made for hire, a copyright endures for a term of 95 years from the year of its first publication or for a term of 120 years from the year of its creation, whichever expires first. 17 U.S.C § 302 (a).

Confusion often arises as to the role of registration in copyright law. A work of authorship is protected when it is fixed in a tangible medium. *See In re World Auxiliary Power Company,* 303 F.3d 1120, 1125 (9th Cir. 2002). It is not mandatory, however, that copyright owners include a copyright notice on the work. 17 U.S.C. § 401 (a). Inclusion of a copyright notice abrogates a defendant's claim of innocent infringement in mitigation of actual or statutory damages. 17 U.S.C. § 401 (d).

While registration is permissive, not mandatory, and not a precondition for protection, it does confer a number of benefits. *Id.* There is a split in authority as to whether an originator must register the copyright with the U.S. copyright office prior to bringing an infringement claim, 17 U.S.C. § 411(a). Registration required: Sixth Circuit: *Hawaiian Village Computer, Inc. v. Print Management Partners,* Inc., 501 F. Supp.2d 951 (E.D. Mich. 2007); Tenth Circuit: *La Resolana Architects P.A. v. Clay Realtors Angel Fire,* 416 F.3d 1195 (10th Cir 2005); Eleventh Circuit: *Stuart Weitzman, LLC v. Microcomputer Resources, Inc.*, 542 F.3d 859 (11th Cir 2008), *M.C.B. Homes, Inc. v. Ameron Homes, Inc.*, 903 F.2d 1486 (11th Cir. 1990). Completed application for copyright registration sufficient: First Circuit: *Foraste v. Brown Univ.*, 248 F. Supp. 71 (D. RI. 2003); Third Circuit: *Wilson v. Mr. Tee's*, 855 F. Supp. 679 (D.N.J. 1994); Fifth Circuit: *Lakedreams v. Taylor*, 932 F.2d 1103 (5th Cir. 1991); Seventh Circuit: *Chicago Bd. of Education v. Substance, Inc.*, 354 F.3d 624 (7th Cir 2003); Eighth Circuit; *Action Tapes, Inc. v. Mattson*, 462 F.3d 1010 (8th Cir 2006); Ninth Circuit; *Cosmetic Ideas*

Inc. v. IAC/Interactive Corp., 606 F.3d 612 (9th Cir 2010). The district courts within the Second, Fourth and D.C. Circuits have issued split decisions, which have not been resolved by the Circuit Courts, while the U.S. Court of Appeals for the Federal Circuit has not decided this issue.

Registration within three months of the publication of the work permits a copyright holder to obtain up to $150,000 in statutory damages for intentional infringement without proof of an actual loss and the right to obtain attorney's fees. 17 U.S.C. §§ 504(c), 412. If the work is published within five years from the date of creation, the registration is prima facie evidence of the validity of the copyright, shifting the burden of proof to the other party. 17 U.S.C. § 410(c); *Gates Rubber Co. v. Bando Chem. Ind., Ltd.*, 9 F.3d 823 (10th Cir. 1993).

The ability to obtain statutory damages and attorney's fees is important as the copyright owner's actual damages and the infringer's profits may be less than the cost of the litigation. The award of attorney's fees is made at the discretion of the court and not automatically to the prevailing party. *Fogerty v. Fantasy, Inc.*, 510 U.S. 517, 537 (1994).

The existence of a contractual agreement gives rise to the question as to whether to bring a claim for breach of contract or for copyright infringement. A copyright claim allows a plaintiff to potentially recover significant penalties as well as its legal fees. A recovery under a breach of contract claim is limited to the actual loss suffered by the breach. Richard A. Lord, 24 Williston on Contracts § 65:1 (4th ed. 2007), Normally, legal fees are not recoverable in a breach of contract claim. *Alyeska Pipeline Svc. Co. v. Wilderness Soc'y*, 421 U.S. 240, 247 (1975).

Courts will carefully evaluate any efforts to restyle a breach of contract claim as a copyright infringement claim. *See generally*, *Eastern Broadcasting Am. Corp. v. Universal Video, Inc.*, 2006 WL 767871 (E.D.N.Y. Mar. 24, 2006); *Marshall v. New Kids on the Block Partnership*, 782 F. Supp. 1008 (S.D N.Y. 1991). Exceeding the scope of a license gives rise to a copyright infringement claim not a beach of contract claim. *Harrell v. Van der Plas*, 2009 WL 3756327 (S.D.N.Y. Nov. 9, 2009).

To bring a successful action for copyright infringement, a plaintiff must establish that the rights violated were copyright, not contractual. *Sun Microsystems, Inc., v. Microsoft Corp.*, 188 F.3d 1115 (9th Cir 1999). "A plaintiff may assert a claim for copyright infringement so long as the alleged distribution was prohibited by a condition restricting that authorized distribution." *Gold Cross Safety Corp. Inc. v. PHH Vehicle Management*, et. al., 2008 WL 2625357 (Letter Opinion June 25, 2008). A dispute over the payment of license fees and the limitation of one user per license are not limitations on the scope of the license, but rather separate contractual promises and are not the basis for a copyright claim. *Netbula, LLC v. Storage Technology Corp.*, 2008 WL 228036 (N.D. Cal. Jan. 18, 2008). Registration also allows the copyright owner to record its registration with the U.S. customs service to protect against infringing copies being imported into the United States.

A copyright holder must bring a claim for copyright infringement "within three years after the claim accrued." 17 U.S.C. § 507(b). A split of authority has arisen, however, over whether the three-year period begins on the date of the injury (the "Injury Rule") or the date the copyright holder knows or should have known of the injury giving rise to the claim (the "Discovery Rule"). A majority of circuits have recognized the Discovery Rule as the correct interpretation. *See Warren Freedenfeld Assocs., Inc. v. McTigue*, 531 F.3d 38, 44–46 (1st Cir. 2008); *Stone v. Williams*, 970 F.2d 1043, 1048 (2d Cir. 1992); Third: *William A. Graham Company v. Hugley*, 568 F.3d 425 (3d Cir. 2009); *Lyons P'ship, L.P. v. Morris Costumes, Inc.*, 243 F.3d 789, 796 (4th Cir. 2001); *Daboub v. Gibbons*, 42 F.3d 285, 291 (5th Cir. 1995); *Roger Miller Music, Inc. v. Sony/ATV Publ'g, LLC*, 477 F.3d 383, 390 (6th Cir. 2007); *Gaiman v. McFarlane*, 360 F.3d 644, 653 (7th Cir. 2004);. *Comcast v. Multi-Vision Elecs., Inc.*, 491 F.3d 938, 944 (8th Cir. 2007); *Polar Bear Prods., Inc. v. Timex Corp.*, 384 F.3d 700, 705-07 (9th Cir. 2004).

For an overview of copyright protection for software, see Buckman, *Copyright Protection of Computer Programs*, 180 A.L.R. FED 1 (2002).

B. The First Sale Doctrine

1. *In General*

The theory of the First Sale Doctrine under the Copyright Act 17 U.S.C. § 101 *et. seq.* is that an individual who *purchases* an authorized copy may use and resell that particular copy free of any restraint by the copyright owner. 17 U.S.C. § 109(a) (emphasis supplied). See *Bobbs Merrill Co. v. Straus*, 210 U.S. 339 (1908). A copyright owner's sale of an authorized copy "exhausts" the copyright owner's exclusive distribution and display rights, such that the purchaser may use, resell, or display that copy free of any claim of infringement. 17 U.S.C. § 109(a).[1] In short, the First Sale Doctrine addresses a *copy owner's rights* as opposed to the *copyright owner's* rights.

The First Sale Doctrine does not apply, however, to the separate exclusive rights of copying, derivative work preparation, and public display or performance. See 17 U.S.C. § 106 (which sets forth five separate and distinct rights). *See, e.g., Red Baron-Franklin Park, Inc. v. Taito Corp.*, 883 F.2d 275, 280 (4th Cir. 1989), and *Columbia Pictures Industries, Inc., v. Aveco, Inc.*, 800 F.2d 59, 64 (3d Cir. 1986). *See also* 17 U.S.C. § 109(e) (which, to legislatively overrule *Red Baron*, permits display of copyrighted video games in coin-operated equipment). The First Sale Doctrine only applies to the *copyright owner's* exclusive rights of distribution and display in its copyrighted work, which are "automatically" conveyed to the buyer or the copy owner upon sale. 17 U.S.C. § 109(a) and (c).[2]

Section 106(3) provides that the copyright owner has the exclusive right to distribute and to authorize distribution of copies or phonorecords of the copyrighted work to the public by sale or other transfer of ownership or by rental, lease, or lending.

---

1. Section 109(a) codifies the First Sale Doctrine, which provides "Notwithstanding the provisions of Section 106(3), the owner of a particular copy or phonorecord lawfully made under this title, or any person authorized by such owner, is entitled, without the authority of the copyright owner, to sell or otherwise dispose of that copy or phonorecord."

2. The owner of a copyright embodying the copyright work receives only the right to display that physical copy where it is located. 17 U.S.C. § 109(a).

Section 106(4) and (5) give the copyright owner the exclusive right to publicly perform or display a literary, musical, dramatic, or choreographic work or a pantomime, motion picture, or other audiovisual work. Section 106(6) gives the copyright owner the exclusive right to perform a sound recording work publicly by means of a digital audio transmission. To prove infringement, the copyright holder must demonstrate only that it possesses a valid copyright, that the copyrighted material was registered for copyright, and that there was unauthorized copying. The principal means of showing unauthorized copying is through access and substantial similarity. *Ford Motor Co. v. Summit Motor Products,* 930 F.2d 277, 290–91 (3d. Cir. 1990) (copying is shorthand for violating any of the five exclusive rights of copyright owners).

The First Sale Doctrine acts as a defense to a claim of infringement. At least one court has held that the defense is available "only to copies legally made and sold in the United States." *Omega S.A., v. Costco Wholesale Corp.*, 541 F.3d 982, 986 (9th Cir 2008), *aff'd Per Curium,* 131 S. Ct. 565 (2010) Interestingly, at least several courts have held that overseas purchases of software manufactured outside of the United States are not entitled to invoke the first sale defense, 17 U.S.C. § 109(a), to a claim of infringement. *Microsoft Corporation v. Big Boy Distribution, LLC,* 589 F. Supp.2d 1308 (S.D. Fla. 2008); *Microsoft Corp. v. Intrax Group, Inc., d/b/a Surplus Computers,* 2008 WL 4500703 (N.D. Cal. Oct. 6, 2008) (rejecting first sale defense for software manufactured and licensed outside of U.S.); *Microsoft Corp. v. Software Wholesale Club, Inc.*, 129 F. Supp.2d 995, 1006 (S.D. Tex. 2000) ("first sale doctrine does not apply to admittedly counterfeit unit").

Software developers, in order to avoid application of the First Sale Doctrine and retain control over redistribution of their programs, have typically distributed even mass-market software under license, rather than through an outright sale, in order to prevent the First Sale Doctrine from severing control over redistribution. See *Microsoft Corp. v. Software Wholesale Club, Inc.*, 129 F. Supp. 2d 995 (S.D. Tex. 2000) (first sale doctrine not applicable to licensed software); *Adobe Systems, Inc. v. One Stop Micro, Inc.*, 84 F. Supp. 2d 1086, 1089 (N.D. Cal. 2000) ("First sale doctrine is only triggered by an actual sale."); *Allen-Myland, Inc. v. International Business Mach. Corp.*, 746 F. Supp. 520 (E.D. Pa. 1990) (first sale doctrine does not apply to computer programs).

For computer software, Section 109(b) limits the First Sale Doctrine and the rights of copy owners in three ways. First, adaptations may not be transferred without permission of the copyright owner. This is true even under the First Sale Doctrine as there is no right to create derivative works. Second, under Section 117 the owner of a program may make an archival copy or an adaptation of the program if such adaptation is essential to the use of the original program by a computer, and that the creator of the copy may only transfer it as part of lease, sale, or other transfer of rights in the underlying program. Exact copies authorized to be made under Section 117 may be transferred without permission of the copyright owner only as part of a transfer of all rights in the underlying program. The distribution right conveyed to the buyer does not, for example, include the right to make further copies for resale.

Third, it provides that the owner of a copy of computer software cannot lend or rent that copy to third parties without permission from the copyright owner. See

Microsoft v. Harmony Computers & Electronics, Inc., 846 F. Supp. 208 (E.D.N.Y. 1994) (unauthorized distributor of a copy of software not entitled to protection under First Sale Doctrine because owner licensed not sold software to distributor's supplier); *Triad Systems Corp. v. Southeastern Express Co.*, 64 F.3d 1330 (9th Cir. 1995), *cert. denied,* 516 U.S. 1145 (1996) (software sold to customers is subject to 17 U.S.C. § 117 protection while copies that are licensed are not); and *Stenograph LLC v. Sims,* 2000 WL 964748, 55 U.S.P.O. 2d 1436 (E.D. Pa. 2000) (first sale doctrine does not apply to gifts).

Known as the Computer Software Rental Amendments Act of 1990, Section 109(b) also addresses computer software rentals. It provides that, unless authorized by the owner of the copyright in a software program (including any tape, disk, or other medium embodying such program), no person in possession of a particular copy of a software program (including any tape, disk, or other medium embodying such program) may, for the purposes of direct or indirect commercial advantage, dispose of or authorize the disposal of the possession of that computer software (including any tape, disk, or other medium embodying such program) by rental, lease, or lending, or any similar act. Section 109(b) specifically excludes nonprofit libraries and nonprofit educational institutions from its prohibitions on renting, leasing, or lending copies of copyrighted software. In short, Section 109 prohibits the rental of a copy of a computer program by the owner of a copy without the permission of the licensor. 17 U.S.C. § 107. See generally, *Central Point Software, Inc v. Global Software & Access, Inc.*, 880 F. Supp. 957 (E.D.N.Y. 1995).

Section 109(d) further limits the scope of application of the First Sale Doctrine by providing that, unless authorized by the copyright owner, the provisions of 17 U.S.C. §§ 109 (a) and (c) do not extend to any person who has acquired possession of the copy or phonorecord from the copyright owner, by rental, lease, loan, or otherwise, without also acquiring ownership of it.

2. Applicability to Software

A software owner needs to consider how it will protect its software. It may be able to protect methods and processes by either trade secret or patent. Patents, however, require revealing the protected process to the public, while trade secret protection requires keeping it confidential. Thus, the same process cannot be protected by both methods. By writing the software, the owner receives copyright protection on the actual expression. This protection does not, however, prevent third parties from independently developing software that performs the same function.

When granting a license to a licensee, a vendor needs to consider what protections it has in the software, and what rights (or sticks in the bundle) it wishes to convey to the licensee. The scope of the license granted will govern the licensee's use. Only if the licensee exceeds the scope may the licensor seek damages or other remedies from a licensee under any intellectual property regimen. Thus, the license grant should be drafted broadly enough to permit use by the licensee, but narrowly enough to enable the intellectual property holder to use copyright, patent, or trade secret law to stop or prevent infringement by the licensee.

There is no uniform test for ascertaining whether a transaction is a sale or a license. In *Vernor v. Autodesk, Inc.*, 621 F.3d 1102 (9th Cir. 2010), the Ninth Circuit established a three part test to determine whether the user is an owner or licensee of the software:

"[A] software user is a licensee rather than an owner of a copy where the copyright owner

1. specifies that the user is granted a license;
2. significantly restricts the user's ability to transfer the software; and
3. imposes notable use restrictions."

Id. at 1111 The first two prongs will usually be satisfied in any dispute, making the third prong the determinative issue. The *Vernor* court cited the governing agreement's restrictions on the transfer of the software and the retention of ownership by Autodesk. The agreement also contained prohibitions "against modifying, translating, or reverse-engineering the software, removing any proprietary marks from the software or documentation, or defeating any copy protection device." *Id.* Thus, it appears, at least in the Ninth Circuit, that language to this effect will satisfy the third prong and allow a court to find the existence of a license and not a sale.

In general, the label placed on the transaction by the parties is not determinative. "[I]n determining whether a transaction is a sale, a lease or a license, courts look to the economic realities of the exchange." *SoftMan Products Co., LLC v. Adobe Systems, Inc.*, 171 F Supp.2d 1075, 1084 (C.D. Cal. 2001). Courts will look to the nature of the transaction itself to reach a decision and will examine such factors as to whether the underlying agreement reserves title with the owner, transfers "limited rights," allows the "purchaser" to permanently retain possession for a single up-front payment or contains restrictions on any future transfers of the software, prohibits resale, or simply requires the payment of an additional fee. *UMG Recordings, Inc. v. Augusto*, 558 F. Supp.2d 1055 (C.D. Cal 2008) (permanent possession without further benefit to copyright owner indicative of sale). Restrictions on the number of users and the number of computers within the licensed entity are indicative of a license. Finally, a court will look to extrinsic evidence to reach a decision. *United States v. Wise*, 550 F.2d 1180 (9th Cir. 1977); *Adobe Systems Incorporated v. One Stop Micro., Inc.*, 84 F. Supp.2d 1086 (N.D. Ca. 2000) (software licensed not sold despite use of terms "purchase," "owned" and "repurchase" in underlying agreement).

In *UMG*, the court found the software had been sold not licensed despite the copyright owners structuring the transactions as a license. In concluding the defendant had not misappropriated the owner's rights under copyright law, the court focused on the fact that the defendants had not made a copy of the copyrighted work prior to reselling their copies. Because the defendant had not made copies, the defendant was simply exercising its rights under the First Sale Doctrine to transfer the single copy in their possession.

For a discussion of several different types of intellectual property protections available for software, see Neelakantan & Armstrong, *Source Code, Object Code, and the Da Vinci Code: The Debate on Intellectual Property Protection for Software Programs*, 23 Computer & Internet Law 1 (Oct. 2006).

C. The Transfer of Intellectual Property Rights

In general, there are two means of conveying intellectual property rights: assignments and licenses. In an assignment, the property owner conveys all of the sticks in the owner's bundle, while in a license the property owner only transfers certain sticks, and retains the rest. Under copyright law, a license applies to *intangible* property rights while a "sale" applies to the transfer of *tangible* property. 17 U.S.C. § 202; see also *Chamberlain v. Cocola Assoc.*, 958 F.2d 282 (9th Cir. 1992).

The First Sale Doctrine, which applies to the sale of a tangible *copy* of software, provides that such sale conveys certain rights to the buyer in the purchased tangible copy of the software, namely the buyer's right to resell the software copy. 17 U.S.C. § 109(a). This right is in derogation of the overall copyright and it is also "automatically" transferred to a new buyer if the copy is resold. 17 U.S.C. § 117. Any transfer of ownership in a copyright must be through an unambiguous written agreement. *Davis v. Meridian Films, Inc.*, 2001 WL 758765 (4th Cir. July 5, 2001).

Typically, the sale of software is not a "sale" of a copy (or anything else) within the meaning of Section 109. The only thing that is sold when software is "sold" at retail is the media on which the copyrighted work is fixed. Certain rights inherent in the work are licensed in conjunction with the sale. A copyright owner who grants a nonexclusive license to use copyrighted material generally waives the right to sue the licensee for a copyright infringement to the extent of the license granted. *Sun Microsystems, Inc. v. Microsoft Corp.*, 188 F.3d 1115 (9th Cir. 1999).

An assignment is an absolute conveyance of the intangible rights and equates to a "sale," with the caveat that a sale typically only conveys the absolute right of distribution and, subject to certain exceptions, the right to display and use. *MacLean Assoc., Inc. v. William M. Mercer-Meidinger-Hanson, Inc.*, 952 F.2d 769 (3d Cir. 1991). A "sale" does not include, for example, the rights of performance or preparation of derivative works rights.

Similar to an assignment, an exclusive license, even if limited in time or place of effect, can amount to a "transfer of copyright ownership." 17 U.S.C. § 201(d)(2). Under the Copyright Act, transfer of an exclusive license is considered to be a conveyance of copyright ownership to the extent granted in the license. 17 U.S.C. § 201(d)(2). In short, entering into a license agreement in which the licensor reserves title is not a "sale" for purposes of the Copyright Act. For example, a licensee cannot distribute the licensor's software without the licensor's authorization, because the licensor is still the owner of the intellectual property. *Relational Design & Technology, Inc. v. Brock*, 1993 WL 191323 (D. Kan. May 25, 1993).

See Chapters 4.A.7 for a more detailed discussion.

CHAPTER **4**

Grant of License

Unless otherwise indicated, all section references (§) refer to the corresponding sections of the Annotated Software License and Services Agreement set forth in Form 23.B.1.

A. Terminology of a License Grant (§ 3.1)

A typical grant of a license contains the following wording:

> "Subject to the provisions of this Agreement, Licensor grants to Licensee a perpetual, personal, non-assignable, nontransferable, nonexclusive object code license to use the Software solely for Licensee's internal business purposes in the United States."

Each of the terms set forth in the above license grant has a specific meaning that fundamentally impacts the rights of the licensor and licensee. Set forth below is a brief discussion of these terms.

1. Definition of the "Licensee" and "Licensor"

(a) "Licensee"

The definition of the "Licensee" is important for both financial and legal reasons. Financially, the broader the definition of the "Licensee," the more entities or individuals who will have access to and use of the licensed software, thus reducing the potential license fees a licensor may receive. A narrow definition potentially acts to restrict the licensee's use of the software including allowing third parties, potentially the Licensor's competitors, from accessing the software.

Some license agreements allow "affiliates" or "subsidiaries" of the licensee to utilize the licensed software as well. See § 1.4. From the licensor's perspective, "Affiliates" and "Subsidiaries" should be narrowly defined. Allowing a later acquired affiliate or subsidiary to "use" the license deprives the licensor of additional license fees while imposing upon the licensor additional obligations and potential liability.

A prudent licensor will seek to define "Licensee" as the licensee and subsidiaries at least 51 percent owned by the licensee. An alternative approach is to limit the definition of "Affiliates" and "Subsidiaries" to those affiliates and subsidiaries in existence at the time the license agreement is executed. Otherwise, the licensor runs the risk that the subsidiaries and affiliates acquired after the execution, or even the expiration of the license agreement, may be covered under the license. *See e.g.*, *Imation Corp. v. Koninklijke Philips Electronics N.V.*, 586 F.3d 980 (Fed. Cir. 2009) (License extends to subsidiaries acquired after expiration of license agreement.)

A more conservative approach is to list in an appendix the authorized users of the software in order to have a definitive limit on the number of users. Alternatively, licenses may use a "common control" definition similar to the definition used in securities transactions. See § 1.4.A. This allows the licensee flexibility in operating its business and reflects the reality that companies are often continually acquiring or divesting business units.

In formulating the definition of "Licensee," the licensee should consider its potential future needs and make sure that the definition is broad enough to encompass the licensee's future needs. The licensee should consider not only the acquisition or divestiture of a business unit but also the outsourcing of certain functions, the retention of third party consultants and the need to relocate its businesses.

A licensee can seek access to the software by its third party consultants by including third party consultants in the license grant or by including third party consultants in the definition of "licensee." The licensee has a better chance of having the licensor accept access by third party consultants if it includes them in the definition of "licensee," rather than including them in the license grant. See Form 23.B.11 § 21 for an example of a license grant allowing third party consultants to access the software.

The licensee's greatest leverage is at the time of contract signature. Once the license has been signed, the licensor will have little incentive other than a financial incentive to expand the scope of the license. If the licensee's enterprise is to be included in the license, and the license fee is paid at the start of the license, the licensor will need to consider the potential impact if the licensee either acquires or is acquired by a large corporation. If the licensor is concerned about the possible lost sales opportunity involved in such an acquisition, the licensor should seek to exclude a potential purchaser from the definition of "licensee" as outside the scope of the license. This position protects the licensor in the event a large corporation acquires or is acquired by the licensee and permits the licensor to price the enterprise license consistent with the licensee's size. However, normal growth of the licensee's business can be included in the scope of the license and the licensor's pricing established accordingly. If the license fee is annual and based upon the number of seats or concurrent users, or some other volume based measure that will increase in the event of such an acquisition, the licensor may not need to seek such exclusion.

"Expanding" the definition of "Licensee" to include affiliates can create a privity issue as to the licensee's ability to bind the affiliate to the terms of the license. If the licensee lacks such authority, the licensor needs to create a mechanism by which the "affiliate" acknowledges that it is bound by the terms of the license. The licensor will want to have the licensee guaranty the performance of the affiliate. Further, if the license is a worldwide license, tax issues may arise from foreign affiliates' license payments to the licensor.

It is also important to distinguish between allowing the "use" of the licensed software by a third party and allowing the licensee to "assign" the license to another entity. With assignment, the assignor relinquishes its license and right to utilize the software. The assignor's right to use the licensed software is transferred to the assignee, preventing both entities from using the software at the same time. Allowing both the licensee and its affiliates to utilize the licensed software may allow numerous distinct legal entities to utilize the software simultaneously, subject to any restrictions on the number of users or other constraints in the license agreement. A smart licensor should take into account the possibility of multiple users when negotiating the license fees and in formulating its general pricing model.

Additionally, the licensor should consider the implications of permitting affiliates and/or third parties to use the software in the event of any dispute related to the software. In the event of a dispute related to the software, the licensor could be sued by all of these parties separately, each asserting that they are third party beneficiaries of the license agreement. The licensor should consider including an express statement that there are no third party beneficiaries. In the event that the licensor permits affiliates to be third party beneficiaries, the licensor should include terms requiring the licensee to consolidate all suits by affiliates. See Chapter 6.J for a more detailed discussion of this issue.

When defining "Licensee," the parties must consider the ramifications, if any, of United States export laws. If a licensee and its affiliates are granted simultaneous use of the licensed software, or the licensee has the unencumbered right to assign the license, and/or use is not restricted to the United States, the licensee's or its affiliate's use of the software outside of the United States may violate U.S. export laws if the appropriate export licenses have not been obtained. Furthermore, the laws of a foreign jurisdiction with which the licensor is unfamiliar, and which may not afford the licensor the same benefits and protections as the laws of the United States, may govern use of the licensed software outside of the United States.

International licenses require the licensor to consider a number of additional issues, such as U.S. export laws (see Chapter 5.M, § 43), import duties and taxes (Chapter 5.M.6), payments, and intellectual property indemnification, as well as moral rights (Chapter 5.A, and Form 23.F.1 § 8). Additionally, local counsel should be consulted in each jurisdiction to verify that the license complies with and is enforceable under local law. See Chapter 9.E for a more detailed discussion.

(b) "Licensor"

The definition of the "Licensor" is important from the licensee's perspective, as the licensee needs to ensure that the licensor has the financial ability to deliver the software/services contracted for and in the event of a breach, the ability to pay for any damages. If the "Licensor" is a subsidiary and lacks the significant assets of its parent, the licensee may seek to have the licensor's parent guaranty the financial performance of the subsidiary. See the Heading and Signature line of Form 23.B.1.

The licensee also wants to ensure that the entity granting any applicable license actually owns the intellectual property or has the right to grant a license and that ownership of the intellectual property is not held by the granting entity's parent, preventing a valid license from being granted.

Some licensors prefer to license their software through resellers. Often reseller agreements disclaim all warranties and indemnities. Since the licensee has no direct arrangement with the licensor, this leaves the licensee with few remedies if there is an issue with the software. Licensees should require that resellers either provide appropriate remedies or pass them through from the manufacturer.

2. *Term of License (§ 4.2)*

The term of the license should begin on delivery of the licensed software, rather than acceptance of the licensed software, to avoid any uncertainties regarding the licensee's obligations or restrictions as to the use of the software prior to acceptance. While many licensees are concerned with the concept of the license beginning upon delivery, the license should clearly state that although the license may begin to protect the licensor's interests upon delivery, acceptance of the software or an obligation of the licensee to pay for the license does not occur until the licensee accepts the licensed software. For the licensee, this issue takes added importance if the term is for a set period of years rather than a perpetual license.

While shrink-wrapped software licenses traditionally have had a perpetual term, other software licenses often had a more limited term, such as 5 or 10 years. Today, the distinction is less important as most software is obsolete within 10 years, and licensors routinely grant perpetual licenses in recognition of the rapid obsolescence of software in general. *But see Apple Computer, Inc. v. Microsoft Corporation,* 35 F.3d 1435 (9th Cir. 1994) (in 1985, Apple granted, in effect, a perpetual license of its Windows visual displays to Microsoft). The term of the license is often linked to price with the licensor's pricing model closely aligned to the "value proposition" of the software. Some lawyers, however, are hesitant to enter into perpetual licenses in the belief they are unenforceable and instead insist on a 99-year license. *See generally,* RAYMOND T. NIMMER, LAW OF COMPUTER TECHNOLOGY §§ 7:94–7:98 (2005).

Interestingly, at least one court, applying New York law, has voided a software license and exclusive distribution agreement as violating the Rule Against Perpetuities. *McAllister Software Systems, Inc. v. Henry Schein, Inc.*, 2008 WL 922328 (E.D. Mo. April 2, 2008) *but see Ultracts, Ltd. v. Wal-Mart Stores, Inc.*, 16 S.W.3d 265, 270 (Ark. Ct. App. 2000).

Generally, if the license for a copyrighted work that is not a work made for hire fails to state a term or contains a term of greater than 35 years, the license will be terminable after 35 years from execution under the Copyright Act, unless state law provides for the license to be terminable in less than 35 years, in which case state law would apply. 17 U.S.C. § 203 (There is a split between the Ninth Circuit with *Rano v. Sipa Press,* 987 F.2d 580 (9th Cir. 1993) on the one hand and the Seventh and Eleventh Circuits on the other with *Walthal v. Rusk,* 172 F.3d 481 (7th Cir. 1999) and *Korman v. HBC Florida, Inc.,* 182 F.3d 1291, 1294–95 (11th Cir. 1999) concerning whether the 35-year provision of Section 203 preempts state law and is therefore a minimum term for contracts). Most commentators, including Nimmer, think *Rano* is wrongly decided. See 3 MELVILLE B. NIMMER & DAVID NIMMER, NIMMER ON COPYRIGHT § 11.01[B] at 11-4–11-9 (2005) and § 10.10[F] at 10-98 (1998) ("Where an assignment or license does not expressly prescribe the period or term of its duration, it will generally be construed (in the absence of evidence of a contrary intent) to be effective for the duration of the then existing copyright term of the work"). *Accord P.C. Films Corp. v. MGM/VA Home Videos, Inc.*, 138 F.3d 453 (2d Cir. 1998); 2 HOWARD ABRAMS, THE LAW OF COPYRIGHT § 13.15 at 13-59 n.28 (2004).

After the 35-year period expires, the license is terminable at will by the author for a period of five years. 17 U.S.C. § 203(3). The licensor must give the licensee, however, advance written notice of at least two but not more than 10 years before such termination. 17 U.S.C. § 203(a)(4)(A). Material breach of the license will also give rise to a right of rescission, which allows the nonbreaching party to terminate the license. *Costello Publishing Co. v. Potell,* 670 F.2d 1035 (D.C. Cir. 1981); 3 MELVILLE B. NIMMER & DAVID NIMMER, NIMMER ON COPYRIGHT § 10.15[A] at 10-118–10-120 (2005). If the license is not terminated, it will continue in effect for the remaining term of the copyright, which protects the software being licensed (17 U.S.C. § 203(b)(6)). Assuming it is an anonymous work or work made for hire, the term of the copyright will be either 95 years from the date of the software's first publication or 120 years from the date of the software's creation, whichever expires first. 17 U.S.C. § 302(c). Under § 2-309 of the Uniform Commercial Code (UCC), however, a contract (license) without a fixed term is valid for a reasonable time and unless otherwise agreed is terminable at will.[1]

The licensor should carefully consider the use of terms such as "perpetual" and "irrevocable" in the license grant as the licensor will likely want to terminate the license upon the breach of the license terms or breach of the agreement by the licensee. By doing so the licensor will avoid any dispute over the interpretation of these terms and whether these terms will prevail over any implied right to terminate the agreement upon the licensee's breach. To negate such arguments, the licensor should preface the license grant with the phrase "Subject to the terms of this Agreement, Licensor grants Licensee . . ." This phrase clarifies any potential ambiguity as to the ability of the licensor to terminate the license. To ensure its ability to terminate the license, the licensor should also include a definitive statement that any license grant may be terminated in the event of the licensee's breach of the terms of the license or contract.

3. *Use (§ 3.1)*

(a) General

Most licensors place restrictions on the licensee as to how the licensed software may be used. Except in the case of open-source software, the principal reason is financial,

1. See Chapter 11.A for a discussion of the applicability of the UCC to software licensing.

causing most restrictions to be strictly an element of price. A licensor may have other, nonfinancial business motives; it may want to restrict the license agreement in the event the licensee is a competitor or the licensor is concerned that the licensee may later be acquired by another company.

To avoid problems of interpretation, the parties should always define "use." See, e.g., § 1.17. Parties who fail to define "use" often later have different interpretations of what it means to "use" the software. *See, e.g., S&H Computer Systems, Inc. v. SAS Institute, Inc.,* 568 F. Supp. 416, 421 (D. Tenn. 1983) (the meaning of "use" as contemplated by the computer industry, (i.e., execute a program) differs from its "normal meaning"); *Kennedy v. National Juvenile Detention Association,* 187 F.3d 690, 694–95 (7th Cir. 1999) ("use" as used in applicable consulting agreement included the right to creative derivative works; dissent: "use" as used in applicable consulting agreement was ambiguous, as the license agreement utilized statutory language of the Copyright Act, i.e., right to reproduce and publish).

By tracking the statutory language of the Copyright Act in defining "use," the licensor will likely avoid the types of disputes set forth in *S&H Computer Systems* and *Kennedy.* The following definition when used with the grant of an object code license (with the right to use source in the event of a triggering event) protects the licensor's interest by clearly delineating the licensee's rights:

> "Use" shall mean the ability to run, execute display, duplicate, and distribute internally the Licensed Software in its Object Code form. In the event that the Source Code for the Licensed Software is released from escrow, then "Use" shall also mean the right to modify and create derivatives of the Source Code.

For a web-based application, the definition might be amended as follows:

> "'Use' shall mean the ability to access, run, execute, and display the Remote Software."

In drafting the language of the license grant, the licensor and licensee should undertake a three-step process to ensure such language meets their needs. First, the parties should consider the fundamental rights a copyright owner is granted: (1) to reproduce the copyrighted work, (2) to prepare derivative works, and (3) to distribute copies of the derivative work. 17 U.S.C. § 106; *Kennedy,* 187 F.3d at 694. Second, they should consider whether there are any rights that are unique to the system such as "access" for a website. Finally, they should consider whether they need to include any industry-specific language such as the right to "create with," in the case with tools.

A corresponding license grant is as follows:

> Licensor grants to Licensee a transferable, nonexclusive right to Use the Licensed Software during the Term and any renewal period.

The licensor should ensure that license restrictions are part of the license grant rather than separate covenants in the agreement. While the breach of a separate covenant is still a breach of contract, such a breach will not constitute a violation of the scope of the license sufficient to support injunctive relief for copyright infringement. *Sun Microsystems, Inc. v. Microsoft Corp.,* 81 F. Supp.2d 1026, 1031 (N.D. Cal. 2001).

To avoid disputes over the scope of use, the licensee should consider future potential changes in its business requirements or those of its customer, as well as the need for third party consultants and the like, for access to the software. *See, e.g., SMC Promotions, Inc. v. SMC Promotions, et al.*, 355 F. Supp. 1127, 1132 (C.D. Cal. 2005) (limited license allowing wholesaler's retail customers to download copyrighted product images was not broad enough to encompass wholesaler's practice of engaging a third party vendor to download images). The licensee should also establish an audit mechanism to track the terms and limitations of the license agreement to ensure the licensee's compliance with the license terms.

(b) Internal Use

Many license grants state that the licensed software may be used for the licensee's "internal business purposes only." The primary objective of this wording is to limit the licensee's use of the licensed software to the licensee's specific business needs and to prevent the licensee from using the software to operate a service bureau or data processing center or from using the software in outsourcing. It is prudent to state this prohibition clearly in the license agreement to avoid a subsequent dispute over the interpretation of the license grant.

Although many licenses utilize the concept of "internal use," many practitioners believe this term by its nature is inherently ambiguous as almost all software is used to directly or indirectly sell the products or services of the licensee. This issue can be resolved by specifically stating the limits on the software's use (e.g., prohibiting the software's use in a service bureau) instead of making a general, amorphous statement regarding the software's use for the licensee's "internal use." Some licensors utilize broader, less specific language to achieve the same result by seeking to contractually prohibit third parties from "accessing the software's functionality" as a means to prevent outsourcing or the use of the software in a service bureau. If the licensee contemplates using third parties or contractors to operate or maintain the software, it should ensure that the license grant affirmatively gives it the right to do so. Regardless of the approach taken, the parties should seek to clearly define how the software may be used or seek other wording to codify this concept.

For a greater discussion of the issues involved, see Marenberg & Brown, *"Scope of Use" Restrictions in Software Licenses*, 10 COMPUTER LAW. 1 (Dec. 1993).

(c) Nonexclusive/Exclusive Use

The term "nonexclusive" is necessary to indicate that the licensor reserves the right to license the same software to other licensees. This is important as some licensees request exclusive use of the licensed software if they believe the software provides them with a competitive advantage. This is especially likely if the licensee paid for the development of the software or educated the licensor about the need for such software in a particular industry. This exclusivity may be for a set period of time or, in the case of distribution rights, for a specific geographic location.

A nonexclusive license can be granted orally or can be implied from the conduct of the parties. *Korman v. HBC Florida, Inc.*, 182 F.3d 1291 (11th Cir. 1999); *Effects Assoc. Inc. v. Cohen*, 908 F.2d 555, 558 (9th Cir. 1990) (nonexclusive copyright licenses do not need to be in writing). An implied license may be created where the author of a work created at the request of a third party provides the work to such party knowing it intends to copy and distribute it. *See MacLean Assoc. v. Wm. M. Mercer-Meidinger-Hansen,* 952 F.2d 769, 779 (3d Cir. 1991) citing *Effects Assoc. Inc. v. Cohen,* 908 F.2d 555, 558–59 (9th Cir. 1990).

A nonexclusive licensee lacks the ability to sue or be joined in a suit. *Ortho Pharmaceutical Corp. v. Genetics Institute, Inc. and Amgen, Inc.*, 52 F.3d 1026 (Fed. Cir.), *cert. denied,* 516 U.S. 907 (1995) (citing *Overman Cushion Tire Co. v. Goodyear Tire and Rubber Co.,* 59 F.2d 998, *cert. denied,* 287 U.S. 651 (1932) (nonexclusive licensee has no right to sue or be joined in a suit)); and *Philadelphia Brief Case Co. v. Specialty Leather Products Co., Inc.,* 145 F. Supp. 425, 429–30 (D.N.J. 1956) (contract clause cannot give right to sue where licensee would otherwise have no such right). Furthermore, the licensor cannot grant such a right where one does not already exist.

Subject to the terms and conditions of the particular license, a copyright owner who grants a licensee a nonexclusive license to use the copyrighted material generally may not sue for copyright infringement and is limited to bringing a claim for breach of contract. *Sun Microsystems, Inc. v. Microsoft Corporation,* 188 F.3d 1115, 1121 (9th Cir. 1999). If the license is limited in scope and the licensor exceeds the scope, a claim of copyright infringement may be brought. *S.O.S., Inc. v. Payday, Inc.,* 886 F.2d 1081, 1087 (9th Cir. 1989).

On occasion a licensor may grant an exclusive license. The exclusivity may go to a geographic region, a specific industry, a set time period, or the use of the entire product itself. Exclusive licenses are uncommon in that they prevent the licensor from re-licensing the software and receiving additional license fees to the extent of the exclusivity. Under the Copyright Act, exclusive licenses must be in writing. 17 U.S.C. §§ 101, 204(a); *MacLean Assoc. v. Wm. M. Mercer-Meidinger-Hansen,* 952 F.2d 769, 778 (3d Cir. 1991). *See generally I.A.E., Inc. v. Sharer,* 74 F.3d 768 (7th Cir. 1996) (a nonexclusive copyright license is granted when (1) the licensee requests creation of a work, (2) the creator/licensor delivers the work to the licensee, and (3) the licensor intends the licensee to copy and distribute the work); *Korman v. HBC Florida, Inc.,* 182 F.3d 1291, 1293 (11th Cir. 1999). Also note that an oral exclusive license creates an implied nonexclusive license. 17 U.S.C. § 204(a); *Gracen v. Bradford Exchange,* 698 F.2d 300, 303 (7th Cir. 1983). Before granting an exclusive license, a licensor must consider whether it needs to reserve any rights. For example, if an exclusive license to distribute is being granted for a particular jurisdiction, a licensor that also distributes via the Internet should consider whether Internet sales should be reserved from the exclusive license.

(d) Scope of Use

Other common limitations include limiting use of the software to a particular central processing unit (CPU), to one class or brand of computer only, to a specific geographic site (§§ 8.B, 8.C), to a specific number of seats or concurrent users, or to a specific time period. This allows the licensor to charge the licensee a fee if the licensee expands or changes its use of the software. *See Equinox Software Sys., Inc. v. Airgas, Inc.,* 1996 WL 278841 (E.D. Pa. May 23, 1996) (soft copies made in violation of license restricting use on a particular CPU constituted copyright infringement); *Apple, Inc. v. Psystar Corp.*, 673 F. Supp.2d 931 (N.D. Cal. 2009) (use of software on computers not manufactured by copyright owner constituted copyright infringement). CPU licenses are increasingly less common as software is licensed to an entity/licensor, not a particular machine. Many manufacturers are moving to subscription licensing because it provides for an annual license fee for the life of the software. Some licensees prefer this model, even though they may pay more in the long run, because it reduces the up-front cost associated with licensing the software. Further, a licensee should carefully consider any limitation on the license it receives. It must contemplate future needs to avoid limiting itself in the future as a court will likely strictly enforce any agreed to license terms. *See, e.g., McRoberts Software, Inc. v. Media 100, Inc.*, 329 F.3d 557 (7th Cir. 2003) (license limited licensee's use of copyrighted software to Macintosh software and licensee exceeded the scope of license by distributing of source code in Windows hardware).

A smart licensee will seek to ensure the license provides a reasonable degree of flexibility as the licensee's needs change. It should seek to anticipate its potential needs and bargain for them at the time the license is entered into. Once the license is executed, the licensee's bargaining power often dissipates. For a discussion of site licenses, see *Software Site Licensing Overview*, 229 COM. L. ADV. 1 (Jan. 2007).

In *Wall Data, Inc. v. Los Angeles County Sheriff's Dept.*, 447 F.3d 769 (9th Cir. 2006), the Ninth Circuit Court of Appeals found that a licensee who purchased 3,663 licenses but installed the software on 6,007 computers was in breach of the license even though it had configured its computers to limit the total number of users that could access the software to the number of licenses the licensee had purchased. In essence, the court held that the mere presence of a software copy on a computer is an infringement even though the software is not accessible to a user.

The decision emphasizes the importance of clearly defining "use" and "seats." In entering into a license, the licensee should clearly understand whether the number of purchased licenses limits the number of users who can access the software concurrently at the same time or the number of users authorized to access the system during the license term.

The *Wall Data* case was also interesting because the court excluded evidence that the licensee's purchase agreement with the software reseller may have allowed such use because the copyright owner was unaware of the reseller's license terms with the licensee. *Id.* at 782–83. This decision creates significant concern for any company that purchases its software through a reseller. For a more detailed discussion, see *Sheriffs' Over-Installation of Licensed Software Was Copyright Infringement, Despite Limited Access or Use of Software*, 23 COMPUTER & INTERNET LAW. 24 (Aug. 2006). Similarly, in *Thoroughbred Software, Int'l v. Dice Corp., et al*, the court found a software distributor liable for all unpaid license fees for all unauthorized copies made even though some copies were not accessible to or used by its customers. 488 F.3d 352 (6th Cir. 2007).

One exception is the licensee's right to make one backup or archival copy or transfer the software to an alternative backup site for a limited period of time (60–90 days) in the case of a catastrophic failure. (§ 20). Some licensors also allow the backup or archival copy to be used at a remote source for disaster recovery and disaster recovery training. Often licensors seek to limit the licensee to a single backup copy for archival purposes. Section 117 of the Copyright Act, which applies only to copy owners (and not licensees), grants the purchaser of a copy of software the right to make archival copies and adapt the software to operate on its computer. This position may be viewed as overly pro-licensor, which may create unnecessary friction with the potential licensee. A more balanced approach takes into account the legitimate needs of the licensee without negatively impacting pricing or the licensor's need for intellectual property protection—ensuring the greater likelihood of entering into an agreement. Note, however, that if the licensee is not a purchaser of the software, such copying may constitute copyright infringement. *See DSC Communications Corp. v. DGI Technologies, Inc.*, 81 F.3d 597 (5th Cir. 1996) (downloading software to hard disk by licensee for compatibility modifications was infringement where licensee had not purchased software).

Some licensors base their license fee on the application involved while other licensors restrict the number of users who can access their software at any one time. This type of restriction is common in a client-server, network environment.

In the event of a dispute regarding a permitted use, the licensor bears the burden of proof that the licensee exceeded the scope of the license agreement. *Netbula, LLC v. Bindview Development Corp.*, 516 F. Supp.2d 1137 (N.D. Cal. 2007).

For a discussion on limiting potential claims for the misuse of a licensor's software, see Hershkowitz & Carroll, *10 Simple Steps to Ensure Software Licensing Compliance*, 37 Law. Brief 13 (No. 16, 2007).

(e) Creation of Derivative Works and the Prohibition of Reverse Engineering (§ 3.4)

(i) General

"Disassembly," "decompilation," and "translation" of software requires making copies of the software program itself and creating "derivative works" in the process based upon the original software. Section 101 of the Copyright Act defines a "derivative work" as:

> a work based upon one or more preexisting works, such as a translation, musical arrangement, dramatization, fictionalization, motion picture version, sound recording, art reproduction, abridgment, condensation, or any other form in which a work may be recast, transformed, or adapted. A work consisting of editorial revisions, annotations, elaborations, or other modifications, which, as a whole, represent an original work of authorship, is a "derivative work".

17 U.S.C. § 101.

Section 106(2) of the Copyright Act prohibits the creation of derivative works without the copyright owner's permission. An author of a derivative work cannot obtain a copyright on any such work if it lacked the permission of the copyright owner to make a derivative work. *Gracen v. Bradford Exchange*, 698 F.2d 300, 303 (7th Cir. 1983); *CMAX/Cleveland, Inc. v. UCR, Inc.*, 804 F. Supp. 337 (M.D. Ga. 1992).

(ii) Derivative Works

In certain situations, the alteration of an original work may create a copyrightable derivative work. To receive copyright protection, a work must be sufficiently original, requiring more than a "modicum of originality." *Waldman Pub. Corp. v. Landoll, Inc.*, 43 F.3d 775, 782 (2d Cir. 1994); *Simon v. Birraporetti's Restaurants, Inc.*, 720 F. Supp. 85 (S. D. Tex. 1989). A derivative work must be substantially different from the underlying work to be copyrightable, *Gracen v. Bradford Exchange*, 698 F.2d 300 (7th Cir. 1983), but yet must be substantially copied from [based on the expression of] prior work. *Apple Computer, Inc. v. Microsoft Corp.*, 759 F. Supp. 1444 (N. D. Cal. 1991), on reconsideration, 779 F. Supp. 133, *aff'd*, 35 F.3d 1435 (9th Cir. 1994); *Litchfield v. Spielberg*, 736 F.2d 1352 (9th Cir.), *cert. denied*, 470 U.S. 1052 (1984). Although the derivative work refers to the entire work, not just the modifications, the copyright in a derivative work applies only to the new work contributed by the author and not to the preexisting material. The new copyright does not imply any exclusive rights in the preexisting copyright. 17 U.S.C. § 103(b); *Moore Pub., Inc. v. Big Sky Marketing, Inc.*, 756 F. Supp. 1371 (D. Idaho 1990). Further, if a derivative work is created using preexisting copyrighted material, copyright protection will not extend to any part of the work in which such preexisting copyrighted material has been used unlawfully. 17 U.S.C. § 103(a).

The right to claim a copyright on a noninfringing, derivative work arises by operation of law, not by the granting of such right by the owner of the original work. Melville B. Nimmer & David Nimmer, Nimmer on Copyright, § 3.06 n.14 (2005). Copyright law does allow, however, the copyright owner of the original work to establish restrictions on preparing any derivative works. *Stewart v. Abend*, 495 U.S. 207, 223 (1990) (It is an "axiomatic copyright principle that a person may exploit only such copyrighted literary material as he either owns or is licensed to use"). Any use of copyrighted material in a derivative work that exceeds the scope of the license constitutes an infringement. *NLFC, Inc. v. Devcom Mid-America, Inc.*, 45 F.3d 235 n.5 (7th Cir. 1995).

Thus, a licensor may contractually require a licensee to assign to the licensor copyright ownership in a derivative work. Any licensee that claims ownership in contravention of a contractual prohibition (i.e., a license) may infringe on the original work. Interestingly, it is not an infringement of copyright to falsely claim ownership of copyright in a derivative work. It may not even be a violation of Lanham Act § 43(a) since copyright ownership does not mean the owner is the source or author of a work. It could be a violation of a license if the license contains a specific restriction regarding attribution.

A license does not always need to explicitly state that a copyright in a derivative work will be the property of the owner of the original work, and the license does not have to be in writing. *Gracen v. Bradford Exchange*, 698 F.2d 300, 303 (7th Cir. 1983); see also 1 Melville B. Nimmer & David Nimmer, Nimmer on Copyright § 3.06 at 3-34 23 n.14 (Perm. Ed. 2000) ("a license may contractually preclude the licensee from obtaining a copyright in a licensed derivative work"). This position is similar to the laws governing a work made for hire that allow an employer to contractually require an independent contractor who is the author of a work to execute an assignment transferring ownership of the work to the employer. See Chapter 5.A.(a).

If a licensor is considering granting a licensee the right to modify and adapt the software, it should do so solely under the provisions of Section 117 of the Copyright Act ("as an essential step in the utilization of the computer program"). The licensor must carefully consider whether the sum of any such modifications will rise to the level of a derivative work. In an abundance of caution, licensors should seek to obtain the copyright for all such modifications and adaptations even if they do not constitute a derivative work. Given that the copyright for a derivative work vests in the author immediately upon the creation of a work, the licensor should contractually require that the author assign the copyright in any derivative it creates to the licensor. See *S.O.S., Inc. v. Payday, Inc.*, 866 F.2d 1081, 1085 (9th Cir. 1989) ("Copyright protection subsists from the moment the work is 'fixed in a tangible medium of expression'"). This will ensure the sanctity of the licensor's software and avoid any disputes regarding ownership if its licensees were to later claim ownership of different portions of the licensor's software.

Conversely, at least one court, without deciding the ownership issue, has rejected the contention that a licensee may not obtain an enforceable copyright on a derivative work unless there was an express authorization in the governing license agreement. *Liu v. Price Waterhouse LLP,* 1999 WL 47025 (N.D. Ill. Jan. 25, 1999).

Further, "a derivative work prepared under authority of the grant [to prepare a derivative work] before its termination may continue to be utilized under the terms of the grant after its termination." 17 U.S.C. § 203(b). Thus, termination only serves to prohibit the licensee from creating future derivative works based on the original work and not on creating additional derivative works based on a derivative work made lawfully during the license agreement. 17 U.S.C. § 203(c)(6)(A) recognizes this right as it grants the copyright owner of the derivative work all the rights of a copyright owner. To avoid problems arising from the creation of derivative works, the licensor should contractually restrict the licensee from utilizing any derivative works in any manner that may be competitive with the licensee.

(iii) Reverse Engineering

Most licensors are very concerned with the licensee reverse engineering the object code provided to the licensee under its license. To alleviate this concern, most licensors include a clause in their licenses stating that the licensee is prohibited from reverse engineering, decompiling, or recompiling the licensed software. In *Bowers v. Baystate Technologies, Inc.,* 320 F.3d 1317 (Fed. Cir. 2003) the court upheld the validity of a contractual clause prohibiting reverse engineering and found that the Copyright Act does not narrow or preempt any such contractual provisions. This decision is consistent with the findings of many other circuits. *Wrench LLC v. Taco Bell Corp.,* 256 F.3d 446, 457 (6th Cir. 2001) (state law contract claim not preempted by federal copyright law); *National Car Rental Sys., Inc. v. Computer Assocs. International, Inc.,* 991 F.2d 426, 433 (8th Cir. 1993); *Taquino v. Teledyne Monarch Rubber,* 893 F.2d 1488, 1501 (5th Cir. 1990), but see *Lipscher v. LRP Publications, Inc.,* 266 F.3d 1305, 1312 (11th Cir. 2001) ("Copyright Act preempts only those state law rights that may be abridged by an act which, in and of itself, would infringe one of the exclusive rights provided by federal copyright law." *Foley v. Luster,* 249 F.3d 1281, 1285 (11th Cir. 2001) (quoting *Computer Assoc. Int'l, Inc. v. Altai, Inc.,* 982 F.2d 693, 716 (2d Cir. 1992)). The right plaintiff "is attempting to protect in its acquisition misconduct claims are copyright rights" and thus preempted.)

The *Bowers* court specifically stated that its opinion "left untouched" its decision in *Atari Games Corp. v. Nintendo of America, Inc.*, 975 F.2d 832 (Fed. Cir. 1992), and those "expressly defined circumstances in which infringement is not copyright infringement under 17 U.S.C. § 1201(f) (section of the Digital Millennium Copyright Act) and 17 U.S.C. § 906." *Id.* at 1325. In *Davidson R. Associates v. Jung,* 422 F.3d 630, 639 (8th Cir. 2005), the Eight Circuit recognized the *Bowers* holding that a party can waive its right to reverse engineer to obtain interoperability through the fair use exception.

Surprisingly, one court has held that the ability to create derivative works may be inferred from the language of the license grant. *Kennedy v. National Juvenile Detention Ass'n.,* 197 F.3d 690 (7th Cir. 1999) (Language permitting licensee to "reproduce, publish and use" any copyright material infers the right to create derivative works).

The Digital Millennium Copyright Act (DMCA), while providing limited exceptions, prohibits reverse engineering. 17 U.S.C. § 1201(a)(1)(A) (prohibiting circumvention of "a technological measure that effectively controls access to a [copyrighted] work.") The DMCA provides three limited exceptions:

1. "[F]or the sole purpose of . . . interoperability" of an independently created computer program. 17 U.S.C. § 1201 (f) (1);
2. To develop and employ a technological means to enable interoperability, 17 U.S.C. § 1201 (f) (2); and
3. To provide information or means for interoperability to others, 17 U.S.C. § 1201 (f) (3).

For an overview of the DMCA, see Lee, *Reverse Engineering Under the DMCA: Recognizing a "Fair Access" Defense,* 20 COMPUTER LAW ASSOC. BULL. 135 (No. 4, 2005); Davidson & Axtell, *Reverse Engineering: The DMCA and the Reverse Engineering of Suspected Infringing Products,* 23 COMPUTER & INTERNET LAW. 1 (Feb. 2006). For a more detailed discussion of the DMCA, see Chapter 5.L.3.

Any prohibition on reverse engineering is not absolute, however, as several courts have ruled that a licensee who makes an intermediate copy of software to the extent necessary to determine how such software works—in order to interface the licensee's or another party's proprietary software to the licensor's software—may fall under the "Fair Use" doctrine of the Copyright Act. *See Sega Enterprises, Ltd. v. Accolade, Inc.*, 977 F.2d 1510 (9th Cir. 1992); *Atari Games Corp. v. Nintendo of America, Inc.,* 975 F.2d 832 (Fed. Cir. 1992). In *Sony Computer Entertainment v. Connectix Corp.,* 203 F.3d 596 (9th Cir. 2000), *cert denied,* 531 U.S. 871 (2000), the court held that the fair use doctrine allows public access to the functional elements and ideas contained in copyright software. If reverse engineering is the only method to access the ideas and functional elements embedded in the software and there is a legitimate reason for such access, reverse engineering/disassembly will constitute fair use of the copyrighted work. *Sega Enterprises Ltd. v. Accolade, Inc.,* 977 F.2d 1510,

1527–28 (9th Cir. 1992) (amended opinion). Thus, in certain situations the fair use doctrine allows the reverse engineering of software. However, any licensee planning to rely upon the fair use doctrine should understand that it is an affirmative defense to a claim of copyright infringement. *Wall Data, Inc. v. Los Angeles County Sheriff's Dept.,* 447 F.3d 769, 776 (9th Cir., 2006). Thus, the burden will be on the defendant to prove that the use was fair.

Additionally, the standard to be met for "fair use" is somewhat subjective. In determining whether a particular use is fair use, courts consider factors including the following: (1) the purpose and character of the use, including whether such use is of a commercial nature or is for nonprofit educational purposes; (2) the nature of the copyrighted work; (3) the amount and substantiality of the portion used in relation to the copyrighted work as a whole; and (4) the effect of the use upon the potential market for or value of the copyrighted work. *Madison River Management Co. v. Business Management Software Corp.,* 387 F. Supp.2d 521, 536 (M.D.N.C. 2005). Thus a licensee cannot be certain in advance that its actions will constitute a fair use. *Id.* (declining to find a fair use when the defendant copied software to "run reports," which took advantage of copyrighted data structure rather than to discover unprotected raw data).

Another limit on reverse engineering prohibitions is that a licensee may modify a software program in order to make the program operate more efficiently for the licensee's internal use, including creating a derivative work. *Aymes v. Bonelli,* 47 F.3d 23 (2d Cir. 1995).

The cases cited above are not cases involving breach of a license. In general, in a negotiated contract a licensee can contractually bind itself not to undertake acts of infringement that others would be able to perform under the fair use doctrine. It is still up in the air whether waivers of fair use rights in click-wrap and shrink-wrap agreements for mass-market software would be enforceable. See *Bowers v. Baystate Technologies, Inc.,* 320 F.3d 1317, 1323 (Fed. Cir.), *cert. denied,* 539 U.S. 928 (2003). In *Bowers,* the Federal Circuit, over a strong dissent, held that a click-wrap waiver of the right to reverse engineer mass-market software (one of the rights generally considered to fall within fair use) was enforceable, even though the agreement was a classic contract of adhesion.

Similarly, European Community (EC) Directive 91/250 allows licensees to reverse engineer software to the extent necessary to create interfaces to the licensor's software. For a more detailed discussion of E.C. Directive 91/250, see Chapter 12.F.1.

The courts have justified these decisions under the "Fair Use" doctrine of copyright law. Under the fair use doctrine, use of a copyrighted work, including use by reproduction of copies for purposes such as criticism, comment, teaching, scholarship, or research, is not an infringement of the owner's copyright. 17 U.S.C. § 107. Factors to be used in determining fair use include the purpose and character of the use, the nature of the copyrighted work, whether the entity possessed an authorized copy of the software, the amount and substantiality of the portion used in relation to the whole, whether the copying was necessary to gain access to the functional elements of the software, whether the reproduction exceeded what was necessary to understand the protected elements, and the effect of the use upon the potential market for or value of the copyrighted work. *Id.* In most situations, verbatim copying of software made for commercial purposes is not fair use. *See, e.g., Compaq Computer Corp. v. Procom Tech., Inc.*, 908 F. Supp. 1409, 1419–21 (S.D. Tex. 1995); *Allen-Myland, Inc. v. Int'l Bus. Machs. Corp.*, 746 F. Supp. 520, 533–35 (E.D. Pa. 1990). *See also, Princeton Univ. Press v. Mich. Document Servs.*, 99 F.3d 1381, 1385–92 (6th Cir. 1996) (verbatim copying of college "coursepacks" was not fair use). For a general discussion, see Rowles, *Reverse Engineering—Can Software Owners License Against It?*, E-Com. Advisor, July 2001.

At the same time, however, an entity will usually not be allowed to reverse engineer software for the purpose of directly competing with the owners of the software. *See Triad Systems Corp. v. Southeastern Express Co.*, 64 F.3d 1330 (9th Cir. 1995), *cert. denied*, 516 U.S. 1145 (1996); *MAI Systems Corp. v. Peak Computer, Inc.*, 991 F.2d 511 (9th Cir. 1993), *cert. denied*, 510 U.S. 1033 (1994). *Triad* did not, however, overrule *Sega*. Reverse engineering remains a fair use even where the defendant displaces sales by the plaintiff, as long as the use is transformative. *See Sony Computer Entertainment v. Connectix Corp.*, 203 F.3d 596 (9th Cir. 2000), *cert denied*, 531 U.S. 871 (2000) distinguishing *Triad*.

Although a *de minimis* defense exists under copyright law, there is not a set standard that allows small portions of computer code to be copied. *See Sandoval v. New Line Cinema Corp.*, 147 F.3d 215 (2d. Cir 1998) quoting *Ringgold v. Black Ent'ment Television, Inc.*, 126 F.3d 70, 74 (2d Cir. 1997) (*de minimis* defense requires that "the copying of the protected material is so trivial 'as to fall below' the quantitative threshold of substantial similarity."); *See also Dun & Bradstreet Software Services, Inc. v. Grace Consulting, Inc.*, 307 F.3d. 197 (3d Cir. 2002) (*de minimis* defense may not be invoked; 27 out of 525,000 lines of code not relevant where qualitative value of copied material is material); *Veritas Operating Corp., v. Microsoft Corp.*, 2008 WL 474248 (W.D. Wa. Feb. 4, 2008) (copying 54 lines of code out of 160,000 lines (0.03%) may constitute copyright infringement); *Marketing Technology Solutions, Inc. v. Medizine LLC.*, 2010 WL 2034404 (S.D.N.Y. May 18, 2010) (rejecting *de minimis* defense where 437 lines of code out of 1,187,363 lines of code in the program were allegedly similar). In general, courts look to the quantitative and qualitative significance of the copied materials in comparison to the completed work. *Dun & Bradstreet Software Servs., Inc. v. Grace Consulting, Inc.*, 307 F.3d 197, 208 (3d Cir 2002) ("A *de minimis* defense does not apply where the qualitative value of the copying is material."); *LeHererse v. World Institute of Scientology Enterprises, Int'l.*, 533 F.3d. 1287 (11th Cir. 2008). See also, 17 U.S.C. § 106 (11). See Chapter 5.L for a more in-depth discussion of the creation of copies of software by independent service organizations (ISOs).

It is important to note that a copyright does not provide the copyright holder rights similar to those held by patent owners. A copyright grants the holder the exclusive right to duplicate the copyrighted material and make derivative works. 17 U.S.C. § 106(1), (2); *CMAX/Cleveland, Inc. v. UCR, Inc.*, 804 F. Supp. 337 (M.D. Ga. 1992). A patent grants the holder the right to prevent others from using, making, or selling the patented subject matter. 35 U.S.C. § 154 (1994). A copyright does not protect against another entity creating similar or even identical software independent from the copyrighted work. For example, it does not protect against the creation of similar screen displays, icons, the method of operation of the software, or the key commands. *See, e.g., Lotus Development Corporation v. Borland International, Inc.*, 49 F.3d 807, 815–18 (1st Cir. 1995), *aff'd per curiam,* 516 U.S. 233 (1996) (menu-command hierarchy was an uncopyrightable method of operation) and *Engineering Dynamics, Inc. v. Structural Software, Inc.*, 26 F.3d 1335, 1342–43 (5th Cir. 1994) (user interface, input formats, and output reports are protectable), *but see Whelen v. Jaslow,* 797 F.2d 1222 (3d Cir. 1986) (concept of program's content not copyrightable but all functions used for implementing the program are protectable).

For a general discussion see, Note, *Locked Out: The Hazards of Reverse Engineering,* 21 J. COMPUTER & INFO. LAW 591 (2003).

(iv) Copyright Protections

Copyrights arise as a matter of law without registration. An author need not affirmatively apply for federal copyright protection. However, a U.S. copyright holder must register the work before bringing an infringement action. 17 U.S.C. § 411(a). Further, owners of registered copyrights who prevail in litigation may receive an award of lawyer's fees and, at their election, statutory damages if the infringement occurs after registration or if the copyrights are registered within three months of publication. 17 U.S.C. § 412. Registering a work within five years of first publication constitutes prima facie evidence of the validity of the copyright and the facts stated in the certificate. 17 U.S.C. § 410 (c) (1994).

Although actual copying is proven in most cases, a copyright holder does not have to affirmatively prove actual copying. Evidence of copying can be inferred by establishing the defendant's access to the program and substantial similarities to the protectable expressions. *Bateman v. Mnemonics, Inc.*, 79 F.3d 1532, 1541 (11th Cir. 1996).

For a general discussion, see Zimmerman, *Baystate: Technical Interfaces Not Copyrightable—On to the First Circuit,* 14 COMPUTER LAW. 9 (April 1997).

4. Geographic Restrictions (§ 3.1)

Most licensors seek to limit the use of the licensed software to a specific country or site; for example, the United States or "Licensee's Wilmington, Delaware site." Limiting location may allow the licensor to charge an additional license fee for each additional foreign affiliate or user not at the authorized site. Alternatively, geographic limitations allow the licensor to grant exclusive rights in a particular or geographic area, potentially segmenting its markets. *See, e.g., Elliott Co. v. Legonda Mfg. Co.*, 205 F. 152 (W.D. Pa. 1913) (license to sell to others for "use" in United States held to limit defendant sales for "use" in United States.)

The failure to limit the use of the licensed software to a particular country may also give rise to a number of export issues. For example, licensing software to a Mexican company that has a subsidiary or affiliate in Cuba would violate the Trading with the Enemy Act if such software were used in Cuba. Furthermore, the use of such software outside of the United States may be governed by the laws of a foreign jurisdiction with which the licensor is unfamiliar and/or which does not grant the same protections to the licensor as the laws of the United States. To protect the licensor's interests, the licensor should insist on receiving a written assurance from the licensee that the licensee will not violate the export laws.

Limitation of geographic scope is closely tied to intellectual property rights indemnification. The intellectual property rights indemnification provision in the license agreement is another important concern. As discussed in Section B.3, below, a domestic licensor should limit the licensor's indemnification to intellectual property infringement of a U.S. intellectual property right and those of the country in which the licensed software will be used. Failure to include a geographic restriction as to the use of the software may expand the scope of indemnification granted by the licensor. If a license is worldwide, the licensor should consider limiting its potential risk by indemnifying the licensee for infringement arising in countries that are signatories to the Berne Convention.

5. Object Code Licenses and Source Code Licenses (§ 3.1)

"Object code" is the binary, machine-readable version of the software. Object code allows the licensee to operate the software but does not enable the licensee to make enhancements or modifications to the software or create derivative works. "Source code" is the human-readable statement in a computer language that, when processed by a compiler, assembler, or interpreter, becomes executable by a computer. Source code allows the licensee to maintain the software, to make modifications and enhancements to the software, and to create derivative works.

If a licensee purchases a source code license it *theoretically* does not need further assistance from the licensor as the licensee itself has the ability to maintain, as well as to modify and enhance the software, or create derivative works from it. The licensing of source code also creates a significant risk of misappropriation and piracy. With the source code, a licensee can become a competitor or intentionally or unintentionally make the source code available to a competitor. Further, routinely granting source code licenses may make it more difficult to enforce trade secret protection on the source code. Consequently, most licensors refuse to sell source code licenses. Those who do sell source code licenses usually charge a significant premium for a source code license over the cost of an object code license.

In granting a source code license, the licensor should restrict the licensee from creating derivative works, enhancements, or modifications. If the licensee obtains the right to do so, it should be prohibited from licensing any such derivative works, enhancements, or modifications. It is important to note that derivative works will generally be owned by the copyright owner unless conveyed. 17 U.S.C. §§ 201(d)(2) and 103(a). The licensor should restrict use of the source code to one physical location and limit access to the source code to the licensee's employees and contractors who have a need for access. The licensee should also be restricted from making additional copies of the source code. Maintaining the confidentiality of the source code is the licensor's most important concern, and the licensor should place strict limitations on the licensee to protect its confidentiality. Finally, the standard limitations on use of the software discussed in Section A.3, above, should be imposed on the licensee.

6. *Irrevocable/Nonterminable Licenses (§ 3.1)*

Licensees often want the terms "irrevocable" or "nonterminable" included in the license grant to ensure that, after they accept the software and pay for the license, the licensor has no basis to revoke the license. The terms "irrevocable" and "nonterminable" imply permanency, however, and as such they cause concern for licensors. Licensors are concerned that the licensee may later violate the terms of the license and that the licensor will lack the ability to terminate the license. This concern is alleviated by prefacing the license grant with the phrase "*Subject to the provisions of this Agreement. . .*" This wording conditions any permanency on the licensee meeting the terms of the license, thus eliminating the licensor's concerns.

In *Nano-Proprietary, Inc. v. Cenn., Inc.*, 537 F.2d 394 (5th Cir. 2008), the Fifth Circuit Court of Appeals held that a court must give effect to the plain meaning of the terms, "fully paid-up," "irrevocable" and "perpetual" and that the patent license granted in this case was nonterminable even in the event of the licensee's material breach. Further, such language may limit the licensor from recovering damages for a breach of the license. *Id* at 400.

Even though the license may unequivocally grant the licensee an "irrevocable" license without any limiting language, the license may be terminable at will by the author after 35 years for a period of five years. 17 U.S.C. § 203(3). See Section A.2, above, for a more detailed discussion of this issue.

7. *Assignability/Transferability/Novation (§ 3.1, § 22)*

(a) By Licensee

Depending on the type of license granted, a licensee may or may not be able to assign its license.

In general, a nonexclusive software license is not assignable unless the license agreement expressly provides that it may be assigned. *See, e.g., Cincom Systems, Inc. v. Novelis Corp.*, 581 F.3d 431 (6th Cir. 2009) (intellectual property licenses nonassignable unless specifically provided for in license agreement); *SQL Solutions, Inc. v. Oracle Corp.*, 1991 WL 626458 (N.D. Cal. Dec. 18, 1991) (assignment of software license by operation of law/merger violates license terms prohibiting assignment); *Harris v. Emus Records Corp.*, 734 F.2d 1329 (9th Cir. 1984) (as to copyright license). *See also Verson Corp. v. Verson International Group PLC,* 899 F. Supp. 358 (N.D. Ill. 1995) (nonexclusive licensee may not assign patent license unless the right of assignment is expressly provided for in the license agreement). This principle is based upon the reasoning that a nonexclusive license is merely a contractual promise not to sue the licensee, which is personal to the licensee and cannot be transferred. Raymond T. Nimmer, The Law of Computer Technology § 7.78 (2005). Nonexclusive licenses are not required to be in writing. *Effects Assocs., Inc. v. Cohen,* 908 F.2d 555, 558 (9th Cir. 1990).

Silence as to assignability will be interpreted in light of federal copyright law prohibiting assignment without the express authorization to make such transfer.

Courts are divided over the ability to assign an exclusive license without consent. *Gardner v. Nike, Inc.*, 279 F.3d 774, 780–81 (9th Cir. 2002) held that exclusive copyright licenses are only assignable with the consent of the copyright owner as a matter of law. It further held that federal law will govern the interpretation of a license where state law conflicts with federal copyright law and policy. *Id. citing S.O.S., Inc. v. Payday, Inc.*, 886 F.2d 1081, 1088 (9th Cir. 1989).

Several courts, however, have held that an exclusive license is assignable by the exclusive licensee, unless the license agreement expressly provides otherwise. The Federal District Court for the Southern District of Indiana took exception to *Gardner*, stating "Exclusive licensees, as copyright owners of their exclusive rights, are free under the [Copyright] Act to transfer those rights to third parties." *Traicoff v. Digital Media, Inc.*, 439 F. Supp.2d 872, 877 (S.D. Ind. 2006). *See also Golden Books Family Entertainment Inc.*, 269 B.R. 311 (Bankr. D. Del. 2001); *In re Sentry Data, Inc.*, 87 B.R. 943 (Bankr. N.D. Ill. 1988); *In re Valley Media, Inc.*, 279 B.R. 105, 135 (Bankr. D. Del. 2002) ("Exclusive licenses grant the licensee a property right in the copyright that is freely transferable . . . ."

This view is shared by the principal treatise on copyrights, *Nimmer on Copyright*, which reasons that an exclusive licensee is considered to be the copyright owner to the extent of the exclusive rights granted by the license and may re-convey such rights absent a contractual restriction. 3 MELVILLE B. NIMMER & DAVID NIMMER, NIMMER ON COPYRIGHT § 10.02 [B][4] at 10-25–10-28 (2005). Another noted expert, Jay Westermeier, believes, however, that exclusive licenses are not assignable without the copyright owner's consent, as a licensor still retains ownership of the copyright even though it has granted the licensee an exclusive license. The transfer of an ownership interest or exclusive right in a copyright must be in writing. 17 U.S.C. § 204(a).

An exclusive license that does not resemble an assignment (e.g., an exclusive license to market the software) is arguably a nonassignable license. *See In re Sentry Data, Inc.*, 87 B.R. 943 (Bankr. N.D. Ill. 1988). Therefore, an exclusive license may convey only certain rights to the licensee, which is similar to the buyer's rights to resell and use the software under the First Sale Doctrine. 17 U.S.C. § 117. See Chapter 3.A.

Several courts, however, have held that a nonexclusive copyright or patent license cannot be transferred without the consent of the licensor. *In re Catapult Entertainment, Inc.*, 165 F.3d 747 (9th Cir. 1999); *Everex Systems, Inc. v. Cadtrak Corp.*, 89 F.3d 673 (9th Cir. 1996); *Harris v. Emus Records Corp.*, 734 F.2d 1329 (9th Cir. 1984); *Unarco Indus., Inc. v. Kelley Co., Inc.*, 465 F.2d 1303 (7th Cir. 1972); *In re Patient Education Media, Inc.*, 210 B.R. 237 (Bankr. S.D.N.Y. 1997).

The federal policy on transfers arises in part from the fact that a nonexclusive license is a personal contractual privilege that does not create a property interest. It is also embedded in policies of encouraging innovation and reserving to the owner of the rights in question the ability to determine to whom and when a license is granted. *See, e.g., Everex Systems, Inc. v. Cadtrak Corp.*, 89 F.3d 673 (9th Cir. 1996).

This area of the law is uncertain, however, as copyright law would appear to conflict with general contract law in this matter. Under Article 2 of the UCC, unless otherwise agreed, contract rights are freely assignable so long as such assignment does not materially change the duty of the other party or materially increase such party's risk or burden. UCC Article 2 § 2-210(2). Similarly, the Restatement (Second) of Contracts provides that a contract is not assignable if it could materially reduce the value received by the obligor, materially increase its burden or risk, materially impair its ability to obtain return performance, or materially reduce the value of the transaction to him. RESTATEMENT (SECOND) OF CONTRACTS, § 317(2)(a).

For a more detailed discussion, see Ziff, *The Effect of Corporate Acquisitions on the Target Company's License Rights,* 57 BUS. LAW. 767 (2002). A related issue in outsourcing is allowing third party contractors to access and maintain the software. See Chapter 5.H and Chapter 11 for a discussion of this issue.

Given the potential uncertainty as to assignment, from the licensor's standpoint, the license should clearly state that the license is not assignable or transferable whether by merger, consolidation, operation of law, or otherwise, and any attempt to do so is void. (See § 22.1). For clarity, the assignment clause should provide that the phrase "operation of law" will include any change of control of the ownership structure of the licensee. See § 22.1 and Form 23.K.1. This will allow the licensor to prevent a transfer or in the alternative charge a transition fee if the licensee is acquired by another company or the customer seeks to outsource the licensor's technology. If the licensor is willing to allow the assignment of the agreement/license to an "affiliate" of the licensee, the licensor should ensure that the licensee remains liable for the affiliate's subsequent breach of the agreement/license.

In *Cincom Systems, Inc. v. Novelis Corp.*, 581 F.3d 431 (6th Cir. 2009), the Sixth Circuit held that a nonexclusive, nontransferable license could not be transferred by merger when an affiliate was merged into a sister entity and out of existence as part of a corporate reorganization. The underlying license agreement licensed the software for use on a designated computer and prohibited the transfer of the license without the licensor's consent. The court emphasized that under federal law, a copyright is unassignable absent express language to the contrary. *Id.* at 437. Further, it stated "[a] transfer is no less a transfer because it takes place by operation of law rather than by a particular act of the parties." *Id.* at 438, *citing PPG Industries v. Guardian Industries Corp.*, 597 F.2d 1090, 1096 (6th Cir. 1979). *See also SQL Solutions, Inc. v. Oracle Corp.*, 1991 WL 626458 (N.D. Cal. Dec. 18, 1991) (assignment of software license by operation of law/merger violates license terms prohibiting assignment). *But see Evolution, Inc. v. Prime Rate Premium Finance Corporation, Inc.*, 2004 WL 1824389 (D. Kan. Aug. 13, 2004) ("whether a merger effectuates an automatic assignment or transfer of license rights is a matter of state law.")

If the license agreement does not contain explicit language defining assignment to include mergers, consolidations, and operation of law, a court may not interpret such actions as an assignment because the assignment arose through the operation of law and not a formal written agreement. In such event, the court may allow the assignment to be concluded and award the licensor monetary damages. *See Rumbin v. Utica Mutual Ins. Co. et al.*, 757 A.2d 526 (Conn. 2000) (Anti-assignment clause did not render assignment ineffective but gave other party right to recover damages for breach). See § 22.1. *See also* RESTATEMENT (SECOND) OF CONTRACTS § 322(2) and comment b (1979).

Some licensees seek to avoid this issue by including language in the license agreement by which the licensor consents to any future outsourcing provided the outsourcer complies with the terms of the license. See § 41. A licensor should carefully consider accepting this type of clause as the outsourcer may be a competitor and may have no incentive to maintain the confidentiality of the licensor's trade secrets.

Farsighted licensees should seek to include language to protect their future business needs, such as in the event that a business unit using the software is sold or otherwise transferred. See § 22.3. Similarly, prudent licensees should also seek the right to use the software on a "beneficial" basis to provide transition services to a third party purchaser of one of its business units to support the transferred assets. See § 42.2.

Licensors should seek to limit assignability to ensure the sanctity of their software. The failure to do so may result in the licensee assigning the software license to a competitor of the licensor or to a party who is much larger than the licensee, preventing the licensor from realizing a larger license fee. Further, the new licensee may lack the creditworthiness of the existing licensee. Finally, when considering the right of assignment, the parties need to distinguish licenses from other ancillary contracts such as software development agreements and support and maintenance agreements when the agreement lacks a limitation on assignment. These ancillary agreements may be governed by common law, not copyright law, potentially resulting in different outcomes for different types of agreements.

See Section A.7.(b), above, and Chapter 3.B 4 for further discussions of this issue.

(b) By Licensor

The licensee should also be concerned with the assignment of the license agreement by the licensor. Specifically, the licensee wants to ensure that any assignee possesses the technical competence and formal resources to support, maintain, and enhance the software. To protect its interests, the licensee should prohibit any assignment of the agreement by merger, consolidation, operation of law, or otherwise without the prior written consent of the licensee. While this right may be qualified by the caveat that the licensee's consent will not be unreasonably withheld or delayed, the licensee should seek the right to immediately terminate the license in the event its consent is not obtained. This will protect the licensee from those assignees who plan to "sunset" the licensed software or seek to contractually exploit the licensee's dependence on the software. Before consenting to any assignment, the licensee should insist on receiving written guarantees that the assignee will continue to support the software at agreed-upon levels and at an agreed-upon pricing for a set period of years.

(c) Novation

A novation is the creation of a new contractual agreement that extinguishes an existing agreement. *I.W. Berman Properties v. Porter Brothers, Inc.*, 344 A.2d 65, 70 (Md. 1975). A new agreement is created on the same terms and condition with only the parties changing. RESTATEMENT (SECOND) OF CONTRACTS § 280. A novation agreement must clearly evidence the intent of all of parties to "extinguish the old obligations and substitute a new one for it." *Adler v. Walker & Dunlop, Inc.*, 225 A.2d 459, 462 (Md. 1967). By entering into a novation, the assigning party extinguishes its liability or at least limits its liability up to the time of the novation, while the other party releases the novating party from future performance. See Chapter 17 for a model Transfer and Novation Agreement. Thus, if a party is interested in transferring its obligations, it may want to consider executing a novation instead of an assignment.

B. Ancillary Clauses

1. *Representations, Warranties, Covenants and Disclaimers (§ 16)*

(a) Representations and Warranties (§§ 16.1, 16A–AE, 16.2)

(i) General

It is generally held that a representation is a statement of a present or past fact and a warranty is a promise that certain existing or future facts will be or are true. *Krys v. Henderson*, 69 S.E.2d. 635, 637 (Ga. Ct. App. 1952). Representations and warranties are not always mutually inclusive and can have different consequences in terms of liability. Thus, the parties should carefully consider the impact of making a representation versus a warranty.

(a) Representations

A "representation" creates a legal risk that the licensor's sales puffery may lead to a claim of fraud in the inducement. *See* Restatement (Second) of Torts §§ 525, 526, and 552C. An action for a fraudulent misrepresentation must be predicated upon a statement relating to a past or an existing fact. Future promises are contractual and do not constitute fraud. *Central On Line Data Systems, Inc. v. Filenet Corp.*, 99 F.3d 1138 (table), 1996 WL 483031 (6th Cir. Aug. 23, 1996) (unpublished disposition). If the plaintiff is successful in proving fraud in the inducement, the contract's limitation of liability will be void. *Accusystems, Inc. v. Honeywell Information Systems, Inc.*, 580 F. Supp. 474 (S.D.N.Y. 1984) (statute of limitations does not apply to claims for fraud in the inducement).

Damages for such fraud may include the amount paid under the contract minus any benefits obtained; the cost of cover; extra labor expenses; the expense related to obtaining different computer services; the costs associated with installing and removing hardware; program conversion costs; and the costs of equipment maintenance, as well as the risk of the rescission of the license agreement without the necessary legal protections for the licensor. *See Applied Data Processing, Inc. v. Burroughs Corp.*, 394 F. Supp. 504 (D. Conn. 1975); *Clements Auto Co. v. Service Bureau Co.*, 298 F. Supp. 115 (D. Minn. 1969), *aff'd as modified*, 444 F.2d 169 (8th Cir. 1971).

In the event of fraud in the inducement, the license agreement's integration clause may be voided allowing previously excluded statements to be considered. *See Financial Times Publications, Inc. v. Compugraphic Corp.*, 873 F.2d 936, 943–44 (8th

Cir. 1990). Further, a party may not escape liability for misrepresentation by invoking a contract's limitation of liability clause. *Vmark Software, Inc. v. EMC Corp.*, 642 N.E.2d 587 (Mass. App. Ct. 1994).

The failure to satisfy a representation does not necessarily give rise to a fraud claim. "[F]raud may not be based on representations of future conduct, on broken promises, or representations of existing intent that are not executed." *Digitech Computer, Inc. v. Trans-Care, Inc.*, 583 F. Supp.2d 984 (S.D. Ind. 2008).

Given that most licensees are willing to accept only a warranty and not require the licensor to provide a representation in the belief one is as good as the other, the licensor should refrain from including any representations in its agreement.

For a general overview of liability for misrepresentations in the sale or lease of computer systems, see Leahy, *Misrepresentation in Sale or Lease of Computer Systems*, 20 Am. Jur. Proof of Facts 3d 621 (1993).

(b) Warranties

Unlike a representation, a beneficiary does not have to rely on a warranty to recover damages. *Rogath v. Siebermann*, 129 F.3d 261 (2d Cir. 1997); *CBS, Inc. v. Ziff Davis Publishing Co.*, 553 N.E.2d 997 (N.Y. 1990). Further, a party's knowledge that a warranty is false does not prevent the party from bringing a claim for breach of warranty unless the party making the warranty informed the beneficiary of such falsehood. *Rogath v. Siebermann*, 129 F.3d 261, 264 (2d Cir. 1997).

(c) Contract versus Tort Claims

A breach of contract does not give rise to a cause of action under tort law. A duty under tort law arises from circumstances extraneous to and not constituting elements of the contract, even though it may be related to and dependent on the contract. *Bristol-Meyers Squibb, Industrial Division v. Delton-Star, Inc.*, 620 N.Y.S.2d 196, 197 (N.Y.A.D. 1994). In short, tort actions arise from the breach of duties imposed by law (e.g., a duty of care) regardless of the contractual terms defining the parties' relationship. Consequently, a claim of fraud will not be allowed where the only alleged fraud arises from the breach of the contract. *Jackson Heights Medical Group v. Complex Corp.*, 634 N.Y.S.2d 721, 722 (1995). By clearly stating or warranting the standard of care or duty in the agreement (e.g., a workmanlike manner; see, e.g., § 16.C) and/or providing for service levels (see, e.g., § 16.B), the licensor should be able to establish the duty it owes the licensee and avoid the implementation of a standard outside the four corners of the license.

In the case of solely economic losses, recovery is limited to contract claims and not tort claims. *Transport Corp. of Amer., Inc. v. International Business Machines Corp.*, 30 F.3d 953, 957 (8th Cir. 1994); *Huron Tool and Engineering Co. v. Precision Consulting Services, Inc.*, 532 N.W.2d 541 (Mich. App. 1995) (fraudulent representations alleged by plaintiff were indistinguishable from terms of contract and warranties, thus plaintiff limited to contractual remedies). See also *Word Management Corp. v. AT&T Info. Sys., Inc.*, 525 N.Y.S.2d 433 (1988).

Courts have used two tests, the economic loss doctrine and the "gist of the action" test, to determine whether tort claims that accompany contract claims should be allowed or rejected as a wrongful attempt to recover additional contract damages. *Bohler v. Uddeholm America, Inc.*, 247 F.3d 79, 103 (3d Cir. 2001). The economic loss doctrine is a judicially created doctrine to preclude a commercial purchaser of a product from suing in negligence (tort) for a loss that is solely economic under the belief that recovery should be had under contract law, warranty, and the UCC. *Prent Corp. v. Martek Holdings, Inc.*, 618 N.W.2d 201 (Wis. 2000). It is unclear, however, whether the doctrine would apply in the case of fraud. A trend has begun to emerge that claims of fraud involving a breach of contract claim will be precluded by the economic loss doctrine. *Werwinski v. Ford Motor Car Company,* 286 F.3d 661 (3d Cir. 2002) (court refused to recognize an exception to the economic loss doctrine where intentional fraud was alleged). A fraud claim that is distinct from a breach of contract claim may survive. *See, e.g., AKA Distributing Co. v. Whirlpool Corp.* 137 F.3d 1086 (8th Cir. 1998) (fraud claim barred by economic loss doctrine); *Huron Tool & Engineering Co. v. Precision Consulting Services, Inc.*, 532 N.W.2d 541 (Mich. App. 1995) (not all fraud claims precluded by the economic loss doctrine). For a more detailed discussion, see Sanford, *Fraud and the Economic Loss Doctrine,* Com. L. Newsl. 3 (Dec. 2000).

Similarly, under the "gist of the action" test, courts have sought to preclude re-characterizing breach of contract claims as tort claims. The doctrine seeks to determine whether the "gist" of the plaintiff's claim lies in contract or tort and bars "plaintiffs from bringing a tort claim that merely replicates a claim for breach of an underlying contract." *Phico Insurance Co. v. Presbyterian Medical Services Corp.*, 663 A.2d 753, 757 (Pa. 1995). At least one court has held that the "gist of the action" test even bars tort claims based upon allegations of intentional fraud. *eToll, Inc. v. Elias/Savion Advertising, Inc.*, 811 A.2d 10 (Pa. Super. 2002).

For a discussion of the use of representations and warranties, see Adams, *A Lesson in Drafting Contracts: What's Up with 'representations and warranties'?,* 15 Bus. L. Today 32 (Nov./Dec. 2005) (author argues that drafters would be better served by using only representation/represents and not warranty/warrants as the term "representation" has a broader meaning), but see Stark, *Another View on Reps and Warranties,* 16 Bus. L. Today 8 (Jan./Feb. 2006).

(ii) Licensor Warranties

Although it has not been definitively determined whether the UCC applies to the licensing of software, many courts have looked to the UCC for guidance in determining warranty issues. See Chapter 11.A for a discussion of the applicability of the UCC to software licensing.

The UCC recognizes to two types of warranties: express warranties and implied warranties. "Express warranties are affirmative promises about the quality and features of the goods being sold. They [can] also include descriptions of the goods being sold or samples shown to the buyer." Cadden & Fuller LLP, *Commercial Law: Express and Implied Warranties Under the Uniform Commercial Code,* http://www.caddenfuller.com/CM/Articles/Articles34.asp (Last viewed October 4, 2010). Implied warranties are presumed to have been made in the sale of a good regardless of whether the seller made any written or verbal affirmative assurances.

(a) Implied Warranties Under Article 2 of the UCC

The UCC provides for two implied warranties: (1) the implied warranty of merchantability (UCC § 2-314) and (2) the implied warranty of fitness for particular purpose. UCC § 2-315. Implied warranties are made whether or not they are affirmatively stated.

(1) Merchantability

The warranty of merchantability is "a warranty that the goods shall be merchantable and is implied in a contract for their sale if the seller is a merchant with respect to goods of that kind." UCC § 2-314. The goods must (i) pass without objection in the trade under the contract description; (ii) in the case of fungible goods, be of fair average quality within the description; (iii) be fit for the ordinary purposes for which such goods are used; (iv) run, within the variations permitted by the agreement, of even kind, quality and quantity within each unit and among all units involved; (v) be adequately contained, packaged, and labeled as the agreement may require; and (vi) conform to the promise or affirmations of fact made on the container or label if any. *Id.* In essence, the warranty requires that a good meet a consumer's reasonable expectations for a good of that kind. Fitness for ordinary purposes is often considered to be part of merchantability but is usually discussed separately to contrast it with fitness for a particular purpose (see below).

The implied warranty of merchantability assures the purchaser that the product falls within the general standards of fitness for ordinary purposes under the product's description. *Vision Graphics, Inc. v. E.I. du Pont de Nemours,* 41 F. Supp.2d 93 (D. Mass. 1999). It does not guarantee that the product will be ideal or ever optimal for a particular use. *Id.*

Use of the phrase "AS IS" is sufficient to disclaim a warranty of merchantability.

(2) Fitness for Particular Purpose

Whereas the warranty of merchantability implies that the goods are fit for the purpose for which they are ordinarily sold in the marketplace, the warranty of fitness for a particular purpose guarantees that the goods are suitable for a specific purpose that may be different from their ordinary purpose. The warranty of fitness for a particular purpose "applies if the seller knows or has reason to know that the buyer will be using the goods he is buying for a certain purpose." Cadden & Fuller LLP, *Commercial Law: Express and Implied Warranties Under the Uniform Commercial Code,* http://www.caddenfuller.com/CM/Articles/Articles34.asp (Last viewed October 4, 2010).

"AS IS" eliminates the warranty for fitness for a particular purpose.

(b) Other Warranties Under Article 2 of the UCC

Under the UCC, two other warranties are read into every contract: (1) the warranty of title, and (2) the warranty of noninfringement. UCC § 2-312. Unlike the implied warranties of merchantability and fitness for a particular purpose (collectively "Implied Warranties"), these warranties are treated somewhat differently. Arguably, the warranties of title and infringement cannot be classified as implied warranties as they are not identified as such under the UCC, and cannot be negated by a general disclaimer of implied warrants. Because the UCC does not identify the warranties of good title and infringement as implied warranties, these warranties may not be disclaimed or modified.

(1) Good Title

In a contract for the sale of goods, a seller is deemed to warrant that (i) the title conveyed is good, and its transfer rightful; and (ii) the goods shall be delivered free from any security interest or other lien or encumbrance of which the buyer at the time of contracting has no knowledge. UCC § 2-312. It implies that the seller of goods has the right to sell those goods.

Stating that a good is provided "AS IS" does not disclaim a warranty of title.

(2) Infringement

The warranty of infringement provides that "the goods shall be delivered free of the rightful claim of any third person by way of infringement." UCC § 2-312.

As with good title, "AS IS" does not disclaim the warranty of infringement.

(c) Express Warranties

For software licenses, there are a number of "standard" express warranties that a licensor typically might make and a number that the licensee should seek. Which warranties to include is dependent on the nature of the transaction and the risk tolerance of the parties. The licensor's willingness to provide warranties will be a function of the size of the transaction but may also be influenced by other factors, such as the licensor's ability to recognize revenue. For example, a licensor that provides a licensee with a warranty based on licensee-defined criteria may find that a right of cancellation is imputed to the licensee, and therefore the licensor may have difficulty recognizing the revenue under the agreement.

General (§ 16.1)

A licensor should warrant that it has valid title to the software it is licensing, that it has the right to grant the license including the license to any third party software, and that the software will operate in all material respects with the functional specifications and current documentation. It is customary, however, for the licensor to state that the operation of the licensed software will not be uninterrupted or error free (§ 16.1.2).

System Warranty (§ 16.A)

When purchasing a software system, the licensee should require the licensor to represent and warrant that the system as a whole will operate within the parameters of certain service levels. A system warranty limits the problems that may arise when each of the individual system components operates properly but when they are combined the resulting performance is less than desired.

Where the software is part of an integrated system being installed by the licensor (i.e., a system integration project), or a group of different vendors, the licensee should require the licensor to expressly warrant that once installed, the system as a whole (versus the independent components) will operate in conformance with certain performance metrics. (Note: UCITA contains an implied warranty regarding integration. See UCITA § 405; Chapter 11.B.3.(i)(iv)).

Licensors should carefully consider any warranty they make as to the software's performance when operated in conjunction with any third party software or certain hardware configurations as they may negatively influence the performance or operation of the licensor's software. Licensees, however, should insist on the inclusion of such a warranty to ensure they receive what they have paid for. If the licensee fails to do so, it may be unable to determine which third party product or service caused the noncompliance and unwittingly assumes the risk of the integrated system being noncompliant with the licensee's needs. The licensee should always seek to have one party or vendor be responsible for the performance of the integrated product, usually through a prime/subcontract relationship.

The customer should insist on the inclusion of detailed performance metrics that set forth the levels to which the individual components and the system as a whole will perform. This usually is done through a warranty. (See § 16.B.)

Software (§ 16.B)

A licensor should warrant that all software will meet certain written performance standards (See §§ 16B, E and § 3.B.) but at the same time the licensor should avoid making broad or exaggerated statements about its software's performance or capabilities. In the extreme, any misrepresentation may void a license agreement's limitation of liability. *Vmark Software, Inc. v. EMC Corp.*, 642 N.E.2d 587 (Ct. App. Mass. 1994). Software by its nature is imperfect. Thus a licensor should never warrant that the software will operate uninterrupted or error-free, as software will always contain "bugs."

Alternatively, many licensees seek to have the licensor warrant that the software is free from defects in design, materials and workmanship. Licensees should carefully consider whether language to this effect is acceptable, as at least one court had held that such a disclaimer excuses the licensor from any obligation to fix all errors. *Info Systems Technology, Inc. v. Logical Software, Inc.*, 835 F.2d 874 (4th Cir. 1987). Further, the term "materials" is ambiguous and arguably is inapplicable to software as software is intangible. The licensor should be willing, however, to give a warranty as to the media on which the software is contained. See the discussion below and § 16.N. Such a warranty creates little risk for the licensor, given that most software is delivered electronically and in the event of a breach, the media can be immediately replaced. The term "design" is also ambiguous although one court has interpreted a warranty as to design to mean the software will have the ability to perform the required functions within a reasonable time frame. *USM Corp. v. Arthur D. Little Systems, Inc.*, 546 N.E. 2d 888 (Mass. 1989).

Licensees should seek a warranty period sufficient to address any inherent problems that may arise after acceptance. Although many licensees seek a warranty of one year, 30 to 90 days is more common. Some practitioners equate an extended warranty to "free" maintenance. It is not free, however, as a prudent licensor will build the cost of any extended warranty into its pricing. From the licensor's perspective, it is better to provide a shorter warranty period and have the licensee execute a separate maintenance agreement under which the licensor can provide free services. See Chapter 5.H for a discussion of the benefits of a separate maintenance agreement.

By having the licensor commit to certain service levels, the licensee is in essence guaranteed that minimum level of performance, and such service level will become the standard of care/duty in the event of any subsequent negligence action. The licensor should ensure that it is excused from liability if the licensor follows the licensee's designated specifications and such specifications do not produce the performance levels the licensee desires or are otherwise set forth in their contract. See Chapter 5.F for a more detailed discussion of service levels.

Usually, the remedy for the breach of this warranty is the provision of pre-agreed service level credits or liquidated damages to the licensee, most likely a small amount. This remedy is also usually accompanied by language stating that if the service credits or liquidated damages reach a certain level, the licensor will be deemed to be in material breach of the underlying agreement and the licensee may terminate the agreement. The licensor has some protection in that the licensor's failure to meet the service levels does not immediately result in a material breach but rather the licensor has some period of time to correct its nonperformance while providing the licensee financial compensation during the period it tries to correct its breach. Most licensors will insist on providing credits instead of actually making a cash payment to the licensee.

The license should include language that the service level credits or liquidated damages are the exclusive remedy of the licensee, to preclude the licensee from also bringing an action for breach. The licensee should insist that there not be separate limitations of liability throughout the contract to ensure the licensee is able to obtain the benefit of the bargain.

Services (§ 16.C)

Where the agreement contemplates a services component, such as for development, support, or maintenance, the licensor should warrant that all services will be rendered in a professional and workmanlike manner. The majority of states hold that under common law there are no implied warranties for the provision of services. FELDMAN & NIMMER, DRAFTING EFFECTIVE CONTRACTS § 5.05[A][2] (2d ed. 2007); *Pearl Investments, LLC v. Standard I/O, Inc.*, 257 F. Supp.2d 326 (D. Me. 2003) (no warranty implied in software development contract); *Gilbert Const. Co. v. Gross*, 129 A.2d 518, 520 (Md. 1957); *Craig v. American Dist. Tel. Co.*, 399 N.Y.S.2d 164, 165 (1977) (implied warranties do not arise from the performance of a service). *But see Adobe Masters, Inc. v. Downey*, 883 P.2d 133, 134 (N.M. 1994); *Continental Dredging, Inc. v. De-Kaizered, Inc.*, 120 S.W.3d 380, 390 n.6 (Tex. 2003). Such licensees should include language in the underlying license agreement that all services will be performed in a "first class manner" or "consistent with the licensor's status as an industry leader." See also RESTATEMENT (SECOND) OF TORTS (1965) § 299A (those who provide professional services will be "required to exercise the skill and knowledge normally possessed by members of that profession or trade in good standing in similar communities."). While no standard is perfect, a more desirable standard from the licensor's perspective is to use a "commercially reasonable manner."

Many lawyers representing licensors believe these standards are ambiguous and can later lead to disputes in interpretation. As such, they seek to avoid these terms in favor of clearly defined standards. Further, the use of the term "professional" raises the issue of whether service personnel are "professionals" and need to be licensed. If so, what professional codes are imported into the license? Similarly, licensors should be careful not to hold themselves out as possessing special skills to avoid creating implied warranties. *Data Processing Services, Inc. v. L.H. Smith Oil Corporation*, 492 N.E. 2d 314 (Ind. 1986) (programmer who held self out as possessing ability and qualification to design and develop computer programs implied by representation possession of skill and diligence possessed by well-informed member of computer programming trade).

Several enterprising plaintiffs have sought to create a higher standard to which all computer services companies and professionals should be held when providing computer services. To date, these attempts have been rejected by the courts. *See Chatlos Systems, Inc. v. National Cash Register Corporation*, 479 F. Supp. 738 (D.N.J. 1979) (court declined to create a new tort of "computer malpractice"); *RKB Enterprises, Inc. v. Ernst & Young*, 582 N.Y.S.2d 814 (1992) (there is no cause of professional malpractice in the provision of computer services); *Metpath, Inc. v. IDS Corporation*, 1991 WL 39617 (Conn. Super Mar. 12, 1991) (allegation of negligence against computer services company does not spawn tort of "computer malpractice").

Documentation (§ 16.D)

The licensor should warrant that the documentation accurately describes the functional and operational characteristics of the software as delivered to the licensee and that the documentation is detailed and complete. Some licensees seek to include language that the documentation will allow a "reasonably skilled" operator to use and operate the software. The use of the term "reasonably skilled" or a similar term is ambiguous and creates significant risk to the licensor. Thus the licensor should resist including language to this effect.

During the warranty period and in any subsequent support agreement, the licensor should agree to promptly provide all updates and enhancements to the software as well as any accompanying documentation to the licensee. Further, all documentation should be contemporaneously updated to reflect any enhancements to the software. Without proper documentation, the licensee will not be able to fully utilize the software. Thus, it is important that the requirements of the documentation are explicitly detailed.

A common question arises as to what is an "update" or "enhancement" as opposed a new version. A vendor will often claim that a customer is not entitled to receive a free copy of a particular improvement to the software, as the improvement constitutes a new version not an enhancement or update. At least two courts have acknowledged that the term "enhancement" is ambiguous and does not have a standard meaning in the technology industry. *Infosystems Technology, Inc. v. Logical Software, Inc.*, 1987 WL 24433 (4th Cir. Nov. 27, 1987); *PRC Reality Systems, Inc. v. National Ass'n. of Realtors*, 766 F. Supp. 972, 453, 459 (E.D. Va. 1991), *aff'd in part, vacated in part*, 972 F.2d. 341, 1992 WL 183682 (4th Cir. Aug. 4, 1992).

Defects in Design, Materials, and Workmanship (§ 16.E)

Many licensees seek to have the licensor warrant that the software is free from defects in materials and workmanship. A licensee may also ask the licensor to warrant defects in design as well. A licensor should think carefully before granting a warranty as to design, as software by its nature is imperfect, creating a potentially significant risk. Defects in materials usually relates to the physical media rather than the intangible software.

The licensor should clarify any warranty regarding "materials" to ensure it is clear that the licensor is only warranting the disk that contains the software to avoid a "bootstrap" argument that a warranty as to materials equates to a "design" warranty. *See, e.g.*, Section B.1 (Media), above; § 16.N. Similarly, the licensor should also clarify the meaning of "workmanship" in any warranty, which arguably includes the design of the software. See Section B.1 (Services), above; § 16.C.

Interface (§ 16.F)

The licensor should warrant/agree that it will assist the licensee in the licensee's development of any application programming interfaces (APIs) between third party systems and the software. Further, the licensor should provide any industry standard APIs that the licensor is evaluating. The licensee should also seek to have the licensor use as many industry-standard protocols as possible. This warranty ensures that the licensee will have the licensor's support in developing APIs. Without the licensor's support, it could be quite difficult and potentially very expensive to develop the necessary interfaces.

If a licensor does not create or publish APIs, the licensee should seek the right to reverse engineer, disassemble, or decompile for the purpose of facilitating interoperability between the licensor's software and third party software products. Without this right, the licensee is at the mercy of the licensor, which could significantly impact the licensee's ability to efficiently operate the licensee's IT systems. Under existing law, the licensee most likely already has this right, but the licensee should seek to have the licensor explicitly acknowledge this right. See Chapter A.3.c.(ii), above.

Open Architecture/Open System Warranty (§ 16.G)

Licensor should also warrant that the software is designed in an "Open Architecture" environment such that the licensor should publish all external interface specifications. Again, this will allow the licensee to create interfaces in a quicker, more cost-effective manner.

Compatibility (§§ 16.H, 16.I)

A prudent licensee should include a warranty that any enhancements to the software will be compatible with the licensee's existing version of the software. The license should also seek a warranty that any enhancement will not degrade the functionality of the existing system. A licensor should be careful about making an open-ended warranty. Rather, the licensor should limit its compatibility obligations to the two most recent versions of the software to avoid the liability of making updated versions compatible with earlier versions in perpetuity.

If the licensor is providing the licensee a complete, integrated system or hardware with the software, the licensor should warrant the compatibility and interoperability of the individual components without modification and with all third party software. A licensor, however, should be hesitant to make such broad open-ended statements. Alternatively, the licensor should warrant that all software and hardware sold by the licensor will be compatible with those third party components set forth in an exhibit attached to the underlying agreement. To the extent the licensor has claimed certain compatibility in its marketing materials, product documentation or RFP response, those products should be included in the attached exhibit.

Data Integrity (§ 16.J)

As part of an ancillary services agreement, a licensee may request that the licensor convert its existing data and have the licensor warrant that the data will be converted accurately and completely. A licensor should think carefully before agreeing to undertake such a conversion or make such a warranty without fully understanding the risk involved. Most prudent licensors will not agree to perform or be responsible for any data conversion as there is significant risk and expense involved in the process.

Software Obsolescence (§ 16.K)

The licensee should seek to obtain a representation and warranty that the licensor is committed to enhancing the software in the future and that the licensor has no plans to discontinue the development, marketing, maintenance, or support of the software. This is especially important if the software will be mission critical to the operation of the licensee's business and the software will be used for a significant period of time. While it is unlikely that a licensor will agree to such a broad commitment, licensors are more receptive to committing to provide maintenance and support services for a set period of time. A more aggressive position is to require the licensor to represent and warrant that it will actually market and license the software for a set period of time. Again, licensors cannot predict changing market demands and thus should be hesitant to do so.

Occasionally, a licensee will seek to have a licensor commit to investing a certain percentage of revenues/profits into the product each year (See § 3.A). A licensor should be hesitant to make this type of commitment as it limits the licensor's flexibility in operating the licensor's business and could significantly reduce its profits. At the same time, however, a licensee has a legitimate interest in knowing that the software/system is not going to be "sunsetted" shortly after the transaction is consummated. An alternate position is to have the licensor covenant that (1) if it ceases to market the licensed software and introduces a new, functionally equivalent software program within a set number of years of the license date or (2) introduces a new software product with a certain percentage of the functionality of the licensed software within a set period of time from the license date, the new software will be licensed free of charge to the licensee.

In addition, the licensee should seek to have the licensor represent and warrant that it will issue a minimum of two updates per year which will address and correct all errors and bugs in the software as of the date of the release. Again, the licensor should be hesitant to commit in writing to an action for which it may lack the resources, finances or business justification to comply.

In addition, the licensee may want the licensor to warrant that the version of the software being delivered to the licensee is the most current version of the software. The intent of this warranty is to ensure the licensor is delivering the licensee the same version of the software it is delivering to its other and perhaps larger customers, and to avoid having the licensee purchase an updated version within a short period of time after it licenses the software.

Disabling Code, Trap Doors, Viruses, and the Like (§ 16.L)

It is common to warrant that, except as documented, there are no trap doors, time bombs, or disabling devices. The failure of a licensee to obtain such a warranty may give the licensor significant leverage in the event of any dispute, as some licenses specifically state that the licensor may disable the software in case of a breach. See *American Computer Trust Leasing v. Jack Farrell Implement Co.,* 763 F. Supp. 1473 (D. Minn. 1991), *aff'd,* 967 F.2d 1208 (8th Cir. 1992) (license permitted licensor to disable software for licensee's nonpayment). As such, the licensee should always seek to include a statement that the licensor will not engage in electronic self-help. A prudent licensor may seek to limit its risk by instituting the caveat "to the knowledge of licensor" under the reasoning that it cannot control the actions of a rogue employee.

At the same time, however, a licensor who disables software without contractual authority may be guilty of an intentional tort and be liable to punitive damages, see, e.g., *Clayton X-Ray Co. v. Professional Systems Corp.*, 812 S.W.2d 565 (Mo. Ct. App. 1991), and may potentially be in violation of the Computer Fraud and Abuse Act (CFAA), 18 U.S.C. § 1030. See *North Texas Preventative Imaging, L.L.C. v. Eisenberg,* 1996 WL 1359212 (C.D. Cal. Aug. 19, 1996) (surreptitious inclusion of time bomb could lead to violation of CFAA). *YourNet Dating, Inc. v. Mitchell,* 88 F. Supp.2d 870 (N.D. Ill. 2000) (unauthorized entry into computer system was violation of CFAA). Courts have interpreted the CFAA broadly. Data Security and Privacy Law: Combating Cyberthreats § 8.42 (Kevin P. Cronin and Ronald N. Weikers eds. 2005).

Licensees should also insist on a virus warranty. Many licensors will seek to give a "knowledge" warranty with respect to viruses or worms and warrant that they will use commercially reasonable efforts to screen the software and media for viruses. *See generally*, Robbins, *Vendor Liability for Computer Viruses and Undisclosed Disabling Devices in Software,* 10 COMPUTER LAW. 20 (July 1993). Licensors should be careful about making an absolute warranty as to the existence of viruses as they are difficult to detect and may enter the software through no fault of the licensor. Many licensors will only warrant that prior to delivery the software was run through a leading virus detection software package. Virus detection always lags behind the identification of the virus, thus it is impossible for the licensor ever to be completely sure the software is virus free. Some licensors seek an additional level of protection by requiring the licensee to run the software through the licensee's own virus detection software prior to installing the software on the licensee's systems.

Compliance with Laws/Regulatory Requirements (§ 16.M)

A prudent licensee should require the licensor to represent and warrant that it is in compliance with all applicable laws, including federal, state, and local labor and employment laws. The licensor should seek to make the representation and warranty mutual, especially if the licensor's employees will be working on the licensee's premises.

To the extent the licensee operates in a regulated industry with which the software interrelates, the licensee will often seek to have the licensor warrant that the software meets all applicable regulatory requirements as specified by the licensee. The licensor should strictly limit the extent of any such warranty, and if the licensor agrees to make such a warranty it should specifically identify the regulatory requirements the software will meet. Further, such warranty should be limited to the regulatory requirements in existence at the time of the contract execution. The licensee should seek to include language stating that the licensor will make the software comply with any new requirements if the licensee pays for such enhancements. Any warranties made by the licensor should be narrowly drawn to avoid unintended liability as the licensee should know the regulatory rules obligation much better than the licensor. See § 1.17 and Form 23.K.1 for definitions of "Regulatory Requirements," which could have a significant impact on the strength and meaning of this warranty.

Media (§ 16.N)

In commercial licenses, the licensor should warrant that the media on which the software is delivered is free from defects. This warranty does not create significant risk to the licensor, provided the license states that the remedy for breach is to simply provide the licensee with a new disk or tape. See Section B.1.(b).(ii), below, for a discussion of the applicability of the Magnuson-Moss Act.

Intellectual Property Infringement (§ 16.O)

Historically, licensors have warranted that the software will not infringe on any third party intellectual property rights. Recently, an increasing number of licensors have ceased giving such warranties in light of the ever-increasing number of software patents and the accompanying risk. Instead, they argue that there is no need to do so because the licensee's risk is mitigated by the licensor's agreement to indemnify the licensee in the event of any infringement. See Section B.3, below. The licensor has no liability until it is sued, which is a remote possibility. While limiting the licensor's risk, this philosophy does not benefit the licensee. While the licensor's indemnity in theory protects the licensee from third party claims, it does not give the licensee the right to declare a breach of the license and sue for direct damages. Even if the licensor defends the suit, the licensee may not want to continue to use the license for a number of business and legal reasons. The licensee should have the right to notice a breach, require a cure, and be able to sue for damages.

It is also possible that a licensee can become aware that the licensor does not have good title or infringes a third party's intellectual property rights without having been sued. In that case, the licensee should be able to confront the licensor without having to wait to be sued. Practically, a licensee does not want to continue to become more and more reliant on a software program when it becomes possible that the licensee will have to switch or accept a less capable version in the future.

In essence, the licensor seeks to allocate the risks of the unknown. The licensee should think carefully before accepting this position and make sure that it is willing to forgo these claims. This is especially important where the indemnification language allows the licensor to simply refund the licensee's license fee where it is impracticable to obtain a license or make the software noninfringing. (See § 14.B.1.) The licensee may want to consider inserting language to allow the licensee to recover its "switching/transition costs" if there is a comparable product the licensee can migrate to. Further, what if a claim is never made against the licensee but the licensee knows the software infringes? Does it have a way to terminate the license?

Alternatively, the risk to the licensor by including such warranty can be mitigated to a degree by stating that the licensee's "sole and exclusive" remedy for the breach of such warranty is limited to the rights contained in the indemnification provision (see § 14.A.5). Stating that it is the "sole and exclusive" remedy seeks to make the warranty a limited warranty and thereby eliminate the licensor's risk from excluding intellectual property infringement from the limitation of liability. For this strategy to work effectively, the licensor must ensure that the indemnification language is clearly written to limit the licensor's liability.

Under the UCC, a purchaser receives an implied warranty that title to the software will be delivered free of any third party claim of infringement. UCC § 2-312. Thus, even if the licensee fails to obtain a warranty of title and against infringement in those states that recognize that UCC Article 2 governs software licensing, the licensee will still theoretically be able to bring a claim against the licensor unless the licensor specifically excluded or modified such warranty in writing or by the circumstances of the sale. UCC § 2-312(2). The warranties of title and infringement must be disclaimed separately. The "AS IS" or "all express and implied warranty" disclaimers are not sufficient. UCC § 2-312(3). In those states where the UCC does not apply, the licensee should seek to obtain an affirmative warranty of title and against infringement.

From the licensee's perspective, the licensee will want to avoid any "sub" limitations from being included throughout the various provisions of the license. The licensee's ability to recover damages is most likely already limited by the license's provisions excluding consequential damages and limiting direct damages.

Third Party Warranties and Indemnities (§ 16.P)

The licensee should require the licensor to assign to the licensee all end-user warranties and indemnities related to any third party software to insure that the licensee receives the benefit of what it has paid for. To the extent the licensor is unable to assign any such warranties or indemnities or they do not run to the end-user licensee, the licensor should agree to enforce all such warranties and indemnities on behalf of the licensee or for its benefit.

Quality (§ 16.Q)

Many licensees require the licensor to certify that the licensor is ISO 9000 compliant, that the software will be developed in compliance with ISO 9000 or that the software will meet certain quality assurance standards. The licensee should insist on the right to inspect the licensor's quality assurance processes and interview its quality assurance team. A few licensees actually seek to insert their own employees into the development process to ensure a quality product. See § 10.

Authority (§ 16.R)

The licensor should warrant that it has the authority to enter into the license agreement, that the individual executing the license is authorized to do so, and that the grant of the license does not violate any third party agreements. Further, if the licensor is providing third party software, it should warrant that it has the right to grant the third party license and pass through all benefits of the third party license.

Pending Litigation (§ 16.S)

The licensee should ask the licensor to warrant that there is no pending or threatened litigation regarding the software of which the licensor has knowledge. This will force the licensor to disclose any existing litigation, which in turn will allow the licensee to learn of any potential defects or claims by other licensees alleging the software is defective. Regardless of whether this representation or warranty is included in the license agreement, the licensee should explore this issue as part of its due diligence.

Change in Control (§ 16.T)

The licensee should insist that the licensor represent and warrant that no "change of control" with the respect to the licensor is being considered, planned, or pending. This protects the licensee from entering into an agreement with the licensor based on the licensor's reputation, size, experience, or the like, and then having the license agreement transferred to a third party—a party that the licensee might otherwise not have been interested in contracting with. A licensor may not be able to make this warranty as the selective disclosure of a potential acquisition/merger may violate any applicable securities laws. Further, the parties negotiating the license for the licensor may be unaware of any potential merger.

In certain rare instances, some licenses contain a provision that to the extent a particular entity may acquire the licensor, the licensee may terminate the license for its convenience without penalty. See § 4.1.B.

Material Misstatements (§ 16.U)

Licensees occasionally seek a representation and a warranty similar to the representations and warranties contained in acquisition agreements that the licensor has not failed to disclose any "material fact" to the licensee or that any of the warranties contained in the agreement are misleading by omission. *See, e.g.*, 17 C.F.R § 240.10b-5. This protects the licensee from the licensor misleading the licensee by omission, but it creates a significant risk for the licensor, as the licensor is obligated to disclose any fact that a reasonable licensee would consider to be "material." From the licensor's perspective, this type of warranty should not be included as it is appropriate only in securities transactions and not software licensing. It potentially creates significant liability and a question of fact as to what was and was not known by the licensor, as well as what is "material."

Interestingly, a warranty of this type raises the issue of whether the licensor is required to disclose any facts of which the licensor has knowledge that would prevent the software from conforming to the stated warranty. A minority of states impose a duty of good faith when entering into a contract. *See, e.g.*, Del.: *Merrill v. Crothall-American, Inc.*, 606 A.2d 96, 102 (Del. 1992); Ill.: *Cuerton v. Abbott Laboratories, Inc.*, 443 N.E.2d 1069, 1071 (Ill. App. 1982) ("As a member of [Illinois] law, every contract includes a duty of good faith and fair dealing;" Mass.: *Anthony's Pier Four, Inc. v. HBS Associates*, 583 N.E.2d 806 (Mass. 1991) ("Neither party shall do anything that will have the effect of destroying or injuring the right of the other party to receive the fruits of the contract."); Mo.: *Insurance & Consulting Assoc. v. ITT Hartford Ins.*, 48 F. Supp.2d 1181, 1191 (W.D. Mo. 1999) ("covenant of good faith and fair dealing is implied in every Missouri contract."); NY: *Jaffe v. Paramount Communications, Inc.*, 644 N.Y.S.2d 43, 47 (1996) ("Implied in every contract is a covenant of good faith and fair dealing. . . .").

At the same time, the licensor must be careful that any statements regarding the performance or capabilities of the software are not misleading. Whether a statement arises to the level of a misrepresentation is a matter of fact and is subjective. Courts generally recognize that the sales process includes a degree of "puffery" and demonstrate some restraint in finding misrepresentation. *See, e.g., Teragram Corporation v. MarketWatch.com, Inc.*, 2004 WL 3086883 (D. Mass Dec. 29, 2004) (licensor's conduct in promoting the capabilities of its products did not constitute misrepresentations; "superior" is sales puffery, not a misrepresentation); *Moses.com Securities, Inc. v. Comprehensive Software Systems, Inc.*, 406 F.3d 1052 (8th Cir. 2005) (general statements made by software developer indicating there would be no problem in meeting launch date for new software system did not establish specific promise respecting system completion or system capabilities).

Fitness for a Particular Purpose (§ 16.V)

Licensors should avoid making statements about future performance or fitness for a particular purpose, as they may unintentionally create an express warranty. If the licensee relied on certain statements by the licensor as to the applicability of the software to the licensee's business needs, the licensee should insist that the licensor warrant that the software is fit for the particular purpose. In *L.S. Heath & Son, Inc. v. AT&T Info. Sys., Inc.*, 9 F.3d 561 (7th Cir. 1993), the court held that a statement that a computer system could meet the buyer's needs induced the buyer to purchase the system, creating an express warranty and becoming part of the bargain. *Id.* at 570.

Data Transfer (§ 16.X)

In conjunction with the provision of ancillary services to the software license, many licensees want the licensor to warrant that the licensor will comply with certain standards in transferring data. With the increased focus on data security, a prudent licensee should insist on the adoption of certain data protection standards (which should be attached to the agreement as an exhibit) and require the licensor to comply with such standards.

Gifts and Gratuities (§§ 16.Y, 45)

Both parties may want to include a warranty that gifts and gratuities were not exchanged by either party in consideration of entering into a contract. This is especially important in international contracts to avoid the ramifications of the Foreign Corrupt Practices Act. See § 45. This warranty assumes special importance when dealing with a governmental entity or a client that is publicly regulated such as utilities or the healthcare industry. For a more detailed discussion of the Foreign Corrupt Practices Act, see Chapter 12.H.

Customer Complaints (§ 16.Z)

The licensee may want to include a warranty that the licensor has not received a systemic number of customer complaints related to the product in question or one aspect of the product in question. This warranty is similar to the warranty set forth in § 16.S, which provides that there has been no material litigation relating to the product in question. This "belt and suspenders" approach seeks to identify those situations where the licensor settled complaints about the software's performance prior to the initiation of litigation.

Open Source Software (§ 16.AA)

An "Open Source" warranty is one of the most important warranties in an agreement. If a vendor were to include open source code in a deliverable to the customer, the customer may lose the ability to charge its end-users a license fee. A number of large, publicly held companies have recognized the risk of open source software to their business and disclosed it in their public filings. *See, e.g.*, Brocade Communications Systems, Inc., Form 10-K filed Jan. 19, 2006, p. 21 ("If we fail to carefully manage the use of 'open source' software in our products, we may be required to license key portions of our products on a royalty free basis or expose key parts of source code.") For an overview of the issues involved with open source software, see Falkowski, *An Innovation in Contract Drafting: Open Source*, MICH. B. J. 30 (May 2005), and Kalina & Czyzcki, *The Ins and Outs of Open Source*, 36 LAW. BRIEF 2 (No. 14, July 2006). See also Davidson, *Open Source Technical Due Diligence*, 23 COMPUTER & INTERNET LAW. 1 (Aug. 2006).

Location of Performance (§ 16.AB)

With greater political sensitivities over the outsourcing of U.S. jobs to foreign countries, the licensee may want to obtain a warranty that all services and work will be performed in the United States or that work cannot be performed offshore without the licensee's consent. The licensee may want to expand its warranty to provide that in the event work is performed overseas, the individuals performing such services may not work from home. See Form 23.K.2.R.5. This warranty is usually related to the provision of services and may be especially important if the licensee is a governmental entity or the work involves sensitive information, such as health or financial records. Most licensors accept this warranty, as it simply is an element of the price charged to the licensee. The licensee should realize that utilizing U.S. labor will increase the cost. Regardless of whether the licensee includes such a warranty, the licensee should always require that the licensor will comply with all U.S. export laws. See Chapter 5.M. See also Form 23.K.2, Section R for additional language regarding the use of foreign labor.

Representations Made in RFI and RFP (§ 16.AE)

Occasionally, licensees seek to have the licensor represent and warrant that all statements made by the licensor during the RFI and RFP process are true and correct as of the date the parties entered into the license agreement. The licensor should never make this representation and warranty, as the product delivered is almost always different from the product requested in the RFI or RFP. The inclusion of a representation of this nature undercuts the validity of the agreement's integration clause. Are the licensee's RFI and RFP, as well as the licensor's RFI response and RFP response, now incorporated into the license agreement? Such language creates ambiguity that in turn increases the likelihood the parties will later enter into a dispute resolution process. As such, the licensee is better off including those statements on which it relied in the agreement, instead of referencing documents that may no longer be valid and may create ambiguity.

Security (See, e.g., §§ 16.AD)

A prudent licensor should disclaim any warranty that the licensor's security methods will be perfect. No system is immune to a determined hacker. At best, a licensor can only warrant that it will use commercially reasonable security procedures and that it will review such procedures on a semi-annually basis to ensure they remain current. See Chapter 10 for a more detailed discussion of data privacy and security related issues.

Other Warranties (See, e.g., §§ 16.AF, AG, AH)

The licensee should also consider whether the nature of the transaction dictates that the licensor make other specialized representations and warranties to the licensee. See, e.g., §§ 16.AF, AG, AH.

Date/Y2K Warranties

While some customers seek to include a Y2K or Year 2000 warranty, such warranties are irrelevant and should not be included. More common are warranties regarding the changing of the date for daylight saving time and whether computer systems will continue to work as a result of such date changes.

Training (§ 16.AI)

Some licensees seek to have the licensor represent and warrant that the training provided by the licensor is sufficient to allow the licensee and its employees to "understand, operate and use" the software. Prudent licensors should be hesitant to make such a representation and warranty as the training provided by the licensor may be sufficient but the licensee's employees are not technically competent. An alternative position is to warrant that technically competent employees will be able to understand and operate the software, but doing so creates an ambiguity as to the meaning of "technically competent" employees.

Existing Installation (§ 16.AJ)

To avoid the issue of sales puffery and vaporware, the licensor should represent that the software is successfully operating in similar production environments at a certain number of customer sites with the same or greater computing requirements as the licensee.

Hardware (§ 16.AK)

To the extent the licensor is also supplying hardware as part of the contracted solution, the licensor should represent and warrant that the recommended hardware configuration will meet the needs of the licensee and the requirements of the contracted solution. Further, the licensor should also represent and warrant that the recommended hardware configuration has the ability to meet a given percentage increase in the licensee's present computing requirements.

The proper sizing of hardware is extremely challenging, as it difficult to predict how a software application will operate a particular hardware configuration especially when the software may have not been fully developed. Further, performance metrics often depend on the individual characteristics of the user. Thus, the licensor should avoid making any such warranties unless it is extremely confident in its methodology for sizing the hardware.

(iii) Licensee Warranties (§ 16.1.2)

The licensor should seek to have the licensee make a number of warranties to the licensor. First, the licensee should warrant that it is a company in good standing in the state in which it is incorporated and that the individual executing the license on behalf of the licensee is authorized to do so (§ 16.2.1). The licensee should warrant that the execution of the license agreement does not violate any other agreement to which the licensee is a party (§ 16.2.2). Further, the licensee should warrant that it has the ability to pay the license fee and its debts as they come due (§ 16.2.3).

If the licensor is developing software to the licensee's specifications, the licensee should warrant that the software will not infringe on any third party intellectual property rights. See § 14.C. The licensor should also consider whether the nature of the transaction dictates that the licensee make other specialized representations and warranties to the licensor. See, e.g., §§ 16AC, 16AD, AE.

For a general discussion of computer warranties, see McKenzie & Roach, *Negotiating Software License Agreements in an Economic Downturn*, 18 COMPUTER & INTERNET LAW 9 (Dec. 2001) and Feldman, *Warranties and Computer Services: Past, Present and Future*, 10 COMPUTER LAW. 1 (1993).

(b) Covenants

A covenant is an agreement by a party to undertake or not undertake a particular act. *Vierk v. Ritenour*, 172 N.E.2d 679 (Ind. App. 1961). It is an assurance that something will be done in the future. In the event of a breach of a covenant, the remedy is an action for damages. *Globe American Corp. v. Miller Hatcheries*, 110 S.W.2d 393 (Mo. 1937).

A covenant may be an express covenant or an implied covenant. Express covenants arise from the specific terms of an agreement, while an implied covenant is inferred from the words of the agreement. *Mercury Inv. Co. v. F.W. Woolworth Co.*, 706 P.2d 523 (Okla. 1985). Implied covenants, however, are not favored in the law. *Id.*

The most common implied covenant is the covenant of good faith and fair dealing implied in all contracts. *Collard v. Incorporated Village of Flower Hill*, 427 N.Y.S.2d 301, *aff'd* 421 N.E.2d 818 (NY. 1981).

(c) Disclaimer of Warranties (§ 16.1.4)

(i) In General

As permitted under UCC § 2-316, the licensor should disclaim all warranties except those expressly made in the license agreement including all implied warranties. If the licensor does not disclaim all other warranties, under UCC §§ 2-313 (express warranties), 2-314 (implied warranty of merchantability), and 2-315 (implied warranty of fitness for a particular purpose), the licensor could be potentially liable for the failure of the licensed software to be merchantable or fit for the purpose for which it is intended by the licensee. Arguably, the warranties of title and infringement cannot be classified as implied warranties as the UCC does not identify the implied warranties and thus they may not be disclaimed or modified.

Under the Uniform Computer Information Transactions Act (UCITA), specialized warranty disclaimers are established to better reflect the "service" and "non-goods" nature of software, but UCITA also allows UCC Article 2 disclaimers to suffice. See Chapter 13.B.3.i (v) for a more detailed discussion and § 16.1.4.A for an example of a UCITA warranty disclaimer. In electing the governing law of the agreement, the parties should carefully consider the implications of UCITA and UCC Article 2, as well as the common law, on the outcome of any potential dispute.

(ii) Magnuson-Moss

Although the Magnuson-Moss Warranty-Federal Trade Commission Improvement Act (the "Act"), 15 U.S.C. § 2301 *et seq;* 16 C.F.R. § 701, primarily addresses consumer products and would appear to be inapplicable to commercial transactions, the Act also applies to products normally used for consumer purposes even if the purchaser plans to use the product exclusively for a commercial use. *Najran Co. v. Fleetwood Enterprises, Inc.*, 659 F. Supp. 1081 (S.D. Ga. 1986).

Further, if the software is to be supplied to consumers who will utilize the software for personal, family, or household purposes (i.e., a "consumer product"), and the license contains any written warranties, the supplier may have to comply with the Act. The Act does not apply if the supplier does not make any express warranties. It is unclear, however, if the Act applies to software at all: the Act applies to "consumer products"—tangible products that are sold. Software is typically intangible and licensed.[2]

The Act broadly defines warranties to include any written affirmations of fact or written promises made in connection with the sale that relate to the nature of the workmanship and that affirm or promise that the material or workmanship is defect free or will meet a specified level of performance over a specified period of time. 15 U.S.C. § 2301(6)(A). It also includes any written undertakings to repair, replace, refund the license, or take other corrective actions if the software fails to meet certain stated functionality. 15 U.S.C. § 2301(6)(B). Functional specifications or a right to return the software are not considered warranties under the Act. The Act requires full and conspicuous disclosure of a warranty's terms and conditions in simple and readily understood language. Furthermore, the Act lists thirteen items whose inclusion may be required by Federal Trade Commission rules. 15 U.S.C. § 2302 (1996).

Under the Act, certain consumer product warranties made in writing must clearly and conspicuously designate the warranty as either a "limited warranty," that is, one that does not meet federal minimum standards set forth in Section 2304 of the Act, or a "full warranty," one that meets minimum federal standards set forth in Section 2304 of the Act. 15 U.S.C. § 2303 (1996). If a full warranty is made, the supplier must correct defects within a reasonable time and without charge and may not limit the duration of implied warranties. Further, after a reasonable number of attempts to remedy a defect, the consumer may elect to receive a refund or replacement. 15 U.S.C. § 2304 (1996). Most companies, however, provide limited, not full, warranties regardless of the industry they are in.

In any case, unlike the UCC and UCITA, the Act prohibits a supplier from disclaiming or modifying any implied warranties of merchantability and fitness for the purpose intended if the supplier makes a written warranty as defined under the Act or the supplier enters into a service contract with the consumer within 90 days of the date of sale. 15 U.S.C. § 2308 (1996). In addition, the Act only allows the supplier to limit the duration of these implied warranties to "the duration of a written warranty of reasonable duration." 15 U.S.C. § 2308(b) (1996).

It is believed the Act applies only to the physical media on which software resides, as opposed to the software program itself, although there has been no judicial decision on this issue as of this writing. Nevertheless, written warranties as to the workings of the software itself may be covered and thus from the licensor's perspective should be avoided. Moreover, warranties as to turnkey systems may fall under the Act, in which case both hardware and software would be covered as a single product. Thus, the careful licensor of software to be licensed to consumers should make no written warranties and should not provide service contracts that become effective less than 91 days from the date of sale.

2. The Federal Trade Commission (FTC) held a hearing on whether the Act applies to software on October 26–27, 2000. The software industry was strongly against any such application. The FTC never issued a staff position, and as of September 11, 2010, the issue is still open at the staff level. For a more detailed discussion, see http://www.ftc.gov/bcp/work shops/warranty/comments/index.html (last viewed September 11, 2010).

For a more detailed discussion on the effects of representations and warranties on software licensing, see Dutton, *Warranties, Time-Bombs and Other Risk Allocation Issues,* 69 COM. L. ADV. 69–102 (Sept. 1993); Friedman & Hildebrand, *Computer Litigation: A Buyer's Theories of Liability,* 4 COMPUTER LAW. 34 (Dec. 1987); Philips, *When Software Fails: Emerging Standards of Vendor Liability Under the Uniform Commercial Code,* 50 BUS. LAW. 151 (1994). See also, Hammond, *Limiting and Dealing with Liability in Software Controls,* 9 COMPUTER LAW. 22 (June 1992).

(iii) Specific Disclaimers (§ 16.5)

Section 2-316(2) of the UCC requires that any warranty disclaimers related to merchantability must mention the word "merchantability," and if in a writing, it must be conspicuous. *See, e.g., Estey. v. Mackenzie Eng'g., Inc.,* 902 P.2d 1220 (Or. 1995). While "conspicuous" is defined under UCC § 1-201(10), whether or not a particular disclaimer is conspicuous is subject to the interpretation of the courts. Printing a disclaimer in block letters has been held to be sufficient. *Window Headquarters, Inc. v. MAI Basic Four, Inc.,* 1994 WL 673519 (S.D.N.Y. Dec. 1, 1994), but see *Sierra Diesel Inj. Service v. Burroughs Corp.,* 656 F. Supp. 426 (D. Nev. 1987), *aff'd,* 874 F.2d 653 (9th Cir. 1989) (disclaimer in bold type not conspicuous when it appeared on reverse of contract).

Those disclaimers relating to fitness for a particular purpose must be in writing and conspicuous. UCC § 2-316.

When disclaiming warranties, the licensor should ensure the disclaimer clause lists the sections which set forth the agreement's warranties; for example. "Except as set forth in *Sections 12 and 13,* Licensor disclaims all other express and implied warranties . . . " The reason for doing so is to definitively identify those warranties that the licensor is making and limit the licensee from claiming the licensor made other warranties in the agreement. If a warranty is not set out in the identified sections it is disclaimed and is of no effect. Of course the licensee should insist on more general language: "Except as set forth in this Agreement, the parties disclaim all other express or implied warranties . . ." as the licensee should be concerned about failing to list all warranties contained in the agreement and thus losing the benefit of its bargain.

The licensor should specifically provide that all warranties are voided by any misuse of the software, modification of the software by the licensee, or the failure to operate the software in the specified environment. Software is temperamental by nature, and its performance can be adversely affected by the failure to run it in the specified environment. Further, the licensee should not be held responsible for misuse of the software or for modifications made by the licensee. The licensor needs to control the integrity of its software to ensure the software meets the stated functional specifications.

(d) Length of Warranty (§ 16.1)

The length of the warranty period for the licensed software is an element of price. Industry standard is to provide a warranty of 60 days to one year (depending on the type of software), effective on the date of delivery or date of acceptance of the software. It is important to recognize when the warranty begins. Many licensors state that the warranty begins on the date of installation or shipment. This is potentially troublesome for the licensee as the warranty may expire prior to acceptance and thus should not be agreed to by the licensee. The equitable solution is to have the warranty run from the date of acceptance. If the licensee requires a warranty longer than the standard warranty offered by the licensor, the licensor can provide one for an increased price. Generally, 12 months of maintenance is priced at an amount equal to 15 to 18 percent of the license fee. Some licensors include the first year's maintenance in the initial license fee.

Licensors must be careful to limit the length of any warranty they give. Many licensees request a one-year warranty. This creates a hidden risk for the licensor as, during the warranty period, the licensee may terminate the license agreement and seek a refund if the licensor is in material breach. During a maintenance period provided under a properly worded and separate maintenance agreement, however, the licensee would only receive a refund of the maintenance fee if the licensor was in material breach. Thus, a prudent solution is for the licensor to grant, for example, a 60-day warranty and 10 months free maintenance under a separate maintenance agreement. At least one major software company provides no warranty period and instead gives the licensee a 90-day period in which to evaluate and test the software prior to acceptance. At the end of the 90-day period, the potential licensee can either accept the software "as is" without a warranty or reject the software without obligation.

2. General Indemnification (§ 15)

(a) Overview

General indemnification clauses usually address the liability of one party to the other for liability the first party incurred to a third party as a result of the second party's actions. It is an attempt to transfer the burden of risk to the party best able to eliminate or control the risk. Indemnification is usually limited to particular types of third party claims, such as personal bodily injury or tangible property damage caused by one of the parties to a third party, including the other party's employees or contractors. Indemnification is not an appropriate remedy for claims between two contracting parties who have a direct claim against the other.

Indemnification clauses traditionally encompass two distinct obligations: the obligation to defend the claim and pay all costs associated with any lawsuit and to indemnify or reimburse the indemnified party for its obligations to the third party claimant. *Trust One Mortgage Corporation v. Invest America Mortgage Corporation*, 134 Cal. App.4th 1302 (Cal. 2005). Indemnification differs from a warranty and a representation in that the entity making the representation or warranty must pay the other party's damages arising from the facts not being as stated.

Although the right of indemnification may arise under common law, indemnification clauses are a common means to contractually allocate risk between the parties. *See, e.g., Novak v. BASF Corporation*, 869 F. Supp. 113, 119 (N.D.N.Y 1994). A correctly worded indemnification clause will also allow for the recovery of lawyer's fees that traditionally are not recoverable in a legal action. The indemnification provisions contained in a license agreement should be mutual for the protection of both parties.

The interaction between the license's indemnification clause and the indemnifying party's insurance policies should be closely scrutinized as the waiver of its insurance company's right of subrogation may raise the indemnifying party's insurance rates.

Usually, the parties will incorporate language to the following effect:

> Licensor shall defend, indemnify and hold harmless Licensee and its Affiliates and their respective officers, directors, agents, lawyers and representatives (collectively the "Indemnified Parties") from and against any and all damages, losses, liabilities, judgments, awards, costs, and expenses of any nature whatsoever, including reasonable attorney's fees and court costs, incurred by any Indemnified Party arising out of or relating to any **non-affiliated third party** claims for: (i) any loss or damage to real property or tangible personal property, or any bodily injury, including death, to the extent caused by the intentional or negligent acts or omissions of Consultant; or (ii) claims, actions, or proceedings brought by any third party alleging infringement by any Software provided to Licensee by Licensor. **Any liability limitations set forth in this Agreement shall not apply to these indemnification obligations.**

Often, however, a party may not understand the true meaning of the language contained in an indemnification clause. The three most important terms are:

> *Indemnify* – to reimburse a party for any liability or loss incurred.
>
> *Defend* – to pay the indemnitee's legal costs in defending a third party claim.
>
> *Hold Harmless* – to protect the indemnitee against harm from a third person.

The term "indemnify" is considered to be an offensive right allowing a party to seek indemnification while the term "harmless" is considered defensive, protecting the indemnified party against claims made by the indemnifying party. *Queen Villas Homeowners Association v. TCB Property Management*, 149 Cal. App. 4th 1 (2007). In the event of an ambiguity, an indemnity provision will be strictly construed against the drafter, or mutually negotiated, against the indemnitee. *Topp Copy Prods., Inc. v. Singletary*, 626 A.2d 98 (Pa. 1993); (ambiguity construed against indemnitee); *Hooper Assocs., Ltd. v. AGS Computers, Inc.*, 548 N.E. 2d 903 (N.Y. 1989). An obligation to indemnify but not defend requires the indemnifying party to act only when the indemnitee has suffered an actual loss. *Larson Mach., Inc. v. Wallace*, 600 S.W.2d (Ark. 1980). An obligation to provide indemnification against liability creates a duty when the liability matures. *Williams v. Johnston*, 442 P.2d 178 (Idaho 1968).

(b) Contributory versus Comparative Negligence

The failure to include an indemnification provision may limit an injured party's recovery under the laws of those states that have not adopted the doctrine of comparative negligence and still recognize the doctrine of contributory negligence. The principle of indemnification seeks to ensure that the standard for the allocation of risk is on a comparative risk basis versus a contributory risk basis. Without an indemnification provision, the parties are subject to the uncertainty of where the action is brought and whether that state utilizes a contributory negligence standard. By including an indemnification provision, the parties can create certainty and eliminate any benefit a party may achieve by bringing a claim in a state whose laws are favorable to its potential claim.

As of October 1, 2010, only Alabama, the District of Columbia, Maryland, North Carolina, and Virginia apply the doctrine of pure contributory negligence.

Some licensees seek to avoid the impact of comparative fault by specifically stating that the obligation to indemnify is absolute, regardless of any comparative fault. See the illustrative language below.

> *"Comparative Fault" shall mean the attribution of fault of each party on a percentage of fault basis where both parties contributed to the cause of the injury."*
>
> *The duty of the Licensor to defend, indemnify and hold harmless the Licensee, its agents and employees under this Section shall exist regardless of whether or not the act giving rise to this duty is caused or claimed to have been caused, in part, by a party indemnified hereunder and such duty shall be determined without regard to any apportionment of liability under the laws relating to Comparative Fault; however, this provision does not apply to claims arising out of or caused by the sole negligence or willful misconduct of any indemnities.*

A more efficient approach is simply to state that the obligation to indemnify exists except to the extent that the indemnified party's injury arose from the indemnified party's *sole* negligence. The inclusion of the word "sole" raises the issue of why the indemnifying party should pay for injuries resulting from the indemnified party's own negligence. Too often, however, the vendor must accept such language to win the transaction.

(c) *Equitable and Implied Indemnification*

An indemnification obligation may arise not only through contract but also through equity. *Smoketree-Lake Murray, Ltd. v. Mills Concrete Construction Company, Inc.*, 234 Cal. App. 3d 1724 (1991). The creation of an equitable indemnification obligation arises as a result of language contained in an agreement unrelated to the indemnification clause or "by the equities of the particular case." *Id.* at 1736. Implied indemnities are a form of equitable indemnities. In its most common form, equitable indemnities are applied "to proportion loss among tortfeasors in proportion to their relative culpability so there will be an equitable sharing of the loss." *Id.*

A majority of jurisdictions that have addressed the issue of implied indemnification obligations have found that a contractual relationship under the UCC, with its implied warranties, provides a sufficient basis for an implied indemnity claim when the buyer incurs liability to a third party as a result of a defect in goods that would constitute a breach of the seller's implied or express warranties. Majority: California, Maine, Michigan, Minnesota, Missouri, Nebraska, New Hampshire, New York, North Carolina, Pennsylvania, Virginia, Washington. *See, e.g.*, *Central Washington Refrigeration, Inc. v. Barbee,* 946 P.2d 760, 764 (Wash. 1997); *Carrier Corp. v. Detrex Corp.*, 6 Cal. Rptr. 2d 565, 569 (1992); *Cyr v. Michaud,* 454 A.2d 1376, 1385 (Me. 1983). Minority: Idaho, South Dakota, Utah. *See, e.g.*, *Sheehan v. Morris Irrigation, Inc.*, 460 N.W.2d 413 (S.D. 1990); *Perry v. Pioneer Wholesale Supply Co.*, 681 P.2d 214, 219 (Utah 1984).

(d) Drafting Considerations

Indemnification usually covers only third party claims and not the indemnified party's own damages. From the licensor's perspective, the indemnification should not cover all third party claims but only those claims arising from intellectual property infringement (see Section B.3, below, for a more detailed discussion) and those arising from damage to tangible personal property and personal bodily injury, including death. A licensee should seek an indemnity for any claim, loss, costs, damages, and the like, arising from the indemnifying party's gross negligence or willful misconduct in performing under the agreement as opposed to specific indemnified acts. Otherwise, the indemnity may not apply if the negligent act was not specifically addressed in the underlying contract but still resulted in liability on behalf of the indemnified party.

A party should indemnify the officers, directors and employees of the indemnified party but should resist indemnifying a party's contractors and agents as well. The indemnifying party should ensure that the indemnity is tightly drafted and should resist indemnifying the other party for "any act or omission," its general negligence or for damages arising from the breach of the license/agreement, as an injured party always has the right to bring a breach of contract claim in the event of a *negligent* act. If the indemnifying party is willing to indemnify another party for any "act or omissions," such indemnification should be limited to the indemnifying party's *negligent* acts and omissions. Further, the indemnifying party should ensure that it has disclaimed all liability for all third party claims except those for which it is specifically indemnifying the indemnified party. See, e.g., § 16.1. The underlying reasoning for this position is that the indemnified party can limit its liability through its contracts with its own customers.

Similarly, the indemnifying party should limit its indemnification obligations solely to third party claims and claims for tangible personal property for damage and personal bodily injury. A prudent party will also include a corresponding warranty to insure seamless coverage allowing it to recover for any injury it may incur. A licensee may object to limiting the indemnification to tangible personal property in software information/technology agreements as the underlying software is usually of greater importance to the parties.

Usually, indemnification for personal bodily injury or personal property damages is excluded from the contract's limit of liability. In consumer goods transactions, any limit of consequential damages in the event of personal bodily injury is prima facie unconscionable. UCC § 2–719(3). As such, the limitation of liability clause discussed in Section B.4, below, often contains "carve out provisions," excluding the license agreement's indemnification provisions from any limit of liability.

Every indemnification provision should require the indemnified party to give the indemnifying party prompt notice of any claim, to cede control of the defense to the indemnifying party and to assist the indemnifying party in the defense of the claim. Unless set forth in the agreement, notice is not a condition precedent to providing indemnification. *ELRAC, Inc. v. Cruz*, 699 N.Y.S.2d 647 (1999) (notice not required); *Am. Home Assur. Co. v. Int'l Ins. Co.*, 684 N.E.2d 14 (N.Y. 1997) (failure to comply with notice provision may void indemnity obligation). *But see Morris v. Schlumberger, Ltd.*, 445 So.2d 1242 (La. 1984).

The indemnification clause should provide that if the indemnifying party fails to accept control of the dispute or settle the claim in a reasonable manner, the indemnified party may settle the matter on a reasonable basis without the consent of the indemnifying party. ELRAC, 699 N.Y.S.2d at 647. Further, any action or inaction by the indemnified party which prejudices the indemnifying party will negate the indemnifying party's obligations to the extent its interests have been prejudiced. *New Amsterdam Cas. Co. v. Lundquist*, 198 N.W.2d 543 (Minn. 1972).

(e) Indemnifying a Party for Its Own Negligence

The indemnifying party should ensure that the agreement clearly provides that the indemnifying party will control and lead the defense of any claim. Given that the indemnifying party is responsible for paying the cost of the defense and any settlement, it should control the defense. The indemnified party may protect its interests by requiring the indemnifying party to obtain the indemnified party's consent prior to settling the matter if the settlement would financially impact the indemnified party.

Increasingly, licensors are seeking to limit their indemnity and other liability to third party claims arising from the licensor's gross negligence and even have the licensee indemnify the licensor for the licensor's own negligence. Most licensees argue that this is unreasonable, and this point most likely will be a deal killer. Gross negligence is a very difficult standard to meet and would likely leave the licensee without a remedy except in the most egregious cases. See Section B.7.(a)(ii)(y), below, for a more detailed discussion of gross negligence. The licensor controls its own actions not the licensee, thus the licensee cannot be expected to insure the actions of the licensor.

Further, it is unclear whether a provision requiring the licensee to indemnify the licensor for the licensor's negligence is enforceable. *See, e.g., Northwest Airlines, Inc. v. Alaska Airlines, Inc.*, 351 F.2d 253 (9th Cir. 1965) (exculpatory and indemnity provision that excuses party from liability for its own negligence is against public policy and invalid); *City of Santa Barbara v. Superior Court*, 161 P.3d 1095 (Cal. 2007) (release for future gross negligence or intentional misrepresentation is unenforceable); Cal. Civ. Code § 2273. *See also, Burns v. N&L Realty Corp.*, 160 F. Supp. 203 (W.D. Pa. 1958) (contract provisions indemnifying lessor for lessor's negligence will be construed strongly against lessor and in favor of lessee).

Some jurisdictions, however, permit such an indemnification under the express negligence rule, requiring only that any indemnification that releases a party from all liability from its own future negligence "must be expressed in unambiguous terms within the four corners of the contract" and must also be "conspicuous." *Griffin Industries, Inc. v. Foodmaker, Inc.*, 22 S.W.3d 33, 37 (Tex. 2000). *See also Iowa*: *Maxim Technologies, Inc. v. City of Dubuque*, 690 N.W.2d 896 (Iowa 2005) (indemnification of party for its own negligence must be expressed in unambiguous terms and will be strictly construed). Conn: *Dow-Westbrook, Inc. v. Candlewood Equine Practice LLC*, 989 A.2d 1075 (Conn. App. 2010) (indemnity clause releasing a party from its own negligence is not unusual in commercial contracts and should be viewed as a means to allocate risk.) Similarly, New York allows indemnification for a party's own negligence, except to the extent the underlying damages arise from the intentional causation of injury. *Austro v. Niagra Mohawk Power Corp.*, 487 N.E. 2d 267 (N.Y. 1985). Any indemnity for an act known to be unlawful at the time of such indemnification, however, is void. *Lemat v. American Basketball Assn.*, 51 Cal. App. 3d 267 (1975). *But see*, California Civ. Code § 2773 (can indemnify for past wrongful act unless a felony).

The statute of limitations on an indemnity claim begins to run when the claim is settled, even if the statute on the underlying warranty has already expired. *Central Washington Refrigeration Inc. v. Barbee*, 946 P.2d 760, 765 (Wash. 1997).

3. Intellectual Property Indemnification (§ 14)

Intellectual property indemnification protects a licensee if a third party brings a claim that the licensee's use of the licensed software violates such third party's intellectual property rights. Usually, these intellectual property rights are copyright, patent, trademark, and trade secrets. Trade secrets create the greatest risk for the licensor as they are not usually recorded in any location where the licensor would be able to determine whether the intellectual property in question infringed upon a third party's trade secrets. Similarly, some licensors are hesitant to provide patent indemnification for software given the recent proliferation of business method patents, as well as the inability of licensors to know what inventions are disclosed in competitors' patent applications that can take two years or more to issue and become publicly available. In response to the ever increasing number of claims bought by "patent trolls," some licensors have sought to transfer the burden of proof of patent infringement claims from the licensor to the licensee. Licensees should strongly resist such change, as the licensor should have a much more thorough understanding of its owned intellectual property and thus, can better understand and mitigate the risk. Trademark infringement is not as serious a concern in software licensing as only infrequently will the licensee be using the licensor's trademarks.

Upon granting a license to the licensee, a licensee may argue that the licensor is assumed to have made an implied warranty of title under UCC § 2-312(2). Section 2-312(2) of the UCC provides that unless otherwise agreed, a seller who is a merchant regularly dealing in goods of the kind sold, warrants that the goods delivered will be free of any rightful claim of infringement by any third party. It also provides that a buyer who furnishes the specifications must likewise indemnify the seller for any claim arising from the seller complying with the buyer's specifications. UCC § 2-312(2); *Bonneau Co. v. AG Industries, Inc.*, 116 F.3d 155 (5th Cir. 1997). This indemnity is limited to third party rights existing at the time of delivery. *Yttro Corporation v. X. Ray Imaging Assoc., Inc.*, 559 A.2d 3, 5 (N.J. 1989). Any disclaimer of this warranty must specifically disclaim the warranty of infringement such that the buyer has reason to know that the seller does not claim title or that a third party may have a claim of infringement. General disclaimers such as "AS IS" are not sufficient to disclaim the warranties of title and infringement. UCC § 2-312(3).

A licensor is likely to argue, however, that software is not a good and the software is licensed, not sold. Thus, UCC 2-312(2) would be inapplicable. See *DSC Commu-*

nications Corp. v. Pulse Communications, Inc., 170 F.3d 1354 (Fed. Cir. 1999) (court applies common law and does not refer to UCC).

A patent license, however, does not usually contain an implied warranty of noninfringement. DELLER, DELLER'S WALKER ON PATENTS 406 (1981). *See Motorola, Inc. v. Varo, Inc.*, 656 F. Supp. 716 (N.D. Tex. 1986), and *Chevron, Inc. v. Aqua Products*, 830 F. Supp. 314 (E.D. Va. 1993) (under the doctrine of federal preemption, UCC § 2-312(3) does not impose an indemnity obligation on a party that would not otherwise bear infringement liability under federal patent law). *But see Cover v. Hydramatic Packing Co.*, 83 F.3d 1390 (7th Cir. 1996) (UCC § 2-312(3) is not preempted by federal law).

The defense of intellectual property indemnification suits can be costly even if the licensor eventually prevails, and during their pendency the licensee may be prohibited from using the software it needs to operate its business. As such the licensor/indemnifying party should carefully limit the indemnity it offers, while the licensee should make sure it obtains the protection it needs to operate its business.

Some licensors believe the indemnification clause should be limited to *existing* U.S. intellectual property rights at the time the license agreement is executed. This eliminates any right to indemnification for intellectual property rights created subsequent to the grant of the license. At the same time, it limits indemnification only to those U.S. intellectual property rights significantly limiting the licensor's risk. However, a limited intellectual property rights indemnification by the licensor may be shortsighted. If the licensee is sued for intellectual property infringement outside the scope of the licensor's indemnification, the licensee will be forced to defend the suit. The licensee's interest in defending the suit, however, may be greatly different from the licensor's in that the licensee may be motivated to settle the suit on terms favorable to the licensee, but which have a disastrous impact on the licensor's business if the decision voids the intellectual property rights of the licensor or otherwise creates a negative precedent for the licensor that impacts its business in the future.

With foreign transactions, indemnification should be limited to the United States and the country in which the software will be used. If the license is worldwide, the licensor should seek to limit its indemnification to those countries that are signatories to the Berne Convention. The model language below, which favors the licensee by not limiting the licensor's indemnification obligations to a definitive list of international agreements, is illustrative:

> *Licensor hereby agrees to indemnify, defend and hold harmless Licensee from any claim brought against Licensee that the Software infringes any third party's intellectual property rights issued, honored or enforceable under U.S. laws or international convention(s) (including but not limited to the Berne Convention, Paris Convention, Universal Copyright Convention, Patent Cooperation Treaty) including but not limited to patents, copyrights, trademarks, trade names and trade secrets.*

At the same time, any foreign indemnification should be granted only after sufficient due diligence has been performed with respect to the product market in the particular foreign country, and even then it should be limited solely to patent and copyright indemnification, since a number of foreign jurisdictions have "first to file" trademark laws that encourage manipulation of the rights of foreign trademark owners. Including the phrase "finally awarded" limits the licensor's obligation to make payments to the licensee until all appeals have been exhausted. The licensor should also be careful to limit indemnification to a specific licensee and not a broad class of entities, such as "the licensee and its affiliates" or "the licensee and its customers." Obviously limiting the jurisdictions covered by the indemnification has a similar risk to the other scope restrictions discussed above. However, this may be outweighed by the risk of providing legal resources in foreign jurisdictions.

If the licensee is willing to agree to a limited intellectual property indemnification, the licensee should still insist that any attempt to limit indemnification to U.S. intellectual property should be limited only to patents. Copyright infringement, for example, should not be limited solely to U.S. copyrights, as under the Berne Convention a foreign copyright holder may enforce its copyrights in the United States. Berne Convention for the Protection of Literary and Artistic Works art. 4, July 24, 1971, S. Treaty Doc. No. 99-27 at 39 (1986).

If the licensor agrees to allow the licensee's contractors to access to its intellectual property, the licensee should indemnify the licensor for any misuse of the licensor's intellectual property by the licensee's contractors.

An indemnification obligation can be characterized by its "front-end" obligations and its "back-end" obligations. Front-end obligations include the right of the indemnifying party to receive notice of a claim and the right to develop a work around or obtain a license for the indemnified party. The back end includes the indemnifying party's right to control any lawsuit and the right of the indemnified party to participate in the lawsuit. In drafting the provision, the licensor should clearly state that the remedy is the exclusive remedy for a claim of intellectual property infringement.

Indemnification by the licensor should be predicated on several requirements. First, the licensee must promptly notify the licensor of any claim. Second, the licensee must assist and cooperate in the claim's defense (at the licensor's expense). Third, the licensor must control the defense and settlement of the suit as the licensor ultimately bears the financial responsibility. Fourth, upon notice of a claim, the licensor may, at its option, either make the licensed software noninfringing, obtain a license to use such software from the party trying to enforce its rights, or provide functionally equivalent software. Alternatively, if none of these options is practicable, at the licensor's option, the licensor may refund the license fee to the licensee. Usually this refund is reduced by the benefit the licensee received prior to the software's removal, based on a five-year amortization. Although the period of depreciation may range from three to seven years, this remedy is usually in full satisfaction of the licensor's liability to the licensee.

Most licensees will reject any attempt by the licensor to "depreciate" the value of the software. Although the licensee may have had use of the software prior to its removal, the licensee will have to obtain new software and, in the process, may incur potentially significant disruptions of its business, as well as switching costs. As such, most licensees will seek to recover the full cost of the software. If the software has been fully depreciated, some licensors will refund fees paid by the licensee starting when the software has been fully depreciated.

All agreements should exclude indemnification to the extent that the licensor acts on the licensee's direct instructions, the licensee utilizes superseded software, or the licensee uses the software in violation of the license, or if the claim arises from the licensee's use of the software in conjunction with commercially available, third party software. Another common exclusion is a patent, copyright or other intellectual property claim in which the licensee or an affiliate of the licensee has an interest. If the licensor utilizes any of the licensee's intellectual property in the licensor's development efforts, the licensee should indemnify the licensor for any claims that the licensee's intellectual property infringes on a third party's intellectual property rights.

Licensors often seek to exclude from their indemnification obligations any infringement caused by the combination of their software with any data, software, or hardware not provided by the licensor. The practical effect of such an exclusion is to eliminate all indemnification obligations for patents that include a computer or a computer memory as an element of the claim. A licensee should seek to require the licensor to warrant that the software will be noninfringing, whether standing alone or in conjunction with the hardware or software with which it was designed to operate. Licensors, however, may be hesitant to make such a warranty as it is difficult to predict how the licensor's software will perform in conjunction with third party products. Licensors should not agree to a warranty that permits combinations not necessary for the use of the software to be covered by the indemnification.

A licensee must make sure it is comfortable with language that allows a licensor to refund the licensee's license fee, especially if the software is important to the operation of the licensee's business, as the licensee may receive only a refund of its license fee in the event of a claim of infringement. Similarly, if the licensee insists on removing the licensor's option to refund the license fee in full satisfaction of an infringement claim, the licensor must be comfortable with the concept that it could be forced to expend its entire net worth obtaining a work around or a license for a functionally similar software package. The solution will usually be an element of price as the licensor will usually expand its indemnification for an increased license fee.

Finally, the licensee should insist on including language allowing the licensee to assume its own defense at the licensor's cost if the licensor fails to promptly assume any defense. While a reasonable requirement from the licensee's perspective, this creates a significant risk from the licensor's perspective, both in its potential cost and in that the licensee's interests in defending and settling the suit may be vastly different than the licensor's. See the detailed discussion of the parties' different interests earlier in this Section, B.3.

For a more in-depth discussion of the issues surrounding intellectual property indemnification and model clauses, see *Neumeyer, Responding to Patent License and Indemnification Demands*, 27 ACC Docket 45 (Oct. 2009). Ocampo, Curtin & Moss, *Infringement Indemnity*, 14 ACCA Docket 64 (July/August 1996).

4. *Acceptance and Acceptance Test Procedures (§§ 1.14, 7)*

(a) Software

The concept of acceptance and the corresponding acceptance test procedures are extremely important in custom software development contracts. With custom software, the concept of acceptance is not difficult to understand, but in practicality it is difficult to quantify. Too often, the license agreement is unclear as to the standard to which the software must conform to be accepted by the customer. Will the software conform to the contractual specifications, the operational documentation, the acceptance test procedures, or some other standard? Must the software strictly comply with all requirements or simply comply in all material respects to the functional specifications? Further, what differentiates a "bug" from an "error"? What level of bugs is acceptable? It is difficult, if not impossible, to agree on the acceptance tests if the parties do not know what aspects of the software will be tested, much less know the functional specifications of the completed software.

The acceptance test procedures should be objective in nature such that an independent third party should be able to determine whether the licensed software has satisfied the tests. Any acceptance test procedures should be mutually agreed upon by the parties to ensure fairness. The licensor usually drafts the test procedures protocol document, given its familiarity with its own software, and submits this document to the licensee for approval. The licensee then either accepts the document or suggests potential modifications. To ensure that there is mutual agreement as to what constitutes "acceptance," the term should be carefully defined. Otherwise, a court itself may determine what is "acceptable." See *Sha-I Corp. v. City and County of San Francisco,* 612 F.2d 1215 (9th Cir. 1980) (satisfactory completion of 95 percent of acceptance requirements constituted acceptance).

In the event the software fails to pass the acceptance test procedures, the contract should provide a set period of time for the licensor to fix the errors and submit the software to the licensee for retesting. The license should then have a set period of time to retest the software. See § 7.2 for model language.

To avoid disputes as to whether or not the software has been accepted, the licensor should have the customer execute an acceptance certificate, formally accepting the software. Execution of the certificate should be contractually required if the software meets the acceptance test procedures. The certificate should also provide formal notice of the start of the warranty. See the model Certificate of Acceptance, Form 23.C.5.

Software by its nature is considered imperfect, and bugs will always exist in a program's code. Acceptance testing will not eliminate all bugs but will hopefully identify any material problems. Consequently, most agreements contain language to the effect that the software will "substantially conform" to the functional specifications or "comply in all material respects." Thus, many agreements classify and delineate the levels of errors and then quantify how many of each level are acceptable. For an example of the classification of errors, see Appendix A to the Software Maintenance and Services Agreement in Form 23.C.2.

Deemed Acceptance

Like off-the-shelf software, custom software contracts should include a provision that the use of the software in a commercial context shall be deemed acceptance. Otherwise, the licensee may have an incentive not to accept the software while receiving the commercial benefits of using the software without paying for the software, starting the warranty period or having to pay for maintenance. See § 7.3. Many licensees, however, seek to include specific language that the software can be accepted only through the acceptance test procedures, and that use of the software in a live operational environment does not constitute acceptance. See § 7.3 (alternative language).

Smart licensees will require that acceptance of any new releases or enhancements are subject to acceptance testing. New releases or enhancements are just as important to the licensee's system as the core software, and these need to be tested prior to being incorporated in the licensee's existing software or system.

For an overview of the issues involved with acceptance from a UCC perspective, see Vizy, *Managing Acceptance,* 226 Com. L. Adv. 1 (Oct. 2006).

(b) Shrinkwrap Software

Off-the-shelf shrink-wrap licenses are deemed "accepted" when the cellophane packaging of the software has been opened or, alternatively, with the use of the software. While there is a split among the federal circuit courts, the enforceability of off-the-shelf acceptance is the majority rule. *See ProCD, Inc. v. Zeidenberg,* 86 F.3d 1447 (7th Cir. 1996). *But see Step-Saver Data Systems, Inc. v. Wyse Technology,* 939 F.2d 91 (3d Cir. 1991) (shrink-wrap license not enforceable under Section 2-207 of UCC as license terms mutually altered the contract between the parties). See Chapter 9 for a more detailed discussion of the validity of shrink-wrap licenses.

Finally, the customer should ensure that the license clearly states that payment does not constitute acceptance. Any payments made by the customer should be considered an advance payment toward the delivery of an accepted deliverable. See Section 23.B.1 § 8.2 for model language.

(c) Professional Services (§ 16.C)

If professional services are a distinct component of the deliverables, the licensee should ensure that the agreement contains a representation and warranty as to the quality of services delivered. Many licensees insist that the services should be delivered in accordance with the highest industry standards. Prudent licensors should not accept this standard, as it is impossible to ascertain what this language would require without conducting continuous surveys as to what the highest standard in the industry entails. A more measured approach is to require the services to be provided in a professional and workmanlike manner in accordance with industry standards. *See D.B. Feedyards v. Environmental Sciences,* 745 N.W.2d 593, 606 (Neb. App. 2008) (consulting service "owed a duty to perform its services as a reasonable . . . consultant with specialized knowledge, skill, training and expertise would under similar circumstances.")

5. Breach, Cure and Termination/Cancellation (§ 5)

A license's termination provisions are extremely important from both the licensor's and licensee's perspective's as each has different concerns about the ability to terminate the license agreement and the rights of each party upon such termination.

The parties should consider the ramifications of not only a breach arising from negligence but also a willful breach. In most cases, the parties will want to establish a carve out from the agreement's limitation of liability in the event of a willful breach to the extent the governing law does not recognize that a willful breach voids a contract's limitation of liability. *Khulusi v. Southwestern Yellow Pages, Inc.*, 916 S.W.2d 227 (Mo. 1995) (willful and wanton conduct voids contract's limitation of liability). Further, in the event of a willful breach or default, the breaching party is not entitled to receive damages from the other party's breach of contract. *Ficara v. Belleau, et al.*, 117 N.E.2d 287 (Mass. 1954).

(a) Breach

(i) Licensee's Breach (§ 5.2)

Most license agreements set forth a number of criteria that allow the licensor to terminate the agreement and the underlying license. The most common are breach of the license grant, nonpayment of any amounts due the licensor, and breach of the licensee's confidentiality obligations. Aggressive licensors often seek to include other triggers such as a change in the licensee's financial status. Licensees should avoid accepting broad subjective language, such as the language below, as it grants the licensor the unfettered ability to terminate the agreement or license.

> Licensor may terminate this Agreement if in Licensor's reasonable judgment, Customer's financial condition does not justify the terms of payment specified herein, unless Customer immediately pays for all Software and Services which have been delivered, and pays in advance for the balance of Software and Services remaining to be delivered during the term of this Agreement.

Many licensors include language allowing the licensor to terminate the agreement in the event the licensee declares bankruptcy, becomes insolvent or is unable to pay its debts as they become due. These conditions, known as *ipso facto* clauses, are unenforceable under the U.S. bankruptcy laws. 11. U.S.C. § 365(e).

See Chapter 17 for a more detailed discussion of the impact of bankruptcy on software licenses.

(ii) Licensor's Breach (§ 5.1)

A licensee should also ensure the license agreement allows it to terminate the agreement in the event of the licensor's breach. The most common justifications are the failure of the software to comply with the functional specifications, a breach of the agreement's representations or warranties and a breach of the licensor's confidentiality obligations. Some licensees will also seek to include a number of other triggers including changes in the licensor's financial status, the failure to meet agreed service levels as well as the failure of the licensor to meet any other material terms of the agreement.

Some licensees seek to include language in the license that if they terminate the licensor for breach and it is later found that they wrongfully terminated the licensor, the termination shall be treated as a termination for convenience not breach. This provision should be rejected by the licensor as it seeks to excuse the licensee from any liability for wrongfully terminating the license. In essence, it removes any element of risk from wrongful termination.

(iii) General Issues Related to Termination for Breach

A party's right to terminate a license agreement for breach should be for a *material* breach only. Common law recognizes that unless the agreement provides otherwise, an agreement can only be terminated for a material breach and not a minor deviation from a contractual obligation. *Rano v. Sipa Press, Inc.*, 987 F.2d 580 (9th Cir. 1993) (material breach required to rescind/terminate license).

Although the phrase "material" is subject to interpretation, it has been defined as "affect[ing] the purpose of a contract in an important or vital way." *K&K Management, Inc. v. Lee*, 557 A.2d 965 (Md. 1989); WILLISTON ON CONTRACTS § 866. The parties will often seek to include a definitive list of "material" breaches in the contract. Licensees should resist this approach as it may limit their ability to terminate the agreement if the licensor's nonperformance does not fall into one of the enumerated breaches.

Software, especially customized software, is often very complex. Thus, in the event of a failure to meet the functional specifications, it may require quite some time to duplicate and diagnose a problem, code the solution, and then install and test the software. The licensee can protect itself from the resulting late delivery by including a provision for liquidated damages, should the licensor fail to deliver the software in a timely manner or if the software fails to operate in accordance with the functional specifications. However, the amount of liquidated damages must not be so high as to be considered unconscionable, or the agreement will be unenforceable. See UCC § 2-718, comment 1.

Licensees are often hesitant to terminate the agreement for the licensor's *material* breach as it creates a dilemma for the licensee. Even though the licensor has not delivered a working product, if the licensee terminates the agreement its business may be severely affected and it will be forced to restart the procurement process. As such, many licensees seek the option of either receiving the software's source code to complete the project itself, the right to receive monetary damages, or both. To ensure they receive the source code when licensors breach the license agreement, most licensees insist on the execution of an escrow agreement. While this ensures the release of the software's source code to the licensee, receipt of the source code does not necessarily solve the licensee's problems. See Chapter 10 for a more in-depth discussion of this issue.

Licensees should also seek to include language requiring the licensor to correct any nonconformance and prohibiting the licensor from walking away from a contract if it becomes unprofitable to perform. At least one court has recognized that a licensor's failure to perform due to a contract's unprofitability is not an intentional breach of contract that would void the contract's limit of liability. *Metropolitan Life Ins. Co.*

v. Noble Lowndes Int'l. Inc., 643 N.E.2d 504 (N.Y. 1994). In essence, the licensee seeks to ensure a form of specific performance.

(iv) Cure Periods (See e.g. § 5.1 (e), (f), (g), (i), (j))

Both parties should ensure that the agreement contains a cure period allowing the party in breach a period of time during which to cure its performance before the other party may terminate the agreement. Except for a breach of the agreement's confidentiality provisions, almost all breaches by a party should be subject to a cure period, usually no less than 30 days. To avoid a dispute, the agreement should stipulate a definitive cure period such as 30 days from receipt of a notice of breach and avoid subjective language giving the breaching party a "reasonable" amount of time to cure the breach. The parties should make sure that the agreed upon time period is sufficient to allow a resolution to be reached without impacting the other party's business. For example, the licensor will likely need at least thirty days to fix any software problems. The licensee should also avoid accepting language that prohibits the licensee from terminating the agreement as long as the licensor is trying to cure the breach.

Any breach notice should be delivered in accordance with the agreement's notice provision and the notice should set forth in detail the nature of the breach in order to allow the breaching party to cure. See *Jasting v. Wright Medical Technology, Inc.*, 528 F.3d 28, 36 (1st Cir. 2008) ("notice of contract termination must state with reasonable certainty the essential facts required by law or by contract.") See § 52.

In New York, a party's failure to comply with a condition precedent for asserting a claim for breach of contract may constitute a breach itself and, in turn, preclude recovery. *Sweetser v. Netsmart Technologies., Inc.*, 558 F. Supp.2d 108, 113 (D. Me. 2008) (citing *Filmline (Cross Country) Prods., Inc. v. United Artists Corp.*, 865 F.2d 513, 518 (2d Cir. 1989)). Thus, it is imperative that a party seeking to terminate an agreement know the terms of the agreement and abide by them.

Express provisions establishing a requirement of notice and opportunity to cure before commencing legal action must be followed. Typically, a party claiming nonperformance must provide any contractually-secured opportunity to cure prior to terminating the contract. *Sea Tow Int'l, Inc. v. Pontin*, 607 F. Supp.2d 378, 388 (E.D.N.Y. 2009) (citing *Point Prods. A.G. v. Sony Music Entm't, Inc.*, 2000 WL 1006236, at *3 (S.D.N.Y. 2000). Thus, if the contract stipulated that notice and a period of days must be given for an opportunity to cure, the party bringing the claim must perform the contract pursuant to that provision in order to avoid the preclusive effect of noncompliance.

(v) Termination versus Seeking Damages for Breach

Even if an opportunity to cure is afforded, it may not apply to every claim arising under the contract. In *Sweetser v. Netsmart Technologies, Inc.*, the court, applying New York law, drew a distinction between a suit for termination of the contract and one for its breach. 558 F. Supp.2d 108, 115 (D. Me. 2008). The underlying agreement provided that termination could be sought on written notice to the defaulting party if that party had not commenced cure within ten days and effected cure within thirty days of receipt of notice of default. *Id.* at 113. The provision did not require a party to terminate before seeking any legal remedies for breach or default. *Id.* After considering the provision in relation to the entire contract, the court held that the notice and cure requirement of the termination provision did not act as a prerequisite to bringing an action for damages from breach. *Id.* at 115. Thus, the terms of the contract providing for an opportunity to cure must be analyzed to see if the requirement pertains to both a claim for breach of contract and termination. If it does not, then failure to provide an opportunity to cure may not constitute a breach for the party commencing legal action.

A termination provision can preclude a claim for breach. *Needham v. Candie's, Inc.*, 2002 WL 1896892 (S.D.N.Y. 2002) (a party was precluded from suing for breach of contract even though only the termination provision provided for an opportunity to cure because the breach consisted of nonpayment of severance after termination).

(vi) Implied Right to Cure

It is unclear, however, whether there is an implied right to cure a breach in the absence of a contractual provision granting such a right. Some commentators have stated that, at least in construction law, a right to cure "is a fundamental common law right implied in every contract as a matter of law." PHILLIP BRUNER AND PATRICK J. O'CONNOR, JR., 5 BRUNER AND O'CONNOR ON CONSTRUCTION LAW § 18.41 (May 2008). Outside of construction law, there is very little case law on the matter. At least one commentator has stated that no such right exists for services contracts. *The Seller's Right to Cure*, 270 COMM. L. ADV. 1, 2 (June 2010) ("there is no right to cure in service contracts.") Other commentators believe that the right to cure is implied within the Restatement (Second) of Contracts and UCITA but there appears to be no case law addressing the issue. RAYMOND T. NIMMER AND JEFF DODD, MODERN LICENSING § 11.8.

In contracts that do not expressly require an opportunity to cure, the failure to provide one will most likely constitute a preclusive breach. In *Delvecchio v. Bayside Chrysler Plymouth Jeep Eagle, Inc.*, a New York court evaluated an employment contract without a provision requiring an opportunity to cure. 271 A.D.2d 636, 639, 706 N.Y.S.2d 724, 726 (App. Div. 2000). The contract provision required only notice of termination, not a specified chance to cure. *Id.* As a result, and in light of the underlying assertion that the plaintiff employee had been terminated for cause, the court held that the required notice was not a material term of the contract and the termination for cause remained effective. *Id.* The fact that the court reached this conclusion indicates that it is likely that New York does not imply a right to an opportunity to cure. If such a right were implied, the court would have found the failure to provide an opportunity as a breach by the defendant, and the plaintiff's termination would have been rendered ineffective. While the *Delvecchio* holding pertains to employment contracts, it is probable that an implied right to an opportunity to cure does not exist in commercial services contracts as well.

(vii) Cure Provisions

Most contracts include the right to cure a breach upon receipt of notice of such breach from the nonbreaching party. The underlying contract should require the nonbreaching party to notify the party in breach setting forth in detail that nature of the breach.

Usually the parties agree on a thirty-day cure period. In those instances where the breach is of an egregious nature, such as a violation of laws, the parties may agree on a much shorter time frame. In some situations, such as the breach of a confidentiality obligation, the nonbreaching party may have the right to immediately terminate the agreement without providing the breaching party a period in which to cure.

(viii) Practical Consideration in Providing a Notification of Breach

To avoid future problems and the cost of unneeded litigation, a party terminating agreement should follow the terms of the contract's termination provision and not only give the required notice and cure period, but also describe the nature of the breaching party's breach in sufficient detail. *See e.g. Competrol, Inc. v. Newtrend, L.P.*, 203 F.3d 1064 (8th Cir. 2000) (failure to significantly specify nature of breach and provide cure period was breach of contract).

The failure of a party to provide the breaching party a contractually required notice and cure period is itself a breach of the contract. A provision in a contract for the termination thereof upon certain conditions can be enforced only in strict compliance with the terms of these conditions. *Blaine Econ. Dev. Auth. V. Royal Elen. Co., Inc.*, 520 N.W. 2d 473, 479 (Minn. Ct. App. 1994) (plaintiff wrongfully terminated contract by failing to provide written notice to cure pursuant to contract); *National Bankcard Services, Inc. v. Family Express Corporation*, 2006 WL 2480479 (D. Minn. April 29, 2006) (failure to give notice to plaintiff of its alleged breach and provide contractually mandated cure period was breach of contract).

(ix) Incurable Breaches and Futility

Some states allow a party to terminate a contract immediately, without affording the breaching party notice and an opportunity to cure, if the breach is incurable or the cure is futile. *Needham v. Candie's, Inc.*, 2002 WL 1896892, at *4 (S.D.N.Y. 2002) (citing *Wolff & Munier, Inc. v. Whiting-Turner Contracting Co.*, 946 F.2d 1003, 1009 (2d Cir. 1991)); *AAMCO Industries, Inc. v. DeWolf*, 250 N.W. 2d 835 (Minn. 1977) (failure to give plaintiff controlling mandated 24-hour cure period would have been futile gesture). Courts have also held that a material breach going to "the root of the matter or the essence of the contract" would excuse the obligation of a period for cure. *Sea Tow Int'l, Inc. v. Pontin*, 607 F. Supp.2d 378, 389 (E.D.N.Y. 2009) (quoting *Southland Corp. v. Froelich*, 41 F. Supp.2d 227, 246 (E.D.N.Y. 1999)). However, the applied scope of what is futile in New York courts is relatively narrow in order to avoid judicial removal of core provisions from contracts. *Annecca Inc., Lexent, Inc.*, 307 F. Supp.2d 999, 1010 (N.D. Ill. 2004) (citing *Petracca v. Petracca*, 756 N.Y.S.2d 587, 588 (App.Div. 2003)). Therefore, a party will not be in breach if it does not provide an opportunity to cure as long as the situation conforms to the narrow scope of the futility exception.

(x) Breaches for Which a Cure Period is Not Reasonable

Some breaches should not be subject to a cure period if it is clear the breach is incurable. These events include misappropriation or breach of a party's confidentiality obligations or breach of the law. In these events, the agreement should be clear that the nonbreaching party may immediately seek injunctive relief or otherwise terminate the agreement without prior notice.

Licensors are very concerned with the protection of their intellectual property and, to a lesser degree, receiving payment. While a "cure period" of 30 days is standard for most breaches by a licensee, most licensors seek to include a provision allowing the licensor to immediately terminate the license or obtain an injunction if the licensee violates any of the terms of the license grant or the license agreement's confidentiality provisions. The basis for immediate termination stems from the licensor's desire to immediately stop the misuse of its software or confidential information, as these breaches cannot be cured. Other issues such as payment, which are not so critical and can be easily cured, are subject to a standard 30-day cure period.

At the same time, the licensee wants to make sure the licensor can only terminate the license and take possession of the software for a material breach. In addition, the licensee should carefully consider any self-help measures the licensor seeks to include in the license and any language regarding the licensor's ability to disable the software without liability. For a more detailed discussion of the issues involved with self-help, see Section B.6.(b)(iii)(z), below.

Many licensees insist that the license contain a provision allowing the licensee to use the software until any dispute is resolved. Licensees should negotiate to obtain the right to utilize the software for a reasonable time after termination to allow the licensee to migrate to another product. In most cases, the licensor's damages will be monetary and the licensor will not be further damaged by the licensee's continued use of the software for a limited period of time. In certain situations such as breach of the license's confidentiality provisions, an injunction, temporary restraining order and termination without the right of further use would be appropriate.

(b) Termination For Convenience (§ 4.1)

Termination for convenience clauses permit a party to terminate a contract "even in the absence of fault or breach by the other party without suffering the financial consequences of a breach of contract." *See e.g. Harris Corp. v. Giesting & Associates, Inc.*, 297 F.3d 1270, 1271 (11th Cir. 2002). Often, software development contracts will contain a termination for convenience clause, allowing a licensee to terminate a contract without cause. Usually a licensee terminates an agreement for convenience when its business plans change such that it no longer requires the contracted software or services. Licensors do not favor termination for convenience clauses, as they prevent the licensor from recognizing the full value of the agreement and may disrupt their staffing and development plans. In the event a licensee terminates an agreement for convenience, the agreement should protect the licensor financially as the agreement was terminated on the whim of the licensee.

(i) Financial Ramifications

Each party should carefully consider the inclusion of such clauses. If included, the parties should ensure the agreed upon language protects each party financially and clearly delineates how any payments due the licensor will be calculated. Too often the parties incorporate such clauses into their agreement without understanding the financial ramifications. By clearly stating how the licensor will be paid for the work performed, the parties will avoid any potential disputes in the future. Many customers seek to limit payment to all work accepted at the time of termination but this approach fails to compensate the licensor for work that it has performed but has not yet delivered. Further, partially complete work may be ineligible for acceptance as the licensor has not been allowed to complete it. Other customers seek to pay on a percent complete basis; that is, they determine what percentage of the total project was complete at the time of termination and pay the licensor the proportional percentage of the total contract value. This approach, however, does not recognize that in certain projects the licensor's costs may not be directly proportional to the percent of work completed; there may be a significant amount of start up work even before undertaking the development. See the model language below:

> Customer may terminate this Agreement and a SOW without cause upon thirty (30) days prior notice to Licensor. To the extent compensation under a SOW which has been terminated without cause is on a time and materials basis, Licensor will be compensated for all Services performed and expenses incurred up to the effective date of termination of the SOW at the rates and expense reimbursement rules specified in the SOW. If a SOW which has been terminated without cause provides compensation for the Services and expenses on a fixed fee basis, Licensor will receive a prorated amount of the SOW compensation equal to the percentage of Services (and Deliverables) completed as of the termination date of the SOW or as otherwise specified in a SOW.

A more equitable approach is to pay the licensor on a time and materials basis for the hours expended provided that in no event will the amount paid to the licensor exceed the total value of the contract or statement of work. The licensor should also insist that if the licensee terminates for convenience, in addition to payment for services rendered, the licensor shall be entitled to recover its termination costs, which may or may not include lost profits and any costs such as the cost of terminating those employees assigned to the project, as well as any travel and expense cost, such as long term apartment rentals, that cannot be avoided. The model language below is more favorable to the licensor:

> In the event of premature termination of the Agreement, Customer shall pay Licensor for Deliverables performed, on a prorated basis, and shall pay Licensor for any and all travel, lodging and out-of-pocket expenses incurred by Licensor in accordance with the SOW through the date of termination. In no event shall such amount exceed the amount that would have been payable to Licensor had the SOW not been terminated.

In the event the licensee seeks to terminate a maintenance contract, the licensee should not be entitled to a refund, as the licensor calculated its pricing based on the licensee purchasing maintenance for the full term of the maintenance agreement.

(ii) Legal Ramifications of Termination for Convenience

Where a party properly terminates an agreement for convenience, it is unclear whether it may later maintain a claim for breach of contract. While there is copious authority addressing termination for convenience relating to government contracts, there is very little law addressing termination for convenience in a commercial setting. Existing case law appears to support the proposition that an entity that terminates a contract for convenience cannot sustain a cause of action against the nonterminating party for breach of contract. In the event a party attempts to argue that it in fact terminated for breach, it would likely be found to have wrongfully terminated the contract by failing to provide the nonterminating party any contractually required cure period.

A party who terminates for convenience or wrongfully terminates the contract will have a difficult time bringing a successful claim for breach of contract. Maryland law permits a defendant to introduce evidence that a plaintiff breached the contract first and thus, is not entitled to payment. *Hubler Rentals, Inc. v. Roadway Express, Inc.*, 637 F.2d 257 (4th Cir. 1981) (Roadway's termination of contract did not provide defendant opportunity to cure in accordance with contract and constituted a breach of the agreement. Performance of the contract by the party suing is a condition precedent to recovery.)

New York law appears to prohibit defendants from introducing evidence of non-performance by the nonterminating party in defense of a claim. *Tishman Construction Corp. v. City of New York*, 643 N.Y.S.2d 589 (1996) (city's termination for convenience entitled contractor to receive amounts due and payable on the date of termination; city precluded from raising a counterclaim for damages due to alleged breach of the contract); *Koppers Company v. Brunswick Corp.*, 303 A.2d 32 (Pa. Super. 1973) (by terminating contract for convenience Brunswick waived its rights to claim breach for defective goods on the part of Koppers); *Fruin-Colnon Corp. v. Niagara Frontier Transportation Auth.*, 180 A.D.2d 222, 585 N.Y.S.2d 248 (1992) (court dismissed defendant's counterclaims as defendant wrongfully terminated the contract, depriving plaintiff of its contractual right to attempt to cure breach. Under the terms of the contract, the wrongful termination of the plaintiff was deemed a termination for convenience. Because the termination was for the convenience of the defendant, it negated the defendant's right to recover payments made to third parties for liquidated damages.) *See also Fruin-Colnon Corp. v. Niagara Frontier Transportation Auth.*, 180 A.D.2d 222, 585 N.Y.S.2d 248 (1992) (counterclaims for liquidated damages dismissed where contract deemed terminated for convenience) and *Paragon Restoration Group, Inc. v. Cambridge Square Condominiums*, 836 N.Y.S.2d 501 (2006) (invoking a termination for convenience clause limits a party's right to recover on a counter-claim for breach, where the terminated party is not provided an opportunity to cure alleged breaches of contract).

Some courts, however, have allowed the terminating party to proceed with a breach of contract counterclaim. See *United States v. TDC Management Corp., Inc.*, 24 F.3d 292 (D.C. Cir. 1994); *Executive Airlines v. Electric Boat Corp.*, 271 F. Supp.2d 392 (D. Conn. 2003); *G.M. Harston Constr. Co., Inc. v. City of Chicago*, 209 F. Supp.2d 902, 908 (N.D. Ill. 2002) (rejecting the plaintiffs' absolute contention "that termination for convenience necessarily means that offsets for substandard or delayed performance cannot be considered").

The law does not demand the dismissal of a terminating party's counterclaim when the underlying contract is terminated for convenience. *See, e.g., Lisbon Contractors, Inc. v. United States*, 828 F.2d 759, 769 (Fed. Cir. 1987) (noting that the government had the burden of proving the amount of setoff and refusing to "decide the issue on the legal ground urged by Lisbon that a setoff cannot be made for corrective work where a convenience termination is involved").

Harris explains that where a party properly terminates an agreement for convenience, the terminating party "is entitled to judgment on [the terminated party's] breach of contract claim for [the] contract termination." *Harris Corp.*, 297 F.3d at 1274.

Further, a number of courts have held that a party who terminates a contract for convenience "is not bound by its initial rational for [terminating an agreement] provided that (1) it was not acting in bad faith; and (2) the [terminated party] did not change its position in reliance upon the initial reason given for termination." *Millgard Corp. v. E.E. Cruz/Nab/Fronier-Kemper*, 2004 WL 1488534, at *13 (S.D.N.Y. July 2, 2004). *See also, Accart Builder Co., Inc. v. Southwest Concrete Systems, Inc.*, 679 S.W.2d 106, 108 (Tex. App. 1984) (contractor who terminated subcontractor for convenience entitled to present issues of subcontractor's deficient performance to jury.)

(c) Force Majeure (§ 33)

Force majeure (FM) clauses are intended to protect against unforeseen events, such as an act of God. Events that are reasonably foreseeable do not excuse performance. Thus companies purchase business interruption insurance for events like a flood even though they may be seen as an act of God.

An H1N1 pandemic may or may not qualify as an event of FM depending on the extent of the pandemic. The H1N1 virus has been publicized/discussed for months, so no one should be surprised by an outbreak in the workplace. A party's ability to successfully invoke a contract's force majeure clause will depend on the extent of the outbreak. For example, if 25 percent of the work force is out sick, a party will be unlikely to prevail. If 75 percent is out sick, a party would have a strong argument. Of course, a court would closely examine a party's efforts to mitigate the effects of any likely force majeure event in reaching a decision. Many force majeure provisions provide that the impacted party (that is, the party who is awaiting performance) may be entitled to terminate the agreement if the event of force majeure continues for a set period of time.

In the event the agreement is terminated as the result of an event of force majeure, neither party should be forced to incur a financial penalty. The licensor should be paid for the work performed but the licensee should not be forced to pay for work it has not received. See Section 6.D for a more detailed discussion of force majeure.

Under no circumstances should the licensor have the right to exercise the remedy of cover if an agreement is terminated for an event of force majeure. Force majeure arises from an unforeseen event outside the control of either party. As such, neither party should receive a financial benefit or be subject to a financial burden. Allowing a licensee to seek cover unfairly places the risk associated with an event of force majeure on the licensor.

(d) Bankruptcy

Federal Bankruptcy laws prevent a licensor from terminating a licensee in the event the licensee declares bankruptcy. See Chapter 17 for more detailed discussion of the impact of bankruptcy in a licensing transaction.

(e) Expiration (and Termination) of the Agreement

Many parties fail to memorialize in detail the effects of the expiration of the license agreement. For example, upon expiration must the licensee immediately cease using the software? Is there a transition period? Is the licensee required to certify to the licensor it has ceased use of the software? Can the licensor audit the licensee to ensure the licensee's compliance with any termination obligations?

Prudent parties will take the time during the license negotiations to memorialize their respective rights and obligations upon the expiration/termination of the agreement. The parties' relationship will be strongest at the time of contract signature. Thus, they should seek to resolve any issues at that time, as it is less likely they will be able to do so later in their relationship.

6. Remedies (§§ 5.2, 5.3)

To protect itself in the event of a breach, each party should seek to include a number of rights and remedies in the parties' contract. The actual rights and remedies included in a particular contract will be dictated by the needs of the parties and the level of protections each party is willing to concede. Given the uncertainty of whether the UCC applies to software licensing transactions, these rights and remedies should supplement any remedies available under the UCC.

The parties should carefully consider the wording related to the stated remedies. Are the stated remedies exclusive? Are other remedies foreclosed? These questions need to be considered and the answers incorporated into the agreement. For example, the inclusion of a liquidated damages provision in an agreement does not prevent a party from seeking other equitable remedies if the agreement did not expressly foreclose such remedies. *Miller v. United States Naval Institute*, 423 A.2d 283 (Md. 1980). Similarly, unless a termination provision for breach is deemed exclusive, it is considered to be cumulative. *Foster-Porter Enterprises v. De Mare*, 81 A.2d 325 (Md. 1951) (contract requiring 10 days' notice specifying nature of default to terminate for breach did not prohibit immediate termination for a material breach).

(a) Remedies under the UCC

The remedies provided under Article 2 of the UCC for a breach of warranty, while potentially applicable, are not easily applied to software due to its intangible nature. Although two states, Maryland and Virginia, have adopted the Uniform Computer Information Transactions Act (UCITA) to address the difficulty of applying the UCC to software licensing, many courts still look to the UCC as a reference. See Chapter 11 for a more detailed discussion of the applicability of the UCC to software licensing.

Under the UCC, damages for breach of warranty may result in merely a reduction in price; that is, the difference in value between what was warranted and what was delivered. UCC § 2-714(2). A customer may also seek rejection under UCC § 2-601 (the "perfect tender rule") or revocation of acceptance under UCC § 2-608. Section 2-601 illustrates the difficulties of applying the UCC to software transactions, as software by its nature is imperfect. In a literal sense, the software deliverable can almost always be rejected under § 2-601 as there will likely be at least one defect, albeit a minor one, in all software.

In cases where the licensor fails to cure a defect, the licensee may recover the amount paid to the seller. UCC § 2-711(2) (a). If the licensor is in breach of the contract, the licensee may, in addition to other potential remedies, purchase reasonable substitute software and recover the difference between the cost of obtaining the substitute software and the contract price as well as any incidental or consequential damages, or, alternatively, the licensee may recover damages for nondelivery equal to the difference between the market price and the contract price of the software at the time when the licensee learned of the breach. UCC §§ 2-712, 2-713.

Both licensees and licensors should understand the difference between general and limited warranties. Under a general warranty, the party providing the warranty is liable upon breach, and the party receiving the warranty has all available remedies. A limited warranty is a warranty in which the remedy is limited, often to repair or re-performance. For example, purchasers of new automobiles usually receive a limited warranty, normally for several years. If the automobile exhibits problems, the only remedy available to the purchaser is to have the manufacturer repair or replace the automobile.

Thus, a licensee who receives a limited warranty that the software will materially comply with specifications will only be entitled to the specified remedy—normally the repair or replacement of the software. If the warranty were general, the licensee would have all of its remedies available.

(b) Licensee Remedies (§ 5.3)

(i) Termination (§ 5.3.1)

In the event of a "material breach," the licensee should have the right to terminate the agreement and seek monetary damages under traditional contract law. This remedy is standard in most agreements with a large portion of the negotiations between the parties focused on what constitutes a "material breach."

(ii) Equitable Relief

(x) Specific Performance (§§ 5.3.4, 28.A.5)

The licensee should seek to include the right to specific performance. Specific performance protects the licensee from having the licensor cease the performance of its obligations in the event it is no longer profitable to perform. *See, e.g., Metropolitan Life Ins. Co. v. Noble Lowndes Int'l, Inc.*, 643 N.E.2d 504 (N.Y. 1994). The licensor, however, will most likely be unwilling to include such a provision as it creates potentially unlimited liability on its behalf by requiring the licensor to re-perform work on a project until it is completed. Further, given the imperfect nature of software, it gives the licensee significant leverage over the licensor in any dispute.

Many licensees often try to include the remedy of specific performance in their license agreements. Sections 2-711(2)(b) and 2-716 of the UCC specifically identify specific performance as an available remedy. Although the UCC provides that specific performance is available if a party can establish the uniqueness of the software and the contract does not explicitly waive the right, licensees often prefer an affirmative statement of their right to specific performance to remove any uncertainty, especially as it relates to the applicability of the UCC versus the common law.

Some licensees, however, prefer to have the contract remain silent on the issue, and if they later seek to invoke the remedy, argue that specific performance is allowed under the UCC. These licensees believe that seeking an affirmative statement of their right to specific performance will potentially bring the issue to the attention of the licensor, who will in turn seek to contractually exclude specific performance as a remedy available to the licensee.

Licensors are hesitant to contractually agree to specific performance because, if included, a licensee may be able to force the licensor to deliver the software regardless of cost. Given that the risk of a large cost overrun is always present with software development, the risk to the licensor increases if the remedy of specific performance is included. Smart licensees also seek to include a statement that they are entitled to specific performance to force the licensor to comply with the terms of the escrow agreement, including requiring the licensor to place the software in escrow and enforcing the license agreement's indemnification provisions.

Licensors should carefully consider the risks when the licensee seeks to include broad statements such as "the right to obtain equitable relief" in the license agreement. While the equitable remedy of injunctive relief for breach of the agreement's confidentiality provision is important, the phrase "equitable relief" grants the licensee rights to several equitable remedies, not just injunctive relief (e.g., specific performance or reformation). As such, the licensee's rights should be limited solely to injunctive relief. Smart licensors will try to include language in the license agreement that, upon the licensor's breach of the warranty, the licensee shall be entitled to monetary damages only, or licensors will try to specifically state that the licensee is not entitled to obtain an equitable remedy.

There may also be specific aspects of performance for which specific performance is a reasonable remedy. For example, in an application service provider (ASP) arrangement, a licensee may be well advised to seek a right of specific performance for the return of the licensee's data—particularly if a failure to return the data would seriously impact the licensee's ability to conduct its business.

(y) Right to Set Off (§§3.B.2. 5.3.2, 8.7)

Another equitable remedy the licensee should seek to include is the right to set off any damages the licensee incurs against any monies owed to licensor by the licensee. The right of set off can arise from common law, statute and express contractual provisions. Even if the parties' contract fails to include this right, most licensees will exercise "self-help" by refusing to make payment until the issue has been resolved. While a smart licensor will seek to exclude language acknowledging the licensee's right to set off and perhaps even specifically prohibit the right of set off, there is little the licensor can do to prevent the licensee from withholding any money due the licensor.

Under law, a licensee must specifically state that it possesses the right of setoff, as this right is statutorily based and does not exist under common law. 80 C.J.S. Set-Off and Counterclaim 4. *See also Stanley v. Clark,* 159 F. Supp. 65, 66 (D.N.H. 1957) (citing C. J.S.); *Carfoss Const. Corp. v. MMSG Ltd. Partnerships,* 904 F. Supp. 450 (D. Md. 1995) (as right of setoff does not exist under Maryland common law it may be exercised only with respect to statutory authority or incident to a courts' equity jurisdiction). Licensors uncertain as to the status of applicable statutory law should insist on an affirmative statement that the licensee may not offset payment to prevent the licensee from gaining additional leverage over the licensor. Removing the right of offset eliminates the licensee's leverage through the ability to withhold payment. In practice, however, a dissatisfied licensee will offset monies owed to the licensor regardless of any contractual prohibition to the contrary or applicable statutory law.

Although setoff may not be allowed under the applicable state law, the licensee should consider whether the closely related doctrine of recoupment has been recognized. Recoupment, a common law remedy, is a form of setoff for damages claimed by the licensee arising from the same transaction for which a party seeks compensation. *See Lee v. Rutledge,* 51 Md. 311, 318 (1878). In short, a defendant in a breach of contract action may, instead of suing, recoup its damages from the plaintiff's breach. *Warfield v. Booth,* 33 Md. 63, 72 (1870).

(z) Withholding Monies Due

While not truly an equitable remedy, withholding monies due is closely related to set-off. From the licensor's perspective, the contract should be clear that nonpayment can occur only in conjunction with withholding, and withholding can occur only in conjunction with a dispute, and then only when the required contractual protocols are followed; that is, timing, notification and specificity. If there has not been proper notification, there is no dispute. If there is no dispute, there is no right to withhold. If there is no withholding, there is no right to nonpayment. Further, the contract should be clear that only particular and specific charges (i.e., invoice line items) can be disputed, not entire invoices.

(iii) Cover (§ 5.3.5)

A smart licensee will seek to include language allowing the licensee to seek "cover" in the event of the licensor's breach. This provision requires the licensor to be financially liable for any costs, in excess of the contract price, incurred by licensee retaining a third party to fulfill the licensor's contractual obligations. Most licensors will not agree to such a provision as it creates essentially a carte blanche for the licensee and the entity that is hired to perform the work. The licensee will likely argue that the licensor is under a common-law duty to mitigate its damages and must seek cover. At a minimum, the licensor should include language that limits the licensor's liability to the predetermined limits of liability set forth in the agreement. Under the UCC, the licensee automatically has the right to seek cover. UCC § 2-712. See Section B.6.(b)(v), below, for a further discussion of the duty to mitigate and cover.

Licensors should remember that "cover" is considered to be a form of "direct" or "actual" damages. *See* UCC § 2-712; *U.S. ex. rel. Virginia Beach Mechanical Services, Inc. v. SAMCO Const. Co.*, 39 F. Supp. 661, 673 (E.D. Va. 1999) (direct damages usually equal the difference between the contract price and the cost of purchasing of substitute goods or having a third party covering the work to be performed under the contract); *Hess Die Mold, Inc. v. American Plasti-Plate Corp.*, 653 S.W.2d 927, 929 (Tex. App. 1983). Thus, cover is not necessarily excluded by the licensor's limitation of liability clause. As such, a smart licensor should contractually exclude the licensee's right to obtain cover from their license agreement.

For a discussion of a buyer's right to cover see, *Buyer's Right to Cover*, 264 Comm. L. Adv. 1 (Dec. 2009).

(iv) Access to Source Code, Documentation, Employees, and Contractors (§§ 5.3.6, 5.3.7)

A licensee should also include language in the contract allowing the licensee to obtain a free or discounted copy of the software's source code and all available documentation in the event of licensor's material breach. While this provision cannot ensure that the licensee will be able to avoid damages from the licensor's breach, it will provide the licensee a means to further limit its risk. The licensee should also insist on language waiving any prohibition on the licensee soliciting and hiring the licensor's employees and contractors in the event of the licensor's material breach. This is important, as without access to the licensor's employees and contractors, possession and use of the source code and documentation will most likely be of little help to the licensee.

(v) Liquidated Damages (§ 3.C)

Licensees, and occasionally licensors, often seek to include a provision for liquidated damages for the late or early delivery of software in development contracts. Usually these damages amount to 0.5 percent of the contract value—excluding the value of hardware and third party software—for each week a delivery is late for up to 10 percent of the contract value. The licensor must carefully consider what will trigger payment.

Many licensees will try to tie the imposition of liquidated damages to acceptance of the software by a certain date and not the contractual delivery date. This creates significant risk for the licensor as acceptance is totally within the control of the licensee. Liability should be based on late delivery of the software and not acceptance of the software by the licensee. At the same time, a licensee may be hesitant to base such damages on late delivery because the licensor may deliver poor quality software just to avoid paying liquidated damages, believing that the poor quality of the software can be corrected during any cure period. The licensee should include language allowing the right of offset against future progress payments if the licensor does not pay the liquidated damages as required.

Similarly, the agreement's liquidated damages clause should address any potential changes in the delivery date due to changes in the software requested by the licensee. It is rare that the licensee does not request changes to the software as it is being developed. Further, delivery may be delayed by third party contractors under the control of the customer. As such, the agreement should contain a mechanism to address the impact on the delivery date resulting from any potential changes. If the licensor delivers the software after the delivery date, the licensor often responds that the late delivery was due to changes requested by the licensee. Any material delay caused by the customer will likely result in additional cost to the licensor, for which the licensor should be compensated. To maintain the integrity of the liquidated damages provisions, the parties must include a mechanism to address such changes.

Further, the licensor should ensure that the payment of liquidated damages is in full satisfaction of any liability the licensor may have for late delivery. To the extent any delay is caused by the licensee, there should be a one-day extension of the licensor's delivery date for every day the licensee caused delay. The licensee may want to provide further protection by providing for termination of the agreement if the licensor has not delivered the software when the maximum payment amount has been reached to avoid giving the licensor an additional cure period.

The parties should carefully word the liquidated damages provision and set the liquidated damages at a reasonable level to avoid the appearance of a penalty, or if liquidated damages are an exclusive remedy, they should not be set so low that the remedy fails at its essential purpose. *Cognifest Corp. v. Riverside Publishing Co.*, 107 F.3d 493 (7th Cir. 1997) (agreed payment of liquidated damages found to be adequate exclusive remedy). Liquidated damages that are out of proportion to the probable loss or grossly in excess of the actual damages may be considered a penalty and thus unenforceable. *Gordonsville Energy L.P. v. Virginia Electric & Power Co.*, 512 S.E.2d 811 (Va. 1999). At least one court has upheld the validity of a contractual waiver of a party's right to attack a liquidated damages provision. *Id.*

The licensee should be careful, however, to include a provision that provides that if the liquidated damages reach a certain level, the licensor shall be deemed to be in material breach and the licensee may terminate the contract.

Similarly, the licensor should seek to include a combination of liquidated damages and bonuses payable to the licensor in the event of certain licensee actions or inactions. If the customer has certain contractual responsibilities beyond payment, such as site readiness or the obligation to promptly accept the licensor's deliverables, the licensor should insist that the customer pay liquidated damages for the customer's failure to promptly meet its obligations. At the same time, the licensor should receive a bonus for the early delivery of the software or other material deliverables. This bonus counters the damages payable for late delivery and is consistent with the goal of liquidated damages to incent the licensor to deliver on time. Licensors often seek to raise their prices when the licensee asks for liquidated damages, claiming the licensor's initial price did not reflect the additional element the licensee had asked them to assume through the payment of liquidated damages. This argument holds little validity if the customer's initial RFP or the model license contained in the RFP put the licensor on notice that the customer expected the resulting contract to contain a liquidated damages provision. *See generally* UCC § 2-718(1) and Karnezis, *Contractual Liquidated Damages—Provisions under UCC Article 2,* 98 A.L.R.3d 586 (1980).

(vi) Lawyer's Fees (§ 5.4)

In the event the licensee brings a successful legal action as a result of a breach of contract by the licensor, the licensee should be entitled to recover its legal fees. This provision provides a disincentive for the licensor to breach the contract or dispute any issue in bad faith. A licensor that agrees to this provision should make sure that it is mutual. By making the provision mutual, both parties are incented to quickly and fairly settle any matter.

(vii) Transition Rights (§ 5.3.3)

If the software licensed by the licensee is critical to the operation of the licensee's business, the licensee should require that the licensor provide transition services in the event of any termination of the agreement, regardless of whether the contract was terminated for one party's breach. A contractual transition period reduces the licensor's leverage in those situations where the licensee is in breach but the services provided by the licensor are important to the continuing business operations of the licensee. Similarly, it requires the licensor to cooperate in the event the licensor is being terminated, where the licensor might otherwise have no incentive to do so. The contract should address the continuation of services or use of the software, knowledge transfer, the cost and duration of such services, as well as the continuation or termination of any collateral services. Regardless of the cause of breach, the licensor should be willing to provide the required services so long as it is compensated accordingly. The price of such services as well as the duration is often determined on the basis of who was in breach.

(viii) Monetary Damages

In the event the licensor desires monetary damages based on a refund of monies paid, the licensor should set forth the basis on which they will be determined. The damages may be based on the purchase price, the price paid less any depreciation for actual use, or a predetermined damages (liquidated damages) price. Each of these methods will result in a different amount and could be greatly affected by the nature of the breach.

(c) Licensor Remedies (§ 5.2)

(i) Termination (§ 5.3.1)

In the event of a "material breach," the licensor should have the right to terminate the agreement and seek monetary damages under traditional contract law. This remedy is standard in most agreements with a large portion of the negotiations between the parties focused on what constitutes a "material breach." The licensee should carefully consider the licensor's ability to terminate the agreement if the licensee will need to utilize the software on an ongoing basis. The licensor's ability to terminate the agreement gives the licensor significant leverage over the licensee in these situations.

(ii) Lawyer's Fees (§ 5.4)

In the event the licensor brings a successful legal action as a result of a breach of contract by the licensee, the licensor should be entitled to recover its legal fees. This provision provides a disincentive for the licensee to breach the contract or dispute any issue in bad faith. A licensee that agrees to this provision should make sure that it is mutual. By making the provision mutual, both parties are incented to quickly and fairly settle any matter.

(iii) Equitable Relief

Injunctive Relief (§ 28.A.5)

The licensor should include a provision allowing the licensor to obtain injunctive relief in the event the licensee breaches the licensing terms or misuses the software. The ability to obtain injunctive relief is important as the licensor needs to quickly and efficiently prevent the licensee from misusing its software. Requiring the licensor to use traditional dispute mechanisms such as arbitration, mediation, or use of the judicial system may significantly delay the licensor's ability to protect its intellectual property.

Self-Help (§ 5.2) (§29.4)

The licensor should reserve the right to utilize the quasi-equitable relief of "self-help" by retaining the ability to disable the software in the event of the licensee's breach. The licensee, however, will likely seek to include a specific contractual provision prohibiting the licensor from utilizing any self-help until any dispute has been resolved in accordance with the contract's dispute resolution mechanism as self-help provides the licensor with significant leverage in the event of a dispute.

Electronic self-help generally takes one of two forms: the software contains an internal mechanism to automatically prevent the licensee from using the software upon the expiration of the license term, or the licensor electronically terminates the licensee's ability to use the software in the event of the licensee's breach of the license terms. It is the second issue that creates the most concern for licensees, as licensees fear the licensor will unjustly leverage its ability to disable the software in the event of a business dispute.

The use of disabling devices in software is fraught with risk for the licensor as well as the licensee. The presence of such a device creates a significant business risk for the licensee as the licensor has the ability to shut down mission critical software. The licensor also bears substantial risk if it terminates the licensee's ability to use the software, as the licensee will likely bring suit for the licensee's resulting damages. See *Clayton X-Ray Company v. Professional Systems Corporation,* 812 S.W.2d 565, 567 (Mo. App. 1991) (court upheld award of punitive damages, "Seller had no legal right, or any colorable legal right to lock up [buyer]'s computer system"); *Werner, Zaroff, Slotnck, Stern & Askenazy v. Lewis,* 155 Misc.2d 558 (N.Y. 1992) (court awarded $25,000 in punitive and compensatory damages to purchaser whose computer system was disabled by consultant through use of a "time bomb"); *State v. Corcoran,* 522 N.W.2d 226 (Wis. 1994) (independent contractor's conviction for computer tampering upheld where he placed time bombs in customer's computer systems over concern of receiving payment for his services).

A common law cause of action of conversion may arise from any self-help that goes beyond the limited scope of the law. *Thyroff v. Nationwide Mutual Ins. Co.*, 864 N.E.2d 1272 (N.Y. 2007) (insurance agent permitted to bring conversion action against insurance company which took possession of computer leased to agent that contained work related data as well as agent's personal electronic files). Another court found that a domain name can be converted. *Kremen v. Cohen*, 337 F.3d 1024,

1033–34 (9th Cir. 2003). Massachusetts courts have reached opposite conclusions when considering this issue. *See In re TJX Companies Retail Security Breach Litigation*, 587 F. Supp.2d 209 (D. Mass. 2007) (Mass. does not recognize cause of action for conversion of intangible records. Court rejected invitation to adopt holding of *Thyroff*). *But see Network Systems Architects Corp. v. Dimitruk*, 23 Mass. L. Rptr. 339 (2007) ("If paper documents can be converted, as they no doubt can, no reason appears that computer files cannot.").

At least one court has upheld a licensor's right to remotely deactivate a licensee's software for breach of the license's payment provisions. *American Computer Trust Leasing v. Jack Farrell Implement Co.*, 763 F. Supp. 1473 (D. Minn. 1991), *aff'd* 967 F.2d 1208 (8th Cir. 1992). *But see Gomar Manufacturing Co. v. Novelli*, C.A. No. 96–4000 (D.N.J. Jan 28, 1998). The Central District Court of California has held that disabling devices/codes may violate the Computer Fraud and Abuse Act (CFAA), 18 U.S.C. § 1030. *North Texas Preventative Imaging L.L.C. v. Eisenberg*, 1996 WL 1359212 (C. D. Cal. Aug. 19, 1996). *But see Shaw and Moon v. Toshiba et. al.*, 91 F. Supp.2d 926 (E.D. Tex. 1999) (court denied motion for summary judgment as CFAA does not apply to manufacturers inserting disabling codes).

A prudent licensor who desires to retain the remedy of self-help should clearly state in the underlying license that it reserves the right of self-help and/or the right to remotely disable the software in the event of the licensee's breach or the licensor detects unauthorized copying. Further, the license should provide that any attempt by the licensee to circumvent any security/self-help measures within the software is a material breach of the license. The licensor should also retain the contractual right to audit the licensee to ensure its compliance with these terms.

The Uniform Computer Information Transactions Act (UCITA) places significant restrictions on the use of the disabling devices by the licensor, which in practicality, make their use very risky. See Chapter 11.B.3.(j) for a more detailed discussion. Nonetheless, the licensee should insist on a specific warranty disclaiming the existence of any disabling devices, trap door, or the like (see § 16.L).

For a general discussion, see Rowles, *Electronic Software Disablement and Repossession,* 8 E-Commerce Advisor 7 (Aug. 2001); Branscomb, *Rogue Computer Programs and Computer Rogues: Tailoring the Punishment to Fit the Crime,* 16 Rutgers Computer & Tech. L.J. 1 (1990).

(iv) Monetary Damages

Monetary damages are often difficult to ascertain. Section 504 of the Copyright Act allows a copyright holder to recover either statutory damages or its actual damages resulting from any infringement as well as "any profits of the infringer that are attributable to the infringement and are not taken into account in computing the actual damages." 17 U.S.C. § 504(a)(b). Actual damages are generally "measured by the profits lost due to the infringement or the value of the use of the copyrighted work to the infringer." *Polar Bear Prods., Inc. v. Timex Corp.*, 387 F.3d 700, 708 (9th Cir. 2004). One method of ascertaining the value of the loss is to determine the hypo thetical licensee fee that would have been paid had the infringer purchased a license from the copyright owner. *Oracle, USA, Inc. v. SAP AG*, 2010 WL 334446 (N.D. Cal.

Jan. 28, 2010) (copyright holder not precluded from seeking damages in the form of a hypothetical license from infringing party).

In the event the licensor seeks to recover monetary damages for the licensee's breach, the licensee should ensure that the license agreement contains a limit of liability to limit the licensee's liability. Often, licensees are so focused on negotiating the limits on the licensor's liability that they forget to make such limit mutual and limit their own liability.

(v) Duty to Mitigate

All parties have an obligation to mitigate or limit their damages. RESTATEMENT (SECOND) OF CONTRACTS § 350 (1981). This duty forbids an injured party from allowing its damages to balloon when such damages can be limited. *Moran Foods, Inc. v. Mid-Atlantic Market Development Company, LLC,* 476 F.3d 436 (7th Cir. 2007). An injured party is prohibited from recovering any damages that could have been avoided. *Kuhlman, Inc. v. G. Heilman Brewing Company,* 266 N.W.2d 382 (Wis. 1978). The burden of proof is on the breaching party to prove the injured party could have mitigated its damages. *Id.* Under the law of at least one state, however, a nonbreaching party is not obligated to mitigate its damages where the parties' contract contains a valid liquidated damages provision. *Barrie School v. Patch,* 933 A.2d 382 (Md. Ct. App. 2007).

Although implied by law, it is important to include a contractual obligation requiring the parties to mitigate their damages. This is especially important where the parties are utilizing an informal dispute mechanism and are unlikely to discuss implied obligations under the law. If the parties proceed to litigation, the efforts a party took to mitigate its damages will likely become a significant issue in the dispute.

The duty to mitigate includes the ability/right to obtain cover. While the concept of the licensee retaining a third party vendor to complete the licensor's contractual obligations may be unpalatable to a licensor, it is difficult for a licensor to argue that the licensee cannot do so. The principal concern of the licensor is that the licensee may incur significant costs for which the licensor is responsible. The licensor can limit its risk, however, by ensuring that the license clearly states that the licensee's right to cover is limited by the agreement's limitation on liability. See Section B.7.(a), below.

7. Limitation of Liability (§ 17)

Each party can limit its aggregate liability by a number of means including limiting its monetary liability; disclaiming special, incidental, consequential, and punitive damages, etc.; and reducing the statute of limitations under which a claim can be made. Each of these means is an integrated part of the party's defenses and is a significant element of any contractual negotiation. Set forth below is an in-depth look at each of these.

While limitations of liabilities usually focus on the licensor's liability, a savvy licensee will also want to look at these means to limit its own liability.

For a general overview, see Shivers & Brunel, *Contractual Limitations of Liability (a/k/a "LOLs" or Why the Other Party is Laughing Out Loud)*, 19 COMPUTER & INTERNET L. 7 (May 2002).

(a) *Limiting Monetary Liability (§ 17.2)*

(i) Limits of Monetary Liability

Every software license should contain a limitation of liability provision. Limitations of liability in commercial contracts are generally upheld. *Borden, Inc. v. Advent Ins. Co.*, 701 A.2d 255, 262 (Pa. Super. Ct. 1997); *American Nursery Products, Inc. v. Indian Wells Orchards*, 797 P.2d 477 (Wash. 1990). The failure to include a limitation of liability clause potentially subjects the licensor and the licensee to unlimited liability. Although the licensee may not want to accept limits on the licensor's liability, it is unreasonable for a licensor to risk its entire company on a single transaction. The licensor should specifically state that its liability is limited to a set amount regardless of whether the claim is brought under contract, tort, warranty, or otherwise, as many licensees seek to bring claims both under contract and tort. A smart licensee will also limit its own liability, a point many licensees forget to make.

The amount of any cap will vary depending on the value of the underlying contract itself. The licensee will want to set the cap at a level that will create a sufficient financial incentive for the licensor to take the appropriate measures to ensure compliance with its contractual obligations and avoid the liability. A proper set of risk allocations should not be viewed as a means to recoup a party's economic losses as it is unlikely that the offering party will have the financial resources to make the injured party whole even with insurance. Rather, the risk allocation provision should be viewed as a prophylactic attempt to avoid harm in the beginning.

Depending on the type and dollar value of the license agreement, the licensor's liability is usually limited to either a multiple of the total dollar value of the license agreement or the statement of work (SOW) under which the liability arose; the amount of money received by the licensor from the licensee either during the term of the agreement or in a set time period (e.g., all revenue received in the 12-month period prior to the claim of liability); or a predetermined amount. In large systems integration agreements that include the development and significant customization of software that will be implemented by the licensor, the parties will often enter into a master services agreement that serves as an overarching "umbrella" containing master terms and conditions. The parties will then execute statements of work for each distinct segment in the overall project that will contain the terms unique to that segment. Many licensors seek to limit their liability to the value of the individual statement of work under which the liability arose. *See, e.g., Computerized Radiological Services, Inc. v. Syntex Corporation,* 595 F. Supp. 1495, 1510 (E.D.N.Y. 1984) (limit of liability limiting damages to amount paid is reasonable).

Most licensees will reject this approach arguing that a structure that limits liability on a statement of work by statement of work basis does not reflect the nature of the underlying transaction. The licensee is hiring the licensor to be the developer and systems integrator for the entire project (not an integrator of only one statement of work) and the agreement's liability structure should reflect the entire relationship of the parties as well as all sums paid by the licensee to the licensor.

A statement of work by statement of work approach may be appropriate for a staff augmentation engagement, but in such a case the licensor's labor rates would be significantly lower than the rates the licensee is likely paying under a license and systems integration agreement.

To the extent that the licensed software is simply an administrative tool, the licensor may argue that it is providing software with certain functionality, but is up to the licensee to utilize the tool and the data it generates. In these situations, a statement of work by statement of work approach may be appropriate. For these types of transactions, licensors usually argue that they should be liable for complying with the software's specifications and the like, but not for third party liability arising from use of the resulting work product.

To the extent that a product is a diagnostic tool, a licensor may have some sympathy with the licensee seeking protection against third party claims. In these situations, a licensor should only be liable for third party claims to the extent that the licensor established the software's specifications.

If the parties cannot agree on a limitation of liability, a potential solution is for the licensor to purchase insurance to cover the increased liability sought by the licensee and to invoice the licensee for the additional cost. When pricing a project, most licensors assume that the limit of liability will be within industry standard parameters, such as the value of the statement of work or the revenues received by the licensor in the preceding three months. Risk is an element of price and if the licensee wants to shift the burden of risk, it should be willing to pay the cost of doing so.

Like many of the aforementioned issues, licensors often view or will argue that the amount of the cap is an element of price. While most licensors limit their liability to the amount received from the licensee, a few may be willing to increase the limit of their liability in return for an increased license fee from the licensee. A common argument by the licensor against increasing the limit of liability is that the licensor must increase its price in response to the increased risk, as the licensor's original price was based on the initially stated cap.

Some licensees seek the right to terminate the underlying agreement without penalty if the licensee has recovered damages close to the agreement's limitation of liability under the reasoning that the licensee lacks a true remedy because it might be unable to fully recover the extent of its damages in the event of another breach. Licensors should reject this position as it changes the nature of the risk and the nature of the bargain. If the licensor's breach is material, the licensee's remedy is to terminate the contract.

Considerations and Restrictions on the Ability to Limit Liability

Any cap must be reasonable and not be so low as to be considered unconscionable, or it may not be upheld as failing of its essential purpose. *See Wayne Memorial Hospital, Inc. v. Electronic Data Systems Corp.*, 1990 WL 606686 (E.D.N.C. Apr. 10, 1990) ($4,000 limit of liability on a $2 million contract is unconscionable). *See also* UCC § 2-719, comment 1. A provision will likely fail of its essential purpose if the aggrieved party is left without a remedy. *Milgard Tempering, Inc. v. Selas Corp. of America*, 761 F.2d 553 (9th Cir. 1985). At least one court has held that a licensor may not limit its liability for misrepresentations based on a contract's limitation of liability clause. *Vmark Software, Inc. v. EMC Corp.*, 642 N.E.2d 587 (Mass. App. 1994).

Similarly, willful or wanton conduct will negate an agreement's limitation of liability provisions. *Khulusi v. Southwestern Yellow Pages, Inc.*, 916 S.W.2d 227 (Mo. 1995). The same is true for gross negligence. *Anunziation v. Orkin Exterminating Co., Inc.*, 180 F. Supp.2d 353, 360 (N.D. N.Y. 2001). *But see Leprino Foods Co. v. Gress Poultry, Inc.*, 379 F. Supp.2d 659 (M.D. Pa. 2005) (parties may agree to limit their liability for gross negligence in a commercial contract). Many states prohibit contracting parties from limiting their liability for their own fraud, willful injury to a person or property of another or violation of the law. *See e.g.* Cal. Civ. Code. § 1668; 4 Okla. Status § 212. *Manning v. Brannon*, 956 P.2d 156 (Okla. 1997). See Section B.1, above, for a discussion of a licensor's potential liability under tort and contract law theories.

In any license agreement it is also important to include a provision granting the licensee a monetary refund or other remedy if a "repair or replace" remedy fails of its essential purpose. Such remedies should be stated to be exclusive. According to some but not all courts, if a limited or exclusive warranty is deemed to have failed its essential purpose, the limit on consequential damages may be voided. *McKernon v. United Technologies Corp.*, 717 F. Supp. 60 (D. Conn. 1989); *Caudill Seed and Warehouse Company, Inc. v. Prophet 21, Inc.*, 123 F. Supp.2d 826 (E.D. Pa. 2000). See Chapter 4.B.7.b.(i) for a more detailed discussion of the exclusion of consequential damages in the event a remedy fails of its essential purpose. A limitation of a party's liability will likely be upheld even if the agreement's warranty has failed. *Piper Jaffray & Co. v. SunGard Sys. Int'l., Inc.*, 2005 WL 999975 (D. Minn. Apr. 28, 2005). (A license agreement's damages cap is enforceable even if the licensor's warranty to cure the defective software has failed in its essential purpose.) See Chapter 4.B.7.(e) for a more detailed discussion.

In commercial contracts, there is a presumption of conscionability. *Siemens Credit Corp. v. Marvik Colour, Inc.*, 859 F. Supp. 686, 695 (S.D.N.Y. 1995). In determining whether a contract is unconscionable, a court will look at the bargaining power of the parties, whether the terms were actively negotiated and the terms themselves. Adhesion contracts receive greater scrutiny for procedural unconscionability. *Id.* See also *Johnson v. Long John Silver's Restaurant's, Inc.*, 320 F. Supp.2d 656, 666 (M.D. Tenn. 2004); *American Nursery Products, Inc. v. Indian Wells Orchards*, 797 P.2d 477 (Wash. 1990). At the same time, however, a contract between merchants is rarely found to be unconscionable. *D. S. Am. (East), Inc. v. Chromagrafx Imaging Sys., Inc.*, 873 F. Supp. 786 (E.D.N.Y. 1995).

A court seeks to ensure that the innocent party is made whole. *See Ragen Corp. v. Kearney & Trecker Corp.*, 912 F.2d 619 (3d Cir. 1990). Thus, the smart licensor always includes an alternate remedy in the license, such as refunding the purchase price, to avoid a specified remedy failing of its essential purpose. *See Ritchie Enterprises v. Honeywell Bull, Inc.*, 730 F. Supp. 1041, 1047 (D. Kan. 1990).

Every limitation of liability clause should clearly provide that the stated limit applies regardless of whether the licensee brings a claim based on contract, tort, or another theory. The failure to do so may result in the licensee seeking to potentially circumvent the cap (and the economic loss doctrine) by bringing a claim under tort theory by arguing that the licensor's liability is limited only in contract. *See generally, Committee Reports Tort Theories in Computer Litigation,* 38 REC. ASS'N. BAR N.Y. 426 (1983); *Budget Rent A Car Corp. v. Genesys Software Systems, Inc.* 1996 WL 480388 (D.N. Ill. Aug. 22, 1996) (claims for fraud, fraudulent inducement, and negligent misrepresentation allowed even though contract claims were disallowed under the license's integration clause).

Licensees should always insist that a limitation of liability be mutual. While the parties often carve out a party's confidentiality obligations from the agreement's limitation of liability, some licensees are hesitant to do so. A viable solution from the licensor's perspective is to accept a limitation of liability on confidentiality, but carve out (1) any breach of confidentiality relating to the licensor's intellectual property, or (2) the breach of any of the licensor's intellectual property rights.

Any limitation of liability should be conspicuous. While the meaning of "conspicuous" will be determined by state law, at a minimum, the exculpatory language should be in capital letters set off in its own paragraph and be written in plain and clear language. *Morgan Home Fashions, Inc. v. UTI, U.S., Inc.*, 2004 WL 1950370 (D.N.J. Feb. 9, 2004); *Stauffer Chem. Co. v. Curry*, 778 P.2d 1083 (Wyo. 1989). Not all states, however, require a limitation of liability to be conspicuous. *Borden, Inc. v. Advent Ink. Co.*, 701 A.2d 255 (Pa. Super. 1997).

For a detailed discussion of the validity of limitation of liability clauses see Katz, *Caveat Vendor: Limitation Clauses in Software Agreements May Not Withstand Judicial Scrutiny,* 9 COMPUTER L. ASS'N. BULL. 12 (No. 2 1994) and Hammond, *Limiting and Dealing with Liability in Software Contracts,* 9 COMPUTER LAW. 22 (June 1992).

(ii) Exclusions to Limitations of Monetary Liability

Licensors and licensees often negotiate a number of commonly accepted exclusions from any limitation of liability. Licensees should insist on excluding breach of the licensor's confidentiality obligations and the licensor's liability under any indemnification obligations (provided the indemnification obligation is limited to intellectual property, personal bodily injury, and tangible personal property, etc.) from any cap. This position should be acceptable to the licensor, provided the indemnification provisions are narrowly drawn. Regardless of whether indemnification is included under the cap, the cost of defending an indemnification claim should never be included under a cap. Further, many licensors seek to exclude the licensor's failure to comply with any applicable laws. See the following section and Chapter 10 for a more detailed discussion of the failure of a party to comply with data privacy protection.

A licensor should avoid any obligation to indemnify the licensee for general breaches of the contract, as indemnities are traditionally used to protect against *third party* claims. Further, licensor's indemnification obligations are often excluded from any limitation on liability, potentially negating the licensor's limitation of liability. The intellectual property infringement exclusion should be accepted by the licensor only if the remedies in the intellectual property infringement provision of the license agreement are the "sole and exclusive remedy" of the licensee. If not, the licensor potentially has unlimited liability.

(x) Confidentiality vs. Data Protection, Data Breach Issues

With the increased legislative focus on data privacy, greater emphasis has been focused on modifying limitations of liability to reflect the risk arising from a data breach. Data privacy laws differ from the confidentiality provisions contained in most agreements. Confidentiality addresses maintaining the confidential business information and trade secrets of the contracting parties. A breach arises from the wrongful disclosure or misuse of the other party's trade secrets or confidential information. Traditionally, breach of a party's confidential information has been excluded from an agreement's limitation of liability.

Data privacy, however, addresses Personally Identifiable Information (PII) and Personal Health Information (PHI) of third parties, usually customers of the licensee, that a licensor may access in performing its obligations under the agreement. PII may include that information which identifies a particular person, such as an individual's name, address, or social security number, while PHI usually encompasses an individual's medical records and information.

For the most part, customers receive the security services for which they have agreed to pay. When pricing the cost to comply with the customer's data privacy and security requirements, the licensor only takes into account the licensor's costs. The licensor usually does not factor into the price (a) the value of the customer's data, (b) the attractiveness of the data to hackers, (c) the monetary benefits the customer will receive from the software, or (d) any other security services or measures the customer is taking to protect its data. The licensor is usually providing services that are tangential to the customer's data privacy obligations. The licensor cannot insure the misappropriation, the loss or destruction of data or the value of the data to the customer. The licensor also does not include in its prices the loss or damage to data even when due to the licensor's own negligence.

Most licensors are unwilling to accept unlimited liability for a breach of a data privacy obligation, as the risks of breach are significantly greater and can arise from actions outside the licensor's control, such as being hacked or data intrusion. Most licensees recognize that the risks involved with data privacy are greater than those with confidential information but argue that it is exactly for that reason the licensor's liability should not be limited. These licensees argue that they have unlimited liability to their customers and potentially to governmental agencies for a breach, so the licensor should not be able to limit its own liability for the licensor's breach.

An Increased Limit of Liability Tied to Specific Standards (Form 23.K.2.EE.2 § 1.2).

One potential solution is to create a second, larger limitation of liability for claims related to data privacy and security as well as a party's compliance with applicable laws. For example, a party's limitation of liability for any such claim may be limited to an amount equal to twice the limitation of liability for other types of claims. Governmental fines should be excluded from the cap. If the value of this increased cap is significant, the licensor may want to negotiate a lower cap equal to the revenue received by the licensor in the six months preceding the event giving rise to the claim.

A licensor's obligations regarding its security and privacy obligations should be tied to specific standards that a party can price and perform against. For example, specific encryption standards should be set for accessing confidential customer data accessed by a licensor for processing or other services, as opposed to a more general standard of care, such a duty to use reasonable care in handling confidential customer data, which may apply to confidential data such as trade secrets. The limitation of liability for breach of obligations regarding security and privacy of data should be tied to the specific standards, not a "reasonable" or "non-negligent" standard, which is more appropriate for a nondisclosure type of confidential information, such as business plans. Model language is set forth below:

> **Special Liability Cap for Security and Confidentiality.**
>
> The Liability Cap amount solely with respect to all claims that a party has breached any of its obligations under Section __ (Security and Confidentiality), shall be 24 months (such amount the "Special Liability Cap") instead of 12 months and each reference to 12 months set forth in Section ___ (Limitation of Liability) shall mean 24 months solely for purposes of calculating claims that a party has breached any of its obligations under Section __(Security and Confidentiality). Except for this modification, all of the provisions of this Article 1 shall be applicable to claims related to Section __. The Special Liability Cap in this paragraph is inclusive of and not in addition to the Liability Cap. Any amounts paid under the Special Liability Cap shall reduce the remaining amount, if any, available under the Liability Cap and any amounts paid under the Liability Cap shall reduce the remaining amount available under the Special Liability Cap.

See Form 23.K.2.EE.2 for additional language illustrative of this point.

(y) Gross Negligence, Willful Misconduct, and Intentional Acts/Intentional Breach

Most licensees should insist on excluding gross negligence, willful misconduct, and intentional acts from any limitation of liability. In many cases, this exclusion does not significantly increase the licensor's liability as a limitation of liability may not be valid for claims of gross negligence, willful or intentional acts, misrepresentation, or fraud even in a commercial context. *See* Boss & Woodward, *Scope of the Uniform Commercial Code, Survey of Computer Contracting Cases,* 43 BUS. LAW. 1513 (1988). *See also Arthur D. Little International, Inc. v. Dooyang Corp.*, 928 F. Supp. 1189, 1205 (D. Mass. 1996) (under Massachusetts law, a damage limitation clause in a contract does not bar recovery for intentional misrepresentation in the inducement of a contract); *Shelby Mutual Insurance Company v. City of Grand Rapids,* 6 Mich. App. 95, 148 N.W.2d 260 (1967) (a party may contract against liability for harm caused by its negligence but may not do so for gross negligence); *NMP Corp. v. Parametric Technology Corp.*, 958 F. Supp. 1536, 1543 (N.D. Okla. 1997) (under Oklahoma law, a party may not contractually limit damages resulting from its own gross negligence or fraud); *AGIP Petroleum Co., Inc. v. Gulf Island Fabrication, Inc.*, 920 F. Supp. 1330, 1343 (S.D. Tex. 1996) (under Louisiana law, a party may not limit its liability for gross negligence and intentional conduct); *Kalisch-Jarcho, Inc. v. City of New York,* 448 N.E.2d 413, 416–17 (N.Y. 1983) (exculpatory agreement will not exonerate a party from liability for willful or grossly negligent acts).

Gross Negligence

In many states, the standard for a court to find "gross negligence" is exceedingly high. "Gross Negligence must betoken a reckless influence to the rights of others." *Net2Globe International, Inc. v. Time Warner Telecom of New York*, 273 F. Supp.2d 436, 450 (S.D.N.Y. 2003) *citing Sommer v. Federal Signal Corp.*, 593 N.E.2d 1365, 1370–71 (N.Y. 1992). A gross negligence standard sets a high threshold. To rise to the level of gross negligence, an act requires special circumstances and particularly egregious conduct. Thus, only rarely will a party be able to demonstrate gross negligence and negate the contractual limitation of liability. *See e.g. Hunter v. Skate III*, 1999 Mass. App. Div. 274 (1999).

There is usually an express exclusion from the agreement's limitation of liability for gross negligence or willful misconduct. The majority of jurisdictions imply this anyway, as gross negligence does not equate with a right to punitive damages.

Gross negligence will be decided by a jury as it is a question of fact. New York law defines "gross negligence" narrowly—a reason for the licensor to select New York law to govern the agreement. Gross negligence as used in contract law is essentially a contract concept, as opposed to negligence, which is founded in tort.

Willful Misconduct

Licensees should refuse to accept any limit on the licensor's liability for the licensor's intentional breach and should specifically state so in the agreement. At least one court has upheld a limitation of liability where the licensor intentionally failed to perform. *See Metropolitan Life Insurance Co. v. Noble Lowndes Int'l., Inc.*, 84 N.Y.2d 430, 618 N.Y.S.2d. 882 (1994). *But see Hosiery Corp. of America, Inc. v. International Data Processing, Inc.*, 1991 WL 30015 (D.N.J. Feb. 28, 1991) (court failed to dismiss breach claim due to factual issue of whether licensor breached agreement by willfully failing to install latest software). See also § 14.A.5.

The meaning of willful misconduct varies by state. New York has interpreted this term narrowly. In *Metropolitan Life Ins. Co. v. Noble Lowndes Int'l, Inc.*, the New York Court of Appeals held that the term "willful misconduct" does not encompass the vendor's intentional failure to perform. In *Metropolitan Life*, Noble delivered the contractually required core software and the functional specifications without incident. After two sets of enhancements were rejected by Metropolitan Life, Noble demanded an increase in the price of the enhancements. When Metropolitan Life refused, Noble stopped performing and Metropolitan Life brought suit against Noble seeking a refund of all monies paid to Noble plus Metropolitan Life's general and consequential damages. *Id.* at 506.

An exception to the limitation of liability provision in the parties' agreement excluded consequential damages except in the case of "intentional misrepresentations, or damages arising out of [Noble's] willful acts or gross negligence." *Id.* at 505–06. The court held that the term "willful acts" should be interpreted as referring to conduct similar in nature to intentional misrepresentation and gross negligence and thus denied Metropolitan Life's claim to recover its consequential damages. *Id.*

If a licensee negotiates a limitation on its own liability, a smart licensor will want to carve out from any such limitation breach of the license grant, violation of the agreement's confidentiality provisions, and the payment of any monies owed the licensor under the payment provisions of the license.

Finally, where the parties are required to insure against potential risks under the license, the license should clearly state that the parties' liability is not limited to the amount of insurance they are required to obtain under the license.

(z) Tangible Personal Property and Personal Bodily Injury

A licensor should ensure that only its indemnification obligation for tangible personal property damage and personal bodily injuries are excluded from the liability cap. "Personal bodily injuries" are usually excluded from any cap, as limiting consequential damages is *prima facie* unconscionable in consumer transactions. UCC. § 2-719(3) prohibits a party from limiting its own liability for personal bodily injury. Most parties are willing to accept these risks, as any loss will likely be covered under a party's insurance policies. See Chapter 6.C for a discussion of insurance issues. Many licensees seek to modify the wording of such exclusions to exclude "personal injury" and "personal property damages" from the agreement's limitation of liability in an effort to expand the limit of the licensor's liability.

By removing the words "tangible" and "bodily," the licensee can potentially seek to hold the licensor liable for any property damage, including intangible property damage. For example, *tangible* personal property damages are unlikely to include erasing a tape, but such an action may be considered personal property damage.

Existing case law supports the proposition that loss of data is considered intangible property damage. *See e.g., Ward General Insurance Services, Inc. v. Employers Fire Insurance Company*, 114 Cal.App.4th 548 (2004) (loss of database is not a direct physical loss); *St. Paul Fire & Marine Insurance Company v. National Computer Systems, Inc.*, 490 N.W.2d 626 (Minn. 1992) (trade secrets contained in binders is not damage to tangible property); *America Online, Inc. v. St. Paul Mercury Ins. Co.*, 207 F. Supp.2d 459, 468 (E.D. Va. 2007) ("Computer data software and systems are intangible items stored on a tangible vessel on the computer or a disk."); *Seagate Technology, Inc. v. St. Paul Fire and Marine Ins. Co.*, 11 F. Supp.2d 1150 (N.D. Cal 1998) (loss of data alone is not "physical damage to tangible property"). *But see Dechert v. Commonwealth*, 998 A.2d 575 (Pa. 2010) (in tax dispute, canned software found to be tangible personal property).

This distinction is important, as increasing amounts of data is being transferred over the internet, as entities move away from using computer tapes to store and transport data. Thus, the data would have to reside on tangible media such as a computer tape or disk to support a claim for "tangible personal property damage." *See e.g., Retail Systems, Inc. v. CNA Insurance Companies*, 469 N.W.2d 735, 737 (Minn. App. 1991) (Computer tape and resident data "tangible property" as data "was integrated completely with the physical property of the tape.").

Similarly, by removing "bodily," the licensor has assumed significant additional risk. The initial intent of this exclusion was to comply with state law limiting a party's ability to limit its liability for personal bodily injury. The deletion arguably exposes the licensor to any type of personal liability. In essence, these changes significantly dilute or even negate the limitation of liability.

> Each party agrees to indemnify, hold harmless and defend the other party, its officers, directors, employees, agents and representatives from and against any claim, demand, cause of action, loss, expense or liability, including reasonable attorney's fees, arising on account of any injury to or death of person or **damage to personal property** to the extent directly or indirectly caused by the acts or **omissions** of the indemnifying party.

From the licensor's perspective, the above language provides several reasons for concern. The language fails to expressly reference third party claims. Many people wrongly believe that by implication indemnification is limited to third party claims. The licensor should qualify any such language relating to an omission by requiring any omission to be intentional. Some parties are willing to accept that "damage to personal property" provided indemnification is limited to third party claims. A prudent party will reject this language, as the indemnified party has no onus to limit its liability to the third party. Given that the indemnified party is in contractual privity with the injured party, it has the ability to limit its liability (and thus the indemnifying party's liability) through its contract with the third party. As such, the indemnifying party must ensure that the exclusion is limited to "tangible personal property" to fully protect its interests.

Alternatively, some parties seek to specifically define "tangible personal property" to include data and information which are usually considered to be intangible. The language set forth below seeks to avoid any ambiguity and broaden the licensor's potential liability. By expanding the definition of "tangible personal property" to include intangibles, the licensee is inviting the licensor to strike this expansive language. A savvy licensee is more likely to achieve its goal by deleting "tangible" instead of attempting to redefine "tangible," which emphasizes the licensee's intent to expand the licensor's liability.

> Licensor shall promptly and fully defend, indemnify and hold harmless licensee and its affiliates and their respective officers, directors, agents and employees (the "Indemnified Parties") against all claims, demands and judgments made or recovered against them for damages to or loss of real or **tangible personal property, including Licensee's Confidential Information, data files, web content, software applications** or for bodily injury or death to any person arising out of, or in connection with this Agreement, to the extent that such damage, injury or death was caused by an action or omission of licensor, its subcontractor or its employees or agents, or on the issue of infringement of any patent, copyright, trade secret, trademark, or trade dress related to a Deliverable or the Services.

(b) Disclaimer of Consequential/Incidental/Punitive Damages (§ 17.1)

Most parties agree to limit their damages to direct damages, that is, those damages arising directly from the breach and those which are not unique to the injured party, and disclaim all other damages, such as consequential damages, incidental damages and punitive damages.

(i) Consequential Damages

Consequential damages constitute "those damages that, although not an invariable result of every breach, were reasonably foreseeable or contemplated by the parties at the time the contract was entered into as a probable result of a breach and were proximately caused by the breach." *Wartsila NSD North America, Inc. v. Hill International, Inc.*, 530 F.3d 269, 277 (3d Cir. 2008). Often, the common law definition of "consequential" damages is broader than the UCC's, as many common law interpretations encompass the UCC definition of both "incidental" and "consequential" damages.

Under Section 2-719 (1), (3) of the UCC, the parties to a contract may exclude consequential and incidental damages provided such exclusions are not unconscionable and there are no other explicit exceptions. *See e.g., The Colonial Life Insurance Company of America v. Electronic Data Systems Corporation,* 817 F. Supp. 235 (D.N.H. 1993). Consequential damages for personal bodily injury cannot be limited in some circumstances. See UCC § 2-719 (3), comments 1 and 3.

Unlike Section 2-316 of the UCC, which imposes a conspicuousness requirement for disclaimers of warranty related to merchantability and fitness, Section 2-719 (1), (3) does not contain a conspicuousness requirement. Comment 3 to Section 2-719(3), which discusses the exclusion of consequential damages, also fails to address conspicuousness. Nonetheless, to err on the side of caution, any such disclaimer should be conspicuous to avoid a court imposing such a requirement and potentially voiding any limitation of liability. *See generally Krupp PM Eng'g. v. Honeywell, Inc.*, 530 N.W.2d 146 (Mich. 1995). *See also D. S. Am. (East), Inc. v. Chromagrafx Imaging Systems, Inc.*, 873 F. Supp. 786 (E. D. N. Y. 1995) (the failure to make a limitation of consequential damages conspicuous is one factor in determining whether a limitation is unconscionable).

If a court finds that the licensor's warranty "failed of its essential purpose" (i.e., the licensor did not provide the licensee with a viable remedy), some courts will void the contractually agreed-to exclusion of consequential damages, potentially creating unlimited liability on the licensor's behalf; others will not, particularly where the exclusion is independent. See UCC § 2-719(2). There is a dichotomy of opinion as to whether a disclaimer of consequential damages is valid if a remedy fails of its essential purpose. Compare *Fidelity & Deposit Trust Co. of Maryland v. Krebs Eng'rs,* 859 F.2d 501, 504-05 (7th Cir. 1988) (consequential damages automatically recoverable if remedy fails its essential purpose) with *Canal Elec. Co. v. Westinghouse Elec. Corp.*, 578 N.E.2d 182, 185 (Mass. 1990) (consequential damages disclaimer valid even though limited remedy failed of its essential purpose). Two commentators believe the two UCC sections operate independently of each other. J. WHITE AND R. SUMMER, UNIFORM COMMERCIAL CODE § 12-10 at 526–27 (3d ed. 1988).

An issue exists, however, as to whether exclusion of consequential damages is valid when a remedy fails of its essential purpose. Compare *Bishop Logging Co. v. John Deere Indus. Equip. Co.*, 455 S.E.2d 183 (S.C. App. 1995) (permitting consequential damages when remedy failed of its essential purpose) and *McNally Wellman Co. v. New York State Elec. & Gas Corp.*, 63 F.3d 1188 (2d Cir 1995) (allowing consequential damages despite contractual exclusion when remedy failed of its essential purpose) with *Caudill Seed and Warehouse Co., Inc. v. Prophet 21, Inc.*, 123 F. Supp.2d 826 (E.D.

Pa. 2000) and *Int'l. Fin. Serv. v. Franz,* 534 N.W.2d 261 (Minn. 1995) (consequential damage exclusion enforceable notwithstanding failure of remedy's essential purpose). One court has found that a limitation of consequential damages applies only to a breach of warranty and not for nonperformance. *PC COM, Inc. v. Proteon, Inc.*, 906 F. Supp. 894 (S.D. N.Y. 1995).

The Ninth Circuit upheld an award of consequential damages despite a disclaimer contained in the parties' contract where the seller failed to deliver a working software system and the contract contained an exclusive "repair or replace" remedy. *RRX Indus. v. Lab-Con, Inc.*, 772 F.2d 543 (9th Cir. 1985). In a later case, the Ninth Circuit held that a limitation on consequential damages was inapplicable because the limit was tied to the limited repair remedy contained in the contract. The court concluded that because a working software system was never delivered, the limited remedy and limit on consequential damages never came into effect. *Hawaiian Tel. Co. v. Microform Data Sys.*, 829 F.2d 919 (9th Cir. 1987). *See also Caudill Seed and Warehouse Company, Inc. v. Prophet 21, Inc.*, 123 F. Supp.2d 826 (E.D. Pa. 2000) (where seller intentionally or negligently stymies buyer's efforts to take advantage of exclusive remedy, damages disclaimer is rendered void and buyer may seek all remedies under UCC including consequential damages).

A limitation on consequential damages will not be upheld where such limitation is unconscionable and contrary to public policy. *Durham v. Ciba-Geigy Corp.*, 315 N.W. 2d 696 (S.D. 1982).

To strengthen a disclaimer of consequential damages or other limitation of liability, any limitation of liability provision should be distinct from and in a separate section from the warranty/remedy provisions of a contract. See, e.g., § 17.1 and § 16. The reasoning for such separation is that if the warranty/remedy provisions fail their essential purpose, and such provisions are separate and distinct from the limitation of liability, the court will hopefully view the provisions as unrelated and uphold the limitation of liability. At least one court has held that a limitation of liability provision and a remedy provision contained in different sections of an agreement will be viewed as independent of each other. *Colonial Life Ins. Co. v. Electronic Data Systems Corp.*, 817 F. Supp. 235, 241 (D.N.H. 1993). This philosophy has been endorsed by two leading commentators. *See* ROBERT A. FELDMAN & RAYMOND T. NIMMER, DRAFTING EFFECTIVE CONTRACTS 5.06 [A][2] Aspen Law & Business (2d Ed. 2007).

A licensor should resist making any disclaimer of consequential damages mutual. If the licensee breaches the terms of the license, the great majority of the licensor's damages will be consequential damages such as lost profit, lost customers and loss of good will.

For a more detailed discussion of consequential damages see Glenn D. West and Sara G. Duran, *Reassessing the "Consequences" of Consequential Damage Waivers in Acquisition Agreements*, 63 BUS. LAW 777 (2008).

(ii) Incidental Damages

A seller's incidental damages are defined under UCC § 2 710(ii), as:

> "any commercially reasonable charges, expenses or commissions incurred in stopping delivery, in the transportation, care, and custody of goods after the buyer's

> breach, in connection with the return or resale of the goods or otherwise resulting from the breach."

A buyer's incidental damages result "from a seller's breach of contract" and "include expenses reasonably incurred in inspection, receipt, transportation and care and custody of goods rightfully rejected, any commercially reasonable charges, expenses or commissions in connection with effecting cover and any other reasonable expense incident to the delay or other breach."

UCC § 2-715(1).

The UCC definition of incidental damages may not be directly applicable to software licensing as Article 2 does not apply to services, only to "transactions in goods." In any event, the applicable common law definition of incidental damages will likely closely mirror these definitions, and it is likely any court would look to the UCC by analogy.

Some licensees reject any attempt to disclaim incidental damages, arguing that incidental damages, such as cover, are in essence direct damages. Based on the Section 2-715(1) definition, many licensees argue that these types of damages should be recoverable by the licensee in the event of a breach. More importantly, aside from the definition, they argue that if examples of incidental damages were submitted to reasonable business people, they would likely agree that these examples of "reasonable expense incident to the delay or breach" should be recoverable in the event a party breaches.

In any negotiation from the licensor's perspective, the exclusion of consequential damages is the most important exclusion, much more so than incidental damages. Many licensors generally disagree with the inclusion of incidental damages as recoverable damages, as the exclusion of special and incidental damages is standard in license agreements. If incidental damages cross the line into what are direct damages, they would not be excluded. An alternative position is for the licensor to agree to pay the cost of cover. This solution is especially relevant if the agreement involves third party suppliers for which the licensor has overall responsibility in its role as a systems integrator, but for which the licensor lacks contractual privity and lacks the contractual right to control their performance.

If a licensor elects to allow the licensee to recover incidental damages, it should ensure that these damages are included in any limit of liability and that the licensee has the obligation to mitigate its damages.

(iii) Special Damages

Special damages are "those which are the actual, but not the necessary, result of the injury complained of, and which in fact follow it as a natural and proximate consequence in the particular case, that is, by reason of special circumstances or conditions." *Twin Coach Co. v. Chance Vought Aircraft Inc.*, 163 A.2d 278, 286 (Del. 1960). The Restatement (Second) of Torts § 904 (2) defines special damages as "compensatory damages for a harm other than one for which general damages are given."

Special damages are usually defined by jurisdiction. *See e.g.*, Statutorily: Alabama: Ala. Code § 15-18-66(2); California: Cal. Civ. Code § 48(a); Montana: Mont. Code

Ann. § 46-18-243(1)(a); By common law: New York: *Liberman v. Gelstein*, 80 N.Y.2d 429, 434–435 (1992); North Carolina: *Sarda v. City/Cty. of Durham Bd. of Adjust.*, 575 S.E.2d 829, 830–31 (N.C. 2003). *Holtzscheiter v. Thomson Newspapers, Inc.*, 506 S.E.2d 497, 501, 502 n.4 (S.C. 1998). *Ray v. Miller Meester Advertising, Inc.*, 684 N.W.2d 404 (Minn. 2004) (Special damages are those which are the natural but not the necessary and inevitable result of the wrongful act). Special damages are often equated with consequential damages (and incidental damages) in which case they will be excluded by an agreement's limitation/exclusion on consequential damages. *Wartsila NSD North America, Inc. v. Hill International, Inc.*, 530 F.3d 269, 277 (3d Cir. 2008).

Special damages, if allowed, should come under any limitation on damages.

(iv) Punitive Damages

Although an express exclusion of punitive damages is usually included in most disclaimers, punitive damages are generally not allowed in contract actions. *Purdy v. Consumers Distrib. Co., Ltd.*, 648 F. Supp. 980 (S.D.N.Y. 1986) (punitive damages not available where claim lies solely in contract). Nonetheless, an express inclusion should be included as there is a trend toward permitting punitive damages where a party's actions have been egregious.

(c) Deemed Direct Damages (§ 17.4, Form 23. K.2.EE.2 § 1.2.)

Direct damages are those damages that may be fairly and reasonably considered as arising from a breach and that do not arise from any special circumstances applicable to the nonbreaching party. Direct damages would include the cost of purchasing a replacement product or services in the open market, while consequential damages would be the value of lost business due to the breach.

Some licensees seek to specify that certain damages will be "deemed" to be direct damages. This effort arises from consequential damages being disclaimed in an agreement preventing licensees from potentially recovering a significant percentage of their damages. The licensor should closely examine the proposed definition to limit the types of damages that are deemed to be direct damages. The licensor should seek to limit any "deemed" direct damages. In particular, it should be hesitant with respect to reconstructing or reloading data. This liability should be aligned to the related contractual obligations (i.e., this provision would not imply that the licensor has more liability with respect to these items than otherwise set forth in the agreement). Reconstructing data can be extremely expensive. Further, the payment of penalties or fines should be limited to be fines and penalties related to the licensor's failure to comply with applicable law. Reprocurement costs would be considered incidental damages. See e.g., Section 2-715 of the UCC, which defines incidental damages as covering reprocurement costs. Many licensors will also accept a licensee's request to define reprocurement costs as direct damages, but seek to exclude any efforts to include lost profits or goodwill. A prudent licensor should seek to limit any expansion of direct damages to those damages that would likely be excluded under the disclaimer of special, incidental and consequential damages.

Both parties should consider exclusions from any disclaimer of consequential damages. Common exceptions to a disclaimer of consequential damages are for violation of the agreement's confidentiality provisions, violation of any law such as any privacy requirements (e.g., HIPAA, Gramm-Leach Bliley), and any indemnification obligations arising from third party claims. The philosophy behind these carve-outs is that most damages arising from these types of claims will be consequential damages.

For a more in-depth discussion of consequential damages, see note, *Consequential Damage Limitations and Cross-Subsidization: An Independent Approach to Uniform Commercial Code Section 2-719,* 66 S. Cal. L. Rev. 1273 (1973).

(d) Reducing the Statute of Limitations (§ 17.1)

Traditionally, a statute of limitations bars a potential plaintiff from bringing a contract claim after a set period of time after the action that gave rise to the claim. *See, e.g., A.B Alexander d/b/a A.B. Alexander and Associates v. The Perkin Elmer Corp.,* 729 F.2d 576 (8th Cir. 1984). Most states have statutorily codified this time period as three or four years. *See, e.g.,* California: Calif. Stat. Ann. § 337 (1996) (four years), and Maryland: MD. Code Ann Cts & Jud. Proc. J. § 5-101(2006) (three years). By default, Section 2-725(1) of the UCC provides for a four-year statute of limitations beginning when the cause of action first accrues, but allows the parties to reduce the statute of limitations by mutual agreement to a minimum of one year. It is important to remember that the statute of limitations for a contract claim may differ from the statute of limitations for a tort claim. Thus, in agreeing to any reduction of the statute of limitations for a contract claim, the parties need to consider the interrelationship with the statute of limitations for third party torts vis-à-vis the license's indemnity provisions.

By agreeing to a period less than the statutory time period, the licensor may reduce the time period in which the licensee may bring a claim, thus limiting the licensor's risk and, consequently, its liability. *See Gruet v. Care Free Housing Division of Kennschl Enterprises Inc.,* 759 N.Y.S.2d 276 (2003) (one-year contractual statute of limitations upheld); *Action Mailing Corp. v. Hewlett Packard Co.,* 2009 WL 3526658 (W.D. Mo. Oct. 26, 2009) (one year contractual statute of limitations for breach of warranty upheld).

To be valid, a clause should be clearly and unambiguously written. Some states do not favor contractual agreements to reduce a statue of limitations and will strictly construe such an agreement against the party seeking to enforce it. *Western Filter Corp. v. Argan,* Inc. 540 F.3d 947 (9th Cir. 2008) (ambiguous clause found not to reduce limitation period).

A smart licensee will want to carefully consider whether to accept any reduction in the statute of limitations and if the licensee chooses to do so, the licensee should make such clause mutual to also reduce its own risk. Given that all states have a statutory statute of limitations for contracts and tort claims, a licensee should resist reducing the statute of limitations to less than the statutory period. Although the contractual statute of limitations may be mutual, in the great majority of instances such limitation will benefit the licensor.

If the statute of limitations is reduced, licensors need to make sure all of their invoices are submitted to the licensee in a timely manner. The licensor should avoid holding invoices in the event of a dispute only to find its collection efforts barred by the statute of limitations. *See, e.g., Ram Systems of LaCrosse, Wisconsin, Inc., v. Wichita Coca-Cola Bottling Co.*, 1994 WL 476528 (D. Kan. Aug. 5, 1994) (licensee alleged one-year statute of limitations barred collection of monies due licensor). Similarly, if the licensee gives notice of a potential breach and the licensor takes over a year to cure, the licensee's claims may be barred by not bringing suit within a year. *See, e.g., Grus v. Patton,* 790 S.W.2d 936 (Mo. App. 1990) (seller's unsuccessful attempts to repair defects over eight-year period did not toll four-year statute of limitations). Thus, a prudent licensee should enter into a tolling agreement while any attempt to cure is under way. See Form 23.H.1 for a model Tolling Agreement.

Licensors should be careful to review the applicable state law to ensure any proposed reduction does not violate the state's law. Texas, for example, prohibits reducing the statute of limitations in most agreements to less than two years. Texas Civil Practice & Remedies Code § 16.070. The parties should also be careful not to unknowingly extend the statute of limitation. For example, under Maryland law, executing an agreement under seal may extend the statute of limitations from 3 to 12 years. Md. Code Ann Cts. & Jud. Proc. J. § 5-101(2006). See Chapter 6.N for a more detailed discussion. A claim of fraud, however, will not be barred by a contract's statute of limitations. *Invacare Corporation v. Sperry Corporation,* 612 F. Supp. 448 (N.D. Ohio 1984) (seller cannot rely on statute of limitations to bar buyer's claim where alleged contracts were induced by fraud).

Finally, the parties should be cognizant of whether the statute of limitations is tolled by a party's efforts to correct any defect in the software. There is a dichotomy among the courts as to whether efforts to correct a defect will toll the statute of limitations. *Compare Triangle Underwriters, Inc. v. Honeywell, Inc.*, 604 F.2d 737 (2d Cir. 1979) (seller's attempt to repair computer system after malfunction did not toll statute of limitations for breach of contract claim) with *Daley v. Twin Disc, Inc.*, 440 F. Supp.2d 48, 52 (D. Mass. 2006) (attempts to repair defective goods will not normally extend or toll the statute of limitations, but "purposely prolonging the time for repairs beyond the statute of limitations" may justify extension) and *Waddell v. L.V.R.V., Inc.*, 125 P.3d 1160 (Nev. 2006) (period in which buyer may timely revoke acceptance may be extended when seller repeatedly failed to cure breach despite repeated assurances) and *North Am. Lighting, Inc. v. Hopkins Mfg. Corp.*, 37 F.3d 1253 (7th Cir. 1994) (seller's attempts to cure do not go against buyer's period of timely revocation).

(e) Exclusive Remedy

Under United States law, unless a contract states otherwise, a remedy is considered to be nonexclusive. As such, licensors should ensure that their licenses clearly state that the remedies provided in the agreement are the sole and exclusive remedies available to the licensee. See the model language below:

Damages as set forth in this Section __ are the parties' sole and exclusive monetary remedy and the sole and exclusive alternative remedy in the event any other remedy fails of its essential purpose.

The first clause of the above language clearly states that the limit of liability is intended as an exclusive monetary remedy and should be made subject to the article, section or paragraph containing the limitation of liability.

The second clause addresses the remedy's failure of essential purpose, which arises from the Uniform Commercial Code. There are conflicting positions in the courts on the meaning of the provision. If the contract is governed under New York law, the failure of essential purpose language can be deleted, as a failure of a remedy's essential purpose will not negate the contract's exclusion of consequential damages. *McNally Wellman Co. v. New York State Elec. & Gas Co.*, 63 F.3d 1188 (2d Cir. 1995). However, under the law of other jurisdictions, it is imperative to include this language. Some licensees resist including language to this effect because they lack familiarity with the intent of the wording.

This language does not seek to preclude specific performance, injunctive relief, or other nonmonetary remedies. If service levels are provided for under the agreement, it is appropriate to include service level credits however they maybe determined.

8. Price and Payment (§ 8)

Price and payment terms will usually depend on the type of license granted and whether the contract requires any software development work to be performed. Both parties need to focus on when payment is due, as the payment terms can affect the licensor's revenue recognition and provide the licensee with the leverage to pay the licensor as each stage of the work is completed.

(a) Pricing

Software licenses can be priced in many different ways. The principle means are enterprise licenses, seat licenses, and Central Processing Unit ("CPU") licenses including core licenses, as well as a blended mix of these methodologies. Occasionally, a vendor may price its licenses on a contingency basis by taking a percentage of cost reductions realized through the implementation of a software solution, such as a percentage of the recovery of improperly paid claims that have been identified by a software solution. Set forth below is a brief explanation of each of these pricing methodologies and the issues associated with each.

(i) Software Licenses

Enterprise Licenses

Conceptually, enterprise licenses are the easiest to price and enforce. The vendor charges one fee for the entire licensing entity to utilize the software, regardless of the number of employees accessing the software or the number of computers processing the software. There is no need to audit the customer's use of the software, nor to implement a complicated pricing model. The principle issue for consideration is the extent to which the license includes the customer's affiliates and subsidiaries as well as future acquisitions and divestures.

From the licensor's perspective, the license should clearly state the ability of present and future affiliates as well as acquired and divested entities, to utilize the software. In the event the licensor agrees to allow the customer's subsidiaries and affiliates to utilize the software, the underlying license agreement should limit use to those subsidiaries and affiliates set forth on a schedule to the license agreement. In the event the licensee is unwillingly to limit use to a scheduled list of subsidiaries and affiliates, the licensor should carefully define "Affiliates" to quantify/limit the number of entities that can utilize the software.

In the case of a divestiture, the licensor should limit the time in which the divested entity may utilize the software after divestiture before it is required to purchase its own license or cease use of the software. The licensee should require the licensor to provide pricing for any divested entity at the time the license is executed to limit the licensor's leverage at the time of the divesture. The license fee for any divested entity should reflect a significant discount in light of the divested entity's prior use of the software and the fact that the licensor will likely incur insignificant additional costs for training, documentation, and the like. In the event of a divestiture, the licensee's support and maintenance fee should decrease, as the licensor is not responsible for divested business.

As to acquisitions, the licensor should carefully consider whether it will allow the licensee to utilize the software in companies the licensee acquires without the payment of an additional fee. The licensor may be forgoing a significant revenue stream, especially if the licensee acquires a large company. The licensor is also at risk if the licensee merges with another, larger company but the licensee is the surviving entity. Even if the licensor agrees that acquired entities may utilize the software without the payment of an additional license fee, the underlying agreement should clearly provide the licensor the right to increase the relevant maintenance and support fees. Maintenance and support fees should be based on the total number of users which should increase proportionally with the size of the assumed entity. If the licensor negotiates for the right to charge an additional fee in the event the licensee acquires or merges with another entity, the parties should negotiate a pricing schedule at the time the license agreement is executed to limit the licensor's leverage in the event of an acquisition.

A prudent licensor will include language within the license agreement as set forth below to protect itself in the event the licensee acquires or merges with another entity.

> Customer shall use a single logical production copy of the Licensed System only to process data related to the internal operations or the financial services offerings of itself, excluding businesses, blocks of business, or lines of business acquired thereby from a third party after the effective date of this Statement of Work.

Seat Licenses

Seat license fees are determined based on the number of concurrent users who are authorized to access the software at the same time. The licensee purchases a number of "seats" which allows the corresponding number of the licensee's employees to access the software. Seat licenses are increasingly favored by both licensors and licensees as more licensors move to a distributed/networked environment. The licensee must carefully negotiate the license terms, as in the sample language below, as questions often arise as to whether the license grant limits the licensee to an agreed upon number of identified users who may access the software or a set number of users who may access the software concurrently. For example, if a licensee purchases 300 seat licenses, can the licensee install the software on 1,000 computers provided only 300 users access the software at one time? Similarly, if the software is installed on only 300 computers, can 900 people working in three shifts utilize the 300 computers to access the software?

> Licensee shall pay to Licensor the license and support fee specified in this Schedule 1 (the "License & Support Fee") for Licensor Product licensed to Licensee based on the total number of Licensed Users using the Licensor Products in the amount indicated below:

Number of Unique Users	Per Unique User Cost
0 -1000	$100
1001 - 2000	$75
2001 - 9999	$50

> Licensing is based on a Unique User. "Unique User" is defined as an individual user that utilizes **NAME OF SOFTWARE PRODUCT™** as a licensee of the Licensor. Unique Users are individual **employees** of the Licensee. Unique users will be reported by the Licensor on a monthly basis pursuant to Section X.X of the Agreement.

In *Wall Data, Inc. v. Los Angeles County Sheriff's Dept.*, 447 F.3d 769 (9th Cir. 2006), the Ninth Circuit Court of Appeals found that a licensee who purchased 3,663 licenses but installed the software on 6,007 computers was in breach of the license even though it had configured its computers to limit the total number of users that could access the software to the number of licenses the licensee had purchased. In essence, the court held that the mere presence of a software copy on a computer is an infringement even though the software is not accessible to a user. The *Wall Data* case was also interesting because the court excluded evidence that the licensee's purchase agreement with the software reseller may have allowed such use because the copyright owner was unaware of the reseller's license terms with the licensee. *Id.* at 782-83. This decision creates significant concern for any company that purchases its software through a reseller. For a more detailed discussion, see *Sheriffs' Over-Installation of Licensed Software was Copyright Infringement, Despite Limited Access or Use of Software,* 23 COMPUTER & INTERNET LAW. 24 (Aug. 2006). Similarly, in *Thoroughbred Software, Int'l v. Dice Corp., et al*, the court found a software distributor liable for all unpaid license fees for all unauthorized copies made even though some copies were not accessible to or used by its customers. 488 F.3d 352 (6th Cir. 2007).

The *Wall Data and Thoroughbred Software* cases illustrate the importance of carefully negotiating the terms of use for any seat licenses purchased.

Machine, CPU and Core Licenses

CPU licenses have traditionally been utilized for mainframe solutions. The licensee purchases one license for each computer the software is installed on, each of which is identified by serial number. The price is based on the number of machines and their computing power. If the licensee desires to install the software on a new CPU, it must obtain the consent of the licensor and must usually pay a new license fee or a transfer fee. By requiring the licensee to provide the serial number of all CPUs on which the software is installed, the licensor can easily audit the licensee's compliance with the number of CPU licenses it purchased.

As computers have become more sophisticated and technology has progressed, licensors have had to reevaluate their pricing methodologies to reflect advances in technology. Many computers today have multiple "cores," which allow a computer to simultaneously process data (e.g., dual core processing, quad core processing). As a result some licensors, such as IBM and Oracle, have based their pricing on the number of cores in a CPU. For example, the license fee for a dual core processor may be priced at 125 percent of the license fee for a single core CPU. Some licensors such as Microsoft, however, have announced they will not base their pricing on the number of cores contained in a CPU.

Licensors who utilize long-term master agreements with established pricing during the term should ensure that the agreement addresses or anticipates future technology advances to ensure the sanctity of their pricing methodologies. Otherwise, they risk being limited by the pricing set forth in the agreement and risk losing revenue from more efficient technologies. For example, a master agreement that incorporates a fee schedule with per-CPU pricing would contractually limit a licensor's ability to increase its fees based on the number of cores contained in a CPU. Given that many CPU licenses are perpetual, the licensor would be unable to recoup "lost" fees when the underlying agreement is renegotiated.

Site License

Site licenses grant the licensee the right to use the software at a particular location without limitation on the number of users, individual computers or their computing power. As most licensees move to a distributed, networked environment, site licenses will likely become less common. Set forth below is model language applicable for use in a site license.

> [Customer shall install and use the Licensed System only on [**computers**] located at Customer's facilities located at {[**site**]}. All Documentation shall be located and used only at such facilities.] **Option for remote use**: [Customer may remotely use the Licensed System only from any facilities within the same country that are controlled, managed, and either owned or leased by Customer.]

Blended Pricing

An increasing number of licensors utilize a blended methodology for determining the relevant license fee. For example, some vendors determine the license fee based on the product of the number of cores by the number of CPUs by the size of the CPUs. Attached to the license agreement is a schedule of all known processors at the time the agreement is executed along with the associated license fee. A prudent licensor will include language stating that the license fee for use of the software on any processor not set forth in the schedule will be negotiated on a case-by-case basis. This protects the licensor from the advent of any technological advances that may impact its license fee stream.

Alternative Pricing

Occasionally, licensors will propose alternative pricing methods for their software. Usually the software in question has a limited or special purpose, not used by the licensee on a day-to-day basis, or the value of such software to the licensee is uncertain, and the licensee is unwillingly to pay the licensor what the licensor believes the software is worth. One of the most common alternative pricing methodologies is a contingency fee where the licensor's fee is based on the amount of money the software saves the licensee or recovers for the licensee.

An example of this is software that evaluates claims paid by an insurer to identify improperly paid claims. The insurer may be unsure how many claims, if any, were improperly paid. It does not want to pay a license fee if it is unsure it will recover its costs. As such, some licensors are willing to license the software to the licensee for a nominal fee and a percentage of any identified or realized savings. This pricing methodology can be fraught with problems, as the basis for payment and the right to receive payment must be carefully defined, and the licensor must have detailed audit rights. The likelihood of a dispute occurring is high, as the licensor will seek very low thresholds for triggering the licensee's payment obligations, while the licensee will most likely adopt a more conservative approach or interpretation.

For example, in the above illustration, will the licensor be paid on the basis of all claims that have been identified as improperly paid or on the basis of money recovered? The licensee will likely argue that until the licensee has recovered the improper payments it has not benefited from the software. As such, it will only want to pay the licensor a percentage of monies recovered, less the cost of recovery. The licensor will likely argue that it cannot control the actual collection and payment and that the software was successful in identifying improper payments. Thus, it should be paid solely on the basis of the value of improperly paid claims identified by the software. The licensor may further argue that it should not bear the risk if the licensee decides not to seek to recover the improper payments for legal, political, public relations or other reasons. Thus, licensors should carefully consider whether to accept payment on a contingency basis and if they do, clearly set forth the triggers for payment in an unambiguous manner.

Service Bureau Licenses (Form 23.B.2)

Most software license agreements require payment through some form of advance payment and/or milestone payments with final payment due upon installation and acceptance. Service bureau licenses are usually priced and paid on a per "transaction" basis and billed monthly. The actual billing structure is dependent on the type of software involved. For example, with cellular telephone billing software, the license fee may be based on the number of subscriber bills printed, or with electronic medical records, on the number of patients in the database. Service bureau licenses are usually utilized when the software is very expensive and the licensee wishes to conserve cash flow by paying by the transaction instead of purchasing an outright license. On a long-term basis, a service bureau license is usually less cost-effective, although it may allow a licensee to switch vendors more easily as the licensee has less money "invested" in the software.

(ii) Software Development Agreements

Many parties seek to combine software licenses and development contracts and/or maintenance obligations into one agreement. A breach of the development obligations is a breach of the entire agreement. This permits a licensee to make its purchase of the software license contingent upon successful development or customization of the software. However, a risk with this approach is that in the case of the licensor's bankruptcy, the bankruptcy trustee cannot terminate a software license under Section 365(n) if the licensee continues to perform. If the licensee has numerous obligations relating to the license, development requirements, and/or maintenance obligations, it is unclear as to whether a court will allow the trustee to void the license. To avoid this risk, the parties should enter into separate and distinct agreements. For a more detailed discussion of the issues related to bankruptcy, see Chapter 17.

Most license agreements with a software development component provide for payment on a time and materials basis or on the basis of certain pre-agreed milestones. Each structure has certain benefits for both the licensor and the licensee. The ultimate payment structure chosen by the parties will reflect the allocation of risk agreed to by the parties.

Time and Materials vs. Fixed Price vs. Time and Materials with a Cap (§ 8.E)

Time and Materials (T&M). Services are usually provided on a time and material basis or a fixed price basis. Occasionally, a licensee may seek to have the licensor provide services on a time and materials basis with a not-to-exceed price. This is not advantageous to the licensor, as the licensor bears all of the risk. If the licensor can deliver the services in an efficient manner, it has no upside, but if the project takes longer than estimated, its fees are capped. T&M contracts provide for payment to the licensor based on direct labor, paid at specified labor rates; and materials paid at cost. In a T&M contract, a prudent license will seek to limit out of pocket costs to 15 percent of the labor costs.

T&M contracts usually are based on a set menu of labor categories and rates. The negotiated rates for labor vary, based on the level of experience and qualifications of each labor category. The customer specifies the work, usually through a statement of work, and the licensor proposes a mix of labor from the labor categories. Materials usually take the form of travel or equipment purchases incidental to the task, and are usually estimated with the provision that if they exceed the estimated amount, the customer's prior written consent is required. The licensor is paid the fixed hourly rate for each hour worked, regardless of the cost to deliver that hour, plus materials at cost. Often customers require a monthly/daily rate reflecting a discount off the hourly/daily rate and define a "day" as a minimum of eight hours regardless of the number of hours worked. To prevent being billed more than eight hours a day, revenue is booked on a monthly basis based on the number of hours delivered, multiplied by the labor category for each individual, plus materials at cost. The fee is included in the hourly rates, and all hours and materials are billed monthly in arrears.

A time and materials structure is preferable when the scope of work is not definitive to allow the parties to agree on a fixed price. This places the risk on the customer, as there is no limit on the price charged by the licensor and payment is not tied to the receipt of a deliverable. A prudent customer should be hesitant to enter into a time and materials contract. An estimate of the number of hours or price to complete the work should provide the customer little comfort. Estimates are nonbinding and the customer has no protection in the event the work is not completed within the parameters of the estimate. See *Denniston and Partridge Company v. Mingus*, 179 N.W. 2d 748 (Iowa 1970) (estimated cost is not a fixed price); *Beeler v. Miller*, 254 S.W.2d 986 (Mo. App. 1953) (estimate did not constitute contract to furnish labor and materials for a certain price).

A time and materials structure is appropriate for engagements where the contractor provides expert support personnel to a customer on an ongoing basis and the work is subject to change as time passes. In a time and materials contract, the licensor's risk is in staffing the contract with qualified personnel at rates within the negotiated hourly rates, including indirect costs. The licensee's risk comes from the licensee's lack of a fixed price, placing the licensee at risk if the licensor exceeds its budget/estimate or has unanticipated problems.

Fixed Price. A fixed price contract provides for a specific statement of work to be performed at a fixed price. The pricing may be for a product delivery or a specific service at fixed rates over a defined period of performance.

A licensor can perform work for both services and product deliveries on a fixed price basis. Services may include items such as help desk responses, software maintenance services, or reports processed. Products may include a system or software deliverable. Revenue is earned based on delivery of specific services to the customer or in the case of a product, as milestones are met.

A fixed price offers the licensor a greater opportunity for profit because the licensor bears a greater share of performance risk, in return for a higher profit opportunity. At the same time, if the licensor significantly underestimates the scope of work, its losses could be significant.

Payment on a time and materials basis is preferred by the licensor, as the licensor is paid as it renders its services, greatly reducing the risk of nonpayment, while, at the same time, eliminating the risk of underestimating the cost of a project. The greatest risk to a developer in a fixed-price contract is that it significantly underestimates the costs involved. If a large contract experiences overruns in the time and labor to finish the project, the overrun can cost the developer tens of millions of dollars. At the same time, without a fixed price, the licensee can never be certain what the cost of the software will be until acceptance. Cynical licensees believe that the developer/licensor has no incentive to limit costs in the absence of a fixed price contract because it bears no economic risk, thus increasing the cost to the licensee.

The licensee is usually billed on a monthly basis for time and materials contracts. For complex projects, payment on a time and materials basis is not favorable for licensees as the licensee cannot be sure that at the end of the project the services will have been satisfactorily performed. Making substantial contemporaneous or even up-front payments to the licensor greatly reduces the licensee's leverage in the event of a dispute with the licensor.

Time and Materials with a Cap. Some licensees seek to implement a time and materials pricing methodology with a fixed cap on price. From the licensor's perspective, this billing mechanism is undesirable. Unlike a fixed-price contract where the licensor can realize additional profit by delivering the project under budget, under this mechanism, the licensor lacks the ability to realize any additional profit because it is being paid on a time and materials basis. Further, unlike a time and materials contract, the licensor assumes the risk that the project cannot be completed on time and on budget. From the licensee's perspective, the licensee is protected from any cost overruns by the licensor and receives the financial benefit if the licensor delivers under budget. Like a fixed-price contract, the licensee can budget a definitive amount for the project without any concern of a cost overrun.

Milestone Payments (§§ 8.2, 8.3)

Pre-agreed milestones provide greater protection for the licensee while assuring the licensor will receive progress payments necessary to fund its development efforts. This method also provides the licensee greater leverage in the event a dispute arises with the licensor. The use of milestones is not without risk, as the parties must agree on what triggers payment (e.g., delivery, acceptance, etc.), which has ramifications on both parties. A licensee should be wary of payment on delivery before the software has been tested, while the licensor must carefully consider accepting payment upon acceptance, as the licensee has greater leverage in not accepting the milestone. A compromise is to have the licensee make payment on delivery, but state that such payment is only an "advance" and that all such payments are immediately repayable to the licensee if the ultimate deliverable is not accepted. Coupling these payments to the establishment of an advance payment bond in an amount equal to the amount of these "advances" effectively limits the licensee's risks. At the same time, the licensor has complete use of its money, less the minimal cost of the bond.

(b) Price Indexing (§ 8.4)

If a license agreement envisions that ongoing services will be provided on a time and materials basis for an extended period of time, both parties will likely seek to limit their pricing risk by establishing an objective basis for increasing the contracted hourly labor rates. This is usually achieved through indexing the licensor's labor charges to a government index such as the Consumer Price Index (CPI). Often, the parties will negotiate a cap and a floor on such indexes in the event they experience a dramatic increase, a period of remaining flat or even deflation. When selecting an index, the parties should be careful to correctly identify the chosen index in the agreement and provide an alternative index in the event the chosen index is no longer maintained or applicable. *See, e.g., Seattle-First Nat'l Bank v. Earl,* 565 P.2d 1215 (Wash. App. 1988) (agreed-upon index was nonexistent); *Metz Farms v. Fisher Sand & Gravel Co.,* 2006

WL 1047067 (D.S.D. Apr. 17, 2006) (vaguely drafted clause referring to "consumer's price index" litigated for vagueness). See Chapter 5.H.1.(c) for a more detailed discussion of indexing fees and pricing.

Both parties should carefully consider what is the appropriate index to use. Many parties simply select the CPI without realizing that the CPI may not reflect the parties' costs. The CPI includes a wide range of costs including gas, real estate food and other expenses that have no bearing on the cost of labor that the licensor will be providing. As seen by the recent recession, drastic declines in the costs of energy and housing have impacted the overall CPI. If any price increase is tied to the CPI, the licensor should clearly state that its prices cannot decrease in the event the selected index is negative for the period in question. If the services will be performed outside the United States, the parties should select an index from the relevant country such as the all-India Consumer Price Index for Urban Non-Manual Employees (CPI (UNME)) for use with Indian labor. Finally, if prices are not quoted in U.S. dollars, the licensor should hedge any currency risk. See § 8.4 for a number of indexes that may be appropriate to determine any cost increase.

For a discussion of the considerations of international licensing, see Loza, Chotkowski, Stevens & Urbanchuk, *Financial Considerations in International Intellectual Property Licensing Transactions,* 23 COMPUTER & INTERNET LAW. 9 (Sept. 2006).

(c) Revenue Recognition Issues

On October 27, 1997, The American Institute of Certified Public Accountants (AICPA) adopted Statement of Position (SOP) 97-2, which set forth guidelines to apply generally accepted accounting principles to revenue recognition in software transactions. SOP 97-2 also applies to "hosting" agreements, where the customer has the right to take possession of the hosted software.

Under SOP 97-2, if a software transaction does not require material production, modification, or customization, four criteria must be satisfied to recognize the revenue derived from each element of the transaction:

1. Persuasive evidence that the software transaction exists.
2. Delivery has occurred.
3. The cost of the software is fixed or determinable.
4. Collectability of payment is likely.

Persuasive evidence that the software transaction exists. This element is satisfied through the existence of a signed license agreement or a purchase order in the case of a licensor who licenses its software through a shrink wrap license.

Delivery has occurred. This element is satisfied if the license agreement provides for an acceptance period of 30 days or less. Delivery is considered to have occurred upon transfer of the first copy of the software. If undelivered elements such as enhancements, or maintenance in a multiple delivery arrangement are "essential to the functionality" of the delivered software, delivery is deemed not to have occurred.

Electronic delivery occurs when the customer either (a) takes possession via electronic download or (b) the customer has been provided with the software access codes.

The cost of the software is fixed or determinable. The cost of the software is not fixed or determinable until any right of cancellation by the customer has lapsed. Fees based on customer usage or other variable terms are not fixed and determinable until they occur.

Collectability of payment is likely. Fees are likely to be collectible if the purchaser's right to a refund or cancellation does not extend beyond 30 days. Further, payments for partial performance cannot be refundable if the contract is not completed.

SOP 97-2 places increased importance on the language of the license to ensure the licensor can recognize revenue in a timely manner. To ensure prompt recognition of revenue, the licensor should license all elements of a software package separately. The licensor should provide that the license fee is nonrefundable and avoid having the license fee contingent upon the delivery of future software modifications.

If the licensee is licensing software as well as purchasing modifications to such software, the licensor should seek to create two distinct transactions, one for the software license and one for the modifications. As such, there should be separate acceptance tests and separate fees for the licensed software and the modifications, and they should have separate descriptions and documentation.

Acceptance testing should be limited to 30 days, as the license fee may be recognized upon delivery if the acceptance period is 30 days or less after software licensing, and the vendor is able to estimate the number of returns that will result from the failure to achieve acceptance through the acceptance testing. Acceptance testing should be based on a vendor determined standard, such as conformance with the vendor's documentation.

By carefully drafting the terms of the license, the vendor can achieve quicker revenue recognition.

Lawyers reviewing a transaction to ensure compliance with SOP 97-2 should look for a number of warning signs that may indicate an attempt to accelerate revenue recognition in violation of SOP 97-2. Potential red flags include backdating contracts to another fiscal period, side letters that alter business terms or obligations, extended warranties, unusual discounts, upgrades or free services and conditional payment terms such as rebates, payment in advance for uncompleted work and payment subject to extraordinary events or conditions. To avoid any problems, a prudent lawyer should have all payment terms reviewed by the company's accounting department.

For more information on SOP 97-2 see www.aicpa.com. (Last viewed September 30, 2010.)

(d) Payment

(i) Payment Terms and Invoices

All payments should be due within thirty (30) days at receipt of the vendor's invoice. Some vendors seek to require payment within thirty days of the date of the invoice but there is no assurance that the invoice will be properly dated. Many customers seek to include language to the effect that the customer's payment obligation matures once it has received a "proper invoice." What constitutes a "proper invoice" is subject to interpretation, and in its most extreme form, a customer could refuse to make payment based on even the smallest inaccuracy. A more prudent approach from the vendor's perspective is to state that the invoice must be in the proper form and to attach an invoice in the proper format to the agreement as an exhibit.

(ii) Credit Concerns

Licensors should place great emphasis on the credit worthiness of any potential customer. The current recession has placed significant financial stress on many companies. Too often they are unable to pay or refuse to pay after the vendor has provided the contracted deliverable.

Licensors should undertake a number of steps to limit any inherent credit risk in contracting with a particular customer. The licensor should undertake a detailed examination of the potential customer's credit history. Some vendors will tailor their contractual terms, requiring more restrictive financial terms, to reflect any increased financial risk. See Form 23.J.11 for a model credit evaluation process.

In addition, the licensor should insist on including language in the underlying agreement, allowing the vendor to terminate the agreement without cause in the event the customer's credit worthiness declines. In addition, the licensor should obtain the ability to increase its prices if the customer's credit quality slips during the contract term, or in the alternative, require a payment bond at the time of contract signature to ensure payment by the customer.

(iii) Disputed Fees and the Escrow of Disputed Amounts

A prudent licensor will ensure that the contract allows the licensee to withhold payment if it has notified the licensor of the dispute in advance and if the licensor has had the opportunity to respond to the licensee concerns. In the event of a dispute, the customer should be obligated to make payment on the undisputed amount, and if the contract is for a significant amount of money, the amount the licensee can withhold should be limited. The failure to pay undisputed amounts should constitute a material breach and a basis for termination. Undisputed fees should never be withheld.

Licensors should insist that in the event of a dispute, the disputed amounts should be placed in an interest bearing account with a third party, such as a bank. The agreement should clearly state that the licensee is not allowed to simply offset the amount in dispute or allege a dispute and not make payment. Requiring the licensee to place the amount in dispute into escrow will discourage the licensee from specious claims as it will not retain possession of such amounts. The failure to place the disputed amounts into escrow should be a material breach of the agreement. Otherwise, the licensor lacks any leverage to force the licensee to disgorge the amounts in dispute.

(iv) Interest (§ 8.5)

Most agreements provide for the payment of interest in the event a party fails to make timely payment. Usually the parties include language setting forth the agreed upon interest rate but provide that in no event should such rate exceed the maximum amount allowed by law (§ 8.5). Most parties insert this phrase to avoid violating any applicable usury laws. Interestingly, at least one court has held that a state's usury laws do not apply to interest applied to overdue license fees. *Bexer County Ice Cream Co. v. Swenson's Ice Cream Co.*, 859 S.W. 2d 402 (Tex. 1993) (absent a loan of money or loan payments, interest charged on IP license did not meet Texas's definition of a usurious transaction). The party seeking to invalidate the interest provision bears the burden of proof to show it is usurious. *Domizio v Progressive County Mut. Ins. Co.*, 54 S.W.3d 867, 874 (Tex. App. Austin 2001).

Some agreements provide that the interest rate shall be the "Prime Rate." Because there is not an agreed upon Prime Rate, the relevant provision should reference a particular bank. For example, the prime rate offered by Citibank or its successor. Further, because the Prime Rate fluctuates, it is much more complicated to compute the interest due than if the parties used a fixed rate. See Form 23.B.11 § 35 for model language based on the Prime Rate.

Most licensees will seek to remove any interest provision from the agreement, and some licensors will not resist believing that they will be unlikely to collect interest without going to court and that if they do go to court, the court will impose the state's statutory interest rate on any judgment. If a licensee is willing to agree to a contractually stated interest rate, the interest rate should correspond to the licensor's "cost of funds" when borrowing from a bank. The reason for paying interest is that the licensor is losing use of its funds while the amounts in question are unpaid and thus must borrow. Thus, the licensee should pay interest on the past due amounts at a rate close to the licensor's cost to borrow.

9. *Taxes (§ 8.6)*

(i) Sales Tax (Form 23.I.7)

Often considered boilerplate, the "taxes" provision in license agreements has assumed increasing importance due to continuing changes to federal, state, and local tax laws. Traditionally, software was taxed on the value of media on which it resided (the disk or tape) and services were not taxed. As taxing jurisdictions have encountered tighter budgets, they have sought new sources of revenue especially in the area of technology licensing.

Today, many jurisdictions tax not only the sale of software, but also ancillary services such as support and maintenance. *See e.g., Verizon North, Inc. v. Combs*, 308 S.W.3d 1 (Tex. 2009) (computer software is taxable as tangible personal property); *Dechert v. Commonwealth*, 998 A.2d 575 (Pa. 2010); *TekSystems, Inc. v. Chumley*, 2009 WL 1312835 (Tenn. Ct. App. May 11, 2009).

The applicable structure is ever changing and almost impossible for a licensor without an internal tax department or full-time outside auditor to remain current. As such, the licensor should make sure the license agreement clearly establishes that the licensee is responsible to pay all taxes except those taxes on the licensor's net income. The term "taxes" should be defined as broadly as possible to include any new taxes or form of taxes that may be implemented during the term of the agreement.

From the licensee's perspective, the licensee cannot budget with any confidence because it cannot anticipate whether new taxes may be imposed over the life of the contract. Nonetheless, in most cases it is the licensee's responsibility to pay such taxes. The licensee can reduce its risk by contractually requiring the licensor to cooperate with it to limit any tax liability and to appeal any taxes the licensee believes have been wrongly imposed. Further, because it is the licensor's obligation to collect any taxes due, the licensee should seek to have the licensor indemnify it in the event the licensor fails to properly calculate and collect the appropriate taxes. In such case, the licensor should be responsible for paying any interest and penalties due. Given the ever-changing nature of state and local taxes, the licensor should avoid any indemnification of the licensee related to taxes.

Another manner in which the parties can limit the licensee's tax liability is through the allocation of the consideration among the different products and services provided. Often, taxing jurisdictions have varying tax rates for different types of services and products. Tax rates also vary among different jurisdictions. To the extent they are able to do so, the parties should examine the possibility of delivering the products and services in jurisdictions with lower tax rates and allocating the stated consideration to those aspects of the transaction that are taxed at a lower rate. In seeking to limit the licensee's sales tax liabilities, the licensor should be careful not to increase its own income tax liabilities. See Form 23.G.8 for a matrix of the tax rates on various technology-related services and products by state.

(ii) Employee Related Taxes (Form 23.K.2.H 1 and 2)

The licensor should also include language to address Section 162(a) of the Internal Revenue Code, which requires the licensor to recognize reimbursed expenses such as travel, lodging, and related expenses as taxable income to its employees who remain on an assignment outside of their home state for more than 12 months. *See* I.R.C. § 162(a); IRS Revenue Rulings 93-86 and 99-7. While the licensor must reimburse the employee's living expenses and income taxes, it must also gross up the employee's compensation to compensate for the increased tax burden. On a large project with a significant number of employees working at the licensee's site, these costs can be significant. See § 8.6 for model language addressing this issue.

The licensee should be aware that it will be charged these costs and should budget accordingly. It can limit its risk by contractually limiting the licensor's travel and expense costs to a percentage of its professional fees, such as 15 percent, and defining these additional tax costs as part of the licensor's travel and expense cost, not consulting fees.

(iii) Foreign Taxes Based on Use of Foreign Labor (Form 23.K.2.II.4)

Some licensors seek to pass on cost of taxes levied by foreign states arising from the use of offshore resources. They do so under the argument that the licensee is responsible for paying all taxes except for taxes on the licensor's net income. Many licensees reject this position arguing that it was the licensor's decision to utilize foreign labor and thus the licensor should bear the cost of such taxes. This argument is specious if the licensee required the licensor to use offshore resources.

10. Licensee Obligations

Too often licensors focus on negotiating the licensor's obligations with the licensee but fail to memorialize the licensee's obligations in the underlying agreement. The licensee's obligations are no less important than the licensor's obligations and should serve as a condition precedent to the licensor's obligations. The licensor should ensure that the underlying agreement sets forth in detail the licensee's obligations. These may include the required hardware and software to operate the licensor's software, as well as any facilities that will be required. If applicable, the license agreement should clearly set out the licensor's ability to access the licensee's facilities and networks.

At the same time, the agreement should provide that the failure of the licensee to meet these obligations will excuse the licensor's performance, and in the event such failure is material, allow the licensor to terminate the agreement for the licensee's breach. The licensor should avoid relying on general language stating that the licensee will provide reasonable cooperation to support the licensor's efforts.

See Form 23.J.10 for model language setting forth the Licensee's obligations.

CHAPTER **5**

Other Important Issues

A. The Work Made for Hire Doctrine and Moral Rights

1. Work Made for Hire Doctrine

(a) Works Created by Independent Contractors

United States law generally holds that the copyright in a work is initially vested in the person who creates it. 17 U.S.C. § 201(a) (1994). Therefore, an independent contractor, as the "author" of a work, usually retains all copyrights to that work unless he or she assigns its rights to the buyer. 17 U.S.C. § 201(d) (1994). Absent any assignment, the buyer is only deemed to hold a nonexclusive license. *See MacLean Associates, Inc. v. Wm. M. Mercer-Meidinger Hansen, Inc.*, 952 F.2d 769 (3d Cir. 1991) (contracting party had obtained an "implied" but limited nonexclusive license); *Effects Associates v. Cohen*, 817 F.2d 72 (9th Cir. 1987), *aff'd*, 908 F.2d 555 (9th Cir. 1990), *cert. denied sub nom. Danforth v. Cohen*, 498 U.S. 1103 (1991). Nonexclusive licenses "may be granted orally or by implication." *Asset Marketing Systems, Inc. v. Gagnon*, 542 F.3d 748, 754 (9th Cir. 2008).

The extent of the license received by the buyer is determined by "the licensor's objective intent at the time of the creation and delivery of the software as manifested by the parties' conduct." *Id.* at 756 (independent contractor's actions manifested intent to grant customer unlimited, nonexclusive, irrevocable license with the right to retain, use and modify the software). The *Gagnon* court created a three part test for determining a licensor's intent to convey an implied license: (1) the licensee requests the creation of a work, (2) the licensor creates the work and delivers it to the licensee, and (3) the licensor intends for the licensee to copy and distribute the work. *Id.* at 754–55.

As such, an implied, nonexclusive license is limited to the scope of use initially contemplated when the buyer commissioned the work, i.e., the number of users, purpose, and the like, and may be terminated by the copyright holder at any time unless the buyer retained other express or implied contractual rights.

Such a limited and nonexclusive license to use the work may place a buyer at a severe disadvantage vis-à-vis its competitors. A contractor, for instance, could potentially disclose a buyer's proprietary information in licensing the work to others and thereby nullify any competitive advantage the employer gained by commissioning the work. In addition, as the "owner" of the copyright in the work, a contractor could limit a buyer's right to use or distribute the work if such use is outside the scope of the original commission. *See Graham v. James*, 144 F.3d 229 (2d Cir. 1990) (creation of a program by an independent contractor remains the property of the contractor and any unauthorized use is actionable).

An independent contractor retaining ownership in software specified and funded by the buyer may seem counterintuitive. A buyer may invest large sums of money and significant technical input in a project only to find that the contractor claims ownership of the work when the project results in a commercially saleable product. The courts have attempted to soften the effect of this result by implying that the employer will have a fully paid-up license to use the software for all purposes intended in the contract and, importantly, to modify the software as necessary to support those uses. *See, e.g., Clifford Scott Aymes v. Jonathan J. Bonnelli d/b/a Island Swimming Sales, Inc.*, 47 F.3d 23 (2d Cir. 1995). *See also Foad Consulting Group, Inc. v. Musil Govan Azzalino*, 270 F.3d 821 (9th Cir. 2001) (party hiring contractor has implied license to use contractor's work product in all ways intended or expected to retain the work's commercial value *unless* the contractor explicitly provides that there is no implied license to use, modify, and assign its rights).

While these interpretations help avoid the harsh results of the rule granting ownership to independent contractors, the courts ultimately hold that, absent an explicit assignment to the employer, the independent contractor owns software produced pursuant to contractual arrangement. *See e.g., Conwell v. Gray Loon Outdoor Marketing Group, Inc.*, 906 N.E.2d 805 (Ind. 2009). Notably, independent contractors rarely demand additional consideration or concessions for such assignments. Failure to secure an assignment from a contractor may result in the loss of a significant asset to the employer, especially where a product may have commercial value apart from the internal use contemplated by the employer. Further, because ownership remains with the contractor, the independent contractor/author may license or assign its rights in a work to a competitor of the party paying for the work.

(b) The Work Made for Hire Doctrine

There are instances where a company will be presumed to be the owner of a commissioned work under the "work made for hire" doctrine. In the United States, an employer is considered the original author of a commissioned work if the work qualifies as work made for hire under the United States Copyright Act. 17 U.S.C. § 201(b). Section 201 of the act provides that "[i]n the case of a work made for hire, the employer or other person for whom the work was prepared is considered the author for purposes of this title, and, unless the parties have expressly agreed otherwise in a written instrument signed by them, owns all of the rights comprised in the copyright." 17 U.S.C. § 201(b). Classifying the work as work made for hire determines not only the initial ownership of copyright, but also the copyright's duration (§ 302(c)), the owner's renewal rights (§ 304(a)) and termination rights (§ 203(a)). *See* 1 Melville B. Nimmer & David Nimmer, Nimmer on Copyright, § 5.03[A] at 5–11 to 5–12 (2005).

Work made for hire is defined as: "(1) a work prepared by an employee within the scope of his or her employment; or (2) a work (i) specially ordered or commissioned for use as a contribution to a collective work, (ii) as a part of a motion picture or other audiovisual work, (iii) as a translation, (iv) as a supplementary work, (v) as a compilation, (vi) as an instructional text, (vii) as a test, (viii) as answer material for a test, or (ix) as an atlas, if the parties expressly agree in a written instrument signed by them that the work shall be considered a work made for hire." 17 U.S.C. § 101.

In determining whether a work will fall within the employee's "scope of employment," the courts will look at a number of factors including the following:

- the level of skill
- the source of the instruments and tools for creation of the work
- the location of the work
- the duration of the employment relationship
- whether the hiring party has the right to make additional assignments
- the hired party's discretion over when or how long to work
- the method of payment, if any
- the hired party's role in hiring/paying assistants
- the location of where the work was created
- whether the work is part of the hiring party's regular business
- the provision of employee benefits.

See, e.g., Avtec Systems, Inc. v. Peiffer, 67 F.3d 293 (4th Cir. 1995); *Cole v. Control Data Corp.*, 947 F.2d 313 (8th Cir. 1991); *Quin v. City of Detroit* 988 F. Supp 1044 (E.D. Mich. 1991); *Miller v. CP Chems., Inc.*, 808 F. Supp. 1238, 1242–44 (D.S.C. 1992); Restatement (Second) of Agency § 228.

Performing work at home after hours will not allow an employee to establish copyright ownership and avoid the work made for hire doctrine. *Rouse v. Walter & Associates, L.L.C.*, 513 F. Supp.2d 1058 (S.D. Iowa 2007). An employee's conduct may be considered within the scope of employment even if it is found in part to benefit the employee or a third party. *Id.* at 1060. Any agreement to alter the employer's ownership in a work under the work made for hire doctrine must be expressly stated. *Id.* at 1061.

Because most computer software does not automatically fall within the nine types of work enumerated earlier in category two, writing a software program will generally qualify as work made for hire only if it was "prepared by an employee, within the scope of his or her employment."

(c) Independent Contractors

An independent contractor, however, will not usually qualify as an "employee" within the meaning of the Copyright Act. In *Community for Creative Non-Violence v. Reid*, 490 U.S. 703 (1989) (CCNV), the Supreme Court declared that an artist, who was commissioned by a nonprofit organization to create a sculpture, was an "independent contractor" and not an employee within the meaning of the copyright act, even though the nonprofit organization directed enough of the sculptor's work to ensure that he produced a sculpture that met their specifications. *Id.* at 753. The U.S. Supreme Court later unanimously generalized *CCNV* as the appropriate standard for defining an employee outside of the copyright area as well. *Nationwide Mutual Ins.* Co. *v. Darden*, 503 U.S. 318, 322 (1992).

If the independent contractor does not qualify as an employee, the employer can only gain title to the work product of the contractor by having the contractor execute an assignment transferring his or her ownership rights in the work to the employer. *CCNV*, 490 U.S. at 750.

For a general overview of copyright issues involving independent contractors and employees, see Holland, *Copyrights and Consultants*, 36 LAW. BRIEF 2 (May 2006); Brewer, *Who Owns the Invention? Addressing Ownership Claims of Employees and Contractors*, 23 COMPUTER & INTERNET LAW. 17 (Aug. 2006).

(d) Employee Inventions

Although an employer will not receive ownership of any patentable invention created under a general employment context, the employer will receive a nonexclusive, implied license to such patentable material. Known as a "shop right," an employer obtains a nonexclusive limited license to use the patentable invention for its internal purposes if the invention was made on company time with company resources. *United States v. Dubilier Condenser Corp.*, 289 U.S. 178, 188 (1933).

To avoid potential disputes and obtain the intellectual property rights needed to operate their business, most employers require that new employees execute a confidentiality and assignment of inventions agreement, usually in conjunction with a non-competition agreement upon employment. See Form 23.F.4 for a model Non-competition, Confidentiality, and Inventions Agreement.

(e) Execution of an Assignment

In order to receive sole and exclusive ownership of the copyright, a customer would be well advised to have the contractor execute an assignment transferring to the buyer the contractor's entire right, title, and interest in the work. (Forms 23.F.1 and 23.F.2 for model Consulting Agreements with an assignment clause.) The author must actually sign the assignment, as a single signature purchase order will not convey ownership to a buyer.

If a contractor previously executed an agreement without an assignment clause, the employer should have a comprehensive assignment agreement executed by the contractor and should be sure to list the consideration that the contractor is receiving for signing the assignment agreement. (See Form 23.F.4 for a model Assignment Agreement.) For any such assignment to be valid, it must be in writing and signed by both parties prior to the work's creation. *BancTraining Video Systems v. First American Corp.*, 956 F.2d 268 (6th Cir. 1993); *Schiller & Schmidt, Inc. v. Accent Publishing Co., Inc.*, 969 F.2d 410 (7th Cir. 1992) (subsequent writing cannot correct the fact that there was no written agreement as required by statute at the time the work was created). *But see Playboy v. Dumas*, 53 F.3d 549 (2d Cir. 1995), *cert. denied*, 516 U.S. 1010 (1995) (prior oral agreement that work is work made for hire may later be memorialized in writing as the work is created). At least one court, however, has held that a work created by an independent contractor qualified as a "work made for hire" even though the author assigned its rights after the work had been completed.

20th Century Fox Film Corp. v. Entertainment Distributing, 429 F.3d 869 (9th Cir 2005). In reaching its decision to uphold a lower court decision, the Ninth Circuit emphasized that the work had been created at the "insistence and expense" of the commissioning party and that the parties intended the work to be a "work made for hire." *Id.* at 880–82.

Employers should require a contractor to transfer ownership of all intellectual property created during the period of the relevant project to the employer. If the contractor claims ownership of similar or related intellectual property that exists at the time of executing the relevant consulting agreement, he should list and describe such intellectual property in detail as an exception to the employer's right of ownership. The failure to do so may lead the contractor to claim ownership of related work important to the employer's project. *See, e.g., Fowler v. Bell Helicopter Textron, Inc.*, 2005 WL 548076 (N.D. Tex. Mar. 9, 2005) (denying employer's motion for summary judgment of its claimed ownership of intellectual property created by contractor during term of his consultancy). *See also* Payne, *Departing Employees and "Abandoned" Research,* 23 Computer & Internet Law. 7 (Jan. 2006).

(f) Independent Contractor or Employee?

In determining whether a party will be considered an employee or an independent contractor, a court will look at a number of factors including the following:

- The nature and duration of the assignment. Is the work a discrete project or of a continuous nature?
- The level of skill provided.
- Who provides the *tools* necessary to perform the work?
- The degree of control over the creator and how the work will be performed.
- How is the creator compensated?
- Eligibility of the creator for employee benefits.
- The location of the work.

In *JustMed, Inc. v. Byce,* 600 F.3d 1118 (9th Cir. 2010), the Ninth Circuit Court of Appeals appeared to adopt a more lenient standard for start up technology companies when determining whether an individual is an employee or an independent contractor. In *JustMed,* a small technology start-up brought suit against Byce alleging misappropriation of trade secrets and conversion in relation to certain software source code written by Byce. Byce counterclaimed seeking a declaratory judgment that he was the sole owner of the software under the Copyright Act. The Ninth Circuit found that Byce was an employee despite the following:

- He worked from home in another state.
- He provided his own computer/tools.
- He worked with little supervision.
- JustMed did not issue a W-2 to Byce.
- JustMed did not withhold taxes, pay workers compensation or pay unemployment insurance for Byce.
- JustMed did not represent Byce as an employee to the state.
- JustMed did not provide Byce any employee benefits.

Despite these indicia of being an independent contractor, the court found Byce to be an employee based on, among other reasons, the nature of the technology industry and JustMed's status as a start-up company. Specifically, the court found that Byce received input and supervision over the phone, recognizing that the nature of computer programming is such that it can be performed remotely without impacting the quality of the work product or the individual's ability to meet the company's needs. The court cited JustMed's status as a start-up company in finding that JustMed's failure to follow all the legal formalities associated with filing the required paperwork associated with its employees was not determinate of an employer/employee relationship. It stated that the failure to comply with applicable employment laws did not justify "denying that firm [Just Med] its intellectual property." *Id.* at 1128. Further,

> As a small start-up company, JustMed conducted its business more informally than an established enterprise might. This fact can make it more difficult to decide whether a hired party is an employee or an independent contractor, but it should not make the company more susceptible to losing control over software integral to its product.

Id.

Thus, it appears, at least in the Ninth Circuit, that the courts will examine not only the indicia of an employer/employee relationship but also the nature of the employer's industry and the employer's corporate maturity.

It is important to note that the Internal Revenue Service (IRS) moved away from the "Twenty Factor" test and has issued guidelines for determining whether an individual is an employee or an independent contractor. See http://www.irs.gov/businesses/small/article/0,,id=99921,00.html. (Last viewed September 15, 2010). The definition of an "employee" is determined on the ability of the employer to control the method and results of an individual's work.

(g) Tangential Issues Related to Work Made for Hire

Including work for hire language and an assignment provision into an independent contractor agreement to vest ownership of any intellectual property in the customer raises a number of tangential issues that should be considered. Section 3351.5 (c) of the California Labor Code provides that if the underlying agreement between the parties characterizes the deliverables as work made for hire, the customer must include the independent contractor under the customer's workers compensation coverage.

In addition, by characterizing the deliverables as "work made for hire," the copyright for the deliverables will expire the earlier of 95 years from the date of publication or 120 years from the date of creation, as opposed to "work not made for hire," which has a term equal to the life of the author plus 75 years. 17 U.S.C. § 302 (a). Further, the ability of an author to terminate the grant of certain rights after 35–40 years does not exist for works made for hire. 17 U.S.C. § 203. See Chapter 4.A.2 for a more detailed discussion.

For a general discussion, see Holland, *Copyrights and Consultants,* 36 LAW. BRIEF 2 (May 2006); *Intellectual Property Issues in the Employment Setting,* 120 INTELL. PROP. COUNS. 1 (Dec. 2006).

(h) Sale of a Business

A related issue often arises when a business is being sold and the business cannot show ownership of a relevant work (which may be crucial to its business), because the business failed to obtain ownership through an assignment. Often the author cannot be located, creating hesitancy by the purchaser to expend a significant amount of money when it will not obtain clear title to the software. In such cases, the seller usually must indemnify the purchaser against any third party claims of ownership or any third party claims of right of use.

See Form 23.F.3 on the enclosed CD-ROM for a model assignment agreement that may be appropriate in the sale of a business, assigning ownership of all intellectual property created by a contractor to an employee.

2. Moral Rights

Moral rights are the right "to claim authorship of the software, to object to or prevent the modification of any software or to withdraw from circulation or control the publication or distribution of any software, and any similar right, existing under judicial or statutory law of any country in the world, or under any treaty, regardless of whether or not such right is denominated or generally referred to as a 'moral right.'" *Managing Risks in Computer Contracts in* DATA PROCESSING AGREEMENTS § 1.261 (William A Hancock ed., April 1997).

Under the Berne Convention, "moral rights" in a work may exist in the author regardless of the author's status as an employee or contractor. Moral rights are separate and distinct from any other ownership rights generally provided for under copyright law.

Moral rights encompass three rights: integrity, paternity, and disclosure rights. Integrity rights provide that the creator of the work must consent to any change to the work to protect against the derogatory treatment of the work. Paternity rights provide that authorship must be attributed to the author and that a third party cannot falsely attribute development of the work. Further, the author's name cannot be used in association with the work he did not complete. Disclosure rights allow the creator of the work to control the display of his work. For a general discussion see Note, *Moral Rights: A Copyright Conflict Between the United States and Canada,* 1 Sw.J.L & TRADE IN THE AMERICAS 171 (1994); Kwall, *Copyright and the Moral Right: Is An American Marriage Possible?*, 38 VAND. L. REV. 1 (1985).

The Canadian Copyright Act, for instance, considers moral rights to encompass "paternity rights" (the right of the author to have his or her name appear as the author of the work in all public uses) as well as "integrity rights" (the right of an author that his or her work not be mutilated or altered). Revised Statutes of Canada Chapter C-42 (13), (14) and (15) (1985, as amended). Such rights may prove troublesome in the case of software that is continuously modified or where marketing considerations preclude identification of the author.

Articles 8 and 9 of the Berne Convention establish the author's right of ownership at the time of creation. Under the Berne Convention, an author's moral rights are "inalienable," and thus it is unlikely that such rights could be contractually transferred by a contractor to an employer. Berne Convention Article 6 bis. Furthermore, a waiver of such rights may be difficult or impossible to enforce in some jurisdictions. Some countries allow moral rights to be waived but not assigned. In such countries, an employer hiring a contractor to perform work would be well advised to include a waiver provision in any legal document with the contractor to protect against ownership claims by the contractor at a later point in time. In addition, some lawyers require the contractor to affirmatively state that he or she will not assert his or her moral rights.

While signatories to the Berne Convention are typically required to recognize and comply with the Berne Convention's requirements on an author's moral rights, the United States does not recognize broad moral rights. The United States has enacted legislation affording limited moral rights to prevent mutilation or destruction of visual works of art only, and only under certain circumstances. 17 U.S.C. §§ 106, 113, amended by Pub. L. No. 101–650, § 604, Dec. 1, 1990. The unwillingness of the United States to recognize moral rights is evidenced by its insistence that the General Agreement on Tariffs and Trade (GATT) and North American Free Trade Agreement (NAFTA) specifically provide that the United States is under no obligation to recognize such rights.

The question of whether a U.S. employer would have to recognize an offshore contractor's moral rights under the Berne Convention is closely tied to the issue of how the Berne Convention is implemented in countries that do not deem treaties to be self-implementing. See Melville B. Nimmer & Paul E. Geller, International Copyright Law and Practice § 3 pp. 69–76 (1993). The answer to that question is found in Article 36 of the Berne Convention, which provides that:

1. any country party to the Convention undertakes to adopt, in accordance with its constitution, the measures necessary to ensure the application of this Convention; and
2. it is understood that, at the time a country becomes bound by this Convention, it will be in a position under its domestic law to give effect to the provisions of this Convention.

Therefore, the Berne Convention appears to leave the decision about self-implementation of the treaty to each individual member country.

This has also been the position of the United States, which has never viewed the Berne Convention to be self-implementing. The United States acceded to the Berne Convention by means of the Berne Convention Implementation Act of 1988. Pub. L. No. 100–568 (Oct. 31, 1988). In doing so, the United States included an express provision denying the self-implementation of the Berne Convention. *Id.* Because the Berne Convention is not self-implementing, the Berne Convention's provisions are not by themselves enforceable in U.S. courts. Moreover, the United States Copyright Act specifically declares that no right or interest in a work protected under Title 17 may be claimed by virtue of, or in reliance upon, the Berne Convention's provisions or the United States' adherence to the convention. Pub. L. No. 100–568 § 4(c) (Oct. 31, 1988). In other words, neither the Berne Convention itself, nor the fact of adherence to the convention, will affect the current law of the United States. In one of the few U.S. cases addressing moral rights, the Seventh Circuit Court of Appeals rejected their application in the United States. *Vargas v. Esquire Inc.*, 164 F.2d 522 (7th Cir. 1947) (moral rights while recognized by the civil law of foreign countries are not recognized by the laws of the United States).

Because U.S. law does not recognize most moral rights, a U.S. employer hiring an offshore contractor in a jurisdiction that is a signatory to the Berne Convention need be less concerned about the applicability of moral rights if the employer can ensure that U.S. law will govern in case of a copyright dispute between the parties and if the work will only be used in the United States. In an attempt to accomplish this, the U.S. employer may select U.S. law by including in a contract with the offshore contractor a choice of law clause. However, this approach is not entirely free of problems.

3. Patent Rights

As the patenting of software becomes commonplace, employers should have their employees assign ownership in all discoveries and inventions to the employer. The general rule under patent law is that an individual owns the patent rights to the subject matter of which he is an inventor, even though he conceived it or reduced it to practice in the course of his employment. *Banks v. Unisys Corporation,* 228 F.3d 1357, 1359 (Fed. Cir. 2000) (denying summary judgment on implied agreement to assign inventions where employee did not execute assignment agreement and the employer did not pursue the execution of an assignment agreement). Thus, although the copyright act grants the employer ownership as to any copyrights, an employer would not own any resulting patent without an assignment. *Id.* However, if the employee is hired to develop a specific product (e.g., a car engine) the patentable invention belongs to the employer. *United States v. Dubilier Condenser Corp.*, 289 U.S. 178, 187 (1933) (employee employed to make an invention must assign to employer any patent obtained as employee produced what he was hired to invent). This obligation extends to corporate executives as well. *Great Lakes Press Corp. v. Froom,* 695 F. Supp. 1440 (W.D.N.Y. 1987).

Under these guidelines, the IRS has set forth a test involving "categories of evidence." Under this test, a business must divide factors pertaining to a given worker's status into three categories: behavioral control, financial control, and type of relationship.

"Behavioral control" includes facts pertaining to whether or not the business controls how the individual does his or her job (e.g., training and instructions given). "Financial control" comprises evidence related to the business aspects of the worker's job (e.g., the worker's investments and expenses). "Type of Relationship" examines relational indicators (i.e., written contracts and length of association). These "categories of evidence" allow a broader and more flexible examination of an individual's status than the prior 20-point test, as the IRS publication indicates that all evidence about degree of control and independence will be considered. *See* Publication 15-A of the Internal Revenue Service (2010).

For a more detailed discussion of the issues involved with the use of independent contractors from an international perspective, see Classen and Paul, *Increasing Global Competitiveness by Utilizing Offshore Independent Contractors,* 2 INT'L. COMPUTER LAW. 2 (No. 11, 1994); for domestic concerns, see Wood, *Defining Employees and Independent Contractors: Don't Try This at Home!,* 17 BUS. L. TODAY 45 (May/June 2008); Classen, Paul & Sprague, *Increasing Corporate Competitiveness by Utilizing Independent Contractors,* 11 COMPUTER L. ASS'N. BULL. 2 (No. 1, 1996) and Schulze, *Watch Out What You Wish For—You May Get Your Wish or Ownership Issues Continued: More on Applying the Work Made for Hire Doctrine to Computer Programmers,* 8 COMPUTER L. ASS'N. BULL. 12 (No. 2 1993).

B. Ownership of Custom Developed Software (§§ 3.2, 3.5, 12.1)

1. In General

Ownership of software developed by the licensor for a specific customer is often a contentious issue. Usually, the licensee claims ownership based upon the fact that it has paid the licensor to develop the software and that the software would not have been otherwise developed. Further, some licensees are concerned that unless they retain ownership of the intellectual property, they lack standing to bring a claim of intellectual property infringement. The licensor desires to retain ownership to keep the integrity of its software (i.e., the licensor does not want its customers owning portions of its proprietary software, especially parts of the program's core code) and to potentially profit from relicensing the custom piece of software.

Those licensors who consider themselves "consultants," as opposed to product companies, argue that they provide solutions, not deliverables. As such, the licensee is not purchasing a new product but rather is contracting with the licensor to solve an internal technical challenge.

In seeking to resolve any dispute over the ownership of custom developed work, the parties should consider the following questions:

- Why does the customer want to own a technology outside its core competency?
- Is the customer's objective to prevent its competitors from using the software?
- Does the customer simply feel it is entitled to own the work having paid for it?
- Is there another, unstated concern?

To determine the relative importance of ownership to each party, the parties should distinguish between a) software that may be reused for other customers and b) software that is created solely for the licensee's environment and is of little or no value to other potential customers. By doing so, all of these concerns can be addressed in the contract while allowing the licensor to retain ownership.

One argument against the licensee owning any intellectual property created by the licensor is that such work product will not be incorporated into the licensor's standard product and thus the maintenance and support of such product will not be included within the licensor's standard maintenance services. By the licensor retaining ownership, the licensee will benefit from any future enhancements and lower maintenance fees, as many other customers will be paying to support and enhance the module in question.

The licensee will likely be unable to independently maintain or support the work product and will be forced to pay an additional fee to the licensor to maintain and support it. Further, if the licensee is concerned that it will lack standing to bring a claim of intellectual property infringement, it can contractually require the licensor to do so. The licensee should carefully consider whether the benefits of owning any work product outweigh the costs of ownership, which includes any additional maintenance and support fees.

The licensee may want to consider alternative restrictions, such as granting the licensor ownership, but prohibiting the licensor from incorporating the work product into its standard product for a set period of time. In return for granting the licensor ownership, the licensor may provide the licensee with free maintenance and support for the period of time prior to the work product being incorporated into the licensor's standard product.

This issue is often resolved by having the licensor retain ownership of the custom-developed portion of the licensor's software, but also having the licensor pay the licensee a royalty based on future license fees received by the licensor from relicensing the custom portion. (§ 8.I) Another potential solution is to have the licensee retain ownership of the custom software and grant to the licensor the right to market the custom software, and have the licensor pay a royalty to the licensee for each license sold.

These are not the only solutions. If the licensor is solely concerned with the licensee owning part of the licensor's core code, the licensee can retain ownership of the custom portion without the right of sublicense or assignment. See Form 23.K.2.U.3 for illustrative language. The licensee could also be granted an exclusive basis for a set period of time, which would allow the licensee to recoup the benefits of its investment.

2. *Joint Ownership*

Another alternative, but one that is less attractive, is to have the licensor and licensee jointly own the custom software. "Joint Work" is "[w]ork prepared by two or more authors with the intention that their contributions be merged into inseparable or interdependent parts of a unitary whole." 17 U.S.C. § 101. Authors of joint work may independently exercise all rights of a copyright owner.

Joint ownership, however, often creates more issues than it resolves, as copyright law imposes a number of restrictions on co-owners. Co-owners of a copyright are treated as tenants in common. *Davis v. Blige*, 505 F.3d 90 (2d Cir. 2007). Subject to certain limitations, each "owner" is free to license and use the work as it sees fit, as well as transfer its limited rights in the work to a third party. 1 Melville B. Nimmer

& David Nimmer, Nimmer on Copyright § 6.11 (Supp. 2006). A co-owner has standing to bring an action for copyright infringement, *Isbell Records v. DM Records*, 2009 WL 3386546 (5th Cir. Oct. 22, 2009), but cannot grant an exclusive license without the consent of all other co-owners, *Sybersound Records v. UAV Corp.*, 517 F.3d 1137 (9th Cir. 2008) and cannot grant a retroactive license. *Davis v. Blige*, 505 F.3d 90 (2d Cir. 2007). Each co-owner must also provide an accounting to all other co-owners for any profits. *Davis, id.* at 98.

Joint ownership allows each party to market the software to whomever it chooses, while at the same time having the right to make modifications and enhancements. This alternative may be detrimental to the licensor because the licensee may license the software to the licensor's direct competitors. Under joint copyright ownership, however, each owner has a duty to account to the other. 1 Melville B. Nimmer & David Nimmer, Nimmer on Copyright § 6.12[A] at 36.6 (2005); *see, e.g., Oddo v. Ries,* 743 F.2d 630 (9th Cir. 1984). While the right to an accounting exists for jointly owned copyrights, there is no right to an accounting for a jointly owned software patent. 35 U.S.C. § 262. This dichotomy could likely lead to confusion, and potentially litigation, if the jointly owned software is protected by both copyright and patent. At the same time, this approach is probably unrealistic as most likely the custom portion is of little value unless it is licensed in conjunction with the rest of the software.

If the resulting work product will contain pre-existing intellectual property owned by the vendor and intellectual property owned by the customer, the work product should contain a copyright notice to the following effect:

> This contains material which is the confidential, unpublished property licensed to Customer. Receipt or possession of it does not convey any rights to divulge, reproduce, use or allow others to use it without the specific written authorization of Customer and use must conform strictly to the license agreement between user and Customer.
>
> Copyright © 20__ [Vendor Legal Name]. All rights reserved
>
> Copyright © 20__ [Customer Legal Name]. All rights reserved

For a discussion of joint ownership see, E. Scott Johnson, *Avoiding Joint Pain: Treatment of Joint Works of Authorship Conditions,* 43 Md. B. J. 13 (May 2010).

3. Other Alternatives

Other alternatives include having the licensor give the licensee a significant price discount to recognize the intrinsic value the licensor will receive by retaining ownership of the custom-developed software or have the licensor pay the licensee a royalty on future sales of the module.

For a general discussion, see Porter, *Negotiating Rights to a Customer's Improvements and Modifications,* 15 Corp. Couns. Q. 14 (April 1999). For a discussion of the licensor's point of view, see Gard & Bullock, *What's Wrong With the 'I Paid For It, I Own It' Strategy,* 23 ACC Docket 23 (May 2005).

C. Statements of Work, Functional Specifications and Technical Specifications (§ 1.7)

1. Statements of Work

Many license agreements and services agreements are structured as "master" agreements whereby the general legal and business terms are set forth in an over-arching master agreement with the actual work to be performed and the software to be licensed contained in statements of work or work orders attached to the master agreement. By utilizing a master agreement format, the parties can attach numerous statements of work for many different types of services and products over the term of the master agreement without having to negotiate a new agreement each time. Because the principle business and legal terms have been agreed to, the parties only need to document the work to be performed and the price for such work.

The Statement of Work ("SOW") is the most important part of any contract, as it defines what the vendor will deliver. Both parties should avoid the temptation to delegate the drafting and approval of statements of work to junior employees under the belief the master agreement is the principle document governing their relationship. Too often the vendor is able to dilute its contractual obligations set forth in the master agreement or limits its deliverables through creative drafting in the statement of work. At the same time, the vendor should ensure that the customer does not introduce additional terms in the statement of work that were not contemplated by the vendor. As such, each party and its lawyers should carefully review each statement of work prior to its execution.

Depending on the terms of the master agreement, each statement of work usually contains a detailed description of the licensed software and services to be provided, the location where they will be provided, ownership of the deliverables as well as the acceptance criteria and payment terms. A statement of work should also include any terms unique to the particular deliverables, such as specialized warranties and records retention. Most importantly, a statement of work should set forth in detail the functional specifications and technical specifications, the assumptions on which the price and timing of deliverables are based, what is in scope and out of scope as well as the responsibilities of each of the parties. *See* Section C.2 below for a discussion of the functional specifications and technical specifications.

At a minimum, a statement of work should include the following elements:

- A reference to the overarching master agreement
- A Delivery Timetable. The dates should be linked to "go-live" benchmarks or other requirements such as milestone payments.
- A Description of Deliverables. A detailed description benefits both parties.
- Acceptance Procedures and Testing Responsibilities
- Pricing. A prudent customer will set a fixed price or maximum price/hours and will tie payment to the vendor meeting well-articulated milestones.
- Project Assumptions. The statement of work should clearly state the assumptions that each party is making when entering into the statement of work.

For example, is the customer responsible for purchasing all third party software and hardware? A deviation from the stated project assumptions should result in a change order or justify a delay in a party's performance without penalty.

- Optional Services. The parties should confirm that any "optional" services are listed as being out of scope items. In a fixed price transaction, the parties need to be absolutely clear as to what is in scope and what is out of scope.
- The Vendor's Project Management Methodologies. These methodologies provide advance warnings of problems, escalation, and resolution, which should result in either the avoidance of any schedule problem or the ability to address a delay in the spirit of compromise via a change order or amendment.
- Signature Lines. Given that the statement of work serves as an addendum/amendment to the master agreement, it needs to be separately signed by an authorized signatory.

One common issue is how to resolve conflicts between the master agreement and the statement of work. In the majority of agreements, the parties agree that any conflict will be resolved in favor of the statement of work given the statement of work is specific to the unique deliverables and that the master agreement may have been negotiated prior to a particular statement of work even being contemplated. Some parties believe, however, that the master agreement should prevail in an effort to maintain the sanctity of the contractual protections it contains. They believe that these protections should not be negated in a later statement of work, especially where the statement of work may be negotiated and executed by someone who does not understand the risks they are assuming. This philosophy is problematic if the parties desire to incorporate conflicting terms into the statement of work, as they now must not only draft the statement of work, but must also amend the master agreement.

A savvy licensee may seek to characterize the license agreement as the purchase of a product with ancillary services in an effort to obtain the protections offered to purchasers under the Uniform Commercial Code (UCC). Licensors should reject this approach and ensure that the contract does not include language declaring that the contract is subject to the UCC. See § 28.3 for language benefiting licensees by declaring the agreement is subject to the UCC.

See Forms 23.C.10 and 11 for a model statement of work.

2. *Functional Specifications*

The software's functional specifications are the technical architecture that the software must meet once it has been developed to the licensee's requirements, and they are usually set forth in a statement of work (SOW) attached as an exhibit to the agreement.

The functional specifications should be extremely detailed and should be agreed upon prior to execution of the license agreement, as they will determine the cost and extent of the effort exerted by the licensor in the software's development. The functional specifications should set forth any user interfaces, system interfaces, hardware interfaces, software interfaces and communications interfaces. In addition, the functional specifications should discus such issues as the scalability of the solution.

For a more detailed discussion see IEEE 830-1998 "IEEE Recommendation Practice for Software Requirements Specifications."

If the functional specifications have not been agreed upon in detail, it is impossible for the licensor to determine with confidence the price of the development effort as the scope of the development effort has not been limited or fixed. The licensee is also at risk because it does not have a document describing in detail the deliverable it will receive for the fixed price.

Often the functional specifications and the scope of work—if there is a service component—are not reviewed by the lawyers on the negotiating team. Too often the lawyers believe these are "technical issues" best left to the technical staff, or the technical staff never seeks legal input. This is a serious mistake because the lawyers can enhance the specificity of the applicable document and determine whether legal terms have been included in the specifications or the scope of work, which benefits both parties. Occasionally, the parties enter into an agreement without agreeing on the functional specifications, usually because the customer is seeking to meet an internal deadline and/or the vendor does not want to lose a customer. Doing so can be disastrous, as it invites litigation if the parties cannot later reach agreement on the specifications. *See e.g., Bubbajunk.com, Inc. v. Momentum Software,* 2004 WL 904081 (Tex. App. Apr. 29, 2004) (unsigned software specification requirements created after contract signature are not part of the contract).

To avoid future problems, the parties should avoid using language such as the following:

> As soon as mutually practical after the Effective Date, the Parties shall work together diligently and in good faith to reconcile differences between the RFP and the Licensor RFP Response and establish a mutually agreeable document setting forth the technical specifications, functional requirements, project schedule, testing and acceptance procedures (such document being hereinafter referred to as the "Conformed Specification"). Once executed by both Parties, the Conformed Specification shall be automatically incorporated by reference into this Agreement and made a part hereof. In the event that the Parties have not agreed upon and executed a Conformed Specification by [insert date], then either Party may terminate this Agreement [without liability or obligation to the other Party] by providing written notice of such termination to the other Party [in which case Licensor shall invoice Licensee for the time expended by Licensor in developing the Conformed Specification at an hourly rate of $_____].

By doing so, the parties shift the negotiating leverage to that party with the least incentive to execute an agreement. If the customer has a deadline for the implementation of the system, it is placed in a difficult position. If it walks away from the contract, that customer has to identify a new vendor and quickly negotiate a contract to meet the customer's schedule.

A significant amount of litigation has arisen as a result of agreements being executed containing general language that the "parties shall negotiate in good faith the functional specifications immediately upon execution of this Agreement." After execution, a dispute often arises because the parties are unable to agree on the functional specifications, given that the licensor is usually constrained by a fixed price—a limit with which a licensee is usually not concerned. Several courts have recognized the licensee's obligation to provide the licensor with the needed information to develop a system. *See H/R Stone, Inc. v. Phoenix Business Systems, Inc.*, 660 F. Supp. 351 (S.D.N.Y. 1987) (licensee breached implied covenant of good faith and fair dealing by failing to provide sufficient information to allow licensor to undertake development); *Truktax, Inc. v. Hugh M. Gray & Associates, Inc.*, 1987 WL 13150 (Tenn. App. July 1, 1987) (customer breached contract for computer software by hindering its development and installation and owed developer the remainder of contract price). Further, by failing to set forth definitive specifications, the parties run the risk of having a court disregard the contract's integration clause and include the parties' correspondence and other writings. *See L.S. Heath & Son, Inc. v. AT&T Info. Sys., Inc.*, 9 F.3d 561 (7th Cir. 1993) (if allegedly integrated writing does not, without reference to another document or other coordinating information, reveal what the basic transaction entailed, then the writing is not integrated; where master agreement did not identify prices, products, services, software applications, or configurations).

In the extreme, a court may find the lack of a contract under the theory of contractual indefiniteness, that is, the functional specifications were such a material portion of the contract that the contract could not exist without them. *See generally Rates Technology, Inc. v. New York Telephone Co.*, 1995 WL 438954 (S.D.N.Y. July 25, 1995) and UCC § 2-204. This possibility finds support under the UCC, which requires an agreement to (a) evidence a contract for the sale of goods, (b) be signed by the parties, and (c) specify a quantity in order to be legally enforceable. UCC § 2-201 comment 1.

The prudent methods of contracting are to (1) enter into a two-phase contract with the first phase consisting of a fixed price engagement to draft the functional specifications, and assuming that the parties can agree on the functional specifications, a second phase consisting of the development effort at a fixed price; (2) jointly develop the functional specifications prior to execution of a fixed price contract; or (3) enter into a time and materials contract. The first option is less attractive to the licensor because once the functional specifications have been agreed to, the potential licensee can shop the functional specifications to other potential software developers to obtain the best price. The licensor's concerns can potentially be alleviated by contractually mandating that the jointly developed specifications are the confidential information/intellectual property of both parties and cannot be disclosed to a third party without the other party's prior written consent.

The second alternative is less attractive to the licensor's business people who want to obtain a binding commitment from the licensee and who do not want a long, drawn-out process in order to reach a final agreement, during which time the licensee could select another licensor. From the licensee's perspective, the third option does not provide the price protection needed to protect against cost overruns and necessary for its budgeting process. Finally, the parties must decide whether the licensed software, when delivered or accepted, meets the functional specifications or the current documentation for the licensed software. Often the parties will include language allowing for the termination of the agreement without cause if the specifications developed are not satisfactory to the potential license or not completed within a specified time frame.

The parties should also avoid setting forth a long list of responsibilities for one party and then stating the other party is responsible for everything not set forth on the list. This concept is clearly attractive to the customer as it limits the customer's responsibilities to a finite list, while the vendor is responsible for everything else, including hardware and third party software whose use may not have been contemplated. The vendor assumes responsibility for the unknown, significantly increasing its risk.

Placing undue risk on one party is likely to lead to a dispute in the future that may prevent the customer from achieving its goal of receiving a system that meets its needs on time and on budget, as well as the vendor's goals of delivering a project on time and on budget.

3. *Technical Specifications*

The technical specifications describe the physical, programmatic elements of the software including its performance and reliability. Performance should be tied to the licensee's technical environment. The technical specifications should specifically set forth the applicable hardware, operating system, and programming language. While the licensee should seek to insert its intended use of the system into the technical specifications, the licensor should be hesitant to insert such description for fear of creating an implied warranty of fitness for a particular purpose.

D. Change Orders (§ 9.8)

Changes in scope usually arise from the changing needs of the customer over the course of the engagement, which may extend over several years. As the customer's business needs evolve during this period, its information technology needs will likely also change. Occasionally, a change in scope will occur because the vendor proposes a new, more efficient technical approach for achieving the customer's goals.

Altering the customer's requirements or a vendor's commitment to complete deliverables during a project is fraught with risk, as the parties have already likely agreed on a fixed price, a specifically defined deliverable, and a definitive delivery date. If the parties are operating on a time and materials basis, an agreement on a change in scope can likely be reached. If the parties cannot agree on the impact of the change order on the price, or agree on a revised delivery date, the parties have opened Pandora's Box as it will likely be difficult for the customer to switch vendors without materially impacting the customer's costs and schedule. Further, the inability of the parties to reach a mutually agreeable resolution may result in litigation, which benefits neither party.

Any change regarding the work to be performed, including a change in the payment terms, the delivery schedule, or the nature of the deliverables themselves should be made through a signed "change order" executed by both parties. Under no circumstances should the customer orally authorize work to be performed, nor should the vendor perform any work, without a written change order. The likelihood of contractual uncertainty and the risk of creating a new, independent oral agreement under the UCC, whose terms may be supplied by the UCC, creates significant risk requiring a written amendment. *See* UCC § 2-204.

Requiring a change order protects the vendor in the event the customer claims the work was not authorized, while limiting any claim by the vendor that the work was performed at the request of the customer or one of its employees. A change order also protects the vendor from having to rely on a *quantum meruit* argument to recover any monies it believes it is entitled to.

1. Methodology of the Change Order Process

Any change order provision contained in an agreement should provide a detailed methodology for enacting a change to a work order. A time line should be included for responding to a proposed change order by one of the parties. The vendor should reject language providing that the failure of the vendor to respond to a change order request within a set period of time (e.g., seven days) is deemed to be acceptance. Silence is generally not deemed to constitute acceptance under contract law, and the parties' contract should adhere to this principle. 2 WILLISTON ON CONTRACTS § 6:53 (4th ed.); *Bowley v. Fuller,* 115 A. 466 (Me. 1921) (mere silence and inaction does not constitute acceptance). The agreed upon process should also address whether the vendor will be compensated for responding to a change order request if a significant amount of work is involved, such as creating a detailed pricing estimate or undertaking a significant amount of research.

From the vendor's perspective, the vendor should avoid accepting any contractual language requiring the vendor to perform *de minimis* changes without charge. While this language is often proposed by customers, it introduces subjectivity and uncertainty into the contract as to what is meant by "de minimis." See § 9.8 and Form 23.B.3. § 2.2.2 on the enclosed CD-ROM. Further, it requires the vendor to perform additional work without additional compensation.

2. The Contents of a Change Order

A change order should not only clearly state the changes to be made, but it should also clearly identify those segments of the existing statement of work or other governing document that have been superseded. At the same time, the customer should insist on a contractual provision that the vendor cannot perform any work on the customer's behalf without a change order executed by an authorized officer of the customer.

Often, the parties execute a change order delineating the changes in the work to be performed but fail to consider or state how such change order impacts the scope of the overall project and any corresponding change in price. If the parties agree upon a scope change, the resulting change order should clearly state the new deliverable date, if any, as well as the change order's impact on the scope of the project. The parties need to avoid becoming so focused on changes to the functional specifications and price that they fail to consider the impact on the overall project.

3. *The Failure to Agree*

If the parties cannot agree on pricing for the change, the contract should allow the customer to terminate the relevant work order or the contract itself if there are no other work orders. Otherwise, the customer may be forced to pay for work it can no longer use. Thus the customer should ensure that it has the ability to terminate the contract in the event the parties cannot agree on a change order and, for the maximum flexibility, include a termination for convenience provision—also known as a "termination without cause" provision. *See, e.g.*, § 4.1.A. The customer should also ensure that the agreement provides for termination assistance in the event of such a termination, particularly where the customer anticipates that another vendor, or its internal IT resources, will take over ownership of the project. See Section J, below, and § 5.3.3. Termination assistance is much more common in the termination of an Application Service Provider ("ASP") relationship, where customer data and proprietary information need to be kept live and accessible right up to the cut-over point.

To protect its expectation interest in the contract, a vendor may wish to minimize the customer's ability to exploit a "failure to agree" termination right, for example, by eliminating the convenience termination—at least in the absence of an early termination penalty payment—or by linking the termination right to the vendor's unreasonable failure to agree. These can be hard to enforce, and most vendors will balk at agreeing to termination solely for disagreement on a change order. This is particularly true in an ASP context where money has already been spent on hardware, or in a large development context where resources have been diverted and may not be capable of being immediately redeployed on another paid project.

In the event the customer elects to terminate the contract without cause, the vendor should ensure the contract provides that the vendor will be paid for all services that have been provided to the customer, not just those services that have been accepted by the customer, as well as the out-of-pocket costs incurred by the vendor as a result of such early termination. These costs may include the cost of terminating any leases for rental housing or office space in the customer's geographic location. Some vendors also seek to have the customer pay the vendor several weeks' salary for each employee working on the customer's project, based on the reasoning that it will take the vendor several weeks to staff these employees on a new project. See, e.g., § 4.1.A.

E. Audit/Quality Assurance (§§ 9.13, 16.Q; Form 23.K.2.E)

A software license and services agreement may contain many different types of "audit" provisions. Some of the most common types include the following:

- Quality audits such as SAS 70 audits to ensure that the licensor is using appropriate quality assurance mechanisms to deliver a quality product. Forms 23.K.2.E.1 and 2
- Compliance audits to determine if the licensor is complying with all applicable laws and the licensee's policies. Form 23.K.2.E.6
- Financial audits to ensure any services performed on a time and materials basis are billed correctly by the licensor. Form 23.K.2.E.5
- Financial audits to ensure the licensor is paying the licensee any required royalty for software which the licensee paid to develop and which is licensed to a third party (§ 8.I)
- Security audits to ensure the licensor is safeguarding the licensee's data
- Compliance audits by the licensor to ensure the licensee is complying with the terms of the license grant (e.g., the number of licensee's employees accessing the software, CPUs, etc.) (§ 8.J and Form 23.K.2.E.4)

Set forth below is a discussion of the different types of audits that may be contained in a software license agreement.

1. *From the Licensee's Perspective*

A commitment to quality is important to both the licensor and the licensee. The licensee wants to ensure that the products and services it receives conform to the requirements of the license agreement and are delivered error free. The licensor is interested in delivering error-free software and services, because the cost of re-performing defective services and correcting defective software can be significant.

It is important for a licensee to oversee the actions taken by the licensor to ensure that it receives a quality product. Even though the license agreement may contain representations and warranties as to the quality of the services and software to be delivered, those representations and warranties do not provide a definitive benchmark of the licensor's quality assurance efforts. The licensee's best method for ensuring that it receives a quality product is by requiring the licensor to conform to certain quality standards and conducting quality audits. The principal means of doing so is through the ISO 9001 compliance standards and conducting SAS 70 audits.

(a) SAS 70 Audits

The Statement on Auditing Standards (SAS) No. 70-Service Organizations was created by the American Institute of Certified Public Accountants (AICPA) to allow service organizations to represent that the service provider or their auditor has undertaken an in-depth audit of the service provider's control activities including its controls over information technology and related processes. Section 404 of the Sarbanes Oxley Act of 2002 (SOX) makes a SAS 70 audit report an integral party of a service provider's obligation to report on effective internal controls.

A SAS 70 audit provides a service organization's customers a standardized format in which to evaluate the service organization's control activities and processes. It allows the organization's independent auditor to issue an opinion based on the AICPA's requirements for fieldwork, quality control and reporting.

As a result of an audit, an auditor will issue a Service Auditor Report. There are two types of reports: Type I and Type II.

In a Type I report, the service auditor will express an opinion on (1) whether the service organization's description of its controls presents fairly, in all material respects, the relevant aspects of the service organization's controls that were in place in operation as of a specific date, and (2) whether the controls were suitably designed to achieve specified control objectives. http://www.sas70.com/about.htm. (Last viewed September 15, 2010).

In a Type II report, the service auditor will express an opinion on the same items noted above in a Type I report, as well as (3) whether the controls that were tested were operating with sufficient effectiveness to provide reasonable, but not absolute, assurance that the control objectives were achieved during the period specified. *Id.*

For a more detailed description, see http://www.sas70.com/about.htm. (Last viewed September 15, 2010).

Most customers request that the vendor undertake a Type II audit. While a vendor may resist such a request due to the cost and administrative efforts that have to be expended, the customer may be required to undertake a Type II audit under SOX and thus require its subcontractors to do so as well. Many vendors already undertake SAS 70 audits so a customer's request to do so may not be an additional burden.

Vendors should resist, however, a customer's efforts to participate in the planning of such an audit or to have such audits conducted more frequently than annually. See § 9.13(i). For vendors who are not required to undertake an SAS 70 audit, they should agree only to undertake a Type I audit unless the customer itself is required to undertake a Type II audit.

(b) Sarbanes-Oxley Act of 2002 (SOX)

SOX is intended to ensure that companies submit accurate information in their financial reporting and should not involve the licensor. Licensees, however, are increasingly asked to warrant that "the Systems being delivered are 'SOX compliant.'" A licensor cannot warrant that the financial information processed by its system is correct because the information belongs to the licensee. Furthermore, if there is a nonconformity in a system that causes incorrect financial information, this is not the licensor's responsibility since the licensee should be obligated to verify the output of the system. The licensor can warrant that any financial reports issued by the system in accordance with the system's documentation will be verifiable with traceable source data. The following provision should be suggested by licensors to satisfy licensees on this issue:

> Licensor represents and warrants that any financial reports generated by the System in accordance with the Documentation will be verifiable with traceable source data and that any revisions or modifications to the Systems will be documented.

(c) Payment Audits (§ 9.13)

If the licensee is paying the licensor for software development services on a time and materials basis or if it is paying for the licensor's travel expenses, it should include an audit provision allowing it to audit the licensor's time and expenses charges. This is a reasonable request for time and material contracts but is inappropriate for a fixed price contract. In negotiating the audit provision, the licensor should limit the rights of the licensee and specifically state that the licensee is not entitled to obtain any information related to the licensor's profit margin. Further, the licensor should insist on including language forbidding the licensee from retaining an auditor on a contingency basis, as the auditor is more likely to take an aggressive position in auditing the licensor's fees, or from retaining a competitor of the licensor to conduct the audit.

A good audit clause will establish the time, location, and length of the audit as well as the obligation of the licensor to cooperate. Further, the clause should provide for the reimbursement of the licensee's audit costs in the event a material discrepancy (5 percent) or a set dollar amount is identified and confirmed.

(d) Compliance with Applicable Laws and License Policies (§ 23.K.2.E.5)

A prudent licensee should ensure that the licensor is in compliance with its obligations to comply with all applicable laws. This is especially important for licensees in regulated industries such as the healthcare industry and the financial services industry. The licensee should insist on the contractual right to audit the licensor's compliance with all applicable laws as well as the licensee's policies. The underlying reason for doing so is to protect the licensee from liability in the event the licensor fails to comply. For example, a licensee may be liable under HIPAA if the licensor fails to protect any Protected Health Information (PHI) that was provided to the licensor by the licensee. The licensee should undertake these audits semiannually to ensure the licensor's continual compliance.

(e) Payment of Royalties (§ 8.I.4)

To the extent the licensee is entitled to receive a royalty from the licensor for software the licensee paid to develop, the licensee should demand the right to audit the licensor's financial records to confirm the licensor has paid the licensee all royalties due the licensee. The language of the audit provision should require the licensor to produce a quarterly statement within thirty days after the end of each calendar quarter. Each such statement should set forth sufficient detail to allow the licensee to confirm that the royalty payment was properly calculated. At a minimum, each such statement should identify the relevant client, the revenue received from such client and the type of license purchased by the client. The licensee should have the right to audit the licensor's financial records upon thirty days notice twice a year. The audit provision should include punitive language in the event the licensor underreports the royalty due twice in any two-year period.

2. *From the Licensor's Perspective (§ 8.J)*

The licensor should always include the right to audit the licensee's use of the software. While most licensees will not intentionally misuse the software or utilize more copies of the application than it has licensed, copyright infringement and piracy are common. Often such issues arise through the merger of two companies, where the merged company let its licenses lapse even though the applications continued to be used, or a company's employees unlawfully copy the software, instead of going through the procurement department to avoid the inherent delay and cost. Another area for concern is the purchase of used hardware that, unbeknownst to purchaser, has unlicensed software resident on it or for which the purchaser thought it was obtaining a license. As software margins are compressed and maintenance fees fall, licensors are more likely to increase their audits in order to maintain or improve their profits. Each of these scenarios illustrates the lack of proper internal controls by the licensee to prevent the improper use of its third party software. By failing to maintain such controls and ensure the company's compliance with its internal policies, the company risks significant financial exposure.

While a licensee does not have a legitimate basis for refusing to accept an audit provision in its license, it should seek to limit the scope of the audit and resulting disruption of its business. The licensor should never agree to not audit the licensee regardless of the scope of the license grant. By agreeing not to audit the licensee, the licensee has no incentive to abide by the terms of the license. See Form 23.K.2.E.4. on the enclosed CD-ROM for language prohibiting the licensor from auditing the licensee.

Licenses frequently contain language allowing the licensor to install, within the licensee's production environments, something simply referred to as "audit software." This request stems mainly from the use of licensing templates, of which many list it as an item to request, rather than the suggestion coming from a knowledgeable IT professional making the request because of legitimate security concerns. This view is supported by the fact that a significant percentage of potential licensors will drop this request during the negotiation process.

For example, "audit software" can be a simple query of a UNIX box to report out the configuration of the operating system, or audit software can be a very sophisticated application to interrogate the complex security and access control systems associated with multiple SAP applications. Licensor's audit uses such an application with a corporate SAP system, and this application requires its own servers to operate. Prudent licensees should ask the licensor to explain exactly what is their meaning of "audit software" and why they feel it necessary to utilize such software.

Something else to consider is the "audit objective" of the audit software. Licensees should ask the licensor to explain its reasoning and what they hope to accomplish with the audit software. The response will position the licensee to propose alternatives as to how to accomplish the licensor's objective without the necessity of the licensor's audit software.

In the course of discussions with the licensor, the licensee should share information regarding the nature of its own audit software that it maintains and operates for its own environment. Does the licensor collaborate with various security organizations to address improvements for both the service delivery model for its clients and the service delivery model for the corporation, as both environments can benefit from some of the same audit software tools?

Answers to these, and other questions, help to determine whether the licensor is really serious about the request, or just asking to see if they can get it. The licensor's level of desire will indicate how much effort is needed to convince them this is really not a good idea.

Many licensees do not want the licensor's audit software within their production environments, primarily due to the nature of audit software design and operation, particularly the high level of access authority associated with executing the software. To operate effectively, audit software is designed to circumvent security and access control mechanisms. To assist with this objective, the level of system access granted to the application when it runs would typically be considered to be the highest level available. Installation of the audit software in the production environment behind the firewalls and behind the intrusion detection systems, combined with powerful access abilities, would allow the software entry into all sorts of areas, including, possibly, some unintended access to areas where it should not be. Keep in mind that the licensor's request to install audit software also implies the licensee's permission for the licensor to execute the software, generally at its sole discretion. Though licensors do partition a licensee within their respective environments, the worst case scenario when using audit software as described above would entail the licensor attempting to gain, or actually gaining, access to the licensee's environment. Alerts and alarm notices would go off, indicating to the licensee that its confidential data had been compromised.

Audit software may also contribute to reduced system performance or cause other forms of interference with proper system functions. These risks would be considered somewhat secondary to the risks described above.

The vast majority of "audit software" requests are typically resolved within several initial discussion sessions. For the few, more challenging licensors, many licensees have been successful in negotiating away the licensor's requirement by providing further detailed explanations, including some of the concerns described above, or by offering alternative audit measures. For example, some licensees periodically provide copies of reports from their own audit software executed by the licensees on their own environments.

3. Audits by Third Parties

In addition to the licensor, several software industry consortiums, the Business Software Alliance (BSA), and the Software and Information Industry Association

(SIIA) have been granted the right to audit customers for copyright infringement by copyright owners.

While these organizations do not have any independent investigatory power and may lack any contractual rights to audit, many licensees seek to cooperate to avoid litigation costs. Most audits from the BSA and SIIA result from tips by disgruntled customer employees. Although the licensor may have a contractual remedy for breach under the Copyright Act, the customer also has liability of up to $150,000 per violation in the event of a willful infringement. 17 U.S.C. § 501. Further, an officer or director of an infringing corporation who received a financial benefit and who had the ability to control the infringing activity may be held personally liable. *See Shapiro, Bernstein & Co., Inc. v. H.L. Green Co.,* 316 F.2d 304 (2d Cir 1963); *RCA/Ariola Intern., Inc. v. Thomas & Grayston Co.,* 845 F.2d 773 (8th Cir. 1988).

If a licensee receives a request for an audit from the BSA, SIIA, or a similar organization, it should promptly seek legal advice. While such audits are usually amicably resolved, the resulting fees and penalties can be significant.

For a general overview of licensor/third party audits of the licensee, see Scott, *Successfully Defending Software Audits,* 2 SciTech Law. 18 (Issue 3 Winter 2006). For more information about the BSA audit program, see http://www.bsa.org/globalhome.aspx (last viewed September 15, 2010). For more information on the SIIA, including model policies and guidelines for software usage, see http://www.siia.net/ (last viewed September 15, 2010).

F. Service Level Agreements (§ 3.B)

Service level agreements (SLAs) set forth mutually agreed performance metrics to measure the licensor's performance. In a software transaction they usually measure whether the software meets the minimum stated performance standards. They incentivize the licensor to meet the agreed upon standards by assigning penalties for the failure to do so.

SLAs set forth the Service Level Credit (SLC) that the licensee is eligible to receive and the Service Level Bonus (SLB) that the licensor is eligible to receive for performing at or above a set level. These credits are usually more common in outsourcing transactions, Internet service provider agreements (ISPs), and application service provider agreements (ASPs) than in general software license agreements. Common metrics covered by SLAs are application availability (downtime limits), response time, refresh rates, help desk response, network availability and business/operational processes, and mean time to report (MTTR). The nature of the applicable SLAs will depend on the type of transaction.

From the customer's perspective, the principal purpose of SLAs is to ensure that the customer receives the same level of services that it contracted for or received prior to the vendor providing the services in question. Often, however, the customer lacks the necessary information to quantitatively document the prior level of services it received. To the extent the customer can quantify prior performance levels, the data is often not detailed enough to create meaningful benchmarks. As such, customers often agree to SLAs without a full understanding of the performance standards the vendor should meet or of the metrics that should be measured.

The SLA should set forth each party's obligations, such as notifying the other party of its noncompliance, corrective actions and response obligations. Further, the SLA should clearly state the measurement methodologies, such as daily, monthly and yearly calculations, as well as the type of credit. Most licensors will agree only to a credit against future services versus a cash payment to the customer. The SLA needs to be carefully drawn to address any factors outside its control, as the licensor's performance could be affected by a number of factors, such as hardware and collateral third party software.

In defining its obligations, the licensor should exclude from calculating any time-sensitive service level obligations; third party problems such as hardware, telecommunications, and infrastructure links; routine maintenance; emergency maintenance, and the like. Further, the licensor should clearly set forth any requirement or obligation of the customer on which its obligations are premised, for example, a certain hardware configuration.

The payment of service level credits should be in full satisfaction of any liability on the licensor's behalf for the failure to meet the stated metrics. At the same time, the customer should insist that once the service level credits reach a certain level, the customer may terminate the agreement. A common issue is whether service level credits count toward the limit of liability contained in the agreement, or are they in addition to any limit of liability. While the licensor seeks to limit its liability, the customer has a strong argument that service level credits represent liquidated damages for failure to meet short-term SLAs and that the overall limit of liability addresses the failure of the project as a whole. Further, "credits" are not cash. The limit of liability goes to the amount of money a licensee can recover from the licensor in the event of a breach. As such, the customer should insist that any service credits should not count toward any cap.

Many licensees believe that there should not be separate caps on the different types of damages set forth throughout the agreement. This belief is founded on the reasoning that the parties have negotiated a mutually agreeable risk allocation and a cap on direct damages. There should not be separate caps for specific types of failures. By having many "sub" limitations, the parties would be forced to spend a significant amount of time negotiating separate caps for the likely failures of both parties.

The licensor should also insist that the SLAs contain a recapture provision, allowing the licensor to recover credits paid to the customer if the licensor performs at a level higher than contractually required either during the period in question or over the term of the contract.

For a more detailed discussion of service level agreements, see Deckelman, *Negotiating Effective Service Level Agreements (SLAs),* http://www.outsourcing-journal.com/nov1997-legal.html.

G. Disaster Recovery (§ 35)

Depending on the nature and scope of the ongoing services to be provided by the licensor to the customer, a disaster recovery provision can be the most important provision in the agreement after the license grant.

The goal of any disaster recovery plan or effort is to ensure the continuity necessary to allow a licensee to operate its business without interruption. The cause of any interruption is likely to come without warning and is difficult to anticipate, such a sudden blizzard, hurricane or fire, or even a terrorist event. A successful plan involves both the vendor and customer working together to ensure a seamless transition in the event of an interruption.

A customer can take a number of actions to protect itself. It should ensure it has alternative power sources, such as emergency generators, at its principal IT sites and that it backs up data nightly. These tapes should be stored offsite, preferably in a different state. Data centers should contain the most up-to-date monitoring systems with Halon fire suppression equipment. The customer should make sure its software licenses allow it to use the software remotely in the event of a "disaster."

To the extent a vendor operates or maintains the customer's data centers or a segment thereof, or provides access to business critical software via an application service provider arrangement, the vendor should be required to establish a formal disaster recovery plan based upon customer requirements. The customer needs to evaluate how critical each of its applications is to its ability to do business and to determine how long the business could operate without access to each application. This will drive the disaster recovery plan. Critical applications may require a "hot" swap capability. A hot site is a site that operates simultaneously with the impacted data center, allowing the applications functions to transfer to the hot site immediately upon a disruption. A customer's business may be able to operate without access to less critical applications for longer periods of time. In this event a "cold" swap may suffice. A cold site is a site that the vendor is required to have operational within a contractually mandated period after a disaster occurs. The cost to maintain a hot site would be significantly higher than a cold site.

Regardless of the support selected by the customer, the customer should visit and audit these sites to ensure the vendor meets its contractual obligations and is prepared for an interruption. Further, the customer and vendor should jointly run tests to ensure that each party's employees are familiar with their responsibilities and that any real disaster will be handled as smoothly as possible. Testing will often expose unanticipated problems with the party's respective plans.

In the event that the licensee's disaster recovery vendor differs from its software licensors, the licensee must ensure that its license allows it to operate the software from several locations in order to ensure continual/seamless operations. At a minimum, the license should allow the software to reside at two locations, provided the second location is not using the software simultaneously to process the licensee's business needs.

H. Maintenance/Future Development (Form 23.C.2)/(§§ 11, 16K)

When a licensee makes a decision to adopt a certain software platform for a mission critical system, it should receive assurances from the licensor that the licensor will continue to enhance and support the software for some period in the future. The licensee wants to avoid a situation where the licensee adopts a system and the licensor shortly thereafter decides to stop enhancing the system or supporting it, essentially forcing the licensee to purchase a new software system.

1. *Maintenance (§ 16)*

Maintenance is often viewed as an extended warranty. The warranty period and the obligation to perform maintenance really address when the licensee begins to pay for support, upgrades and fixes; the shorter the warranty period, the greater the revenue that will likely flow to the licensor from maintenance.

From the licensor's perspective, a maintenance provisions should be separate and distinct from the warranty in the license agreement and should ideally be in a separate agreement. This is important due to the difference in the licensor's liability for breach of the warranty contained in the license agreement and for breach of a separate maintenance agreement. The licensee also benefits from separate agreements as it has the ability to terminate the maintenance agreement while continuing to utilize the software.

Under some license agreements, maintenance begins upon acceptance. Under others, maintenance does not occur until the expiration of the warranty. During the warranty, the licensee may terminate the license agreement if the software does not meet the functional requirements or perform in accordance with the licensee's other requirements and may potentially receive a refund of the entire license fee. If the software does not meet the functional specifications during the maintenance period or the licensor fails to maintain the software in accordance with the contractual requirements, the licensee can terminate the maintenance agreement but will usually only be entitled to receive a refund of the maintenance fee, provided the maintenance provisions are contained in a separate agreement. In short, by utilizing separate agreements, assuming industry standard limits of liability—the amount of the license fee for the license and 180 days trailing revenue for the maintenance agreement—the licensor will most likely be able to reduce its liability in the event of a breach, as the warranty under the license agreement will likely be 90 days or less.

(a) Licensor Obligations

Given the complexities of software, the licensee should receive a commitment from the licensor that the licensor will support and maintain the software for a minimum of five years (see § 11.3). It is not unreasonable to have the licensor agree to a minimum support period, unless the licensor is planning to "sunset" the software and release the employees supporting the software. Further, any agreement should address the length and type of notice that must be given to the licensee in the event the licensor stops supporting the software. The maintenance agreement should explicitly state the scope and nature of the support.

Licensees should insist that the licensor's level of support under the maintenance agreement be the same as the licensor's level of support under the warranty provisions of the license agreement. The licensee should not accept a lesser level of support. This is especially true for any functionality that was not tested or implemented during the warranty period. The maintenance standards should specifically provide the response times and repair times, as well as the licensee's remedies if the licensor fails to properly support the software. Often licensors will implement a "bypass" to correct a problem, as it is often quicker, easier, and cheaper to circumvent an issue than to fix it.

Usually, maintenance agreements classify errors into three classes based on severity with a shorter response time corresponding to the seriousness of the issue. See the model Software Maintenance and Services Agreement, set forth in Form 23.C.2 on the enclosed CD-ROM which contains illustrative language.

A Level 1 error usually means that the software will not function and that the licensor will respond immediately to the licensee's notification of an error and will work continuously until the problem is resolved. A Level 2 error usually means that a material aspect of the software's functionality is inoperable. The licensor will usually commit to work continuously during normal business hours until the issue has been resolved. A Level 3 issue usually means there is a noncritical "bug" for which a work-around exists. The licensor usually commits to fix all Level 3 errors in the next update.

Many maintenance agreements provide that if the licensor ceases to provide maintenance, the licensor will provide the licensee with a copy of the software's source code so that the licensee can maintain the source code itself. In this situation, the licensee should insist on the right to have a third party maintain the software. The parties should distinguish situations where the software has reached the end of its commercial viability or there is no longer a demand for maintenance and support, versus situations in which the licensor simply decides to no longer support the software. If the licensee insists on maintaining the software itself, the licensor may want to consider having the licensee indemnify it for any liability arising from the licensee's continued use of the software and for any claims for any modifications the licensee may make to the software. Licensees should realize, however, that it may be impractical to maintain the system themselves given the complex nature of many large software systems and the large learning curve necessary to master the system.

Finally, all maintenance agreements should require the licensor to update the product documentation in connection with any enhancement or alteration to the software and ensure the documentation is consistent with the licensed software. An aggressive licensee will also seek to require that the licensor's software, as maintained, will be compatible with all third party software and hardware upgrades. This additional requirement creates great risk for the entity providing maintenance, given the uncertainty of when such upgrades will occur and the cost to make the licensor's software compatible.

Many licensors include language in their agreements that they are only obligated to fix those errors that can be duplicated. These provisions protect licensors from having to devote resources to try to identify and fix "ghost" errors that are not easily reproducible.

In the event of a dispute between the parties regarding maintenance and support, the governing agreement should provide an escalation procedure to try to resolve the issue.

(b) Licensor Exclusions

A licensor can keep its costs low only by maintaining a standard version of the software and amortizing its costs over a large number of customers. As such, licensors should always state that they will maintain only the last two versions of the software to avoid increased costs from maintaining too many versions. The licensor should clearly state that while the licensor will support other versions, there will be an additional cost to do so. See Form 23.C.2, Section 3.4, Software Maintenance and Services Agreement.

Most maintenance agreements void any obligation to maintain the software if the licensee or its agents modify the software in any way or if any problems with the software result from the negligent or unauthorized actions by the licensee or from the use of the software in conjunction with a third party product. A smart licensor will claim ownership of any modifications, enhancements, or derivative works created by the licensor while performing maintenance for the licensee. Finally, the licensor should clearly state that any services not explicitly listed as being part of maintenance is outside the scope of maintenance and will be charged on a time and material basis.

(c) Pricing (§ 8.4)

Maintenance has traditionally been priced at 10 to 25 percent of the original license fee. Some licensors calculate the maintenance fee on the aggregate of the license fee plus the cost of any enhancements or modifications made by the licensor, while others consider any enhancements or modifications to be consulting services or professional services and not included in the base amount for calculating the maintenance fee.

Maintenance/support is usually very profitable for a licensor if the software is well written and widely distributed, allowing the cost of support to be amortized over a large number of customers. Some licensors generate margins as high as 85% on software maintenance. The cost/risk of ongoing support rises significantly if the installation becomes more of a project than a product, that is, the software becomes so customized that it cannot be maintained consistent with the versions utilized by other customers.

Licensees usually want the licensor to agree to offer maintenance for a set period of time, such as 5 to 10 years from acceptance, without committing to actually purchasing maintenance from the licensor. The requirement to offer maintenance for a minimum period is reasonable as an expensive software system is worthless unless it is properly maintained. At the same time, a reasonable licensee cannot expect the licensor to fix or project its prices 10 years into the future.

The licensee should seek to have the licensor fix its price for support during an initial five-year period, in which case the licensor will assume the risk of a significant increase in the cost to deliver the support. From the licensor's perspective, the solution is to include language that the licensor will provide such services at "licensor's then-existing price." The licensee should be wary of accepting a commitment to provide support without fixing the price. Without a fixed price, the licensee does not have a true commitment from the licensor, as the licensor may raise its support and prohibitively make the purchase of support services financially unfeasible for the licensee.

A solution that may be mutually agreeable is to increase the cost annually by an escalator. This usually gives rise to an animated discussion as to which index properly reflects the actual increase in the licensor's costs. Two common indexes used are the Consumer Price Index (CPI) and the Employment Cost Index, Civilian Workers, Not Seasonally Adjusted, Compensation Costs (ECI), published by the Bureau of Labor Statistics, U.S. Department of Labor. The CPI is a broad-based index that reflects a large "basket" of goods while the ECI is focused solely on labor costs. The parties should carefully consider whether either index reflects the nature of their agreement or whether they should explore other labor/cost indexes published by the Department of Labor that may more closely mirror the costs incurred in supporting the underlying software. Licensees should seek a mechanism to reduce the licensor's fees if the licensor's costs decrease. This is not unrealistic, as costs in the information technology services industry have historically fallen over time.

Each index carries its own risks. In the 1970s and 1980s, the CPI rose significantly, driven by higher real estate prices, while technology salaries remained constant. In the late 1990s, technology salaries quickly outpaced the rate of inflation, causing many licensors with fixed price obligations to suffer significant losses in providing support. Before agreeing to tie fee increases to the CPI, the licensor should consider the likelihood that the CPI will decline. The recent recession has brought the CPI nearly to zero. If the CPI goes negative, will the licensor be obligated to decrease its prices? A prudent licensor will ensure to include language that its prices are not subject to decrease.

A mutually agreeable resolution may be for the licensor to commit to provide support for a period of five to seven years with a fixed price for the first two or three years. For the remainder of the term, the licensor may increase the price annually based on an agreed upon index but with a minimum increase and a maximum cap. Alternatively, the parties may agree after an initial period to tie future price increases to a very specific index, reflecting the licensor's labor costs. See, e.g., § 8.4E. (i.e., the Syntec salary index that tracks technology labor costs in France).

Licensees should also seek to include a most favored nation clause. It is often difficult to have a licensor accept this type of clause except in the case of its largest and best customers. For a detailed discussion of most favored nation clauses, see Section Q, below.

Maintenance fees should be nonrefundable and priced on an annual basis. Occasionally, licensees seek to terminate their maintenance agreement for convenience during the stated term and receive a pro rata refund for the remaining term of the agreement. This request is unreasonable from the licensor's perspective because the licensor staffs its help desk based on the number of customers it has and amortizes the cost of such support over those customers. If the licensor loses a customer, it is unable to increase its prices to the remaining customers to cover the lost revenue, as the licensor is usually contractually precluded from raising its prices until each contract is renewed. Thus, from the licensor's perspective, maintenance agreements should be terminable only for cause or upon written notice 90 days prior to the anniversary date of the agreement.

2. *Future Development (§ 16K)*

The licensee should seek to require that the licensor continue to update and upgrade the software for a set period of time. See § 11.3. Some licensees seek to have the licensor commit to invest a certain percentage of the licensor's revenue into the software on an annual basis. See § 3.A. This request is usually unacceptable to the licensor as it places the licensee in the position of operating the licensor's business or at least making important business decisions.

The licensee usually seeks these types of commitments to ensure that the licensor does not "sunset" the product in question. The licensee, however, should take comfort from the licensor's support commitment and should base its purchasing decision on the software's functionality at the time of contract execution. If the licensor has committed to the future development of a particular function or module, this commitment should be set forth in the functional specifications or a Statement of Work.

3. *Independent Service Organizations (ISOs) (§ 3.6)*

One issue of great concern to licensors is when the licensee seeks to maintain the software through the use of independent service organizations (ISOs). Many licensors are concerned that these independent third parties, who are often their competitors, will learn the licensors' trade secrets or siphon off the licensors' maintenance revenue, which is usually a significant portion of their profits. *See, e.g., Hodge Business Computer Systems, Inc. v. U.S.A. Mobile Communications, Inc.*, 910 F.2d 367 (6th Cir. 1990). Further, any changes made by an ISO may have an unanticipated impact on any future updates or enhancements created by the licensor. See § 14.A.4.(d) for model language limiting the licensor's liability in the event a third party makes changes to the licensor's software.

To limit third party access to the license or its software and thus prevent the retention of ISOs by the licensee, the license should clearly state that the licensee may not grant a third party access to the software. See § 3.6 for an example of such language. The failure to be explicit may allow a third party to assume responsibility for maintenance of the software. *See, e.g., Hogan Systems, Inc. v. CyberSource Int'l, Inc.*, 158 F.3d 319 (5th Cir. 1998). In the event the licensee seeks to allow an ISO or other contractor access to the licensor's intellectual property and trade secrets, the licensor should require the licensee to indemnify the licensor for any misuse by the licensee. The issue of third party access is complex, as the failure to allow third parties to provide maintenance support potentially raises antitrust concerns. For a more detailed discussion of these antitrust issues, see Section L, below. *See* Johanson & Zollman, *Computer Maintenance Raises Antitrust Issues*, NAT'L. L. J., May 20, 1996, at C 40. The utilization of an ISO should serve as a basis for terminating an existing warranty relating to intellectual property indemnification as the licensor cannot be responsible for the ISO's actions. The licensor should also be relieved of any responsibility for future enhancements, updates or continuing maintenance, or bug fixes.

4. *Maintenance versus New Versions*

A common issue in the provision of maintenance services is what actually constitutes an "update," which would be considered maintenance and covered under the annual maintenance plan, and what constitutes a new "version" of the software for which the licensor could levy an additional fee. Given that maintenance is usually charged on an annual basis, licensors have financial incentive to characterize substantial improvement to the software as a new version and outside the scope of maintenance. As such, the licensor would be able to charge the licensee an additional fee. A licensee should seek to clearly define the scope of "maintenance" to ensure that it receives the benefit of what it has paid for and seek to limit the licensor's claim that an "update" is a new "version." See Form 23.C.2 for a description of services usually covered under maintenance.

I. Training and Documentation (§§ 11, 13.1)

1. *Training (§ 11)*

A detailed description of the training to be provided by the licensor is important to both the licensor and the licensee. The licensor wants to put distinct limits on the training to be provided to the licensee to fix the licensor's cost. This is especially important when both parties want to use a "train the trainer" approach to reduce costs. The description should set forth absolute time limits, class size, class location, materials to be provided, and the language in which the classes will be taught. A licensor will also want to delineate prerequisite skills the attendees must have to attend the specific training. This is to ensure that the licensor does not spend time teaching basic programming skills that the attendees should already possess. The licensor also wants to carefully state which skills will be taught and which skills the attendees will possess upon completion of the course. For example, training should teach the attendees how to operate the software, but the licensor should not make statements to the effect that the licensee's attendees will be able to maintain the software unless such training will be provided.

At the same time, the licensee wants to clearly state that upon completion of training, the licensee will be able to fully operate the software; that future training will be available at a mutually agreed upon time if the licensee desires to purchase extra training; and that all documentation and training provided by the licensor to the licensee will be accurate and current. Further, the licensee's attendees will receive copies of all documentation used during the course. Smart licensees will distribute the training materials several days before classes begin so that students are familiar with the materials, and in addition they will seek to videotape and audiotape the training sessions to educate other employees. However, some licensors are hesitant to allow the licensees to audiotape or videotape the training if the training incorporates the licensor's trade secrets or if the licensor believes it will lose training revenue.

2. Documentation (§ 13.1)

All documentation provided by the licensor should be in sufficient detail to allow a reasonably skilled programmer to operate and use the software. The licensor should warrant that the documentation is the most current version, complete and free from any errors and omissions, and that it corresponds to the licensee's current version of the software installed at the licensee's site and is not a baseline version of the software. Further, the licensor should promptly provide the licensee with updated documentation reflecting any changes made to the software used by the licensee.

Unless the licensor desires to make a profit on duplicating the documentation, the licensee should be free to reproduce the documentation without cost, provided the licensee reproduces the licensor's protective marks (i.e., copyright notices) and does not modify the documentation.

J. Transition/Continuing Services (§ 42.2)

Customers should ensure that the underlying agreement between the parties addresses the vendor's ongoing obligations to provide any ongoing services and support to the customer in the event that the agreement is terminated. By addressing these issues in the agreement, the customer can avoid being held hostage by the vendor.

The biggest concern for the customer is that the vendor ceases to provide support if either the vendor or the customer terminates the contract for breach. The customer should require the vendor to provide support services for no less than six months from the date of termination at the rates set forth in the contract. If the contract is terminated for the vendor's breach, savvy customers seek to have the vendor provide such services at a significant discount from the vendor's existing rates. While a vendor may agree to a discount for its best customers, such a discount is justified by the vendor's breach. In the event of the vendor's breach, the customer should also seek to require that the vendor transfer to the customer all necessary licenses needed by the customer to conduct its business, including any third party licenses.

The vendor should also limit its post-termination obligations to the customer, especially if the vendor has terminated the contract for the customer's breach. In the event the agreement was terminated without cause or for the customer's breach, the vendor should resist providing services beyond 60 or 90 days from the termination date and should charge market rates for its services. If the customer has breached the contract, the vendor will likely want to assign its employees to new accounts as quickly as possible, especially if it can obtain higher rates for their services. Thus, the vendor should not agree to retain specified "key" employees on the account after the termination date. The vendor should also require the customer to pay the vendor's fees monthly in advance to avoid any payment disputes.

K. Benchmarking (§ 8.B)

Closely associated with the concept of "most favored customer pricing" is benchmarking. Benchmarking is the process of evaluating an existing contract and comparing it to the current market environment. Benchmarking usually focuses on pricing and the scope of any applicable service level agreements.

The first issue for consideration is if and when there will be benchmarking. Licensors usually resist benchmarking because it has the effect of increasing their performance metrics while reducing their profit margins. Further, many licensors believe that services are not an easily compared commodities and that the data necessary to make a valid comparison is not easily obtained. Further, cost models are not easily analyzed in great detail. As such, licensors are hesitant to enter into an obligation that will likely lower their margins over the term of the agreement. Licensees, however, usually require benchmarking as a condition to entry into a contract, as they believe they are entitled to receive the benefit of falling prices and increased quality representative of the IT market today. Many contracts require benchmarking every few years depending on the length of the contract. The parties should carefully consider the frequency of any benchmarking, as it is expensive and time-consuming, and it often creates significant tensions between the parties.

The parties should clearly identify the methodology for identifying the third party hired to perform the benchmarking, who pays for the cost of the benchmarking, and how the parties will act on the results. The licensor should avoid having the licensee select the party undertaking the benchmarking. A better solution is to have the licensee identify three well-respected independent vendors, such as Gartner, who perform benchmarking and have the licensor select the actual party to undertake the benchmarking from the three identified vendors. The cost of the resulting study should be divided evenly between the parties.

The licensor should insist that the results of any study be kept confidential. Publishing the results of a study may have a negative impact on the licensor's reputation and/or serve as a floor in any subsequent negotiations with any future client. While this is a reasonable request, the licensee should resist any other restriction on the use of such data by the licensee.

Most licensors generally do not try to restrict use of the benchmark results beyond confidentiality. Each contract is unique in its approach to benchmarking (mandatory, discretionary, frequency, automatic adjustments, guidelines for "acceptable" performance, etc.), but once the licensee receives the results, it is hard to keep it from using the results for whatever purpose it sees fit within the bounds of confidentiality. For example, if the benchmark somehow revealed service level failures not previously known to the licensee, the licensor would be hard pressed to prevent the licensee from assessing any associated credits.

The parties should also clearly delineate the standard against which the licensor's performance will be judged. The two biggest benchmark issues for the licensor are the desire of the customer to use a "best quartile" standard and the desire of the licensee to use "tower-specific" benchmarks. Having benchmark results considered in the aggregate is a material benefit to the licensor in dealing with post-benchmark contractual remedies. When negotiating benchmarking provisions, the licensor should strive to maintain the concept of benchmarking in the aggregate—across all towers and geographies and against a similar scope of services for similarly positioned customers. Otherwise, the vendor runs the risk of having the prices it charges on a small transaction benchmarked against competitors' pricing on a larger-volume transaction. Similarly, benchmarking on cost alone is not fair to the licensor, as contractual terms and service requirements will drive deal costs. Thus, for example, it would be unfair to compare the cost of hosting services between two vendors without making adjustments for the fact that one contract specified 99.999 percent uptime (requiring the vendor to establish redundant hardware), and the other specified only 98.5 percent uptime.

The licensor should also seek to use the concept of the benchmarker's definition of "a good deal" instead of the prevalent "top quartile" standard. Most third party benchmarking consultants have a "good deal" standard in their benchmark process. If the top quartile standard is to be used, the vendor should still seek to have a materiality standard of 5–10 percent difference before any adjustment in their fees is required.

To fairly assess the benchmarked services, the benchmarker must take into consideration the specifics of the underlying transaction, such as the quality of the service provider, any underlying assets purchased, any employees assumed, the volume of services, and the geographic location of the services being provided. In considering the totality of these requirements, it will be difficult to obtain similar comparators. Thus, the results may be open to interpretation. Likely areas for dispute are the scope and timing of any survey, the sample size of the benchmarked peer group, and where the service provider should fall within the benchmarked comparators.

Given the number of variables in attempting to compare different transactions across different providers, benchmarking can be a complex and expensive process that can lead to a dispute between the parties. Because it is a tool to test the contract against the current market, it is most useful in a long-term arrangement. In shorter-term arrangements, the cost and distraction of benchmarking may not be worthwhile because the market may not have changed significantly.

For model language, see Form 23.C.7. The language set forth in Form 23.C.7 is well balanced, limiting the list of potential benchmarking companies with performance measured against the mean, and all adjustments are transparent.

For a discussion of benchmarking, see Stuckey, *Contractual Items to Consider Before You Outsource Your Company's Data Center,* 25 ACC DOCKET 70, 79 (Jan./Feb. 2007).

L. Antitrust and Copyright Misuse Issues (§ 3.6)

A licensor may restrict the licensee's use of the licensed product so long as the restrictions imposed on the licensee do not violate antitrust law, constitute copyright misuse, or violate another doctrine. Set forth in the following paragraphs is a brief discussion of several issues that should be considered in determining the enforceability of any license restrictions.

1. Antitrust Issues

Traditionally, the provision of maintenance, enhancement, and support services has been very lucrative for licensors, due to the high margins involved with such work. Licensees are often at the mercy of the licensor, as the licensor has the familiarity with the software and the necessary proprietary software tools to provide these services. With the advent of outsourcing, the proliferation of competent third parties to maintain proprietary software, and the increasing desires of licensees for other alternatives, some licensors have sought injunctions to prohibit third party access to licensors' proprietary software without a license. *See, e.g., Triad Systems Corp. v. Southeastern Express Co.,* 64 F.3d 1330 (9th Cir. 1995), *cert. denied,* 516 U.S. 1145 (preliminary injunction granted and affirmed on appeal); *Independent Services Organizations Antitrust Litigation,* 910 F. Supp. 1537 (D. Kan. 1995) (counterclaim for preliminary injunction against ISO granted). Or they have sought damages for such use. *See Data General Corp. v. Grumman Systems Support Corp.,* 36 F.3d 1147 (1st Cir. 1994) (jury awarded damages for copyright infringement for unlicensed use of diagnostic software). The licensors' actions are based on their claims that their software is a copyrightable, proprietary asset, and that the third party has not purchased a license to use or access the software.

Similarly, courts have held that the antitrust laws do not negate a patent holder's right to exclude others from licensing a patent. *Intergraph Corp. v. Intel Corp.,* 195 F.3d 1195 (9th Cir 1997). *See also In re Indep. Serv. Org. Antitrust Litig. v. Xerox,* 203 F.3d 1322 (Fed. Cir. 2000) (patent holders' decision not to sell or license patented parts nor to sell or license copyrighted materials and software did not violate antitrust laws).

At the same time, however, a licensor's attempt to exploit its software may be subject to liability based on the antitrust laws. Antitrust claims are usually based on illegal tying or monopolization. Licensees and other third parties have often claimed that licensors "tie" the use of their software to the purchase of maintenance services from the licensor in a violation of the antitrust laws. A tying arrangement is "an agreement by a party to sell one product only on the condition that the buyer also purchase a different product, *or at least agree not to purchase that product from any other supplier.*" (Emphasis supplied.) *Northern Pacific Ry. v. United States*, 356 U.S. 1, 5–6 (1958).

In order to have a cause of action for tying, the party imposing the tie must have market power in the tying product and use that market power to leverage into the tied products market, creating a competitive disadvantage for the other competitors in the tied product market. *Jefferson Parish Hosp. Dist. No. 2 v. Hyde*, 466 U.S. 2, 16–17 (1984). As always, a key issue is how to define the "market." A patent per se is sufficient to establish market power. *United States v. Loew's, Inc.*, 371 U.S. 38, 45–47 (1962); *United States Steel Corp. v. Fortner Enterprises, Inc.*, 429 U.S. 610, 619 (1977). A copyright is also sufficient to establish market power. *Independent Ink, Inc. v. Illinois Tool Works, Inc.*, 396 F.3d 1342, 1348–49 (Fed. Cir. 2005). One way to avoid a tying allegation is to sell each product separately as well as together. As long as the pricing does not cause an "economic tie," one should avoid violating the law.

In *Data General Corp. v. Grumman System Support Corp.*, 36 F.3d 1147 (1st Cir. 1994), Data General sued Grumman for using its copyrighted diagnostic software that had been provided to Data General's customers on the specific condition that the customers not allow access to a third-party service provider, such as Grumman. Grumman in turn counter-claimed that Data General's actions violated the antitrust laws. The First Circuit held that Data General as a copyright holder had presumptively a valid business reason for refusing to license its copyrighted software. *Id.* at 1187. This holding is consistent with other similar cases in this area. *See MAI Systems Corp. v. Peak Computing, Inc.*, 991 F.2d 511 (9th Cir. 1993), *cert. denied*, 510 U.S. 1033 (1994); *Advanced Computer Services of Michigan v. MAI Systems Corp.*, 845 F. Supp. 356 (E.D. Va. 1994),. *But see, Electronic Data Systems Corp. v. Computer Associates Int'l., Inc.*, 802 F. Supp. 1463 (N.D. Tex. 1992) (allegation of tying of licenses for certain software to licenses for maintenance software is a valid claim of action). *See also Service and Training, Inc. v. Data General Corp.*, 963 F.2d. 680 (4th Cir. 1992) (refusal of the licensor to license maintenance software, except to computer purchasers who self-maintained, held not to be an antitrust violation or a violation of copyright policy, but rather the right of a copyright owner to exercise control over its copyright).

At least one court has held, however, that the mere refusal to license a patented invention or copyrighted work may give rise to liability if the holder does so with an "anticompetitive" interest. *Image Technical Services, Inc. v. Eastman Kodak Co.*, 125 F.3d 1195 (9th Cir. 1997). *But see Intergraph Corp. v. Intel Corp.*, 195 F.3d 1346 (Fed. Cir. 1999) (termination of advance disclosure agreement by industry leader as a result of customer's suit for patent infringement did not violate antitrust laws as vendor had no obligation to disclose proprietary information).

For a detailed discussion of the issues associated with tying the purchase of computer hardware to the purchase of computer software and maintenance, see Robert S. Chaloupka, *Tying in the Computer Maintenance Context*, 24 CORP. COUNS. Q. 395 (July 2008).

2. Copyright Misuse Issues

A copyright owner may not seek monopolies beyond those granted under the copyright statute. *Broadcast Music, Inc. v. Columbia Broad. Sys., Inc.*, 441 U.S. 1 (1979); *Lasercomb Am. Inc. v. Reynolds*, 911 F.2d 970 (4th Cir 1990). Copyright misuse arises when the copyright holder seeks an exclusive right or monopoly beyond those granted by copyright law and against public policy. *Lasercomb*, 911 F.2d at 977. A finding of copyright misuse prevents the enforcement of the copyright or any copyright license from such misuse but does not invalidate the copyright itself. *Alcatel USA, Inc. v. DGI Technologies, Inc.*, 166 F.3d 772 (5th Cir. 1999). Thus, a licensor must be careful not to violate public policy by placing unlawful prohibitions on a licensee.

Courts have been quick to recognize the copyright misuse defense when the copyright owner uses its copyright in a manner that violates public policy. *See, e.g., Alcatel USA, Inc. v. DGI Technologies, Inc.*, 166 F.3d 772 (5th Cir. 1999) (copyright license limiting use of operating software system software to the copyright owner's hardware constituted copyright misuse); *Lasercomb Am. Inc. v. Reynolds*, 911 F.2d 970 (4th Cir. 1990) (prohibiting licensee from developing competing software program during term of 99-year license is copyright misuse); *Practice Mgmt. Info. Corp. v. Am. Medical Ass'n.*, 121 F.3d 516, 520 (9th Cir. 1997) (requiring licensee not to buy products that compete with licensed product is copyright misuse).

At the same time, however, courts recognize that a copyright holder has the right to protect its copyright, provided it is done in such a way not to violate public policy. In *Apple, Inc. v. Psystar Corp.*, 673 F. Supp.2d 931 (N.D. Cal. 2009), on a motion for summary judgment, the court denied a claim that Apple's practice of requiring that its operating system only be used on Apple computers was misuse. The court noted: "[t]he question is not whether the copyright is being used in a manner violative of antitrust law (such as whether the licensing agreement is 'reasonable'), but the question whether the copyright is being used in a manner violative of the public policy embodied in the grant of a copyright." It emphasized that Apple did not prohibit others from independently developing and using their own operating systems and did not prohibit purchasers of Mac OS X from using competitor's products. Instead, Apple simply prohibited purchasers from using Mac OS X on competitors' products. *See also, Video Pipeline v. Buena Vista Home Entertainment*, 342 F.3d 191 (3d Cir. 2003) (prohibition on licensee websites from making disparaging comments regarding licensor, motion picture industry or movies not copyright misuse).

A copyright licensor may not continue to collect royalties from the licensee after the copyright underlying the licensed software has expired. *April Productions, Inc. v. G. Schirmer, Inc.*, 126 N.E.2d 283 (Ct. App. N.Y. 1955). Attempts to collect such payments after the copyright has expired may be considered copyright misuse and a violation of the antitrust laws. See *DSC Communications Corp. v. DGI Technologies*, 81 F.3d 597 (5th Cir. 1996). *See also Brulotte v. Thys Co.*, 379 U.S. 29, 33 (1964) (attempts to collect royalties under expired patent constituted an improper use of patent monopoly, analogous to tying purchase or use of patented article to purchase or use of unpatented one).

For a more in-depth discussion, see Holland, *Copyright Misuse*, 87 Intell. Prop. Couns. 7 (Mar. 2004); Hemnes, *Restraints on Alienation, Equitable Servitudes, and the Feudal Nature of Computer Software Licensing*, 71 Denv. U. L. Rev. 577 (1994); Davidson & Enisch, *A Survey of the Law of Copyright Misuse and Fraud on the Copyright Office: Legitimate Restraints on Copyright Owners or Escape Routes for Copyright Infringers*, Intellectual Property Antitrust 489 (Practicing Law Institute 1996).

For a general discussion of the antitrust issues in maintenance, enhancement, and support services, see Soobert, *Antitrust Implications of Bundling Software and Support Services*, 21 U. Dayton L. Rev. 63 (1995); Hamilton, *Software Tying Arrangements Under the Antitrust Laws: A More Flexible Approach*, 71 Denv. U. L. Rev. 607 (1994); Johanson & Zollman, *Computer Maintenance Raises Antitrust Issues*, Nat'l. L. J., May 20, 1996 at C40; Rosenhouse, *Sufficiency of Copyright Misuse Defense to Allegations of Copyright Infringement Pursuant to Federal Copyright Law*, 185 A.L.R. Fed 123 (2003).

3. Digital Millennium Copyright Act – Computer Maintenance Competition Assurance Act

On October 28, 1998, Congress enacted legislation known as the Computer Maintenance Competition Assurance Act ("CMCAA"), 17 U.S.C. § 117, to partly overturn the MAI Systems case and make it easier for ISOs to service computer hardware. Incorporated as Title III of the Digital Millennium Copyright Act ("DMCA"), the law is directed solely to the copying of software as part of the act of servicing computer hardware. Under the law, the making of a RAM copy of a computer program by an ISO as part of servicing computer hardware will not be an act of copyright infringement. The law provides a limited immunity to copyright infringement only and does not address the ISO maintaining and modifying the software in and of itself. 17 U.S.C. § 117. As interpreted by at least one court, the CMCAA applies retroactively. *Telecomm Technology Services, Inc. v. Siemens Rolm Communications*, 1999 WL 696011 (N.D. Ga. July 6, 1999).

In a case of first impression, the U.S. Court of Appeals for the Federal Circuit held that an ISO was likely to prevail on its maintenance and repair defense (17 U.S.C. § 117(c)) under the DMCA in an infringement action based on its circumvention of an encryption system of the manufacturer's copyrighted maintenance code, done solely for the purposes of maintenance or repair. Further, the court read the right to "repair and maintain" broadly. *Storage Tech. v. Custom Hardware Engin. & Consult., Inc.*, 421 F.3d 1307 (Fed. Cir. 2005) (absent proof that circumvention of manufacturer's encryption system facilitated copyright infringement, ISO's circumvention to access system codes did not violate DMCA).

For an overview of the DMCA, see *Corporate Counsel's Primer on the Digital Millennium Copyright Act*, 39 Law. Brief 1 (July 2009); Lee, *Reverse Engineering Under the DMCA: Recognizing a "Fair Access" Defense*, 20 Computer Law Assoc. Bull. 133 (No. 4. 2005); Davidson & Axtell, *Reverse Engineering: The DMCA and the Reverse Engineering of Suspected Infringing Products*, 23 Computer & Internet Law. 1 (Feb. 2006).

M. Export/Import Issues (§ 43)

1. General

Under U.S. export regulations, an individual may "undertake transactions subject to the Export Administration Regulations[1] (EAR) without a license or other authorization, unless the regulations affirmatively state such a requirement." 15 C.F.R. § 736.1. The EARs are consistent with the position of many European governments that anything not prohibited is allowed, in contrast to the Bureau of Industry and Security's (BIS) (known prior to April 18, 2002 as the Bureau of Export Administration) previous position that everything is prohibited unless an exception exists. Under the EAR, licenses are not required for most shipments to Canada and to U.S. territories, possessions, and commonwealths. The export regulations can be found at http://www.bis.doc.gov (last viewed September 15, 2010).

For a general overview, see Blageff, *Overview of Export Controls*, 239 Com. L. Advisor 1 (Nov. 2007).

2. Definitions

Section 734.2(b)(1) of the EARs defines "export" as:

(i) an actual *shipment or transmission* of items subject to the EAR out of the United States; or

(ii) "release" of technology or software subject to the EAR to a foreign national in the United States.

Section 734.2(b)(2) defines "export of technology or software" as:

(i) any "release" of technology or software subject to the EAR in a foreign country; or

(ii) any release of technology or software subject to the EAR to a foreign national.

In the context of this definition, Section 734.2(b)(3) of the EARs defines "release" as:

(i) visual inspection by foreign nationals of U.S. origin equipment and facilities;

(ii) oral exchanges of information (with foreign nationals) in the United States or abroad; and

(iii) the application to situations abroad of personal knowledge or technical experience acquired in the United States.

---

1. The Export Administration Regulations are issued by the Department of Commerce and administered by the Bureau of Industry and Security (BIS) to implement the Export Administration Act of 1979, as amended.

3. Export of Software and Technology

The export and re-export of technology and software from the United States is under increasing scrutiny by the U.S. government. Special attention is focused on encryption technology and satellite technology. Exports are controlled by BIS and the Department of State's Directorate of Defense Trade Controls (DDTC). BIS usually governs goods, software, and technology with civilian applications, while the DDTC governs goods, software, and technology with military applications and satellite technology. The first step in exporting any software or technology is to determine whether an export license is needed. Under 15 C.F.R. 736.2(b), the exporter must apply a 10-step process to determine whether the exporter's software or technology requires a license under the EAR. Based on the results, software or technology will fall into one of three categories:

1. *No License Required* (NLR). If software or technology to be exported is either not subject to the EAR or does not require a license as a result of the 10-step process under 15 C.F.R. 736.2(b), it is considered to be "No License Required" or NLR. Software and technology classified as EAR 99 fall into this category.

2. *License Exceptions.* If a determination is made that the software or technology requires a license under the EAR, the exporter must determine whether a "License Exception" is available. A License Exception is the authorization to export under stated conditions that would otherwise require a license. 15 C.F.R. 740.1(a). For software and technology, two potential License Exceptions are available under Section 740:

   (a) *Technology and Software under Restriction (TSR).* Section 740.6 allows export and re-export of software and technology, subject to national security controls, to Country Group B upon receipt of a Letter of Assurance.

   (b) *Technology and Software-Unrestricted (TSU).* Section 740.13 of the EAR provides a License Exception for certain "Operation Technology" and software, software updates, and mass-market software, permitting their export without a license. This License Exception covers certain mass-market software, such as software sold over the counter through mail order transactions and telephone call transactions, sales technology, and software updates. Operation Technology is defined as "the minimum technology necessary for the installation, operation, maintenance (checking), and repair of those commodities that are lawfully exported or re-exported under a license, a License Exception or NLR." 15 C.F.R. 740.13(a)(1).

3. If a License Exception does not exist, the exporter must apply for a license under 15 C.F.R. 748.

In addition, the United States and United Nations maintain comprehensive economic embargoes against certain countries. 15 C.F.R. § 746 (2008). Sanctioned countries, as of March 1, 2008, include Cuba, Iran, Iraq, North Korea, Sudan, and Syria.

For a detailed explanation of the export laws, see CORPORATE COUNSEL'S GUIDE TO EXPORT CONTROLS (2d ed. 2009).

4. Deemed Exports

Both parties must also be aware of the "deemed" export rules. The EARs prohibit the export or release of Technical Data to an entity's foreign offices, employees, customers, and its customer's employees without a valid license or license exception. Except in certain limited situations or with the existence of a license exception, a valid export license is required for aliens to view Technical Data, as this is a "deemed" export. This restriction applies to Technical Data and source code provided to aliens inside the United States, whether oral, written, or through other media. Visual inspections also constitute the provision of Technical Data. As such, a party may violate the export laws if it discloses Technical Data to foreign aliens within the United States or to individuals overseas who are employees of the disclosing party.

Further, both parties should not allow IT managers who are foreign aliens to have administrator rights that would allow them to access to export-controlled files.

The penalties for non-compliance are significant: civil penalties of up to $250,000 per incident or two times the value of item involved, as well as loss of export privilege and criminal penalties of up to $1,000,000 and two years in prison. 18 U.S.C. § 1001.

5. Contractual Considerations (§ 45)

The licensor should make sure the license includes language requiring the licensee to comply with all U.S. export laws. The licensee should acknowledge that the software and all related materials are subject to U.S. export controls and that it agrees to comply with all applicable laws. The failure to do so may subject the licensor to significant liability.

Under the export laws, the licensor may have the obligation to place certain export-related notices on its invoices and on the bill of lading. *See, e.g.*, 15 C.F.R. 758.6 (2000). Further, the license should specifically state that the licensor has no liability for its failure to obtain a U.S. export license to export the software.

For additional information on export licensing, see the Bureau of Industry and Security's website: http://www.bis.doc.gov (Last viewed September 15, 2010); the Office of Foreign Asset Control's website: http://www.treas.gov/ofac (Last viewed September 15, 2010); the MIT Technology Licensing Office's website: http://web.mit.edu/tlo/www/ (Last viewed September 15, 2010); and Microsoft's licensing website: http://www.microsoft.com/exporting (Last viewed September 15, 2010).

6. Customs

In addition to complying with U.S. export laws, the licensor also needs to be concerned with the custom duty laws of the importing country. And, likewise, U.S. import laws must be abided by when software is imported into the United States. Recently, U.S. Customs and Border Protection issued a ruling that importers must pay duty on the value of royalty payments made in connection with licensing the patented technology incorporated into the goods imported into the United States. HQ W548692 March 2, 2001. These issues are often quite complicated and require serious attention. Not only can there be a significant financial impact as a result of customs duties, but several countries restrict the importation of encryption software or require the source code to be made available to the government. For an overview of the issues involved with customs duties, see Lyverse, MacLennan and Apker, *Cracking the Customs Code: How to Export to Europe Effectively*, ACC DOCKET 24 (June 2006) at 40.

N. Bonds, Parent Guarantees, and Letters of Credit (§§ 8.H, Exhibit 8H, 34)

1. Bonds (§ 34)

(a) Bid Bonds

Occasionally, a licensee issuing an RFP will require potential bidders to post a bond upon submission of their bid, often equal to 5 percent of the bidder's price. This requirement is to ensure that a bidder is serious about its bid and will enter into an agreement with the licensee if it is selected as the provider of choice. These bonds usually expire once a contract is executed.

(b) Performance Bonds/Payment Bonds (§ 34.1)

Performance bonds and payment bonds are often used when there is concern as to one party's ability to meet its financial obligations. Performance bonds are not favored by licensors as they must be obtained from a bank or insurance company at an additional cost. Payment bonds are often required where there is concern with the ability of the licensee to pay. In such cases, a letter of credit drawn on a U.S. bank payable at sight may be more attractive to the licensor. At a minimum, the party required to obtain a bond should seek to pass the cost of the bond on to the benefiting party and carefully review the terms that instigate payment of the bonds.

2. Parent Guarantees (§ 8.H, Exhibit 8H, Signature Line) (Form 23.I.2)

An alternative to a performance bond or payment bond is a parent guaranty. Parent guarantees are appropriate where there is some concern that either the licensor or licensee may lack the resources to meet its contractual obligations. Guarantees are applicable only where the party in question is the subsidiary of a larger financially solvent parent, and they are attractive to the party required to obtain a guaranty in that they usually do not involve any cost unlike a performance bond or payment bond. In the event the license allows the licensee's affiliates to utilize the software or the licensee can add any of its affiliates to the license as a matter of right, the licensor should insist on a parent guaranty by the licensee. If the parent agrees to give

Q. Compliance with Laws (§ 25)

Most licensees seek to include a provision in the underlying license agreement requiring the licensor to comply with all applicable laws. On its face, this statement seems innocuous, as every party has a pre-existing duty to comply with valid, applicable laws. A closer examination raises a number of issues. Most important, from the licensor's perspective, is who pays for any changes in the law that impact the licensor's performance and increase its costs. Licensees must recognize that licensors cannot assume unlimited liability for unknown risks. Licensors lack the ability to predict future legislation, preventing them from fairly pricing their products and services to reflect the cost of such future changes.

1. Utilizing the Change Order Process

Many licensors seek to qualify their obligations to comply with changes in the law by expressly subjecting any such obligation to the change order process, which allows the licensor to increase its prices if justified. The licensor's remedy in the face of the licensee's rejection of a proposed regulatory driven change order is to initiate the dispute resolution process, given the licensor most likely lacks the contractual right to refuse the change and terminate the agreement. The licensor is then faced with proceeding with undertaking the change at its cost and then seeking to recover such costs from the licensee.

While language proposed by a licensor to make a change in law subject to the change control process may be unacceptable to the licensee, a licensor should look to other provisions in the agreement for protection. One such protection is a covenant by both parties regarding their respective obligations to comply with the law. (See e.g., § 25.) Further, the licensor should seek to include language in the agreement that provides that if the licensee fails to approve a licensor's proposed change required to respond to changes in law, the licensee will hold the licensor harmless from any losses the licensor incurs in connection with such noncompliance.

In the event of a dispute, the licensor may have to undertake changes to the software and subsequently seek compensation as part of a protracted dispute. To the extent there is ambiguity with respect to the actions the licensor is obligated to undertake at the licensor's cost to respond to changes in the law, the licensor may lose any such dispute and end up financing such changes as well as potentially incur significant legal costs. Further, to the extent there is any lack of clarity in a statement of work on this issue, such ambiguity may provide additional risk.

Many licensees reject the licensor's position, arguing that the licensor has an existing obligation to comply with all applicable laws, and that the licensee's use of the software cannot be disrupted by a dispute between the licensor and the licensee as to who should pay for the cost of any required changes. They argue that as an industry expert, the licensor is better able to track changes in the law and spread the cost of any required changes across its many customers. A critical factor for the vendor in deciding whether to accept this risk is whether the required charges can be made simultaneously, accessing all of its clients, or whether each client's system must be modified individually.

Licensors argue that the licensee would have incurred the cost of any change in the law had the underlying transaction not occurred and thus it is inequitable for the licensee to expect the licensor to assume this cost. Ordinarily, a licensor's remedy in the face of having to absorb costs for which it believes it is not responsible would be to terminate the agreement. Most licensors lack such a termination right, however, and most licensees are unwilling to grant one. Licensees emphasize that the licensor is providing a product that must be current and competitive with market demands (i.e., complying with all laws), and that market forces, that is, the licensor's competitors, will force the licensor to have a compliant product.

2. A Compromise

A compromise is to have the licensor assume responsibility for the costs of all changes affecting its industry (i.e., the information technology industry) and have the licensee assume all costs affecting the licensor's industry, (e.g., the healthcare industry). In this manner, each party is responsible for the costs it would have incurred had a transaction had not been entered into. For laws such as HIPAA and Sarbanes-Oxley, the licensor should agree only that it will follow the client's directives set forth in a specific statement of work or other contractual agreement.

Many licensees seek to contractually transfer the risk of future changes in the law to the licensor. This is true especially for licensees in regulated industries, such as the healthcare and financial industries, as well as in outsourcing contracts where the licensor may be providing services for a significant period of time during which it is likely that the applicable laws may change.

3. Contractual Language

As discussed, a vendor should be hesitant to agree that the software and services it provides will be compliant with all future laws, as the cost to do so may be great and difficult to estimate. It should avoid accepting language similar to the following:

> Vendor, at no additional cost to Customer, shall make all modifications that are recommended, mandated, or required to meet federal and state governmental and quasi-governmental regulatory requirements, statutes, ordinances, policies, edicts, rules, guidelines, or standards related to Customer's use of the software.

This language creates significant risks for the vendor as the vendor is contractually obligated to bring the software and services into compliance with all future laws without additional compensation. It is very rare, however, to see language that so expressly and comprehensively addresses this issue as set forth above. Vendors are more likely to encounter language that discreetly shifts the burden:

> Vendor agrees that [or represents and warrants that] the Software shall comply with all applicable laws.

A more balanced approach is to include language similar to that set forth in Section 25 of Form 23.B.1. While an improvement over the language set forth in the previous paragraphs, it is ambiguous and will likely lead to a dispute. More equitable language is as follows:

> Each party hereby agrees to bear the cost of complying with all requirements of its particular industry and each party agrees to equally bear the cost of any subsequent changes in the law outside of each industry such as data privacy laws and security.

A vendor must consider that without limiting its covenant to the time of delivery, this language may obligate the vendor to deliver updates responsive to future changes in the law. Similarly, a customer must consider whether it is protected by language to this effect or whether it should seek more explicit language as set forth above in the first example.

In *County of Mercer v. UniLect Corporation*, 612 F. Supp.2d 638 (W.D. Pa. 2009), the court considered this issue. The County of Mercer brought suit against UniLect alleging UniLect breached its duty to keep UniLect's voting machines in compliance with state certification standards. The contract between the parties contained the following warranty:

> UniLect warrants the products, as delivered, will conform with and perform according to the specifications required by the State of Pennsylvania . . . . If any programs should not so perform, they shall be corrected or replaced by UniLect in a timely manner as mutually agreed.

The County argued the UniLect breached its obligations to keep the voting machines in compliance with state standards when, three years after delivery date, the machines were found not too be in compliance with new certification standards. The court found that the warranty did not create an express warranty that the machines would meet the specifications beyond the date of delivery even though the contract stated that the life of the machines was 20–25 years. *Id.* at 644–46. The court's decision was founded on the principal that the warranty expired on delivery and did not extend beyond delivery. Thus the licensor had no ongoing obligation to keep the voting machines compliant with state standards.

From the licensee's perspective, it should clearly state in the license agreement that all representations and warranties shall survive for the desired period and shall identify such representations and warranties in the survival clause.

A prudent vendor should agree only that the software and services will be in compliance with all applicable laws in effect on the date of contract execution or the time of delivery. A vendor may also agree to bring the software and services in to compliance with future laws at the vendor's then-existing time and material rates.

See Chapter 6.L for a more detailed discussion on survival clauses and § 18.

4. Monitoring Changes in the Law

Vendors should neither agree to monitor potential or actual changes in the law nor notify the customer of any such potential change that may affect the customer's business, even if the customer agrees to pay for such compliance monitoring, as the risk to the vendor may be great. Software and technology vendors are not law firms that can opine on legal matters. Further, many vendors provide services across many different industries and lack the ability to track potential legislation for a particular industry. It would be a Herculean task to track legislation nationwide at the local, state, and federal levels much less internationally. Customers are better suited through their internal legal department, outside counsel, independent auditors, industry trade groups, and consultants to monitor legislation that affects their business.

Further, a licensor should not agree to notify the licensee of any changes in the law that it becomes aware of and should never agree to provide its interpretation of the law, as it is not a law firm. Any request for an interpretation of a law or ordinance should be referred to the licensee's law firm.

5. Ensuring Compliance

If a vendor does agree to assume the risk of a customer's compliance obligations, the customer should be sure to investigate how the vendor plans to ensure compliance.

In the event that there is a change in the law that impacts a broad spectrum of a vendor's business, such as the Health Insurance Portability and Accountability Act (HIPAA) or identity theft laws, a vendor will likely make its software and services compliant without additional cost to its customers. Without a HIPAA-compliant product, a vendor would quickly go out of business, as its competitors would almost certainly offer a compliant product. A savvy vendor may ask a customer to share the vendor's development costs depending upon the magnitude of the required changes, given that the customer will have to pay new money to migrate to another new, compliant vendor. If a customer is concerned about assuming the risk of future changes in the law, the vendor can alleviate those concerns by contractually agreeing to amortize the cost of any needed changes across all of the vendor's customers using the software. See Section 23.K.2 E.6. for model language allowing a customer to audit the licensor's obligation to comply with all applicable laws.

Another approach is for the vendor to assume responsibility for all laws affecting the vendor's industry and for the customer to assume all liability for those laws affecting the customer's industry. While this concept appears straightforward, it is often difficult to put into practice because many laws may affect both parties. Shared responsibility is likely to lead to future disputes. Thus, this approach should be avoided unless a strong demarcation can be created dividing the parties' responsibilities.

R. Best Efforts, Good Faith Efforts, and Commercially Reasonable Efforts

1. General

Licensees often seek to require the licensor to exercise its "best efforts" in performing the licensor's obligations under the agreement while licensors usually seek to negotiate a "good faith efforts" standard in the belief that "good faith efforts" requires a lesser standard of effort than "best efforts," and that good faith is implied in every contract. See Chapter 4.B.1.(a)(i) (Material Misstatements). In practicality, however, these terms are ambiguous without a commonly accepted meaning under the law. Prudent parties should not affix any expectation that one standard dictates a higher level of performance in comparison to the other.

2. Good Faith

"Good Faith" is generally interpreted as requiring the parties to deal openly and honestly with each other and is dependent on the facts of the situation. *Hamlin v. Steward*, 622 N.E.2d 535 (Ind. App. 1993) ("A good faith effort is . . . what a reasonable person would determine is a diligent and honest effort under the same set of facts or circumstances."). "The covenant of good faith and fair dealing does not include the requirement to use best efforts." *Liu v. Beth Israel Med. Ctr.*, 2003 WL 1488081, at *7 (S.D.N.Y. June 26, 2003). Unlike "good faith," which takes on the mantle of dealing fairly with the other party, "best efforts" is generally interpreted as encompassing a performance or diligence standard.

On the other hand, "Bad Faith" has been defined as the "evasion of the spirit of the bargain, lack of diligence and slacking off, willful rendering of imperfect performance, abuse of a power to specify terms, and interference with or failure to cooperate in the other party's performance. *Foseid v. State Bank of Cross Plains*, 541 N.W.2d 203, 213 (Wis. Ct. App. 1995).

The law of most states implies an obligation of good faith in the performance of a party's obligation under an agreement. *See e.g.*, Cal.: *Kransco v. American Empire Surplus Lines Ins., Co.*, 2 P.3d 1 (Cal. 2000); Penn.: *Fraser v. Nationwide Mut. Ins. Co.*, 135 F. Supp.2d 623 (E.D. Pa. 2001); Wis.: *Ubelacker v. Paula Allen Holdings, Inc.*, 464 F. Supp.2d 791 (W.D. Wis. 2006). *See also* Restatement (Second) Contracts § 205 ("Every contract imposes on each party a duty of good faith and fair dealing in its performance and enforcement.").

An implied covenant of good faith, however, does not "prohibit a party from doing what is expressly permitted by the agreement itself," even if it is to the detriment of the other party. *Wolf v. Walt Disney Pictures and Television*, 162 Cal. App. 4th 1107, 1120 (2008).

Although state law may infer an obligation of good faith and fair dealing, it does not necessarily create an independent cause of action. *Compare Automed Technologies, Inc. v. Eller,* 160 F. Supp.2d 915, 925 (N.D. Ill. 2001) (implied duty of good faith "does not create independent duties or give rise to an independent cause of action. It is used more as a canon of construction for interpreting a contract's other terms.") *with MacPhee v. Verizon Communications, Inc.*, 2008 WL 162899, at *7 (S.D.N.Y. Jan. 15, 2008) ("New York courts have recognized a separate cause of action for breach of the covenant of good faith and fair dealing in cases involving efforts by one party to a contract to subvert a contract to itself").

3. Best Efforts

The meaning of "best efforts" has been recognized by many courts as ambiguous. *Martin v. Monumental Life Ins. Co.*, 240 F.3d 223, 233 (3d. Cir 2001); *Carlson Distributing Co. v. Salt Lake Brewing Co.*, 95 P.3d 1171, 1179 (Utah App. 2004) ("'best efforts' is primarily a subjective standard"). Its meaning is generally dependent on the factual circumstances surrounding an agreement. *Carlson Distributing Co.*, 95 P.3d at 1179. At least one court has acknowledged the lack of clarity in distinguishing good faith and best efforts. In *Ashrokan Water Services, Inc. v. New Start LLC,* 111 Misc. 3d 686 (N.Y. 2006), the court stated "[i]t is still unclear . . . the relationship between 'best efforts' and 'good faith' . . . ."

"Best efforts" has been found to require "greater care and diligence than ordinary care and diligence." *Allen v. Williamsburgh Sav. Bank,* 69 N.Y. 314, 322 (1877). It requires more than good faith, which is implied in all contracts, *Kroboth v. Brent,* 215 A.D.2d 813, 814 (3d Dept. 1995), and generally requires diligence and an elevated duty of good faith. *National Data Payment Systems v. Meridian Bank,* 212 F.3d 849, 854 (3d. Cir. 2000). A party is obligated to do the best it can, regardless of the abilities of others. *Carlson Distributing,* 95 P.3d at 1179. The court in *Bloor v. Falstaff Brewing Corp.*, 454 F. Supp. 258 (S.D.N.Y 1978), *aff'd,* 601 F.2d 609 (2d. Cir 1979) held that "best efforts" requires a party to perform "to the extent of its own total capabilities."

Some courts seek to impose a reasonable efforts standard. "Best efforts" requires "a party to make such efforts as are reasonable in the light of that party's ability and the means at its disposal and of the other party's justifiable expectations." *T.S.I. Holdings, Inc. v. Jenkins,* 924 P.2d 1239, 1250 (Kan. 1996). *Kroboth,* 215 A.D.2d at 814 ("'Best efforts' requires that plaintiffs pursue all reasonable methods for" meeting its contractual obligations); *Timberline Dev. v. Kronman,* 263 A.D.2d 175, 178 (1st Dept. 2000) ("The requirement to employ reasonable efforts or 'best efforts,' as it is generally expressed in the performance of contractual obligations is deemed to be implicit in every agreement."); *Permanence Corp. v. Kennametal, Inc.*, 908 F.2d 98 (6th Cir. 1990) (the exercise of due diligence or reasonable efforts).

"Best efforts" does not require a party to ignore its own interests. *First Union National Bank v. Steele Software Sys. Corp.*, 838 A.2d 404 (Md. App. 2003); *Macksey v. Egan,* 633 N.E.2d 408, 414 n.16 (Mass. 1994) ("best efforts" requires a good faith effort to meet a party's obligations with the right to consider its own interests). Further, it does not require success or the "single minded pursuit of the objective." *Mark Technologies v. Utah Resources Intern.*, 147 P.3d 509, 512 (Utah App. 2006). *See also Triple-A Baseball Club Assocs. v. Northeastern Baseball, Inc.*, 832 F.2d 214, 225–26 (1st. Cir. 1987), *cert. denied,* 485 U.S. 935 (1988) ("best efforts" equates to good faith but does not require every conceivable effort).

Given the ambiguity surrounding the concept of best efforts, the parties should avoid adopting a "best efforts" standard unless it is clearly defined. By defining "best efforts," the parties can ensure certainty in the interpretation of their contract. A potential definition is "Reasonable diligence necessary to further the intentions of the parties hereunder."

4. Commercially Reasonable Efforts

A common compromise between the use of a "good faith" standard and a "best effort" standard is the use of a "commercially reasonable efforts" standard. Again, the meaning of "commercially reasonable" is ambiguous unless it is defined. General contract law, however, will impose a reasonableness standard unless it is explicitly disclaimed. *Durham v. Warner Elevator Mfg. Co.*, 139 N.E.2d 10 (Ohio 1956); Restatement (Second) of Torts § 324A (1965).

For a more detailed discussion, see Farnsworth, *On Trying to Keep One's Promises: The Duty of Best Efforts in Contract Law*, 46 U. Pitt. L. Rev. 1 (1984) and Best Efforts Clauses, 236 Com. L. Advisor 1 (Aug. 2007). Randolph Stuart Sergent, *Do Your Best with "Best Efforts": Using Open Contract Terms*, 40 Md. B. J. 49 (March 2007).

CHAPTER **6**

Boilerplate

"Boilerplate" has been defined as "standard clauses lifted from other agreements on file or in form books." E. ALLAN FARNSWORTH, CONTRACTS § 7.1 at 426 (3rd ed. 1999). Many practitioners consider boilerplate those provisions that appear at the end of an agreement. Boilerplate has assumed increasing importance, such that at least one book has been written on the subject, and the University of Michigan Law School held a symposium on boilerplate, "Boilerplate: Foundations of Market Contracts Symposium" at the University of Michigan Law School September 23–24, 2005. *See* 104 MICH. L. REV. (March 2006). *See, e.g.*, STARK, NEGOTIATING AND DRAFTING CONTRACT BOILERPLATE (2003).

Practitioners often pay scant attention to these boilerplate clauses. Subtle nuances in an agreement's boilerplate, however, can have important and unrealized ramifications on the parties. *See* Van Puymbrouck and Zinski, *When Boilerplate Gets Hot*, BUS. L TODAY 16 (Nov./Dec. 2006) at 43; Ahdieh, *The Strategy of Boilerplate*, 104 MICH. L. REV. 1033 (2006). Although parties never enter into an agreement with the expectation of litigation, a skilled lawyer can significantly reduce its client's risk in the event of litigation through thoughtful drafting.

The discussion set forth in this chapter is intended to guide readers through the thought process they should undertake when reviewing and drafting the "boilerplate" provisions of an agreement.

A. Recitals and Headings (§ 53)

1. *Recitals*

The recitals of an agreement are often viewed as a perfunctory necessity of little value. While recitals are not mandatory, they can be very important. The recitals give the parties the opportunity to set forth their respective intents for entering into the agreement. A properly drafted recital may provide a subtle advantage to a party in the event of a dispute. In general, the recitals are not considered to be a substantive part of the contract, but rather they describe the parties' purposes or objectives and are used in the interpretation and construction of the contract. *Jones v. City of Paducah*, 142 S.W.2d 365, 367 (Ky. 1940).

While each party should be free to set forth their individual intent, licensors should reject any attempt by the licensees to insert overbroad, self-serving statements designed to place the licensor at a significant disadvantage in the event of litigation. Licensors should not agree to statements of fact that essentially serve as additional representations and warranties, such as the following:

> **Whereas** Licensor is the world leader in the implementation of Enterprise Resource Planning Systems (ERP). Whereas Licensor has the expertise and experienced employees to install and support a worldwide, world-class ERP system. Whereas Licensee has relied on Licensor's skill in selecting Licensor to implement the system.

The Licensor should be especially concerned in those states where recitals involving a statement of fact are considered to be conclusive evidence of the facts stated. *See, e.g., Detroit Grand Park Corp. v. Turner,* 25 N.W.2d 184 (Mich. 1946).

A prudent licensor will ensure that the agreement states that the recitals do not expand the licensor's obligations under the agreement beyond those set forth in the body of the agreement. If the licensee insists on including self-serving recitals, the licensor should insert a recital stating it is the parties' intent that the licensor make a reasonable profit and that the recitals only be looked to in the event of an ambiguity within the agreement.

2. *Headings (§ 53)*

Section headings can also have importance. At least one court has held that a contractual provision containing a warranty disclaimer—set forth under a misleading section heading—was void. *See Blankenship v. Northtown Ford, Inc.,* 420 N.E.2d 167 (Ill. App. 1981). As such, the parties should ensure that each section heading clearly reflects the provision it contains and include language that clearly indicates the section headings are for convenience of reference only and are not intended to have any substantive significance.

Similarly, the parties should use caution in "defining" the parties and other entities in the agreement. A party may later claim that such short hand definition modified the parties' intent or could otherwise have unintended consequences. *See, e.g., Roanoke Engineering Sales Company, Inc. v. Rosenbaum,* 290 S.E.2d 882, 884 (Va. 1982) (defendant, who was an officer and director of plaintiff corporation, claimed use of the term "Employee" to identify defendant in his employment agreement and limited the applicability of his non-compete obligations.)

B. Definitions (§ 1 and Form 23.K.1)

The "Definitions" section and the definitions contained therein are one of the most important but overlooked parts of an agreement. Creating a definition specific to a contemplated transaction allows the parties to avoid subjecting themselves to the "ordinary" meaning of the word in question as determined by a third party. A carefully drafted definition may limit or even shift liability. The definitions set forth § 1 and in Form 23.K.1 are no exception. Some have been drafted to benefit the licensor and some the customer. A skilled lawyer must read each definition carefully to ensure that it does not place the lawyer's client at a disadvantage. Further, each definition must be read in light of the contemplated transaction as the meaning of each definition may vary with each transaction. Defined terms evolve to recognize the changes in the technology industry. For example, the definition of "source code" used 25 years ago would not necessarily protect the licensee's interests today, as it would likely fail to encompass new technologies such as html, web browsers, and so on.

The definitions set forth in Form 23.K.1 serve as examples of how a lawyer should seek to draft definitions to benefit its clients. Further, a review of these definitions may raise issues not initially contemplated by a party or that may have been overlooked. Form 23.K.1 should serve as a starting point in creating or reviewing a definition. The parties should resist the temptation to utilize a form definition from a prior transaction and instead craft definitions that capture the unique nature of the transaction they are negotiating.

C. Insurance (§ 38)

1. General Liability Insurance

The allocation of contractual risk can be achieved through a number of mechanisms, including the assignment of contractual responsibilities, indemnification, limitations of liability and the use of insurance. Insurance is a means to transfer or reduce financial risk, as it allows a third party to assume the risk that otherwise would be borne by one of the contractual parties.

(a) Types of Insurance

Most licensees seek to require the licensor to purchase minimum amounts of insurance. Usually, the licensor is required to carry the following coverage:

- General (public) liability;
- Automobile liability, which covers third party bodily injury and property damage;
- Workers' compensation/employer's liability, which covers work related injuries to the licensor's employees;
- Umbrella/excess insurance, which provide higher limits above the primary limits for general and automobile liability insurance;
- Crime (employee dishonesty insurance) for dishonest acts of employees, including computer fraud, theft of money or property, including the client property.
- Professional liability insurance (errors & omissions) to respond to claims for wrongful acts arising out of professional services. Most professional liability policies are "claims-made" policies which require that a claim be reported during the current policy period.
- "All risk" property insurance, which covers a licensor's property and the property of clients in a licensor's custody.

(b) Additional Insureds

During the term of the agreement, many licensees seek to be named as an "additional insured" on the policies the licensor is required to maintain. The licensor should resist adding the licensee as an additional insured to its errors and omissions insurance unless pressured by the licensee. A customer can be named as an additional insured under the licensor's general, umbrella and automobile liability insurance policies, but cannot be named under the licensor's workers compensation policy, as the licensor's employees are not employed by the licensee. Further, the customer cannot be an additional insured under the licensor's professional liability policy, as the customer is the party bringing the claim.

A customer should not be a "named insured" or "additional named insured." A named insured can order changes to the policy, is responsible for payment of policy premiums and deductibles, and is obligated to perform certain duties, such as making representations in application, reporting and cooperating with claims, maintaining records, and allowing audits. While the terms are used interchangeably throughout the insurance industry since there is no industry-wide accepted standard, licensors prefer to use "additional insured" for consistency in its contracting practices.

The licensee may be a loss payee under a property insurance policy if the policy holder has custody of the licensee's property. Usually, the governing insurance policy requires the policy holder to report the location and value of the licensee's property in its possession. A party can also be a loss payee under a crime insurance policy if the policy holder's employees hold positions where the client's property could be stolen.

(c) Licensor Obligations

The licensee should also seek to contractually require the licensor to notify the licensee prior to making any material changes in the licensor's coverages or terminating or cancelling any policy. While these demands are reasonable, the licensor should carefully consider any additional demands that may impact the licensor's ability to operate its business in a prudent manner.

Some licensees seek to dictate in detail the parameters of the licensor's insurance coverages, including the type of coverages carried, the dollar amount of such coverages, the credit rating and financial size of the carrier through which the insurance is purchased, as well as requiring the chosen carrier to be licensed in a particular state. Licensors should not allow the licensee to select the insurer to provide the required coverages or require that the licensor's insurer be licensed to do business in a particular state as long as the insurer is able to pay any claims submitted on the licensee's behalf and is legally authorized to do business in the state in question. Further, licensors should be hesitant to allow the licensee to establish a minimum credit rating that the insurer must maintain.

Prudent licensees should require the licensor to submit proof of insurance prior to execution of the license agreement and again prior to the execution of any statement of work to ensure the licensor has obtained the required insurance and has maintained the policy in good stead. Licensors should not provide the licensee with copies of its insurance policies, only certificates of insurance, as the insurance policies are the proprietary information of the licensor. The licensee has no need to see the actual policies. Most policies contain similar standard language, thus the licensor can easily provide a summary of the policy's principal terms in lieu of providing the licensee with a copy of the actual policy. To avoid any unintended cap on its ability to recover from a licensor, licensees should make sure the license agreement clearly states that the licensee's recovery is not limited by the amount of the licensor's insurance. (§ 38)

The licensee should require the licensor to maintain the agreed upon insurance beyond the termination of the contract. This requirement is inapplicable to "occurrence" policies such as general liability insurance, but is applicable for "claims made" policies such as errors and omissions insurance.

(d) Coverage

Failure to maintain any required insurance coverages should not be treated as a material breach of the agreement, as the licensee has not suffered an actual loss from the failure to maintain such coverages. From the licensee's perspective, it is faced with the issue of how to enforce its rights if the licensor's failure to comply does not constitute a material breach. Licensors will argue that the licensee is not at risk as long as the licensor has a net worth sufficient to satisfy any claim. In essence, the licensor is self-insuring and the breach should be treated as an immaterial breach. The licensee is not prejudiced and is essentially in the same position as if the licensor were contractually allowed to self-insure.

Occasionally, a licensee will seek the right to purchase the contractually required coverages and pass on the cost to the licensor or offset the cost of any such premiums against money owed to the licensor. It is unlikely that the licensee would be able to purchase insurance to cover the licensor's nonperformance. What insurance company would be willing to insure an unrelated third party's performance? The licensee would be unable to purchase worker's compensation insurance, as the employees in question would not be employed by the licensee. The licensee would also be unable to purchase professional liability insurance for the licensor's performance. Further, to the extent the licensee is able to obtain the desired insurance, this right to "cover" may create a financial risk to the licensor, as the licensee may not act in the licensor's best interest financially. The licensor may mitigate this risk by limiting the licensee to purchasing such insurance from a well respected broker representing a highly rated insurance company or requiring the licensee to obtain three quotes and accepting the lowest price.

(e) Self Insurance

Many large companies self-insure a certain level of their risk. If a licensor seeks to negate any requirement to maintain a certain insurance coverage because it self-insures, the licensee should make sure it understands the nature of the licensor's self-insurance and the licensor's ability to pay any claim. Does the licensor self-insure all of its risk, only a certain portion, or only a certain type of risk? For example, the licensor may self-insure up to $10 million of liability and purchase third party insurance for any liability above that amount, or it may only self-insure for its automobile coverage.

Only by thoroughly understanding the nature and limits of the licensor's coverages will the licensee be able to quantify the licensee's risks.

(f) Subcontractors

The licensee should make sure the licensor flows down all insurance requirements to its subcontractors to insure the licensee is protected. A licensor should not agree to add it subcontractors to its own policies and should not name its subcontractors as additional insured.

(g) Indemnity

A party should not indemnify the client for injuries to its own employees caused by the client's negligence. The licensor most likely pays for no fault workers compensation, and the licensor pays the general liability claim for the client. In essence, the licensor is paying twice.

(h) Subrogation

A waiver of subrogation is a waiver of the common law right to recover damages from a responsible party. Waivers of subrogation can apply to general and automobile liability, workers compensation, crime and property insurance. The result is that a party is responsible for its own loss and is usually extended to the party's insurers. Any waiver should be reciprocal.

2. *Intellectual Property Infringement Claims*

Generally, a licensor's comprehensive or commercial general liability ("GCL") policy includes coverage for "advertising injuries." A claim for intellectual property infringement may fall under the coverage for advertising injury. *See e.g., Hyundai Motor America v. National Union Fire Insurance*, 600 F.3d 1092 (9th Cir. 2010) (insurer must indemnify patent infringement claim as advertising injury).

A prudent licensor should carefully evaluate its CGL policy and errors and omissions policy to ascertain whether its existing policy will provide coverage in the event of a claim of intellectual property infringement. Insured should carefully examine the definition of a "claim" under its policies to ensure the definition is broad enough to encompass any potential risks or factual circumstances that may arise. Policies will be read strictly. *See e.g., FirePond Liquidating Trust v. Vigilant Insurance Co.*, 2007 W.L. 2695642 (D. Minn. Sept. 11, 2007) (information errors and omission policy does not cover contract dispute). Given the increasing costs to defend such claims, many insurers are modifying their policies to exclude coverage for claims related to intellectual property, advertising and internet related claims. To the extent the insured lacks the breath of coverage it desires, it may want to obtain specialized insurance for internet and cyberspace related claims.

In the event of a claim, a party should carefully read its policy and promptly place its carrier on notice. The carrier is likely responsible for paying not only any award entered against the insured, but also the cost of defense.

For a more detailed discussion of insurance coverage for claims of intellectual property insurance, see Kenneth W. Brothers, Edward A. Meilman, Bradley J. Olson, and Ranga Sourirajan, *Coverage for IP-Related Risks*, http://www.dicksteinshapiro.com/ipnewsfall2008/coverage/ (Last viewed September 15, 2010).

D. Force Majeure (§ 33)

Force majeure clauses are intended to excuse a party's performance in the event the party's ability to perform is thwarted by unforeseen events outside of its control, such as an act of God. Events that are reasonably foreseeable do not constitute an event of force majeure and do not excuse performance. *See URI Cogeneration Partners, L.P. v. Board of Governors for Higher Educ.*, 915 F. Supp. 1267 (D. RI. 1996); *Watson Labs., Inc. v. Rhone-Poulenc Rorer, Inc.*, 178 F. Supp. 2d 1099 (C.D. Cal. 2001). Force majeure clauses are narrowly construed. *Kel Kim Corp. v. Central Markets, Inc.*, 519 N.E. 2d, 295 (N.Y. 1987). To invoke the protections of a force majeure clause, the event must be beyond a party's control and not due to its own fault or negligence. *Gulf Oil Corp. v. Federal Energy Regulatory Commission*, 706 F.2d 444 (3d Cir. 1983), cert. denied 464 U.S. 1038 (1984). Because of these limitations, companies carry business interruption insurance even though their injuries may arise from an act of God such as a flood.

For example, a H1N1 pandemic may not qualify as an event of force majeure, depending on the extent of the pandemic. The impact of the HIN1 virus has been publicly discussed for months, so no one should be surprised by an outbreak in the workplace. In the event of an H1N1 outbreak, a party's ability to successfully invoke a contract's force majeure clause would depend on the extent of the outbreak. For example, if 25 percent of the work force were ill, a party would be unlikely to prevail. If 75 percent were ill, a party would have a stronger argument. Of course, a court would closely examine a party's efforts to mitigate the effects of any foreseeable event in reaching a decision.

Both parties should pay careful attention to a contract's force majeure clause as a typical clause sets forth a laundry list of events whose occurrence are deemed to constitute an event of force majeure. Each party should carefully review such list to ensure that each event is truly an event of force majeure and is not simply an effort to expand a party's ability to limit its risk and avoid performance. Some courts will only excuse performance to the extent an event is set forth in an agreement's force majeure clause. *Kel Kim Corp. v. Central Markets, Inc.*, 519 N.E. 2d, 295, 296 (N.Y. 1987). A more prudent approach is to utilize general language referencing acts of God. See §33. Of course, this ambiguity itself may lead to a dispute.

For the most part, such clauses excuse only the licensor's performance, as usually the licensee's only affirmative obligation is to pay the license fee. Nonetheless, the licensee should insist on making any such clause mutual.

Generally, a party's performance is excused only from those obligations impacted by an event of force majeure. *Idaho Power Co. v. Cogeneration, Inc.*, 9 P.3d 1204 (Idaho 2000. An event of force majeure does not terminate an agreement but rather excuses a party's performance during the period the event of force majeure is in existence. *Commonwealth Edison Co. v. Allied-Gen Nuclear Servs.*, 731 F. Supp. 850 (N.D. Ill. 1990). A party seeking to invoke the protection of a force majeure clause can do so only after using its skill, diligence and good faith to perform. *Oosten v. Hay Haulers Dairy Employees and Helpers Union*, 291 P.2d 17, 20-21 (Cal. 1955); Corbin on Contracts § 1342. Both parties should insist on having the right of termination if the event of force majeure continues for a set period of time. While this right to terminate may be a hollow right, if every vendor is affected by same the event of force majeure, it could be a significant benefit to the licensee if a third party could deliver the contracted for software or services. From the licensor's perspective, the licensor does not want to keep a project fully staffed while it waits for the event of force majeure to abate. If the licensor is unable to terminate its performance after a set period, it may have to staff a project for which it will not be compensated. The parties should also address whether an event of force majeure that continues for a set period of time triggers the release any source code escrow.

The licensee should give careful consideration to the wording of any clause as an overly broad force majeure clause could undercut any service level agreements or performance obligations of the licensor. Additionally, the licensee should include an exclusion of the licensor's disaster recovery obligations from the force majeure provision. At the same time, the licensor should seek to ensure that the clause is not so narrowly drawn as to restrict the licensor's ability to excuse performance for conditions beyond its control.

For example, many licensees are hesitant to include labor strife or strikes within the list of events constituting an event of force majeure as theoretically they are within the control of the respective employer. Further, the nonperformance of the licensor's subcontractors should also not be considered an event of force majeure. Thus, a prudent licensee should specifically state that the failure of a licensor's subcontractors to perform shall not excuse the licensor's performance. One way to address this issue is to draft the agreement's force majeure clause in such a way that it addresses the different obligations of the licensor. Thus, a licensor may be excused from performing one aspect of a contract but not another upon the occurrence of the same event.

The parties should also definitively state that a change in the economic conditions underlying a contract's performance does not constitute an event of force majeure. While this position is clearly supported in the case law, it does not hurt to include an affirmative statement to this effect in the contract. *U.S. v. Panhandle Eastern Corp.*, 693 F. Supp. 88, 98 (D. Del. 1988) ("economic hardship due to market fluctuations in the natural gas industry did not constitute a force majeure event."); *Chainworks, Inc. v. Webco Indus.*, Inc., 2006 WL 1521946 (W.D. Mich. May 31, 2006).

To the extent a licensor claims it is excused from performance by an event of force majeure, a customer who has paid for undelivered services may be entitled to recover any monies paid to the licensor under the theory of *quantum meruit*. *See Facto v. Pantagis*, 915 A.2d 59 (N.J. Super 2007) (plaintiff entitled to recover monies paid for event cancelled by force majeure).

For a more detailed discussion of the doctrine of force majeure, see Klein & Glazer, *The Lowly Force Majeure: Why It Shouldn't Be Neglected*, START-UP & EMERGING COMPANIES 5 (Nov. 2000).

Commercial impracticality is a concept arising under the UCC and the Restatement (Second) of Contracts closely related to the doctrine of force majeure that applies in the event a party's performance is thwarted by events outside its control that was not anticipated by the parties. *See* UCC § 2-615; RESTATEMENT (SECOND) CONTRACTS § 261. For a more detailed discussion including the doctrine of commercial impracticality, see *Commercial Impracticality as an Excuse for Contract Performance*, 38 THE LAW. BRIEF 1 (Sept. 15, 2008); H. Ward Classen, *Judicial Intervention in Contractual Relationships Under the Uniform Commercial Code and Common Law*, 42 S.C. L. REV. 379 (1991).

E. Public Disclosures and References (§§ 44, 50)

1. Public Disclosures (§ 44)

Often the licensee seeks to limit the licensor's right to publicize the fact that the licensee is a customer. The reason for doing so may stem from an unwillingness to appear to endorse the licensor's product, especially when it is unknown at the time of contract signature that the software implementation will be successful. Further, the licensee's trademarks and service marks are valuable assets that require a written license to fully protect and maintain their value.

On the other hand, the licensor may be required to disclose the existence of the contract if it is a publicly held company. As a result, the parties should carefully negotiate the wording of any publicity clause. The licensee may allow the licensor to publicize the existence of the contract, only to the extent necessary to satisfy any applicable securities laws or retain the right to approve any press release or use of the licensee's marks. Any consent granted by the license should address all applicable uses of the licensee's mark. For example, the agreed upon language should address not only written press releases and filings, but also the use of the licensee's name and marks on websites, product brochures, public speeches, and trade shows.

The vendor should ensure that it obtains the approvals and licenses necessary to use the customer's name and marks. The failure to do so may result in the vendor's infringement of the customer's trademarks and service marks. To avoid any potential problems, some customers prohibit the vendor from disclosing, in any manner, that the customer has a relationship with the vendor. The vendor should be careful, however, to ensure that it has the right to disclose whatever information is necessary to comply with any applicable laws or regulatory obligations, such as the disclosure obligations placed upon publicly held companies.

To avoid uncertainty, the parties should negotiate a joint press release prior to the execution of the agreement and attach it as an exhibit to the license. This will allow the parties to issue the press release simultaneously with the execution of the license and to surface any wording issues prior to the execution of the license.

2. *References (§ 50)*

Potential customers should ask the vendor for a list of all of the vendor's customers and seek the right to contact them to discuss their level of satisfaction with the vendor. Vendors will usually provide a potential customer with a vetted list of loyal customers who can be counted upon to provide excellent references. Discussions with these customers provide little value to the potential customer. The potential customer should seek to discuss the vendor's capabilities with a variety of customers, including disgruntled customers, to obtain a complete assessment of the vendor's capabilities.

Some customers require the vendor to use them as a reference on all future bids. The reasoning for doing so is that the vendor will likely make sure the customer is satisfied if it is required to use the customer as a reference. While this philosophy is rare, it does create incentive to produce the customer's deliverables on time and on budget. To enforce this obligation, some customers require a vendor to pay the customer a fee each time the vendor fails to use the customer as a reference. Vendors should resist including this language in their agreement as it grants the customer undue leverage.

F. Waiver (§ 31)

All agreements should contain a waiver clause that provides that a party's forbearance in enforcing a term of an agreement does not prohibit the party from enforcing it in the future. The intent is to avoid a claim by one party that the other's actions or inactions waived that party's right to enforce a particular term of the agreement. *See Klipsch, Inc. v. WWR Technology, Inc.*, 127 F.3d 729 (8th Cir. 1997); *S.H.V.C. v. Roy*, 450 A.2d 351 (Conn. 1982).

G. Waiver of Right to Jury Trial (§ 32)

With the increase in large jury awards that often include a significant component of punitive damages, many licensors seek to include jury trial waivers in their license agreements. Many licensors believe that juries are incapable of understanding complex software/copyright matters and that judges are less likely to award punitive damages. Further, jurors may be influenced by the size of the licensee and its relationship with the community, as well as the number of people the licensee employs in the geographic area. The concern of punitive damages may be overemphasized, as punitive damages are only rarely awarded in contract disputes. Further, the risk of any award of punitive damages can be mitigated by disclaiming such damages in the agreement's limitation of liability clause. See, e.g., § 17.1 and Chapter 4.B.3(b).

Licensees should carefully consider waiving their right to a jury trial. Many licensees would prefer to utilize some form of alternative dispute resolution before waiving their right to a jury trial. Both parties should avoid the temptation to believe they can "shop" for a good judge. An exception may be the recent efforts undertaken by some states to create specialized business and/or technology courts to hear business/technology disputes in the belief such courts will make their states a more attractive place for businesses to locate. *See* Robert L. Haig, *New York's New Business Court*, 26 Colorado Law. 65 (May 1997). *See also* http://www.courts.state.md.us/businesstech (Maryland) (Last viewed September 15, 2010); http://www.ncbusinesscourt.net/final%20 rules.htm (North Carolina) (Last viewed September 15, 2010).

The validity of pre-litigation jury waiver clauses is uncertain, as at least two states have held that pre-litigation contractual jury waiver clauses are unenforceable. *See, e.g.*, *Bank South N.A. v. Howard*, 444 S.E.2d 799 (Ga. 1994). The California Supreme Court found that a contractual agreement to waive the right to a jury trial, entered into prior to any dispute between the contracting parties, is unenforceable under the California Constitution and Section 631 of the California Code of Civil Procedure. *Grafton Partners LP v. Superior Court*, 88 P.3d 24 (2004), *aff'd* 116 P.3d 479 (Cal. 2005).

Further, to limit any claim of unconscionability, the parties should make any waiver conspicuous and print such waiver in capital letters.

For a general discussion, see McGuire & Belzberg, *Are Jury Trial Waivers Coming of Age?*, 38 Md. B.J. 25 (Nov./Dec. 2005).

H. Governing Law and Venue (§ 28)

1. Governing Law

(a) In General

Copyright disputes are usually adjudicated under state law, subject to the provisions of federal copyright law. Federal law will govern the interpretation of a license where state law conflicts with federal copyright law and policy. *S.O.S., Inc. v. Payday, Inc.*, 886 F.2d 1081, 1088 (9th Cir. 1989). As such, a choice of the law of a particular state may not have a material impact on those disputes involving copyright, patent and other intellectual property rights as opposed to contractual disputes. In recognition of this fact, many savvy practitioners preface their choice of law provision with "Except where governed by federal law . . . ."

Although most parties instinctively seek be governed by the laws and venue of their own jurisdiction, the parties should carefully consider the benefits offered through the election of the governing laws of other jurisdictions. To be enforceable, however, many states require a nexus between the agreement and the choice of law. *See, e.g.*, *Airgo, Inc. v. Horizon Cargo Transport, Inc.*, 670 P.2d 1277 (Haw. 1983); *Navasota Resources Ltd. v. Heep Petroleum, Inc.*, 212 S.W.3d 462 (Tex. App. 2006); Restatement (Second) Conflicts of Laws § 187 (1) (1971).

In selecting the governing law, the parties should seek the existence of a well-developed body of law relating to software licensing and evaluate the state's other laws, such as whether the state is a contributory or comparative negligence state. A well-developed body of law increases the likelihood of a predictable outcome and in turn reduces litigation costs while increasing the likelihood of settlement. Similarly, some states allow contracting parties to require arbitration and contractually prohibit class action suits, while other states limit their ability to do so. *See Parrish v. Cingular Wireless, LLC*, 2005 WL 2420719 (Cal. App. Oct. 3, 2005), *cert denied*, 547 U.S. 1188 (2006) (arbitration agreement unconscionable because its class action waiver operated as an exculpatory clause under California law); *Riensche v. Cingular Wireless*, 2006 WL 3827477 (W.D. Wash. Dec 27, 2007) (court determined that the prohibition against class actions was "unconscionable" and denied the defendant's motion to compel arbitration); *Vasquez-Lopez v. Beneficial Oregon, Inc.* 153 P.3d 940 (Ore. 2007) (prohibition on class actions, in part, rendered the otherwise mandatory arbitration agreement unenforceable).

The parties should also consider the impact of the governing law on all aspects of their agreement beyond licensing. For example, some license agreements include non-solicitation restrictions and non-competition covenants. Parties seeking to enforce non-compete agreements should avoid the laws of California and Georgia, which have held non-compete agreements to be void. California: West's Ann. Cal. Bus. & Prof. Code § 16600 (2007); Georgia: *Jenkins Brick Company v. Bremer*, 321 F.3d 1366, 1369 (11th Cir. 2003) ("Georgia's courts rarely uphold blanket non-compete agreements"). The parties should be cognizant of the fact that some states such as Georgia will apply Georgia law to certain aspects of an agreement, such as a covenant of non-competition, even if the parties have contractually agreed to the laws of another state. *See Nasco, Inc. v. Gimbert*, 238 S.E.2d 368, 369 (Ga. 1977).

Many licensors seek to avoid Texas law, as it has strong consumer protection laws and prohibits reducing the statute of limitations to less than two years, while favored jurisdictions include New York, which generally benefits licensors. *See, e.g., Metropolitan Life Insurance Company v. Noble Lowndes International, Inc.*, 643 N.E.2d 504 (N.Y. 1994) (limitation of liability valid when vendor intentionally fails to perform for its own economic self-interest); *Gruet v. Care Free—Housing Division of Kennschl Enterprises, Inc.*, 759 N.Y.S.2d 276 (2003) (court upheld contract reducing statute of limitations to one year).

For entities licensing their software to consumers, the laws of some states may allow the licensor to contractually prohibit class action lawsuits or to indirectly do so by requiring the parties to resolve all disputes through arbitration. Alabama, Alaska, Georgia, Kentucky, Louisiana, Mississippi, Montana and Virginia do not permit consumers to assert a class action to enforce their rights. *See* Ala. Code §8-19-10(a)(1); Alaska Stat. §45.50.531(a); Ga. Code Ann. §10-1-399(a); Ky. Rev. Stat. Ann. §367.170; La. Rev. Stat. Ann. §51:1409(A); Miss. Code Ann. §75-24-15(4); Mont. Code Ann. §30-14-133(1); Va. Code Ann. §59.1-204(A). The courts are divided as to the legality of class action exclusions, but a court's willingness to uphold an exclusion may make the laws of a particular state more attractive. *See Johnson v. West Suburban Bank*, 225 F.3d 366 (3d Cir. 2000) (arbitration clause in an agreement enforceable even though it may exclude class action); *Randolph. v. Green Tree Financial Corp.*, 244 F.3d 814 (11th Cir. 2001) (contractual provision requiring arbitration enforceable even if it precludes class actions); *Pick v. Discover Financial Service Corp.*, 2001 WL 1180278 (D. Del. Sept. 28, 2001) (arbitration clauses not unconscionable because they exclude class actions).

(b) Trade Secrets (§ 28.1.B)

Occasionally, the licensor is flexible as to the choice of governing law but wants to ensure that the law of a particular state governs any trade secret dispute. Given the licensor's trade secrets/intellectual property is its greatest asset; it is understandable that the licensor wants certainty especially when some states have not enacted the Uniform Trade Secrets Act (UTSA). See Chapter 3.A.2.(b) for a detailed discussion of the UTSA and § 28.1.B for model language addressing this issue.

(c) Uniform Computer Information Transactions Act (UCITA)

If the license is governed by the laws of Virginia or Maryland, the parties need to consider whether to opt out of the Uniform Computer Information Transactions Act, which has been adopted by both states. Proponents of UCITA believe it brings certainty to software licensing transactions, while others believe UCITA is overly pro-licensor. Many parties opt out of UCITA because there are very few court decisions based on UCITA, creating an air of uncertainty. See Chapter 11.B for a more detailed discussion of UCITA and § 28.2 for a UCITA disclaimer.

If the parties elect Maryland or Virginia law but opt out of UCITA, a question arises as to what law governs the transaction. The Maryland and Virginia legislatures superseded existing state laws to enact their respective versions of UCITA. By opting out of UCITA, it is unclear how the contract will be interpreted under Maryland or Virginia law. Thus, it is best to select a governing law other than Maryland or Virginia rather than choosing to opt out of UCITA and retaining Maryland or Virginia as governing law.

(d) International Considerations/UN Convention on Contracts for the International Sale of Goods

Internationally, it is imperative to utilize the laws of the United States, the United Kingdom, Sweden, or other western countries, as most third world countries do not have well-developed software laws or case law for software licensing. If the license is governed by the laws of a country other than the United States, the parties may want to consider binding arbitration as an alternative. Further, the parties should consider opting out of the United Nations Convention on Contracts for the International Sale of Goods ("UN Convention").

If the license is between parties domiciled in two different countries, and both countries are signatories to the UN Convention, the convention automatically applies unless the parties opt out. UN Convention, Article 1. Simply selecting the law of a particular state is not enough to opt out of the convention. *See BP Oil Int'l, Ltd v. Empresa Estatal Petroleos de Ecuador*, 332 F.3d 333, 337 (5th Cir. 2003). The parties must specifically state that they are opting out of the convention. *See Modius, Inc. v.*

PsiNaptic, Inc., 2006 WL 1156390, at *5 (N.D. Cal. May 2, 2006). *But see American Biophysics Corp. v. Dubois Marine Specialties*, 411 F. Supp.2d 61 (D. R.I. 2006) (UN Convention did not apply to agreement with forum selection clause that contained mandatory venue language). Many parties opt out believing case law based on the UN Convention is not well developed, creating uncertainty. As a federal treaty, the UN Convention preempts any application of the UCC or other applicable law. *De Geofroy v. Riggs*, 133 U.S. 258 (1890).

See http://www.cisg.law.pace.edu for a discussion of the UN Convention and a list of member countries. See also § 28.2 for model language opting out of the Convention. For a more detailed discussion of the UN Convention, see Chapter 12.G.

2. *Venue*

Venue is equally important as governing law because it is in both parties' interest to have the case decided by a sophisticated, knowledgeable trier of facts and/or jury. Further, for smaller parties the location of any action or claim can significantly increase the cost of litigation or dispute resolution.

Forum selection clauses "are prima facie valid" and will be enforced unless they are found to be "unreasonable under the circumstances." *The Bremen v. Zapata Off Shore Co.*, 407 U.S. 1 (1972). A forum selection agreement will be honored or enforced by a court "so long as they are procured freely and voluntarily, with the place chosen having some logical nexus to one of the parties or the dispute. . . ." *America Online, Inc. v. Superior Court*, 108 Cal. Rptr. 2d 699, 707 (2001); *See also*, *AC Controls Co. v. Pomeroy Computer Resources, Inc.*, 284 F. Supp.2d 357 (W.D.N.C. 2003) (forum selection clause enforceable unless it is unreasonable).

The party opposed to the forum bears the burden to show why the forum selection clause should not be enforced. *George Jumara and Evangelina Jumara v. State Farm, Inc. Co.*, 55 F.3d 873, 880 (3d Cir. 1995).

The forum selection clause does not need to include the words "sole" or "exclusive" for a court to construe the clause as mandatory. *Scotland Memorial Hospital, Inc. v. Integrated Informatics, Inc.*, 2003 WL 151852 (M.D. N.C. 2003) ("specific reference to the venue indicates mandatory language"). To avoid any potential dispute, the parties should include a statement of the venue and affirmative consent of the stated jurisdiction. The parties should also include such words as "sole" or "exclusive" to further limit potential disputes over the enforceability of such clauses, and the contractual language should state that the forum selection clause applies to "any dispute arising out of or related to the agreement," which would include tort as well as contract claims. *See Terra International, Inc. v. Mississippi Chemical Corp.*, 922 F. Supp. 1334 (N.D. Iowa 1996).

To settle any dispute as to the forum prior to entering into a contract, some licensors and licensees include language in their license agreements stating that the forum will be the licensor's choice if the licensee elects to arbitrate or litigate, and that the forum will be the licensee's choice if the licensor elects to bring an action. The benefit is that such language serves to discourage parties from bringing claims.

This solution is not viable for the choice of governing law as there must be one pre-agreed governing law to interpret the license agreement prior to any action being commenced. If the parties agree on a mandatory venue, the respective contract language should state that the chosen venue is the "exclusive" venue to avoid any later claim that the language is permissive and not exclusive. In adopting this approach, the parties must ensure that the language is tightly drafted and clearly sets forth the selected venue. *See Micro Focus v. Bell Canada*, 686 F. Supp.2d 564 (D. Md. 2010) (court declined to enforce "non-sensical" forum selection clause).

Interestingly, it is not uncommon for parties to agree to a "non-exclusive" jurisdiction when the parties cannot agree on an exclusive jurisdiction. From the vendor's perspective, agreeing on a non-exclusive jurisdiction allows the vendor to bring an action in the stated jurisdiction while providing the customer a venue the vendor will accept without a fight, should the customer initiate legal action. This reasoning, in essence, causes a party to waive any claim that the stated non-exclusive jurisdiction is improper. At the same time, it provides a party a semblance of flexibility, while reserving the right to challenge any other jurisdiction. Set forth below is model language reflecting this principle.

> Customer agrees to the non-exclusive (emphasis added) jurisdiction of the courts of Baltimore County, Maryland for any action or proceeding arising out of or in relation to this Agreement.

Internationally, an exclusive forum selection clause is also important as many local courts have a bias against foreign licensors and do not always enjoy the same level of competency as the judiciary in the United States.

For a general discussion and sample clauses, see Vizy, *Forum Selection Clauses*, 219 Com. L. Adv. (Nov. 2006) and Kobayashi & Ribstein, *Uniformity, Choice of Law and Software Sales*, 8 Geo. Mason L. Rev. 261 (1999) (comparing the choice of law provisions under the UCC, UCITA, and common law).

I. Notices (§ 52)

Notice provisions are not usually highly negotiated but, as electronic communication becomes more prevalent and accepted, the parties should carefully consider how "notice" should be delivered. Most notice provisions provide for delivery by registered mail or over-night courier. An increasing number provide for notice through facsimile and email.

Facsimile notices should be discouraged as there are significant risks. The notice may be received, picked up by an employee other than the recipient, and not delivered to the recipient. Further, the notice may be retained in the machine's memory due to a lack of paper or other problem and never printed out or inadvertently deleted. In each of these instances, the notice could be contractually satisfied and the cure period started without the intended recipient ever realizing it. Finally, privacy issues create additional concerns as a breach notice may be read by any employee passing by the fax, creating a confidentiality issue.

Emails are equally problematic. The receiving party's spam filter may block the email after its receipt without ever notifying the receiving or sending party. If the email's heading does not clearly reflect its content, the email may be deleted by the receiving party. Further, the receiving party may leave the company or be assigned a new email address preventing receipt of the message.

At a minimum, notice should be effective upon receipt, and the sending party should be obligated to send copies to at least two other individuals, at least one of which should be outside of the receiving party (i.e., their lawyer). Further, if notice is sent electronically, a written confirmation copy should also be sent. This will hopefully ensure the notice will be received.

Despite the strongest precautions, disputes will arise. At least one court has found that when parties identify the mode of notification, they are indicating an intention to consider the communication "received" when the notice is dispatched in accordance with such requirement. *United States v. Continental Casualty Co.*, 245 F. Supp. 871, 873 (E.D. La. 1965). Similarly, a Maryland court has found that notice was effective upon its mailing. *Grubbs v. Prince George's County*, 297 A.2d 754 (Md. 1972). As such, the parties should include language that notice is effective only upon receipt.

J. Third Party Beneficiaries (§ 40)

The Restatement (Second) of Contracts and common law recognizes two types of third party beneficiaries: incidental third party beneficiaries and intended third party beneficiaries. *See e.g.*, RESTATEMENT (SECOND) OF CONTRACTS §302; *F. O. Bailey Co., Inc. v. Ledgewood, Inc.*, 603 A.2d 466, 468 (Me. 1992). An intended beneficiary is a party who has the ability to enforce the rights and receive the benefits of a contract. Incidental third party beneficiaries are those who can benefit from a contract but cannot sue to enforce it. *Id.* The Restatement (Second) of Contracts § 302 (2) defines an incidental beneficiary as one who is not an intended beneficiary.

As a general rule, under common law, a third party who is not an intended beneficiary cannot assert a claim for breach of warranty. *OFW Corp. v. City of Columbia*, 893 S.W.2d 893 (Mo. App. 1995); *see also* RESTATEMENT (SECOND) OF CONTRACTS, Chapter 14 (1979). The determination of whether a party is an incidental or intended beneficiary is made by looking within the "four corners" of the contract.

This general rule has at least three recognized exceptions. The first is for personal injury or tangible damage to property. In such incidences, contractual privity is not required. See Prosser, *The Fall of the Citadel*, 50 MINN. L. REV. 791 (1996).

The second is that under Article 2 of the UCC, warranty protection extends under UCC Section 2-318 to one of three classes of persons injured in their person, depending on which alternative the respective state enacted. Two classes are narrow with the third broader. This warranty extension cannot be contractually waived.

The third is created by those states that have abolished privity requirements, even when the loss is only economic. *See, e.g., Dual Building Restoration, Inc. v. 1143 East Jersey Avenue Assocs., Inc.*, 652 A.2d. 1225 (N.J. 1995) (building owner could sue paint manufacturer for peeling paint even though owner's contract was only with his painting contractor).

In many states, the creation of an intended beneficiary is not favored. *MCI Telecommunications Corp. v. Texas Utilities Elec. Co.*, 995 S.W.2d 647 (Tex. 1999).

Except in the case of a sublicense, a licensor should always ensure the license disclaims the creation any of third party beneficiaries. This is especially important when viewed in light of any representations or warranties granted by the licensor under the license agreement. To be recognized as a third party beneficiary, the underlying agreement must expressly recognize the third party as an intended beneficiary of the contract. *Sovereign Bank v. BJ's Wholesale Club*, 533 F.3d 162 (3d Cir. 2008). A prudent party may want to provide a limited exception to allow those who claim under an indemnification provision to be recognized as a third party beneficiary. See the model language below

> Nothing in this Agreement, express or implied, is intended to or shall confer upon any Person (other than the parties hereto) any right, benefit or remedy of any nature whatsoever under or by reason of this Agreement; provided, however, that after the Effective Time, the Indemnified Person shall be third party beneficiaries of, and entitled to enforce, Section ___ (Indemnification of Directors and Officers).

Occasionally, a licensee will seek to include language in a master agreement, providing that its affiliates are third party beneficiaries of the agreement and can license software and purchase services under the agreement. While this language serves as a convenient means for related parties to take advantage of an existing contract and pricing structure, the licensor should limit its risk by clearly stating in the agreement that an affiliate is a third party beneficiary only to the extent that it is a party to a particular work order and then only with respect to that particular work. By doing so, the licensor will hopefully limit the licensee's affiliates' ability to enforce the agreement to only those situations where they are receiving software and services directly from the licensor.

If the licensor is allowing a licensee to sublicense the licensor's software to a third party, the licensor should require the licensee to name the licensor as a third party beneficiary in the sublicense to allow the licensor to enforce the terms of the license if the licensee chooses not to do so. Without the inclusion of such language, the licensor lacks a meaningful remedy to protect its intellectual property, as monetary remedies are insufficient.

K. Legal Fees (§ 49)

Under the "American rule" of litigation, each party is responsible for paying its own legal fees. *Alyeska Pipeline Svc. Co. v. Wilderness Soc'y*, 421 U. S. 240, 247 (1975). Some licensors seek to include provisions in the license agreement allowing the prevailing party in any dispute to recover its legal fees from the losing party. A more aggressive position from the licensor's perspective is to include unilateral language, allowing the licensor to recover its legal costs if it brings legal action to protect its intellectual property. Many licensees seek to include a prevailing party clause in their agreement in the belief that the licensee is more likely to bring a claim against the licensor than the licensor bringing a claim against the licensee.

A prevailing party clause provides the parties an incentive to settle a matter prior to bringing suit, as the cost of litigation can be quite large, thereby increasing the risk in the event a party loses the dispute. Given that a large number of litigation matters settle before trial without determining a prevailing party, these clauses are often moot. Similarly, most arbitrations are not clearly decided in favor of one party, as it is rare for arbiters to declare one party the prevailing party and award attorney's fees.

L. Survival (§ 18)

1. General

A survival clause identifies certain provisions in the agreement as surviving the termination of the agreement for any reason. There are two philosophies in drafting survival clauses. One is to specifically list those sections that survive by section number and name. By doing so, the parties avoid any ambiguity and any dispute over whether a particular provision survives termination. The risk in this approach is that the parties fail to include a particular section that should survive. See § 18 for language reflecting this approach.

The second is to use very general language such as "all sections that by their nature should survive the termination of this Agreement shall survive." The lack of specificity avoids the issue of failing to identify a particular section but is potentially problematic as the identity of the surviving clauses is open for interpretation and likely to increase the chance of litigation. Do the warranties survive? The indemnification provisions? In the event of a dispute, it is likely that the parties will have conflicting views as to their intent at the time of contract signature. Typical language reflecting this approach is as follows:

> Any provision of this Agreement which contemplates performance or observance subsequent to termination or expiration of this Agreement shall survive termination or expiration of this Agreement and continue in full force and effect (provided that if a provision has an express time period that such provision is to be in effect, then such provisions shall survive only for the applicable time periods).

The above language creates more ambiguity than it resolves. As such, the parties should strive to eliminate ambiguity and should take the time to carefully review the contract and list by section number every clause they want to survive.

See § 18, Alternative Language, for additional language reflecting this approach.

Under New York law, a court deciding which terms survive the termination or cancellation of a contract will look at the language of the contract as a whole. *See generally, Primex Int'l Corp. v. Wal-Mart Stores, Inc.*, 89 N.Y.2d 594, 679 N.E.2d 624 (1997); *Scientific Components Corp. v. Raytheon Co.*, 2005 WL 1561508 (S.D.N.Y. June 21, 2005). The fact that specific terms are not identified in the survival clause does not necessarily mean that they do not survive.

Some courts have adopted a "redundancy" approach as one factor in deciding the intention of the parties. In *Scientific Components Corp. the* court interpreted a manufacturing agreement and its survival clause. *Id.* The agreement included a broad arbitration clause that was not listed as surviving in the survival clause. The court agreed with the arbitration panel and found that the broad arbitration clause already encompassed termination-related issues and that "it would have been redundant to expressly list it in the Survival Clause." *Id.*, at *3.

A Colorado court reached a similar conclusion in *Shams v. Howard*, holding that an arbitration clause survives when a dispute arises under the contract if there is not "clear intent to the contrary." 165 P.3d 876, 879 (Colo. App. 2007). In *Smyx Techs., Inc. v. Stargate Mobile, L.L.C.*, a Michigan court considered the entirety of the contract and held that it would be "strained reading" to suggest that the arbitration clause and other provisions would not survive simply because they were not mentioned in the survival clause. 2006 WL 2943301, at *2 (E.D. Mich. Oct. 13, 2006). However, if the survival of the provisions in *Smyx Techs.* had not been supported throughout the contract itself, the court admitted that the failure to include the provisions in the survival clause could indicate an intent not to survive. *Id.* Thus, even the presence of a survival clause does not necessarily make the identification of terms that survive termination an easy task. Thus, a court will look to the "four corners" of the document as a guide in determining the intent of the parties.

2. *Lack of a Survival Clause*

The intention of the parties also governs when the contract does not contain a survival clause. The lack of a survival clause helps to strengthen the argument that the terms were not intended to survive termination, but it is not conclusive. In *Primex Int'l Corp. v. Wal-Mart Stores, Inc.*, a New York court held that the choice of law provision and arbitration clause in two separate contracts without survival clauses survived the natural expiration and unilateral termination under a notice of cancellation provision or breach. 89 N.Y.2d 594, 598-99 (N.Y. 1997).

If a party can demonstrate, however, that it was the intention of the parties that a clause not survive termination, then the obligation will end the contract. In *Aberdeen Golf & Country Club v. Bliss Const., Inc.*, a Florida court held that an alternative dispute resolution provision was intended only during performance of a construction contract and terminated when the contract expired. 932 So.2d 235, 241 (Fla. Dist. Ct. App. 2005). The court viewed the contract in light of the entire text, context, structure and performance in order to determine the intention of the parties. *Id.* at 236. The intent not to survive was demonstrated by the facts that performance involved many tasks over a long duration and an alternative dispute resolution provision would postpone litigation for sake of progress on the construction project. *Id.* at 237. Because the contract did not have a survival clause, "the ADR provision went down with the whole." *Id.* at 241.

The *Aberdeen* court's approach is analogous to professional services agreements requiring many tasks over a long duration. Arguably, specific provisions, like an audit clause, were included in the contract for the sake of progress on the entire project and were meant to terminate along with the contract. While *Aberdeen* was decided in Florida, the conclusion reached by the court seems consistent with New York's practice of determining and upholding the intention of the parties.

M. No Construction Against Drafter (§ 51)

As a general principal, ambiguous contractual provisions that cannot be resolved from the four corners of the agreement or through parol evidence are interpreted against the drafter. *Truck Ins. Exchange v. Marks Rentals, Inc.*, 418 A.2d 1187 (Md. 1980). Individual terms will be given their ordinary meaning unless a technical meaning is clearly intended. *Id.*

Not all courts are in agreement as to interpreting ambiguity against the drafter. At least one court has found that where both parties to an arm's length agreement are sophisticated parties and have been represented by counsel, any ambiguities arising from the agreement should not be automatically construed against the drafter. *Western Sling and Cable Co. v. Hamilton*, 545 So.2d 29 (Ala. 1989). This potential dichotomy extends to specific industries. *Compare Truck Ins. Exchange v. Marks Rentals, Inc.*, 418 A.2d 1187, 1197 (Md. 1980) (Maryland rejects rule that ambiguous insurance policies are to be interpreted against insurer) and *Lindsay Mfg. Co. v. Hartford Acc. & Indem. Co.*, 118 F.3d 1263, 1269 (8th Cir. 1997) (ambiguous language will be construed against insurer).

To avoid potential problems, the parties should include a clause acknowledging that the parties have been represented by counsel, that they are sophisticated commercial parties, and that any ambiguity should not be interpreted against one party or the other. See § 51. The licensee may reject the notion that it is a sophisticated commercial party as it relates to software licensing and may seek to exclude this provision. If the terms of the license were not broadly negotiated, the licensee may be justified in its position. Notwithstanding the licensee's belief, the licensor should never accept language interpreting any ambiguity against the licensor. See, e.g., Form 23.K.MM.5.

N. Integration/Entire Agreement (§ 58)

1. General

An "Integration" or "Entire Agreement" clause provides that the entire agreement between the parties is set forth within the four corners of the document and that all provisions, discussions, agreements, statements, etc., not set forth within the agreement shall be of no force and effect. In short, integration clauses limit the rights and obligations of the parties to the actual terms set forth in the license agreement. Negotiations are presumed to be merged into the agreement and oral testimony is inadmissible to explain or vary the agreement. *National Cash. Reg. Co. v. Modern Transfer Co., Inc.*, 302 A.2d 486 (Pa. 1973) (integration clause contained in a computer lease agreement prevented the lessee from introducing evidence as to oral representations made by the lessor's agent prior to the execution of the agreement which were not included in the agreement). Integration clauses prevent a party from agreeing in a clearly worded integration clause that it did not rely on statements and representations outside of the agreement then later claiming that it did rely. *Abry Partners V, L.P. v. F & W Acquisition L.L.C.*, 891 A2d 1032 (Del. 2006).

Integration clauses protect the licensor from claims that sales "puffery" made by the licensor's sales force in the sales process constitutes fraud. From the licensee's perspective, however, the license agreement needs to ensure that all statements made by the licensor and relied on by the licensee in making its decision to select the licensor are included in the agreement. If these statements are not included, they are moot.

Most courts will enforce a well articulated integration clause between sophisticated parties. *MBIA Ins. Corp. v. Royal Indemnity Co.*, 426 F.3d 204, 218 (3d Cir. 2005) ("When sophisticated parties include a broad but unambiguous anti-reliance clause in their agreement, the Delaware Supreme Court will likely indulge the assumption that they said what they meant and meant what they said."). Some courts, however, will strictly interpret such clauses to limit broad exclusions. *Texas Taco Cabana, L.P. v. Taco Cabana of New Mexico*, 304 F. Supp.2d 903 (W.D. Tex. 2003) (non-reliance clause will bar claims to extent the clause specifically identified statements not relied on but will not always bar claims on other issues not expressly disclaimed in agreement).

Courts are divided as to whether an integration clause will bar a claim for fraudulent inducement. *Compare Northwest Bank and Trust, Co. v. First Illinois National Bank*, 354 F.3d 721 (8th Cir. 2003) (contractual disclaimer ineffective to bar claim for fraudulent inducement) and *Contractor Utility Sales Co., v. Certain-Teed Corp.*, 748 F.2d 1151, 1154 (7th Cir. 1984) ("Integration rule yields to a properly established demonstration of fraud inducing and vitiating the execution of the written agreement.") *with Rosen v. Watermill Development Corp.*, 1 A. D.3d 424 (N.Y. App. 2003) (integration clause must specifically disclaim basis of alleged misrepresentations to defeat claim of fraud). Under New York law, the specificity requirement is lowered where the integration clause resulted from extensive negotiations between sophisticated parties. *Citibank, N.A. v. Plapinger*, 495 N.Y.S.2d 309, 311-12 (N.Y. 1985).

Prudent licensors, however, will insist on the inclusion of an integration clause to defeat a claim of fraud by the customer arising from the sales process. *See i2 Technologies, Inc. v. DARC Corporation*, 2003 WL 22205091 (N.D. Tex. 2003).

The importance of an integration clause is illustrated by *BSkyB Ltd. v. H.P. Enterprise Sources UK Ltd.*, 2010 WL 20033 (E.W.H.C. B.D. Jan. 26, 2010). Although decided in the United Kingdom, the case provides insight as to the risk that can arise from improper behavior. In *BSkyB*, a company subsequently acquired by HP entered into a contract with BSkyB to design, build and provide systems integrations services for a new Customer Relationship Management (CRM) system. The integration clause in the underlying agreement specifically identified fraudulent misrepresentations as not being excluded by the clause. BSkyB subsequently brought suit against HP for breach of contract in failing to deliver the contractually agreed upon CRM system.

The court found that HP had made fraudulent misrepresentations when HP stated that it had studied BSkyB's requirements and could deliver the required system within the contractually required time frame. HP eventually settled the matter for

$459,400,000, an amount more than ten times the contract's $45,294,000 limitation of liability.

To avoid similar claims, licensors should include a statement in the agreement's integration clause to the effect that the licensee has not relied on any representation, warranty or statement other than as set forth in the agreement. The following language is illustrative:

> Each party acknowledges that, in entering into this Agreement, it has not relied on, and shall have no right or remedy in respect of, any statement, representation, assurance or warranty (whether made negligently or innocently) other than as expressly set out in this Agreement.

If the parties are entering into or have entered into multiple agreements, the parties should reference the other agreements in the integration clause to avoid any argument that one agreement superseded another. Another means of avoiding an "unintended consequence" is to include language to the effect that the document reflects the entire agreement between the parties "on the subject matter hereof." *See e.g., G.M. Persey and Associates v. Britt/Paulk Insurance Agency, Inc.*, 2008 WL 203747 (D. Md. May 6, 2008).

2. *Collateral Agreements*

To the extent other documents are intended to be included within the terms of the agreement, they should be attached to the agreement as exhibits. The agreement should specifically state that all exhibits and schedules are specifically incorporated into and made part of the agreement. At least one court has held that the "mere reference to another document is not sufficient to incorporate that other document into a contract, particularly where the incorporating document makes no specific reference that it is 'subject to' the collateral documents." *Monfiston v. State of Florida,* 920 So.2d 1286, 1288 (Fla. 2006). Simply stating that an agreement is subject to a collateral document is not necessarily sufficient to bind a party to a collateral agreement. *Id.* See, e.g., § 53. The parties should ensure that these collateral documents do not in turn reference other documents, such that the effect of the integration clause is effectively mooted by a continuing "daisy chain" of documents.

The parties should be careful when including integration clauses in dependent agreements, that is, agreements that are either incorporated into a separate agreement or attached as an exhibit. At least one court has found that where both an agreement and an exhibit to such agreement contain distinct integration clauses, such agreements should be interpreted as independent agreements. *Baldwin Piano, Inc. v. Deutche Wurlitizer GMBH,* 2004 WL 46243 (N.D. Ill. Jan. 7, 2004) ("The presence of the integration clauses in each of the agreements therefore indicates the parties' intent that each document should stand on its own and be interpreted as a complete agreement into itself."). Courts will seek to read and construe the various documents together "as a evidencing the intention of the parties in regard to a single transaction . . . even though the instruments were executed at different times and do not in terms refer to each other." *Rocks v. Brocius,* 217 A.2d 531, 545 (Md. 1967).

O. Seals (Penultimate Paragraph and Signature Line)

The use of seals arises from ancient times when many people could not read and write. Their "seal" indicted their acceptance or endorsement of the relevant document. For a brief history of the use of seals in the legal contract, see *From the History of Seals and Signatures*, Information Security Solutions Europe Conference 2000 (Barcelona, Sept. 28, 2000). Many practitioners often overlook the ramifications of including the word "(SEAL)" after the signature line or including the phrase "executed under seal" in the agreement. It is often believed that such terms are an archaic reminder from earlier times, or that such terms are an acknowledgment that many corporations no longer have a corporate seal.

Sealed instruments or contracts do not require consideration to be binding. Restatement (Second) Contracts §95. *See e.g., Warten v. Moore*, 366 S.E.2d 666 (Ga. 1988). Further, the use of the term "seal" may significantly extend the statute of limitations and the analogous period for laches. *See e.g. Whittington v. Dragon Group, L.L.C.*, 991 A.2d 1 (Del. Supr. 2009) (typing word "Seal" on signature line was sufficient to extend statute of limitations and analogous period for laches from 3 to 20 years). Under Maryland law, for example, use of the term "seal" extends the statute of limitations from 3 to 12 years. Md Code Ann. Cts & Jud. Proc. § 5-102(a) (5) (2006). The requirements for a sealed instrument vary by state. Under Maryland law, the signature lines need only to contain the term "(SEAL)" to be considered sealed. *Warfield v. Baltimore Gas and Electric Company*, 512 A.2d 1044 (Md. 1986). Under New York law, however, the agreement itself must contain an acknowledgment of the parties' intent to have a sealed agreement. *Transbel Inv. Co., Inc. v. Venetos*, 18 N.E.2d 129 (NY 1938).

P. Signatures, Signature Lines and Signature Pages

Although customary, no specific language is required to precede a signature line. Often the parties include language similar to that set forth in Form 23.B.1 to indicate that there are no further contractual provisions and that the signature lines follow.

A party should avoid signing blank signature pages prior to negotiating the final agreement. Every effort should be made to have the signature lines appear on the same page as the last contractual provisions. Doing so limits the potential for fraud through the addition of additional clauses without the knowledge of the other party. Further, if signature pages are attached to the agreement by a lawyer without the review of the client, the agreement will likely be binding on the client under the theory that the client's lawyer had the actual or apparent authority to approve the agreement and attach the signature pages. While such actions may give rise to a claim of malpractice against the lawyer, a malpractice claim is a hollow remedy for the affected client.

Since the adoption of the Electronic Signatures in Global and National Commerce Act (E-SIGN) in 2000, 15 U.S.C. § 7001 *et seq.*, to recognize the validity of electronic signatures, a small but vocal group of practitioners have been promoting the use of electronic signatures. Electronic signatures, however, are not without their own issues.

Among the most common concerns is the need to ensure that the chosen e-signature software allows the parties to authenticate the user's identity/signature and ensure that the "executed" document is the same agreement that the parties had agreed on. Further, the integrity of the document must be guaranteed through a chain of custody so that in the event of a dispute, the document can later be entered into as evidence of the document governing the relationship between the parties. The parties must comply with the compliance obligations set forth in E-SIGN. Thus, prior to agreeing to utilize electronic signatures, the parties should clearly understand the risks and obligations of doing so.

Finally, the parties should ensure that they each maintain proper security for their computer networks, allowing the parties to prove that each executed the agreement electronically. At least one court has refused to enforce an agreement because the party seeking to enforce the agreement could not prove that the other party had electronically executed the agreement. *See Kerr v. Dillard Store Services, Inc.*, 2009 WL 385863 (D. Kan. Feb. 17, 2009).

Q. Dating the Agreement

The parties should be careful when stating the date that the contract was executed. While the parties are free to choose an effective date, back dating a contract may be fraudulent and even criminal. As such, the parties should clearly indicate the date on which the agreement was executed and the effective date of the agreement.

CHAPTER 7

Licensing Issues Arising from Alternative Delivery Models

Many licensors and licensees are utilizing alternative delivery models for providing and accessing software applications. Most commonly illustrated through the use of "cloud computing," these delivery models raise many of the same issues involved in traditional software licensing, while at the same time creating issues unique to the respective delivery model. Additionally, many software licensors and licensees are delegating the management of their software to third parties who "host" and maintain the software on the hosting provider's servers. Known as "managed hosting," this model allows both end users and software vendors to potentially reduce their costs while increasing the efficiency in which the software is utilized.

The discussion below provides a brief overview of cloud computing and the licensing issues associated with SaaS in particular, as well as, the most common forms of hosting.

A. Overview of Cloud Computing

Traditionally, most software has been licensed for use on the licensee's internal computer systems resident on the licensee's premises. An increasing number of licensors and licensees, however, are seeking to provide and access their software through cloud computing. The "cloud" is a metaphor for the internet.

Cloud computing allows a user to access an application, data storage and processing power from any computer with a web browser, eliminating the need to provide applications and the attendant hardware. Data is accessed and transferred over the internet instead of through a fixed transmission line. The U.S. National Institute of Standards and Technology ("NIST") has defined cloud computing as a "model for enabling convenient, on-demand network access to a shared pool of configurable computing resources….that can be rapidly provisioned and released with minimal management effort or service provider interaction." http://csrc.nist.gov/groups/SNS/cloud-computing/cloud-def-v15.doc. (Last viewed September 15, 2010.)

1. Characteristics of Cloud Computing

Cloud Computing has several characteristics:

- On-demand self-service
- Broad network access
- Shared infrastructure and applications
- Rapid scalability
- Consumption billing

By standardizing technology, a customer is able to benefit from economies of scale for common technologies such as core applications and development platforms. Pricing for most cloud computing service offerings is determined by consumption, that is, the amount of services utilized by the customer.

Scalability is another characteristic of a cloud computing, as clients have the ability to generally scale their infrastructure needs while paying only for their required capacity, giving the customer greater flexibility and limiting financial outlays. Finally, cloud services are accessed through web browsers, allowing a customer to access an application without any specific operating system requirements. Customers are able to manage their service requirements without significant vendor involvement.

Cloud computing is largely unregulated, although a number of industry leading companies such as IBM, Cisco, SAP and EMC created the Open Cloud Manifesto to address data protection in the cloud. See www.opencouldmanefesto.org for more information.

2. Delivery Models

Cloud services may be delivered through several different models:

(a) Public Cloud

A public cloud is operated by a vendor where the applications and data of many different clients are resident on a common infrastructure. Public clouds are usually are hosted at the vendor's facility and not at the customer's facility. A public cloud allows customers to incur lower costs through shared infrastructure and the flexibility to increase their infrastructure requirements on an as needed basis.

(b) Private Cloud

A private cloud is created for a particular client providing the client with increased control over its data and greater security. The client owns the infrastructure and determines how the purchased applications are deployed. The applications and infrastructure may be resident at the vendor's facilities or at a client facility.

(c) Hybrid Cloud

Hybrid clouds combine aspects of both a public cloud and a private cloud. They provide increased flexibility in meeting a client's applications and infrastructure needs.

Hybrid clouds are most commonly used for the storage of data in the support of web 2.0 applications.

(d) Community Cloud

In a community cloud model, infrastructure and applications are shared by several organizations with common aspects such as similar security risk profiles or similar business models.

3. Service Models

Cloud services generally fall within one of four distinct offerings:

- **Business Process as a Service** where an entire business process is accessed through the cloud.
- **Platform as a Service** allows a client to deploy client created or acquired applications over the vendor's cloud infrastructure, including the network, servers and storage, which are controlled and managed by the vendor.
- **Infrastructure as a Service** where the client has access to provision processing, storage, networks and other fundamental computing resources.
- **Software-as-a-Service (SaaS)** allows a user access a vendor's applications on a cloud infrastructure.

4. Benefits and Concerns of Cloud Computing

Cloud computing provides a number of tangible benefits including reducing a client's infrastructure investment, lowering its costs of entry into the marketplace, and increasing innovation in the marketplace by allowing enhancements to be brought to the market quicker. The user is able to quickly increase or decrease the scope of its information technology needs. Cloud computing also allows users to meet their "green" computing goals by increasing utilization of the vendor's data center and lowering energy costs.

Cloud computing does raise several reasons for concerns, the most important of which is data security. Accessing highly sensitive data over the internet exposes the user to the risk of loss or misappropriation. In addition, a client cannot forgo a software upgrade as all users are on the same version of the software.

B. Software as a Service

1. An Overview of "Software as a Service"

"SaaS" is a business model under which a software application is delivered to the customer as a service usually over the Internet. The end user does not purchase a copy of the software, but accesses it on a time-sharing basis via a subscription. In essence, the end user "rents" the software on an as-needed basis. SaaS has superseded Application Service Provider (ASP) and "Utility Computing" as the industry's preferred name for purchasing software on a service basis.

From a software vendor's perspective, SaaS allows the vendor to reduce its support costs by maintaining a single version of its software on a single platform. A SaaS model allows vendors to monitor how their customers use the application, bring improvements to the market, and address any problem that has arisen. The vendor's support staff is able to evaluate a customer's problem as each customer is using the same application on the same platform. Updates are automatically made available to customers instead of customers having to wait to receive, and pay for, the newest update. In addition, SaaS allows the vendor to sell to customers who may not be able to afford to purchase the software and/or the infrastructure to support it.

From the end user's perspective, the end user is able to reduce its information technology costs by eliminating the purchase of the application, the hardware required to run it, as well as fees for updates and technical support. All of these are built into the cost of accessing the application. SaaS allows the end user to invest its technology budget in those technologies that will give it a competitive advantage in its industry, instead of investing in infrastructure.

The user also avoids the significant time and cost of installing applications. In essence, application management has been outsourced, allowing the end user's IT staff to focus on other projects. Because the software is already operating on the vendor's system, the time to begin using the new application is dramatically reduced. The customer's usage of software is fully monitored by the vendor, allowing the vendor to instantaneously receive "feedback." Instant feedback quickens the pace of improvements to the software while customers can benchmark against their peers. Further, the end user is able to automatically access the most recent updates and enhancements to the software without the risks inherent in moving to a new version.

SaaS does have several limitations or reasons for concern. The greatest basis for concern is that the customer has relinquished control over its IT to a third party. The customer is totally dependent on the third party to consistently deliver access without interruption while using a secure environment. See Section B.4, below, for a more detailed discussion of the security issues associated with SaaS. The customer also lacks the ability to customize the applications for its needs as most vendors will only modify the application for very large customers.

2. *Pricing*

Customers are charged through various means, including on a per-user per-month basis, on a monthly subscription for the customer's entire company, or based on the use of the application (e.g., a marketing software company is paid according to the number of solid leads generated through the customer's use of the software).

The end user's cost to use the software should be reduced as the price is amortized among several users and the subscription fee is often based on usage. By paying only for the time it uses, the customer avoids paying for excess capacity. The usage fee is amortized over the period of the customer's use as opposed to the purchase of a software license where payment in full is usually due immediately upon acquisition of the license. This payment mechanism evens out the user's payments over the course of a year, potentially helping with cash flow.

3. Delivery

SaaS may be delivered through two similar mechanisms: a hosted application model or a software-on-demand model. In the hosted application management model, a hosting provider hosts the desired software and delivers it to its customers over the Internet. Under the software-on-demand model, the provider gives its customers network based access to a single copy of an application modified for SaaS over a network. Software on demand is also known as the "application service provider" model. In both cases, the end user is paying for access to the application. The vendor may choose to have someone else host it, but delivery is the same. Both are basically "on-demand."

The vendor may choose to deliver Software-as-a-Service either by hosting the application itself or by outsourcing the hosting of the application to a hosting provider. See Section 7.C for a more detailed discussion of managed hosting. Usually, the vendor will license the use of the software to its own clients. However, in some cases, a hosting provider will license a copy of the software from the vendor and set up a SaaS model with its own customers. In the latter case, the hosting provider would acquire rights from the software vendor to sub-license the access and use of the software to end users.

4. Security Concerns

Security is always an important concern when utilizing a SaaS model, but it is especially important for those clients utilizing a public cloud. By centralizing a party's data in a secure data center, a party may actually increase its security. On the other hand, the client has ceded control over its data and now is dependant on the vendor for protection. A prudent customer will address its concerns with the vendor and incorporate its security requirements in the underlying agreement. Depending on the size of the contract and the importance of the application, the customer should visit the facility from which the SaaS services are provided, if applicable, and request a written copy of the vendor's security protocol for the building's physical security and the security of the network from intrusion, viruses, and the like. The customer should closely examine and vet the vendor's policies. The customer should also ascertain the specific type of infrastructure used by the vendor to provide the hosting services.

When considering SaaS, the client must carefully evaluate the vendor's security protections. The customer should understand who has access to its confidential information and data and under what circumstances. Who has the ability to modify such data? What controls are in place to protect the client from an unauthorized individual accessing and modifying the client's data? Where is the vendor's data center located? Does the data center have adequate physical and virtual security? Does the vendor have appropriate virus protection software and appropriate security measures to protect the customer's data and internal systems?

A prudent customer should contractually require that all customer data remain within the continental United States to avoid subjecting the customer to the laws of those jurisdictions in which the data resides, including the jurisdiction's privacy laws, data transfer laws and jurisdictional discovery rules. The European Union has very restrictive laws as to data protection and prohibits the transfer of data to countries with inadequate data protection laws. To the extent a customer allows its data to be removed from the United States, a customer should monitor the data's location to avoid any potential prohibition by the jurisdiction in which the data now resides on relocating the data back to the United States.

The customer should ensure the required protections are maintained 24x7x365 days a year. The vendor should utilize advanced software to detect intrusions to its network, as well as eliminate viruses and similar problems. The vendor should undertake an external and internal security analysis several times a year. The results of these efforts should be provided to the customer without the customer's having to request it.

A client should require that its data be encrypted not only during storage but also during transmission. Not all vendor applications are encrypted, making data stored on such applications vulnerable to misappropriation or theft. A client should insist that the vendor comply with the client's security standards and that a vendor comply with all applicable data protection obligations. The parties should also establish specific encryption standards for the encryption of the client's data. See the language below for model language:

> Customer will encrypt the Data using the AES-256 standard and store on Vendor Simple Storage Service (S3) devices within the Vendor east coast and west coast data centers. When needed, the encrypted Data will be replicated to Elastic Band Storage (EBS) devices and made available during the boot process to server instances and associated server user accounts with proper credentials. The credentials will be stored and maintained within the Customer-managed data center and presented to the Vendor server instances only during the boot process. No credentials will be stored in the Vendor cloud environment.

Finally, the contract should address the parties' respective responsibilities for complying with all federal, state and local data breach notification laws. The vendor should be obligated to notify the client immediately in the event of a data breach and provide a detailed written explanation of the nature of such breach and the actions its has taken to remedy such breach. The agreement should also clearly provide which party has responsibility for paying for any costs associated with complying with new laws enacted after the execution of the agreement.

5. Disaster Recovery

The vendor's disaster recovery plans should be carefully reviewed by the client. The parties should include in the contract the level of redundancy for the application, i.e., the availability of the application in the event of a failure of the primary server or application (such as a geographically diverse "hot" site) as well as the vendor's protocol for backing up data, the storage of such data offsite, and the period for which it will retain the backups. See Chapter 5.G for a more detailed discussion of disaster recovery issues. The vendor should be able to provide a detailed plan addressing a power outage, natural disaster, equipment failure, and so on, as well as service level agreements for uptime and the ability to log onto the application. The customer should also ask the vendor about any previous security problems or service interruptions. Finally, the vendor should disclose any audit protocols it has adapted to ensure its existing protocols and methodologies are adhered to.

6. Performance Standard/Service Level Agreements (SLAs)

When entering into a SaaS agreement, the customer should seek to include performance standards/SLAs to ensure the promised services meet the customer's needs. Common measurements include availability, response time and scalability. Vendors should be hesitant, however, to be measured on customer dependent elements such as location processing capability.

Perhaps the most important metric from the customer's perspective is unplanned outages. Many clients require system availability of 99.99 percent per month and that all maintenance will be scheduled in advance and limited to the hours of 12 a.m. to 4 a.m. during weekdays and on weekends. Unplanned outages are unavoidable, requiring the client to develop a detailed plan to mitigate its inability to access needed applications and data during any outage. The client should specifically evaluate any required redundancies to continue operating during a period of outages. Prudent customers will require the vendor to provide historical data on system availability. For a convenient chart converting uptime percentages to minutes, hours and days, see http://royal.pingdom.com/2009/03/24/a-handy-uptime-and-downtime-conversion-cheat-sheet/. (Last viewed September 17, 2010.)

Any penalties or credits should be carefully delineated. The agreement should include examples of how any such penalties or credits should be calculated and applied. If a service interruption occurs, the contract should stipulate how quickly the customer will be notified and how quickly the problem will be resolved. Many vendors, however, do not offer meaningful SLAs, arguing the software must meet the demands of multiple customers. In the event the vendor fails to meet an SLA, most vendors will seek to provide future credits instead of a refund to avoid revenue recognition issues.

7. Contractual Protections

Most vendors seek to have the client sign pro forma contracts without change with little contractual protection for their clients. A typical contract disclaims almost all warranties, disclaims liability for any outages or data loss and limits the vendor's liability to the damages set forth in any service level agreement with an overarching cap tied to a multiple of the monthly fees. Many vendors argue that pro forma contracts are industry standard and reflect the nature of lower margin, shared services thus negating the need to negotiate the contract.

Clients should carefully evaluate a contract's pricing model to ensure the pricing structure is clearly delineated and that the client has the ability to independently verify any amounts it is billed by the vendor. Many pricing models are based on the number of subscribers or users, placing great importance on how these terms are defined. One leading vendor defines a user as an identified individual accessing the system on January 1. Thus if a user quits his employment after January 1, and a replacement employee is hired, the customer is required to purchase two licenses. Like a traditional license, the price should be fixed for a set period of time and the amount of any future price increases should be capped.

The client should think carefully before accepting the law of a particular jurisdiction to govern the agreement. Agreeing to the laws of a particular jurisdiction will subject the customer to that jurisdictions' data protection and data breach laws, and this may greatly impact the client's rights and remedies.

To the extent that it is able to do so, a prudent client should require the vendor to represent and warrant that the contracted for application will be interoperable with the client's legacy systems and that the format of the client's data will be compatible with the vendors' information technology standards. The customer should ensure that the data created by the application will be compatible with the client's legacy systems and thus avoid any potentially costly and time-consuming data migration project. The vendor should also be willing to make written a commitment as to the application's future features and functionality that will be made available to the clients. A prudent vendor is hesitant to do so, however, to retain the maximum flexibility to operate its business. At a minimum, a vendor should be willing to warrant that there will be no material reduction in functionality during the term of the license/service agreement.

The underlying agreement should provide that the client's data should at all times be exclusively owned by the client and shall be immediately returned to the client upon its request.

Finally, a prudent customer will ensure the underlying agreement sets forth in detail the client's rights upon the termination of the agreement. The client wants to ensure that any such transition will not interrupt its business and that the vendor will cooperate with the replacement vendor to ensure the transition is a smooth one. To that end, the client should obtain a contractual commitment regarding its right to continue to use the services during the transition period, the right to the immediate return of its data, an agreement on a rate card establishing the rates for any transition assistance fees and the vendor's commitment to cooperate with any new vendor.

From the vendor's perspective, the vendor should require the customer to indemnify the vendor against any third party claims that data placed in the cloud by the customer infringes a third party's intellectual property rights. In addition, customers should indemnify the vendor in the event the customer breaches the terms of the service agreement, as well as in the event the customer fails to follow the contractually required security procedures.

8. *Litigation and E-Discovery Considerations*

An increasing concern is the ability of a party utilizing the cloud to comply with its e-discovery obligations, as a party is required to preserve and disclose all information within its control, even if it resides on a third party's servers. *Pension Committee of the University of Montreal Pension Plan et. al v. Bank of America Securities, LLC*, 685 F. Supp. 2d 456, 465 (S.D.N.Y. 2010). Courts have interpreted "control" broadly to include not only information in a party's possession, but also information that a party has the right to access or obtain. *See Rock v. Stripling*, 736 F.2d 650 (11th Cir. 1984). For example, will the client be able to conduct a forensic evaluation to establish the authenticity of any data stored in the cloud? Will the client have the ability to preserve any data in its custody and control? Can the vendor implement and comply the client's document retention policies?

Another consideration is the impact of storing data and documents in the cloud on the attorney client privilege. How will storing data and documents in the cloud affect the client's ability to claim the attorney client privilege? By doing so, has the client waived the attorney client privilege?

9. *Export Issues*

Clients also need to be concerned as to the application of U.S. export laws to the remote storage of data and the remote access to applications. In January 2009, the Bureau of Industry and Security issued an advisory opinion on the applicability of the Export Administration Regulations ("EAR") to the transfer of data through cloud computing. The opinion stated that providing computation capacity services though the cloud is "not subject to the EAR as the service provider is not shipping or transmitting any commodity, software or technology to the user," but that shipping or transferring software that is subject to the EAR would constitute an export. The opinion stated that in the event data was transferred via the cloud, the customer/user bears the responsibility for complying with all export requirements. http://www.bis.doc.gov/policiesandregulations/advisoryopinions/jan13_2009_ao_on_cloud_grid_computing.pdf. (Last viewed September 15, 2010.)

10. Bankruptcy Concerns

One concern for customers is that, in the event of the vendor's bankruptcy, the customer may be unable to take advantage of the protections offered under Section 365(n) of the bankruptcy code. Under Section 365(n), if a bankrupt vendor rejects an executory contract/license, the licensee retains its license rights to the underlying intellectual property.

SaaS may be considered a service and thus outside the purview of Section 365(n). If the agreement grants access to the software by means of a service contract, the customer will not necessarily receive a license to the underlying intellectual property, and will lack the right to retain its use of the software. To protect its interests, the customer should ensure that the underlying agreement includes language stating that the customer is licensing the software and that the "license grant" falls under Section 365(n).

Including such language does not necessarily protect the customer in the event of the vendor's bankruptcy and the vendor's subsequent rejection of the license. While the customer would still have rights to the software, the vendor would not be obligated to provide hosting, maintenance, and support services. It may be difficult for the customer to obtain such services, much less on short notice. To limit the impact of any interruption, the customer should require the vendor to escrow the software and grant the customer the right to host and maintain the software in the event of the vendor's bankruptcy. This language also serves to support the customer's position that the underlying agreement is a license of intellectual property, in the event the vendor contests the customer's right to access the software. While this is not a perfect solution, it will likely lessen the impact of the vendor's bankruptcy and any subsequent rejection of the underlying agreement.

For a more detailed discussion of the issues involved with the bankruptcy of software vendors, see Chapter 17. See also Form 23.C.3 § 3.1.2.

C. Hosting

1. An Overview of Hosting

In a hosting model, the customer pays the hosting provider to provide some combination of (1) facilities, network and security, (2) hardware and software, and (3) the management of such hardware and software.

The simplest form of hosting is collocation, where the client retains ownership of all hardware and software, and the hosting provider supplies rack space and power within a data center, Internet connectivity, and basic monitoring that the equipment is online—commonly known as "power, pipe, and ping." From a software licensing perspective, the collocation model differs little from the traditional licensing model between vendor and customer. The hosting provider is merely providing housing for the equipment on which the software resides; the client is solely responsible for the purchase, maintenance, and use of both the equipment and the software as well as all content the client places on the site/hosting environment. However, since the hosting provider has physical access to the application, the client may want this acknowledged in its license agreement with the vendor.

In a managed hosting model, the hosting provider is responsible for managing and maintaining the customer's equipment and/or software in the hosting provider's data center, as well as for providing security services (e.g., firewalls, vulnerability testing), high availability services, monitoring services, Internet and/or dedicated access to the customer's hosted sites, and the like. The customer's hosting environment may consist of equipment and software dedicated to the customer's use, or the customer may purchase segments of a shared physical environment with logical partitioning ("virtual servers").

Additionally, many software vendors and licensees are delegating the management of their software to third parties who "host" and maintain the software on the "hosting provider's" servers. Known as "managed hosting," this model allows both clients and software vendors to potentially reduce their costs while increasing the efficiency in which the software is utilized. The discussion that follows focuses on managed hosting, where the hosting provider has license rights and/or responsibilities with regards to the licensed software that is part of the customer's hosting environment.

2. *Licensing Models*

There are two principal models for a software license used in a managed hosting environment:

(a) Hosting Provider Licenses the Software from the Third Party Vendor

(i) Hosting Provider as Licensee

Under the most common model, the hosting provider licenses proprietary software from a third party software vendor (e.g., Microsoft) and provides its hosting customers with access to and use of the application in its data centers. The hosting provider obtains from the third party software vendor the right to re-license copies of the software to its customers. The hosting provider may receive rights under its license agreement with the software owner that are not passed on to the hosting provider's clients, such as right to copy the software onto different servers.

From the hosting provider's perspective and for most software vendors, the right to re-license required by the hosting provider is different from granting the hosting provider the right to resell the software. The hosting provider is not a sales channel for the software vendor, and the hosting provider's customers do not have the right to the use the software outside of their contract with the hosting provider.

(ii) Hosting Provider as Licensor

In its agreement with its customer, the hosting provider is the licensor of the software vendor's application. The hosting provider grants its customer a limited license to use the software in the hosting provider's data center for the term of the hosting agreement. The underlying software license does not necessarily transfer to the customer upon the termination of the hosting agreement.

(b) Hosting Customer Licenses the Software Directly from the Third Party Vendor for Use in the Hosting Provider's Data Center

In this case, the customer obtains the right from the software owner to place its software on the hosting provider's servers. The customer must obtain this right under its license agreement as the owner/licensor is not in contractual privity with the hosting provider, which has physical access to the software and may have logical access as well. For software provided by the customer, the hosting provider relies on the customer to obtain the rights necessary for the hosting provider to fulfill its responsibilities under the hosting contract. Under this model, the customer may also have the hosting provider provide maintenance and/or technical support for the software.

3. Dedicated versus Shared Hosting

The two principal types of hosting are dedicated hosting, also known as outsourced managed hosting, and shared hosting.

(a) Dedicated Hosting

Under a dedicated hosting model, the hardware/server and software architecture provided by the hosting provider is dedicated solely to the use of a particular customer.

The hosting provider may provide a variety of services including security services, monitoring of the hardware and software, technical support, as well as backup services. By leasing the entire server, the customer can exercise greater control over its environment, including selecting the operating system, hardware, and the parameters under which support will be provided. Services offered by a vendor may include updates to the operating system and application, technical support, security, firewall and anti-virus updates, disaster recovery and backups, load balancing, and database administration.

(b) Shared Hosting

Under a shared hosting model, a hosting infrastructure (network, security, server hardware) is shared by multiple clients. Partitions are created on a shared server ("server virtualization") so that client data and other software applications can be dedicated to each client. Because the server is shared, system administrative services are included. This model is attractive for small customers who may not be able to afford a dedicated hosting environment.

4. The Benefits and Drawbacks of Hosting

(a) Benefits

From the customer's perspective, hosting allows the customer to reduce or avoid making a large financial investment in infrastructure technology and IT support staff. The hosting provider is responsible for the support and maintenance of the servers and their software, technical support, security, and disaster recovery and backups. The hosting provider can usually provide a higher level of expertise and technology than the customer would be able to do on its own (e.g., providing highly available, geographically diverse environments, data centers that meet regulatory standards for security and 24x365 support and response to security incidents).

In some scenarios, hosting lowers the cost of technology services as it allows licensees to "share" expensive hardware and software, theoretically allowing the cost to be amortized over a large number of licensees. In short, the customer pays only for the services it uses. Even when the customer bears the cost of dedicated hardware and software, the cost may be less than if the customer purchased them itself. The hosting provider often has vendor contracts that provide significant discounts based on volume purchases. Customers who have their own enterprise-wide agreements with the applicable vendors may choose to provide the hardware and/or software themselves.

(b) Drawbacks

One drawback to hosting is that the customer does not "control its destiny." The customer's software applications, which may be critical to the success of the customer's business, are, at least to some extent, under the control of the hosting provider. The customer is now dependent on the hosting provider meeting its contractual obligations. If the hosting provider has significant down time or the hardware or software is not properly maintained, the customer may be left with very few practical remedies. This is especially true if the hosting provider's liability is limited under its contract with the customer.

Hosting does not always result in a lower cost to the customer. Many customers require their own servers for security purposes, requiring the cost of such hardware to be directly borne by the customer, increasing its costs. Further, software licensors are often unwilling to give discounts beyond those already offered for volume purchases. Unless the customer retains a qualified technology staff, the customer may be forced to use the hosting provider's staff to maintain its site, usually at an increased cost.

5. Issues for Consideration in Hosting Agreements

When entering into a hosting agreement, a customer should ensure that the scope of services to be provided by the vendor is clearly delineated. The scope should also include performance metrics for the vendor's hosting services, as well as its obligations to update and enhance its services. Those events that allow the vendor to terminate the agreement should be stated in detail, along with any transition services and the notice period for any termination of services. The customer should seek to negotiate a large limitation of liability to protect itself in the event of a breach. The vendor will usually seek to limit its liability to an inconsequential amount. The customer should require the vendor to commit to those metrics that are important to the customer, including uptime, server response time, help desk response time, and security.

6. *Licensing Concerns in a Hosting Environment*

(a) As between the Software Owner and Hosting Provider

(i) The Software Owner's Perspective

License Grant

Licensors should grant the licensee/hosting provider a nonexclusive, nontransferable license to (1) copy and install the software in object code form only on servers owned or managed by the hosting provider in the hosting provider's data centers (or owned by hosting provider or the hosting provider's customers and installed in hosting provider's data centers), and (2) re-license copies of the software to its customers under an end-user license agreement.

In all cases, the licensor should prohibit reverse engineering, decompiling, or otherwise trying to obtain the source code of the software.

To maintain strict control over its software, the licensor may want to grant a license to use, without the right to copy except for backup and archival copies and without any further right to re-license. In this case, the hosting provider may need to require its customer to license the software directly from the vendor.

The licensor may want to grant the right to transfer the licensed software from one computer to another, and/or from one client to another, provided the number of copies does not increase.

Pricing

The license grant is partly dependent on how the software is priced. How is the software licensed? On a per copy basis? Per Central Processing Unit (CPU)? Per client accessing the software (seat license)? The licensor needs to gauge how to maximize its profitability and/or the desires of its customers and structure both its license and its pricing accordingly.

If the software is priced on a per user basis, the licensor may grant the hosting provider the right to copy the software on as many computers as it wants. If pricing is on a per copy basis, the licensor may not want to grant the hosting provider the right to copy and instead grant the right to install and use. This way, the licensor controls the number of copies, and the hosting provider has to seek the licensor's consent for each additional copy. Alternatively, the licensor may make copies of the software freely available (e.g., the software can be downloaded from the vendor's website), but production use of the software is subject to a license key, so that the copies can be tracked. Other vendors make their software freely available, but charge for support and maintenance.

Other Contract Terms

In general, most other contract terms follow the same principles as standard software licensing. Usually, the licensor disclaims all warranties. The hosting provider should insist, however, on a warranty of title or indemnification for infringement, the latter being preferable. See Chapter 4.B.3. Like any licensor/licensee relationship, the licensor will likely prefer to give a warranty instead of an indemnification.

The licensor should seek an indemnification for any claim resulting from the hosting provider's agreement with the client (e.g., if the hosting provider decides to grant a better warranty than what the licensor has given to the hosting provider or disclaimed in the end-user license).

If the licensor permits the hosting provider to assign the license in the event of a merger/acquisition without the prior written approval of the licensor, the license grant should not allow increased use without appropriate payment. For example, a license grant for the software to be copied and used in the hosting provider's two data centers for one flat fee would potentially allow the purchaser to increase the number of clients without additional payment to the licensor. If a small client merges with a much larger company, software can potentially be used in many more data centers by many more users without any additional compensation payable to the licensor.

The software owner should provide the hosting provider with an end-user license agreement (EULA) as an exhibit to their contract and require the hosting provider to incorporate such license into the hosting provider's contract with the client. If the EULA is incorporated into the hosting provider's agreement with its clients, the vendor is in essence dictating the terms that apply to the particular application.

The licensor should also require that the hosting provider's agreement with its clients contain at a minimum the following clauses or substantially similar terms:

- identify the licensor as a third party beneficiary
- Have the client acknowledge the proprietary nature of the licensor's software. This point is less important if the EULA becomes part of the agreement between the client and the hosting provider.

Support

The licensor should carefully consider the level of support it expects to provide. Is the software licensor willing to provide any support directly to the clients? If so, can the clients call the software licensor directly, or does the vendor want the hosting provider to triage the calls first?

If the hosting provider is allowed to transfer the license to the client at the end of the contract between the hosting provider and the client, does support transfer with the license? Both technical support and help-desk support? If so, this could greatly increase the number of calls the software licensor will receive.

Will the software owner provide technical support? On what basis (normal business hours (if so, what time zone)? 24x7x365?) Hosting providers usually require 24x7, or at least pager access 24x7. Is support included in the price of the license, or is it priced separately? If the licensor grants the right to make derivative works, the licensor needs to make sure support does not include fixing problems caused by the licensee's scripts, etc. A smart licensor will limit its support obligations to the hosting provider to avoid being inundated by clients. Its maintenance support agreement should provide that clients cannot call the licensor for technical support, only the hosting provider's technical team.

What about client help desk support (e.g., can someone call to ask how to do a mail merge in Word or only call if the software is crashing the server)? If help desk/user support will not be provided, the contract should explicitly state so.

(ii) Hosting Provider's Perspective

License Grant

From the hosting provider's perspective, its license with the licensor should allow the software to be installed on multiple servers in different data centers and to be re-licensed to different clients. This avoids the hosting provider having to seek the licensor's permission each time a client wants to add servers or the hosting provider adds customers or data center locations.

In all cases, the hosting provider should be allowed to make copies for backup and archival purposes at no additional fee. Hosting providers should also seek to obtain additional copies for internal testing purposes at no cost. The right to transfer a copy of the software from one server/computer to another (e.g., if the hardware is upgraded) is also important to hosting providers. The hosting provider should also have the right to transfer a copy from one client to another client. For example, if a client has paid for a year's license and the client leaves the hosting provider, the hosting provider should have the right to use that license for another client for the balance of the license term. Some licensors do not allow this and require a new fee to be paid for each client. This position is unreasonable from the hosting provider's perspective as the license fee has already been paid. The licensor will not suffer a financial loss if the number of copies, CPU, or other metric does not increase.

Other Contract Terms

When representing a hosting provider, counsel should ascertain whether the hosting provider (or the client) wants to write scripts or port the software to a different operating system. Although some software licensors expect all derivative works to belong to the licensor, it makes more sense, consistent with federal copyright law, from the client's perspective if the new code belongs to the party who writes it, subject to the rights of the owner in the original work. *See* 17 U.S.C. § 101. See also Chapters 4.A.3(e) and 5.B.

The software licensor is unlikely to accept this position, however, as usually it seeks to own all enhancements and modifications to maintain the integrity of its software. Often licensors are concerned that if third parties own portions of their software, they will lose their ability to control their software.

The hosting provider should seek the right to resell the license to the software (and/or copy and distribute the software in object code form only) to its clients upon termination of the hosting agreement between the hosting provider and client or upfront—so long as the client will be hosting the software with the hosting provider and they can only use it on the client's premises after termination of the agreement between the client and hosting provider. In practice, however, the licensor is unlikely to agree to allow the hosting provider to resell the license.

The hosting provider will not want to attach the software vendor's EULA to each customer's agreement. Even small hosting architectures can require more than a dozen different applications residing on the customer's servers. Attaching each individual EULA makes the customer's contract unnecessarily long. Instead, the hosting provider should negotiate wording in its agreement with the licensor that states the hosting provider's agreement with the client will contain licensing terms that are no less protective of the licensor's rights than the terms of the agreement with the licensor. This allows the hosting provider to fold the licensor's limitations of liability and limitations of warranty under the general terms of the hosting provider's agreement with the customer and to include a general license grant that will cover all vendor agreements. Alternatively, the hosting provider may want to negotiate the minimum terms that need to be included in the sublicense to the client.

Support

The hosting provider should carefully consider the level of support it expects the licensor to provide. The hosting provider should definitively determine what is included in the licensor's license fee. The license should detail whether upgrades, patches, maintenance, and the like are included. For those services that are likely to be needed but are not included, the license should clearly set forth the applicable pricing to avoid later pricing disputes when the hosting provider lacks leverage.

Since uptime is very important to a hosting provider's customers, hosting providers should insist on access to 24x7 support, at least by pager. From the customer's perspective, the hosting provider is managing the software. If the software crashes, the hosting provider may need immediate access to the vendor in order to meet its uptime service level agreement with its customer.

(b) As between the Hosting Provider and the End User

(i) The Hosting Party's Perspective

While the hosting provider usually seeks to disclaim all warranties, the client should insist on a warranty of title or indemnification for infringement, the latter being preferable from the client's perspective. See Chapter 4.B.3. Special, incidental, consequential, punitive, and similar damages are usually disclaimed by the hosting provider. The hosting provider's damages are usually limited to the amount received in payment *or* the amount received in the one year prior to the event that gave rise to the claim. The hosting provider should ensure that it flows down the licensor's terms to the client. The "license grant" set forth below addresses a majority of the required flow down terms typically imposed by licensors:

> In the event we provide any software to you in connection with the Services, we grant you a personal, non-exclusive, non-transferable license, for the duration of your Service Period, to use such software in object code form only on the hardware on which it is installed for the sole purpose of enabling you to use the Services.

> We represent and you acknowledge that the software is copyrighted, that title to such software remains with us or our suppliers, and that the content and design of such software are valuable trade secrets. You agree not to (a) disclose or make available to third parties any portion of such software without our advance written permission; (b) copy or duplicate such software; (c) reverse engineer, decompile, or disassemble such software; or (d) modify or make derivative works of such software. You agree not to use such software after the Service Period without obtaining a valid license from us or from the third-party supplier.

(ii) The End User's Perspective

From the client's perspective, the client should insist that the hosting provider transfer ownership of the license to the client upon termination of its agreement with the hosting provider. It may be argued that this position is equitable only given that the client has paid for the license. The hosting provider, however, may consider the underlying agreement a services agreement and thus take the position that the client is not entitled to receive the software. While the cost of the software license is taken into account in pricing the hosting provider's services, the relationship is analogous to an ongoing lease rather than payment for ownership. If the parties agree to a transfer, the hosting provider needs to ensure the client pays the cost of any transfer fees. The parties also need to determine whether support and maintenance can be transferred along with the license. Usually this is even more difficult.

The client should insist on an indemnification for infringement from the hosting provider, even though the hosting provider is not the owner of the software. The hosting provider should be receiving the indemnity from software owner. Further, technical support for the software will usually be provided by the hosting provider, rather than having the client contact the vendor directly. Will the hosting provider assume responsibility for the software if it causes downtime (i.e., are all problems included for purposes of SLAs)? The hosting provider should seek an exclusion for defects in the software for which fixes have not been provided by the vendor.

CHAPTER **8**

Open Source Software

A. Overview

Ignored a decade ago as the purview of counter-culture programmers, open source software has assumed greater prominence in commercial software licensing. The myth that open source software has little commercial value for or strategic impact on software vendors or their customers has been proven false. With an increasing number of industry leaders, such as IBM and Sun Microsystems, developing open source software products and a growing number of for profit service providers, such as Red Hat, whose business model is founded on supporting open source software, the importance of open source software can no longer be ignored or disputed. The Gartner Group has projected that by 2011 80 percent of all commercial software will incorporate open source software to some degree. *See* http://www.gartner.com/it/page.jsp?id=593207 (Last viewed September 15, 2010).

Open source is developed through a number of means, including core developers who determine project direction and approve changes made by others, contributors who supply fixes and enhancements, deployment of source code management ("SCM") tools (sometimes themselves open source, like the popular Subversion and CVS tools), virtual development teams sometimes supported by commercial companies, and users who submit bug reports and enhancement requests. Open source software has achieved popularity in many categories, including user-ready products for operating systems (e.g., Linux, BSD), desktop applications (e.g., Open Office, Firefox Browser), servers (e.g., Apache, Tomcat), development tools and code components.

B. Definition

While there is no one definitive definition of "open source software", the term generally refers to software with source code that is made freely available to the public without charge and which may be further distributed. The Free Software Foundation ("FSF") and the Open Source Institute ("OSI"), the two oldest and most influential and longest-active bodies advocating, respectively, free and open source software, have adopted differing definitions. The OSI definition sets forth ten criteria that the software must satisfy. *See http://www.opensource.org/docs/definition.php* (Last viewed September 15, 2010). The FSF definition sets forth five criteria, and notably requires the software to be licensed under the mandatory "copyleft" license in order to be considered open source. *See* http://www.fsf.org/licensing/essays/free-sw.html. (Last viewed September 15, 2010).

Open source software is generally assumed to have the following traits:

- The software including the source code is made publicly and freely available
- The licensee is able to modify the source code
- The licensee is able to redistribute the software including its source code
- The software is subject to a license agreement
- Protection is provided through copyright, patent and contract protection, not trade secret protection

Open source software differs from other categories of noncommercial third party software such as shareware, freeware, and public domain software. Shareware is generally considered to be software available in object code that requests the payment of a license fee for its use. Freeware is similar to shareware but the licensor does not require a license fee. Public domain software is software for which the author has waived all rights of ownership including copyright claims and the right to receive license fees. Public domain software is usually distributed in source code form.

C. Costs Associated with Using Open Source Software

The belief that open source software is "free" is a misconception as there are many costs associated with using open source software. Foremost is the cost of complying with the license requirements and obligations. The licensee must review the underlying licensing terms to ensure its compliance and in turn expend management costs to educate its employees and guide later usage activities (particularly software modification and/or redistribution) as to the user's compliance obligations.

Many also pay support fees to third party specialist entities that support open source software (and usually are intimately involved with the prior and ongoing development of some particular application[s] or tool[s]). First line support is usually provided by the user's in house development staff. Most users outside very large companies lack the infrastructure or ability to provide higher levels of support. Further, redistribution of the software is not necessarily free as it is subject to the terms of the underlying license. Perhaps the greatest cost is haphazard use of open source software modules that could infect proprietary code with unwanted publication and redistribution requirements.

D. Advantages and Disadvantages of Using Open Source Software

1. Advantages

Open source software provides a number of potential advantages, depending on a particular prospective user's goals, operating culture, and resources. In addition to the obvious benefit of no license fees for the software itself, users can obtain enhanced functionality by adding new features to existing development projects and support for new platforms. Standardization is another potential advantage, as some long established open source software, such as Apache, has become the *defacto* standard for certain industries and applications. Further, open source software may improve consistency and reuse through improved quality, assuming the particular code has enjoyed refinement through many capable individuals and versions. In theory, a large number of contributors may mean that a greater number of bugs will be identified and resolved and that there will be more testing and validation (hence the assertions by open source advocate Eric S. Raymond that "Given enough eyeballs, all bugs are shallow"). Open source is immediately available as it can be downloaded almost instantaneously from the Internet. Finally, open source encourages agreement on common standards and interoperability.

2. Risks of Using Open Source Software

Open source software is not the panacea many programmers hear and believe. Most open source software comes without a warranty of any kind, including a warranty against infringement or viruses. Further, under some license types, owners of proprietary software that integrate open source software into their product are prohibited from charging for the further distribution of their proprietary software and may be required to distribute source code.

There is no guarantee of support for open source software. Because the underlying code may be the product of many different authors, there is little accountability and certainly no service level standards or guarantee of future enhancements. Any enhancements are subject to the whim of the user community and the software may be abandoned by its authors, leaving the user on its own. In these cases, the user will have to rely on its own in-house support or have to move to a new third party product. Finally, documentation is often weak with little or no training materials available.

3. Legal Concerns

There are many legal issues associated with the use of open source software. The most prominent is the mandatory (so-called "viral") provisions contained in some licenses (e.g., the GPL and LGPL licenses). The term "viral" refers to the provisions contained in these licenses requiring users who integrate the open source software into their proprietary software to offer the combined product as open source software with the right of further distribution. Often referred to as "copyleft" provisions, in contrast to the protections provided by a copyright, these provisions seek to prevent the redistribution of the integrated open source software as so-called closed (no source code available and with traditional proprietary licensing) commercial software.

Open source licenses may also provide reason for concern as they often are not written by lawyers and may be vague, confusing, and contain conflicting terms that are open to interpretation. Licensees should carefully review the license terms for all third party software that they utilize. For example, some third party licensors, such as Microsoft, may prohibit use of their software with open source products in an attempt to protect their products from viral open source. *See* http://news.cnet.com/2100-1001-268889.html (Last viewed September 15, 2010). Many open source licenses require the user to disclose the existence of open source software in the user's proprietary product and to provide the end user with a copy of the underlying open source software license. *See* Form 23.E.1 § 2 and Form 23.E.2 § 1. For a general discussion, *see* Bouscaren & Parker, *Notice and Attribution: A Crucial Component of Proper Open Source Software Redistribution,* 27 ACC Docket 66 (Sept. 2009); Murray, *Attribution Requirements* in *Free and Open Source Software Licensing,* 25 Computer and Internet Law. 10 (May 2008); Bouscaren and Parker, *Notice & Attribution: A Crucial Component of Proper Open Source Software Redistribution*, ACC Docket 66 (Sept. 2009).

One of the biggest issues for licensors that incorporate open source into their proprietary products is attempting to ascertain initial ownership of the open source software and quantifying the risk of intellectual property infringement, including patent and copyright infringement. Most open source licenses disclaim any liability for intellectual property infringement and do not provide any accompanying indemnity. The party's risk is accentuated by the lack of a clear chain of title due to the communal nature of development. Those licensors that accept liability (i.e., the few, large corporations that offer enhanced versions of software, usually with extra services, for a subscription or other fee) usually limit their liability to the cost of the software. The risk of litigation regarding intellectual property allegations over software that is key to the infrastructure and operations of a business may be exploited by a competitor in an effort to discourage the user's potential customers from purchasing the user's products. One of the most well known examples (though not regarding open source software) is *NTP, Inc. v. Research in Motion, Ltd.*, 418 F.3d. 1282 (Fed. Cir. 2005) where NTP claimed that certain software used by Research in Motion ("RIM") infringed on NTP's patents. NTP sought an injunction to prevent RIM from utilizing the subject, software, which would have shut down RIM's business. At one point in the litigation RIM agreed to pay NTP $450M even before the matter was settled. *See* http://news.cnet.com/BlackBerry-getting-squeezed/2009-1047_3-6042243.html (Last viewed September 15, 2010).

Occasionally, a licensor may offer both an open source license and a commercial license for its application. The licensor does so as it likely believes the open source license it is offering is not commercially friendly. In those cases, the safest path for the licensee planning to commercially exploit the software is to license the software under the traditional commercial license terms.

E. License Types

As of September 15, 2010, there are 67 types of open source licenses that have been recognized by the Open Source Institute ("OSI") despite an effort in recent years by the OSI to reduce the number of approved licenses to reduce complexity and its possible impediment to open source adoption. *See* http://www.opensource.org/licenses/alphabetical (Last viewed September 15, 2010). Each of these licenses reflects the personality of the particular software's author. In general, each of these licenses can be placed into one of two categories: permissive licenses and non-permissive licenses. Set forth below is a general discussion of each of these license types and the issues associated with each.

1. Permissive Licenses

Permissive licenses are generally defined as those open source licenses that do not require the licensor to place derivative works into the public domain or provide source code to downstream users. The licensor may distribute source code or object code provided it provides the underlying open source software copyright notice and license terms (including liability disclaimer) to the end user. Further, the user may not represent the software's contributors as endorsing the user's products. Modifications and enhancements may be claimed as trade secrets (i.e., if distributed in only object code form) and be owned by the licensor. Examples of permissive licenses are the Apache license, the MIT license and the Berkeley Software Distribution ("BSD") license. *See* Form 23.E.1 for a copy of the MIT license.

2. Non-permissive Licenses ("Viral" Licenses)

Non-permissive licenses are those that include "copyleft" provisions which require the licensor, in certain circumstances, to make available improvements or enhancements to the underlying open source software on terms identical (historically, though possibly somewhat varied with the still relatively new GPLv3 license) to those under which the licensor licensed the open source software. This may include making the source code available without charge to end users.

Viral provisions in non-permissive licenses may be activated if the licensor modifies the underlying open source code and seeks to distribute the code as an integrated part of the licensor's proprietary software. If the licensee simply links its software to the open source software without commingling or integration, the viral provisions may not apply. The viral provisions in non-permissive licenses are complicated, and care should be taken to understand these terms, the relative integration of the open source software into the proprietary software, and the anticipated distribution strategy for the software. Examples of non-permissive licenses are the GPL license (both v2 and v3), the Lesser General Public License ("LGPL") license, and the NGPL license. *See* Form 23.E.2 for a copy of the GNU license.

F. Negotiating Licenses for Software Which Incorporates Open Source Software

The negotiation of license agreements where open source software is incorporated into the licensed product is complex and is presently evolving and immature in the marketplace. A prudent licensee will seek at least indemnification and warranties flowing to the integrated product which licensors are likely hesitant to give. Some particularly vigilant customers may seek specific contractual assurances regarding the particular contents, tools, and development history of the software (e.g., if the application is only available from one vendor, is mission-critical to the customer's entire operations, or implicates regulatory compliance in the customer's industry). Further, licensors must be ever vigilant to ensure open source software is not incorporated into their proprietary software without their knowledge, while prudent licensees must be careful to try to assure that open source software is not included into the licensed software without their knowledge. Monitoring the presence of open source software in a particular program is a difficult task for both licensors and licensees. Set forth below is a discussion of several of the issues that licensors and licensees should consider when negotiating a license involving open source software.

1. Incoming Licenses

In evaluating the risk of accepting acknowledged open source software in a licensed product, licensees can take a number of actions to limit their risk. For example, a licensee should require the licensor to represent and warrant that the software delivered to the licensee contains no open source software, or, if open source is incorporated into the deliverables, that all open source software (and its corresponding license and the particular Website and page from which it was downloaded) is set forth accurately in a detailed schedule to the underlying software license. This should not be an issue for the well-managed, well-informed licensor as all open source software licenses recognized by the Open Source Institute require users to attribute authorship of the open source software contained in their deliverables and provide the licensee with copies of the relevant licenses for the incorporated open source software. To protect against unknowingly receiving open source code, the licensee should also consider scanning (or, requiring scanning by the vendor of) the deliverables with a software program to detect the presence of open source software, such as using products and/or services from Black Duck Software, Palamida, or SourceAdvisor, or even newer, evolving open source tools like FOSSBazaar with proper direction from knowledgeable employees or consultants.

Licensees should also seek to have the licensor represent and warrant that the deliverables, including the open source software incorporated within the deliverables, do not infringe on any third party intellectual property. The licensee also should seek to have the licensor indemnify the licensee against any ownership disputes, breach of open source obligations, or third party intellectual property infringement. However, the licensor may argue that the licensee is receiving a reduced license fee by incorporating open source software and is thus unwillingly to provide such an indemnity. Many informed software vendors presently decline to give broad intellectual property warranties or indemnifications related to open source software. If the licensee is unable to secure proper indemnification, representations, or warranties, then the licensee (with full cooperation from the licensor) should carefully review any incorporated open source software and associated licenses to assess the risk of future claims. Licensors incorporate open source software into their product without any representation, warranty, or indemnity from the community of developers, so they typically will not pass any assurances along to their licensees. *See* Chapter 4.B.1 and 4.B.3.

See Form 23.E.4 for a model licensee oriented warranty applicable to open source software.

2. *Outgoing Licenses*

Because most open source licenses disclaim all warranties, especially the warranty of noninfringement, licensors usually avoid making any representations or warranties to the licensee relating to any open source software delivered with their product (or software tools used to design and develop the product). Licensors often carefully define "Deliverables" or "Licensed Software" to mean the licensor's proprietary software products and exclude any third party products (including open source software) incorporated into the deliverables. By doing so, the licensor can avoid assuming liability arising from third party products where it cannot quantify its risk.

See Form 23.E.3 for model language limiting the licensor's representations and warranties to its own proprietary software, and excluding third party software including open source software.

Some licensors will warrant that the deliverables, including any open source software incorporated therein, will operate in substantial conformance with the delivered documentation. In the event a licensor is willing to make such a warranty, it should clearly limit the licensee's remedy to replacing the nonconforming software with comparable software within a reasonable period of time. The stated time period should reflect the period of time the licensor believes it will take to develop a replacement product.

Most open source licenses require the user to provide its licensees with a copy of the underlying open source license agreement. *See* e.g. Forms 23.E.1 and Form 23.E.2 § 4. To satisfy this requirement, the licensor can attach actual copies of the relevant licenses or provide a link to the relevant open source licenses in the licensor's license.

Another issue for licensors who utilize open source software is the lack of internal procedures for incorporating open source software into their proprietary software. As such, the licensor assumes the risk that the software is defective or infringes on a third party's intellectual property rights. Thus the licensor should carefully weigh the benefits of utilizing open source software against the risks of potential liability for intellectual property infringement and the software's failure to operate properly. Sophisticated licensors that use open source software have rigorous procedures to review the need for such software, the relevant license terms, and the attendant risks of incorporation. Ideally, as discussed below, these procedures lie in the legal function of the organization that has experience in open source software issues.

Savvy licensees will argue that they are entitled to receive a representation and warranty against infringement and that the software is virus free. Most licensors will respond that the use of open source software saves the licensee a significant amount of money in development costs and that the licensee must balance the lack of representations and warranties against reduced costs. For well developed, widely used open source products, tool, or components, the risk may be small, but for unknown products downloaded from the Internet with little or no operating history, the risk could be great to both the licensor and the licensee. Both the licensor and the licensee should undertake significant due diligence on the product in question before utilizing the software, including an investigation of the modular nature of the software and its documentation to assess the feasibility of future substitution of the open source software to mitigate risk.

G. Quantifying the Risk

In trying to quantify the risk, licensors and licensee should examine several factors. First, a party should determine what percentage of the delivered code is made up of open source software. Further, how is the open source software linked to the licensor's proprietary product? How quickly and effectively could the functionality provided by the open source software be recreated or replaced? How important to the operation of the deliverables is the open source software? Is the open source product proven in the industry? Has the licensor used the open source software for a significant period of time? What is its reputation? Is the particular open code a "dying tree," with few recent upgrades, bug fixes, or comments at its project base Website? How closely managed and documented have been code additions over time (given the variety of options in setting up and administering source code maintenance systems)? The smaller the impact of open source on the entire product, the smaller the risk. Similarly, if other products are available to replace the open source software, the risk is smaller.

1. Open Source Review Board for Software Development

To limit their risks and maintain the integrity of their product, vendors incorporating open source software into their proprietary product should establish an open source review board to approve the incorporation of open source software into their products. Thus it will allow the vendor to map the "genealogy" of their product and provide a disciplined, possibly evolving, and documented approach to the inclusion of open source. The review board should include representatives of the vendor's software developers, lawyer(s) "fluent" in open source theory, history, culture, and concepts, and business people to ensure that a balanced and well-reasoned decision is made. The software developers should determine, in consultation with the vendor's lawyer(s), whether any non-permissive/viral provisions of the underlying open source license are triggered based on the nature of incorporation and distribution of the open source software. The business people should periodically evaluate whether the cost savings achieved through the incorporation of open source software outweighs the then-perceived risk of incorporating open source software into the vendor's proprietary software. Such internal "policy and process" entities are often deployed to handle related issues, such as determining if and when employees can participate in or start open source projects. *See* Forms 23.E.5 and 23.E.6.

2. Open Source Software Audits for Licensees

On the licensee side, a code audit can determine how the proprietary code has been used historically (not just currently) with the open source software to confirm whether the proprietary code has to be made publicly available pursuant to the GPL license. The GPL license is written not from a legal perspective but from a technical view. Hence, many references will require a technical explanation, e.g., static vs. dynamic linking. Typically, GPL licenses require, among other things, that the source code of the combined product be made publicly available.

If the code has been "combined" with the open source software, the combined code becomes subject to the terms and conditions of the GPL license. This technical analysis will give the licensee the information it needs to decide whether to take a license to the software. The licensee should speak with the licensor's technical staff and actually review the code itself, not just rely on the licensor's technical staff. The licensor should identify each open source software program, state whether the program has or has not been used in a manner that would require the proprietary code to become open source code, and explain whether the program qualifies for an exception to the GPL requirements.

Additionally, the GPL code is protected through copyright law. If the licensee were to use it in violation of the terms of the GPL license, it would be considered misappropriation of copyrighted material, which is illegal and has both civil and criminal penalties.

Lastly, all open source licenses exclude performance warranties, infringement warranties and indemnification obligations. If the licensee were to sublicense code that contains the GPL open source software with infringement and indemnification warranties, the licensee would be liable both to upstream contributors and downstream users—significant intellectual property exposure.

H. Legal Challenges

A modest number of legal challenges have been brought against authors of open source software challenging the validity of the underlying open source software licenses and the restrictions they contain. These claims have been based both in contract law and copyright law.

1. *Contract Based Claims*

The Free Software Foundation acting through its Software Freedom Law Center ("SFLC") recently filed a number of complaints against users of the Busy-Box software utilities for their failure to comply with the licensing terms contained in the GPLv2 license agreement. Most of these cases were quickly settled by the defendant. In general, the defendants agreed to make a payment to the licensor, contact all prior recipients of the licensor's software to offer them source code, and appoint an open source compliance officer (a term not required by the GPLv2).

2. *Copyright Based Claims*

In a case of first impression, the United States Court of Appeals for the Federal Circuit, in *Jacobsen v. Katzer*, 535 F.3d 1373 (Fed. Cir. 2008), hearing an appeal from the Federal District Court for the Northern District of California held that open source software is entitled to the available protections under copyright law. The *Jacobsen* court was the first court to uphold the validity of open source software licenses under both contract and copyright law.

Jacobsen bought suit against Matthew Katzer and Kamind Associates alleging among other claims that the defendants had failed to include the required notice of attribution required by the open source license agreement under which they licensed Jacobsen's software. The District court held that open source licenses were founded on contract law, ignoring the underlying copyright issues, and thereby limiting Jacobsen's recovery to monetary damages.

The Federal Circuit court, however, held that "[c]opyright holders who engage in open source licensing have the right to control the modification and distribution of copyrighted material." *Id.* at 1381. It emphasized that "[t]he choice to extract consideration in the form of compliance with the open source requirements of disclosure and explanation of changes, rather than as a dollar-denominated fee, is entitled to no less legal recognition." *Id.* at 1382. It distinguished a copyright claim and a contract claim in finding that the restrictions contained in Jacobsen's license were necessary "to accomplish the objectives of the open source licensing collaboration, including economic benefit." *Id.* at 1381. In reaching its decision, the *Jacobsen* court found that the licensor's terms were conditions on the scope of the license thus giving rise to a claim for copyright infringement. *Id.*

The ruling was the first to recognize that violating the terms of an open source license could constitute copyright infringement. By doing so, the *Jacobsen* court exposed licensees to potential liability of up to $150,000 per work in statutory damages and the payment of the licensor's legal fees (assuming the plaintiff owner received copyright registration before or within three months of the initial infringement) as well as allowing licensors the right to seek injunctive relief in addition to monetary damages for breach of contract.

For a more detailed discussion, *see* Hines and Robin, *Federal Court Rules that Open Source Licenses are Enforceable Under Copyright Law*, 143 Intell. Prop. Couns. 13 (Nov. 2008).

I. Going Forward

Open source software can significantly benefit both licensors and licensees through the reduction of development costs and time, increased quality and compatibility, and efficient delivery of marketable features and functions. Prudent parties should undertake an in-depth due diligence process to identify and limit the potential risks of incorporating open source software into any deliverables. With increasing sensitivity to open source issues from their customers, licensors should establish a well-documented process to approve and map the incorporation of open source software into their proprietary software. An open source review board with experienced technical personnel and legal counsel with particular open source experience can identify the risks and benefits of potential incorporation of open source software. Licensees should insist on specific representations, warranties, and indemnification relating to open source software to limit their risks or, absent such assurances, perform a code scan or other diligence on the delivered software to assess the risk and assure compliance with all open source obligations.

For a more In-depth overview of open source software, *see* Rosen, Open Source Licensing (Addison-Wesley, Prentice Hall 2005); Davidson and Kumagai, *Developments in the Open Source Community and the Impact of the Release of GPLv3*, 25 Computer and Internet Law. 1 (Jan. 2008); Falkowski, *Open Source Licensing: An Innovation in Contract Drafting*, 84 Mich. B. J. 30 (May 2005); Kubelka and Fawcett, *No Free Beer – Practice Tips for Open Source Licensing*, 22 Santa Clara Computer & High Tech. L. J. 797 (2006); González de Alaiza Cardona, *Open Source, Free Software, and Contractual Issues*, 15 Tex. Intell. Prop. L. J. 157 (2007); *Kennedy, A Primer on Open Source Licensing Legal Issues; Copyright, Copyleft and Copyfuture*, 20 St. Louis U. Pub. L. Rev. 345 (2001).

CHAPTER **9**

Shrink-wrap, Click-wrap and Browse-wrap Licenses

A. Shrink-wrap Licenses

Shrink-wrap licenses derive their name from the practice of containing them on (or currently in) a shrink-wrap package that also contains the software and documentation. The license is visible through the cellophane packaging, and it usually provides that the purchaser is bound by the terms of the license upon opening the shrink-wrap. If the licensee does not agree with and therefore does not wish to be bound by the terms of the license, it should return the unopened package to the licensor for a full refund. There is no opportunity to negotiate the terms of the license.

Initially, courts were hesitant to enforce shrink-wrap licenses. Courts upholding shrink-wrap licenses also use the Uniform Commercial Code (UCC) as well as other laws. *See generally Step-Saver Data Systems, Inc. v. Wyse Technology,* 939 F.2d 91 (3d Cir. 1991) (shrink-wrap license not enforceable under Section 2-207 of UCC as license terms mutually altered the contract between the parties); *Arizona Retail Systems v. Software Link, Inc.,* 831 F. Supp. 759 (D. Ariz. 1993) (shrink-wrap license not binding under UCC Sections 2-207 and 2-209). *See also Vault Corporation v. Quaid Software, Ltd.,* 847 F.2d 255 (5th Cir. 1988) (provisions of shrink-wrap license unenforceable to the extent their validity is based on Louisiana Software License Enforcement Act that is preempted by federal copyright law).

In *ProCD, Inc. v. Zeidenberg,* 86 F.3d 1447 (7th Cir. 1996), the Seventh Circuit held that "shrink-wrap licenses are enforceable unless their terms are objectionable on grounds applicable to contracts in general" (i.e., unconscionable). The court rejected the applicability of UCC § 2-207 stating that a battle of the forms could not exist if only one form existed. Thus, there was initially a stark dichotomy of opinion as to the enforceability of shrink-wrap licenses. *See also Hill v. Gateway 2000, Inc.,* 105 F.3d 1147 (7th Cir. 1997), *cert. denied,* 522 U.S. 808 (1997) (contract terms in computer box enforceable, including arbitration clause); *M.A. Mortenson Co. v. Timberline Software Corp.,* 998 P.2d 305 (Wash. 2000), *aff'd,* No. 67796-4, 2000 Wash. LEXIS 287 (Wash. Sup. Ct. May 4, 2000); *Bowers v. Baystate Technologies, Inc.,* 320 F.3d 1317 (Fed. Cir. 2003) (Copyright Act does not preempt or narrow contractual prohibition on reverse engineering contained in shrink-wrap license).

Since *ProCD,* many federal and state courts have upheld licenses given to the customer after payment of the license fee, provided the licensee has the right to cancel the transaction once it receives the license terms and is unwilling to accept them. *See Meridian Project Systems, Inc. v. Hardin Const. Co.,* 42 F. Supp. 2d 1101 (E.D. Cal. 2006) (shrink-wrap EULA not unconscionable because buyer did not see license prior to purchasing software; EULA not preempted by Copyright Act.). *See also Hill v. Gateway 2000, Inc.,* 105 F.3d 1147, 1149–50 (7th Cir. 1997), *cert. denied* 522 U.S. 808 (1997); *O'Quin v. Verizon Wireless,* 256 F. Supp. 2d 512 (M.D. La. 2003); *Lozano v. AT&T Wireless,* 216 F. Supp. 2d 1071, 1073 (C.D. Cal. 2002); *i.LAN Systems, Inc. v. NetScout Service Level Corp.,* 183 F. Supp. 2d 328, 337–38 (D. Mass. 2002); *Moore v. Microsoft Corp.,* 741 N.Y.S.2d 91 (2002); *Brower v. Gateway 2000, Inc.,* 676 N.Y.S.2d 569 (1998); *M.A. Mortenson Co. v. Timberline Software Corp.,* 970 P.2d 803, 809 (Wash. 1999).

Given that most shrink-wrapped software is utilized in the consumer market, it is possible that it is subject to the Magnuson-Moss Act. The contrary is also possible. Consequently, to avoid coverage under the Magnuson-Moss Act, and the accompanying limitations, a licensor must be very careful as to the warranties it makes. See Chapter 4.B.1(b)(ii) for a detailed discussion of the Magnuson-Moss Act.

Section 209 of the Uniform Computer Information Transactions Act (UCITA) recognizes the validity of shrink-wrap licenses with certain limitations. See Chapter 11.B.3(k) for a more detailed discussion.

For a more detailed discussion, see Lemley, *Intellectual Property and Shrink-wrap Licenses,* 68 S. CAL. L. REV. 1239 (1995); Moore and Hadden, *On-Line Software Distribution: New Life for "Shrink-wrap" Licenses?,* 13 COMPUTER LAW. 1 (April 1996); *Recent Legal Developments in Shrink Wrap License Agreements,* 12 COMPUTER L. STRATEGIST 1 (April 1996); Miller, *The Enforceability of Shrink-wraps as Bare Intellectual Property Licenses,* 9 COMPUTER LAW. 15 (August 1992).

For a general discussion, see Kim, *Clicking and Cringing,* 86 OR. L.R. 797 (2007); Rowles, *Shrink-Wrap and Click-Wrap Agreements Under the Uniform Computer Information Transactions Act,* 17 E-COMMERCE ADVISOR 3 (May 2001); Rowles, *Enforceability of Shrink-Wrap and Click-Wrap Licenses—Revisited,* 18 E-COMMERCE ADVISOR 1 (June 2002).

B. Click-wrap Licenses

Click-wrap licenses are similar to shrink-wrap licenses except that they are viewed online and the user must click on an icon to accept the terms of the license. Requiring the user to manifest its assent provides a licensor with a stronger argument for enforcing a license than otherwise may be made in the case of a shrink-wrap license. Click-wrap licenses are generally held to be enforceable when the license terms are viewed prior to the software's purchase or installation. *See, e.g., i.LAN Systems, Inc. v. NetScout Service Level Corp.,* 183 F. Supp. 2d 328 (D. Mass. 2002); *Davidson & Assocs. v. Jung,* 422 F.3d 630 (8th Cir. 2005). *See generally Caspi v. Microsoft Corp.,*

743 A.2d 851 (N.J. App. Div. 1999) (forum selection clause in click wrap agreement was enforceable); *A.V. v. iParadigms, LLC,* 544 F. Supp. 2d 473 (E.D. Va. 2008) (minors bound by terms set forth in click-wrap agreement). A click-wrap agreement will generally be enforced if the user is given the opportunity to read the digital license agreement prior to delivery of the software. *Moore v. Microsoft Corp.*, 293 A.D.2d 587 (N.Y.A.D. 2002). For a general discussion, see Rowles, *Shrink-Wrap and Click-Wrap Agreements Under the Uniform Computer Information Transactions Act,* 17 E-COMMERCE ADVISOR 3 (May 2001); Rowles, *Enforceability of Shrink-Wrap and Click-Wrap Licenses—Revisited,* 18 E-COMMERCE ADVISOR 1 (June 2002).

However, licensors must be careful in structuring the click-through process. At least one court refused to enforce the provisions of a click-wrap agreement when the user had to scroll down below the "download" button to see the license terms and where the "download" button did not indicate unambiguous assent to the terms. *See Specht v. Netscape,* 306 F.3d 17, 35 (2nd Cir. 2002). Rather than use language such as "please review and agree to the terms" on the button, the licensor should use language that indicates assent, such as "by clicking, I agree to the terms." Cunningham & Witkow, *Click with Caution: Liability for Breach of Click-Wrap and Browse-Wrap Agreements,* 23 COMPUTER & INTERNET LAW. 1 (June 2006).

For an overview of electronic transactions, see RAYMOND T. NIMMER & HOLLY K. TOWLE, THE LAW OF ELECTRONIC COMMERCIAL TRANSACTIONS, Thompson * West (2010).

For a general overview of the enforceability of click-wrap and shrink-wrap licenses, see Rowles, *Shrink-Wrap and Click-Wrap Agreements Under the Uniform Computer Information Transactions Act,* 17 E-COMMERCE ADVISOR 3 (May 2001); Rowles, *Enforceability of Shrink-Wrap and Click-Wrap Licenses—Revisited,* 18 E-COMMERCE ADVISOR 1 (June 2002); Grierson, *Enforceability of "Click-wrap" or "Shrink-wrap" Agreements Common in Computer Software, Hardware, and Internet Transactions,* 106 A.L.R. 5th 309 (2003); Dessent, Browse-wraps, Click-Wraps and Cyberlaw: Our Shrinking (Wrap) World, 25 T. JEFFERSON L. REV. 1 (2002); Kunz *et. al., Browse-Wrap Agreements: Validity of Implied Assent in Electronic Form Agreements,* 59 BUS. LAW. 279 (2003); and Kunz *et al., Click-Through Agreements: Strategies for Avoiding Disputes on Validity of Assent,* 57 BUS. LAW. 401 (2001).

C. Browse-wrap Licenses

Browse-wrap licenses are licenses posted on website that are usually accessed through a hyperlink and that do not require a user to affirmatively indicate his/her acceptance of the license terms. *See Pollstar v. Gigmania, Ltd.*, 170 F. Supp. 2d 974, 981 (E.D. Cal. 2000) ("[A] browse wrap license is part of the website and the user assents to the contract when the user visits the website."). Browse-wrap licenses are generally enforceable even if the user did not read the license terms, provided that the terms were available to the user prior to acceptance. *Druyan v. Jagger,* 508 F. Supp. 228 (S.D.N.Y. 2007). "The validity of a browsewrap license turns on whether a website user has actual or constructive knowledge of a site's terms and conditions prior to using the site." *Southwest Airlines Co. v. BoardFirst, L.L.C.*, 2007 WL 4823761 *5 (N.D. Tex. Sept. 12, 2007).

For a general overview, see Ian Rambarran & Robert Hunt, *Are Browse-Wrap Agreements All They Are Wrapped Up to Be?*, 9 TUL. J. TECH. & INTELL. PROP. 173 (Spring 2007); Christina L. Kunz et al., *Browse-Wrap Agreements: Validity of Implied Assent in Electronic Form Agreements*, 59 Bus. Law. 279 (Nov. 2003).

CHAPTER **10**

Privacy and Security Issues

Unlike confidentiality clauses and agreements which traditionally have sought to protect the proprietary trade secrets of the contracting parties, data privacy and security provisions address the parties' compliance with applicable data privacy/security laws and the parties' contractually required standards and safeguards to protect their Personally Identifiable Information ("PII") Protected Health Information ("PHI"), which is a subset of PII as well as Non-Public Personal Information ("NPI"). From a licensor's perspective, this usually involves protecting a third party's PII in compliance with all applicable law and other mutually agreeable standards including the licensee's data security and data privacy policies. For a general discussion of the impact of a party's bankruptcy on data protection/security, see Claypoole & Benoit, *Protecting Data in a Business Failure*, 27 ACC DOCKET 21 (Sept. 2009).

See Form 23.L.1 for a model Data Privacy/Security Checklist and Chapter 22.L.2 for a checklist for reviewing Business Associate Agreements ("BAAs").

A. Data Privacy and Security

Data privacy and security obligations are assuming greater importance in those license negotiations where the licensor has access to PII. Licensee data, personal information, data security, data privacy and confidentiality all, to some degree, relate to PII. Protection requirements for PII now extend beyond the terms of the underlying agreement to include the ever-increasing number of state, federal and local laws. As of September 2010, forty-seven states and the District of Columbia had enacted data breach notification laws. These laws focus on the obligations to report once a breach has occurred. Increasingly, states are also enacting laws that focus on requiring appropriate security safeguards to prevent breaches from happening to begin with (see, for example, Massachusetts comprehensive law that mirrors NIST and ISO standards). Some of these laws create causes of action on behalf of third parties such as the licensee's customers and employees who lack contractual privity with the licensor. As such, both parties should carefully negotiate each party's obligations as to data privacy and security. By carefully considering and allocating risk, the parties can quantify their risk while limiting the impact of unforeseen consequences.

For a general discussion regarding data privacy, see Jonathan T, Rubens, *So Many Privacy Rules! The Developing Standard of Care for Data Security and Identity Theft Protection,* 18 BUS. L. TODAY 55 (July/Aug. 2009).

Set forth below is a discussion of several issues that should be considered by both parties to ensure the relevant risks related to data privacy and security have been identified and mitigated to the greatest extent possible.

1. Evaluation of the Underlying Risks

Prior to entering an agreement, both the licensor and licensee should evaluate the level of risk and likelihood of a data or security breach. The level of risk is determined by a number of factors: (i) the type of data involved; (ii) the respective responsibilities of the parties related to the data; (iii) the operational safeguards imposed by the licensee; and (iv) the licensor's own data security safeguards. Risk is also dependent upon the nature of the violation and the data disclosed or otherwise compromised. In one of the largest known cases of a data breach, TJ Maxx settled with the Master Card and VISA associations for approximately $65 million and paid an aggregate fine of $9.7 million to the attorneys general of 33 states. http://www.businesswire.com/portal/site/tjx/?ndmViewId=news_view&newsId=20080402006143&newsLang=en (last viewed September 20, 2010); http://www.businesswire.com/portal/site/tjx/?ndmViewId=news_view&newsId=20080402006143&newsLang=en (last viewed September 20, 2010). In the largest case, *Heartland Payment Systems*, the breach affected more than 130 million credit card numbers. See http://www.privacyrights.org/data-breach. (last viewed September 20, 2010).

If the licensor will be providing data processing services, information technology support services such as help desk services, or managing and performing general infrastructure services, the licensor may have access to PII. The licensee can reduce its risk by limiting the licensor's access to PII, and negotiating strict security obligations. By implementing and maintaining rigorous physical security protections at its data and service centers, as well as by conducting background checks on its employees who will have access to PII, the licensor can further limit its liability. To the extent possible, the licensor should ensure PII removed from the United States is properly protected and controlled in the destination jurisdiction.

(a) Types of Data the Licensor Will Be Transmitting, Processing or Storing

The parties should carefully evaluate the types of data the licensor will be transmitting, processing and/or storing. If the licensor will have access to any regulated PII, PHI or credit card information, the licensee should ensure the licensor implements proper safeguards, including limiting access to a need-to-know basis, and complies with any industry standards (*i.e.*, the Payment Card Industry ("PCI") standards), requiring background checks, implementing procedural and operational safeguards, as well as conducting periodic audits.

The parties should determine whether the licensor has access to the PII of any non-U.S. citizen. If the PII relates to an EU citizen, the EU Directive on Data Protection (95/46/EC) may be applicable and certain standards may be imposed on both parties by European or other foreign laws. See Chapter 12.F.2 for a more detailed discussion of the laws relating to the management of European data.

(b) Respective Responsibilities of the Licensor and Licensee for Data Protection

The licensor and licensee should clearly delineate each party's responsibilities for protecting any PII. The respective responsibilities should be unambiguous. In addition to establishing written policies, the parties should evaluate the operational aspects of the transaction to assign responsibilities.

The agreement should set forth the contractual standard for the protection of a party's information and data. The contractually agreed upon standard may be the legally required standard, the licensor's standard, the licensee's standard or a third party standard such as the International Organization for Standardization ("ISO") ISO/IEC 27001: 2005 – Information Technology – Security Technique. ISO 27001 mandates specific requirements allowing an organization's security process to be audited and certified as compliant.

The license agreement should clearly require the licensor to comply with the licensee's policies and procedures for data protection/privacy and physical protection at the licensee's facilities. These standards should supplement the licensor's own security standards.

If applicable, the licensee should determine where the mainframe environment, if any, is located and if it or any applicable servers are located inside the licensee's firewall perimeter. The licensee should ensure the licensor possesses stringent controls and maintains its own firewall perimeter. Further, the parties should ascertain whether the relevant data resides inside the firewall perimeter architected and controlled by the licensee. It is important to determine whether there is access by the licensor for remote services, such as reporting, which is outside the licensee's firewall perimeter. The services provided by the licensor should be provided over a secure network specified by the licensee and approved by the licensor. The license agreement should also clearly state which party retains responsibility, if applicable, for security including intrusion detection.

The licensee should reserve the right to amend its security standards during the term of the agreement although this right raises the issue of who bears any increased costs arising from any subsequent amendment. A prudent licensor will seek to attach the agreed upon data privacy/security standards to the license agreement to ensure the standards are static. The licensor should not agree to comply with a fluid standard, such as a policy accessed through a URL, which may change during the term of the agreement, without allocating the assumption of risk for the incremental cost of complying with a revised standard. *See Margae, Inc. v. Clear Link Technologies, LLC,* 2008 WL 2465450 (June 16, 2008 D. Utah 2008) (amendment of contract between two sophisticated parties by one party posting modifications online not unconscionable).

The recent information security standards adopted by the state of Massachusetts are the most detailed information security standards adopted to date by any state.

http://www.mass.gov/Eoca/docs/idtheft/201CMR1700reg.pdf (last viewed September 20, 2010).

Cloud computing (where there are often multiple layers of subcontractors, and environments as well as licensors placing data from multiple licensees on the same server) also gives rise to concern. Licensees must make risk-based decisions whether to utilize these more cost-effective solutions while contemplating contractually implementing detailed and thoughtful privacy requirements or the vendor. For a more detailed discussion see Chapter 7 and http://csrc.nist.gov/groups/SNS/cloud-computing/ (Last viewed September 20, 2010).

(c) Operational Safeguards

The licensee should impose its own physical security measures on the operation of the licensor's data and service centers, if any, as well as the transfer of data and communications between the parties. To ensure a secure environment, the licensee should require that the licensor's equipment be dedicated solely to the licensee and physically separated from those of other customers. Licensors should be willing to provide dedicated servers/hardware provided the licensee is willing to pay the additional cost. A separate data transmission line should be used for transmitting the licensee's data. All transmitted data must be encrypted. If such transmitted data will be stored on mobile devices (such as laptops, PDAs, phones, etc.), those devices should also encrypt the data at rest.

The licensee should also undertake an independent assessment of the licensor's security architecture. The licensor should be obligated to obtain written confidentiality obligations with its subcontractors. All individuals supplying services including the licensor's employees and subcontractors should undergo background checks and, to the extent possible, all work should be performed in the United States to reduce the risk of misappropriation.

In addition to adequate encryption and password protection, a party should ensure the existence of adequate physical security. Monitoring and good record keeping are also important. Strong records retention/destruction policies and procedures should be implemented to ensure that all data is destroyed in a safe and controlled environment. Finally, each party should have adequate controls for reporting the enforcement of its obligations.

Operational safeguards cannot definitively protect against a security lapse. A failure to install an antivirus patch, an unaccounted-for tape or an employee who makes an inadvertent or intentional disclosure in violation of confidentiality obligations can still occur. Nonetheless, detailed policies and procedures can reduce the level of overall risk.

(d) Data Breach Plan

Each party should have a detailed data breach plan. The plan should include how to detect a breach, how to collect and retain evidence in the event of such a breach, and should include any contractual requirements to notify the licensee, the relevant regulatory authorities and the impacted individuals. The plan should take into consideration the likelihood of a lawsuit and seek to protect the entity's interests while complying with its contractual obligations. The plan should also identify the party responsible for undertaking each action set forth in the plan in the event of a breach. The plan should be updated quarterly to reflect changes in the law as well as any changes in the contract.

2. Contractual Provisions Addressing Data Privacy and Security

(a) Use Clear and Unambiguous Language

Agreeing to comply with stated security standards and the resulting liability arising from the failure to comply with such standards creates a significant risk for a licensor. The licensor should ensure that the data privacy/security standards to which it must comply are stated in an objective manner without ambiguity. Further, a licensor should never agree to comply with a standard or policy set forth in a URL that can change without notice or without compensation for any increased costs associated with complying with the new standards. For example, it should be clarified whether the licensor would be required to keep the licensee's PII/data confidential, or to simply use the same standard of care that the licensor uses to protect its own information, but no less than a reasonable level of care. It should also be clear whether the licensor is required to comply with stated security procedures and/or required to comply with all applicable laws. Finally, it should be clear whether the licensor simply is required to encrypt the licensee's data prior to transmission or whether there will be more subjective obligations. Clearly stating a party's obligations will protect both the licensor's and licensee's interests.

Prudent licensors should seek to tie their liability to their failure to comply with a specific standard stated in the license agreement or if applicable, the statement of work. Licensors should avoid assuming liability for any data disclosure in absence of its failure to meet a contractually agreed standard. For example, if there is a release of data and the licensor's obligation was only to encrypt the data, the licensor should not be liable in the event of a release provided the data was encrypted. If the licensor was obligated to encrypt the PII and unencrypted PII was released, the licensor would be liable.

(b) Limitations of Liability

(i) Generally

While ten years ago little thought would have been given to a party assuming unlimited liability for a breach of the party's confidentiality obligations, the changing landscape for liability related to breaches of data privacy/protection has caused licensors to re-examine limits of liability. Many savvy licensors now seek to limit their liability based on the cause and nature of the breach. Prudent licensors should think carefully before accepting unlimited liability for breaches of their data privacy and security obligations.

For general negligence claims, prudent parties seek to limit their liability to a stated amount, as no entity should risk insolvency over the failure to perform a single contract. See Chapter 4.B.7 for a more detailed discussion on limitations of liability for general negligence. Licensees are increasingly arguing that any claims arising from a breach of a licensor's obligations related to PII, especially those in violation of a law, should not be subject to a limitation of liability. Given the significant liability that may arise from the loss or theft of PII, licensors should carefully consider any cap on liability.

Although the amount of a direct damages cap is important, of equal importance is the exclusion of consequential damages as the majority of damages arising from a breach of a party's data privacy/security obligations will likely be consequential damages. As such, many licensors, who may be willing to accept unlimited liability for direct damages, seek to include a cap on consequential damages. In the event of a data breach or loss, it is likely that the majority of the resulting damages will be consequential damages, not direct damages. To the extent the agreement contains a waiver or limitation on consequential damages, a licensee should insist on an exception for data breach or loss. Without such an exception, the injured party may be barred from recovering a significant portion of its damages.

Common contractual exclusions from an agreement's limitation of liability include breach of a party's confidentiality obligations, willful misconduct, gross negligence, and compliance with laws. For breach of a data privacy or security obligation, the parties usually exclude notification expenses, (i.e., the cost to notify parties whose PII has been wrongly disclosed) from any limitation of liability. That being said, reasonableness should be the standard when negotiating notification processes and determining whether one party will have exclusive say over how the notification should be accomplished.

The two most commonly negotiated exceptions from an agreement's limitation of liability are those for breaches related to compliance with laws and breaches of a party's confidentiality obligations, which are often defined as including breaches of data security and data privacy.

Claims for breaches of confidentiality, compliance with laws, data security and data privacy are to some degree related. A claim for a data breach or loss will likely be made under one or more of these exclusions.

As the risk of liability from data breaches increases, licensors are increasingly seeking to negotiate a bifurcated approach based on the nature of the breach with a supplemental cap for PII claims and claims related to compliance with laws that is larger than the cap for other types of claims. While it is unreasonable to expect the licensor to assume unlimited liability in all cases, it is reasonable for the licensor to agree to an increased limit of liability for breaches of its data privacy/security obligations arising from an "operational" breach, as the standard is clearly set and any failure to comply should be able to be proven easily.

"Operational" breaches are often defined to include the following: (i) the licensor's failure to follow an agreed upon standard operating procedure; (ii) the licensor's failure to utilize antivirus software resulting in an infection; (iii) the inability to account for all tapes in the licensor's possession (often caused by a failure to follow a check-in, check-out procedure); (iv) a hacker's penetration of a firewall server if licensor personnel failed to perform a duty preventing penetration; and (v) the inadvertent disclosure of the licensee's business data.

An "operational" breach may also arise from a licensor's employee stealing the licensee's data. A theft would most likely not be viewed as an operational error, thus exposing the licensor to a higher limitation of liability. The theft might also be deemed attributable to gross negligence, which, depending on the terms of the agreement, exposes the licensor to unlimited liability. However, if the theft would not have occurred but for a failure to follow an operational procedure, the licensor could argue that this was an operational error. If the theft was made possible because of a flaw in the licensee's security procedures, the licensor would likely argue that the theft would not have taken place but for the security flaw and the liability should remain with the licensee.

A two-tiered approach limiting the licensor's liability for data breaches caused by a contracted-for "operational" breach to a multiple of the contract's general limitation of liability is a reasonable compromise. For example, if the license agreement contains a limitation of liability equal to 12 months' fees for a general negligence claim, the parties may agree to limit the licensor's liability to an amount equal to 24 months' worth of fees for "operational" breaches.

(ii) Liability Associated with Specific Types of Breaches

Uncapped liability for direct and consequential damages for breaches of confidentiality was traditionally accepted in license agreements and professional services agreements. This position remains today although, as discussed above, licensors are seeking to bifurcate those damages arising from the disclosure of a party's trade secrets and those damages resulting from a security breach involving PHI or PII. Often, an indemnification obligation for breaches of confidentiality is uncapped; however, liability for breaches of confidentiality between the parties more often than not is capped. There is usually a carve-out for consequential damages arising from the breach of a party's confidentiality/data obligations, but such damages are subject to any applicable cap.

(1) Confidential Information Including Protected Health Information

Licensors should be careful to define confidential information as narrowly as they can. For example, one concept that is well tolerated is to include a sentence at the end of the confidential information definition that says something to the following effect: "If there is a BAA, all categories of information covered by the BAA will be dictated by the terms of the BAA exclusively, and not be considered under the terms of the master services agreement." While such acts may not limit the licensor's exposure, it provides clarity to the applicable standards for the different categories of information.

(2) Indemnities Arising from a BAA

Many licensors typically accept full uncapped and consequential damages in connection with any agreed-to indemnity, including indemnities arising in the context of a BAA (i.e., for third party claims associated with wrongful dissemination of PHI). Licensees believe that unlimited liability for breach of PII and PHI are dictated by the nature of an indemnity. That is, if you are going to hold a party harmless, you must do so without regard to limits. From a licensor's perspective, it is important to ensure that the indemnity is limited to third party claims and, in the case of the BAA, to include a "no third party beneficiary" provision.

Many licensors agree to accept full damages for an indemnity obligation to a third party relating to breaches of confidentiality, including consequential damages if such damages are awarded as part of a judgment or settlement. These claims would include indemnities arising in the context of a BAA.

If the licensor takes on full uncapped and consequential damages in connection with an agreed indemnity, the licensor will logically expect to assume control of the defense, something that the licensee may not be entirely comfortable with if indeed there is reputational harm or licensee/licensor relationships at issue.

(3) Breach of Business Associate Agreements ("BAAs")

An increasing number of licensees are seeking full, uncapped and consequential damages in connection with any breach of a BAA (this means accepting uncapped liability for direct damages owed to the other party in connection with inadequate mitigation, reputational damage, etc.). In turn, many licensors are accepting this risk anytime they enter into a stand-alone BAA that has no express limits in it—most do not.

Customers usually define a PHI "breach" as the "unauthorized" acquisition, access, use or disclosure of Protected Health Information in a manner not permitted by the (HIPAA) Privacy Rule or (HIPAA) Security Rule, which compromises the security or privacy of such Protected Health Information, but excludes such acquisition, access, use or disclosure described in 45 C.F.R. § 164.402—so it should be limited. Most BAAs are silent on this subject. If they are entered into under an existing master services agreement or other umbrella agreement, in most instances the liability cap of that agreement will be applicable. There is no private right of action under HIPAA, although HHS and states' attorneys general can impose monetary penalties and bring suit for damages. HITECH now imposes civil and criminal fines on Business Associates for certain security and privacy violations under HIPAA. Furthermore, the lack of a private right of action by a third party under HIPAA does not preclude causes of action for breach of privacy statutes under state law.

(4) Loss or Damage to Business Data

Many licensors do not accept uncapped and consequential damages in connection with damage to business data generally, particularly if the breach does not involve a public disclosure. To protect themselves, licensors should limit the carve-out from any applicable limit of liability to tangible personal property (not data), and make sure the terms are (i) not so broad as to constitute every type of business data as confidential information; and (ii) truly limited to public disclosure scenarios, so that negligent use that does not involve disclosure (e.g., loss of data due to a system crash) is not covered.

Vendors may accept uncapped liability or liability subject to a supplemental cap in the event a licensor fails to follow certain data security measures set forth in an agreement.

(5) Loss or Damage to PHI

The trend is to carve out any breach of a BAA from any applicable limit of liability protections, provided (i) the BAA mirrors the legal requirements under HITECH as closely as possible and does not otherwise contain heightened standards imposed by the licensee; and (ii) the carve out is limited to breach of the BAA and not mere acts or omissions involving PHI.

The primary focus of HIPAA and HITECH is not loss or damage to data, including PHI, but rather on the improper use or disclosure of PHI. Therefore, if a system fails and the PHI is lost (and cannot be recovered), HIPAA is not directly implicated, although the Business Associate may still face liability if it cannot perform its objectives under the BAA, such as providing an accounting, as well as liability under any tangential agreement requiring back-up and disaster recovery. Further, there are requirements embedded in the HIPAA security rule to maintain the availability of data, and to establish contingency plans. See 45 C.F.R § 164.306 and § 164.308(a)(7).

(iii) Governing Law

Governing law may have an important impact on the adjuctication of any dispute. New York, for example, strictly construes "gross negligence" and "willful misconduct," thus limiting a plaintiff's potential recovery. At the same time, California prohibits limiting a party's liability for breach of law.

(c) Indemnities

The licensee should seek to have the licensor indemnify the licensee against third party claims arising from a breach of the licensor's data security and privacy obligations as well as violations of law. From the licensee's perspective, liability for third party claims should be unlimited. Licensors often argue, however, that liability for such indemnity obligations should be capped, as the licensee is able to limit its liability with its customers by inserting an appropriate limitation of liability in the parties' contract.

3. Potential Damage Claims for Privacy and Security Breaches

A breach of the licensor's obligations may give rise to a number of damage claims. Set forth below is a discussion of types of the claims that would likely be brought in the event of a privacy or security breach. Nonetheless, the courts have consistently upheld the proposition that a plaintiff must have actual damages to pursue a data breach claim even in consumer friendly states such as California. *See Ruiz v. Gap, Inc.*, 2010 WL 2170993 (9th Cir. May 28, 2010).

(a) Direct Damages

A licensee whose data or customer's data has been lost or compromised will likely seek to recover the cost of reconstructing the lost data, the loss in value of any secret, technical or other information and the cost of notification of and monitoring any third party data that was released or lost, as well as all damages directly flowing from the loss. The cost to restore data can be very expensive and the licensee must ensure that it is fully protected to avoid a significant disruption of its business or a significant financial loss.

(b) Consequential Damages

The great majority of damages are likely to be consequential damages—those damages that flow from the licensor's actions.

(c) Third Party Claims by Affected Individuals and Other Third Parties

A significant concern for licensees is the possibility of a class action lawsuit being filed against it for the unauthorized disclosure of personal information. While these types of claims have been largely unsuccessful, the ever increasing number of federal, state and local laws makes the possibility of success more likely. The likelihood of a third party claim makes it very important that the savvy licensee seek indemnification from the licensor for third party claims.

(d) Governmental Fines

Various federal, state and local agencies such as the Federal Trade Commission ("FTC"), Health and Human Services ("HHS") and the state attorneys general have the ability to impose fines or require enhanced security which may not be contemplated by the licensor at the time the license agreement is executed. While historically, fines have generally been well under a million dollars, in the much publicized *TJ Maxx* case the TJ Maxx Companies settled with 33 state attorneys general for a fine of $9,750,000. It is likely that in the future fines levied by governmental entities will increase both in number and dollar value. Given that liability arises from the failure to comply with applicable laws, the licensor should assume all liability for all penalties, fines, interest and other costs arising from the breach. There should be no limit on the licensor's liability for government levied fines.

4. Insurance

Data breaches can be very expensive to mitigate and a prudent licensee should ensure that it will be able to collect any judgment it obtains against the licensor. To that end, prior to execution of the license, the licensee and the licensor should ascertain the amount of the licensor's insurance coverage for data breaches under the licensor's Errors and Omissions policy or General Liability Policy and ensure that the policy limit is large enough to satisfy any potential claim. The licensee should also determine the amount of any retention or deductible to make sure the licensor can satisfy that amount. To the extent the licensor's existing policies do not cover any potential claim and the licensor lacks the financial resources to pay all potential claims, the licensor should be required to obtain insurance in an amount sufficient to cover the licensee's likely losses.

For a general discussion of the legal issues associated to data security, see J.T. Westermeier, *Managing the Legal Risks Related to Information Security*, 2 COMPUTER L.R. INT'L. 43 (2008); Jonathan M. Cohen and Elise Dieterich, *Five Steps for Managing the Risks Associated with Sensitive Data*, 25 CORP. COUNS. 1 (No. 2 June 2010); W. Scott Blackmer, *Code or Clear? Encryption Requirements Under Information Privacy and Security Laws*, 159 INTELL. PROP. COUNSEL (March 2010); and Theodore E. Claypoole and Danielle M. Benoit, *Protecting Data in a Business Failure*, 27 ACC DOCKET 21 (Sept. 2009).

B. HIPAA and HITECH

1. Applicability

The Standards for Privacy of Individually Identifiable Health Information and Security Standards (the "Standards") were adopted as a result of the Administrative Simplification provisions under the Health Insurance Portability and Accountability Act of 1996 ("HIPAA"). 42 U.S.C. §§ 1320d–1320d-8 (2009). The Standards require "Covered Entities" and their "Business Associates" to protect the privacy and security of certain individually identifiable health information, referred to as "protected health information" ("PHI") in accordance with specified procedures. The primary focus of HIPAA and HITECH is not loss of or damage to data, including PHI, rather the improper use or disclosure of PHI. Thus, if a system fails and the PHI is deleted, HIPAA is not directly implicated although the Business Associate may face liability if it cannot perform under the relevant BAA or contract. Further, there are requirements embedded in the HIPAA security rule to maintain the availability of data, and to establish contingency plans. *See* 45 C.F.R. § 164.306 and § 164.308(a)(7).

As defined in 45 C.F.R. § 160.103, a "Business Associate" is a person or entity that performs or assists a Covered Entity in the performance of a function or activity involving the use or disclosure of PHI.

A "Covered Entity" is defined as (1) a health plan, (2) a health care clearinghouse, or (3) a health care provider who transmits any health information in electronic form in connection with a transaction covered by this subchapter (e.g., HIPAA Administrative Simplification transaction standards). 45 C.F.R. § 160.103.

Although what constitutes arranging, performing or assisting a Covered Entity in the use or disclosure of confidential information has been broadly construed, there may be circumstances, especially in a multi-licensor environment, where the services that are in-scope do not include the use or disclosure of PHI and thus do not require entering into a Business Associate Agreement ("BAA").[1] This issue has

1. For ease of reference and consistency in this section, the licensor shall be referred to as the Business Associate and the licensee as the Covered Entity.

renewed importance because, pursuant to the HITECH provisions of the American Recovery and Reinvestment Act of 2009 ("ARRA"), Pub. L. No. 111-5, 123 Stat. 115 (2009) (codified in scattered sections of 6, 19, 26, 42, and 47 U.S.C.), as of February 17, 2010, Business Associates are directly subject to and required to comply with certain HIPAA Security Standards; that is, Business Associates will have direct obligations under HIPAA.

Under HITECH, civil penalties for violators were increased to up to $1.5 million while criminal sanctions can result in fines up to $250,000 and/or ten years in prison. HITECH, Pub. L. No. 111-5 § 13410 (d)(3); 123 Stat. 226, 467 (2009) (stating tiers of civil liability); 42 U.S.C. § 17931 (b) referencing application of 42 U.S.C. § 1320d-6 to business associates for criminal penalties. See also, 42 U.S.C. § 17934 (c). Fines are mandatory in the event of a violation arising from "willful neglect." 42 U.S.C. § 17939 (a). In addition, HITECH grants state attorneys general the right to enforce the provisions of HIPAA and allows enforcement actions to be brought against employees of healthcare institutions. HITECH, Pub. L. No. 111-5 § 13410 (e); 123 Stat. 226, 467 (2009). HITECH also implemented a security breach notification obligation requiring notification in the event of a breach of any type of unencrypted personal information. The notification does not set forth any threshold for the risk involved and thus notification must be given in all events.

The HHS regulations, in their final form, establish a threshold that a "compromise" of data occurs if there is a "significant risk of financial, reputational, or other harm to the individual." See 45 C.F.R § 164.402. HITECH also expanded beyond the typical Covered Entities and Business Associates, and also established rules applicable to those who provide direct to consumer medical record hosting services. The FTC has promulgated rules regarding such "protected health records," and interestingly enough, the FTC's breach notification rules under HITECH for these actors does not include any threshold (e.g., similar to substantial risk of harm) for what constitutes a breach. As of August 23, 2010, HHS has withdrawn the final rule ("Final Rule") from OMB review until it does further review. http://www.hhs.gov/ocr/privacy/hipaa/administrative/breachnotificationrule/finalruleupdate.html (Last viewed September 20, 2010).

Finally, HITECH extended the applicability of HIPAA to Business Associates regardless of whether they access electronic health records. Interestingly, in one of the few cases examining the relationship between HIPAA and state law, the Federal District Court for the Northern District of Ohio found that HIPAA did not preempt an Ohio state law prohibiting the disclosure of medical records. *Turk v. Oiler*, 2010 WL 446566 (N.D. Ohio Feb. 1, 2010) (HIPAA exception allowing the disclosure of medical records in response to subpoena does not preempt Ohio law prohibiting testimony as to patient-physician "communications" where communication defined to include patient records).

2. Description of Services

If the parties determine that a BAA is necessary, the next consideration is whether it is possible to precisely describe which services, if any, provided under the licensing agreement constitute arranging, performing or assisting a Covered Entity in the use or disclosure of PHI. Although some BAAs describe this obligation more generally, the Business Associate should define the subset of the services provided under the licensing agreement that trigger the HIPAA obligations as precisely as possible (and this subset of services is typically referred to as the "Affected Services"). This will enable a Business Associate to subsequently use the defined term of Affected Services to more precisely define (i.e., narrow) mitigation activities, as well as the scope of any reporting and/or indemnity obligations. Although this approach is not always successful, the rationale is that only a portion of the services under the licensing agreement trigger the obligations related to handling and protecting PHI and that other data and information may not be handled and protected in the same manner (by agreement or otherwise). It is important to clearly state that the limitations regarding Affected Services are not intended to limit a Business Associate's ability to perform the services specified in the licensing agreement.

3. Business Associate Agreements

The obligation to execute a BAA applies when the party to whom the data is disclosed is performing a function on behalf of the covered entity (it does not apply broadly to the disclosure of data, e.g., to another covered entity). *See* 45 C.F.R. § 160.103; 164.308(b). An entity receiving PHI from a Covered Entity is known as a Business Associate. *See* 45 C.F.R. § 160.103(1)(i)(A) (2009). BAAs are essentially specialized non-disclosure agreements. Covered Entities usually seek to impose one-sided BAAs on Business Associates. Set forth below is a discussion of some of the most important issues contained in a BAA.

(a) Mitigation

BAAs increasingly impose a mitigation obligation on the Business Associate to mitigate any deleterious effects from improper disclosure of PHI. The scope of the mitigation obligation is often undefined, but can reasonably be expected to include detailed notices to a very large pool of affected individuals, call-in hotlines and, depending on the obligations under the licensee's policies, credit watch services. Mitigation of the harmful effects is a requirement under HIPAA, but the rules do not define what actions must be taken or the scope of mitigation. *See* 45 C.F.R. § 164.530(f) (2009). The proposed language below obligates the Business Associate to use "reasonable efforts" to limit "additional losses" but expressly disclaims any obligations that would result in the Business Associate incurring a material financial expense. This language favors the Business Associate, but it is likely unacceptable to the Covered Entity, which usually wants to have its damages mitigated regardless of cost.

> Business Associate agrees to mitigate, to the extent practicable, any harmful effect that is actually known to Business Associate of a Security Incident, caused by Business Associate or its subcontractor(s) arising from its provision of the Services. Business Associate's obligation to mitigate shall consist of reasonable efforts to limit additional losses after a Security Incident has occurred. Business Associate shall not be required to undertake any actions which would be unduly burdensome in terms of time or resources or cause Business Associate to incur a material financial expense. [For purposes of this BAA, a material financial expense shall mean an expense which will cost in total an amount which is equal to or exceeds five percent (5%) of the fees under the Agreement associated with the provision of Covered Services in the immediately preceding three (3) months.]

Note that this language does not establish a defined cure period in which a breach must be cured. Although many covered entities seek a definitive period, a cure period may not be practical depending on the nature of the breach, for example, disclosure of information versus noncompliance with a policy and procedures.

(b) Indemnity

The scope of indemnity in BAAs is typically cast very broadly beyond the failure to comply with laws, to include any act or omission under the BAA which gives rise to a claim. A broadly worded indemnity is reason for concern as indemnities have traditionally served as a remedy for third party claims and not as a substitute for a breach of contract claim. See Chapter 4.B.2. At a minimum, Business Associates should insist on including in the agreement a "No Third Party Beneficiary" provision to attempt to insulate the Business Associate from claims by the owner of the PHI.

From the Business Associate's perspective, an indemnity should not be provided. HIPAA does not require that a BAA include an indemnity. Most, if not all, Covered Entities however, maintain that an indemnity is "market standard." In response, the Business Associate should propose a specific indemnity. The indemnity set forth below requires that the indemnified claim be both a violation of the Privacy Regulations and a material breach of the Affected Services. In addition, it excludes third party claims arising from instructions received from a Covered Entity.

> Business Associate agrees to indemnify, defend and hold harmless Covered Entity against all actual direct losses claimed by *unaffiliated* third parties arising directly from the use or disclosure of PHI by Business Associate or its agents which is both an express violation of the [Applicable Laws] and a material breach of this Agreement ("Business Associate Indemnified Claim"). Said responsibility adheres only to violations solely attributable to the actions/inactions of Business Associate and/or its agents. The foregoing indemnity will not cover any third party claims arising from any action or inaction of Business Associate taken or not taken by Business Associate at the request of Covered Entity or to action or inactions of Business Associate that are permitted under [Applicable Laws] and/or this Agreement. For the avoidance of doubt, a Business Associate Indemnified Claim may not be asserted under any other indemnity provided by Business Associate to Covered Entity.

> Covered Entity agrees to indemnify, defend and hold harmless Business Associate against all actual direct losses claimed by an *unaffiliated* third party arising from any action or inaction of Business Associate taken or not taken by Business Associate

at the request of Covered Entity or to actions/inactions of Business Associate that are permitted under the [Applicable Laws] and/or this Agreement.

Although inconsistent with the approach set forth above, another approach is to maintain that the general indemnities in the license agreement already address this issue, and therefore it is not necessary for the BAA to include a separate indemnity. This approach is dependent on the specific terms of the license agreement, but such an indemnity could be based on (i) an indemnity for breach of any representation and warranties (the license agreement is likely to include a representation that the Business Associate is in compliance with all material laws); (ii) an indemnity for breach of obligations related to data; (iii) an indemnity for fines and penalties imposed by law (although this would not address third-party claims); and/or (iv) an indemnity related to breach of the Business Associate's obligations related to confidential information. The risks associated with this alternative are (i) the scope of the indemnities in the license agreement are most likely much broader (i.e., not limited to Affected Services); (ii) the indemnities in the license agreement do not require an actual violation of the Privacy Regulations; (iii) indemnified claims under the license agreement; and (v) the right to terminate in the licensing agreement may not expressly provide for the opportunity to cure that is specified in the BAA.

(c) Immediate Termination

Business Associates should reject language giving the Covered Entity an immediate right of termination in the event of a breach of the BAA and should insist on a right to cure in the event it breaches the BAA. If the Covered Entity exercises its right to immediate termination, it could cause a corresponding termination of the license agreement and even unrelated statements of work without notice. Set forth below is model language providing the Business Associate a right of cure.

> Termination for Cause. Upon Covered Entity's knowledge of a material breach by Business Associate, Covered Entity shall provide Business Associate written notice of the existence of the alleged material breach and provide Business Associate thirty (30) days from the delivery of such notice within which to cure the breach or end the violation. Covered Entity may terminate this Agreement [and the _________ Agreement/sections ____ of the _______________ Agreement] if Business Associate does not cure the breach or end the violation within such thirty (30) day time period by Covered Entity.
>
> If neither termination nor cure is feasible as reasonably determined by Business Associate and Covered Entity, Covered Entity shall report the violation to the Secretary. Covered Entity's report to the Secretary shall be limited to the specific information giving rise to the breach.

The template BAA developed by the Department of Health and Human Services Office of Civil Rights expressly provides a cure right. See http://www.hhs.gov/ocr/privacy/hipaa/understanding/coveredentities/contractprov.html. (Last viewed September 20, 2010.) *See also* 45 C.F.R. § 314(a)(1)(i)(B) (2009).

The OCR Privacy Guidance provides the following:

> Where a covered entity knows of a material breach or violation by the business associate of the contract or agreement, the covered entity is required to take reasonable steps to cure the breach or end the violation, and if such steps are unsuccessful, to terminate the contract or arrangement. If termination of the contract or agreement is not feasible, a covered entity is required to report the problem to the Department of Health and Human Services (HHS) Office for Civil Rights (OCR).

Id. §§ 164.502(e), 164.504(e), 164.532(d)-(e).

The Privacy Rules similarly contemplate a cure right and only require termination where the Covered Entity took reasonable steps to cure the breach or end the violation, as applicable, and such steps were unsuccessful. *Id.* § 164.504(e)(1)(ii).

(d) Notice

(i) In General

From the licensee's perspective, the Business Associate should be required to notify the Covered Entity within 24 hours of any breach. In actuality, notification within 24 hours is very fast, and may not be realistic. Although California and the Connecticut Insurance Commissioner have issued rules requiring notification to the individuals affected within five days, as a commercial matter, it may make more sense to go with "immediately" or a comparable term for the licensor agreement. Notice should set forth in detail the nature of the breach and the corrective actions that are being taken to mitigate the risk.

(ii) U.S. Department of Health and Human Services

Many Covered Entities seek broad rights to disclose breaches to the Secretary of HHS. These rights extend far beyond what is contemplated under HIPAA and these rights extend without any requisite notice to the Business Associate or consultation with the Business Associate as to the scope of a breach and the content of any statement. The potential for damage to a Business Associate's reputation is significant.

Notice to the Secretary of HHS is required where neither termination of the underlying agreement nor cure of the breach is feasible. 45 C.F.R. § 164.504(e)(1)(ii)(B) (2009). Notice to the Secretary of HHS is also required under Section 13402 of HITECH by Covered Entities of unsecured PHI that has been acquired or disclosed in a breach. If the breach was with respect to five hundred or more individuals, the Final Rule requires notification "without unreasonable delay, and no later than 60 days after discovery." If the breach was with respect to less than five hundred individuals, the licensee may maintain a log and annually submit the log to the Secretary documenting such breaches occurring during the year involved. 42 U.S.C. § 17932(e)(3) (2009).

(e) Treatment as Confidential Information/Failure to Comply with Laws

A breach of a BAA is often cast as a breach of a party's obligations related to Confidential Information and/or a failure to comply with laws, both of which potentially expose the Business Associate to unlimited liability depending on the terms of the license agreement. Similarly, claims brought under the indemnity also are potentially uncapped.

The obligations in a typical license agreement related to Confidential Information and/or compliance with laws are not specific. HIPAA, however, imposes specific obligations and remedies for failure to properly use or disclose PHI. *See* 42 U.S.C. §§ 1320d-5–1320d-6 (stating the penalties for noncompliance); 45 C.F.R. § 164.502 (2009) (identifying the general rules for use and disclosure of PHI). Not all Confidential Information will have the same handling and protection obligations imposed by HIPAA for PHI. Therefore, the BAA should be used as the comprehensive document where the parties have specified their obligations with respect to such information. Similarly, compliance with laws provisions are usually not specific and instead allocate compliance responsibility by category (e.g., laws affecting the licensee business, laws affecting the Business Associate's business). HIPAA is treated differently because it already specifies the obligations of a Covered Entity and a Business Associate, and the BAA specifies not only the mitigation responsibilities but also the liability of each party. Accordingly, a breach of a BAA should not be subject to the same treatment as a breach of Confidential Information or a general compliance with laws provision.

(f) Increasing Scope of Laws

Many Covered Entities seek to expand BAAs to cover not only HIPAA but also all "applicable" state laws, whatever those may be under a given engagement. Business Associates should carefully examine references to other categories of personal information included in a BAA such as Gramm Leach Bliley.

The Privacy Standards require that if the laws of a particular state apply more stringent standards than the federal regulations with regard to the privacy of protected health information, the state's laws, or the portion of the state's laws that are more stringent will apply instead of the federal regulations. 45 C.F.R. § 160.203(b) (2009). Therefore, instead of agreeing to be bound by applicable state laws, the preferred position is to require a Covered Entity to specify what state laws applicable to its operation are more stringent than the applicable federal regulations. Otherwise, the obligation would impose an ongoing obligation to be aware of all applicable state laws, and more importantly, to make a determination if such state laws are more stringent than applicable federal laws or regulations.

(g) Amendment to Comply with Changing Laws

Many BAAs contain a provision which seeks to automatically amend the BAA so that the BAA remains in compliance with changing laws. Business Associates should resist these provisions and base compliance on signed amendments containing proposed textual changes. An automatic amendment assumes the Business Associate is fully informed of all changes in law and fully compliant at all times, including with respect to variable interpretations of the law as may be imposed by the licensee on the Business Associate, without any regard to the consequent costs associated with compliance.

HIPAA and HIPAA Regulations now apply to Business Associates. Presumably, therefore, Business Associates monitor any changes to HIPAA and HIPAA Regulations. The license agreement should address how the Business Associate will comply with HIPAA and HIPAA Regulations as of the effective date of the license agreement. Any changes to HIPAA and/or HIPAA Regulations made after the effective date of the license agreement should be addressed in a collaborative manner, with the licensee specifying how it wants to comply with the changes (in most instances the manner in which it complies with any change to a law or regulations depends upon their tolerance for risk and how such licensee interprets the changes to the applicable law or regulation). The preferred language described above places the monitoring and notice obligations on the licensee and requires that any changes to HIPAA and/or HIPAA Regulations be governed by a change control process. It is important to note that the Business Associate should not suggest that compliance with the changes to HIPAA and/or HIPAA Regulations is discretionary, but rather that the parties must agree on the manner in which those changes are implemented.

(h) Data Retention

The requirements for the secure destruction/return of PHI and related data retention requirements and procedures vary by BAA. The Business Associate should liaise with the Business Associate's compliance department to ensure that compliant record retention tools are available and that it retains data in accordance with the variable timeframes required by each licensee.

The Privacy Rules require the following:

> At termination of the contract, if feasible, return or destroy all protected health information received from, or created or received by the business associate on behalf of, the covered entity that the business associate still maintains in any form and retain no copies of such information or, if such return or destruction is not feasible, extend the protections of the contract to the information and limit further uses and disclosures to those purposes that make the return or destruction of the information infeasible.

45 C.F.R. § 164.504(e)(2)(ii)(I) (2009).

This language is consistent with these requirements, but places the decision of whether destruction or return is feasible with the Business Associate.

(i) Audit

The audit provisions contained in many BAAs are very broad, extending not only to books and records, but facility audits, and audits of practices and procedures. Usually, the BAA provides that audits need not be triggered by a breach and are not necessarily subject to appropriate controls. This is of particular concern to a Business Associate when an audit of a facility or systems could expose other licensee data and/or short-term deficiencies that the Business Associate may have identified in its compliance.

The only audit requirement under HIPAA is that the Covered Entity must obligate the Business Associate to make its internal practices, books, and records relating to the use and disclosure of PHI received from, or created or received by the Business Associate on behalf of the Covered Entity available to the Secretary for purposes of determining the Covered Entity's compliance with the privacy rules. 45 C.F.R. § 164.504(e)(2)(ii)(H) (2009). Note that the purpose of the disclosure of books and records is not to assess the Business Associate's compliance, but rather the Covered Entity's. No other audit requirements are imposed by the HIPAA rules. The language set forth below provides the Covered Entity a limited audit right, but one that satisfies the requirements of HIPAA.

> Business Associate agrees to make those internal practices, books, and records specifically relating to the use and disclosure of Confidential Information received from, or created or received by Business Associate on behalf of Covered Entity available to Covered Entity, or at the request of Covered Entity to [third party auditor], in a reasonable time and manner agreed to by Covered Entity and Business Associate, for the purpose of [Insert limited purpose]. Such books and records shall exclude any legally privileged information, as well as non-relevant personal data or Confidential Information of other Business Associate licensees.

(j) Attendant Imposition of Obligations on the Covered Entity

There are legitimate obligations which a Business Associate may impose on a licensee, although these are often not included in a BAA. A better understanding of the evolving laws would improve the Business Associate's position in terms of gaining some reciprocal protections and, in some cases, a legitimate basis for any failure to comply.

A Covered Entity's obligations with respect to the BAA are fairly limited and consist only of the following requirements: provide a notice of privacy practices, 45 C.F.R. § 164.520 (2009); notify the Business Associate of changes by the patient in permitted uses and disclosures, *see id.* § 164.504(e)(2)(i); and, under HITECH, provide notice of security breaches, 42 U.S.C. § 17932(a) (2009). The language set forth below imposes upon the licensee the requirement to notify the Business Associate in the event of a change in the law. Licensors believe this language is appropriate as the licensee provides services in the healthcare field and is thus better positioned to track changes in the law. Licensees, however, are likely hesitant to accept this language as it excuses the Business Associate from complying with the law in the event the licensee fails to notify the Business Associate of a change in the law.

> Licensee shall provide Business Associate with licensee's Notice of Privacy Practices that licensee produces in accordance with 45 CFR 164.520 on or before the effective date of this BAA, as well as written notice of any changes to such Notice of Privacy Practices prior to such changes taking effect to the extent that any changes may affect the Business Associate's use or disclosure of PHI.
>
> Licensee shall provide Business Associate with immediate written notice of any changes in, or revocation of, permission by an Individual to use or disclose PHI, if such changes may affect Business Associate's permitted or required uses and disclosures.
>
> Licensee shall be responsible for all notification requirements associated with breach of unsecured PHI as required by law.

ALTERNATIVELY:

> Business Associate will comply with the following state privacy laws [OPTION: as directed by Covered Entity] but only to the extent such laws are applicable to the Services and to the extent Covered Entity was in compliance with such laws at the time Business Associate commenced providing services: [SPECIFY STATE STATUTES].
>
> Covered Entity shall monitor and promptly identify and notify Business Associate of all changes in Applicable Laws occurring on or after the Effective Date and all noncompliance existing as of the date Business Associate commences services (collectively "Legal Changes"). Covered Entity and Business Associate will work together to identify the effects of Legal Changes on the provision or receipt of the Services. With respect to Legal Changes, the parties will discuss, in a timely manner, what modifications to the Services, if any, are necessary to comply with such Legal Changes. Business Associate shall promptly thereafter propose any amendments or change orders to the Agreement associated with such Legal Changes including applicable charges necessary to implement such Legal Changes. Upon the parties' agreement to the relevant amendment or change order, Business Associate shall implement the changes to the Services in a timely manner.

(k) Third Party Beneficiaries

From the Business Associate's perspective, protective language should be added to a BAA to protect the Business Associate from liability to third parties whose PHI may be disclosed. Although HIPAA does not provide a private cause of action against Business Associates, the Business Associate should seek to take protective action from an activist court. Model language is set forth below:

> Nothing express or implied in this Agreement is intended to confer, nor shall anything herein confer, upon any person other than the parties who sign this Agreement any rights, remedies, obligations or liabilities whatsoever. There are no intended third party beneficiaries. [OPTIONAL – the parties might want to state that there are no third party beneficiaries other than as specified in the indemnification provisions.]

(l) Compliance

The Business Associate should make sure it can comply (from an operational perspective) with any security/privacy standards required by the license agreement. If the Business Associate has any questions regarding its current privacy and security policies and procedures, it should be in a position to rectify them so it can be in a position to certify compliance at the licensee's request.

The Covered Entity should ensure that the BAA restricts the transfer of its PHI to an offshore location unless the Business Associate receives the Covered Entity's prior approval. Approval may be conditioned upon specific compliance to the Covered Entity's satisfaction with the Covered Entity's policies and procedures. The Covered Entity should require that it be notified of any wrongful disclosure in violation of the BAA within 24 hours of discovery and the notice must contain all of the details required by the underlying BAA.

The Business Associate should ensure that in the event of a material breach of the BAA, which would not necessarily be a wrongful disclosure, but could be noncompliant policies and procedures, the Business Associate has a reasonable cure period, whereupon the Covered Entity can terminate the BAA, the underlying Agreement and any project work. Upon termination, expiration, or the like, the Covered Entity should ensure the BAA contains certification requirements the Business Associate must satisfy with respect to the return of PHI.

See Form 23.G.7 for a model BAA favoring the Covered Entity's position which has been marked to show changes from the Business Associate's perspective. See Form 23.L.2 for a model Checklist for reviewing and commenting on a BAA.

(m) Limitation of Liability

Many Business Associates enter into a BAA as part of a larger transaction, which is usually documented through an independent agreement separate and distinct from the BAA. Covered Entities are often concerned that the limitation of liability contained in such separate agreement may have the unintended consequence of limiting the Business Associate's liability for the breach of the BAA. To avoid any such unintended consequence, a Covered Entity should include language to the following effect in the BAA:

> Exclusion from Limitation of Liability. To the extent that Business Associate has limited its liability under the terms of a separate agreement, whether with a maximum recovery for direct damages or a disclaimer against any consequential, indirect or punitive damages, or other such limitations, all limitations shall exclude all damages to Covered Entity arising from Business Associate's breach of its obligations relating to the use and disclosure of Protected Health Information.

To further protect its interests, the Covered Entity should ensure that each agreement's integration clause provides that the agreement covers all matters related to the subject matter of the agreement. See Chapter 6.N. for a more detailed discussion of integration clauses.

(n) Other Issues to Consider

A Covered Entity may want to restrict the Business Associate from sharing any PHI with an offshore location without the Covered Entity's specific approval. From the Covered Entity's perspective, approval should be conditioned upon the Business Associate's strict compliance with a mutually agreed set of policies and procedures at the offshore location.

The Covered Entity may also want to include the right to audit the Business Associate's facilities as well as its books and records to assess not only the Business Associate's compliance with terms of the BAA but also the reasons for any failure to comply.

4. *Mitigating the Risk*

To mitigate any potential risk, both parties should evaluate each party's overall security plans to ensure that the plans comply with all applicable laws and regulations, as well as their underlying contractual obligations. Both parties should continually update and provide security awareness training and education to their employees and contractors. Such education and training should be included in every employee orientation program. The parties should also review the Centers for Medicare and Medicaid Services ("CMS") document entitled *Interview and Document Request List for HIPAA Security Onsite Investigations and Compliance Reviews,* http://www.hipaacertification.net/hipaa-audit-security-compliance.htm (Last viewed September 20, 2010), to ensure they comply with all of the requirements of such document.

C. Compliance with Other Privacy Standards

The licensor should think carefully before agreeing to comply with "all applicable laws" regarding the processing, storage, handling, collection, and transmission of licensee data, including the Safe Harbor Principles outlined in the Safe Harbor Agreement between the U.S. Commerce Department and the European Commission and similar international agreements. *See* Issuance of Safe Harbor Principles and Transmission to European Commission, 65 Fed. Reg. 56,534 (Sept. 19, 2000); Issuance of Safe Harbor Principles and Transmission to European Commission, 65 Fed. Reg. 45,666 (July 24, 2000); *see also* European Union Safe Harbor Documents, http://www.export.gov/safeharbor/eu/eg_main_018493.asp (providing access to documents of the safe harbor privacy framework) (Last viewed September 20, 2010).

The reference to the Safe Harbor Principles in the Safe Harbor Agreement is somewhat unusual. The licensee should not treat the Safe Harbor Agreement as law. Any company that participates in the Safe Harbor program must satisfy two requirements: (i) identify a publicly available privacy policy that complies with the Safe Harbor Principles; and (ii) acknowledge to the U.S. Commerce Department that it complies with the Safe Harbor Principles. It is unclear whether the reference to the Safe Harbor Agreement is intended to require that the licensor satisfy the above-described requirements or whether it is instead intended to require a Service Provider to comply with the licensee policies that comply with the Safe Harbor Principles. In either case, they should not be treated as a law.

Licensors may wish to consider joining the Safe Harbor program as an approach to addressing concerns from European licensees about the "adequacy" of the protection offered by the licensor.

CHAPTER 11

Applicability of the Uniform Commercial Code (UCC) and the Principles of Law and Software Contracting

A. Article 2 of the Uniform Commercial Code

Article 2 of the UCC applies to "transactions in goods" and is the fundamental contract law applied in commercial transactions. UCC § 2-102. At the time Article 2 was adopted in 1951, the use of software was not foreseen and certainly was not a significant part of commercial business transactions as it is today. As such, businesspeople and lawyers have not had a uniform law to look to in commercial transactions involving software, creating uncertainty as to how business disputes involving software should be resolved.

Software is neither fish nor fowl as it looks like it is bought and sold like a good, but it is licensed. Nor is it a tangible product. In the past, some courts have looked to whether a software transaction was primarily the sale or license of software (in which case software has been found to be a good) or the provision of services such as software development (*See, e.g., Micro Managers Inc. v. Gregory,* 434 N.W.2d 97, 100 (Wis. Ct. App. 1988)) to determine whether the UCC Article 2 would apply to a particular transaction. If the contract is primarily for the provision of a software program, the UCC will apply. The trend has been to recognize that the UCC governs software transactions, *Wachter Management Co. v. Dexter & Chaney,* 144 P.3d 747, 750 (Kan. 2006) ("without the purchase of the software, the services would have been unnecessary"); *Advent Sys. Ltd. v. Unisys Corp.,* 925 F.2d 670, 674–75 (3d Cir. 1991); *RRX Indus., Inc. v. Lab-Con, Inc.,* 772 F.2d 543, 546 (9th Cir. 1985); *Triangle Underwriters, Inc. v. Honeywell, Inc.,* 604 F.2d 737, 742–43 (2d Cir. 1979) including those transactions involving customized software. *See, e.g., Advent, Id.* at 674; *Colonial Life Inc. Co. v. Electronic Data Systems,* 817 F. Supp. 235, 239 (D.N.H. 1993). *But see Mortgage Plus, Inc. v. DocMagic, Inc.,* 2004 WL 2331918 (D. Kan. Aug. 23, 2004) (software worthless without technical services which were predominate purpose of contract). *See also Computer Software as Sales Law Problem,* 41 UCC L. Letter (No. 6 Aug. 2007), Note, *Computer Software as a Good under the Uniform Commercial Code; Taking a Byte out of the Intangibility Myth,* 65 B.U.L. Rev. 129 (1985), Note, *Computer Programs as Goods under the UCC,* 77 Mich. L. Rev. 1149 (1979).

On the other hand, courts have also completely ignored UCC Article 2 and have looked to the common law. *DSC Communications Corp. v. Pulse Communications, Inc.,* 170 F.3d 1354 (Fed. Cir. 1999). Other courts have expressly held that UCC Article 2A, at least, does not apply. *Rhone-Poulenc Agro, S.A. v. DeKalb Genetics Corporation,* 284 F.3d 1323, 1333 (Fed. Cir. 2002). Other courts have begun to question the holdings of those courts who assume UCC Article 2 will apply. *Specht v. Netscape Communications Corp.,* 306 F.3d 17 n.13 (2d Cir. 2002). This dichotomy is the reason for the development of the Uniform Computer Information Transactions Act discussed in Section B below.

The application of UCC Article 2 to software transactions creates significant unforeseen liability for the licensor. *See* Phillips, *When Software Fails: Emerging Standard of Vendor Liability Under the Uniform Commercial Code,* 50 Bus. Law. 151 (1994). Numerous sections of Article 2 on their face appear to be inapplicable to software, or at least fail to recognize the nature of software. For example, the perfect tender rule under Section 2-601 would require that the software tendered by the licensor be in total conformity with the contract. In *RRX Industries, Inc. v. LAB-CON, Inc.,* 772 F.2d 543 (9th Cir. 1985), the court looking to the "essence of the agreement" found that the software system in question was a good governed by the terms of the UCC and struck the exclusion of consequential damages.

To provide certainty, some licensors seek to state definitively that the governing agreement shall not be governed by the UCC. Some licensees, in an effort to take advantage of the protections offered to purchasers by the UCC, seek to affirmatively state that the agreement is subject to the applicable governing law's UCC provisions. A licensor should avoid at all costs accepting such a statement as it places the licensor at considerable risk as previously indicated. See § 28.3 for model language opting in and out of the UCC.

See generally Cohn, Kirsh & Nimmer, *License Contracts Under Article 2 of the Uniform Commercial Code: A Proposal,* 19 Rutgers Computer & Tech. L.J. 281 (1994); Brennan, *Why Article 2 Cannot Apply to Software Transactions,* 38 Duq. L. Rev. 459 (2000); *Scope of Article 2 of UCC,* 251 Comm. L. Advisor 1 (Nov. 2008).

B. The Uniform Computer Information Transactions Act (UCITA)

1. History of Attempts to Apply UCC Article 2 to Software Licensing

(a) Massachusetts Model

In 1990, a committee headed by Stephen Y. Chow in conjunction with the Business Law Section of the Massachusetts Bar Association drafted a model UCC Article 2B to serve as a discussion point for adapting the UCC to software licensing. The committee created a completely new article by modifying those sections of Article 2, which it thought were inapplicable to software, while maintaining the majority of Article 2. Although this article was widely circulated, there was no attempt to adopt it under Massachusetts law or elsewhere.

(b) Hub and Spoke Approach

As a result of the increasing need for a uniform law for software licensing, the National Conference of Commissioners for Uniform State Laws (NCCUSL) began to create plans to adapt Article 2 to software. The committee discussed utilizing a hub and spoke approach to apply UCC Article 2 to software licensing.

Under a hub and spoke approach, existing UCC Article 2 would serve as a "hub" and from that hub, spokes (i.e., those portions of UCC Article 2 that needed to be amended for software licensing, such as the perfect tender rule), would protrude. In August of 1995, after reviewing several drafts of a revised Article 2 using the hub and spoke approach, the NCCUSL board decided not to pursue the hub and spoke approach but instead to support a totally new Article 2B to directly address software licensing. For a general discussion of the hub and spoke concept, see Nimmer, *Intangibles Contracts: Thoughts of Hub, Spokes and Reinvigorating Article 2,* 35 WM. & MARY L. REV. 1337 (1994) and Feldman, *A New Draft of UCC Article 2: A High Tech Code Takes Form,* 12 COMPUTER LAW. 1 (Feb. 1995).

(c) UCC Article 2B

In September 1995, the NCCUSL board in conjunction with the American Law Institute (ALI) began discussing a proposed UCC Article 2B. Article 2B was to be a completely new article drafted along the lines of the Massachusetts model. When approved in final form, the Article needed to be voted on by the full NCCUSL board and ALI, and then sent to the individual states to adopt into law. After going through many revisions and being subject to much criticism involving arguments about and beyond UCITA regarding contract law, consumer law, as well as intellectual property law, the proposed Article "died" in March 1999 when it became clear that NCCUSL and ALI lacked a consensus to approve its ratification. On April 17, 1999, NCCUSL announced that there would be no proposed Article 2B of the UCC. Shortly thereafter, NCCUSL revamped a committee that had been revising UCC Article 2 because of similar controversy there regarding contract law and consumer law.

For a more detailed discussion of this process, see Graff, *The Evolution of the Uniform Computer Information Transactions Act,* 14 COMPUTER L. ASS'N BULL 47 (Nov. 1999).

Prior drafts of Article 2B are available from the University of Pennsylvania Law School's website at http://www.law.upenn.edu/search/search.aspx?q=ucc+drafts (Last viewed September 15, 2010).

2. Present Status of UCITA

NCCUSL decided to move forward without ALI creating a model law (instead of a UCC article) from the proposed UCC Article 2B, the "Uniform Computer Information Transactions Act" (UCITA). NCCUSL approved UCITA in July 1999. In August 2002, NCCUSL modified certain provisions of UCITA in response to criticism of the American Bar Association.

In March 2000, Virginia enacted UCITA effective July 2001 (VA. CODE ANN. §§ 59.1-501.1 *et. seq.*). Maryland enacted UCITA effective October 1, 2000 (MD. CODE ANN. COMM. LAW §§ 22-101 *et. seq.*). A number of other states, including Arizona, Delaware, the District of Columbia, Illinois, Maine, New Hampshire, New Jersey, Oregon, and Texas, have considered adopting UCITA, but there has not been overwhelming support to adopt it. Many states have been hesitant to do so in light of the controversies previously mentioned. NCCUSL revised UCITA in 2002 to address some of the concerns raised by consumer groups.

NCCUSL believes that a uniform law is needed given the considerable diverse legislative activity within the states regarding electronic commerce issues. The diversity of legislation is particularly troublesome since electronic transactions can, and frequently are, conducted across state lines. NCCUSL sees the UCITA as an intermediate step that will bring uniformity and clarity to this area of law until it can develop further. UCITA and the official comments are available at http://www.law.uh.edu/ucc2b.

For a detailed discussion of UCITA, see BRENNAN, TOWLE & WOLFSON, THE COMPLETE UCITA, Glasser LegalWorks (2004).

3. Significant Provisions of UCITA (2002 Version)

Section references set forth herein refer to the relevant sections of UCITA.

(a) Scope

UCITA applies to all "computer information transactions," which is defined as "an agreement or the performance of it to create, modify, transfer or license computer information or informational rights in computer information." UCITA §§ 103(a); 102(11). "Computer Information" is defined as "information in electronic form which is obtained from or through the use of a computer or which is in a form capable of being processed by a computer." UCITA § 102(10).

UCITA governs software licenses and sales, computer games, contracts and licenses, online databases, and information systems. It does not govern transactions involving print media, such as printed books, magazines, newspapers, or goods such as television sets, cars, movies, or computers, as well as employment agreements. UCITA § 103(d) comment 3. Where a computer program is imbedded in a good, UCITA will not apply to the imbedded software unless the good is a computer or peripheral or obtaining access or use of the computer program is a material purpose of the transaction. UCITA § 103(b). Embedded software that is excluded from UCITA cannot be used as a basis to opt into UCITA. UCITA § 103 comment (4)(b)(3).

UCITA provisions are "default" or "background law" provisions that apply only in the event the governing agreement does not contain contrary language (i.e., when the parties are silent as to a topic, UCITA attempts to supply a rule). Except for the provisions set forth in § 115(b) (such as conscionability), UCITA's provision can be varied by agreement. UCITA § 115 comments 2, 3. Under UCITA, the parties to an agreement for computer information may opt out of or into UCITA. UCITA § 106(b); 115(a). See § 28.2 of the Annotated Software License and Services Agreement in 23.B.1 for language opting out of UCITA. UCITA provides that any decision to opt into or out of the act does not alter certain obligations, such as the obligations of good faith, diligence, reasonableness, or the limitations on enforceability in the event of unconscionability or public policy. UCITA §§ 105(b)(c); 115(b). Opting out is often viewed as beneficial by licensees who assume the controversy surrounding UCITA was accurate. In fact, opting out can have significant adverse consequences for licensees.

Any portion of UCITA that is preempted by federal law is unenforceable to the extent of the preemption. UCITA § 105(a). Laws regarding trade secrets and unfair competition are considered to supplement UCITA and not preempt it. UCITA § 105(c). Similarly, UCITA does not preempt any consumer protection statute. UCITA § 104(b).

(b) Electronic Contracting

UCITA recognizes the validity of electronic contracts. *See, e.g.*, UCITA § 107; § 202(a); §§ 212–214 ("A contract may be formed in any manner sufficient to show agreement . . ." UCITA § 202(a)). It incorporates the term "record" instead of the word "writing" in recognition of the inclusion of electronic records. UCITA § 102(55). Similarly (and like the revised articles of the UCC, such as revised UCC Article 9), UCITA uses the word "authenticate" in place of the word "signature" to include electronic processes and symbols used to indicate an intent to sign a record. UCITA § 102(6).

(c) Acceptance (§ 203)

UCITA Section 203(4) reverses the mailbox rule for electronic messages by making acceptance effective upon receipt, in contrast to the traditional rule that makes acceptance effective upon deposit of the means of acceptance in the mailbox. See comment 5 of § 203 of The Official Comments to UCITA.

(d) License Terms/Background Rules (§§ 306, 307)

(i) Number of Users

Under UCITA, if the license does not specify the number of users, UCITA holds that the license will be viewed to allow a reasonable number of users "in light of the commercial circumstances existing at the time of the agreement." UCITA § 306.

(ii) Right to Enhancements or Modifications

Section 307(d) provides that a licensee is not automatically entitled to any new enhancements, versions, or modifications and that any agreement to provide new enhancements, versions, or modifications imposes such duty (as a background law matter) only to those as developed and made generally available from time to time. UCITA § 307(c).

(iii) Right to Source Code

Unless otherwise provided in the agreement, neither party is entitled to receive copies of the other party's source code, schematics, design material, or other similar materials. UCITA § 307(d).

(iv) Term

If a license is silent as to the term of the license, the term will be deemed for a commercially reasonable period. UCITA § 306 comment 2.

(v) Statute of Limitations

Any action for breach of contract must be brought within "the later of four years after the right of action accrues or one year after the breach was or should be been discovered, but not later than five years after the right of action accrues." UCITA § 805(a). Section 805(b)(1) provides that the statute of limitations may be reduced to not less than one year, but cannot be extended. Consumer contracts may not reduce the statute of limitations. UCITA § 805(b)(2).

(e) Assignability (§ 503)

Under § 503(1), a party may generally assign its contractual interest, other than for copyrights, unless (a) the transfer is prohibited by law or (b) "would materially change the duty of the other party, materially increase the burden or risk imposed on the other party, or materially impair the other party's property or its likelihood or expectation of obtaining return performance." A prohibition on assignment will generally be enforced as a breach of contract and void. UCITA § 503(2). A prohibition on the transfer of a licensee's contractual interest under a mass-market license must be conspicuous. UCITA § 503(4) comment 5.

(f) Choice of Law (§ 109)

Under §109(a), the parties may choose the governing law of the agreement, provided that in a consumer contract such choice does not violate the laws of the jurisdiction whose laws would apply in the situations below. In the absence of an agreement in the governing contract, UCITA sets forth three rules for determining which jurisdiction's law governs:

1. Internet transactions for the electronic transfer of information are governed by the laws of the state where the licensor was located when the contract was entered into. UCITA § 109(b)(1).
2. Transactions for the physical delivery of a tangible copy in a consumer transaction are governed by the law of the state where the delivery is made. UCITA § 109(b)(2).
3. In all other situations, the transaction is governed by the law of the state with the most significant relationship to the transaction. UCITA § 109(b)(3).

In a case of first impression, a Virginia court has upheld the election of the contracting parties to be governed by the terms of the underlying agreement and not UCITA. *Pilar Services, Inc. v. NCI Information Systems*, 569 F. Supp.2d 563 (E.D. Va. 2008).

(g) Choice of Forum (§ 110)

Under § 110 of UCITA, a choice of an exclusive judicial or arbitral forum will be upheld unless it is considered to be unreasonable or unjust. UCITA § 110(a). To ensure an exclusive judicial forum, the parties must specifically state that the selected venue is the exclusive judicial forum. UCITA § 110(b).

(h) Survival of Obligations (§ 616)

Except as set forth in § 616(b) below, all executory obligations of both parties are discharged upon termination of the license. UCITA § 616(a).

Under § 616(b), 11 rights and obligations will survive the termination of a contract:

1. a right based on a previous breach or performance;
2. confidentiality, nondisclosure, and non-competition obligations;
3. terms applicable to the use of licensed copies or information not returned to the other party;
4. an obligation to deliver or dispose of information, documentation, or copies; an obligation to destroy copies; or a right to obtain information from an escrow agent;
5. a choice of law or forum;
6. arbitration or alternate dispute resolution obligations;
7. terms limiting the time for commencing an action or giving notice;
8. certain indemnity obligations;
9. a limitation of remedy or modification or disclaimer of warranty;
10. an obligation to provide an accounting and make payments due under the accounting; and
11. any terms that the contract provides will survive.

(i) Warranties

(i) Implied Warranty of Non-Interference and Non-Infringement (§ 401)

Under § 401(a), a licensor who is a merchant dealing in the type of information licensed, "warrants that the information will be delivered free of the rightful claim of any third person by way of infringement or misappropriation. . . ." A licensor will be held harmless for liability arising from its conformance to the detailed specifications and the method required for meeting such specifications provided by the licensee, unless such claim arises from the licensor's failure to adopt or notify the licensee of a non-infringing alternative of which the licensor had reason to know. UCITA § 401(a).

Under Section 401(b)(1), a licensor is deemed to warrant that for the duration of the license, except for a claim of infringement or misappropriation, no person has a valid claim to or interest in information that arose from an act or omission of the licensor that will interfere with the licensee's use or interest. Further, as to an exclusive license, the licensor is deemed to warrant that the "informational rights are valid and exclusive for the information as a whole to the extent exclusivity and validity are recognized by the law applicable to the licensed rights. . . ." UCITA § 401(b)(2)(B).

(ii) Implied Warranty of Merchantability of Computer Program (§ 403)

Unless the warranty is disclaimed or modified, a merchant that is a licensor of the program type licensed, warrants to the end user that the "program is fit for the ordinary purposes for which such computer programs are used," and that "the program conforms to any promises or affirmations made on the container or label." UCITA § 403(a)(2),(3).

(iii) Implied Warranty of Informational Content (§ 404)

Under UCITA § 404, a merchant in a special relationship of reliance with a licensee who collects, processes, provides, or transmits informational content is deemed to warrant to the licensee that "there is no inaccuracy in the informational content caused by the merchant's failure to perform with reasonable care." UCITA § 404(a).

(iv) Implied Warranty of System Integration (§ 405)

Under UCITA § 405(a), a licensor providing systems integration services is deemed to warrant that the information provided by the licensor is fit for a particular purpose, if the licensor at the time of contracting has reason to know of the particular purpose for which the computer information is required and that the licensee is relying on the licensor's expertise to select, develop, or furnish the needed information.

If the licensor is required to provide or select a system of computer software and goods, and the licensor has reason to know that the licensee is relying on the skill of the licensor in making such selections, there is an implied warranty that the components provided or selected will function together as a system. UCITA § 405(c).

(v) Disclaimer, Modification, or Warranty (§ 406) (§ 16.1.4.A of Chapter 23, Form 23.B.1)

Section 406 sets forth the language necessary to disclaim the express and implied warranties set forth in Part 4 of UCITA. The language necessary to disclaim a warranty is different from the UCC, but the use of UCC Article 2 language will suffice. *See* UCITA § 406 comments 1, 2, 4, and 5. In any case, the parties should carefully consider the appropriate language to ensure their intent is met. See § 16.1.4.A of Chapter 23, Form 23.B.1 for model language.

Any attempt to disclaim an express warranty must be construed wherever reasonable as consistent with language creating the express warranty. To the extent any construction is unreasonable, the disclaimer or modification is void. UCITA § 406(a). To disclaim or modify an implied warranty arising under Section 403, the language must include the words "merchantability" or "quality" or words of similar meaning and if contained in a record, must be conspicuous. UCITA § 406(b)(1)(A).

To disclaim or modify an implied warranty arising under Section 404, the language in a record must include the word "accuracy" or similar wording. UCITA § 406(b)(1)(B). To disclaim or modify an implied warranty under Section 405, the disclaimer or modification must be in a record and conspicuous. UCITA § 406(b)(2).

A disclaimer is sufficient to disclaim all implied warranties if it individually disclaims each implied warranty or, except for the implied warranty in Section 401, if the following language or similar language is conspicuously stated: "Except for express warranties stated in this contract, if any, this 'information' 'computer program' is provided with all faults, and the entire risk as to satisfactory quality, performance, accuracy, and effort is with the user." UCITA § 406(b)(3). Unless the facts indicate otherwise, all implied warranties other than the warranty created under Section 401 are disclaimed by the expressions "as is," "with all faults," or other language that calls the licensee's attention to such disclaimer and makes it clear there are no implied warranties. UCITA § 406(c).

If an agreement requires ongoing performance or a series of performances by the licensor, any proper disclaimer under UCITA is effective as to all subsequent performances. UCITA § 406(f). The parties may limit the remedy for breach of warranty with respect to the limitation of damages and the contractual modification of remedies. UCITA § 406(g).

(vi) Modification of a Computer Program (§ 407)

A licensee that alters, deletes, or adds code to or from a computer program, other than by using one of the program's capabilities intended in the ordinary purpose, does not invalidate any performance warranties of the unmodified copies but rather invalidates only those of the modified copy. UCITA § 407.

(vii) Third Party Beneficiaries of Warranty (§ 409)

A warranty to a licensee extends to any third person for whose benefit the licensor provides the information or informational rights that rightfully use the information in the manner reasonably expected by the licenser. UCITA § 409(a). A warranty to a consumer extends to the consumer's immediate family or household if such person's use of the product could be reasonably foreseen by the licensor. UCITA § 409(b).

A licensor may disclaim third party beneficiaries except to a consumer's immediate family in a consumer transaction. UCITA § 409(c). A disclaimer or modification of a warranty or remedy that is effective against a licensee is also effective against any third party to which a warranty extends. UCITA § 409(d).

(j) Self-Help (§§ 605, 815, 816)

Three sections within UCITA govern the licensor's use of self-help. Section 605 addresses electronic regulation of performance while Sections 815 and 816 address electronic self-help procedures implemented as a result of the termination of the contract for breach.

Section 605(b) sets forth four situations where a licensor may utilize an "automatic restraint." Automatic restraint is not truly "self-help" because it has nothing to do with breach of the license. A licensor may use an automatic restraint:

1. if the agreement permits the use of a restraint;
2. to prevent a licensee's use inconsistent with a contractual provision;
3. to prevent use of the software after the expiration of the stated duration or a stated number of uses; and
4. after the contract's termination other than set forth in item three above and upon reasonable notice to the licensee before preventing access.

The licensor is not required to give prior notice under the first two situations.

An "automatic restraint" is defined as "a program, code, device, or similar electronic or physical limitation the intended purpose of which is to prevent use of information contrary to the contract or applicable law." UCITA §605(a).

A licensor who meets the requirements set forth in Section 605(b) or (c) is protected from losses due to using the automatic restraint. UCITA § 605(d). A licensor is free to implement an update of a software program that incorporates an automatic restraint to disable an earlier version. UCITA § 605(e). Under Section 605(f), an automatic restraint cannot be used to enforce a remedy for breach of contract or cancellation for breach. Because UCITA defers to federal law (§ 105(a)), UCITA's rules should be read in light of the rules regarding "technological measures" under the Federal Digital Millennium Copyright Act that imposes fewer burdens on licensors than under UCITA. Sections 815 and 816 of UCITA govern the use of electronic self-help (i.e., use of self-help after breach). Under § 816(b), upon the cancellation of a license, electronic self-help is prohibited. This provision may not be waived or varied by an agreement before the breach of the license. UCITA § 816(d). Under Section 815(b), a licensor who exercises its rights without judicial process, without breach of the peace, must respect the licensee's information (i.e., it cannot delete the licensee's information).

(k) Mass-Market Licenses (§ 209)

UCITA defines a "mass-market transaction" as a consumer contract or a transaction with an end-user licensee for information or informational rights directed to the general public under substantially the same terms for the same information. UCITA § 102(44). This includes transactions in a retail market, such as shrink wrap licenses, but excludes contracts for the display of public works, a contract for information that is customized, a site license, or access contract. UCITA § 102(43). A "mass-market license" is defined as "a standard form used in a mass-market transaction."

To be valid, the license terms must be presented prior or at the time the licensee first uses the information and the licensee manifests its assent. UCITA § 209(a). A term is not part of the license if it is unconscionable or conflicts with a term that the parties have expressly agreed. UCITA § 209(a)(1), (2). If the licensee refuses the mass-market license after having an opportunity to review the license, the licensee has the right to return the information for a refund and the reasonable cost of return must be paid by the licensor. UCITA § 209(b). The licensee is also entitled to receive compensation for any actual damages caused by the installation of the information for purposes of reviewing or removing the software. *Id.* Further, the terms of a mass-market license cannot alter contract terms that have been expressly agreed by the parties. UCITA § 209(a)(2).

4. *Rejection of UCITA (Bomb Shelters)*

To date, the vast majority of states have chosen simply not to enact UCITA. However, some states have gone so far as to enact legislation designed to reject the application of UCITA to their residents. The group Americans for Fair Electronic Commerce Transactions (AFFECT) has published draft legislation that has been termed "bomb shelter" legislation because it protects a state's citizens from the application of UCITA. As discussed in part (f) of this chapter, UCITA permits the parties to choose the law of any state "provided that in a consumer contract such choice does not violate the laws of the jurisdiction whose laws would apply" in certain situations. AFFECT is concerned that the parties to a license could specify that Maryland or Virginia law would govern the agreement, even if both parties reside in another state. So-called bomb shelter legislation voids any contractual choice of law provision that would result in the application of UCITA to an agreement. As of September 2010, bomb shelter legislation has been enacted in four states: Iowa (IOWA CODE § 554D.104), North Carolina (N.C. GEN. STAT. § 66-329), Vermont (9 VT. STAT. ANN. § 2463a (2003) and West Virginia (W. VA. CODE § 55-8-15).

C. Principles of the Law of Software Contracts

In May 2009, the American Law Institute approved the Principles of the Law of Software Contracts ("Principles"), which provide many recommendations for reforming the laws applicable to software licensing. Whether these recommendations are ever adopted by the state legislators or the judiciary remains to be seen. UCITA, which was approved in July 1999, has only been adopted in two states as of September 15, 2010. See Chapter 11.B, above, for a discussion of UCITA.

The Principles are perceived as licensee oriented and as incorporating consumer protections into commercial transactions. Many argue the Principles limit the freedom of contract, increasing vendor costs and uncertainty, leading to an increase in litigation.

The Principles focus on the transfer of software, defining "transfer" as "a conveyance of rights in software or an authorization to access software, including by way of sale, license, lease or access agreement." Principles § 101 (m) . The Principles address a number of significant issues that a prudent practitioner should address if and when the Principles are adopted by the state legislators or judiciary.

From the licensor's perspective, the most controversial provision addresses a non-disclaimable warranty of no hidden material defects (§ 3.05). Section 3.05 provides that a licensor who receives money in return for use of its software warrants that the software contains no "material hidden defects." This warranty may not be disclaimed. *Id.* The warranty extends "to any party in the normal chain of distribution." *Id.* Thus the licensor could potentially be obligated to correct any defective software regardless of where or when it was purchased.

Another important provision is an implied obligation to indemnify against infringement (§ 3.01). Although most licensors agree to indemnify the licensee against infringement, the indemnification included in the Principles is broader then the indemnification offered by most licensors. Other notable provisions include a disclaimer of warranties (§§ 3.02, 3.06 and 4.01), as well as the "Standard Form of Transfers" (§ 2.02), which likely extends consumer protections to commercial businesses.

As mentioned earlier, it remains to be seen whether the Principles will be adopted. Until the Principles are judicially interpreted, it is difficult to predict their impact on software licensing and the actions a prudent licensor and licensee should take to protect their interests. The controversial nature of the Principles, however, ensures that its provisions will be debated for some time to come.

CHAPTER **12**

Representing the Global Entity

Although this book focuses on the issues arising in the licensing of software domestically, counsel must consider whether the underlying licensing agreement and the provision of related services raise any international issues. These issues may arise even when both parties are incorporated and headquartered in the United States. The consideration of these issues assumes greater importance as more software development and information technology services are performed outside of the United States. If the underlying licensing and related services transaction are considered to be a consumer transaction, the licensor must also consider the implications of the various consumer laws of each applicable country.

The issues that may arise and thus require consideration will depend on the type of software being licensed and the services being provided. The parties must ascertain where the software will be used; whether the software and technical data will be accessed by the customer from outside the United States; and where the services will be performed, as the failure to comply with U.S. export laws may lead to criminal penalties, civil penalties, and the revocation of the licensor's export privileges. 15 CFR § 763.3 (2007). Customers should ascertain where the software will be used, whether the customer will access the software from outside the United States and what, if any, services will be provided from outside of the United States. Services may include development services, application support and maintenance services, help desk/call center services and data processing, as well as database management.

To quantify the level of risk involved, the customer should require the licensor to represent and warrant to the customer where the services will be performed. See Chapter 4.B.1. This representation and warranty should be accompanied by a mirrored indemnification, indemnifying the customer for any claims or liability arising from work performed outside of the United States. If all work is to be performed within the United States, the licensor should make a representation and warranty to that the effect. Further, from the customer's perspective, the contract should provide that no work may be performed outside of the United States without the prior written consent of the customer. See § 16.AB.

Set forth in the following paragraphs is a brief overview of some of the specific issues that prudent parties should consider when entering into a contract where services will be or may be performed outside of the United States, or where the customer may access or use the licensor's software and technical data outside of the United States.

A. Access and the Scope of Use

As discussed in Chapter 5.M, U.S. export/import laws, rules, and regulations may have an important impact on transferring or accessing software and technical data internationally. From the licensor's perspective, it is important to ascertain what rights the customer requires (such as the ability/right to access the licensed software remotely from outside of the United States) and to draft the license grant accordingly. While software licenses often restrict where the software can be installed (i.e., at a facility/data center within the United States) to the extent the software is accessible by the licensee from outside the United States, the applicable license should address this contingency. The licensor must be careful not to grant the customer rights that would violate U.S. export laws.

The first issue for the licensor to consider is whether or not the software will be accessed remotely. For instance, certain software is used in facility-based applications, without the need to be remotely accessed. For many administrative and production systems serving the global needs of organizations, however, companies need to provide remote access to these systems for their employees.

The second issue is whether the software application, or portions of it, is required to reside on a laptop or other portable electronic device (known sometimes as "fat client" architecture). If the software, or portions thereof, is required to reside on a computer in order to facilitate remote access, then an export event will occur when the laptop or other portable device is taken out of the United States. In that event, U.S. export laws would apply and must be complied with. In addition, other import laws may apply as well. For example, if the software is situated on computer servers located in the United States with Internet access capabilities, the question arises whether accessing and displaying the software on a laptop or another portable device is an "export" for purposes of compliance with U.S. export laws. On a theoretical basis, since the software is being displayed remotely, one could argue that the export laws apply. In practice, however, many practitioners do not believe that such access triggers the applicability of U.S. export laws. The correct answer will depend upon whether the source code or technical data is accessible from outside of the United States.

U.S. export authorities take a fairly expansive view of the applicability of U.S. export laws, particularly if the software has capabilities that are considered sensitive. For example, if a customer in Russia sends data to a location in the United States and later accesses pieces of software located in the United States, such actions are likely to be considered an "export" and subject to U.S. export controls, even though the software does not leave the United States. The trigger is the customer's access to the software. If the Russian customer simply provides the data that is processed in the United States and the Russian customer later receives only the processed data, the transaction is unlikely to be considered an export.

When drafting a software license agreement where the customer will be accessing the software from outside of the United States, a prudent licensor should incorporate a "scope of use" clause that recognizes that the software may be accessed remotely from outside of the United States, and, to the extent compliance with U.S. export laws is required, require the licensee to comply with all applicable laws. A sample license provision protecting the licensor's interests is as follows:

> Licensor grants to Customer a nonexclusive, perpetual, non-assessable, fully paid, unlimited user type, multi-site and non-transferable license for Customer to use and install the Software in the United States, and to permit its Affiliates and other Authorized Users to use the Software and Documentation in accordance with the Agreement, and by remote access worldwide provided that Customer shall be responsible for compliance with any applicable laws, rules and regulations related to access of the Software outside of the United States.

B. Provision of Technical Data to Non-U.S. Citizens

The U.S. export laws apply to the "export" of technical information whether it is an actual export to a location outside of the United States or a "deemed" export where a foreign national accesses the technical information from within or outside of the United States. Thus, the customer and licensor must determine not only whether the work will be performed outside of the United States, but whether any "technical data" will be accessed by a foreign national from outside as well as inside of the country.

If the work is performed by an individual who is not a U.S. citizen, export control law issues need to be considered. Under U.S. export control laws, all "technical data" exported from the United States to any country that does not fall under a license exception generally requires an export license. 15 CFR § 736.2 (2007). This includes technical data provided by an employer to an alien who is not a permanent resident of the United States, regardless of his or her location (i.e., even if the alien is in the United States when receiving the information) and regardless of whether the alien is an independent contractor or employee. 15 CFR § 734.2(b)(2) (2007). The Code of Federal Regulations broadly defines "technical data" as including, but not limited to, "blueprints, plans, diagrams, models, formulae, tables, engineering designs and specifications, manuals and instructions written or recorded on other media or devices such as disk, tape, read only memories." 15 CFR § 772.1 (2007).

The approval period for an export license may be several months depending on the type of information to be exported. Furthermore, as of October 2010, the United States maintains comprehensive trade sanctions against certain countries. The export of technical data to citizens of certain countries, including Cuba, Iran, North Korea, Sudan, and Syria, regardless of its use, may be impermissible. *See* 15 CFR § 746 (2007). In order to avoid any potential violations of U.S. export control laws, a party who provides technical information to another party should ascertain the citizenship of the individuals who will have access to such information. The disclosing party should require the receiving party to represent and warrant the receiving party's compliance with U.S. export laws. Further, the disclosing party should keep detailed records of exactly what technical information is provided to the recipient. To protect its interest, the disclosing party may want to have each of its subcontractors verify the nationality of each of its employees with access to the disclosing party's technical information.

See Chapter 5.M for a more detailed discussion of the issues created by U.S. export laws.

C. Ownership of Developed Work

Ownership of the work to be developed is a significant concern for the customer. To ensure that it obtains ownership of the developed intellectual property, the customer must understand the laws of the jurisdiction in which the work will be performed. Many countries recognize moral rights under the Berne Convention. Unlike an author's rights under the "work made for hire" doctrine, which can be assigned, moral rights can only be waived. Thus, the customer should ensure that the licensor obtains the necessary waivers from its employees and subcontractors to validly transfer ownership to the customer. For a more detailed discussion of ownership rights for software development outside of the United States, see Chapter 5.A.2, Chapter 5.A.4, and Chapter 12.F.

For a discussion of the issues involved with the retention of international independent contractors, see Classen and Paul, *Increasing Global Competitiveness by Utilizing Offshore Independent Contractors*, 2 INT'L. COMPUTER LAW. 2 (Nov. 11, 1994).

D. Taxes and Import/Export Duties

Both parties should determine what foreign taxes and/or import/export duties may be applicable to the provision of the services and/or licenses contemplated under the agreement. Given that most agreements require the customer to pay any such levies, the customer should exert its best efforts to quantify the amount of such levies and should not rely on any claims by the licensor that no duties or taxes are payable. Foreign customers should reject any attempt by a U.S. licensor to have the customer pay any local income taxes levied on the licensor's income when the licensor is licensing and installing its software outside of the United States. See § 8.6. If the customer agrees to pay any such taxes on the licensor's income, it should require the licensor to provide the customer with a valid receipt to allow the customer to receive a tax deduction.

Many countries tax royalties, dividends, services, software, and hardware at different rates. As such, the agreement between the parties should require the parties to cooperate to limit the amount of such duties or taxes and agree on the allocation of any consideration payable to the licensor among royalties, dividends, services, software, and hardware. See § 8.6.A.3. Further, the contract should obligate the licensor to contest any such duties or taxes on the customer's behalf and at the customer's expense if the customer requests the licensor to do so.

E. Governing Law Provisions

It is a generally accepted principle of international law that intellectual property rights are governed by the laws of the country in which the work is created or used. *See* Melville B. Nimmer & Paul E. Geller, International Copyright Law and Practice § 1 (1993). *See also* Melville B. Nimmer & David Nimmer, Nimmer on Copyrights § 17.02 (1990). A choice of law provision may be effective in selecting U.S. law to govern an agreement between a U.S. entity and a foreign entity and may thereby help minimize an offshore software developer's claim of ownership in the commissioned work, but it may not be adequate to override local statutory intellectual property law. Melville B. Nimmer & Paul E. Geller, International Copyright Law and Practice § 6 p. 189 (1993).

In *Bragance c. Michel de Grece,* an author asked a French court to enforce a French copyright law provision that makes moral rights inalienable and grants to authors a share of the proceeds from exploitation of their work. The author had signed a contract under which the parties agreed to have U.S. law govern the contract. The court granted relief to the author on the basis that moral rights set out a French law copyright rule, which overrode the otherwise valid U.S. contract. The court then distinguished French statutory provisions governing moral rights from provisions assuring authors a share of the proceeds for use of their product. It found the latter to constitute a French law contract rule, which did not override the U.S. contract insofar as the contract stipulated terms of payment for the transfer. *Bragance c. Michel de Grece,* Paris, 1 ere ch., Feb. 1, 1989, 142 R.I.D.A. 301 (1989). For a more in-depth discussion of this case, see Melville B. Nimmer & Paul E. Geller, International Copyright Law and Practice § 6 p.188 (1993).

In light of the *Bragance* decision, contracting parties should recognize the possibility that a choice of law clause may not always guarantee the application of U.S. law, especially in the intellectual property area, and that "no over-riding choice of law system determines which copyright-contracts rules are subject to which conflicts principles worldwide." Melville B. Nimmer & Paul E. Geller, International Copyright Law and Practice § 6 p. 189 (1993).

Under Chinese law, Chinese contracts must be governed by domestic law, if the contracting parties are exclusively local entities and the services are to be provided in mainland China. Only when a contract qualifies as a "foreign-related contract" may the contracting parties select a foreign law as the governing law. Art. 126 of the People's Republic of China Civil Code and Contract Law. According to the Chinese Supreme Court, a contract qualifies as a "foreign-related contract" if one of the following three factors is present:

1. at least one of the contracting parties is a foreign party; or
2. the object of the contract is located outside of China; or
3. legal facts that create and/or change and/or terminate the contract take place outside of China.

Art. 178 of the *Opinions of the Supreme People's Court on Several Issues regarding the Implementation of the General Civil Code of the People's Republic of China,* issued by the Supreme People's Court on January 26, 1988. The word "foreign" also pertains to Hong Kong SAR, Macao SAR, and Taiwan.

According to the Chinese Supreme Court, the foreign law selected by the contracting parties as the governing law shall not apply if the contracting parties intended to avoid the "mandatory/ prohibitive legal provisions of China." *Id.*

The existence of a master agreement between the foreign parents of two entities incorporated under the laws of the People's Republic of China (PRC) who signed a local contract and the commercial link between the master agreement and the local contract, constitute a "foreign-related factor." Therefore the local contract may not be governed by the laws of a foreign jurisdiction, although certain terms and conditions in the master agreement may be governed by the local contract. If the domestic parties to a contract without a foreign-related factor use a foreign arbitration to settle any dispute between the two PRC entities utilizing foreign laws, an arbitration award made by the foreign arbitration institute will not be recognized and enforced by PRC courts.

Two PRC entities cannot choose foreign laws as the "governing laws" of a contract signed between them, even if the contract is signed for the purpose of performance of a master agreement signed between their foreign parents. Arbitration awards made by foreign arbitration organizations on disputes between two PRC entities under foreign laws may not be enforceable in the PRC. In some cases where foreign law could be applied, a U.S. licensor may be better off under Chinese law. If the claim is governed by foreign law, a foreign licensor loses certain rights and protections under Chinese law. Further enforcement of a foreign judgment in China is difficult.

Thailand has similar laws. For a bill of sale used in an outsourcing contract, the Thai Conflict of Laws Act dictates Thai law as the governing law, so long as the assets (whether movable or immovable) are situated in Thailand. BE 2481 § 9 (1938). To be prudent, the parties should assume that the laws of less developed countries, such as Myanmar, Laos, and Cambodia have similar provisions.

Licensors should recognize that even if the court does recognize the applicability of U.S. law, a local court may lack experience in interpreting and applying U.S. law. As such, any outcome may be uncertain.

F. Applicability of Local Laws

Local laws may also have a significant unforeseen impact on the contract. These laws may not be well known and may not only increase the vendor's costs but may (if abused by the licensee) also place the vendor's intellectual property at risk. Set forth in the subsequent paragraphs are several examples of the types of laws that a customer and vendor must consider when licensing software and providing services internationally.

1. European Council (EC) Directive 91/250/EEC

Under EC Directive 91/250, a licensee is deemed to have the right to create such copies as are necessary to utilize a software program for the licensed purpose and to revise the program within its licensed purpose for the correction of errors. (Art. 5). Further, similar to the Digital Millennium Copyright Act, 17 U.S.C. § 1201(f), the licensee may reverse engineer the software, but only as strictly necessary to ensure interoperability with the licensee's other software. (Art. 6). The licensee may not, however, reverse engineer the software for any other purpose. *See also* EC Directive 2001/29/EC.

For a copy of EC Directive 91/250, see http://eur-lex.europa.eu/LexUriServ/LexUriServ.do?uri=CELEX:31991L0250:EN:NOT (Last viewed September 15, 2010.)

2. European Union (EU) Data Protection Directive 95/46/EC

In October 1988, the EU through the European Commission (EC) adopted Directive 95/46/EC to protect the personal data (including electronic copies of personal data). The directive defines personal data as "any information related to an identified or identifiable natural person" and deems the protection of such data to be a human right. The Directive prohibits the transfer of personal data outside of the EU to any country or entity that does not maintain adequate safeguards. The adequacy of any protection is evaluated on the basis of six principles.

1. Personal data should be processed only for the stated purpose.
2. All personal data should be correct, accurate, and accumulated only to the extent necessary for the stated purpose.
3. Individuals should be notified of the reason for processing the personal data and the identity of the person controlling the personal data. (Art. 6).
4. Adequate security procedures should be implemented to protect the personal data.
5. The affected individual should have the right to obtain a copy of all processed personal data and the right to ensure its accuracy.
6. Subsequent transfer of the personal data should only be permitted if the transferee is subject to the obligation to provide adequate security.

This obligation applies to third party vendors who may access such information through the provision of the contracted services.

For a more detailed discussion, see Tarr, *The Nuts and Bolts of the EU Safe Harbor*, 27 ACC DOCKET 107 (Nov. 2009); Sotto *et al.*, *European Union Data Protection*, 130 INTELL. PROP. COUNSELOR 1 (Oct. 2007); Chaloupka, *Documenting International Privacy Issues*, 26 CORP. COUNS. Q. 193 (2008).

3. Canadian Legal Issues

Canada's federal and provincial laws have similar origins to those of the United States. Canada's IP laws and technology law decisions are sometimes modeled on them, the exception being the provincial laws of Québec, which, like Louisiana, is a civil code jurisdiction. There are few surprises awaiting a licensor in Canada, but needless to say, as with any foreign jurisdiction, the advice of local counsel should be sought.

While no particular case definitively supports the enforceability of shrink-wrap licenses, click-through licenses have been enforced by the courts. If the terms of a license are effectively brought to the consumer's attention before a sale is final, it is unlikely that a court would refuse to enforce the contract simply because acceptance was evidenced by tearing shrink-wrap or another indication of consent short of signature. Canada's copyright law has been updated to deal with computer software, and licensees are prohibited from renting computer software and are allowed to make backup copies to protect against the loss of the work, a right that can be waived.

The protection of data in Canada, while expressed in subtly different ways, is essentially the same as that in the United States. Canada's copyright law includes moral rights, and moral rights attached to a piece of computer software can be waived but not assigned. A copyright-protected work made in the course of employment belongs to the employer. This rule is, however, applicable only to a true employment relationship. When a programmer is working under a consulting contract, unless a written assignment of his interest is given, in the end result the work belongs to the programmer, although a court can find an implied license for the customer's benefit. Any such assignment must be in writing. A contract for the use of computer software, like other choices in action, is presumptively assignable under Canadian law. However, where a contract is silent on the issue of assignment, the court will enquire into the nature of the rights and obligations represented by the contract and whether assignability is appropriate in the particular case.

Finally, Canada has an increasingly complex environment relating to privacy. A federal privacy law governs exchanges of personal data in the private sector, but its application is limited where provinces have enacted their own data protection laws. In other words, the situation is the reverse of the United States. It is unclear that the federal government has the statutory authority to regulate privacy, so it willingly cedes jurisdiction if a province chooses to. So far, the federal privacy law has not yet been judged unconstitutional. Several Canadian states, such as Québec, British Columbia, and Alberta, have enacted private sector data protection laws that supersede the jurisdiction of the federal law. Ontario has done so, but only with respect to personal health information. Finally, it is worth noting that specific public sector laws and rulings of privacy commissioners in the private sector limit, or require notice of, exporting data for outsourced data processing and even software maintenance purposes.

4. *Indian Legal Issues*

Utilizing Indian resources to reduce costs is not without risk. Licensors and licensees knowingly or unknowingly may assume additional risk from having the services provided in India, negating the financial benefits of Indian labor.

(a) Intellectual Property Issues

(i) Assignments

Any copyright assignment must specify the rights assigned. Under Section 19 of the Indian Copyright Act, if the period of assignment of the copyright is not stated in the assignment, the assignment is deemed to be for five years from the date of the agreement. Further, if the territorial extent of the assignment is not specified in the agreement, it is presumed to extend only within India. If the assignee does not exercise the rights assigned to it within one year from the date of assignment, then the assignment in respect of such rights is deemed to have lapsed after the expiry of that one year period unless otherwise specified in the assignment agreement.

To ensure a comprehensive transfer of all rights to the licensor or licensee as the case may be, an assignment should:

- Identify the copyrighted work;
- Specify the term;
- Specify the territory (i.e. worldwide);
- Specify the rights assigned;
- Provide that the rights will not cease if they are not exercised;
- State the purpose of the assignment and acknowledge that any use in accordance with that purpose will constitute sufficient exercise of those rights; and
- Provide for proper consideration if dealing with the employee/author, as this is the most likely basis to demonstrate that the terms of the assignment are inequitable to the author (which may form valid grounds for revocation of the assignment).

(ii) Patent Rights

Regarding protection of a vendor's intellectual property rights, such as copyrights, inventions, ideas, source and object code, it must be specifically contemplated in the underlying agreement. Indian patent law does not contain automatic assignment provisions, as provided under the Copyright Act, and thus inventions must be assigned by both employees and consultants. The vendor and its employees must assign any new invention to the client during the course of the contract, as well as execute an assignment of the final work product.

(iii) Confidential Information

Under many agreements, the customer provides the vendor with third party confidential information to enable the vendor to perform the contracted services. The customer must ensure that the vendor maintains the confidentiality of such information and uses the information only for the contractually agreed purposes. Moreover, the customer should ensure the vendor's employees have executed confidentiality agreements providing that they will not infringe the proprietary and intellectual property rights of the customer or third parties.

(iv) Work Product and Related Inventions

The vendor should agree to maintain the confidentiality of all work products developed under the agreement and the vendor should grant the customer an exclusive, royalty-free, irrevocable, perpetual, worldwide assignment, to any new invention developed under the contract. The vendor should not retain any right to use the work product or the ability to challenge the validity of the customer's exclusive rights to the work product.

For a more detailed discussion of intellectual property rights in India, see Hane and Hanson, *Selected Intellectual Property Law Issues for Consideration in Licensing in India*, 139 INTELL. PROP. COUNS. 1 (July 2008).

(b) Dispute Resolution/Enforcing Foreign Judgments

In selecting a dispute resolution process, the parties should remember that foreign judicial awards are very difficult to enforce in Indian courts. As such, the parties should carefully consider selecting arbitration to resolve any dispute.

(i) Enforcing Judicial Award

A foreign judgment can be enforced in India in one of two ways:

"Reciprocating" Territories

Judgments from courts in "reciprocating territories" can be enforced directly by filing an Execution Decree before an Indian court. A "reciprocating territory" is defined as: "Any country or territory outside India which the Central Government may, by notification in the Official Gazette, declare as a reciprocating territory." Explanation 1 to Section 44A of India's Civil Procedure Code. Presently, the United States is not recognized as a "reciprocating territory" by the government of India.

"Non-Reciprocating" Territories

Judgments from "non-reciprocating territories," such as the United States, can be enforced only by filing a lawsuit in an Indian court seeking a judgment based on the foreign judgment. The foreign judgment is considered only evidentiary. The time limit to file such a lawsuit in India is within three years of the date of the foreign judgment.

A foreign judgment is considered conclusive by an Indian court if such decision was (i) heard by a court of competent jurisdiction; (ii) reached on the merits of the case; (iii) based on international law; (iv) not fraudulently obtained; and (v) the initial claim was not in violation of any Indian law.

The Indian court system is notoriously slow. Enforcing a foreign judgment in India can take years, depending upon the complexity of the issues in dispute.

(ii) Arbitration

The Indian Arbitration and Conciliation Act (the "Act") governs the enforceability of arbitration agreements and awards made outside India pursuant to the United Nations' 1958 Convention on the Recognition and Enforcement of Foreign Arbitral

Awards ("NY Convention") wherein the parties may contractually agree on the venue of arbitration and governing law in the underlying agreement. Under the Act, any matter that can be decided by a civil court can be referred to arbitration except for antitrust matters and matters dealing with the dissolution of a company. The parties to an agreement must establish the governing law, venue, procedures, etc., for arbitration. For companies conducting business in India, arbitration is often preferable to litigating in the Indian courts.

G. U.N. Convention on Contracts for the International Sale of Goods

The parties should also be cognizant of the potential application of the United Nations Convention on Contracts for the International Sale of Goods ("UN Convention"), as it automatically applies to all contracts for the sale of goods between two parties who are domiciled in different countries, both of which are signatories to the UN Convention.[1] The UN Convention, adopted by the United States on January 1, 1988, provides a substantive framework for the formation of international contracts for the sale of goods and governs the rights of the buyer and seller. Even though the UN Convention does not define the term "good," it is written broadly enough to potentially include services for the development of software rendered by an independent contractor.

Computer software is not specifically included in the UN Convention, but is also not identified in the exclusionary provisions. UN Convention Arts. 2 and 4. The UN Convention does provide that if a "good" is regulated by a signatory country, the UN Convention will not govern its sale, because such action would interfere with the domestic laws of that particular country. UN Convention Art. 4. In the United States, the development and sale of software may be considered a "good" within the meaning of the Uniform Commercial Code (UCC) and may also be considered to be part of a non-regulated industry. *See, e.g., RRX Industries, Inc. v. Lab-Con, Inc.*, 772 F.2d 543, 546 (9th Cir. 1985); *Communications Group, Inc. v. Warner Communications, Inc.*, 527 N.Y.S.2d 341, 343–44 (1988); *Schroeders, Inc. v. Hogan Systems, Inc.*, 522 N.Y.S.2d 404 (1987). Thus, in the case of software development, a court could use the UCC definition of a "good" to justify the applicability of the UN Convention to the agreement.

If the parties wish to ensure that U.S. domestic law governs their agreement, the agreement must specifically opt out of coverage by the UN Convention. UN Conven-

1. As of January 1, 2011, the following signatories have partially or fully adopted the UN Convention: Albania, Argentina, Armenia, Australia, Austria, Belarus, Belgium, Bosnia & Herzegovina, Bulgaria, Burundi, Canada, Chile, China, Columbia, Croatia, Cuba, Cyprus, Czech Republic, Denmark, Dominican Republic, Ecuador, Egypt, El Salvador, Estonia, Finland, France, Gabon, Georgia, Germany, Ghana, Greece, Guinea, Honduras, Hungary, Iceland, Iraq, Israel, Italy, Japan, Republic of Korea, Kyrgyzstan, Latvia, Lebanon, Lesotho, Liberia, Lithuania, Luxembourg, Macedonia, Mauritania, Mexico, Moldova, Mongolia, Montenegro, Netherlands, New Zealand, Norway, Paraguay, Peru, Poland, Romania, Russian Federation, Saint. Vincent and Grenadines Serbia, Singapore, Slovakia, Slovenia, Spain, Sweden, Switzerland, Syria, Turkey, Uganda, Ukraine, United States, Uruguay, Uzbekistan, Venezuela, and Zambia.

tion Art. 6. Whether it is advisable to opt out of the UN Convention depends on the particular circumstances surrounding the contract. The fact that domestic courts are often unfamiliar with the UN Convention due to the lack of a fully developed body of case law (particularly as to its potential application to the software field) may prompt the contracting parties to opt out of its coverage. It may not be prudent for a party to subject itself to a legal regime that is still largely untested. However, if a party in a developing country will not agree to select U.S. law as the governing law of the agreement, the UN Convention may provide an acceptable alternative to both parties. In such cases, the UN Convention may be preferable to the uncertainties resulting from the application of conflict-of-laws rules or the risk of being subjected to less developed legal systems.

In sum, the parties must first determine if the country where the work will be performed is a signatory to the UN Convention. The party should then determine whether the UN Convention would cover the services/software to be provided under the relevant contract. If the parties wish to avoid any uncertainties resulting from the application of the UN Convention, the parties should opt out of the UN Convention and specify which country's laws govern the contract. See § 28.1 model language opting out of the UN Convention. The agreement should specifically exclude the application of any conflicts of laws principles. It should be noted that it is not entirely clear under U.S. law whether parties can choose to "opt in" to the UN Convention where the convention does not otherwise apply to the transaction in question.

In some instances, it may be technically unnecessary to opt out of coverage by the UN Convention. The United States implementing legislation adopting the UN Convention contains a reservation limiting its applicability to situations where the contracting U.S. party has a place of business in the country of the other party. Isaak Dore, *Choice of Law under the International Sales Convention, a U.S. Perspective,* 77 AM. J. INTL. L. 521, 525–26 (1980). If the U.S. party has no place of business in the country in which the other party is domiciled, an opt-out clause may not be required, although it would be prudent to include one whenever possible for the sake of certainty.

For a more detailed discussion, see *Guide to the International Sale of Goods Convention*, Thomson * West (2010); Karambelas, *United Nations Convention on International Sale of Goods: An International Law as Domestic Law*, WASH. LAW. 27 (April 2009); Nicholas, *Teach an Old UCC Dog New Tricks - An Overview of the UN Convention on International Sale of Goods,* BUS. L. TODAY 39 (Sept./Oct. 2008). *See also Recent Cases Interpreting The Convention on Contracts for the International Sale of Goods*, 272 COM. L. ADVISER (Aug. 2010).

H. The Foreign Corrupt Practices Act

The U.S. Foreign Corrupt Practices Act ("FCPA") is a federal criminal statute enforced by the U.S. Department of Justice (the "DOJ") and the U.S. Securities and Exchange Commission (the "SEC"). The FCPA contains separate "anti-bribery" provisions and "books and records" provisions.

1. Anti-Bribery Provisions

(a) Statutory Elements

The FCPA's anti-bribery provisions prohibit certain entities and individuals from "corruptly" offering or paying anything of value to a foreign official for the purpose of influencing an act or decision in his or her official capacity or securing any improper business advantage in order to obtain or retain business. *See* 15 U.S.C. §§ 78dd-1(a)(1), 78dd-2(a)(1), 78dd-3(a)(1).

Because the FCPA prohibits only payments or offers made "*corruptly*," an offer or payment is unlawful only if made with wrongful intent to influence the recipient. *See* 15 U.S.C. § 78dd-1(a). According to the FCPA's legislative history, a payment is made "corruptly" if it is "intended to induce the recipient to *misuse his official position* . . . ." S. Rep. No. 95-114, 95th Cong., 1st Sess., at 10 (1977) (emphasis added); *see also United States v. Liebo*, 923 F.2d 1308, 1312 (8th Cir. 1991) (citing Senate Report). The legislative history also suggests that the domestic bribery statute, 18 U.S.C. § 201, may be useful in interpreting the FCPA. *See* H.R. Conf. Rep. 100-576, 95th Cong., 1st Sess., at 918 (1977). Under the domestic bribery statute, the evidence must show that the bribe was made as part of a *quid pro quo* for a tangible benefit from the government. It is not sufficient to show that a party conferred something of value upon an official simply because of his or her official position. The value must be offered or given in connection with a specific action from that official. *See United States v. Sun-Diamond Growers of California*, 526 U.S. 398, 414 (1999).

"Anything of value" is broadly construed to encompass currency, securities, and currency equivalents (such as coupons or gift cards), tangible items, and intangible benefits (including travel, entertainment, and valuable favors). The FCPA does not contain any exception for *de minimis* expenditures; accordingly, giving or offering things of little value for an improper reason may create liability.

The FCPA defines the term "foreign official" to include "any officer or employee of a foreign government or any department, agency, or instrumentality thereof." *See* 15 U.S.C. §§ 78dd-1(f)(1), 78dd-2(f)(1), 78dd-3(f)(1). This broad definition encompasses employees of state-owned businesses.

The FCPA prohibits not only payments intended to obtain business directly from government, but also efforts to obtain favorable legal or regulatory treatment. *See, e.g., United States v. Kay*, 359 F.3d 738 (5th Cir. 2004) (payments allegedly made to Haitian government officials for purpose of reducing corporation's customs duties and taxes were potentially within the FCPA's prohibition against payments to foreign officials to secure an "improper advantage" in order to "obtain or retain" business).

The FCPA also prohibits "corruptly" giving anything of value to "any person" while "knowing" that all or a portion of such thing of value will be given, directly or indirectly, to a foreign official for the purpose of influencing an act or decision in his or her official capacity or securing any improper business advantage in order to obtain or retain business. *See* 15 U.S.C. § 78dd-1(a)(3). The FCPA defines a "knowing" state of mind as being aware, or having a firm belief that a result is substantially certain to occur. *See* 15 U.S.C. § 78dd-1(f)(2)(A). Specifically, knowledge of circumstances "is established if a person is aware of a high probability of the existence of such circumstance, unless the person actually believes that such a circumstance does not exist." *See* 15 U.S.C. § 78dd-1(f)(2)(B). Accordingly, conscious disregard of indications that a third party intermediary is making prohibited payments may give rise to liability, even absent actual knowledge of such payments.

(b) Affirmative Defenses

The FCPA allows two affirmative defenses for conduct that might otherwise satisfy the elements of an offense. Under the "local law defense," payments to government officials that are lawful under the "written laws and regulations" of the recipient's country do not violate the FCPA. *See* 15 U.S.C. § 78dd-1(c)(1). Under the "promotional expenses defense," payments to government officials do not violate the FCPA if they constitute "reasonable and bona fide expenditures" that "directly relate" to the "promotion, demonstration, or explanation" of products or services or performance of contracts. *See* 15 U.S.C. § 78dd-1(c)(2). As these are affirmative defenses, a party defending against FCPA allegations bears the burden of establishing their elements.

2. Books and Records Provisions

The FCPA's books and records provisions contain two components, an accounting component and an internal controls component, both flowing from the Securities Exchange Act of 1934 (the "Exchange Act"). The books and records provisions apply only to "issuers" of U.S. securities.

The FCPA's accounting provisions require issuers to "make and keep books, records, and accounts, which, in reasonable detail, accurately and fairly reflect the transactions and dispositions of the assets of the issuer." *See* 15 U.S.C. § 78m(b)(1)(A). This requirement mandates that all reported information be "reasonably current" and "in reasonable detail" or maintained at "such level of detail and degree of assurance as would satisfy prudent officials in the conduct of their own affairs." *See* 15 U.S.C. § 78(b)(7). Essentially, this provision makes it illegal to falsify, misrepresent, or omit information in the records kept under the FCPA. Records are "inaccurate" and violate the Act if they fail to record illegal or even improper transactions, or falsify or disguise such transactions. There is no materiality threshold.

The internal-controls component of the FCPA requires a U.S. issuer to implement a system of controls to prevent and detect improper accounting for transactions. Specifically, the provision requires issuers to "devise and maintain a system of internal accounting controls sufficient to provide reasonable assurances" that transactions are executed according to management's general or specific authorization, that transactions are recorded as necessary to permit preparation of financial statements according to generally accepted standards; and that the recorded accountability for assets is compared with the existing assets at reasonable intervals, and appropriate action is taken with respect to any differences. *See* 15 U.S.C. § 78m(b)(2)(B).

Because the books and records provisions apply only to U.S. issuers, the SEC has primary enforcement authority over these provisions. However, the DOJ enforces the sections of these provisions that provide criminal liability for U.S. issuers who "*knowingly* circumvent or *knowingly* fail to implement a system of internal accounting controls or knowingly falsify any book, record, or account." *See* 15 U.S.C. § 78m(b) (5) (emphasis added). The legislative history for the 1988 amendments to the FCPA make clear that "criminal penalties shall not be imposed for failing to comply with the FCPA's books and records or accounting provisions. This provision is meant to ensure that criminal penalties would be imposed where acts of commission or omission in keeping books or records or administering accounting controls have the purpose of falsifying books, records, or accounts, or of circumventing the accounting controls set forth in the Act. This would include the deliberate falsification of books and records and other conduct calculated to evade the internal controls requirement." Summary of Legislative History of the 1988 Amendments to the FCPA, available at http://www.justice.gov/criminal/fraud/fcpa/history/ (Last viewed September 15, 2010).

3. Applicability of FCPA

(a) Jurisdictional Limits

The jurisdictional limits of the anti-bribery provisions and the books and records provisions (and the extent of their applicability to foreign subsidiaries) differ.

The anti-bribery provisions of the FCPA are predicated on a variety of possible jurisdictional bases linking the conduct to the United States. First, the anti-bribery provisions apply to U.S. issuers, or officers, directors, employees, agents or stockholders of an issuer acting on behalf of a U.S. issuer. *See* 15 U.S.C. § 78dd-1(a). Second, the anti-bribery provisions apply to "domestic concerns," or a domestic concern's officers, directors, employees, agents or stockholders. *See* 15 U.S.C. § 78dd-2(a). Domestic concerns include U.S. citizens, nationals or residents, or corporations that are incorporated in, or have their primary place of business in, the United States. *Id.* at § 78dd-2(h)(1). Third, any action by any other person within the United States in furtherance of improper activity triggers the anti-bribery provisions. *See* 15 U.S.C. § 78dd-3. Merely transferring funds to, from, or through the United States may be sufficient to confer jurisdiction under this provision. In addition, the FCPA applies whenever a "United States person" commits any act, anywhere in the world, in furtherance of a prohibited payment. *See* 15 U.S.C. § 78dd-3(i). Thus, the applicability of the FCPA anti-bribery rules in specific circumstances requires analysis of the involvement of U.S. issuers and U.S. persons (both natural and corporate) as well as a determination of whether there was U.S. activity.

On its face, the FCPA does not make a U.S. issuer directly liable for improper payments by its foreign subsidiaries. However, the Department of Justice has interpreted expansively the three jurisdictional links outlined above and has been willing to assert corporate liability on the basis of virtually any nexus with the United States. Under a literal reading of the statute, a foreign subsidiary of a U.S. company does not appear to fall within the anti-bribery provisions of the FCPA, provided that its principal place of business lies overseas, it is not itself a U.S. issuer, and it does not act within the United States or make use of U.S. mail or wires. However, U.S. enforcement authorities take the position that a parent company in the United States may be held liable for the acts of its foreign subsidiary if it "authorized, directed, or controlled the activity in question." *See* DOJ, Foreign Corrupt Practices Act Anti-bribery Provisions, P3 (March 2002), *available at* http://www.justice.gov/criminal/fraud/fcpa/docs/lay-persons-guide.pdf (Last viewed September 15, 2010). More often, however, the U.S. enforcement authorities simply rely on evidence that directors, officers, or employees of the parent company knew about the foreign subsidiary's illicit payments or ignored clear evidence that the foreign subsidiary was violating the anti-bribery provisions of the FCPA.

Unlike the FCPA's anti-bribery provisions, the books and records provisions of the FCPA explicitly apply to majority-owned subsidiaries. *See* 15 U.S.C. § 78m(b)(6). Thus, when U.S. issuers own a majority of shares, foreign subsidiaries must comply with the FCPA record-keeping requirements in the same manner as their parent corporations, who effectively face strict (civil) liability for any violations by their subsidiaries.

4. *Risks under FCPA Anti-bribery Provisions*

(a) Business Gifts, Travel, and Entertainment

The principal risk with respect to the FCPA related to the anti-bribery provisions is the practice of providing extensive travel, gifts, and entertainment for employees of state-owned enterprises and government agencies.

Such recipients would qualify as "foreign officials" for purposes of the FCPA, even if they do not qualify as public officials for purposes of, for example, Chinese law. Providing travel, gifts, and entertainment to foreign government officials thus constitutes the provision of "things of value" to foreign officials. The entertainment of employees of customers and prospective customers is usually undertaken to "assist" in "obtaining or retaining business."

Providing gifts, travel, and entertainment for government officials may be consistent with the FCPA to the extent that either: (1) the other elements of an anti-bribery offense requiring corrupt intent to influence improperly the official conduct of a government official in connection with the company's business are not satisfied; or (2) the conduct qualifies for the affirmative defense for as a "reasonable and bona fide" expenditures "directly related" to the promotion or demonstration of products and services of the performance of a contract. Evidence of "corrupt intent" or of the "reasonable and bona fide" nature of an expense may be inferred from the circumstances. U.S. enforcement authorities are likely to conclude that any gifts or entertainment for employees of state-owned customers which are *not* reasonable and bona fide promotional expenses constitute corrupt payments intended to influence the recipient to act improperly.

(i) Relevant Enforcement Actions and DOJ Guidance

The FCPA itself does not define acceptable promotional activities or business entertainment, and there are no judicial decisions that do so. Indeed, there have only been two enforcement actions brought on grounds that payment of travel and entertainment expenses alone violated the anti-bribery provisions of the FCPA.

(a) *U.S. v. Metcalf & Eddy, Inc.*

In *U.S. v. Metcalf* & *Eddy, Inc.*, No. 99CV12566-NG, (D. Mass. 1999), the DOJ initiated a civil enforcement action against an engineering consulting firm, alleging that it had provided travel advances and accommodation upgrades for the chairman of an Egyptian sanitation authority and his family. Without admitting or denying the allegations of the complaint, the company consented to a permanent injunction from future violations of the FCPA, agreed to make specific improvements to its compliance program and to submit to periodic audits, and agreed to pay a $400,000 civil penalty and $50,000 costs of investigation.

(b) *U.S. v. Lucent*

More recently, Lucent entered settlements with the SEC and DOJ to resolve allegations that it had violated the FCPA in connection with travel and entertainment practices involving employees of Chinese state-owned telecommunications companies.

In a civil complaint filed in the U.S. District Court for the District of Columbia, the SEC alleged that Lucent, a global communications solutions provider, paid for Chinese government officials to travel to the United States and elsewhere for sightseeing, entertainment, and leisure purposes. According to the government, Lucent hosted approximately 315 trips and spent over $10 million on travel and entertainment expenses from 2000 to 2003 for approximately 1,000 employees of state-owned or state-controlled telecommunications enterprises in China that were prospective or existing Lucent customers. Although many of the approximately 315 trips were ostensibly to provide training or to allow inspection of Lucent's factories, the foreign officials spent little or no time in the United States visiting Lucent's facilities. Instead, they visited tourist destinations, such as Hawaii, Las Vegas, New York City, Niagara Falls, the Grand Canyon, Disney World, and Universal Studios. Some visits had only a day or half-day of business activities, followed by up to two weeks of tourist activities.

One visit described in the complaint involved five days of visiting Lucent facilities followed by nine days of traveling and sightseeing across the country at Lucent's expense. Another visit included five days of training in Florida followed by sixteen days of sightseeing in California, Nevada, Arizona, New York, Washington D.C., and Hawaii, again, at Lucent's expense. In addition, Lucent was alleged to have paid per diems of $500 to $1,000 per day, even though it was already paying for all lodging, transportation, food, and entertainment expenses. The SEC Complaint noted Lucent's apparent focus on the capacity of trip participants to influence the award of specific contracts in approving or declining requests for travel, and also highlighted evidence that Lucent personnel were aware of the impropriety of the trips (e.g., by providing itineraries overstating the business purpose of the trips in connection with visa applications).

The government also alleged that Lucent improperly recorded the expenses in its books and records. For example, over 160 trips were charged to Lucent's "factory inspection account," even though the officials did not visit a Lucent factory at any time during their trips. Indeed, during much of the time period at issue, Lucent did not have any factories in the United States. Similarly, expenses were often recorded as "Service Rendered - Other Services," an expense account that Lucent normally used for crediting "other service" expenses rather than as a repository for travel expenses. Another set of expenses was recorded as "Transportation International," which Lucent normally used for international freight transportation costs where a product crosses country borders. In addition, the government alleged that Lucent lacked internal controls to detect and prevent trips intended for sightseeing, entertainment, or leisure, rather than business purposes.

The SEC filed a settled complaint, alleging that Lucent had violated the record-keeping and internal controls provisions of the FCPA. Lucent did not admit or deny the allegations as part of the settlement, but consented to the entry of a final judgment ordering it to pay a $1.5 million civil penalty and permanently enjoining it from future violations of Sections 13(b)(2)(A) and 13(b)(2)(B) of the Securities Exchange Act of 1934. Lucent also entered into a non-prosecution agreement with the DOJ. Lucent agreed to pay a $1 million fine and to implement more rigorous internal controls to ensure compliance with the FCPA. The DOJ agreed not to prosecute Lucent if it complied with the terms of the agreement over the next two years.

(c) DOJ Opinion Releases

In addition to these two published enforcement actions, the DOJ has issued a series of "Opinion Releases" addressing promotional activities and business entertainment for foreign officials. Through the Opinion Releases, the DOJ provides prospective guidance on the DOJ's intent to take enforcement actions with respect to future activities based on facts and circumstances as represented by the requesting party. Since 2004, the DOJ has issued five Opinion Releases concerning travel, entertainment, promotional activities, and gifts involving foreign government officials in different industries and commercial contexts. *See* Opinion Procedure Releases 07-01, 07-02, 04-01, 04-03, and 04-04, *available at http://www.usdoj.gov/criminal/fraud/fcpa/opinion/* (Last viewed September 15, 2010).

In each instance the DOJ indicated that it would not bring an enforcement action in light of the commercial circumstances, the business purpose for the activity, and the precautions taken to promote transparency and avoid impropriety (or the appearance thereof). Together, these Opinion Releases suggest a set of best practices for promotional activities and business entertainment for government officials.

In each of these Opinion Releases, the proposed activity was directly related to a demonstrably legitimate business activity. Opinion Release 07-02 involved a tour of a U.S. company's operating facilities to demonstrate its operations and capabilities and help establish the company's business credibility. The other Opinion Releases involved educational tours for foreign regulators to learn about relevant U.S. regulatory practices.

Where the proposed activity has a legitimate business purpose at its core, the following practices can further reduce the risk of improper payments:

- Limiting covered expenses to lodging, meals, local transport, and airfare directly related to the legitimate activity.

- Not funding, organizing, or hosting any entertainment or leisure activities for the officials, *apart from meals and receptions connected to substantive meetings, speakers, or events.* Any such entertainment or leisure activities should be incidental and proportionate to the core business activity. (For example, the DOJ approved a "modest four-hour city sightseeing tour" incidental to a five-day education seminar).
- Allowing the government entity to select individual participants rather than inviting specific government officials to participate
- Limiting participation to relevant personnel with legitimate business purpose for participating in the activity
- Not paying for any expenses for spouses, family, or other guests of the officials
- Funding appropriate expenses through direct payment to the vendor (e.g., hotel, airline, restaurant) rather than to the government entity or to the individual government official
- Where reimbursement of appropriate expenses is necessary, limiting reimbursement to modest amounts upon presentation written receipts and paying reimbursements through means other than cash (e.g., check, wire transfer)
- Limiting souvenirs or gifts to items of nominal value (hats, shirts, tote bags) featuring the host company's name and logo
- Not compensating or paying foreign officials to participate
- Not providing any per diems or pocket money to foreign officials
- Obtaining written assurances for a reputable law firm that the sponsorship of the event and payment for disclosed expenses is not contrary to the law of the foreign country
- Obtaining written assurances from the government entity that the sponsorship of the event and payment for disclosed expenses is not contrary to the law of the foreign country

While a promotional event need not necessarily conform to each of these practices in order to qualify as a reasonable and bona fide business expense, following these practices reduces the risk of an actual or apparent violation of the anti-bribery provisions of the FCPA.

Additionally, these Opinion Releases suggest that promotional activities involving foreign officials are less likely to raise concerns under the FCPA when the host company either has no current or planned business (e.g., bids, product approvals, license applications) before the relevant agencies or its current or planned business before the relevant agencies is limited to routine activities involving little or no discretionary action by government authorities.

From an FCPA perspective, it is prudent to obtain certifications of compliance with the FCPA from foreign contractors and agents—especially sales agents and distributors. A prudent licensor should require local contractors and agents to complete a questionnaire that demonstrates that it is a valid and qualified contractor and agent, and is not simply a conduit for funneling funds to the local government in violation of the FCPA. See Form 23.G.12 on the CD-ROM for a model FCPA questionnaire.

For a more detailed discussion of the FCPA, see *Overview of the Foreign Corrupt Practices Act Bribery Provisions and Recent Enforcement Actions*, 39 The Law. Brief 1 (Jan. 15, 2009); Gantz, *The Foreign Corrupt Practices Act: Professional and Ethical Challenges for Lawyers*, 14 Ariz. J. Int'l & Comp. Law 97, n.66 (1997); Chang, *Legal Issues Relating to Transacting Business Abroad: What Every Lawyer Should Know about the Foreign Corrupt Practices Act*, 35 Hous. Law. 16, 18–19 (1997).

I. The USA Patriot Act (Public Law 107-56)

On October 26, 2001, President George W. Bush signed into law the Uniting and Strengthening America by Providing Appropriate Tools Required to Intercept and Obstruct Terrorism Act ("Patriot Act") as a direct result of the September 11, 2001 terrorist attacks. The Patriot Act expands the federal government's ability to access customer data maintained by Internet service providers (ISPs) as part of their business operations. The Patriot Act was amended in 2006 in two ways that create greater transparency over this process of obtaining evidence from companies. The amendments provide for congressional oversight by requiring the U.S. Department of Justice to report to Congress every six months about how many business record subpoenas it seeks. They also permit companies that receive these subpoenas to challenge any government order to keep the request secret.

Many non-U.S. companies operating outside of the United States fear that by using a vendor incorporated in the United States, the U.S. government will have unfettered access to their customers' data under the Patriot Act. In reality, U.S. law enforcement does not have unfettered access to data under the Patriot Act, and even under its broadest provision, the Foreign Intelligence Surveillance Act (FISA) business records ex parte subpoena must still follow a legal process in obtaining information and must swear to the issuing court that the information is "sought for an authorized investigation conducted accordance with [Department of Justice guidelines] . . . to obtain foreign intelligence information . . . or to protect against international terrorism or clandestine intelligence activities." 50 U.S.C. § 1861(b)(2). In fact, this authority is comparable to the powers of law enforcement authorities in many European jurisdictions.

Many customers seek to limit the U.S. government's access to their data by requiring the vendor to store their data outside of the United States. While the desire of the vendor to protect its clients' data is understandable, there is little a U.S. company can do to limit governmental access pursuant to lawful process, short of challenging the constitutionality of the Patriot Act. *See, e.g., Doe v. Ashcroft*, 334 F. Supp. 2d 471 (S.D.N.Y. 2004); *Doe v. Gonzales*, 386 F. Supp. 2d 66 (D. Conn. 2005)), *aff'd*. 449 F.3d 415 (2d Cir. 2006).

J. Availability of a Meaningful Remedy

When entering into an agreement with a foreign entity, a party must consider whether it will have a meaningful remedy in the event of a breach of contract by the foreign entity. Many parties that are domiciled outside of the United States have only a small sales operation in the United States with the great majority of their assets outside of this country. The ability to obtain a meaningful remedy is especially important in the event of a third party claim of intellectual property infringement or if a party breaches its confidentiality obligations. If a customer has retained an Indian company to develop an important piece of software, and the Indian entity fails to deliver, will the customer have the ability to obtain an adequate remedy for such breach? Similarly, if a licensor licenses its software to the U.S. subsidiary of a foreign company, and the subsidiary breaches the license agreement, does the licensor have a meaningful recovery? In these situations, the domestic party should ensure that the foreign entity has sufficient resources in the United States in the event of a breach of contract. If the foreign entity lacks sufficient assets, the domestic entity should require the foreign entity to establish a performance bond or establish a letter of credit for the benefit of the domestic party.

To avoid these types of issues, prudent customers include language in their agreements and/or a Request for Proposal (RFP) to the following effect:

> Customer requires that the Vendor entity that is party to the Agreement be a U.S. entity. If the services required under the Agreement will be provided by an entity other than the Vendor's ultimate Parent Company, the Vendor must provide a guarantee from its ultimate parent company in a form and substance satisfactory to Customer, which irrevocably and unconditionally guarantees the complete and proper performance of the contract and the financial liabilities of the Vendor. If the Parent Company is not a U.S. entity, Customer requires Parent Company to provide a performance bond acceptable to Customer.

CHAPTER **13**

Escrow Agreements

A. Release Events

1. In General

Escrow agreements are usually entered into to protect the licensee by providing access to the licensed software's source code in the event of a "release event." The definition of a release event is one of the most important aspects of a properly drafted escrow agreement. To avoid future disputes and ensure that the licensee is able to promptly access the source code, it is important that the parties clearly define what constitutes a release event. Common release events include (i) a material breach of the license agreement by the licensor; (ii) the failure of the licensor to properly maintain the software or offer maintenance for a contractually agreed period of time (at least five years); (iii) the acquisition of or a change in control of the licensor; and (iv) the bankruptcy/insolvency of the licensor.

A prudent licensor should ensure that the licensee does not have the unilateral right to declare a release event and trigger the release of the source code. In the event the licensee believes a release event has occurred, the licensee should be obligated to provide the escrow agent written notice describing the relevant event, and the licensor should have a reasonable time period in which to respond. If the licensor cannot show that a release event has not occurred or the licensor does not contest the licensee's claim, the source code should be released. A well-drafted escrow agreement will also establish in detail the dispute resolution process in the event the parties dispute the existence of a release event.

From the licensee's perspective, the licensee should have the automatic right to receive the source code once it files a claim with the escrow agent, without having to arbitrate or invoke the dispute resolution process. Most licensors, however, are unwilling to agree to such an automatic release. *See e.g., Vemics, Inc. v. Radvision, Ltd.*, 2007 WL 1459290 (S.D.N.Y. May 16, 2007).

A savvy licensor will seek to include a liquidated damages provision in the event the licensee inappropriately uses/releases the source code. See *Mid-Michigan Computer Systems Inc. v. Marc Glassman, Inc.*, 416 F.3d 505 (6th Cir. 2005) (licensee required to pay licensor $50,000 for each site using software in the event source code wrongfully accessed).

2. In the Event of Bankruptcy

To the extent the licensee seeks to include the licensor's bankruptcy as a release event, the licensor should ensure that the bankruptcy be in conjunction with a material breach of the licensor's obligations in order for the release to be triggered. It is inequitable to dictate a release solely for the licensor's insolvency if the licensor continues to perform its obligations under the license and is not otherwise in material breach. Further, the ability to enforce an automatic release in the event of bankruptcy is of questionable legality. 11 U.S.C. § 365(e)(i). See Chapter 17 for a more detailed discussion.

It is critical from the licensee's perspective that the escrow agreement include a "license grant" to use the source code. Many license agreements grant the licensee an object code license while requiring the escrow of the source code, but yet the license does not address the use of the source code in the event it is released. Without such a license grant and specific terms regarding use of the source code, the licensee may have no "intellectual property right" subject to Section 365(n) of the U.S. Bankruptcy Code as described in Chapter 17. Moreover, the license grant should not be conditioned upon the existence of a bankruptcy related event. Section 365(n) only applies to intellectual property "as such rights existed immediately before the case commenced." 11 U.S.C. § 365(n)(1)(B). Thus, a license grant to the source code, which is conditioned upon the licensor seeking bankruptcy protection, may not be protected by Section 365(n).

From the licensee's perspective, the escrow provision should provide for the release of the source code prior to the licensor declaring bankruptcy. Once an escrow dispute is before a bankruptcy court, it could take up to 18 months to resolve. Even if the licensee ultimately prevails, the release of the source code will likely come too late to be of value to the licensee. See the language in Form 23.C.3 § 3.2, which seeks to avoid having the release of the escrow deposit delayed in the bankruptcy hearings. For a more detailed description of the issues associated with bankruptcy, see Chapter 17.

The licensee should seek to include language in the escrow agreement releasing the source code upon the occurrence of any significant financial warning signs as specifically identified in the license agreement, such as a debt downgrade, the licensor being placed on a credit watch, or the licensor publicly announcing that it has retained an investment bank to explore "strategic options." The licensee should also negotiate a "self reporting" obligation for the licensor, obligating the licensor to report any warning signs of a triggering event (e.g., the licensor's liabilities exceeding its assets). In short, the licensee should endeavor to include language in the agreement to allow it to avoid appearing before the bankruptcy court to enforce its rights.

B. Use of Third Party Escrow Agents

1. In General

Disputes often arise as to whether the software to be "escrowed" must be placed with an independent third party, an escrow agent, or held by the licensor. The licensor is often hesitant to place its source code in the possession of a third party, where the licensor is unable to control access to the source code and the release of the source code. The licensee should insist on the use of an independent third party as the licensor may wrongfully refuse to release the source code in contravention of the escrow agreement.

In selecting an escrow agent, a licensee and licensor should look for an entity specializing in technology escrows with a technical staff to verify the deposit. No reasonable law firm would (or should) agree to assume the responsibilities of the escrow agent. The escrow agent should carry errors and omissions insurance; be ISO 9000 certified; and employ significant security measures both as to the vault and the deposit material. The agent should be financially stable such that it will still be in the business if the licensee ever needs to exercise its rights under the escrow agreement. For a more detailed discussion of the issues involved in escrowing software, see http://www.ironmountain.com/ipm/ (Last viewed September 15, 2010).

The parties should include the escrow agent in the negotiation process. Escrow agents have their own forms of escrow agreements and often will not agree to terms solely because the licensee and licensor have agreed to them. The escrow agent can potentially be liable for wrongfully releasing the source code, and thus it will want its obligations to be clearly stated, while at the same time seeking to limit its liability.

2. Verification of Escrowed Materials

Regardless of whether the source code is escrowed with a third party, the licensee should verify that the licensor has escrowed all the materials it is required to escrow which may include not only the source code but documentation, manuals, tools and other collateral materials. Licensees should seek to include an affirmative statement granting the licensee the remedy of specific performance to force the licensor to meet its escrow obligations, including but not limited to placing the software in escrow. See Chapter 4.B.6.(a)(ii)(x) for a more detailed discussion of specific performance. A smart licensee will include language in the escrow agreement requiring the licensor to release the software directly to the licensee upon the licensee's written request, if the licensor fails to place the required materials or any updates in escrow. See § 5.3.6. Although the licensor would likely not comply, such a requirement provides leverage to the licensee in the event it seeks a judicial remedy.

At the time escrowed materials are deposited, the third party escrow agent should be contractually obligated to verify that the materials are the complete and most recent version, the media is readable and virus free, that the deposited materials duplicate the licensee's development environment with the required information on the relevant utilities, compilers and operating systems. The escrow agent should also verify that the source code can be compiled and that the compiled materials are identical to the licensee's licensed technology. See Section 3 below for a more detailed discussion of the materials to be escrowed.

These duties should be an ongoing obligation, performed on a periodic basis, as the software and escrowed materials are "living" items that will continue to change during the term of the escrow agreement. Because of liability concerns, however, some escrow agents will not agree to evaluate the escrowed materials—they will only report what they are told they received, as well as the results of a visual inspection. A prudent licensee should seek to use a "full service" escrow agent that can provide verification services.

Escrow agents usually offer several levels of verification. Under the first level, the agent will confirm receipt of the software, that the software deposited is what is required to be deposited, and that the source code is readable. The second level requires the agent to confirm that the source code can be compiled into object code and that the software is identical to the software being utilized by the licensee. Under the most comprehensive level, the agent will confirm that the software will process data in the identical fashion as the licensed software.

Licensors should carefully review the agreement's verification provisions. Licensees occasionally try to include the right to participate in the verification process and thereby obtain access to the licensor's source code. Most licensors, however, are unwilling to allow the licensee to participate in the verification process.

3. Materials to be Escrowed

A smart licensee will require that the licensor escrow not only the software but also the tools, logic diagrams, programmer notes, encryption keys, compilers, and documentation necessary to operate the software. The licensor should be required to update all escrowed materials and software no less than quarterly and warrant that the software escrowed is the current version of the software presently utilized by the licensee.

The licensor should also be required to escrow all tools needed by the licensee to operate and support the software if the licensee takes possession of the software. In addition, the licensee may want to seek an express right to recruit and hire the licensor's employees in the event the source code is released, as many licenses and employment agreements contain non-solicitation provisions. Similarly, the licensee should allow the licensee to utilize third party contractors to access and maintain the source code if the original license grant does not allow third party access. Finally, the licensee should require the licensor to escrow the names, phone numbers, and addresses of the licensor's programmers so that the licensee can contact and hire them if need be.

If the software/source code is known to be complex and confusing (the proverbial "spaghetti code"), some licensees seek to have the licensor include a video tutorial with the escrowed materials to explain how the software works. A video can be very valuable if the source code is later released to the licensee and the licensor fails to cooperate with the licensee.

Each party should appoint one person within its organization to be responsible for the party's obligations under the escrow agreement and to monitor the other party's compliance. The failure to do so will invariably lead to one party's failure to comply with its obligations. A serious issue may arise if the licensee later seeks access to the escrowed materials only to discover that the materials are not current or do not provide the expected level of protection.

4. *Escrow Fees*

Verification and escrow fees can be quite expensive, sometimes costing tens of thousands of dollars. This cost should be allocated between the parties in the escrow agreement. Usually, the licensee will assume financial responsibility for any third party escrow fees as the licensee requested that the source code be escrowed. It is inequitable to require the licensor to pay for such fees especially if the licensor has already established a centralized escrow for all of its customers. A licensee should not balk at paying such fees if it believes the source code will be of value if a release event occurs. The licensee should resist the temptation to save money and allow the licensor to "self escrow."

C. Restrictions on Use of Escrowed Materials

Use of the licensed software's source code, which is released under an escrow agreement, should be subject to the terms of the license agreement, and such use should be restricted to maintaining the licensee's copy of the software for its internal purposes only. The license agreement/escrow agreement should contain a specific license grant clearly establishing the limitations on the licensee's use of the software and the licensor's ability to terminate such source code license in the event the licensee breaches the terms of use. In addition, strict confidentiality restrictions should apply.

D. Execution of the Escrow Agreement

The escrow terms are not an insignificant part of the transaction and must be addressed at the time the license is entered into. Any escrow agreement should be executed prior to or contemporaneously with the license agreement to avoid having the licensor later refuse to execute the escrow agreement, having the parties fail to agree on its terms, or having the licensor fail to escrow the required materials. Too often the parties fail to execute an escrow agreement contemporaneously with execution of the license agreement. The licensee then loses its leverage, as there is no incentive for the licensor to execute the escrow agreement after the license has been signed.

E. Third Party Software

Another issue for consideration is whether the escrowed software incorporates third party software and how the incorporation of third party software may affect the licensee's ability to maintain and support the source code if a release event occurs. To fully utilize the escrowed software, the licensee may need to obtain a license from the third party to use the third party's software. Most third parties have little or no incentive to grant such a license. Some licensees require that the licensor not use any third party software whose source code cannot be placed in escrow, without the licensee's prior written consent. See § 5.3.6 for a more detailed discussion.

F. Practical Nature of Software Escrow

Escrowing source code is not the panacea many licensees believe it to be. Often a release is delayed by litigation or arbitration over whether a release event has occurred. Even the timely release of the source code may not provide the desired solution for the licensee's problems. Placing fully documented software in escrow does not immediately allow a licensee to support the system. Licensees usually lack the needed expertise to use the source code, and it may take a significant amount of time and investment for the licensee to understand the operation of the software and make the software operational.

In actuality, the source code is probably of little value without an employee/programmer of the licensor to support it and explain the software's operation to the licensee's IT staff. Unless the software is extremely important to the operation of the licensee's business, it is unlikely that the licensee will spend the money to understand the code and keep it upgraded and current. Finally, there is the administrative burden on the licensee to ensure that the licensor has indeed placed a current, working copy of the source code and documentation in escrow and that the licensor has also subsequently escrowed all enhancements, modifications, etc.

In sum, a source code escrow may not provide meaningful protection from the licensor's failure to perform. However, as licensors tend to be extremely concerned as to the possible release of their source code, a well-drafted escrow provision can provide an incentive for a licensor to meet its contracted performance.

For a general discussion of technology escrow, see Watzke, *Technology Escrow: Protect Your Company's IP Assets and Technology Investments,* ACC Docket 22 (Apr. 2004) at 110–23, and Meeker, *Thinking Outside the Lock Box: Negotiating Technology Escrows,* 20 Computer & Internet Law 6 (Sept. 2003).

See Forms 23.C.3 and 23.C.4 (C.4 on CD-ROM only) for model Escrow Agreements.

CHAPTER **14**

Confidentiality Provisions and Trade Secret Protection

Protecting a party's intellectual property and trade secrets is important if an entity is to enjoy a competitive advantage in the marketplace. The type of protection available and the protections an entity should seek will depend on the nature of the intellectual property. Set forth in this chapter is a discussion of the different protections available and the advantages and disadvantages of each. For a general discussion, see *Programmers' Dilemma: What Protection Is Best?*, N.L.J. July 24, 2000 at C6.

A. Proprietary Information Clauses and Agreements (§ 12)

1. General

Proprietary information agreements, which are also known as confidentiality agreements or nondisclosure agreements, are essential when dealing with intellectual property. While trade secrets are often protected under state trade secret laws, which are usually based on the Uniform Trade Secrets Act (UTSA), proprietary information agreements provide an added level of protection. In the absence of an express confidentiality agreement, a confidential relationship does not exist between a licensee and licensor. *Seatrax, Inc. v. Sonbeck Int'l, Inc.*, 200 F.3d 358 (5th Cir. 2000).

A proprietary information agreement may protect information a licensor or licensee desires to keep confidential but which may not constitute a trade secret. These agreements provide a level of contractual protection as opposed to statutory protection under the trade secret laws. Proprietary information agreements allow a party to obtain a level of protection not offered by trade secret laws. While Section 7(a) of the UTSA provides that it "displaces" all conflicting state law providing civil remedies for the misappropriation of trade secrets, Section 7(b) clearly states that it "does not affect contractual remedies, whether or not based upon misappropriation of a trade secret. . . ." *See IDX Sys. Corp. v. Epic Sys. Corp. et al.*, 285 F.3d 581 (7th Cir 2002) (claim for breach of nondisclosure agreement not preempted by Wisconsin UTSA); *Celeritas Technologies, Ltd. v. Rockwell Int'l Corp.*, 150 F.3d 1354 (Fed. Cir. 1998) (California UTSA does not preempt plaintiff's claim for breach of nondisclosure agreement). One commentator believes that if the breach of contract/nondisclosure claim simply restates a party's obligation not to disclose trade secrets, the court may view such claim as being preempted by Section 7(a) of the UTSA. Voltchenko, *Software Development Outsourcing: NDAs Go Beyond Intellectual Property Laws—But How Far?* 20 Computer L. Ass'n. Bull. 98, 101 (No. 3, 2005). Thus, a proprietary information agreement can potentially prevent two customers from comparing their respective relationship with a licensor or exchanging any information that falls outside the definition of a trade secret.

While it is not required that this legal protection appears in a separate agreement from the license agreement, it is preferable that a separate and distinct agreement exists. A separate agreement avoids any claim that the parties' confidentiality obligations do not survive the termination of the license agreement. This is especially important for the licensor.

To limit the potential for misappropriation of a party's confidential information, the parties should not disclose confidential information at an initial meeting. Only after the parties have determined the each other's interest in entering into a potential transaction should confidential information be disclosed. This will reduce the amount of information disclosed and limit the risk of misappropriation or inadvertent disclosure.

Licensors and licensees often have no choice but to release proprietary information to the other. Release of such information could, for instance, be incidental to instructing the licensor to the specific requirements a product must meet or to specific functions a product must perform. In such cases, the execution of a proprietary information agreement is imperative to protect the licensee's proprietary information.

Proprietary information agreements provide the terms and conditions under which one party's proprietary information will be provided to another party, and also limitations on the use of such information by the receiving party. By executing a proprietary information agreement, the parties may agree upon what information will be exchanged; under what conditions the information will be returned to the disclosing party; the period of time for which the information will be kept confidential; and the right of the disclosing party to obtain equitable as well as monetary relief if the receiving party breaches its obligations under the agreement. Often, the agreement requires the receiving party to have its employees and contractors execute nondisclosure agreements if they are to receive the confidential information. It is not practical to have a party's employees and contractors execute new confidentiality agreements every time a new customer agreement is entered into. To avoid an undue burden on the receiving party, most parties will accept the confidentiality agreements the employees executed when they began employment with the receiving party. These agreements should protect the disclosing party's confidential information, but the disclosing party should review the agreement to make sure it provides adequate protection. See, e.g., Form 23.G.3. Thus, the receiving party can have its employees execute individual agreements or provide copies of the confidentiality agreement the employee should have executed when he or she started work.

Of principal importance to the licensor is an acknowledgement by the customer that the licensor's software is a trade secret and an agreement not to disclose such trade secrets. See Chapter 14.B for a further discussion of this issue. At the same time, the licensor should be required to protect the confidentiality of the customer's trade secrets, including the way the customer operates its computer system and any information about the licensee's own customers. The parties should carefully consider what is considered to be "proprietary" and "confidential" under the agreement, as collateral information may also be considered confidential. For example, the licensor may consider its pricing confidential and would not want the licensee shopping the licensor's price. The licensee, however, may want a very narrow definition so that it may discuss its experiences with other users (i.e., user conferences). Similarly, some licensors seek to classify customer feedback and evaluations as confidential information. A licensee, however, may want the right to discuss this information with third parties such as other vendors it is considering working with and thus should resist classifying such information as confidential information.

Many parties seek to use the definition of "trade secrets" under Section 1839(c) of the Economic Espionage Act of 1996 to define confidential information in their confidentiality agreements with the belief that, in the event of a breach of the agreement, they may be able to interest the U.S. Attorney's office in pursuing an action against the breaching party. See Chapter 14.B.6, below, for a discussion of the Economic Espionage Act of 1996.

Most agreements provide for either a "strict liability" standard or "commercially reasonable" standard for the protection of confidential information; that is, some agreements provide that the receiving party *will not* disclose any confidential information, while others provide the receiving party will use the same standard of care to protect its own confidential information but no less than a reasonable standard of care. The first creates a strict liability standard, creating liability on the receiving party's behalf if information is disclosed, while the later requires the disclosing party to prove the receiving party did not exercise a reasonable standard of care to find it liable. Any breach of a party's confidentiality obligations should be tied to the respective standard contained in the agreement.

The receiving party must carefully consider accepting a strict liability standard, especially if it is responsible for unauthorized disclosures made by its employees, consultants, or agents. Any such breach could create significant liability for the receiving party with little basis for a defense. Many agreements seek to avoid disclosure by prohibiting disclosure to anyone but the receiving party's employees on a need-to-know basis. This may be unacceptable to a receiving party if its third party consultants need access to the information. At the same time, the disclosing party has a legitimate concern as the third party consultants may be competitors of the disclosing party and may have little incentive not to later disclose or use the confidential information. Thus, the disclosing party should insist that the confidential information not be disclosed to third parties unless they are not competitors and have signed a nondisclosure directly with the disclosing party. See Chapter 14.A.2, below, for a more detailed discussion of third party access to the licensor's confidential information.

Some licensees seek to avoid this issue by including a clause in the license where the licensor acknowledges that the licensee may allow third parties access to the licensor's software or deliverables. See § 41. The licensor should carefully consider whether to accept the inclusion of this type of clause. Licensors should never agree to the disclosure of their confidential information to a third party by their customer without the right to directly enforce their rights against such party (i.e., become a third party beneficiary to any confidentiality agreement between the customer and third party). See Chapter 6.J. and § 40.

A significant issue for both parties is the period for which the receiving party must keep the information received confidential. This period is different from the term of the agreement, as the obligation of confidentiality will most likely survive the termination of the agreement. The parties should specifically state that the confidentiality provisions and any other provisions necessary to adjudicate a dispute survive the termination of the confidentiality agreement.

Careful consideration should be given to the length of any confidentiality obligation. Many confidentiality agreements provide for a set period of confidentiality, such as three to five years from the date of last disclosure, but a more prudent approach is to provide that trade secrets will remain confidential as long as they are entitled to trade secret protection. This protects a disclosing party from the risk of losing trade secret protection for its confidential information at the end of the stated term. See, e.g., Form 23.G.2 § 7, Form 23.G.3 § 7.and Form 23.G.2 § 9.3.8. Too often, the parties impose an artificial term of five or seven years, or until the occurrence of a particular event (i.e., for so long as licensee is using the software) to keep information confidential, when in fact the information may remain confidential well after the expiration of such term or the occurrence of the cited event.

Proprietary information agreements cannot actually prevent an independent contractor from disclosing an employer's proprietary information. Rather, proprietary agreements should be viewed as providing a framework for enforcing the employer's rights upon the contractor's breach. Every agreement should, therefore, include a provision for equitable relief, which would allow the injured party to obtain injunctive relief without prejudicing its rights to obtain other remedies. The availability of equitable relief is very important, since it entitles an injured party to immediate relief when a breach of the proprietary information agreement occurs. This is especially important as monetary damages alone can be inadequate once proprietary information has been widely disseminated.

A proprietary information agreement should also include clauses addressing governing law, choice of forum, personal jurisdiction, and the survival of the obligation of confidentiality beyond the termination of the agreement. Some agreements require that individuals who receive the confidential information be prohibited from working for a competing entity for a set period of time. The parties may also want to consider including a prohibition of assignment to prevent their confidential information from being assigned to a competitor and a requirement that any permitted successors to the receiving party be bound by the confidentiality obligations contained in the agreement.

Further, the parties should consider the need for an integration clause if they have executed a number of confidentiality agreements over the course of their relationship. The parties should try to ensure the consistent treatment of their confidential information throughout the various confidentiality agreements.

The agreement should also provide that all information should be considered confidential regardless of how it is disclosed (e.g., in writing, electronically, orally or visually) Some agreements require a disclosing party to identify any confidential information so that there is not inadvertent disclosure by the receiving party, especially to information that is orally disclosed. In such instances, the disclosing party would be required to identify in writing within a set time period (e.g., 10 days after disclosure) any orally disclosed information as confidential.

Most agreements provide that for any information to be considered proprietary and confidential, it must be marked as such. Further, any confidential information disclosed orally must be reduced to writing and submitted to the receiving party within 30 days of its disclosure. Recently, an increasing number of parties have sought to include language to the effect that any information that the receiving party should have known by its nature to be confidential should be treated as confidential whether or not it has been marked. Many parties reject this broad language as creating too much uncertainty as to what is confidential and thus subject to the agreement's obligations. See the model language below that may be applicable:

Notice of Confidentiality

> This document contains confidential information belonging to **[Licensor/Customer]** or one of its subsidiaries. This information is protected by civil and criminal trade secrecy law and such information is intended only for the use of the recipients named above. Disclosure of any information included herein to anyone else is expressly prohibited. If you are not the intended recipient, you are hereby notified that any disclosure, copying, distribution, use, or the taking of any action in reliance on the contents of this information is unauthorized and strictly prohibited.

It is important to make sure that the agreement provides that all software shall be considered proprietary and confidential, regardless of whether or not it is marked as such. This is important because, although most agreements require confidential and proprietary information to be marked, the media (disk or tape) containing the software is often not marked by the programmer who may be unfamiliar with the confidentiality agreement or the importance of marking the media.

To avoid this issue, companies may want to have custom disk labels pre-printed with the term "Proprietary and Confidential, ©Copyright [Company Name] all rights reserved," so that the company is protected if its employees fail to properly mark the software. Further, although counterintuitive, licensors should insist that any open source software provided to the licensee be considered the confidential information of the licensor as the licensor may be able to claim copyright protection. For a detailed discussion, see Davidson & Holloway, *Protecting Trade Secrets in an Open Source Environment,* 23 Computer & Internet Law. 1 (Jan. 2006).

Proprietary information agreements may be unilateral or bilateral. A unilateral agreement protects only one party's information, while a bilateral agreement would protect both parties' information. (See Forms 23.G.1 and G.2 for model unilateral and bilateral proprietary information agreements). Given that it is likely that both parties will be exchanging confidential information, it is prudent to sign a bilateral agreement. Some parties seek to limit their liability by only entering into a unilateral non-disclosure agreement that protects their confidential information and not the information of the other party. They often proclaim that they do not want to receive the other party's confidential information and that the other party must seek their consent prior to disclosing such party's confidential information. Further, any information disclosed to such party without its consent will not be considered confidential. Often the party seeking to prohibit the disclosure of confidential information is a large company that argues that it cannot adequately protect the other party's information. This argument is specious as each party should agree to protect and acknowledge the confidential nature of the other's information. A more likely reason is that these companies want to avoid a claim by a smaller disclosing party that the receiving party's intellectual property was developed from the disclosing party's intellectual property. Prohibiting disclosure reduces any potential misappropriation claim by the disclosing party.

Licensees should be cognizant that a licensor may transfer trade secret material as part of the deliverable work. Occasionally, cases of trade secret infringement arise out of criminal acts, such as trespass and larceny against the premises or property of another, usually a direct competitor. However, the fact that no clandestine raids on competitors' source code or design documents have occurred should not lure the licensee into believing that trade secret misappropriation has not taken place. Software engineers and programmers carry so-called tool kits around in their heads and in their personal files. They consider stock routines to handle common programming exercises, such as input/ output, disk access, data capture, and graphics generators, to be the building blocks of their work. The suggestion that such software would be proprietary to the entity that paid the development costs associated with the routines is often a radical departure from what they consider fair and equitable. The fact that they may be subject to confidentiality and invention assignment agreements does not always change their point of view on this issue.

Consequently, licensees should exercise caution when retaining licensors to avoid unwittingly committing trade secret misappropriation from one of the licensor's previous customers. The licensor should be interviewed and screened to ensure that its engagements did not involve the licensee's direct competitors or products likely to tempt the contractor into taking shortcuts by copying prior work. The licensor should be cautioned against using stock routines, and the contractor's reputation within the industry should be verified. The licensee should obtain a representation and warranty from the licensor that the deliverables will not include the intellectual property of any third party and that the licensor will indemnify the licensee for all damages incurred by the licensor for the breach of any such warranty. Similarly, if the customer licenses any intellectual property to the licensor for use in the deliverables, the customer should indemnify the licensor for any intellectual property infringement.

Courts tend to interpret confidentiality agreements strictly. *See Rainbow Nails Enterprises, Inc. v. Maybelline, Inc.*, 93 F. Supp. 808 (E.D. Mich. 2000) (failure to label information "confidential" as required by agreement negates confidentiality obligation); *Confold Pacific v. Polaris Industries*, 433 F.3d 952 (7th Cir. 2006) (claim by plaintiff for unjust enrichment and breach of confidentiality agreement denied where title, preamble, and merger clause all indicated limited nature of NDA and information in dispute was provided to defendant two months after NDA was executed and was not contemplated at time of initial discussions). For a more detailed discussion, see Bowden, *Drafting and Negotiating Effective Confidentiality Agreements*, 14 CORP. COUNS. REV. 155 (Nov. 1995).

The parties should carefully consider any requirement to certify that all copies of any confidential information have been returned to the disclosing party or destroyed. See Form 23.G.6 for a model certification. Some parties believe that it is better to allow each party to retain one copy of the confidential information it received from the disclosing party. The reasons for doing so include the need to meet the receiving party's audit requirements, and the receiving party's desire to know what information it received to defend itself from a subsequent claim by the disclosing party that it misappropriated the confidential information. If copies are retained, they should be kept in a single archive in the office of the party's lawyers to ensure the information is not later disseminated.

Prior to making this certification, the receiving party must ensure that any "soft" copies have been identified and destroyed. This would include reviewing all archived email files and removing such documents. This could be a burdensome task as most entities back up their email files on a nightly basis and often store these files for years. Thus, to comply, the receiving party would have to review the contents of each of these files. Similarly, if this information was circulated to the receiving party's offices around the world, this search would have to be repeated many times. To avoid this problem, the receiving party should carefully consider whether to agree to this requirement and should limit the distribution of any confidential information it receives. Further, the parties should carefully consider whether to exchange confidential information in an electronic format. Exchanging information in hard copy will eliminate the problem of identifying and destroying all electronic copies.

Both parties should review their internal policies relating to the receipt of confidential information prior to receiving the other party's confidential information. At a minimum, a receiving party must use "reasonable efforts" to protect another party's confidential information. Without the proper standards in place, a receiving party risks significant liability.

A receiving party should have a very specific, detailed written policy regarding the preservation of a third party's confidential information. Such a policy should contain prohibitions on the reproduction of information and the safeguards required to keep it confidential. These limitations may include limiting dissemination of confidential information on a need-to-know basis; keeping written records of who accessed such information; securing it at night, not discussing the information in public areas, and limiting access to those areas where the information is stored. Individuals with access to confidential information should be required to reaffirm their agreement to follow company policies regarding third party information on an annual basis, and the company should circulate semi-annual reminders to its employees and consultants. Finally, the company should document in writing all of its efforts and policies.

For a general discussion, see Barish and Caslin, *Before Signing Your Next Nondisclosure Agreement, Count to 10,* 24 ACC DOCKET 24 (Jan. 2006) at 24. For a general overview of proprietary information agreements, see Vizy, *Confidentiality Agreements,* 227 Com. L. Advisor 8 (Nov. 2006).

2. *Third Party Access*

A licensor should seek to insure that its confidential information is not disclosed except as is reasonably necessary. It is, of course, necessary for the licensor to disclose its confidential information to its prospects and customers. Customers, however, frequently request that the licensor permit them to disclose the licensor's confidential information not only to their employees, but also to other third parties, such as third party consultants. Such disclosure is for a variety of purposes, but is solely for the benefit of the customer. A licensor has an incentive to work with its customers within certain reasonable boundaries to allow its customers to make such disclosure, provided it does not create an unreasonable risk of loss or misappropriation of the licensor's confidential information or other intellectual property rights.

To protect its information, a licensor may adopt several procedures to provide reasonable safeguards for the continued protection of its confidential information and trade secrets. The first safeguard is that the customer requesting the disclosure must execute a proprietary information agreement and thereby agree to monitor such third party's use of the confidential information; to limit disclosure of such information on a need-to-know basis, and finally to guarantee such third party's compliance with the terms and conditions of the proprietary information agreement. The licensor should also seek to have the third party execute a nondisclosure agreement with the licensor so that the licensor is in contractual privity with the third party.

The guarantee serves several purposes. First, it serves as a measure of how trustworthy the customer believes the third party is. In a case where the customer objects to executing the proprietary information agreement, it is a clear signal the customer views such disclosure as an unacceptable risk. In such a case, the licensor's position is as follows: (a) the customer (not licensor) selected the third party, has worked with the third party, and therefore is in a better position to judge the risk associated with disclosing the information to the third party; (b) based on the customer's knowledge and experience with the third party and its business practices, the customer's objections to executing the proprietary information agreement are some of the best evidence of the third party's ability to protect the licensor's intellectual property rights; (c) the customer (not the licensor) receives all the benefits from such disclosure and, as such, should bear the risk associated with the disclosure to third parties. When the customer objects to executing the proprietary information agreement, the licensor should deem the risk to be too great and refuse to allow such disclosure.

The second purpose of the guarantee is to allow the licensor to proceed against both the customer and the third party for a breach of the proprietary information agreement. The licensor, like most businesses, is not in the habit of suing its customers. However, the customers, who are the paying clients of third parties, are in a better position to get the third parties to cease any wrongful activity. If there is a problem, the licensor will work with its customer to try and get the customer to resolve such breach with its third party business partner. Without the guarantee, the customer is loath to get involved, making it harder, if not impossible, for the licensor to amicably resolve issues arising out of the proprietary information agreement.

The second procedure or safeguard that the licensor should adopt for the continued protection of its confidential information and trade secrets is that the licensor should not allow disclosure of such information to direct competitors. However, even in this case, a licensor should try to work with its customers to create alternative solutions so that disclosure is not necessary. In very rare circumstances where alternative solutions cannot be created, a licensor may be willing to allow disclosures to direct competitors, subject to the proprietary information agreement including special provisions to ensure the third party employees receiving disclosure to the licensor's confidential information are identified and are not put in a position to use such information for a two-year period. Absent such additional protection, the risk is likely too great and the disclosure should be prohibited.

3. *Employees*

(a) Licensee Employees

Some licensors also seek to have the customer's employees execute a nondisclosure agreement with the licensor. Prudent customers will not allow their employees to sign a nondisclosure agreement directly with the licensor to avoid any potential liability on the employee's behalf. To support this position, the customers will likely argue that the employee has already signed a nondisclosure with the customer as a condition of employment.

(b) Licensor Employees

(i) Nondisclosure Agreements

Licensors should also require their employees to execute nondisclosure agreements as a condition of employment to protect the licensor's confidential information, especially in the event the employee leaves the licensor's employment.

A comprehensive nondisclosure agreement should include an agreement to keep the licensor's and its customers' confidential information confidential; an obligation to return any confidential information upon the termination of the employee's employment; the assignment of any inventions made by the employee to the licensor; an agreement to assist the licensor in obtaining and enforcing any patents or copyrights, and an acknowledgment by the employee of the licensor's right to obtain injunctive and equitable relief in the event of the employee's actual or threatened breach of the agreement. The licensor may also want to include a covenant of non-competition and a covenant not to solicit the licensor's employees and customers. The employer should require all of its employees to attend regular training sessions to "refresh" their commitment to abide by their nondisclosure obligations.

An employee's obligation of confidentiality may also arise out of common law. *Jostens, Inc. v. National Computer Systems, Inc.*, 318 N.W.2d 691, 701 (Minn. 1982).

(ii) Civil/Common Law Actions

At least one court has held that a common law cause of action of conversion applies to intangible records resident on a computer hard drive. *Thyroff v. Nationwide Mutual Ins. Co.,* 864 N.E.2d 1272 (N.Y. 2007) (insurance agent permitted to bring conversion action against insurance company, which took possession of computer leased to agent that contained work related data as well as agent's personal electronic files). Another found a domain name can be commuted. *Kremen v. Cohen,* 337 F.3d 1024, 1033–34 (9th Cir. 2003). Massachusetts courts have reached opposite conclusions when considering this issue. *See In re TJX Companies Retail Security Breach Litigation,* 587 F. Supp. 2d 209 (D. Mass. 2007) (Mass. does not recognize cause of action for conversion of intangible records. Court rejected invitation to adopt holding of *Thyroff*). *But see Network Systems Architects Corp. v. Dimitruk,* 23 Mass. L. Rptr. 339 (2007) (If paper documents can be converted, as they no doubt can, no reason appears that computer files cannot).

(iii) Criminal Actions

Licensors may also have the ability to bring a criminal complaint against present or former employees for the theft of trade secrets. In 2007, an employee of Duracell and an employee of Coca-Cola were sentenced for the theft of trade secrets. Duracell: http://wombletradesecrets.blogspot.com/2007/05/sentencing-in-duracell-trade-secrets.html (Last viewed September 15, 2010); Coca-Cola: http://money.cnn.com/2007/05/23/news/newsmakers/coke/ (Last viewed September 15, 2010).

Almost all states have enacted legislation making the theft of a trade secret a crime. For example, Section 499(c) of the California Penal Code (Crimes Against Property) prohibits the theft of trade secrets and broadly defines "theft" to including making copies of trade secrets or using trade secrets without authorization of the owner. Similarly, Section 31.05 (b)(2) of the Texas Penal Code makes the theft of a trade secret and the unauthorized copying of a trade secret a crime. V.T.C.A. Penal Code § 31.05 (b)(2). For a listing of state statutes making the theft of a trade secret a crime, see *Protecting Trade Secrets* § 3:21, Thompson* West (2007).

For a general discussion, see Gray & O'Rourke, *Preventing Employee Trade Secret Misuse from Derailing Your Company,* 132 Intell. Prop. Couns. 1 (Dec. 2007); Newman, *Protecting Trade Secrets: Dealing With the Brave New World of Employee Mobility,* Bus. L. Today 25 (Nov./Dec. 2007).

B. Trade Secret Laws/Protections

1. General

Trade secrets are generally governed by state law in contrast to other intellectual property rights such as copyrights and patents, which are governed by federal law. Trade secret protection encompasses broader protection than is otherwise available for copyright and patent protection. *Salsbury Laboratories, Inc. v. Merieux Laboratories, Inc.,* 735 F. Supp. 1537, 1542 (M.D. Ga. 1987) ("a trade secret does not require the uniqueness and novelty of a patent.") Unlike patent protection, trade secret protection does not prevent other parties from developing similar inventions or reverse engineering the technology in question.

To maintain a concept's or information's status as a trade secret, the owning entity must undertake reasonable steps to protect the confidential nature of the information of trade secrets. *Incase, Inc. v. Timex Corp.*, 488 F.3d 46, 52–53 (1st. Cir. 2007) (owner must take regular steps to maintain secrecy of trade secrets); *Arcor, Inc. v. Haas*, 842 N.E.2d 265 (Ill. App. 2005) (reasonable affirmative steps must be taken to maintain secrecy); *CMBB LLC v. Lockwood Mfg., Inc.*, 628 F. Supp.2d 881 (N.D. Ill. 2009) (employer not entitled to protections of Illinois Trade Secret Act due to its failure to take reasonable protections to protect claimed trade secrets). Whether a piece of information is in actuality a trade secret is a question of fact to be determined by a trier of fact. *Hoffman-La Roche, Inc. v. Voder*, 950 F. Supp. 1348 (S.D. Ohio 1997).

If a dispute arises, the owner must prove it considered the relevant information as a trade secret and that it took appropriate action to protect such information. A trade secret does not lose protection if it has been memorized. *Al Minor & Assoc., Inc. v. Martin*, 881 N.E.2d 850 (Ohio 2008).

A party may be liable for trade secret misappropriation even if it does not comprehend the information or cannot decipher it. *ClearOne Communications, Inc. v. Chiang*, 2007 WL 4376125 (D. Utah Dec. 13, 2007) (party may be liable for trade secret misappropriation even if it cannot understand or decipher object code constituting trade secrets). Computer software has been found to be a trade secret where source code is not easily copied or ascertained. *LinkCo, Inc. v. Fujitsu, Ltd.*, 230 F. Supp.2d 492, 499 (S.D.N.Y. 2002); *Q-Co Indus., Inc. v. Hoffman*, 625 F. Supp. 608 (S.D.N.Y. 1985).

Trade secrets can take many forms including customer lists and information, sales and marketing strategies, pricing, methodologies, functional specifications, technical specifications, object code and source code and employee names.

Actions that demonstrate taking reasonable actions to protect a party's trade secret include marking all tangible property containing such confidential information, including any disks or tapes, as "Secret" or "Proprietary and Confidential." Trade secret protection also provides an owner with protection for potentially an unlimited duration in comparison to copyright and patent protection. *See Jostens Inc. v. National Computer Systems, Inc.*, 318 N.W.2d 691 (Minn. 1982) (employer failed to take reasonable steps to protect its intellectual property by failing to mark software tapes and documents "secret" or "confidential").

All employees, consultants, vendors, and customers should execute a confidentiality agreement prior to their access to confidential information, *See MAI Sys. Corp. v. Peak Computer, Inc.*, 991 F.2d 511, 521 (9th Cir. 1993), and the owning entity should limit the dissemination of the information to a need-to-know basis. *Surgidev Corp. v. Eye Technology, Inc.*, 828 F.2d 452, 455 (8th Cir. 1987). Further, the owning entity should secure the business premises with locks, controlled entryways, visitor logs, etc. *Wyeth v. Natural Biologics, Inc.*, 2003 WL 22282371, at *3 (D. Minn. 2003). All persons and bags entering and leaving a facility should be subject to search.

All documentation should be shredded after use, while all white boards and writing surfaces should be erased and cleaned. Confidential information should not be faxed to unattended machines. Fax machine memories should be purged/cleaned daily. All access to soft copies of all the information should be computer-password restricted with prohibitions on copying or forwarding such information electronically or downloading on to personal digital assistants. The company's technology department should insure that the appropriate firewalls are in place and that adequate encryption technology is being used. Further, employees should be informed that there is no expectation of privacy for their corporate email.

A company should ensure that all locations where the information is stored are secure, not just the electronic files that may contain the information. *See Nationwide Mutual Ins. Co. v. Mortensen*, 606 F.3d 22 (2d Cir. 2010) (company not entitled to trade secret protection for client information as company failed to take reasonable precautions for all locations where information stored).

In addition, the owning entity should have written policies and procedures on protecting and the non-dissemination of its trade secrets/confidential information. Semiannual reminders of this policy should be distributed, and all of the company's efforts should be documented. *Centrol, Inc. v. Morrow*, 489 N.W.2d 890, 894–95 (S.D. 1992). For extremely confidential documents, each document should receive a special tag or footer to allow the company to identify to whom each copy was distributed, and provide the ability to trace any copies that are wrongfully circulated. An employee incentive program should be created to encourage the development and maintenance of intellectual property. All intellectual property including trade secrets should be documented and cataloged.

Upon an employee's resignation, the employee's access to the employer's computer networks and intellectual property should be frozen. If technically feasible, the employer should send the ex-employee a "kill e-mail" which, when opened, will automatically delete any of the employer's files on the ex-employee's computer. *See e.g., Haggard v. Spine*, 2009 WL 1655030 (D. Colo. June 12, 2009) (Employers protective measures including sending a "kill e-mail" demonstrated the value the employer placed on its trade secrets and the efforts it took to protect them). The employee's network and computer access for the ninety days prior to resignation or termination should be reviewed to ensure the employee did not improperly access or download any of the employer's intellectual property. An exit interview should be conducted with all departing employees to remind them of their continuing obligation to maintain the confidentiality of the employer's confidential information.

An employer should also evaluate whether special protections need to be implemented if a great number of its employees work remotely or use laptops or memory sticks that contain the employer's trade secrets. The employer may want to establish an internal committee to identify potential risks arising from employees who work remotely and seek to implement appropriate safeguards. Appropriate security procedures should be implemented to protect the computer systems accessed by those employees and to address the use of memory sticks.

All actual or potential disclosures should be documented through the execution of a nondisclosure agreement. Execution of a nondisclosure agreement is not, however, per se required to uphold the existence of a trade secret. *Marshall v. Gipson Steel, Inc.*, 806 So. 2d 266, 272 (Miss. 2002).

To avoid potential disputes over the proprietary nature of their intellectual property, many licensors have the customer acknowledge in their license that the licensor's intellectual property is a trade secret. This may prevent the customer from later claiming the intellectual property was not a trade secret and focuses any dispute on whether the customer breached its confidentiality obligations and the amount of damages suffered. Contractually agreeing, however, that a piece of information is a trade secret will not in and of itself grant trade secret status to such information. *Thompson v. Impaxx, Inc.*, 113 Cal. App. 4th 1425, 1430 (2003) ("Labeling information as a trade secret . . . does not conclusively establish that the information fits this description."). A customer should carefully consider the implications of acknowledging whether something is a trade secret. The customer most likely does not know whether the information in question is a trade secret. A reasonable solution is for the customer to acknowledge that the licensor treats the information as a trade secret. At a minimum, the licensor should also acknowledge that the customer's information is a trade secret.

Having one party acknowledge that certain information is a trade secret is not dispositive. In *Computer Associates International, Inc. v. American Fundware, Inc.*, 831 F. Supp. 1516, 1530 (D. Colo. 1993), the U.S. District Court for Colorado held that the defendant was not estopped from contesting the existence of trade secrets, even though it had signed a license acknowledging that the information in question constituted trade secrets. *See also Gary Van Zeeland Talent, Inc. v. Sandas*, 267 N.W.2d 242, 249 (Wis. 1978) (public policy prohibits estoppel based on contractual acknowledgment of trade secrets in restraint of trade case). Courts have found, however, that where the defendant acknowledged over several years the proprietary nature of the information, estoppel may be appropriate, *In re Uniservices, Inc.*, 517 F.2d 492 (7th Cir. 1975), or where the estopped party had directly developed the trade secrets in question. *Ultra-Life Laboratories, Inc. v. Eanes*, 221 S.W.2d 224 (Mo. 1949).

Federal patent law does not prevent state trade secret and breach of contract claims where an inventor seeks trade secret protection and not patent protection. *Russo v. Ballard Medical Products*, 550 F.3d 1004 (10th Cir. 2008). *See also Kewanee Oil Company v. Bicron Corporation*, 416 U.S. 470 (1974); *Bonito Boats, Inc. v. Thunder Craft Boats, Inc.*, 489 U.S. 141 (1989).

For a general overview of data protection and developing confidentiality systems, see Catanzariti, *Keeping Secrets—Developing Confidentiality Systems*, ACC DOCKET 24 (Oct. 2006) at 22; Spenser, *Tips and Insights on Data Protection*, ACC DOCKET 24 (Oct. 2006) at 114. Fine, *7 Steps to Information Protection*, 134 INTELL. PROP. COUNS. 1 (Feb. 2008).

For a detailed discussion of trade secrets, see R. MARK HALLIGAN & RICHARD F. WEYAND, TRADE SECRET ASSET MANAGEMENT—AN EXECUTIVE'S GUIDE TO INFORMATION ASSET MANAGEMENT, INCLUDING SARBANES-OXLEY ACCOUNT REQUIREMENTS FOR TRADE SECRETS, Aspatore Books (2007).

2. *The Inevitable Disclosure Doctrine*

The inevitable disclosure doctrine provides that it is inevitable that an employee will disclose his former employer's trade secrets if he or she accepts employment with a competitor. *See PepsiCo., Inc. v. Redmond,* 54 F.3d 1262 (7th Cir. 1995) (unless the employee "possesses an uncanny ability to compartmentalize information" he would be making decisions at his/her employee based on knowledge of his former employer's trade secrets. *See also Strata Marketing, Inc. v. Murphy,* 740 N.E.2d 1166 (Ill. 2002); *Merck & Co., Inc. v. Lyon,* 941 F. Supp. 1443 (M.D.N.C. 1996); *Uncle B's Bakery, Inc. v. O'Rourke,* 920 F. Supp. 1405 (N.D. Iowa 1996); *B.F. Goodrich Co. v. Wohlgemuth,* 192 N.E.2d 99 (Ohio Ct. App. 1966); *Allis-Chalmers Mfg. Co. v. Continental Aviation & Eng'g Corp.,* 255 F. Supp. 645 (E.D. Mich. 1966); *E.I. du Pont de Nemours & Co. v. American Potash & Chem. Corp.,* 200 A.2d 428 (Del. Ch. 1964).

Not all courts have accepted the doctrine of inevitable disclosure. In *Marrietta Corp. v. Fairhurst,* 754 N.Y.S.2d 62 (N.Y. App. 2003), a New York court refused to apply the doctrine stating, "the doctrine of inevitable disclosure is disfavored." *See also Whyte v. Schlage Lock Co.,* 101 Cal.App.4th 1443 (2002) (rejecting inevitable disclosure doctrine); *Del Monte Fresh Produce Co. v. Dole Food Co.,* 148 F. Supp.2d 1326 (S.D. Fla. 2001) (Under Florida law, injunction to bar employment under theory of inevitable disclosure doctrine requires demonstration of actual trade secret appropriation); *Le Jeune v. Coin Acceptors,* 849 A.2d 451 (Md. 2004) (court "declines" to adopt doctrine of inevitable disclosure).

For an overview of the doctrine of inevitable disclosure see Comment, *An Overview of Individual States' Application of Inevitable Disclosure: Concrete Doctrine or Equitable Tool?* 55 SMU L. Rev. 621 (2002); John M. Murphy, *Managing the Risk of Inevitable Trade Secrets Disclosure,* 26 Corp. Couns. Q. 58 (Jan. 2010).

For a discussion of employee trade secret obligations see Chapter 18.B.

3. *Uniform Trade Secret Act*

The Uniform Trade Secret Act (UTSA) was approved in 1979 by the National Conference of Commissions on Uniform State Laws and has subsequently been adopted by every state, and the District of Columbia, except for Massachusetts, New Jersey, New York, and Texas.

Section 4 of the UTSA defines a "trade secret" as:

> [I]nformation, including a formula, pattern, compilation, program, device, method, technique, or process, that: (i) derives independent economic value, actual or potential, from not being generally known to, and not being readily ascertainable by proper means by other persons who can obtain economic value from its disclosure or use; and (ii) is the subject of efforts that are reasonable under the circumstances to maintain its secrecy.

This definition is broader than the traditional meaning under common law as, under the UTSA, the trade secret does not need to be presently used in the owner's business. Trade secret status will be granted to information that will be used in a contemplated business activity.

To receive protection under the UTSA, a trade secret must meet three criteria:

- it must have independent economic value as a result of its confidentiality;
- it must not be generally known or readily ascertainable; and
- the owner must take reasonable efforts to maintain its secrecy.

UTSA § 1(4). An owner's efforts to maintain secrecy must be reasonable under the circumstances and need not be extreme. *E.I. DuPont de Nemours & Co., Inc. v. Christopher*, 431 F.2d 1012 (5th Cir.1970).

Some states require that any misappropriation be known. *See e.g.*, Ga. Code Ann. § 101-761. *See Southern Nuclear Operating Co., Inc. v. Electric Data Systems Corp.*, 2008 WL 1700204 (11th Cir. April 14, 2008).

Under the UTSA Section 3(a), an injured party is entitled to recover monetary damages for lost profits and unjust enrichment. *See e.g., Ice Corp. v. Hamilton Sunstrand Corp.*, 615 F. Supp.2d 1256 (D. Kan. 2009) (plaintiff in successful misappropriation claim entitled to recover lost profits). In the alternative, the UTSA also allows the aggrieved party to receive a royalty. A party is also entitled to injunctive relief for both actual and threatened misappropriation. Injunctive relief remains in place until the affected party seeks its removal, because the information in question is no longer a trade secret. Further, in the event of a willful and malicious misappropriation, an injured party can receive exemplary damages equal to two times its actual damages. UTSA § 3(b). Finally, the prevailing party may also obtain lawyer's fees. UTSA § 4. *See e.g., FLIR Systems, Inc. v. Parrish*, 174 Cal.App.4th 1270 (Cal. 2009) (affirming award of legal fees under California UTSA).

Any claim for misappropriation of a trade secret must be brought within three years after the misappropriation has been discovered. UTSA § 6. California courts have interpreted the statute of limitations as beginning to run "when the plaintiff has any reason to suspect that the third party knows or reasonably should know that the information is a trade secret." *Cypress Semiconductor Corp. v. Superior Court*, 77 Cal. Rptr. 3d 685, 687 (Cal. 2008).

A dichotomy exists among the courts as to whether the UTSA preempts a right of recovery under common law. The majority holds that the UTSA preempts all common law and statutory recovery rights for theft including unfair competition, conversion, breach of fiduciary duty, tortuous interference with a contractual relationship, and *quantum meruit*. *See, e.g., Thomas & Betts Corp. v. Panduit Corp.*, 108 F. Supp. 2d 968, 971 (N.D. Ill. 2000); *AutoChannel, Inc. v. Speedvision Network, LLC*, 144 F. Supp. 2d 784, 788-89 (W.D. Ky. 2001) (allowing both common law and UTSA claims to be asserted "would undermine the uniformity and clarity that motivated the creation and passage of the Uniform Act."); *K.C. Multimedia, Inc. v. Bank of America Tech. & Oper., Inc.*, 171 Cal. App.4th 939, 958 (Cal. 2009) quoting *Digital Envoy, Inc. v. Google, Inc.*, 370 F. Supp.2d 1025, 1035 (N.D. Cal. 2005) (California UTSA "prevents common law claims that are based on the same nucleus of facts as the misappropriation of trade secret claims for relief."); *Composite Marine Propellers,*

Inc. v. Van Der Woude, 962 F.2d 1263, 1265 (7th Cir. 1992) (Illinois Trade Secrets Act abolished all common law theories of misuse of confidential information). The minority holds that the UTSA preempts common law causes of action for misappropriation of trade secrets but allows a party to seek remedies based in tort for the theft of a trade secret. *See e.g., Accuimage Diagnostics Corp. v. Terarecon, Inc.*, 260 F. Supp.2d 941, 953-54 (N.D. Cal. 2003) (common law trade secret misappropriation claim preempted); *Mortgage Specialists, Inc. v. Davey*, 904 A.2d 652, 666 (N.H. 2006) (UTSA preempts conversion).

Independently developing knowhow that constitutes a trade secret is recognized by the UTSA as a defense to a claim of trade secret misappropriation. One means of utilizing this defense is to show that the allegedly infringing knowhow was developed in a "clean room" by individuals without knowledge or access to the trade secret in question. Such efforts are not always enough, however, to prevent a preliminary injunction from being issued. *See e.g., Computer Associates International v. Quest Software, Inc.*, 333 F. Supp.2d 688 (N.D. Ill. 2004).

For a more detailed discussion of the Independent Development Defense see, Michael L. Katz, *The "Independent Development" Defense under the Uniform Trade Secrets Act"*, 140 INTELL. PROP. COUNS. 1 (Aug. 2008); Randall E. Kahnke and Kerry L. Burdy, *Clean Rooms Are Not Just For Kids: How to Demonstrate Independent Development to Avoid a Trade Secret*, http://www.faegre.com/articles.aspx (last viewed September 15, 2010).

Interestingly, the UTSA recognizes that independent parties who develop the same trade secret can own the rights to the same trade secret and both parties are entitled to trade secret protection for the same information. Only the party from whom the information was misappropriated, however, can collect damages. Comment Sections 1 and 3 to UTSA. Further, a party is free to disclose the secret to the public, thus destroying its value. In the event a trade secret becomes public, a licensee's obligation to pay royalty fees is not necessarily negated, *See Warner-Lambert Pharmaceutical Co. v. John J. Reynolds, Inc.*, 178 F. Supp. 655 (S.D.N.Y. 1959), *aff'd* 280 F.2d 197 (2d Cir. 1960), but a hybrid trade secret-patent would be invalid. *Meehan v. PPG Industries, Inc.*, 802 F.2d 881 (7th Cir. 1986); *Pitney Bowes, Inc. v. Mestre*, 701 F.2d 1365 (11th Cir. 1983).

4. Computer Fraud and Abuse Act

The Computer Fraud and Abuse Act (CFAA), 47 U.S.C. § 1030, offers another means for an employer to bring an action against a former employee. The CFAA prohibits the theft of computer data, the unauthorized access to protected computer information, and the knowing transmission of a command that intentionally damages an employer's computer. CFAA § 1030(a). An injured party must prove that it suffered a "loss" of at least $5,000 in damages.

Courts are divided as to whether an employee still employed by the employer violates the CFAA when he steals information from the employer or damages the employer's computer hardware or software. See Chapter 18.F for a more detailed discussion of the CFAA and its application to employee misconduct.

5. Restatement (Third) of Unfair Competition

Section 39 of the Restatement (Third) of Unfair Competition sets forth two factors to determine whether a concept or information is a trade secret: (1) the extent to which the information can be used in the operation of a business or other enterprise, and (2) whether it is sufficiently valuable and secret to afford an actual or potential economic advantage to others. Thus, the determination of whether a piece of information is a trade secret depends on whether it meets these requirements. The definition of "trade secret" under the Restatement is consistent with the definition of trade secret in § 1(4) of the UTSA.

6. Economic Espionage Act of 1996

The Economic Espionage Act of 1996 ("Act") makes certain misappropriations of a trade secret a federal crime and provides enhanced penalties for the theft of trade secrets. 18 U.S.C. § 1831 *et. seq.* (1996). The Act has two principal objectives, to prevent the theft of trade secrets by an agent of a foreign government or instrumentality or a person acting on behalf of a foreign government, and the protection of trade secrets from theft in general.

Under this law, anyone who seeks to steal a trade secret related to or included in a product that is produced for or placed in interstate or foreign commerce that injures the owner of that trade secret shall be subject to a fine not more than $5 million or imprisonment of not more than 10 years, or both. 18 U.S.C. § 1832. The requirements of the Act are similar to the requirements of UTSA, with the added requirement that the trade secret be related to a product placed into interstate commerce.

The Economic Espionage Act defines "trade secrets" broadly as:

> all forms and types of financial, business, scientific, technical, economic, or engineering information, including patterns, plans, compilations, program devices, formulas, designs, prototypes, methods, techniques, processes, procedures, programs or codes, whether tangible or intangible, and whether or how stored, compiled or memorialized physically, electronically, graphically, photographically, or in writing if—(A) the owner thereof has taken reasonable measures to keep such information secret; and (B) the information derives independent economic value, actual or potential, from not being generally known to, and not being readily ascertainable through proper means, by the public . . . .

18 U.S.C. § 1839(3) (1996). The Act defines "trade secrets" more broadly than common law or the Restatement. See *United States v. Martin*, 228 F.3d 1 (1st Cir. 2000) (Act defines "trade secret" broadly to include tangible property and intangible information). This law is also applicable to anyone who receives, buys, or possesses such information knowing that it has been stolen or appropriated, obtained, or converted without authorization. 18 U.S.C. § 1832(a)(3). The Economic Espionage Act does not preempt or displace any other remedies, whether civil or criminal, provided by U.S. federal, state, commonwealth, or territory law for the misappropriation of trade secrets. 18 U.S.C. § 1838. Individuals who violate the act are subject to fines of

$500,000 and 10 years in prison, while a corporation may be fined up to $5 million. 18 U.S.C. § 1832(a).

While the Economic Espionage Act contains criminal penalties unlike the UTSA, a plaintiff under the Act must prove guilt "beyond a reasonable doubt." Further, the due process requirements for criminal acts must be satisfied. Approximately six cases are brought a year under the Act. Since its enactment in 1996, only one defendant has been sentenced to prison, receiving a 24-month prison sentence. http://www.justice.gov/criminal/cybercrime/OwSent.htm (last viewed September 15, 2010).

For a general overview of potential criminal liability for the staff of software and electronic data, see Gross, *Criminal Liability for Theft of, Interference with, or Unauthorized Use of Computer Programs, Files or Systems,* 51 ALR 4th 971 (1987).

7. State Laws

Employers may also be entitled to protection from an employee's theft of the employer's trade secrets under various state laws. See, e.g., *New Jersey: New Jersey Computer Related Offenses Act,* N.J.S.A. 2A:38A-3; Georgia OCGA § 16-9-93 (Computer Theft), *DuCom v. State,* 654 S.E.2d 670 (Ga. App. 2007). These laws vary by state and their applicability will depend on the location of the employer and whether the employee is a resident of the relevant state or working in an office in such state. A prudent employer should seek to utilize the benefits of all laws to protect its intellectual property rights.

For a further discussion, see Chapter 14.A.3. See also Chapter 18.D, E and F.

CHAPTER 15

When Problems Arise

Parties to a contract can be so focused on signing the agreement that they are unprepared for problems that may arise thereafter. The ability to anticipate and quickly address potential problems is essential for ensuring a successful project. Too often, a lack of foresight creates a downward spiral resulting in litigation. Litigation benefits neither party as it creates additional expense without satisfying the original goals of the parties. At least one survey has found that a staggering 71 percent of major information technology projects were unsuccessful. In a 2004 survey, The Standish Group International, Inc. found that 18 percent of larger projects completely failed, 53 percent were "challenged," and only 29 percent succeeded. *The CHAOS Report*, 2004, The Standish Group International, Inc; *See also* Tom Field, *When Bad Things Happen to Good Projects*, CIO MAGAZINE, Oct. 15, 1997, and Steve McConnell, *Rapid Development—Taming Wild Software Schedules*, p. 81, MICROSOFT PRESS ("The odds of a large project finishing on time are close to zero. The odds of a large project being cancelled are an even money bet"); *Enterprise Licensing Agreement: The State Failed to Exercise Due Diligence When Contracting with Oracle, Potentially Costing Taxpayers Millions of Dollars*, Apr. 2002, California State Auditor, Bureau of State Audits.

A. Addressing Issues That May Arise

Problems usually arise in one of three areas: (i) failure by the vendor to meet the agreed upon project milestones; (ii) failure of the deliverables to meet the agreed upon specifications; and (iii) cost overruns by the vendor in a fixed price environment and by the customer in a time and materials engagement. Frequently problems in one area trigger problems in one or both of the other areas. For example, failure of deliverables to meet agreed upon specifications will often delay the delivery schedule, both of which generate unanticipated project costs.

While each of these issues may have a different genesis, they all should be addressed in the same manner.

1. Be Proactive

The first step to a successful relationship is for each party to closely monitor the progress of the contract and each party's performance from the date the contract is signed. Each party should appoint a contract manager, who monitors compliance with the contract and, for the vendor, insists on change orders when the customer requests features/functions not covered by the contract. A strong change order procedure will avoid "scope creep" and hopefully limit any potential disputes among the parties. The parties should hold weekly meetings to ascertain their progress and to identify potential issues before they mature. By proactively monitoring the project, the likelihood of problems arising is reduced and the impact of those problems is minimized. Early identification of problems also allows the parties greater time to resolve the issue, develop work-arounds, and maintain the parties' original delivery schedule.

2. *Maintaining the Attorney-Client Privilege/Attorney Work Product Doctrine*

The Attorney Client Privilege and Attorney Work Product Doctrines are designed to protect legitimate exchanges of information between attorney and client from disclosure to an opposing party in litigation. If a party cannot keep a truthful and probing assessment of its performance (or, similarly a plain discussion of its legal rights and obligations) protected from potential claimants, it would present an almost insurmountable impediment to forthright communications between a client and his/her attorney.

(a) Attorney Client Privilege

The Attorney-Client Privilege (Legal Professional Privilege in the United Kingdom and Canada) is a long-standing legal concept that was created to protect from disclosure confidential communications between lawyers and their clients. The privilege is based on several fundamental considerations:

- clients are encouraged to be completely open, honest and truthful with their attorneys so that the attorney's legal advice can be based on all relevant facts; and
- clients would be reluctant to seek an attorney's advice if they feared that their communications would be revealed to others such as opposing parties.

Communications between a client and an attorney are privileged whether oral or written, irrespective of whether litigation is anticipated or in progress at the time. However, not all communications between attorneys and clients are protected—only communications that are intended to be confidential and which are for the purpose of seeking or rendering legal advice. The Attorney-Client Privilege applies to corporations as well as individuals.

Thus, communications between employees and a company's in-house and external counsel that are made in confidence for the purpose of seeking legal advice concerning corporate legal matters are protected by the Attorney-Client Privilege.

In this context, legal advice is not confined to receiving pure legal advice regarding legal rights and obligations (e.g., whether a party is in breach of a contract or other legal obligation) it can, subject to circumstances, include practical, strategic advice as to what actions can and should be done in the relevant legal context.

For example, not every internal report can be protected by the Attorney-Client Privilege, but a draft of a project report could be protected if upon completion it is sent to a party's attorneys for the genuine purpose of legal review with a request for legal advice as to content, legal risks arising for the party from the findings, etc.

The applicability of the Attorney-Client Privilege is dependant on the facts of the situation, but protection only will result if a party is sincerely seeking legal advice and not simply trying to protect its communications from being discoverable.

It is important to remember that confidentiality is the key to preserving the privileged nature of the communication. If the substance of an attorney-client communication is disclosed to people outside of the company (other than external legal counsel) or even to people within the company who are not directly involved in a specific legal matter, the privilege may be lost. Therefore, confidential communications with a company's attorneys must not be discussed with anyone outside of the company or with individuals within the company who are not involved in the specific matter nor have a business need to know.

For the privilege to exist, the communication must be to, from, or with a licensed attorney with a company's legal department or the company's outside law firm. Discussing a matter with a company employee who has a law degree but is not part of the company's legal department will not be privileged. The only exception is a company employee or law firm paralegal working under the direction of counsel. Moreover, often in-house counsel wears two hats—one legal and one business. If the communication with in-house counsel was for a business rather than legal purpose, or if in-house counsel was acting in his role as a business person rather than lawyer, the communications may not be protected.

Vendors should carefully consider asserting any claim of privilege as placing "privilege" on a document may have no impact at all. A careful examination of the applicable state laws on privilege, which usually require a communication be made in seeking legal advice, is essential. By placing "privilege" on a document and subsequently producing it, under the laws of some states a party may waive the privilege for all lawyer–client communications related to the matter. As such, a party should carefully consider the ramifications of its actions before asserting any claim of privilege. For a more detailed discussion on the subject of preserving privilege in connection with internal investigations, see Roberts and Rodriquez, Preserving Attorney-Client Privilege in Internal Investigations, http://www.faegre.com/2695. (Last viewed September 15, 2010). See also *Upjohn Co. v. United States,* 449 U.S. 383 (1981).

An investigation that a vendor's quality assurance group undertakes at an attorney's request should be protected by the attorney-client privilege. While expanding the disclosure of the content of these reports unnecessarily is not desirable, any such materials should be used for the legitimate purpose of addressing delivery issues on a client account and remedying the issues, which may prevent litigation from arising.

The parameters listed below should be adhered to in facilitating any exchange between a party's quality assurance team examining contractual compliance and the use of best practices and the business people associated with the account:

- Only those portions of the quality assurance investigation reports that are relevant to the efforts of the account team should be shared.
- All information provided to the account team is provided on a confidential basis, and should be kept confidential. The account team should be advised as to the requirements of the confidentiality agreements they signed at the time of their employment.
- Any reports generated by quality assurance team should be marked "Confidential."
- Only those members of the account team necessary to the further investigation who need access to the quality assurance report should be provided with a copy. Such copies should not be further distributed by them to anyone.
- Under no circumstances should any information in the quality assurance report be shared with the customer, and if possible that information should not be brought on to the customer site.

(b) Attorney Work Product Doctrine

The Work Product Doctrine is more expansive than the Attorney-Client Privilege as it applies to materials created in anticipation of litigation, at which time an obligation to maintain a party's documents may arise. The Work-Product Doctrine is not limited to communications between an attorney and his/her client, but rather encompasses documents created by any person in preparation of potential litigation. It also encompasses interrogatories, materials acquired to bring or defend a matter, as well as any documents, records or information created by an attorney *Hickman v. Taylor*, 329 U.S. 495 (1947). The intent of the doctrine is to allow a client and his attorney to "prepare and develop legal theories and strategy 'with an eye toward litigation,' free from unnecessary intrusion by his adversaries." *United States v. Adlman*, 134 F.3d 1194, 1196 (2d. Cir 1998) (quoting, in part, from *Hickman v. Taylor*, 329 U.S. 495, 510-11 (1947).

The Work-Product Doctrine provides in general that "a party may not discover documents and tangible things that are prepared in anticipation of litigation or for trial by or for another party or its representative." Rule 26(b)(3) of the Federal Rules of Civil Procedure. Unlike the Attorney-Client Privilege, the Work Product Doctrine is not absolute. Rule 26(b)(3) permits the discovery of documents, even if they otherwise would be protected by the work product privilege, if the moving party can show that it has substantial need for the requested documents and that it cannot obtain the needed information by other means without undue hardship. Rule 26(b)(3)(A) However, "mental impressions . . . opinions, or legal theories" receive heightened protection. Rule 26(b)(3).

However, the doctrine applies only to work done *in contemplation* of or preparation for litigation or other formal dispute resolution. Documents prepared in the ordinary course of business are not protected. What, precisely, is meant by litigation being "in contemplation" has never been clearly and objectively defined, but case law indicates it is clear that there has to be a "reasonable prospect" of litigation, but that "reasonable prospect" does not necessarily mean greater than a 50 percent chance. The party's lawyer always should advise on this issue in light of the relevant circumstances in each case.

Proper preparation by an attorney for litigation requires that he or she assemble information, review that information to determine what is relevant, prepare legal theories, plan strategy, and present the case. This work is reflected in interviews, statements, memoranda, technical expert evaluations, correspondence, briefs, mental impressions, personal beliefs, and many other tangible and intangible ways.

As mentioned previously, although "factual" work-product may be discoverable upon a showing of substantial need for the information sought, the protection afforded to "opinion" work-product—which reflects counsel's subjective beliefs, impressions, and strategies regarding a case—is nearly absolute. Thus, to the extent that work product reveals the opinions, judgments, and thought processes of counsel, it receives some higher level of protection, and a party seeking discovery must show extraordinary justification.

The doctrine also protects material prepared by the attorney, whether or not disclosed to the client, and it protects material prepared by the attorney's agents, such as paralegals and technical experts. When an employee is asked to work under the direction of an in house or external attorney to support litigation, that person becomes an agent of the attorney. As such, the work the employee performs in this capacity is subject to the same protection as if the attorney performed the work him or herself.

It is important to distinguish between collecting existing data for an attorney and creating original documents that analyze the data for the attorney. In the former situation, the data collected from the files or computer systems of a party is not attorney work product. The data existed before a litigation case was ever conceived. For example, if an attorney asks an employee to extract financial data from a company computer system, the data that he or she extracts and provides to the attorney is not protected. However, if the attorney asks an employee to extract and analyze the data—providing the attorney with a memorandum containing an analysis of the data in the context of the case—the memorandum to the attorney is subject to the attorney work product doctrine.

To ensure the protection of the doctrine, all documents should contain a header that reads: "SUBJECT TO THE ATTORNEY WORK PRODUCT DOCTRINE." Distribution of any documents should be limited to only those who need to know relative to the impending litigation or mediation, and all distributions should in all instances include an attorney representing the party's interests.

For a more detailed discussion, see John K. Villa, *Work Product Protection for Document Collections: A Quarter Century After Sporck v. Peil*, 28 ACC Docket 106 (May 2010).

3. Meet to Discuss an Issue

Once a potential issue has arisen, the parties immediately should meet to discuss the issue in detail. The parties should agree on the specific nature of the problem, including its cause; its impact on the project from a cost, time, and functionality perspective; as well as a resolution or a course of action to fix it. The proposed solution should receive "buy in" from both parties, and both parties should be responsible for its implementation.

Managing a customer's expectations and maintaining a strong relationship with the customer is critical for a successful project. In every discussion, the vendor should be forthright about explaining to the customer the nature of the challenges the vendor faces in trying to resolve the problem. Failing to address the problem honestly and openly only creates larger problems later, particularly if the customer concludes that the vendor was not forthright about the extent of the problems and the project is delayed or has greater costs than previously anticipated.

Although it is critical to consider involving legal counsel early in the process (as discussed later), the parties' lawyers alone will not be able to resolve most problems. Resolution of the problem and maintenance of the customer relationship only can be accomplished by the parties themselves. It is best to have the parties' technical staff meet first to define the problem and undertake a root cause analysis. The business-people should then join the discussion to evaluate potential solutions. Both of those meetings should focus on the problem and resolution without assigning blame. The nature of software requires that the parties be as specific and detailed as possible in defining the problem and the solution.

4. Document the Process

Both parties should document their meetings, the actions agreed to be taken by the parties, and their progress in resolving the issue. Minutes of all meetings should be kept. These minutes should be reviewed, approved, and signed by both parties. A written record ensures that at a later date an independent third party can evaluate whether each party undertook to meet its responsibilities under the agreements of the parties and how diligent and timely each party was in seeking to resolve the problem. The parties should remember, however, that these documents and records are discoverable if litigation arises and are often some of the most critical pieces of evidence in determining which party will bear the cost of the problem.

Given that litigation may arise, each party may want to retain their own legal counsel early in the process to review any minutes or other documents prior to execution, and otherwise establish protocols for the creation and maintenance of documents. The parties also may want to agree that, in order to foster an open atmosphere that is crucial to address the issue, their discussions and any documents produced by the parties may not be used in any subsequent litigation. Any such agreement should be in writing, and it is important to remember that the agreement only binds the parties to it. A third party subcontractor who may provide software or services is not bound by an agreement between the vendor and the customer and would be free to use any and all documents should either the customer or vendor bring a claim against it.

5. Quality Assurance Audits

The parties' contract often requires the vendor to undertake quality audits of the project's status and provide the customer with any resulting reports. See, e.g., Chapter 4.B.9 and 10 and §§ 8.B, 9.3. The vendor's quality assurance team is charged with identifying actual or potential problems in the vendor's development process so that they may be corrected prior to delivery.

These quality audit reports frequently support the customer's breach of contract claims and undercut the vendor's defense that the software met the contract requirements. The requirement to produce the audit reports places the vendor in a quandary: it needs to undertake quality audits to ensure a quality product, but at the same time it wants to avoid creating a report that is critical of its development efforts and may be used against it in any litigation.

Similarly, some customers seek to require the vendor to notify the customer in the event the vendor becomes aware of a problem or anticipates that a problem is likely to arise. See, e.g., Chapter 4.B.9 and § 9.13. A broad reading of this obligation may require the vendor to notify the customer of any issues identified by the vendor's quality audits. Savvy customers also will seek to review the vendor's quality audit reports to determine when the vendor realized that a problem existed.

To avoid such problems, some vendors seek to have their quality audit reports prepared under the direction of the vendor's lawyers, and claim protection under the lawyer-client privilege and the lawyer-client work product doctrine. See, e.g., Form 23.H.4 on the CD-ROM for a model memo requesting the production of internal confidential information. It is unclear whether privilege would protect the report, and moreover if the reports are provided to the customer, the vendor is unlikely to prevail in any dispute over a claim of privilege.

6. Prepare for the Possibility of Litigation

Although the parties seek to avoid litigation, they should be prepared for that possibility. Litigation counsel should be contacted as soon as a party suspects a dispute cannot be amicably resolved. Legal counsel should notify all employees and consultants associated with the project to retain all documents regarding the project whether written, electronic, or oral (voice mail). See Form 23.H.5 on the CD-ROM for a model Document Preservation memo. There is not a consensus as to when legal counsel should send such notice. Some believe that notice should be sent when a party believes it may sue another party, while others argue that notice should be sent when a notice is received from the other party. The party's information technology department should be notified to retain all emails that may otherwise be destroyed as part of the company's document retention policy.

Counsel also should consider placing the other party on notice that it may be bringing a legal claim and remind the other party of its obligation to preserve all documentation related to the project, given that litigation is contemplated. Consideration also should be given as to whether to recommend that the other party notify its insurance carrier regarding a potential claim. Although this may cause the other party to take a more aggressive position (possibly including bringing a lawsuit for a declaratory judgment), early notification may be advantageous if a party believes the other may not otherwise retain documentation that may support the party's case.

B. Potential Claims, Defenses, and Counterclaims

Information technology litigation is often like kabuki, the ritualized Japanese theatre. Although the nature of every dispute is different, most disputes are related to the vendor's delivery obligations (both quality and timeliness), costs, functionality of the software to be delivered, and scope creep. An experienced practitioner will recognize an atmosphere of *déjà vu* with information technology disputes as the vendor and customer exchange common claims and defenses that repeat from one dispute to another.

1. Customer Claims

The majority of customer claims arise from disputes over the vendor's failure to provide the deliverables in accordance with the agreed upon specifications in a timely manner. As such, most claims are based on breach of contract, fraud, or similar claims.

(a) Breach of Contract

(i) Failure to Deliver Required Functionality

Perhaps the most common problems alleged by customers are that the software lacks the required functionality, fails to operate in a stable manner, fails to perform the required functions in a timely manner, and/or is filled with bugs.

Disputes over functionality often arise when the technical specifications have not been drafted in sufficient detail. Although each party may have had a thorough understanding of what it expected would be delivered at the time the contract was entered into, the failure to include detailed technical specifications in the agreement may result in a product that does not meet the customer's expectations or needs. If the specifications included in the agreement are not detailed, the vendor may be able to correctly claim that it met its contractual obligations. This scenario benefits neither the customer nor the vendor as the parties likely will enter into a lengthy, time consuming, and expensive dispute resolution process to resolve the issue.

Most of these issues are identified through acceptance testing procedures. Once identified, the vendor likely will have a "cure period" in which to make any allegedly necessary corrections. If the vendor is unable to do so, the customer is left with little recourse but to bring a claim under the contract's dispute resolution provision.

An inability of the vendor to satisfy the contractually agreed-to acceptance tests provides a strong incentive for the vendor to reach a settlement with the customer. Failure to be able to meet the acceptance tests is rare, however, and the typical response by the vendor is that it has met the contractually required functionality and that the demands of the customer are outside the scope of the contract.

(ii) Failure to Deliver in a Timely Manner

Customers seek to implement their technology solution as quickly as possible. During the negotiation process, they often encourage the vendor to compress the proposed development schedule to meet the desired delivery date. Although many customers realize the problems that may arise by shortening the development and delivery cycle, they believe that these problems are the vendor's issue and that the customer need not be concerned. Fearing that it may lose the business, vendors often accept a tight schedule that leaves little room for error. Although the customer may be happy in the short term, this strategy can be catastrophic, with the customer missing its published implementation date and ending up in litigation with the vendor: a steep price for pressing the vendor to reduce its development cycle.

When the inevitable delay occurs, both the vendor and customer are placed in a difficult spot. To meet the required delivery date, the vendor may be forced to expend additional resources/labor that was not contemplated, creating cost overruns that must be absorbed by the vendor. A rush to complete the project likely will increase the number of bugs in the software, causing further delays when the software needs to be rewritten. In turn, the customer suffers by receiving the late delivery of an unstable product, which may harm its business. As such, customers are better served by accepting a realistic delivery schedule, with agreed-upon incentives to encourage the vendor to deliver early. Depending on the terms of the agreement, the vendor may be subject to liquidated damages for failure to deliver on time, in addition to absorbing the additional labor costs necessary to complete the project. See, e.g., § 3.C. The vendor is confronted with the options of delivering late, asking the customer for additional funds to pay for additional resources, or reducing the functionality of the deliverables. These options are unlikely to be well received by the customer.

To mitigate the efforts of any potential delay, most savvy customers contractually obligate the vendor to promptly notify the customer if the vendor foresees any delay in the delivery schedule. See § 9.6.4.

(iii) Failure to Deliver for Contracted Price

In a fixed-price contract, the parties contractually agree on both the scope of the deliverables and the price to be paid. Vendors usually seek to avoid fixed-price contracts as they allocate the risk of cost overruns to the vendor. Customers, however, often require that the contract have a fixed price in order to estimate the project cost and to place the burden on the party that should have better knowledge of what is necessary to develop and implement the software.

If a vendor has underestimated the work effort involved, its only option under a fixed-price contract, other than to assume the loss or be held in default, is to approach the customer to seek an increase in the contract price. Most customers, however, are unlikely to accept an increase in the contract price—leaving the vendor to bear any loss.

(b) Fraud

Customers often allege fraud in an attempt to void the contract's limit of liability. Fraud is one of the few claims that will allow a court to negate a carefully negotiated limit of liability. *See Vmark Software, Inc. v. EMC Corp.,* 642 N.E.2d 587 (Ct. App. Mass. 1994) (vendor's misrepresentation voided contract's limitation of liability). Without voiding the limit of liability, a customer often is contractually limited to a refund of the monies it has paid under the statement of work that created the liability. For statements of work (SOWs) with a large dollar value, the vendor's liability often is limited to a percentage of the full contract price, for example those monies received by the vendor under the relevant statement of work in the 90 days prior to the event giving rise to the claim of breach.

A fraud claim is usually founded on allegations that the vendor made a misrepresentation to induce the customer to enter into the agreement, or that the vendor knew at the time the agreement was executed that it could not meet a particular contractual obligation, such as a delivery date, or that the vendor misrepresented the software's functionality or capabilities. Although fraud cases are very difficult to win, the fear of negating the contract's limit of liability may cause the vendor to settle. The recent *BSkyB Ltd. v. H.P. Enterprise Sources UK Ltd.*, case in the United Kingdom illustrates this issue. By bringing a claim for fraud, BSkyB was able to defeat the agreement's limitation of liability and receive a judgment in excess of $450M. See Chapter 6.N.1 for a more detailed discussion of the *BSkyB* case.

To bring a successful claim for fraud, a party must demonstrate the following:

1. false representation or concealment of fact;
2. knowledge of its falsity;
3. the intent to induce reliance;
4. justifiable reliance; and
5. damages.

A vendor should carefully consider a choice of law provision in the contract that (i) explicitly applies to any fraud claims arising out of the execution or performance of the contract and, (ii) selects a forum whose laws are unfriendly to fraud in the inducement claims, such as New York. In addition, a carefully worded merger clause is important in defending against a fraud claim. Finally, a vendor should never misrepresent the status of a project by assuring the client that a project is on track when in actuality the project is behind schedule.

2. *Customer Actions*

(a) Setoff and Recoupment

Setoff and recoupment are types of counterclaims that may be asserted by a defendant in response to a plaintiff's initial complaint seeking recovery. *Stulz v. Boswell*, 307 Pa.

Super. 515, 520 (1982) ("A counterclaim is defined as a claim presented by a defendant in opposition to, or deduction from, the claim of the plaintiff; a counterclaim encompasses both set off and recoupment.") (internal quotation marks omitted); *see also J.B. Hunt Transport, Inc. v. Falcon Transport, Co.*, 723 F. Supp. 359, 361 (W.D. Pa. 1989) ("Pennsylvania law draws a distinction between a counterclaim that seeks affirmative relief (known as a "set off") and a counterclaim that 'involves only the claims averred by the plaintiff and raises no possibility of affirmative relief' (known as 'recoupment')") (quoting *Harmer v. Hulsey*, 321 Pa. Super. 11 (1983)).

A defendant's counterclaim does not turn the plaintiff into a defendant. *See Shuman v. Colsano*, 1978 WL 283 (Pa. Ct. Com. Pl. 1973) (rejecting the plaintiff's contention that they should be treated as "defendants" since they are responding to a counterclaim because "the rules ... do not countenance such an interpretation"). By invoking the doctrines of set off and recoupment, the plaintiff, in effect, seeks to assert a counterclaim to the defendant's counterclaim. "There is, however, no provision for a reply containing a counter-counterclaim." *Id.*

(i) Setoff

Set off arises under common law allowing "every creditor, to apply the appropriated moneys of his debtor, in his hands, in extinguishment of the debts due him." *Boers v. United States*, 44 Fed. Cl. 725, 733 (1999). The common law right of set off is not forfeited in the absence of language to the contrary or the absence of a reservation of rights clause. *Applied Companies v. United States*, 144 F.3d 1470 (Fed. Cir. 1998).

In the case of bankruptcy, the debtor's claim against the creditor and the creditor's claim against the debtor must both arise pre-petition. A party cannot setoff a post-petition payable against a pre-petition receivable and cannot exercise its right of setoff without first obtaining relief from the automatic stay in the bankruptcy court by filing a motion. The bankruptcy code recognizes the existence of a creditor's setoff rights. 11 U.S.C. § 553.

(ii) Recoupment

Recoupment is "not in the nature of a cross demand, but rather it lessens or defeats any recovery by the plaintiff." *Algrant v. Evergreen Valley Nurseries Ltd. P'ship*, 126 F.3d 178, 184 (3d Cir. 1997). Recoupment is a defensive claim that "must be related to the nature of the demand brought by the plaintiff." *Id.*

Like the doctrine of setoff, the doctrine of recoupment allows a creditor that owes a debt to a debtor to reduce the amount of its debt by the amount of a debt owed by the debtor to the creditor. The doctrine of recoupment only exists where the two debts arise out of the same transaction (i.e., the same contract). For recoupment to apply, the defendant's claim must arise from the same transaction. *See Koken v. Legion Ins. Co.*, 900 A.2d 418, 428 (Pa. Commw. 2006) (discussing the "same transaction" requirement for recoupment); *see also Cohen v. Goldberg*, 554 Pa. 201, 205 (1998) ("Recoupment is the setting up of a demand arising from the same transaction as the plaintiff's claim or cause of action, strictly for the purpose of abatement or reduction of such claim.") (internal quotation marks omitted). The "same transaction" requirement has been narrowly construed. *Cohen*, 554 Pa. at 205. The same transaction requirement exists because recoupment originated as an equitable remedy, intending that "a transaction which is made the subject of a suit by a plaintiff ...be examined in all aspects and a judgment rendered that does justice in view of the one transaction as a whole." *Stulz*, 307 Pa. Super. at 521.

Unlike setoff, the right of recoupment is not limited to pre-petition debts. The right of recoupment is not codified in the Bankruptcy Code. It has been established through case law.

(iii) Preclusion/Waiver of Rights

Although recoupment and waiver may be available to a party at common law, the party may contract away its rights to set-off or recoupment. *Lytle v. CitiFinancial Service, Inc.*, 2001 WL 34644548 (Pa. Com. Pl. 2001); *see also Pearce v. Utah Athletic Foundation*, 179 P.3d 760, 765 (Utah 2008) ("In two recent cases, we reaffirmed our position with the majority of states that people may contract away their rights to recover in tort for damages caused by the ordinary negligence of others."); *CPI Phipps, LLC v. 100 Park Avenue Partners, L.P.*, 654 S.E.2d 690, 693 (Ga. App. 2007) ("[I]t is clear that two parties may contract away or extend their rights as they please . . . so long as public policy is not violated."). It is not against public policy to contract away those rights.

In evaluating a party's ability to exercise the common law remedies of set off and recoupment, a party must examine whether they are precluded by the contractual terms of the underlying license agreement. Although a license agreement may address equitable remedies, that language in and of itself does not preclude the rights of set off or recoupment. *See Bender*, 493, A.2d at 760, 763 (refusing to read exclusion of all remedies into a contract). An integration clause that provides that the contract represents the "entire agreement and understanding between the licensee and licensor relating to the subject matter herein" does not exclude a remedy. *Id.* A party may not read language into the agreement that is not included within its plain terms. The question of whether the parties intended to contract away their equitable remedies is a question of fact for the court to interpret.

3. Vendor Defenses

(a) Desired Functionality is Out of Scope

In response to a customer's claim that the vendor did not deliver the contracted functionality, the vendor often will respond that it has met the requirements of the contract and that the customer is seeking functionality outside the scope of the contract. In short, the customer is seeking to increase the scope of the deliverables without paying for the vendor's increased costs.

To avoid disputes, a vendor should never agree to change in functionality or scope without a written agreement. A vendor that acts otherwise is inviting a customer to claim that the work done was in scope, because otherwise a new agreement would have been executed.

(b) Vendor's Failure to Perform Caused by Customer's Breach

In response to a customer's allegations that the vendor breached the contract by its failure to deliver in a timely manner, the vendor often will respond that any such delay was, in fact, caused by the customer. Delivery delays may arise from many factors, including customer-demanded changes in scope; the failure of the customer to promptly approve the functional specifications; the failure of the customer to provide access to its third party legacy software systems; the failure of the customer to provide qualified employees; the failure of the customer to provide necessary assistance; and the failure of the customer to perform any other contractual obligations.

Under a fixed-price contract, if the customer fails to meet its contractual obligations, the contract should provide for financial compensation to the vendor for the impact of any delay caused by the customer. See, e.g., § 21.

Customer-caused delays also can arise from the failure of third party vendors retained directly by the customer to meet their contractual obligations, when the vendor's performance is contingent on the successful performance of such third parties. Because the other vendors have contracted directly with the customer and the vendor lacks the ability to control their performance, the customer must be contractually responsible for their impact on the vendor.

To protect the vendor's interests, the contract should set forth the customer's obligations and provide that they are conditions precedent to the vendor's obligations. The customer's obligations should include assigning knowledgeable employees to the project and promptly responding to any requests by the vendor. See, e.g., §§ 9.5, 21, 37. Too often, customers claim that their only obligation is to pay the vendor. That is never true in major technology contracts, and vendors should ensure during negotiation of the agreement that the customer's responsibilities are defined clearly.

Customers frequently fail to address the impact of their other vendors on the vendor's obligations. A prudent customer will retain a prime contractor, requiring all third party vendors to contract directly with the prime contractor to avoid any potential liability on the customer's behalf when a vendor other than the prime contractor fails to perform. A prudent vendor should identify specifically those third parties on whom the vendor's performance is contingent and specify that the vendor is excused from performing in the event the customer's other vendors fail to perform.

Finally, when faced with customer-caused delays or non-payment, a vendor should notify the customer in writing, in conformance with the contract's notice provisions that the vendor is ready, willing, and able to perform. See, e.g., § 52. This will protect the vendor when seeking compensation for any such delay and will provide protection in the event the customer claims the vendor was unable to perform or that the vendor was not materially harmed. See Form 23.H.8 for a model letter stating the vendor's ability to perform.

(c) The Gist of the Action Doctrine

Plaintiffs often bring multiple claims against defendants based in contract and tort in an effort to maximize their recovery. The tort claims are often founded on negligent and/or intentional misrepresentation. These multiple claims usually are duplicative and under the laws of many states violate the gist of the action doctrine. Specifically:

> [T]he [gist of the action] doctrine bars tort claims: (1) arising solely from a contract between the parties; (2) where the duties allegedly breached were created and grounded in the contract itself; (3) where the liability stems from a contract; or (4) where the tort essentially duplicates a breach of contract claim or the success of which is wholly dependent on the terms of the contract.

Etoll, Inc. v. Elias/Savion Advertising, Inc., 811 A.2d 10, 19 (Pa. Super. 2002) (internal citations and quotations omitted); *Caudill Seed & Warehouse Co. v. Prophet 21, Inc.*, 123 F. Supp.2d 826 (E.D. Pa. 2000).

Many plaintiffs' tort claims fall within all of the categories set forth in *Etoll.* It is clear that a plaintiff's misrepresentation claims all alleged statements or omissions supposedly made by the defendant during the course of the project and about the performance on the project. Those are exactly the types of claims that are barred by the gist of the action doctrine because they are directly related to the contractual obligations of the parties.

Second, the allegations in support of the negligent and/or intentional misrepresentation claim are the same allegations that form the basis for plaintiff's breach of contract claim.

Third, any liability stems from the underlying contract. The only relationship between most parties is their contractual relationship. Without the contract, most defendants would have no duty whatsoever to plaintiff. In *Etoll*, 811 A.2d at 23, the court affirmed the dismissal of the plaintiff's complaint, in part because it held that no special relationship existed that would create a duty outside of the parties' contract. The court reasoned: "If parties to routine arms length commercial contracts for the provision of needed goods or services were held to have a 'special relationship,' virtually every breach of such a contract would support a tort claim." *Id.* The court refused to permit tort claims to usurp the law of contracts.

Fourth, the success of a plaintiff's tort claims is wholly dependent upon the terms of the contract.

The law is clear—allegations that stem from the performance under a contract, regardless of whether they are couched in terms of misrepresentation, properly can be brought as breach of contract claims, but not as tort claims. As such, the plaintiff's tort claims must be dismissed.

(d) The Economic Loss Rule

The economic loss rule similarly bars a plaintiff's misrepresentation claim. *Werwinski v. Ford Motor Co.*, 286 F.3d 661, 675 (3d Cir. 2002). The economic loss doctrine provides that a party who suffers purely economic loss as a result of another's conduct cannot recover that loss under tort law, but rather must seek redress under contract law. *Apollo Group, Inc. v. Avnet, Inc.*, 58 F.3d 477, 479 (9th Cir. 1995). Economic loss is a term of art used to distinguish commercial injury from physical or personal injury. *Rich Products Corp. v. Kemutec, Inc.*, 66 F. Supp.2d 937, 968 (E.D. Wis. 1999). A claim to recover commercial injuries must be brought as a breach of contract action; whereas a claim for personal injuries may be brought in tort.

Usually, the damages sought by the plaintiff are for economic loss only and are based upon the plaintiff's allegations that the defendant failed to perform its contractual obligations.

(e) Professional Negligence Is Not a Recognized Cause of Action

Although plaintiffs often allege "professional negligence," no such tort exists for providers of computer consulting services. *Rapidigm Inc. v. ATM Mgmt. Servs. LLC*, 2003 WL 23146480 (Pa. Com. Pl. July 10, 2003) (dismissing claim for professional negligence against a computer consultant because Pennsylvania law does not recognize such a cause of action). *See also Chatlos Systems, Inc. v. National Cash Register Corp.*, 479 F. Supp. 738 (D.N.J. 1979) (declining to find tort for computer malpractice); *RKB Enterprises, Inc. v. Ernst & Young*, 582 N.Y.S.2d 814 (1992) (no cause of action for malpractice arising from computer services); *Metpath, Inc. v. IDS Corp.*, 1991 WL 39617 (Conn. Super. Mar. 12, 1991) (same).

4. Vendor Claims/Counterclaims

In almost all disputes that reach litigation, the vendor will bring counterclaims against the customer, if for no other reason than to gain leverage in any settlement negotiation or to "muddy the waters" if the matter ultimately goes to trial. Vendors should avoid bringing a claim against a customer unless it lacks any other option, as suing a customer likely will have a chilling effect on the vendor's business. The three most common claims are breach of contract, *quantum meruit,* and copyright infringement.

(a) Breach of Contract

Like the customer, the vendor will respond to the customer's claim with a counterclaim alleging a breach of contract by the customer. Such claims can encompass a broad range of factual theories, including the customer's failure to pay the vendor's invoices; the failure of the customer to provide needed hardware and software; the failure of the customer to provide the vendor access to the customer's third party legacy systems; and the failure of the customer to make decisions critical to the success of the project in a timely fashion. Further, an aggressive vendor may consider filing a declaratory judgment action seeking to have the customer's demands declared outside the scope of the contract. Seeking a declaratory judgment likely will irreparably harm the relationship. Nonetheless, this strategy may be attractive to a vendor who believes that the customer is planning to sue for breach of contract and believes the relationship cannot be salvaged. The exact nature of these claims will depend on the requirements of the contract, but the essence of the vendor's claim is that the customer failed to meet its contractual obligations or that what the customer is demanding is outside the scope of the contract.

Customers often fail to limit their own liability in their contracts. See, e.g., § 17.2. In these cases, the vendor will seek to leverage this oversight by seeking a significant recovery including its full profit. The vendor hopes to cause the customer to rethink its suit, given the customer's unlimited liability and the vendor's contractually limited liability.

(b) Quantum Meruit

The vendor may bring a counterclaim under the quasi-contract doctrine of *quantum meruit. Quantum meruit,* is an equitable remedy that attempts to prevent unjust enrichment. Under this theory, the vendor seeks to recover the value of the services it provided to the customer. The vendor is alleging that the customer has been unjustly enriched by receiving services for which the customer has not paid. To bring a successful quantum meruit claim, the vendor must demonstrate the following:

1. the vendor provided services or materials of value;
2. to the person or entity from whom the vendor seeks to collect;
3. the services or materials were accepted by such person who used such services or materials; and
4. under circumstances where the beneficiary of such services or materials was aware that the vendor expected to be paid for such services or materials.

Vortt Exploration Co. v. Chevron USA Inc., 787 S.W.2d 942, 944 (Tex. 1990). *Quantum meruit* usually is not available as a remedy if there is an existing agreement between the parties. *Truly v. Austin*, 744 S.W.2d 934 (Tex. 1988).

From the customer's perspective, a *quantum meruit* argument may seem specious if the customer does not want to continue using the deliverables/software because the vendor failed to meet its contractual obligations. A *quantum meruit* claim is likely to be successful where the vendor successfully delivered the deliverable (or some independently valuable portion thereof) and the customer lacks a valid basis for its failure to pay. In many jurisdictions, however, a *quantum meruit* claim is not viable if there is a valid contract. *See, e.g.*, Georgia: *Blue Soft Inc. v. Advanced Computing Technologies, Inc.*, 616 S.E.2d 816 (Ga. 2005); Ohio: *Daniels v. National Employee Ben. Services, Inc.*, 877 F. Supp. 1067 (N.D. Ohio 1995); South Dakota: *Mooney's v. South Dakota Dept. of Finance*, 482 N.W.2d 43, 47 (S.D. 1992) ("Quantum meruit does not provide a basis for recovery when a valid express contract exists. . . ."); Texas: *Sherman Acquisition II, LP v. Garcia*, 229 S.W.2d 802 (Tex. 2007). In such a case, breach of contract is the proper claim. Nevertheless, the *quantum meruit* counterclaim provides a potentially valuable defensive countermeasure to the customer's fraud claim, because if the fraud claim voids the contract then the *quantum meruit* claim may survive and may provide the vendor with damages to offset the customer's claims.

(c) Copyright Infringement

A vendor also may respond by filing a copyright infringement claim against the customer. Under U.S. law, copyright is created in the name of the author at the time a written work is created. *In re World Auxiliary Power Company*, 303 F.3d 1120, 1125 (9th Cir. 2002). Because computer software frequently (though not always) fails to meet one of the nine enumerated exceptions of the "work made for hire" doctrine, the deliverables typically are owned by the vendor until and unless ownership is assigned to the customer. See Chapter 5.A.1 for a more detailed discussion of the work made for hire doctrine. Although the agreement between the vendor and the customer most likely will contain an assignment transferring ownership of the deliverables created under the agreement to the customer, it is not uncommon for customers to start negotiations by insisting that ownership vests in the customer at the time of creation. A prudent vendor, however, should insist on language that ownership not transfer to the customer until the vendor has been paid in full.

If the governing agreement provides that the vendor shall retain ownership, the customer's continued use of the software without a license is a copyright infringement and provides the vendor leverage in the event there is a dispute (including the possibility of an injunction against the customer's continued use of the software—see, e.g., §§ 5.2, 29.5). This is true even if the vendor did not register its copyright in the work, although remedies for infringement are limited if the infringement arose before registration. *See Conwell v. Gray Loon Outdoor Marketing Group, Inc.*, 906 N.E.2d 805 (Ind. 2009). See Chapter 3.A.2(c) for a more detailed discussion of copyright law.

Note also that under the Copyright Act, the copyright must be registered before a copyright claim may be brought in court, although some courts have sought to create a limited exception to this statutory requirement. Section 411(a) of the Copyright Act requires that registration or pre-registration must occur before a plaintiff can assert a valid claim. 17 U.S.C. § 411(a) ("no action for infringement of the copyright in *any* United States work *shall be instituted* until pre-registration or registration of the copyright claim has been made in accordance with this title."); 17 U.S.C. § 501(b) ("The legal or beneficial owner of an exclusive right under a copyright is entitled, subject to the requirements of Section 411, to institute an action for any infringement."). A copyright claim cannot exist without registration or pre-registration. As such, courts lack subject matter jurisdiction over claims that do not yet exist. *See, e.g., Bowles v. Russell,* 551 U.S. 205 (2007) ("Because Congress decides within constitutional bounds, whether federal courts can hear cases at all, it can also determine when, and under what conditions, federal courts can hear them.").

Some courts have found that the submission of the application with all the required items is sufficient for a suit, even if the application has not been granted or rejected, as a suit is permitted after rejection as well. Other courts have interpreted "registration" as meaning submitting the application for registration—not actually becoming registered. *See e.g., La Resolana Architects, PA v. Clay Realtors Angel Fire,* 416 F.3d 1195 (10th Cir. 2005) (decision from Copyright Office required prior to filing suit). *See also Prunte v. Universal Music Group,* 484 F. Supp. 2d 32 (D.D.C. 2007) (submission of the application is "registration"). For a more detailed explanation see Chapter 3.A.2.(c).

(d) Amount of Vendor Claim

Often in the event of a dispute, vendors seek to recover the value of all services performed for a client including the value of unbilled services. Many times the vendor has not billed the customer for services it performed for a variety of reasons, including the vendor is trying to placate the customer, the contract was a fixed-price contract or the contract limited the vendor's employees to billing eight hours a day. Courts usually are unpersuaded by a vendor's efforts to recover for unbilled services, questioning why the vendor is entitled to recover when it never planned to bill for such services.

A savvy vender may be more likely to recover such fees if it bills the client for all work performed and notifies the customer that it will issue a credit for the fees in question upon the customer's acceptance of the software or services. This approach should strengthen a vendor's claim, as it has not reduced the amount of its claim. If the customer never accepts the deliverables, the licensor will be able to bring a claim for the total value of its services.

(e) Injunctive Relief

A savvy vendor will seek injunctive relief to prevent the licensee from using its software while the dispute is being resolved. Doing so not only protects the vendor's intellectual property rights but also increases the vendor's leverage over the licensee, as the licensee can no longer use the vendor's software. In *Salinger v. Colting*, 607 F.3d 68 (2d. Cir 2010), the Second Circuit, citing *eBay, Inc. v. MercExchange*, 547 U.S. 388 (2006), found that the party seeking injunctive relief must demonstrate irreparable injury. Prior to *Salinger*, the courts utilized a "presumption of harm" standard, which set a much lower hurdle for seeking an injunction.

5. Termination for Convenience (§ 4.1.A)

Occasionally, a customer may consider terminating an agreement or statement of work for "convenience" instead of breach to avoid expending the effort and cost to prove the vendor's breach. Although that strategy may appear to be the best solution in the short term, it can cause the customer significant problems. "Termination for convenience" or "without cause" means the vendor is without fault. Once the customer provides written notice that it is terminating the agreement or statement of work for convenience, it is difficult for the customer to later claim that the vendor failed to meet its performance obligations. A savvy vendor will point out the inconsistency of the customer's earlier statement that the vendor was not at fault. A termination for convenience potentially provides the vendor the leverage to claim not only payment for the services already provided but also for the vendor's costs of winding down the project. The customer usually lacks a contractual basis for making a counterclaim and is left to negotiate the amount of compensation due the vendor. As such, customers should carefully consider terminating the agreement for convenience if the vendor is at fault.

C. The Negotiation Process

1. Tolling Agreement

One of the first actions the parties should take when seeking to settle a dispute is to execute a tolling agreement to preserve their respective rights. See, e.g., the model Tolling Agreement set forth in Form 23.H.1. Settlement negotiations may take a significant period of time and will likely last longer than expected. A tolling agreement is especially important if the parties have agreed to contractually limit the time to bring litigation. See generally Chapter 4.B and § 17.1. The vendor should ensure that the tolling agreement is mutual because its claims should remain viable as well as those claims that could be asserted by its customer.

2. Settlement Negotiations

(a) Deciding to Settle

In almost all situations, a negotiated settlement is preferable to entering into litigation or an alternative dispute resolution process. The dispute process can be lengthy and expensive, and prevent the parties from achieving the goals each party hoped to achieve at the time the agreement was signed.

Prior to meeting with the other party, each party should decide whether it wants to terminate the agreement and enter into a settlement agreement, or whether it wants to renegotiate the original agreement and continue the relationship. Parties usually renegotiate an agreement when both parties bear some culpability and the customer believes the vendor can successfully complete the project.

In considering whether to enter into a settlement, the customer must first determine whether it wants to continue its relationship with the vendor. If the vendor failed to successfully meet its initial contractual obligations, what makes the customer believe that the vendor will meet the new commitments?

(b) Structuring the Settlement

In negotiating a settlement, vendors are generally loath to make a cash payment to the customer. More often, the vendor will offer a discount on, or a credit against, future work. These structures are favored by vendors because the vendors usually will not have to take a write-off. By offering a discount or a credit, the vendor also ensures a continuing working relationship with the customer. The cost to the vendor is limited as the offered discount is often less than the vendor's margins. Further, the customer may not use the full credit, especially if the vendor has imposed a limited time period in which the customer may use the credit.

If the vendor offers a credit against or a discount on future services, the customer should make certain that it will be able to receive the full benefit of its bargain. Is the future discount offered by the vendor of value to the customer? Will the customer be able to fully use any credit offered? After the discount, are the vendor's services priced lower or higher than other similar vendors?

In exploring the possibility of a settlement, a party should discuss the parameters of any proposed settlement with not only their lawyers, but also their accountants and businesspeople to avoid any unintended consequences, including an unforeseen financial impact, especially as to previous financial reporting periods. The businesspeople will advise on whether any credit or discount given to the customer would violate the terms of any agreement with any other customer, such as a most favored nation clause, and the accountants will be able to advise whether the credit or discount will impact prior, current, or future period financial statements.

The terms of any resulting settlement agreement should reflect the needs and goals of the parties. The agreement may combine the elements of both a settlement and a termination, where the customer retains a license to the deliverables and will perhaps employ the services of a third party to complete the vendor's work as well as receive a cash payment in return for releasing the vendor from all liability. In short, the structure is limited only by the imagination of the parties.

(c) Leverage

(i) Customer Leverage

The customer's principal leverage is the ability to withhold payment or set-off monies due the vendor. Withholding payment, however, usually will not incent the vendor to complete the work on time. See Chapter 4.B.6(a) and §§ 5.3.2, 8.7. The customer may express its dissatisfaction with the vendor in the marketplace, which may impact the vendor's ability to obtain future work. In doing so, the customer should be mindful of defaming the vendor.

(ii) Vendor Leverage

Although the customer possesses the ability to withhold payment, the vendor also may hold significant leverage if the customer continues to use the deliverables after the dispute has ripened. Savvy vendors usually provide in the agreement between the parties that ownership of the deliverables only transfers to the customer upon full payment. Thus, even if the vendor does not exercise the remedy of self-help (see Chapter 4.B.6.(b)(iii)(z)), the vendor has the ability to bring a claim against the customer for copyright infringement and seek injunctive relief to prevent the customer from using the deliverables. See, e.g., §§ 5.2, 29.5. For more detailed discussion, see Chapter 15.B.4(c). If successful, injunctive relief may seriously impact the customer if the software is critical to the customer's business.

To avoid this problem, savvy customers should refuse to include language transferring ownership to the customer only upon full payment or include language in the contract requiring the vendor to continue to provide services and allow the customer to use the deliverables while any contract dispute is adjudicated. See, e.g., §§ 5.5, 8.7. *See e.g., IKL, Inc. v. Adoutlet.com, Inc.*, 2001 WL 315219, at *10 (N.D. Ill. March 29, 2001) (court denied motion for preliminary injunction where agreement did not provide customer "will be considered the author of the source code and the owner of its copyright only after full payment . . . .") Most vendors will accept language allowing the customer to continue to use deliverables but many are hesitant to continue working if they believe they may not be paid. Prudent vendors should provide that non-payment by a customer is a contractually permitted basis for ceasing work. Even without explicit language, unexcused non-payment is a basis for claiming material breach.

An additional area of vendor leverage is withholding maintenance and support. Even if the customer retains the right to use the deliverables, without support and maintenance the deliverables may be useless.

(d) The Settlement Agreement

Once the parties have reached a settlement, the resulting agreement should set forth the concessions made by each party. If the vendor is going to provide a credit or discount to the customer, the settlement agreement should provide specific examples of how such credit or discount will be applied. See, e.g., the model Settlement Agreement and Mutual Release set forth in Form 23.H.2.

Further, the parties should make sure that any release is carefully drafted to avoid releasing the parties from obligations that were meant to survive.

Of equal importance is the confidentiality provision, if any. Most licensors seek to publicize any settlement as a warning to others that may be in violation of their licenses. The Business Software Alliance, which pursues copyright violations on behalf of its members, who are principally large software companies, will include a confidentiality provision in its settlement agreements only if the offending party agrees to pay a significantly higher settlement fee.

Licensees who have brought a claim against the licensor are less concerned with publicity, as their primary concern is to be compensated for damages. In these situations, the licensor should insist on including a confidentiality provision in any settlement agreement to protect its image in the market. In addition, it should not admit guilt in any settlement, as the settlement agreement may ultimately become a public document. The agreement simply should state that a disagreement arose between the parties and that the parties are settling their dispute to avoid the cost of litigation.

3. Renegotiating the Contract

If both parties bear some responsibility for the problem in question, the parties may seek to renegotiate the contract. A renegotiation may be as simple as a one-page contract amendment or as complicated as a complete redrafting of the agreement. Regardless of which approach is taken, the parties should keep in mind a number of issues when undertaking the renegotiation.

Each party should form a "well-rounded" team experienced in renegotiating contracts. A typical team should include the business sponsor, the relevant information technology employees, an experienced information technology lawyer, and a finance person. Each person's perspective is necessary to ensure that neither party negotiates a contract that best serves its interests. The failure to field a well-rounded team creates the risk that the resulting contract will neither meet the needs of the party nor will be approved by management.

The new agreement should address the prior actions of the parties under the original agreement and, if appropriate, release one or both parties for actions taken prior to the date of the amended contract. Further, if appropriate, it should release the parties from their duties to perform their obligations under the previous contract. See, e.g., the model Settlement Agreement and Mutual Release set forth in Form 23.H.2. If consideration is given for the release of obligations under the original agreement, the new agreement should clearly state such consideration. The vendor should avoid making a concession while being held to its original obligations under the old contract.

D. If Litigation Arises

If litigation is unavoidable, the parties should retain litigators with extensive information technology (IT) litigation experience. IT litigation differs from other litigation in that the facts of the case must be viewed in light of the underlying technology and industry practice. It is extremely difficult, if not impossible, for a lawyer without a background in technology litigation to obtain the requisite knowledge quickly enough to successfully represent a party in a complicated IT dispute. In addition, litigators with experience in IT disputes know the patterns of failure (on both sides) in such projects and know what "rocks to look under" to uncover the weak points of the other side's case. They also will have experience working with the kinds of experts who are necessary in such cases and can help to advance the case and make it understandable to a judge or jury without the significant learning curve (and associated cost) that litigators without IT experience often face.

Ideally, the parties should seek to have as part of their legal team lawyers who were computer programmers prior to practicing law or who at least have a degree in computer programming. Many IT lawyers started their careers as computer programmers. An experienced IT lawyer will be able to quickly judge the strength of a party's case and spot the weaknesses in its opponent's case. The value of an experienced IT practitioner cannot and should not be underestimated.

Finally, if applicable, the parties should place their insurance carriers on notice as to the likelihood of a potential claim. The parties should make sure they understand the required procedures under their insurance policy for making a claim. Further, if a party believes it is entitled to make a claim for indemnification, it should understand and follow the procedures for doing so.

CHAPTER **16**

Alternative Dispute Resolution (§§ 29, 30)

Given the large number of disputes arising in the development and installation of complex computer systems, each party should carefully consider the benefits of alternative dispute resolution (ADR) for the resolution of any disputes. ADR can take many forms, including but not limited to mediation, arbitration, mini trials, and neutral evaluation. Each has its benefits and drawbacks, all of which are magnified in intellectual property disputes. Given the ever-increasing expense of litigation, the uncertainty of juries, and the diversion of corporate resources even when a party prevails, an increasing number of parties are choosing ADR. The parties can utilize ADR in an escalating fashion to resolve any disputes. The two principal forms of ADR, arbitration and mediation, are discussed next.

For a general overview, see Chaloupka, *Overview of Alternative Dispute Resolution Techniques*, 37 Law. Brief (Nov. and Dec. 2007); Jamar, *Resolving Intellectual Property License Disputes Out of Court*, 24 Computer & Internet Law. 24 (Sept. 2007).

A. Mediation (§ 29)

Mediation is an attractive alternative in those cases where (i) the relationship between the parties can be repaired or continued; (ii) the law is well settled and there is no need for additional discovery; (iii) the positions of both parties have merit making the outcome difficult to predict; and (iv) the cost of litigation is likely to be great. Mediation is unlikely to be a viable alternative where (i) one party has a significant advantage; (ii) there is no factual issue in dispute; (iii) one party seeks to delay resolution of the issue; (iv) a vital corporate interest is at stake; or (v) the dispute is emotionally charged with each party's position being irretractable.

Mediation is usually a much quicker process than arbitration due to limited, if any, discovery and the desire of the parties to move quickly through mediation because of its nonbinding nature. This is extremely important if the nature of the dispute is time sensitive. Mediation is usually used as a last step prior to litigation or during litigation if the parties believe a compromise can be reached. Many parties include an informal mediation process to allow the escalation of disputes, thereby permitting the parties to continue working constructively while the dispute is addressed at higher levels in their respective organizations.

Mediation does not impact the ability of either party to pursue litigation. Rather, it allows the parties to attempt to resolve their differences at a number of different levels prior to initiating the litigation process. At the same time, each party can educate itself as to the strength of the other party's case.

The absence of discovery avoids potentially damaging admissions, the production of damaging documentation and the costs associated with discovery. Further, the use of a qualified expert as the mediator ensures a decision maker well versed in the law governing the issues in dispute. Mediation also offers lower costs and greater confidentiality due to the limited discovery and the fact that any decision is not publicly reported. Finally, the often acrimonious nature of litigation is usually avoided due to the more relaxed nature of the proceedings.

For a comparison of the benefits of mediation versus arbitration, see *Cause for Alarm,* ABA J. 19 (Nov. 2006).

For a more in depth discussion of international mediations, see Rogers & Dawson, *Unchartered Waters: Ten Considerations to Crafting the International Mediation Clause,* 26 ACC DOCKET 78 (Oct. 2008).

B. Arbitration (§ 30)

1. General Benefits and Drawbacks

Like most things in life, arbitration has its advantages and disadvantages. Arbitration is, generally, quicker than the court system, but may provide an ineffective means of resolving certain legal issues. For example, a licensee would not want to arbitrate whether a licensor must indemnify the licensee for an alleged intellectual property infringement since the passage of time involved in reaching the decision could be highly damaging to the licensee's financial position. Alternatively, a court can quickly issue an injunction in the licensor's favor if the licensee breaches the terms of the license grant. For a discussion of the issues involved in obtaining an injunction, see Friedman & LaMotta, *When Protecting Software Through an Injunction, How Do You Spell Relief?,* 11 COMPUTER LAW. 18 (March 1994).

While there is strong public policy in favor of arbitration, a court cannot compel the parties to arbitrate a matter that they did not agree to submit to arbitration. *Shopsmith Woodworking Promotions, Inc. v. American Woodworking Academy, Inc.,* 1995 WL 614355 (Ohio App. Oct. 18, 1995). As such, if the parties desire to arbitrate, the governing agreement should clearly indicate that intent.

Arbitration is often advantageous in terms of cost, particularly when used in smaller disputes. With large matters, cost savings may be achieved if an extensive and protracted discovery process can be avoided and the appeals process is curtailed by a well-drafted arbitration provision. Often, there is no need for hiring court reporters for depositions or expert witnesses, as most arbiters are themselves experts in the field. Arbiters are not bound by legal precedent and need not articulate a rationale for their decision. Thus arbitration may result in an outcome much more efficiently and without the time and expense associated with having to address every legal nuance that a court would.

Large arbitrations can take years to reach their conclusion, during which time each party will incur significant expense. Because the outcome of arbitration is not dictated by legal precedent and therefore less predictable, arbitration may not be a prudent choice if the dispute is one commonly dealt with by the courts. There are no evidentiary rules in arbitration. If there is crucial evidence in the dispute that would not likely be admissible in court and would negatively impact the party in question, a court may be the better choice. Further, many arbiters are reluctant to rule on pre-hearing dispositive motions.

Arbitration may benefit a breaching party due to the potentially greater time period needed to reach a resolution, and the fact that there is no possibility of summary judgment. Furthermore, an entity must disclose its claims in arbitration, which puts a licensor at a disadvantage assuming the licensee is in breach. Finally, under arbitration all actions must be by mutual agreement, allowing one party to potentially delay the proceedings if it chooses.

Another consideration is the business relationship between the parties to the dispute. An ongoing relationship, i.e., in the performance of long-term contracts, is often more likely to be preserved through an arbitration proceeding than by litigation. Arbitration is less stressful on the parties and it is confidential. The lack of public exposure can help protect the present and future business relationship between the parties as well as their relationships with other clients or vendors.

A common complaint about arbitration is that the arbiters will often try to "split the baby" without a real resolution of the issue, leaving neither party satisfied.

Another potential benefit of arbitration arises in the context of enforcement of an injunction in a foreign jurisdiction. Most courts are hesitant to enter a court order for injunctive relief based on a decision of a foreign jurisdiction. On the other hand, a court may be more likely to support an arbitral award for injunctive relief. As of September 15, 2010, The New York Convention on the Recognition and Enforcement of Foreign Arbitral Awards ("NY Convention") has been adopted by 144 countries and requires courts of member states to recognize the validity of arbitration agreements and reject a party's efforts to litigate a matter that is subject to a contractual agreement to arbitrate. Further, the courts of member states are required to recognize and enforce foreign arbital decisions. Under the NY Convention, judicial review of the merits of an award is prohibited. As a result of the widespread acceptance of the NY Convention, arbitration in some situations may be preferable to a judicial decision for injunctive relief.

In consumer transactions, a properly drafted arbitration clause may allow a licensor to eliminate the ability of a licensee to bring a class action suit or to serve as a class representative. See Chapter 6.H.1 for a more detailed discussion.

For a comparison of the benefits of arbitration to litigation, see Freeman & Wilson, *Arbitration or Litigation?* 24 ACC Docket 37 (Oct. 2006).

2. *Legal Concerns*

Federal policy favors arbitration as a means to resolve disputes. *Shearson/ American Express, Inc. v. McMahon*, 482 U.S. 220, 225–26 (1987). Any challenges to the underlying agreement and not specifically the arbitration clause within such agreement must be resolved by the arbiter(s). *Buckeye Check Cashing, Inc. v. Cardegna*, 546 U.S. 440, 449 (2006). See also *Qualcomm v. Nokia*, 466 F.3d 1366, 1374 (Fed. Cir. 2006) (if parties indicated intent to delegate authority to arbiter, any claim for arbitral relief that is not wholly groundless must proceed).

For any arbitration clause to be enforceable, it cannot be procedurally and substantively unconscionable. Even if the agreement is procedurally unconscionable, it may be enforceable if the substantive terms are reasonable. *Comb v. PayPal, Inc.*, 218 F. Supp. 1165 (N.D. Cal. 2002). The procedural aspect requires the parties to have equal bargaining positions and to avoid terms reflective of an adhesion contract. *Id.* at 1172. The substantive aspect looks to whether the agreement is one sided and "shocks the conscience." *Id.* To be enforceable, the terms of the arbitration agreement cannot be so one sided that the agreement is unconscionable. Unequal bargaining power alone, however, will not cause an agreement to be found procedurally unconscionable. *Zimmer v. Cooperneff Advisors, Inc.*, 523 F.3d 224 (3d Cir. 2008).

The parties should avoid agreements where (i) one party must pay a significant portion of the arbitration costs; (ii) the forum for the arbitration is inconvenient for one party; (iii) the obligation to arbitrate is not mutual; and (iv) there is a prohibition against the consolidation of claims. An arbitration clause should be broadly drafted so that it encompasses all of the parties' potential claims, not simply a portion of their claims. *See, e.g.*, *Tres Jeanee v. Brolin Retail Systems Midwest, Inc.*, 2007 WL 3118482 (W.D. Ky. Oct. 22, 2007) (software licensor's motion to compel arbitration under clause requiring mandatory arbitration of software disputes denied because dispute involved software and hardware issues); *Holt Co. v. Ohio Machinery Co.*, 2007 WL 1674023 (Ohio App. June 12, 2007).

3. *Practical Concerns*

To avoid any potential problems that arbitration may create, the parties should set forth specific language in the contract to assuage such problems. See § 30 for model language addressing some potential concerns.

To be effective, the language should provide that the arbitration is the *exclusive* means to resolve any dispute. Any exceptions should be specifically listed. By specifically stating the scope of the disputes to be arbitrated, the parties can avoid further disagreements when seeking arbitration. The location of the arbitration should be stated along with the governing law. To ensure prompt action, the parties should include the time period in which an action must be filed and the period in which the action must be resolved. This will prevent the arbitration from extending for an indefinite period. The parties should also clearly identify the arbitration rules under which the arbitration will take place. In addition, the parties should state any parameters for the use and protection of the parties' confidential information.

The parties should limit the number of witnesses, document requests, interrogatories, and depositions and their length. By setting forth such restrictions in detail, the parties can significantly reduce future costs and any potential disputes. The agreement should also establish the number and qualifications of the panel member(s). For example, do the panel member(s) need to be lawyers or have experience in software licensing or a particular industry? By requiring the panel to have specific, relevant experience and expertise, the arbitration will move quicker and more likely result in a well-reasoned decision. The parties should avoid identifying a specific arbiter or arbitral body if they cannot ensure that the identified individual or body will be able to hear the dispute. At least one court has refused to enforce an arbitration agreement where the arbitral body identified in the agreement no longer heard the type of dispute in question. *See Khan v. Dell, Inc.*, 2010 WL 3283529 (Aug. 18, 2010) (court denied motion to compel arbitration where contractually agreed arbitral body no longer heard consumer disputes).

While many agreements require three arbiters, one chosen by each party and a third "neutral" arbiter chosen by mutual agreement of the parties, the use of three arbiters significantly increases the cost of the arbitration, principally as a result of the arbiter's collective fees. Further, coordinating the schedule of three arbiters can significantly delay any resolution of the matter. The parties may want to consider the retention of a single, neutral arbiter as a means to reduce bureaucracy and costs.

Finally, the parties should enumerate any limitation on the awarding of damages. Many entities select arbitration to avoid large, punitive damages awards. The arbitration agreement should clearly set out any limits on the arbiters' ability to award damages and any limits on the types of damages that may be awarded. It is unclear whether punitive damages can be awarded when the overarching agreement is silent as to punitive damages. See *Mastrobuono v. Shearson Lehman Hutton*, 514 U.S. 52 (1995); *Garity v. Lyle Stuart, Inc.*, 40 N.Y.2d 354 (1976). To avoid any uncertainty and to eliminate the possibility of the arbiters awarding punitive damages, the parties should include language to the following effect:

> In any arbitration arising out of or related to this Agreement, the arbiter(s) are not empowered to award punitive damages or other damages in excess of compensatory damages, except where required by statute, and the parties waive any right to recover any such damages.

The arbitration agreement should clearly set forth the form any decision will take. For example, is a signed opinion sufficient or do the parties want a detailed explanation of the arbiters' rationale and the basis for the decision? The parties may want the arbiters to set forth their findings of fact. The lack of a detailed opinion may make it more difficult to challenge any decision that is clearly erroneous as to law. Nonetheless, arbitration agreements are subject to judicial review in only a limited number of situations. *See Hall Street Associates, LLC v. Mattel*, 552 U.S. 576 (2008).

A well drafted arbitration clause will address the following:

- The location of the arbitration
- The governing law
- The number of arbiters

- The arbiters' qualifications
- The scope of matters subject to arbitration
- Limitations on discovery
- The availability of judicial review
- Payment of arbitral costs and legal fees
- Limitations on the award of damages
- Punitive damages
- Injunctive relief
- Specific performance
- The format of the opinion issued by the arbiters (e.g., an order, a detailed opinion)

Inclusion of an arbitration provision in a license may impact other collateral agreements. At least two courts have held that an arbitration provision in a license agreement is enforceable as to a separate services agreement. *See Armed Forces Insur. Corp. v. Allenbrook, Inc.*, 2001 WL 699735 (D. Kan. June 11, 2001); *LDS, Inc. v. Metro Can. Logistics, Inc.*, 28 F. Supp.2d 1297 (D. Kan. 1998) (arbitration clause in license agreement encompasses all matters in dispute including maintenance agreement). For a comparison of relative advantages and disadvantages of arbitration and litigation, see Freeman & Wilson, *A Tale of 2 Cases: Arbitration or Litigation?*, 24 ACC DOCKET 24, 36–46 (October 2006). The parties should carefully consider the impact of ancillary documents having conflicting dispute resolution mechanisms to avoid a protracted and expensive resolution of the collective dispute. *See e.g. Brennan v. Global Safety Labs*, 2008 WL 2234830 (N.D. Okla. May 29, 2008).

For a general discussion on the arbitration of intellectual property disputes, see Arnold, *Suggested Form of Contract to Arbitrate a Patent or Other Commercial Dispute Annotated,* 2 TEX. INTELL. PROP. L.J. 205 (1994). Ytterberg, *Beyond The Stock Arbitration Clause: Tailoring Arbitration to Match Business Needs and Commercial Realities,* 26 ACC DOCKET 77 (Jan./Feb. 2008); *Purchaser's Guide to Commercial Arbitration,* 24 COMM. L. ADV. 1 (Aug. 2008).

4. International Arbitration

International arbitration offers an alternative to subjecting a U.S. domiciled party to the uncertainty of a foreign court proceeding and may be an attractive alternative, given increasing global hostility toward the United States and the judicial corruption that exists in many developing countries. By carefully selecting the arbitral body, the arbiters, the venue of the arbitration and the governing law, a U.S. entity can avoid many risks inherent in international disputes.

International arbitration may also be attractive to a foreign entity that is reluctant to adjudicate a matter in the United States due to significant legal costs and the potential for "hometown" prejudice. The most popular venues for international arbitration are England, France and Switzerland. Choosing the venue is one of the most important decisions a party will make as some countries may not enforce the arbiter's decision. Thus it is important that the country chosen for the venue is a signatory to the NY Convention.

The selection of the arbiter(s) is an equally important decision as the arbiters should have a thorough understanding of the industry from which the dispute arises as well as the area of law in question. The arbiters' schedule should be flexible so that the arbitration may be held promptly and a decision rendered quickly. It is important that the arbiters are fluent in the language of the arbitration, not only conversationally, but also in the technical terms of the industry. If possible, the agreement should contain a requirement for impartial arbiters who were previously unaware of, and not otherwise impacted by, the dispute.

At a minimum, a well-drafted international arbitration agreement will identify the following:

- The venue
- The governing law
- The qualifications of the arbiters
- The number of arbiters
- The parties' confidentiality obligations
- The scope of discovery
- The scope of testimony
- The scope of the panel's authority
- The rights and powers of the arbiters
- The rules that govern the arbitration
- The language in which the arbitration will be conducted
- The finality of the decision
- The availability of injunctive relief
- The scope of damages (e.g. the award of punitive damages)
- The enforcement of any decision through the NY Convention.

There are a number of well-respected arbitral organizations outside the United States, including the International Chamber of Commerce (ICC), the London Court of International Arbitration (LCIA), the Singapore International Arbitration Centre, and the Stockholm Chamber of Commerce. While the American Arbitration Association (AAA) has a division devoted to international arbitration, it is not as well known or utilized as these other arbitral organizations. Each of these organizations has its own rules and procedures. As such, a potential party should familiarize itself with the rules and procedures of the different organizations before agreeing to be bound by the decisions of a particular arbitral organization. For a comparison of the rules of the AAA, ICC, and LCIA, see Horn, *Choosing the Right Form of International Arbitration in London*, TRENDS 7 (May 2007); Chaloupka, *International Distribution and Licensing*, 70 DISTRIBUTION COUNS. 1, 9–12 (Oct. 2006). Shanks, Chedid & Chao, *Tools that Create Successful Resolutions in International Arbitration*, 25 ACC DOCKET 50 (June 2007).

For an overview of the advantages and disadvantages of international arbitration, including instruction on drafting an international arbitration clause, see *International Arbitration*, 40 THE LAW BRIEF 1 (June 30, 2010). Wilburn, *Mix and Match:*

Divergent Legal Traditions in International Arbitration, 53 Md. M.J. 4 (July 2010); Constable, *International Commercial Arbitration*, 53 Md. B.J. 12 (July 2010). Swanton, *A Survival Guide to International Arbitration*, Inside Couns. 43 (Jan. 2008); Shanks, Chedid & Chao, *Tools that Create Successful Resolutions in International Arbitration*, 25 ACC Docket 50 (June 2007); *The Neutral Zone: A Practical Guide to International Arbitration*, 24 ACC Docket 64 (June 2006).

CHAPTER **17**

Bankruptcy Issues[1]

Software has assumed an omnipresent existence in our society. It is so pervasive and intertwined with the operation of most businesses that it would be impossible to successfully operate without it. At the same time, software companies rely on their contracts to protect the sanctity of their ownership interests.

The present economic uncertainties require that both licensors and licensees place greater emphasis on protecting their rights under their existing software licenses and focus on mitigating any potential risks when negotiating a new license. This chapter examines the risks and liabilities that may arise from the financial instability or bankruptcy of a licensor or a licensee. It discusses several means by which licensors and licensees can reduce their potential exposure to business risk or financial liability.

A. The Treatment of Software Licenses in Bankruptcy

The treatment to be accorded a software license when the licensor or licensee files for bankruptcy depends upon whether the license is executory or nonexecutory. 11 U.S.C. § 365. Title 11 of the United States Code (the "Bankruptcy Code") treats executory agreements very differently from nonexecutory agreements. Section 365 of the Bankruptcy Code, which governs the treatment of executory agreements, generally permits a debtor to do one of three things: (1) assume the agreement, (2) assume and assign the agreement to a third party, or (3) reject the agreement. *Id.* Generally speaking, a debtor may not enjoy the full benefits of an executory agreement unless it assumes all of the obligations under the agreement, including the curing of all prepetition defaults under the agreement. *Id.* The same is not true with respect to a nonexecutory agreement.

Although the Bankruptcy Code does not define the term "executory", most bankruptcy courts use the definition formulated by Professor Vern Countryman,

1 An earlier version of this chapter was published as Classen and Sullivan, *Software Licensing in a Troubled Environment*, 19 Bus. Law Today 23 (No. 2 Nov./Dec. 2009). Mr Sullivan is a partner in the law firm of Moses & Singer LLP and can be reached at jsullivan@mosessinger.com

> . . . a contract under which the obligations of both the bankrupt and the other party to the contract are so far unperformed that the failure of either to complete performance would constitute a material breach excusing the performance of the other.

Vern Countryman, *Executory Contracts in Bankruptcy, Part I*, 57 MINN. L. REV. 439, 460 (1973). Thus, where performance has been substantially completed by one or both parties to the contract, the license is nonexecutory.

Whether a bankruptcy court will find a software license to be executory will depend upon a very fact-based analysis of the license agreement and the remaining obligations of each party under the license agreement. Although most software licenses with ongoing payment obligations by the licensee will likely qualify as an executory contract, the courts will look to the substance of the license agreement rather than the form in determining whether a contract is executory. *See Waterman v. Mackenzie*, 138 U.S. 252, 256 (1891) (differentiating between nonexclusive license of patent rights and exclusive assignment of such rights); *Microsoft Corp. v. Dak Indus.*, 66 F.3d 1091, 1095 n.2 (9th Cir. 1995). Thus, a royalty-free or fully paid-up license of software may not in fact be a license at all, but an assignment of a property interest that is nonexecutory. *See, e.g., Chesapeake Fiber Packaging Corp. v. Sebro Packaging Corp.*, 143 B.R. 360, 374–75 (D. Md. 1992), *aff'd*, 8 F.3d 817 (4th Cir. 1993); *In re Stein*, 81 B.R. 263, 266–67 (Bankr. S.D.N.Y. 1988); *In re Monument Record Corp.*, 61 B.R. 866, 868–69 (Bankr. M.D. Tenn. 1986).

Some examples of types of continuing obligations that may render a software license executory are continuing obligations to account for and pay royalties; duty to notify licensor or licensee of infringement suits; duty of licensor to defend licensee against infringement claims; obligation to forbear from making sales or licenses of the software to others; obligation to forbear from engaging in certain activities in certain territories or markets; duty to pursue infringement claims against third parties; obligations to provide maintenance and software upgrades; obligation to cross-license software or other intellectual property; indemnity and warranty obligations; training obligations; obligation to maintain records and permit inspections; confidentiality obligations; duty to pay fees for maintenance or ancillary services; obligations to provide most-favored nation treatment; and development and commercialization obligations. *See, e.g., Lubrizol Enters., Inc. v. Richmond Metal Finishers, Inc.*, 756 F.2d 1043, 1045 (4th Cir. 1985); *Fenix Cattle Co. v. Silver*, 625 F.2d 290, 292 (9th Cir. 1980).

B. The Licensor's Bankruptcy

1. Nonexecutory License

When a licensor files for bankruptcy, a licensee may be left in a precarious position, especially if its license agreement is nonexecutory. That is because the licensor may seek to breach the license by refusing to provide necessary support or software upgrades, or even worse by relicensing the software to a third party. The Bankruptcy Code offers little protection to a licensee that is a party to a nonexecutory contract with a debtor. In fact, a licensee's sole recourse may be to file a general unsecured claim against the debtor. Accordingly, a licensee should seek to protect itself from a licensor's bankruptcy to the greatest extent possible. Some techniques include getting a security interest in the licensed software, getting a technology escrow, drafting the license in such a way to ensure that it will be treated as an executory contract entitled to the protections of Section 365(n) of the Bankruptcy Code, and/or drafting the license to include equitable remedies that will survive the licensor's bankruptcy. See Section B.3 below for a description of these drafting techniques.

2. *Executory License*

In response to the concern of the software industry and licensees in particular, the federal bankruptcy laws were rewritten in 1987 to protect licensees in the event of a licensor's bankruptcy. Section 365(n) of the Bankruptcy Code (11 U.S.C. § 365(n)) ("Section 365(n)"), provides that in the event the debtor/licensor rejects the license agreement, the non-debtor/licensee has two options. First, it can bring a claim for damages to the extent the rejection caused the licensor to fail to meet the licensor's obligations under the license agreement. 11 U.S.C. § 365(n)(1)(A). Under this option, the licensee forgoes any right to use the licensed technology/software in the future. *Id.* Second, it can retain the rights to use the software/intellectual property for the period provided for under the license and any contractual extension periods. 11 U.S.C. § 365(n)(1)(B).

The trustee in bankruptcy can still reject the license agreement causing any executory provisions to become null and void, but the licensee can elect to retain its rights under the software license. If the licensee elects to retain its intellectual property rights, it must continue to pay the license fees due the licensor and must forego certain remedies otherwise available under the Bankruptcy Code (e.g., rights of setoff or to assert a § 503(b) administrative priority claim). Under Section 365(n), the licensee does not need to affirmatively elect to retain its intellectual property rights to preserve its license. 11 U.S.C. § 365(n)(1)(B). *But see In re E.I. International*, 123 B.R. 64, 67 (Bankr. D. Idaho 1991) (failure of licensee to elect to retain benefits of license caused license to be treated as terminated).

Most licensees elect the second option, to continue using the software. Although the licensee may continue using the software, it cannot compel the licensor to perform other contractual obligations except for any exclusivity provisions in the contract. The licensor is relieved of its obligations to provide any ancillary services, such as training, maintenance, support, documentation, or updates. The licensee is able to require the trustee to turn over any embodiments of the licensed technology, provided they were stated in the license, including any exclusivity right. 11 U.S.C. §§ 365(n)(1)(B) and 365(n)(3). The licensee must continue, however, to pay all royalties due the licensor. 11 U.S.C. § 365(n)(2)(B). This is a good reason to have separate agreements or payment schedules for the software license and any ancillary obligations, such as development as well as maintenance and support services. Utilizing a single contractual document, rather than multiple documents, will make the agreement appear executory in nature because of the existence of long term ongoing obligations. Separate agreements or payment schedules lessen the risk of an agreement being rejected because each obligation is compartmentalized and associated with a specific payment and a licensor will not be entitled to receive the separate fee unless it performs the separate service.

Other executory provisions of the contract are not enforceable by the licensee, such as maintenance and any unfinished development work. The licensee is able to require the trustee to turn over any embodiments of the licensed technology, provided they were stated in the license, including any exclusivity right. 11 U.S.C. §§ 365(n)(1)(B) and 365(n)(3).

3. Drafting Techniques

To ensure the protections of Section 365(n) are available to the licensee, the licensee should make sure the license specifically provides that the licensed software is "intellectual property" under § 101(56) and that the license is governed by Section 365(n) in the event the licensor files for bankruptcy protection.

Set forth below is model language that a licensee should include in its license agreement to ensure that it may avail itself of the protections set forth in Section 365(n).

> **Affirmation of rights.** All rights and licenses granted pursuant to any section of this Agreement are, and will otherwise be, for purposes of Section 365(n) of the U.S. Bankruptcy Code and/or any similar or comparable section of the U.S. Bankruptcy Code (as such sections may be modified, amended, replaced, or renumbered from time to time), executory licenses of rights to "intellectual property," as defined under **Section 101 (35A)** of the U.S. Bankruptcy Code and/or any similar or comparable section of the U.S. Bankruptcy Code (as such sections may be modified, amended, replaced, or renumbered from time to time). The parties will retain and may fully exercise all of their respective rights and elections under the U.S. Bankruptcy Code. Accordingly, the licensee of such rights shall retain and may fully exercise all of its rights and elections under the U.S. Bankruptcy Code. Upon the commencement of bankruptcy proceedings by or against either Party under the U.S. Bankruptcy Code, the other Party shall be entitled to retain all of its license rights and use rights granted under this Agreement.

Under the Bankruptcy Code, "intellectual property" is defined as "(A) trade secrets; (B) invention, process, design or plant protected under title 35; (C) patent application; (D) plant variety; (E) work of authorship protected under title 17; or (F) mask work protected under chapter 9 of title 17; to the extent protected by applicable non-bankruptcy law." 11 U.S.C. § 101 (56). It is clear that software will fall under this definition. As such, software will usually be governed by Section 365 of the Bankruptcy Code.

In addition, to further ensure that Section 365(n) is available to the licensee, the licensee should be sure to include sufficient continuing obligations in the license by both sides. See Section A above for examples of such obligations, to ensure that the license will be deemed an executory agreement. A licensee should also clearly state the contractual obligations that are deemed material, such that the breach by one party of such provision would excuse continued performance by the other party. Doing so will assist a bankruptcy court in applying the *Countryman* standard for determining whether an agreement is executory or the point at which an executory agreement becomes nonexecutory.

To limit its financial risk, the licensee should delineate the payments made for collateral obligations, such as training and support, from general royalty/license fees. The licensee should seek to have such collateral obligations contained in a separate agreement or payment schedule. By lumping all fees together, the licensee could be obligated to pay for collateral services that the licensor is no longer providing.

Many licensees seek to further limit their risk in the event of a licensor bankruptcy through the use of a source code escrow. Such an escrow will ensure that the licensee will have access to the source code for the licensed software if the licensor rejects the license and refuses to perform its obligations under the license agreement. Set forth below is model language than a licensee should include in its escrow agreement to ensure that it may avail itself of the protections set forth in Section 365(n)

> ***Supplementary Agreement***. This Escrow Agreement is "supplementary" to the License Agreement within the meaning of § 365(n) of the U.S. Bankruptcy Code (11 USC § 365 (n)) and/or any similar or comparable section of the U.S. Bankruptcy Code (as such sections may be modified, amended, replaced, or renumbered from time to time). If this Escrow Agreement and/or the License Agreement are/is rejected by Licensor as a debtor in possession or a trustee or by any other person or entity under the U.S. Bankruptcy Code, then the Licensee may elect to retain its right as provided in § 365(n). The Parties intend that no bankruptcy or bankruptcy proceeding, petition, law or regulation (and no other proceeding, petition, law or regulation of a similar nature in any state or foreign jurisdiction) will impede, delay or prevent the release of Deposit Materials to Licensee in accordance with the provisions of this Agreement, and the Licensor hereby conveys to Escrow Agent such rights (including intellectual property rights) as are necessary to allow Escrow Agent to lawfully make such release and perform this Agreement.
>
> Any licenses granted under this Agreement or which are provided pursuant to this Agreement are intended to be executory licenses of rights in intellectual property as contemplated by Section 365(n) of the U.S. Bankruptcy Code, 11 U.S.C. § 365(n), and/or any similar or comparable section of the U.S. Bankruptcy Code (as such sections may be modified, amended, replaced, or renumbered from time to time). In the event that Licensor becomes a debtor under the U.S. Bankruptcy Code, it is the intent of the Parties that Licensee shall have all benefits granted to licensees under the provisions of the U.S. Bankruptcy Code including, without limitation, Section 365(n) of the U.S. Bankruptcy Code (11 U.S. 365(n)) and/or any similar or comparable section of the U.S. Bankruptcy Code (as such sections may be modified, amended, replaced, or renumbered from time to time).

Another option is for the licensee to obtain a security interest in the licensor's software. In addition to protecting the licensee's interest in the software, the security interest will also secure any rejection damages claim available to the licensee in the event the debtor rejects the license agreement. Because the security interest will limit the benefits available to a debtor upon rejecting the license, it will incentivize the debtor to assume the license agreement. In order to perfect a security interest in a licensor's software, the licensee must comply with both the Uniform Commercial Code and copyright law, which require that a notice be filed with the Copyright Office. The grant of a security interest is considered to be the transfer of copyright ownership. *In re Avalon Software, Inc.*, 209 B.R. 517 (Bankr. D. Ariz. 1997).

Finally, the licensee should include equitable remedies in the license agreement, such as the right to enforce any exclusivity provisions in favor of the licensee with an injunction against infringement. Such remedies are particularly important where the license is not executory and thus not entitled to the remedies available under Section 365(n). The majority of courts will enforce such a provision where such remedy is not an alternative or substitute for money damages. *See, e.g., Kennedy v. Medicap Pharmacies, Inc.*, 267 F.3d 493, 497 (6th Cir. 2001) (holding that an equitable remedy for breach of an agreement that is not an alternative to monetary remedy is not a "claim" that can be discharged in bankruptcy); *In re Udell*, 18 F.3d 403 (7th Cir. 1994) (same); *In re Gilpin*, 391 B.R. 210 (Table) (6th Cir. BAP 2008) (same). *But see, e.g., In re Ward*, 194 B.R. 703, 709-15 (Bankr. D. Mass. 1996) (holding that equitable remedies can be discharged if breach of agreement can be remedied with monetary damages, even where equitable remedies are also available); *In re Brown*, 31 Bankr. Ct. Dec. (CRR) 1055, 1997 WL 786994 (E.D. Pa. 1997) (adopting middle ground approach that requires the court to consider the nature of relief available under applicable state law in determining whether equitable remedies should be discharged). One method that can be used to increase the likelihood that a court will enforce the equitable remedies is to include a provision in the agreement that the parties agree that a breach cannot be adequately addressed through monetary damages and an agreement that equitable relief, such as an injunction, is needed to protect the licensee's rights in the software.

For a more detailed discussion, see Agin, *Reconciling Commercial Law and Information Technology: An Essay on Bankruptcy Practice During the Next Business Cycle*, 4 J. of INTERNET L. (October 2000) and Kupetz, *Beware When Dealing With Licensor's of Intellectual Property: Avoiding Potential Pitfalls Facing Licensees and Lendors When Bankruptcy Intervenes*, 17 COMPUTER LAW. 21 (Jan. 2000); Kupetz, *Dealing With Issues in Chapter 11 Cases Filed by Licensors of Intellectual Property*, 16 E-COMMERCE & STRATEGY 1 (Jan. 2000). *See also*, Sommer, *Bankruptcy and Intellectual Property Contracts*, 21 LICENSING J. 11 (Jan. 2001); Bartlett, *Effects of Bankruptcy on Licensing Under 11 U.S.C. § 365(n)*, 5 J. PROPRIETARY RTS. 20 (July 1993); *The Protection of Intellectual Property Rights of a Licensee When a Licensor Goes Into Bankruptcy Under the Amended 11 U.S.C. 11 § 365*, 73 J. PAT. & TRADEMARK OFF. SOC'Y. 893 (1991); Brown, Hansend, & Salerno, *Technology Licenses under Section 365(n) of the Bankruptcy Code: The Protections Afforded the Technology User*, 95 COM. L.J. 170 (1990).

It is important to note that Alternative Service Provider ("ASP") licenses do not receive the same protection under the Bankruptcy Code as other software licenses. *See* RAYMOND T. NIMMER & HOLLY K. TOWLE, LAW OF ELECTRONIC COMMERCIAL TRANSACTIONS § 8.14 Thompson*West (2003).

C. The Licensee's Bankruptcy

1. Nonexecutory License

A software licensor's primary concern when a licensee files for bankruptcy is payment. If the license is considered to be nonexecutory, for example where the licensor has already substantially performed its obligations under the agreement, then the licensor's sole recourse may be to assert a general unsecured claim against the licensee's estate. Accordingly, a licensor should seek to protect itself from a licensee's bankruptcy to the greatest extent possible. One technique is obtaining a security interest in the licensed software and/or other assets, which will incentivize the licensee to honor its commitments under the license agreement. Another technique is to draft the license in such a way to ensure that it will be treated as an executory contract, which, as described in Section C.2.(c) below, may make it difficult for the licensee to assume or assign the license without the licensor's consent and thus provide the licensor with greater leverage. See Section B.2 above for a description of these drafting techniques. As described in Section C.2.(c) below, although the restrictions on assignment of an executory software license may also apply to the assignment of a nonexecutory software license, a court might treat a nonexecutory license as a sale or assignment of the software rather than a license, in which case the court may not be inclined to apply the exception to assignment provided for under Section 365(c) of the Bankruptcy Code.

2. Executory License

(a) Termination of License

Many licensors include language in their license agreements automatically terminating the license agreement upon a licensee's bankruptcy. Such provisions, sometimes referred to as *ipso facto* clauses, are not enforceable. 11 U.S.C. § 365(e). Section 365(e)(1) of the Bankruptcy Code provides that an executory contract of the debtor may not be terminated or modified after a bankruptcy filing because of a provision in the license agreement that is conditioned on the insolvency or financial condition of the debtor or the commencement of a bankruptcy filing. 11 U.S.C. § 365(e)(1). Any attempt by the non-bankrupt party to unilaterally terminate a contract covered by the provisions of the Bankruptcy Code without first seeking relief from the automatic stay may expose such party to significant liability. *See, e.g., In re Computer Communications, Inc.*, 824 F.2d 725 (9th Cir. 1987) (unilateral termination of agreement to buy hardware and software from bankrupt debtor violates bankruptcy code as ability to terminate stayed by bankruptcy filing; debtor awarded over $4 million in damages).

Although *ipso facto* clauses are generally not enforceable, their inclusion in a license agreement may provide a party leverage in the event the other party is insolvent and does not declare bankruptcy or a bankruptcy court rejects the insolvent party's bankruptcy petition. To the extent a party has received a parent guaranty for the performance of the other party and the parent declares bankruptcy, the beneficiary of the guaranty would be able to terminate the agreement.

To provide a greater level of protection, a licensor can include certain performance requirements in the license agreement that would allow the licensor to terminate the license agreement if the licensee fails to abide by such requirements. These may include requiring the licensee to continue operating, maintain a minimum amount of sales, or expend a minimum amount on marketing or promotion. These rights are separate and distinct from those provisions typically placed in a license agreement allowing the licensor to terminate the license for the licensee's bankruptcy.

The language below illustrates a potential basis for terminating a license without violating the *ipso facto* prohibitions of the Bankruptcy Code. Only covenants that do not relate solely to the financial condition of the debtor are capable of being enforced.

> (a) If Licensee (i) fails to continue operating its material businesses, (ii) fails to maintain monthly sales of $__________; (iii) fails to expend at least $________ per month on marketing and promotion of _______
>
> (b) then Licensor may by giving written notice to Licensee, terminate this Agreement in whole or in part and without charge, as of the date specified in such notice of termination

In addition, a licensor may terminate a license prior to a licensee's bankruptcy filing provided the termination is effectuated prior to the licensee's bankruptcy filing. *See, e.g., Moody v. Amoco Oil Co.*, 734 F.2d 1200 (7th Cir. 1984). The fact that the effective date of any notice of termination does not occur until after the licensee files for bankruptcy should not affect the result so long as the termination is complete and not subject to cure or reversal, either under the terms of the contract or under state law. *Id.* at 1213 (holding that automatic stay does not toll mere running of time under contract and does not prevent automatic termination of contract, nor does it give debtor greater rights under contract, and debtors could not rely upon it to prevent termination of contracts as to which 90-day notice had been given before filing of petition). Where the termination is subject to cure or reversal at the time of the bankruptcy filing, however, the licensee will have an opportunity to cure the default under section 365 of the Bankruptcy Code and prevent the termination from occurring. *Id.* at 1215 (where debtors filed for bankruptcy before expiration of 15-day cure period allowed by termination notice, debtors could elect to assume the contract, and, if they did so determine, they could cure default at any time prior to the assumption).

(b) Assumption or Assignment of Executory License

Under Section 365(b) of the Bankruptcy Code, a software licensee who declares bankruptcy and desires to assume an executory license agreement must cure all breaches, fully perform its obligations under the license agreement, and provide adequate assurances that it will perform in the future. If the licensee fails to do so, it must reject the license agreement and relinquish all rights to the underlying intellectual property.

Furthermore, there is a limit on a debtor licensee's ability to assign a software license to a third party. For example, it appears that a debtor licensee cannot assign a nonexclusive software license to another entity without the licensor's consent even where there is no prohibition to such assignment under the license agreement. *See, e.g., In re Alltech Plastics, Inc.*, 71 B.R. 686 (Bankr. W.D. Tenn. 1987) (holding that patent licenses cannot be assigned by licensee under section 365 of the Bankruptcy Code without licensor's consent because under federal common law the duties and obligations of a licensee are personal and nondelegable and thus not assignable without the licensor's consent); *In re CFLC, Inc.*, 89 F.3d 673, 679 (9th Cir. 1996) (prohibiting assignment of nonexclusive patent license without licensor's consent); *In re Patient Educ. Media, Inc.*, 210 B.R. 237, 242-43 (Bankr. S.D.N.Y. 1997) (prohibiting nonexclusive copyright license without licensor's consent); 11 U.S.C. § 365(c) (providing exception to assignment of contracts under section 365 of the Bankruptcy Code where "applicable law" excuses a nondebtor party to an executory contract from accepting its assignment).

The same limitations may not apply to the assignment of an exclusive software license, which may be characterized as an assignment of a property interest rather than the license of limited rights to use the software. *See In re Golden Books Family Entertainment, Inc.*, 269 B.R. 311 (Bankr. D. Del. 2001) (assignability of copyright license turns on whether it is exclusive or nonexclusive; exclusive copyright license of children's book character was assignable by debtor); *In re Supernatural Foods, L.L.C.*, 268 B.R. 759 (Bankr. M.D. La. 2001) (holding that trustee could assume and assign exclusive patent license, despite provision to contrary in agreement because generally applicable law did not prohibit assignment). *But see Gardner v. Nike, Inc.*, 279 F.3d 774 (9th Cir. 2002) (holding that licensee did not have right to transfer its rights in exclusive copyright license without licensor's consent); *ProteoTech, Inc. v. Unicity Intern., Inc.*, 542 F. Supp.2d 1216 (W.D. Wash. 2008) (holding that licensee did not have right to transfer its rights in exclusive patent license without licensor's consent); cf. *In re Hernandez*, 285 B.R. 435 (Bankr. D. Ariz. 2002) (holding that licensee could not assume exclusive patent license notwithstanding lack of debtor's intention to transfer license).

Similarly, at least one court has held that a licensee cannot use a nonexclusive license after its bankruptcy reorganization absent the licensor's consent. *In re Catapult Enter., Inc.*, 165 F.3d 747, 754–55 (9th Cir. 1999) ("where applicable non-bankruptcy law makes an executory contract non-assignable because the identity of the non-debtor is material, a debtor in possession may not assume the contract absent consent of the non-debtor party."). *But see Institut Pasteur v. Cambridge Biotech Corp.*, 104 F.3d 489 (1st Cir. 1997) (holding that debtor is not to be prevented from assuming license unless it actually intended to assign license to third party); *In re Hernandez*, 287 B.R. 795 (Bankr. D. Ariz. 2002) (holding that exclusive patent license need not be assumed or rejected by debtor, but may "ride through" the bankruptcy case).

Licensees also need to be concerned about their right to assume a license in the event of their bankruptcy as there is a dichotomy among the federal circuit courts. In *In re Sunterra Corporation*, 361 F.3d 257 (4th Cir. 2004), Sunterra licensed certain software and cross-licensed any enhancements Sunterra made to the software back to the licensor. Prior to declaring bankruptcy, Sunterra spent approximately $38 million to enhance the software. When Sunterra later declared bankruptcy and subsequently tried to assume the license, the licensor claimed that under 11 U.S.C. § 365 (c), the licensee was precluded from assuming the contract without the licensor's consent even though the license agreement permitted the debtor to assign the license.

The Fourth Circuit Court of Appeals held that Section 365(c) of the Bankruptcy Code precluded the debtor licensee from assuming the contract without the licensor's consent even though the license agreement permitted the debtor to assign the license. *Id.* This position, which emphasizes the literal meaning of the statutory language to evaluate the assumption of executory contracts (also known as the "hypothetical test") has been adopted by the Third, Fourth, Ninth and Eleventh Circuits. The hypothetical test provides that the courts should follow the plain meaning of the statute (§ 365(c)) when the terms of the statute are unambiguous. Third: *In re West Elec., Inc.*, 852 F.2d 79, 83 (3d Cir. 1988); Fourth: *In re Catron*, 158 B.R. 629, 633–38 (E.D. Va. 1993), *aff'd. without op.* 25 F.3d 1038 (4th Cir. 1994); Ninth: *In re Catapult*, 165 F.3d at 750; Eleventh: *In re James Cable Partners*, 27 F.3d 534, 537 (11th Cir. 1994) (in dicta).

The First Circuit along with a majority of bankruptcy courts, however, has adopted the "actual" test, which it believes represents the intent of Congress. *Institut Pasteur v. Cambridge Biotech Corp.*, 104 F.3d at 493; *In re Footstar, Inc.*, 323 B.R. 566, 569 n.2 (Bankr. S.D.N.Y. 2005). See *In re Footstar*, 323 B.R. at 569 n.2 and *In re Catapult*, 165 F.3d at 749 n.2 for a summary of bankruptcy courts that have adopted the "actual" test. Under the "actual test," a court will examine, on a case by case basis, whether the non-debtor would be required to accept performance from a party other than the party with which it initially contracted. Further, a debtor is not to be prevented from assuming a license unless it actually intends to assign the license to a third party.

Thus, a prudent licensee should include language in its license that in the event of the licensee's bankruptcy, and subsequent decision to assume the license, the licensor agrees that it will consent to and accept the assumption. The ramifications of not having such a provision in the license agreement may be so big that it ultimately could affect a licensee's decision on where to file for bankruptcy protection or whether to file for bankruptcy protection at all. A licensor who agrees to such a provision may wish to limit a consent to assumption provision to situations that do not involve a change in control of the licensee.

In addition, a personal services contract cannot be assigned or assumed by a debtor under the Bankruptcy Code. 11 U.S.C § 365(c); *In re Catron,* 158 B.R. 624 (Bankr. E.D. Va. 1992), *aff'd,* 158 B.R. 629, *aff'd,* 25 F.3d 1038. *But see In re Fastrax, Inc.*, 129 B.R. 274 (Bankr. M. D. Fla. 1991) (subcontract for installation of storage, retrieval, and distribution computer center not a personal service contract and could be performed by another computer software company).

For a more detailed discussion, see Agin, *Reconciling Commercial Law and Information Technology: An Essay on Bankruptcy Practice During the Next Business Cycle,* 4 J. of INTERNET L. (October 2000).

For a general overview of the bankruptcy process in the event of a customer's bankruptcy, see Sullivan & Ravert, *A Vendor's Guide to Bankruptcy,* 1 BLOOMBERG CORP. L.J. 494 (2006).

CHAPTER **18**

Employee Issues

A tangential but important consideration in software licensing is ensuring that appropriate safeguards have been taken by the licensor in relation to its employees and contractors. These actions are important not only to protect the licensor's business but also the interests of the licensor's customers.

A. Assignment of Intellectual Property Rights

From the employer's perspective, it is important to ensure that the employer owns its employee's work product in order to maintain the integrity of the licensor's products and to ensure that the licensor has the right to transfer ownership of any intellectual property it creates, particularly if it is contractually obligated to do so.

Generally, an employer has an interest in the inventions of an employee by an implied contract if the employee is "employed to invent." *See Standard Parts Co. v. Peck*, 264 U.S. 52, 59–60 (1924). The meaning of "employed to invent" is a matter of state law and will vary by state. For example, some states require only that the employee's job description generally include innovation or improvements. In other states, however, the employee must be employed to invent specific innovations or improvements that must be detailed in advance. *Standard Parts Co. v. Peck*, 264 U.S. 52, 59–60 (1924); *Teets v. Chromalloy Gas Turbine Corp.*, 83 F.3d 403 Fed. Cir. 1996); *Cahill v. Regan*, 157 N.E.2d 505 (N.Y. 1959). Thus, the choice of law governing a person's employment contract or related confidentiality and inventions agreements signed upon hiring is a very important consideration. *See* Van Slyke and Friedman, *Employer's Rights to Inventions and Patents of its Officers, Directors and Employees,* 18 Am. Intell. Prop. L. Q.J. 127 (1990).

An employer must carefully document its ownership of an employee's work product to avoid future disputes. At the time the employee begins his/her employment, he/she should be required to execute an agreement assigning ownership of all work created during the scope of his/her employment to the employer. To the extent the employee claims to own intellectual property existing at the time of employment, all such intellectual property should be listed in detail on a schedule attached to the agreement. See e.g. Form 23.G.5. The agreement should provide that the failure to identify and list any such intellectual property is conclusive evidence that the employee lacked any intellectual property at the time of his/her employment. Some employers seek to state that *all* intellectual property created by an employee during the period of his/her employment with the employer or within a set period of time following the termination of the employee's employment will be owned by the employer. Given that this intellectual property may be created outside of the scope of the employee's employment, it is unclear whether or not this language is enforceable. *See Applied Materials, Inc. v. Advanced Micro-Fabrication Equip., Co.*, 630 F. Supp.2d 1084 (N.D. Cal 2009) (assignment clause assigning ownership of employee work created outside of employment unenforceable).

An employer should carefully define the inventions and other materials that are being assigned to the employer to avoid any ambiguity as to what is being transferred. The description should be as broad as possible. The failure to clearly describe the nature of what is being assigned to the employer may provide the opportunity for the employee to claim that he or she did not assign all ideas and concepts related to such materials to the employer, and in fact retained certain "ideas." *See e.g., Mattel v. MGA Entertainment, Inc.* 616 F.3d 904 (9th Cir. 2010) (employment agreement did not unambiguously require assignment of employee's idea for a new doll to employer).

Employers also should pay careful attention to the language used to transfer ownership of any employee's work to the employer to ensure that it creates an immediate assignment of intellectual property rights at the time the intellectual property is created. In *DDB Technologies, L.L.C. v. MLB Advanced Media L.P.*, 517 F.3d 1284 (Fed. Cir. 2008), the United States Court of Appeals held that if an employee agreement grants the employer all rights in future inventions, the assignment arises automatically upon creation of the work, and the transfer occurs by operation of law. The court focused on the fact that the agreement contained an actual assignment, not an agreement to assign. *Id.* at 1287, 1290. ("Employee agrees to and does **hereby grant and assign** to Company or its nominee his entire right, title and interest in and to ideas, inventions and improvements . . . .") (emphasis supplied). It contrasted the language contained in the employee agreement to an *agreement to transfer* any future invention, which does not automatically vest title in the employer since it requires the execution of an assignment in the future. *Id.*

Similarly, in *Board of Trustees of Leland Stanford Junior University v. Roche*, 583 F.3d 832 (Fed. Cir. 2009) the court found that the language used by Stanford University in its employment agreement was inadequate to assign ownership in an employee's invention to the University. In *Roche* an employee executed an employment agreement which provided: "I agree to assign or confirm in writing to Stanford . . . that right, title and interest in . . . such inventions as required by Contracts or Grants." *Id.* at 837. The employee entered into a subsequent agreement with Cetus as part of Stanford's collaboration with Cetus. As a condition to accessing Cetus's confidential information, he executed a Visitor Confidential Agreement ("VCA"), which provided that he "will assign and do[es] assign to Cetus, my right, title, and interest in each of the ideas and improvements" developed as a result of his work at Cetus.

A dispute subsequently arose as to the ownership of patents developed by the employee. Stanford claimed ownership as a result of the employee executing the Stanford agreement, while Cetus claimed ownership based on the VCA. The United States Court of Appeals found that the language of the Stanford agreement did not assign ownership to Stanford, as it was only an agreement to assign and thus Stanford did not immediately gain title to the invention. One the other hand, the court found the Cetus VCA effected an immediate assignment of the researcher's invention to Cetus. *Id.* at 841–42. Thus, ownership vested in Cetus, not Stanford.

To avoid potential disputes and ensure ownership of its employee's work, a prudent employer should ensure that its employment agreement actually assigns all of the employee's rights in all copyrights, patents and other intellectual property created by the employee. See Form 23.G.5 § 5 for model language.

To the extent the employer seeks to have the employee execute an agreement after the start of his employment, the employer should provide the employee additional consideration beyond the employee's continued employment to ensure such agreement will be binding. *See e.g., Lucht's Concrete Pumping, Inc. v. Homer*, 224 P.3d 355 (Colo. App. 2009).

B. Protection of Employer and Client Confidential Information

As a condition of employment, all employees also should be required to sign an employee confidentiality agreement that is tailored to the employee's state of residence. These agreements should provide that during and after the termination of his or her employment, the employee will treat all employer and customer information as confidential and that the employee will not disclose any such confidential information other than is required in the performance of his or her duties for the employer. The confidentiality provisions should be broadly written to protect the parties' confidential information and strictly identify and limit the use of any confidential information. Doing so will protect the parties in the event an employee misuses the information. *Marketing Technology Solutions, Inc. v. Medizine LLC.*, 2010 WL 2034404 (S.D.N.Y. May 18, 2010) (employee's access of employer's computer system exceeded authorized use under employee's employment agreement).

Unlike covenants of non-competition, which must be of reasonable duration, courts do not generally restrict covenants of confidentiality to a set time period. *See, Ashland Management Inc. v. Altair Investments NA, LLC*, 869 N.Y.S.2d 465 (N.Y. 2008) (court enforced confidentiality agreement of unlimited duration). Further, all states recognize an employer's right to protect its confidential information. *See e.g. Majestic Marketing, Inc. v. Nay*, 2010 WL 338966, at * 5 (Cal.App Jan. 29, 2010) ("Despite California's broad prohibition against noncompetition agreements, covenants not to compete may be enforced to the extent that enforcement is necessary to protect a company's trade secrets.")

Some customers seek to have the vendor's employees sign a confidentiality agreement directly with the customer. Vendors should not agree to have their employees execute a confidentiality obligation directly with the customer, as it exposes the employee, personally, to potential liability for breach. Instead, the underlying license agreement between the vendor and customer should provide that the employees will sign a confidentiality agreement with the vendor that is as restrictive or more restrictive than the agreement between the vendor and the customer.

All employees should be informed of the employer's Code of Ethics and Standards of Conduct with the expectation they will be adhered to. At the start of each new customer project, all employees working on the project should complete an "onboarding" process during which the employee team is briefed on the project, including any requirements of confidentiality particular to such project. To the extent possible, the employer should keep a record of those in attendance and have the employees sign an acknowledgement of their obligations.

Employees also should be required to complete annual online ethics training, and the employer's human resources department should circulate periodic ethics related articles to all of the employer's employees. These should include reminders of each employee's obligations in regard to the customer's confidential information. Additionally, if the employer publishes an employee newsletter, the employer should include an ethics and confidentiality reminder in the newsletter.

Employers should only bring a good faith claim against an employee and should refrain from bringing a claim solely to have a chilling effect on its employees, especially those employees seeking to leave the employer's employ. Employers should only bring a claim in the event of an actual trade secret misappropriation and should avoid the tendency to sue first and develop facts to support their case afterwards. *See FLIR Systems, Inc. v. Parrish*, 174 Cal.App.4th 1270 (Cal.App 2009) (Court awarded ex-employees $1.6M for claim brought in bad faith by former employer alleging trade secret misappropriation under doctrine of inevitable disclosure, despite the fact the doctrine had been rejected in California. Court found suit had been brought to stifle competition and there was no evidence of trade secret misappropriation).

Potential employers also can be held liable if a new employee brings his or her former employer's confidential information to their new employer. *See e.g., William A. Graham Co. v. Haughey*, 484 F. Supp.2d 324 (E.D. Pa. 2007) (use of former employer's copyrighted templates brought by ex-employee to new job constituted copyright infringement by new employer). To that end, employers should have all new employees execute an acknowledgment, acknowledging their obligation to abide by any agreements entered into with former employers and requiring the employee to provide the new employer with a copy of any such agreement. See Form 23.I.11 for a model acknowledgment.

For a general discussion of trade secret misappropriation by employees, see Thomas J. Gray and Peter O'Rourke, *Preventing Employee Trade Secret Misuse from Derailing Your Company*, 24 Corp. Couns. Q. 205 (April 2008); Mark D. Weller and Ronald J. Shaffer, *Employee Theft of Trade Secrets*, 26 ACC Docket 87 (Oct. 2008); Michael Starr and Christopher N. Franciose, *Disloyalty and the USTA*, Nat'l L.J. Apr. 20, 2009, at 13.

C. Non-solicitation of Employees by Former Employees (§§ 5.3.7, 9.14)

As part of the hiring process, prudent employers should require their employees to execute a covenant of non-solicitation, prohibiting an employee, upon departure, from soliciting his or her former co-workers to leave the employment of the employer. Prohibitions on soliciting co-workers protect an employer's interest in its employees, as employers make a significant financial investment in training and developing their employees.

Practically, non-solicitation provisions are difficult to enforce, but they do provide the employer with some leverage in the event a former employee tries to entice a former co-worker to leave the employer. Enforcement is difficult, as both the soliciting employee and the solicited employee will likely deny one solicited the other. It is almost impossible to prove solicitation without a paper trail or an admission.

Employee referral programs may provide the necessary paper trail and a motivation. Many employers have an "employee referral program" that provides existing employees a "referral fee" for referring potential candidates for open positions. Too often an employee seeks to encourage his former co-workers to join him at the new employer in order to receive a referral fee. By subpoenaing the new employer's records, the former employer will be able to determine if the employee received a referral bonus, and thus by implication, violated his non-solicitation covenant.

A less confrontational means of addressing the issue is to send the employee a letter reminding the employee of his non-solicitation obligation and copying his new employer. It puts both the employee and the new employer on notice that the prior employer plans to enforce its rights in the event of a breach. For the same reason, every employee leaving the company should be required to have an exit interview. During the exit interview the employee should be given a copy of his/her non-competition agreement and reminded of his/her obligations under the agreement. To the extent it is able to do so, the employer should have the soon to be ex-employee execute an acknowledgement, acknowledging his/her obligations. See Form 23.G.12 for model language.

To avoid potential problems, a new employer should have each employee represent and warrant that he or she is not subject to any contractual obligation that would prohibit him or her from accepting employment with the employer, and that there are no limitations on the employee fulfilling his or her duties as an employee. The new employer should remind the employee not to bring any materials or information from the employee's previous employer to the new job. All electronic media from the employee's personal equipment should be deleted/erased. See Form 23.I.11 for a model certification requiring the prospective employee to disclose any actual or potential conflict. *See Southwest Stainless L.P. v. Sappington*, 582 F.3d 1176 (10th Cir. 2009) (finding that former employee and new employer tortuously interfered with ex-employer's contractual relationship with its employees by soliciting an employee known to be subject to a non-competition agreement).

Employers should carefully select the governing law for any non-solicitation agreement, as some courts have found covenants of ex-employees not to solicit former co-workers to terminate their employment an illegal restraint of trade. *Schmersahl, Treloar & Co., P.C. v. McHugh,* 28 S.W.3d 345 (Mo. App. 2000).

D. Non-Competition Agreements

Most software vendors require their employees to execute a covenant of non-competition, prohibiting the employee from competing with the employer for a period of time after the employee leaves the employer's employ. To increase the likelihood that the covenant will be upheld by a court, prudent employers will draft the limitation narrowly, limiting the employee from working directly or indirectly for, or providing services to, those customers with whom the employee interacted or had access to their confidential information in the 12 months prior to the termination of his or her employment. *See Unisource Worldwide, Inc. v. Carrara*, 244 F. Supp.2d 977 (C.D. Ill. 2003). The prohibition on soliciting customers and employees should be limited to no more than two years and limited to those customers with whom the employee was involved in the two years prior to the termination of his or her employment. The underlying agreement should provide that the period of non-competition will be tolled for a stated period of time each time the signatory violates the restrictive covenant. *See e.g., Proudfoot Consulting Co. v. Gordon*, 576 F.3d 1223 (11th Cir. 2009).

The enforceability of any covenants of non-competition and any non-solicitation covenants will depend on the state of residency of the employee in question and the governing law of the underlying agreement. Employers should avoid having the agreement governed by the laws of California and Georgia, which have held non-compete agreements to be void. California: West's Ann. Cal. Bus. & Prof. Code § 16600 (2007); *Edwards v. Arthur Anderson LLP*, 189 P.3d. 285 (Cal 2008) (restrictive covenant of limited duration prohibiting solicitation of specific client unenforceable); Georgia: *Jenkins Brick Company v. Bremer*, 321 F.3d 1366, 1369 (11th Cir. 2003) ("Georgia's courts rarely uphold blanket non-compete agreements."). The parties should be cognizant of the fact that some states, such as Georgia, will apply Georgia law to certain aspects of an agreement affecting its residents, such as a covenant of non-competition, even if the parties have contractually agreed to the laws of another state. *See Nasco, Inc. v. Gimbert*, 238 S.E.2d 368, 369 (Ga. 1977). The courts of Texas, for example, will enforce a choice of venue provision against a Texas resident where the venue is outside of Texas, but they will not enforce the choice of another state's law against a Texas resident. *See In re AutoNation, Inc.*, 228 S.W.3d 663 (Tex. 2007) (enforcing Florida venue in matter to enforce non-competition agreement against a Texas resident); *DeSantis v. Wackenhut Corp.*, 793 S.W.2d 670 (Tex. 1990) (Texas law, rather than contractually selected Florida law, used to interpret non-competition agreement signed by Texas resident). To ensure certainty, an employer should always select the state of the employee's residence to govern the interpretation of the agreement, but the employer may select its desired venue to hear any dispute.

The courts of some states will "blue pencil" any overly broad provision and thus, such states should be viewed favorably at least as compared to those that will void the entire agreement. *See e.g., Fowler v. Printers II*, 598 A.2d 794 (Md. 1991) *cert. denied* 602 A.2d 710 (Md. 1992).

Prudent employers should considering having employees execute new non-competition agreements upon their promotion, as some courts have held that a promotion may void an employee's non-competition agreement because the terms of employment changed as a result of the employee's new role. *Lycos, Inc. v. Lincoln Jackson,* 18 Mass. L. Rptr. 256 (2004).

Some employers will waive a covenant of non-competition if the employee is involuntarily terminated, as it is difficult to argue that the employee should be prohibited from working for another employer or that the employee's subsequent employment is a threat to the former employer's business when the employer did not deem the employee worthy of being retained.

A tangential question that often arises is whether a non-competition agreement may be assigned by the employer without the employee's consent. A dichotomy of opinions exist on this issue. Ohio and Minnesota courts have held that non-competition agreements without an assignment clause may be assigned by the employer. *Haughen v. Sundseth*, 118 N.W. 666 (Minn. 1908); *Artomick Int'l, Inc. v. Koch*, 759 N.E.2d 385 (Ohio Ct. App. 2001). Hawaii and Virginia, among others, prohibit the assignment of non-competition agreements. *UARCO Inc. v. Lam*, 18 F. Supp.2d 1116 (D. Haw. 1998); *Reynolds and Reynolds Co. v. Hardee*, 932 F. Supp. 149, 153 (E.D.Va.1996) ("contracts for personal services are not assignable unless both parties agree to the assignment.")

Pennsylvania, however, has adopted a more tempered approach interpreting the right of assignment narrowly but allowing assignment in some cases. *All-Pak, Inc. v. Johnston*, 694 A.2d 347, 351 (Pa. Super 1997) ("absent an explicit assignability provision, courts should be hesitant to read one into the contract."). Those agreements requiring the employer to obtain the employee's consent to assignment likely will be strictly construed. *Guy Carpenter & Co. v. John B. Collins & Assocs.*, 2006 WL 2502232 (D. Minn. Aug. 29, 2006) (failure of employer to obtain employees' consent prior to assignment of non-competition agreement rendered non-competition provision unenforceable).

Based on the disparate holdings of the different jurisdictions, a prudent employer should include an explicit assignment clause permitting the employer to assign an employee's non-competition agreement. See, e.g. Form 23.G.5 § 11.

For a general overview, see Trepanier & MacGillis, *Non-Compete Agreements: Are They Assignable Under Minnesota Law? http://trepanierlaw.com/whatsnew.asp?id=70520090113* (last viewed September 15, 2010).

For an overview of covenants not to compete, see Michelle L. Evans, *Enforceability of Covenant Not to Compete*, 39 Law. Brief 1 (April 2009); Megan M. Belcher and Tracey M. Gullickson, *Fencing the Herd: Protecting Your Company's Proprietary Interests with Restrictive Covenants,* 27 ACC Docket 55 (Dec. 2009).

E. Non-Solicitation of Employees of Licensor/Licensee

Many licensors and IT services vendors include language in their license/services agreements prohibiting the licensee/customer from hiring its employees. They do so to protect their investment in their employees and to protect their revenue stream. A well-worded prohibition will prevent the licensee/customer from hiring only those employees who provided services to the licensee/customer for a set period of time, or alternatively, proscribing liquidated damages in the event the prohibition is breached.

In reality, non-hire provisions are difficult to enforce if the licensee is a large or profitable customer and the enforcement of the provision may damage the business relationship. In the event of a dispute with a customer over a non-solicitation provision, most licensors are hesitant to enforce such provisions to avoid alienating the customer. Many customers recognize the leverage they hold over the licensor/vendor, and thus can negotiate an "exception" to any non-hire prohibitions. Often the licensee/customer will seek to include an exception granting it the right to hire the employee after the employee has been assigned to the licensee/customer's project for a minimum period of time, such as three months, or include a liquidated damages provision that provides for reduced payments the longer the employee provides services to the customer.

If the licensee is willing to accept a non-solicitation clause, it should seek to negotiate any desired exceptions for which it would need to hire the licensor's employees, such as in the event of the licensor's breach of the contract, the licensor declaring bankruptcy or the licensor ceasing support of the software. Many licensees exclude from any prohibition hiring an employee through a general solicitation such as a newspaper advertisement or internet job posting. This exclusion creates a very large loop hole, as any claim that a licensee specifically targeted a desired employee can be readily refuted by reference to the advertisement and any screening of responses received in connection with the advertisement.

The licensee should insist that any non-hire provision in the license agreement be mutual to protect its own employee population, especially for those employees with hard-to-find expertise. Very few licensees seek to include a non-solicitation provision in their agreements, which is a serious oversight. For licensors, a customer's employee population is a fertile recruiting ground for employees with scarce skill sets, especially if the licensor has trained the employees at the customer's expense as part of the implementation. Further, many licensee employees are underpaid in comparison to salaries paid by licensors, making the opportunity to join the licensor financially attractive.

F. Theft/Destruction of Employer Property—Computer Fraud and Abuse Act

The Computer Fraud and Abuse Act, 18 U.S.C. § 1030 ("CFAA") potentially provides an employer a means to bring an action against a former employee who has stolen or destroyed employer property through the use of a computer. An employer may seek civil damages and criminal penalties. The CFAA prohibits intentionally accessing computer data without authorization or accessing computer data that exceeds the individual's authorized access. 18 U.S.C. § 1030(a).

An injured party must prove that it suffered a "loss" of at least $5,000 in damages. 18 U.S.C. § 1030(c)(4)(A)(i)(l). The CFAA has adopted a broad definition of "loss" allowing a plaintiff to recover for a broad array of damages. "Loss" is defined as:

> [a]ny reasonable cost . . . including the cost of responding to an offense, conducting a damage assessment, and restoring the data, program, system, or information to its condition prior to the offense, and any revenue lost, cost incurred, or other consequential damages incurred because of interruption of service.

18 U.S.C. § 1030(e)(8)(11).

Notwithstanding the potentially broad remedy the CFAA might otherwise have provided, the majority of courts have concluded that trade secrets and the revenue associated therewith do not constitute a loss as contemplated under the CFAA, but instead must arise from accessing the injured party's computers, such as an interruption of service. *ResDev v. Lot Builders*, 2005 WL 1924743 (M.D. Fla. Aug. 10, 2005); *Nexans v. Sark-USA, Inc.*, 319 F. Supp.2d 468 (S.D.N.Y. 2004).

Other courts have limited the reach of the CFAA more literally by reading the definition of "loss" very strictly. *American Family Mut. Ins. Co. v. Rickman*, 554 F. Supp.2d 766 (N. D. Ohio 2008) (Losses incurred from employee's theft of data do not constitute "losses" as defined under CFAA). *See also*, *Modis Inc. v. Bardelli*, 531 F. Supp.2d. 314 (D. Conn. 2008). The CFAA "treats lost revenue as a different concept from incurred costs," and permits recovery of lost revenue only when connected to "an interruption in service." *Nexans Wires S.A. v. Sark-USA, Inc.*, 166 Fed. Appx. 559, 562 (2d Cir. 2006). "[T]he costs of responding to the offense" are recoverable, regardless of whether there is an interruption in service, and federal courts have sustained actions based on allegations of costs to investigate and take remedial steps in response to a defendant's misappropriation of data. *P.C. Yonkers, Inc. v. Celebrations! The Party and Seasonal Superstore, L.L.C.*, 2007 WL 708978 (D.N.J. March 5, 2007).

Courts are divided as to the applicability of the CFAA to bring suit against employees who have stolen an employer's confidential information. The First and Seventh Circuits, as well as several district courts recognize a cause of action arising under the CFAA. They do so under the reasoning that an employee owes a fiduciary duty to his or her employer, and is granted access to the employer's computer systems to further the employer's business goals. When the employee accesses the computer system to harm the employer's business interests, the employee has breached his or her fiduciary duty and exceeded the scope of his or her authority. *See Int'l Airport Centers*

LLC v. Citrin, 440 F.3d 418, 420–21 (7th Cir. 2006) (employee exceeded "authorized access" when he accessed employer information for allegedly improper purpose); *EF Cultural Travel B.V. v Explorica, Inc.* 274 F.3d 577 (1st Cir. 2001); *Shurgard Storage Centers, Inc. v. Safeguard Self Storage, Inc.,* 119 F. Supp. 2d 1121, 1123, 1125–28 (W.D. Wash. 2000); *Ervin & Smith Advertising and Public Relations, Inc. v. Ervin,* 2009 WL 249998 (D. Neb. Feb. 3, 2009). *See also, Mintel Int'l. Group, Ltd. v. Neergheen,* 2008 WL 2782818 (N.D. Ill July 16, 2008) (employee's emailing to himself employer's confidential information may have exceeded authorized access).

The Ninth Circuit and a number of district courts reject this conclusion, holding that employees who are authorized to access an employer's computer system cannot be found in violation of the CFAA, as they are authorized to access the system and their intent is irrelevant under the CFAA. *LVRC Holdings, LLC. v. Brekka,* 581 F.3d 1127 (9th Cir. 2009) (employee did not violate CFAA, as he had company authorization to access information he emailed to himself); *Shamrock Foods Co. v. Gast,* 535 F. Supp.2d 962 (D. Ariz. 2008) (employee's copying of employer's confidential information to his personal email was not "unauthorized" under CFAA). *Diamond Power Int'l, Inc. v. Davidson,* 540 F. Supp.2d 1322 (N.D. Ga. 2007) (employee did not violate CFAA in forwarding former employer's confidential information to new employer because he was authorized to access hardware and specific data in question); *Condux International, Inc. v. Haugum,* 2008 WL 5244818 (D. Minn. Dec. 15, 2008) (employee's downloading of employer's confidential information in anticipation of resignation did not constitute "unauthorized access" under CFAA); *Orbit One Communications, Inc. v. Numerex Corp.,* 692 F. Supp.2d 373, 386 (S.D.N.Y. 2010) (corporate executives did not violate CFAA as they had been "granted unfettered access to . . . computer system" and data it contained); *B&B Microscopes v. Armogida,* 532 F. Supp.2d 744 (W.D. Pa. 2007) (employee did not violate CFAA when he deleted computer files because he was employed at time of access and has authorization to use laptop). *ReMedPar, Inc. v. AllParts Med., LLC,* 683 F. Supp.2d 605 (M.D. Tenn. 2010) (employee's alleged conduct did not violate CFAA, as he was authorized to access computers and thus did not exceed authorization); *Bridal Expo, Inc. v. Van Florestein,* 2009 WL 255862 (S.D. Tex Feb.3, 2009) (employees who copied employer's databases on last day of employment did not violate the CFAA, as they were authorized to access the employer's computer system).

The courts rejecting the application of the CFAA to employees have interpreted the CFAA as "generally aimed towards outside, third parties or other 'high-tech' criminals, rather than the rouge employee." *Lasco Foods, Inc. v. Hall and Shaw Sales, Marketing, and Consulting, LLC,* 600 F. Supp.2d 1045, 1049 (E.D. Mo. 2009).

See also, Modis, Inc. v. Bardelli, 531 F. Supp. 2d 314 (D. Conn. 2008) (departing employee who accessed employer's client database may have violated CFAA, as the employee's employment agreement limited use of the database to those activities in furtherance of the employer's business).

1. Contractual Protections

To avoid problems related to unauthorized systems access, the employer should insert language to following effect in any employment agreement its employees may sign:

> **Authorized Access.** I understand that the Company maintains information systems for business purposes and that my authorization to access and use the Company's business information stored on the Company's information systems is limited to such business purposes for the benefit of Company. I agree that any access to the Company's information on the Company's information systems that I undertake for my personal use or for any third-party for other than the Company's business purposes exceeds my authorization to access and use the Company's information systems. I agree I am not entitled to obtain or alter any Company information that I access, or assist others in accessing, in excess of the limited scope of my authorized access as set forth in this Agreement.[1]

Language to this effect will strengthen a case against an employee who steals his employer's valuable information. At least one company has been able to obtain a preliminary injunction for violation of the CFAA against former employees who violated their confidentiality agreements. *EF Cultural Travel B.V.v Explorica, Inc.* 274 F.3d 577 (1st Cir. 2001).

2. *Corporate Policies*

Any policies for accessing and using the employer's information and data should specifically prohibit any use other than for the employer's direct benefit. Access should be limited to a "need to know" basis and be compartmentalized to limit access to only those areas that the employee needs to know. Security protocols should be reviewed and updated regularly. Upon termination of employment, an employee's access should immediately be revoked and the employee's hard drive and email scanned for any unusual activity.

An employer should include language in its employee handbook explaining the company's expectations as to the protection of its confidential information, and state that employees have no expectation of privacy in the use of their computers. In *Bank v. Mario Industries of Virginia, Inc.*, 650 S.E.2d 687 (Va. 2007) an employer brought suit against two ex-employees who left to start a competing business. Prior to leaving, one employee wrote a memo to his attorney on the employer's computer, which included the employer's confidential information. The employer sought to introduce the memo into court and the employee objected, claiming the protection of the attorney-client privilege. The Supreme Court of Virginia found that the memo was not protected by the attorney-client privilege, as it was written on the employer's computer, and the employer's handbook clearly stated that while its employees could use work computers for personal matters there was no expectation of privacy. *See also Sims v. Lakeside School*, 2007 WL 2745367 (W.D. Wash. Sept 20, 2007) (relying on school policy, court concluded school employee did not have reasonable expectation of privacy as to emails created on school laptop).

---

1. This language was drafted by Jay Westermeier of the Finnegan, Henderson, Farabow, Garrett & Dunner, LLP law firm in Reston, Virginia.

CHAPTER **19**

Best Practices for Contract Drafting and Successful Implementation

One means of limiting contractual risk is to implement a quality assurance program to apply industry best practices to ensure an entity's contracts meets the entity's internal standards and those of a prudent party. A robust program will include creating uniform terms and conditions, eliminating ambiguity in the agreement, implementing peer review, using an authority matrix and auditing compliance after contract execution. Set forth below is a discussion of these methods and the benefits that may be achieved through their use.

A. Create Uniform Terms and Conditions

The first step in reducing contractual risk is to create a standard set of terms and conditions that can be used as a starting point for all negotiations throughout the contracting entity. Utilizing standard terms ensures that the entity's employees are starting the negotiation process with terms that are favorable to the entity and that have been approved by the entity's legal counsel. Through repeated use, the entity's employees will gain familiarity with an agreement's terms and the risks involved in accepting alternative language. Further, the entity can update its terms to reflect lessons learned from other negotiations and projects. Ideally, all employees involved in the contracting process should understand the meaning and purpose of the agreement's contractual terms. Detailed knowledge of an agreement's terms will allow the employees to better assess the risks involved.

Realistically, it is unlikely that a licensor or licensee will be able to utilize its preferred terms as the start of every negotiation. In many situations, but particularly in large transactions, the customer has greater leverage, and thus is able to require the vendor to use the customer's terms as a starting point. It is unlikely; however, that the customer will have standard terms for every contemplated transaction, as cost and time considerations will dictate the creation of standard terms only for those transactions that arise on a frequent basis, such as non-disclosure agreements.

To the extent practical, a licensor or licensee should create a matrix setting forth its acceptable, preferred and minimum positions for all material terms in an agreement. The preferred position is the position a party seeks to allow it to meet its contractual obligations with a comfortable margin of error and thus a small amount of risk. The acceptable position is the position that is acceptable to a party although the level of risk is higher than the party would like to accept. The minimum position represents the maximum level of risk a party is willing to accept before walking away from the contract. Providing a guideline as to acceptable and preferred positions allows a licensor's or licensee's negotiation team to know their limits of authority. While there will always be the tendency to accept the "minimum" position to get the deal done, a minimum position ensures that the individuals negotiating the agreement can only promote a position acceptable to the entity.

In creating a matrix, it should be clearly stated that an individual negotiating an agreement cannot accept a term less favorable then the minimum position without obtaining prior approval from a higher authority. While the licensor or licensee may ultimately accept a position less favorable than the stated minimum position, the matrix ensures that the decision to do so will be made outside of the negotiating sales team, which may have a financial incentive to assume an unacceptable amount of risk.

See Section D below for a discussion on the use of authority matrices and Form 23.I.7 for a model authority matrix.

B. Eliminate Ambiguity

Eliminating ambiguity is perhaps the most important element for reducing risk in an agreement. Both parties should strive to create a contract that is clear, concise, and easily understandable, as well as one that can be easily adjudicated by an unrelated third party, such as a judge or an arbiter. Too often, parties draft a contract based on their common understanding of the underlying transaction, which arises through many months of negotiations and meetings without providing sufficient contractual detail or clarity. Ambiguity can arise in many forms:

- The failure to clearly define terms, leading each party to ascribe their own definition to terms in question. *See e.g.*, *JA Apparel Corp. v. Abboud*, 568 F.3d 390 (2d Cir. 2009) (agreement ambiguous as term "name" could be interpreted in two different manners)
- The failure to contemplate and address potential future problems/issues
- The failure to address in detail the parties' rights upon termination. *See e.g.*, *Topps Co., Inc. v. Cadbury Stani S.A.L.C.*, 526 F.3d 63 (2d Cir. 2008) (license agreement ambiguous as licensee's rights upon termination open for interpretation)
- Vagueness in the agreement's wording
- The failure to use precise language in any change order or a statement of work
- Lack of detail in eliminating conflicting terms within the same agreement
- The failure to establish clear lines of communication
- The failure to ensure adequate levels of accountability

One means of reducing ambiguity is to include, if appropriate, diagrams or examples. Examples may be appropriate in illustrating the calculation of license fees and royalty payments. The inclusion of these aids may not eliminate a dispute but they will guide a third party adjudicating any dispute in ascertaining the parties' intent. For a more detailed discussion, see Henry W. (Hank) Jones, III, *Envisioning Visual Contracting: Why Non-Textual Tools and Content Will Improve Your Contracting*, International Association for Contract and Commercial Management (IACCM), 2 CONTRACTING EXCELLENCE 27 (No. 6 Aug. 2009) available at http://www.iaccm.com/contractingexcellence.php?storyid=949 (last viewed September 15, 2010).

Often in the event of a dispute over a contract's interpretation or the parties' intent after a contract's execution, the parties find that the contract does not clearly address the issue in question. The likelihood of a dispute is foreseeable, as the parties often enter into extended negotiations, the result of which is that each party clearly understands the desires of the other party and the deal at the time of contract signature. While each party previously understood the issues at the time of contract execution, problems can arise when the individuals involved in the negotiation are no longer involved in the transaction, and their successors lack the detailed knowledge of their predecessors. *See e.g. Upper Deck Co., LLC v. BreaKey Int'l.*, 2004 WL 2980190, at *3 (S.D.N.Y. Dec. 22, 2004) (language requiring developer to deliver source code "necessary to enable consumers to use the product . . . in the same manner as the Product is presently operated" is ambiguous).

The parties' relationship is usually strongest at the time of contract signature. After execution, the individuals involved usually transition from the negotiation team to a new group of individuals that is usually responsible for delivering the deliverables and managing the contract. Often, the new individuals lack the historical knowledge arising from the negotiation. Thus, the parties should make every effort to document all aspects of the transaction in minute detail and resist the temptation to address and document an issue after contract signature.

The question of whether a contract is ambiguous is a question of law to be resolved by a court. *Leprino Foods Co. v. Gress Poultry, Inc.*, 379 F. Supp.2d 659 (M.D. Pa. 2005). In the event of an ambiguity, most courts will look to the "four corners" of the agreement to resolve the ambiguity. Individual clauses will be subordinated to the overall intent of the parties by reading the contract as a whole. RESTATEMENT (SECOND) CONTRACTS §§ 202(2), 230, 233. Courts will look to commercial reasonableness in attempting to interpret an ambiguous contract and will examine the conflicting interpretations of the parties to ascertain which "interpretation fits both the language of the contract and the contract's commercial setting . . . ." *Sutter Insurance Company v. Applied Systems, Inc.*, 393 F.3d 722, 726 (7th Cir 2004). The intent of the parties must be ascertained from the entire agreement. *Waldman v. Shoemaker*, 80 A.2d. 776 (Pa. 1951). Greater weight will be placed on the specific terms of the agreement over general language. *County of Suffolk v. Alcorn*, 266 F.3d. 131 (2d Cir. 2001); RESTATEMENT (SECOND) CONTRACTS § 203(c)(1981). Terms will be interpreted to give "the meaning that would be ascribed to it by a reasonably intelligent person who was acquainted with all of the usages and circumstances surrounding the making of the writing." *Unihealth v. U.S. Healthcare, Inc.*, 14 F. Supp.2d 623, 633 (D.N.J. 1998).

If the court is unable to resolve the ambiguity, it will be construed against the drafter or the person who supplies the words and meaning that serves the public interest. *See Current Tech. Concepts v. Irie Enterprises*, 530 N.W.2d 539 (Minn. 1995); RESTATEMENT (SECOND) OF CONTRACTS §§ 206, 261(c). As such, the party drafting the agreement should include language to the effect that each party was involved in the drafting and negotiation of the agreement and that neither party should be deemed to be the drafter of the agreement. See §51.

For an excellent discussion of drafting ambiguity-free contracts, see ROBERT A. FELDMAN & RAYMOND T. NIMMER, DRAFTING EFFECTIVE CONTRACTS: A PRACTITIONER'S GUIDE, 4th Ed. (2009).

C. Implement Peer Review

All entities should implement a peer review process to allow for an independent review of the negotiated terms during the negotiation process. A robust Institutional Review Team ("IRT"), consisting of cross-functional employees, is crucial to providing an independent opinion on the risks inherent in a particular transaction. IRTs should be involved early on in the process. If the IRT is engaged only at the end of the process, the parties' negotiation may be too developed to allow a change in position or the identified problem may be unable to be fixed without alienating the other party or causing the other party to walk away from the transaction.

The delivery of a successful project requires the involvement of many functions, each of which has its own perspective. It is important that IRTs contain a broad cross-section of functions to ensure a well rounded review. All functions that will be involved in the delivery process should be included. To ensure an unbiased review, the IRT members should be independent of the negotiation team. For example, IRT members should not have a reporting relationship to members of the negotiating team, members of the sales team or those with a financial incentive to close the transaction. At a minimum, legal, contracts, finance, delivery assurance, project management and technology should be included to ensure the transaction receives a thorough vetting. As an independent group, unrelated to the negotiation process, IRTs also limit "second guessing."

D. Use an Authority Matrix

All entities should create an authority matrix to ensure any agreement receives the appropriate level of scrutiny prior to execution. A prudent entity will require the agreement to be approved by all functions involved with the delivery or acceptance of the deliverables to ensure all aspects of the agreement meet the entity's requirements. The level of approvals will usually depend on the dollar value of the contract and the risk involved. From the licensor's perspective, risk is usually an element of cost, functionality and the time in which the deliverables must be provided. As such, at a minimum, representatives from the following areas should be required to review and/or approve the agreement: finance, project management/information technology, delivery assurance/quality assurance and the business sponsor.

Ideally, depending on the size of the deal and the size of the company, the division president or the division CFO should be the only party who can execute an agreement. It is important that there should be clear guidance as to who is authorized to sign an agreement. Requiring a senior officer to sign the agreement will increase accountability by having the senior person accept responsibility for the terms of the agreement. Too often when a problem arises, managers are quick to point the finger at others. Having a senior person execute the agreement will likely cause that person to implement quality measures and have the authority to enforce them.

Finally, many companies have issues with document control and often cannot locate a contract after it has been executed. If signature authority is vested in only a small number of people, it is much easier to track the executed contracts after contract signature. Creating a central repository to which all executed agreements must be sent will help eliminate document control issues.

See Form 23.I.7 for a Model Authority Matrix.

E. Audit Compliance After Contract Execution

After the contract has been executed, both parties should audit the delivery team's compliance with its internal standards on a regular basis. For example, the licensor's finance department should undertake regular audits to ensure statements of work, project plans, change orders and/or other contractually required documentation necessary to authorize and get paid for work have been executed for all work being performed by the licensor and that the customer is billed in accordance with the contract's milestones. Large unbilled or unpaid receivables are often a sign of problems. In such an event, the finance team should question the project management team to understand why the customer has not been billed for or paid such receivables. Further, the auditors should confirm the licensor's delivery team is utilizing the contract's change order process to capture any changes in scope.

During the audit process, the auditors should examine the following questions:

- Have all contractual documents (License Agreement, Statements of Work, Program Definitions, Change Orders, etc.) been signed by both parties?
- Have all contractual agreements been scanned and/or filed in the appropriate locations (e.g., central repository)?
- Is the licensor performing work without a signed statement of work, a signed change order or other contractually authorizing document?
- Have any deliverables been rejected due to quality or content issues?
- Has there been a change in the licensor's or customer's sponsorship or licensor/customer's senior executives?
- Has a project review been conducted within the past 90 days, and has it been reviewed with senior management?
- Has the project team received any negative indications (verbal, email, letter, etc.) from the customer?
- Are all invoices being paid consistent with all payment terms?

- Have any project milestones or other time-sensitive items been missed, or are any forecasted to miss, the contractual delivery dates?
- Has the project exceeded, or is it forecasted to exceed, time schedule estimates by more than 5 percent?
- Has the project exceeded, or is it forecasted to exceed, the budget/cost estimates by more than 5 percent?

Regular technical reviews should be scheduled to track the delivery team's progress against the deliverable time line. The licensor wants to avoid any deviation that will create significant risk and additional cost. Similarly, the licensee wants to avoid waiting until the delivery date to learn that there is a delivery problem. As such, the licensee should monitor the licensor's progress to ensure the licensor is meeting the time line to provide the deliverables within the contractual required time. Further, the licensor should be obligated to promptly inform the licensee if the licensor knows or suspects that the project is behind schedule or that the deliverables will be late (§ 9.6.4).

F. Create an Early Warning System

The licensor should create an "early warning system" to monitor its progress in completing the deliverables within the parameters of the contract. The intent of an early warning system is to identify problems before it is too late to fix them. The licensor should establish a process to identify contracts with the following traits:

- Significant costs in excess of revenues during the initial phases
- Significant proposed cost deferrals
- Large billed and unbilled receivables
- Pricing modifications
- Proposed capitalization of software development costs
- On-going losses
- Legal disputes/settlements
- Write-offs
- The licensing of software/provision of services in overseas locations
- Corporate reports, such as delivery assurance, internal audit or Sarbanes Oxley, that identify material deficiencies
- Potential regulatory changes that may impact the cost of delivery
- Change in management impacting relationship

A cross-functional team of legal, finance, delivery assurance and business representatives should meet on a monthly basis to review and resolve any potential issues that have been identified by the early warning system. Each issue should be coded red, yellow, or green to indicate the severity of the issue and allow the members of the team to easily track the progress of the issue from month to month. The team should be careful not to include any attorney-client privileged information within the matrix to avoid potentially waiving any claim of privilege. See Form 23.H.9 for a model Early Warning Report.

CHAPTER 20

Recommended Resource Materials

JIM E. BULLOCK, THE IP LICENSING LAWYER'S JOB: A SURVIVAL GUIDE (2008).

LORIN BRENNAN, HOLLY K. TOWLE, & JOEL ROTHSTEIN WOLFSON, THE COMPLETE UCITA (2004).

MICHAEL A. EPSTEIN & FRANK L. POLITANO, DRAFTING LICENSE AGREEMENTS, 4th ed. (2010).

ROBERT A. FELDMAN & RAYMOND T. NIMMER, DRAFTING EFFECTIVE CONTRACTS: A PRACTITIONER'S GUIDE, 2nd ed. (2009).

MELVIN F. JAGER, TRADE SECRET LAW (2010).

KURTIS A. KEMPER, COMPUTER AND INFORMATION LAW DIGEST, 2nd ed. (2010).

L.J. KUTTEN, COMPUTER SOFTWARE: PROTECTION/LIABILITY/LAW/FORMS (2010).

GENE LANDY, THE IT/DIGITAL LEGAL COMPANION (2008).

RAYMOND T. NIMMER, THE LAW OF COMPUTER TECHNOLOGY, 4th ed. (2010).

RAYMOND T. NIMMER & HOLLY K. TOWLE, THE LAW OF ELECTRONIC COMMERCIAL TRANSACTIONS (2010).

RAYMOND T. NIMMER & JEFF C. DODD, MODERN LICENSING LAW, 4th ed. (2009).

PETER C. QUITTMEYER, CLARENCE H. RIDLEY, & JOHN MATUSZESKI, COMPUTER SOFTWARE AGREEMENTS, 3rd ed. (2010).

MICHAEL D. SCOTT, SCOTT ON COMPUTER LAW, 3rd ed. (2010).

VIRGINIA V. SHUE & JAMES VERGARI, STATE COMPUTER LAW: COMMENTARY, CASES AND STATUTES (2010).

THOMSON*WEST EDITORIAL STAFF, CORPORATE COUNSEL'S GUIDE TO SOFTWARE TRANSACTIONS (2010).

TINA L. STARK, NEGOTIATING AND DRAFTING CONTRACT BOILERPLATE (2003).

Useful newsletters include THE COMPUTER & INTERNET LAWYER published by Wolters-Kluwer Law & Business, phone: (800) 638-8437; THE ITECH LAW BULLETIN, phone: (781) 876-8877; and INTELLECTUAL PROPERTY COUNSELOR published by Thomson*West, phone: (800) 328-4880.

CHAPTER **21**

Technology Acronyms

AAA	American Arbitration Association
ADR	Alternative Dispute Resolution
AFFECT	Americans for Fair Electronic Commerce Transactions
AICPA	American Institute of Certified Public Accountants
ALI	American Law Institute
API	Application Programming Interface
ARC	Additional Resource Charge
ASP	Application Service Provider or Alternative Service Provider
AUP	Acceptable Use Policy
BPO	Business Process Outsourcing
BSA	Business Software Alliance
BSI	Bureau of Industry and Security
BXA	Bureau of Export Control
CAD/CAM	Computer Aided Design/Computer Aided Manufacturing
CCL	Commerce Control List
CFAA	Computer Fraud and Abuse Act
CGI	Common Gateway Interface
CISG	United Nations Convention on Contracts for the International Sale of Goods
CMMI	Capability Maturity Model Integration
CO	Central Office
COE	Consistent or Common Operating Environment
COLA	Cost of Living Adjustment
COPA	Child Online Protection Act
COTS	Commercial off the Shelf (as it relates to software)
CPI	Consumer Price Index
CPU	Central Processing Unit
CRM	Customer Relationship Management (software)
Db	Database
DBA	Database Administrator
DBMS	Database Management System
DFAR	Defense Federal Acquisition Regulations
DMCA	Digital Millennium Copyright Act
DMS	Desktop Managed Services

DSL	Digital Subscriber Line
EAR	Export Administration Regulations
ECCN	Export Control Classification Number
ECI	Employment Cost Index
EDI	Electronic Data Interchange
EMEA	Europe, Middle East and Africa
ERP	Enterprise Resource Planning (software or systems)
ETL	Extraction, Transformation and Loading
EULA	End User License Agreement
FAR	Federal Acquisition Regulations
FCPA	Foreign Corrupt Practices Act
FFP	Firm Fixed Price
FTC	Federal Trade Commission
FTE	Full Time Equivalent
FTP	File Transfer Protocol
4GL	Fourth Generation (computer) Language
GAAP	Generally Accepted Accounting Principles
Gb	Gigabyte
GLB	Gramm-Leach-Bliley Act
GUI	Graphical User Interface
HIPAA	Health Insurance Portability and Accountability Act
HITECH	The Health Information Technology for Economic and Clinical Health Act
HTML	Hyper Text Markup Language
HTTP	Hyper Text Transfer Protocol
ISO	Independent Sales Organizations or Independent Service Organizations
ISP	Internet Service Provider
ISV	Independent Service Vendor
IT	Information Technology
IP	Intellectual Property
ISDN	Integrated Services Digital Network
LAN	Local Area Network
LOI	Letter of Intent
LAWN	Local Area Wireless Network
Mb	Megabyte
MDE	Managed Desktop Environment
MHS	Managed Hosting Services
MIP	Million Instructions per Second
MOE	Managed Operating Environment,
MSA	Master Services Agreement
MTTR	Mean Time to Report
NLR	No License Required
NTE	Not to Exceed
OEM	Original Equipment Manufacturer

OCR	Optical Character Recognition
OEM	Original Equipment Manufacturer
OS	Open Source
OS	Operating System
OSI	Open Source Initiative
QOS	Quality of Service
RAS	Route Access System
RFI	Request for Information
RFP	Request for Proposal
RRC	Reduced Resource Credit/Charge
RTU	Right to Use
SaaS	Software-as-a-Service
SDE	Standard Desktop Environment
SDLC	Systems Development Life Cycle
SIIA	Software and Information Industry Association
SL	Service Level
SLA	Service Level Agreement
SLB	Service Level Bonus
SLC	Service Level Credit
SOE	Server Operating Environment or Standard Operating Environment
SOP	Statement of Position
SOW	Statement of Work
SOX	Sarbanes-Oxley Act
SQL	Structured Query Language
3GL	Third Generation (computer) Language
T&M	Time and Materials
TCV	Total Contract Value
TSR	Technology and Software under Restriction
TSS	Technical Support Services
TSSG	Technical Support Guidelines
TSU	Technology and Software–Unrestricted
UCC	Uniform Commercial Code
UCITA	Uniform Computer Information Transactions Act
UETA	Uniform Electronic Transactions Act
UTSA	Uniform Trade Secret Act
VAR	Value Added Reseller
VPN	Virtual Private Network
WAN	Wide Area Network
WSDL	Web Services Description Language
XML	eXtensible Markup Language
XSD	XML Schema Definition

CHAPTER 22

Glossary

Acceptance Testing—formal testing to determine whether a system works according to specifications and should be accepted.

Actual Business Run Test—use of the software in the licensee's business environment during a test period in which the software vendor corrects all identified errors.

Additional Resource Charge (ARC)—the charge for an additional resource that is above and beyond the fee associated with the services baseline. Usually used in conjunction with an outsourcing contract. Resources are typically measured in units of full time equivalents (FTE).

Alpha Testing—internal testing conducted by a software developer; the first of two pre-release phases.

Application Service Provider (ASP)—a service provider who provides shared access to proprietary software through a hosted environment.

Applications Software or **Applications**—a software program, or in the case of outsourcing those programs and programming—including the supporting documentation, media, online help facilities, and tutorials—that perform, in the conduct of the services, specific user-related data processing and telecommunications tasks.

Baseline—a specific quantity of resources for a resource category included within an annual base charge when pricing an outsourcing agreement.

Benchmark(ing)—the process of comparing the vendor's service levels, results, and pricing against a pre-agreed industry standard.

Best Efforts—a standard of performance that is typically thought to be the highest and hardest to satisfy. Best efforts are generally interpreted to require more effort than merely reasonable efforts or good faith efforts. Effort-based clauses can be useful in dealing with situations where a party is uncertain as to their ability to meet a specific objective.

Best Practices—the process of identifying the practices, processes, and standards that are utilized in a particular industry (i.e., the information technology industry) and considered to be the gold standard of the industry. The vendor is subsequently obligated to adopt such practices in delivering its services/products.

Beta Testing—testing conducted by select users of the software under normal operating conditions; the second phase of pre-release testing.

Business Process Outsourcing (BPO)—the transfer of discrete business functions, such as billing, claims processing, etc., to an external vendor.

Call Center—an organization that provides customer support usually over the phone, although their support services may be provided over the Internet.

Central Processing Unit (CPU)—the principal processing unit of a computer that processes the computer application in question. Many license agreements will limit the number of CPUs that can be used to access a particular computer program at one time. Some license agreements may be CPU specific.

Change Control Procedure—the procedure that the parties follow to implement a change order.

Change Order—a change to a party's contractual obligations, such as deliverable, time of delivery, or price, that may be requested by either the vendor or customer.

Cloud Computing—allows a user to access an application, data storage and processing power from any computer with a web browser, eliminating the need to provide applications and the attendant hardware. Data is accessed and transferred over the internet instead of through a fixed transmission line.

Customer Relationship Management (CRM) Software—the generic name for proprietary software that can manage an entity's relationship with its customer, such as billing, shipping, payments, etc.

Database (Db)—a collection of records that are organized in such a manner as to be easily searchable, sortable, and updatable. There are many commercially available database products. There are many different types of databases, but relational databases are the most commonly used. Relational databases use a specific set of instructions referred to as Structured Query Language (SQL).

Derivative Work—"a work based upon one or more preexisting works, such as a translation, musical arrangement, dramatization, fictionalization, motion picture version, sound recording, art reproduction, abridgment, condensation, or any other form in which a work may be recast, transformed, or adapted. A work consisting of editorial revisions, annotations, elaborations, or other modifications which, as a whole, represent an original work of authorship, is a 'derivative work.'" 17 U.S.C. § 101. Some derivative works may include relatively minor derivations from the original work on which the derivative work is based, while other derivative works may include substantial derivations from the original work.

Disabling Device—a piece of computer code that disables a user's ability to use a software application. Often inserted by a vendor to allow the vendor to prevent the end user from using the software after the license has expired. It may also refer to a virus, spider, worm, etc., that disables the software. Disabling code is often referred to as malicious code.

Disaster Recovery—the process by which an entity's data systems are returned to operating order in the event of a disruption.

Disentanglement Services—the provision of services by the vendor to provide customer assistance and services in the event of termination of the applicable agreement and to facilitate the orderly transition and migration of the services. May require the vendor to continue to provide services until all of the customer's data files have been completely converted and transferred to the customer's alternative system provider. The vendor usually provides for the prompt and orderly conversion of all the customer's data files on the vendor system and the conclusion of all work—as the customer may reasonably direct—including completion or partial completion of some projects, documentation of work in process, and other measures to ensure an orderly transition to the customer. The work is usually performed by the vendor at no additional cost to the customer beyond what the customer would pay for the services absent the performance of the disentanglement services. For services provided after the expiration date of the contract, the vendor may charge the customer a premium to the amounts normally charged.

Dual Core Processor(s)—two independent computer processors on a single computer chip enhancing the computer's performance.

End User—the user of the vendor's services or the application software, such as an employee, agent, and authorized third party of the customer, as well as other users of similar services.

End User License Agreement (EULA)—a contract between an end user and the manufacturer or distributor of an application software product. End user license agreements can be executed in a variety of nontraditional ways, such as communicating acceptance to the agreement by clicking on an "I Accept" button on a computer screen.

Enhancements—any new software releases, versions, improvements, modifications, upgrades, updates, fixes, and additions to the software that the applicable vendor markets or makes available to its customers who are eligible to receive maintenance support services. Enhancements usually include any re-platformed software, whether on different operating systems or equipment, except, however, that enhancements do not include new, separate product offerings.

Enterprise Resource Planning (ERP) Software—the generic name for proprietary software that can manage an entity's infrastructure needs, such as its accounting system, payroll, sales pipelines, purchasing, human resources, and inventory management.

eXtensible Markup Language—a simplified version of SGML that is used to facilitate the exchange of documents on the World Wide Web. XML allows for the marking of a document according to content rather than by format.

Firmware—software embedded on a computer chip or hard disc, often referring to the computerized element in consumer electronics and other programs.

Flat Files—a file for which there is no embedded structure used to manage information and govern relationships between records. A flat file database uses a single table, in contrast to a relational database that utilizes different tables with different columns and data relationships.

Freeware—software that is licensed to the licensee for free. Although the license agreement for freeware does not involve the payment of a fee, the license agreement will often include limitations and restrictions similar to those found in fee-based licensing arrangements.

Functional Specifications—the specifications to which the developed/licensed software must contractually conform.

Functionality—the capabilities of a program.

Gigabyte (Gb)—a measurement of digital data. A gigabyte equates to 1,000 megabytes.

Good Faith—honest intentions without any intent to defraud. In Section 1-201 of the Uniform Commercial Code (UCC) good faith is defined generally as "honesty in fact in the conduct or transaction concerned."

Gramm-Leach-Bliley Act (15 U.S.C. §§ 6801-6810)—regulates the sharing of personal information about individuals who obtain financial products or services from financial institutions. It attempts to inform individuals about the privacy policies and practices of financial institutions so that consumers can make choices about financial institutions with which they wish to do business. The law gives consumers limited control, via opt out provisions, over how financial institutions use and share the consumers' personal information.

Graphical User Interface (GUI)—a visual computer environment that uses visual representations and tools, such as menus, icons, and buttons, to represent programs, files, and options.

Help Desk—a vendor-maintained technical support usually offered over the phone and Internet.

Hosting (a.k.a Managed Hosting Services)—See ***Managed Hosting Services***.

Hyper Text Transfer Protocol (HTTP)—the communications protocol used on the World Wide Web to carry requests from a web browser to a web server, and to transport pages from web servers back to the requesting browser.

Integrated Databases—facilitating the ability of multiple databases to exchange information with each other. The phrase is typically used in the context of integrating non-relational databases with relational databases.

Interfaces—software that allows two, third party software applications to "interface" or communicate with each other (i.e., an Oracle Database and another third party proprietary application).

Local Network System—multiple, interactive user terminals connected to a single-processing or multi-processing, micro-computing unit that is owned, leased, or operated by the customer.

Maintenance—the continued support provided by a software licensor after it has delivered its product. Maintenance may or may not include enhancements, a help desk, and new editions of the software.

Managed Hosting Services (MHS)—a service in which software applications that would otherwise be hosted on the servers of a particular organization are instead hosted by a third party provider, such as a vendor of IT outsourcing services.

Megabyte (Mb)—a measurement of digital data. A megabyte equates to 1,048,576 bytes.

Methodology—refers to a party's proprietary methodology that is used in implementing the deliverables.

Milestone—a scheduled event, accomplishment, or achievement (including delivery of a deliverable) as specified in a contract.

Multi-Core Processor(s)—multiple independent computer processors on a single computer chip enhancing the computer's performance. For example, a quad core processor has four independent computer processors on a single computer chip.

Network Configuration—the hardware and software arrangements that define a computer or telecommunications system, such as LAN and WAN, and thus determine what the system will do and how effectively and efficiently it functions.

Object Code—the machine-readable version of the source code after it has been compiled.

Open Source (Software)—a framework for licensing software in which the source code is made free to interested users and developers, even though they were not involved in creating the original product and do not have a relationship with the originator of the software. An open source license is typically embedded within the source code. The underlying exchange in many open source licenses is that the licensee is given free access to software, in exchange for the licensee agreeing not to charge a license fee to a third party sub-licensee for any software applications made by the licensee using the open source code components. Many open source licenses are referred to as copyleft licenses because they utilize copyright laws to prevent open source licenses from charging a license fee to third parties.

Operating System (OS)—the underlying computer software on which a computer's operation is founded, such as Windows 98® and Windows NT®.

Original Equipment Manufacturer (OEM)—with respect to computers and software, this term is used interchangeably with VAR and ISO. An OEM generally purchases computers and customizes them with software applications for end users.

Parallel Run Testing—running a process concurrently using the old and new software, and then comparing the results.

Performance Standards—the quantitative and qualitative performance standards and commitments for the vendor's services, including the service levels, which are usually contained in the applicable agreement.

Prime Rate—a particular rate of interest charged by a particular bank from time to time.

Reduced Resource Credit/Charge (RRC)—a credit to be provided by a vendor to a customer in the event a customer uses fewer resources than the vendor is contractually obligated to provide. Usually used in conjunction with a contract for outsourced services.

Residuals—the vendor's general knowledge, skills, and experience, and any ideas, concepts, know-how, methodologies, and techniques that are not protected or susceptible of protection under U.S. patent or copyright laws, but that are used by the vendor within the scope of the vendor's business practice and may be used by it in the course of providing the services. Residuals usually do not include any work product, customer data, or customer confidential information.

Response Time—the time it takes for a computer to process a particular transaction once the "Enter" button is pressed.

Reverse Engineering—with respect to software, the process of recreating, extracting, decompiling, or otherwise determining the source code of a software program from the object code or machine code form.

Right to Use—a license grant that allows the end user the right to use the software.

Root Cause Analysis—the formal process used by a vendor to diagnose the underlying cause of problems at the lowest reasonable level so that corrective action can be taken to eliminate repeat failures.

Sample Data Test—testing conducted by running typical and atypical functions on a sampling of user data.

SAS 70—an auditing standard created by the American Institute for Certified Public Accountants in response to the requirements of the Sarbanes-Oxley Act. See Chapter 5.E and Chapter 23, Form 23.B.1 § 9.13 for a more detailed description of SAS 70.

Seat License—a means of calculating the license fee charged to a licensee based on the number of users accessing the application, i.e., on a per seat basis. The fee may be calculated based on the number of concurrent users or on the aggregate number users with access to the system; i.e., each individual would be required to purchase a license even though they are all not accessing the application at the same time.

Server or **Servers**—a computer connected to a local- or wide-area network serving one or more desktop devices or peripherals, including application servers, domain servers, file servers, print servers, fax servers, and data servers.

Service Bureau—another name for hosting.

Service Level—contractual technical standard that a service provider must meet in the provision of its technical services. For example, the time in which a vendor must answer a call to a help desk or the time in which a computer must process a particular transaction once the "Enter" button is pressed.

Service Level Agreement (SLA)—an agreement setting forth the standards to which the vendor's services must comply.

Service Level Credit (SLC)—a credit that may be granted to a customer in the event the vendor does not meet a contractual obligation to provide its services at a certain level. Usually used in conjunction with an outsourcing contract.

Shareware—software provided on a trial basis without charge. If the customer decides to use such software on a continuing basis, the customer would then pay for a license.

Source Code—computer software in the form of electronic and printed human-readable, mnemonic or English-like program listings. Printed and online descriptions of the design of such software including data definition models, indices, structure tables, system flow charts, program flow charts, defined terms, file layouts, program narratives, global documentation (including global variables), and program listings.

Specifications—in software development, a written statement or outline for the development of software, indicating the functions or tasks that the software should accomplish and/or the hardware, programming techniques, or algorithms that must be used.

Statement of Work (SOW)—a detailed explanation of the work to be performed by the vendor and the standards it must meet for acceptance, as well as any related contractual obligations of the vendor and customer.

System Integrator—a vendor responsible for integrating a customer's hardware, software, and network into an integrated working system.

Terabyte—a measurement of digital data. A terabyte equates to 1,000 gigabytes.

Termination/Expiration Assistance—assistance provided by a vendor when a customer is transitioning from one vendor to another or as the contract is terminated.

Third Party Software—applications software and systems software used by a systems integrator to provide the services under license to the customer or vendor by a third party. They often include ongoing services (e.g., maintenance and support services, upgrades, subscription services) provided by third parties (e.g., vendor, manufacturer, lessor) in the same license covering such software.

Tools—reusable code components used by software developers to develop software applications and customizations to software applications.

Transition Plan—a plan between a service provider and customer to transition the customer to or from the service provider's products or services.

Turn-key System—a complete hardware and software system, preassembled and preconfigured for the user, so that the user does not need to program or configure the system in order to use it.

Updates—a compendium of "fixes" that the licensor releases to the users of the software.

Upgrades—a new release or version of the software constituting a compendium of enhancements.

Value Added Reseller (VAR)—a reseller of a third party's products after having improved them. For example, a software vendor may resell third party hardware after having installed its proprietary software on the hardware. The VAR usually buys the third party products at a discount and marks them up. See, e.g., Chapter 23.F.2 § 7.4.

Virus—a program code, programming instruction, or set of instructions intentionally constructed with the ability to damage, interfere with, or otherwise adversely affect computer programs, data files, or operations.

Web Services Description Language (WSDL)—an XML format for describing network services as a set of endpoints operating on messages containing either document-oriented or procedure-oriented information. The operations and messages are described abstractly, and then bound to a concrete network protocol and message format to define an endpoint. Related concrete endpoints are combined into abstract endpoints (services). WSDL is extensible to allow description of endpoints and their messages regardless of what message formats or network protocols are used to communicate. However, the only bindings described in this document describe how to use WSDL in conjunction with SOAP, HTTP GET/POST, and MIME.

XML Schema Definition (XSD)—specifies how to formally describe the elements in an Extensible Markup Language (XML) document. This description can be used to verify that each item of content in a document adheres to the description of the element in which the content is to be placed.

Software License and Services Agreement (Annotated)

The model license that follows is not intended to be used verbatim. Instead, it is intended to be used as a guide to potential clauses that may be included in an agreement while providing an explanation of the ramifications of including such clauses.

CONTENTS

APPENDICES AND EXHIBITS REFERENCED IN SOFTWARE LICENSE

Appendix 3.1	Central Processing Units
Appendix 3.B	Service Level Standards and Credits
Appendix 3.C	On-site Inspection Certificate
Appendix 5.3.6	Source Code License Terms
Appendix 8	Model Pricing Schedule for Time and Materials Contracts
Appendix 8.C	CPU License Fees
Appendix 9.2	Key Personnel
Appendix 9.2.3	Information Technology Support and Maintenance Services
Appendix 9.6.1	Expense Guidelines
Appendix 9.6.4	Performance Reports
Appendix 9.9	Project Terms and Conditions
Appendix 11.2	Installation Services
Appendix 11.3	Hardware and Support Services
Appendix 16.Q	Quality Standards
Appendix 35	Disaster Recovery
Exhibit 7.1	Certificate of Acceptance
Exhibit 8.H	Form of Parent Guarantee
Exhibit 9.15	Confidentiality and Nondisclosure Agreement
Exhibit 16.C	Standards of Conduct
Exhibit 34	Form of Performance Bond and Payment Bond
Exhibit 43	Letter of Assurance

APPENDIX A	Customer Affiliates
APPENDIX B	Price Schedule

Software License and Services Agreement

THIS SOFTWARE LICENSE AND SERVICES AGREEMENT is made this ______ day of ______, 20___ by and between ________________________, a ________________ corporation with its principal address at __________________ (hereinafter "Licensor") and ___________, a __________ corporation with offices located at ________________ (hereinafter "Customer").

- ***Who are the appropriate contracting entities?***
- ***Who is the Customer? Is the Customer financially stable and able to pay Licensor, or is a parent guarantee needed? (See Section 8.H, the signature line and Chapter 17.G.4)***
- ***Is a parent guarantee or performance bond needed to ensure the Licensor's performance? (See Sections 8.H and 34)***
- ***Consider the Licensor's and Customer's addresses as they may have income tax implications for the Licensor, sales tax implications for the Customer, and impact any dispute over venue and governing law.***

BACKGROUND

Licensor has developed and owns certain proprietary software for use in the __________ industry. Customer desires to obtain a license to use such software and have Licensor develop certain modifications and enhancements for such software. Licensor desires to license such software to Customer and perform the services on the terms and conditions set forth herein.

- ***Think carefully about the wording contained in any recital, as the laws of some states such as Michigan treat recitals involving a statement of fact as conclusive evidence of the facts stated.* See, Detroit Grand Park Corp. v. Turner, 25 N.W.2d 184 (Mich. 1946).**
- ***Avoid incorporating by reference the Customer's RFP or the Licensor's RFP response as this may create an internal conflict with the terms of the Agreement and the functional specifications contained in the Agreement.***

IN CONSIDERATION of the foregoing and the mutual covenants set forth herein, and intending to be legally bound, the parties agree as follows:

Alternatively:

NOW, THEREFORE, in consideration of the foregoing Recitals, **which shall be deemed to be a substantive part of this Agreement**, and the mutual covenants, agreements, representations, and warranties hereinafter set forth, the parties hereto do hereby agree, as follows:

- ***Licensors should be hesitant to accept language acknowledging the recitals to be a substantive part of the agreement. From the customer's perspective if the licensor is willing to acknowledge the facts of the recitals, it should be willing to stand behind such statements. The risk to the licensor is that the recitals are now part of the agreement even in those states that have not adopted the position of Michigan.***

1. Definitions

Whenever used in this Agreement, any Schedules, Exhibits, or Addenda to this Agreement, or the Source Code Escrow Agreement, the following terms shall have the meaning ascribed to them below. Other capitalized terms used in this Agreement are defined in the context in which they are used and shall have the meanings ascribed therein. The terms defined in this Schedule include the plural as well as the singular.

- ***See Chapter 23.K.1 for additional and/or alternative definitions that may be more applicable for your transaction.***

1.1 **Acceptance** for the System shall occur only when: (a) Licensor has provided to Customer all Deliverables required to be provided to Customer; and (b) (i) Customer notifies Licensor in writing that all testing for the System has been completed successfully in accordance with the terms of this Article, or (ii) Licensor provides to the applicable Customer Project Manager a written notice of completion stating that all Critical Defects and Medium Defects have been corrected. Nothing else, including Customer's use of the System, or any portion thereof, in a live, operational environment, shall constitute Acceptance (under contract law or the Uniform Commercial Code of [STATE]) of any portion of the applicable system.

1.2 **Affiliate(s)** or **Affiliate Company** shall mean those companies that are initially listed on Appendix 1.2 attached hereto, which may be amended from time to time with the prior written consent of an authorized executive officer of Licensor.

- ***Think about who is going to be able to use the Software and how the usage by those entities may affect Licensor's revenues and pricing. The Customer may want to provide software to all of its "Affiliates" including those overseas. The licensor will often want to restrict the license to the Customer alone or to the Customer's then existing "Affiliates" who are listed on an attached Appendix. By listing the Affiliates, the Licensor is able to limit the license to a finite number of entities avoiding any potential misunderstanding as to who is included. The Customer may not add an entity to the list of Affiliates without Licensor's***

permission. The breadth of this definition is often an element of price. In addition to pricing concerns, the Licensor may want to limit use of the software to ensure compliance with U.S. export laws.

1.2.A **Affiliate** shall mean, as to a Party, any other Person that directly or indirectly controls or is controlled by such Party. The term "control" (including, with correlative meanings, the terms "controlled by" and "under common control with") as applied to any Person means the possession, direct or indirect, of the power to direct or cause the direction of the management and policies of such Person, whether through the ownership of voting securities or other ownership interest. For the purposes of this definition, "Person" means any individual, partnership, corporation, limited liability company, unincorporated organization or association, any trust, or any other business entity.

- ***The definition of "Affiliate" set forth in Section 1.2.A offers greater flexibility to reflect the ever changing nature of a large corporation's relationship with its affiliates. The definition of "Affiliate" is not fixed as of a particular time allowing additional users without modifying the license agreement. This definition more closely tracks the definition of affiliates used under the securities laws and from a Securities and Exchange Commission perspective.***

1.3 **"Consolidated Net Worth"** means, at any time, (a) the total assets of the Customer [and its Affiliates] that would be shown as assets on a consolidated balance sheet of the Customer [and its Affiliates] as of such time prepared in accordance with GAAP, after eliminating all amounts properly attributable to minority interests, if any, in the stock and surplus of Affiliates, minus (b) the total liabilities of the Customer and its Affiliates that would be shown as liabilities on a consolidated balance sheet of the Customer and its Affiliates as of such time prepared in accordance with GAAP.

1.4 **Critical Error(s)** shall mean a failure of the Software that severely impacts Customer's ability to provide service or has a significant financial impact on Customer for which an alternative temporary solution or work around [acceptable to Customer] may not be accomplished.

- ***This definition favors the Customer as it includes not only those errors that impact Customer's ability to provide services but also any that have a "financial impact" on the Customer.***

1.5 **Custom Software** means those Deliverables that are classified in Appendix 1.5 hereto as Custom Software, as well as the documentation related thereto; an exhaustive list of Custom Software is set forth in Appendix 1.5 hereto.

1.6 **Deliverable** means the Hardware, Software, and Documentation to be delivered hereunder; an exhaustive list of all Deliverables is set forth in Appendix 1.6 hereto.

1.7 **Direct Damages** means the damages incurred by the claiming Party to this Agreement directly resulting from a breach of this Agreement by another party to this Agreement and specifically excludes: (a) loss of interest, profit, or revenue; failure to achieve cost savings or business interruption and (b) any incidental, consequential, punitive, multiple, or indirect damages of any kind or nature. Direct Damages include by way of example but without limitation, (i) the costs incurred by Customer to obtain software or services that are the same as or substantially similar to (but not broader in scope than) the Software or Services being replaced, that is, the charges to be paid to another services provider(s) to the extent such costs are commercially reasonable and exceed the Fixed Charges hereunder for such Software or Services; (ii) the costs to correct any deficiencies in the Software or Services rendered that result in a failure of the Deliverables to meet Service Levels or the specifications set forth in the applicable Statement of Work, after Licensor has failed or refused to correct such deficiencies; (iii) the costs incurred to transition the Software or Services to another provider(s) of services; (iv) any payments, fines, penalties, or interest imposed by a governmental body or regulatory agency for failure to comply with requirements or deadlines; and (v) the reasonable out-of-pocket costs and fees incurred by Licensor to collect from Customer any fees payable to Licensor under the Agreement.

- ***Alternatively the parties may want to include a section similar to Sections 17.3 and 17.4.***

1.8 **Divested Business** means any business unit, as determined by Licensee, that Licensee sells or of which it otherwise transfers the assets or ownership. The term "Divested Business" shall mean such business unit or the acquirer thereof, as applicable.

1.9 **Documentation** means collectively: (a) all of the written, printed, electronic, or other format materials published or otherwise made available by Licensor that relate to the functional, operational, and/or performance capabilities of the ABC System and/or any Software; (b) all user, operator, system administration, technical, support, and other manuals and all other written, printed, electronic, or other format materials published or otherwise made available by Licensor that describe the functional, operational, and/or performance capabilities of the ABC System and/or any Software including but not limited to the Functional Specifications and Software Acceptance Plan; and (c) any other Deliverable that is not Hardware or Software. Documentation shall not include Source Code.

1.10 **Error(s)** shall mean a failure of the Software to substantially conform to the Documentation or the Functional Specifications, which materially impacts the Software's operational performance or functional performance.

- ***The definition of "Error" is written to recognize that software by its nature is imperfect. The Customer, however, may want a tighter definition to ensure the software's performance meets the Customer's needs.***

1.11 **Functional Specifications** shall mean those specifications to which the Software shall conform as set forth Appendix 1.11.

- ***The Functional Specifications should be set out in detail prior to execution of the Agreement to avoid later disagreements. Agreement in advance may not be feasible depending on the nature of the development undertaken by Licensor. Without agreeing upon the Functional Specifications, the Licensor cannot give***

the Customer a fixed price for any software development. At the same time, it is unwise for either party to agree to a fixed price with the intent on negotiating the Functional Specifications later.

1.12 **Hardware** means those Deliverables that are classified in Appendix 1.5 hereto as Hardware, as well as the documentation furnished therewith in the normal course of business; an exhaustive list of Hardware is set forth in Appendix 1.12 hereto.

1.13 **License(s)** shall mean any personal, nonexclusive, nontransferable, non-assignable license or licenses for Customer's internal use only granted by Licensor to Customer to use the Software under this Agreement.

1.14 **Object Code** shall mean the binary machine-readable version of the Software.

1.15 **"Open Source Materials"** shall mean any software, library, utility, tool, or other computer or program code (collectively, **"Code"**) that is licensed or distributed as "free software," "freeware," "open source software," or under any terms or conditions that impose any requirement that the Code or any software using, linked with, incorporating, distributed with, based on, derived from or accessing the Code: (i) be made available or distributed in source code form; (ii) be licensed for the purpose of making derivative works; (iii) be licensed under terms that allow reverse engineering, reverse assembly or disassembly of any kind; or (iv) be redistributable at no charge. Open Source Materials include without limitation any Code licensed or distributed under any of the following licenses or distribution models or similar licenses or distribution models: the GNU General Public License (GPL), GNU Lesser General Public License or GNU Library General Public License (LGPL), Mozilla Public License (MPL), BSD licenses, the Artistic License, the Netscape Public License, the Sun Community Source License (SCSL) the Sun Industry Standards License (SISL) and the Apache License).

- ***Licensees and Licensors need to ensure the definition of "open source" reflects the contemplated use of the software and any changes in technology. The parties should not ignore the risk of utilizing language such as "includes without limitation" or "including but not limited to."***

1.16 **Performance Standards** means collectively the warranties and performance standards set forth in Section 16 and all associated Exhibits, Appendixes, Attachments, and Addenda referenced therein.

1.17 **Regulatory Requirements** is defined in Appendix 3.B "Service Level Standards and Credits," Attachment 8 "Information Technology Support."

1.18 **Services** shall mean the work done by Licensor in support of the Software, including but not limited to development services, installation services, training, consulting, support, telephone support, and such other services.

1.19 **Site** shall mean a Customer's computer facility located in one specific geographic location.

1.20 **Software** means the aggregate of the Standard Software and the Custom Software including all physical components that are provided by Licensor, including but not limited to, magnetic media, job aids, templates, and other similar devices; an exhaustive list of all Software is set forth in Appendix 1.20.

1.21 **Software Acceptance Plan** shall mean that plan set forth in Appendix 1.21.

- ***The Software Acceptance Plan should be set out in detail prior to execution of the Agreement to avoid later disagreements. Agreement in advance may not be feasible, however, depending on the nature of the development undertaken by Licensor. Any plan should be objective in nature to protect both parties.***

1.22 **"Source Code"** means computer software in the form of source statements for the Software (excluding all Third Party Software) including, without limitation, all software in the form of electronic and printed human-readable, mnemonic or English-like program listings, including printed and on-line descriptions of the design of such software including, without limitation, data definition models, indices, structure tables, system flow charts, program flow charts, defined terms, file layouts, program narratives, global documentation (including global variables) and program listings.

1.23 **Standard Software** means those Deliverables that are classified, in Appendix 1.23 hereto as Standard Software, as well as the documentation furnished therewith by Licensor or its subcontractors in the normal course of business; an exhaustive list of the Standard Software is set forth in Appendix 1.23.

- ***The "Definitions" section of any agreement is very important, as this is where the Customer or Licensor may try to insert a definition, which has a favorable implication later in the Agreement, based upon its use. For example, many Customers try to define the "Agreement" to include the RFP. This is dangerous as the deliverables may have changed from the RFP or Licensor may never have intended to meet certain requirements of the RFP by listing such requirements in the "Exceptions" portions of Licensor's RFP response. Further, if the RFP and RFP response are incorporated in the Agreement, the two documents may be inconsistent, leading to internal inconsistencies and potential problems of interpretation.***

2. Scope of This Agreement

2.1 **Scope.** This Agreement defines the terms and conditions under which Licensor will design, develop, integrate, deliver, install, and support the Software and the Deliverables.

2.2 **Turn-key Basis.** The Parties hereto acknowledge that the performance by Licensor of its obligations hereunder is to be done on a "turn-key" basis. This expression is understood to mean that Licensor is fully responsible, pursuant to the terms and conditions hereof, for the delivery of the Deliverables in full conformity with the terms and conditions hereof, and that the said Deliverables shall function in conformity with the performance criteria stipulated herein upon delivery and up to and including the date on which the acceptance certificate is issued.

- ***From the Customer's prospective, it is important that the Licensor be responsible for providing the entire software system. Otherwise, if there is a defect each individual vendor will affix blame for the problem on the other vendors. The Customer wants to place the responsibility on the Licensor to deliver a complete, integrated working system and if required fix any problem that arises regardless of whether it arises from the hardware, operating system, proprietary software, data base software, etc. For assuming this additional risk, the Licensor should be entitled to receive a higher fee.***

2.3 **Modification of Delivery Date.** Either Party hereto may submit a request to the other to modify the delivery date for one or more Deliverable(s) if it believes that such a modification of a delivery date is necessary or appropriate given circumstances external to this Agreement or the failure of the other Party to perform in strict conformity with the terms hereof. It is nonetheless acknowledged that the other party shall have full power and authority to accept or reject such a request.

3. Software and Services

3.1 **License Grant**. Subject to the provisions of this Agreement as well as the payment of all applicable license fees for the term of such license, Licensor grants Customer and Customer accepts a limited, personal, nonexclusive, nontransferable, non-assignable Object Code [Source Code] license to use the [Standard] Software for Customer's internal use only in the United States [on the Central Processing Units (CPUs) listed on Appendix 3.1.]

- ***Customer—Who is the Customer?***
- ***License—Licensor "licenses" its software; Licensor does not "sell" it. "Selling" indicates a transfer of ownership, meaning the Customer could potentially "resell" the Software to a third party.***
- ***Limited—Customer has only limited rights in the software.***
- ***Personal—Use of the software is "personal" to the Customer only.***
- ***Nonexclusive—Other customers may receive a license to use the same software.***
- ***Nontransferable—The Software cannot be transferred to other entities.***
- ***Non-assignable—The Software cannot be assigned to other entities.***
- ***Object code—Unless source code is being licensed, the Customer will receive object code only.***
- ***Internal use—The Software cannot be used for outsourcing, timesharing, service bureaus, etc.***
- ***United States—To avoid export issues and the potential diversion of the Software, the Customer may use the Software only in the United States.***

- ***This Section assumes that the Licensor shall own all Software including the Custom Software in contradiction of Sections 6.4 and 12.1, which assume that the Customer will own the Custom Software. Section 3.1.A below provides additional language, which allows the Licensor to retain ownership, but grants the Customer an exclusive license to use the Custom Software.***
- ***The entire license grant is preceded by the clause "Subject to the provisions of this Agreement," which allows Licensor to terminate the license grant if the Customer breaches any other terms of the Agreement.***
- ***The scope of the license grant is directly related to pricing. For example, while Licensor may not initially grant a source code license that could potentially limit Licensor's ability to earn revenue from maintaining the software or developing enhancements, licensors will often license source code for an appropriately larger license fee.***

Additional Language Granting the Customer an Exclusive License in Return for Funding Development

3.1.A **Exclusive License Grant.** In consideration of the Customer funding the development of the Custom Software, the Customer is hereby granted the exclusive license and right to utilize the Custom Software for five years from the date Customer accepts the Software (the "Exclusivity Period"). During the Exclusivity Period, Licensor shall not license or sell the Custom Software or allow any other individual or entity to utilize the Custom Software. Further, the Licensor shall not develop, create, or license any other software functionally equivalent to the Custom Software.

- ***This language provides a compromise to the Customer claiming ownership of the Custom Software. It allows the Licensor to retain ownership of the Custom Software while providing the Customer with the benefit of any competitive advantage that the Custom Software may provide. This language is too broad from the Licensor's perspective. Not only does it provide the Customer with an exclusive license, but it also prohibits the Licensor from developing any functionality equivalent software. This prohibition may severely impact the Licensor's ability to sell future work. Section 8.H provides alternative language allowing the Customer to recoup its investment in funding the development of the Custom Software from royalty payments for future licenses of the Custom Software granted by the Licensor.***

Additional Language Granting the Customer the Right to Copy the Software

3.1.B **Right to Copy.** Customer may copy the Software only in so far as strictly necessary for the intended use of the Software. Customer explicitly agrees that in the foreseeable future the intended use of the Software does not require copies of the Software other than for archival and/or backup purposes should at any time occur that the intended use of the Software implies the necessity of copies for other purposes than archival and/or backup purposes, Customer shall immediately notify Licensor in writing and provide Licensor with all information necessary in order to enable Licensor to evaluate the actual necessity of such copies.

3.2 **Software Related Materials.** All Software used in, for, or in connection with the software, parts, subsystems, or derivatives thereof (the "ABC System"), in whatever form, including, without limitation, source code, object code, microcode, and mask works, including any computer programs and any documentation relating to or describing such Software, such as but not limited to logic manuals and flow charts provided by Licensor, including instructions for use of the Software and formulation of theory upon which the Software, is based are furnished to Customer only under a personal, nonexclusive, nontransferable, non-assignable Object Code license solely for Customer's own internal use.

3.3 **No Licenses.** Except as explicitly provided in Section 3.1 of this Agreement, no license under any patents, copyrights, trademarks, trade secrets, or any other intellectual property rights, express or implied, are granted by Licensor to Customer under this Agreement.

3.4 **Reverse Engineering.** Customer shall not and shall not permit its Affiliates or any third party to translate, reverse engineer, decompile, recompile, update, or modify all or any part of the Software or merge the Software into any other software.

Additional/Alternative Language Benefiting Customer

Customer shall not otherwise, in whole or in part, sublicense, copy, rent, loan, transfer, prepare derivatives of the Software or any copy of the Software. Customer shall not decompile the Software for other purposes than creating interoperability of the Software and Customer shall not create interoperability without having approached Licensor in order to obtain from Licensor the necessary information and data to do so, provided that Licensor does not provide Customer with such information and data within a reasonable time, Customer shall have the right to decompile the Software.

Customer shall not modify the Software for other purposes than correcting errors of the Software. Customer acknowledges that all Improvements and Modifications, not made contrary to the terms of this Agreement, of the Software or any part thereof (whether developed by Licensor, Licensor, Customer or any third party acting on behalf of them at any time during the term of this agreement) shall be deemed to be part of the Software and shall be and remain the sole and exclusive property of Licensor, subject to the terms and conditions of the Agreement and any additional agreements concluded and maintenance contracts permitted by this Agreement.

- ***Section 3.4 restricts the Customer from modifying or enhancing the Software. It is essential this paragraph remain in the Agreement, otherwise the Customer (and potentially the Customer's other vendors) would under the* Sega, Atari, *and* Bateman *decisions have the right to reverse engineer the Software to create its own interfaces, etc. It is also important that the Customer is forbidden from merging the Software with other software, which in turn may create a new work, which could be copyrighted in the Customer's name.***

3.5 **Ownership of Materials.** All patents, copyrights, circuit layouts, mask works, trade secrets, and other proprietary rights in or related to the Software are and will remain the exclusive property of Licensor, whether or not specifically recognized or perfected under the laws of the jurisdiction in which the Software is used or licensed. Customer will not take any action that jeopardizes Licensor's proprietary rights or acquire any right in the Software or the Confidential Information, as defined in Section 12 herein below. Unless otherwise agreed on a case-by-case basis, Licensor will own all rights in any copy, translation, modification, adaptation, or derivation of the Software or other items of Confidential Information, including any improvement or development thereof. Customer will obtain, at Licensor's request, the execution of any instrument that may be appropriate to assign these rights to Licensor or perfect these rights in Licensor's name.

- ***Section 3.5 provides that even if the Customer creates a derivative work or a modification or enhancement, in contradiction to Section 3.4, Licensor will have sole and exclusive ownership of such work. The Licensor needs to be careful that any restrictions placed on the Customer do not amount to copyright misuse.***

3.6 **Third Party Access.** Customer shall not allow any third party to have access to the Software without Licensor's prior written consent. Further, Customer shall neither engage in nor permit any use of the Software such that a copy would be made of such Software solely by virtue of the activation of a machine containing a copy of the Software.

- ***Section 3.6 prevents the Customer from utilizing outside contractors and consultants from utilizing, maintaining, or supporting on the Software. This protects Licensor from the Customer hiring Licensor's competitors or outsourcing the software and its maintenance. The second sentence seeks to negate the effect of The Computer Maintenance Competition Assurance Act, 17 U.S.C. § 117.***

3.7 **Service Locations**. To the extent applicable, each specific Statement of Work shall identify (i) the Customer Locations that shall receive Services under such Statement of Work, and (ii) the Licensor Service Locations that shall provide such Services. Customer acknowledges that Licensor may utilize non-U.S. based operations in connection with the performance of this Agreement. Licensor shall be entitled, upon obtaining prior written consent from Customer (such consent to be granted or withheld in Customer's sole discretion) and subject to compliance with all applicable Laws, including all Data Protection Laws, to move the Services and related obligations from a Licensor Service Location to another location and, if such move is from one country to another country, from one Local Agreement to another Local Agreement. Notwithstanding Customer's approval of such transfer of Services, Licensor shall remain liable and responsible for the performance of all Services by it and all its Affiliates hereunder and Licensor shall be responsible for any expenses and price increases (including, but not limited to additional taxes) resulting from any transfer from one Licensor Service Location to another Licensor Service Location unless expressly otherwise agreed by Customer in a Change Order.

"**Data Protection Laws**" shall mean any data protection or privacy Laws.

"**Local Agreement**" shall mean a separate agreement between (i) Customer or a Customer Affiliate, and (ii) Licensor or a Licensor Affiliate in a jurisdiction in which the Services shall be provided by Licensor or an Affiliate of Licensor that shall modify the terms and conditions of this Agreement as necessary to address the requirements of local laws. A Local Agreement for a particular jurisdiction shall govern the Statement of Work under which Services are provided in such jurisdiction.

- ***See Section 16.AB for a representation and warranty as to the location of where the services will be performed.***

3.8 **Improvements and New Technology.**

3.8.1 **Continuous Improvement.** Licensor will explore opportunities on an ongoing-basis to reduce Customer's total cost of receiving the Services (including but not limited to the charges) and to improve Licensor's performance of the Services and Service Levels and shall be required, throughout the Term, to implement such measures. Such opportunities may include economies of scale and greater efficiencies developed by Licensor and technological changes and other developments affecting delivery of the Services. Prior to the execution of a Statement of Work hereunder, Licensor will present a continuous improvement program with respect to the Services to be provided under such Statement of Work. The continuous improvement program will include short-term initiatives (0-6 months) with detailed business cases and demonstrable business benefit to Customer, medium-term initiatives (6-12 months) with high-level business cases, and long-term initiatives (12 months on).

3.8.2 **New Technology and Reengineering.** During the Term, Licensor shall keep itself informed of new technology and improvements in current technology that may facilitate or improve the Services to result in cost savings, improvement in Licensor's performance of the Services and Service Levels, and other benefits to Customer. Licensor shall promptly advise Customer of such new technology or improvements about which it is aware and promptly advise Customer of their prospective benefits to Customer. In addition, Licensor shall review the operations required to support Customer and shall recommend to Customer certain reengineering procedures, processes and tools. In the event that the reengineering opportunity would require Customer to modify its methods, practices or policies, Licensor shall (i) present the changes to Customer, (ii) discuss with Customer the requirements of implementation, and (iii) identify the projected benefits to both Customer and Licensor. The Parties shall work in good faith to determine the costs, benefits, and proper level of commitment by both Customer and Licensor for implementing such reengineering projects. Either Party may request implementation of any of the foregoing in accordance with the procedures for Changes set forth in Article ___, and Licensor shall not implement any of the foregoing without Customer's prior written consent.

3.9 **Customer Authorized User Satisfaction.**

3.9.1 **Baseline Customer Authorized User Satisfaction Survey.** In the time frames set forth in Exhibit _____ (Critical Deliverables), an independent third party selected by Customer shall conduct a baseline Customer Authorized User satisfaction survey for affected users at each Customer Service Location and/or Customer Site Approved by Customer measuring their satisfaction with their receipt of the Services. This Customer Authorized User Satisfaction Survey shall be mutually agreed upon by the Parties, and shall be administered as determined by the selected organization and shall be the initial baseline for measurement of user satisfaction improvement described in Section ____ (Customer Authorized User Satisfaction Survey).

3.9.2 **Customer Authorized User Satisfaction Survey**. Every six (6) months during the first four (4) years of the Term and annually thereafter (unless otherwise agreed in writing by the Parties), an independent third party selected by Customer shall conduct a Customer Authorized User Satisfaction Survey for each Customer Service Location and/or Customer Site. The survey shall, at a minimum, cover at least the following classes of users: (1) sample of end users of the Services, and (2) all senior management of Customer. The content, scope, and method of the survey shall be consistent with the baseline Customer Authorized User Satisfaction Survey conducted pursuant to Section ____ (Baseline Customer Authorized User Satisfaction Survey) and the timing of the above surveys are subject to Customer's Approval. It is the goal of Licensor to increase Customer Authorized User satisfaction for each class of Customer Authorized Users. The baseline for determining the initial gap shall be the results of the surveys conducted pursuant to Section _____ (Baseline Customer Authorized User Satisfaction Survey). The baseline for determining subsequent gaps will be the results of the Customer Authorized User Satisfaction Survey compared to the immediately prior Customer Authorized User Satisfaction Survey. Licensor agrees that increasing measured Customer Authorized User satisfaction shall be a key performance incentive for compensation for key executives assigned to Customer's account. The costs for all Customer Authorized User Satisfaction Surveys shall be borne solely by Customer. Notwithstanding the foregoing, in the event that any Customer Authorized User Satisfaction Survey fails to meet the applicable Service Level, the cost of all surveys following such failure shall be borne solely by Licensor until the Service Level failure has been remedied by Licensor (after a survey Service Level failure is remedied Customer again shall bear the costs of the subsequent survey); provided, however, that the first Customer Authorized User Satisfaction Survey immediately following any Service Level failure shall be conducted no earlier than six (6) months, and no later than seven (7) months, after such failure.

3.10 **Data Maps**

Licensor shall provide current data dictionaries and maps to Licensee both with the initial installation and with each Update of the Licensed Software, so that all data managed by the Licensed Software can be readily located, searched, extracted, and exported in whole or in part by Licensee personnel as Licensee deems appropriate, with or without the use of tools provided by Licensor.

Alternative/Additional Language

3.A **Commitment to Research and Development.** Licensor acknowledges that research and development is an integral part of being able to continue to improve functionality and meet the increasing business needs of the [name of] industry in the future. Having acknowledged the foregoing, Licensor shall invest on a yearly basis a minimum of [XX] percent (XX%) of the gross revenues it collects from all customers using and receiving services related to the Software into research and development efforts related to the Software. In the event that Licensor fails to invest the required amount into the research and development of the Software, Customer shall: (a) have the right to migrate to the new services or system that Licensor offers to its customers, which migration shall be at no additional cost to Customer and shall include the retro-fitting of all custom programming, or (b) have the right, at any time, to terminate this Agreement and: (i) obtain all Source Code and other deposit material to all Software and/or to provide Services to Customer; and/or (ii) transition to a new software vendor, pursuant to Customer's rights under Section 5.3.3. [Transition Rights in the event of Licensor breach.] All Services provided by Licensor during any such transition period shall be provided at no cost to Customer.

- ***When purchasing a mission critical software system, a customer should obtain a commitment from the Licensor that the Licensor will continue to invest in the product to keep the product competitive during the customer's use of the product. This protects the customer from the Licensor "sunsetting" the product by failing to invest in the product and to keep the product competitive with market requirements. The language set forth above provides the customer the right to migrate to any new product the Licensor offers to replace the licensed software at no additional cost or terminate the Agreement and obtain the source code and/or transition to a new vendor. This clause provides complete protection in the event the Licensor creates a new product shortly after the customer enters into the license agreement. At the same time, the clause creates significant risks for the Licensor and will likely be hotly debated in most licensing negotiations.***

3.B **Service Level Standards**

3.B.1 **General.** Licensor shall provide the Software, and any other Services, as applicable, according to the performance criteria and at the service level standards ("Service Level Standards") set forth in Appendix 3.B. Licensor and Customer shall meet on a semi-annual basis to discuss whether changes to the Service Level Standards are necessary due to any changes business needs of Customer. Any changes to the Service Level Standards agreed upon in writing by both parties shall replace the then existing Appendix 3.B.

- ***Almost all license agreements from the Customer's prospective should include service level standards. Service level standards establish the minimum level of acceptable performance such as response times and refresh rates. While a general warranty may include broad generalizations as to the software's performance, service level standards provide specific standards that the Licensor's***

software must meet. This creates greater risks for the Licensor but the Customer is only asking the Licensor to commit in writing to the standards the Licensor has most likely already agreed to or stated in its marketing materials.

3.B.2 **Service Level Credits.** In the event Licensor fails to meet the Service Level Standards, Customer shall be entitled to receive from Licensor service level credits ("Service Level Credits"), which shall be: (a) in the amounts and according to the terms set forth in Appendix 3.B, all of which shall be based on Licensor's monthly performance as set forth in the monthly performance reports prepared by Licensor pursuant to Section X.6.3 (attached as an alternative section); and/or (b) in the amount imposed upon Customer by [Regulatory Agency] for failing to comply with a State standard where such failure is caused by a Licensor failure to meet the Service Level Standards or any other performance standard or requirement set forth in this Agreement. Customer shall have the right to set off any undisputed amounts owed to Licensor against any Service Level Credits assessed by Customer against Licensor.

- ***Service Level Credits flow directly from the failure of the software to meet the Service Level Standards. The Customer has a significant amount of money and effort invested in the implementation of the software. Termination of the license agreement for the failure of the software to meet the Service Level Standards is not always a practical solution. Further, a regulatory agency or end-user may have imposed penalties on the Customer causing the Customer to incur out-of-pocket costs. Consequently, Service Level Credits provide the Customer with a way to incent the Licensor short of terminating the Agreement. The Customer should provide, however, that if the Service Level Credits exceed a certain threshold that the Customer shall have the right to terminate the Agreement (See § 5.1(d)). The Licensor should ensure that the level of credits is acceptable and that the Service Level Standards are realistic. Further, the Licensor should insist that each set of credits be capped in the aggregate and on a monthly basis.***

3.C **Liquidated Damages**

3.C.1 **Liquidated Damages Payable by Licensor.**

(a) In the event that Customer refuses, as per the provisions of Appendix 3.C hereto, to issue the On-Site Acceptance Certificate on or before a day which is twenty (20) calendar days after the Delivery Date for Milestone Nos. ___ or ___ (On-Site Acceptance Certificates), respectively (hereinafter referred to as the "LD Date"), liquidated damages shall be payable by Licensor pursuant to the conditions set forth in Section 3.C hereof. Such liquidated damages shall be imposed on a daily basis, as from and including the day immediately following the LD Date up to and including the date on which the aforesaid On-Site Acceptance Certificate is issued. The amount of such liquidated damages shall be __________ (____) per calendar day, subject to a maximum amount of ___________ (____).

(b) In the event that Customer refuses, as per the provisions of Appendix 3.C hereto, to issue the Provisional Acceptance Certificate on or before a day which is twenty (20) calendar days after Milestone Nos. ____ or __ (Provisional Acceptance Certificates), respectively (hereinafter referred to as the "LD Date"), liquidated damages shall be payable by Licensor pursuant to the conditions set forth in Section 3.C hereof. Such liquidated damages shall be imposed on a daily basis, as from and including the day immediately following the LD Date up to and including the date on which the aforesaid Provisional Acceptance Certificate is issued. The amount of such liquidated damages shall ______ (___) per calendar day, subject to a maximum amount ____ (____).

(c) Notwithstanding the provisions of Sections 3.C.1 (a) hereof, in the event that the On-Site Acceptance Certificate is issued on a date that is more than twenty (20) calendar days after Milestone No. ___ (On-Site Acceptance Certificate), Milestone No. ___ (Provisional Acceptance Certificate) shall be deemed to be moved forward in time by the number of calendar days equal to a number of calendar days between Milestone No. _____, plus twenty (20) days, and the date on which the On-Site Acceptance Certificate is issued, provided, however, that in no event shall the number of days by which the aforesaid Milestone No. ___ shall be moved forward in time exceed one hundred (100).

3.C.2 **Liquidated Damages Payable by Customer**

(a) In the event that Licensor refuses, as per the provisions of Appendix 3.C hereto, to issue the Acceptance Test Cases Acceptance Certificate on or before a day which is twenty (20) calendar days after Milestones Nos. __ or __ (Acceptance Tests Cases Certificates), respectively (hereinafter referred to as the "LD Date"), liquidated damages shall be payable by Customer pursuant to the conditions set forth in Section 3.C.3 hereof. Such liquidated damages shall be imposed on a daily basis, as from and including the day immediately following the LD Date up to and including the date on which the aforesaid Acceptance Test Cases Acceptance Certificate is issued. The amount of such liquidated damages shall be _______ (_______) per calendar day, subject to a maximum amount of ____ (___).

(b) In the event that Licensor refuses, as per the provisions of Appendix 3.C hereto, to issue the Site Ready Acceptance Certificate on or before a day which is twenty (20) calendar days after Milestone No. ___ (Site Ready Acceptance Certificate) (hereinafter referred to as the "LD Date"), liquidated damages shall be payable by Customer pursuant to the conditions set forth in Section 3.C.3 hereof. Such liquidated damages shall be imposed on a daily basis, as from and including the day immediately following the LD Date up to and including the date on which the aforesaid Site Ready Acceptance Certificate is issued. The amount of such liquidated damages shall be ___ (___) per calendar day, subject to a maximum amount of ____ (____).

(c) Notwithstanding the provisions of Section 3.C.2 (a) hereof, in the event that the Acceptance Tests Cases Acceptance Certificate is issued on a date that is after Milestone No.___ (Acceptance Tests Cases Acceptance Certificate), Milestones Nos. ___, ___ and ___ (On-Site Delivery, On-Site and Provisional Acceptance Certificates) shall be deemed to be moved forward in time by a number of calendar days equal to the number of calendar days between Milestone No. ___ and the date on which the Acceptance Tests Cases Acceptance Certificate is issued, provided, however, that in no event shall the number of days by which the aforesaid Milestones Nos. ___, ___ and ___ shall be moved forward in time exceed one hundred (100). Notwithstanding the provisions of Section 3.C.2 hereof, in the event that the Site Ready Acceptance Certificate is issued on a date that is after Milestone No. ___, subsequent impacted Milestones shall be deemed to be moved forward in time by a number of calendar days equal to the number of calendar days between Milestone No. ___ and the date on which the Site Ready Acceptance Certificate is issued, provided, however, that in no event shall the number of days by which the aforesaid subsequent impacted Milestones shall be moved forward in time exceed one hundred (100).

3.C.3 **Payment of Liquidated Damages.** If Customer is entitled to receive liquidated damages pursuant to Section 3.C.1 hereof, it shall notify Licensor thereof in writing and Licensor shall cause a credit to appear on the next invoice it issues hereunder. If Licensor is entitled to receive liquidated damages pursuant to Section 3.C.2 hereof, it shall notify Customer thereof in writing and shall cause a debit to appear on the next invoice it issues to Customer hereunder.

3.C.4 **Termination in Lieu of Liquidated Damages.** In the event that the maximum amount of liquidated damages prescribed by Sections 3.C.1 or 3.C.2 is reached, the Party that would otherwise be entitled to receive liquidated damages shall have the right, but not the obligation, to terminate this Agreement pursuant to the provisions of Section 5 hereof by sending a notice to that effect to the other Party.

- ***Liquidated damages are a predetermined good-faith estimate of damages the Customer will incur as a result of Licensor's breach or that the Licensor will incur as a result of the Customer's breach, which eliminates the necessity that the injured party prove its damages. For example, once the Customer demonstrates that the Licensor breached its obligations, it is entitled to collect the pre-agreed damages. If there are concerns about the ability to collect payment, each party can require the other to establish an irrevocable bond or letter of credit.***
- ***Any provision for liquidated damages should be mutual as the Licensor may also suffer damages, for example if the Customer's performance is delayed.***
- ***To the extent one party's performance is delayed by the action or inaction of the other party and as a result is liable for liquidated damages, the party whose performance has been delayed shall be entitled to one extra day for each day its performance has been delayed by the other party.***

4. *Term of Agreement and License*

4.1 **Term of Agreement.** The term of this Agreement shall commence upon the execution of this Agreement, and shall continue for ____ years unless terminated upon the breach of this Agreement by either party [or as otherwise provided herein].

- ***This "term" relates to the term of the Agreement although the term of individual licenses granted under the Agreement may be different.***

Additional Language Allowing Customer to Terminate for Convenience

4.1.A **Termination without Cause.** Upon written notice to Licensor, Customer shall have the right to terminate this Agreement without cause. In such event: (a) Licensor shall discontinue its Services with respect to this Agreement, and (b) Customer shall be obligated to pay to Licensor a termination fee in an amount equal to the Services Fees paid or payable for the two (2) month period immediately preceding the effective date of such termination.

- ***This clause usually benefits the Customer as it allows the Customer to terminate the agreement at the Customer's convenience and depending on the wording it may not allow the Licensor to recover its termination costs, investment, etc. The Licensor should make sure that if the Licensor accepts such a clause that the negotiated termination fee allows the Licensor to recover its investment, expenses, and the cost of money. The Licensor may have significant termination costs including employee termination costs, subcontract termination costs, leases, travel, etc. The language set forth above does not favor the Licensor as the termination fee is not specifically stated and is tied to revenues. This creates the risk of an unanticipated event that reduces the agreement's revenues and in turn lowers the termination fee the Licensor is entitled to receive.***
- ***This clause must be carefully worded to clearly state how any termination fee will be determined. Usually the Customer must pay for work completed, Licensor's termination costs and Licensor's lost profit. The Licensor must determine whether the Customer should compensate Licensor for work performed based on Licensor's costs (a cost plus model) or on a percent complete (of the project) basis. In either case, the agreement should provide that Licensor is entitled to recover Licensor's lost profit or at least a pro rata portion of its lost profits.***

4.1.B **Termination upon Acquisition by XYZ Software Company**. Upon written notice to Licensor, Customer shall have the right to immediately terminate this Agreement if Licensor is acquired by XYZ Software Company of one of its Affiliates. In such event: (a) Licensor shall discontinue its Services with respect to this Agreement; and (b) Customer shall be obligated to pay to Licensor a termination fee in an amount equal to the Services Fees paid or payable for the two (2) month period immediately preceding the effective date of such termination.

4.2 **Term of Licenses.** Subject to the limitations contained in this Agreement, the term of each individual License granted under this Agreement begins on the date of delivery of the Software, and shall terminate on the date set forth herein, unless earlier terminated as provided in this Agreement.

- ***The term of the "License" should begin on "delivery" and not on "acceptance" otherwise the Customer would have no legal obligations as to the use of the Software prior to "acceptance." Binding the Customer to the terms of the license upon delivery does not indicate the Customer's acceptance or create an obligation for the Customer to pay the applicable license fee.***

5. Events of Default and Remedies

5.1 **Events of Default.** Licensor and Customer acknowledge and agree that the following shall constitute events of default ("Events of Default") and that the occurrence of one (1) or more of such Events of Default shall constitute a material breach of this Agreement, which shall allow a party, as applicable, to seek the rights and remedies set forth in this Section:

(a) Licensor's failure to deposit the Deposit material as required by the Source Code Escrow Agreement within the time frames specified therein;

(b) Licensor's breach of the Regulatory Requirements warranty set forth in Section 16.M, and in no event shall such failure be subject to a cure period;

(c) Except for breaches that constitute a Section 5.1.(d) Event of Default, Licensor's material breach of any license obligation as provided in Section 3 provided that such breach is not cured within thirty (30) calendar days following written notice of such breach;

(d) Licensor's failure to materially conform to the Service Level Standards set forth in Appendix 3.B, or the occurrence of Service Level Credits for any three months during a twelve (12) month period in the amount of ____________________ ($) or more per month; provided that Customer shall have provided Licensor with written notice of Licensor's non-compliance after the second month of non-compliance with such written notice being provided to Licensor within thirty (30) calendar days of the second month of Licensor's non-compliance of Service Level Standards;

(e) Licensor's continuous failure to timely provide to Customer monthly performance reports regarding Licensor's performance in relation to the Service Level Standards as set forth in Section 9.6.4.;

(f) Licensor's failure to maintain insurance coverage as specified in Section 36, provided that such failure is not cured within thirty (30) calendar days following receipt of written notice of such failure;

(g) Customer's failure to timely pay any undisputed amount owed to Licensor, provided that such failure is not cured within thirty (30) calendar days following receipt of written notice of such failure;

(h) Customer's breach of Sections 3, 12, or 13 or if Customer otherwise misuses the Software in contravention of this Agreement;

(i) Either party's material breach of any representation or warranty set forth in this Agreement, provided that such breach, if curable, is not cured within the time frames specified in Section 16, if applicable, or if such Section 16 does not apply to the breach, then within thirty (30) calendar days following receipt of written notice of such breach;

(j) Failure of a party to perform any other material obligation under this Agreement, provided that such failure is not cured within thirty (30) calendar days following receipt of written notice of such failure;

(k) The institution of bankruptcy, receivership, insolvency, reorganization, or other similar proceedings by or against either party under any section or chapter of the United States Bankruptcy Code, as amended, or under any similar laws or statutes of the United States or any state thereof, if such proceedings have not been dismissed or discharged within thirty (30) calendar days after they are instituted; or the insolvency or making of an assignment for the benefit of creditors or the admittance by either party of any involuntary debts as they mature or the institution of any reorganization arrangement or other readjustment of debt plan of either party not involving the U.S. Bankruptcy Code; or any corporate action taken by the Board of Directors of either party in furtherance of any of the above actions;

(l) Appointment of a receiver for all or substantially all of either party's assets or any corporate action taken by the Board of Directors of either party in furtherance of the above action; and

- ***While many parties include language similar to the language set forth in subsections (k) and (l) in their agreements, these provisions are unenforceable as contrary to the provisions of the U.S. Bankruptcy Act, which provides that an executory contract may not be terminated solely because of a party's seeking protection under the bankruptcy laws.***

(m) If, but for the application of Section __ [Limitation of Liability] Licensor would be liable for damages in excess of the applicable Cap, Customer may terminate for material breach of this Agreement upon not less than thirty (30) days notice; provided, however, that if Licensor agrees in writing, within thirty (30) days after receiving notice of Customer's intention to terminate this Agreement, to reset such Cap to an amount equal to the payments made by Customer to Licensor for Services during the twenty-four (24) months prior to the occurrence of the first event that is the subject of the first claim with respect to any liability arising after receipt of such notice, Customer may, at its option, choose not to terminate the Agreement and the Cap shall be so reset.

- ***Some Customers seek to insert language allowing them to terminate the agreement if the Licensor's maximum liability under the agreement has been reached unless the Licensor agrees to increase its limit of liability. This demand is unreasonable as the parties previously negotiated a limit of liability that was agreeable to both parties. The Customer should not be allowed to unilaterally renegotiate the agreement or otherwise be allowed to terminate the agreement if the Licensor does not agree to amend it.***
- ***A Customer should carefully consider what actions or inactions on the Licensor's behalf should constitute a material breach. Some issues such as (e) and (f) are not as important as the failure to deliver a working product. At the same time, the Licensor should seek to limit the number of events of default to limit its risk.***

- ***Licensor must have the immediate right to terminate the Agreement without granting a cure period if the Customer breaches the Agreement by misusing the Software. This position is justifiable because a cure period cannot "absolve" the breach.***
- ***Licensor must have a time period in which to "cure" any defaults. The time period must be long enough to allow Licensor to be able to do so. Given the nature of software, this period can be no less than 30 days.***

5.2 **Rights and Remedies of Licensor upon Default of Customer.** Upon the occurrence of an Event of Default by or with respect to Customer, subject to Customer's rights set forth in **Section 5.3.3**, Licensor shall be entitled to any of the following remedies:

(a) terminate, in whole or in part, this Agreement; and/or
(b) subject to the terms of Section 17, seek to recover damages from Customer; and/or
(c) if applicable, seek to obtain the additional rights and remedies set forth in Section 29.5 [Equitable Relief]; and/or
(d) [exercise the right of self-help]

Notwithstanding anything contained herein to the contrary, Licensor expressly waives and disclaims any right or remedy it may have to discontinue the performance of the Services or any portion thereof or terminate the License without due process of law.

- ***This clause seeks to prevent the Licensor from exercising any form of "self help," such as stopping the delivery services or disabling its software without following the dispute resolution procedure set forth in Section 29. Note that Section 5.3.2 specifically allows the Customer to exercise a form of self-help. This limitation conflicts ideologically with Customer's right of setoff in Section 5.3.2. and 3.B.2. Consequently, the Licensor should insist on parity for self help.***

5.3 **Rights and Remedies of Customer upon Default of Licensor**

5.3.1 **General.** Upon the occurrence of an Event of Default by or with respect to Licensor, Customer shall be entitled to any of the following remedies:

(a) terminate, in whole or in part, this Agreement; and/or
(b) subject to the terms of Section 17, seek to recover damages from Licensor; and/or
(c) if applicable, obtain the additional remedies described in Sections 5.3.2–5.3.7; and/or
(d) if applicable, seek to obtain the additional rights and remedies set forth in Section 29.5 [Equitable Relief].

5.3.2 **Right to Set Off.** Customer shall have the right to set off any undisputed amounts owed to Licensor against any damages or charges including, without limitation, Service Level Credits, assessed by Customer against Licensor.

- *Note that this section allows the Customer to set off only* **undisputed** *amounts owed to Licensor.*
- ***The parties should specifically state and agree as to whether they have the right of set off against the other. The common law of many states allows the right of set off even if it is not set forth in the contract. The Licensor is more likely to be concerned, as the Customer will want to offset any payments due the Licensor in the event of the Licensor's breach.***

5.3.3 **Transition Rights**

(a) **Termination by Customer.** In the event Customer terminates this Agreement pursuant to the terms of this Agreement in whole or in part, Customer shall provide to Licensor a written notice of transition ("Transition Notice"), setting forth the target date on which Customer plans to cut-over from Licensor's system to a new system or otherwise not require the future services of Licensor (the "Target Cut-Over Date"). At least thirty (30) days prior to the actual cut-over date ("Actual Cut-Over Date"), Customer shall provide Licensor with written notice of the Actual Cut-Over Date. Licensor shall continue to provide to Customer all Services required by Customer ("Transition Period"). Services provided by Licensor during the Transition Period shall include all conversion and other Services necessary for an orderly transition to another system. Customer shall place the Services Fees that accrue from and after the date of Transition Notice to the Actual Cut-Over Date into a Customer reserve account, and such reserved funds shall be disbursed as follows: (i) fifty percent (50%) of the reserve funds shall be distributed to Licensor on a pro-rata monthly basis over the first twelve (12) months after the Actual Cut-Over Date, and (ii) the remaining fifty percent (50%) of the reserve funds shall be paid to Licensor in one lump sum upon the completion of all Outsourcing Services obligations under this Agreement relating to the Prior Claims.

(b) **Termination by Licensor.** In the event Licensor terminates this Agreement pursuant to the terms of this Agreement, and provided Customer pays all undisputed amounts owed to Licensor, Licensor shall provide to Customer a minimum of twelve (12) months of all Services. Services provided by Licensor during this period shall include all conversion and other Services necessary (at Licensor's Service Rates) for an orderly transition to another system.

- ***In both 5.3.3(a) and (b), the parties should carefully negotiate the payment terms. In the event of 5.3.3(b), the Licensor may want to require the Customer to make payment in advance. At the same time, the Licensor may want to soften the payment terms in Section 5.3.3(a).***

Alternative Language Benefiting the Customer

Termination/Expiration Assistance Services

Termination/Expiration Transition Plan. Licensor understands and agrees that Customer's business operations are dependent on the Services, and that Customer's inability to receive the Services would result in irreparable damages to Customer. Therefore, upon the expiration of this Agreement or its termination by either Party for any reason, including the breach of this Agreement by the other Party, Termination Assistance Services shall be provided as set forth in this Section ___ (Termination/Expiration Assistance Services). If no Termination Transition Plan has yet been agreed to at the time of termination, the rights of Customer upon any expiration or termination of this Agreement shall be as set forth in this Section ___ (Termination/Expiration Assistance Services). If a Termination Transition Plan has been agreed to, then the rights of Customer upon any expiration or termination of this Agreement shall be as set forth in the most recent approved Termination Transition Plan, and also as set forth in this Section ____ (Termination/Expiration Assistance Services). In the event of any inconsistency between this Section ____ (Termination/Expiration Assistance Services) and the applicable Termination Transition Plan, this Section shall govern. If no Termination Transition Plan has been agreed to by the Parties at the time of any termination of this Agreement, then Licensor shall provide the professional services staff necessary to provide (1) the Services (as requested by Customer in accordance with Section ____ (Termination Transition Period) at performance standards and Service Levels in effect at the time of termination or expiration, and (2) the Termination Assistance Services.

Performance of Services. Licensor and Customer acknowledge and agree that their mutual cooperation is important to an effective transition of technology services provided by Licensor to Customer or its designated provider(s). As requested by Customer in accordance with Section ___ (Termination Transition Period), Licensor shall provide Customer with all of the Services, including all of the Termination Assistance Services set forth in this Section ___ (Termination/Expiration Assistance Services) and in the then most recent version of the Termination Transition Plan. Licensor shall have no right to withhold or limit any of the Services (including the Termination Assistance Services) on the basis of any alleged breach of this Agreement by Customer, other than a failure by Customer to timely pay the amounts due for the Services (including Termination Assistance Services) rendered during the Termination Transition Period (as set forth in Section ___ (Termination Transition Period). Customer shall have the right to seek specific performance of this Section ___ (Termination/Expiration Assistance Services). In addition to the Services as set forth in this Agreement, the Termination Assistance Services shall include, at a minimum, (i) converting data; (ii) providing parallel services until transition to a new system; (iii) providing on-site technical support; (iv) cooperating with Customer or its designated vendor in developing required interfaces; (v) meeting with Customer as soon as practicable after a notice of termination or notice of a decision to not extend this Agreement has been given, to discuss any potential modifications to the then most current Termination Transition Plan; (vi) using all commercially reasonable efforts to assist Customer in effecting a transition of the Services, in accordance with best practices, to Customer or another vendor chosen by Customer; (vii) providing the number and types of resources necessary to complete the transition in accordance with the Termination Transition Plan; and (viii) such other services as shall be necessary or appropriate to facilitate, without interruption to the Services, the orderly transition of the Services to Customer or its new provider of services in accordance with best practices. If Licensor is providing any Services hereunder at the time of such transition utilizing any software license from a Third Party Vendor, the responsibility for obtaining and paying for the transfer of such licenses shall be in accordance with Section ___ (Consents). Notwithstanding anything in this Agreement to the contrary, Customer shall be entitled to increase and/or decrease the scope of the Services and Termination Assistance Services in its sole discretion during any Termination Transition Period. Licensor shall be compensated on a time and material basis or fixed fee basis (as agreed by the Parties) for all Termination Assistance Services by payment by Customer, with respect to time and materials charges, in accordance with the rates set forth in this Agreement or, if applicable rates for time and materials charges are not contained in this Agreement, and for all fixed fee charges, at commercially reasonable rates, it being understood that the charges for the Termination Assistance Services are not included in the Charges.

Termination Transition Period. Unless otherwise directed by Customer, commencing: (i) six (6) months prior to the expiration of the Agreement; (ii) upon any notice of termination or non-renewal of the Agreement; or (iii) six (6) months prior to any other ceasing of Service under the Agreement, and continuing for a period defined in the Termination Transition Plan but in no event less than twelve (12) months following the expiration or termination of this Agreement (unless a shorter time period is requested by Customer), Licensor will continue to provide the Services (including the Termination Assistance Services) as requested by Customer. After such twelve (12) month period (or such shorter time period as requested by Customer), unless otherwise directed by Customer, Licensor shall provide extensions of the Services (including the Termination Assistance Services) as requested by Customer in serial thirty (30) day extension terms for up to an additional six (6) months (such period, the "Termination Transition Period"). The total Termination Transition Period shall not exceed eighteen (18) months.

In addition to the Services as set forth in this Agreement, the Termination Assistance Services shall include, at a minimum, converting data, providing parallel services until transition to a new system, providing on-site technical support, cooperating with Customer or its designated vendor in developing required interfaces, and such other services as shall be necessary or appropriate to facilitate, without material or extended interruption to the Services, the orderly transition of the Services to Customer or its new provider of services in accordance with Licensor's best practices. Customer shall have the same rights to Software and such other intellectual property rights as provided in Section ____ (Intellectual Property) during the transition period as it does during the Term.

Transition Services. Licensor will provide the following Termination Assistance Services at Customer's request:

A. Licensor shall (i) assist Customer in developing a written transition plan for the transition of the Services to Customer or Customer's designee, which shall include capacity planning, facilities planning, human resources planning, and data transport/telecommunications planning necessary to effect the transition; (ii) perform programming and consulting services as requested to assist in implementing the transition plan; (iii) train personnel designated by Customer in the use of any Equipment, Software, materials, or processes to be transferred; (iv) catalog all Software, Customer Data and Equipment used to provide the Services, provide machine readable and printed listings of source code for Software in accordance with Section ____ (Intellectual Property) to the extent such source code is generally made available for such Software, and assist in its reconfiguration; (v) analyze and report on the space required for the Customer Data and the Software needed to provide the Services; (vi) assist in the execution of a parallel operation, data migration, and testing process until the transition to Customer or Customer's designee has been successfully completed; (vii) create and provide copies of the Customer Data in the format and on the media reasonably requested by Customer and, when directed by Customer to do so, delete (and certify in writing such deletion) all Customer Data in Licensor's possession or control from any tapes or other data storage media, including written records, in Licensor's possession or control except archival records as necessary for documentation of Licensor's engagement with Customer; (viii) provide a complete and up-to-date, electronic copy of the Policy and Procedures Manual, in the format and on the media reasonably requested by Customer; (ix) identify, and assist Customer in Provisioning, a suitable functionally equivalent replacement for any shared hardware or software then used by Licensor to provide the Services, and (x) provide other technical assistance as requested by Customer.

B. Customer or Customer's designee shall be permitted to undertake, without interference from Licensor or Licensor Affiliates (including counter-offers), to hire, effective after the later of the termination of the Term or completion of any Termination Assistance Services, any employees of Licensor or Licensor Affiliates primarily assigned to the performance of Services within the twelve (12) month period prior to the expiration or termination date by providing Licensor with written notice of its intent to hire any such employees no later than the latter of (i) forty-five (45) days prior to the expiration of the Term, or (ii) forty-five (45) days prior to the completion of any Termination Assistance Period. Licensor shall waive, and shall cause its Affiliates to waive, their rights, if any, under contracts with such personnel restricting the ability of such personnel to be recruited or hired by Customer or its designee. Customer or its designee shall have reasonable access to such employees of Licensor or Licensor Affiliates for interviews, evaluations, and recruitment. Customer shall conduct the above-described hiring activity in a manner that is not unnecessarily disruptive of the performance by Licensor of its obligations under this Agreement or any of the Implementation Agreements.

C. To the extent Customer or its designee is entitled under Section ____ (Intellectual Property) to a license, sublicense, or other right to use any Software or other IP utilized in performing the Services, Licensor shall provide Customer or its designee with such license, sublicense, or other right, including, Source Materials (where Customer has the right to such Source Materials), Object Code and Documentation related to Software (where Customer has the right to such Documentation), in Licensor's possession or control in a form reasonably requested by Customer. Notwithstanding anything in this Agreement to the contrary, Licensor shall have no obligation to provide Customer any Software that is Source Materials other than where the Source Material is Custom IP.

D. Customer or its designee shall have the right (but not the obligation, except as set forth in Sections ____ (Failure to Comply with the Transition-In Plan), _____ (Change of Control), ____ (Termination for Insolvency), or ____ (Termination for Convenience)) upon reasonable notice to purchase any Equipment owned by Licensor and which, on the date of expiration or termination of this Agreement, Licensor is using on a dedicated basis to perform the Services. In addition, at Customer's request, Licensor shall use commercially reasonable efforts to provide Customer with the right to either (i) lease directly from the applicable third party lessor (other than a Licensor Affiliate) any leased Equipment that on the date of expiration or termination of this Agreement Licensor is using on a dedicated basis to perform the Services; or (ii) assume Licensor's lease for any such Equipment (other than as to Equipment provided by a Licensor Affiliate), provided that Licensor shall use commercially reasonable efforts to minimize any costs associated with the exercise of any such right by Customer and any transfer, assumption or termination fees or expenses associated with the exercise of any such right shall be the responsibility of, and paid for by, Customer. Customer shall assume such lease obligations (or pay for the applicable lease buy-out) if obligated to do so in accordance with Exhibit ___ (Fees). Customer shall execute such documents as necessary for Licensor to be relieved of Licensor's obligations under such assumed leases after the transfer date. In the case of leases entered into specifically to provide the Services, Licensor shall use commercially reasonable efforts to obtain such rights in advance and shall not enter into any such lease not offering such rights without Customer's prior written consent, which shall not be unreasonably withheld or delayed (provided that the withholding of consent shall not preclude Licensor from then using a lease not entered into specifically for this engagement to acquire such Equipment). In all cases, such owned or leased Equipment shall be transferred in good working condition, reasonable wear and tear excepted, as of the expiration or termination date or the completion of any Services associated with such Equipment requested by Customer under this Agreement, whichever is later. In the case of Licensor-owned equipment, Licensor shall grant to Customer a warranty of title and a warranty that such Equipment is free and clear of all liens and encumbrances. Such conveyance by Licensor to Customer shall be at net book value (not to exceed fair market value at the time placed in service) calculated in accordance with generally accepted accounting principles using the depreciation schedule customarily used by Licensor for the applicable type of equipment (including equipment dedicated to Licensor internal use, used at shared Licensor service facilities and dedicated to specific Licensor customers). In the case of leased Equipment, Licensor shall represent and warrant that the lease is not in default and that all payments thereunder have been made through the date of transfer.

E. Licensor shall return to Customer, if not previously returned, all Customer Equipment, in condition at least as good as the condition thereof on the Reference Date, ordinary wear and tear accepted. Such Equipment shall be returned at the expiration or termination date or the completion of any Services or Termination Assistance Services associated with such Equipment requested by Customer under this Agreement, whichever is later.

F. Licensor shall inform Customer of Subcontracts or Third Party Vendor contracts primarily dedicated by Licensor, Licensor Subcontractors or Licensor Affiliates to perform the Services. Customer shall retain the right to contract directly with any such Subcontractor or Third Party Vendor. In addition, Licensor shall use commercially reasonable efforts to provide Customer with the right to contract directly with any Subcontractor or Third Party Vendor previously utilized by Licensor to perform any Services or to assume Licensor's contract with such Subcontractor or Third Party Vendor.

In the event that Licensor is able to obtain the right for Customer to assume such Subcontracts and Third Party Vendor contracts in accordance with the Subsection (F) above, Licensor shall assign the designated Subcontracts and Third Party Vendor contracts to Customer or its designee as of the expiration or termination date or the completion of any Services associated with such Subcontracts or Third Party Vendor contracts, whichever is later. There shall be no charge or fee imposed by Licensor on Customer related to such assignment and Licensor shall use commercially reasonable efforts to minimize or eliminate any such charges or fees imposed by any Subcontractors or Third Party Vendor. To the extent charges or fees are imposed by any Subcontractors or Third Party Vendor, such costs shall be paid by Customer. Licensor shall (i) represent and warrant that it is not in default of such Subcontracts and Third Party Vendor contracts; (ii) represent and warrant that all payments have been made thereunder through the date of assignment; and (iii) notify Customer of any defaults by Subcontractors or Third Party Vendor contractors with respect to such Subcontracts and Third Party Vendor contracts of which Licensor is then aware. Subject to Licensor's compliance with the requirements of this subsection, Customer shall represent and warrant to Licensor that, from the date of assumption, it will assume all contractual responsibilities and liability associated with such Subcontracts and Third Party Vendor contract assigned to Customer hereunder.

5.3.4 **Specific Performance.** Licensor acknowledges that, in the event it breaches (or attempts or threatens to breach) its obligation to provide [the services and software contemplated under this Agreement] [termination/expiration assistance] as provided in Section 6.6.3, Customer will be irreparably harmed. In such a circumstance, Customer may proceed directly to court. If a court of competent jurisdiction should find that Licensor has breached (or attempted or threatened to breach) any such obligations, Licensor agrees that without any additional findings of irreparable injury or other conditions to injunctive relief, it shall not oppose the entry of an appropriate order compelling performance by Licensor and restraining it from any further breaches (or attempted or threatened breaches).

- ***See Chapter 23.K.2 (15) for language allowing both parties to utilize the remedy of specific performance.***
- ***A Licensor should carefully consider the risks before including any language that allows the Customer to invoke the remedy of specific performance. Specific performance may have a significant impact on the Licensor's profitability and may serve to circumvent the limits of liability set forth in the agreement.***

5.3.5 **Cover.** In the event that this Agreement is terminated in whole or part for Licensor's breach, Customer shall have the right, at Licensor's expense, to engage third parties to correct Licensor's breach and to deliver any software or services that Licensor failed to deliver. Licensor shall continue performance of this Agreement to the extent not terminated.

- ***The Licensor should limit its liability for cover to the overall limit of liability of the contract and seek to prevent the Licensee from retaining the Licensor's competitors to complete the work.***

5.3.6 **Access to Source Code.**

- ***Each of the clauses set forth below seeks to address the release of source code to the customer, albeit each in a different way. A customer should review each clause to determine which best fits its needs. Often, a customer will utilize a combination of these approaches.***

In the event that this Agreement is terminated for Licensor's breach, Customer shall have the right to obtain, and Licensor shall have the obligation to grant to Customer, [upon payment to Licensor by Customer of a fee of _______________ U.S. Dollars (U.S.$ __________),] such nonexclusive, [royalty-free], non-transferable, personal, Source Code license for the Software as may be necessary in order to permit Customer to complete the development, installation, deployment, operation, and maintenance of the Software system as contemplated hereby. Set forth in Paragraph X of Appendix 5.3.6 is the terms and conditions of the Source Code license contemplated by this Section 5.3.6.

- ***This provision grants the Customer a Source Code license in the event of the Licensor's breach. It provides the option of requiring the Customer to purchase the license, which is unreasonable given the fact the Licensor has breached the contract. This language is fairly standard but the Customer need to carefully review the terms of any license to ensure such terms meet its needs.***

Alternatively:

In the event that this Agreement is terminated for Licensor's breach, all rights, title, and interest and all copyrights and other intellectual property rights including the right to use, reproduce, adapt, enhance, and commercialize the same, in and to the Custom Software or any part thereof, therefore developed pursuant hereto, shall immediately vest in Customer upon the effective date of termination agreed between the parties.

- ***This language transfers actual ownership of the custom software to the Customer as opposed to simply granting the Customer a license to use the source code. This provision would be utilized when the Licensor developed custom applications to the Licensor's core software and retained ownership of such enhancements under the term of the license. It would also be applicable***

in the unlikely event the Licensor custom developed a new application for the Customer and retained ownership under the terms of the development agreement.

and/alternatively:

Direct Access to Licensor Source Code. If the parties do not conclude an agreement with a Escrow Provider, of if Licensor fails to deposit conforming Source Materials including updates as required, then upon the occurrence of the conditions described in Section 5.3.6 above, Licensor shall provide Customer with all Source Materials immediately upon Customer's written request, subject to the same limitations on use set forth in Section 5.3.6.

- ***This provision addresses the issue of what happens if the parties fail to reach agreement on the terms of an escrow agreement or if the Licensor fails to deposit the required materials with the escrow agent. It seeks to provide a remedy outside of those set forth in the escrow agreement. In reality, however, if the Licensor breaches the terms of the escrow agreement, the Licensor will likely not provide the source code to the Customer as required under this language.***

and/alternatively:

Third Party Software. If Licensor is providing Third Party Software to Customer and the applicable third party license does not provide Customer with rights to Source Code, Licensor shall obtain an appropriate software escrow agreement from the third party licensor for Customer's benefit, or if unable to do so, shall obtain Customer's prior written consent that the Third Party Software may be provided without such an escrow agreement.

- ***This language seeks to ensure the Customer will have access to the source code for any third party software. By requiring the Licensor to obtain the Customer's consent prior to utilizing any third party software, the Customer will be aware and can ascertain the risks it faces in the event of the Licensor's breach.***

and/alternatively:

Customer Completion of Payment: Access to Software and Equipment Customer shall have the right to obtain, and Licensor shall have the obligation to grant to Customer, such nonexclusive, world-wide, permanent licenses as may be necessary or appropriate in order to permit Customer, or a third party engaged by Customer for such purpose, to complete the development, installation, deployment, operation, and maintenance of the Software system as contemplated hereby. The licenses so granted shall (a) be to all such Standard Software and other software, tools, and materials, in object and/or source form, as may be necessary and appropriate as aforesaid, and (b) be limited to the exclusive purposes of the completion of the obligations assumed by Licensor hereunder. The royalties payable by Customer with respect to the licenses so granted shall be equal to fifty percent (50%) of the royalties charged by Licensor in the normal course of business. At Customer's request, Licensor shall: (a) obtain any required consents from third parties and thereafter assign to Customer or its designee leases for some or all of the Equipment that was used primarily in providing the Services as of the date of termination/expiration of this Agreement, and Customer shall assume all obligations under such leases that relate to periods after such date, and (b) sell to Customer or its designee, at the lower of Licensor's then current book value, unrecovered capital payments, or fair market value, some or all of the Equipment owned by Licensor that was used primarily in providing the Services as of such date. Licensor shall also provide all user and other documentation relevant to such Equipment which is in Licensor's possession. Customer will assume responsibility under any maintenance agreements for such Equipment to the extent such responsibilities relate to periods after the date of termination/expiration of this Agreement. Licensor shall obtain any necessary rights and thereafter make available to Customer or its designee, pursuant to reasonable terms and conditions, any third party services then being utilized by Licensor in the performance of the Services including services being provided through third party service or maintenance contracts on Equipment and Software. Licensor will be entitled to retain the right to utilize any such third party services in connection with the performance of services for any other Licensor Customer.

- ***This language favors the Licensor, as it requires the Customer to pay royalty for use of the software in the event of the Licensor's breach.***

5.3.7 **Licensor Employees and Contractors.** In the event that this Agreement is terminated for Licensor's breach, Customer or Customer's designee shall be permitted to undertake, without interference from Licensor, to hire any Licensor employees primarily performing the Services as of the date Licensor receives notice of termination, or, in the case of expiration, within the six (6) month period (or longer period requested by Customer) prior to expiration. Licensor shall waive, and shall cause its subcontractors to waive, their rights, if any, under contracts with such personnel restricting the ability of such personnel to be recruited or hired by Customer. Customer or its designee shall have reasonable access to such personnel for interviews and recruitment. If Customer is entitled pursuant to this Agreement to a sublicense or other right to use any Software owned or licensed by Licensor and utilized in performing the Services, Licensor shall provide such sublicense or other right.

- ***In the event of the Licensor's breach, it is important that the Customer have access to the Licensor's employees and contractors. Access to the source code alone will usually not permit the Customer to maintain, support, or modify the software. The Customer's ability to do so will be significantly greater if it is allowed to hire the Licensor's employees and contractors. Thus, any prohibition on their solicitation should be waived in the event of the Licensor's breach.***

5.4 **Attorneys' Fees.** In the event of an alleged breach of this Agreement, the prevailing party shall be entitled to reimbursement of all of its costs and expenses, including reasonable attorneys' fees, incurred in connection with such dispute, claim, or litigation, including any appeal therefrom. For purposes of this Section, the determination of which party is to be considered the prevailing party shall be decided by the court of competent jurisdiction or independent party (i.e., mediator or arbitrator) that resolves such dispute, claim, or litigation.

5.5 **Services Not to Be Withheld**

5.5.1 **Prohibition.** Licensor shall not "Abandon" the Services. Unless otherwise specified in a Statement of Work, for the purposes of this Agreement, "Abandon," or "Abandonment" means: Licensor's actual willful non-performance of any material aspects of the Services in breach of the Agreement, and which results in a material adverse effect on (i) the ability of Customer to timely and properly receive and/or use the Services including the Services Transfer Assistance, or (ii) critical aspects of Customer's internal operations or financial reporting requirements, to be performed and provided by Licensor for Customer. For avoidance of doubt, an Abandonment will not have occurred, if Licensor has properly terminated, or has the right to terminate this Agreement, or if Licensor's performance is excused by Force Majeure Event in accordance with Section 32.

5.5.2 **Termination.** In the event of an Abandonment, Customer may, but shall not be required to, (i) terminate this Agreement for cause upon notice to Licensor pursuant to Section 12.1(a) (without observing the cure period set forth therein) and (ii) require Licensor to provide Services Transfer Assistance for a period of up to twelve (12) months from the effective date of the termination effected pursuant to this Section 5.5.2., provided that such Services Transfer Assistance is fully paid for by Customer in accordance with the terms of this Agreement. The exercise of Customer's right to require Licensor to provide the Services Transfer Assistance under this Section 5.5.2. shall not waive or release any rights, claims, or remedies that Customer may have for the Abandonment of the Services for the entire remaining portion of the Term.

5.5.3 **Injunctive Relief.** If Licensor breaches or threatens to breach Section 5.5.1., Licensor agrees that Customer will be irreparably harmed and shall be entitled to apply to a court of competent jurisdiction for an injunction compelling specific performance by Licensor of its obligations under this Agreement without the necessity of posting bond.

- ***As the result of Metropolitan Life Insurance, Co. v. Noble Lowndes Int'l, Inc., 643 N.E.2d 504 (NY App. 1994), which held that an intentional failure to perform did not pierce the limitation of liability, many cautious customers have insisted on including clauses similar to Section 5.5 above to mitigate their potential damages in such event. See Chapter 6.H.1 for a discussion of the issues involved in the selection of a governing law.***

6. Delivery of Deliverables—Risk of Loss—Title

6.1 **Delivery by Licensor of Deliverables.** Licensor shall deliver the Deliverables to Customer at __________ ("Delivery Place") on the Delivery Dates.

6.2 **Risk of Loss of Deliverables.** The risk of loss appurtenant to all Deliverables shall be transferred to Customer upon the issuance of an Acknowledgment of Receipt with respect thereto at the Delivery Place.

6.3 **Title to Standard Software.** It is hereby acknowledged and agreed that Customer shall not obtain title to any Standard Software. In lieu thereof, Customer shall obtain the license rights relating thereto stipulated in Section 3 hereof.

- ***Generally the Customer does not have a legitimate basis for claiming ownership of the Licensor's core software that the Licensor owned prior to entering into the license agreement. It is common, however, to negotiate ownership of any custom developed software as discussed in Section 6.4 below.***

6.4 **Title to Custom Software.** Without prejudice to the provisions of Section 3 hereof, Customer shall obtain good and clear title in and to the Custom Software upon the due payment by Customer of the sums relating thereto. Licensor hereby agrees to provide to Customer, upon its written request, with such title certificates, acknowledgments, and other documents as may be necessary or appropriate to establish Customer's good and clear title in and to the Custom Software.

- ***Section 6.4 and Section 12.1 assume that the parties have agreed that the Customer will own any Custom Software. See Sections 3.1 and 3.1.A, which assume the Licensor will retain sole ownership of all software.***
- ***Ownership of any Custom Software is often one of the most negotiated sections in a software license. The Licensor usually insists on retaining ownership to ensure the sanctity of its product while the Customer usually believes that because it has paid for the development, it should own the resulting product. A compromise can usually be reached based upon the needs of each party. For example, if the Licensor wants to retain ownership to ensure it owns its products, the Customer may be willing to accept royalty payments for future licenses granted by the Licensor as a tradeoff to ownership. If, however, the Customer wants to own the Custom Software to ensure its competitors do not receive a license to the software, the Customer may be willing to accept an exclusive license to the Custom Software and allow the Licensor to retain ownership. This exclusive license may or may not be limited to a set time period. See Section 3.1.A for an example of an exclusive license.***

6.5 **Title to Hardware.** Customer shall obtain good and clear title in and to the Hardware upon the payment in full by Customer of the sums relating thereto. Licensor hereby agrees to provide to Customer, upon its written request, with such title certificates, acknowledgments, and other documents as may be necessary or appropriate to establish Customer's good and clear title in and to the Hardware.

6.6 **Title to Documentation, Contractual Documents, and Deliverables other than those Prescribed by Sections 6.1–6.5 Hereof.** It is hereby acknowledged and agreed that Customer is, and shall remain, the owner of (a) all Documentation other than [list exceptions], (b) the Functional Specifications hereto, and (c) any and all information contained therein. Licensor shall obtain the license rights relating thereto stipulated in Section 12.1 hereof.

- ***This section assumes that the Customer will own the intellectual property rights developed by Licensor.***

7. Acceptance of Software and Services

7.1 **Acceptance Tests.** Licensor and Customer shall jointly conduct Software and Services acceptance tests in accordance with the Software Acceptance Plan during the installation process at a Customer designated location(s) during a thirty (30) day acceptance period. The acceptance period will commence once the Software is operational in the Customer designated location(s). The Software and Services shall (1) materially comply with the Functional Specifications; (2) function substantially in accordance with Licensor's specifications; (3) be compatible and substantially conform to the Documentation; and (4) substantially comply with the Software Acceptance Plan. Upon Acceptance, the Customer shall immediately execute a Certificate of Acceptance, substantially in the form attached hereto as Exhibit 7.1.

- ***Because the Licensor has greater familiarity with its own software, the Licensor should create the first draft of the Software Acceptance Plan. The licensee should then modify it to make sure the plan reflects the parties' intent.***

7.2 **Failure to Comply.** If, during the acceptance period, Customer determines that the Software and/or Services do not substantially meet the above requirements, Customer shall so notify Licensor in writing, specifying in detail the area of noncompliance. Licensor shall use its good faith efforts to correct all conditions that prevent the Software and/or Services from substantially meeting the requirements within fifteen (15) calendar days following receipt of notice from Customer. If all Customer reported conditions that prevent the Software and/or Services from substantially complying with the acceptance criteria are not corrected by the end of acceptance period, the Customer will notify the Licensor, in writing, within two (2) calendar days following the end of the acceptance period identifying the specific areas of noncompliance. Failure to notify Licensor in writing will constitute acceptance of the Software and/or Services. Upon receipt of written notice of noncompliance, an extension period of sixty (60) calendar days begins, which will supply Licensor with the time necessary to correct the deficiencies identified in the notice. Within five (5) days after such sixty (60) day period, the Customer will provide written notice to Licensor indicating Customer's acceptance of the Software and/or Services, Customer's desire to extend the "extension period" or the Customer's intent to terminate this Agreement without penalty or further financial obligation.

7.3 **Deemed Acceptance.** Notwithstanding anything contained herein, Customer shall be deemed to have accepted the Software or Services if Customer uses the Software or Services in the operation of Customer's business prior to accepting the Software.

- ***From the Licensor's perspective, the Agreement must provide that use of the Software in the operation of the Customer's business constitutes acceptance.***

Otherwise there is no incentive for the Customer to start or complete acceptance test procedures. If the Customer is using the software in conducting its business, the software most likely meets the Customer's requirements. Note that the definition of Acceptance under Section 1.1 disclaims any "deemed" acceptance.

Alternative Language Benefiting the Customer

Nothing else, including Customer's use of the Services and/or Software, or any components thereof, in a live, operational environment for limited testing-related purposes, shall constitute Acceptance (under applicable state contract law, the Uniform Commercial Code (UCC) or the Uniform Computer Information Transactions Act (UCITA), as adopted by any state) of any portion of the Services and/or Software, and/or the applicable Statement of Work.

- ***This language protects the Customer from any claim by the licensor that the Customer has constructively accepted the software while testing the software in a live environment or while it is being run in parallel with the legacy system.***

The language set forth below is additional language, albeit in more detail to be considered for inclusion.

Certification Testing Provision for Software

Pre-live testing for the Software ("Pre-Live Testing") shall commence on the date specified in the applicable Implementation Work plan, including the execution of the test suites as provided for in the applicable Test Plan. Customer shall have a period of thirty (30) calendar days (the "Pre-Live Testing Period") to conduct Pre-Live Testing pursuant to the Test Plan and the provisions of this Section. In order for Customer to determine whether the Software operates in accordance with the testing criteria set forth in the Test Plan, Pre-Live Testing shall include the following types of testing:

(a) Functionality Testing—the Software shall be tested on an individual basis for functional capabilities and characteristics;
(b) Integration Testing—the Software shall be tested for integration by testing the information flows to and from the Software and between and among the various modules of such Software; and
(c) Stress Testing—the Software shall undergo load testing by transmitting and processing high-volume operational data in a production-simulated environment to verify and confirm that the Software is integrated into the operating environment.

If any Defects are discovered as a result of Pre-Live Testing, Licensor shall promptly correct such Defects. When all Defects identified during Pre-Live Testing have been corrected by Licensor, Customer shall give Licensor written notice thereof and the Software shall thereafter be ready for Live Testing. Customer shall have a period of not less than sixty (60) calendar days following successful completion of all Pre-Live Testing (the "Live Testing Period") to test the Software under actual, everyday operating conditions to assess whether such Software operates in accordance with the applicable

Documentation, Specifications, Performance Standards, and Regulatory Requirements ("Live Testing"). (Defects defined as "High" and "Medium" defects.)

Defect Correction Provision

In the event any Defects are discovered during the Pre-Live Testing Period or Live Testing Period, Customer shall report such Defects to Licensor, and Licensor shall promptly correct all such Defects. Upon Licensor's receipt of notice from Customer of any Defects, the Pre-Live Testing Period or Live Testing Period (but not Customer's use of the Software) shall be suspended temporarily and shall recommence upon Licensor's receipt of written notice from Customer that such Defects have been corrects; provided, however, that Customer shall in no event have less than fifteen (15) calendar days to verify any correction provided by Licensor. Subject to the terms of Section [____] (the failure to achieve project acceptance section), such process shall repeat as often as necessary until all Defects have been corrected. Successful Live Testing shall occur when the Software: (a) has been operating for the Live Testing Period and all High Defects and Medium Defects have been corrected, and (b) has been operating during the last ten (10) calendar days of the Live Testing Period without experiencing any High Defects or any Medium Defects.

Post-Acceptance Remedy

Following Acceptance, if Customer discovers that the Software fails to comply with any of the functional or performance representations and warranties, within ten (10) calendar days of Customer's notice to Licensor of such breach, Licensor shall repair, replace, or correct the applicable Software and/or provide corrective equipment and/or software without any cost to Customer as required to repair, replace, or correct such defective Software. If Licensor is not able to repair, replace, or correct the Software with such ten (10) calendar day period, Customer shall be entitled, in its sole discretion, to: (a) seek monetary damages from the Licensor; (b) terminate in whole or part the Agreement and or the applicable Statement of Work for such Software; (c) receive a refund of all monies paid to Licensor for the defective Software; and/or (d) seek any other legal and equitable rights and remedies Customer may have.

8. Price and Payments

8.1 **Price.** Without prejudice to the other provisions of Section 8, in consideration of the development and delivery by Licensor of the Deliverables and the provision of the Support Services pursuant to Section 11 hereof, Licensor shall invoice Customer and Customer shall pay Licensor, pursuant to the terms and conditions of this Section 8, the following aggregate sums:

	U.S. Dollars
For Hardware:	
For Standard Software:	
For Custom Software:	
Grand Total:	

The aforesaid aggregate sums shall be paid in _______ (___) installments, ____ (___) of which are to be made pursuant to Section 8.2 hereof and ______ (___) of which are to be made pursuant to Section 8.3 hereof.

Additional Language that May Be Applicable for Overseas Development

8.1.A **Remote Network Connectivity.** Licensor's offshore rates include only Licensor's standard VPN "Client-to-Site" remote connectivity, in which (1) VPN software is installed directly on the individual developer's desktop computer in India and (2) a secure VPN network connection is established, utilizing the Internet, between the desktop and Customer's VPN network termination point. Additional remote networking components are available at additional cost. For the avoidance of doubt, such additional components include but are not limited to:

- ***A scalable, site-to-site VPN network connection between Licensor's Global Network and Customer,***
- ***Design, installation, and testing of the above,***
- ***Managed firewall services,***
- ***India-based printers,***
- ***Additional network equipment, and user authentication tokens or certificates.***

8.2 **Cash Advances.** The Parties have agreed that Customer is to make the following cash advances in order to provide Licensor with some of the working capital necessary to perform hereunder:

Cash Advance Number	Event Giving Rise to the Cash Advance	Amount of the Cash Advance
1	Letter of Intent	
2	Contract Signature	
3	Milestone 1	
4	Milestone 2	
5	Delivery	
TOTAL		

All cash advances so paid by Customer shall not, when paid, be deemed to have been earned by Licensor, either for accounting purposes or for purposes of this Agreement. Consequently, each cash advance shall be deemed to constitute an advance payment for the Deliverables to be delivered by Licensor subsequent thereto and shall be deemed to be "earned," in part or in full, if and when the payment against which it is taken as a credit is made pursuant to said Section 8.3 hereof. In the event that this Agreement is terminated, by Licensor, Customer, or operation of law, Licensor shall forthwith place in escrow, pursuant to the terms and conditions of the Escrow

Agreement attached hereto and made a part hereof as Appendix 8.2, that portion of the cash advances theretofore paid which have not then been earned.

- ***Section 8.2 characterizes progress payments or milestone payments as "advances." By characterizing these payments as an "advance," the Customer seeks to undercut any claim by the Licensor that the Licensor is entitled to retain any monies in the event Licensor breaches the contract. The advances are matched against the payment schedule set forth in Section 8.3.***
- ***Section 8.2 provides a mechanism for the Customer to advance money to the Licensor for cash advances to help the Licensor eliminate cash flow problems.***

8.3 **Payments to Be Made with Respect to Deliverables.** Licensor shall issue invoices for the amounts set forth in the following table upon the occurrence of the following events, at which time the payments corresponding to such events shall be deemed "earned"; Customer shall remit the net payment stipulated in said table pursuant to the provisions of Sections 8.1 and 8.2 hereof:

Payment Number	Event Giving Rise to Payment	Amount of Payment	Credit from Cash Advance Earned	Net Payment
1	Deliverable A	X	Cash Advance A and B	X - (A+B)
2	Deliverable B	Y	Cash Advance C	Y - C
3	Final Acceptance Certificate	Z	N/A	Z
TOTALS				

- ***The amounts in the foregoing table that are marked with an asterisk (*) are subject to adjustment pursuant to the provisions of Section 8.4 hereof.***
- ***Section 8.3 corresponds with Section 8.2. Section 8.3 provides the mechanism to vest payment in the Licensor after Licensor's successful performance.***

8.4 **Adjustment of Prices.** The amounts expressed in Payments Number _____, in the table set forth in Section 8.3 hereof that are marked with an asterisk (*) shall be subject to adjustment pursuant to the following formula:

$$P = P_0 \, (0.15 + 0.7 * S_1/S_0 + 0.15 * Psdc_1/Psdc_0)$$

P	Amount of Net Payment after adjustment
P_0	Amount of the Net Payment prescribed in the table set forth in Section 8.3 hereof prior to adjustment
S_1	Syntec salary index value for the month of invoicing
$Psdc_1$	Syntec products and services index value for the month of invoicing
S_0	Syntec salary index value for MONTH 2011
$Psdc_0$	Syntec products and services index value for MONTH 2011

Notwithstanding the foregoing, in the event that Licensor is obligated to pay liquidated damages with respect to the late issuance of the Acceptance Certificates or the Provisional Acceptance Certificates, the payment to be made upon the issuance of one of the aforesaid Acceptance Certificates shall not be adjusted pursuant to this Section 8.4 with respect to the period extending from the Delivery Date for the issuance of the Acceptance Certificate in question up to and including the date on which the invoice for the said payment is issued.

This section is illustrative of a mathematical formula to adjust the licensor's prices to reflect the impact of inflation. The actual methodology adopted should reflect the geographic region where the majority of the licensor's employees will be located or employed. The formula above is specific to France as the "Syntec salary index" is a salary index compiled by "Syntec Informatique," a French consortium of software services companies (including many U.S. companies) established in 1970 to track French technology salaries, products, and services. Two common indexes used for the United States are the Consumer Price Index (CPI) and the Employment Cost Index, Civilian Workers, Not Seasonally Adjusted, Compensation Costs (ECI), published by the Bureau of Labor Statistics, United States Department of Labor. The CPI is a broad based index that reflects a large "basket" of goods while the ECI is focused solely on labor costs. The parties should carefully consider which index best reflects the nature of their agreement. See Chapter 3.C.8(iii).

For transactions involving international cost/pricing, refer to the Foreign Labor Statistics section of the U.S. Department of Labor, Bureau of Labor Statistics website (http://www.bls.gov/fls), and/or (http://www.bls.gov/bls/other.htm#International).

Currently, consumer price indices are available on this site for the following countries outside the United States: Canada, Australia, Japan, Austria, Belgium, Denmark, France, Germany, Italy, Netherlands, Norway, Spain, Sweden, Switzerland, and the United Kingdom. If you require a country that is not on this list, there are links on the website to the various statistical agencies around the world. Two other sources on the Internet where international inflation data can be found are http://www.oecd.org, which publishes inflation data for its member countries, or http://laborsta.ilo.org/, which provides consumer price indices for almost every country in the world.

Examples of some of the common indices are provided below:

- ***For work performed from India:***

  The all-India Consumer Price Index for Urban Non-Manual Employees, CPI (UNME) on base 1984–85=100, as released by the Government of India, Ministry of Statistics and Programme Implementation, Central Statistical Organisation (CSO). This data can be referenced at the website (http://www.mospi.nic.in).
- ***For work performed from North America:***

  Employment Cost Index (ECI), Not Seasonally Adjusted, Total Compensation, Professional, Specialty, and Technical Occupations, Private Industry (U.S. Department of Labor, Bureau of Labor Statistics).

- ***For work performed from Germany:***
  Index of Collectively Agreed Wages of Wage Earners (Federal Statistical Office—Germany).
- ***For work performed from Switzerland:***
  Index of Real Wages Adjusted for est. Inflation (Swiss Federal Statistical Office).
- ***For work performed from the United Kingdom:***
  Average Earnings Index: Service Industries (National Statistics Office).
- ***For work performed from Canada:***
  Statistics Canada, Canadian Statistics, The Economy, Latest Indicators, Labour (Employment by major industry groups, and province, seasonally adjusted).

Alternative Language to Section 8.4

8.4.A **Fees Charged by Licensor.** The fees charged by Licensor for the Services may be increased by Licensor once annually commencing on the date one (1) year from the Effective Date; provided, however, that such annual increases shall not exceed the percentage increase in the ECI for the applicable Service period. In no event shall such increases exceed the following percentages over the previous year rates, nor shall such increases be cumulative from year to year:

Date	Maximum Percentage Increase
September 1, 2005 to August 31, 2006	X%
September 1, 2006 to August 31, 2007	X%
September 1, 2007 to August 31, 2008	X%
September 1, 2008 to August 31, 2009	X%

On or after September 1, 2007, Licensor shall have the right to request a meeting between the parties to propose a fee adjustment. If the parties cannot agree upon a fee adjustment within ten (10) business days of the request, Customer shall have the right to: (a) terminate this Agreement and Customer shall have no termination fee obligations, or (b) continue this Agreement by paying Licensor adjusted Service fees based on the actual ECI increase for the fiscal years commencing September 1, 2007 and September 1, 2008, respectively and as applicable. Any invoice relating to fees for any Services shall detail: (a) the Services performed (i.e., each activity, task, and/or milestone), (b) the identity of the Licensor personnel performing the Services, and (c) the number of hours and corresponding fees attributable to each such person's performance of the Services.

If you use this Section 8.4.A, insert this definition in the "Definitions" Section of your agreement: "'**ECI**' shall mean the official Employment Cost Index, Civilian Workers, Not Seasonally Adjusted, Compensation Costs, published by the Bureau of Labor Statistics United States Department of Labor."

Alternatively:

Renewal Pricing Terms. No more than once every twenty-four (24) months, but in no event earlier than twenty-six (26) months from the Effective Date, Licensor may propose an increase in the fees listed on Schedule __. Such proposed increases must be negotiated by the parties in good faith, with any resulting increases not exceeding the lesser of (a) 105 percent of the applicable fee charged by Licensor for comparable services during the immediately preceding twenty-four (24) month period, or (b) percentage increases in the Consumer Price Index (Workers) (CPI-W) of the U.S. Department of Labor for the relevant geographical area of the position for the relevant time period.

8.5 **Interest.** Licensor may charge Customer a one and one-half percent (1½%) monthly finance charge to be calculated monthly with respect to all outstanding amounts not paid within thirty (30) days following the date of Licensor's invoice(s), but in no event shall any finance charge exceed the maximum allowed by law.

- ***Licensor must have the right to charge interest on unpaid balances, otherwise the Customer may not have a motivation to pay its bills on time. If a dispute occurs, Licensor may be unable to charge the Customer interest while the dispute is being resolved or afterwards if Licensor is successful in its claim. The interest rate should be high enough so that the Customer does not view the Licensor as a bank. At the same time, the Customer should include a license provision allowing the Customer to charge interest on any unpaid amounts the Licensor owes the Customer.***

8.6 **Taxes.** There shall be added to the charges provided for in this Agreement amounts equal to any taxes, whether federal, state, or local, however designated, that may be validly levied or based upon this Agreement or upon the Software, Hardware, and Services furnished hereunder, excluding, however, taxes based on or measured by Licensor's net income, and any taxes or amounts in lieu thereof paid or payable by Licensor in respect of the foregoing. Taxes payable by Customer shall be billed as separate items on Licensor's invoices and shall not be included in Licensor's prices. Customer shall have the right to have Licensor contest with the imposing jurisdiction, at Customer's expense, any such taxes that Customer deems are improperly levied.

- ***The Customer as the purchaser is required by law to pay sales taxes where applicable. Traditionally, sales taxes were not collected on services but as states have looked for additional sources of revenue they have sought to tax services. To protect itself from unanticipated costs or a change in the law, Licensors should insist on including language requiring the customer to pay all taxes except taxes on Licensor's income. If the Customer claims a tax exemption it must produce the appropriate documentation to prove its exemption. See Chapter 23. Form 23.I.4 for a matrix of the different types of taxes collected by each state on technology transactions.***

As to Licensor personnel that ultimately remain or have intent to remain on the assignment for more than 12 months, or who perform services in states/countries other than where they are permanently assigned, or in other certain limited situations, there may be an increased tax burden pursuant to home and work jurisdiction tax laws. Customer will be responsible for, and will pay, the increased expenses related to federal, state, and local tax assistance provided by Licensor to the affected Licensor personnel. Application of the appropriate tax rules will be determined by Licensor in accordance with Internal Revenue Service guidelines. The charges will be billed, when appropriate, with the travel and living expenses affected and incurred in the performance of the Services detailed in this Agreement or a Work Order attached hereto. In the case of services performed outside the individual's permanent work country, there may be additional charges as a result of the international assignment program.

Licensor will invoice Customer for Services and applicable taxes directly where appropriate and may provide estimated payment schedules in advance to address the potential tax impact. In addition, Licensor will invoice Customer monthly for actual travel and living expenses, applicable taxes, and other reasonable expenses incurred in connection with the Services. Invoices are payable upon receipt.

Alternatively:

Customer shall also reimburse Licensor for any incremental taxes incurred by the employee due to Customer's requirements that the Licensor employee provide Services from another tax jurisdiction other than Licensor's employee's domicile.

- ***Section 162 of the Internal Revenue Code requires an employer to include as income on an employee's W-2 any monies paid to such employee for travel and living expenses for any assignment in which the employee provides services in a location outside if its home state for more than 12 consecutive months. The employer in most instances will "gross up" such payments to the employee to mitigate the financial impact to the employee. The employer needs to include the language set forth above to avoid incurring significant un-reimbursable costs in the provision of the services. The parties can limit their exposure to such costs by rotating the employees assigned to a project and having the employees work remotely.***

Alternative Language Benefiting Customer

8.6.A **Taxes**

8.6.A.1 **Responsibility.** The charges described in Section 8.1 to be paid by Customer are inclusive of all applicable income, sales, use, gross-receipts, excise, personal property, real property, intangibles, or other similar taxes based upon or measured by (i) Licensor's cost in acquiring or providing Equipment, materials, supplies, or services furnished to or used by Licensor in providing and performing the Services; (ii) the value or cost or use of all Licensor Equipment, Licensor Software, and other Licensor resources however described; and (iii) Licensor's revenues, income, and/or profit. Licensor shall be solely responsible for remitting all the applicable taxes to the appropriate taxing authority in each jurisdiction. Each Party shall bear sole responsibility for all taxes, assessments, and other real or personal property-related levies on its owned or leased real or personal property, for franchise or similar taxes on its business, for employment taxes on its employees, and for intangible taxes on property it owns or licenses.

8.6.A.2 **Taxes on the Services.** Notwithstanding Section 8.6.A.1, if a value added tax or tax on services is assessed solely and directly with respect to Charges to Customer for the provision of the Services by Licensor to Customer under this Agreement, Customer shall be responsible for and pay the amount of any such tax to Licensor, or as the law otherwise requires, in addition to the Charges.

8.6.A.3 **Cooperation to Minimize Tax Liability.** The Parties agree to reasonably cooperate with each other in good faith to more accurately determine and reflect each Party's tax liability. Each Party shall provide and make available to the other any resale certificates and other exemption certificates or information reasonably requested by either Party. The Parties will also work together to segregate the Charges, reimbursements, expenses, and other amounts payable hereunder, into separate payment accounts charged under separate invoices, as appropriate, for Services and the components of the Services (i.e., components that are taxable and non-taxable, including those for which a sales, use, or similar tax has already been paid by Licensor and for which Licensor functions merely as a paying agent for Customer in receiving goods, supplies, or services including licensing arrangements that otherwise are non-taxable or have previously been subjected to tax, components that are capitalized, and components that are expensed).

8.7 **Disputed Amounts.** If an invoiced amount is disputed in good faith by Customer then, until resolution of the dispute occurs pursuant to Article 29, Customer may suspend disputed payments and toll the running of time for default by: (a) paying the undisputed amount, if any, and (b) sending a written statement of exceptions to Licensor. All of Licensor's obligations shall continue unabated during the duration of the dispute resolution. In the event that, as a result of the dispute resolution process, Customer is found to have inappropriately withheld payment two (2) times in any twelve (12) month period, Customer shall pay interest to Licensor on the second withheld payment and any subsequent withheld payments at a rate equal to the then-applicable Prime Rate plus ____ percent as published in the *Wall Street Journal.*

- ***To protect against the Customer wrongfully withholding payment from the Licensor, the Licensor should include language allowing the Licensor to charge interest for any amounts wrongfully withheld. See also Section 8.5 providing for interest on undisputed amounts.***

8.8 **Discounts**

All fees paid by customer or any of its affiliates to supplier, regardless of the agreement governing the services, shall be aggregated for the purpose of calculating discounts under this agreement. Unless expressly prohibited by a separate agreement, the existence of such separate agreement shall not preclude any customer business unit or affiliate from obtaining services under this agreement. All services provided by supplier, regardless of the line of business, business unit, or the legal relationship between supplier and the entity/unit that is providing the service, shall be governed by the terms of this agreement, and to the extent separate implementation agreements are approved in writing by customer, such implementation agreements shall not change, alter, or modify any term of this agreement, except as required by the law of the country in which services are to be provided under such implementation agreement or as set forth in Section ____ (terms and conditions). Other than modifications required to comply with the law of the country in which services are to be provided under such implementation agreement or as set forth in Section ____ (terms and conditions), no negotiation or counter proposals by supplier of terms contained in this agreement is permissible in connection with the execution of an implementation agreement. Supplier commits to acting as the sole interface with customer in connection with the negotiation of implementation agreements, regardless of the nature of the legal relationship between supplier and an "in-country" affiliate. This provision is specifically intended to eliminate efforts to renegotiate the terms of this agreement in the context of executing implementation agreements.

Additional Language Favoring Customer

8.A **Most Favored Customer.** Licensor represents and warrants to Customer that all of the pricing terms set forth in this Agreement are comparable to or better than the equivalent pricing terms being offered by Licensor to any present customer of Licensor of the same or lesser [insert limiting factors] as customer licensing similar Software and Services. If, during the term of this Agreement, Licensor enters into arrangements with any other customer of the same or lesser [insert limiting factors] as Customer to receive similar Software and Services and provides such customer more favorable pricing terms than those set forth herein, Licensor shall immediately provide Customer with a detailed written notice of such terms (without disclosing Licensor's customer) and, upon such notice, this Agreement shall be deemed amended to provide the same pricing terms to Customer.

or

Most Favored Customer. In no event shall Customer pay a fee for any Services, whether such Services are provided on a Fixed Fee basis or on a time and materials basis, that exceeds the fees paid by any of Licensor's other customers for services comparable to the Services. On an annual basis Licensor's auditor shall certify in writing that (1) no Fixed Fee arrangement and no rate or price set forth in Exhibit D exceeds this limitation, and (2) any fee that would exceed this limitation has been reduced to be the same as or less than the lowest price charged to any of Licensor's other customers for comparable services. Licensor's compliance with this provision shall be subject to audit pursuant to Section ___. ***[Insert Cross Reference to relevant audit language.]***

- ***Customers usually desire "Most Favored Customer" wording to ensure they receive the best price offered by the Licensor. The Licensor, however, should avoid the insertion of this language to avoid having its prices ratcheted down to the lowest common denominator. Licensors often try to dilute the effect of such language by inserting qualifying language (i.e., "if Customer purchases like quantities, under similar terms and conditions") that makes it difficult for the Customer to ever claim the benefit of its perceived bargain. The language set forth above is self initiating and benefits the Customer as it requires the Licensor to take the affirmative step of notifying the Customer that the Customer is entitled to a lower price rather than having the Customer have to claim the benefit from the Licensor.***

8.B **Benchmarking.** On the first anniversary of the Effective Date and each anniversary thereafter, Customer shall be entitled at its option to select a third party (the "Benchmarker") to compare Licensor's Services and fees with other arrangements of Licensor or other consultants of a similar nature, size, and significance ("Similar Arrangements") to ensure that (i) Licensor is providing the Services at a level equal to or greater than the level at which Similar Arrangements are performed, and (ii) Licensor's fees are competitive with the fees for which Similar Arrangements are performed. Customer shall attempt in good faith to select a Benchmarker agreeable to both parties, but if the parties are not able to agree upon a Benchmarker within a reasonable amount of time then Customer shall have sole discretion to select the Benchmarker, provided that Customer shall not select a Benchmarker that is a direct competitor of Licensor without Licensor's express written consent. Each party shall pay half of the cost for the services of the Benchmarker. In the event the Benchmarker determines Customer is not receiving (a) Services at a level equal to or greater than the level at which Similar Arrangements are performed, or (b) fees that are competitive with the fees for which Similar Arrangements are performed, then the parties shall revise the Services or adjust the fees, as applicable, in accordance with such determination, provided that in no circumstance shall the level of Services be diminished or decreased nor shall the fees payable by Customer be increased.

Alternative Language Favorable to Customer

Benchmarking

8.B.1 **Benchmarking Procedure.** Licensor shall improve the quality of the Services during the term of this Agreement. Customer shall have the right, at any time during the Term and at its cost, to benchmark any of the Services to ensure that the Services are competitive with respect to price, quality, service, performance standards, and technology. Customer shall consult with Licensor in advance concerning the definition and specifications of each Service provided by Licensor that Customer desires to subject to the benchmarking process, but the final decision on such definition and specifications shall be made by Customer. Licensor shall, at Customer's request, prepare and provide, or cooperate with Customer's reasonable requests, given the nature of the Services pursuant to the applicable Work Process Agreement, in the preparation of comparative competitive information and data verifying the competitive nature of the Services delivered or offered in such frequency, methodology and detail as required by Customer. The benchmark procedure shall be performed by a third party selected by Customer. Such third party shall not be a direct competitor of Licensor. The benchmarker will deliver the benchmark results to Customer in a written report. If the results of the benchmark show, in Customer's reasonable judgment, that Services provided by Licensor are not competitive with respect to price, quality, service, performance standards and technology, then Customer shall provide Licensor with a copy of the benchmark results.

8.B.2 **Licensor Review of Benchmarking Results.** Upon receipt of the benchmarking results, Licensor shall be given a thirty (30) day period (or such other period as may be agreed in writing) to review the results and discuss with Customer any disagreement with the benchmark results. At the end of such review period, Licensor shall be given the opportunity to propose a plan to address any or all of the benchmark results that Licensor agrees show Licensor not to be competitive. Such plan will be delivered to Customer within thirty (30) days of the end of the review period specified above or such other period as shall be agreed between by Customer and Licensor in writing.

8.B.3 **Customer's Acceptance or Rejection of Licensor's Plan.** Customer must accept or reject the plan within thirty (30) days of receipt. If accepted, Licensor must implement the plan in strict accordance with its terms. If Customer accepts the plan and Licensor fails to deliver in line with the plan, or if Customer does not accept the plan, Customer may terminate the Services upon sixty (60) days' written notice and such termination shall be deemed to have occurred pursuant to Section [Termination for Convenience].

Additional Language Where Appropriate

8.C **CPU License.** The machine class of each Software License, where applicable, shall be determined at the time of execution of this Agreement, **in accordance with Licensor's then current price list as may be amended from time to time [and initially set forth in Appendix 8.C]**. Unless Customer moves the Software to a higher class Central Processing Unit (CPU), said machine class shall not change for any existing License and Licensor shall not restructure machine classes or License fees in any way that will cause an increase in any License fees for Licenses already acquired by Customer, other than in accordance with this Section.

- ***Pricing should be determined by the type of license granted.***
- ***Depending on the type of pricing utilized by Licensor paragraphs 8.B, 8.C, 8.D, or 8.E may not be applicable.***
- ***Licensor must have the ability to amend its pricing, otherwise the Customer may claim the price is fixed for the duration of the license or the Agreement.***

8.D **CPU Upgrade.** If Customer moves the Software to a higher machine class CPU, Customer shall notify Licensor in writing thirty (30) days prior to the move and shall incur and pay an upgrade charge that will be the difference between the License fee charged for functionally identical Software placed on the higher class CPU, after any associated discounts are applied, and the License fee paid by Customer for the Software being moved.

8.E **Transfer Fees.** If Customer desires, subject to obtaining Licensor's prior written consent, to operate the Software subsequent to a change in control of Customer, other than with the designated CPU's or other than at Customer's site identified in this Agreement, Customer will be required to pay Licensor a transfer fee according to Licensor's then-existing fee structure.

- ***Section 8.E allows Licensor to charge the Customer a transfer fee for a change of control. See Section 22.2 for alternative language for the Customer's rights upon a change of control.***

8.F **Service Fees.**

8.F.1 **Fixed Fee Services.** All Services identified in a purchase order or statement of work as Services to be paid at a fixed rate shall be invoiced according to the following:

% of Services Fee	**Event**
25%	Execution of the Purchase Order/ Statement of Work
50%	Spread equally among no less than two (2) Critical Path Milestones
25%	Project Acceptance

8.F.2 **Time-and-Materials Services.** All Services identified in a purchase order or statement of work as Services to be paid on a time-and-materials basis shall be invoiced in accordance with the terms set forth in this Section. Licensor shall invoice Customer for an amount equal to eighty-five percent (85%) of the fees for all Services rendered by Licensor as such Services are rendered. The remaining fifteen percent (15%) of such fees shall be invoiced by Licensor upon Acceptance.

8.G **Customer Credit Risk.** If in Licensor's reasonable judgment, Customer's financial condition does not justify the terms of payment specified above, unless Customer immediately pays for all Software, Software Products, and Services that have been delivered, and pays in advance for the balance of Software, Software Products, and Services remaining to be delivered during the term of this Agreement, Licensor may terminate this Agreement without further liability to Customer.

8.H **Parent Company Guarantee.** [Concurrently with the execution of this Agreement,] Licensor/Customer shall within twenty-one (21) days from the date hereof provide a guarantee from its parent company **[List Name]** and in the form of Exhibit 8H. The cost of obtaining the guarantee shall be at the sole expense of Licensor/Customer. The parent company guarantee shall be valid from the date of this

Agreement until **[final payment] [thirty (30) days after the expiry of the warranty period of the software]**.

8.I **Customer Royalty.** In consideration of Customer partially funding the development of the Custom Software, Licensor shall pay Customer a royalty on the future licensing of the Software as set forth in this Section 8.I. Licensor shall pay to Customer a royalty based on the "Gross License Fee" ("Fee") of the Custom Software for all third party licenses of Custom Software by Licensor made within _______ ( ) months from the earlier of [**Acceptance**] or the Licensor licensing such module to any third party.

8.I.1 **Fee.** Subject to the limitations of Section 8.I above, Customer shall receive five percent (5%) of the Fee received by Licensor for all licenses of the Custom Software licensed by the Licensor.

- ***Both parties should carefully review any language describing the Customer's right to receive a royalty. For example, the Licensor would want to revise the above language to limit the Customer's right to receive a royalty to those funds actually received by the Licensor. The above language places the risk of a bad debt on the Licensor, as the Licensor may be obligated to pay the Customer a royalty on license fees the Licensor did not receive.***

8.I.2 **Fee Cap**. Notwithstanding anything contained in this Section 8.I, Customer shall not be entitled to receive royalties once it has received an aggregated _____________ ($ ________) in royalties from Licensor's licensing of the Custom Software.

- ***The Licensor should seek to place an absolute cap on the royalties payable to the Customer. The Customer should be happy with recovering an amount equal to the fees it paid the Licensor. An alternative is to cap the Customer's recovery at a multiple of the fees paid by Customer to the Licensor for the module's development. In no event should the Licensor allow the royalty payments to be unlimited in either the amount or the period of time in which the Customer is entitled to receive them.***

8.I.3 **Payment**. On or before the last business day of the first month following the end of each calendar quarter, Licensor shall generate a report that shall document the number of licenses of the Custom Software granted by the Licensor in the previous calendar quarter and all license fees received by the Licensor from the licensing of the Custom Software in the previous calendar quarter. Licensor shall calculate the fees, if any, that are due to Customer under the terms of this Section 8.H. and within thirty (30) days of such date, Licensor shall pay to Customer all such monies due Customer.

8.I.4 **Audit**. Licensor shall keep all usual and proper books and records pertaining to the licensing and use of the Custom Software. During the Term of this Agreement and for three years thereafter, Customer and/or its designated representatives shall have the right to audit (including by inspecting and copying any such books and records) Licensor, in order to verify its compliance with the terms of this

Agreement. Customer shall conduct such audits during the Licensor's normal business hours and in such a manner as not to interfere unreasonably with Licensor's normal business operations. Customer may conduct such audits from time to time, as Customer deems necessary, but shall use any information obtained or observed during the course of the audit solely for the purposes of determining (i) whether the Licensor is making the proper royalties in compliance with the terms of this Agreement, and is otherwise in compliance with this Agreement and any applicable laws, and (ii) of enforcing its rights under this Agreement and any applicable laws. Except to the extent necessary to enforce its rights, Customer and its representatives will hold all such information in confidence.

- ***In contracts where the customer is entitled to receive a royalty or is being charged on a time and materials basis, the contract should always provide for the Customer's right to audit the Licensor even if the Customer never plans to invoke it. Audit clauses are not appropriate for fixed price contracts under which the Customer is not entitled to a royalty.***

8.J **Reports, Payments, Accounting, and Inspections**

8.J.1 **Periodic Accounting Reports.** On or before the last business day of the first month following the end of each calendar quarter, Licensee shall generate a report using functionality provided by the system that shall document Licensee's user count. If the user count provided by the report is greater than the current license limitation, Licensee shall report the current user count to Licensor. Licensor shall determine what fees are due to Licensor under the terms of this Agreement and Licensor shall invoice Licensee for the appropriate amount.

8.J.2 **Payments.** Within thirty (30) days of receipt of any invoice referenced in the preceding Paragraph, Licensee shall pay to Licensor all payments due and payable pursuant to Article Y of this Agreement.

8.J.3 **Books and Records.** Licensee shall maintain at its principal place of business full, accurate, and complete books of account and records reflecting all activities and transactions subject to or covered by this Agreement. Licensee shall keep such books and records in at least sufficient detail as will permit the written reports provided for in this Agreement to be made and the licensee fees payable hereunder to be determined. These books and records shall be open to inspection and/or audit during usual business hours, from time to time, upon reasonable advance notice, by Licensor or by Licensor's designated representatives, who shall be entitled to copy extracts therefrom. Licensor's right to inspect shall include any of Licensee's records reflecting information either provided to or maintained for any regulatory agencies or authorities or industry associations pertaining to the Software or to Licensee's operations under the License. Such books and records shall be maintained for at least three (3) years after the period to which they pertain for the purposes, e.g., of verifying the accuracy of the payments by Licensee. Licensee shall cause its appropriate employees and agents to cooperate with Licensor in connection with such inspections or audits.

8.J.4 **Audit.** In the event that Licensor requests an independent audit of Licensee's books and records pursuant to this Agreement, all audit expenses shall be borne by Licensor. However, should such audit reveal a deficiency in the licensee fees paid by Licensee of greater than five percent (5%) of any payment thereof, then Licensee shall bear the entire cost of the audit.

8.J.5 **Inspections by Licensor.** Licensor shall have the right at any time during normal business hours, upon reasonable advance notice, to visit and inspect Licensee's facilities, and all operations by Licensee conducted under the License, and all equipment and materials utilized by Licensee in so doing. Licensee shall cause its appropriate employees and agents to cooperate with Licensor and to provide reasonable facilities and assistance to Licensor in connection with such visits or inspections.

9. Personnel, Management, New Projects, and Testing

- ***The Sections set forth below generally favor the Customer in that the Licensor is contractually obligated to commit certain individuals to the project. By doing so, the Licensor potentially limits its ability to operate and manage its overall business. Consequently, the Licensor may want to delete some of the provisions set forth below.***

9.1 **Cooperation with Customer.** Licensor shall cooperate fully with Customer as necessary to provide the Services and shall disclose such information to Customer relating to Licensor, the ABC System, and Software as may be required or necessary to provide the Services. The parties agree that joint planning and experienced personnel are critical factors for successfully providing the Services.

9.2 **Licensor Personnel**

9.2.1 **General.** Licensor shall provide sufficient qualified personnel to perform Licensor's obligations hereunder, which personnel shall have a minimum of twelve (12) months of experience similar or related to the tasks to which they are assigned to perform. All Licensor personnel described in this Agreement shall be intimately familiar with Customer, its networks, operations, needs, and requirements. Additionally, all such personnel shall be intimately familiar with [industry] functions and the regulatory requirements of the [Regulatory Agency] with respect to [industry] functions. Such individuals shall be equipped with all necessary infrastructure in terms of tools, networks, and documentation regarding the ABC System and the Services and shall be sufficiently mobile to allow on-site assistance at Customer's location at any time. The individuals described in Sections 9.2.2, 9.2.3, and 9.2.4 below are designated as key personnel ("Key Personnel") and are identified in Appendix 9.2.

- ***The Licensor should limit the number of individuals identified as key personnel to retain the greatest degree of flexibility in allocating its employees among the many different projects it is performing. The Customer, however, should insist that any Licensor employee who is important to the project be listed. This prevents the Licensor from transferring an important member of the production team to another client's project if that customer's project were to need assistance. A complete listing of all important employees will give the Customer***

greater leverage if the Licensor ever sought to reassign those employees important to the Customer's project.

- ***NOTE: Appendix 8 sets forth a model Pricing Schedule for Time and Materials Contacts.***

9.2.2 **Licensor Services Manager**. The Licensor manager for the Services ("Licensor Services Manager") is identified in Appendix 9.2. The Licensor Services Manager shall act as a liaison between Licensor and Customer for all matters related to this Agreement and shall have overall responsibility for ensuring Licensor's performance of its responsibilities and obligations as set forth in this Agreement.

9.2.3 **Licensor Services Support Team**. The individuals identified in Appendix 9.2 shall serve as a designated group of experts experienced with the ABC System and Licensor's Services who shall be available via telephone or pager continuously (twenty-four (24) hours per day, seven (7) days per week, three hundred sixty-five (365) days per year) for Customer to consult with regarding issues related to the ABC System and/or the Services ("Licensor Services Support Team"). The Licensor support representative identified in Appendix 9.2 ("Licensor Services Support Representative") shall serve as the liaison between Customer and Licensor with respect to Support matters, which shall include attending all Planning/Review Meetings. The Licensor Services Support Team shall provide the Information Technology Support and Maintenance Services described in Appendix 9.2.3, which shall include, without limitation:

(a) Answering ABC System related technical, functional, and operational questions and resolving all ABC System problems reported by Customer;
(b) Coordinating all activities of Licensor personnel and Third Party personnel to implement appropriate actions and resolve ABC System problems;
(c) Serving as the single point of contact for any Equipment-related problems;
(d) Providing any on-site Support and Maintenance Services, and
(e) Such other items and/or matters as may be requested by either Customer or Licensor.

9.2.4 **Licensor Technical Support Team.** The individuals identified in Appendix 9.2 shall serve as a select number of highly qualified technical staff to assist Customer in all technical matters related to the ABC System and/or the Services ("*Licensor* Technical Support Team"). The Licensor technical support representative identified in Appendix 9.2 ("Licensor Technical Support Representative") shall serve as the liaison between Customer and Licensor with respect to technical support matters, including providing input at all Planning/Review Meetings. The Licensor Technical Support Team shall be knowledgeable about and capable of discussing with Customer the following subjects, without limitation:

(a) The design and architecture of the ABC System;
(b) Licensor's current research and development efforts and activities;

(c) Suggestions made by Customer representatives as to future Licensor research and development efforts;
(d) Changes to Licensor's preferred equipment platforms for the ABC System;
(e) Emerging technologies and the role such technologies can and should play in future research and development efforts;
(f) Licensor short-term and long-term business strategies vis-à-vis Licensor's decisions to invest in the development of certain products or services over others;
(g) Licensor's internal research and development budget proposals (before finalized) for the future fiscal year; and
(h) Such other items and/or matters as may be requested by either Customer or Licensor.

9.3 **Selection and Continuity.**

9.3.1 **Selection.** For any new or additional Licensor personnel, Licensor shall provide Customer with a listing of the qualifications required of the personnel who will be assigned to accomplish the tasks described in this Agreement and a list of the personnel Licensor proposes to assign to perform such tasks. Licensor shall notify Customer if any of the proposed individuals have less than twelve (12) months' experience related to such tasks. The list shall include the professional qualifications of each individual, along with their proposed role. Customer shall have the right to review the qualifications of the proposed Licensor personnel, interview all such personnel and reject any personnel whom Customer reasonably determines to be unqualified to perform the tasks assigned to them under this Agreement. Any Licensor personnel who are assigned or designated to perform such tasks who have less than the required twelve (12) months of experience shall be clearly identified by Licensor to Customer as "Trainees." Licensor shall obtain Customer's written consent prior to deploying any Trainees to work under this Agreement and shall not charge Customer for the services of any such Trainees.

9.3.2 **Continuity**. Except for changes in personnel due to resignation, termination, promotion, geographic transfers, or leaves of absence, Licensor shall maintain the same Licensor Services Manager and other Key Personnel throughout the term of this Agreement. Licensor shall not reassign away from Customer the Licensor Services Manager or any member of the Licensor Services Support Team or the Licensor Technical Support Team. Licensor shall not promote an employee for the purpose of avoiding its obligations under this Section. For any transfers approved by Customer, any required transitions will be accomplished in an orderly and businesslike manner upon four (4) weeks advance written notification and with on-going telephone consultation with the departing individual in order to achieve a seamless transition and minimize any disruption that may be experienced by Customer as a result of such transitions.

- ***Although the Customer may seek to limit the transfer of certain key employees it is unreasonable to prevent the Licensor from operating its business in the normal course. Consequently, the contract should provide for the ability of***

the Licensor to replace certain key employees upon the occurrence of certain events.

9.3.3 **Succession Plan.** Licensor will maintain detailed written substitution and succession plans and replacement procedures for the Licensor Services Manager in such a manner so as to assure an orderly succession if the Licensor Services Manager takes a leave of absence or must be replaced. Upon request, Licensor will make such plans and procedures available to Customer.

9.4 **Replacement.** Customer shall have the right to require Licensor to replace the Licensor Services Manager and other Key Personnel whom Customer deems to be unfit or otherwise unsatisfactory to perform Licensor's duties hereunder. In the event Customer requests that Licensor replace any such Licensor personnel, Licensor promptly shall replace such personnel with qualified replacement personnel. For the purpose of this Section, "qualified" means that the proposed replacement personnel possess comparable experience and training as the Licensor personnel being replaced. At no additional cost to Customer, such replacement personnel shall work with the replaced Licensor personnel for a transition period that will be specified by Customer, the duration of which shall be based upon the duties and responsibilities of the person being replaced and any other applicable criteria. In addition to the foregoing, and provided the replaced Licensor personnel remain in the employ of Licensor, such personnel shall continue to be available by telephone to answer any project-related questions in order to achieve a seamless transition and minimize any disruption that may be experienced by Customer as a result of such replacement. The cost and expenses associated with the replacement of any Licensor personnel shall be paid by Licensor. Race, gender, age, religion, national origin, and other legally discriminatory characteristics shall not be valid grounds for any such request by Customer.

9.5 **Customer Personnel.** Customer shall provide personnel to perform its responsibilities under this Agreement, including a manager for the Services (the "Customer Services Manager"), who shall act as a liaison between Licensor and Customer, coordinate Customer resources, coordinate Customer personnel and have overall responsibility for meeting Customer's responsibilities and obligations.

9.6 **Meetings and Reports.**

9.6.1 **On-site Readiness Meetings.** On a bi-weekly basis, the Licensor Services Manager and the Customer Services Manager shall be available to meet at Customer's facility to review the status of Licensor's performance under this Agreement including, without limitation, the timely and accurate generation of all required reports as set forth in Attachment ___ to Appendix 9.6.1. Customer shall reimburse Licensor for all reasonable travel and out-of-pocket expenses incurred by the Licensor Services Manager in connection with such meetings, provided that such expenses conform to Appendix 9.6.1.

9.6.2 **Contract Management Meetings.** On a monthly basis, or more often if Customer requests, the Licensor Services Manager and other applicable Key Personnel, the Customer Services Manager, other appropriate representatives of the parties and any necessary Third Parties shall meet at a Customer-designated site to discuss Licensor's compliance with the terms and conditions of this Agreement, and to review, without limitation, the following items:

(a) All financial arrangements; including invoices submitted by Licensor;
(b) A detailed status report as described in Section 9.6.4, including, without limitation, reporting on Licensor's compliance with all Service Level Standards and the status of any Project;
(c) Any specific difficulties or issues that may exist; including any personnel issues and any proposed changes to the Agreement or any Service Level Standards, and
(d) Such other matters as may be requested by either party.

Licensor shall keep minutes of all Contract Management Meetings in form and substance reasonably satisfactory to Customer, and Licensor shall issue copies of the minutes to all meeting attendees within forty-eight (48) hours of each meeting.

9.6.3 **Planning/Review Meetings.** On a quarterly basis, or more often if Customer requests, the Licensor Services Manager, the Customer Services Manager, the Licensor Technical Support Representative, the Licensor Technical Support Representative, any other appropriate representatives of the parties and any necessary Third Parties, shall meet at a Customer-designated site to review Licensor's compliance with the terms and conditions of this Agreement and to plan for Customer's acquisition of any new services and to discuss, without limitation, the following items:

(a) Performance of the ABC System and plans for improving Licensor's performance;
(b) Performance of the Licensor Services Support Team and plans for improving Licensor's performance;
(c) Performance of the Licensor Technical Support Team and plans for improving Licensor's performance;
(d) The status of any Projects, including Custom Programming Projects;
(e) A description of any change in recommended Equipment platforms, and
(f) Such other matters as may be identified for discussion by either party.

The parties jointly shall prepare and distribute a meeting agenda for each quarterly Planning/Review Meeting at least ten (10) calendar days prior to the date of the Planning/Review Meeting. Each party shall be responsible for its own travel or out-of-pocket expenses incurred in connection with attending the Planning/Review Meeting.

9.6.4 **Reports.** Licensor shall provide to Customer the specific reports listed in Attachment ___ to Appendix 9.6.4 in accordance with the terms and conditions set forth therein. In addition, at least five (5) business days before each monthly Contract Management Meeting, Licensor shall present to Customer written reports of the performance of the ABC System and the Services in forms substantially similar to the forms attached as Appendix 9.6.4. The report shall include a summary, in such detail as Customer shall reasonably request, of: (a) the monthly performance of the ABC

System and Services in relation to the Service Level Standards, (b) any accomplishments and difficulties encountered during the prior reporting period, (c) suggestions and proposed actions for dealing with and resolving any identified difficulties and the anticipated results during the next reporting period, and (d) a comprehensive and consolidated log of all outstanding support and technical problems identified by Customer and Licensor that remain to be resolved. Customer shall have the right to assume that Licensor does not know of any problems, difficulties, or issues that may have an adverse impact on the Services (whether from a timing, cost, or performance standpoint) unless Licensor specifically identifies such problems, difficulties, or issues in its written performance reports. Licensor's failure to provide such reports within the time frames set forth in this Section shall result in a \$1,000/day per report late charge to be paid by Licensor to Customer.

9.7 **Administration of the Agreement.** The Customer Services Manager and the Licensor Services Manager shall administer the Change Order process set forth in Section 9.8 and all decisions requiring the consent and/or approval of the other party, except for those decisions requiring the consent and/or approval of Customer pursuant to the terms set forth in Sections 22 and 40, which consent and/or approval shall be effective only upon a written notice signed by a Vice President or higher-level officer of Customer. All consents and/or approvals made in contravention of the terms set forth in this Section shall be void and of no force and effect. Such Managers shall be responsible for identifying within their respective organizations the individual(s) authorized to sign a Change Order based on the dollar value of such Change Order.

9.8 **Change Order Procedure.** If either party believes that a change in the Services and/or a Project (whether in time frames, costs, or deliverables) is necessary or desirable, such party shall submit a written change request to the other (a "Change Request"). Licensor represents to Customer that it has factored into Licensor's fee adequate contingencies for *de minimis* change orders. Accordingly, if Change Requests are made, they will be presumed not to impact the fees under this Agreement; provided, however, that if the Change Request consists of other than a *de minimis* deviation from the scope of the Services and/or Project, Licensor shall provide Customer with written notification of such other deviation within five (5) business days after receipt of the Change Request. If agreed to by Customer, a change in the fee shall be made. In the event of a Customer-initiated Change Request, within five (5) business days of Licensor's receipt of such Change Request, Licensor shall provide to Customer a written statement describing in detail: (a) the impact on the ABC System performance, if any, and the modifications to the ABC System that will be required as a result of the Change Request including, without limitation, Change in Software, Equipment, if any, and Services, and (b) an estimate of the cost to implement each Change Request (collectively, the "*Change Response*"). If Licensor submits a Change Request to Customer, such Change Request shall include the information required for a Change Response. Customer shall accept or reject any Change Response or Licensor-initiated Change Request, as applicable, within five (5) business days after receipt of same from Licensor. If Customer accepts a Change Response or Licensor initiated Change Request in writing, such Change Response, together with Customer's Change Request or such Licensor-initiated Change Request, shall be deemed to be a "*Change Order*" and shall become part of this Agreement. If Customer rejects Licensor's Change Response or Licensor-initiated Change Request, Licensor shall proceed to fulfill its obligations under this Agreement.

- ***The change order procedure section is one of the most important sections in any license, but yet it often receives little attention in the negotiation process. Many disputes that arise under a software license are directly related to "scope creep," changes to the functional specifications or other delivery obligations. The process for implementing these or other similar changes should be clearly documented to eliminate the potential for future disagreements. Licensors should avoid language like that above, which allows the customer to make* de minimis *changes without additional cost to the customer. This subjective standard can create many problems of interpretation potentially leading to litigation. See Chapter 23.K.2 (J) for alternative language.***

9.8.A **Mandatory Changes.**

9.8.A.1 **Commencement of Required Changes.**

If the Parties have not agreed in writing on the terms of a Change Request that consists primarily of modified or additional services that are of a type that is the same as or similar to the Services, and Customer determines that the Change is a Required Change, then Customer may, by written notice, **require** Licensor to commence with such Change prior to reaching agreement on the applicable Change Request. Customer shall reimburse Licensor for reasonable costs, if any, that Licensor incurs in implementing such Change at the rates set forth in Exhibit __ until the Parties agree on Licensor's charges for such Change, if any, through the Change control procedures set forth in this Article 9.8.

9.8.A.2 **Significant Event.**

Customer shall notify Licensor as soon as reasonably possible with respect to any event or set of events that Customer believes constitutes a Significant Event, subject to Customer's obligations relating to confidentiality and any applicable Laws. If, as a result of a Significant Event, Customer requires Licensor to perform Significant Event Additional Services, Licensor shall provide the Significant Event Additional Services as soon as reasonably possible. To the extent there is a charging methodology or pricing metric for such additional Services in the applicable Work Process Agreement, Licensor shall charge Customer for the Significant Event Additional Services at such rate. In the event there is no such charging methodology or pricing metric for such additional Services in the applicable Work Process Agreement, the Parties shall agree upon any pricing changes to reflect adequately and equitably such Significant Event Additional Services in accordance with the procedures set forth in this Article 9.8. Notwithstanding the foregoing, if such Significant Event Additional Services are included in the scope of Services set forth for the then-current pricing in the applicable Work Process Agreement, Licensor shall provide such Significant Event Additional Services at no additional cost to Customer. To the extent that the Significant Event Additional Services adversely affect Licensor's ability to meet the applicable Service Levels, Licensor shall notify Customer, in advance, of such adverse effect and shall use its best efforts to mitigate such effect. Licensor shall not be subject to affected Service Level Credits for such length of time as is reasonably necessary for Licensor to accommodate the Significant Event Additional Services so as to meet the affected Service Levels, which period may be specified in a Change Order to be approved in connection with, or subsequent to, the commencement of the Significant Event Additional Services. Such Change Order may also set forth new Service Levels intended to apply to Licensor's provision of Significant Event Additional Services.

9.8.A.3 **Changes in Law. If Customer reasonably determines that a Change is necessary or advisable due to a change in applicable Law, Licensor shall, promptly upon notice from Customer regarding the necessity of such a Change, implement any such Change. Licensor shall, promptly upon becoming aware of any change in Laws applicable to the Services, notify Customer of such change in Law and promptly implement any Change that Customer reasonably determines is necessary or advisable due to such change in Law. Licensor shall be financially responsible for any Change required due to changes in Laws (i) that apply to Licensor's principal business as a service provider, (ii) that apply to Licensor's customers generally, or (iii) that Licensor makes available to any other customer without charge.** The Parties shall negotiate in good faith with respect to the allocation of costs, if any, associated with a Change required due to a change in Law other than the types set forth in the preceding sentence. If the scope of Services set forth in the applicable Work Process Agreement includes adequate resources to implement a Change required by changes in Law or otherwise allocates the costs associated with such Change to Licensor, Licensor shall bear the costs associated with such Change.

- ***The licensor should be careful about committing to pay for any modifications necessary due to changes in the law without knowing the potential cost. A more practical solution is to agree to amortize the cost over all of the licensor's customers and charge the customer its pro rata portion.***

"**Significant Event**" shall mean a circumstance in which an event or discrete set of events has occurred or is planned with respect to the business of Customer that results or shall result in a significant change in the scope or nature of the Services that shall be required from Licensor. By way of illustration and not limitation, examples of the kinds of events that might cause such significant changes are: (i) changes in the method of Customer's service delivery, or (ii) a substantial acquisition or divestiture.

9.9 **New Projects.** Licensor shall provide any new product and/or functionality to Customer as part of a project (each a "Project") to be implemented and managed pursuant to the terms and conditions set for in Appendix 9.9.

9.10 **Testing Process.** Customer shall have the right to test all new Services, Software and Custom Programming obtained or licensed from Licensor, as applicable, and shall have the right to test any and all Enhancements thereto in accordance with the terms set forth in Appendix 9.10.

9.11 **Time Tracking.** At the end of each week during which Licensor provides Services on site at a Customer location, Licensor shall report in a Customer time tracking system all hours that it and its employees worked pursuant to this Agreement and any individual project during such week. Customer shall review such reports and notify Licensor of its acceptance of such reports or its good faith dispute of any of the information provided in such reports. Customer shall not be obligated to pay Licensor for any of Licensor's time that is the subject of such a dispute, and the provisions of Section 8.7 relating to disputed invoices shall also apply to any disputes under this Section 9.11. The parties may agree that employees of Licensor who provide Services from a location other than a Customer location will have access to the time tracking system and, in such event, such employees' use of the time tracking system shall be governed by the provisions of this Section 9.11.

9.12 **Competitors.** Licensor acknowledges that any work performed by Licensor for competitors of Customer could implicate the proprietary rights of Customer. In order to avoid disputes concerning infringement of Customer's proprietary rights, during the term of any Project Agreement and for a period of one (1) year thereafter, Licensor shall not, without the prior written consent of Customer, provide consulting services to any company or entity whose business competes with any [describe product] product of Customer or whose interests are adverse to those of Customer.

Alternative Language Benefiting Vendor

Licensor shall not be precluded by this Agreement from rendering services or developing work products that are competitive with, or functionally comparable to, the services rendered and Deliverables provided hereunder. Licensor shall not be restricted in its use of ideas, concepts, know-how, and techniques acquired or learned in the course of activities hereunder. The provisions of this Section 9.12 shall not be construed to alter Licensor's obligations under the [Nondisclosure Agreement **or** Section 12. Proprietary Rights, Confidentiality, and Security].

9.13 **Audit/Quality Control.**

(a) **Contract Records.** Licensor shall, and shall cause its Subcontractors and suppliers to, maintain complete and accurate records of and supporting documentation for all Charges, all Customer Data and all transactions, authorizations, changes, implementations, soft document accesses, reports, filings, returns, analyses, procedures, controls, records, data, or information created, generated, collected, processed or stored by Licensor in the performance of its obligations under this Agreement ("**Contract Records**"). Licensor shall maintain such Contract Records in accordance with applicable Laws. Licensor shall retain Contract Records in accordance with Customer's record retention policy (as such policy may be modified from time to time and provided to Licensor in writing) and in all events in compliance with Internal Revenue Code Section 6001 and regulations and revenue procedures issued thereunder, and successor provisions, during the Term and any Termination Assistance Services period and thereafter through the end of the second full calendar year after the calendar year in which Licensor stopped performing Services (including Termination Assistance Services requested by Customer under Section ______) (the "**Audit Period**"); provided, however, the Audit Period shall in all events not be shorter than the records retention period provided under federal or other governmental programs applicable in Customer's or the Eligible Recipients' business operations.

(b) **Operational Audits.** During the Audit Period (as defined in Section ________), Licensor shall, and shall cause its Subcontractors and suppliers to, provide to Customer (and internal and external auditors, inspectors, regulators, and other representatives that Customer may designate from time to time, including customers, vendors, licensees, and other third parties to the extent Customer or the Eligible Recipients are legally or contractually obligated to submit to audits by such entities) access at reasonable hours to Licensor Personnel, to the facilities at or from which Services are then being provided and to Licensor records and other pertinent information, all to the extent relevant to the Services and Licensor's obligations under this Agreement. Such access shall be provided for the purpose of performing audits and inspections to (i) verify the integrity of Customer Data; (ii) examine the systems that process, store, support, and transmit that data (including system capacity, performance, and utilization); (iii) examine the internal controls (i.e., financial controls, human resource controls, organizational controls, input/output controls, system modification controls, processing controls, system design controls, and access controls) and the security, disaster recovery and back-up practices and procedures; (iv) examine Licensor's performance of the Services; (v) verify Licensor's reported performance against the applicable Service Levels; (vi) examine Licensor's measurement, monitoring and management tools; and (vii) enable Customer and the Eligible Recipients to meet applicable legal, regulatory, and contractual requirements (including those associated with the Sarbanes-Oxley Act of 2002 and the implementing regulations promulgated by the United States Securities and Exchange Commission and Public Company Accounting Oversight Board). Licensor shall (A) provide any assistance reasonably requested by Customer or its designee in conducting any such audit, including installing and operating audit software; (B) make requested personnel, records, and information available to Customer or its designee; and (C) in all cases, provide such assistance, personnel, records, and information in an expeditious manner to facilitate the timely completion of such audit. If an audit reveals a breach of this Agreement, Licensor shall promptly reimburse Customer for the actual cost of such audit and any damages, fees, fines, or penalties assessed against or incurred by Customer or an Eligible Recipient as a result thereof.

(c) **Financial Audits**. During the Audit Period (as defined in Section _______), Licensor shall, and shall cause its Subcontractors to, provide to Customer (and internal and external auditors, inspectors, regulators, and other representatives that Customer may designate from time to time, including customers, vendors, licensees, and other third parties to the extent Customer or the Eligible Recipients are legally or contractually obligated to submit to audits by such entities) access at reasonable hours to Licensor Personnel and to Contract Records and other pertinent information to conduct financial audits, all to the extent relevant to the performance of Licensor's obligations under this Agreement. Such access shall be provided for the purpose of performing audits and inspections to (i) verify the accuracy and completeness of Contract Records; (ii) verify the accuracy and completeness of Charges and any Pass-Through Expenses and Out-of-Pocket Expenses; (iii) examine the financial controls, processes, and procedures utilized by Licensor; (iv) examine Licensor's performance of its other financial and accounting obligations; and (v) enable Customer and the Eligible Recipients to meet applicable legal, regulatory and contractual requirements, in each case to the extent applicable to the Services and/

or the Charges for such Services. Licensor shall (A) provide any assistance reasonably requested by Customer or its designee in conducting any such audit; (B) make requested personnel, records, and information available to Customer or its designee; and (C) in all cases, provide such assistance, personnel, records, and information in an expeditious manner to facilitate the timely completion of such audit. If any such audit reveals an overcharge by Licensor, and Licensor does not successfully dispute the amount questioned by such audit in accordance with Article ___, Licensor shall promptly pay to Customer the amount of such overcharge. In addition, if any such audit reveals an overcharge of more than one percent (1%) of the audited Charges in any Charges category, Licensor shall promptly reimburse Customer for the actual cost of such audit (including auditors' fees).

(d) **Audit Assistance**. Customer and certain Eligible Recipients may be subject to regulation and audit by governmental bodies, standards, or certification or accreditation organizations, other regulatory authorities, customers, payors, or other parties to contracts with Customer or an Eligible Recipient under applicable Laws, rules, regulations, standards, and contract provisions, including certification or accreditation requirements of JCAHO. If a governmental body, standards or certification or accreditation organization, other regulatory authority or customer, payor, or other party to a contract with Customer or an Eligible Recipient exercises its right to examine or audit Customer or an Eligible Recipient pursuant to such Laws, rules, regulations, standards or contract provisions, Licensor shall provide all assistance (including such assistance as contemplated in Sections _____ and ___ requested by Customer or the Eligible Recipient in responding to such audits or requests for information and shall do so in an expeditious manner to facilitate the prompt closure of such audit or request.

(e) **General Procedures.**

(i) Licensor shall obtain audit rights equivalent to those specified in this Section 9.13 from all Subcontractors and will cause such rights to extend to Customer.

(ii) Notwithstanding the intended breadth of Customer's audit rights, Customer shall not be given access to (A) the proprietary information of other Licensor customers; (B) Licensor locations that are not related to Customer, the Eligible Recipients or the Services; or (C) Licensor's internal costs, except to the extent such costs are the basis upon which Customer is charged (i.e., reimbursable expenses, Out-of-Pocket Expenses, Pass-Through Expenses, or cost-plus Charges) and/or are necessary to calculate the applicable variable Charges.

(iii) In performing audits, Customer shall endeavor to avoid unnecessary disruption of Licensor's operations and unnecessary interference with Licensor's ability to perform the Services in accordance with the Service Levels.

(iv) Following any audit, Customer shall conduct (in the case of an internal audit), or request its external auditors or examiners to conduct, an exit conference with Licensor to obtain factual concurrence with issues identified in the review.

(v) Customer shall be given adequate private workspace in which to perform an audit, plus access to photocopiers, telephones, facsimile machines, computer hook-ups, and any other facilities or equipment needed for the performance of the audit.

(f) **Licensor Internal Audit**. If Licensor determines as a result of its own internal audit that it has overcharged Customer, then Licensor shall promptly pay to Customer the amount of such overcharge.

(g) **Licensor Response**. Licensor and Customer shall meet promptly upon the completion of an audit conducted pursuant to this Section 9.13 (i.e., an exit interview) and/or issuance of an interim or final report to Licensor and Customer following such an audit. Licensor shall respond to each exit interview and/or audit report in writing within thirty (30) days, unless a shorter response time is specified in such report. Licensor and Customer shall develop and agree upon an action plan to promptly address and resolve any deficiencies, concerns and/or recommendations identified in such exit interview and/or audit report and Licensor, at its own expense, shall undertake remedial action in accordance with such action plan and the dates specified therein to the extent necessary to comply with Licensor's obligations under this Agreement.

(h) **Licensor Response to External Audits**. If an audit by a governmental body, standards organization or regulatory authority having jurisdiction over Customer, an Eligible Recipient or Licensor results in a finding that Licensor is not in compliance with any applicable Law or standard, including any generally accepted accounting principle or other audit requirement relating to the performance of its obligations under this Agreement, Licensor shall, at its own expense and within the time period specified by such auditor, address and resolve the deficiency(ies) identified by such governmental body, standards organization, or regulatory authority, in the manner approved by Customer.

(i) **SAS70 Audit**. In addition to its other obligations under this Section 9.13, Licensor shall cause a Type II Statement of Auditing Standards (SAS) 70 audit (or equivalent audit) to be conducted on an annual or more frequent basis for each Licensor shared services facility at or from which the Services are provided to Customer and/or the Eligible Recipients. Licensor shall permit Customer to participate in the planning of each such audit, confer with Customer as to the scope and timing of each such audit, and accommodate Customer's requirements and concerns to the extent practicable. Unless otherwise agreed by the Parties, each SAS 70 audit shall be designed and conducted to facilitate periodic compliance reporting by Customer and the Eligible Recipients under the Sarbanes-Oxley Act of 2002 (and implementing regulations promulgated by the United States Securities and Exchange Commission and Public Company Accounting Oversight Board) and comparable Laws in other jurisdictions. To the extent the resulting audit report is relevant to Customer and/or the Eligible Recipients, Licensor shall provide a copy of such report to Customer and its independent auditors for review and comment as soon as reasonably practicable and in all events within thirty (30) days of completion. Licensor shall respond to such report in accordance with Section _____.

To the extent Customer provides reasonable notice and requests that, in addition to the Type II SAS 70 audit described above, Licensor conduct a Customer-specific Type II SAS 70 audit, Licensor shall do so and Customer will be financially responsible for the third party auditors fees and expense for such audit (provided, Licensor notifies Customer of such fee and expense, obtains Customer's approval, and uses commercially reasonable efforts to minimize such fees and expense). If, however, Licensor undertakes additional or different Type II SAS 70 audits (or equivalent audits) of Licensor Facilities at, from or through which Services are provided to Customer and/or the Eligible Recipients (other than customer-specific audits requested and paid for by other Licensor customers), Licensor shall accord Customer the rights described in the preceding paragraph with respect to such audits.

(j) **Audits Costs.** Licensor and its Subcontractors and suppliers shall provide the Services described in this Section 9.13 at no additional charge to Customer.

Alternative SAS 70 Language Benefiting Customer

SAS-70 COMPLIANCE:

A. Each year during the Term (and the Termination/Expiration Assistance Period) Licensor shall obtain the SAS 70 Type 2 Report applicable to Services being rendered under this Agreement. Licensor shall provide Customer with a copy of the SAS 70 Type 2 Report within 15 days of Licensor's receipt thereof from the Service Auditor. Licensor shall bear all costs and expenses associated with obtaining and delivering each SAS 70 Type 2 Report.

B. If any Services are provided or related systems are operated by a Licensor subcontractor, and if such Services or Systems (or any controls or other aspects of such Services or Systems) would fall within the scope of the SAS 70 Type 2 Report had such Services or Systems been provided directly by Licensor, then Licensor shall cause each such subcontractor to comply with the requirements of Section ____ and, if applicable, Section ____.

C. As requested by Customer, Licensor shall either (1) certify to Customer in writing that during the applicable SAS 70 Gap Period no changes have been made to the Services or the Systems, the manner in which the Services or Systems are provided or operated, applicable controls, or the Control Objectives that could reasonably be expected to have any impact on the contents of, or opinions set forth in, the applicable SAS 70 Type 2 Report; or (2) provide Customer with a written description of any such changes.

D. The SAS 70 Type 2 Report shall be Confidential Information of Licensor (or the applicable Licensor subcontractor); provided, however, that notwithstanding the foregoing or the confidentiality provisions of this Agreement, Customer (and Customer's independent auditors) shall be permitted to disclose the SAS 70 Type 2 Report (or any of the content thereof) to any person, entity or governmental authority as necessary for Customer to comply with the Sarbanes-Oxley Requirements or any other applicable Law.

E. As of the Effective Date, the Control Objectives include those set forth in Exhibit __ to this Agreement. Customer may update the Control Objectives set forth in Exhibit __ to this Agreement at any time during the Term (or the Termination/Expiration Assistance Period) provided that, subject to the Change Control Procedure, Customer shall be responsible for any additional costs incurred by Licensor in complying with the updated Control Objectives to the extent that such updated Control Objectives apply only to Customer and not to any other customer of Licensor. To the extent that such updated Control Objectives apply to other customers of Licensor, then the costs associated with compliance with such updated Control Objectives will be, subject to the Change Control Procedure, equitably allocated among Customer and such customers.

Alternative Language Benefiting Licensor

Licensor shall provide all Work Products and Services in conformance with any quality control requirements Customer may provide to Licensor from time to time and shall provide to Customer such documentation as Customer may request, demonstrating that such Work Products and Services have been provided in conformance with such requirements. Customer may visit Licensor's facilities to audit Licensor's adherence to any such quality control requirements provided by Customer.

- ***Licensors should avoid language as set forth immediately above as it leaves the licensor's obligation open ended. Instead, licensors should commit to meet certain industry standard requirements such as SAS 70 or ISO 9001. See § 16.Q.***

9.14 **Non-solicitation of Employees.** During the term of this Agreement and for a period of 180 days thereafter, neither party shall solicit for employment or hire employees of the other party and its subcontractors who have been involved in rendering or receiving services under this Agreement without obtaining the prior written consent of the other party; provided, however, that this restriction shall not prohibit either party from conducting general solicitations in newspapers in connection with its hiring. Accordingly, if either Licensor or Customer, at any time during the term and 180 days thereafter, hires any employee of the other party and its subcontractors who has been involved in rendering or receiving services hereunder, the hiring party shall pay to the other party a fee, equal to one hundred percent (100%) of the annualized gross compensation, reportable on a Form W-2 to the Internal Revenue Service, that was most recently earned by such person as an employee of the other party. The provisions of this Section 9.14 shall not restrict the hiring of any person who: (a) has not been involved in rendering or receiving services, on behalf of Licensor or Customer, under this Agreement; or (b) has not been an employee of the other party for one hundred eighty (180) or more days. This Section 9.14 sets forth the exclusive remedy of Licensor and Customer in each instance in which a party hires a present or former employee of the other. The parties expressly agree that a fee calculated in accordance with this Article is reasonable and adequate compensation for the costs that would be incurred in each such instance. Further, Licensor shall provide Customer with written notice before hiring any person who has been employed by Customer at anytime in the 12 months prior to such notice.

- ***Both parties should insist on the inclusion of a non-solicitation clause or the execution of a separate nondisclosure agreement as they both have made significant investments in their employees. The Licensor does not want the Customer hiring its employees directly to save money or create internal expertise. At the same time, the Customer does not want the Licensor hiring its employees after they have been trained. Agreeing to a set liquidated damages amount serves as a significant deterrent. See Chapter 18.E.***

9.15 **Approval of Subcontractors.** Licensor shall obtain Customer's prior written consent, which Customer may withhold in its sole discretion, before entering into an agreement with any subcontractor who may be retained by Licensor to supply any Software, Services, or provide any Deliverables hereunder. Customer shall not be bound by the terms of such agreements entered into by Licensor and such agreements shall not contain any obligation with respect to Customer including, without limitation, a guarantee of payments to such subcontractor. Any approval of Licensor's right to use a subcontractor shall be conditioned upon Customer's ability to obtain a full assignment of such agreement upon written notice by Customer to Licensor and the subcontractor following any default by Licensor under this Agreement including, without limitation, any warranties contained therein. Licensor agrees that assignment of any subcontractor agreement to Customer shall in no way diminish, reduce, modify, or affect Licensor's duties or warranties to Customer hereunder, except with respect to the future performance of the subcontractors subsequent to such assignment. All subcontractors and their representatives, agents, and employees must sign a Confidentiality and Nondisclosure Agreement, in substantially the form set forth in Exhibit 9.15.

9.16 **Screening of Licensor Personnel.** Licensor acknowledges that Customer must comply with VCCA and the OFAC SDN Requirements. Licensor shall, at Licensor's expense and prior to assigning any Personnel to provide Services hereunder, perform all background checks and any other applicable testing on its Personnel as necessary or desirable to ensure compliance and, in addition, such checks and testing as indicated on the applicable Statement of Work. Such background checks and testing shall include, at a minimum, an initial review and subsequent periodic reviews of the SDN Lists against its Personnel lists. Upon Customer's request, Licensor shall provide Customer information regarding the methods and safeguards utilized when conducting such background checks and screening Licensor shall not bring upon Customer premises, or assign to provide the Services, any Personnel or Third Party Personnel whose background check revealed: (i) the appearance of such individual's name on, and/or such individual's association with, persons, companies, other entities or countries on the SDN Lists; (ii) a felony (or equivalent) conviction; or (iii) any other pertinent information indicating that such individual poses a significant risk to the health or safety of others.

Upon determining that any of the foregoing conditions apply to any Personnel or Third Party Personnel, Licensor shall: (i) not assign such Personnel or Third Party Personnel to provide the Services, if such Personnel or Third Party Personnel has not yet been assigned to provide Services hereunder; or (ii) immediately notify Customer of the existence of such conditions and provide relevant information concerning the role of such Personnel or Third Party Personnel in providing the Services to date and such other information as Customer may reasonably request, if such Personnel or Third Party Personnel had previously been assigned to provide Services and such conditions were found to exist pursuant to a subsequent background check.

Additional Language Relating to the Screening of Licensor Personnel in Compliance with U.S. Export Laws.

Prohibited Persons and Entities. All Licensor personnel performing the Services, regardless of their location, shall be validated by Licensor upon assignment, to have not been on any list published and maintained by the government of the United States of America of persons or entities with whom any U.S. person or entity is prohibited from conducting business. Presently, the lists of such persons or entities include without limitation the following websites: (i) Denied Persons List on the Bureau of Industry and Security at http://www.bis.doc.gov/dpl/default.shtm, or (ii) the Specially Designated Nationals and Blocked Persons List of the Office of Foreign Assets Control Department of Treasury at http://www.ustreas.gov/offices/enforcement/ofac/sdn/index.html. In the event of either Party becoming aware of any Licensor Personnel involved in providing Services being included in the list of prohibited persons or entities, Licensor shall promptly remove such personnel from the provision of Services under this Agreement. Licensor shall conduct a quarterly review of the lists mentioned above and shall provide to Customer results of such reviews. Licensor shall report to Customer immediately if the name of any of Licensor Personnel is placed on any list published by the government of the United States of America of persons or entities with whom any U.S. person or entity is prohibited from conducting business and shall immediately, at Licensor's sole expense, remove such person(s) from performing any Services and as soon as possible and replace such person(s) with qualified person(s) whose names do not appear on such lists.

9.17 **Licensor Management.** In Customer's sole discretion, Customer may elect to use a third party Licensor management company ("Management Company") to administer certain activities on Customer's behalf (i.e., time collection, expense reimbursement and fee and invoice management, collectively "Licensor Management Services"). Licensor acknowledges that in order to supply Services to Customer, it may be required to enter into an agreement with Customer's Management Company and Licensor will timely do so upon Customer's request. SUCH LICENSOR MANAGEMENT SERVICES AGREEMENT BETWEEN THE LICENSOR AND MANAGEMENT COMPANY MAY INCLUDE A FEE TO BE PAID BY LICENSOR TO THE MANAGEMENT COMPANY FOR THESE SERVICES. As between this Agreement and the Licensor's Management Company agreement, for any conflicting terms other than those concerning Licensor Management Services, this Agreement shall supersede. "Statement of Work" as defined herein shall include any "job description" documentation received by Licensor from either Customer and/or the Management Company that outlines, in lieu of a Statement of Work, the Licensor's expected duties and services hereunder.

- ***While many Customers are outsourcing their contracts administration functions and requiring their vendors to underwrite the cost of doing so, a licensor should never agree to do so, especially if it has a unique solution in the market. The language set forth above is more applicable to the provision of temporary labor or "body-shopping."***

9.18 **Technology Changes.** If a Technology Change (defined below) occurs, Customer and Licensor will identify the efficiencies, economies, and net savings resulting from such Technology Change and will, in good faith, evaluate the affected Services including Charges and negotiate equitable adjustments (including, as applicable, increases or decreases) to the Charges specified in Exhibit ___ (Fees) as to the affected Service(s). "Technology Change" shall mean a material change to the Customer IT Environment resulting from the implementation of (1) planned efficiencies (e.g., server consolidation); (2) process improvements; or (3) new technology advances, Customer investments or delivery model changes that result in demonstrable and material reductions in Licensor's cost of providing the Services. For purposes of this Section 9.18 (Technology Changes), an increase in Licensor Personnel providing Services off shore or near shore by ten (10) or more shall be deemed a delivery model change. The Parties agree that delivery by Licensor of the technology solutions detailed in Exhibit ____ (Transition/Transformation Projects Overview), including server consolidation and the global resourcing solution shall not be deemed a Technology Change under this Section.

10. Involvement of Customer Employees in Licensor's Team

10.1 **Involvement of Customer Employees/Consultants in Licensor's Development Team.**

10.1.1 In order to permit a transfer of know-how relating to the Custom Software, Customer shall have the right, but not the obligation, to cause up to three (3) of its employees and/or consultants to work at Licensor's offices in [Location] as part of each of the Licensor teams that develop the Custom Software and Licensor hereby agrees to welcome such Customer employees/consultants into such teams pursuant to the terms and conditions of Sections 10.1.1–10.1.3 and 10.3.1–10.3.6 hereof. If Customer wishes to avail itself of this possibility, it must notify Licensor, no later than thirty (30) calendar days before the date on which the said Customer employees/consultants will join the Licensor development team(s). The said employees/consultants shall join Licensor's development team(s) no earlier than the date of issuance of the Functional Specifications Acceptance Certificate, as the case may be, and shall cease to work with Licensor no later than the date on which the Acceptance Certificate is issued.

10.1.2 Customer shall ensure that its aforesaid employees/consultants possess a minimum level of engineering competence in (a) the general field of software and documentation development, in particular, as concerns UNIX systems, telecommunications protocols, local area networks (LANs), and wide area network systems (WANs), and (b) Type B technology or EDI or 9.400 technologies.

10.1.3 During the time of involvement of the aforesaid Customer employees/consultants, Licensor shall have full authority to direct such employees/consultants.

10.2 **Involvement of Customer Personnel in Licensor's Integration and Acceptance Team.**

10.2.1 In order to permit the training of Customer employees/consultants with respect to the use and operation of the Deliverables, Customer shall have the right, but not the obligation, to cause up to two (2) of its employees/consultants to work at Licensor Licensor's offices in the [Location], or at the Site, as part of each of the Licensor integration and acceptance teams. Licensor hereby agrees to welcome such Customer employees/consultants into such teams pursuant to the terms and conditions of Sections 10.2.1–10.3.6 hereof. If Customer wishes to avail itself of this possibility, it must notify Licensor, no later than fifteen (15) calendar days before the date on which Licensor commences the factory tests at its premises with respect to the project on which the said employees/consultants will work; in this connection, Licensor hereby agrees to give Customer no less than thirty (30) calendar days prior written notice of the date on which it intends to commence its factory tests. The said Customer employees/consultants will join Licensor's integration and acceptance team(s) no earlier than the date on which Licensor commences its factory tests for the project in question and shall cease to work with Licensor no later than the date on which the Delivery Acceptance Certificate is issued.

10.2.2 Customer shall ensure that its aforesaid employees/consultants possess a minimum level of engineering competence in (a) the general field of software integration and acceptance, in particular, as concerns Unix systems, telecommunications protocols, local area networks (LANs), and wide area network systems (WANs); (b) Type B or 9.400; or (c) the content of the Acceptance Tests.

10.2.3 During the time of involvement of the aforesaid Customer employees/consultants, Licensor shall have full authority to direct such employees/consultants.

10.3 **General.**

10.3.1 Notwithstanding the foregoing, Licensor shall have the right, (a) prior to Customer employee's/consultant's relocation to Licensor, to reject said employee/consultant on the basis of his credentials, or (b) subsequent to an employee's relocation to Licensor, to require Customer to recall the said employee on the basis of his job performance. In the event of a rejection or recall of a Customer employee/consultant, Customer shall have the right but not the obligation to provide a replacement for such employee/consultant. In no event shall any such rejection or recall diminish or void Customer's assurance relating to the technical competence of its employees/consultants, as aforesaid.

10.3.2 Each of the aforesaid Customer employees/consultants shall, before commencing any work, execute and deliver to Licensor and Customer a Nondisclosure Agreement in the form of Appendix 10.3.2 attached hereto. Customer acknowledges that a material breach by one of its employees/consultants of the aforesaid Nondisclosure Agreement shall, for the purposes of this Agreement, constitute a breach by Customer under Section 5 of this Agreement.

10.3.3 Licensor shall be responsible for any and all work performed by the aforesaid Customer employees/consultants; in no event shall Licensor be relieved of any of its obligations hereunder, as a result of (a) any rejection/replacement of a Customer employee/consultant pursuant to Section 10.3.3 hereof; (b) the activities of Customer employees/consultants, except where such activities are in direct opposition to instructions given by Licensor or constitute intentional or grossly negligent acts or omissions that affect Licensor's performance hereunder; or (c) the election by Customer not to cause any of its employees/consultants to be integrated into the Licensor team. In no event shall Licensor be liable for the tortuous acts or omissions of any Customer employee/consultant and Customer shall indemnify and hold harmless Licensor from any third party claims, actual losses, costs (including reasonable attorneys fees), and direct damages or liabilities arising therefrom.

10.3.4 The Parties hereto expressly agree that the Customer employees/consultants relocated to Licensor as per above shall not be considered to be employees/consultants of Licensor. Customer shall, at all times, be responsible for any compensation, insurance, or other employee benefits to which such employees/consultants are, or may become, entitled and, under no circumstances, shall Licensor be required to make payment of any kind to any such employee/consultant on Customer's behalf.

10.3.5 The Parties hereto further expressly agree that said Customer employees/consultants shall not have the authority (a) to make representations on behalf of or to otherwise bind Customer or Licensor in any manner whatsoever, and (b) to convey any information or Deliverable to Licensor for or on behalf of Customer. Consequently, if Licensor relies on any representations and statements of the aforesaid Customer employees/consultants, it shall do so at its own risk.

- ***A Customer should insist on inserting into its contract language similar to that set forth in this Section 10 to avoid the Licensor selling a project with its experienced personnel and later staffing the Customer's project with less experienced people. It is unlikely, however, that a Licensor would accept the language as written.***
- ***The language set forth above allows the Customer's employees to participate in the development process. The Customer's goal is two-fold. The first is to allow the Customer's employees to become educated in the operation and development of the software. This will reduce the Customer's dependency on the Licensor's employees. To some extent, it will also allow the Customer's employees to provide maintenance, potentially reducing the Customer's maintenance costs. The second is to allow the Customer to keep closer track of the development process. If problems develop, the Customer will have an unbiased view of the nature of the problem and its significance. It will avoid any lack of candor on behalf of the Licensor if a problem arises. The Licensor may have concerns about including this language, but there are no legitimate reasons for not including it if the Customer's employees sign appropriate nondisclosure agreements and the Customer's assumes responsibility for any delays caused by its employees.***

11. Support and Maintenance Services

11.1 **Training Services.** In addition to the training prescribed by Section 10 hereof, Licensor undertakes to provide training services to Customer personnel with a view to permitting them to operate, administer, and maintain the ABC System. In the event that Customer wishes to obtain such training services, Customer and Licensor shall agree upon a statement of work pursuant to the provisions of Section 11.4 hereof. Customer shall designate, in this regard, such members of its personnel that are sufficiently qualified and skilled to participate in such training, and the said training shall take place in compliance with the conditions to be defined at a later date by mutual agreement between the Parties.

11.2 **Installation Services.** It is hereby acknowledged and agreed that Licensor shall provide such installation services as are classified, pursuant to the provisions of Appendix 11.2 hereto, as prerequisites for the appropriate Acceptance Procedures. In the event that Customer wishes to receive installation services above and beyond same, Customer and Licensor shall agree upon a statement of work pursuant to the provisions of Section 11.2 hereof.

11.3 **Hardware and Software Support Services.** Provided Customer is not then in default of its obligations under this Agreement, Licensor agrees to make Hardware support services, Standard Software support services, and Custom Software support services available to Customer on an annually renewable basis **for a period of ______ (__) years from [the Effective Date, the date of this Agreement, or an event such as acceptance]** pursuant the terms and conditions of Appendix 11.3 hereto.

Alternative Language Benefiting Licensor

Maintenance support may be ordered by Customer and upon payment of Maintenance Fees, will be provided under Licensor's Customer Support Programs policies in effect at the time the services are ordered. Following the first anniversary of the Agreement date, as long as Licensor is offering Maintenance, Customer may at Customer's option renew Maintenance. In the event Customer allows Maintenance to lapse, it may thereafter renew such support for the affected Software by paying, in addition to the then current annual Maintenance Fee, an amount equal to the aggregate Maintenance Fee that would have been payable for the affected Software during the period of lapse. Licensor agrees that the Maintenance support will be conducted from the Licensor location, which is geographically closest to the Customer location eligible for such Maintenance support.

Alternative Language Benefiting Customer

Maintenance Commitment. Subject to the provisions of this Agreement allowing for suspension or termination of Maintenance or this Agreement, Licensor agrees to make Maintenance available to Licensee for at least five (5) years beyond the date of this Agreement.

No Automatic Installation of Updates. Licensee may elect to defer or decline installation of Updates or to install Updates in a test environment before applying them in its production systems. Licensor shall not install or attempt to install any Update on any Licensee system without Licensee's prior written consent.

Obsolescence. Licensor acknowledges that Licensee is making a significant resource commitment to acquire the Licensed Software and that it does not want to move involuntarily to a new system or a new hardware or operating environment in order to be able to continue using the Licensed Software. Accordingly, provided that Licensee continues to purchase Maintenance and Support from Licensor, and subject to Sections ___ (Maintenance Commitment) and ___ (Support Commitment), Licensor shall continue to make Maintenance and Support available to Licensee for each version, release, or Update of the Licensed Software installed by Licensee for at least five (5) years after the installation date. Within that time period, Licensor shall not require Licensee to migrate to a new version, release, or Update of the Licensed Software or new versions, releases, or Updates of third party Software or database platforms, as a condition of continued Maintenance or Support.

- ***Most software is of little value if it is not supported and maintained. The Customer is usually unable to provide such support and maintenance as it lacks access to the software's source code and the Customer lacks the requisite knowledge to provide such support. As such, the Customer should require the Licensor to commit to provide support for a set number of years for a set price. Without a set price, the Licensor has significant leverage over the Customer as the Customer has no practical choice but to purchase support regardless of price.***

11.4 **Additional Support Services.** In the event that Customer wishes to receive services above and beyond those contemplated by Section 11.1–11.3 hereof, Customer and Licensor shall agree upon a statement of work pursuant to the provisions of Appendix 3 hereto.

12. Proprietary Rights, Confidentiality, and Security

12.1 **Ownership of Intellectual Property.** Pre-existing intellectual property and all improvements thereto that Licensor uses in connection with performing the Services, providing any Deliverables and performing any other Services hereunder shall remain the sole and exclusive property of Licensor, and Licensor shall mark any such written materials as "confidential" and/or "proprietary." Any Custom Programming, including all source code and materials developed by Licensor, all intermediate and partial versions thereof, as well as all specifications, program materials, flow charts, notes, outlines, and the like created in connection therewith (collectively, "Custom Programming Materials") shall be the sole and exclusive property of Customer. All written reports, requirements documents (including newly created technical and non-technical data embodied therein), specifications, program materials, flow charts, notes, outlines, and the like that are developed, conceived, originated, prepared, or generated by Licensor in connection with Licensor's performance under this Agreement including, without limitation, all copyright, trademark, trade secret, and all other proprietary rights therein and derivative works created therefrom (collectively, "Written Deliverables"), shall be the sole and exclusive property of Customer. Such ownership of Custom Programming Materials and Written Deliverables shall inure to the benefit of Customer from the date of the conception, creation, or fixation of the Custom Programming Materials and Written Deliverables in a tangible medium of expression, as applicable. All newly created copyright aspects of the Custom Programming Materials and Written Deliverables shall be considered a "work-made-for-hire" within the meaning of the Copyright Act of 1976, as amended. If and to the extent the Custom Programming Materials and Written Deliverables, or any part thereof, are found by a court of competent jurisdiction not to be a "work-made-for-hire" within the meaning of the Copyright Act of 1976, as amended, Licensor agrees that all exclusive right, title, and interest in and to those newly created copyrightable aspects of the Custom Programming Materials and Written Deliverables, and all copies thereof, are hereby expressly assigned automatically to Customer without further consideration. Any agreement entered into by Licensor and a Third Party in connection with Services related to Custom Programming Materials and Written Deliverables under this Agreement shall require the prior consent of Customer as set forth in Section 12.3, and shall further include substantially the same terms as those appearing in this Section to ensure that Customer obtains the same rights in the Custom Programming Materials and Written Deliverables generated under such Third Party agreement as those set forth in this Section. Licensor agrees to assist Customer in obtaining and enforcing all rights and other legal protections for the Custom Programming Materials and Written Deliverables and to execute any and all documents that Customer may reasonably request in connection therewith, including any copyright assignment document(s). Licensor shall ensure that all Custom Programming Materials and Written Deliverables created hereunder (including each page of any document produced) will be marked as follows:

Confidential and Proprietary
*© Copyright **[20__/Year Developed]** Customer*
All Rights Reserved

Licensor shall not reuse the Custom Programming Materials or Written Deliverables, or any intermediate or partial version thereof, or any derivative work based upon the Custom Programming Materials or Written Deliverables without Customer's express written consent, which consent may be withheld by Customer in its sole discretion.

- ***This language assumes that the Customer will own the work product created by the Licensor under this Agreement. The Licensor should think carefully before agreeing to give up ownership rights as this decision may limit the Licensor's ability to perform similar work in the future or may impact the Licensor's future profit margins by limiting its ability to reuse the code.***
- ***Alternately, allow IP rights to be assigned according to statute / common law and provide as follows:***

Nothing contained in this Agreement will restrict either party from using any ideas, concepts, know-how, methodologies processes, technologies, algorithms, or techniques relating to the Services that either party, individually or jointly, develops or discloses under this Agreement, provided that in doing so the party does not breach its obligations under Section 12 (Proprietary Rights, Confidentiality, and Security) or infringe the intellectual property rights of the other party or third parties who have licensed or provided materials to the other party. Nothing in this Agreement will prevent either party from independently developing any software that is the same or similar to any software owned by the other party so long as the developing party does not infringe or misappropriate any intellectual property rights of the other party.

12.2 **Confidential Information.** "Confidential Information" means any material, data, or information in whatever form or media of a party to this Agreement that is provided or disclosed to the other, except for any information that is: (a) publicly available or later becomes available other than through a breach of this Agreement; (b) known to the Receiving Party or its employees, agents, or representatives prior to such disclosure or is independently developed by the Receiving Party or its employees, agents, or representatives subsequent to such disclosure; or (c) subsequently lawfully obtained by the Receiving Party or its employees, agents, or representatives from a Third Party without obligations of confidentiality. Confidential Information shall include the following categories of information whether disclosed orally or not marked as confidential: Written Deliverables, network configurations, network architecture, Services rendered by Licensor to Customer, financial and operational information, and other matters relating to the operation of the parties' business, including information relating to actual or potential customers and customer lists, customer usage or requirements, business and customer usage forecasts and projections, accounting, finance or tax information, pricing information, and any information relating to the corporate and/or operational structure of Customer and its Affiliates, Software, Equipment, Deliverables, or Services rendered under the Letter Agreement and any amendments thereto, any information exchanged between the parties pursuant to the Nondisclosure Agreement, and all information and materials relating to Third Party vendors, systems integrators, or consultants of Customer that have provided or that may provide in the future any part of Customer's information or communications infrastructure to Customer. The party that has received Confidential Information (the "Receiving Party") shall exercise the same degree of care and protection with respect to the Confidential Information of the party that has disclosed Confidential Information to the Receiving Party (the "Disclosing Party") that it exercises with respect to its own Confidential Information and shall not directly or indirectly disclose, copy, distribute, republish, or allow any Third Party to have access to any Confidential Information of the Disclosing Party. Notwithstanding the above: (i) Customer may disclose Licensor Confidential Information to Authorized Users who have a need to know; (ii) Licensor may disclose Customer's Confidential Information to its employees and agents who have a need to know, provided that for Licensor's agents, such agent is acceptable to Customer in its sole discretion and the agent has previously executed the Confidentiality Agreement as set forth in Exhibit 2 ("Confidentiality Agreement"); and (iii) either party may disclose Confidential Information if so required by law (including court order or subpoena), provided that such disclosure is made in accordance with the terms of Section 12.5.

12.3 **Privileged Information.** Licensor shall keep and maintain all Privileged Information in strict confidence and shall protect all such Privileged Information from disclosure to third parties without the prior written consent of Customer.

12.4 **Return of Confidential Information.** Unless otherwise authorized, upon the earlier of termination of this Agreement or request of the Disclosing Party, with respect to the Disclosing Party's Confidential Information and/or Privileged Information (except for any Software licenses and related Documentation paid for by Customer, which Customer shall have the right to retain) the Receiving Party shall promptly either: (a) return such Confidential Information and/or Privileged Information and provide certification to the Disclosing Party that all such Confidential Information and/or Privileged Information has been returned; or (b) destroy such Confidential Information and/or Privileged Information and provide certification to the Disclosing Party that all such Confidential Information and/or Privileged Information has been destroyed.

12.5 **Notification Obligation.** If the Receiving Party becomes aware of any unauthorized use or disclosure of the Confidential Information and/or Privileged Information of the Disclosing Party, the Receiving Party shall promptly and fully notify the Disclosing Party of all facts known to it concerning such unauthorized use or disclosure. In addition, if the Receiving Party or any of its employees or agents are requested or required (by oral questions, interrogatories, requests for information or documents in legal proceedings, subpoena, civil investigative demand, or other similar process) to disclose any of the Confidential Information and/or Privileged Information of the Disclosing Party, the Receiving Party shall not disclose the Confidential Information and/or Privileged Information without providing the Disclosing Party at least twenty-four (24) hours prior written notice of any such request or requirement so that the Disclosing Party may seek a protective order or other appropriate remedy and/or waive compliance with the provisions of this Agreement. Notwithstanding the foregoing, the Receiving Party shall exercise its best efforts to preserve the confidentiality of the Confidential Information and/or Privileged Information including, without limitation, by cooperating with the Disclosing Party to obtain an appropriate protective order or other reliable assurance that confidential treatment will be accorded the Confidential Information and/or Privileged Information by such tribunal.

12.6 **Non-Aggregation of Data**. Licensor shall not compile and/or distribute statistical analyses and reports utilizing aggregated data derived from information and data obtained from Company; provided that upon Company's written request and direction, Licensor may compile Company data for the sole and exclusive purpose of preparing statistical analysis for Company and Licensor shall be prohibited from sharing, directly or indirectly, any data, whether compiled or non-Company specific, with any third party.

- ***The Licensor should think carefully before including language similar to Section 12.6 in the Agreement as it prevents the Licensor from compiling data that***

may help the Licensor later in the development or enhancement of the software. The Customer should have no objection if the compilation is undertaken in such a way that the Customer's proprietary information and/or identity are not disclosed.

12.7 **Residuals.** Licensor will not be precluded by this Agreement from rendering services or developing work products that are competitive with, or functionally comparable to, the services rendered and Deliverables provided hereunder. Licensor shall not be restricted in its use of ideas, concepts, know-how, methodologies, and techniques acquired or learned in the course of activities hereunder. The provisions of this Section 12.7 shall not be construed to alter Licensor's obligations under any nondisclosure agreements between the parties.

Alternatively:

Residuals. Notwithstanding anything herein to the contrary, either party may use Residuals resulting from this Agreement for any purpose, including without limitations use in the development, manufacture, acquisition, promotion, sale, or maintenance of the party's products and/or services; provided, however, that this right to Residuals does not represent the grant of any license under any valid patents, copyrights, or other intellectual property rights of the disclosing party. The term "Residuals" shall mean any information that is retained in the unaided memories of the receiving party's employees who have had access to the disclosing party's information pursuant to the terms of this Agreement. An employee's memory is unaided if the employee has not intentionally memorized the information for the purpose of retaining and subsequently using or disclosing it.

- ***The Licensor will want to include language similar to Section 12.7 into the agreement so that the Licensor may utilize the intangible knowledge that it obtains during this project on future projects. If the agreement provides that the Licensor retains ownership of all deliverables this section is moot.***

12.8 **Employee/Agent Acknowledgment.** Licensor and Customer shall not disclose Confidential Information or Privileged Information to any of their employees, agents, or representatives unless and until such employee, agent, or representative has been made aware that his or her obligations under this Agreement are subject to confidentiality restrictions and unless such employee, agent, or representative is the subject of a written confidentiality or nondisclosure agreement and has executed the Confidentiality Agreement.

12.9 **Survival; No Limitation of Liability.** The terms of this Article shall survive the expiration or termination of this Agreement. Notwithstanding anything contained in this Agreement to the contrary, the terms of any limitation of liability set forth in this Agreement shall not apply to any breach by a party of its confidentiality obligations under this Article.

- ***Additional language for use when the Licensor will be performing services internationally or will have access to personal data for individuals who reside outside of the United States.***

12.10 **Customer Information.** Licensor shall comply with all U.S. and international Laws governing or relating to privacy, data security and the handling of data security breaches. All information pertaining to a former or current customer or applicant of Customer, including but not limited to such person's address, telephone number and other contact information, image, gender, age, social security number, account or other identifying numbers or attributes, and financial, health and insurance information, and other information about an individual, including the fact that the individual is or was a customer or applicant of Customer ("Customer Information"), shall be deemed to be Confidential Information, subject to the obligations and restrictions set forth in this subsection and Customer's Health Insurance Portability and Accountability Act of 1996 (HIPAA) requirements, attached hereto as Schedule 12.10.

12.11 **International Privacy Laws.** In addition to the above, if any country where Services are to be rendered under the Agreement has or enacts a data protection-related law that requires the execution of a data export agreement, then Licensor shall, upon Customer's request, execute and cause any subcontractors to execute such supplemental agreement promptly on such terms and conditions as shall be mutually agreed.

Alternative Language for Use When the Parties Desire to Have an Independent Nondisclosure Agreement

Notwithstanding the previous paragraphs, all information provided by either party to the other under this Agreement shall be kept confidential in conformance with and subject to the terms of a certain Proprietary Information Agreement dated __________, 20__ by and between the parties hereto.

- ***The parties may want to execute a separate proprietary information agreement to eliminate any survivability issues arising upon the termination of the license agreement.***

Additional Language Setting Forth Specific Security Requirements

Security Procedures. Licensor shall employ reasonable security measures for itself and the Licensor Personnel, which shall include, but not be limited to:

A. Prohibiting of the disclosure of Proprietary or Confidential Information within Licensor's organization except to individuals identified as requiring access to such information to perform Licensor's obligations under this Agreement pursuant to Section __ hereto;

B. Precluding access to Proprietary and Confidential Information by any Licensor Personnel until such individual has been trained with regard to the handling of the Proprietary or Confidential Information, and use of security measures identified herein;

C. Requiring all new Licensor Personnel who are not employees of Licensor to execute a confidentiality agreement with terms no less restrictive than those in Section __;

D. Providing each individual authorized to access Proprietary or Confidential Information with a unique access code and notifying such individual that disclosure of any password, access code, or security device shall result in disciplinary action, including termination;

E. Promptly canceling any password or security access code when Licensor Personnel is terminated or transferred;

F. Locating display screens, keyboard devices, and other desktop devices in a way that access and visualization is restricted to authorized users only;

G. Physically safeguarding all telecommunication switches, computer rooms, and tape libraries, as well as restricting access to such sites to authorized personnel through card access system (CAS) badges or comparable security mechanisms;

H. Ensuring audit trails are maintained with regard to access to all Licensor premises and computers. Without limitation, Licensor shall utilize sufficient access control applications to enable it to identify and authenticate Licensor's users with access to Licensor's or Customer's data, and to record and investigate security related events and data. Licensor shall investigate any security breach in Licensor's premises and computers resulting in unauthorized access to such data, and provide additional security protections, at no additional charge to Customer;

I. Reporting to Customer immediately any breaches of security or unauthorized access to Customer's systems that Licensor detects or becomes aware of. Licensor will use diligent efforts to remedy such breach of security or unauthorized access that is caused by Licensor in a timely manner and deliver to Customer a root cause assessment and future incident mitigation plan with regard to any such breach of security or unauthorized access affecting Protected Health Information; and

J. Understanding that Licensor may receive access to Customer's computers and electronic communications systems ("Communication Systems"), including, but not limited to, voicemail, email, customer databases, and Internet and intranet systems. Such Communication Systems are intended for legitimate business use related to Customer's business. Licensor acknowledges that Licensor does not have any expectation of privacy as between Licensor and Customer in the use of or access to Customer's Communication Systems and that all communications sent over, received by or from, or stored in any such systems by or on behalf of Licensor are subject to Customer's scrutiny, use and disclosure (subject to the protections of Proprietary and Confidential Information herein), at Customer's sole discretion. Customer reserves the right, for business purposes, to monitor, review, audit, interpret, access, archive, and/or disclose (subject to the protections of Proprietary and Confidential Information herein) materials sent over, received by or from, or stored in any of its Communication Systems. This includes, without limitation, email communications sent by users across the Internet and intranet from and to all domain names maintained by Customer. This also includes, without limitation, any electronic Communication Systems that has been used to access any of Customer's systems. Licensor further agrees that Licensor will use all appropriate security, such as, for example, encryption and passwords, to protect Customer's Proprietary or Confidential Information from unauthorized disclosure (internally or externally) and that the use of such security does not give rise to any privacy rights in the communication as between Licensor and Customer. Customer reserves the right to override any security passwords to obtain access to voicemail, email, computer (and software or other applications), and/or computer disks in connection with its Communication Systems. Licensor also acknowledges that Customer reserves the right, for legitimate business purposes, to search all work areas on Customer Sites (for example, offices, cubicles, desks, drawers, cabinets, computers, computer disks, and files) and all personal items brought onto Customer property.

13. Reproduction of Documentation, Object Code, and Source Code

13.1 **Documentation.** Customer shall have the right, at no additional charge, to reproduce solely for its own internal use, all Documentation furnished by Licensor pursuant to this Agreement regardless of whether such Documentation is copyrighted by Licensor. All copies of Documentation made by Customer shall include any proprietary notice or stamp that has been affixed by Licensor. Licensor shall furnish for each License purchased by Customer, and at no additional charge to Customer, one (1) copy of the Documentation sufficient to enable Customer to operate the Software. All Documentation shall be in the English language.

- ***Licensor usually does not make money from reproducing its manuals, thus Licensor is not concerned that the Customer makes copies so long as the Customer incorporates Licensor's protective notices. The Licensor should be careful about including language that the Documentation will allow the Customer to operate the software. At the same time, the Customer should insist on the inclusion of language that provides some level of comfort as to the level of detail of the Documentation.***

13.2 **Object Code.** One copy of the Object Code may be reproduced by Customer, at no additional charge, only for backup or archival purposes. Customer shall notify Licensor in writing of its methods and procedures for archiving the Object Code prior to doing so.

13.3 **Source Code.** Upon purchase of a Source Code license, one additional copy of the Source Code may be reproduced by Customer, at no additional charge, only for backup or archival purposes. Customer shall notify Licensor in writing of its methods and procedures for archiving the Source Code prior to doing so.

- ***When a Customer purchases a Source Code license it buys only one copy of the Source Code with the right to make a backup copy for archival purposes. The***

Customer must buy a second copy of the Source Code if it wants to modify the Source Code while using the original copy in production.

- ***The Customer is prohibited under Section 3.4 from reverse engineering the Software.***

14. Patent and Other Proprietary Rights Indemnification

14.1.A **Language that Favors Licensor.**

14.A.1 **Third Party Infringement Claims.** Licensor will defend at its own expense any action against Licensee brought by a third party to the extent that the action is based upon a claim that the Software directly infringes any U.S. copyright or misappropriates any trade secret recognized as such under the Uniform Trade Secret Law, and Licensor will pay those costs and damages finally awarded against Licensee in any such action that are specifically attributable to such claim or those costs and damages agreed to in a monetary settlement of such action.

- ***This language favors the Licensor as the Licensor's obligations are extremely limited. The Licensor is obligated only to defend a third party claim and not to indemnify the Licensee. Its obligation to defend is limited only to third party claims that the software directly infringes on any U.S. copyright or the misappropriation of "trade secrets" as The Uniform Trade Secret Law defines such term. This language does not address patent claims or claims made under any laws other than those of the United States.***
- ***"Finally awarded" limits Licensor's obligation to pay for the costs and damages incurred until all appeals have been exhausted. Further, it only addresses "monetary settlements" and not other types of settlements.***
- ***The infringement is limited to U.S. copyrights. With foreign transactions, indemnification should be limited to the United States and the country in which the software will be used.***

14.A.2 **Conditions.** Licensor's obligations under the preceding paragraph with respect to an action are conditioned on (a) Licensee notifying Licensor promptly in writing of such action; (b) Licensee giving Licensor sole control of the defense thereof and any related settlement negotiations; and (c) Licensee cooperating with Licensor in such defense (including, without limitation, by making available to Licensor all documents and information in Licensee's possession or control that are relevant to the infringement or misappropriation claims, and by making Licensee's personnel available to testify or consult with Licensor or its attorneys in connection with such defense).

14.A.3 **Licensor's Options.** If the Software becomes, or in Licensor's opinion **is likely to become, the subject of an infringement or misappropriation claim,** Licensor may, **at its option** and expense, either (a) procure for Licensee the right to continue using the Software; (b) replace or modify the Software so that it becomes non-infringing; **or** (c) terminate Licensee's right to use the Software and give Licensee a refund or credit for the license fees actually paid by Licensee or Licensor for the infringing components of the Software less a reasonable allowance for the period of time Licensee has used the Software.

- ***This language gives the Licensor significant leeway as it allows the Licensor to modify the software if, in the Licensor's opinion, the software may potentially infringe a third party's intellectual property. Further, the Licensor maintains control over the remedy chosen. If the software is mission critical, the Licensee should retain the right to select the appropriate remedy.***

14.A.4 **Exclusions**. Notwithstanding the foregoing, Licensor will have no obligation or otherwise with respect to any infringement or misappropriation claim based upon (a) any use of the Software not in accordance with the Agreement or for purposes not intended by Licensor; (b) any use of the Software in combination with other products, equipment, software, or data not supplied by Licensor; (c) any use of any release of the Software other than the most current release made available to Licensee; or (d) any modification of the Software made by any person other than Licensor.

- ***The Licensor's stated exclusions should only be effective to the extent that one of the enumerated events causes a claim of infringement or misappropriation. The Licensor should not be excused from its obligations if one of the enumerated events occurs but the claim of infringement or misappropriation does not arise as a result of such excluded event.***
- ***The Customer should indemnify Licensor if an infringement claim arises from modifications or uses undertaken by the Customer that were not authorized by the license and that cause any infringement.***

14.A.5 **Entire Liability.** This section states licensor's entire liability and licensee's sole and exclusive remedy for infringement and misappropriation claims and actions.

- ***The language set forth in 14.A.5 protects the licensor from unlimited liability and should be contained in any agreement where intellectual property indemnification is excluded from the limit of liability.***

14.1.B **Language that Favors Licensee.**

14.B.1 **Indemnification.** Licensor will indemnify and hold Licensee harmless from and against any and all claims, losses, liability, damages, costs, and expenses (including attorney's fees, expert witness fees, and court costs) directly or indirectly arising from or related to any actual or alleged infringement (including contributory infringement), misappropriation, or violation of any third party's patents, copyrights, trade secret rights, trademarks, or other intellectual property or proprietary rights of any nature in any jurisdiction in the world, resulting from the use of the Software by Licensee. If Licensee's continued use of the Software is restricted or prohibited as a result of any such infringement, misappropriation, or violation of third party rights, Licensor shall, at Licensee's option and at no charge to Licensee, and in addition to Licensee's other rights and remedies, (a) secure for Licensee the right to continue using the Software as allowed under this Agreement, (b) modify or replace the infringing components of the Software so that they are non-infringing with no loss or degradation of features, functionality, or performance, or (c) refund to Licensee all amounts paid by Licensee for the Software.

- ***This language favors the Licensee, as the Licensor must indemnify the Licensee for any claim directly or indirectly related to any actual or alleged infringement. Further, it grants the Licensee the option to select the remedy that meets the Licensee's business needs, including a full refund of all amounts paid, not a pro-rated refund.***
- ***Licensor must be careful to limit indemnification to a specific entity and not a broad class of entities, i.e., all Affiliates of Licensee.***
- ***Including "attorney's fees" allows the indemnified party to collect attorney's fees, which are usually not recoverable under common law.***
- ***Licensor always needs the option to refund the Licensee's money if Licensor cannot alter the software to make it non-infringing or obtain a license for the Licensee to use the Software. Otherwise Licensor could potentially be obligated to provide a software fix/license regardless of cost or Licensor's ability to do so.***
- ***The Licensee should include language that if the Licensee must convert off the Licensor's system to a third party system, the Licensor will pay all costs incurred by the Licensee in such conversion.***

14.B.2 **Exclusions.** Notwithstanding the foregoing, Licensor will not be obligated to indemnify Licensee to the extent that an infringement or misappropriation claim is based upon (i) use of the Software in breach of this Agreement, if such infringement or misappropriation would not have occurred but for such breach; (ii) use of the Software in combination with other products not supplied or recommended by Licensor or specified by Licensor as being compatible with the Software, if such infringement or misappropriation would not have occurred but for such combined use; (iii) use of any release of the Software other than the most current release made available to Licensee, if the most current release was furnished to Licensee specifically to avoid such infringement or misappropriation and if such infringement or misappropriation would have been avoided by use of the most current release; or (iv) any modification of the Software made by Licensee (other than at Licensor's direction), if such infringement or misappropriation would not have occurred but for such modification.

14.B.3 **Defense of Third Party Suits.** Licensee will use reasonable efforts to notify Licensor promptly of any third party claim, suit, or action (a "Claim") for which Licensee believes it is entitled to indemnification under this Section 14 and which Licensee desires Licensor to defend. However, Licensee's failure to provide such notice or delay in providing such notice will relieve Licensor of its obligations under this Section 14 only if and to the extent that such delay or failure materially prejudices Licensor's ability to defend such Claim. If Licensee tenders the defense of a Claim to Licensor, Licensor will have the right and the obligation to defend such Claim with counsel of its choice; however, Licensee may participate in the defense of the Claim with its own counsel and at its own expense. Once Licensor assumes defense of a Claim, it will be conclusively presumed that Licensor is obligated to indemnify Licensee for such Claim, and Licensee will cooperate with Licensor, at Licensor's reasonable request and at Licensor's expense, in the defense of the Claim. No settlement of a Claim will be binding on Licensee without Licensee's prior written consent.

- ***This language favors the Licensee in that the Licensee must only use reasonable efforts to promptly notify the Licensor of any third party claim. Further, the Licensee may notify the Licensor of those claims "which Licensee desires Licensor to defend" regardless of Licensor's legal obligation to actual defend the Licensee. Further, the Licensee failure to give prompt notice will only excuse the Licensor's obligation to defend to the extent the Licensor's interest have been materially prejudiced, which will be hard to prove.***
- ***Further, once the Licensor assumes defense of a claim, the Licensor is conclusively presumed to be obligated to defend such claim. This prevents the Licensor from later claiming it did not have a legal obligation to defend such claim, significantly increasing its risks.***
- ***The Licensor may bind the Licensee under any settlement without the Licensee's consent. From the Licensee's perspective, this is prudent, as the Licensee cannot allow its business interest to be determined by the Licensor.***

[*Alternative Language Dependant on Prior Language Accepted*]

14.2 **Assumption of Defense.** If the indemnifying party fails to assume the defense of any actual or threatened action covered by this Section 14 within the earlier of (a) any deadline established by a third party in a written demand or by a court, and (b) thirty (30) days of notice of the claim, the indemnified party may follow such course of action as it reasonably deems necessary to protect its interest and shall be indemnified for all costs reasonably incurred in such course of action; provided, however, that the indemnified party shall not settle a claim without the consent of the indemnifying party.

- ***This language allows a party to undertake its own defense if the indemnifying party fails to do so.***
- ***Although intellectual property indemnification is usually excluded from any limit of liability, in actuality the Licensor is protected by the limits set forth in subsections (a), (b), and (c).***
- ***Traditionally, there is no limitation of liability for patent indemnification claims.***

14.3 **Cessation of Fees.** In no event shall Customer be liable to Licensor for any charges after the date that Customer no longer uses the item because of actual or claimed infringement.

14.4 **Licensee Indemnification of Licensor.** Except as otherwise expressly provided in Section 14.1 of this Agreement, Customer shall indemnify and defend Licensor, its directors, and its officers, and shall hold such parties harmless from and against any and all claims, liabilities, damages and expenses, including reasonable attorneys' fees, arising from any third party claim in connection with (a) any Customer supplied intellectual property, (b) any Functional Specifications supplied by Customer, or (c) Customer's transaction of business through the use of any web page or website. The provisions of this Section 14.4 shall not apply to any third party loss or damage caused by Licensor's gross negligence or willful misconduct.

15. General Indemnity

15.1 **Indemnity.** Subject to the limitations contained in this Agreement, Licensor agrees to indemnify and hold harmless Customer, and Customer agrees to indemnify and hold harmless Licensor respectively, from any liabilities, penalties, demands, or claims **finally awarded** (including the costs, expenses, and **reasonable attorney's fees** on account thereof) that may be made **by any third party** for **personal bodily injuries, including death, resulting from the indemnifying party's gross negligence or willful acts or omissions or those of persons furnished by the indemnifying party, its agents, or subcontractors or resulting from use of the Software, Software Products, and/or Services furnished hereunder**. Licensor agrees to defend Customer, at Customer's request, and Customer agrees to defend Licensor, at Licensor's request, against any such liability, claim, or demand. Customer and Licensor respectively agree to notify the other party promptly of any written claims or demands against the indemnified party for which the indemnifying party is responsible hereunder. The foregoing indemnity shall be in addition to any other indemnity obligations of Licensor or Customer set forth in this Agreement.

- ***Indemnification by its nature acts as a risk-shifting device usually with respect to third party liability. As such, it usually addresses intellectual property infringement, personal bodily injury, and property damage. In some cases, indemnification may include damages resulting from intentional acts and willful misconduct. Many Customers today seek to have the Licensor indemnify the Customer for any liability arising from or related to the agreement. The Licensor should strictly limit its indemnification obligations to addresses intellectual property infringement, personal bodily injury, and property damage. The Customer already has a remedy for the Licensor's breach through a breach of contract claim. Thus, there is no need for the Licensor to indemnify the Customer for the Licensor's breach of the agreement. The alternative language below favors the Customer by significantly expanding the nature of the Licensor's indemnification obligations and hence the Licensor's risk.***
- ***The first clause limits Licensor's liability to the amounts set forth in Section 16 (i.e., to the amount of money received from the Customer). Most licensees will want to exclude indemnification from any limit of liability.***
- ***"Finally awarded" limits Licensor's obligations to pay the Customer until all appeals have been exhausted.***
- ***An indemnification clause may allow a recovery in those states that recognize the doctrine of contributory negligence and not the doctrine of comparative***

negligence. It also allows for the recovery of attorneys' fees, which are usually not recoverable.

Alternative Language Benefiting the Customer

Indemnification. Licensor hereby agrees to indemnify and hold Customer and its Representatives harmless from and against all claims, liabilities, losses, damages, and expenses (including reasonable attorneys' fees and expenses) incurred or suffered by any of them as a result of or in connection with (a) any breach by Licensor or any of its Representatives of any of their obligations under this Agreement or any Representative Agreement, or (b) the negligence or willful misconduct of Licensor or any of its Representatives.

or:

Indemnification. Licensor shall indemnify, defend and hold Customer's (its directors, officers and employees) harmless from and against any and all suits, proceedings at law or in equity, claims, loss, liabilities, costs, payments, injury, damage and expenses of any nature (including attorney's fees and court costs) to the extent such damages result from or arise out of (1) failure of Licensor or its Personnel, servants or subcontractors to comply with the terms and conditions of this Agreement; (2) failure of Licensor or its Personnel, servants or subcontractors to comply with applicable laws; (3) negligent acts or willful misconduct of Licensor or its Personnel, servants or subcontractors; (4) any obligation of Licensor to its Personnel, servants or subcontractors including any payment or worker's compensation claim; (5) claims of intellectual property infringement arising from the Services performed hereunder; or (6) any injury or death to any person or damage to property caused by or sustained by Licensor its Personnel, servants, or subcontractors as a result of being on, at or in Customer's facility or entering or leaving therefrom.

15.2 **Assumption of Defense.** If the indemnifying party fails to assume the defense of any actual or threatened action covered by this Section 15 within the earlier of (a) any deadline established by a third party in a written demand or by a court, and (b) thirty (30) days of notice of the claim, the indemnified party may follow such course of action as it reasonably deems necessary to protect its interest and shall be indemnified for all costs reasonably incurred in such course of action; provided, however, that the indemnified party shall not settle a claim without the consent of the indemnifying party.

- ***This language allows a party to undertake its own defense if the indemnifying party fails to do so.***

16. Warranty and Warranty Disclaimer

- ***Because Section 2-316 of the UCC requires that warranty disclaimers be "conspicuous" this paragraph is broken into several shorter paragraphs to allow***

ease of reading and comprehension. Further, Section 16.1.4, which contains the actual disclaimer, is in block letters.

16.1 **Licensor Warranties**

16.1.1 **General Warranties.** Licensor warrants that it owns all rights, title, and interest in and to the Software, or that in the case of any third party software that it has the right to grant a sublicense to use such third party software, that all Software shall substantially conform to the Functional Specifications, and that the Software and Services shall be free from material defects in workmanship and materials that prevent them from substantially meeting the aforementioned criteria. Licensor further warrants that any Services provided by Licensor under this Agreement shall be performed in a workmanlike manner and in accordance with the prevailing professional standards of the software industry. This warranty coverage shall include any modifications made to the Software by Licensor. Such warranty shall extend for sixty (60) days from acceptance and shall survive inspection, test, acceptance, use, and payment.

- ***Licensor carefully limits what it warrants. Licensor only warrants that (1) Licensor owns the Software or has the right to license the software, (2) the software substantially conforms to the Functional Specifications, and (3) the Software is free from material defects in workmanship and materials. By using the phrases "substantially conforms" and "material defects," Licensor allows itself a small level of error as software by its nature is imperfect.***
- ***Licensor's warranty is sixty (60) days. Warranty is an element of price. If the Customer wants a one-year warranty, Licensor can provide one at an increased price.***
- ***Avoid stating "Licensor represents and warrants." A breach of a "representation" gives rise to a claim under tort. By making only warranties, the Licensor limits any claim to contract with a substantially smaller risk of a large recovery.***

16.1.2 **Operation of Software.** Licensor does not warrant that the operation of the Software or the operation of the Software Products will be uninterrupted or error free.

- ***The licensor should always state that the operation of the software will be neither error free nor uninterrupted to avoid creating any implied warranties.***

16.1.3 **Remedy**. In the event of any breach of the warranties set forth in this Agreement, Licensor's sole and exclusive responsibility, and Customer's sole and exclusive remedy, shall be for Licensor to correct or replace, at no additional charge to Customer, any portion of the Software or Services found to be defective; provided, however, that if within a commercially reasonable period Licensor neither corrects such defects nor replaces the defective Software or Services, then Customer's sole and exclusive remedy shall be to receive direct damages not to exceed the license fees paid to Licensor for use of the defective Software or Services. In the event of any breach of any provision of this Agreement other than the warranties set forth in this

Agreement, Customer's sole and exclusive remedy shall be to receive direct damages not to exceed the amounts received by Licensor pursuant to this Agreement. For the avoidance of doubt, Customer's monetary remedies for any breaches of any provision of this Agreement (including, without limitation, the warranty provisions) shall not, in the aggregate, exceed an amount equal to the amounts actually received by Licensor from Customer.

16.1.4 **Warranty Disclaimer.**

EXCEPT AS SET FORTH **IN THIS SECTION 16**, LICENSOR MAKES NO EXPRESS OR IMPLIED REPRESENTATIONS OR WARRANTIES WITH RESPECT TO THE SOFTWARE, OR SERVICES OR THEIR CONDITION, MERCHANTABILITY, FITNESS FOR ANY PARTICULAR PURPOSE OR USE BY CUSTOMER. LICENSOR FURNISHES THE ABOVE WARRANTIES IN LIEU OF ALL OTHER WARRANTIES, EXPRESSED OR IMPLIED, INCLUDING THE WARRANTIES OF MERCHANTABILITY AND FITNESS FOR A PARTICULAR PURPOSE.

- ***UCC Section 2-316 requires all warranty disclaimers to be "conspicuous." Therefore the disclaimer should be in capital block letters.***
- ***From the Licensor's perspective, it is important to specifically reference the section(s) of the agreement that contains the representations and warranties being made by the Licensor. The failure to do so may result in the inclusion of certain implied representations and warranties that may be located elsewhere in the agreement that were never intended to be part of the agreement. The customer, however, should insist on more general language, such as "Except as set forth in this Agreement," or should carefully review the agreement to ensure all representations and warranties are included and referenced by section number. For example, Section 35 contains additional representations and warranties related to disaster recovery, which may be excluded by the reference to "Section 16" set forth above.***

To avoid any attempt to limit the Licensor's warranties to a specific section, some customers seek to include language to the following effect:

Representations and Warranties throughout Agreement. It is understood and agreed by the Parties that Supplier's representations and warranties are set forth throughout this Agreement and are not confined to this Section ___ (Representations, Warranties, and Covenants).

- ***If Licensor does not disclaim all other warranties, Licensor may be liable for certain implied warranties including the failure of the software to function as the Customer thought it would.***

Alternative Language to Meet UCITA Requirements

16.1.4.A **UCITA Warranty Disclaimer.**

The Parties hereby agree that, in respect of information and computer programs provided by one Party to the other Party under this Agreement, and except for the express warranties set forth in Section 16.1 of this Agreement: THERE ARE NO

WARRANTIES (A) AGAINST INTERFERENCE WITH ENJOYMENT OF INFORMATION, (B) AGAINST INFRINGEMENT, (C) THAT INFORMATON, EITHER PARTY'S EFFORTS, OR SYSTEMS, AS EACH MAY BE PROVIDED UNDER THIS AGREEMENT, WILL FULFILL ANY OF EITHER PARTY'S PARTICULAR PURPOSES OR NEEDS, AND (D) WITH RESPECT TO DEFECTS IN THE INFORMATION OR SOFTWARE THAT AN EXAMINATION SHOULD HAVE REASONABLY REVEALED. THE PARTIES HEREBY EACH DISCLAIM IMPLIED WARRANTIES OF MERCHANTIBILITY, QUALITY, AND ACCURACY. THE INFORMATION AND COMPUTER PROGRAMS PROVIDED UNDER THIS AGREEMENT ARE PROVIDED "AS IS" WITH ALL FAULTS, AND THE ENTIRE RISK AS TO SATISFACTORY QUALITY, PERFORMANCE, ACCURACY, AND EFFORT IS WITH THE USER OF SUCH INFORMATION AND COMPUTER PROGRAMS.

- ***Language similar to that set forth in Section 16.1.4.A should be used in those contracts governed by the laws of those states that have adopted UCITA. UCITA's warranty disclaimer requirements are different than the UCC, thus the parties must carefully evaluate whether UCITA applies and ensure that the disclaimers included in the contract are appropriate for the type of damages the Licensor seeks to limit.***

16.1.5 **Voiding of Warranties.** Any and all warranties and indemnifications shall be void as to Services or Software where the non-compliance is caused by or related to (1) the acts or omissions of non-Licensor personnel, its agents, or third parties; (2) misuse, theft, vandalism, fire, water, or other peril; (3) moving or relocation not authorized by Licensor; (4) any alterations or modifications made to any Software by the Customer, it representatives, or agents; (5) use of the Software other than in the operating environment specified in the technical specifications; or (6) coding, information, or specifications created or provided by client.

- ***Licensor should not be held liable for a breach of warranty or an indemnity if the Customer was the cause of any such breach.***
- ***While the Licensor wants to limit its liability in the event the Licensee modifies the software, the Licensee should insist or more limiting/exacting language that excuses the Licensor's performance only to the extent any failure was caused by the Licensee's modifications (i.e., to protect against those cases where the infringement was not caused by the modification but rather by the Licensor's existing code). The limiting language should mirror the language for any intellectual property infringement set forth in Section 14.1.***
- ***The Licensee may also take exception to the voiding of the warranty. The Licensee should insist that the warranty not apply and not be totally voided.***
- ***It is important to note that there is a difference between warranty and maintenance. Warranty is much more comprehensive including modifying the software to make it work. Maintenance involves only maintaining an ongoing operating system to a lesser standard. Breaches of the maintenance provisions will usually result in a refund of the maintenance fees paid to Licensor, but a breach of warranty may entitle Customer to a refund of all development***

and services fees paid to Licensor, which usually is a much larger amount. As such, maintenance should always be addressed in a separate and distinct agreement.

Additional Warranties Benefiting the Customer

16.A **System.** Licensor represents and warrants to Customer that the ABC System shall function without Critical Error in accordance with the applicable Specifications, Performance Standards, Documentation, and Regulatory Requirements.

- ***This warranty ties together all of the appropriate items that set forth the performance of the software system as a whole. This warranty is much broader and goes to the collective operation of the hardware, the Licensor's proprietary software, and any third party software. This is a significant risk for the Licensor as it is essentially warranting the operation of the system as a whole as well as any third party components over which it potentially has no control. By tying together the specifications, performance standards, documentation, and regulatory requirements, if any, the Customer has guaranteed that is will receive the complete benefit of its bargain.***

16.B **Software Performance.** Licensor represents and warrants to Company that the Software or System, as applicable, shall meet the Performance Standards set forth in this Agreement when operating in the operating environment described therein, including the maximum response times and availability ("Operating Environment"). Licensor shall correct any failure of the applicable Software and/or System to operate in accordance with the performance warranties set forth in this Section by providing all additional software, equipment, and/or services to Company at no additional cost to Company. In the event Licensor is unable to correct such failure within a forty-eight (48) hour period [an event of "Default" shall be deemed to have occurred.] **OR** [Customer shall receive from Licensor credits in the amounts set forth in Appendix 3.B.2. In the event Licensor is unable to correct such failure within thirty (30) calendar days, an Event of Default shall be deemed to have occurred.]

Customer and Licensor shall jointly assess, on an annual basis commencing on the first anniversary of Project Acceptance, or more frequently if necessary, whether Customer is operating the Software and/or System in accordance with the Operating Environment. In the event the parties determine that (a) the Operating Environment has changed so that Customer is no longer operating the Software and/or System in accordance with the Operating Environment; and (b) Customer wants to continue the performance warranties set forth in this Section, Licensor shall make such adjustments and recommendations that it deems reasonably necessary to ensure that the Software and/or System will continue to operate in accordance with the warranties set forth herein while operating within the re-established Operating Environment including, without limitation, a recommendation that Customer purchase additional equipment and/or license additional software from Licensor or a third party. If Customer implements such recommendations, the warranties set forth in this Section shall remain in effect. The process described in this Section shall, at Customer's option, repeat for as long as Customer continues to receive Support and Maintenance Services and wants to maintain the performance warranties set forth in this Section. Licensor represents and warrants to Customer that the Software provided under this Agreement shall function without Defect in accordance with the applicable Specifications, Performance Standards, Documentation, and Regulatory Requirements (Defect being defined as a "High" and/or "Medium" Defect).

- ***The warranty contained in Section 16.B contains an additional remedy if the Licensor fails to meet the performance standards. In addition to the Customer's right to receive service level credits and to terminate the agreement, the Licensor has the obligation to purchase all necessary hardware, software, and services necessary to meet the performance standards. This place significant risks and financial burden on the Licensor.***

16.C **Services.** Licensor represents and warrants to Customer that it shall perform the Services and provide the Deliverables required by this Agreement in a workmanlike manner, in accordance with the standards of care and diligence and the level of skill, knowledge, and judgment normally practiced by nationally recognized information technology services firms in performing services of a similar nature, and in accordance with the standards of conduct attached hereto as Exhibit 16.C provided, however, that where this Agreement specifies a particular standard or criteria for performance, this warranty is not intended to and does not diminish that standard or criteria for performance. Further, Licensor represents, warrants, and covenants that it shall provide the Services or create any Deliverables using only proven current technology or methods unless otherwise mutually agreed by the parties [in a particular Statement of Work].

16.D **Documentation.** Licensor represents and warrants to Customer that it has provided to Customer all Documentation for the ABC System and that such Documentation is detailed and complete and accurately describes the functional and operational characteristics of the ABC System. Licensor further represents and warrants that it will provide to Customer updated versions of all such Documentation when it provides to Customer Enhancements to the ABC System and that all such updated Documentation will be complete and accurate and will be at least as detailed as the Documentation issued to Customer with the initial version of the ABC System. The warranty and commitments contained in this Section shall remain in full force and effect for as long as Company continues to receive Support and Maintenance Services from Vendor.

Additional Language that Benefits Licensee

Licensee represents and warrants that it shall at all times document the operation of the Software in a manner consistent with the best practices of the software development industry, and such Documentation shall accurately reflect the operation of the Software and enable a person reasonably skilled in computer programming and in possession of the Software source code to use and maintain the Software fully and completely. Licensee further represents and warrants that it shall control and identify all adaptations, upgrades, and enhancements of the Software by means of a version number, and all lesser modifications by means of a release number.

- ***The Licensor should warrant that not only is the initial Documentation detailed and complete but that the Documentation should reflect any customizations or modifications made to the Customer's system. Licensor should also warrant that any subsequent documentation delivered with any modifications or enhancements is complete and accurate and as detailed as the documentation initially delivered to Customer.***

16.E **Defects.** Licensor warrants that the Software will be free of defects in design, materials, and workmanship.

- ***A prudent Licensor should avoid making any warranty as to the software's design. System architecture/design is a very complex area and thus creates a significant level of risk for the vendor who makes this type of warranty. See*** **USM Corp. v. Arthur D. Little Systems, Inc.,** ***546 N.E.2d 888 (Mass. 1989) (warranty against defects in design required that computer system be able to perform necessary functions in a reasonable time period).***

16.F **Interfaces.** Licensor acknowledges that Customer is working with a number of third parties in developing, maintaining, and supporting Customer's various systems and that Customer's use of the Software may involve the development and/or use of one or more application programming interfaces (APIs) between such third party systems and the Software. Licensor agrees that it will fully cooperate with the Customer and third parties to develop, maintain, and support such APIs. Licensor further agrees that Licensor shall communicate to Customer the industry-standard APIs that Licensor is evaluating and/or implementing, and shall reasonably cooperate and work with Customer and such third parties in good faith to identify industry-standard APIs and, if mutually agreed to by the parties, develop such APIs using as many industry-standard protocols as possible.

[Optional—where Licensor does not create or publish APIs]

Licensor acknowledges and agrees that Customer shall be entitled, for Customer's internal use only, to reverse engineer, disassemble, or decompile the Software licensed hereunder for the purpose of creating interoperable computer programs that facilitate interoperability between Licensor's Software and third party software products.

16.G **Open Architecture/Open System.** Licensor represents and warrants to Customer that the Software systems are designed and shall continue to be designed to operate in an Open Architecture environment and, as such, all external Licensor interface specifications shall be published and generally available. For purposes of the foregoing, an "Open Architecture" is an architecture that adheres to a publicly known set of interface specifications so that any applications that have been implemented to those interface specifications shall be able to interoperate with any other third party applications that adhere to the same interface specifications.

16.H **Compatibility.** Licensor represents and warrants to Customer that the Software is fully operational on the Equipment. Licensor further represents and warrants that non-Licensor supplied third party software is capable of being loaded on the Equipment with no upgrades or modifications to the Equipment or any Software (operating system or otherwise) relating to the Equipment.

Additional Language that Benefits Licensee

Licensor warrants that the Software will be compatible with the Licensee's technical environment, including hardware, operating system(s), software application(s), CPUs, and networks specified by Licensee in the applicable Request for Proposal or Work Order.

16.I **Future Compatibility.** Licensor warrants that all updates, upgrades, and revisions to the Software furnished hereunder will be implemented in such a manner as to maintain backward compatibility with the previous version or release of the Software furnished hereunder, under the Agreement, or under any other agreement issued pursuant to this Agreement, so that such previous versions or releases shall continue to be operable with the Software as updated, upgraded, or revised, in materially the same manner and with materially equivalent performance.

- ***See Chapter 23.K.2.FF.16 for additional language benefiting licensee.***

16.J **Data Integrity.** Licensor represents and warrants to Customer that all data types, structures, formats, and content will be converted completely and accurately such that the Customer will be able to reconcile the original data with the converted data without any loss to or deviation from the original data. **In the event of data loss caused by the Software or Software failure, including, but not limited to, a Software failure resulting from an error, malfunction, or overloading, Licensor shall undertake its best efforts to restore or recover any data or results at no cost to Customer within a commercially reasonable time.**

- ***The highlighted language benefits the Licensor as the licensor is required to use its "best efforts" to remediate any problem, but it is not definitively obligated to resolve the problem.***

Alternative Language Benefiting Customer

In the event that Customer's data is corrupted or lost as a result of any action by the Licensor, Customer may, in addition to the other remedies that may be available to it, require the Licensor at the Licensor's expense to restore or procure the restoration of Customer's data by whatever means necessary to ensure its integrity.

- ***Licensors should be hesitant to make this warranty or to convert data in general. Data conversion can be very expensive and result in corrupted data. It is prudent to have the Licensee convert its own data.***

16.K **Software Obsolescence.** Licensor acknowledges that Customer is making a significant resource commitment in order to acquire the Software and that Customer does not want to move involuntarily to a new system *[at a later date OR prior to a specified date]*. Having acknowledged the foregoing, Licensor represents and warrants to Customer that it will continue to enhance the Software (meaning adding new features and functionality, in addition to ordinary course defect corrections), as long as Customer continues to receive Software support services from Licensor.

additionally/alternatively:

Latest Versions. All Software as delivered will be the most current release or version that Licensor has made commercially available to its customers, unless Customer, after being advised by Licensor of the availability of a newer release or version, expressly elects to acquire and deploy and older one.

- ***The Customer should ensure that the Licensor commits to continually enhance the software. Otherwise, the Customer may make a significant investment only to find that the Licensor plans to "sunset" the software requiring the Customer to purchase a new software system.***

16.L **Disabling Code.** Licensor represents and warrants to Customer that in connection with the licensing of the Software, Customer will not receive or experience any virus, worm, trap door, back door, timer, clock, counter, or other limiting routine, instruction, or design that would erase data or programming or otherwise cause any Customer system to become inoperable or incapable of being used in the full manner for which it was designed and created (collectively, a "Disabling Code"). In the event a Disabling Code is identified, Licensor shall take all steps necessary, at no additional cost to Customer, to restore and/or reconstruct any and all data lost by Customer as a result of such Disabling Code.

- ***This warranty favors the customer in that it is impossible for the licensor to ensure that the software is free of viruses, etc. Virus detection software is issued and updated only after the latest viruses have been identified. Thus all a licensor can state is that it will use commercially reasonable virus software prior to delivering the software to the customer. The language set forth below is more balanced language, which the licensor should be willing to accept.***

alternatively:

Viruses. Licensor warrants that it will use commercially reasonable virus detection computer software programs to test the Software licensed hereunder for viruses prior to delivery to Customer and that Licensor will continue to take such step with respect to any code delivered to Customer to correct any identified error. Customer hereby warrants that it will use commercially reasonable virus detection computer software programs to test the Software licensed hereunder for viruses prior to installation and that Customer will continue to take such step with respect to any code delivered to Customer to correct any identified error. Licensor warrants that it will maintain a copy of the current version and the one (1) immediately preceding version of the Software, which have been tested as set forth herein. Upon Customer's request, Licensor agrees to make such copy of the Software available to Customer, for Customer's comparison with Customer's copy of the Software. Licensor further warrants to Customer that it is not the policy of Licensor to intentionally include disabling mechanisms or computer viruses into software provided to its customers and that should such policy change, Licensor will advise Customer in advance and, upon Customer's request, will provide Customer with the code(s) necessary to defeat any such disabling mechanisms or computer viruses, intentionally inserted by Licensor or its employees into the Software.

Unauthorized Code. Unauthorized Code means computer instructions that alter, destroy, or inhibit the Customer's processing environment, including, but not limited to, data storage and computer libraries. Unauthorized Code includes, but is not limited to, programs that self-replicate without manual intervention, instructions programmed to activate at a predetermined time or upon a specified event, and programs purporting to do a meaningful function but designed for a destructive function. During the Term, Licensor warrants that it shall take reasonable steps to test all releases furnished to Customer for the presence of Unauthorized Code. The determination of "reasonable tests" shall be based on then current industry standards for testing for such Unauthorized Code on the applicable hardware platform. However, Customer may not use said releases until Customer has similarly tested all releases on Customer's computers after delivery. If Customer notifies Licensor in reasonable detail of a breach of the foregoing warranties that occurred in the sixty (60) days prior to such notice, then Licensor shall provide a release conforming with this warranty as soon as reasonably possible but within ten (10) business days. THIS SHALL BE CUSTOMER'S SOLE REMEDY FOR ANY SUCH BREACH, TO THE EXCLUSION OF ALL OTHER REMEDIES, EVEN IF SUCH LIMITATION CAUSES THIS WARRANTY OR ITS REMEDY TO FAIL OF THEIR ESSENTIAL PURPOSES.

- ***This warranty should be mutual, as it is possible that the Customer's employees or consultants may introduce Disabling Code into the system.***

16.M **Regulatory Requirements.** Licensor represents and warrants to Customer that the Software meets and satisfies all Regulatory Requirements. Licensor further warrants that the Licensor, its employees, agents, and subcontractors shall comply with the Regulatory Requirements [set forth in the Business Associate Addendum] attached hereto as Exhibit 16.M.

- ***To the extent the Customer is subject to any regulatory requirements such as in the healthcare, insurance, or telecommunications industries, the Licensor should warrant that the software meets and satisfies all applicable regulatory requirements.***

16.N **Media.** Licensor warrants that for a period of 90 days from the date of delivery of the Software that the media used to store and deliver the Software to the Customer shall be free from defects in manufacture and material. Should the media fail to be free of defects in manufacture or material during the 90-day warranty period, Licensor shall replace the defective media. Defective media shipped to the Licensor with a shipping date within the 90-day warranty period will be replaced at no charge including shipping.

16.O **Intellectual Property.** Licensor represents and warrants to Customer that Customer's use of the Software does not and shall not infringe upon any [U.S.] patent, trademark, copyright, trade secret or other intellectual property, or proprietary right of any Third Party, and there is currently no actual or threatened suit against Licensor by any Third Party based on an alleged violation of such right. This warranty shall survive the expiration or termination of this Agreement.

- ***Given the explosion of patent infringement suits involving software, many licensors no longer want to make a representation or warranty as the intellectual property infringement. They argue that because the licensor agrees to indemnify the customer as the result of such infringement (See Section 14), the customer does not need a warranty. While a Customer may insist on a "belt and suspenders" approach, the Customer does not usually gain a significant level of greater protection.***
- ***If the licensor does give such a warranty, the Licensor will want to reduce its potential risks by limiting liability to the infringement of U.S. intellectual property rights.***

16.P **Third Party Warranties and Indemnities.** For any Third Party Software provided by Licensor to Customer, Licensor hereby assigns to Customer all end user warranties and indemnities relating to such Third Party Software. To the extent that Licensor is not permitted to assign any of such end user warranties and indemnities through to Customer, Licensor shall enforce such warranties and indemnities on behalf of Customer to the extent Licensor is permitted to do so under the terms of the applicable Third Party agreements.

16.Q **ISO 9001.** Licensor warrants that during the term of this Agreement, Licensor shall utilize a quality system in accordance with Appendix 16.Q. This quality system shall also be in accordance with ISO 9001.

16.R **Authority.** Each party represents and warrants to the other that it has the right to enter into this Agreement. Licensor further represents and warrants that there are no outstanding assignments, grants, licenses, encumbrances, obligations, or agreements (whether written oral or implied) that are inconsistent with this Agreement and the rights granted or transferred herein. This warranty shall survive the expiration or termination of this Agreement.

16.S **Pending Litigation.** Licensor represents and warrants to Customer that there is no action, suit, claim, investigation or proceeding pending, or to the best of Licensor's knowledge, **threatened** against, by or affecting Licensor or the ABC System which, if adversely decided, might adversely affect Licensor's ability to enter into this Agreement, Licensor's performance of its obligations herein, or Customer's use of the Software. As of the date hereof, Licensor further represents and warrants that it does not know of any basis for any such action.

- ***This warranty protects the Customer by requiring the Licensor to disclose any threatened or pending litigation that may interfere with the Customer's license***

rights. This is especially important with regard to any third party intellectual property infringement claims. A prudent Licensor would not agree to this warranty because it is so broad.

16.T **Change of Control.** Licensor represents and warrants to Customer that no Change of Control with respect to Licensor is being considered, planned, or pending by the Board of Directors, shareholders or management of Licensor or by any Affiliate of Licensor.

- ***A prudent Licensor would not agree to this warranty because it is so broad and may place the Licensor in the position of inadvertently violating the securities laws or breaking the agreement.***

16.U **Material Misstatements or Omissions.** No representation or warranty by Licensor that is contained in this Agreement or in any Appendix, Exhibit, or other Attachment hereto contains any untrue statement of a material fact or omits to state a material fact necessary to make the statements and facts contained herein or therein not materially misleading.

- ***A prudent Licensor would not agree to this warranty, as it is so broad that it creates a significant level of risk for the Licensor.***

16.V **Fitness for a Particular Purpose.** Licensor warrants that the Software will be fit for [describe purpose] by the Customer under normal use and service.

- ***A prudent Licensor should avoid giving this warranty as it creates a significant risk of liability on the Licensor's behalf by promising the software will be fit for the Licensee's intended use or purpose.***

16.W **Privacy/HIPAA.** Licensor acknowledges that the Licensee Data may contain personal data, health data, and/or medical records data, the use of which data is subject to various Privacy Laws, including all state, federal, and international laws and regulations and state, federal, and national government agency orders and decrees to which Licensee may be subject ("Privacy Laws"), as well as certain restrictions imposed on the Licensee Data by the data subjects or other third party data providers. Licensor agrees to strictly abide by all such restrictions pertaining to the Licensee Data, as they are promulgated and applied, currently and in the future. Furthermore, Licensor shall in good faith execute any and all agreements that Licensee is required to have Licensor execute in order that Licensee may comply with any Privacy Laws. If Licensor's use (whether directly or indirectly) of the Licensee Data is contrary to any Privacy Law, or contrary to any of the restrictions set forth in this Agreement, Licensee shall have the right to (i) terminate this Agreement for cause if such breach has not been cured within five (5) days of receipt by Licensor of written notice, and (ii) pursue any other legal and equitable remedies.

16.X **Data Transfer.** Licensor represents and warrants that it will only transfer (including internal Licensor transfers that occur beyond the internal firewalls of Licensor) Licensee Data in a secure and confidential manner, including at a minimum, encrypting the data with no less than 128 bit encryption or through establishing a virtual private network with Licensee and shall comply with all security provisions and procedures set forth in Licensee's Information Asset Protection Policies and Licensee's Consumer Data Protection Policies and Procedures.

16.Y **Gifts and Gratuities.** Licensor, its employees, and agents shall not give or offer to give any material gifts or gratuities of any kind whatsoever to any Licensee employee or members of their families. In the event that Licensor is approached by anyone suggesting fraudulent or unethical behavior with regard to Licensor's business activities with Licensee, or if any request is made to Licensor, its employees, or agents by any Licensee employees or members of their families for gifts or gratuities of any kind, Licensor agrees to immediately notify Licensee's legal department. Licensor certifies by execution of this Agreement that it knows of no material gifts or gratuities, or any kind whatsoever, paid to Licensee employees or members of their families by Licensor, Licensor's employees, or agents during the past two (2) years, except as otherwise set forth in writing to Licensee's legal department as an exhibit to this Agreement. Licensor agrees to immediately notify Licensee legal department in writing of any violations of this subsection.

16.Z **Customer Complaints.** There is no existing pattern or repetition of customer complaints regarding the Programs or Services, including functionality or performance issues, and that Licensor's engineers have not currently identified any repeating adverse impact on the Programs or Services, including functionality or performance, for which the root cause is believed to be a flaw or defect in the Programs or Services. The foregoing warranty shall not extend to any specifications provided by Customer.

16.AA **Open Source Materials.** Licensor represents and warrants to Customer that Licensor has not (i) incorporated Open Source Materials into, or combined Open Source Materials with, the Deliverables or Software, (ii) distributed Open Source Materials in conjunction with any Deliverables or Software, or (iii) used Open Source Materials, in such a way that, with respect to the foregoing (i), (ii), or (iii), creates obligations for the Licensor with respect to any material Deliverables or grant, or purport to grant, to any third party, any rights or immunities under any material Deliverables (including, but not limited to, using any Open Source Materials that require, as a condition of use, modification and/or distribution of such Open Source Materials that other material software included in Deliverables incorporated into, derived from or distributed with such Open Source Materials be (A) disclosed or distributed in source code form, (B) be licensed for the purpose of making derivative works, or (C) be redistributable at no charge).

Alternatively:

Open Source. Licensor represents and warrants to Customer that the Work Product provided pursuant to this Agreement shall not contain any "Open Source." For purposes of this Agreement, "Open Source" means any software code that: (a) contains, or is derived in any manner (in whole or in part) from, any software that is distributed as free software, open source software, shareware (e.g., Linux), or similar licensing or distribution models; and (b) is subject to any agreement with terms requiring that such software code be (i) disclosed or distributed in Source Code or Object Code form, (ii) licensed for the purpose of making derivative works, and/or (iii) redistributable. Open Source includes, but is not limited to, software licensed or distributed under any of the following licenses or distribution models, or licenses or distribution models similar to any of the following: (A) GNU's General Public License (GPL) or Lesser/Library GPL (LGPL); (B) the Artistic License (e.g., PERL); (C) the Mozilla Public License(s); (D) the Netscape Public License; (E) the Berkeley Software Design (BSD) license including Free BSD or BSD-style license; (F) the Sun Community Source License (SCSL); (G) an Open Source Foundation License (e.g., CDE and Motif UNIX user interfaces); (H) the Apache Server license; and (I) any licenses listed at http://www.opensource.org/licenses.

16.AB **Location of Performance.** Licensor further warrants that all Services shall be performed and rendered within the continental United States.

- ***See Section 3.7 for language acknowledging that the Licensor will be performing services offshore.***

16.AC **Usability of Source Code.** Licensor represents and warrants that the Source Code is and shall be understandable and useable by a trained computer-programming contractor who is familiar with similar systems, though not necessarily those incorporating the Software. Licensor further represents and warrants that the Software does not involve any proprietary languages or programming components that such contractor could not reasonably be expected to understand, except to the extent the source code contains sufficient commentary to enable such contractor to understand and to use such languages or components. Licensor further represents and warrants that the source code includes all of the devices, programming and documentation necessary for the maintenance of the Software by the Customer upon release of the source code pursuant to this Escrow Agreement, except for devices, programming and documentation commercially available to the Customer on reasonable terms through readily known sources other than the Licensor.

16.AD **Security.** Licensor warrants and represents to Customer and its Affiliates that (i) the provision of the Services shall not permit any unauthorized access to or cause any loss or damage to Customer Systems, Customer Pre-existing Intellectual Property, any Work Products (where such Work Products are owned by Customer in accordance with this Agreement) or Confidential Information belonging to Customer; and (ii) it shall comply with any Customer Security Policies in place from time to time during the term of this Agreement.

16.AE **Representations Made in RFI and RFP.**
Licensor represents and warrants that all statements and representations made in Licensor's response to each of Customer's Request for Information dated as of ________, 20__ and Customer's Request for Proposal dated as of _____, 20__ were true and correct at the time made and remain true and correct as of the date of this Agreement.

The Following Clauses Are Typical of Those Used in the Pharmaceutical and Healthcare Industries

16.AF **Debarment.** Licensor represents and warrants that Licensor and its officers, directors, employees, and agents have not been debarred under any federal, state or local law, regulation, rule, or order, including, but not limited to, the Generic Drug Enforcement Act of 1992. In the event any pending proceeding or threatened debarment of Licensor or its officers, directors, employees, or agents, Licensor shall immediately notify Licensee of such proceeding or threatened debarment.

16.AG **Recording Devices.** Licensor, subcontractors, and their respective employees shall not bring video or audio recording devices, including, but not limited to, cameras, PDAs, or similar devices with video or audio capabilities into Licensee's facilities without the express written permission of Licensee's security department. Licensor, subcontractors, and their respective employees shall not make audio or video recordings inside Licensee's facilities without the express written permission of Licensee's security department.

16.AH **Drug Testing/Criminal Background Investigation.** Licensor represents and warrants that all Licensor personnel and its subcontractor personnel that will be providing services at a Licensee facility have received and passed a pre-assignment drug test within thirty (30) days of beginning an assignment at a Licensee facility and at least annually thereafter. Licensor represents and warrants that Licensor personnel and its subcontractor personnel used to perform services for Licensee under this Agreement have not been convicted of the following crimes: felony or misdemeanor fraud conviction, felony or misdemeanor theft conviction, felony drug conviction, felony firearms conviction, or felony convictions of crimes of a violent or serious nature (e.g., battery, sexual offenses, robbery). In addition, Licensor shall not use Licensor personnel or subcontractor personnel on the Licensee project that have multiple convictions (i.e., three or more) for offenses less serious than those listed above (other than minor traffic offenses) during the last five years.

Other Warranties to Consider

- ***A Licensee should consider whether any other warranties are required depending on the nature of the underlying transaction. These may include complying with future regulatory changes and scalability, etc.***

16.2 **Customer Warranties**

- ***The Licensor should also insist on the inclusion of certain representations and warranties by the Customer, the most important of which are the customer's representation that it has the authority to enter into the agreement and that it has the ability to pay the licensee fee. The Licensor should consider whether any special representations or warranties are needed i.e., in international transactions, that the Customer has received approval for the licensor to repatriate any fees received by it.***

16.2.1 **Authority**. Customer represents and warrants to the Licensor that Customer has all requisite power and authority to execute and deliver this Agreement and to perform the Customer's obligations hereunder. This Agreement has been duly and validly executed and delivered by the Customer, and constitutes a valid and binding obligation of the Customer, enforceable against the Customer in accordance with its terms.

16.2.2 **Conflict with Other Agreements.** Customer represents and warrants to the Licensor that neither the execution and delivery of this Agreement by the Customer nor the consummation by the Customer of the transactions contemplated by this Agreement will (i) conflict with or violate any provision of the Certificate of Incorporation or bylaws of the Customer; (ii) require on the part of the Customer any filing with, or any permit, authorization, consent, or approval of, any court, arbitrational tribunal, administrative agency or commission, or other governmental or regulatory authority or agency (a "Governmental Entity"); (iii) conflict with, result in a breach of, constitute (with or without due notice or lapse of time or both) a default under, result in the acceleration of, create in any party the right to accelerate, terminate, modify, or cancel, or require any notice, consent, or waiver under, any agreement, instrument, contract, or arrangement to which the Customer is a party or by which the Customer or any of its properties is bound; or (iv) violate any order, writ, injunction, decree, law, statute, rule, or regulation applicable to the Customer.

16.2.3 **Financial Ability.** Customer represents and warrants to the Licensor that it presently has sufficient funds and will have sufficient funds available to timely pay Licensor all amounts due or that will come due under this Agreement. The Customer further represents and warrants to Licensor that Customer will not, at any time, permit its Consolidated Net Worth to be less than $[___].

17. Limitation of Liability

17.1 **DISCLAIMER OF LIABILITY.**

LICENSOR SHALL NOT BE LIABLE FOR ANY (A) SPECIAL, INDIRECT, INCIDENTAL, PUNITIVE, OR CONSEQUENTIAL DAMAGES, INCLUDING LOSS OF PROFITS, ARISING FROM OR RELATED TO A BREACH OF THIS AGREEMENT OR ANY ORDER OR THE OPERATION OR USE OF THE SOFTWARE AND SERVICES INCLUDING SUCH DAMAGES, WITHOUT LIMITATION, AS DAMAGES ARISING FROM LOSS OF DATA OR PROGRAMMING, LOSS OF REVENUE OR PROFITS, FAILURE TO REALIZE SAVINGS OR OTHER BENEFITS, DAMAGE TO EQUIPMENT, AND CLAIMS AGAINST CUSTOMER BY ANY THIRD PERSON, EVEN IF LICENSOR HAS BEEN ADVISED OF THE POSSIBILITY OF SUCH DAMAGES; (B) DAMAGES (REGARDLESS OF THEIR NATURE) FOR ANY DELAY OR FAILURE BY LICENSOR TO PERFORM ITS OBLIGATIONS UNDER THIS AGREEMENT DUE TO ANY CAUSE BEYOND LICENSOR'S REASONABLE CONTROL; OR (C) CLAIMS MADE A SUBJECT OF A LEGAL PROCEEDING AGAINST LICENSOR MORE THAN TWO YEARS AFTER ANY SUCH CAUSE OF ACTION FIRST AROSE.

- ***Licensor should disclaim all "speculative" and "third party" damages. Damages recoverable by the Customer should be limited to Customer's actual direct damages. The Uniform Commercial Code does not require that any disclaimer be "conspicuous" although the courts may impose this requirement. Therefore this section should be in large block letters.***
- ***Licensor will not be liable for any damages suffered by the Customer's customers or any other third party.***
- ***By requiring claims be brought within two years, Licensor limits its risk/liability by shortening the statute of limitations which may be up to 12 years.***

17.2 LIMITATION OF LIABILITY.

NOTWITHSTANDING ANY OTHER PROVISION OF THIS AGREEMENT, BUT EXCLUDING ANY CLAIMS FOR INDEMNIFICATION UNDER SECTION 14.1 LICENSOR'S LIABILITIES UNDER THIS AGREEMENT, WHETHER UNDER CONTRACT LAW, TORT LAW, WARRANTY, OR OTHERWISE SHALL BE LIMITED TO DIRECT DAMAGES NOT TO EXCEED THE AMOUNTS ACTUALLY RECEIVED BY LICENSOR [**UNDER THIS AGREEMENT OR IN THE ______ MONTHS PRIOR TO THE DATE OF THE ACTION GIVING RISE TO THE CLAIM**].

Additional Language Benefiting Customer

NOTWITHSTANDING THE FOREGOING, IF ANY CLAIM AGAINST LICENSOR IS A CLAIM COVERED BY ANY INSURANCE POLICY MAINTAINED BY LICENSOR, ANY RECOVERY OF PROCEEDS UNDER SUCH POLICY SHALL BE PAID TO CUSTOMER TO THE EXTENT CUSTOMER'S DAMAGES EXCEED THE FOREGOING LIMITATION OF LIABILITY.

- ***Licensor seeks to limit its liability under both contract and tort theories, which have different statues of limitations, and different bases for which a recovery can be made.***
- ***The customer should seek to carve out a number of claims from the licensor's limit of liability including patent indemnification, personal bodily injury and personal property damage, breach of the licensor's confidentiality obligations, gross negligence, and intentional misconduct. For public policy reasons, many jurisdictions forbid tortfeasors from limiting their liability for personal injuries arising from consumer goods. See UCC § 2 719(13).***
- ***Licensor should limit its liability (to the amount received from the Customer) or it could potentially be liable for Licensor's entire net worth. (Traditionally, there is no limitation of liability for patent indemnification claims and in consumer transactions, for personal bodily injury). The Licensor will want to limit its liability to the amount received so that it is never out of pocket, while the Customer will want to ensure that it recovers its actual losses, which may exceed the amounts paid to the Licensor. The Customer may want to agree to limit the Licensor's liability to a multiple of the amount paid to the Licensor or a multiple of the value of the contract regardless of the amount paid. To protect itself during the early periods of the agreement when it is likely that only a small amount of money has been paid to the Licensor, the Customer may***

want to insist that the Licensor's liability is limited to the greater of a set dollar amount or the value of the contract.

- ***Limitation of liability is an element of price. Licensor has based its pricing on limiting Licensor's liability at the amount received from the Customer or alternatively the contract value. If the Customer wants a higher limitation of liability, Licensor can raise its limit of liability but: (a) the license fee must increase because Licensor is now bearing more risk; or (b) Licensor must buy errors and omissions insurance and charge the Customer for the cost.***
- ***It is important to retain a default remedy provision, otherwise a court may find Licensor's warranty "failed of its essential purpose" (i.e., did not provide the Customer with an adequate remedy) and void Licensor's limitation of liability and disclaimer for consequential damages.***

17.3 **Items Not Considered Damages.** The following shall not be considered damages subject to, and shall not be counted toward the liability cap specified in, Section 17.1:

(i) amounts withheld by Customer in accordance with this Agreement due either to incorrect Charges by Licensor or nonconforming Services; or

(ii) amounts paid by Customer but subsequently recovered from Licensor due either to incorrect Charges by Licensor or nonconforming Services.

17.4 **Acknowledged Direct Damages.** The following shall be considered direct damages and neither Party shall assert that they are indirect, incidental, collateral, consequential, or special damages or lost profits to the extent they result directly from either Party's failure to perform in accordance with this Agreement:

(a) Reasonable costs and expenses of recreating or reloading any lost, stolen, or damaged Customer data;

(b) Reasonable costs and expenses of implementing a work-around in respect of a failure to provide the Software or Services or any part thereof;

(c) Reasonable costs and expenses of replacing lost, stolen, or damaged equipment, software, and materials;

(d) Reasonable costs and expenses incurred to procure the Software or Services or corrected Software or Services from an alternate source, to the extent in excess of Licensor's Charges under this Agreement;

(e) Reasonable straight time, overtime, or related expenses incurred by either Party, wages and salaries of additional employees, travel expenses, overtime, expenses, telecommunication charges, and similar charges due to failure of Licensor to provide all or a portion of the Software or Services incurred in connection with (a) through (d) above;

(f) Reasonable costs and expenses incurred to bring the Services in-house or to contract to obtain the Software or Services from an alternate source, including the costs and expenses associated with the retention of external consultants and legal counsel to assist with any re-sourcing; provided that, with respect to external consultants and legal counsel, Customer shall act and in a manner consistent with that historically used by Customer or customarily used by other customers in procuring similar services in similar transactions;

(g) Payments, fines, penalties, or interest imposed by a governmental body or regulatory agency for failure to comply with requirements or deadlines;

(h) Liquidated damages assessed under (Transition Services); or

(i) Service Level Credits assessed against Licensor.

18. Obligations that Survive Termination

The parties recognize and agree that their obligations under Sections 8, 12, 14, 15, 17, 28, 30, 34, and 35 of this Agreement survive the cancellation, termination, or expiration of this Agreement or the License granted under Section 3.1.

- ***The obligations of the parties that will survive termination of the Agreement, i.e., payment to Licensor, confidentiality, limitation of liability, governing law etc., should be specifically listed because these obligations would otherwise "terminate" with the Agreement. As a result, Licensor may be unable to get paid or protect its proprietary information since the Agreement is no longer in existence and thus the Customer is no longer bound by the terms of the Agreement. Avoid use of imprecise language such as "Any terms of this Agreement that would, by their nature, survive the expiration or termination of this Agreement shall so survive" to avoid disputes over the intent or meaning of this or similar language.***

Alternative Language:

The terms, provisions, representations and warranties contained in this Agreement shall survive completion or other termination of this Agreement unless otherwise provided.

- ***The above language creates more ambiguity than it resolves. As such, the parties should strive to eliminate ambiguity and should take the time to carefully review the contract and list by section number every clause they want to survive.***

19. Error Correction under Warranty

19.1 **Notification of Errors.** During the warranty period, Customer will notify Licensor verbally of Errors and provide written notification to Licensor within seventy-two (72) hours of such verbal notification. Licensor shall provide Customer with a telephone number that is answered from 9:00 a.m. to 6:00 p.m. Washington, D.C. time, Monday through Friday, except for Licensor holidays, a list of which is set forth on Appendix 19.1. Customer shall have access via this telephone number to individuals who shall accept Error reports and are qualified to assist Customer with the verification of suspected Errors and who may provide solutions for said Errors. Customer shall be provided with a telephone number that is answered for all hours outside of Monday through Friday, 9:00 a.m. to 6:00 p.m. Washington, D.C. time by individuals who shall accept Error reports.

19.2 **Correction of Errors.** During the warranty period, Licensor shall use its good faith efforts to immediately correct any Critical Errors affecting Customer's continued business use of the Software after Licensor's notification of the Error. Licensor will use its good faith efforts to correct all other Errors within twenty (20) days after Licensor's notification of the Error.

20. Right to Move [If Applicable]

Any Software License may be temporarily transferred to a backup computer while the licensed computer is inoperative or for emergency testing purpose. The backup computer may be at the same Customer Site, another Customer Site, or an off-site location under emergency conditions and after sufficient advance notice has been given to Licensor of the name and location of the off-site operator. Customer may re-designate the Site or the CPU on which the Software will be used for on-going operations with Licensor's consent. Customer shall be permitted concurrent operation at the new and old Site or CPU for not more than thirty (30) days and such operation will require no additional fees. Customer shall provide Licensor written notice of the re-designation within a reasonable length of time of the Software being moved to the new Site or CPU. In the event Licensor consents to the Customer moving the Software to another Customer Site or CPU, or Customer assigning the Software licensed under this Agreement, Licensor agrees that it shall continue the warranty and assist in its transfer to such other Site, CPU, or assignee.

21. Customer Preparation

If the Software is to be installed by Licensor, the Customer shall have all things in readiness for installation, including, but not limited to, other equipment, connections, and facilities for installation at the time the Software is delivered. In the event the Customer shall fail to have all things in readiness for installation on the scheduled installation date, the Customer shall reimburse Licensor for any and all expenses caused by Customer's failure to have things in readiness, unless Customer has notified Licensor at least thirty (30) business days prior to the scheduled installation date. Customer agrees to provide and bear the cost of all communications costs incurred by Licensor from the Customer site and the costs of a dedicated dial-up communications facility equipped with 56 KB Hayes compatible modem for the purposes of remote access and support by the Licensor consultant or phone support group. In addition, Customer shall fully cooperate with Licensor during the term of this Agreement.

- ***The contract should set forth in detail any actions the Customer is obligated to undertake to prepare for the installation of the software. This list should be very detailed and include any physical requirements such as air conditioning, modem lines, etc. The Customer should be subject to liquidated damages for its failure to meet these obligations.***

22. Assignment and Transfer

22.1 **Prohibition on Assignment.** Customer may not assign or transfer its interests, rights, or obligations under this Agreement by written agreement, merger, consolidation, **operation of law**, or otherwise, without the prior written consent of an authorized executive officer of Licensor. Any attempt to assign this Agreement by Customer shall be null and void. Furthermore, for the purposes of this Agreement the acquisition of an equity interest in Customer of greater than 25 percent by any third party shall be considered an "assignment."

- ***Licensor must limit the ability of the Customer to assign the Agreement to avoid losing potential license fees. In a merger or acquisition, the entity being acquired will seek to assign its pre-merger contracts to the acquiring party to avoid paying a transfer or license fee. By stating that any assignment is "void" a court will not allow the assignment. In the absence of such language the court will permit the assignment and allow the Licensor to seek recovery of monetary damages.***
- ***To protect itself in the event that it believes it may be acquired, the customer may want to include language to the following effect:***

Notwithstanding the foregoing, Customer may assign its rights and obligations under this Agreement, in whole or part, without the approval of Licensor to (a) an entity acquiring, directly or indirectly, Customer through a Change of Control of Customer; (b) an entity into which Customer is merged; or (c) an entity acquiring all or substantially all of Customer's assets to which this Agreement relates, in any case provided the acquirer or surviving entity agrees in writing to be bound by the terms and conditions of this Agreement. Without limiting the generality of the foregoing, the phrase "by operation of law" shall include a Change of Control.

Additional Language Benefiting Customer

22.2 **Remedy.** In the event that Licensor, with Customer's written consent, assigns, or otherwise transfers this Agreement, or any part hereof, or delegates any of its duties hereunder, whether by operation of law or otherwise, to any Third Party or Affiliate and, within eighteen (18) months after such transfer, Customer, in its sole discretion, is not satisfied with the level of service provided under this Agreement, Customer shall have the right to terminate this Agreement and, pursuant to Customer's rights under Section 4.1.A, [Termination/Termination for Convenience] transition to a new software vendor. All Services provided by Licensor's transferee during the Transition Period shall be provided at no cost. Customer may assign this Agreement to any Affiliate at any time upon written notice to Licensor. Any rights granted to Customer under this Agreement to use the Software and Documentation shall inure to the benefit of any acquirer of, or successor in interest to, Customer, whether by merger, consolidation, purchase, operation of law, or otherwise.

- ***This language attempts to protect the Customer in the event that a new entity provides services or software in the Licensor's stead. While the language as written gives the Customer broad discretion as to whether the quality of services has degraded under the new provider a more objective standard should be selected such as a material increase in the failure to meet the service level standards.***

22.3 **Transfer.** Licensee may assign or transfer the License, in whole or in part, to any Affiliate or Divested Business that agrees in writing to be bound by the terms of this Agreement; provided such transferee's primary business is not licensing similar software. After any such assignment or transfer and with respect to such portion of the Software assigned or transferred, (i) Licensee will not continue to use that portion of the Software; (ii) Licensor will have recourse only to the transferee and will not have recourse to Licensee or Affiliates, and the transferee will be solely responsible and liable, for breaches by the transferee with respect to any such transferred rights, the License, or this Agreement.

23. Amendments, Modifications, or Supplements

Amendments, modifications, or supplements to this Agreement shall be permitted, provided all such changes shall be in writing signed by the authorized representatives of both parties, and all such changes shall reference this Agreement and identify the specific articles or sections of this Agreement or the particular order that is amended, modified, or supplemented.

24. Independent Contractor

All work performed by Licensor in connection with the Software and/or Services described in this Agreement shall be performed by Licensor as an independent contractor and not as the agent or employee of Customer. All persons furnished by Licensor shall be for all purposes solely Licensor's employees or agents and shall not be deemed to be employees of Customer for any purpose whatsoever. Licensor shall furnish, employ, and have exclusive control of all persons to be engaged in performing Services under this Agreement and shall prescribe and control the means and methods of performing such Services by providing adequate and proper supervision. Licensor shall be solely responsible for compliance with all rules, laws, and regulations relating to employment of labor, hours of labor, working conditions, payment of wages and payment of taxes, such as employment, Social Security, and other payroll taxes including applicable contributions from such persons when required by law.

25. Compliance with Laws/Changes in Laws

Licensor and Customer each shall comply with the provision of all applicable federal, state, county and local laws, ordinances, regulations, and codes [as of the date of this Agreement] including, but not limited to, Licensor's and Customer's obligations as employers with regard to the health, safety, and payment of its employees, and identification and procurement of required permits, certificates, approvals, and inspections in Licensor's and Customer's performance of this Agreement.

- ***It is unclear whether this language requires the Licensor to conform its software and services to any applicable changes in the law. Both parties should agree on which party will bear the responsibility and cost for ensuring that the software and services will comply with all applicable laws. Most licensors will accept responsibility to ensure all software and services comply with all laws in effect as of the date of the agreement. Licensors should be hesitant to agree to comply with all laws in the future with out additional compensation as the vendor cannot quantify the price of ensuring its compliance with unknown future changes. A reasonable compromise is to require the licensor to make all such changes at the customer's expense unless the cost of such changes can be amortized over all of the licensor's customers. See the language set forth in Section 9.8.A that specifically addresses this issue.***

Alternative Language that Benefits the Customer:

Changes in Law and Regulations.

Licensor represents warrants and agrees that it shall identify the impact of changes in Licensor Regulatory Requirements on its ability to deliver the Services and perform its obligations under the Agreement. Licensor shall notify Customer of such Licensor Regulatory Requirements within ten (10) days after it learns of the enactment of any such Licensor Regulatory Requirements and shall work with Customer to identify the impact of such changes on how Customer uses the Services or on how Licensor delivers the Services. Customer and Licensor shall promptly make any resulting modifications to the Services as reasonably necessary as a result of changes in such Licensor Regulatory Requirements. Licensor shall comply with changes to all Licensor Regulatory Requirements and shall implement any necessary modifications to the Services prior to the deadline imposed, or extensions authorized by, the regulatory or other governmental body having jurisdiction for such Licensor Regulatory Requirements. All costs associated with identification and compliance with Licensor Regulatory Requirements shall be borne by Licensor. Upon Approval by Customer of an applicable change request pursuant to the Change Control Procedures, Licensor shall (i) implement Customer Regulatory Requirements, and (ii) shall implement any necessary modfications to the Services, in accordance with Customer's Policies and Procedures and/or an applicable Statement of Work, as applicable. Except as provided in this Section, Licensor shall have no obligation to identify regulatory changes.

Alternative Additional Language that May Be Appropriate Depending on the Customer's Business

For Customers subject to SEC regulation:

SEC Requirements. Licensor hereby undertakes to furnish promptly to the U.S. Securities and Exchange Commission ("Commission"), its designees or representatives, any self-regulatory organization of which Customer is a member, or any State securities regulator having jurisdiction over Customer, upon reasonable request, such information as is deemed necessary by the staffs of the Commission, any self-regulatory organization of which Customer is a member, or any State securities regulator having jurisdiction over Customer to download information kept on electronic storage media for Customer to any medium acceptable under Rule 17a-4. Furthermore, Licensor hereby undertakes to take reasonable steps to provide access to information contained on such electronic storage media, including, as appropriate, arrangements for the downloading of any record required to be maintained and preserved by Customer pursuant to Rules 17a-3 and 17a-4 under the Securities Exchange Act of 1934 in a format acceptable to the staffs of the Commission, any self-regulatory organization of which Customer is a member, or any State securities regulator having jurisdiction over Customer. Such arrangements will provide specifically that in the event of a failure on the part of Customer to download the record into a readable format and after reasonable notice to Customer, upon being provided with the appropriate electronic storage medium, the Licensor will undertake to do so, as the staffs of the Commission, any self-regulatory organization of which Customer is a member, or any State securities regulator having jurisdiction over Customer may request.

With respect to any books and records maintained or preserved on behalf of Customer, Licensor hereby undertakes to permit examination of such books and records at any time or from time to time during business hours by representatives or designees of the Securities and Exchange Commission, and to promptly furnish to said Commission or its designee true, correct, complete and current hard copy of any or all or any part of such books and records.

Licensor further represents that the media with which the books and records of Customer are maintained by the undersigned meet the requirements of Rule 17a-4(f) (2).

For a publicly held company:

Sarbanes-Oxley Requirements: Licensor recognizes that Customer will be subject to Sarbanes-Oxley Requirements. Licensor shall provide whatever assistance is necessary to ensure Customer is able to comply with such requirements with respect to its outsourced information technology functions. Licensor will comply with Customer's financial reporting process as set forth in the Policies and Procedures Guide (and as such process is revised from time to time by Customer) and provide Customer with copies of all related records, reports and data as necessary for Customer to satisfy Sarbanes-Oxley Requirements. Licensor shall recommend and, subject to Customer approval, implement compliance measures to satisfy Sarbanes-Oxley Requirements.

26. Security, Access, and Safety Requirements

Licensor shall instruct its employees, agents, and subcontractors that they shall comply with Customer's security, access, and safety requirements for the protection of Customer's facilities and employees while on Customer's premises.

27. Releases Void

Neither party shall require waivers or releases of any personal rights from representatives of the other in connection with visits to Licensor's and Customer's respective premises. No such releases or waivers shall be pleaded by Licensor or Customer or third persons in any action or proceeding against an employee.

28. Governing Law and Venue

28.1 **Governing Law and Venue.** The validity, construction, interpretation, and performance of this Agreement shall be governed by and construed in accordance with the domestic laws of the State of [________] except as to its principals of conflicts of laws and the parties hereto irrevocably submit to the exclusive jurisdiction and venue of the Federal District Court for the District of [________] to resolve any disputes arising hereunder or related hereto.

The parties hereto hereby (a) submit to the exclusive jurisdiction of any state or federal court sitting in [______________] for the purpose of any Action arising out of or relating to this Agreement brought by any party hereto, and (b) irrevocably waive, and agree not to assert by way of motion, defense, or otherwise, in any such Action, any claim that it is not subject personally to the jurisdiction of the above-named courts, that its property is exempt or immune from attachment or execution, that the Action is brought in an inconvenient forum, that the venue of the Action is improper, or that this Agreement may not be enforced in or by any of the above-named courts.

The parties may bring any actions seeking specific performance, equitable relief or other non-monetary remedies in any state or federal court of competent jurisdiction.

Alternative Language for Alternating Choice of Venues

28.1.A **Alternating Venue.** The validity, construction, interpretation, and performance of this Agreement shall be governed by and construed in accordance with the domestic laws of the State of [________] except as to its principals of conflicts of laws, and the parties hereto irrevocably submit to the exclusive jurisdiction and venue of the Federal District Court for the District of [**Licensee's desired venue**] if the Licensor shall bring an action hereunder or related hereto provided, however, Customer agrees to submit to the exclusive jurisdiction of [**Licensor's desired venue**] for any action brought by Licensor alleging a violation by Customer's confidentiality obligations hereunder. If the Licensee shall bring an action hereunder or related hereto, the parties hereto irrevocably submit to the exclusive jurisdiction and venue of the Federal District Court for the District of [**Licensor's desired venue**] to resolve any disputes arising hereunder or related hereto.

Alternative Language for Differing Venues Based on Trade Secret Concerns

28.1.B. **Governing Law.** This Agreement shall be deemed to have been entered into and executed in the State of **(CUSTOMER'S REQUESTED STATE)** and shall be construed, performed, and enforced in all respects in accordance with the laws of that State, except as to the definition and protection of trade secrets and confidential information which shall be determined pursuant to the laws of the State of **(LICENSOR'S REQUESTED STATE).**

Alternative Language for Opting Out of the United Nations Convention on Contracts for the International Sale of Goods

28.1.C. **The United Nations Convention on Contracts for the International Sale of Goods.** The United Nations Convention on Contracts for the International Sale of Goods shall not govern or be used to construe this Agreement. OR

It is hereby stipulated that the "Convention Relating to a Uniform Law on the International Sale of Goods" shall not apply to this Agreement. OR

The application of the United Nations Convention on Contracts for the International Sale of Goods is expressly excluded.

- ***If the parties to the agreement are incorporated under the laws of two different countries, both of which are signatories to the UN Convention, the UN Convention automatically governs the agreement unless the parties affirmatively opt out of the UN Convention. Given that case law interpreting the UN Convention is not well developed and its impact on software licenses is unclear, the parties should opt out.***

28.2 **UCITA Disclaimer.** Pursuant to Md. Code Ann. Section 21-104, the parties hereby expressly agree to opt out of application of the Maryland Uniform Computer Information Transactions Act (MUCITA), Md. Code Ann. Commercial Law Sections 22-101 through 21-816, except to the extent that Section 22-104(2) of the Act applies. The parties further agree that this Agreement shall be governed by the common law of Maryland relating to written agreements and Maryland statutes other than MUCITA which may apply.

Alternative Language to Address UCITA Where It Has Not Been Adopted

The parties agree that, in the event that the Uniform Computer Information Transaction Act, any version thereof or a substantially similar law (collectively UCITA) is enacted as to be applicable to a party's performance under the Agreement and this Addendum, said statute shall not govern any aspect of the Agreement and this Addendum, any license granted hereunder, nor any of the parties' rights and obligations arising pursuant to the Agreement and this Addendum. The applicable law shall be the law as it existed prior to the enactment of UCITA.

- ***Licensor would like the Agreement to be governed by the laws of the state where it has the majority of its operations although there is some flexibility as to the particular state law. It is also important to have the venue (the location of any trial) be in the same state. Some states such as Texas favor the Customer while others such as New York favor the Licensor. To ensure the choice of law is upheld, there must be a nexus between that state and the parties. Usually, it is where the Customer site is located or where a majority of the work is performed.***
- ***Make sure you review the law of the state chosen and understand its ramifications. For example, has the state in question adopted UCITA? (see Section 28.2 if you do not want the contract to be governed by UCITA. Make sure you include language opting out of UCITA) and if so have you utilized the UCITA required warranty disclaimer (see Section 16.1.4.A.).***
- ***Be certain to use the word "exclusive" to ensure that the relevant venue is the exclusive venue and the clause is not interpreted to be the "permissive" venue.***
- ***Licensor wants to avoid arbitration or alternative dispute resolution (ADR) because arbitrators tend to "split the baby." In addition, it may be very difficult to get an immediate injunction to halt the misuse of Licensor's Software. Advantages of arbitration are quicker resolution, lower cost, and lower profile.***

Potential Language to Resolve Any Question as to the Applicability of the UCC

Favoring Licensee:

28.3 **Applicability of Uniform Commercial Code.** To the extent this Agreement or any SOW entails the delivery of Software or Software Products, such Software or Software Products shall be deemed "goods" within the meaning of Article 2 of the Uniform Commercial Code, except when deeming services as "goods" would cause an unreasonable result. This Agreement or an SOW shall control where there is a conflict with the UCC.

Favoring Licensor:

28.3 **Applicability of Uniform Commercial Code.** The parties agree that this contract is not a contract for the sale of goods; therefore, this Agreement shall not be governed by any codification of Article 2 or 2A of the Uniform Commercial Code, or any codification of the Uniform Computer Information Technology Act (UCITA), or any references to the United National Convention on Contracts for the International Sale of Goods.

- ***Occasionally, licensees will seek to include language "declaring" software to be a good in an attempt to create certainty in the event of a dispute and to take advantage of the protections the UCC offers to the purchasers of goods. This language often has the opposite effect as the language itself is unclear and adds further uncertainty. Further, the applicability of the UCC, as opposed to UCITA, places the licensor at a significant disadvantage.***

29. Non-Binding Dispute Resolution

Additional Language Related to Dispute Resolution

29.1 **Manager Level Performance Review.** The applicable Licensor Manager and Customer Manager shall meet as often as shall reasonably be required to review the performance of the parties under this Agreement and to resolve any disputes. Written minutes of such meetings shall be kept by Licensor for review and approval by Customer. If these representatives are unable to resolve a dispute within ten (10) calendar days after the initial request for a meeting, then the dispute shall be submitted to an executive level performance review as described in Section 29.2.

29.2 **Executive Level Performance Review.** Face-to-face negotiations shall be conducted by senior executive officers of Customer and Licensor. If these representatives are unable to resolve the dispute within ten (10) calendar days after the representatives have commenced negotiations, or twenty (20) calendar days have passed since the initial request for negotiations at this level, then the parties may agree in writing to submit the dispute to mediation.

29.3 **Voluntary, Non-binding Mediation.** If executive level performance review is not successful in resolving the dispute, the parties may, but shall not be obligated to, mutually agree in writing to submit the dispute to non-binding mediation. Mediation must occur within five (5) business days after the parties agree to submit the dispute to mediation, and the duration of the mediation shall be limited to one (1) business day. The parties mutually shall select an independent mediator experienced in commercial information systems contract disputes, and each shall designate a representative(s) to meet with the mediator in good faith in an effort to resolve the dispute. The specific format for the mediation shall be left to the discretion of the mediator and the designated party representatives and may include the preparation of agreed-upon statements of fact or written statements of position furnished to the other party.

29.4 **Continued Performance.** Except where clearly prevented by the area in dispute, both parties shall continue performing their obligations under this Agreement while the dispute is being resolved under this Section unless and until the dispute is resolved or until this Agreement is terminated as provided herein. Except for disputes relating to the payment of Licensor invoices as described in Section 8.7, the time frame for a party to cure any breach of the terms of this Agreement shall not be tolled by the pendency of any dispute resolution procedures.

29.5 **Equitable Relief.** Notwithstanding anything contained in this Agreement to the contrary, the parties shall be entitled to seek injunctive or other equitable relief whenever the facts or circumstances would permit a party to seek such equitable relief in a court of competent jurisdiction.

- ***The language set forth above in Section 29.5 favors the Customer and should be limited. While injunctive relief is commonly accepted, other potential equitable remedies including specific performance are not. Thus, the language set forth above should be reduced in scope to limit equitable relief solely to injunctive relief. See Section 5.3.4 for a discussion of Specific Performance.***

30. Arbitration

Alternative Language When the Parties Agree to Arbitration

30.1 **Binding Nature.** Any claim or controversy arising out of or relating to this Agreement or the alleged breach hereof must be submitted and settled as set forth in this section.

30.2 **Escalation Procedure.** If any party to this Agreement alleges that any other party to this Agreement has breached [**or may breach**] any of the terms of this Agreement, then the party alleging breach shall inform the other party or parties of their breach in writing pursuant to the notice provisions of this Agreement. Upon receipt of such notice, the allegedly nonperforming party shall have ten (10) days to cure the alleged breach. If the parties do not agree that effective cure has been accomplished by the end of the ten (10) day period, then the parties' Project Coordinators shall meet in person and confer in good faith to resolve the dispute within fifteen (15) days of the expiration of the prior ten (10) day period. If the parties do not agree that effective cure has been accomplished by the end of the fifteen (15) day period, then upon written request of any party Licensor's Chief Operating Officer and Customer's Chief Financial Officer shall meet in person and confer in good faith to resolve the dispute within fifteen (15) days of the expiration of the prior fifteen (15) day period. If the parties do not resolve the dispute through a meeting of Licensor's Chief Operating Officer and Customer's Chief Financial Officer, then the parties agree jointly to retain a mediator from a professional mediation organization (such as the American Arbitration Association, JAMS/Endispute, or the CPR Institute for Dispute Resolution) and to mediate the dispute within the next thirty (30) days.

30.3 **Filing of Claim.** If, after the above procedures, the dispute remains unresolved, then the dispute shall be submitted to the office of the American Arbitration Association located closest to [City, State], and shall be settled by arbitration to occur in [City, State], said arbitration to be administered by the American Arbitration Association in accordance with its Commercial Arbitration Rules in effect at the time of the arbitration and the laws of the State of ________ governing such arbitrations. Such arbitration must be filed within twelve (12) months of the first accrual of the cause of action, and the parties agree that the statute of limitations for any cause of action brought pursuant to, in connection with, or relating to the provision of the

Services or any other subject matter of this Agreement shall be twelve (12) months from the first accrual of the cause of action.

30.4 **General Rules.** The arbitration shall be heard and decided no later than seven (7) months after the notice of arbitration is filed with the American Arbitration Association. The arbitrators shall hear and determine any preliminary issue of law asserted by a party to be dispositive of any claim, in whole or in part, in the manner of a court hearing a motion to dismiss for failure to state a claim or for summary judgment, pursuant to such terms and procedures as the arbitrators deem appropriate. No witness or party may be required to waive any privilege recognized under [State] law. The hearing shall not last longer than four (4) days unless all parties agree otherwise, with time to be divided equally between Licensor and Customer. In the event of such arbitration each party shall select an impartial arbitrator and the parties' impartial arbitrators shall select a chief arbitrator from a list provided by the American Arbitration Association.

30.5 **Discovery.** For good cause shown, the arbitrators may permit each side to serve no more than fifteen (15) document requests (including subparts) and ten (10) interrogatories (including subparts) on the opposing parties. For good cause shown, the arbitrators may permit each side to subpoena no more than two (2) third party witnesses for testimonial depositions (each deposition not to exceed two (2) hours of examination by __________ and not to exceed two (2) hours of examination by __________) if the witnesses cannot be compelled to attend the arbitration, and no more than two (2) current (at the time of the subpoena) employees of each opposing party for testimonial depositions (each deposition not to exceed two (2) hours of examination by __________ and not to exceed two (2) hours of examination by __________) if the witnesses cannot be compelled to attend the arbitration. Any discovery as set forth above shall be governed by the Federal Rules of Civil Procedure and the precedents applicable to cases brought in the United States District Court for the __________ District of [State]. No other discovery shall be permitted except by written agreement of all parties. The parties and the arbitrators shall treat all aspects of the arbitration proceedings, including, without limitation, discovery, testimony and other evidence, briefs, and the award, as strictly confidential and not subject to disclosure to any third party or entity, other than to the parties, the arbitrators, and the American Arbitration Association. The arbitrators must give full effect to the applicable law and to all terms of this Agreement, and are specifically divested of any power to render decisions in derogation thereof or *ex aequo et bono.*

30.6 **Decision.** The arbitrators shall issue written findings of fact and conclusions of law, the decisions of the arbitrators will be binding and conclusive upon all parties involved, and judgment upon any decision of the arbitrators may be entered in the highest court of any forum, federal or state, having jurisdiction thereof.

31. Waiver of Breach

No waiver of breach or failure to exercise any option, right, or privilege under the terms of this Agreement or any order on any occasion or occasions shall be construed to be a waiver of the same or any other option, right, or privilege on any other occasion.

- ***This provision states that if Licensor fails to enforce any of its rights now, Licensor is not prohibited from enforcing such rights at a later date.***

32. Waiver of Right to Jury Trial

THE PARTIES HEREBY UNCONDITIONALLY WAIVE THEIR RESPECTIVE RIGHTS TO A JURY TRIAL OF ANY CLAIM OR CAUSE OF ACTION ARISING DIRECTLY OR INDIRECTLY OUT OF, RELATED TO, OR IN ANY WAY CONNECTED WITH THE PERFORMANCE OR BREACH OF THIS AGREEMENT, AND/OR THE RELATIONSHIP THAT IS BEING ESTABLISHED AMONG THEM. The scope of this waiver is intended to be all encompassing of any and all disputes that may be filed in any court or other tribunal (including, without limitation, contract claims, tort claims, breach of duty claims, and all other common law and statutory claims). THIS WAIVER IS IRREVOCABLE, MEANING THAT IT MAY NOT BE MODIFIED EITHER ORALLY OR IN WRITING, AND THE WAIVER SHALL APPLY TO ANY SUBSEQUENT AMENDMENTS, RENEWALS, SUPPLEMENTS, OR MODIFICATIONS TO THIS AGREEMENT, AND RELATED DOCUMENTS, OR TO ANY OTHER DOCUMENTS OR AGREEMENTS RELATING TO THIS TRANSACTION OR ANY RELATED TRANSACTION. In the event of litigation, this Agreement may be filed as a written consent to a trial by the court.

Each of the parties hereto (a) certifies that no representative, agent, or attorney of any other party has represented, expressly or otherwise, that such other party would not, in the event of litigation, seek to enforce that foregoing waiver, and (b) acknowledges that it and the other parties hereto have been induced to enter into this Agreement, as applicable, by, among other things, the mutual waivers and certifications in this Section 32.

Alternatively:

EACH PARTY ACKNOWLEDGES AND AGREES THAT ANY CONTROVERSY WHICH MAY ARISE UNDER THIS AGREEMENT IS LIKELY TO INVOLVE COMPLICATED AND DIFFICULT ISSUES, AND THEREFORE IT HEREBY IRREVOCABLY AND UNCONDITIONALLY WAIVES ANY RIGHT IT MAY HAVE TO A TRIAL BY JURY IN RESPECT OF ANY LITIGATION DIRECTLY OR INDIRECTLY ARISING OUT OF OR RELATING TO THIS AGREEMENT AND ANY OF THE AGREEMENTS DELIVERED IN CONNECTION HEREWITH OR THE TRANSACTIONS CONTEMPLATED HEREBY OR THEREBY. EACH PARTY CERTIFIES AND ACKNOWLEDGES THAT (A) NO REPRESENTATIVE, AGENT OR ATTORNEY OF ANY OTHER PARTY HAS REPRESENTED, EXPRESSLY OR OTHERWISE, THAT SUCH OTHER PARTY WOULD NOT, IN THE EVENT OF LITIGATION, SEEK TO ENFORCE EITHER OF SUCH WAIVERS, (B) IT UNDERSTANDS AND HAS CONSIDERED THE IMPLICATIONS OF SUCH WAIVERS, (C) IT MAKES SUCH WAIVERS VOLUNTARILY, AND (D) IT HAS BEEN INDUCED TO ENTER INTO THIS AGREEMENT BY, AMONG OTHER THINGS, THE MUTUAL WAIVERS AND CERTIFICATIONS IN THIS SECTION 32.

- ***Before agreeing to a contractual waiver to a trial by jury be sure to confirm that a pre-litigation jury waiver clause will be upheld under the governing law chosen by the parties as at least two states have held that pre-litigation contractual jury waiver clauses are unenforceable.* See Bank South N.A. v. Howard, *444 S.E.2d 799 (Ga. 1994); Grafton Partners LP v. Superior Court, 88 P.3d 24 (2004), aff'd 116 P.3d 479 (2005).***

33. Force Majeure

Neither party shall be responsible for any delay or failure in performance of any part of this Agreement to the extent that such delay or failure is caused by fire, flood, explosion, war, embargo, government requirement, civil, or military authority, act of God, act or omission of carriers, or other similar causes beyond its control. If any such event of force majeure occurs and such event continues for ninety (90) days or more, the party delayed or unable to perform shall give immediate notice to the other party, and the party affected by the other's delay or inability to perform may elect at its sole discretion to (a) terminate this Agreement upon mutual agreement of the parties; (b) suspend such order for the duration of the condition and obtain or sell elsewhere Software or Services comparable to the Software or Services to have been obtained under this Agreement; or (c) resume performance of such order once the condition ceases with the option of the affected party to extend the period of this Agreement up to the length of time the condition endured. Unless written notice is given within thirty (30) days after the affected party is notified of the condition, option (c) shall be deemed selected.

Alternatively:

Except for monetary obligations hereunder, neither party shall be liable for any failure or delay in performance due in whole or in part to any cause beyond the reasonable control of such party or its contractors, agents or suppliers, **including but not limited** to utility or transmission failures, failure of phone lines or phone equipment, power failure, strikes or other labor disturbances, acts of God, acts of war or terror, floods, sabotage, fire, natural or other disasters ("Force Majeure").

- ***The parties should always exclude monetary obligations from a force majeure event to avoid having a party claim it cannot perform (pay any monies due) due to an economic downturn and thereby be excused form making payment.* See e.g., Marionneaux v. Smith, *163 So. 206 (La. 1935) (unforeseen economic depression is not an event of force majeure).***
- ***The Licensee should ensure that the list of force majeure "events" is narrowly drawn such that the Licensor cannot invoke the clause to avoid meeting its service level agreements or other obligations. Usually, the agreed upon events only pertain to the entity's day-to-day operations. While the licensee may desire to agree upon a specific list that will excuse nonperformance, force majeure clauses by their nature are designed to protect against an unanticipated contingency***

and should not be limited to a list of specific events. The Licensee should specifically exclude the licensor's subcontractor's nonperformance. Given the nature of the contract, it may be appropriate to have different force majeure clauses for different events.

- ***All force majeure clauses must be carefully reviewed to ensure that the Customer cannot automatically terminate the Agreement. It is preferable that the Agreement be put on hold until the force majeure dissipates.***

34. Bonds

Licensor shall provide Customer with the bonds set forth in this Section. The bonding companies providing such bonds must be acceptable to Customer, in its sole discretion, and be authorized to do business in the State of ________. In the event the bonding company providing such bonding does not have an A.M. Best rating of A or better, Customer may require Licensor to obtain bonds required under this Section 34 from another bonding company. The premium for all bonds required below shall be paid solely by Licensor.

34.1 **Performance and Payment Bonds.** Licensor shall obtain, or cause to be obtained, a performance bond (a "Performance Bond") and a payment bond (a "Payment Bond"). The Performance Bond shall continue through the term of the Agreement and the Payment Bond shall continue until the earlier to occur of the following: (a) when Licensor has obtained all applicable releases from all subcontractors (and provided copies of such releases to Customer); or (b) when Licensor has satisfied in full any and all obligations and amounts due and owing to all subcontractors for work performed pursuant to this Agreement and provided Customer with satisfactory evidence of such payment. Licensor shall secure a Payment Bond and Performance Bond, each in an amount equivalent to the value of the Agreement. Licensor shall deliver such Performance Bond and Payment Bond to Customer on or prior to the Effective Date hereof and such Performance Bond and Payment Bond shall be attached as Appendix 34.

34.2 **Requirements.** Unless otherwise agreed to by the parties, the Performance Bond and Payment Bond shall: (a) name Customer as obligee; (b) be in a form and be issued by a licensed surety satisfactory to Customer, its sole discretion, and not subject to mediation or arbitration; and (c) be in the amounts described in Section 34.1 above.

35. Business Continuity Plan (Disaster Recovery) [If Applicable]

Upon the Commencement Date for Services to be performed by Licensor under certain Statements of Work, Licensor shall apply Licensor's business continuity and disaster recovery plans (as approved by Customer and as modified pursuant to this Agreement) to such Services. An outline and executive summary of Licensor's Business Continuity Plan shall be exchanged. The Business Continuity Plan for all such Services shall (i) be designed (a) to continue all Licensor business operations that are critical to the overall operation and functionality of such Services, and (b) to ensure Licensor's compliance with the information security requirements set forth in Exhibit __ notwithstanding the occurrence of a Crisis; (ii) specify procedures and frequency of testing; (iii) be compatible with Customer's own business continuity and disaster recovery plans, as such plans are provided and amended from time to time by Customer, and ensure business reasonable integration with such Customer plans in the event of a Crisis; and (iv) be, and shall be maintained, consistent with then-current highest generally accepted industry standards and Customer's then-current business continuity plan. The Business Continuity Plan shall specifically address the ability of Licensor to provide each such Service in the event of a Crisis. The Business Continuity Plan shall provide, among other things, a mechanism for the redundancy or backup of business operations designed to keep such Services from becoming unavailable for a significant amount of time due to a Crisis and to permit the related business operations of Customer to be re-instituted in a time period that permits the ongoing operation and functionality of Customer's business to which such Services relate. Without limiting the generality of the foregoing, the Business Continuity Plan shall address all of the computer software, computer hardware (whether general or special purpose), telecommunications capabilities (including all voice, data and video networks) and other similar or related items of automated, computerized, and/or software system(s) and any other network(s) or system(s) that are used, or relied on, by Licensor in the provision of such Services and the manner in which Licensor will re-institute the processing of relevant information in a time period that permits the ongoing operation and functionality of Customer's business to which such Services relate. Notwithstanding the foregoing, if a Crisis prevents Licensor from providing such Services to Customer, Licensor shall allocate its efforts and resources to restoring Customer's Services no less favorably to Customer than it allocates to any of its other customers affected by the Crisis.

Upon the occurrence of a Crisis and at vendor's sole expense, Licensor shall promptly (but in any event in less than twenty-four (24) hours) implement the Business Continuity Plan. The occurrence of a Crisis (including any Force Majeure Event) will not relieve Licensor of its obligation to implement the Business Continuity Plan and to provide disaster recovery Services. If the Services are not restored within the period specified in the Business Continuity Plan, Customer may terminate the applicable Work Process Agreement and such termination will be deemed to have occurred under Section ___.

"Crisis" shall mean (i) any extraordinary event affecting Licensor that requires emergency response measures to be taken, including any event that may result in the Services becoming unavailable for a significant amount of time, or (ii) any event that, **in the Customer's reasonable determination**, requires emergency measures to be taken.

- ***The Licensor should avoid agreeing to perform any services or take any action based on the Customer's sole determination regardless of whether it is subject***

to a reasonableness standard unless the Customer has agreed to pay for such services.

Alternatively:

Disaster Recovery: As part of this Agreement, if Licensor maintains any Customer information on its computer system or in databases, Licensor will maintain a Disaster Recovery plan that defines the tasks and timeframes to expeditiously overcome any disability that causes a system outage. The Disaster Recovery plan will adequately address the backup of hardware, software, and facilities during a service outage. Licensor agrees that the Disaster Recovery Plan will provide, without limitation, the following: (i) in the event of any incidence of system failure (other than a catastrophic system failure as determined by Customer), Licensor will define the problem and present a plan of resolution to Customer within four (4) business hours of identification of the system failure; and (ii) Licensor will use its best efforts to correct any system failure in no more than eight (8) business hours and to ensure that multiple incidents of system failure will occur no more than twice in a single calendar month. Supplier must provide Customer with a written Contingency Plan, which outlines how the Supplier will provide continuity of Products in the event of a disaster, catastrophe or pandemic. Supplier will provide an update once per year or as often as changes are made whichever is more frequent. In the event that Supplier fails to provide a plan or provides a plan which does not meet Customer's approval, Customer reserves the right to take its own measures to ensure continuity of Product. Such measures may include contracting with alternate suppliers for backup supply, altering the volume allocation previously given to Supplier, and/or termination of this Agreement.

- ***The Customer should make certain that the Licensor provides reasonable assurances as to the Licensor's disaster recovery plans. These plans should be set forth in detail in an exhibit. If the Licensor is unwilling to do so, the Licensee should retain another vendor.***

36. Covenant of Good Faith

Each Party agrees that, in its respective dealings with the other Party under or in connection with this Agreement, it shall act in good faith.

- ***This paragraph is important as it imposes a duty of good faith in those jurisdictions that do not already do so. The implementation of such a duty may create additional obligations and risks for the parties. See § 16.U.***

37. Time Is of the Essence

The Parties hereto acknowledge that the performance by Licensor and Customer of their obligations hereunder is to be done on a "time is of the essence" basis. This expression is understood to mean that Licensor and Customer are to deliver their respective Deliverables no later than the Delivery Dates therefore and that any delay in connection therewith will cause the other Party damage; it is for this reason that the Parties have agreed, pursuant to Section 3.C hereof, that liquidated damages will be imposed if delays are experienced.

Alternatively:

Time is of the essence with respect to Licensor's performance of all of its obligations under License/Service Schedules, SOWs, and implementation plans. ***Licensor shall not be entitled to any increase in fees or any other adjustment caused by delay attributable in whole or in part to Licensor, or any delay as to which Licensee did not receive timely notice. Licensor agrees to make no claim for damages for delay occasioned by an act or a failure to act by Licensee or any of its representatives.*** Licensor's sole remedy for such delay shall be an extension of its deadlines for performance, provided such extension is otherwise agreed to in advance in writing by the parties.

- ***The first clause provides that Licensor will deliver the Software on time. If Licensor is even one minute late, the delay is considered material allowing the Customer to terminate the Agreement and collect damages from Licensor. Consequently, the Licensor should think carefully before including this language. Licensor should clearly state that any times lines are good faith estimates and contingent on licensee timely meeting all of its obligations. At a minimum, the language should be made mutual.***
- ***The second clause seeks to limit the Licensor's ability to collect additional fees or hold the Customer liable for any delay caused by the Customer.***

38. Insurance

Licensor shall maintain in effect at all times during the term of this Agreement insurance with a carrier with an A.M. Best rating of A or better. Such insurance shall include, without limitation, worker's compensation in statutory amounts, and products/completed operations liability, errors and omissions, business interruption, comprehensive general liability, and automobile insurance in amounts not less than $10 million per occurrence and $25 million annual aggregate for all claims against all losses, claims, demands, proceedings, damages, costs, charges, and expenses for injuries or damage to any person or property arising out of or in connection with Licensor's performance or non-performance under this Agreement and shall designate Customer and its Affiliates as "additional insurers" on such insurance policies. Licensor shall, on or before the Effective Date and thereafter upon Customer's reasonable request, provide Customer with certified copies of all applicable endorsements and certificates of insurance, both evidencing such coverage, which shall also state that Customer shall be provided a minimum of thirty (30) calendar days prior written notice of any proposed cancellation, or expiration without renewal, and five (5) business days prior written notice of any proposed change in carriers or material terms of coverage. Upon Customer's request, Licensor shall also provide Customer with certified copies of the involved insurance policy or policies within fifteen (15) calendar days of such request.

Licensor shall obtain or otherwise arrange for appropriate levels of insurance coverage for all subcontractors. Licensor shall maintain, in its files, evidence of all subcontractors' insurance coverage and shall provide proof of such coverage to Customer upon Customer's request. In the event coverage is denied or reimbursement of a properly presented claim is disputed by the carrier for insurance provided as described above, upon written request, Licensor shall provide Customer with a certified copy of the involved insurance policy or policies within ten (10) business days of receipt of such request. Customer may withhold an amount equal to fifty percent (50%) of all monies due and to become due to Licensor under this Agreement should Licensor not comply with any terms of this Section. The terms of this Section shall not be deemed to limit the liability of Licensor hereunder, or to limit any rights Customer may have including, without limitation, rights of indemnity, or contribution.

- ***Most Customers require Licensor to provide a certificate of insurance evidencing Licensor has the required insurance from an acceptable company. Language should also be included that Licensor has the right to self-insure. Do not waive Licensor's/Licensor's insurer's right of subrogation (the right of Licensor or its insurer to sue any co-tortfeasor for their pro rata portion of any damages award) as the waiver of this right may raise Licensor's insurance rates. This paragraph should be mutual if the Licensor is working on the Customer's property as the Licensor's employees may be injured by the Customer's employees, agents, or contractors. The Licensor should never accept language that allows the Customer to purchase insurance for the Licensor or allow the Customer to offset money due Licensor for the Licensor's failure to obtain insurance.***

39. Third Party Software

Customer shall have sole responsibility to obtain and pay for any third party software necessary or desirable to operate the Software or ABC System.

- ***Licensor will not provide any third party software unless the cost of third party software was included in Licensor's pricing.***

40. Third Party Beneficiaries

This Agreement is entered into solely for the benefit of Licensor and Customer. No third party shall have the right to make any claim or assert any right under it, and no third party shall be deemed a beneficiary of this Agreement. The foregoing notwithstanding, the Parties acknowledge and agree that **[list exception]** is the intended third party beneficiary of this Agreement and, as such, **[list exception]** is entitled, subject to the terms and conditions of this Agreement, to all remedies entitled to third party beneficiaries under law.

- ***A licensor must be careful to disclaim any third party beneficiaries to avoid a third party claiming the benefit of a warranty granted under the license. This is especially important when the software will process information or tasks for a third party.***

and/or

The parties acknowledge that the Software may include software licensed by Licensor from Licensor's licensors. Licensor's licensors may be direct and intended third party beneficiaries of this Agreement and may be entitled to enforce it directly against Customer to the extent (a) this Agreement relates to the licensing of Licensor's licensors' software products, and (b) Licensor fails to enforce the terms of this Agreement on their behalf.

41. Outsourcing

Licensor acknowledges that Customer has entered into information technology services agreements with International Business Machines Corporation ("IBM") and Keane, Inc. ("Keane") for the provision of information technology, data processing, and related services, to Customer. Licensor hereby agrees that, at no additional charge to Customer, (i) Customer may disclose to IBM and Keane all hardware, software, and related products and documentation that are licensed or transferred to Customer pursuant to this Agreement (the "IT Systems"); (ii) IBM and Keane shall have the limited right to use the IT Systems for the sole purpose of delivering information technology, data processing, and related services to Customer; and (iii) upon notice to Licensor, all or part of the IT Systems may be installed or relocated to a facility controlled by IBM or Keane. Notwithstanding clauses (i) or (ii) above, neither IBM nor Keane shall use the IT Systems in a manner that is inconsistent with Customer's rights under this Agreement.

Licensor further acknowledges that Customer may at any time during the term of this Agreement enter into an arrangement with other third parties ("Outsourcer(s)") for the provision of information technology, data processing, and related services. Customer shall notify the Licensor of the name and location of the Outsourcer(s), and the Licensor consents to the use of the IT Systems by the Outsourcer(s) at any time during the term of this Agreement for the purpose of providing information technology, data processing, and related services to Company so long as use of the IT Systems by the Outsourcer(s) is not inconsistent with the other terms of this section.

42. Divestiture and Transition

42.1 **Divestiture.** In the event of an assignment or transfer to a Divested Business, Licensor shall enter into a separate agreement with the Divested Business upon the same terms and conditions (including fees) as this Agreement.

42.2 **Transition.** Licensee shall have the right to use Software to provide services to Divested Businesses as part of any such divestiture, as Licensee directs, for a period of two (2) years after the completion of each such divestiture, at no additional cost other than the compensation provided for in this Agreement. In addition, Licensee shall have the right to use Software to provide such services for an additional one (1) year period (or any longer period as Licensee and Licensor agree), subject to reasonable terms and license fees to be agreed upon.

43. Export

Licensor and Customer each shall comply with the provision of all applicable federal, state, county, and local laws, ordinances, regulations, and codes including, but not limited to, Licensor's and Customer's obligations as employers with regard to the health, safety, and payment of its employees, and identification and procurement of required permits, certificates, approvals, and inspections in Licensor's and Customer's performance of this Agreement.

Customer and Licensor acknowledge that the Software and all related technical information, documents, and materials are subject to export controls under the U.S. Export Administration Regulation. Customer and Licensor will (i) comply strictly with all legal requirements established under these controls; (ii) cooperate fully with the other party in any official or unofficial audit or inspection that relates to these controls; and (iii) not export, re-export, divert, transfer, or disclose, directly or indirectly, any Software or related technical information, document, or material or direct products thereof to any country so restricted by the U.S. Export Administration Regulations, as modified from time to time, or to any national or resident thereof, unless Customer has obtained the prior written authorization of Licensor and the U.S. Commerce Department and any relevant local governmental authority. Furthermore, Customer recognizes and agrees that concurrently with the execution of this Agreement it shall provide Licensor with a Letter of Assurance, substantially in the form of Exhibit 43 attached hereto. Customer agrees Licensor shall have no liability for the failure to obtain a U.S. export license to export the Software to **[COUNTRY NAME]**.

- ***Both parties should ensure that their license agreement provides the necessary protections under the U.S. export laws. The U.S. Commerce Department has taken an aggressive position to ensure compliance. The failure to include the appropriate language, especially in an agreement with a foreign entity, may expose the Licensor to significant liability.***

44. Publicity and Use of Customer Marks

44.1 **Publicity**

Both parties hereby agree to make best endeavors to issue a mutually agreed press release or similar publicity statement within six (6) weeks of the date of this Agreement. Thereafter, neither party shall issue a press release or other similar publicity of any nature regarding this Agreement without the other party's prior written approval, which shall not be unreasonably withheld. Notwithstanding the foregoing, each party hereby agrees the other party may use its name, URL, and logo on its website and in its customer and partner lists for corporate and financial presentations.

Alternatively:

Neither party shall issue a press release or similar public announcement of any kind regarding the Parties' relationship established hereunder without the prior written approval of the other Party. Other than expressly set forth herein, neither Party shall use publicly the other Party's name or refer to the other Party in any way in or with the media, including, but not limited to, in advertising, without the other Party's prior written consent as required herein, provided, however, that either Party may make disclosures or filings required to comply with applicable laws, including filings with regulatory agencies, such as the United States Securities and Exchange Commission, or disclosures or filings required to comply with the rules of a national securities exchange or automated quotations systems such as the National Association of Securities Dealer's Automated Quotations. A VIOLATION OF THIS PROVISION SHALL CONSTITUTE A MATERIAL BREACH OF THIS AGREEMENT.

Alternatively:

Without the prior written consent of the other Party, neither Party shall issue or release any statement, article, advertisement, public or private announcement, media release or other similar publicity relating in any manner to: (a) any aspect of this Agreement, including Statement of Works; (b) any aspect of any Services and/or Deliverables; or (c) the fact that the Parties have engaged in any discussions or negotiations regarding any of the foregoing. Neither Party shall use the name or any business name, trade name, trademark, service mark or logo of the other Party without the prior written consent of the other Party.

Alternatively:

Promotions Referring to Customer. Licensor agrees that Customer shall be entitled to review and Approve any and all promotional materials that contain a reference to Customer as contemplated herein before publication or distribution of same. No public disclosures by Licensor relating to this Agreement, except for internal announcements or disclosures required to meet legal or regulatory requirements, shall be made without the prior written approval of authorized representatives of the other Party.

Demonstration and Promotions Not Warranties. In no event shall any demonstration or any promotional materials pursuant to this Section constitute an endorsement, representation or warranty, express or implied, by Customer. In the event of a dispute between Customer and Licensor, Customer's agreement to participate in promotions and demonstrations under this Section and all statements made by Customer in connection with such activities shall not be deemed an admission or declaration against interest of Customer in any trial or dispute resolution proceeding between the Parties.

- ***Set forth above are four examples of potential "publicity" clauses reflecting differing degrees of restrictions on publicizing the underlying contract. Publicly held companies must at a minimum have the right to disclose any information necessary to comply with any applicable securities laws. The licensor usually wants to publicize its client list especially if it has prestigious clients. A customer may not want to have the licensor use the customer's name in the licensor's marketing campaign to avoid giving the appearance that the customer is endorsing the licensor's products. If the customer does grant the licensor the right to use the customer's name and trademark/service marks in the customer's marketing and sales activities, the customer should make sure that it clearly delineates the terms under which the licensor may use the customer's name and marks.***
- ***Set forth below is Model language to license the vendor to use the Customer's trademarks and service marks.***

44.2 **Use/License of Customer Marks.**

44.2.1 Subject to the terms and conditions specified in this Agreement, Customer hereby grants to Licensor (and Licensor's Affiliates), for the term of this Agreement, a non-exclusive, non-transferable license to use the Customer licensed marks setforth in Exhibit __ ("the Customer Licensed Marks") exactly as depicted in the graphic configuration or as subsequently modified by Customer. Customer may, in its sole discretion, at any time add to or delete from the Customer Licensed Marks and change the graphic configuration of the Customer Licensed Marks.

44.2.2 Licensor agrees that the style of use of the Customer Licensed Marks shall be in the form and style conforming to the trademark usage guidelines as provided to Licensor in writing. Licensor shall not use any of the Customer Licensed Marks as part of its corporate name, trade name, business name or Internet domain name.

44.2.3 Licensor shall submit to Customer for review and approval, at least ten (10) business days prior to proposed use, any web pages or other Internet locations, and all marketing, advertising, press releases or other Promotional Materials in which the Customer Licensed Marks are used. Customer shall approve or disapprove such materials at least five (5) business days after its receipt of such materials; Customer will not unreasonably withhold or delay the granting of its approval thereof. Licensor shall not publish, distribute or use any such web pages or other Internet locations, or any such marketing, advertising, press releases or other Promotional Materials in which the Customer Licensed Marks are used, without the prior written approval of Customer.

44.2.4 Notwithstanding the foregoing, Licensor may designate at the time of submission that the requested approval is for multiple/repetitive, identical uses on the same medium. Customer may request approval for such multiple/repetitive, identical use through the end of the Initial Term or any Renewal Term of this Agreement, or six (6) months, whichever is less. Such multiple/repetitive, identical use shall be in accordance with this Agreement and shall be subject to revocation by Customer upon written notice to Licensor.

44.2.5 Licensor further acknowledges and agrees that all use of the Customer Licensed Marks by Licensor and all goodwill developed therefrom shall inure to the benefit of and be on behalf of Customer except for the goodwill associated or derived from the Licensor Licensed Marks.

44.2.6 Licensor agrees that nothing in this Agreement shall give Licensor any right, title, or interest in or to the Customer Licensed Marks other than the right to use the Customer Licensed Marks in the manner contemplated by this Agreement, and only for so long as this Agreement is in force or as otherwise permitted under this Agreement (unless such Customer Licensed Marks are licensed pursuant to a separate agreement).

44.2.7 **Infringement.**

44.2.7.1 Licensor agrees to use commercially reasonable efforts to notify Customer promptly of any unauthorized use of the Customer Licensed Marks by others, to the extent Licensor has actual notice of such use. Customer and its parent and affiliated companies shall have the sole right to engage in infringement or unfair competition proceedings involving the Customer Licensed Marks.

44.2.7.2 Any recovery obtained in connection with or as a result of any infringement action contemplated under this section, whether by settlement or otherwise, shall be retained by Customer.

45. Appointment of Agent for Service of Process

During the Term of this Agreement and for a period of two (2) years thereafter, Licensor shall maintain, for each Affiliate rendering Services under this Agreement, registered agents authorized to receive service of process within the State of _______, and shall provide the name and street address of such registered agents to Customer within thirty (30) days of the date of this Agreement and any change during the Term.

46. Electronic Transfer of Intellectual Property

Whenever practical, Licensor agrees to deliver any Software deliverable under this Agreement including any updates or patches, via download, file transfer protocol (ftp), or through the use of Licensor's copy of the tangible Software media. Notwithstanding anything to the contrary in Section _____ (Documentation), upon completion of such delivery, Licensor shall remove the tangible Software media and not provide any of the tangible Software media to Customer.

47. Electronic Documents and Transmissions

Each party, at its own expense, provides and maintains the equipment, software, services, and testing necessary to send and receive electronic documents effectively and reliably and shall maintain audit trails with respect thereto. Electronic documents shall not be considered to have been properly received, and no document shall give rise to any obligation, until accessible to the receiving party at such party's receipt computer. Posting of information by Customer on any Licensor discussion boards, user groups or online forums does not place any material associated with this Agreement in the public domain nor constitute any waiver by any part of any Customer Intellectual Property in such material, nor grant any express or implied right or license to Licensor. Licensor is responsible for data backup and recovery of data held by, or on, facilities or hardware under Licensor's control, and shall ensure that processing can be properly resumed in the event of failures, which include but are not limited to power, mechanical, electronic or communication failure.

48. Liens

Licensor agrees to keep customer, all of the real and personal property of customer, and the services free and clear of all liens or lien claims. Should any lien or lien claim be asserted for any reason, customer may, at its sole discretion (i) pay the amount of such lien or lien claim; (ii) deduct such amounts from payments due to Licensor; and/or (iii) require Licensor to obtain a properly executed release of lien satisfactory to Customer.

49. Legal Fees

In the event of litigation relating to the enforcement of this Agreement, the prevailing party shall be entitled to recover its reasonable attorneys' fees from the non-prevailing party.

50. Mandatory References

Effective at the beginning of the second calendar quarter after the Reference Date, Customer will be provided the option to be a reference for new Licensor offshoring business of significant value to Licensor (determined by anticipated annual fees of $50 million or more, or in the event that there is not a Licensor transaction of such size to provide as a reference in a calendar quarter, then Licensor shall use the transaction that most closely approximates the $50 million anticipated annual fee requirement as a reference) within the United States. At a minimum, the Customer Applications Partnership Executive and Customer Chief Information Officer will be afforded this opportunity on a calendar quarterly basis. If Licensor elects not to provide the reference opportunity to Customer in any calendar quarter ("Non-Referral Quarter"), Customer shall be entitled to withhold one percent (1%) of the amount of invoices to be paid subsequent to such Non-Referral Quarter. In the event Customer is provided the option to be a reference as required in this Section in the calendar quarter subsequent to a Non-Referral Quarter, the accumulated withhold amount attributable to that Non-Referral Quarter under this Section shall be paid to Licensor with the payment of the next invoice, without interest. In the event Customer is not provided the option to be a reference as required in this Section in the calendar quarter subsequent to the Non-Referral Quarter, the withhold amounts under this Section shall be retained by Customer and converted from a withhold to an applied credit to undisputed amounts owed by Customer to Licensor in the next invoice.

51. No Construction against Drafter

The parties agree that any principle of construction or rule of law that provides that an agreement shall be construed against the drafter of the agreement in the event of any inconsistency or ambiguity in such agreement shall not apply to the terms and conditions of this Agreement.

52. Notices

All notices, demands, or other communications herein provided to be given or that may be given by any party to the other shall be deemed to have been duly given when made in writing and delivered in person, or upon receipt, if deposited in the United States mail, postage prepaid, certified mail, return receipt requested, as follows:

Notices to Licensor:	*Notices to Customer:*
____________________	____________________
____________________	____________________
____________________	____________________
Attn:______________	Attn:______________

With a required copy to:

____

____

____

____

Attn: General Counsel

or to such address as the parties may provide to each other in writing from time to time.

- ***All notices should be effective upon receipt, not mailing, because the notice may get lost in the mail or delayed, potentially allowing the one party to terminate the Agreement without the other party ever knowing it was in breach.***
- ***Always include the business person and the legal department in the notices to avoid any notice "falling through the cracks." By requiring a second copy be***

delivered to the General Counsel, Licensor limits the risk that a notice could be misplaced or lost.

53. Background, Enumerations, and Headings

The "Background," enumerations, and headings contained in this Agreement are for convenience of reference only and are not intended to have any substantive significance in interpreting this Agreement.

54. Incorporation of Appendices and Exhibits

Appendices [list] referred to in this Agreement and attached hereto are integral parts of this Agreement and are incorporated herein by this reference.

55. Severability

If any of the provisions of this Agreement shall be invalid or unenforceable under the laws of the jurisdiction where enforcement is sought whether on the basis of a court decision or of arbitral award applicable to the entire Agreement, such invalidity or unenforceability shall not invalidate or render unenforceable the entire Agreement but rather the entire Agreement shall be construed as if not containing the particular invalid or unenforceable provision or provisions and the rights and obligations of Licensor and Customer shall be construed and enforced accordingly.

56. Counterparts

This Agreement and any Appendix hereto, may be executed simultaneously in two (2) or more counterparts, each of which will be considered an original, but all of which together will constitute one and the same instrument.

57. Facsimile Execution

The parties agree that transmission to the other party of this Agreement with its facsimile signatures shall suffice to bind the party transmitting same to this Agreement in the same manner as if an original signature had been delivered. Without limitation of the foregoing, each party who transmits this Agreement with its facsimile signature covenants to deliver the original thereof to the other party as soon as possible thereafter.

58. Entire Agreement

This Agreement, the appendices, and subordinate documents referenced in this Agreement constitute the entire agreement between the parties with respect to the subject matter contained herein, superseding all previous agreements pertaining to such subject matter, and may be modified only by an amendment executed in writing by the authorized officers of both parties hereto. All prior agreements, representations, warranties, statements, negotiations, understandings, and undertakings are superseded hereby **and Customer hereby represents and acknowledges that in entering into this Agreement it did not rely on any representations or warranties other than those explicitly set forth in Section 16 of this Agreement**. Both parties hereto represent that they have read this Agreement, understand it, agree to be bound by all terms and conditions stated herein, and acknowledge receipt of a signed, true, and exact copy of this Agreement.

- ***This statement prevents the Customer from trying to hold Licensor to any statements by Licensor's salespeople or those contained in Licensor's RFP response that are not specifically included in the Agreement.***
- ***The acknowledgment that Customer did not rely on any representations or warranties other than those set forth in Section 16, attempts to avoid any liability for tort claims as well as contract claims.***
- ***Avoid incorporating by reference the Customer's RFP or the Licensor's RFP response as this may create an internal conflict with the terms of the Agreement including the functional specifications.***

59. Contingent Agreement

The parties agree and acknowledge that this Agreement has been signed by an officer of Customer subject to the approval of the Board of Directors of Customer (the "Board"). The parties agree that neither party will be bound by the terms of this Agreement until the Board approves this Agreement and that upon such approval, this Agreement will be binding against both parties. Customer agrees to give Licensor prompt written notice of the Board's approval or rejection of this Agreement.

- ***This language may be used when one party requires Board consent or the consent of third party prior to their entering into the agreement. While such language may be acceptable, the other party must be careful to impose a strict time limit for receiving such approval to ensure that such consent or rejection is quickly received and does not interfere with the other party's business.***

IN WITNESS WHEREOF, the parties have executed this Agreement **under seal** as of the day and year first written above.

- ***An actual corporate "seal" is not necessary, as the word (seal) is legally valid because many corporations no longer have actual "seals." The use of a "seal" may have a beneficial impact. For example in Maryland, the use of a "seal" extends the statute of limitations from the three to twelve years.***

ATTEST:	CUSTOMER
________________	By: ________________(SEAL)
ATTEST:	LICENSOR:
________________	By: ________________(SEAL)

[USE IN LIEU OF SECTION 8H]

The performance of Licensor's\Customer's obligations under this Agreement, including the Statements of Work, is hereby guaranteed by:

NAME OF COMPANY MAKING GUARANTY
By:________________

or

Parent hereby (i) guarantees the payment and performance by Licensor\Customer of all its liabilities and obligations under this Agreement and all documents, instruments, and agreements delivered hereunder, and (ii) consents to the jurisdiction of the U.S. District Court for the _______ District of _______ with regard to any claim under this guarantee as provided in Section 12(h) of this Agreement. This guarantee is a guarantee of payment and not of collection and shall continue to be effective or shall be reinstated if any payment of a guaranteed obligation is rescinded or must otherwise be returned by Licensor\Customer because of the insolvency, bankruptcy, or reorganization of Parent, all as though such payment had not been made.

PARENT/ NAME OF COMPANY MAKING GUARANTY
By:________________________________
Name:
Title:

- ***Always sign the agreement in non-black ink so that the original is clearly identifiable.***
- ***To be legally binding, persons signing for the Customer and Licensor must be authorized and have "signing authority."***
- ***Always use "By" and your title to indicate you are signing in your corporate capacity and limit your personal liability.***
- ***"Attest" is used for a corporate signatory, "Witness" for an individual signatory.***

- ***See the Agreement's preamble for issues as to when a corporate guarantee may be appropriate.***
- ***Check the date of the form to make sure the draft you begin with is the most recent and the "original" form, not a negotiated contract.***

SCHEDULES

The Appendixes are very important as they may contain the crucial details of the Agreement, i.e., payment, deliverables, acceptance test procedures, etc. The deliverables should be set forth in great detail. Avoid incorporating the deliverables in a high level requirements document.

DO NOT UNDER ANY CIRCUMSTANCE FAIL TO READ OR UNDERSTAND THE SCHEDULES

[The salesperson must decide whether Licensor will provide pricing in advance or whether all prices will be at Licensor's then-existing rates.]

APPENDIX 8

Model Price Schedule For Time and Materials Contracts

Prices as of _________, 20__

I. SOFTWARE

A. LICENSES

1. TERM OF LICENSES AVAILABLE: Licensor may offer Customer a Software License for any term listed in this Section. Such License shall continue for the period of time indicated, so long as Customer is not in default under this Agreement. The provisions for each term are as follows:

i. **Perpetual.** For payment of a one-time perpetual License fee, Customer shall be granted a perpetual License to use the Software for ninety-nine (99) years or until discontinued by Customer in accordance with this Agreement.

ii. **Annual.** For payment of an annual License fee, Customer shall be granted a one (1) year License to use the Software. Customer shall notify Licensor in writing at least thirty (30) days in advance of the pending expiration if Customer desires to discontinue said License. Otherwise, said annual License will be automatically renewed for another term of one (1) year until discontinued by Customer in accordance with this Agreement. If perpetual Licenses are offered by Licensor, Customer may elect to convert an annual License to a perpetual License by providing Licensor thirty (30) days written notice in advance of the perpetual License effective date and Customer shall receive a credit in the amount of fifty percent (50%) of all annual license fees already paid for the particular License being converted. Such credit shall be applied toward payment of the perpetual License fee then currently in effect under this Agreement.

iii. **Monthly.** For payment of a monthly License fee, Customer shall be granted a License to use the Software on a monthly basis until discontinued by Customer in accordance with this Agreement. If Customer elects to convert a monthly License to a perpetual or annual License, Customer shall so notify Licensor in writing by providing Licensor thirty (30) days written notice in advance of the perpetual or annual License effective date. Customer shall receive a credit in the amount of fifty percent (50%) of all monthly License fees paid for the particular License being converted. Such credit shall be applied toward payment of the perpetual or annual License fee then currently in effect under this Agreement.

2. TYPES OF SOFTWARE LICENSES AVAILABLE: The types of Licenses that may be offered by Licensor to the Customer are as follows:

i. **Corporate License.** A Corporate License grants Customer, including all Affiliated Companies listed, the right to duplicate the Software and Software

Products for use at as many Customer locations and on as many leased Central Processing Units (CPUs) as Customer desires. Customer shall pay only one (1) Corporate License fee for this type of license. If Customer orders Software Maintenance for Software under a Corporate License, then Customer shall pay only one (1) Software Maintenance fee for said Software.

ii. **Site License.** Each Site License grants Customer the right to use the Software on any or all CPU's located at the facility indicated on the Order as the Site License address. Customer must obtain a separate Site License for each site where the Software is located.

iii. **CPU License.** Each CPU License grants Customer the right to use the Software on a single CPU designated by type and serial number. A separate CPU License is required for each CPU on which the licensed Software will be used.

3. License Fees: A one-time perpetual "Right To Use" Site License for ______________. **[FILL IN PRICE SCHEDULE]**

II. SERVICES

A. **System Installation:** This support service option provides initial Software installation as follows:

Prices for system installation include instructor and training materials. Licensor's reasonable and customary travel expenses will be billed separately.

Installation Charges. The installation cost for the Customer is a one time fee of $_____________ exclusive of all reasonable and customary travel charges. An invoice for this fee will be sent once Licensor begins the installation process. Should the installation exceed the time period specified herein, due to elements beyond Licensor's control, an additional charge of $___________ per week will be applicable.

B. **Telephone Support:** Licensor maintains a group of highly trained phone support specialists who will be familiar with your application. If there is a problem or even a question that requires our attention, we can remotely access your system through the telephone line and modem that was installed with the system. This capability allows us to assist you as if we were sitting locally in the service center. Licensor's phone support specialists can resolve system problems, answer questions, dispatch a hardware support team, or assist your field consultant in support activities.

This support service provides a reasonable number of calls to Licensor's telephone support organization from a single point of contact at each installed location. This group will assist Customer in testing, evaluating, diagnosing, and directing Customer personnel via telecommunication to make the Software function substantially in accordance with the installed generic release specification. The phone support group will report all Software bugs to the appropriate. Licensor personnel and can report suspected hardware problems to the appropriate Customer Contact.

Under this support service option, Licensor will receive phone calls from Customer representatives during the hours of 8 a.m. to 7 p.m. Eastern Standard Time, Monday through Friday excluding Licensor holidays.

Telephone Support Charges: The Telephone Support cost for the Customer is a one time fee of $_______________ exclusive of all reasonable and customary travel charges. An invoice for this fee will be sent once Licensor begins the Telephone Support process. Should the Telephone Support exceed the time period specified due to elements beyond Licensor's control, an additional charge of $_____________ per week will be applicable.

C. **Consulting Support:** This support service option provides a dedicated consultant to assist the Customer with Software questions, work with local users on establishing site specific operational procedures, assume all table maintenance responsibility, discuss system enhancement alternatives, provide follow up training, and work with Customer to prepare Software user guides.

After initial training is completed and daily on-site support is no longer needed, Licensor will continue to be responsive to Customer's needs by maintaining a Licensor consultant dedicated to your account. The consultant will answer any questions that arise, assist in problem resolution, and make any necessary table modification. Customer will have up to thirty (30) hours a month of consultant availability included in the basic monthly charge. Consultant hours used in excess of thirty per month will be billed at the rate of $________/hour. All reasonable and customary travel expenses incurred by Licensor in rendering such services will be billed separately.

Customer Support Charges: The Customer Support charges for the Customer is a one time fee of $_____________ exclusive of all reasonable and customary travel charges. An invoice for this fee will be sent once Licensor begins the Customer Support process. Should the Customer Support exceed the time period specified due to elements beyond Licensor's control, an additional charge of $_____________ per week will be applicable.

D. **Follow-up Training:** This support service option will provide follow up training to assist Customer in the use of Software and Software Products. Two classes of follow up training are available.

[DESCRIBE TRAINING] Training $___________/year

E. **Enhancements:**

i. Generic Releases: Licensor will price Generic Releases consisting of Customer requested software enhancements in accordance with the price schedule specified in this Appendix C. Once a Generic Release has been priced, Customer will receive a proposal for the release which will be valid for thirty (30) days. The proposal will consist of a price quote and a delivery interval from the time the Licensor receives written approval to begin work from Customer. Licensor will not begin work on any Generic Release until receiving written authorization from Customer to proceed with the development activity. Licensor will use the lowest rate possible when multiple enhancements are requested for a specific generic release. Licensor's reasonable and customary travel charges will be invoiced separately.

ii. Generic Release Charges: Licensor will provide prices for all Enhancement requests in accordance with the following schedule of charges:*

(a) Hourly rate: $______ per hour. This applies to anything less than eight hours. The minimum is four hours.

(b) Daily rate: $______ per day. This applies to anything less than forty hours. The minimum number of hours at this rate is eight.
(c) Weekly rate: $______ per week. This applies to anything less than 160 hours and greater than 39 hours.
(d) Monthly rate: $_______ per month. This rate is for 160 hours; anything beyond 160 hours will be billed at the rate of $______ per hour.

*** Licensor will use the lowest rate possible when multiple enhancements are programmed at one time.***

III. HARDWARE

A. **System Hardware:** Customer will supply all necessary system hardware to run the Software in Customer designated locations. The selection of system hardware will be contingent upon Licensor approval. This includes, but is not limited to, computer hardware, peripheral devices, modems, and cables. Licensor agrees to assist Customer in the selection of suitable system hardware necessary to operate the Software. Customer will acquire all hardware maintenance services necessary to support the Software implementation. Licensor agrees to work with Customer to provide all Software modifications necessary to support upgrades or changes to Customer owned hardware within a mutually agreed upon time frame.

B. **Hardware Maintenance**: Customer is responsible for all ongoing maintenance charges for all system hardware.

IV. SYSTEM SOFTWARE

A. **System Software:** Customer will supply all necessary system software to run the Software in Customer designated locations. The selection of system software will be contingent upon Licensor approval. This includes, but is not limited to, operating system software, communications software, and firmware, and other system software that may facilitate the use of the Software. Licensor agrees to assist Customer in the selection of suitable system software necessary to operate the Software. Customer will acquire all system software maintenance services necessary to support the Software implementation. Licensor agrees to work with Customer to provide all Software modifications necessary to support upgrades or changes to Customer supplied system software within a mutually agreed upon time frame.

B. **System Software Maintenance:** Customer is responsible for all system software maintenance.

V. NETWORK COMMUNICATION

A. **Network Communications:** Customer will supply all networking required to implement the Software. All networking will be contingent upon Licensor approval. This includes, but is not limited to, data circuits, communications equipment, modems, and cabling. Licensor agrees to assist Customer in the determination of network communication requirements necessary to implement the Software. Customer agrees to provide all network communications maintenance services required to support the Software implementation. Licensor agrees to work with Customer to provide all Software modifications necessary to support upgrades or changes to Customer supplied

Networking within a mutually agreed upon time frame. All Software modifications will be provided as part of a Generic Release for a fee that is calculated based upon the price schedule listed in this Appendix B as amended from time to time. The Generic Release programming activity will begin upon receiving written authorization from Customer complete with all necessary technical information on the new network architecture. Customer agrees to provide and bear the cost of a dedicated dial up communications facility equipped with 56KHayes Compatible modem at Customer's CPU hardware for the purposes of remote access and supporting the Licensor's consultant or phone support group.

B. **Network Communications Maintenance**: Customer is responsible for all network communications maintenance.

VI. MISCELLANEOUS

A. **Price Changes:** All prices set forth in this Appendix B are subject to change upon thirty (30) days prior written notice to Customer.

B. **Other Costs:** Customer agrees to pay all of Licensor's reasonable, actual, out of pocket costs, including but not limited to travel expenses incurred by Licensor in project management, system analysis, and consulting during the term of this Agreement, such expenses will be billed to Customer separately at cost.

APPENDIX 3.B

Service Level Standards and Credits

The Services consist of the terms and conditions set forth herein and in the Attachments identified below.

Attachment 1	Benefit Plan Administration
Attachment 2	Member Eligibility Administration
Attachment 3	Provides/Capitation Management
Attachment 4	Claims Processing
Attachment 5	Case Management
Attachment 6	Reporting
Attachment 7	Customer Service
Attachment 8	Information Technology Support

The Service Level Standards and Credits identified in Attachments 1 through 8 represent the basic service levels and credits provided by Licensor to Customer. In the event Customer negotiates a contract with a substantial customer with increased Service Level Standards and/or Credits, Customer shall communicate such increased service level standards and/or credits to Licensor thirty (30) calendar days prior to the effective date of such standards and credits and such standards and credits for such Customer shall become effective at the end of the thirty (30) day period.

ATTACHMENT 1

Benefit Plan Administration

1. **Licensor Obligations.** Licensor shall establish and maintain the integrity and accuracy of the Customer benefit plans by timely processing routine updates and performing quality control audits. Licensor's Services shall include the following:

(a) Define with Customer the data requirements for benefit plan definition. Licensor will identify system requirements for benefit plan data.

(b) Develop source format requirements and submission procedures for benefit plan maintenance.

(c) Perform benefit plan maintenance:

(i) Establish new lines of business

(ii) Establish and verify new benefit plans

(iii) Log, track, process, and verify routine plan updates

(iv) Initiate and drive resolution of benefit plan maintenance issues

(d) Perform quality control audits on benefit plan. Initiate and drive resolution of discrepancies identified through results of regular claims processing sampling audits.

(e) Correct all errors and inaccuracies in the benefit plan database and validate, on a monthly basis, the information contained therein.

(f) Validate the completeness of the benefit plan data provided by Customer.

(g) Participate with Customer in developing Test Data and a Test Plan pursuant to Schedule ____ in order to validate the accuracy of the Customer benefit plans. The Test Plan for the benefit plans shall include various benefit plan scenarios, which shall be updated and refined from time to time.

2. **Customer Responsibilities.** Customer shall cooperate with Licensor in the performance of Licensor's above-listed obligations by performing the tasks set forth below; provided, however, that in no event shall any failure by Customer to act as described below be construed as or result in a breach of this Agreement:

(a) Define with Licensor the data requirements for benefit plan definition. Customer will identify their requirements for benefit plan data.

(b) Define benefit plans for Members.

(c) Provide benefit plan source documents, communicate completeness criteria to Licensor.

(d) Participate in the verification of benefit plan maintenance.

3. **Service Level Standards/Credits.**

Standard	Credit
Successfully process fully tested routine benefit plan update within three (3) calendar days of receipt of complete maintenance request.	$1,000/day for the first seven (7) calendar days past due. $2,000/day for each day thereafter.
Successfully process up to twenty-five (25) new benefit plans loaded in the system within thirty (30) calendar days of receipt of complete source documents. At Customer's option, additional plans will be either (i) processed in the current period for an additional fee, or (ii) processed in the next period.	$2,000/day for the first seven (7) calendar days that standard is not met. $5,000/day for each day thereafter.

ATTACHMENT 2

Member Eligibility Administration

[Customer to Provide Descriptions]

1. **Licensor Obligations.** Licensor shall __________________________.
Licensor's Services shall include the following:

(a)

(b)

2. **Customer Responsibilities.** Customer shall cooperate with Licensor in the performance of Licensor's above-listed obligations by performing the tasks set forth below; provided, however, that in no event shall any failure by Customer to act as described below be construed as or result in a breach of this Agreement.

(a)

(b)

3. **Service Level Standards/Credits.**

ATTACHMENT 3

Provider/Capitation Management

1. **Licensor Obligations.** As requested by Customer and at no additional charge or expense to Customer, Licensor shall establish providers within the system, create and maintain provider fee schedules, price rules, generate capitation reports, reconcile with payer, and perform periodic quality assurance on capitation models. Licensor's Services shall include the following:

(a) Define with Customer the data requirements for provider fee schedules. Licensor will identify system requirements for provider fee schedule data.

(b) Develop source format requirements and submission procedures for provider fee schedule maintenance.

(c) Perform provider fee schedule maintenance:

(i) Establish and verify new provider fee schedules and institutional pricing as submitted,

(ii) Log, track, process, and verify provider fee schedule and institutional pricing updates as submitted;

(iii) Initiate and drive resolution of provider fee schedule and institutional pricing maintenance issues.

(d) Provide notice to Customer within two (2) business days of any incompleteness in source document information.

(e) Perform quality control audits on provider fee schedules and reimbursement formulas. Initiate and drive resolution of discrepancies identified through results of regular claims processing sampling audits.

(f) Process withholds in accordance with contractual arrangements.

(g) Provide retroactive processing.

2. **Customer Responsibilities.** Customer shall cooperate with Licensor in the performance of Licensor's above-listed obligations by performing the tasks set forth below; provided, however, that in no event shall any failure by Customer to act as described below be construed as or result in a breach of this Agreement:

(a) Define and provide provider reimbursement plans/fee schedule methodologies for providers and hospitals.

(b) Participate in the verification of reimbursement formulas and follow-up with the appropriate source documents for missing information.

(c) Define financial requirements (bank accounts, etc).

(d) Receive payments from payers for reconciliation.

3. **Service Level Standards/Credits.**

Standard	Credit
Successfully process routine participating provider fee schedule updates and price rules within three (3) calendar days of receipt of maintenance request.	$250/day per provider schedule or provider contract for which standard is not met.
Successfully establish up to fifty (50) new participating provider fee schedules and price rules in system within fourteen (14) calendar days of receipt of complete source documents.	$250/day per provider schedule or provider contract for which standard is not met.

ATTACHMENT 4

Claims Processing

1. **Licensor Obligations.** Licensor shall administer the processing and adjudication of claims to ensure that submitted claims are processed in a timely manner. Licensor's Services shall include the following:

(a) Define with Customer the claims format and procedures for claims receipt, routing, and verification.

(b) Define with Customer the procedures for fixing holes in pricing, forwarding unclean claim information to Customer for resolution, handling COB, and resolving denied claims.

(c) Define with Customer the procedures for management of third party liability, subrogation processes, and pre-existing conditions.

(d) Log, track, and process submitted claims.

(e) Adjudicate claims for payments, which shall include DRG Grouper processing.

(f) Resolve pended claims.

(g) Receive Remittance Advice (RAs) and explanation of benefits (EOBs) and process accordingly. Produce claims checks, process weekly or as requested by Customer and distribute to Customer within 24 hours.

(h) Respond to customer service personnel inquiries.

(i) If requested by Customer, print RAs with checks.

(j) Administer HPR Code Review to detect and correct claim unbundling and fraudulent billing.

(k) Processing of unique requirements, i.e., special turnaround time for large clients.

(l) Maintain physical copies of claims for a minimum of seven (7) years unless otherwise required by Customer.

(m) Produce copies of microfilm images for Customer on a monthly basis.

(n) Identify and correct voided checks, refunds, and claim overpayment recoveries.

(o) Maintain sufficient internal payment audit process to ensure claims payment accuracy, to include the development and implementation of corrective action plans.

(p) Accept and process electronic data interchange ("EDI") transmissions.

(q) Define EOBs text.

(r) Verify and distribute withholds.

(s) Verify and approve checks and EOBs.

(t) Provide financial report/statement and/or data files for close-of-period (including annual) reconciliation.

2. **Customer Responsibilities.** Customer shall cooperate with Licensor in the performance of Licensor's above-listed obligations by performing the tasks set forth below; provided, however, that in no event shall any failure by Customer to act as described below be construed as or result in a breach of this Agreement:

(a) Define with Licensor the claims format and procedures for claims receipt, routing, and verification.

(b) Assist Licensor with the procedures for correcting pricing issues, forwarding unclean claim information to Licensor for resolution, handling COB, and resolving denied claims.

(c) Define correspondence text for claims, EOB/request, and or letters.

(d) Verify and approve claims checks/RAs.

3. **Service Level Standards/Credits.**

Standard	**Credit**
Produce checks within two (2) business days of Customer sign off.	
Enter new claims into ABC System within two (2) business days of receipt.	
Adjudicate 99 percent of claims within fifteen (15) calendar days of receipt. Adjudicate 99 percent of claims within thirty (30) calendar days of receipt. Adjudicate 99 percent of claims within sixty (60) calendar days of receipt. Licensor shall produce a detailed written explanation as to why any claims are not adjudicated by the thirty (30) day mark, which explanation shall include, without limitation, the reason(s) for such delay and the individuals responsible for and necessary to achieve adjudication.	$100 per claim not adjudicated within sixty (60) calendar days.
Provide resolution to "Hot Claim" issue within three (3) business days from date of input for Licensor attention, unless information provided is incorrect, then Licensor shall provide response within three (3) days.	If less than 99 percent of issues are not resolved or responded to, as applicable, in a given thirty (30) day period, Customer shall receive from Licensor $2,500 for that period.

Standard	Credit
Complete online or daily processing of HPR within twenty-four (24) hours of adjudication and make adjustments prior to next check run.	
9 percent random of experienced examiners. Audit and correct prior to claims payment or audit plan acceptable to Customer.	
9 percent manager review of all claim payments in excess of $10,000 billed Customer prior to payment.	
Process held claims within forty-eight (48) hours of client direction.	
9 percent error-free clerical accuracy on claims processed.* For purposes hereof, "clerical accuracy" shall mean data entry that does not cause a financial impact. *Based on Customer's internal audit.	If Licensor does not meet required standard in a given thirty (30) day period, the following credit structure shall apply for that period: Licensor Performance — Credit 95% to 100%: $0 91% to <95%: 5,000 81% to <90%: 10,000 <80%: 20,000
99 percent financial accuracy.* For purposes hereof, "financial accuracy" shall mean data entry that causes any adjudication resulting in an over or under payment. *Based on Customer's internal audit	If Licensor does not meet required standard in a given thirty (30) day period, the following credit structure shall apply for that period: Licensor — Performance 99% to 100% $25,000 bonus (to Licensor) 98% to <99%: 0 96% to <98%: 25,000 credit 91% to <95%: 50,000 credit <90%: 100,000 credit

ATTACHMENT 5

Case Management

1. **Licensor Obligations.** Licensor shall establish and maintain remote system access to allow Customer personnel to perform required case management responsibilities. Licensor's Services shall include the following:

(a) Provide access to claims history and utilization history files, both online and archived files for ad hoc reporting and case management.

(b) Provide capability to develop screening criteria and protocols online.

(c) Define and develop with Customer interfaces with critical resource directories.

2. **Customer Responsibilities.** Customer shall cooperate with Licensor in the performance of Licensor's above-listed obligations by performing the tasks set forth below; provided, however, that in no event shall any failure by Customer to act as described below be construed as or result in a breach of this Agreement:

(a) Define case management requirements for all functionality (e.g., CM responsibilities, pre-certification validation criteria, screening criteria, protocols, and reports).

(b) Define and develop with Licensor interfaces with critical resource directories.

(c) Create authorizations for service.

ATTACHMENT 6

Reporting

1. **Licensor Obligations.** Licensor shall assist Customer in the development and on-going generation of necessary reports and downloaded files. Licensor's Services shall include the following:

(a) Provide/download the necessary files to generate ad hoc reports, labels, and correspondences, as requested.

(b) Provide ad hoc reporting capabilities to support Customer requests. [______] Ad hoc reports shall be provided to Customer per month at no additional charge.

(c) Restart printer queues following any scheduled or unscheduled reboot of system.

(d) Provide management, performance, and other reports to Customer at the frequencies specified below to include the following:

(i) Management Reports: **[TBD]**

(ii) Performance Reports: See Schedule 4.6.4.

(iii) Other Reports: **[TBD]**

(e) Assist Customer in downloading of data for Customer internal reports at mutually agreed-upon frequencies.

(f) Provide the capabilities to run month-end financial reporting by the third working day after month end.

(g) Facilitate Customer's downloading of data from ABC System into report formats.

2. **Customer Responsibilities.** Customer shall cooperate with Licensor in the performance of Licensor's above-listed obligations by performing the tasks set forth below; provided, however, that in no event shall any failure by Customer to act as described below be construed as or result in a breach of this Agreement:

(a) Define membership profile reporting requirements.

(b) Define capitation reporting requirements.

(c) Develop format with Licensor and define frequencies for generation of reports.

3. **Service Level Standards/Credits.**

Standard	Credit
Complete report request within five (5) business days of sign-off of report specifications.	
Complete closing schedule within three (3) business days from end of month.	
Provide monthly performance reports on data specified.	$1,000/day per report late charge
Report data accuracy and consistency.	$5,000/day per finance report from date of discovery to date of correction

ATTACHMENT 7

Customer Service

1. **Licensor Obligations.** Licensor shall establish and maintain remote system access to allow Customer personnel to perform required Customer Service responsibilities. Licensor's Services shall include the following:

(a) Develop with Customer a mechanism to report back to Customer Service the results of processing events.

2. **Customer Responsibilities.** Customer shall cooperate with Licensor in the performance of Licensor's above-listed obligations by performing the tasks set forth below; provided, however, that in no event shall any failure by Customer to act as described below be construed as or result in a breach of this Agreement:

(a) Develop with Licensor a mechanism to report back to Customer Service the results of processing events.

(b) Log provider/Member inquiries, complaints, and grievances.

ATTACHMENT 8

Information Technology Support

1. **Licensor Obligations.** Licensor shall provide Services and otherwise maintain the ABC System (including all Custom Programming) so that such services and system function without Material Defects in accordance with the Specifications, Performance Standards, Documentation, and Regulatory Requirements, and Licensor shall provide the following additional Support and Maintenance Services to Customer:

1.1 **Telephone Hotline/Help Desk.** Licensor shall continuously (twenty-four (24) hours per day, seven (7) days per week) provide a telephone number for Customer personnel to call for all purposes regarding Support and Maintenance Services for the ABC System. Customer's help desk shall be monitored exclusively by members of the Licensor Support Team. At Customer's option, Licensor shall only provide such telephone hotline support from 7 a.m. to 7 p.m., Eastern Time (i.e., business hours); provided, that if Customer elects such option: (a) the Support and Maintenance Services fees attributable to continuous 24–7 telephone hotline support shall be decreased on a pro-rata basis according the hours of support provided; (b) Licensor shall make call-out support services available during non-business hours, which services shall be charged at the Services Rates designated in Schedule _____, and Customer shall be charged only for call-out services that Licensor actually provides to Customer (i.e., no "on-call" charges); and (c) Customer may revert back to continuous 24–7 telephone hotline support at any time upon notice to Licensor.

1.2 **Modem Support.** Licensor shall provide modem support to Customer twenty-four (24) hours per day, seven (7) days per week. Customer shall maintain a dial-up modem with unique dial back identification passwords for each individual assigned by Licensor to provide modem support to Customer. Customer may disconnect the dial-up modem, at its sole discretion, during the hours of operation. Customer acknowledges that disconnection of its modem may adversely affect the Defect resolution time frames.

1.3 **Support and Maintenance History and Tracking System.** Licensor shall maintain a current record of Customer's Support and Maintenance Services history. Upon Customer's request, Licensor shall provide a detailed history of all Support and Maintenance Services performed by Licensor. Customer shall own all such records. On a monthly basis, Licensor shall provide to Customer a report detailing: (a) the number of calls to the support center received by Licensor during the reporting period; (b) the date, time, day of the week, and duration of each call; (c) the subject matter of each call; and (d) the resolution of the matter.

1.4 **Software Information Network.** Customer shall have online access to Licensor's software information network, if any, for online software information and questions. Licensor shall provide to Customer phone number for purposes of accessing Licensor's software information network. Customer shall not be charged an access fee to such network, but Customer shall be responsible for any connect-time charges to the public telecommunications carrier.

1.5 **Enhancements and New Features.** Licensor shall provide all Enhancements to the ABC System including, without limitation, all Enhancements necessary to operate the ABC System on the current versions of the Equipment and all Enhancements necessary to maintain compatibility with all Embedded Third Party Software. Enhancements requested by Customer shall be performed by Licensor by the Programmers at no additional cost to Customer.

1.6 **Regulatory Requirements.** Regulatory modifications to the ABC System shall be provided by Licensor, at no additional cost to Customer, whenever such modifications are recommended, mandated, or required to meet federal and state governmental and quasi-governmental regulatory requirements, statutes, ordinances, policies, edicts, rules, guidelines, or standards related to Customer's use of the Services or the functions of the ABC System including, without limitation, all standards or guidelines established by committees, agencies, or other standard-setting organizations implementing regulatory requirements, policies, or operating standards adopted by the [name] industry and any other such modifications or changes that may be required to meet the then-current, industry-accepted specifications or standards for Third Party Software with which the ABC System interfaces and all federal, state, and regulatory requirements that relate to Customer's provision of [industry] services (collectively, "**Regulatory Requirement**"). Without limiting the generality of the foregoing, Regulatory Requirements shall mean those requirements as set forth in the State Contract and shall include, without limitation, all federal and state standards and regulations regarding electronic data interchange transactions (including, without limitation, 45 CFR Part 142 and any other standards or regulations addressing the mandates of Section 262 (Administrative Simplification) of the Health Insurance Portability and Accountability Act of 1996). Before the date on which Customer is required to comply with such Regulatory Requirements and with sufficient time in which to test, Licensor shall provide to Customer and install and test all such Regulatory Requirements modifications. Licensor represents to Customer that the ABC System and Services currently operate in accordance with all Regulatory Requirements and that the ABC System and Services and all future Enhancements to the ABC System will operate in accordance with all Regulatory Requirements. Licensor shall provide to Customer all Regulatory Requirements, including, without limitation, Regulatory Requirements for components of the ABC System and Services that currently are not regulated but that may, in the future, be regulated by Regulatory Requirements prior to the date on which Customer is required to comply with such Regulatory Requirements.

1.6.1 **Annual Updates.** For changes required to the federal DRG Grouper, the ICD9CM Codes and the CPT Codes on an annual basis, Licensor shall ensure delivery within fifteen (15) business days of receipt of third party software from 3M (DRG Grouper), HCFA (DRG Pricer), HCIA (ICD9CM Codes), and AMA (CPT Codes) or other electronic provider, except that, when annual regulations require major Licensor system revisions to accommodate major federal changes, such as for century date compliance, reimbursement methodology revisions, or massive coding system alterations, Licensor will ensure that all personnel responsible for applicable regulatory programming changes are assigned to provide the changes in a timely manner, as their highest priority project.

1.6.2 **DRG** Window Rule. Licensor shall cause its software to comply with the federal regulations set forth in Fed. Reg. 63 No. 28, February 11, 1998 (**"DRG Rule Regulations"**). Any changes needed to Licensor Software to implement changes associated with the DRG Rule Regulations will be provided by Licensor at no additional charge to Customer.

1.6.3 **EDI** Regulations. The Licensor Software shall comply with all Federal and State standards and regulations regarding electronic data interchange (**"EDI"**) transactions (including 45 CFR Part 142). If any of the Licensor Software currently does not comply with any newly enacted Federal and/or State regulations, Licensor shall ensure that such Software does comply within the time frames/windows for compliance allowed by such regulations.

1.7 **Obligation to Generally Improve the ABC System.** Licensor shall generally enhance and improve the ABC System for as long as Customer elects to receive and pays for the Services.

1.8 **Documentation and Specifications.** Licensor shall provide any and all updated Documentation and/or Specifications, as applicable, for the ABC System, any Enhancements or Custom Programming provided to Customer in accordance with the Agreement as such Documentation and/or Specifications are generally released, or more frequently if significant errors and/or discrepancies are discovered in such Documentation and/or Specifications.

2. **Customer Responsibilities.** Customer shall cooperate with Licensor in the performance of Licensor's above-listed obligations by performing the tasks set forth below. Provided however, that in no event shall any failure by Customer to act as described below be interpreted as or result in a breach of this Agreement:

(a) Assist Licensor in the development of support procedures.

(b) Define with Licensor process for submission, qualification, approval, and implementation of functionality modification requests.

(c) Ensure end users follow established support procedures.

(d) End users will employ reasonable efforts to solve problems/address requests before calling the Help Desk.

(e) Work with Licensor to define and establish telecommunication links necessary to exchanges data electronically among all parties for enrollment, eligibility, benefit plans, encounters for PCPs claims, back-end files, and reconciliation.

(f) Maintain local network and devices.

(g) Work with payers to define file formats for required/desired interfaces.

(h) Assist in the development of disaster recovery plan per item (k) above.

(i) Assist in development of system capacity planner.

(j) Assist in development/modification of backup and archive strategy.

3. **Resolution of Defects**

3.1 **Defect Levels.** Customer shall classify, or reclassify, as applicable, all Defects as Critical Defects, Medium Defects, and Low Defects pursuant to the definitions set forth below in **Section 3.3.**

3.2 **Reporting of Defects.** Reports of Defects (an "Incident Report") will be made through Licensor's Customer Support Center via telephone, fax, or email at numbers to be provided by Licensor to Customer. Licensor shall provide to Customer Support Center coverage twenty-four (24) hours per day, seven (7) days per week, as follows:

(a) Customer Support Center Peak Coverage Hours: 6 a.m. to 6 p.m., Eastern Time, Monday through Friday, excluding New Year's Day, Memorial Day, July 4, Labor Day, Thanksgiving Day, and Christmas Day, or the days on which Licensor observes any of these holidays. Calls of a non-emergency nature (requests not involving a Critical Defect or a Medium Defect) should be reserved to peak coverage hours. During peak coverage hours, a member of the Licensor Support Team will answer the call. Incident Reports of Critical Defects and Medium Defects should be made by telephone during peak coverage hours to facilitate a timely response.

(b) Customer Support Center On-Call Coverage Hours: All periods not included as peak coverage. During on-call coverage hours, an on-call support contact will contact Customer within thirty (30) minutes after Customer's report of a Defect. Incident Reports of Critical Defects and Medium Defects should be made by pager number during on call coverage hours to facilitate a timely response.

The Licensor Customer Support Center will log the reported Defect and provide Customer with an incident tracking number to refer to when making follow-up inquiries. The Incident Report shall contain, to the extent known, applicable and/or possible: (c) the name/type of affected equipment; (d) Customer contact name, email address if available, telephone number, and fax number; and (e) the nature of the Defect, a description of the Defect and Customer's classification of the Defect. Customer will exercise commercially reasonably efforts to limit Incident Reports concerning Low Defects to peak coverage times. If Customer makes a call to the Customer Support Center during on-call coverage hours, Customer personnel shall remain available to receive a reply from Licensor's personnel. Customer will provide Licensor with as much information as possible to enable Licensor to investigate and attempt to identify and verify the reported maintenance issue. Customer will work with Licensor support personnel during the problem isolation process, as reasonably needed. Customer will notify Licensor of any configuration charges, such as network installation/expansion, upgrades, relocations, etc.

3.3 **Response Procedures.** Based upon a Defect's severity level, Licensor shall correct such Defect in accordance with the procedures set forth in this Section.

Severity of Defect	Response
"**Critical Defect**" means any Defect that severely impacts Customer's ability to receive or Licensor's ability to provide Services, or any Defect that has a significant financial impact on Customer or a direct impact on Customer's managed care services, or the failure of any network element, such as a printer, to be operable.	Licensor shall: (i) Provide a Defect Analysis for a Critical Defect within one (1) hour of receipt of an Incident Report; (ii) Provide an Interim Resolution for a Critical Defect as soon as possible, and in no event later than four (4) hours of receipt of an Incident Report, and Licensor shall provide progress reports every one (1) hour; and (iii) Provide a Final Resolution for a Critical Defect within five (5) calendar days after notice thereof.
"**Medium Defect**" means any Defect that adversely affects Customer's ability to receive or Licensor's ability to provide Services but for which an alternative temporary solution or workaround acceptable to Customer may be accomplished.	Licensor shall: (i) Provide a Defect Analysis for a Medium Defect as soon as possible, but in no event later than four (4) hours of receipt of an Incident Report; (ii) Provide an Interim Resolution to a Medium Defect within forty-eight (48) hours after notice thereof; and (iii) Provide a Final Resolution for a Medium Defect within thirty (30) calendar days of notice thereof.
"**Low Defect**" means any Defect that is of de minimis nature.	Licensor shall respond to a Low Defect within forty-eight (48) hours of receipt of an Incident Report and resolve a Low Defect in the next release of the affected Software.

For purposes of this Section:

"Defect Analysis" means a fax, email, or telephone call from Licensor acknowledging that an Incident Report has been received, details on what Licensor has learned about the Defect as of the time of communication that appropriate technical personnel have been assigned to work on the Defect, and Licensor's initial analysis of and action plan for resolving the reported Defect.

"Final Resolution" means Licensor provides a correction or modification of the ABC System that corrects the Defect.

"Interim Resolution" means Licensor: (a) reinitiates or restarts, as applicable, the ABC System, or affected part thereof, if the reported Defect caused the ABC System to be inoperative; (b) enables Customer to access the ABC System, if the reported Defect caused Customer to be unable to access the ABC System; or (c) provides

Customer with an acceptable workaround that solves or mitigates a reported Defect, which workaround can be provided with minimal Customer inconvenience.

4. **Time-and-Materials Support.**

4.1 **General.** Customer shall have the right, at any time upon thirty (30) calendar days written notice to Licensor, to obtain Support and Maintenance Services on a time-and-materials basis ("Time-and-Materials Support") at the Service Rates set forth in an applicable purchase order, which rates shall not exceed the Service Rates set forth in Schedule ____. In the event Customer elects to obtain Time-and-Materials Support: (a) Licensor shall credit any pre-paid, but unearned Support and Maintenance Services fees, which fees shall be applied against any amounts invoiced for Time-and-Materials Support; and (b) Customer shall have the right, at any time upon thirty (30) calendar days written notice to Licensor, to return to obtaining Support and Maintenance Services on an annual basis for the Support and Maintenance Services fees set forth in an applicable purchase order, which fees shall not exceed the Support and Maintenance Services fees set forth in Schedule ____.

4.2 **Enhancements.** At the time of Customer's election to obtain the Time-and-Materials Support, the parties shall negotiate in good faith a fixed fee, if any, for Customer to obtain Enhancements under Section 1.5 of this Attachment 8.

Source Code License Agreement

(Short Form)

THIS SOURCE CODE LICENSE AGREEMENT is made this _____ day of __________, 20__, by and between ________________, a _____________ corporation, having its principal place of business at ____________________________(hereinafter referred to as "Licensor"), and ______________________________, a __________________ corporation, having its principal place of business at __________________________ __________________ (hereinafter referred to as "Licensee").

BACKGROUND

Licensee has previously licensed the object code version of Licensor's ______________ software (the "Software"). Licensee now desires to license a source code copy of the Software, as more fully described in Exhibit A. It is Licensor's desire to grant Licensee a source code license, upon the terms and conditions hereinafter set forth.

IN CONSIDERATION of the mutual covenants set forth herein, and for other good and valuable consideration, the receipt and sufficiency of which are hereby acknowledged, Licensor and Licensee hereby agree as follows:

1. **License.**

1.1 Subject to the terms of this Agreement, Licensor grants Licensee a perpetual, limited, nonexclusive, non-assignable, nontransferable, personal, source code license without the right to sublicense during the term of this Agreement, solely to [**describe use**].

1.2 Subject to the terms of this Agreement, Licensor grants Licensee a royalty-bearing, nonexclusive, nontransferable license to make, use, sell, offer for sale, reproduce, distribute, disclose, import, and prepare derivative works of the object code. The rights to distribute, sell, offer for sale, and import is granted only in conjunction with the Software.

1.3 Subject to the terms of this Agreement, Licensor grants Licensee a royalty-free, nonexclusive, nontransferable license to make, use, sell, offer for sale, reproduce, distribute, disclose, import, and prepare derivative works of documentation, together with the right to sublicense others to do the same.

2. **Consideration.**

2.1 In consideration for the rights granted under this Agreement, Licensee shall pay Licensor:

(a) a paid-up license fee of $______________ for the rights granted in Section 1.1 above; and

(b) a royalty of $________________ for each copy of object code that is sold, distributed, or otherwise disposed of, either internally or externally, by Licensee. However, no royalty shall be due for any copy used or distributed by Licensee for reasonable demonstration, training, or support purposes.

2.2 Payments due Licensor shall be made within thirty (30) days after the end of each calendar quarter, reflecting royalties for all copies of object code programs shipped during the previous quarter, less a credit for any returns.

2.3 Licensor may, at its expense and no more frequently than once a year, engage an independent auditor to verify royalty payments. The auditor may take abstracts from the relevant records of Licensee to determine compliance with this Agreement.

2.4 Licensee shall be solely responsible for any taxes on royalties and other fees paid to Licensor under this Agreement, including state and local use, sales, property (*ad valorem*), and similar taxes, but excluding taxes calculated solely on Licensor's income.

3. **Delivery.** Delivery of the Software will be made by Licensor and Licensee shall pay all shipping, insurance, and freight charges as well as all other costs incurred by Licensor in shipping the Software. Risk of loss or damage to the Software shall be assumed by Licensee upon delivery of the Software by Licensor to the common carrier.

4. **Licensee Responsibilities.** Licensee shall pay all installation and operation costs incurred by Licensee in utilizing the Software. Licensee shall pay $______________ per day per person for each Licensor employee or agent required to install, operate, and maintain the Software as well as all reasonable actual out-of-pocket and travel expenses incurred by Licensor's employees or agents. Licensee shall maintain in effect all times during the term hereof insurance (including, without limitation, workman's compensation, public liability, product liability, property damage, and automobile liability insurance) against all losses, claims, demands, proceedings, damages, costs, charges, and expenses for injuries or damage to any person or property arising out of or in connection with this Agreement that are the result of the fault or negligence of Licensee, its agents, and subcontractors.

5. **Title.** Title to the Software shall at all times remain with Licensor and Licensee's interest therein is only that of having temporary possession of the Software. Licensee shall provide and pay for all maintenance necessary to maintain the Software during the term of this Agreement.

6. **Payment.** Licensor shall bill Licensee on a monthly basis for all costs incurred by Licensor during the previous thirty (30) day period. All invoices shall be paid by Licensee within thirty (30) days of their receipt. All amounts past due over thirty (30) days shall accrue interest from the due date at a rate of eighteen percent (18%) per annum but no more than the maximum permissible under applicable law.

7. **Proprietary Information.** Both Licensor and Licensee acknowledge and agree to be bound by the terms and conditions of a certain Proprietary Information Agreement by and between the parties hereto dated ______________, 20__.

8. **Term.** This Agreement shall begin _________________, 20__ and continue until ___________________, 20__, unless otherwise terminated as provided herein.

9. **Termination.**

(a) "Default"—Either party has the right to terminate this Agreement if the other party breaches or is in default of any obligation hereunder which default is incapable of cure or which, being capable of cure, has not been cured within thirty (30) calendar days after written receipt of notice of such default (or such additional cure period as the non-defaulting party may authorize). Notwithstanding the previous sentence, if Licensee breaches Sections 1, 4, or 6 of this Agreement, Licensor may immediately terminate this Agreement without prior notice.

(b) "Acts of Insolvency"—Either party may terminate this Agreement by written notice to the other and may regard the other party as in default of this Agreement, if the other party becomes insolvent, makes a general assignment for the benefit of creditors, files a voluntary petition of bankruptcy, suffers or permits the appointment of a receiver for its business or assets, or becomes subject to any proceedings under any bankruptcy or insolvency law, whether domestic or foreign, or has wound up or liquidated, voluntarily or otherwise. In the event that any of the above events occurs, that party shall immediately notify the other party of its occurrence.

(c) "Force Majeure Event"—In the event that either party is unable to perform any of its obligations under this Agreement or to enjoy any of its benefits because of natural disaster, actions, or decrees of government bodies or communication line failure not the fault of the affected party (hereafter referred to as "Force Majeure Event"), the party who has been so affected shall immediately give notice to the other party and shall do everything possible to resume performance. Upon receipt of such notice, all obligations under this Agreement shall be immediately suspended until such "Force Majeure" is resolved.

(d) "Return of Properties"—Upon the termination of this Agreement by either party, or its expiration, each party forthwith shall immediately return to the other all papers, materials, and other properties of the other held by it in connection with the performance of this Agreement.

10. **"Limitation of Liability."** ALL SOFTWARE IS PROVIDED "AS IS" WITHOUT WARRANTY OF ANY KIND. LICENSOR MAKES NO EXPRESS OR IMPLIED REPRESENTATIONS OR WARRANTIES WITH RESPECT TO THE SOFTWARE, SOFTWARE PRODUCTS, OR SERVICES TO BE PROVIDED HEREUNDER OR THEIR CONDITION, MERCHANTABILITY, FITNESS FOR ANY PARTICULAR PURPOSE, OR USE BY LICENSEE. LICENSOR SHALL NOT BE LIABLE FOR ANY (I) SPECIAL, INDIRECT, INCIDENTAL, PUNITIVE, OR CONSEQUENTIAL DAMAGES, INCLUDING LOSS OF PROFITS, ARISING FROM OR RELATED TO THE OPERATION OR USE OF THE SOFTWARE AND SOFTWARE PRODUCTS INCLUDING BUT NOT LIMITED TO DAMAGES ARISING FROM LOSS OF DATA OR PROGRAMMING, LOSS OF REVENUE OR PROFITS, FAILURE TO REALIZE SAVINGS OR OTHER BENEFITS, DAMAGE TO EQUIPMENT, AND CLAIMS

AGAINST LICENSEE BY ANY THIRD PERSON, EVEN IF LICENSOR HAS BEEN ADVISED OF THE POSSIBILITY OF SUCH DAMAGES; OR (II) CLAIMS MADE A SUBJECT OF LEGAL PROCEEDING AGAINST LICENSOR MORE THAN TWO YEARS AFTER ANY SUCH CAUSE OF ACTION FIRST AROSE. NOTWITHSTANDING ANY OTHER PROVISION OF THIS AGREEMENT, LICENSOR'S TOTAL LIABILITIES HEREUNDER SHALL NOT BE GREATER THAN THE AMOUNTS ACTUALLY RECEIVED BY LICENSOR FROM LICENSEE PURSUANT TO THE TERMS OF THIS AGREEMENT.

11. **Copyright and Trade Notices.**

11.1 Licensee shall assure that all object code and documentation distributed by Licensee will include the following notice:

"Copyright **Licensor, Inc.**, 2008. All Rights Reserved."

11.2 The notice shall be:

(a) affixed in a prominent location on the media, in the documentation on the media packaging, and in a readable file in the code; and

(b) will appear on at least one display screen for at least two seconds during execution of the object code.

11.3 Licensee shall assure that all source code has the following legend affixed to it in a prominent location on the media, and in a readable file in the code:

"Unpublished Confidential Information of Licensor, Inc. Do not disclose. Copyright Licensor, Inc., 2008. All Rights Reserved."

12. **Grant back of Enhancements.**

12.1 Licensee shall keep complete and accurate records of all enhancements.

12.2 Licensee shall disclose all enhancements to Licensor promptly, but in any event no later than ninety (90) days after such works are made commercially available to Licensee's customers.

12.3 Licensee hereby grants Licensor a nonexclusive, worldwide, irrevocable, royalty-free license to all such enhancements to make, use, sell, offer for sale, import, reproduce, distribute, disclose, and prepare derivative works of such enhancements.

13. **Binding Effect.** This Agreement shall be binding upon and inure to the benefit of the parties hereto, their successors, and permitted assigns or other legal representatives.

14. **Governing Law.** This Agreement shall be construed in accordance with the laws of the State of _______, excluding its principles of conflicts of laws. The parties hereto agree that any action related to this Agreement shall be venued solely in the Federal District Court for the State of __________, and the parties hereby irrevocably submit to the jurisdiction and venue of said court to resolve any dispute arising hereunder or relating hereto.

15. **Export Regulations.** Licensee acknowledges its obligations to control access to technical data under the U.S. Export Laws and Regulations and agrees to adhere to such laws and regulations with regard to any technical data received under this Agreement.

16. **Waiver of Breach.** No term or provision hereof shall be deemed waived and no breach excused unless such waiver or consent shall be in writing and signed by the party claimed to have waived or consented.

17. **Notices.** Any notice or other communication pursuant to this Agreement shall be in writing and shall be deemed to have been fully given or made when personally delivered by registered or certified mail, postage prepaid, to the following address or such other addresses as the parties may provide in writing to the other from time to time:

If to Licensee:

____

____

____

Attention:__________________

If to Licensor:

____

____

____

Attention:__________________

18. **Amendments.** This Agreement and terms and conditions contained herein may be amended only in writing by an authorized executive officer of each respective party to this Agreement.

19. **Background, Enumerations, and Headings.** The "Background," enumerations, and headings contained in this Agreement are for convenience of reference only and are not intended to have any substantive significance in interpreting this Agreement.

20. **Publicity.** No release shall be made to the news media or to the general public relating to this Agreement without the prior written approval of an authorized executive officer for the other party.

21. **Assignment.** Licensee shall not assign this Agreement whether by operation of law or otherwise, or any interest therein, without the prior written consent of an authorized executive officer of Licensor and any attempt to make such an assignment in violation of this Section shall be void.

22. **Survival.** The parties recognize and agree that their obligations under Sections 2, 3, 6, 10, 11, 14, 17, and 22 of this Agreement survive the cancellation, termination, or expiration of this Agreement.

23. **Entire Agreement.** This Agreement and the Exhibits attached hereto shall constitute the entire agreement between the parties hereto and supersede all existing contracts or agreements, written or oral, between the parties hereto relating to the subject matter hereto.

IN WITNESS WHEREOF, the parties have executed this Agreement under seal as of the day and year set forth above.

ATTEST:	LICENSEE
____________________	By:__________________ (SEAL)
	LICENSOR
____________________	By:__________________ (SEAL)

EXHIBIT A

Software to be Supplied by Licensor

EXHIBIT B

Proprietary Information Agreement

Demonstration License Agreement

THIS DEMONSTRATION LICENSE AGREEMENT is made this ________ day of ______________, 20___, by and between __________________, a ____________ corporation, having its principal place of business at ____________________________ (hereinafter referred to as "Licensor"), and ______________________________, a ____________ corporation, having its principal place of business at ______________ ___________________________________ (hereinafter referred to as "Licensee").

BACKGROUND

Licensee desires to demonstrate and test Licensor's software (the "Software") on Licensee's hardware. Licensee has requested that Licensor license to Licensee a copy of the Software, as more fully described in Exhibit A, to use in such demonstration. It is Licensee's desire to demonstrate the Software and Licensor's desire to participate in such a demonstration, upon the terms and conditions hereinafter set forth.

IN CONSIDERATION of the mutual covenants set forth herein, and for other good and valuable consideration, the receipt and sufficiency of which are hereby acknowledged, Licensor and Licensee hereby agree as follows:

1. **License.** Subject to the terms of this Agreement, Licensor grants Licensee a limited, non-exclusive, non-assignable, non-transferable, personal, object code license during the term of this Agreement to demonstrate the Software to Licensee's customers. Licensee agrees not to make any modifications, copies, changes, or enhancements to the Software without the express prior written consent of an authorized executive officer of Licensor. The license fee for the use of the Software during the term of this Agreement is $10.00 payable upon execution of this Agreement.

The Software shall be kept and used in conformance with the intended purposes and application hereunder to which both parties have agreed. Licensee agrees to keep Licensor informed at all times as to the location of the Software. Licensee agrees to provide a site, all third party software, and all other requirements necessary to operate the Software in conformance with Licensor's standard requirements.

2. **Delivery.** Delivery of the Software will be made by Licensor and Licensee shall pay all shipping, insurance and freight charges as well as all other costs incurred by Licensor in shipping the Software. Risk of loss or damage to the Software shall be assumed by Licensee upon delivery of the Software by Licensor to the common carrier. During the period of time that the Software is in the possession of Licensee, Licensee shall take good care of the Software and Licensee shall be solely responsible for any and all damages to the Software.

3. **Licensee Responsibilities.** Licensee shall pay all installation and operation costs incurred by Licensee in utilizing the Software. Licensee shall pay $_______________ per day per person for each Licensor employee or agent required to install, operate and maintain the Software as well as all reasonable actual out-of-pocket and travel expenses incurred by Licensor's employees or agents. Licensee shall maintain in effect at all times during the term hereof insurance (including, without limitation, workman's compensation, public liability, product liability, property damage and automobile liability insurance) against all losses, claims, demands, proceedings, damages, costs, charges and expense for injuries or damage to any person or property arising out of or in connection with this Agreement which are the result of the fault or negligence of Licensee, its agents and subcontractors.

4. **Title.** Title to the Software shall at all times remain with Licensor and Licensee's interest therein is only that of having temporary possession of the Software. Licensee, subject to the limited license granted in Section 1 of this Agreement, shall utilize the Software solely for the purpose of demonstrating the Software to its customers. Licensee shall provide and pay for all maintenance necessary to maintain the Software during the term of this Agreement.

5. **Payment.** Licensor shall bill Licensee on a monthly basis for all costs incurred by Licensor during the previous thirty (30) day period. All invoices shall be paid by Licensee within thirty (30) days of their receipt. All amounts past due over thirty (30) days shall accrue interest from the due date at a rate of eighteen percent (18%) per annum but no more than the maximum permissible under applicable law.

6. **Proprietary Information.** Both Licensor and Licensee acknowledge and agree to be bound by the terms and conditions of a certain Proprietary Information Agreement by and between the parties hereto dated ___________________, 20__. Upon demand by Licensor, Licensee shall immediately return all of Licensor's confidential information to Licensor. Furthermore, Licensee agrees to have all of its customers to whom it demonstrates the Software execute a non-disclosure agreement substantially in the form of Exhibit B.

7. **Term.** The Agreement shall begin ___________________, 20__ and continue for ______________________ (______) days until ______________________, 20__, unless otherwise terminated as provided herein. Notwithstanding the previous sentence, either party may terminate this Agreement upon seven (7) days' prior written notice to the other party.

8. **Termination.**

(a) *Default* - Either party has the right to terminate this Agreement if the other party breaches or is in default of any obligation hereunder which default is incapable of cure or which, being capable of cure, has not been cured within thirty (30) calendar days after written receipt of notice of such default (or such additional cure period as the non-defaulting party may authorize). Notwithstanding the previous sentence, if Licensee breaches Sections 1, 4 or 6 of this Agreement, Licensor may immediately terminate this Agreement without prior notice.

(b) *Acts of Insolvency* - Either party may terminate this Agreement by written notice to the other and may regard the other party as in default of this Agreement, if the other party becomes insolvent, makes a general assignment for the benefit of creditors, files a voluntary petition of bankruptcy, suffers or permits the appointment of a receiver for its business or assets, or becomes subject to any proceedings under any bankruptcy or insolvency law, whether domestic or foreign, or has wound up or liquidated, voluntarily or otherwise. In the event that any of the above events occurs, that party shall immediately notify the other party of its occurrence.

(c) *Force Majeure Event* - In the event that either party is unable to perform any of its obligations under this Agreement or to enjoy any of its benefits because of natural disaster, actions or decrees of government bodies or communication line failure not the fault of the affected party (hereafter referred to as "Force Majeure Event") the party who has been so affected shall immediately give notice to the other party and shall do everything possible to resume performance. Upon receipt of such notice, all obligations under this Agreement shall be immediately suspended until such "Force Majeure" is resolved.

(d) *Return of Properties* - Upon the termination of this Agreement by either party, or its expiration, each party forthwith shall immediately return to the other all papers, materials and other properties of the other held by it in connection with the performance of this Agreement.

9. **Limitation of Liability.** ALL SOFTWARE PROVIDED "AS IS" WITHOUT WARRANTY OF ANY KIND. LICENSOR MAKES NO EXPRESS OR IMPLIED REPRESENTATIONS OR WARRANTIES WITH RESPECT TO THE SOFTWARE, SOFTWARE PRODUCTS OR SERVICES TO BE PROVIDED HEREUNDER OR THEIR CONDITION, MERCHANTABILITY, FITNESS FOR ANY PARTICULAR PURPOSE OR USE BY LICENSEE. LICENSOR SHALL NOT BE LIABLE FOR ANY (I) SPECIAL, INDIRECT, INCIDENTAL, PUNITIVE, OR CONSEQUENTIAL DAMAGES, INCLUDING LOSS OF PROFITS, ARISING FROM OR RELATED TO THE OPERATION OR USE OF THE SOFTWARE AND SOFTWARE PRODUCTS INCLUDING BUT NOT LIMITED TO DAMAGES ARISING FROM LOSS OF DATA OR PROGRAMMING, LOSS OF REVENUE OR PROFITS, FAILURE TO REALIZE SAVINGS OR OTHER BENEFITS, DAMAGE TO EQUIPMENT, AND CLAIMS AGAINST LICENSEE BY ANY THIRD PERSON, EVEN IF LICENSOR HAS BEEN ADVISED OF THE POSSIBILITY OF SUCH DAMAGES; (II) DAMAGES (REGARDLESS OF THEIR NATURE) FOR ANY DELAY OR FAILURE BY LICENSOR TO PERFORM ITS OBLIGATIONS UNDER THIS AGREEMENT DUE TO ANY CAUSE BEYOND ITS REASONABLE CONTROL; OR (III) CLAIMS MADE A SUBJECT OF LEGAL PROCEEDING AGAINST LICENSOR MORE THAN TWO YEARS AFTER ANY SUCH CAUSE OF ACTION FIRST AROSE. NOTWITHSTANDING ANY OTHER PROVISION OF THIS AGREEMENT, LICENSOR'S TOTAL LIABILITIES HEREUNDER SHALL NOT BE GREATER THAN THE AMOUNTS ACTUALLY RECEIVED BY LICENSOR FROM LICENSEE PURSUANT TO THE TERMS OF THIS AGREEMENT.

10. **Publicity.** No release shall be made to the news media or to the general public relating to this Agreement without the prior written approval of an authorized executive officer for the other party.

11. **Assignment.** Licensee shall not assign this Agreement whether by operation of law or otherwise, or any interest therein, without the prior written consent of an authorized executive officer of Licensor.

12. **Binding Effect.** This Agreement shall be binding upon and inure to the benefit of the parties hereto, their successors and permitted assigns or other legal representatives.

13. **Governing Law.** This Agreement shall be construed in accordance with the laws of the State of _________, excluding its principles of conflicts of laws. The parties hereto agree that any action related to this Agreement shall be venued solely in the Federal District Court for the District of __________, and the parties hereby irrevocably submit to the jurisdiction and venue of said court to resolve any dispute arising hereunder or relating hereto.

14. **Export Regulations.** Licensee acknowledges its obligations to control access to technical data under the U.S. Export Laws and Regulations and agrees to adhere to such laws and regulations with regard to any technical data received under this Agreement.

15. **Waiver of Breach.** No term or provision hereof shall be deemed waived and no breach excused unless such waiver or consent shall be in writing and signed by the party claimed to have waived or consented.

16. **Notices.** Any notice or other communication pursuant to this Agreement shall be in writing and shall be deemed to have been fully given or made when personally delivered by registered or certified mail, postage prepaid, to the following address or such other addresses as the parties may provide in writing to the other from time to time:

If to Licensee:

If to Licensor: with a copy to:

17. **Amendments.** This Agreement and terms and conditions contained herein may be amended only in writing by an authorized executive officer of each respective party to this Agreement.

18. **Background, Enumerations and Headings.** The "Background", enumerations and headings contained in this Agreement are for convenience of reference only and are not intended to have any substantive significance in interpreting this Agreement.

19. **Entire Agreement.** This Agreement and the Exhibits attached hereto shall constitute the entire agreement between the parties hereto and supersede all existing contracts or agreements, written or oral, between the parties hereto.

IN WITNESS WHEREOF, the parties have executed this Agreement under seal as of the day and year set forth above.

ATTEST:	LICENSEE
______________________	By:______________________ (SEAL)
ATTEST:	LICENSOR
______________________	By:______________________ (SEAL)

EXHIBIT A

Software to be Supplied by Licensor

EXHIBIT B

Proprietary Information Agreement

Software License and Support Agreement (Seat License with Informal Tone)

THIS SOFTWARE LICENSE AND SUPPORT AGREEMENT is between ___________, a _____________ corporation located at _________________________ ("Licensor"), and ____________________________, with an office at _______________ ("you" or the "client"). Intending to be legally bound, you and Licensor agree to the terms and conditions stated in this Agreement, including its Schedules and any exhibits, addenda, appendices or amendments (collectively, the "Agreement").

LICENSED PROGRAMS AND MODULES:

1. **[PRODUCT NAME]®**

PERMITTED USERS FOR THE PROGRAMS/MODULES ABOVE:

____ Administrative Users
____ Full Time Users
____ Occasional Users
1 Host Computer

SCOPE OF LICENSE: The license granted hereunder is for the limited use of the Programs and Materials including for configuring, system testing, and training purposes for Customer's internal use in a non-production environment and to assist its clients in such non-production environment.

LICENSE FEE: The License Fee shall be $___________ for the licensed Program(s) listed above.

SUPPORT FEES: There shall be no support or maintenance fees for the Programs, however, in the event you request support in accordance with Section 3.0 herein, such shall be billable at Licensor's then current rates.

YOUR SHIP TO ADDRESS

Ship to Name:
Address:
E-mail:
Telephone Number:

The parties agree to the terms and conditions of this Software License and Support Agreement as of the later date written below "(Effective Date").

LICENSOR	**LICENSEE**
By: ____________________	By: ____________________
Date: ____________________	Date: ____________________

TERMS AND CONDITIONS

PART I. SOFTWARE LICENSE TERMS

Capitalized terms are defined in Section 13.

1.0 **LICENSE AND PROGRAM USE**

1.1 Licensor grants you a non-exclusive, royalty-bearing license to install and use the *Program(s)* in object code form and to the *Materials*, as described on the initial pages of this Agreement.

1.2 You may:

A. Install the Programs on the number of *Host Computers* specified on the initial pages of this Agreement to process information internally for your business.

B. Use the Programs subject to the limitations on the number of users, computers, servers, sites, business units, websites or networks specified on the initial pages of this Agreement.

C. Make an appropriate number of backup copies of the Program to protect against malfunction or damage to your computer systems or the media on which the Programs are stored. Install on an appropriate number of backup computers for purposes of backup systems in case of operational problems with primary computers.

D. Make and install an appropriate number of copies of the Program and Materials for internal training and testing purposes.

If you desire to use any Program or Materials for purposes that exceed the restrictions set forth in this Agreement, then an additional license will be required.

1.3 You may not:

A. License, sell or lease the Programs or Materials to, or permit the use of the Programs by or for the primary benefit of, any third party.

B. Modify the Programs or any part of them.

C. Reverse engineer, decompile or disassemble the Programs under any circumstances.

D. Copy any part of the Programs or Materials unless this Agreement permits it.

E. Remove or destroy any proprietary markings or legends, including copyright and trademark notices, appearing on or contained within any Program or Materials.

1.4 Licensor and its Third-Party Software Providers (if any) retain all right, title and interest in the Programs and Materials (including copies made by you), except for those rights expressly granted to you under this Agreement. You acknowledge that Licensor, its Third-Party Software Providers (if any), and their successors and assigns own all proprietary rights in the Program and Materials, including copyrights and valuable trade secrets.

1.5 If requested by Licensor, you will submit an annual certification, signed by an officer or authorized representative, specifying the number of users and number and location of all copies of the Programs that you have. Licensor may also, once annually, upon reasonable notice and during regular business hours, audit compliance with the license restrictions.

2.0 **SERVICES.** No training, implementation or on-site service is included under this Agreement. You are responsible for the installation of the Programs unless you have agreed separately to purchase installation or other professional services from Licensor.

PART II. SUPPORT AND MAINTENANCE TERMS

3.0 **SUPPORT.** During the term of this Agreement, Licensor may, in its discretion, provide you with the following Software Support:

Telephone, web and e-mail consultation services, for up to one Support Environment (hereinafter defined) including problem solving, bug reporting, documentation clarification and technical guidance for the Program at the latest "x.0" revision level (or revision level immediately preceding the most recent revision level for 180 days after its release). "Support Environment" includes Program instances at client's site location(s). Telephone and e-mail consultations will be available during the hours of 8:00 a.m. to 8:00 p.m. Eastern Time, Monday through Friday, exclusive of Licensor holidays, and pager support for *Critical Errors* will be available at all other times. Web support will be available 24x7.

4.0 **TERMS OF PERFORMANCE OF SOFTWARE SUPPORT SERVICES.** In Licensor's discretion, Enhancements (defined below) and related documentation made generally available at no additional charge to all licensees of Licensor who have purchased support and maintenance may also be provided to you at no charge. "Enhancements" are new releases and versions, error corrections, minor updates and modifications of the Program(s).

PART III. PAYMENT AND OTHER GENERAL TERMS

5.0 **FEES AND INVOICES.**

5.1 The license fee for additional users will be billed at the then current rate, unless a different rate is contained in this Agreement. You must notify Licensor no later than thirty (30) days after the number of users exceeds the contracted number. The license fee for users added will be due and payable within 30 days after the number of users exceeds the contracted number.

5.2 All invoices are due and payable upon receipt in U.S. dollars. Late payment charges will be imposed at the rate of 1.5% per month, including any fees overdue for an increase in the number of users.

5.3 Software Support Fees for any additional users will be 18% of the user fee paid and will be prorated for any partial year from the date on which the number of users exceeded the contracted number.

5.4 All fees and charges listed on the initial pages of this Agreement do not include sales, use, value-added and similar taxes, which are your responsibility.

6.0 **TERM**

6.1 The term of the license set forth in Part I and the term of this Agreement shall be for one (1) year from the date of execution and can only be terminated as specifically set forth herein.

7.0 **TERMINATION**

7.1 This Agreement may be terminated as set forth in this Section 7 (or Section 9 below). In addition, any license to a particular Program licensed under this Agreement may be terminated as set forth in this Section 7 or in Section 9.

7.2 If either party defaults in the performance of any material obligations under this Agreement, and such default is not corrected within ten (10) days after receipt of written notification of the default from the non-defaulting party, then the non-defaulting party may terminate this Agreement (or, if applicable, individual Program license(s)) including the license granted in Part I immediately upon delivery of the written notice of termination to the defaulting party. Nonpayment of any Support Fee shall not constitute a material default with regard to the license granted in Part I.

7.3 Licensor may terminate this Agreement and any license granted under Part I: (a) immediately if you materially violate Section 1 or 11 of this Agreement or (b) upon 30 days' notice to you for any reason or without reason, in Licensor's discretion. In addition, and not withstanding anything to the contrary herein, this Agreement shall automatically terminate immediately upon termination of the Joint Marketing Agreement between the parties, entered into on or about the same date as this Agreement.

7.4 If you are obligated to pay any future fees under this Agreement, then this Agreement and license granted under Part I shall terminate, immediately and without notice, if you: (a) file in any court pursuant to any statute of the United States or any individual state, a petition in insolvency or for the appointment of a receiver or trustee of you or of your assets; (b) are served with an involuntary petition against you, filed in any insolvency proceeding, and such petition shall not be dismissed within 60 days after the filing thereof; (c) propose or become a party to any dissolution or liquidation; or (d) make an assignment for the benefit of creditors.

7.5 Within one month after the date of termination of this Agreement and/or license granted under Part I, you will return to Licensor or destroy (at Licensor's option) the original and all copies, in whole or in part as then remaining, in any form, of all Programs and Materials that are the subject of such termination, and an executive of your company will certify to the foregoing in writing delivered to Licensor.

7.6 You will pay all charges required under this Agreement incurred prior to the date of termination.

8.0 **ASSIGNMENT**

8.1 Without the prior written consent of Licensor, your rights to any Programs and Materials under this Agreement may not be assigned, sublicensed, or otherwise transferred, voluntarily or otherwise, by you, except to your affiliates.

8.2 Without your prior written consent, Licensor's obligations under this Agreement may not be assigned or otherwise transferred, voluntarily or otherwise, except in connection with the sale of its business by merger, stock sale or transfer of a substantial portion of its assets.

9.0 **WARRANTY AND INDEMNITY**

9.1 Licensor warrants that the Program, when used within the scope of this Agreement, does not infringe any United States patent, copyright or trade secret. Licensor will defend at its expense any action brought against you to the extent based on a claim that the Program, when used within the scope of this Agreement, infringes a U.S. patent, copyright or trade secret. Licensor will pay any costs and damages finally awarded against you in such action that are attributable to such claim, provided that you promptly notify Licensor in writing of the claim, allow Licensor to control the defense, provide Licensor with the information and assistance necessary for the defense and/or settlement of the claim, and do not agree to any settlement without Licensor's prior written consent. Should the Program become, or in Licensor's opinion be likely to become, the subject of any claim of infringement, Licensor may at its option (i) procure for you the right to continue using the Program, (ii) replace or modify the Program so as to make it non-infringing, or, if (i) and (ii) are not commercially reasonable, (iii) terminate the license granted hereunder and refund the amounts paid for such license. Licensor will have no liability for any claim of infringement based upon (i) use of other than the latest unmodified release of the Program available to you if such infringement would have been avoided by the use of such release and you were notified that use of the release would avoid such infringement, (ii) use or combination of the Programs with other programs or data if such infringement would not have occurred without such use or combination except where such use or combination is typical for the Programs or Materials, or (iii) use of the Programs after receiving notice from a third party or Licensor that the Programs infringe a patent, copyright or trade secret right of a third party unless prompt written notice thereof is given to Licensor. The forgoing states the exclusive remedy of you and Licensor's entire liability with respect to infringement of patents, copyrights, trade secrets or other proprietary rights.

10.0 **LIMITATIONS**

10.1 **THE PROGRAMS ARE LICENSED TO YOU "AS IS."** OTHER THAN THE WARRANTIES EXPRESSLY STATED IN THIS AGREEMENT, LICENSOR NEITHER MAKES NOR GRANTS ANY WARRANTIES, REPRESENTATIONS OR CONDITIONS, EXPRESS OR IMPLIED. LICENSOR EXPRESSLY EXCLUDES ALL IMPLIED WARRANTIES, REPRESENTATIONS AND CONDITIONS, INCLUDING SPECIFICALLY ANY AND ALL IMPLIED WARRANTIES, REPRESENTATIONS OF MERCHANTABILITY, MERCHANTABLE QUALITY, OR FITNESS FOR ANY PURPOSE, PARTICULAR, SPECIFIC OR OTHERWISE.

10.2 EXCEPT FOR ANY MATERIAL VIOLATION OF SECTION 11, YOUR SOLE AND EXCLUSIVE REMEDY FOR ANY DAMAGE OR LOSS IN ANY WAY CONNECTED WITH THE PROGRAM, THIS AGREEMENT, SOFTWARE SUPPORT OR ANY OTHER MATERIAL, INFORMATION OR SERVICES FURNISHED BY LICENSOR HEREUNDER, WHETHER OR NOT CAUSED BY LICENSOR'S BREACH OF WARRANTY, NEGLIGENCE OR ANY BREACH OF ANY OTHER DUTY, SHALL BE, AT LICENSOR'S OPTION, REPLACEMENT OF THE LICENSED PROGRAM, MATERIALS OR ENHANCEMENTS, REPERFORMANCE OF THE SOFTWARE SUPPORT OR SERVICES, OR RETURN OR CREDIT OF THE APPROPRIATE PORTION OF ANY AMOUNTS RECEIVED BY LICENSOR FROM YOU. EXCEPT FOR LICENSOR'S INDEMNITY OBLIGATIONS IN SECTION 9.2, IN NO EVENT SHALL EITHER PARTY'S LIABILITY EXCEED THE AMOUNTS RECEIVED BY LICENSOR FOR THE PROGRAM AND MATERIALS OR FOR SOFTWARE SUPPORT UNDER THIS AGREEMENT DURING THE TWELVE (12) MONTH PERIOD IMMEDIATELY PRECEDING YOUR CLAIM FOR RECOVERY, EVEN IF LICENSOR IS ADVISED OF THE POSSIBILITY OF SUCH DAMAGES. EXCEPT FOR INSTANCES OF INTENTIONAL VIOLATION OF THE OTHER PARTY'S CONFIDENTIALITY OR INTELLECTUAL PROPERTY RIGHTS, NEITHER PARTY SHALL BE LIABLE FOR ANY SPECIAL, INDIRECT, PUNITIVE OR CONSEQUENTIAL DAMAGES HEREUNDER, INCLUDING, BUT NOT LIMITED TO, LOSS OF USE OR THE LOSS OF DATA OR INFORMATION OF ANY KIND, HOWEVER CAUSED, OR FAILURE OF THE PROGRAM TO WORK OR PERFORM IN ANY WAY, OR ANY LIABILITY TO END-USERS OR TO THIRD PARTIES (EXCEPT AS SET FORTH IN SECTION 9.2).

11.0 **CONFIDENTIALITY.** Each party may disclose to the other party information that it designates as confidential or which should be reasonably understood to be confidential under the circumstances ("Confidential Information"). Each party agrees to hold such Confidential Information of the other party in confidence and to protect it with at least the same degree of care with which it protects its own similar confidential information, which in no event shall be less than reasonable care. Licensor's Confidential Information includes, without limitation, its technology, processes, specifications, developments and software programs, whether or not designated as Confidential Information. In addition, any Third Party Software shall be included as Confidential Information, whether or not designated as Confidential Information. Nothing in this Agreement shall prohibit or limit either party's use of information (including, but not limited to, ideas, concepts, know-how, techniques, and methodologies) (i) previously known to it without an obligation of confidence, (ii) independently developed by or for it, (iii) acquired by it from a third party which is not, to its knowledge, under an obligation of confidence with respect to such information, or (iv) which is or becomes publicly available through no breach of this Agreement. This Section 11 does not negate or supersede the terms of any other confidentiality agreement between you and Licensor. Neither party may disclose the financial terms of this Agreement to any third party other than its counsel or accountants or as required by law.

12.0 **GENERAL**

12.1 This Agreement will be governed by and interpreted in accordance with the laws of the State of _______________, excluding its principles relating to conflicts of laws.

12.2 This Agreement constitutes the entire understanding between the parties with respect to the subject matter of this Agreement and supersedes any and all other prior understandings, statements, warranties, representations and agreements, oral or written, relating to them, except that the terms of any earlier nondisclosure or confidentiality agreement shall remain in full force and effect. You are not relying on any representations about the Program(s) or any future releases of the Program(s) other than the Materials, unless such representations are attached in writing to this Agreement. Any amendment to this Agreement must be in writing and signed by both parties. Printed or standard terms on any order form submitted by you shall not apply if, and to the extent that, they are inconsistent with this Agreement. This Agreement may be executed in multiple counterparts, which may be exchanged via electronic facsimile machines or electronic signature devices.

12.3 Except for actions initiated by either party to this Agreement for injunctive relief to enforce its rights pursuant to Section 11 above or, at the election of the party seeking collection, for the collection of any payments due in the normal course of business, any dispute or claim arising in connection with this Agreement will be adjudicated in the appropriate courts located in the State of New Jersey.

12.4 You will comply with, and at all times cooperate promptly with Licensor to enable Licensor to comply with, the provisions of the United States Export Administration Act, War Powers Act, or other law or Executive Order relating to control of exports or transfer of technology, and the regulations of the United States Departments of State, Commerce and Defense relating to them (in present form or as they may be amended in the future).

12.5 Notices delivered under the terms of this Agreement will be in writing and sent by prepaid certified mail, return receipt requested, or by a nationally recognized overnight courier service to the respective addresses of the parties set forth in the recitals to this Agreement. In the case of Licensor, such notices will be directed to the attention of the General Counsel; and, in your case, such notices will be directed to the attention of the individual named above executing this Agreement on your behalf. Notices will be effective on the date received.

12.6 No term or provision of this Agreement will be deemed waived and no breach of this Agreement will be deemed consented to or excused, unless such waiver, consent or excuse will be expressed in writing and signed by the party claimed to have so waived, consented or excused such term or provision.

12.7 The application to this Agreement of the United Nations Convention on Contracts for the International Sale of Goods is hereby expressly excluded.

12.8 To the extent that terms of the base Agreement conflict with terms of an Exhibit, Addendum or Schedule, the relevant Exhibit, Addendum or Schedule will control with respect to the relevant Program or service.

12.9 After expiration or termination of this Agreement, all provisions relating to payment shall survive until completion of required payments. In addition, all provisions regarding scope of the license granted in Part I, audit, indemnification, warranties, liability and limits thereon, assignment and confidentiality or protection of proprietary rights and trade secrets, shall survive indefinitely.

13.0 **DEFINITIONS.** For purposes of this Agreement, the following terms shall be defined as follows:

"Administrative User" each Administrative User has full end user access to the Program. The Administrative User has the rights of all other User types as well as the ability to define security parameters, including granting and denying user access, defining user roles, configuring business logic, defining workflows for each Program and performing maintenance on the Program.

"Critical Error" means an Error which causes the Program production system to go down or prevents you from working in the system.

"Error" means a failure of the Programs to conform to the specifications therefor as set forth in the Materials resulting in the inability to use or a considerable restriction in use of the Programs.

"Error Correction" means either a software modification or addition that, when made or added to the Programs, corrects the Error, or a procedure or routine that, when observed in the regular operation of the Program, eliminates the practical adverse effect of the Error on End User.

"Full Time User" each Full Time User has the rights of an Occasional User as well as the ability to configure limited ad hoc business logic and workflows, full search capabilities and the ability to manage, create, view, approve, reject, comment, modify and edit (including deleting any data) data in the Program's application.

"High Error" means an Error which represents a failure of expected functionality that causes serious degradation to your use of the Program production system.

"Host Computer" means a single production database server.

"Maintenance Release" means a subsequent version of a Program that includes Error Corrections and/or Upgrades.

"Materials" means the user guide and technical guide related to the Programs, and any related support material specified in a Schedule.

"Occasional User" Each Occasional User has the ability to search, view (read only access), approve, reject and comment on data and receive email alerts regarding any such actions required under a workflow related to data within the Program. In addition, an Occasional User has the ability to generate pre-approved templates and route them for approval and comment.

A ***"Production User"*** is each person assigned a unique log in to access the Programs who has update privileges (that is, the ability to add, change, or delete data base information on any Base Table) for any module.

"Programs" means all of the programs and modules listed on the initial pages of this Agreement, as they may be upgraded, enhanced, and/or modified by Licensor, in machine-readable, object code form only. The Programs include any *Third-Party Software* products and related documentation listed on the initial pages of this Agreement or in a Schedule.

"Third-Party Software" means software of companies other than Licensor that Licensor has licensed to you under this Agreement.

"Third-Party Software Provider" means a company, other than Licensor, that has licensed Third Party Software to Licensor, which Licensor sublicenses to you under this Agreement.

"Users" All Users under this Agreement are named users assigned a unique login to access the Program, and they do not have concurrent user rights to use the Program.

Sublicense Agreement (Annotated)

(Per Core License Fee)
Sublicensor Oriented

THIS SUBLICENSE AGREEMENT is dated as of _________, 20__, by and between ___________________________, a _______________corporation with its principal offices at ___________________________ ("Sublicensee"), and ___________________, a __________ corporation with its principal offices at ___________________________ ("Sublicensor").

BACKGROUND

_______________ ("Company") has granted Sublicensor a world-wide license, with the right to sublicense to Company's proprietary __________________ software. Sublicensee desires to acquire a sub-license from Sublicensor to use the Software. Sublicensor is willing to grant the Sublicensee a non-exclusive, non-transferable **world-wide** license to use the Software as set forth in this Agreement.

NOW THEREFORE, in consideration of the mutual covenants and promises set forth herein the parties hereto agree as follows;

1. **Definitions.**

1.1 ***"Documentation"*** means all user and administrator manuals, operating instructions, installation guides, help files, and other printed, electronic, and online material generally made available to Sublicensor's customers with respect to the Software, and all other printed, electronic, or online materials provided or made available to Sublicensor, that describe the features, functions, or operation of the Software.

1.2 ***"Processor"***[1] means as all processors where the Software is installed and/or running.

1.3 ***"Software"*** means Company's proprietary _______________ software as more fully described in Exhibit A.

1.4 ***"Technical Support"*** means the technical support offered by Company under a separate agreement.

---

1. Each sublicense must be structured to mirror the terms of the primary license. For example, is the pricing for the sublicense based on an entity license, site license, seat license or CPU/core license? Based on the answer, at a minimum Sections 1.2, 2.1 and 3 of this sublicense will have to be modified.

1.5 ***"Use"***[2] is the right of Sublicensee: (i) to copy, including without limitation, to transmit, any portion of the Software onto CPUs, networks, desktops, servers, processors, storage units or media; (ii) to transfer any portion of any Software for use on a network between desktops, CPUs, servers, and other units in the network; and (iii) to use the Software in accordance with the Documentation and this Agreement.

2. **License.**

2.1 Subject to the terms of this Agreement, Sublicensor grants Sublicensee a perpetual,[3] non-exclusive, non-transferable, worldwide, royalty bearing object code license[4], without the right of further sublicense, to Use the Software. Software licensed hereunder may be accessed by Sublicensee's internal users (including agents and contractors) and by Sublicensee's third party users.

2.2 The Software is provided to Sublicensor pursuant to a license agreement with Company, its subsidiaries and its third-party suppliers. Sublicensee understands that Company may, without consultation with or consent from Sublicensor, terminate this Agreement if and when Sublicensor violates the terms of the license agreement between Sublicensor and Company. In such event, the license granted to Sublicensee under this Agreement shall immediately terminate and be transferred to Company.

2.3 Sublicensee agrees that it may install, use, and execute the Software only on Sublicensee's equipment and hardware. Sublicensee may make one (1) copy of the Software for nonproduction backup purposes only, provided that it retains or affixes the equivalent of Company's proprietary legend and copyrights to the copy and in no event shall Sublicensee copy the Software onto any public or distributed network. Sublicensee may not decompile, decrypt, reverse engineer, disassemble, or otherwise translate the Software. Sublicensee is prohibited from making modifications, adaptations or derivative works of the Software or permitting third parties to do so.

2.4 Title in and ownership in the Software and Documentation, and all enhancements and modifications thereto thereof, shall remain at all times vested in Company.

3. **License Fees.**[5]

3.1 Upon execution of this Agreement, Sublicensee shall promptly pay Sublicensor an initial non-refundable license fee of $ ______ for _____ cores.[6]

3.2 The number of required licenses shall be determined by multiplying the total number of cores of each Processor by a core Processor licensing factor specified on the Company Processor Core Factor Table, which can be accessed at http://xxxxx.com/contracts. All cores on all multi-core chips for the Software are to be aggregated before multiplying by the appropriate core processor licensing factor, and all fractions

2. The definition of "Use" will depend on the purpose for which the software will be utilized and the means by which the software will be distributed to the users.

3. The length of the license will dictate the term set forth in section 9.1 (Term).

4. The license grant should be a sub-set of the license grant set forth in the master license agreement.

5. Make sure to review the payment terms with the sublicensor's finance department to ensure there are no issues relating to revenue recognition.

6. Consistent with the prior footnote, pricing may be structured in many ways including on an entity basis, site basis, per user basis, CPU/core basis, etc.

of a number are to be rounded up to the next whole number. When licensing the Software, a Processor is counted equivalent to an occupied socket; however, in the case of multi-chip modules, each chip in the multi-chip module is counted as one occupied socket.

3.3 Within thirty (30) days following the end of each calendar quarter, Sublicensee will calculate any additional license fees due Sublicensor and shall wire transfer, in United States Dollars, the full amount of license fees due for any additional Processors added during such quarter to an account specified by Sublicensor. Simultaneously with paying such license fees, Sublicensee shall submit a report, whether or not any license fees are due, in a form reasonably acceptable to Sublicensor, which shall be certified by an authorized representative of Sublicensee and which shall state, by CPU ID number, the Software licensed by Sublicensee, the number of Processors included in each such CPU and the license fees due to Sublicensor thereon. The proper format of this report is attached hereto as Exhibit B.

3.4 There shall be added to the charges provided for in this Agreement amounts equal to any taxes, whether federal, state, or local, however designated, that may be validly levied or based upon this Agreement or upon the Software and services furnished hereunder, excluding, however, taxes based on or measured by Sublicensor's net income, and any taxes or amounts in lieu thereof paid or payable by Sublicensor in respect of the foregoing. Taxes payable by Sublicensee shall be billed as separate items on Sublicensor's invoices and shall not be included in Sublicensor's prices. Sublicensee shall have the right to have Sublicensor contest with the imposing jurisdiction, at Sublicensee's expense, any such taxes that Sublicensee deems are improperly levied.

3.5 Sublicensee agrees that any payments required under the terms of this Agreement which are not paid when due will accrue interest at the lesser of: (i) the prime lending rate established by Citibank, New York plus 5%, or (ii) the highest rate permitted by applicable law; such interest commencing to accrue thirty (30) days after the date such monies are due Sublicensor. The right to collect interest on such late payments shall be in addition to any other rights that Sublicensor may have.

4. **Audit Rights and Obligations.**

4.1 Sublicensor shall have the right, upon at least five (5) days written notice, to inspect Sublicensee's books and records and all other documents and material in the possession of or under the control of Sublicensee with respect to the subject matter of this Agreement, at the place where such records are normally retained by Sublicensee, which place shall be within the continental United States. Sublicensor shall have free and full access thereto for such purposes and shall be permitted to make copies thereof and extracts there from.

4.2 In the event that such inspection reveals a discrepancy between the license fee owed Sublicensor and that which was actually paid, Sublicensee shall pay such discrepancy, plus interest, as set forth above. In the event that such discrepancy is in excess of five percent (5%) over a period of at least two quarters [**as determined by**

an independent certified public accountant working on a non-contingency basis[7]]. Sublicensee shall also reimburse Sublicensor for the cost of such inspection including any accountants' or attorneys' fees incurred in connection therewith.

4.3 All books and records relative to Sublicensee's obligations hereunder shall be maintained and kept accessible and available to Sublicensor for inspection, within the Continental United States, for at least two (2) years after termination of this Agreement. In addition Sublicensee shall retain for a reasonable period of time such records as may be necessary in order to enable Sublicensee and Sublicensor to defend lawsuits which may be instituted by third parties.

4.4 In the event that an investigation of Sublicensee's books and records is made, certain confidential and proprietary business information of Sublicensee may necessarily be made available to the person or persons conducting such investigation. It is agreed that such confidential and proprietary business information shall be retained in confidence by Sublicensor and shall not be used by Sublicensor or disclosed to any third party without the prior express written permission of Sublicensee unless required by law. It is understood and agreed, however, that such information may be used in any proceeding based on Sublicensee's alleged failure to pay its license fee obligation(s). Sublicensor shall have the right to inspect any record only once, and shall not conduct more than one audit per year.

5. **Warranty[8], Limitation of Liability.[9]**

5.1 Sublicensor warrants to Sublicensee that Sublicensor has the right to grant to Sublicensee the sublicense granted hereunder.

5.2 [**Flow down those warranties from the master license agreement that are appropriate.**]

5.3 Sublicensor does not warrant that the operation of the Software will be uninterrupted or error free.

5.4 SUBLICENSOR SHALL NOT BE LIABLE FOR ANY (A) SPECIAL, INDIRECT, INCIDENTAL, PUNITIVE, OR CONSEQUENTIAL DAMAGES, INCLUDING LOSS OF PROFITS, ARISING FROM OR RELATED TO A BREACH OF THIS AGREEMENT OR THE OPERATION OR USE OF THE SOFTWARE AND SERVICES INCLUDING SUCH DAMAGES, WITHOUT LIMITATION, AS DAMAGES ARISING FROM LOSS OF DATA OR PROGRAMMING, LOSS OF REVENUE OR PROFITS, FAILURE TO REALIZE SAVINGS OR OTHER BENEFITS, DAMAGE TO EQUIPMENT, AND CLAIMS AGAINST SUBLICENSEE BY ANY THIRD PERSON, EVEN IF SUBLICENSOR HAS BEEN ADVISED OF THE POSSIBILITY OF SUCH DAMAGES; (B) DAMAGES (REGARDLESS OF THEIR NATURE) FOR ANY DELAY OR FAILURE BY SUBLICENSOR TO PERFORM ITS OBLIGATIONS UNDER THIS AGREEMENT DUE TO ANY CAUSE BEYOND SUBLICENSOR'S REASONABLE

7. Some parties seek to exclude accounting firms working on a contingency basis under the belief that they have a financial incentive to find an underpayment.

8. Make sure to review the sublicensor's warranty obligations with the sublicensor's finance department to ensure there are no issues relating to revenue recognition.

9. The limitation of liability should mirror the limitation of liability language set forth in the master license agreement so that the sublicensor is "back to back" with the Company.

CONTROL; OR (C) CLAIMS MADE A SUBJECT OF A LEGAL PROCEEDING AGAINST SUBLICENSOR MORE THAN TWO YEARS AFTER ANY SUCH CAUSE OF ACTION FIRST AROSE.

5.5 NOTWITHSTANDING ANY OTHER PROVISION OF THIS AGREEMENT, SUBLICENSOR 'S LIABILITIES UNDER THIS AGREEMENT, WHETHER UNDER CONTRACT LAW, TORT LAW, WARRANTY OR OTHERWISE SHALL BE LIMITED TO DIRECT DAMAGES NOT TO EXCEED THE AMOUNTS ACTUALLY RECEIVED BY SUBLICENSOR FROM THE SUBLICENSEE PURSUANT TO THIS AGREEMENT.

6. **Infringement.**[10]

6.1 Sublicensor will defend, at its expense, and will indemnify Sublicensee against any loss, cost, expense or liability arising out of any claim by a third party against Sublicensee asserting that the Software infringes upon or violates any United States patent, copyright, or trade secret or other intellectual property right of any third party. Sublicensor's obligations under this Section shall be contingent on Sublicensee's providing to Sublicensor (i) prompt written notice of such claim, (ii) sole control and authority over the defense and settlement thereof, and (iii) reasonable information and assistance to settle and/or defend any such claim or action.

6.2 If an injunction or order is obtained against Sublicensee's use of the Software, or if Sublicensor determines that the Software is likely to become the subject of a claim of infringement or violation of a patent, copyright or trade secret of a third party, Sublicensor shall, in its sole discretion, (a) procure for Sublicensee the right to continue using the Software, or (b) replace or modify the same so that it becomes noninfringing provided such modification or replacement does not materially and adversely affect the specifications for or the use of the Software by Sublicensee, or (c) accept the return of the Software and refund the fees paid hereunder with respect thereto.

6.3 Notwithstanding anything above to the contrary, Sublicensor shall have no liability or obligation to defend and/or indemnify if the alleged infringement or violation is based upon: (a) the combination of the Software with any product or technology not furnished by Sublicensor to the extent such combination causes the infringement or violation; (b) the modification of the Software other than by Sublicensor to the extent such modification causes the infringement or violation; or (c) compliance with Sublicensee's specifications, designs or instructions.

6.4 This Article 6 sets forth Sublicensor's sole liability, and Sublicensee's sole remedy, arising out of any actual or alleged infringement or violation of any third party intellectual property rights in connection with its use of the Software.

6.5 Sublicensee agrees to defend or at its option settle any suit or proceeding brought against Sublicensor and/or Company concerning Sublicensee's use of the Software, except for claims for which Sublicensor is obligated to provide defense and indemnity as provided in Sections 6.1 and 6.2 above. Sublicensee's obligations

10. The infringement language should mirror the infringement language set forth in the master license agreement so that the Sublicensor is "back to back" with the Company.

under this Section shall be contingent on Sublicensor providing to Sublicensee (i) prompt written notice of such claim, (ii) sole control and authority over the defense and settlement thereof, and (iii) reasonable information and assistance to settle and/or defend any such claim or action.

7. **Technical Support.** Sublicensee may acquire Technical Support services for the Software from Company at Company's rates in effect at the time the Technical Support Services Agreement is entered into between the parties.

8. **Confidentiality.** Sublicensee acknowledges that the Software is owned by Company or its suppliers or licensors and is protected by United States copyright laws and international treaty provisions. The Software constitutes the valuable, confidential and proprietary information of Company. Sublicensee shall take all reasonable steps to protect the value and confidentiality of the Software, including without limitation limiting disclosure thereof to employees who have agreed to protect their value and confidentiality and who need access thereto to exercise Sublicensee's rights under this Agreement. In the event either party breaches, or threatens to breach any of the covenants expressed herein, the damages to the non-threatening or non-breaching party may be great and irreparable and difficult to quantify; therefore, the non-threatening or non-breaching party may apply to a court of competent jurisdiction for injunctive or other equitable relief to restrain such breach or threat of breach, without disentitling such party from any other relief in either law or equity.

All information provided by either party to the other under this Agreement shall be kept confidential in conformance with and subject to the terms of a certain Proprietary Information Agreement dated _______________, 20 __ by and between the parties hereto.

9. **Term and Termination.**

9.1 The term[11] of this Agreement shall commence as of the date first set forth above and shall continue until _______________, 20___ unless sooner terminated as provided herein.

9.2 Either party may terminate this Agreement if the other party commits any material breach or default and fails to provide an acceptable remedy of such breach or default within thirty (30) days (in all other cases) after written notice of such breach or default from the non-breaching or non-defaulting party. Without limiting the generality of the foregoing, any failure to meet the obligations of Section 3 shall be considered a material breach of this Agreement.

9.3 The parties recognize and agree that their obligations under Sections 3, 4, 5.4, 5.5, 6, 8, 9.3, 10, 12, 13, 16 and 17 of this Agreement survive the cancellation, termination or expiration of this Agreement and the License granted hereunder.

11. The term of the agreement should tie to the term of the license set forth in Section 2.

10. **Governing Law and Venue**[12]**.** This Agreement and matters connected with its performance shall be governed by, construed, and interpreted in accordance with the laws of the State of ____________, without reference to its conflict of laws provisions. Any suit or proceeding relating to this Agreement shall be brought only in the courts, state and federal, located in ____ County, _____ and the parties hereby consent to the exclusive personal jurisdiction and venue of such courts.

11. **Publicity.** Sublicensee may not use the Company's name in advertisements or any other marketing or publicity activities, nor otherwise disclose the existence or content of this Agreement without the Company's prior written consent.

12. **Third Party Beneficiaries.** Sublicensee understands and agrees that Company shall be considered an intended third party beneficiary with the right to enforce the provisions of this Agreement.

13. **Notices.** All notices required or permitted to be given hereunder shall be in writing and shall be delivered by hand, or dispatched by prepaid air courier or by registered or certified airmail, postage prepaid, addressed as follows:

If to Sublicensor	If to Sublicensee

All notices shall be effective upon receipt.

14. **Assignment.** Neither this Agreement nor any right or obligation hereunder is assignable by Sublicensee, whether in conjunction with a change in ownership, merger, acquisition, the sale or transfer of all, substantially all, or any portion of Sublicensee's business or assets or otherwise, either voluntarily, by operation of law, or otherwise, without the prior written consent of Sublicensor, such consent not to be unreasonably withheld. Any such purported assignment or transfer shall be deemed a breach of this Agreement and shall be null and void.

15. **Relationship of the Parties.** Nothing in this Agreement shall be construed to make the parties partners or joint venturers or to make either party liable for the obligations, acts, omissions or activities of the other.

16. **Severability.** If any provision of this Agreement is held illegal, void or unenforceable, to any extent, in whole or in part, as to any situation or person, the balance shall remain in effect and the provision in question shall remain in effect as to all other persons or situations, as the case may be.

17. **Entire Agreement and Waiver.** This Agreement is intended to be the entire agreement between the parties with respect to matters contained herein, and supersedes all prior or contemporaneous agreements, discussions and negotiations with respect

12. The governing law and venue should be consistent with the master license agreement between the Company and Sublicensor.

to those matters. No waiver of any breach or default shall constitute a waiver of any subsequent breach or default.

IN WITNESS WHEREOF, the parties hereto have signed this Agreement as of the date first above written.

SUBLICENSEE

By: ______________________________

SUBLICENSOR

By: ______________________________

EXHIBIT A

Software Description

EXHIBIT B

Licensee Fee Report

Software Maintenance and Services Agreement

THIS SOFTWARE MAINTENANCE AND SERVICES AGREEMENT is made this ________ day of ________________, 20__ by and between ____________ a ______________________ corporation, with its principal place of business at ________________________________ (hereinafter "Company") and ___________, a ______________ corporation, (hereinafter "Customer"), with offices located at ____.

BACKGROUND

Company has licensed Customer Company's proprietary ___________ software as modified to meet Customer's needs in accordance with the Software License and Services Agreement dated __________________, 20__ by and between Company and Customer (the "Software License Agreement"). Customer desires to have Company maintain and support such software and Company desires to maintain and support such software for Customer under the terms and conditions set forth herein.

IN CONSIDERATION of the foregoing and the mutual covenants set forth herein, and intending to be legally bound, the parties agree as follows:

1. **DEFINITIONS.** The following words shall have the following means when used in this Agreement:

1.1 "Bypass" shall mean a procedure communicated by Company to Customer, which permits Customer to avoid Error(s) by implementing the same when using the Software.

1.2 "Enhancement(s)" shall mean a modification to the Software that alters the functionalities described in the Functional Specifications without materially degrading the functionalities or performance of the Software prescribed by the Functional Specifications.

1.3 "Error(s)" shall mean a failure of the Software to conform to the Functional Specifications.

1.4 "Error Report" shall mean the document to be created by Company, pursuant to Article 3 hereof, each time that Customer reports an Error.

1.5 "Fix(es)" shall mean the document to be created by Company pursuant to this Agreement in order to correct Errors.

1.6 "License(s)" shall mean any license or licenses granted by Company to Customer to use the Software under the Software License Agreement.

1.7 "Object Code" shall mean the binary machine readable version of the Software.

1.8 "Maintenance Services" shall mean the services to be provided under this Agreement.

1.9 "Optional Maintenance Services" means the services that Customer may elect to receive from Company pursuant to the provisions of Article 4 hereof; it is hereby agreed that if Customer elects to receive any Optional Maintenance Services, the said Optional Maintenance Services shall thenceforth be deemed to constitute Maintenance Services.

1.10 "Severity Level" shall mean the level of severity assigned to a reported Error with the Software, in accordance with the Severity Level definitions set forth in Appendix A to this Agreement.

1.11 "Site" shall mean a Customer computer facility located in one specific geographic location.

1.12 "Software" shall mean Company's proprietary _________ software as modified with Customer's specified enhancements, including Bypasses, Fixes, Enhancements, Updates, and Upgrades. The term "Software" includes Software Products.

1.13 "Software Products" shall mean all physical components, other than program codes that are offered by Company, including but not limited to, manuals, documentation, magnetic media, job aids, templates, and other similar devices.

1.14 "Update" shall mean a compendium of Fixes that Company releases to the users of the Software from time to time and which Company shall supply to Customer pursuant to the terms of this Agreement.

1.15 "Upgrades" shall mean a new release or version of the Software constituting a compendium of Enhancements.

Any capitalized terms not defined in this Agreement shall have the meaning set forth in the Software License Agreement.

2. **COMPANY'S OBLIGATIONS**

2.1 In consideration of Customer's performance hereunder, Company shall, in addition to the other obligations imposed on Company hereby, render the Maintenance Services pursuant to Article 3 hereof, and render such Optional Maintenance Services as Customer may elect to purchase pursuant to the provisions of Article 4 hereof.

2.2 All Maintenance Services performed by Company under this Agreement shall be performed by Company in a professional manner in accordance with industry standards. If Company receives notice of defects in the Maintenance Services, Company shall re-perform said Maintenance Services. Company does not warrant that the Maintenance Services or Software will be uninterrupted or error free.

2.3 The parties acknowledge and agree that, notwithstanding anything to the contrary herein contained, Company shall not maintain the Hardware or the Third Party Software.

Optional language:

2.4 In the event Customer allows Maintenance to lapse, it may thereafter renew such support for the affected Software by paying, in addition to the then current annual Maintenance Fee, an amount equal to the aggregate Maintenance Fee that would have been payable for the affected Software during the period of lapse. Company agrees that the Maintenance support will be conducted from the Company location that is geographically closest to the Customer location eligible for such Maintenance support.

3. **MAINTENANCE SERVICES**

3.1 By rendering the Maintenance Services, Company shall correct all Errors, regardless of how such Errors are brought to the attention of Company, in accordance with this Agreement, and, in particular, Appendix A hereto. During the term of this Agreement, Company shall provide the following types of Maintenance Services:

3.1.1 Telephone Support. Company telephone support representative(s) shall be available to receive Customer telephone calls between the hours of 8:30 a.m. and 5:30 p.m., Washington, D.C. time, Monday through Friday, excluding public holidays. Company shall provide Customer with a telephone number that is answered at all other times by an individual who will accept Error Reports. Such telephone support representative(s) shall serve as the Customer's interface with Company and shall ensure that reported Errors are handled in a timely manner as specified in Appendix A hereto. Company shall provide to Customer in writing, the name(s) and telephone number(s) of such telephone support representative(s) within ten (10) days of the later of the execution of this Agreement or the acceptance of the Software by Customer under the Software License Agreement. All Errors shall be investigated and if the Error relates to the Software, or is directly caused by the Software, (a) an Error Report shall be opened, (b) the Error shall be assigned a Severity Level as per the provisions of Exhibit A hereto, and (c) the Error shall be resolved in accordance with the procedures and processes set forth in Appendix A hereto.

3.1.2 Installation Assistance. Company shall provide to Customer telephone assistance for the implementation or installation of Bypasses, Fixes, and Updates between the hours of 8:30 a.m. and 5:30 p.m., Washington, D.C. time, Monday through Friday, excluding public holidays.

3.1.3 Bypasses. Company shall provide to Customer such Bypasses as are necessary to ensure the resolution of Errors that can be resolved by a Bypass.

3.1.4 Fixes. Company shall provide to Customer such Fixes as are necessary to ensure the resolution of Errors that can be resolved by a Fix.

3.1.5 Updates. Company shall, as soon as they are made available, provide to Customer such Updates as it provides to the users for the Software from time to time.

3.1.6 Enhancements. Company shall provide to Customer such Enhancements as it provides to the users for the Software from time to time.

3.1.7 Upgrades. Company shall provide, as soon as they are made available, to Customer such Upgrades as it provides to the users for the Software from time to time.

3.2 Other Software Products. Company shall provide to Customer, at no additional cost, any Software Products relating to the Software made generally available to other Software users without charge. Any Software Products so made available at a given cost to the other Software users shall be offered to Customer at Company's then-existing rates.

3.3 Regular Activity Reports. Upon written request by Customer, Company shall provide: (a) a status report of Error resolution activities; and (b) a status report of all outstanding Error Reports. Such status reports shall contain Company's tracking number, Error description, Error resolution status, and a definitive resolution time frame and release number for all Errors.

3.4 Limitation on Maintenance Services. Notwithstanding any other provisions in this Maintenance and Services Agreement, Company shall provide Maintenance Services only with respect to the two (2) most recent Upgrades of the Software.

3.5 Intellectual Property Rights. Title to all Bypasses, Fixes, Updates, Enhancements, and Upgrades shall remain solely and exclusively with Company. It is hereby acknowledged and agreed that the former shall be deemed to constitute Software for purposes of the application of the Software License Agreement.

4. **OPTIONAL MAINTENANCE SERVICES**

4.1 Customer shall be entitled to purchase from Company the following Optional Maintenance Services at the rates set forth in Appendix B of this Agreement:

4.1.1 Consultant Support. Software Maintenance can be extended to include up to eighty (80) hours per month of on-site or off-site consultant support to assist with the operations and support of the Software. Such consultant shall offer training, support, and consultation to optimize the Software system and the Customer's practices. The consultant will also act as liaison between Customer and Company. All travel and expenses arising from consultant support shall be billed to the Customer at Company's actual cost, provided all such travel and expenses shall be approved by Customer in advance.

4.1.2 Dedicated Telephone Support. Company shall provide the number of any dedicated telephone representatives ordered by Customer. Such dedicated telephone representative(s) shall be available between the hours 8 a.m. and 6 p.m., Washington, D.C. time, Monday through Friday, excluding public holidays. Such dedicated telephone representatives shall, in addition to telephone support services, answer application questions (i.e., how to run reports, etc.) and system questions (i.e., what system precautions should be taken during month end processing, UNIX-related questions, etc.).

4.1.3. Proactive System Checks. Should Customer purchase the services of a dedicated telephone representative, such representative shall perform weekly proactive system checks. The dedicated telephone representative shall check the Software for possible problems (i.e. runaway processes, dbspace, file system space, etc.). If problems are found they shall be reported to the Customer's designated system administrator at the affected Site within two (2) hours.

5. **OUT OF SCOPE PROBLEMS**

5.1 Any time incurred by Company in diagnosing or fixing problems that are not caused by the Software, or are not covered by this Agreement are billable to the Customer at Company's then-existing rates that are initially set forth in Appendix B of this Agreement, with a one-hour minimum per call.

5.2 Any travel and expenses incurred in conjunction with out of scope maintenance and support shall be billed to Customer at Company's actual costs, provided all such travel and expenses shall be approved by Customer in advance.

6. **TERM OF AGREEMENT.** This Agreement shall become effective ______________ and continue for a __________ (__________) year term (the "Initial Term"). Thereafter, it shall continue on a year-to-year basis, until terminated by either party ninety (90) days prior to the anniversary date of this Agreement.

7. **FEES FOR MAINTENANCE AND SERVICES**

7.1 During the Initial Term, Customer shall pay Company for the Maintenance Services set forth in Section 3 an amount calculated as follows: an annual fee equal to 15 percent of the sum of (i) the undiscounted RTU Fee, as set forth in Section ______________ of the Software License Agreement; (ii) the price of the development work as set forth in Section __________ of the Software License Agreement; and (ii) the price of any other enhancements or modifications to the Software undertaken by Company at the written request of Customer, including any change orders received under the Software License Agreement (collectively, the "Agreed Maintenance Fee").

7.2 Company shall charge Customer its then existing rates for all optional services. Such rates are initially set forth in Appendix B of this Agreement.

8. **DESIGNATED CUSTOMER PERSONNEL.** The Customer shall identify by name and location all Customer personnel who may contact the Company representatives as set forth in Sections 3 and 4. The personnel identified shall have authority to authorize an investigation of software problems and have knowledge of the rules of engagement for maintenance and support. The list of authorized Customer contact personnel is set forth in Appendix C of this Agreement, provided that such list may be revised by Customer at any time as long as Company is informed in writing and such list does not exceed a maximum of fifteen (15) Customer contact personnel.

9. **CONFIDENTIALITY.** Information provided by either party to the other under this Agreement shall be kept confidential in conformance with and subject to the terms of the Nondisclosure Agreement dated ___________________, 20__ by and between the parties hereto.

10. **REPRODUCTION OF MANUALS, DOCUMENTATION, AND OBJECT CODE**

10.1 Customer shall have the right, at no additional charge, to reproduce solely for its internal use, all manuals and documentation furnished by Company relating to the Software, regardless of whether such manual or documentation is copyrighted by Company. All copies of manuals or documentation made by Customer shall include any proprietary notice or stamp that has been affixed by Company. Company shall furnish to Customer and at no additional charge to Customer, one (1) hard copy of the relevant documentation sufficient to enable Customer to maintain and operate the Software. All documentation shall be in the English language.

10.2. One (1) copy of the Object Code may be reproduced by Customer, at no additional charge, only for back up or archival purposes. On written request by Company, Customer shall notify Company in writing of its methods and procedures for archiving of Object Code software prior to doing so.

11. **LIMITATION OF LIABILITY AND DISCLAIMER OF WARRANTY**

11.1 In no event shall Company be liable for any special, indirect, incidental, punitive, or consequential damages, including loss of profits arising from or related to the breach of this Agreement, even if Company had been advised of the possibility of such damages.

11.2 NOTWITHSTANDING ANY OTHER PROVISION OF THIS AGREEMENT, IN THE EVENT ANY REMEDY FAILS OF ITS ESSENTIAL PURPOSE, COMPANY'S LIABILITIES UNDER THIS AGREEMENT, WHETHER UNDER CONTRACT LAW, TORT LAW, OR OTHERWISE, SHALL BE LIMITED TO DIRECT DAMAGES NOT TO EXCEED THE AMOUNT ACTUALLY RECEIVED BY COMPANY PURSUANT TO THIS AGREEMENT.

11.3 EXCEPT AS SET FORTH IN SECTION 2.2, COMPANY MAKES NO EXPRESS OR IMPLIED REPRESENTATIONS OR WARRANTIES WITH RESPECT TO THE SOFTWARE OR MAINTENANCE SERVICES OR THEIR CONDITION, MERCHANTABILITY, FITNESS FOR ANY PARTICULAR PURPOSE, OR USE BY CUSTOMER. COMPANY FURNISHES THE WARRANTIES IN SECTION 2.2 IN LIEU OF ALL OTHER WARRANTIES, EXPRESSED OR IMPLIED, INCLUDING THE WARRANTIES OF MERCHANTABILITY AND FITNESS FOR A PARTICULAR PURPOSE.

11.4 No action, regardless of form, arising under this Agreement, may be brought more than one year after the cause of action has arisen, except that an action for nonpayment may be brought within two (2) years after the date of the most recent payment.

12. **INDEPENDENT CONTRACTOR.** All work performed by Company in connection with the Software and/or Maintenance Services described in this Agreement shall be performed by Company as an independent contractor and not as the agent or employee of Customer. All persons furnished by Company shall be for all purposes solely the Company's employees or agents and shall not be deemed to be employees of Customer for any purpose whatsoever. Company shall furnish, employ, and have exclusive control of all persons to be engaged in performing maintenance services under this Agreement and shall prescribe and control the means and methods of performing such maintenance services by providing adequate and proper supervision. Company shall be solely responsible for compliance with all rules, laws, and regulations relating to employment of labor, hours of labor, working conditions, payment of wages, and payment of taxes, such as employment, Social Security, and other payroll taxes including applicable contributions from such persons when required by law.

13. **FORCE MAJEURE.** Neither party shall be responsible for any delay or failure in performance of any part of this Agreement to the extent that such delay or failure is caused by fire, flood, explosion, war, embargo, government requirement, civil, or military authority, act of God, act or omission of carriers, or other similar causes beyond its control. If any such an event of force majeure occurs and such event continues for ninety (90) days or more, the party delayed or unable to perform shall give immediate notice to the other party, and the party affected by the other's delay or inability to perform may elect at its sole discretion to: (a) terminate this Agreement or the affected order solely upon mutual agreement of the parties; (b) suspend such order for the duration of the condition and obtain or sell elsewhere Software, Software Products, or Maintenance Services comparable to the Software, Software Products, or Maintenance Services to have been obtained under the order; or (c) resume performance of such order once the condition ceases with the option of the affected party to extend the period of this Agreement up to the length of time the condition endured. Unless written notice is given within thirty (30) days after the affected party is notified of the condition, option (c) shall be deemed selected.

14. **ASSIGNMENT.** This Agreement shall be binding on the successors and assigns of both parties, provided, that neither party may assign or transfer its interests, rights, or obligations under this Agreement or any order by written agreement, merger, consolidation, operation of law, or otherwise without the prior written consent of an authorized executive officer of the other party, which consent shall not be unreasonably withheld. It shall be reasonable to withhold consent to such assignment or transfer if the assignee or transferee is in direct competition with the other party. Any purported assignment of this Agreement in violation of this Section 14 shall be null and void.

15. **AMENDMENTS, MODIFICATIONS, OR SUPPLEMENTS.** Amendments, modifications, or supplements to this Agreement shall be permitted, provided all such changes shall be in writing signed by the authorized representatives of both parties, and all such changes shall reference this Agreement and identify the specific articles or sections of this Agreement that is amended, modified, or supplemented.

16. **NOTICES.** All notices, demands, or other communications herein provided to be given or that may be given by any party to the other shall be deemed to have been duly given when made in writing and delivered in person, or upon receipt, if (a) deposited in the U.S. mail, postage prepaid, certified mail, return receipt requested, or (b) sent by reputable overnight courier addressed as follows:

Notices to Company:	**Notices to Customer:**
With a required copy to:	With a required copy to:

or to such address as the parties may provide to each other in writing from time to time.

17. **OBLIGATIONS THAT SURVIVE TERMINATION.** The parties recognize and agree that the obligations of the other party under Sections 9, 11, 16, and 19 of this Agreement, shall survive the cancellation, termination, or expiration of this Agreement.

18. **EXPORT REGULATIONS.** Customer and Company acknowledge that the Software and all related technical information, documents, and materials may be subject to export controls under the U.S. Export Administration Regulations and, to the extent applicable, Customer and Company shall (a) comply with all requirements set forth in such regulations, and (b) cooperate fully with each other in any official or unofficial audit or inspection that relates to such export requirements.

19. **GOVERNING LAW.** The validity, construction, interpretation, and performance of this Agreement shall be governed by and construed in accordance with the domestic laws of the State of __________ except as to its principles of conflicts of laws. The parties acknowledge and agree that the United Nations Convention for the Sale of Goods shall not apply to this Agreement. The parties irrevocably submit to the jurisdiction of the Federal District Court for the District of __________ to resolve any disputes arising under or related to this Agreement.

20. **BACKGROUND, ENUMERATIONS, AND HEADINGS.** The "Background" enumerations and headings contained in this Agreement are for convenience of reference only and are not intended to have any substantive significance in interpreting this Agreement.

21. **ENTIRE AGREEMENT.** This Agreement shall constitute the entire agreement between the parties hereto and replaces and supersedes all prior agreements, written and oral, relating to the subject matter hereof, between the parties to this Agreement.

IN WITNESS WHEREOF, the parties have executed this Agreement under seal as of the day and year first written above.

ATTEST:	[CUSTOMER]
______________________________	By: ____________________ (SEAL)
ATTEST:	[COMPANY]
______________________________	By:____________________ (SEAL)

APPENDIX A

Escalation Procedures and Processes for Software Error Resolution

Classification of Errors

All Errors reported by Customer to Company shall be assigned a Severity Level jointly agreed upon by Customer and Company. The point of contact throughout this initial Error reporting procedure shall be the applicable Company support representative available to Customer under the terms of this Agreement. Reported Errors shall be classified as follows:

Severity Level 1—Severity Level 1 implies that the Software is not functioning. Some examples of Severity Level 1 Errors are as follows:

1. Production System down and will not restart;
2. Production Software not able to communicate with external systems (including the network control center) that halts online and other processing and no Bypass is available; and
3. Production Software is generating a data corruption condition that halts online and other processing and no Bypass is available.

Severity Level 2—Severity Level 2 implies that the Software is running but that Customer is unable to use major portions of the Software, and no Bypass is available. Some examples of Severity Level 2 Errors are as follows:

1. Intermittent Error in a live, production system that continues processing with no Bypass; and
2. Major functional component is unavailable with no Bypass.

Severity Level 3—Severity Level 3 implies that the Software is operating close to normal, but there is a non-critical Error for which an operational Bypass exists for such Error. Severity Level 3 Errors will be fixed in the next scheduled Update.

Severity Level 4—Severity Level 4 includes purely cosmetic Errors and documentation anomalies.

Out-of-Scope—A reported problem is out-of-scope when it is determined not to be related to the Software and is beyond the bounds of Company's responsibility. Examples of such unrelated problems include, but are not limited to, Customer host or applications software, Customer hardware and cabling, power or environmental conditions, and human error.

Severity Level 1

Error Resolution—Immediate steps shall be taken toward solving the Error. Company shall work to resolve Severity Level 1 Errors on a twenty-four (24) hour basis until the Error is resolved. If required, Company staff shall be moved off of lower Severity Level Errors to service Severity Level 1 Errors.

Resource Commitment—When a Severity Level 1 Error is reported, Company shall assign all resources required to correct the Error. Work on the Error shall be continuous until a Fix is found. If system access is required, Customer shall provide a contact available to Company and access to its system and software for the duration of the Error correction procedures.

Completion Goal—The completion goal shall be to resolve 100 percent of all Severity Level 1 Errors with a Fix or Bypass within eight (8) hours of receipt of the Error Report.

Escalation and Status Thresholds—When a Severity Level 1 Error Report is opened, the following escalation and status procedures shall be followed.

Hour 1–Hour 3

1. The Error shall be resolved by Company first line support; or
2. The Error will be referred to the maintenance engineering group. All log files and a description of the work done by Company will be transferred to this group. The report will receive an Error Report number that will be entered into the SMS. The error will be passed to the maintenance engineering group via the SMS as well as by email.

The Customer will be notified of the status of the Error.

Hour 3

1. The maintenance engineering point of contact will resolve the Error; or
2. It will be decided that more resources are required to work on the Error.

The Customer will be notified of the status of the Error.

Hour 4–Resolution

1. Company shall continue to work on the Error, on a twenty-four (24) hour basis, until a resolution is found. All available resources shall be used to assist the person who is responsible for the resolution of the Error; and
2. The Project Manager and Operations Support Manager shall be notified that a Severity Level 1 Error has reached a critical time frame.

Severity Level 2

Error Resolution—Severity Level 2 Errors will be analyzed in the order that they are reported. Severity Level 1 Errors will take priority over Severity Level 2 Errors.

Resource Commitment—Appropriate technical resources will be assigned to Severity Level 2 issues as long as Severity Level 1 Errors are not open.

Completion Goal—The completion goal will be to resolve 100 percent of all Severity Level 2 Errors with a Fix or Bypass within forty-eight (48) hours of receipt of the Error Report. If it is a Bypass, a Fix will be applied within sixty (60) days.

Escalation and Status Thresholds—When a Severity Level 2 Error Report is opened, the following escalation and status procedures will be followed.

Hour 1–Hour 24

1. The Error shall be resolved by Company; or
2. The maintenance point of contact person will be contacted. All log files and a description of the work done by Company will be transferred to this group. An Error Report number will be assigned and entered in the trouble tracking system.

The Customer will be notified of the status at this stage.

Hour 25–Hour 48

1. The maintenance engineering point of contact will resolve the Error; or
2. The maintenance engineer will continue working the Error until it is fixed.
3. A date will be estimated upon when this Error will be fixed.

The Customer will be notified of the status at this stage.

Severity Level 3

Error Resolution—Severity Level 3 errors shall be researched after Severity Level 1 and Severity Level 2 Errors. The majority of the Severity Level 3 Errors shall be scheduled for correction and be resolved as part of the next scheduled Update.

Resource Commitment—Severity Level 3 Fixes shall be included in the next scheduled Update.

Completion Goal—The completion goal and objective shall be to correct Errors in the next scheduled Update.

Escalation and Status Thresholds—The status of Severity Level 3 Errors shall be available on demand. A monthly report will be distributed that will reference any uncorrected Errors that are over ninety (90) days old.

Severity Level 4

Error Resolution—Severity Level 4 Errors shall be addressed at Company's discretion after Severity Level 1, Severity Level 2, and Severity Level 3 Errors are corrected. All Severity Level 4 Errors shall be scheduled for correction and be resolved as part of the next scheduled Update.

Resource Commitment—Severity Level 4 Fixes shall be included in the next scheduled Update.

Completion Goal—The completion goal and objective will be to correct issues in the next scheduled Update.

Escalation and Status Thresholds—The status of Severity Level 4 Errors shall be available on demand.

APPENDIX B

Optional Services and Standard Rate Schedule Effective Through [DATE]

(all prices are in U.S. Dollars)

BILLING RATES	
Classification	$ Monthly
Senior Consultant	
Consultant	
Project Manager	
Project Leader	
System Analyst	
Training Manager	
Trainer	
Senior Programmer	
Programmer	
Documentation Specialist	

Travel and Expenses are not part of the standard rate and are to be paid by the Customer.

OPTIONAL SUPPORT SERVICES
Consultant Support $/year
Dedicated Telephone Support $/year
Off-Hour Support $/year
Consultant Support/Annual Maintenance Fee Adjustment Reduction

If any one individual or combination of the Consultant Support, Dedicated Telephone Support, and Off-Hour Support options listed above is ordered by Customer simultaneously with the Annual Software Maintenance and Software Support Fee, the Annual Software Maintenance and Software Support Fee will be reduced to __% of the Delivered Software per Annum for that particular year.

Out-Of-Scope / Secondary Authorized Rate $/hour

To be used in conjunction with support delineated under Sections 2, 3, and 4.

Training $/program

A comprehensive training program to "train the trainers" shall be offered to Customer by Company. This instructor led program requires a total of fifteen (15) days to complete and will accommodate up to five (5) attendees. Training shall be conducted at a designated Customer location. An outline of the "train the trainer" program shall be provided by Company on request. Reasonable travel and expenses are not part of the training fee and shall be billed to Customer at Company's actual cost.

APPENDIX C

Designated Customer Personnel

The following Customer personnel shall be designated by Customer to contact Company in accordance with the terms of this Agreement and shall have authority to authorize an investigation of software errors and have knowledge of the terms and conditions set forth therein:

Source Code Escrow Agreement (Annotated)

THIS SOURCE CODE ESCROW AGREEMENT ("Escrow Agreement"), is made and entered into this _____ day of ___________, 20__, ("Effective Date") by and among ____________________ (hereinafter, "Licensor"), ___________________ (hereinafter, "Licensee"), and ___________, as escrow agent (hereinafter, the "Escrow Agent").

WHEREAS, Licensor and Licensee have entered into a Software License Agreement dated as of _______________, 20__ (the "Services Agreement"), which provides for, among other things, the provision of certain services to Licensee utilizing Licensor's computer software programs ("Computer Programs") in accordance with the terms and provisions thereof; and

WHEREAS, the availability and provision of such services utilizing Licensor's Computer Programs is critical to Licensee in the conduct of its business and, as a consequence, Licensor has agreed to deposit in escrow a machine-readable copy of source code, object code, source code specifications, and other items required by Licensee and identified and defined in Attachment A to this Escrow Agreement, to operate, support, and maintain the Computer Programs without reliance on or support from Licensor (such items referred to in Attachment A shall individually be referred to as a "Deposit," and collectively referred to as the "Deposits" or "Deposit Materials"); and

- ***Licensors should avoid agreeing to self-serving statements with no relationship to the agreement itself.***

WHEREAS, the Deposits are to be held by the Escrow Agent in accordance with the terms and conditions of this Escrow Agreement.

NOW, THEREFORE, in consideration of the promises and the mutual covenants contained herein, the parties agree to the foregoing and as follows:

ARTICLE 1
CREATION AND MAINTENANCE OF ESCROW; ESCROW AGENT OBLIGATIONS

1.1 **Creation and Maintenance of Escrow.** Licensor hereby agrees to deposit with Escrow Agent the current release of the Deposits for the Computer Programs ("Initial Deposits") **within thirty (30) calendar days following the Effective Date.** Licensor further agrees that it shall deposit current copies of the items described in Attachment A ("Supplemental Deposits") with Escrow Agent thirty (30) calendar days after the close of each calendar quarter, provided that the parties may mutually agree in writing to have the Supplemental Deposits deposited less frequently. Licensor shall package the items comprising the Deposits separately and label each package in accordance with the definitions in Attachment A so that each of the items can be separately and easily identified by Escrow Agent and Licensee. Along with each Deposit, Licensor shall prepare and submit to Escrow Agent a Description of the Deposit Materials in the form attached hereto as Attachment B.

- ***The licensee should require the licensor to deposit the Deposits at the time of the executing of the Escrow agreement or on the date the software is accepted. By allowing the licensor to deposit the software 30 days after the Escrow Agreement was signed creates the risk of breach and having to sue the licensor to require it to deposit the software.***
- ***Licensee should set forth in detail the manner in which the deposits will be delivered. By setting forth the licensor's obligations, the escrow agent will be more likely able to determine if the required deposits have been delivered and help the Licensee utilize the deposits in the event of a release.***

1.2 **Escrow Agent Obligations.** In addition to the other duties and obligations imposed upon Escrow Agent in connection with the terms of this Escrow Agreement:

(a) Escrow Agent shall notify Licensee as to the receipt of the Deposit or Deposits described in Attachment A according to the procedures specified in Section 1.2(b). Escrow Agent's responsibilities under this provision shall be limited to checking the label and quantity of the Deposits that are shipped to identify whether the items described in Attachment B have been received, and shall not include determining whether the purported contents of such boxes or packages actually contain the necessary information Licensor is required to submit as part of the Deposits; provided that Escrow Agent's responsibilities under this provision shall not be reduced or diminished by Licensor's submission of a Description of Deposit Materials as described in Attachment B.

(b) Upon the acceptance of the Initial Deposit and each Supplemental Deposit, Escrow Agent shall notify Licensee and Licensor by issuing an executed copy of Attachment B within ten (10) calendar days of such acceptance. If no quarterly Deposit has been made by Licensor, Licensor shall certify to Licensee that the Deposit Materials contain the current copies of the items identified in Attachment A. Licensor shall use the form attached hereto as Attachment B for such notification.

- ***To avoid having the quarterly deposits "fall through the cracks," the referenced form will allow the Licensee/escrow agent to track the licensor's actions even if a deposit does not need to be made.***

(c) Escrow Agent shall separately identify the Deposits through a deposit account number and shall segregate the Deposits from any of Licensor's other materials that may be in the possession of Escrow Agent.

(d) Escrow Agent shall store the Deposits in defined units of space ("Storage Units"). The cost of the first Storage Unit is included in the Deposit Fee. Costs for additional Storage Units are detailed in Attachment D.

(e) Escrow Agent shall safeguard, safekeep and maintain the Deposits in accordance with industry standards applicable to an escrow company. Escrow Agent shall secure insurance covering its obligations to safeguard, safekeep, and maintain the Deposits and shall, upon request of Licensee, procure reasonable evidence of such insurance. The parties agree that under no circumstances shall the Escrow Agent be liable for breach or delay in performance due to hostile or warlike action in time of peace or war, including action in hindering, combating or defending against an actual, impending or expected attack, military action or governmental action or other peril not ordinarily covered by typical property insurance maintained by a trust company in accordance with industry standards and not covered by the insurance actually maintained by Escrow Agent. The parties agree that the amount of liability insurance that the Escrow Agent shall secure for the Deposits shall be at least One Million Dollars ($1,000,000), and that such insurance shall: (i) cover Licensee against damages incurred as a result of the destruction of the Deposits (which Deposits cannot be replaced), and (ii) name Licensee as an additional insured. Licensee shall notify the Escrow Agent in writing of any need to increase the amount of such insurance, which may be required after the date hereof. The cost for such additional insurance shall be borne by Licensee.

(f) Except as provided in this Escrow Agreement, Escrow Agent agrees that it will not divulge or disclose or otherwise make available to any third person whatsoever, or make any use whatsoever, of the Deposits, without the express prior written consent of Licensor.

1.3 **Limitation of Liability.** ESCROW AGENT SHALL NOT BE LIABLE TO LICENSOR OR LICENSEE UNDER THIS ESCROW AGREEMENT FOR ANY INDIRECT, CONSEQUENTIAL, INCIDENTAL, SPECIAL OR PUNITIVE DAMAGES.

ARTICLE 2
TERM OF ESCROW AGREEMENT

Upon payment of the initial fee, this Escrow Agreement shall remain in full force and effect for an initial period of seven (7) years unless earlier terminated by the Licensor and Licensee upon a joint, written notice to the Escrow Agent or otherwise as provided herein. This Escrow Agreement shall be renewed automatically thereafter on an annual basis, provided Escrow Agent receives the renewal fees prior to the last day of the initial period or any subsequent renewal period ("Expiration Date"). Escrow Agent may, however, extend the period of the Escrow Agreement to cover the processing of any outstanding instruction made during any period of the Escrow Agreement. Licensee shall pay renewal fees and other related fees in accordance with Article 10. In the event Licensor is of the opinion that a renewal should not occur, Licensor may so notify Escrow Agent and Licensee in writing; provided, however, that Escrow Agent may not terminate this Escrow Agreement based on Licensor's notice that the renewal should not occur. If the Escrow Agreement is not renewed or is otherwise terminated in accordance with the terms and conditions set forth herein at the end of any initial or renewal period: (a) all duties and obligations of Escrow Agent to Licensor and Licensee will terminate; and (b) if Licensor requests return of the Deposit, Escrow Agent shall return the Deposit to Licensor only after any outstanding or due and payable invoices and the Deposit return fee as provided in Attachment D are paid by Licensor. Escrow Agent's obligations to hold and maintain the Deposits shall immediately cease upon delivery of the Deposits to Licensee or to Licensor in accordance with the provisions of this Escrow Agreement.

ARTICLE 3
DISCLOSURE EVENTS

An event requiring the release of the Deposits to Licensee ("Disclosure Event") shall be deemed to have occurred under this Escrow Agreement in the event of:

3.1 An Licensor Event of Default as set forth in the Software License Agreement; or

3.2 Licensor's uncured material breach of any of its support and maintenance obligations under the Software License; or

3.3 Licensor's discontinuation of any part of the Software or support and maintenance services under the Software License Agreement for any reason other than Licensee's uncured material breach of its obligation to pay Licensor for such services; or

3.4 The institution of bankruptcy, receivership, insolvency, reorganization, or other similar proceedings by or against Licensor under the Federal Bankruptcy Code, if such proceedings have not been dismissed or discharged within thirty (30) calendar days after they are instituted; the insolvency or making of an assignment for the benefit of creditors or the admittance of any involuntary debts as they mature by Licensor; or the taking of any action by the Board of Directors of Licensor in furtherance of any of the foregoing.

3.5 **[LIST ANY "WARNING SIGNS" applicable to the Licensor's business, the existence of which would trigger a deposit release and hopefully allow the licensee to avoid being subjected to bankruptcy court proceedings to obtain access to deposited materials.]**

- ***The Licensee should include a "laundry list" of potential concerns that will trigger the release of the source code and deposit materials. The Licensee should seek to identify those events that are likely to occur not only in the near future but in the distant future as it is unlikely the Licensor will agree to amend the escrow agreement once it has been executed. The Licensor should seek to limit this list to avoid having the source code released and potentially lose the ability to control its dissemination.***

ARTICLE 4
NOTICE OF DISCLOSURE EVENT AND DELIVERY OF DEPOSITS

4.1 In the event Licensee believes that a Disclosure Event has occurred, Licensee shall provide written notice of such Disclosure Event to Licensor. Within seven (7) calendar days after receiving such notice, Licensor shall either: (1) cure the Disclosure Event; or (2) provide a written explanation and corrective plan to Licensee that is satisfactory to Licensee in its sole discretion explaining why the Disclosure Event has not occurred. If Licensor fails to either cure the Disclosure Event or provide an explanation and corrective plan to Licensee that is satisfactory to Licensee as provided in this Section 4.1, Licensee may, by written notice to Licensor and Escrow Agent (the "Notice"), demand that the Deposits be delivered to Licensee by Escrow Agent. Such demand shall be accompanied by an affidavit signed by an officer of Licensee attesting:

(a) To a full description of the Disclosure Event; and
(b) That the specific Disclosure Event has occurred and, in the case of a material breach by Licensor of its support and maintenance obligations under the Services Agreement, that the breach has continued for more than thirty (30) calendar days from Licensor's receipt of written notice from Licensee and that the breach is continuing; and
(c) That Licensee is not in breach of the Services Agreement; and
(d) That the Deposits shall continue to be the sole property of Licensor and shall be subject to the confidentiality provisions of the Services Agreement; and

(e) That the Deposits shall be used solely for Licensee's support and maintenance, modification or correction of the Computer Programs used by Licensor to provide services to Licensee; and

(f) That Notice and said affidavit has been provided to Licensor in accordance with the provisions of this Escrow Agreement.

Said affidavit must be dated and sworn to within the seven (7) calendar-day period prior to receipt of the Notice by the Escrow Agent. Escrow Agent shall send Licensor a copy of each request and any related materials received from the Licensee (including the affidavit) within three (3) business days of receipt.

4.2 Unless Escrow Agent receives an original order or certified copy of an order of a court of competent jurisdiction as described in Section 4.3 restraining Escrow Agent from making delivery of the Deposits to Licensee, then Escrow Agent shall deliver the Deposits to Licensee on the twenty-first (21st) calendar day after the date of the Notice; provided that Escrow Agent shall not be required to deliver the Deposits until Licensee has made all payments to Escrow Agent for any fees described under Section 10.1 that remain unpaid at the time the Deposits are due to be delivered to Licensee. In no event shall Licensee be required to pay for any legal fees incurred by Escrow Agent except as stated in Article 6.

4.3 Licensor's exclusive and only right to challenge Licensee's demand for delivery of the Deposits shall be through: (a) instituting an appropriate action in a court of competent jurisdiction; and (b) within the twenty (20) calendar day period after the date of the Notice, causing the delivery and receipt by Escrow Agent of an order of such court to Escrow Agent restraining Escrow Agent from making delivery of the Deposits to Licensee. Licensor and Licensee agree that the sole basis for the entry of such an order shall be the absence of a Disclosure Event as described in Sections 3.1 or 3.2 or Licensor's cure of a Section 3.3 Disclosure Event within the time provided.

* ***Section 4.3 seeks to limit the licensor's ability to wrongfully delay or challenge a release of the deposit materials.***

4.4 **In the event Licensee receives the Deposits pursuant to the provisions of this Article 4, Licensee agrees that it shall maintain the confidentiality of the Deposits and shall use the Deposits in accordance with the terms of this Escrow Agreement and the Services Agreement.**

- ***The Licensor should include language to ensure that the terms of the license grant in the original license agreement govern the Licensee's use of the source code. The failure to do so may grant the Licensee unlimited rights.***

4.5 Escrow Agent's sole responsibility is to review the affidavit from Licensee for execution in accordance with this Escrow Agreement. Escrow Agent shall have no duty to investigate the facts set forth in the affidavit including, without limitation, whether a Disclosure Event and lack of cure as described in Section 3.3 exists, or any other document, and may act upon receipt of a properly executed affidavit.

ARTICLE 5
TERMINATION OF SOFTWARE LICENSE AGREEMENT

In the event the Software License Agreement is terminated by Licensee in accordance with the terms of the Software License Agreement, Licensor may by written notice to Escrow Agent and Licensee demand return of the Deposits by Escrow Agent to the Licensor, and Escrow Agent shall deliver said Deposits to Licensor on the thirtieth (30th) calendar day following receipt of such notice, unless Escrow Agent has received a second notice from Licensor canceling the first notice or a notice from Licensee stating that Licensee is entitled to an extension in accordance with its transition rights as set forth in the Services Agreement. Such notice and demand for return of the Deposits by Licensor shall include written acknowledgment or other instructions satisfactory to the Escrow Agent that the Services Agreement has been terminated. Such notice shall also be accompanied by the Deposit return fee.

ARTICLE 6
INDEMNIFICATION OF ESCROW AGENT

Escrow Agent, by reason of its execution of this Escrow Agreement, shall not assume any responsibility or liability for any transactions between Licensor and Licensee other than for the performance of Escrow Agent's obligations with respect to the Deposits held by it in accordance with this Escrow Agreement. The party on whose behalf, or pursuant to whose direction, Escrow Agent acts, shall indemnify, defend and hold harmless Escrow Agent from any and all liability, damages, costs or expenses, including reasonable attorneys' fees, which may be sustained or incurred by Escrow Agent as a result of taking such action. Absent any such direction, the parties hereto shall jointly and severally indemnify and hold harmless the Escrow Agent from any and all liability, damages, costs or expenses, including reasonable attorneys' fees, except for any liability, damages, costs or expenses that may be sustained or incurred by the gross negligence or willful misconduct on the part of Escrow Agent, its employees or agents, and except for the breach by Escrow Agent of Escrow Agent's duties under Section 1.2. Escrow Agent is not a party to, or bound by, any provisions contained in the Services Agreement, and with respect to the Deposits acts as a depository only and is not responsible or liable in any manner whatever for the sufficiency, correctness, genuineness or validity of the Services Agreement, or with respect to the form or execution of the same, or the identity, authority or right of any person executing the same or depositing the Deposits. This indemnification shall survive the termination of this Escrow Agreement.

ARTICLE 7
COMPLIANCE WITH ORDERS OF COURT

Escrow Agent is hereby expressly authorized to comply with and obey any and all orders, judgments or decrees of any court of competent jurisdiction as determined by counsel of the Escrow Agent's choosing, and in case the Escrow Agent complies with any such order, judgment or decree, it shall not be liable to the parties hereto or to any other person or entity by reason of such compliance. In complying with the foregoing, if Escrow Agent becomes or is made a party to any court proceeding that affects this Escrow Agreement or the parties hereto or the Deposits, Escrow Agent shall promptly give notice of such order or directive to Licensor and Licensee and comply therewith. Licensor or Licensee, as the case may be, shall hold the Escrow Agent harmless from any loss or expense incurred by the Escrow Agent as a result of following the instructions given by Licensor or Licensee. To the extent possible in any such proceedings, Escrow Agent shall interplead Licensor and Licensee, and Licensor and Licensee shall take all actions necessary to assume complete responsibility for such proceedings.

ARTICLE 8
LOCATION AND CONDITION OF DEPOSITS

The parties hereby acknowledge that the Deposits will be stored in accordance with Escrow Agent's standard escrow operating procedures. Escrow Agent shall maintain the environmental conditions within the vault within normal operating temperatures and humidities. For purposes of this Escrow Agreement, normal operating temperatures and humidities shall mean temperatures and humidities at or near the range usually maintained for ordinary computer media storage. Licensor and Licensee hereby agree not to hold Escrow Agent liable for any damages or claims resulting from loss of data that may occur: (a) solely as a result of self-destruction or disintegration of a tape or disk; (b) solely because of defects of the tapes or disks on which the data is stored; or (c) solely because such tapes or disks are sensitive to the normal operating temperatures and humidities in the vault.

* ***Both licensor and licensee should insist on incorporating the Escrow Agent's "standard operating procedures" into the Escrow Agreement.***

ARTICLE 9
RESIGNATION OF ESCROW AGENT

In the event the Escrow Agent wishes to resign for any reason, it shall give the other parties sixty (60) calendar days prior written notice of such resignation and within said sixty (60) calendar day period Licensor and Licensee, jointly shall appoint and designate a successor Escrow Agent to stand in the place and stead of the Escrow Agent under this Escrow Agreement, and following such appointment and designation, Escrow

Agent shall forthwith deliver the Deposits to the successor Escrow Agent. If the parties do not appoint a successor Escrow Agent within said sixty (60) calendar day period, the Escrow Agent may apply to a court of competent jurisdiction for the appointment of a successor Escrow Agent and any costs incurred in connection therewith shall be borne by Licensee and Licensor equally. This Escrow Agreement shall terminate when the Escrow Agent delivers the Deposits to the successor Escrow Agent.

ARTICLE 10
FEES AND EXPENSES OF THE ESCROW AGENT

10.1 Licensee hereby agrees to pay Escrow Agent in accordance with this Article 10 and the fee schedule set forth in Attachment D or the then-current fee schedule of Escrow Agent, which such new fee schedule shall be in accordance with the terms set forth in Attachment D and shall be provided to Licensor and Licensee ninety (90) calendar days prior to any fee change. Such fees are subject to periodic review by the management of the Escrow Agent in accordance with its pricing policies.

10.2 Notwithstanding anything in this Escrow Agreement to the contrary, except for any acts taken by Escrow Agent at the direction of Licensee or Licensor pursuant to Article 6, Licensor and Licensee shall each reimburse the Escrow Agent for fifty percent (50%) of any extraordinary costs which Escrow Agent may incur including, without limitation, the costs of hiring or retaining any agents or attorneys; provided, however, that Escrow Agent shall provide written notice to Licensor and Licensee before incurring any extraordinary costs.

10.3 Initial fees shall be invoiced by Escrow Agent upon the Effective Date. In the event the initial fees are not paid within thirty (30) calendar days of the Effective Date, Escrow Agent shall notify Licensee and Licensor with a notice in the form of Attachment C. Such notice shall be sent in accordance with the notice procedures specified herein. If the initial fees are not received within thirty (30) calendar days following Licensee's and Licensor's receipt of such notice, Escrow Agent may terminate the Escrow Agreement without further notice or liability to Licensor or Licensee.

10.4 Yearly renewal fees are due in full upon the receipt of invoice, unless otherwise specified in the invoice. Each year during the term of this Escrow Agreement, Escrow Agent shall invoice Licensee for the renewal fees ninety (90) calendar days prior to the anniversary of the execution date of this Escrow Agreement. In the event the renewal fees are not received thirty (30) calendar days prior to the anniversary of the execution date of this Escrow Agreement, Escrow Agent shall notify Licensor and Licensee that the renewal fees have not been received by providing Licensor and Licensee with a notice in the form of Attachment C. Such notice shall be sent in accordance with the notice procedures specified herein. If the renewal fees are not received by the anniversary of the execution date of this Escrow Agreement, Escrow Agent may terminate the Escrow Agreement without further notice or liability to Licensor or Licensee.

- ***In general, the Licensee usually agrees to pay for the cost of the escrow as the escrow benefits the Licensee.***

ARTICLE 11
ANNUAL REPORTS

Escrow Agent agrees to keep records of the activities undertaken and materials prepared pursuant to this Escrow Agreement. Escrow Agent shall issue to Licensor and Licensee an annual report profiling the Deposit account or otherwise make the information described in this Article available to Licensor and Licensee. Such annual report shall identify the Licensor, Licensee, the current designated contacts, selected special services, and the Deposit history which includes all Initial Deposits, Supplemental Deposits and/or releases of the Deposits and any instructions related thereto. Upon reasonable notice, during Escrow Agent's normal business hours and during the term of the Escrow Agreement, Licensor or Licensee shall be entitled to inspect the records of Escrow Agent pertaining to this Escrow Agreement. The Deposit may not be changed during the audit period.

ARTICLE 12
VERIFICATION RIGHTS

Licensor grants to Licensee the option to verify the Deposit for accuracy, completeness, and sufficiency and upon reasonable notice during Escrow Agent's normal business hours, Licensee shall be entitled to inspect the physical status and condition of the Deposit. Further, Licensor agrees to permit Escrow Agent and/or at least one (1) employee or agent of Licensee to be present at Licensor's facilities to verify, audit and inspect the Deposit held by Escrow Agent to confirm the quality and/or content of the Deposit for the benefit of Licensee. If Escrow Agent is present or is selected to perform the verification, Escrow Agent will be paid by Licensee according to Escrow Agent's then-current verification service hourly rate and any out-of-pocket expenses; provided, however, that in the event that such inspection indicates that Licensor has failed to keep the Deposits current in accordance with the terms of this Escrow Agreement, then Licensor shall be solely responsible for the payment of Escrow Agent's verification fees as set forth herein.

- ***The right of verification is the most important right the licensee has. The licensee should make sure to use it.***

ARTICLE 13
MISCELLANEOUS

13.1 **Further Assurances.** Each of the parties hereto shall from time to time execute and deliver all such further documents and instruments and do all acts and things as any other party may reasonably require to effectively carry out the intent and meaning of this Escrow Agreement.

13.2 **Amendments and Waiver.** No modification of or amendment to this Escrow Agreement shall be valid or binding unless set forth in writing and duly executed by the parties hereto. No waiver of any breach of any term or provision of this Escrow Agreement shall be effective or binding unless made in writing and signed by the party against whom enforcement is sought and, purporting to give the same and, unless otherwise provided, shall be limited to the specific breach waived.

13.3 **Assignment.** This Escrow Agreement shall not be assigned by any party except with the written consent of the other parties and any such attempt shall be null and void. This Escrow Agreement shall inure to the benefit of and be binding upon the respective successors and permitted assigns of the parties hereto.

13.4 **Notices.** Any demand and/or notice to be given in connection with this Escrow Agreement shall be given in writing and may be given by ordinary mail, except for demands and/or notices required to be given in connection with Sections 4 and 5 of this Escrow Agreement, which shall be given by registered or certified mail, or by overnight courier addressed to the recipient as follows:

If to Licensee:	If to Escrow Agent:
Attention: Telecopier:	Attention: Telecopier: email:

If to Licensor:

Telecopier:
email:

or to such other address or individual as may be designated hereafter from time to time by notice given by any party to the other parties. Any demand, notice or other communication given by personal delivery shall be deemed to have been given on the business day of actual delivery thereof or, if given by overnight courier, the next business day, or if given by registered, certified or ordinary mail, on the third (3rd) business day following the deposit thereof in the mail.

13.5 **Severability.** If any provisions of this Escrow Agreement shall for any reason be held illegal or unenforceable, such provision shall be deemed separable from the remaining provisions of this Escrow Agreement and shall in no way affect or impair the validity or the enforceability of the remaining provisions of this Escrow Agreement.

13.6 **Headings.** The division of this Escrow Agreement into Sections and the insertion of headings are for convenience of reference only and shall not affect the construction or interpretation of this Escrow Agreement. The terms "this Escrow Agreement," "hereof," "hereunder" and similar expressions refer to this Escrow Agreement and not to any particular Section or other portion hereof and include any agreement supplemental hereto. Unless something in the subject matter or context is inconsistent therewith, references herein to Sections are to Sections of this Escrow Agreement.

13.7 **Attorneys' Fees.** In the event that Licensor or Licensee shall commence a proceeding or bring an action to enforce the provisions of this Escrow Agreement, the prevailing party shall be entitled to be reimbursed for its reasonable attorneys' fees, disbursements and all applicable court costs.

- ***From the Licensee's perspective, this may be a moot point if the Licensor is in bankruptcy. Nonetheless, it serves as a deterrent against the Licensor filing frivolous motions to prevent the release of the deposit materials.***

13.8 **Governing Law; Exclusive Jurisdiction.** This Escrow Agreement, and all the rights and duties of the parties arising from or relating in any way to the subject matter of this Escrow Agreement or the transaction(s) contemplated by it, shall be governed by, construed, and enforced in accordance with the laws of the State of ______ (excluding any ________ conflict of laws rules that would refer to and apply the substantive laws of another jurisdiction). Any suit or proceeding relating to this Escrow Agreement shall be brought only in the courts, state and federal, located in ____ County, _____ and the parties hereby consent to the exclusive personal jurisdiction and venue of such courts.

13.9 **Attachments.** The following are Attachments annexed hereto and incorporated by reference and deemed to be part hereof:

Attachment A - Deposits
Attachment B - Description of Deposit Materials
Attachment C - Notice
Attachment D - Escrow Fees

13.10 **Counterparts.** This Escrow Agreement may be executed in any number of counterparts, each of which shall be deemed to be an original and all of which taken together shall be deemed to constitute one and the same instrument.

13.11 **Defined Terms.** As used in this Escrow Agreement, capitalized terms shall have the meanings specified in this Escrow Agreement or as specified in Definitions Section of the Software License Agreement.

13.12 **Supplementary Agreement.** This Escrow Agreement is "supplementary" to the License Agreement within the meaning of § 365(n) of the U.S. Bankruptcy Code (11 USC § 365 (n)). If this Escrow Agreement and/or the License Agreement are/is rejected by Licensor as a debtor in possession or a trustee or by any other person or entity under the U.S. Bankruptcy Code, then the Licensee may elect to retain its right as provided in § 365 (n). The Parties intend that no bankruptcy or bankruptcy proceeding, petition, law, or regulation (and no other proceeding, petition, law, or regulation of a similar nature in any state or foreign jurisdiction) will impede, delay, or prevent the release of Deposit Materials to Licensee in accordance with the provisions of this Agreement, and the Licensor hereby conveys to Escrow Agent such rights (including intellectual property rights) as are necessary to allow Escrow Agent to lawfully make such release and perform this Agreement.

13.13 **Entire Agreement.** This Escrow Agreement constitutes the entire agreement between the parties hereto with respect to the subject matter hereof and cancels and supersedes any prior understandings and agreements between the parties hereto with respect thereto. There are no representations, warranties, terms, conditions, undertakings or collateral agreements, express, implied, or statutory, between the parties other than as expressly set forth in this Escrow Agreement.

IN WITNESS WHEREOF, the parties have executed this Source Code Escrow Agreement on the day and in the year as set forth above.

LICENSOR:

____

By: ______________________________

Title: ______________________________

LICENSEE:

____

By: ______________________________

Title: ______________________________

ESCROW AGENT:

____

By: ______________________________

Title: ______________________________

ATTACHMENT A

Deposits

- ***The Licensee should carefully review this list to ensure that it is a comprehensive list of the materials and information the Licensee needs to operate and maintain the software in the event of the Licensor's breach.***

A. Description of Deposits

1. All Licensor-developed or owned source code for the Computer Programs used to provide services to Licensee under the Services Agreement, including all source code listings in human-readable and machine-readable form.

2. All Custom Programming modifications to the Computer Programs and all Documentation associated with such Custom Programming modifications.

3. All Enhancements to the Computer Programs and Custom Programming modifications thereto to which Licensee is entitled under the Services Agreement, to the extent the source code for such Enhancements is not provided to Licensee pursuant to the terms of the Services Agreement.

4. All available sub-programs, routines, program files, data files, file and data definitions and relationships, data definition specifications, data models, program and system logic, interfaces, algorithms, program architecture, design concepts, system designs, program structure, sequence and organization, screen displays and report layouts related to interacting with or a part of the Computer Programs and Custom Programming modifications thereto, whether in human-readable or machine-readable form (collectively, "Additional Programs").

5. All initial program load and start-up instructions, directions, information, and material that will enable a reasonably skilled programmer to load and execute (including compiling if necessary), the source code without the assistance of Licensor or any other person or reference to other materials (collectively, "Load Instructions").

6. Licensor-developed or owned maintenance and support tools, utilities, diagnostic programs, and supporting programs used or utilized by Licensor internally in the support or maintenance of the Computer Programs, or externally in connection with supporting other customer locations, whether or not such items are made available to Licensees generally or at an additional fee, whether in human-readable or machine-readable form (collectively "Support Tools").

7. All documentation and source code specifications including, without limitation, a list of all the names and business addresses and telephone numbers of key programmers or authors currently employed by Licensor, of any portion of the Computer Programs and the items referenced in paragraphs 2, 3, 4, 5 and 6 above ("Programmer List").

8. A complete list of third party products, including versions, incorporated in the Computer Programs and Custom Programming modifications thereto.

9. Third party system utilities (compiler and assembler descriptions). A description of the system/program generation, and descriptions and locations of programs not owned by Licensor that are required for use and/or support of the Computer Programs and Custom Programming modifications thereto.

10. Any other information and technical materials in Licensor's possession that are required for a reasonably skilled computer programmer to maintain, modify or enhance the Computer Programs and Custom Programming modifications thereto without the aid of Licensor or any other person and without reference to any other materials.

B. Usability of Source Code

Licensor represents and warrants that the source code is and shall be understandable and useable by a trained computer-programming contractor who is familiar with similar systems, though not necessarily those incorporating the Computer Programs. Licensor further represents and warrants that the Computer Programs do not involve any proprietary languages or programming components that such contractor could not reasonably be expected to understand, except to the extent the source code contains sufficient commentary to enable such contractor to understand and to use such languages or components. Licensor further represents and warrants that the source code includes all of the devices, programming, and documentation necessary for the maintenance of the Computer Programs by the Licensee upon release of the source code pursuant to this Escrow Agreement, except for devices, programming, and documentation commercially available to the Licensee on reasonable terms through readily known sources other than the Licensor.

ATTACHMENT B

Description of Deposit Materials

Licensee Name and Address

Re: Account No. [**Account No.**]; Computer Programs of ____________

Ladies and Gentlemen:

This writing is to inform you of the receipt of the following items of Deposit under the terms of that certain Escrow Agreement by and among ________________ ________________, ________________ and ________________, as Escrow Agent, dated as of __________, 20__ ("Escrow Agreement"). All capitalized terms herein shall have the meanings ascribed to them in the Escrow Agreement and the Attachment(s) attached thereto. The items marked or checked below have been received as of the dates indicated below:

Received	*Label Description Item of Deposit*	*Quarterly Updates*	*Date Received*
_______	1. Source Code	_______	____________, ____
_______	2. Custom Programming	_______	____________, ____
_______	3. Enhancements	_______	____________, ____
_______	4. Additional Programs	_______	____________, ____
_______	5. Load Instructions	_______	____________, ____
_______	6. Support Tools	_______	____________, ____
_______	7. Specifications including Source Code Specifications and Programmer List	_______	____________, ____
_______	8. List of third party products	_______	____________, ____
_______	9. Third party system utilities	_______	____________, ____
_______	10. Other information and materials	_______	____________, ____

Please check as applicable:

Deposit Type: Initial _____ Supplemental ______

Environment: ______________________________________

Special Instructions: ______________________________________

____

I received and deposited the above described Deposit Materials pursuant to the terms and conditions of this Escrow Agreement.

Escrow Agent

By: ______________________________

Title: ______________________________

Date: ______________________________

I certify that the above described Deposit Materials were forwarded to Escrow Agent.

Licensor

By: ______________________________

Title: ______________________________

Date: ______________________________

ATTACHMENT C

Notice

____

____

____

Attention:_____________________________

RE: Escrow Agreement #

Dear Sir or Madam:

In accordance with your escrow agreement, the **[SPECIFY EITHER "INITIAL" OR "RENEWAL"]** fees are due by **[INSERT APPLICABLE DUE DATE].** If such fees are not received by the date set forth above, [Escrow Agent] may terminate the escrow agreement without further notice or liability to you.

If you have any questions, please contact me at (__)-____________.

Sincerely,
Escrow Agent

____

Name

____

Title

____

Date

ATTACHMENT D

Escrow Fees

Initialization fee (one time only)	$ _____
Annual maintenance/storage fee	$ _____
• Includes four (4) Deposit Material updates	
• Includes one (1) cubic foot of storage space	
Additional Updates (above four (4) per year)	$ _____
Additional Storage Space	$ _____ /cubic foot
Due Upon Licensee's Request for Release of Deposit Materials	$ _____ for initial 2 hrs

A 10 percent discount is credited towards the initialization fee for current Escrow Agent clients. Fees due in accordance with **Article 10** and shall be paid in U.S. Dollars. Fees shall be subject to then-current pricing, provided that the prices set forth above shall not increase by more than 10 percent per year. An invoice for all renewal fees will be issued on the anniversary of the initial invoice. If other currency acceptance is necessary, please contact your Account Manager to make arrangements. For any service not listed on this fee schedule, Escrow Agent shall provide a quote prior to rendering such service.

Certificate of Acceptance – Software

THIS CERTIFICATE OF ACCEPTANCE is issued this ______ day of ________, 20__ by ______________________, a ______________ company with offices located at ______________________________________ ("Customer").

BACKGROUND

Customer and ______________________ ("Licensor") have entered into a certain Software License, Development, and Services Agreement executed the ______ day of _____, 20__ (the "Agreement"). Under the Agreement, Licensor undertakes to license, customize, and install on behalf of Customer, Licensor's proprietary ______ software (the "Software"). The Agreement sets forth certain procedures and requirements to be conducted by Customer together with Licensor for the acceptance testing of the Software. The Agreement stipulated that upon completion of such Acceptance Tests when the Software or a substantial part thereof has passed the test procedures set forth in the Acceptance Tests, Customer shall issue to Licensor a Certificate of Acceptance.

IN CONSIDERATION of the foregoing and of the covenants herein contained, Customer intending to be legally bound certifies as follows:

1. Customer together with Licensor has conducted the Acceptance Tests as contemplated in Section ____ of the Agreement, and detailed in Appendices ____ and ____ of the Agreement.

2. Customer together with Licensor has determined, after conducting the Acceptance Tests, that as set forth in Section ____ of the Agreement, the Software:

(a) complies with the functionality and complies with the other provisions of the Customer's Requirement and Specifications,

(b) functions in accordance with Licensor specifications,

(c) is compatible with and conforms to the functionality in accordance with user documentation and operating manuals furnished by Licensor; and

(d) complies with the relevant Acceptance Tests that have been mutually agreed upon and have been developed and agreed to in writing by Customer and Licensor.

3. The warranty set forth in Section ___ of the Agreement began on _________, 20__.

4. This Certificate of Acceptance, when executed by an officer of Customer, shall indicate fulfillment by Licensor of all of Licensor's obligations under the Agreement, excluding Licensor's ongoing maintenance and support obligations as set forth in the Agreement and clarified in certain Software Maintenance and Software Support Agreements.

5. Capitalized terms not otherwise defined in this Certificate of Acceptance, shall have the meanings ascribed to them in the Agreement.

IN WITNESS WHEREOF, Customer has executed this Certificate of Acceptance under seal effective the date first written above.

ATTEST:	CUSTOMER:
______________________________	By: ________________________(SEAL)

Certificate of Acceptance – Services

Vendor Name:

Contract:

Work Order #:

PO #:

Internal Customer Name:

Submitted Deliverable(s):

Date Submitted	Description	Date Rejected	Acceptance Date	Acceptance on behalf of Customer (Printed Name)	Signature

Rejected Submissions:

Date Submitted	Description	Date Rejected	Acceptance Date	Acceptance on behalf of Customer (Printed Name)	Signature

TERMS AND CONDITIONS MAY NOT BE ADDED TO THIS DOCUMENT

Client Name
Project Name

Statement of Work (SOW)

________, 20__

DRAFT

This Statement of Work is incorporated
into the Master Professional Services Agreement
dated ____________________, 20__.

Accepted By:	
CLIENT:	**VENDOR:**
Name:	**Name:**
Title:	**Title:**
Date:	**Date:**
Signature:	**Signature:**

Table of Contents

1. Current Situation

2. *Objectives*

Client's Business Objectives

Project Objectives

Phase Objectives

Constraint Prioritization

This phase of the project will be governed by the following prioritization of the three key constraints of scope, elapsed time, and budget:

High -
Medium - x
Low - x

This prioritization will drive the manner in which the project is managed, the way Changes of Scope will be handled, and the approach to resolving issues. These approaches are described in Section 5.1.

3. Scope

The scope of this project can be defined most clearly by breaking it down into specific categories. Vendor describes these categories as domains. There are three domains related to business scope:

Business Process Scope describes the work activities
Organization Scope describes the people, teams, and departments
Location Scope describes the physical locations or facilities

There are three domains related to technical scope:
Application Scope describes specific business software applications
Data Scope describes the specific data items, structures, relationships, and business rules for information
Technology Scope describes the hardware, system software, communication components, and development tools

The following scope definitions, Sections 3.1–3.6, define the areas that are in and out of scope. Any areas not specifically identified as "in scope" are assumed to be "out of scope." Specific items listed as "out of scope" are presented for clarity.

3.1 **Business Process Scope**

In Scope

Out of Scope

3.2 Organization Scope

In Scope

Out of Scope

3.3 Location Scope

In Scope

Out of Scope

3.4 Application Scope

In Scope

Out of Scope

3.5 Data Scope

In Scope

Out of Scope

3.6 Technology Scope

In Scope

Out of Scope

4. *Approach*

4.1 Approach Overview

4.2 Project Activities

Activity	Description/ Purpose	Associated Work Product	Responsibility

4.3 Deliverables

Deliverable	Description	Responsibility

5. *Project Management*

5.1 Management Approach

Vendor and Client are jointly responsible for the management of the project and for providing the necessary resources to the project. Our joint management objectives are focused on tightly monitoring, controlling, and balancing the project's three key constraints: Scope (or Product), Budget, and Schedule. To be effective in achieving this primary management objective, we must establish:

An agreed-upon baseline,
A process to monitor progress,
A clear means of communication,
An open approach for dealing with issues,
An objective change control procedure,
A process to recognize and manage risks,
An approach for accepting project deliverables, and
A definition of what constitutes project completion.

This section describes the basic approaches that we will use to provide this type of control.

5.1.1 Agreed-Upon Baseline

This Statement of Work is the foundation or baseline for all the key project management activities on the project. It identifies the work activities that will be tracked, defines the boundaries for scope control, identifies responsibilities, and clarifies many of the areas where issues may arise that need to be managed.

The Statement of Work is then used as the basis for creating a detailed project plan for all the work activities to be performed on the project. Every activity will have an estimate of work effort. All project team members, from Vendor and Client, will be assigned these activities, and this will determine the cost of the activity based on the cost of the individual team members assigned to it.

Once all the activities are allocated to team members, the project plan is leveled and loaded against the calendar. This completed plan represents the baseline plan. This plan will provide the key milestone dates to track schedule progress.

The summation of all activity costs from the baselined project plan, plus expenses, plus the costs of purchased items like hardware, software, and other services, will represent the budget that the Vendor/Client management team will track against.

5.1.2 Process to Monitor Progress

The detailed project plan is the key vehicle for measuring progress. The specific activities that each team member works on, and their progress against completing those activities, are the only objective measure of where the project stands against the schedule and budget. To capture this information every team member, both Vendor and {Client}, will record and report their actual hours spent on project activities against the budgeted time in the project plan. In addition, each team member will provide estimates of the effort remaining on activities that have not been completed.

This information will be recorded on a weekly time sheet and given to the appropriate manager along with a status report that provides a brief description of work accomplished, issues/problems, and planned work. The management team will determine where the project stands versus the schedule and budget by analysis of this information.

5.1.3 **Means of Communication**

Because Vendor and Client are responsible for managing this project, it is important that we use a formal process to support timely and accurate communication between the organizations. There are two key vehicles for providing this communication: a weekly status report and a weekly status meeting.

As mentioned earlier, all team members will report progress and status weekly. This information, and the analysis of it, will be summarized into a project status report for Client and Vendor Management. This report contains the following information:

Significant Problems/Actions Taken,
Progress Summary,
Accomplishments,
Planned Accomplishments,
Budget Status, and
Issues Log (discussed later).

The weekly project status meeting will be used to review the project status and open issues in the status report. The Vendor and Client management team must be committed to having this meeting and making it effective. The keys to making the meeting worthwhile are the following:

Have the meetings often enough so that timely information is available;
Focus the meeting on major issues or areas where management action or intervention is required; and
Make sure that the information provided is accurate and objective.

5.1.4 **Approach for Dealing with Issues**

Every project has issues that hinder progress. It is important that these issues are identified and resolved quickly by the right person. The first step in effectively dealing with these issues is to make the entire team aware of the importance of identifying issues and getting proper resolution. We will then use the following procedure to track the identified issues:

Identify issues. When the project begins, we will start identifying any issues that could hinder our ability to meet the objectives of the project. Issues can be identified by anyone involved with the project.

Document the issue. The person who identifies the issue must document it.

Assign responsibility for resolving issues. The Vendor/Client management team will determine the appropriate individual who will be responsible for resolving each issue. The responsible person must be an individual who has the knowledge and authority to make decisions regarding the issue. The management team will also assign a priority to the issue.

Monitor and control progress. All issues will be tracked on an issues log that will be maintained to formally track the status and resolution of the issues.

Report progress on issue resolution. As mentioned earlier, the issues log will be a part of the weekly status report and discussed in the weekly status meeting.

Communicate issue resolution. The issues log and documented resolutions of issues will be made available to all team members.

In the event that an issue cannot be resolved in a reasonable time-frame, to the mutual satisfaction of Vendor and Client, we will determine a mutually acceptable approach to escalating it to the next level of management.

5.1.5 Change Control Procedure

The Change Control Procedure is a crucial mechanism that can affect the success or failure of this project. This process is the primary vehicle for containing scope and giving management the opportunity to make timely trade-offs between the three key project variables of cost, time, and scope. It is important that potential changes are identified early, documented carefully, and resolved at the appropriate levels of responsibility.

Changes are broadly defined as work activities or work products not originally planned for as defined by this Statement of Work. More specifically, changes will include the following:

Any scope items not listed in this Statement of Work (Section 3),

Participation in activities not previously included in this Statement of Work's list of work activities (Section 4.2),

Provision or development of deliverables not included in this Statement of Work (Section 4.3),

A change in responsibilities, as defined in this Statement of Work (Sections 4, 5, or 6) between Vendor and Client, including reallocation of project staffing,

Any rework of completed activities or accepted deliverables,
Investigative work to determine the impact of major changes,
Assumptions not remaining valid,
Risks that actually occurred,
Delays caused by schedule slippage, and
Variances of actual work effort from estimated effort.

In order to manage change properly, a Change Control Process will be established to identify, record, assess, and approve changes to the project. Vendor and Client will follow this process to classify, prioritize, approve, or reject changes. Change requests need to be clearly defined, including cost and schedule implications, to allow Vendor and Client management to make appropriate decisions. Vendor will always need prior authorization and approval of expenditures by Client before starting work on changes.

This information will be identified and tracked as part of the monitoring and reporting processes defined in Sections 5.1.2 and 5.1.3.

At the beginning of the project Vendor and Client management will institute a mutually acceptable change control procedure.

5.1.6 Acceptance of Deliverables

All of the completed deliverables identified in this SOW will be formally submitted for final review and approval. This section outlines the key components to this acceptance process. Vendor and Client at the start of the project will mutually agree to a more detailed acceptance procedure and specific acceptance criteria. The key components are:

There will be only one person identified as the designated acceptor for each deliverable;

The deliverables will include an acceptance form for signature;

Each deliverable will have clearly documented, objective acceptance criteria;

There will be a specified time-frame for acceptance/rejection of each deliverable; and

Deliverables will be deemed accepted if the acceptance time-frame is exceeded.

In order to avoid delays in the schedule and the associated increased cost due to slow deliverable review, deliverables not reviewed and approved within a review period of NN work days will be considered accepted. Feedback supplied after the review period will be evaluated as a change of scope.

5.1.7 Project Completion Criteria

The project will be completed when all of the deliverables identified in Section 4.3 have been accepted.

5.2 Project Organization

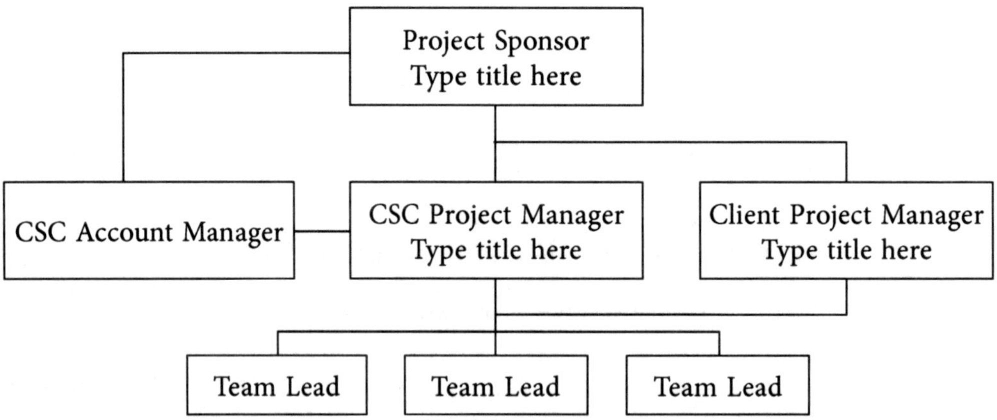

5.3 Roles and Responsibilities

During this engagement, Client PROJECT MANAGER NAME will be performing the role of Client Project Manager and Vendor PROJECT MANAGER NAME will be performing the role of Vendor Project Manager. In order to eliminate duplicate effort or gaps, the following table defines the separation of responsibilities:

Responsibility	Person
Budgets/Funding	
Authorize Funding/Budget	CLIENT PROJECT MANAGER NAME
Adherence to Budget	CLIENT PROJECT MANAGER NAME
Track/Report Client Costs	CLIENT PROJECT MANAGER NAME
Track/Report Vendor Costs	Vendor PROJECT MANAGER NAME
Schedules	
Planning	Vendor PROJECT MANAGER NAME
Planning Support	CLIENT PROJECT MANAGER NAME
Adherence	CLIENT PROJECT MANAGER NAME
Track/Report	Vendor PROJECT MANAGER NAME
Issues	
Identify	Entire Project Team
Track/Report	Vendor PROJECT MANAGER NAME
Resolve Client Issues	Client PROJECT MANAGER NAME
Resolve Vendor Issues	Vendor PROJECT MANAGER NAME
Changes of Scope	
Identify	Vendor PROJECT MANAGER NAME
Track/Report	Vendor PROJECT MANAGER NAME
Approve	Client PROJECT MANAGER NAME
Deliverables	

Responsibility	Person
Track Status	Vendor PROJECT MANAGER NAME
Review for Quality	Client PROJECT MANAGER NAME
Present for Acceptance	Vendor PROJECT MANAGER NAME
Approval and Sign-off	Client PROJECT MANAGER NAME
Team Management	
Team Structure	Both
Acquiring Resources	Each is responsible for its part of the team
Management of Third Parties	Client PROJECT MANAGER NAME
Allocation of Resources	Each is responsible for its part of the team
Overall Direction	Client PROJECT MANAGER NAME
Specific Direction to Client Team	Client PROJECT MANAGER NAME
Specific Direction to Vendor Team	Vendor PROJECT MANAGER NAME
Methodology & Management Procedures	
Development	Vendor PROJECT MANAGER NAME
Approval	Client PROJECT MANAGER NAME
Monitoring	Vendor PROJECT MANAGER NAME
Adherence	Each is responsible for its part of the team
Status Reports	
Collect Information	Vendor PROJECT MANAGER NAME
Write–Draft	Vendor PROJECT MANAGER NAME
Review	Client PROJECT MANAGER NAME
Write–Final	Vendor PROJECT MANAGER NAME
Distribute	Vendor PROJECT MANAGER NAME

The following table describes the roles and responsibilities of other key team members.

Resource/Role	Time Required	Description	Firm

6. Assumptions

Project Assumptions are those expectations upon which the Project "path forward" is based and which, if proven incorrect, result in a significant Project Issue that could invalidate the Project Budget Estimates, Schedules, and Approach. Such an invalidated Project Assumption will usually result in processing of a Change Request to the Project.

6.1 General Exclusions

1.
2.

6.2 General Assumptions

1.
2.

6.3 Business Process

1.
2.

6.4 Organization

1.
2.

6.5 Location

1.
2.

6.6 Application

1.
2.

6.7 Data

1.
2.

6.8 Technology

1.
2.

7. Fees and Expenses

Vendor will conduct this project on a Time & Materials basis.

7.1 Professional Fees

Vendor will be paid for all hours worked on the project at the rates listed in this section. There will be no maximums or minimums and no premium rate for overtime work, which is defined as hours worked by one person exceeding 40 hours in one week (Sunday through Saturday).

The hourly rates that will be used for this project are:

Person or Role or Category	Hourly Rate

7.2 Travel-Related Expenses

Client will pay all reasonable travel-related expenses incurred by employees of Vendor in connection with this project. These charges will be billed at cost, plus an administrative fee of 3 percent of expenses.

7.3 Other Expenses

Client will pay all reasonable and mutually agreed-upon expenses incurred by Vendor.

7.4 Payment Schedule

Vendor will submit bi-weekly invoices for all services provided and for travel-related and other expenses. Invoices are due upon receipt.

8. Appendices

Statement of Work (Alternate Form)

This Statement of Work ("**SOW**"), effective as of _____________, 20__ by and between _____________________ ("**Licensor**") and ____________________________(for purposes of this SOW, the "**Customer**"), is executed pursuant to and as part of that certain Software license and Professional Services Agreement by and between Customer and Vendor, dated as of ______________, 20__ (the "**Agreement**").

The parties have entered into the Agreement for the provision of certain rights, services, resources, and deliverables to Customer by Vendor. The Agreement contemplates that the parties may enter into specific SOWs describing detailed terms and conditions applicable to specific services, resources, and deliverables to be provided.

NOW, THEREFORE, for and in consideration of the foregoing premises, and the agreements of the parties set forth below, Customer and Vendor agree as follows:

1. Services.

[INSERT DESCRIPTION OF SERVICES TO BE PROVIDED, INCLUDING (1) APPLICABLE CUSTOMER ENTITY OR DIVISION FOR WHICH SERVICES WILL BE PERFORMED, (2) LENGTH OF PROJECT IF T&M SERVICES ARE TO BE PROVIDED, AND (3) ANY SPECIFIC MAINTENANCE SERVICES TO BE PROVIDED IN CONNECTION WITH DELIVERABLES, IF APPLICABLE]

2. Service Project Location.

[INSERT NAME OF APPLICABLE CUSTOMER ENTITY OR DIVISION AND PHYSICAL LOCATION WHERE SERVICES ARE TO BE PROVIDED]

3. Deliverables; Vendor Proprietary Information; Open Source.

[INSERT DESCRIPTION OF ANY DELIVERABLES TO BE PROVIDED. ALSO: (1) SPECIFICALLY DESCRIBE ANY BACKGROUND TECHNOLOGY AND/OR THIRD PARTY TECHNOLOGY (SUCH AS THIRD SOFTWARE OR REUSABLE TOOLS VENDOR IS PROVIDING) TO BE USED BY VENDOR (IF ANY), OR, IF DELIVERABLES WILL NOT INCORPORATE ANY VENDOR PROPRIETARY INFORMATION, STATE "No Vendor Proprietary Information"; and (2) IDENTIFY ANY OPEN SOURCE CODE TO BE INCORORATED INTO THE DELIVERABLES (IF ANY) AND ATTACH THE APPLICABLE OPEN SOURCE LICENSE(S) TO

THIS SOW, OR, IF DELIVERABLES WILL NOT INCORPORATE ANY OPEN SOURCE CODE, STATE "No Open Source Code".]

4. *Vendor Personnel.*

[INSERT NAME AND JOB TITLE OF SPECIFIC CONSULTANTS TO BE ENGAGED (IF ANY), OR STATE "Not Applicable".]

5. *Schedule and Milestones (If Any).*

Project Start Date: ______________________________

Estimated Project Completion Date: ___________________________

[ALSO INSERT DESCRIPTION OF TIMETABLE FOR COMPLETING SERVICES, MEETING MILESTONES AND/OR SUPPLYING DELIVERABLES, IF APPLICABLE]

6. *Charges.*

[INSERT: (1) EITHER (A) FOR T&M PROJECTS, APPLICABLE DAY RATES, ESTIMATED EXPENSES (IF ANY) AND MAXIMUM ESTIMATED COST FOR TOTAL PROJECT, *OR* (B) FOR FIXED FEE PROJECTS, FIXED FEE, ESTIMATED EXPENSES (IF ANY) AND TIMETABLE FOR PAYMENTS; *AND* (2) ANY APPLICABLE DISCOUNTS OR PERFORMANCE-RELATED INCENTIVES OR PENALTIES.]

Vendor shall send all invoices under this SOW to the following address:

[INSERT: CUSTOMER ADDRESS AND CONTACT INFORMATION FOR RECEIPT OF INVOICE]

7. *Project Managers.*

For Customer:	For Vendor:
Name:	Name:
Phone:	Phone:
Email:	Email:

8. Testing and Acceptance Procedures.

(**NOTE:** if no testing/acceptance procedures are set forth in this Section, the testing and acceptance procedures set forth in the Agreement shall govern.)

[INSERT DESCRIPTION OF ANY NECESSARY TESTING AND ACCEPTANCE PROCEDURES, OR STATE "As per the Agreement".]

9. Individualized Reports; Status Meetings.

[INSERT DESCRIPTION OF ANY INDIVIDUALIZED/ SPECIAL REPORTS OR STATUS MEETINGS RELATED TO THIS PROJECT, OR STATE "As per the Agreement".]

10. Other Specifications.

[INSERT ANY OTHER SPECIFICATIONS APPLICABLE TO WORK TO BE PERFORMED UNDER THIS STATEMENT OF WORK, FOR EXAMPLE, SPECIFICATIONS FOR DELIVERABLES OR OTHER WORK PRODUCT TO BE PROVIDED HEREUNDER]

11. Flow-Down Provisions for Subcontractors.

[INSERT ANY PROVISIONS THAT SHOULD FLOW DOWN FROM THE AGREEMENT TO VENDOR'S AGREEMENTS WITH ITS SUBCONTRACTORS RELATED TO WORK TO BE PERFORMED UNDER THIS SOW.]

Except to the extent otherwise expressly set forth in this SOW, this SOW is governed by the terms and conditions of the Agreement. Any defined terms not otherwise defined herein shall have the meanings set forth in the Agreement. This SOW may be modified or amended only by a writing signed by both parties. The parties hereto acknowledge having read this SOW and agree to be bound by its terms.

IN WITNESS WHEREOF, the parties have each caused this SOW to be signed and delivered by their duly authorized officers, all as of the date first set forth above.

______________________________	______________________________
By: ____________________	By: ____________________
Name: __________________	Name: __________________
Title: ___________________	Title: ___________________

Change Order

This Change Order No. __ ("**Change Order**"), effective as of ______ __, 20__, is made pursuant to and a part of that certain Software License and Professional Services Agreement, dated as of ______________ __, 20__, by and between ______________ ("Licensee") and ______________________ ("Licensor") (the "**Agreement**"), and Statement of Work thereto, by and between ______________________________ and ______________________________ dated as of ________________________ (the "**SOW**").

This Change Order is governed by the terms and conditions of the Agreement. Any defined terms not otherwise defined herein shall have the meanings set forth in the Agreement. Except to the extent otherwise expressly set forth in this Change Order, the terms of the SOW shall remain in full force and effect. The parties hereto acknowledge having read this Change Order and agree to be bound by its terms.

The modification(s) set forth below will impact the following terms of the SOW (please check all that apply):

[ ] Services [ ] Deliverables [ ] Estimated completion date

[ ] Fees [ ] Schedule [ ] Other: ________ (please specify)

Please provide a detailed description of the proposed modification(s) and their impact on the SOW:

[ADD DESCRIPTION OF CHANGES]

IN WITNESS WHEREOF, the parties hereto have each caused this Change Order to be signed and delivered by their duly authorized officers, all as of the date first set forth above.

[LICENSEE]	[LICENSOR]
By: ____________________________	By: ____________________________
Name: __________________________	Name: __________________________
Title: ___________________________	Title: ___________________________

Software as a Service ("SaaS") Subscription Agreement*

SaaS SUBSCRIPTION AGREEMENT*

This SaaS Subscription Agreement, is made and entered into this ____ day of __________, 20__, by and between ____________________ (hereinafter, "Vendor") with its principal address at __________________________ and ____________________ (hereinafter, "Customer") with its principal address at __________________________.

BACKGROUND

Vendor is in the business of providing software for the ________ industry. The parties desire that Vendor make such software available to Customer under the terms and conditions of this Agreement. Each order defined in an Order Form will be performed under these terms and conditions.

In consideration of the mutual promises and covenants set forth herein and for other good and valuable consideration, the receipt and sufficiency of which are hereby acknowledged, the parties agree as follows:

1. Definitions

As used in this Agreement and in any Order Forms, the following terms shall have the following meaning:

"Agreement" means these online terms of use, any Order Forms, whether written or submitted online via the Online Order Center, and any materials available on the Vendor website specifically incorporated by reference herein, as such materials, including the terms of this Agreement, may be updated by Vendor from time to time in its sole discretion.

"Content" means the audio and visual information, documents, software, products, and services contained or made available to Customer in the course of using the Service.

"Customer Data" means any data, information, or material provided or submitted by Customer to the Service in the course of using the Service.

"Effective Date" means the earlier of either the date first set forth above or the date Customer begins using the Service.

"Initial Term" means the initial period during which Customer is obligated to pay for the Service equal to the billing frequency selected by Customer during the subscription process (e.g., if the billing frequency is quarterly, the Initial Term is the first quarter).

"Intellectual Property Rights" means any unpatented inventions, patent applications, patents, design rights, copyrights, trademarks, service marks, trade names, domain name rights, mask work rights, know-how and other trade secret rights, and all other intellectual property rights, derivatives thereof, and forms of protection of a similar nature anywhere in the world.

"License Administrator(s)" means those Users designated by Customer who are authorized to purchase licenses online using the Online Order Center or by executing written Order Forms and to create User accounts and otherwise administer Customer's use of the Service.

"License Term(s)" means the period(s) during which a specified number of Users are licensed to use the Service pursuant to the Order Form(s).

"Order Form(s)" means the form evidencing the initial subscription for the Service and any subsequent order forms submitted online or in written form, specifying, among other things, the number of licenses and other services contracted for, the applicable fees, the billing period, and other charges as agreed to between the parties, each such Order Form to be incorporated into and to become a part of this Agreement (in the event of any conflict between the terms of this Agreement and the terms of any such Order Form, the terms of this Agreement shall prevail).

"Online Order Center" means Vendor's online application that allows the License Administrator, among other things, to add additional Users to the Service.

"Vendor Technology" means all of Vendor's proprietary technology (including software, hardware, products, processes, algorithms, user interfaces, know-how, techniques, designs, and other tangible or intangible technical material or information) made available to Customer by Vendor in providing the Service.

"Service(s)" means the specific edition of Vendor's online customer relationship management, billing, data analysis, or other corporate ERP services identified during the ordering process, developed, operated, and maintained by Vendor, accessible via http://www.____________ or another designated website or IP address, or ancillary online or offline products and services provided to Customer by Vendor, to which Customer is being granted access under this Agreement, including the Vendor Technology and the Content.

"User(s)" means Customer employees, representatives, consultants, contractors, or agents who are authorized to use the Service and have been supplied user identifications and passwords by Customer (or by Vendor at Customer's request).

2. License Grant and Restrictions

Vendor hereby grants Customer a nonexclusive, nontransferable, worldwide right to use the Service, solely for Customer own internal business purposes, subject to the terms and conditions of this Agreement. All rights not expressly granted to Customer are reserved by Vendor and its licensors.

Customer may not access the Service if Customer is a direct competitor of Vendor, except with Vendor's prior written consent. In addition, Customer may not access the Service for purposes of monitoring its availability, performance or functionality, or for any other benchmarking or competitive purposes.

Customer shall not (i) license, sublicense, sell, resell, transfer, assign, distribute, or otherwise commercially exploit or make available to any third party the Service or the Content in any way; (ii) modify or make derivative works based upon the Service or the Content; (iii) create Internet "links" to the Service or "frame" or "mirror" any Content on any other server or wireless or Internet-based device; or (iv) reverse engineer or access the Service in order to (a) build a competitive product or service, (b) build a product using similar ideas, features, functions or graphics of the Service, or (c) copy any ideas, features, functions or graphics of the Service. User licenses cannot be shared or used by more than one individual User but may be reassigned from time to time to new Users who are replacing former Users who have terminated employment or otherwise changed job status or function and no longer use the Service.

Customer may use the Service only for Customer's internal business purposes and shall not: (i) send spam or otherwise duplicative or unsolicited messages in violation of applicable laws; (ii) send or store infringing, obscene, threatening, libelous, or otherwise unlawful or tortuous material, including material harmful to children or violative of third party privacy rights; (iii) send or store material containing software viruses, worms, Trojan horses, or other harmful computer code, files, scripts, agents, or programs; (iv) interfere with or disrupt the integrity or performance of the Service or the data contained therein; or (v) attempt to gain unauthorized access to the Service or its related systems or networks.

Certain editions of the Service offer integration capabilities via an application programming interface (API). The number of API calls Customer can make per account is limited as follows (excluding calls resulting from use of Vendor client applications and Vendor-certified [third party] applications):

1,000 calls/day/User (aggregated over all Users under the account), up to an aggregate maximum of 1,000,000 calls/day/account.

3. Customer Responsibilities

Customer is responsible for all activity occurring under Customer's User accounts and shall abide by all applicable local, state, national, and foreign, laws, treaties and regulations in connection with Customer's use of the Service, including those related to data privacy, international communications, and the transmission of technical or personal data. Customer shall: (i) notify Vendor immediately of any unauthorized use of any password or account or any other known or suspected breach of security; (ii) report to Vendor immediately and use reasonable efforts to stop immediately any copying or distribution of Content that is known or suspected by Customer or Customer Users; and (iii) not impersonate another Vendor user or provide false identity information to gain access to or use the Service.

4. Account Information and Data

Vendor does not own any Customer Data. Customer, not Vendor, shall have sole responsibility for the accuracy, quality, integrity, legality, reliability, appropriateness, and intellectual property ownership or right to use of all Customer Data, and Vendor shall not be responsible or liable for the deletion, correction, destruction, damage, loss or failure to store any Customer Data. In the event this Agreement is terminated (other than by reason of Customer's breach), Vendor will make available to Customer a file of the Customer Data within 30 days of termination if Customer so requests at the time of termination. Vendor reserves the right to withhold, remove, and/or discard Customer Data without notice for any breach, including, without limitation, Customer's non-payment. Upon termination for cause, Customer's right to access or use Customer Data immediately ceases, and Vendor shall have no obligation to maintain or forward any Customer Data.

5. Intellectual Property Ownership

Vendor (and its licensors, where applicable) shall exclusively own all right, title, and interest, including all related Intellectual Property Rights, in and to the Vendor Technology, the Content and the Service and any suggestions, ideas, enhancement requests, feedback, recommendations, or other information provided by Customer or any other party relating to the Service. This Agreement is not a sale and does not convey to Customer any rights of ownership in or related to the Service, the Vendor Technology or the Intellectual Property Rights owned by Vendor. Vendor's name, Vendor's logo, and the product names associated with the Service are trademarks of Vendor or third parties, and no right or license is granted to use them.

6. Third Party Interactions

During use of the Service, Customer may enter into correspondence with, purchase goods and/or services from, or participate in promotions of advertisers or sponsors showing their goods and/or services through the Service. Any such activity, and any terms, conditions, warranties, or representations associated with such activity, is solely between Customer and the applicable third party. Vendor and its licensors shall have no liability, obligation, or responsibility for any such correspondence, purchase, or promotion between Customer and any such third party. Vendor does not endorse any sites on the Internet that are linked through the Service. Vendor provides these links to Customer only as a matter of convenience, and in no event shall Vendor or its licensors be responsible for any content, products, or other materials on or available from such sites. Vendor provides the Service to Customer pursuant to the terms and conditions of this Agreement. Customer recognizes, however, that certain third party providers of ancillary software, hardware, or services may require Customer's agreement to additional or different license or other terms prior to Customer's use of or access to such software, hardware or services.

7. Charges and Payment of Fees

Customer shall pay all fees or charges to Customer's account in accordance with the fees, charges, and billing terms in effect at the time a fee or charge is due and payable. The initial charges will be equal to the current number of total User licenses requested times the User license fee currently in effect. Payments must be made annually in advance unless otherwise mutually agreed upon in an Order Form or through the Online Order Center. All payment obligations are non-cancelable and all amounts paid are nonrefundable. Customer is responsible for paying for all User licenses ordered for the entire License Term, whether or not such User licenses are actively used. Customer must provide Vendor with valid credit card or approved purchase order information as a condition to signing up for the Service. An authorized License Administrator may add licenses by executing an additional written Order Form or using the Online Order Center. Added licenses will be subject to the following: (i) added licenses will be coterminous with the preexisting License Term (either Initial Term or renewal term); (ii) the license fee for the added licenses will be the then current, generally applicable license fee; and (iii) licenses added in the middle of a billing month will be charged in full for that billing month. Vendor reserves the right to modify its fees and charges and to introduce new charges at any time, upon at least 30 days prior notice to Customer, which notice may be provided by email. All pricing terms are confidential, and Customer agrees not to disclose them to any third party.

8. Excess Data Storage Fees

The maximum disk storage space provided to Customer at no additional charge is (i) 5 MB per User license for [Version], (ii) 1 GB per 5-User license package for

[Version], or (iii) the greater of 1 GB or an aggregate of 20 MB per User license, for [Version]. If the amount of disk storage required exceeds these limits, Customer will be charged the then-current storage fees. Vendor will use reasonable efforts to notify Customer when the average storage used per license reaches approximately 90 percent of the maximum; however, any failure by Vendor to so notify Customer shall not affect Customer's responsibility for such additional storage charges. Vendor reserves the right to establish or modify its general practices and limits relating to storage of Customer Data.

9. Billing and Renewal

Vendor charges and collects in advance for use of the Service. Vendor will automatically issue an invoice to Customer each year on the subsequent anniversary or as otherwise mutually agreed upon. The renewal charge will be equal to the then-current number of total User licenses times the license fee in effect during the prior term, unless Vendor has given Customer at least 30 days prior written notice of a fee increase, which shall be effective upon renewal and thereafter. Fees for other services will be charged on an as-quoted basis. Vendor's fees are exclusive of all taxes, levies, or duties imposed by taxing authorities, and Customer shall be responsible for payment of all such taxes, levies, or duties, excluding only U.S. (federal or state) taxes based solely on Vendor's income.

Customer agrees to provide Vendor with complete and accurate billing and contact information. This information includes Customer's legal company name, street address, email address, and name and telephone number of an authorized billing contact and License Administrator. Customer agrees to update this information within 30 days of any change to it. If the contact information Customer has provided is false or fraudulent, Vendor reserves the right to terminate Customer's access to the Service in addition to any other legal remedies.

If Customer believes its bill is incorrect, Customer must contact Vendor in writing within 60 days of the invoice date of the invoice containing the amount in question to be eligible to receive an adjustment or credit.

10. Nonpayment and Suspension

In addition to any other rights granted to Vendor herein, Vendor reserves the right to suspend or terminate this Agreement and Customer's access to the Service if Customer's account becomes delinquent. Delinquent invoices and accounts are subject to interest of 1.0 percent per month on any outstanding balance, or the maximum permitted by law, whichever is less, plus all expenses of collection. Customer will continue to be charged for User licenses during any period of suspension. If Customer or Vendor initiates termination of this Agreement, Customer will be obligated to pay the balance due on Customer's account computed in accordance with Section 9 above. Customer agrees that Vendor may bill Customer for such unpaid fees.

Vendor reserves the right to impose a reconnection fee in the event Customer is suspended and thereafter request access to the Service. Customer agrees and acknowledges that Vendor has no obligation to retain Customer Data and that such Customer Data may be irretrievably deleted if Customer's account is 30 days or more past due.

11. Termination upon Expiration/Reduction in Number of Licenses

This Agreement commences on the Effective Date. For Vendor Personal Edition licenses, the term is indefinite and may be terminated at any time in Vendor's sole discretion. For all other editions, the Initial Term will be as Customer elects during the online subscription process or as otherwise mutually agreed upon in an Order Form, commencing on the date Customer agrees to pay for the Service by completing the online subscription form, or on the start date of the Order Form.

Upon the expiration of the Initial Term, this Agreement will automatically renew for successive one-year terms at Vendor's then current fees. Either party may terminate this Agreement or reduce the number of licenses, effective only upon the expiration of the then current License Term, by notifying the other party in writing at least thirty (30) days prior to the expiration of the term. In the case of free trials, notifications provided through the Service indicating the remaining number of days in the free trial shall constitute notice of termination. In the event this Agreement is terminated (other than by reason of Customer's breach), Vendor will make available to Customer a file of the Customer Data within 30 days of termination if Customer so requests at the time of termination. Customer agrees and acknowledges that Vendor has no obligation to retain the Customer Data, and may delete such Customer Data, more than 30 days after termination.

12. Termination for Cause

Any breach of Customer's payment obligations or unauthorized use of the Vendor Technology or Service will be deemed a material breach of this Agreement. Vendor, in its sole discretion, may terminate Customer's password, account or use of the Service if Customer breaches or otherwise fails to comply with this Agreement. In addition, Vendor may terminate a free account at any time in its sole discretion. Customer agrees and acknowledges that Vendor has no obligation to retain the Customer Data, and may delete such Customer Data, if Customer has materially breached this Agreement, including but not limited to failure to pay outstanding fees, and such breach has not been cured within 30 days of notice of such breach.

13. Representations and Warranties

Each party represents and warrants that it has the legal power and authority to enter into this Agreement. Vendor represents and warrants that it will provide the Service in a manner consistent with general industry standards reasonably applicable to the provision thereof and that the Service will perform substantially in accordance with the online Vendor help documentation under normal use and circumstances. Customer represents and warrants that Customer has not falsely identified Customer nor provided any false information to gain access to the Service and that Customer's billing information is correct.

14. Mutual Indemnification

Customer shall indemnify and hold Vendor, its licensors and each such party's parent organizations, subsidiaries, affiliates, officers, directors, employees, attorneys, and agents harmless from and against any and all claims, costs, damages, losses, liabilities, and expenses (including attorneys' fees and costs) arising out of or in connection with: (i) a claim alleging that use of the Customer Data infringes the rights of, or has caused harm to, a third party; (ii) a claim, which if true, would constitute a violation by Customer of Customer's representations and warranties; or (iii) a claim arising from the breach by Customer or Customer Users of this Agreement, provided in any such case that Vendor (a) gives written notice of the claim promptly to Customer; (b) gives Customer sole control of the defense and settlement of the claim (provided that Customer may not settle or defend any claim unless Customer unconditionally releases Vendor of all liability and such settlement does not affect Vendor's business or Service); (c) provides to Customer all available information and assistance; and (d) has not compromised or settled such claim.

Vendor shall indemnify and hold Customer and Customer's parent organizations, subsidiaries, affiliates, officers, directors, employees, attorneys, and agents harmless from and against any and all claims, costs, damages, losses, liabilities, and expenses (including attorneys' fees and costs) arising out of or in connection with: (i) a claim alleging that the Service directly infringes a copyright, a U.S. patent issued as of the Effective Date, or a trademark of a third party; (ii) a claim, which if true, would constitute a violation by Vendor of its representations or warranties; or (iii) a claim arising from breach of this Agreement by Vendor; provided that Customer (a) promptly gives written notice of the claim to Vendor; (b) gives Vendor sole control of the defense and settlement of the claim (provided that Vendor may not settle or defend any claim unless it unconditionally releases Customer of all liability); (c) provides to Vendor all available information and assistance; and (d) has not compromised or settled such claim. Vendor shall have no indemnification obligation, and Customer shall indemnify Vendor pursuant to this Agreement, for claims arising from any infringement arising from the combination of the Service with any of Customer products, service, hardware or business process(s).

15. Disclaimer of Warranties

VENDOR AND ITS LICENSORS MAKE NO REPRESENTATION, WARRANTY, OR GUARANTY AS TO THE RELIABILITY, TIMELINESS, QUALITY, SUITABILITY, TRUTH, AVAILABILITY, ACCURACY, OR COMPLETENESS OF THE SERVICE OR ANY CONTENT. VENDOR AND ITS LICENSORS DO NOT REPRESENT OR WARRANT THAT (A) THE USE OF THE SERVICE WILL BE SECURE, TIMELY, UNINTERRUPTED, OR ERROR-FREE OR OPERATE IN COMBINATION WITH ANY OTHER HARDWARE, SOFTWARE, SYSTEM, OR DATA; (B) THE SERVICE WILL MEET CUSTOMER'S REQUIREMENTS OR EXPECTATIONS; (C) ANY STORED DATA WILL BE ACCURATE OR RELIABLE; (D) THE QUALITY OF ANY PRODUCTS, SERVICES, INFORMATION, OR OTHER MATERIAL PURCHASED OR OBTAINED BY CUSTOMER THROUGH THE SERVICE WILL MEET CUSTOMER'S REQUIREMENTS OR EXPECTATIONS; (E) ERRORS OR DEFECTS WILL BE CORRECTED; OR (F) THE SERVICE OR THE SERVER(S) THAT MAKE THE SERVICE AVAILABLE ARE FREE OF VIRUSES OR OTHER HARMFUL COMPONENTS. THE SERVICE AND ALL CONTENT IS PROVIDED TO CUSTOMER STRICTLY ON AN "AS IS" BASIS. ALL CONDITIONS, REPRESENTATIONS AND WARRANTIES, WHETHER EXPRESS, IMPLIED, STATUTORY OR OTHERWISE, INCLUDING, WITHOUT LIMITATION, ANY IMPLIED WARRANTY OF MERCHANTABILITY, FITNESS FOR A PARTICULAR PURPOSE, OR NON-INFRINGEMENT OF THIRD PARTY RIGHTS, ARE HEREBY DISCLAIMED TO THE MAXIMUM EXTENT PERMITTED BY APPLICABLE LAW BY VENDOR AND ITS LICENSORS.

16. Internet Delays

VENDOR'S SERVICES MAY BE SUBJECT TO LIMITATIONS, DELAYS, AND OTHER PROBLEMS INHERENT IN THE USE OF THE INTERNET AND ELECTRONIC COMMUNICATIONS. VENDOR IS NOT RESPONSIBLE FOR ANY DELAYS, DELIVERY FAILURES, OR OTHER DAMAGE RESULTING FROM SUCH PROBLEMS.

17. Limitation of Liability

IN NO EVENT SHALL EITHER PARTY'S AGGREGATE LIABILITY EXCEED THE AMOUNTS ACTUALLY PAID BY AND/OR DUE FROM CUSTOMER IN THE TWELVE (12) MONTH PERIOD IMMEDIATELY PRECEDING THE EVENT GIVING RISE TO SUCH CLAIM. IN NO EVENT SHALL EITHER PARTY AND/OR ITS LICENSORS BE LIABLE TO ANYONE FOR ANY INDIRECT, PUNITIVE, SPECIAL, EXEMPLARY, INCIDENTAL, CONSEQUENTIAL, OR OTHER DAMAGES OF ANY TYPE OR KIND (INCLUDING LOSS OF DATA, REVENUE, PROFITS, USE, OR OTHER ECONOMIC ADVANTAGE) ARISING OUT OF, OR IN ANY WAY CONNECTED WITH THIS SERVICE, INCLUDING BUT NOT LIMITED TO THE USE OR INABILITY TO USE THE SERVICE, OR FOR ANY CONTENT OBTAINED FROM OR THROUGH THE SERVICE, ANY INTERRUPTION, INAC-

CURACY, ERROR, OR OMISSION, REGARDLESS OF CAUSE IN THE CONTENT, EVEN IF THE PARTY FROM WHICH DAMAGES ARE BEING SOUGHT OR SUCH PARTY'S LICENSORS HAVE BEEN PREVIOUSLY ADVISED OF THE POSSIBILITY OF SUCH DAMAGES.

18. Additional Rights

Certain states and/or jurisdictions do not allow the exclusion of implied warranties or limitation of liability for incidental, consequential, or certain other types of damages, so the exclusions set forth above may not apply to Customer.

19. Local Laws and Export Control

Vendor provides services and uses software and technology that may be subject to U.S. export controls administered by the U.S. Department of Commerce, the U.S. Department of Treasury Office of Foreign Assets Control, and other U.S. agencies and the export control regulations of Switzerland and the European Union. Customer acknowledges and agrees that the software and Services shall not be used, and none of the underlying information, software, or technology may be transferred or otherwise exported or re-exported to countries on which the United States, Switzerland, and/or the European Union maintains an embargo (collectively, "Embargoed Countries"), or to or by a national or resident thereof, or any person or entity on the U.S. Department of Treasury's List of Specially Designated Nationals or the U.S. Department of Commerce's Table of Denial Orders (collectively, "Designated Nationals"). The lists of Embargoed Countries and Designated Nationals are subject to change without notice. By using the Service, Customer represents and warrants that Customer is not located in, under the control of, or a national or resident of an Embargoed Country or Designated National. Customer agrees to comply strictly with all U.S., Swiss, and European Union export laws and assume sole responsibility for obtaining licenses to export or re-export as may be required.

The software and Service may use encryption technology that is subject to licensing requirements under the U.S. Export Administration Regulations, 15 C.F.R. Parts 730–774 and Council Regulation (EC) No. 1334/2000.

Vendor and its licensors make no representation that the Service is appropriate or available for use in other locations. Customer is solely responsible for compliance with all applicable laws, including without limitation export and import regulations of other countries. Any diversion of the Content contrary to U.S., Swiss, or European Union (including European Union Member States) law is prohibited. None of the Content, nor any information acquired through the use of the Service, is or will be used for nuclear activities, chemical, or biological weapons, or missile projects, unless specifically authorized by the U.S. government or appropriate European body for such purposes.

20. Notice

Vendor may give notice by means of a general notice on the Service, email to Customer address on record in Vendor's account information, or by written communication sent by first class mail or pre-paid post to Customer address on record in Vendor's account information. Such notice shall be deemed to have been given upon the expiration of 48 hours after mailing or posting (if sent by first class mail or pre-paid post) or 12 hours after sending (if sent by email). Customer may give notice to Vendor (such notice shall be deemed given when received by Vendor) at any time by any of the following: letter sent by confirmed facsimile to Vendor at the following fax number: (___) ___-____ ; letter delivered by nationally recognized overnight delivery service or first class postage prepaid mail to Vendor at the following address:

21. Modification to Terms

Vendor reserves the right to modify the terms and conditions of this Agreement or its policies relating to the Service at any time, effective upon posting of an updated version of this Agreement on the Service. Customer is responsible for regularly reviewing this Agreement. Continued use of the Service after any such changes shall constitute Customer's consent to such changes.

22. Assignment; Change in Control

This Agreement may not be assigned by Customer without the prior written approval of Vendor but may be assigned without Customer's consent by Vendor to (i) a parent or subsidiary, (ii) an acquirer of assets, or (iii) a successor by merger. Any purported assignment in violation of this section shall be void. Any actual or proposed change in control of Customer that results or would result in a direct competitor of Vendor directly or indirectly owning or controlling 50 percent or more of Customer shall entitle Vendor to terminate this Agreement for cause immediately upon written notice.

23. General

This Agreement shall be governed by ________ law and controlling U.S. federal law, without regard to the choice or conflicts of law provisions of any jurisdiction, and any disputes, actions, claims, or causes of action arising out of or in connection with this Agreement or the Service shall be subject to the exclusive jurisdiction of the state and federal courts located in __________, ________.

No text or information set forth on any other purchase order, preprinted form, or document (other than an Order Form, if applicable) shall add to or vary the terms and conditions of this Agreement. If any provision of this Agreement is held by a court of competent jurisdiction to be invalid or unenforceable, then such provision(s) shall be construed, as nearly as possible, to reflect the intentions of the invalid or unenforceable provision(s), with all other provisions remaining in full force and effect. No joint venture, partnership, employment, or agency relationship exists between Customer and Vendor as a result of this agreement or use of the Service. The failure of Vendor to enforce any right or provision in this Agreement shall not constitute a waiver of such right or provision unless acknowledged and agreed to by Vendor in writing. This Agreement, together with any applicable Order Form, comprises the entire agreement between Customer and Vendor and supersedes all prior or contemporaneous negotiations, discussions or agreements, whether written or oral, between the parties regarding the subject matter contained herein.

IN WITNESS WHEREOF, the parties have executed this SaaS Subscription Agreement on the day and in the year as set forth above.

VENDOR:

BY: ______________________________

By: ______________________________

Title: ______________________________

CUSTOMER:

By: ______________________________

By: ______________________________

Title: ______________________________

* Based on the salesforce.com, inc. Master Subscription Agreement.

Consulting Agreement

(Neutral)

THIS CONSULTING AGREEMENT is made this _____ day of ___________, 20__, by and between ____________________, a ________________________ corporation, with its principal place of business at ______________________________ ______ ("Company") and ________________, [a _______________ corporation] [individually], with [its][his] principal place of business at ___________________ ____ ("Consultant").

BACKGROUND

Company is engaged in the development, licensing, and marketing of proprietary computer software. Consultant has expertise and experience in the areas listed in Exhibit A attached hereto and desires to consult with Company in its area of expertise. Based on Consultant's experience, Company desires to retain the services of Consultant and Consultant desires to render such services on the terms and conditions set forth below.

In consideration of the foregoing and of the mutual covenants herein contained, the parties, intending to be legally bound, agree as follows:

1. **Retention as Consultant.** Company hereby retains Consultant, and Consultant hereby agrees to render consulting services to Company, upon the terms and conditions set forth herein.

2. **Duties.** Consultant covenants and agrees that it will, as an independent contractor, perform all services as set forth in Exhibit A attached hereto.

3. **Independent Contractor Status.** The parties recognize that Consultant is an independent contractor and not an employee, agent, partner, joint venturer, covenantor, or representative of Company and that Company will not incur any liability as the result of Consultant's actions. Consultant shall at all times represent and disclose that it is an independent contractor of Company and shall not represent to any third party that Consultant is an employee, agent, covenantor, or representative of Company. [Company shall not withhold any funds from Consultant for tax or other governmental purposes, and Consultant shall be responsible for the payment of same. Or Consultant shall be considered to be a "casual employee" of Company and as such Company shall withhold all required taxes from Consultant's compensation.] Consultant shall not be entitled to receive any employment benefits offered to employees of Company including workers' compensation insurance coverage. Company shall not exercise control over Consultant.

4. **Compensation.** Company shall pay to Consultant, as compensation for the services to be rendered, the amount set forth in Exhibit B attached hereto.

5. **Term.** This Agreement shall commence on the date first written above and shall continue for ______________, unless otherwise terminated as provided herein.

6. **Termination.** Notwithstanding Section 5 of this Agreement, Company may immediately terminate Consultant for cause without prior notice.

7. **Covenant of Nondisclosure.** Consultant shall not, at any time during or after the term of this Agreement, in any manner, either directly or indirectly, divulge, disclose, or communicate to any person, firm, corporation, or other entity, or use for its own benefit or for the benefit of any person, firm, corporation, or other entity, and not for the benefit of Company, any information acquired from Company, its parent or subsidiaries, without the express prior written consent of an authorized executive officer of Company, as more fully set forth in a certain Proprietary Information Agreement between Company and Consultant dated __________________________________, 20____. In addition, Consultant shall ensure that Consultant's employees, officers, directors, agents, and representatives shall execute similar agreements protecting Company's proprietary information and agree to be bound by the terms and conditions contained therein.

8. **Rights to Work.** The parties acknowledge that any work performed by Consultant for Company is being created at the insistence of Company and shall be deemed "work made for hire" under the U.S. copyright law.

Company shall have the right to use the whole work, any part of parts thereof, or none of the work, as it sees fit. Company may alter the work, add to it, or combine it with any other work or works, at its sole discretion. Notwithstanding the foregoing, all original material submitted by Consultant as part of the work or as part of the process of creating the work, including but not limited to programs, listings, printouts, documentation, notes, flow charts, and programming aids, shall be the property of Company whether or not Company uses such material. No rights are reserved by Consultant.

All programs, specifications, documentation, and all other technical information prepared by Consultant in connection with the performance of its services hereunder will become and remain Company's sole property. Title to all material and documentation, including, but not limited to systems specifications, furnished by Company to Consultant or delivered by Company into Consultant's possession shall remain with Company. Consultant shall immediately return all such material or documentation within seven (7) days of any request by Company or upon the termination or conclusion of this Agreement, whichever shall occur first.

Whenever an invention or discovery is made by Consultant either solely or in collaboration with others, including employees of Company under or relating to this Agreement, the Consultant shall promptly give Company written notice thereof and shall furnish Company with complete information thereon including, as a minimum, (1) a complete written disclosure of each such invention, and (2) information concerning the date and identity of any public use, sale, or publication of such invention made by or known to Consultant or of any contemplated publication by Consultant. As used herein, the term (1) "invention" or "discovery" includes any art, machine, manufacture, design, or composition of matter or any new and useful improvement thereof where it is or may be patentable under the patent laws of the United States or of any foreign country; and (2) "made," when used in relation to any invention or discovery, means the conception of the first actual or constructive reduction to practice of such invention.

Consultant hereby grants, assigns, and conveys to Company all right, title, and interest in and to all inventions, works of authorship, and other proprietary data, and all other materials (as well as the copyrights, patents, trade secrets, and similar rights attendant hereto) conceived, reduced to practice, authored, developed, or delivered by Consultant or its employees, agents, consultants, contractors, and representatives either solely or jointly with others, during and in connection with the performance of services under this Agreement with Company. Consultant agrees that it will not seek, and that it will require its employees, agents, consultants, contractors, and representatives not to seek patent, copyright, trademark, registered design, or other protection for any rights in any such inventions, works or authorship, proprietary data, or other materials. Consultant shall have no right to disclose or use any such inventions, works of authorship, proprietary data, or other materials for any purpose whatsoever and shall not communicate to any third party the nature of or details relating to such inventions, works of authorship, proprietary data, or other materials. Consultant agrees that it shall do and that it will require its employees, agents, consultants, contractors, and representatives to do, at Company's expense, all things and execute all documents as Company may reasonably require to vest in Company or its nominees the rights referred to herein and to secure for Company or its nominees all patent, trademark, or copyright protection.

Consultant's obligations under this Agreement shall survive expiration or termination of this Agreement and any amendments thereto. Furthermore, Consultant irrevocably waives its moral rights in any work created, developed, or delivered hereunder.

Consultant agrees it will not disclose to any third party, without the prior written consent of Company, any invention, discovery, copyright, patent, trade secret, or similar rights attended hereto, made under or relating to this Agreement or any proprietary or confidential information acquired from Company under this Agreement, including trade secrets, business plans, and confidential or other information that may be proprietary to Company.

Consultant warrants and represents that it has or will have the right, through written agreements with its employees, to secure for Company the rights called for in this Section. Further, in the event Consultant uses any subcontractor, consultant, or other third party to perform any of the services contracted for under this Agreement, Consultant agrees to enter into and provide to Company such written agreements with such third party, and to take such other steps as are or may be required to secure for Company the rights called for in this Section. Consultant further agrees to provide the names and addresses of all agents, contractors, consultants, representatives, or other third parties who perform work on behalf of Consultant under this Agreement.

9. **Legal Relief.** In the event Consultant breaches, or threatens to breach any of the covenants expressed herein, the damages to Company will be great and irreparable

and difficult to quantify; therefore, Company may apply to a court of competent jurisdiction for injunctive or other equitable relief to restrain such breach or threat of breach, without disentitling Company from any other relief in either law or equity. In the event that any or all of the covenants expressed herein shall be determined by a court of competent jurisdiction to be invalid or unenforceable, by reason of its geographic or temporal restrictions being too great, or by reason that the range of activities covered are too great, or for any other reason, these covenants shall be interpreted to extend over the maximum geographic area, period of time, range of activities, or other restrictions to which they may be enforceable.

10. **Export Regulations.** Consultant acknowledges its obligations to control access to technical data under the U.S. Export Laws and Regulations and agrees to adhere to such laws and regulations with regard to any technical data received under this Agreement.

11. **Adherence to Laws.**

11.1 Consultant agrees that in carrying out its duties and responsibilities under this Agreement, it will neither undertake nor cause, nor permit to be undertaken, any activity which either (i) is illegal under any laws, decrees, rules, or regulations in effect in [**either**] the United States [**or foreign country if applicable**]; or (ii) would have the effect of causing Company to be in violation of any laws, decrees, rules, or regulations in effect in [**either**] the United States [**or foreign country if applicable**].

11.2 Consultant agrees that in connection with this Agreement or with any resultant contract or subcontract, it will not, directly or indirectly, give, offer or promise, or authorize to tolerate to be given, offered, or promised, anything of value to any entity or individual with the intent to (i) influence any act or decision of such entity or individual, or (ii) induce such entity or individual to use their influence to affect or influence any act or decision in order to assist Company in obtaining or retaining business or in directing business to any person.

11.3 Consultant agrees to notify Company immediately of any extortive solicitation, demand, or other request for anything of value, by, or on behalf of any entity or individual, relating to the subject matter of this Agreement.

12. **Covenant of Noncompetition.** Consultant agrees that for the period of this Agreement and for two (2) years thereafter, it and its employees and agents performing work hereunder will not directly or indirectly represent, be employed by, consult for or otherwise be associated with any other supplier of telecommunications software or software consulting services in the same capacity for which Consultant is providing services under this Agreement nor will Consultant be employed by or consult for any client of Company for which Consultant performs work for under this Agreement. Furthermore, Consultant agrees that Consultant and any individual or entity under Consultant's direct or indirect control will not solicit, hire, or retain as an employee or independent contractor any employee or former employee of Company without the prior written consent of an authorized executive officer of Company.

13. **Indemnification.** Consultant shall defend, indemnify, and hold harmless Company and its officers, directors, employees, agents, parent, subsidiaries, and other affiliates, from and against any and all damages, costs, liability, and expense, whatsoever (including attorneys' fees and related disbursements) incurred by reason of

(a) any failure by Consultant to perform any covenant or agreement of Consultant set forth herein; (b) the death or injury to any individual, or damage to or loss of Company property or the property of Company's client due to the negligence and/or willful acts of Consultant or Consultant's personnel; or (c) any breach by Consultant of any representation, warranty, or covenant under this Agreement. Company shall have the right of offset against fees or commissions due Consultant under this Agreement in the amount of any indemnification which Company is entitled under this Section 13.

14. **Warranty.** As an inducement for Company to enter into this Agreement, Consultant makes the following representations and warranties:

14.1 **Qualifications.** Consultant hereby represents and warrants to Company that all statements and materials regarding its qualifications to perform the work contemplated under this Agreement are true and correct and are not misleading or incomplete for any reason including by reason of omission. Consultant recognizes and agrees that Company may immediately terminate this Agreement if Consultant has misstated its qualifications or the qualifications of its employees, consultants, contractors, agents, or representatives to perform the work contemplated under this Agreement or otherwise breached its representations and warranties set forth in this Section 14.

14.2 **Quality of Services.** Consultant hereby represents and warrants to Company that all services, work, and deliverables to be performed hereunder shall be performed by qualified personnel in a professional and workmanlike manner, in accordance with the highest industry standards.

14.3 **Good Title.** Consultant hereby represents and warrants to Company that Company will receive good and valid title to all deliverables delivered by Consultant to Company under this Agreement, free and clear of all encumbrances and liens of any type.

15. **Miscellaneous.**

15.1 **Cooperation.** Consultant agrees that at any time and from time to time, upon the request of Company, to do, execute, acknowledge, and deliver, or cause to be done, executed, acknowledged, and delivered, all such further acts, documents, and instruments as may be required to effect any of the transactions contemplated by this Agreement.

15.2 **Assignment or Amendment.** This Agreement is not assignable by either Consultant or Company and all obligations hereunder shall terminate automatically upon the death of Consultant should such death occur prior to the termination of this Agreement. No alteration, modification, amendment, or other change of this Agreement shall be binding on the parties unless in writing, approved and executed by Consultant and an authorized executive officer of Company.

15.3 **Notices.** Any notice or other communication pursuant to this Agreement shall be in writing and shall be deemed to have been fully given upon receipt to the following addresses or such other addresses as the parties may provide in writing to the other from time to time:

If to Company: If to Consultant:

Attn: General Counsel

15.4 **Governing Law.** This Agreement shall be construed in accordance with the domestic laws of the state of ___________, excluding its principles of conflicts of laws. The parties hereto agree that any action related to this Agreement shall be venued solely in the Federal District Court for the District of ___________ and the parties hereby irrevocably commit to the jurisdiction of the said court.

15.5 **Invalidity.** The terms of this Agreement shall be severable so that if any term, clause, or provision hereof shall be deemed invalid or unenforceable for any reason, such invalidity or unenforceability shall not affect the remaining terms, clauses, and provisions hereof, the parties intending that if any such term, clause, or provision were held to be invalid prior to the execution hereof, they would have executed an agreement containing all the remaining terms, clauses and provisions of this Agreement.

15.6 **Waiver of Breach.** The waiver by either party hereto of any breach of the terms and conditions hereof will not be considered a modification of any provision, nor shall such a waiver act to bar the enforcement of any subsequent breach.

15.7 **Background, Enumerations, and Headings.** The "Background," enumerations, and headings contained in this Agreement are for convenience of reference only and are not intended to have any substantive significance in interpreting this Agreement.

15.8 **Company Property.** All Company property in the possession or control of Consultant including, but not limited to specifications, documentation, source code, magnetic media, and building entry keys and cards, as well as all material developed or derived by Consultant in performing its duties under this Agreement will be returned by Consultant to Company on demand, or at the termination of this Agreement whichever shall come first.

15.9 **Time.** Time is of the essence in the performance of Consultant's duties under this Agreement.

15.10 **Entire Agreement.** Except for the Proprietary Information Agreement referenced in Section 7, this Agreement shall constitute the entire agreement between the parties hereto and replaces and supersedes all prior agreements, written and oral, relating to the subject matter hereof, between the parties to this Agreement.

IN WITNESS WHEREOF, the parties have executed this Agreement under seal effective the date first written above.

ATTEST:	COMPANY:
______________________________	By: ____________________________(SEAL)
WITNESS/ATTEST:	CONSULTANT
______________________________	[By:] __________________________(SEAL)

Federal Tax Id. No./Social Security Number_______________

EXHIBIT A

Duties of Consultant

Consultant shall, upon the request of Company, perform the following tasks to the satisfaction of Company:

EXHIBIT B

Compensation

Company shall pay to Consultant, as compensation for the services to be rendered, the sum of $________ per hour for hours actually worked for a maximum of ______ hours per year. Consultant shall work the hours required, but Company shall not be obligated to provide a minimum number of hours of work to Consultant, nor shall Consultant be entitled to receive any compensation for hours not worked.

Consultant shall not be reimbursed by Company for Consultant's expenses. Consultant shall report to ____________________________.

Consultant shall not be paid for travel time.

Company shall pay Consultant all undisputed invoices presented by Consultant under this Agreement within thirty (30) days of the receipt of such invoices.

Master Services Agreement (Customer Oriented)

This Master Services Agreement (**"Agreement"**) is made and entered into this ___ day of _______, 20___ (**"Effective Date"**), by and between _____________________________, a _____________ corporation, with its principal place of business at _____________ ___________________________ (**"Customer"**), and ____________, a _______ corporation having a place of business at ____________ (**"Service Provider"**) (Customer and Service Provider sometimes are individually each referred to as a **"Party"**, and collectively referred to herein as the **"Parties"**).

RECITALS

WHEREAS, Service Provider submitted to Customer a proposal dated ___________, as supplemented (the "***Service Provider Proposal***", and attached as **Exhibit 3 (Service Provider Proposal)**), and represented to Customer that it had the expertise, personnel, services, and skills required to meet the requirements of Customer.

WHEREAS, Customer, in reliance on the information set forth in the Service Provider Proposal, other information provided by Service Provider and subsequent discussions, has selected Service Provider over other service providers to provide the Services and/or Deliverables (later defined herein) described in this Agreement.

WHEREAS, Customer and Service Provider want to specify the terms and conditions under which Service Provider shall provide the Services and/or Deliverables to Customer.

NOW, THEREFORE, in consideration of the agreements, representations, warranties, promises and covenants contained herein, and other good and valuable consideration, the receipt, sufficiency and adequacy of which are hereby acknowledged, the Parties, intending to be legally bound, agree to the foregoing and as follows:

ARTICLE 1—GENERAL

1.1 ***Overview of Agreement.*** This Agreement represents the terms and conditions under which Service Provider shall provide the mutually agreed to Services and/or Deliverables to Customer.

1.2 ***Definitions.*** Capitalized terms used in this Agreement, including in any Schedules, Exhibits, Attachments and/or other documents attached to or otherwise made a part of this Agreement, shall have the meanings ascribed to them in **Schedule 1.2 (Definitions)**. Other capitalized terms used in this Agreement are defined in the context in which they are used and shall have the meanings ascribed to them therein. SOW-specific definitions, if any, shall be included in the applicable Statement of Work. All defined terms include the plural as well as the singular.

1.3 ***Captions, References, and Construction.*** Captions, titles, and headings to articles and sections of this Agreement are inserted for convenience of reference only and are not intended to affect the interpretation or construction of this Agreement. Any reference herein to a particular Section number (e.g., "Section 2"), shall be deemed a reference to all Sections of this Agreement that bear sub-numbers to the number of the referenced Section (e.g., Sections 2.1, 2.1.1, etc.). The terms "this Agreement," "herein," "hereof," "hereunder," and similar expressions refer to this Agreement and not to any particular article, section or other portion hereof. Unless otherwise specified, "days" means calendar days. Any use of the term "including" in this Agreement shall be construed as if followed by the phrase "without limitation" or "but not limited to."

1.4 ***Conflicts in Interpretation.***

1.4.1 ***General Rules.*** The following order of precedence shall be followed in resolving any inconsistencies between the terms of this Agreement and the terms of any Schedules, Exhibits, Attachments and/or other documents attached hereto: (a) first, the terms contained in the body of this Agreement; (b) second, the terms of the Schedules, Exhibits, Attachments and/or other documents attached to this Agreement (excluding Schedules, Exhibits, Attachments, and/or other documents that constitute or are part of a Statement of Work), provided that no order of precedence shall be applied among such Schedules, Exhibits, Attachments, and/or other documents; (c) third, the terms of any Statements of Work, including all Schedules, Exhibits, Attachments, and/or other documents thereto; (d) fourth, the terms of any purchase order signed and issued by an authorized representative of Customer, including all Schedules, Exhibits, Attachments, and/or other documents thereto; (e) fifth, the Service Provider Proposal; and (f) sixth, the Documentation (excluding Service Provider Proposal).

1.4.2 ***Exception for Statements of Work.*** Unless the Parties specify in the applicable Statement of Work that a particular provision of the Statement of Work is to supersede a provision of this Agreement, in which case the superseding Statement of Work provisions shall be applicable only to such Statement of Work and shall be effective for such Statement of Work only if such provision expressly references the applicable Section of this Agreement that is to be modified and clearly states that such provision supersedes the conflicting or inconsistent provision in this Agreement, any attempt to alter or amend the terms and conditions contained in this Agreement through conflicting or inconsistent terms in a Statement of Work or any other document shall be void and of no force and effect.

1.5 ***Benefits of Agreement.*** All rights and benefits granted under this Agreement to Customer may be exercised, used, and enjoyed by any Affiliate of Customer. Further, for purposes of calculating discounts (if any) available under this Agreement that are based on volume, quantity, or other measurement factor, the total volume, quantity, or other measurement factor of all Customer Affiliates shall be counted to determine whether the applicable volume, quantity, or other measurement factor has been achieved.

1.6 ***References to Service Provider.*** As used in this Agreement, references to "Service Provider" also shall apply to Service Provider Affiliates, subcontractors and Service Provider Personnel in accordance with the following: (a) references to Service Provider shall mean at all times that Service Provider is responsible for ensuring and causing the compliance of Service Provider Affiliates, subcontractors, and Service Provider Personnel with the terms and conditions of this Agreement; (b) with regard to complying with the terms and conditions of this Agreement, references to Service Provider include Service Provider Affiliates and subcontractors to the extent that such Service Provider Affiliates and/or subcontractors are providing the Services to Customer as permitted by this Agreement; and (c) with regard to complying with the terms and conditions of this Agreement, references to Service Provider include the applicable Service Provider Personnel who are providing the Services. Notwithstanding the foregoing, under no circumstances shall Service Provider Affiliates and subcontractors and Service Provider Personnel shall be eligible for or exercise, use, or enjoy any rights or benefits of Service Provider under the terms and conditions of this Agreement unless otherwise explicitly stated otherwise in the applicable term or condition of this Agreement.

1.7 ***Statutory Rights.*** Nothing in this Agreement affects any statutory rights granted or terms required, in either case, by mandatory statutory law that cannot be waived or limited by contract. If there is a conflict between the terms and conditions of this Agreement and mandatory statutory law, mandatory statutory law will prevail.

1.8 ***Neither Party Considered Drafter.*** Despite the possibility that one Party may have prepared the initial draft of this Agreement and/or played the greater role in the preparation of subsequent drafts, the Parties agree that neither of them shall be deemed the drafter of this Agreement, and that, in construing this Agreement in case of any claim that any provision hereof may be ambiguous, no such provision shall be construed in favor of one Party on the ground that such provision was drafted by the other Party.

ARTICLE 2—STATEMENT(S) OF WORK

2.1 ***Statements of Work.***

2.1.1 ***General.*** Service Provider shall provide Services and/or Deliverables to Customer pursuant to one (1) or more Statements of Work in accordance with the terms set forth in this Agreement and this Article 2 (Statement(s) of Work).

Customer shall not be responsible to pay for any Services and/or Deliverables under this Agreement unless such Services and/or Deliverables are the subject of a written Statement of Work or a duly authorized Change Order. Each Statement of Work shall be attached to this Agreement as Exhibit 1 – __ (Statements of Work).

2.1.2 ***Contents of a Statement of Work.*** In preparing a Statement of Work, Service Provider shall propose to Customer, for its review and approval, the initial draft, which shall include: (a) a detailed description of the Services, including (i) identification of all milestone events, (ii) identification of all critical path milestones ("Critical Path Milestones") and the commencement and completion dates for such Critical Path Milestones, (iii) a detailed description of all activities to be performed by Service Provider and Customer, (iv) the number of Service Provider personnel-hours required to perform each task and Critical Path Milestone, (v) a detailed description of all activities, if any, to be performed by Third Parties, (vi) the dates and locations of scheduled status meetings, pursuant to **Section 2.4 (Status Meetings and Reports)**, and (vii) commencement and completion dates for any critical tasks related to or in connection with the Services; (b) the pricing of such Services and payment schedule; (c) the Deliverables (if any) to be generated by such Services; (d) the benchmarks or levels against which the quality, completeness, timeliness, and accuracy of the Services will be and the metrics used to measure Service Provider's performance of the Services ("Service Levels"); (e) personnel designated to perform the Services; and (f) a transition/implementation schedule detailing how the Services will be transitioned from the current provider of the Services, if any, to Service Provider.

2.2 ***Service Provider's Responsibilities for Equipment and Labor.*** Service Provider will furnish and pay for all labor, materials, services, tools, software, equipment, and other resources (including, without limitation, computer resources) necessary to perform the Services, except as otherwise expressly specified in a Statement of Work.

2.3 ***Change Order Procedures.***

2.3.1 ***Change Request.*** If either Party believes that a change (whether in the processes, procedures, standards, Service Levels, time frames, costs or deliverables) is necessary or desirable, such Party shall submit a written change request to the other Party (a "Change Request"). Service Provider represents to Customer that it has factored into Service Provider's fee adequate contingencies for de minimis change orders. Accordingly, if Change Requests are made, they will be presumed not to impact the fees under this Agreement; provided, however, that if the Change Request consists of other than a de minimis deviation from the scope of the SOW, Service Provider shall provide Customer with written notification of such other deviation within five (5) business days after receipt of the Change Request.

2.3.2 ***Change Response.*** In the event of a Customer-initiated Change Request, within five (5) business days of Service Provider's receipt of such Change Request, Service Provider shall provide to Customer a written statement describing in detail: (a) the impact on any Customer System performance, if any, and the modifications to the Customer System that will be required as a result of the Change Request including changes in Services and/or Deliverables; (b) the effect of the Change Request on the applicable SOW plans and tasks including any impact on any Critical Path Milestone dates; and (c) an estimate of the cost to implement each Change Request (collectively, the "Change Response"). If Service Provider submits a Change Request to Customer, such Change Request shall include the information required for a Change Response. Customer shall accept or reject any Change Response or Service Provider-initiated Change Request, as applicable, within five (5) business days after receipt of same from Service Provider.

2.3.3 ***Change Order.*** If Customer accepts a Change Response or Service Provider-initiated Change Request in writing, such Change Response, together with Customer's Change Request, or such Service Provider-initiated Change Request, shall be deemed to be a "Change Order" and shall become part of this Agreement and the applicable Statement of Work. If Customer rejects Service Provider's Change Response or Service Provider-initiated Change Request, Service Provider shall proceed to fulfill its obligations under this Agreement and the applicable Statement of Work. Without first obtaining Customer's prior written approval in accordance with the Change Order procedures set forth in this **Section 2.3 (Change Order Procedures)**, which approval Customer may withhold in its sole discretion, Service Provider shall make no Change which may: (a) increase Customer's total cost of the Services and/or Deliverables; (b) require changes to Customer's Systems, facilities, software, utilities, tools or equipment; (c) require Customer to install a new version, release, upgrade of, or replacement for, any software or equipment or to modify any software or equipment; (d) have an adverse impact on the functionality, interoperability, performance, security, accuracy, speed, responsiveness, quality, or resource efficiency of the Services and/or Deliverables; (e) have an adverse impact on the schedule for and the delivery of services and/or products by Customer to its clients and customers; or (f) violate or be inconsistent with the Customer Policies and/or applicable Laws.

2.4 ***Delays.*** If Customer reasonably determines that Service Provider is likely to fail to meet a Critical Path Milestone and/or the Interoperability Requirements, or if Service Provider has failed to meet a Critical Path Milestone and/or the Interoperability Requirements, then in addition to any other rights and remedies that may be available to Customer as provided in this Agreement and/or the applicable Statement of Work, at no additional cost or expense to Customer and at Customer's option, Service Provider shall provide to Customer all necessary additional Service Provider Personnel to accelerate performance as may be required or necessary to meet the Critical Path Milestone and/or the Interoperability Requirements or, if Service Provider has already failed to meet one (1) or more Critical Path Milestones and/or the Interoperability Requirements, complete the Critical Path Milestone and comply with the Interoperability Requirements within a re-adjusted time frame established by Customer. In addition to the foregoing, and subject to the terms of **Article 8 (Term and Termination)**, Customer shall be entitled to withhold any and all payments due from Customer to Service Provider until such Critical Path Milestone and/or the Interoperability Requirements are achieved.

2.5 ***Status Meetings and Reports.*** On the dates and at the locations specified in the SOW, and in any event no less than monthly, the Service Provider SOW Manager and other Key Personnel, the Customer SOW Manager, other appropriate representatives of the Parties and any necessary Third Parties shall meet at a Customer-designated site or by telephone conference, as determined by Customer, to discuss the status of each SOW, the development or implementation of any individual tasks within each SOW and any difficulties or issues that may exist, including personnel issues and any proposed changes to any Critical Path Milestones and/or changes to any date or other item set forth in the applicable SOW. The Parties acknowledge that any change of a Critical Path Milestone date shall require a mutually agreed Change Order. Service Provider shall keep minutes of all status meetings in form and substance reasonably satisfactory to Customer, and Service Provider shall issue copies of the minutes to all meeting attendees within forty-eight (48) hours of each meeting. At least five (5) business days before each status meeting, Service Provider shall present to Customer a written report of the status of each SOW in substantially the form attached as **Schedule 2.5 (SOW Status Report)**. The report shall include a summary, in such detail as Customer shall reasonably request, of: (a) the accomplishments and difficulties encountered during the prior reporting period; (b) suggestions and proposed actions for dealing with and resolving any identified difficulties and the anticipated results during the next reporting period; (c) a comprehensive and consolidated log of all outstanding SOW-related problems identified by Customer and Service Provider that remain to be resolved; and (d) if applicable, identification of any Customer or Third Party delays or other circumstances that Service Provider claims have impacted or will impact its ability to meet any Critical Path Milestone. Customer shall have the right to assume that Service Provider does not know of any problems, difficulties and/or issues that may have an adverse impact on the SOW (whether from a timing, cost or performance standpoint) unless Service Provider specifically identifies such problems, difficulties or issues in its written SOW Status Reports.

2.6 ***Rights of Divested Entities.*** A "***Divested Unit***" shall mean any Affiliate or any business, division, department, or group of assets of Customer or any Customer Affiliate which: (a) was, immediately prior to a particular date ("***Divestment Date***"), using or entitled to use the Deliverables, or receiving or entitled to receive the Services under this Agreement or to otherwise gain or derive some benefit from this Agreement ("***Benefit***"); (b) would not, on or after the Divestment Date, be entitled (other than by virtue of this provision) to use the Deliverables, receive the Services or otherwise gain that Benefit; and (c) as of the Divestment Date, is either acquired by a legal entity or, in the case of any business, division, department or group of assets, is constituted as a separate legal entity, or, in the case of an Affiliate, ceases to be an Affiliate as defined in this Agreement for any other reason. In the event that any of the events specified in **subsection (c)** above occurs, the rights and benefits under this Agreement shall be extended to the affected Divested Unit, without payment of any transfer or other fees, to enable that Divested Unit to continue to benefit from this Agreement or to gain the Benefit for a transition period not to exceed twelve (12) months from the Divestment Date. The Parties understand and agree that the purpose of such extension is to permit the Divested Unit to use the Deliverables, receive the Services or to otherwise gain the Benefit on a temporary basis during the transition to alternative Third Party service providers.

2.7 ***Limited Exceptions to Performance.***

2.7.1 ***Service Provider's Failure to Perform.*** Service Provider's failure to perform its responsibilities under this Agreement and/or a Statement of Work shall be excused if and only to the extent such Service Provider non-performance is directly caused by Customer's wrongful action or failure to perform its obligations under this Agreement and/or the applicable Statement of Work, but only if: (a) Service Provider notifies Customer in writing and expeditiously (under the circumstances) of such wrongful action or failure to perform and Service Provider's consequent inability to perform under such circumstances; (b) Service Provider provides Customer with every reasonable opportunity to correct such wrongful action or failure to perform and thereby avoid such Service Provider non-performance; and (c) Service Provider uses its best efforts to perform notwithstanding Customer's wrongful action or failure to perform.

2.7.2 ***References to Customer Responsibilities.*** References to Customer's responsibilities under this Agreement and/or a Statement of Work (other than Customer's obligation to pay for the Services and/or Deliverables in accordance with this Agreement), are intended solely for purposes of identifying what is not Service Provider's responsibility and will not under any circumstance constitute grounds for a claim that Customer has breached the applicable Statement of Work or this Agreement.

ARTICLE 3—SERVICES

3.1 ***Types of Services.*** As mutually agreed by the Parties and set forth in a Statement of Work to this Agreement, Service Provider shall provide any professional or other services that may be requested by Customer including consulting, design and build, implementation, hosting, integration, testing, development, custom programming, conversion, transition training, and support and maintenance services (individually or collectively, the "***Services***").

3.2 ***General Criteria for the Performance of Services.*** Service Provider shall perform the Services in a manner that shall: (a) avoid any adverse impact on the business, operations, financial condition and/or prospects of Customer; and (b) not degrade the services then being received by Customer from other Third Parties or provided internally by Customer. Prior to undertaking any Services-related activity or task, Service Provider shall discuss with Customer all known material risks and shall not proceed with such activity or task until Customer is satisfied with the plans with regard to such risks (provided, however, that, neither Service Provider's disclosure of any such risks to Customer, nor Customer acquiescence in Service Provider's plans, shall operate or be construed as limiting Service Provider's responsibilities under this Agreement). Service Provider shall identify and resolve any problems that may impede or delay the timely completion of each task in the SOW that is Service Provider's responsibility and shall use its best efforts to assist Customer with the resolution of any problems that may impede or delay the timely completion of each task in the SOW that is Customer's responsibility.

3.3 ***Compatibility and Interoperability.*** As part of the Services, Service Provider shall ensure that all Customer Systems shall be successfully integrated, interfaced, and compatible with the Services and Deliverables and that adequate and appropriate (as determined by Customer) architectural functions and structural integration exists between and among Customer Systems and the Services and Deliverables such that the Services and Deliverables have the capability to communicate, execute programs, or transfer data seamlessly. Further, Service Provider shall use its best efforts to ensure that the Services and/or Deliverables shall not adversely affect the Customer Systems, whether as to functionality, speed, service levels, interconnectivity, reliability, availability, performance, response times, or similar measures. The requirements of this **Section 3.3 (Compatibility and Interoperability)** shall be referred to as the "***Interoperability Requirements***".

3.4 ***Transition of Services.***

3.4.1 ***Transition Generally.*** During the period beginning on the Effective Date and ending on or before ____________, Service Provider shall plan, prepare for and conduct the transition of certain operations all in accordance with the Transition Plan (the "Transition"). Service Provider's responsibilities with respect to the Transition include: (a) performing the tasks set forth in the Transition Plan in accordance with the Transition Milestones; (b) performing the Services without interruption and without disrupting Customer's business operations; (c) paying all costs associated with the Transition, except to the extent otherwise set forth in the Statement of Work; and (d) performing such other transition and migration tasks as are necessary to enable Service Provider to complete the Transition and provide the Services.

3.4.2 ***Transition Plan.*** The Transition shall be conducted in accordance with a written plan which shall include: (a) a description of the operations being transitioned; (b) a description of the methods and procedures, personnel and organization that Service Provider will use to perform the Transition; (c) a schedule of transition activities; (d) a detailed description of the respective roles and responsibilities of Customer and Service Provider; and (e) such other information and planning as are necessary to ensure that the Transition takes place on schedule and without disruption to Customer operations (the "Transition Plan"). The draft of the Transition Plan as of the Effective Date is attached to the Agreement as Schedule 3.4.2 (Transition Plan). Service Provider shall be responsible for revising and finalizing the Transition Plan; provided that: (A) Service Provider shall cooperate and work closely with Customer in finalizing the Transition Plan (including incorporating Customer's reasonable comments); and (B) the final Transition Plan (and any changes thereto) shall be subject to written approval by Customer.

3.4.3 ***Completion of Transition.*** Customer reserves the right to monitor, observe, and participate in the Transition and, to the extent applicable, test any technical elements of the Transition. Service Provider will notify Customer without delay if such monitoring, participation or testing has caused (or if Service Provider expects it to cause) a problem or delay in the Transition, and will work with Customer to prevent or circumvent the problem or delay. If any Transition Milestone is not completed on or before the given date for such Transition Milestone due primarily to the fault of Service Provider, then for the period of delay: (a) Service Provider shall pay to Customer the applicable out of pocket costs Customer incurs as a result of the delay until such Transition Milestone is completed; (b) if Service Provider's charges to Customer are greater than they would have been if the delayed Transition Milestone had been completed on schedule, Customer will receive a credit against Service Provider's monthly charges in an amount equal to the difference between Service Provider's actual charges and what Service Provider's charges would have been if the delayed Transition Milestone had been completed on schedule; and (c) Service Provider shall pay to Customer actual costs incurred by Customer as a result of such delay, including costs incurred in having to extend Third Party contracts.

3.5 ***Service Provider Cooperation with Consultants; APIs; Know-How Transfer.***

3.5.1 ***Cooperation with Consultants.*** Service Provider acknowledges that Customer is now and will be, during the Term of this Agreement, working with a number of Third Parties in developing, installing, implementing, maintaining, and supporting the Customer Systems, and that Customer's use of the Services and/or any Deliverables is likely to involve the development and/or use of one or more APIs between such Customer Systems and the Services and/or any Deliverables. Service Provider shall cooperate with Customer and such Third Parties as may be necessary in connection with the foregoing, including using industry-standard APIs or developing APIs using as many industry-standard protocols as possible. Service Provider shall provide to Customer in written and, if available, electronic format API Documentation and other similar information for each API or modification thereof provided to Customer. In addition, Service Provider shall disclose API Documentation and other Service Provider Confidential Information as requested by Customer to Third Parties who have a need to know such Service Provider Confidential Information in order to perform services for Customer related to Customer's Systems, provided that such Third Parties are subject to written confidentiality obligations with Customer protecting Service Provider Confidential Information.

3.5.2 ***API Development and Modifications.*** As required by Customer in order to meet the Interoperability Requirements, Service Provider shall develop one (1) or more APIs and such APIs shall be considered a Deliverables hereunder and will be provided pursuant to Article 3 (Services). If an API problem occurs, or if a modification to an API is required, Service Provider agrees that it will cooperate with all applicable Third Parties to modify the API as necessary so that the API performs in accordance with the applicable Specifications and Documentation. If an API modification is required because of a Third Party system change or problem, Service Provider shall implement such modification pursuant to a Statement of Work or, in the event such modification relates to an existing Statement of Work, such modification shall be implemented in accordance with the Change Order procedure described in **Section 2.2 (Change Order Procedures)**. If such modification is required due to a failure of the Service Provider portion of the API to operate in accordance with the applicable Specifications or Documentation, Service Provider shall implement such modification at no additional cost or expense to Customer.

3.5.3 ***Know-How Transfer.*** During the Term of this Agreement, during the course of performance of the Services, Service Provider shall, at no additional cost to Customer, transfer knowledge, ideas, concepts, information and the like regarding the Services and/or Deliverables in order that Customer shall become self-reliant with respect to the day-to-day operation and provision of the Services and/or Deliverables and will be able to develop and implement all necessary interfaces between the Services and/or Deliverables and Customer's Systems (collectively, "Know-How"). The transfer of Know-How may include attendance by Customer-designated employees at Vendor's training programs that relate to the Services and/or Deliverables. In addition, Vendor's transfer of Know-How shall include information and/or programs, tools and other materials, which may include knowledge relating to the following: (a) data files, file and data definitions and relationships, data definition specifications, data models, interfaces, program architecture, program structure, sequence and organization, screen displays, reference and user manuals, design and functional specifications relating to the Services and/or Deliverables; (b) maintenance, support utilities, and tools relating to the Services and/or Deliverables; (c) security requirements and methodologies relating to the Services and/or Deliverables; and (d) such other material to which the Parties mutually agree in writing.

3.6 ***Service Levels.***

3.6.1 ***Service Level Commitment and Reporting.*** Service Provider commits to provide the Services in accordance with the Services Levels as set forth in the applicable Statement of Work. Service Provider shall provide monthly reports to Customer regarding its performance relative to the Service Levels. If Service Provider fails to meet a Service Level in a month, Service Provider shall: (a) report that failure to Customer; (b) promptly investigate the causes of the problem; (c) prepare a report identifying the causes and the methods to be used by Service Provider to correct the problem and prevent a recurrence; (d) take commercially reasonable actions necessary to correct the problem and begin meeting the Service Levels as soon as practicable; (e) advise Customer of the status of the remedial efforts being undertaken with respect to such problem; and (f) if requested by Customer due to the nature of the problem or its recurrence, make available for meetings and consultation with Customer those personnel within Service Provider who are the recognized experts with respect to the problem. Service Provider shall utilize the necessary measurement and monitoring tools and procedures to measure and report Service Provider's performance of the Services against the applicable Service Levels to Customer on a monthly basis. Such measurement and monitoring shall permit reporting at a level of detail sufficient to verify compliance with the Service Levels, and shall be subject to audit by Customer in accordance with **Section 9.5 (Audits)** of this Agreement.

3.6.2 ***Service Level Credits.*** Service Provider recognizes that its failure to meet the Service Levels may have a material adverse impact on the business and operations of Customer and that the damage from Service Provider's failure to meet a Service Level cannot be precisely determined. Accordingly, in the event that Service Provider fails to meet a Service Level, then, in addition to any non-monetary remedies available to Customer under this Agreement, in equity or at law, Customer shall recover, the corresponding "Service Level Credit" specified in the applicable Statement of Work as liquidated damages and not a penalty. Service Provider shall not be required to pay Service Level credits to the extent that failure to meet Service

Levels is caused solely: (a) by the actions of Customer; or (b) circumstances that constitute a Service Provider Force Majeure Event.

3.7 ***Included Services.*** If any services, functions, or responsibilities not specifically described in this Agreement and/or the applicable Statement of Work are an inherent, necessary, or customary part of the Services, or are required for proper performance or provision of the Services in accordance with this Agreement and/or the applicable Statement of Work, they shall be deemed to be included within the scope of the Services to be delivered for the Fees, as if such services, functions, or responsibilities were specifically described in this Agreement, unless such services, functions, or responsibilities are expressly excluded in this Agreement or designated in a writing approved by Customer to be the responsibility of Customer. Except as otherwise agreed in writing by the Parties as a Customer responsibility, Service Provider shall procure or otherwise provide, at Service Provider's cost and expense, all Service Provider Personnel with the hardware, software, network facilities, and the other materials, resources, and items required to provide the Services and otherwise perform its obligations under this Agreement.

3.8 ***Services Evolution.*** Throughout the Term, Service Provider will seek to improve the quality, efficiency, and effectiveness of the Services to keep pace with advances or improvements in business processes or technology, and support Customer's efforts to maintain its competitiveness in the markets in which it competes. Service Provider will do this by: (a) identifying and applying best practice techniques and methodologies in performing and providing the Services; (b) training Service Provider Personnel in new techniques, methodologies, and technologies used generally within Service Provider's organization or the IT services industry and approved by Customer for use in the Services; (c) training Service Provider Personnel in new techniques, methodologies, and technologies used within Customer's organization, or used generally in the IT services industry; and (d) making investments to maintain the currency of the processes, methodologies, tools, infrastructure, and other resources used by Service Provider to provide the Services.

3.9 ***Right to In-Source and Re-Source the Services.*** Customer has the right to perform itself, or retain Third Parties to perform, any of the Services. To the extent Customer performs any of the Services itself, or retains Third Parties to do so, Service Provider shall cooperate with Customer or such Third Parties, which cooperation shall include: (a) providing access to the facilities being used by Service Provider to provide the Services (as necessary for Customer or a Third Party to perform its work); (b) providing access to the systems involved in providing the Services; and (c) providing such information regarding the business processes and methodologies, system constraints and other operating parameters as a person with reasonable commercial skills and expertise would find reasonably necessary for Customer or a Third Party to perform its work. Third Parties retained by Customer shall comply with Service Provider's reasonable security and confidentiality requirements and with Service Provider's reasonable work standards, methodologies and procedures, as these have been provided by Service Provider in writing.

ARTICLE 4—PERSONNEL

4.1 ***Minimum Personnel Requirements.*** All Service Provider Personnel shall have experience, training, and expertise sufficient to perform Service Provider's obligations under this Agreement, including Service Provider's obligations with respect to the Specifications, Performance Standards, Interoperability Requirements, and/or Service Levels. All costs and expenses associated with equipping, training, and retaining Service Provider Personnel and other staff is included within the fees. Customer shall not be required to pay for Services provided by any Service Provider Personnel who does not possess the represented levels of experience and expertise.

4.2 ***Service Provider SOW Manager.*** Each Statement of Work shall designate the Service Provider SOW manager ("***Service Provider SOW Manager***") and any Key Personnel for that SOW. The Service Provider SOW Manager shall: (a) act as a liaison between Service Provider and Customer for all matters related to this Agreement and the applicable Statement of Work; (b) manage the relationship with Customer and will be Customer's primary point of contact for all questions and issues relating to the SOW; (c) provide such information and data as is reasonably necessary to enable Customer to perform its duties, responsibilities or obligations hereunder; and (d) have overall responsibility for ensuring Service Provider's performance of its responsibilities and obligations as set forth in this Agreement and in the applicable SOW.

4.3 ***Removal of Service Provider Personnel by Customer.*** Customer shall have the right to require Service Provider to replace the Service Provider SOW Manager and other Service Provider Personnel whom Customer deems to be unfit or otherwise unsatisfactory to perform Service Provider's duties, responsibilities or obligations hereunder. Without limiting the foregoing, during the forty-eight (48) hour period immediately following Customer's notice to Service Provider of such request for replacement, designated representatives from each Party shall meet to discuss the request and any alternative solutions. Race, gender, age, religion, national origin, and other legally discriminatory characteristics shall not be valid grounds for any such request by Customer.

4.4 ***Removal/Reassignment by Service Provider.*** Service Provider shall not remove or temporarily reassign the Service Provider SOW Manager or other Key Personnel: (a) without providing at least ten (10) days prior written notice to Customer; and (b) until such time as the Parties have agreed to the replacement personnel. If Service Provider replaces or reassigns the Service Provider SOW Manager or other Key Personnel as permitted hereunder, the proposed replacement personnel shall possess comparable experience and training as the individual whom Service Provider proposes to replace. At no time shall there be a vacancy or gap in the position of Service Provider SOW Manager or other Key Personnel unless otherwise agreed to by the Parties in writing. Customer may withhold an amount equal to fifty percent (50%) of all monies due and to become due to Service Provider under this Agreement until the position of Service Provider SOW Manager or other Key Personnel is filled by a qualified employee, as approved by Customer. Service Provider shall not charge Customer for the costs associated with educating any individuals replacing the Service Provider SOW Manager or other Key Personnel (e.g., costs resulting from a replaced

Service Provider SOW Manager educating a new Service Provider SOW Manager). Provided the replaced individual remains in the employ of Service Provider, such individual shall continue to be available by telephone to answer any SOW-related questions. Either Party's request for removal or reassignment of personnel shall not excuse Service Provider from meeting any Critical Path Milestones.

4.5 ***Approval of Subcontractors.*** Service Provider shall obtain Customer's written consent, which Customer may withhold in it sole discretion, before entering into agreements with or otherwise engaging any subcontractors (including Affiliates of Service Provider) who may supply any part of the Deliverables and/or or Services to Customer. At Customer's request, Service Provider shall provide information regarding the subcontractors' qualifications and a listing of the subcontractors' key personnel including, if requested by Customer, resumes of proposed Service Provider Personnel. Service Provider shall remain directly responsible to Customer for its subcontractors and shall indemnify Customer for the actions or omissions of its subcontractors under the terms and conditions specified in **Section 10.1 (Service Provider Indemnifications)**. All subcontractors and their representatives, agents and employees must sign a Confidentiality and Nondisclosure Agreement, in materially the form set forth in **Exhibit 2 (Confidentiality and Nondisclosure Agreement)**, prior to and as a condition of becoming an authorized subcontractor, and shall be subject to the provisions of this Agreement applicable to Service Provider Personnel, including removal pursuant to **Section 4.3 (Removal of Service Provider Personnel by Customer)**.

4.6 ***Compliance with Customer Policies.*** In performing the Services and while at any Customer facilities, Service Provider Personnel shall: (a) conduct themselves in a businesslike manner; (b) comply with the policies, procedures, and rules of Customer regarding safety and health and personal, professional and ethical conduct; (c) comply with the finance, accounting, banking, Internet, security, and/or other applicable standards, policies, practices, processes, procedures, and controls of Customer; and (d) abide by all Laws applicable to the Customer facilities and/or the provision of the Services, and all additions and modifications to each of **subsections (b)**, **(c)**, and **(d)** (collectively, "***Customer Policies***"). Customer Policies, and additions or modifications thereto, may be communicated orally or in writing to Service Provider or Service Provider Personnel or may be made available to Service Provider or Service Provider Personnel by conspicuous posting at a Customer facility, electronic posting, or other means generally used by Customer to disseminate such information to its employees or contractors. Service Provider shall be responsible for the promulgation and distribution of Customer Policies to Service Provider Personnel to the extent necessary and appropriate.

4.7 ***Service Provider Personnel Are Not Customer Employees; Responsibility for Service Provider Personnel.*** Except as otherwise expressly set forth in this Agreement, the Parties intend to create an independent contractor relationship and nothing in this Agreement shall operate or be construed as making Customer and Service Provider partners, joint venturers, principals, joint employers, agents, or employees of or with the other. No Service Provider Personnel retained by Service Provider to perform work on Customer's behalf or for Customer hereunder shall be deemed to be an officer, director, employee, agent, Affiliate, contractor, or subcontractor of Customer for any purpose. Service Provider, not Customer, has the right, power, authority, and duty to supervise and direct the activities of the Service Provider Personnel and to compensate such Service Provider Personnel for any work performed by them on the behalf of or for Customer pursuant to this Agreement. Service Provider, and not Customer, shall be responsible and therefore solely liable for all acts and omissions of Service Provider Personnel, including acts or omissions constituting negligence, gross negligence, willful misconduct, and/or fraud.

4.8 ***Background Checks for Service Provider Personnel.*** Service Provider shall ensure that Service Provider Personnel: (a) are authorized to work in the jurisdiction in which they are assigned to perform Services; (b) have not been convicted of a felony and are not proven substance abusers; and (c) are not otherwise disqualified from performing the Services under applicable Laws. If requested by Customer and not in violation of applicable Law, Service Provider shall conduct a background check on all Service Provider Personnel to verify compliance with the preceding requirements and shall review the results of the background check of each Service Provider Personnel to verify that the Service Provider Personnel meets Service Provider's standards for employment. Such background check shall be in the form generally used by Service Provider in its initial hiring of employees or contracting for contractors or, as applicable, during the employment-screening process but must, at a minimum, have been performed within the preceding twelve (12) month period. Service Provider Personnel who do not meet criteria acceptable to Customer, in Customer's sole discretion, shall not be assigned to work hereunder, and Customer shall have the right, at its sole option, to refuse access to any Service Provider Personnel to any Customer facility.

4.9 ***Customer Personnel.*** Customer shall provide personnel to perform its obligations under this Agreement and any Statement of Work, including a SOW manager for each SOW ("***Customer SOW Manager***"), who shall act as a liaison between Service Provider and Customer, coordinate Customer resources, coordinate Customer personnel and have overall responsibility for meeting Customer's responsibilities and obligations.

ARTICLE 5—TESTING PROCESS

5.1 ***Test Plan.*** Service Provider shall be responsible for testing the Services and/or Deliverables, or components thereof, as applicable, in accordance with a test plan to be mutually developed and agreed to by the Parties in writing ("***Test Plan***"), which Test Plan will incorporate testing methodologies to confirm that the Services and/or Deliverables, or components thereof, as applicable, operate in accordance with the applicable Documentation, Specifications, Service Levels, Interoperability Requirements, and Performance Standards. The Test Plan will be developed in accordance with the time frame specified in the applicable SOW, and the date to complete development of the Test Plan shall, unless otherwise agreed to by the Parties, be a Critical Path Milestone. In addition to the above, each Test Plan shall describe the exact scope, methodologies, and procedures (including expected performance results) for testing the Services and/or Deliverables, or components thereof. When approved by Customer in writing, the Test Plan will be attached to the applicable Statement of Work. Customer may modify or amend the scope, methodologies, and procedures for executing the testing process to include additional testing criteria as may be reasonably necessary to conduct the testing in accordance with the Change Order process set forth in **Section 2.2 (Change Order Procedures)**.

5.2 ***Pre-Live Testing.*** Pre-live testing for the Services and/or Deliverables, or components thereof, as applicable ("***Pre-Live Testing***") shall commence on the date specified in the applicable SOW, including the execution of the test suites as provided for in the applicable Test Plan. If any Defects in the Services and/or Deliverables, or components thereof, are discovered as a result of Pre-Live Testing, Service Provider shall promptly correct such Defects. When all Defects identified during Pre-Live Testing have been corrected, Customer shall give Service Provider written notice thereof and the Services and/or Deliverables, or components thereof, shall thereafter be ready for Live Testing.

5.3 ***Live Testing.*** Following successful completion of all Pre-Live Testing, Customer shall have the period specified for Live Testing in the applicable Statement of Work ("***Live Testing Period***") to test the Services and/or Deliverables, or components thereof, under actual, everyday operating conditions to assess whether such Services and/or Deliverables, or components thereof, operate in accordance with the applicable Documentation, Specifications, Service Levels, and Performance Standards ("***Live Testing***"). In the event any Defects in the Services and/or Deliverables, or components thereof, are discovered during the Live Testing Period, Customer shall report such Defects to Service Provider, and Service Provider shall promptly correct all Defects in the Services and/or Deliverables, or components thereof. Upon Service Provider's receipt of notice from Customer of any Defects, the Live Testing Period (but not Customer's use of the Services and/or Deliverables, or components thereof) shall be suspended temporarily and shall recommence upon Service Provider's receipt of written notice from Customer that such Defects have been corrected; provided, however, that Customer shall in no event have less than fifteen (15) days to verify any correction provided by Service Provider. Subject to the terms of **Section 5.5 (Failure to Achieve Acceptance)**, such process shall repeat as often as necessary until all Defects have been corrected. Successful Live Testing shall occur when the Services and/or Deliverables, or components thereof: (a) has been operating for the Live Testing Period and all Material Defects have been corrected; and (b) has been operating during the last ten (10) days of the Live Testing Period without experiencing any Material Defects.

5.4 ***Acceptance.*** "***Acceptance***" for the applicable Services and/or Deliverables, or components thereof, shall occur only when: (a) Service Provider has corrected, to Customer's satisfaction, all Material Defects identified by the Parties during testing; (b) Service Provider has provided to Customer all Services and/or Deliverables, or components thereof, required to be provided to Customer pursuant to the applicable Statement of Work, and each of the Parties has completed all tasks required to be completed by such Party that are identified by the Parties as a pre-condition to Customer's acceptance; and (c) either (i) Customer notifies Service Provider in writing that all testing for the Services and/or Deliverables, or components thereof, as applicable, has been completed successfully in accordance with the terms of this

Section 5.4 (Acceptance) and the applicable Statement of Work and that the requirements of **subsections (a)** and **(b)** above have been satisfied to Customer's satisfaction, or (ii) Service Provider provides to the Customer SOW Manager a written notice of completion stating that Service Provider believes all testing for the Services and/or Deliverables, or components thereof, has been completed successfully in accordance with the terms of this **Section 5.4 (Acceptance)** and the applicable Statement of Work and that the requirements of **subsections (a)** and **(b)** above have been satisfied, unless Customer provides Service Provider with notice to the contrary within fifteen (15) days following the date of receipt by the Customer SOW Manager of Service Provider's written notice of completion, in which case Acceptance shall not occur and the Parties shall continue the applicable testing in accordance with this **Article 5 (Testing Process)**. With respect to Statements of Work involving more than one phase or rollout, the testing and acceptance process may be conducted on a per-phase/rollout basis, with final Acceptance occurring only upon successful completion and acceptance of each phase/rollout, as mutually agreed by the Parties and set forth in the applicable Statement of Work. Nothing else, including Customer's use of the Services and/or Deliverables, or any components thereof, in a live, operational environment, shall constitute Acceptance (under applicable state contract law, the Uniform Commercial Code (UCC) or the Uniform Computer Information Transactions Act (UCITA), as adopted by any state) of any portion of the Services and/or Deliverables, and/or the applicable Statement of Work.

5.5 ***Failure to Achieve Acceptance.*** In the event Acceptance is not achieved within ninety (90) days following commencement of Live Testing, Customer shall have the right to declare an Event of Default and seek the rights and remedies available to it under **Article 8 (Term and Termination)**. Without limiting the foregoing, the Parties hereby acknowledge and agree that, upon the occurrence of such event with respect to the Statement of Work, Customer shall be entitled to a full refund of any and all fees, expenses and amounts paid to Service Provider in connection with or related to the applicable SOW.

5.6 ***Post-Acceptance Correction of Defects.*** Service Provider shall correct any Defects in the Services and/or Deliverables, or any components thereof, remaining to be corrected following Acceptance under the applicable Statement of Work.

ARTICLE 6—REPRESENTATIONS AND WARRANTIES

6.1 ***Deliverables Functionality and Performance.*** Service Provider represents and warrants to Customer that the Deliverables provided under this Agreement shall: (a) contain the functionality specified in the applicable Documentation, Specifications, Service Levels and Performance Standards; and (b) for the period of time specified in the applicable Statement of Work or, if no time frame for a warranty is specified therein, one (1) year from the date of Acceptance (the "***Warranty Period***") operate without Defect in accordance with the applicable Documentation, Specifications, Service Levels, Interoperability Requirements and Performance Standards. Service Provider further represents and warrants that Deliverables shall perform in accordance with the purposes for which the Deliverables were designed and intended to be used by Customer (as such intended use is generally described in the Service Provider Proposal and in the applicable Statement of Work), it being acknowledged and agreed that Customer selected Service Provider to provide the Deliverables based, in part, on Service Provider's representations that the Deliverables is capable of meeting Customer's needs. Service Provider shall correct, at no additional cost or expense to Customer, any failure of the applicable Deliverables to operate in accordance with the warranties set forth above. If additional software, equipment and/or services are required to remedy the failure, Service Provider shall provide to Customer, at no additional cost or expense to Customer, the additional software, equipment and/or services required for the Deliverables to operate in accordance with the warranties set forth above. In the event Service Provider is unable to correct such failure within thirty (30) days after receiving notice thereof, an Event of Default shall be deemed to have occurred. This warranty shall survive the expiration or termination of this Agreement for the applicable Warranty Period.

6.2 ***Performance of the Services.*** Service Provider represents and warrants to Customer that Service Provider has the skills, resources, and expertise to provide and shall provide all Services in accordance with the terms and conditions of this Agreement. Without limiting the generality of the foregoing, Service Provider represents and warrants to Customer that: (a) all Services provided under this Agreement shall be provided in a timely, professional, and workmanlike manner consistent with the highest industry standards of quality and integrity; provided, however, that where this Agreement specifies a particular standard or criteria for performance, this warranty is not intended to and does not diminish that standard or criteria for performance; and (b) other than the applicable fees set forth in **Article 7 (Price and Payment)**, no additional cost or expense shall be required of Customer in order for Service Provider to be able to provide the Services as required under this Agreement.

6.3 ***Intellectual Property.*** Service Provider represents and warrants to Customer that the Services and/or Deliverables and Customer's use of the Services and/or Deliverables does not and shall not infringe upon any Intellectual Property Rights of any Third Party, and there is currently no actual or threatened suit against Service Provider by any Third Party based on an alleged violation of such Intellectual Property Rights. This warranty shall survive the expiration or termination of this Agreement.

6.4 ***No Violation of Laws.*** Service Provider represents and warrants to Customer that Service Provider is not, and covenants that it shall not be, in violation of any Laws to which it is subject, and has not failed, and shall not fail, to obtain any licenses, permits, franchises or other governmental authorizations necessary for the performance of the Services, ownership of its properties or the conduct of its business, which violation or failure, either individually or in the aggregate, might adversely affect its business, properties or financial condition, the consummation of the transactions contemplated by this Agreement, or the performance of its obligations hereunder. Service Provider further represents and warrants that it is compliant with all applicable anti-money laundering laws, including the USA Patriot Act, and the laws administered by the U.S. Treasury Department's Office of Foreign Assets Control, including Executive Order 13224. Service Provider further represents and warrants that it is not owned or controlled by any person or entity, on the SDN List published by the U.S. Treasury Department's Office of Foreign Assets Control. Service Provider agrees that it will notify Customer immediately in writing of the occurrence of any event which renders the foregoing warranties and representations incorrect.

6.5 ***Disabling Code.*** Service Provider represents and warrants to Customer that the Licensed Products do not contain and will not receive from Service Provider's data transmission via modem or any other Service Provider medium any virus, worm, trap door, back door, timer, clock, counter or other limiting routine, instruction or design that would erase data or programming or otherwise cause the Deliverables to become inoperable or incapable of being used in the full manner for which it was designed and created (collectively, a "***Disabling Code***"). In the event a Disabling Code is identified, Service Provider shall take all steps necessary, at no additional cost or expense to Customer, to: (a) restore and/or reconstruct any and all Confidential Information and data lost by Customer as a result of such Disabling Code; (b) furnish to Customer a new copy of the Deliverables without the presence of Disabling Codes; and (c) install and implement such new copy of the Deliverables. This warranty shall survive any expiration or termination of this Agreement until Customer discontinues its use of the applicable Deliverables.

6.6 ***Open Source.*** Unless otherwise agreed by the Parties in writing, Service Provider represents and warrants to Customer that the Deliverables provided pursuant to this Agreement shall not contain any "***Open Source***". For purposes of this Agreement, "Open Source" means any software code that: (a) contains, or is derived in any manner (in whole or in part) from, any software that is distributed as free software, open source software, shareware (e.g., Linux), or similar licensing or distribution models; and (b) is subject to any agreement with terms requiring that such software code be (i) disclosed or distributed in Source Code or Object Code form, (ii) licensed for the purpose of making derivative works, and/or (iii) redistributable. Open Source includes, but is not limited to, software licensed or distributed under any of the following licenses or distribution models, or licenses or distribution models similar to any of the following: (A) GNU's General Public License (GPL) or Lesser/Library GPL (LGPL); (B) the Artistic License (e.g., PERL); (C) the Mozilla Public License(s); (D) the Netscape Public License; (E) the Berkeley software design (BSD) license including Free BSD or BSD-style license; (F) the Sun Community Source License (SCSL); (G) an Open Source Foundation License (e.g., CDE and Motif UNIX user interfaces); (H) the Apache Server license; and (I) any licenses listed at http://www.opensource.org/licenses.

6.7 ***Legal and Corporate Authority.*** Service Provider represents and warrants to Customer that: (a) Service Provider is a ____________ **[corporation]**, and is qualified and registered to transact business in all locations where the performance of its obligations hereunder would require such qualification; (b) Service Provider has all necessary rights, powers and authority to enter into and perform this Agreement, and the execution, delivery and performance of this Agreement by Service Provider have been duly authorized by all necessary corporate action; (c) the execution and performance of this Agreement by Service Provider shall not violate any Law and shall not breach any agreement, covenant, court order, judgment, or decree to which Service Provider is a party or by which it is bound; and (d) Service Provider has, and promises that it shall maintain in effect, all governmental licenses and permits necessary for it to provide the Services and/or Deliverables contemplated by this Agreement. Service Provider further represents and warrants to Customer that Service Provider owns or leases and promises that it shall own or lease, free and clear of all liens, claims, encumbrances, or demands of Third Parties, all right, title, and interest in and to the tangible property and technology and the like that Service Provider intends to use or uses to provide the Services and/or Deliverables, and in and to the related Intellectual Property Rights, or has received appropriate licenses, leases or other rights from Third Parties to permit such use. These warranties shall survive the expiration or termination of this Agreement.

6.8 ***Information Furnished to Customer.*** Service Provider represents and warrants to Customer that all written information (including financial information) furnished to Customer prior to the Effective Date by or on behalf of Service Provider in connection with this Agreement, including in the Service Provider Proposal, and all the information made a part of this Agreement is true, accurate and complete, and contains no untrue statement of a material fact or omits any material fact necessary to make such information not misleading.

6.9 ***Pending Litigation Warranty.*** Service Provider represents and warrants to Customer that there is no action, suit, claim, investigation or proceeding pending, or to the best of Service Provider's knowledge, threatened or anticipated against, by or affecting Service Provider or the Services and/or Deliverables which, if adversely decided, might adversely affect: (a) Service Provider's ability to enter into this Agreement; (b) Service Provider's performance of its obligations herein; or (c) Customer's use of the Services and/or Deliverables. Service Provider further represents and warrants that it does not know of any basis for any such action. At all times during the Term, Service Provider shall notify Customer, within fifteen (15) days of Service Provider's knowledge of any such action, suit, claim, investigation, or proceeding initiated by or against Service Provider that may adversely affect Service Provider's ability to perform under this Agreement, including where amounts in dispute may result in a material adverse change in the financial status of Service Provider.

6.10 ***Third Party Warranties and Indemnities.*** For any Third Party software provided by Service Provider to Customer, Service Provider hereby assigns to Customer all end-user warranties and indemnities relating to such Third Party software. To the extent that Service Provider is not permitted to assign any of such end-user warranties and indemnities through to Customer, Service Provider shall enforce such warranties and indemnities on behalf of Customer to the extent Service Provider is permitted to do so under the terms of the applicable Third Party agreements. The Service Provider obligations set forth in this **Section 6.10 (Third Party Warranties and Indemnities)** are in addition to and not in lieu of Service Provider's warranty and indemnification obligations, responsibilities and liabilities with regard to such Third Party software under this **Article 6 (Representation and Warranties)** and **Article 11 (Indemnification and Insurance)**. This warranty shall survive the expiration or termination of this Agreement.

6.11 ***Warranty Disclaimer.*** THE REPRESENTATIONS AND WARRANTIES SET FORTH IN THIS AGREEMENT AND IN ANY STATEMENT OF WORK ARE

EACH PARTY'S ONLY REPRESENTATIONS WARRANTIES AND NO OTHER REPRESENTATIONS OR WARRANTIES, EXPRESS OR IMPLIED, WILL APPLY. EXCEPT AS OTHERWISE PROVIDED FOR HEREIN, SERVICE PROVIDER SPECIFICALLY EXCLUDES THE IMPLIED WARRANTIES OF MERCHANTABILITY AND FITNESS FOR A PARTICULAR PURPOSE.

ARTICLE 7—PRICE AND PAYMENTS

7.1 ***Total Charges.*** Service Provider's charges for the Services shall all be set forth in the applicable Statement of Work. The charges specified in the Statement of Work are the total charges for the Services on a particular Statement of Work, and no other fees, costs, or expenses may be charged to Customer except as set forth in the Statement of Work.

7.2 ***Time and Method of Payment.*** All fees payable to Service Provider under this Agreement shall be detailed, categorized, and clearly stated on an invoice in accordance with the terms and conditions set forth in this **Article 7 (Price and Payments)**. Unless otherwise agreed by the Parties in the applicable Statement of Work or otherwise, all amounts payable under this Agreement shall be payable in U.S. Dollars. Service Provider shall invoice Customer as set forth in this Section, and Customer shall pay all net undisputed amounts due to Service Provider under this Agreement within forty five (45) days of Customer's receipt of Service Provider's invoice. Service Provider shall submit invoices on a monthly basis (but not until the last day of each month during which Services and/or Deliverables were delivered), or as may be otherwise specified in this Agreement, in a form provided by Customer or as otherwise mutually agreed to by the Parties.

7.3 ***Services.*** The rates for all Services rendered by Service Provider to Customer shall be payable as set forth in the applicable Statement of Work. Any invoice relating to fees for any Services shall detail: (a) the Services performed (e.g., each activity, task and/or Critical Path Milestone); (b) the identity of the Service Provider Personnel performing the Services; (c) the number of hours and corresponding fees attributable to each such person's performance of the Services; and (d) such other information as reasonable requested by Customer. Unless other payment terms are specified in the applicable Statement of Work, Customer and Service Provider agree that payments to Service Provider for Services shall be invoiced as follows:

7.3.1 ***Fixed Fee Services.*** All Services identified in a Statement of Work as Services to be paid at a fixed rate shall be invoiced in accordance with the payment schedule set forth in the applicable Statement of Work. If no payment schedule is set forth in the applicable Statement of Work, such Services fees shall be invoiced as follows:

% of Services Fee	Event
20	Execution of the Statement of Work
60	Spread equally among no less than three (3) Critical Path Milestones
20	Acceptance

7.3.2 ***Time-and-Materials Services.*** All Services identified in a Statement of Work as Services to be paid on a time-and-materials basis shall be invoiced in accordance with the terms set forth in this Section. The applicable Statement of Work shall identify no less than three (3) Critical Path Milestones. Upon Service Provider's successful completion of each Critical Path Milestone and delivery to Customer of any Deliverables corresponding to such Critical Path Milestone, Service Provider shall invoice Customer for an amount equal to seventy five percent (75%) of the fees for all Services rendered by Service Provider for completion of the applicable Critical Path Milestone. The remaining twenty five percent (25%) of such fees for each Critical Path Milestone shall be invoiced by Service Provider upon Acceptance. Service Provider shall cause its personnel to promptly record or report their hours worked performing Services under this Agreement on a weekly basis, either manually or online as may be reasonably requested by Customer.

7.3.3 ***Not to Exceed Services.*** Under a not to exceed amount payment structure, Customer's obligations with respect to Services performed under the applicable Statement of Work (other than to reimburse for pass-through charges, travel and other expenses in accordance with this Article 7 (Price and Payments) shall not exceed such amount (the "Not to Exceed Amount"), regardless of the amount of time and materials expended by Service Provider.

7.3.4 ***SOW Budget.*** Each Statement of Work to be paid on a time and materials basis or based on a Not to Exceed Amount shall contain a budget for the overall Services to performed under the applicable SOW ("Budget"). If a SOW fails to identify the payment structure (i.e., time and materials, not to exceed, etc.), the Budgeted amount shall be deemed to be a fixed fee. Service Provider shall notify the Customer SOW Manager with each invoice for Services as to the Percentage of Completion and the Incurred Cost Percentage (for Time and Materials and for Not To Exceed Amounts) or the Incurred Fixed Fee Percentage (for fixed fee amounts) through the end of the period covered by the invoice. The Customer SOW Manager also shall report to the Service Provider SOW Manager the Customer SOW Manager's estimate of the Percentage of Completion as of the end of such period. Failure to agree on the Percentage of Completion shall be treated as dispute under Article 11 (Dispute Resolution). Customer shall not pay any portion of any invoice for Services that represents an Incurred Cost Percentage or an Incurred Fixed Fee Percentage in excess of the Percentage of Completion for the period of the invoice. At any time that the Incurred Cost Percentage or the Incurred Fixed Fee Percentage exceeds the Percentage of Completion for a SOW, or at any time that the Service Provider SOW Manager or the Customer SOW Manager determines that a cost overrun in relation to the Budget is probable, the Service Provider SOW Manager shall provide a written assessment to the Customer SOW Manager as to whether the SOW can be completed by Service Provider within Budget. If the written assessment indicates that the SOW will not be completed within Budget, the Service Provider SOW Manager also shall include in such written assessment the reasons why the Budget will not be met and recommendations for how to complete the SOW within Budget (e.g., reallocating priorities, etc.). If Customer is not satisfied with the written assessment, Customer shall have the right, in its sole discretion, to: (a) revise the scope of the SOW so that the Budget will not be exceeded; (b) reforecast the Budget; (c) terminate the SOW immediately without liability or penalty; or (d) take such other action as will result in the Budget not being exceeded. Customer shall have the right to withhold any payments due to Service Provider until such written assessment has been provided to Customer.

7.4 ***Pass-Through Charges.*** Customer shall not be responsible for any pass-through charges unless Customer has agreed to such charges in a Statement of Work. Before submitting an invoice to Customer for any pass-through charges, Service Provider shall: (a) review and validate the invoiced charges; (b) identify any detectable errors or omissions; and (c) communicate with the applicable supplier to correct any errors or omissions, resolve any questions or issues, and obtain any applicable credits for Customer. Service Provider shall deliver to Customer the original supplier invoice, together with any documentation supporting such invoice and a statement that Service Provider has reviewed and validated the invoiced charges, within five (5) days after Service Provider's receipt thereof. Service Provider shall not charge any handling or administrative charge in connection with its processing or review of such invoices. In addition, if the supplier's invoice offers a discount for payment prior to a specified date, Service Provider shall use best efforts to deliver such invoice and associated documentation to Customer at least ten (10) days prior to such date. To the extent Service Provider fails to comply with its obligations hereunder, it shall be financially responsible for any discounts lost or any late fees or interest charges incurred by Customer. In addition, to the extent Service Provider fails to process any invoice for pass-through charges in accordance with this provision within ninety (90) days after receipt, Service Provider shall be financially responsible for the payment of all such invoiced amounts.

7.5 ***Travel Policy, Out-of-Pocket Expenses and Other Charges.*** Customer shall reimburse Service Provider for all reasonable travel and out-of-pocket expenses incurred by Service Provider, provided that such expenses conform to the travel and out-of-pocket expenses policy attached hereto as **Schedule 7.5 (Expense Policy)** (as may be modified by Customer upon reasonable notice to Service Provider) or are otherwise pre-approved by Customer in writing. Such travel and out-of-pocket expenses shall not include Service Provider's overhead costs (or allocations thereof), general and/or administrative expenses or other mark-ups, and shall be calculated at Service Provider's actual incremental expense and shall be net of all rebates and allowances.

7.6 ***Disputed Amounts.*** If an invoiced amount is disputed in good faith by Customer then, until resolution of the dispute occurs pursuant to **Article 11 (Dispute**

Resolution), Customer may suspend disputed payments and toll the running of time for default by: (a) paying the undisputed amount, if any; and (b) sending a written statement of exceptions to Service Provider. All of Service Provider's obligations shall continue unabated during the duration of the dispute resolution. Customer shall have the right to set off any undisputed amounts owed to Service Provider against any credits due Customer by Service Provider.

7.7 ***No Charge for Reperformance.*** At no additional cost or expense to Customer, Service Provider will reperform (including any required backup or restoration of data from scheduled backups or, if not available on such backups, restoration by other means with Customer's reasonable cooperation) any Services and/or reprovide any Deliverables that result in incorrect outputs due to an error or breach by Service Provider, and the resources required for such performance or provisioning will not be counted in calculating the fees or charges payable or resources utilized by Customer hereunder.

7.8 ***Taxes.***

7.8.1 ***Responsibility for Taxes.*** Each Party will be responsible for any taxes on property it owns or leases, for any franchise or privilege tax on its business, and for any tax based on its gross or net income or gross receipts. Service Provider will be responsible for all sales, service, value-added, lease, use, personal property, excise, consumption, and other taxes and duties, including VAT, payable by Service Provider on any goods or services used or consumed by Service Provider in providing the Services and/or Deliverables (including services obtained from Service Provider subcontractors and/or Service Provider Affiliates). Service Provider will be responsible for all Service Taxes. If required under applicable Laws, Service Provider will invoice Customer for the full amount of such Service Taxes, as separately stated items, and then credit or reimburse Customer for that portion of such Service Taxes for which Service Provider is financially responsible under this Agreement.

7.8.2 ***Minimizing Taxes; Liability for Taxes.*** The Parties will cooperate to more accurately determine and minimize their respective tax liability. Each Party will provide tax information or tax documents reasonably requested by the other Party. Each Party will promptly notify the other of any claim for taxes asserted with respect to this Agreement or a Statement of Work by a taxing authority with jurisdiction over either Party. With respect to any claim arising out of a tax form or return signed by a Party to this Agreement, the signing Party may control the response to and settlement of the claim, but the other Party shall have the right to participate to the extent it may be liable.

7.9 ***Set Off.*** Customer may set off against any and all amounts otherwise payable to Service Provider pursuant to any of the provisions of this Agreement any and all amounts owed by Service Provider to Customer under the provisions of this Agreement or any other agreements between the Parties including Service Level credits. Within thirty (30) days following any such set off, Customer shall provide to Service Provider a written accounting of such set off and a written statement of the reasons therefor.

ARTICLE 8—TERM AND TERMINATION

8.1 ***Term.***

8.1.1 ***Term of Agreement.*** This Agreement shall remain in effect until the Parties no longer have any unfulfilled obligations under this Agreement ("Term").

8.1.2 ***Term of Statement of Work.*** Each Statement of Work shall remain in effect until the earlier to occur of: (a) termination of such Statement of Work by either Party in accordance with this Article 8 (Term and Termination); or (b) completion of all Services and the acceptance of all Services and/or Deliverables by Customer required thereunder.

8.1.3 ***Survival.*** Notwithstanding the foregoing, any terms and conditions of this Agreement expressly identified (including [TBD]) or that would by their nature survive the expiration or termination of this Agreement and/or the applicable Statement of Work (including any terms pertaining to Service Provider's grant to Customer of any perpetual licenses hereunder) shall so survive.

8.2 ***Termination for Convenience.*** Upon the provision of thirty (30) days prior written notice to Service Provider, Customer shall have the right to terminate without cause any Statement of Work and Service Provider shall discontinue its Services with respect to such Statement of Work. In such event, Customer shall be obligated to pay to Service Provider the cost of any Services already provided by Service Provider but not paid by Customer, pro-rated as appropriate for any fixed-fee SOW, and the cost of the actual out-of-pocket expenses incurred by Service Provider, in each case as of the date of Service Provider's receipt of Customer's written notice of termination. Except as set forth in this **Section 8.2 (Termination for Convenience)**: (a) Customer shall in no event be required to pay any other fees, costs, or expenses to Service Provider with respect to any such termination; and (b) Customer shall have no further liabilities or obligations to Service Provider under this Agreement.

8.3 ***Termination for Force Majeure.*** In the event a portion of the Services, or Service Provider's performance of the Services, is delayed or interrupted because of a Force Majeure Event as described in **Section 12.3** for a period of five (5) consecutive days or more, and such delay or interruption materially, adversely impacts Customer's business and Service Provider fails to provide a temporary alternative reasonably acceptable to Customer, Customer shall have the right, in its sole discretion without liability prior to the date Service Provider corrects the problem causing the material, adverse impact, or provides a temporary alternative reasonably acceptable to Customer, to: (a) terminate the Agreement; (b) terminate the affected Statement of Work; or (c) terminate the affected portion of the Services by providing Service Provider with written notice of termination and paying Service Provider for any accrued fees for such portion of the affected Services pro-rated to the effective date of termination. If Customer terminates only the affected portion of the Services pursuant to subsection (b) above, and performs such services itself or contracts for an alternate provider to provide such services, upon Service Provider's request Customer may transfer such services back to Service Provider; provided that Service Provider pays all costs (including fees imposed by the alternate provider) relating to such transfer. Except as set forth in this **Section 8.3 (Termination for Force Majeure)**: (d) Customer shall in no event be required to pay any other fees, costs, or expenses to Service Provider with respect to any such termination; and (e) Customer shall have no further liabilities or obligations to Service Provider under this Agreement.

8.4 ***Events of Default.*** Service Provider and Customer acknowledge and agree that the following shall constitute events of default ("***Events of Default***") and that the occurrence of one (1) or more of such Events of Default shall constitute a material breach of this Agreement which shall allow a Party, as applicable, to seek the rights and remedies set forth in this **Section 8.4 (Events of Default)**. Except as set forth in this **Section 8.4 (Events of Default)**: (a) Customer shall in no event be required to pay any other fees, costs or expenses to Service Provider with respect to any such termination; and (b) Customer shall have no further liabilities or obligations to Service Provider under this Agreement.

8.4.1 Subject to **Section 2.3 (Delays)**, Service Provider's failure to achieve a Critical Path Milestone, Transition Milestone or to deliver a key Deliverable to Customer within the time frame specified in the SOW, and in no event shall such failure be subject to a cure period.

8.4.2 Failure of Service Provider to complete successfully any testing or re-testing or failure of a SOW to achieve SOW Acceptance, and in no event shall such failure be subject to a cure period.

8.4.3 Unless different criteria are set forth in the applicable SOW, Service Provider's failure to meet any Service Level: (a) in any one (1) month to such an extent as to adversely affect in a material manner Customer's ability to perform a critical business function; (b) for three (3) consecutive months; or (c) for four (4) months out of any consecutive six (6) month period, and in no event such any such failure be subject to a cure period.

8.4.4 Service Provider's material breach of any representation or warranty set forth in this Agreement or in any Statement of Work, provided that such breach, if curable, is not cured within the time frames specified in Article 6 (Representations and Warranties), if applicable, or if such Article 6 (Representations and Warranties) does not apply to the breach, then within thirty (30) days following receipt of written notice of such breach.

8.4.5 Service Provider's failure to maintain insurance coverage as specified in **Section 10.4 (Insurance)**, provided that such failure is not cured within thirty (30) days following receipt of written notice of such failure.

8.4.6 Failure of Service Provider to perform any other material obligation under this Agreement and/or a Statement of Work, provided that such failure is not cured within thirty (30) days following receipt of written notice of such failure.

(i) Customer's intentional and willful material breach of Service Provider's intellectual property rights as set forth in **Section 9.1 (Proprietary Rights)** that is not cured within forty five (45) days following receipt of written notice of such breach;

8.4.7 Customer's intentional and willful material breach of any of the terms, conditions, and/or requirements of **Section 9.3 (Confidential Information)** that is not cured within forty five (45) days following receipt of written notice of such breach.

8.4.8 Customer's failure to timely pay any undisputed amount owed to Service Provider, provided that such failure is not cured within thirty (30) days following receipt of written notice of such failure.

8.4.9 The institution of bankruptcy, receivership, insolvency, reorganization, or other similar proceedings by or against Service Provider under any section or chapter of the U.S. Bankruptcy Code, as amended, or under any similar laws or statutes of the United States or any state thereof, if such proceedings have not been dismissed or discharged within thirty (30) days after they are instituted; the insolvency or making of an assignment for the benefit of creditors or the admittance by Service Provider of any involuntary debts as they mature; the institution of any reorganization arrangement or other readjustment of debt plan of Service Provider not involving the U.S. Bankruptcy Code; appointment of a receiver for all or substantially all of Service Provider's assets; or any corporate action taken by the Board of Directors of Service Provider in furtherance of any of the above actions.

8.5 ***Rights and Remedies of Service Provider Upon Default of Customer.*** Upon the occurrence of an uncured Event of Default by or with respect to Customer, Service Provider shall be entitled to: (a) discontinue performance of its obligations under the affected Statement(s) of Work; (b) subject to the terms of **Section 8.9 (Limitations of Liability)**, seek to recover damages from Customer; and/or (c) if applicable, seek to obtain the additional rights and remedies set forth in **Section 8.7 (Equitable Relief)**.

8.6 ***Rights and Remedies of Customer Upon Default of Service Provider.*** Upon the occurrence of an Event of Default by or with respect to Service Provider, Customer shall be entitled to any of the following remedies: (a) terminate, in whole or in part, any affected Statement(s) of Work and/or this Agreement; (b) subject to the terms of **Section 8.9 (Limitations of Liability)**, seek to recover damages from Service Provider; (c) receive a refund of any prepaid but unearned fees, which refund shall be paid by Service Provider to Customer within thirty (30) days following Service Provider's receipt of Customer's notice of such discontinuation; (d) if applicable, seek to obtain the additional rights and remedies set forth in **Section 8.7 (Equitable Relief)**; and/or (e) if elected by Customer, receive the Termination Assistance described in **Section 8.11 (Termination Assistance Rights)**.

8.7 ***Equitable Relief.*** Notwithstanding anything contained in this Agreement to the contrary, the Parties shall be entitled to seek injunctive or other equitable relief whenever the facts or circumstances would permit a Party to seek such equitable relief in a court of competent jurisdiction.

8.8 ***Attorneys' Fees.*** In the event of an alleged breach of this Agreement, the prevailing Party shall be entitled to reimbursement of all of its costs and expenses, including reasonable attorneys' fees, incurred in connection with such dispute, claim or litigation, including any appeal therefrom. For purposes of this Section, the determination of which Party is to be considered the prevailing Party shall be decided by the court of competent jurisdiction or independent party (i.e., mediator or arbitrator) that resolves such dispute, claim or litigation.

8.9 ***Limitations of Liability.***

8.9.1 ***Limitation Upon Types of Recoverable Damages.*** EXCEPT AS OTHERWISE PROVIDED IN THIS AGREEMENT, NEITHER PARTY SHALL BE LIABLE FOR ANY CONSEQUENTIAL, INCIDENTAL, INDIRECT, EXEMPLARY, SPECIAL, OR PUNITIVE DAMAGES, INCLUDING LOSS OF USE, REVENUE, OR PROFIT, ARISING IN CONTRACT, WARRANTY OR IN TORT (INCLUDING NEGLIGENCE) OR ANY OTHER LEGAL THEORY, EVEN IF SUCH PARTY HAS BEEN ADVISED OF THE POSSIBILITY OF SUCH DAMAGES.

8.9.2 ***Cap on Damages.*** EXCEPT AS OTHERWISE PROVIDED IN **SECTION 8.9.3 (EXCLUSIONS FROM LIMITATIONS OF LIABILITY)**, EACH PARTY'S LIABILITY TO THE OTHER FOR ANY CAUSE OF ACTION ARISING OUT OF OR RELATING TO THIS AGREEMENT SHALL NOT EXCEED THE FEES PAID OR TO BE PAID BY CUSTOMER FOR THE DELIVERABLES AND SERVICES PROVIDED UNDER THIS AGREEMENT.

8.9.3 ***Exclusions from Limitations of Liability.*** Notwithstanding anything contained herein to the contrary, the limitations of liability contained in this Section shall not apply to: (a) damages arising out of or relating to a Party's failure to comply with its confidentiality obligations under **Section 9.3 (Confidential Information)**; (b) either Party's indemnification obligations under **Section 10.1 (Service Provider Indemnifications)** or **Section 10.2 (Customer Indemnifications)**; (c) personal injury, including death, and damage to tangible property caused by the negligent, willful or intentional acts of a Party or its employees, agents, or subcontractors; (d) damages arising out of any loss of data or other damage to data caused by any Disabling Code; (e) amounts paid as late charges pursuant to **Section 2.3 (Delays)** for failure to achieve timely a Critical Path Milestone; (f) Service Provider's wrongful termination of this Agreement and/or a Statement of Work or repudiation or wrongful abandonment of all or any part of the Services; and (g) either Party's obligation to pay litigation costs and attorneys' fees incurred by the other Party in enforcing the terms of this Agreement as set forth in **Section 8.8 (Attorneys' Fees)**.

8.10 ***Remedies Not Exclusive.*** Except as otherwise expressly provided herein, the rights and remedies set forth in this Agreement shall not be exclusive and are in addition to any other rights and remedies provided by law or this Agreement. Notwithstanding the foregoing and anything contained herein to the contrary, Service Provider expressly waives and disclaims any right or remedy it may have to de-install, disable, or repossess any Deliverables without due process of law.

8.11 ***Termination Assistance Rights.*** Upon written notice of termination of a Statement of Work or this Agreement for any reason, Customer shall have the option, for up to six (6) months ("***Termination Assistance Period***") beyond the termination date, to continue to use the Services for the purposes set forth in the applicable Statement of Work and upon payment of the fees set forth in such Statement of Work as and when due. The terms and conditions of this Agreement, including Service Levels, shall apply to the Services during the Termination Assistance Period. Service Provider and Customer will cooperate during the Termination Assistance Period in order to facilitate Customer's transition either to a new service provider or to perform the Services on its own, and Service Provider shall provide such reasonable assistance as may be requested by Customer to effectuate such transition. After the Termination Assistance Period Service Provider shall answer questions from Customer regarding the Services on an "as needed" basis at rates to which the Parties will mutually agree, provided such rates do not exceed the then-current standard billing rates of Service Provider.

ARTICLE 9—PROPRIETARY RIGHTS, CONFIDENTIALITY, AND AUDIT RIGHTS

9.1 ***Proprietary Rights.***

9.1.1 ***Service Provider Materials.*** All information and materials, including computer software, provided to Customer by Service Provider or otherwise used by Service Provider in connection with the Services, that Service Provider developed or acquired prior to or independently of this Agreement (the "Service Provider Materials") are and shall remain the property of Service Provider or its licensors, which shall retain all Intellectual Property Rights therein. Service Provider Materials shall also include derivative works created to the foregoing, even if the derivative works were created as part of the Services, to the extent such derivative works do not incorporate any Deliverables, Customer Confidential Information, and/or Customer Materials.

9.1.2 ***Licensed Service Provider Materials.*** "Licensed Service Provider Materials" shall mean Service Provider Materials that are incorporated in any Deliverables. Service Provider hereby grants to Customer a nonexclusive, irrevocable, world-wide, perpetual, fully paid-up and royalty-free license to use, copy, modify, maintain, support, and create derivative works of the Licensed Service Provider Materials solely as a part of the Deliverables, for the benefit of Customer and its Affiliates. Customer may not extract Licensed Service Provider Materials from the Deliverables for use separately therefrom, unless so permitted by Service Provider. The foregoing license shall include use by Customer's employees, Third Party service providers, consultants, auditors, agents, and representatives, to the extent providing services to or on behalf of Customer. Any additional license terms and conditions shall be as mutually agreed in a Statement of Work. The Parties acknowledge that Licensed Service Provider Materials created under a Statement of Work may be considered by Customer to have competitive value to Customer (e.g., they are based on Customer's Confidential Information and/or specific know how). Accordingly, with respect to Licensed Service Provider Materials that are identified as "Competitive Materials" in a Statement of Work, the license granted under this **Section 9.1.2 (Licensed Service Provider Materials)** shall be deemed to be exclusive to Customer.

9.1.3 ***Customer Information and Materials.*** All information, materials and technology, including computer software, provided to Service Provider by Customer or otherwise used by Customer in connection with the Services, including modifications, changes and derivatives thereto whether or not created as part of the Services (the "Customer Materials") are and shall remain the property of Customer or its licensors, which shall retain all Intellectual Property Rights therein. Service Provider obtains no right, title, or interest therein, except that during the Term Service Provider may use the Customer Materials for the sole, exclusive, and limited purpose of performing the Services in compliance with the terms and conditions of this Agreement. Service Provider shall comply with the terms of any license or other agreement applicable to such Customer Material. All Customer Materials shall be subject to the confidentiality provisions of this Agreement. Service Provider shall not encumber the Customer Materials in any way, and promptly shall return to Customer any and all Customer Materials in Service Provider's possession or control upon Customer's request and, in any event, upon termination or expiration of the applicable Statement of Work.

9.2 ***Ownership of Deliverables.***

9.2.1 ***Definition of Deliverable; Customer Ownership Rights.*** The Parties hereby agree that all software programming (including all Object Code, Source Code, and Source Code Materials pertaining thereto), work product and other deliverables (including APIs), and all related written reports, requirements documents (including newly created technical and non-technical data embodied therein), specifications, program materials, flow charts, notes, outlines and the like, and all intermediate and partial versions thereof, that are developed, authored, conceived, originated, prepared, or otherwise created by Service Provider or its employees, agents, or subcontractors for or on behalf of Customer in connection with Service Provider's performance of Services under this Agreement (collectively, "Deliverables"), and all Intellectual Property Rights in and thereto and derivative works created therefrom, shall be the sole and exclusive property of Customer. Such ownership shall inure to the benefit of Customer from the date of the conception, creation, or fixation of the Deliverables in a tangible medium of expression, as applicable. All newly created copyright aspects of the Deliverables shall be considered a "work-made-for-hire" within the meaning of the Copyright Act of 1976, as amended. If and to the extent the Deliverables, or any part thereof, is found by a court of competent jurisdiction not to be a "work-made-for-hire" within the meaning of the Copyright Act of 1976, as amended, Service Provider agrees that all exclusive right, title, and interest in and to those newly created copyrightable aspects of the Deliverables, and all copies thereof, are hereby expressly assigned automatically to Customer without further consideration. Notwithstanding the foregoing, all Intellectual Property Rights in and to the Deliverables and any of the ideas contained therein shall be automatically assigned to Customer without further consideration. Service Provider hereby waives and quitclaims to Customer any and all claims of any nature whatsoever which Service Provider now or may hereafter have for infringement of any Intellectual Property Right assigned to Customer. Service Provider shall ensure that all Deliverables created hereunder (including each page of any document produced) will be marked as follows:

Confidential and Proprietary

Copyright © 20 [Insert Customer Name].

All Rights Reserved.

9.2.2 ***Prohibitions and Limitations on Service Provider.*** Any agreement entered into by Service Provider and a Third Party in connection with Services related to Deliverables under this Agreement shall require the prior consent of Customer as set forth in **Section 4.5 (Approval of Subcontractors)**, and shall include substantially the same terms as those appearing in this Section to ensure that Customer obtains the same rights in the Deliverables generated under such Third Party agreement as those set forth in this Section. Service Provider agrees to assist Customer in obtaining, registering, maintaining, and enforcing all rights and other legal protections for the Deliverables and to execute any and all documents that Customer may reasonably request in connection therewith, including any patent, trademark, and copyright assignment document(s). Service Provider shall not reuse the Deliverables, or any intermediate or partial version thereof, or any derivative work based upon the Deliverables without Customer's express written consent, which consent may be withheld by Customer in its sole discretion. Without limiting the foregoing, Deliverables shall not be incorporated by Service Provider into Service Provider's technology or otherwise made available to other Service Provider customers, unless otherwise specifically approved by Customer in writing in its sole discretion. Service Provider shall furnish to Customer, concurrently with the delivery of the Deliverables and any thereto, the Source Code for the Deliverables and all related Documentation and Source Code Materials.

9.3 ***Confidential Information.***

9.3.1 ***Definition of Confidential Information.*** "Confidential Information" means: (a) all information marked confidential, restricted or proprietary by either Party; and (b) any other information that is treated as confidential by the Disclosing Party and would reasonably be understood to be confidential, whether or not so marked or disclosed orally. In the case of Customer, Confidential Information also shall include software provided to Service Provider by or through Customer, Customer Systems, Deliverables, Personal Information, Customer data, attorney-client privileged materials, attorney work product, Customer lists, Customer contracts, Customer costs and pricing, actual or potential customers and customer lists, customer requirements, business forecasts and projections, information with respect to competitors, strategic plans, account information, research information, financial/accounting information (including assets, expenditures, mergers, acquisitions, divestitures, billings collections, revenues and finances), human resources and personnel information, marketing/sales information, information regarding businesses, plans, operations, Third Party contracts, all information and materials relating to Third Party service providers or Service Providers of Customer that have provided or that may provide in the future any part of Customer's Systems or infrastructure, licenses, internal or external audits, law suits, regulatory compliance, or other information or data obtained, received, transmitted, processed, stored, archived, or maintained by Service Provider under this Agreement.

9.3.2 ***Exclusions from Confidentiality.*** Except with respect to Customer data and Personal Information, Confidential Information does not include any information that is: (a) publicly available or later becomes available other than through a breach of this Agreement; (b) known to the Receiving Party or its employees, agents, or representatives prior to such disclosure or is independently developed by the Receiving Party or its employees, agents, or representatives subsequent to such disclosure; or (c) subsequently lawfully obtained by the Receiving Party or its employees, agents, or representatives from a Third Party without obligations of confidentiality.

9.3.3 ***Personal Information.*** "Personal Information" means all personally identifiable information (e.g., name, address, credit card number, email address, static IP address, etc.) that is generated, collected, or obtained as part of this Agreement, including transactional and other data pertaining to individuals. Service Provider will comply with all applicable privacy and other laws and regulations relating to protection, collection, use, and distribution of Personal Information. Service Provider will also comply with the provisions of Customer's privacy statement or policies relating to Personal Information. Personal Information is the exclusive property of Customer and will be deemed Customer Confidential Information under the applicable provisions of this Agreement. Service Provider will not, without the prior written consent of an authorized representative of Customer, use Personal Information for any purpose other than to provide the Services under this Agreement. In no event may Service Provider: (a) use Personal Information to market its services or those of a Third Party; (b) sell or transfer Personal Information to Third Parties, or otherwise provide Third Parties with access thereto; or (c) merge or aggregate Personal Information obtained through the Services with information not obtained through the Services, except as may be expressly authorized by Customer. Without limiting its other obligations under this Agreement, Service Provider agrees that all such information will be secured from unauthorized access, use, disclosure, and loss using commercially acceptable security practices and technologies. If there is a suspected or actual breach of security involving Personal Information, Service Provider will notify Customer within two (2) hours of becoming aware of such occurrence. Service Provider shall provide Customer with access to Personal Information at any time as Customer may request. Upon termination or expiration of this agreement all Personal Information in the possession of the Service Provider will be provided to Customer in a manner reasonably requested by Customer and all copies will be permanently removed from Service Provider's system, records, and backups and all subsequent use of such information by Service Provider will cease.

9.3.4 ***Obligations of Confidentiality.*** The Party that has received Confidential Information (the "Receiving Party") shall exercise the same degree of care and protection with respect to the Confidential Information of the Party that has disclosed Confidential Information to the Receiving Party (the "Disclosing Party") that it exercises with respect to its own Confidential Information, but in no event shall the Receiving Party exercise less than a reasonable standard of care. The Receiving Party shall not directly or indirectly disclose, copy, distribute, republish, or allow any Third Party to have access to any Confidential Information of the Disclosing Party. Notwithstanding the above: (a) Customer may disclose Service Provider Confidential Information to its employees, Third Party service providers, consultants, auditors, agents, and representatives, to the extent providing services to or on behalf of Customer; (b) Service Provider may disclose Customer's Confidential Information to its representatives, agents, and employees who have a need to know, provided that for Service Provider's representatives and/or agents, such representatives and/or agents are acceptable to Customer in its sole discretion and each such representative and/or agent has previously executed a Confidentiality and Nondisclosure Agreement, in materially the form set forth in Exhibit 2 (Confidentiality and Nondisclosure Agreement), prior to and as a condition of receiving or getting access to Customer's Confidential Information; and (c) either Party may disclose Confidential Information if so required by Law (including court order or subpoena), provided that such disclosure is made in accordance with the terms of **Section 9.3.5 (Notification Obligation)**.

9.3.5 ***Notification Obligation.*** If the Receiving Party becomes aware of any unauthorized use or disclosure of the Confidential Information of the Disclosing Party, the Receiving Party shall promptly and fully notify the Disclosing Party of all facts known to it concerning such unauthorized use or disclosure. In addition, if the Receiving Party or any of its employees or agents are requested or required (by oral questions, interrogatories, requests for information, or documents in legal proceedings, subpoena, civil investigative demand, or other similar process) to disclose any of the Confidential Information of the Disclosing Party, the Receiving Party shall not disclose the Confidential Information without providing the Disclosing Party at least twenty-four (24) hours prior written notice of any such request or requirement so that the Disclosing Party may seek a protective order or other appropriate remedy and/or waive compliance with the provisions of this Agreement. Notwithstanding the foregoing, the Receiving Party shall exercise its best efforts to preserve the confidentiality of the Confidential Information including by cooperating with the Disclosing Party to obtain an appropriate protective order or other reliable assurance that confidential treatment will be accorded the Confidential Information by such tribunal.

9.3.6 ***Notification and Mitigation.*** In the event of any impermissible disclosure, loss or destruction of Confidential Information, the Receiving Party shall immediately notify the Disclosing Party and take all reasonable steps to mitigate any potential harm or further disclosure, loss or destruction of such Confidential Information.

9.3.7 ***Return/Destruction of Confidential Information.*** Upon the expiration or termination of this Agreement and/or a Statement of Work, as applicable, and at any other time upon written request by the Disclosing Party, the Receiving Party shall return to the Disclosing Party all Confidential Information (including all documentation in any medium that contains, refers to, or relates to the Confidential Information) of the Disclosing Party then in its possession or control, in whatever form, or, in the case of a written request by the Disclosing Party, the Confidential Information specified in such request as then in the Receiving Party's possession or control, in whatever form, in any case within thirty (30) days. In addition, unless the Disclosing Party otherwise consents in writing, the Receiving Party also shall deliver to the Disclosing Party or, if requested by the Disclosing Party, shall delete or destroy, any copies, duplicates, summaries, abstracts, or other representations of any such Confidential Information or any part thereof, in whatever form, then in the possession or control of the Receiving Party. Notwithstanding the foregoing: (a) Service Provider may retain one (1) copy of documentation and data, excluding Customer data or Personal Information, for archival purposes or warranty support; provided, however, that any subsequent disclosure of such archived data shall comply with this **Section 9.3 (Confidential Information)**; and (b) Customer may retain copies of Service Provider Confidential Information to the extent required by Law, to the extent otherwise permitted under this Agreement and for legal archival purposes.

Each Party shall deliver to the other Party written certification of its compliance with this **Section 9.3.7 (Return/Destruction of Confidential Information)** signed by an authorized representative of such Party.

9.3.8 ***Restricted Period.*** These restrictions upon disclosure and use of Confidential Information shall continue during the Term of this Agreement and shall extend beyond the Term of this Agreement for a period of ten (10) years; provided, however, that with respect to any Confidential Information that constitutes a trade secret (as determined under applicable law), such restrictions on disclosure and/or use shall survive the termination, expiration or non-renewal of this Agreement for as long as such Confidential Information remains a trade secret but, in no event, shall such restrictions on disclosure and/or use cease prior to the expiration of ten (10) years following the termination, expiration or non-renewal of the Term of this Agreement.

9.4 ***Safeguarding of Customer Materials and Property.*** Service Provider shall establish and maintain reasonable safeguards against the destruction, loss, alteration, or unauthorized use of Customer Confidential Information, Customer Materials and other Customer property in the possession or control of Service Provider that are consistent with the standards of other companies providing similar services and that in any event are no less rigorous than those used by Service Provider to safeguard its own materials and property. Customer shall have the right to establish backup security for data and to keep backup data and data files in its possession if it chooses. Without limiting the generality of the foregoing, Service Provider Personnel shall not attempt to access, or allow access to, any Customer Confidential Information, Customer Materials to which they are not entitled under this Agreement. If such access is attained, Service Provider shall immediately report such incident to Customer, describe in detail any accessed information and/or materials and return to Customer any copied or removed information and/or materials.

9.5 ***Audits.***

9.5.1 ***Compliance Audits.*** Upon notice from Customer, Service Provider shall provide Customer, its auditors (including internal audit staff and external auditors), inspectors, regulators, and other reasonably designated representatives as Customer may from time to time designate in writing (collectively, the "Customer Auditors") with access to, at reasonable times, to any facility or part of a facility at which either Service Provider or any of its subcontractors is providing the Services, to Service Provider Personnel, and to data and records relating to the Services for purposes of verifying compliance with this Agreement (including Service Provider's compliance with its physical and data privacy and security obligations and other terms of this Agreement) and to support Customer's audits of the business of Customer relating to the Services. Service Provider will provide any assistance that Customer Auditors may reasonably require with respect to such audits. All financial and non-financial transactions resulting from this Agreement shall be documented by Service Provider and subject to audit by the Customer Auditors. Service Provider and Customer shall meet to review each audit report promptly and to agree upon an appropriate and effective manner in which to respond to the deficiencies identified and changes recommended by such audit report.

9.5.2 ***Customer-Initiated Control and Procedure Audits.*** Service Provider agrees to provide any assistance reasonably requested by Customer relating to disclosure controls and procedures (pursuant to Sections 302 and 404 of the Sarbanes-Oxley Act of 2002, or otherwise), including but not limited to: (a) Customer's review of any documented Service Provider's controls and procedures related to the Services; (b) cooperating with the Customer Auditors in connection with the testing of such controls and procedures; (c) informing Customer on a timely basis regarding any material changes to such controls and procedures; (d) remediating any material weakness or significant deficiency in complying with Service Provider's controls and procedures related to the Services, at Service Provider's expense, and (e) permitting Customer to perform an audit of the Services (including the internal control environment relating to thereto). It is hereby understood that, except as otherwise stated above, any fees or costs incurred by Customer Auditors, or any incremental costs incurred by Service Provider in complying with Customer's audit requirements in connection with this Section (to the extent that such requirements cause Service Provider to provide services that it does not routinely provide to its clients), shall be the responsibility of Customer.

9.5.3 ***Service Provider-Initiated Control Audits.*** Throughout the Term of this Agreement, Service Provider shall provide Customer, at Customer's written request, copies of reports resulting from audits performed by independent, qualified external auditors engaged by Service Provider that assess the internal controls and information security related to the Services ("Service Provider Audits"). The reports from such Service Provider Audits ("Service Provider Audit Reports") will comply with current industry standards, including generally accepted auditing standards such as, without limitation, the American Institute of Certified Public Accountants Statement on Auditing Standards Number 70 (SAS 70). More specifically such Service Provider Audit Report will comply with the requirements of a "Type II" report as defined by SAS 70.

9.5.4 ***Fee Audits.*** Upon notice from Customer, Service Provider shall provide Customer Auditors with access to such financial books and records and supporting documentation (excluding Service Provider's cost data and internal cost analysis) as may be requested by the Customer Auditors. Customer Auditors may audit Service Provider's charges to Customer to determine if such charges are accurate and in accordance with this Agreement. If, as a result of such audit, Customer determines that Service Provider has overcharged Customer, Customer shall notify Service Provider of the amount of such overcharge and Service Provider shall (in addition to any and all other remedies that may be available to Customer) promptly pay to Customer the amount of the overcharge, plus interest, calculated from the date of receipt by Service Provider of the overcharged amount until the date of payment to Customer. If Customer determines that Service Provider has undercharged Customer, Customer shall notify Service Provider of such undercharge. In addition to Customer's rights set forth in this **Section 9.5.4 (Fee Audits)**, in the event any such audit reveals an overcharge to Customer of three percent (3%) or more for any Statement of Work, Service Provider shall (in addition to any and all other remedies that may be available to Customer) reimburse Customer for the cost of such audit associated with the particular Statement of Work.

ARTICLE 10—INDEMNIFICATION AND INSURANCE

10.1 ***Service Provider Indemnifications.***

10.1.1 ***General Indemnifications.*** Service Provider shall indemnify, defend, and hold Customer, its Affiliates and their respective directors, officers, shareholders, members, employees, representatives, agents, attorneys, successors, and assigns (collectively, "Customer Indemnified Parties") harmless from and against, and shall pay, any and all Losses sustained or incurred by any of the Customer Indemnified Parties, based upon, relating to or arising from, any and all Third Party claims, actions, suits, proceedings, or investigations in connection with or pertaining to any of the following:

(a) Any actual or alleged bodily injury or death, damage to personal or real property, including computer data, data loss, or any other related damage, notwithstanding the form in which any such action is brought (e.g., contract, tort, or otherwise), to the extent such injuries or damages arise directly or indirectly from acts, errors, or omissions that constitute negligence, willful misconduct, or violations of Law, by Service Provider and/or any Service Provider Personnel;

(b) Any actual or alleged breach of the Service Provider's representations and warranties set forth in Article 6 (Representations and Warranties);

(c) Any actual or alleged breach of any agreement between Customer and Third Party, to the extent the claim, suit or proceeding is a result of (i) Service Provider's failure to fulfill its obligations under this Agreement, and/or (ii) Service Provider's breach of any term or condition of this Agreement;

(d) Service Provider's breach or failure to perform any of the obligations set forth in Article 9 (Confidential Information) relating to Customer Confidential Information or the protection of the security or privacy of Customer data or Personal Information;

(e) Any improper disclosure, misuse, and/or theft of Customer Confidential Information, Customer data, or Personal Information by Service Provider or Service Provider Personnel;

(f) Any introduction by Service Provider or Service Provider Personnel of Disabling Code in Customer's Systems, environment or networks;

(g) Any breach or failure by Service Provider to comply with its obligations under **Sections 6.4 (Compliance with Law)**;

(h) Fines, penalties, sanctions, underpayments, and/or other remedies to the extent such fines, penalties, sanctions, underpayments, and/or other remedies relate to any breach of any Laws by Service Provider or any Service Provider Personnel or any other failure by Service Provider or Service Provider Personnel to perform Service Provider's responsibilities under this Agreement; and

(i) Any failure by Service Provider to pay applicable taxes, together with any interest and penalties, assessed or imposed against Customer for which Service Provider has responsibility pursuant to **Section 7.8 (Taxes)** or applicable Laws.

10.1.2 ***Intellectual Property Rights Indemnification.*** Service Provider shall indemnify, defend, and hold the Customer Indemnified Parties harmless from and against, and shall pay, any and all Losses sustained or incurred by any of the Customer Indemnified Parties, based upon, relating to or arising from, any and all Third Party claims, actions, suits, proceedings, or investigations alleging that the Services and/or Deliverables misappropriates, infringes and/or violates and/or Customer's use of the Services and/or Deliverables in accordance with the terms of this Agreement constitutes a misappropriation, infringement, and/or violation of any Intellectual Property Right of any Third Party. If Customer's right to receive and use the Services and/or Deliverables, or any part(s) thereof, is enjoined or interfered with in any manner or appears likely to be enjoined or interfered, Service Provider promptly (but in any case within thirty (30) days of such injunction or interference) shall, at Service Provider's sole cost and expense and in such a manner as to minimize the disturbance to Customer's business activities and rights under this Agreement, do one of the following: (a) obtain for Customer the right to continue receiving and using such Services and/or Deliverables free of claims of infringement, misappropriation and/or violation; (b) modify the Services and/or Deliverables so that they no longer infringe, misappropriate and/or violate (provided that such modification does not degrade the performance or quality of the Services and/or Deliverables or adversely affect Customer's use or intended use of the Services and/or Deliverables as contemplated by this Agreement); or (c) replace the Services and/or Deliverables with non-infringing, non-misappropriating, and non-violating Services and/or Deliverables of equivalent or greater functionality that is acceptable to Customer. In the event Service Provider is unable, after exercising its best efforts to implement one of the options set forth in subsections (a), (b), or (c) above, accept return of the Deliverables at Service Provider's sole cost and expense and refund to Customer an amount equal to the amounts paid by Customer to Service Provider for the Deliverables and Services under the applicable Statement of Work, plus all out-of-pocket expenses and costs incurred by Customer in connection with procuring substitute deliverables and services, to the extent such costs and expenses exceed the refunded amount. This Section shall survive the expiration or termination of this Agreement.

10.2 ***Customer Indemnifications.*** Customer shall indemnify, defend and hold Service Provider, its Affiliates and their respective directors, officers, shareholders, members, employees, representatives, agents, attorneys, successors, and assigns (collectively, "***Service Provider Indemnified Parties***") harmless from and against, and shall pay, any and all Losses sustained or incurred by any of the Service Provider Indemnified Parties, based upon, relating to or arising from, any and all Third Party claims, actions, suits, proceedings, or investigations in connection with or pertaining to any of the following:

(a) any actual or alleged bodily injury or death, damage to personal or real property, excluding computer data, data loss or any other related damage, notwithstanding the form in which any such action is brought (e.g., contract, tort, or otherwise), to the extent such injuries or damages arise directly or indirectly from acts, errors, or omissions that constitute negligence, willful misconduct, or violations of Law, by Customer;

(b) Customer's breach or failure to perform any of the obligations set forth in Article 9.3 (Confidential Information) relating to Service Provider Confidential Information;

(c) Fines, penalties, sanctions, underpayments, and/or other remedies to the extent such fines, penalties, sanctions, underpayments, and/or other remedies relate to any breach of any Laws by Customer; and

(d) Any failure by Customer to pay applicable taxes, together with any interest and penalties, assessed or imposed against Service Provider for which Customer has responsibility pursuant to **Section 7.8 (Taxes)** or applicable Laws.

10.3 ***Indemnification Procedures.*** In connection with any claim, action, suit, proceeding, or investigation for which the Customer Indemnified Parties or the Service Provider Indemnified Parties, as applicable, seeking indemnification ("***Indemnified Party***") from the other Party (the "***Indemnifying Party***") in accordance with this **Article 10 (Indemnification and Insurance)**, the Indemnified Party: (a) shall give the Indemnifying Party prompt written notice of the claim, action, suit, proceeding, or investigation; provided, however, that failure to provide such notice shall not relieve the Indemnifying Party from its liabilities or obligations hereunder, except solely to the extent of any material prejudice as a direct result of such failure; (b) shall cooperate with the Indemnifying Party, at the Indemnifying Party's sole cost and expense, in connection with the defense and settlement of the claim, action, suit, proceeding, or investigation; and (c) shall permit the Indemnifying Party to control the defense and settlement of the claim, action, suit, proceeding, or investigation; provided, however, that the Indemnifying Party may not settle the claim, action, suit, proceeding, or investigation without the Indemnified Party's prior written consent, which shall not be unreasonably withheld or delayed, in the event such settlement materially adversely impacts the Indemnified Party's rights or obligations. Further, the Indemnified Party, at its cost and expense, may participate in the defense of the claim, action, suit, proceeding, or investigation through counsel of its own choosing. This Section shall survive the expiration or termination of this Agreement.

10.4 ***Insurance.***

10.4.1 Service Provider shall maintain in effect at all times during the Term of this Agreement and for three (3) years thereafter insurance from an insurance company or companies having a Best's Financial Performance Rating ("FPR") of A+/A++ and a minimum Financial Size Category (FSC) of VIII or higher (if FPR is A/A-, then FSC must be IX or higher). Such insurance shall include the requirements set forth in this Section and in Schedule 10.4 (Insurance) and shall designate Customer and its Affiliates as "additional insureds" as specified in Schedule 10.4 (Insurance).

10.4.2 Service Provider shall, on or before the Effective Date and thereafter upon Customer's reasonable request, provide Customer's Risk Management Department with certified copies of all applicable endorsements and certificates of insurance, both evidencing such coverage, which also shall state that Customer shall be provided a minimum of thirty (30) days prior written notice of any proposed cancellation, or expiration without renewal, and five (5) business days prior written notice of any proposed change in carriers or material terms of coverage. Upon Customer's request,

Service Provider shall also provide Customer with certified copies of the involved insurance policy or policies within fifteen (15) days of such request.

10.4.3 Service Provider shall obtain or otherwise arrange for appropriate levels of insurance coverage for all of Service Provider's subcontractors. Such insurance shall name Customer and its Affiliates as "additional insureds" and shall satisfy the requirements set forth in this Section and in Schedule 10.4 (Insurance) unless Service Provider obtains the prior written approval of Customer's Risk Management Department with respect to the limits of insurance the subcontractors should carry. Service Provider shall provide Customer with certified copies of all applicable endorsements and certificates of insurance evidencing such coverage prior to any subcontractor commencing work.

10.4.4 In the event coverage is denied or reimbursement of a properly presented claim is disputed by the carrier for insurance provided as described above, upon written request, Service Provider shall provide Customer with a certified copy of the involved insurance policy or policies within ten (10) business days of receipt of such request.

10.4.5 The terms of this Section shall not be deemed to limit the liability of Service Provider hereunder, or to limit any rights Customer and/or its Affiliates may have including rights of indemnity or contribution. Failure to maintain such insurance (including subcontractor's insurance) or provide certificates of insurance as required above shall not relieve Service Provider of any or all liability. Additionally, any approval by Customer of any of Service Provider's insurance policies or limits shall not relieve Service Provider or its subcontractors of any obligation obtained in this Agreement.

ARTICLE 11—DISPUTE RESOLUTION

11.1 ***SOW Manager Level Performance Review.*** The applicable Service Provider SOW Manager and Customer SOW Manager shall meet as often as shall reasonably be required to review the performance of the Parties under the applicable Statement of Work and to resolve any disputes. Written minutes of such meetings shall be kept by Service Provider for review and approval by Customer. If these representatives are unable to resolve a dispute within ten (10) days after the initial request for a meeting, then the dispute shall be submitted to an executive-level performance review as described in **Section 11.2 (Executive-Level Performance Review)**.

11.2 ***Executive-Level Performance Review.*** If a SOW Manager-level review is not successful in resolving the dispute, face-to-face negotiations shall be conducted by senior executive officers of Customer and Service Provider. If these representatives are unable to resolve the dispute within ten (10) days after the representatives have commenced negotiations, or twenty (20) days have passed since the initial request for negotiations at this level, then the Parties may agree in writing to submit the dispute to mediation pursuant to **Section 11.3 (Voluntary, Non-Binding Mediation)**.

11.3 ***Voluntary, Non-Binding Mediation.*** If an executive-level review is not successful in resolving the dispute, the Parties may, but shall not be obligated to, mutually agree in writing to submit the dispute to non-binding mediation. Mediation must occur within five (5) business days after the Parties agree to submit the dispute to mediation, and the duration of the mediation shall be limited to one (1) business day. The Parties mutually shall select an independent mediator experienced in commercial technology contract disputes, and each shall designate a representative(s) to meet with the mediator in good faith in an effort to resolve the dispute. The specific format for the mediation shall be left to the discretion of the mediator and the designated Party representatives and may include the preparation of agreed-upon statements of fact or written statements of position furnished to the other Party.

11.4 ***Continued Performance; No Tolling of Cure Periods.*** Except where clearly prevented by the area in dispute, both Parties shall continue performing their obligations under this Agreement and the applicable Statement(s) of Work while the dispute is being resolved under this Article unless and until the dispute is resolved or until this Agreement is terminated as provided herein. The time frame for a Party to cure any breach of the terms of this Agreement shall not be tolled by the pendency of any dispute resolution procedures.

ARTICLE 12—MISCELLANEOUS

12.1 ***Notices.*** Any written notice required or permitted to be delivered pursuant to this Agreement shall be in writing and shall be deemed delivered: (a) upon delivery if delivered in person; (b) three (3) business days after deposit in the U.S. mail, registered or certified mail, return receipt requested, postage prepaid; (c) upon transmission if sent via telecopier, with a confirmation copy sent via overnight mail; or (d) one (1) business day after deposit with a national overnight courier, in each case addressed to the addresses below or to such other address as may be specified by either Party hereto upon notice given to the other.

If to Customer: ____________	If to Service Provider:
Attn: ____________	Attn: ____________
With a copy to: ____________	With a copy to: ____________
Attn: ____________	Attn: ____________

12.2 ***Bankruptcy.*** In the event Service Provider voluntarily or involuntarily becomes subject to the protection of the Bankruptcy Code and Service Provider or the trustee in bankruptcy rejects this Agreement under Section 365 of the Bankruptcy Code, Customer shall have the right to: (a) treat this Agreement as terminated; or (b) retain Customer's rights under this Agreement, specifically including the right to exercise its rights granted herein to the Deliverables (and to all work-in-progress relating thereto). Failure by Customer to assert its right to retain its benefits to the intellectual property embodied in the Deliverables pursuant to Section 365(n)(1)(B) of the Bankruptcy Code with respect to an executory contract rejected by Service Provider or the trustee in bankruptcy shall not be construed by the courts as a termination of such contract by Customer under Section 365(n)(1)(A) of the Bankruptcy Code.

12.3 ***Force Majeure.***

12.3.1 ***Definition.*** Subject to **Section 12.3.3 (Use of Alternate Providers by Customer)** below, neither Party shall be liable for any failure or delay in the performance of its obligations under this Agreement or any Statement of Work, if any, to the extent such failure or delay both: (a) is caused, without fault of the non-performing Party, by fire, flood, earthquake, elements of nature, or acts of God; acts of war, riots, civil disorders, rebellions or revolutions; quarantines, embargoes, and other similar governmental action; or any other similar cause beyond the reasonable control of such Party; and (b) could not have been prevented by reasonable precautions and cannot reasonably be circumvented by the non-performing Party through the use of alternate sources, work-around plans or other means.

12.3.2 ***Excused Performance.*** Events meeting both of the criteria set forth in subsections (a) and (b) of **Section 12.3.1 (Definition)** above are referred to collectively as "Force Majeure Events". Subject to **Section 12.3.3 (Use of Alternate Providers by Customer)** below, upon the occurrence of a Force Majeure Event, the non-performing Party shall be excused from its non-performance or observance of the affected obligation(s) for as long as such circumstances prevail and such Party continues to attempt to recommence performance whenever and to whatever extent possible without delay. Any Party so delayed in its performance will immediately notify the other by telephone or by the most timely means otherwise available (to be confirmed in writing within two (2) business days of the inception of such delay) and describe in reasonable detail the circumstances causing such delay.

12.3.3 ***Use of Alternate Providers by Customer.*** If a Force Majeure Event causes a material failure or delay in the performance of any Services for more than five (5) consecutive days, Customer shall have the right, at its sole election, and in addition to any rights Customer may have pursuant to **Section 8.3 (Termination for Force Majeure)**, procure such Services from an alternate source until Service Provider is again able to provide such Services. Customer shall continue to pay Service Provider the applicable fees for Services actually rendered by Service Provider, less any amounts payable by Customer to the alternate source, but Service Provider shall not be entitled to any additional payments as a result of the Force Majeure Event. Notwithstanding any other provision of this **Section 12.3 (Force Majeure)**, a Force Majeure Event shall not relieve Service Provider of its obligation to implement successfully all of the Services relating to disaster recovery and business continuity services that are included in any Statement of Work within the time period described in such Statement of Work.

12.3.4 ***Allocation of Resources.*** Without limiting Service Provider's obligations under this Agreement, whenever a Force Majeure Event causes Service Provider to allocate limited resources between or among Service Provider's customers, Customer shall receive at least the same treatment as comparable Service Provider customer. In no event will Service Provider redeploy or re-assign any Service Provider Personnel to another customer or account in the event of the occurrence of a Force Majeure

Event without the prior written consent of Customer, which consent may be withheld in Customer's sole discretion.

12.4 ***Assignment.*** Service Provider shall not assign or otherwise transfer this Agreement, or any part hereof, nor delegate any of its duties hereunder, whether by operation of law or otherwise, to any Third Party or Affiliate without the prior written consent of Customer. Without limiting the generality of the foregoing, the phrase "by operation of law" shall include a Change of Control. Any attempted assignment in contravention of this provision shall be void. Any rights granted to Customer under this Agreement to use the Deliverables, Services and/or Documentation shall inure to the benefit of any acquirer of, or successor in interest to, Customer, whether by merger, consolidation, purchase, operation of law or otherwise. Customer also shall have the right to assign this Agreement, in whole or in part, to any Third Party. Subject to the foregoing, this Agreement shall be binding on the Parties and their successors and permitted assigns.

12.5 ***Media Releases and Public Disclosures of Agreement.*** Without the prior written consent of the other Party, neither Party shall issue or release any statement, article, advertisement, public or private announcement, media release, or other similar publicity relating in any manner to: (a) any aspect of this Agreement, including Statement of Works; (b) any aspect of any Services and/or Deliverables; or (c) the fact that the Parties have engaged in any discussions or negotiations regarding any of the foregoing. Neither Party shall use the name or any business name, trade name, trademark, service mark, or logo of the other Party without the prior written consent of the other Party.

12.6 ***Counterparts; Facsimile Signatures.*** This Agreement and any Statement of Work may be executed in one or more duplicate originals, all of which together shall be deemed one and the same instrument. This Agreement and any Statement of Work shall be binding on the Parties through facsimile signatures, with originals to follow by regular mail or overnight courier.

12.7 ***Severability.*** If any provision of this Agreement or any Statement of Work is found by a court of competent jurisdiction to be invalid or unenforceable, such invalidity or unenforceability shall not invalidate or render unenforceable any other part of this Agreement or any Statement of Work, but the Agreement and/or Statement of Work shall be construed as not containing the particular provision or provisions held to be invalid or unenforceable.

12.8 ***Waiver.*** No delay or omission by either Party hereto to exercise any right occurring upon any noncompliance or default by the other Party with respect to any of the terms of this Agreement shall impair any such right or power or be construed to be a waiver thereof. A waiver by either of the Parties hereto of any of the covenants, conditions or agreements to be performed by the other shall not be construed to be a waiver of any succeeding breach thereof or of any covenant, condition or agreement herein contained.

12.9 ***Governing Law; Exclusive Jurisdiction.*** This Agreement, and all the rights and duties of the Parties arising from or relating in any way to the subject matter of this Agreement or the transaction(s) contemplated by it, shall be governed by, construed and enforced in accordance with the law of the State of ________ (excluding any conflict of laws provisions that would refer to and apply the substantive laws of another jurisdiction). The Parties hereby agree to waive and opt-out of any application of the Uniform Computer Information Transactions Act (UCITA), or any version thereof, adopted by any State in any form. Any suit or proceeding relating to this Agreement, including arbitration proceedings, shall be brought only in ________. **EACH OF THE PARTIES CONSENT TO THE EXCLUSIVE PERSONAL JURISDICTION AND VENUE OF THE COURTS, STATE AND FEDERAL, LOCATED IN ________.**

12.10 ***Relationship of Parties.*** The Parties acknowledge that they are independent contractors, and nothing set forth in this Agreement shall be deemed or construed to render the Parties as joint venturers, partners or employer and employee. Under no circumstances shall Customer be considered the employer of any Service Provider personnel, nor shall Service Provider have any right with respect to any employee of Customer.

12.11 ***Entire Agreement; Modification.*** This Agreement, together with all of the Schedules, Exhibits (including Statement of Works), Attachments and Addenda hereto, sets forth the entire, final, and exclusive agreement between the Parties as to the subject matter hereof and supersedes all prior and contemporaneous agreements, understandings, negotiations, and discussions, whether oral or written, between the Parties. This Agreement may be modified only pursuant to a writing executed by authorized representatives of Customer and Service Provider. Service Provider expressly agrees that all amendments to this Agreement executed by Customer after the Effective Date must be signed by a Vice President or higher-level officer of Customer in order to be effective and enforceable against Customer. The Parties expressly disclaim the right to claim the enforceability or effectiveness of: (a) any amendments to this Agreement that are not executed by a Vice President or higher-level officer of Customer; (b) any oral modifications to this Agreement; and (c) any other amendments that are based on course of dealing, waiver, reliance, estoppel, or other similar legal theory. The Parties expressly disclaim the right to enforce any rule of law that is contrary to the terms of this Section.

IN WITNESS WHEREOF, authorized representatives of the Parties have executed this Master Services Agreement effective as of the Effective Date.

CUSTOMER	**SERVICE PROVIDER**
By: ____________________	By: ____________________
Name: ____________________	Name: ____________________
Title: ____________________	Title: ____________________

SCHEDULE 1.2

DEFINED TERMS

"***Acceptance***" is defined in **Section 5.4.**

"***Affiliate(s)***" means any person, corporation, or other entity that now or in the future, directly or indirectly, controls, is controlled with or by or is under common control with a Party. For purposes of the foregoing, "control" shall mean, with respect to: (a) a corporation, the ownership, directly or indirectly, of fifty percent (50%) or more of the voting power to elect directors thereof or, for purposes of foreign corporations, if less than fifty percent (50%), the amount allowed by applicable law; and (b) any other entity, the power to direct the management of such entity.

"***Agreement***" means this Master Services Agreement by and between Customer and Service Provider, inclusive of all Statement of Works, Schedules, Exhibits, Attachments, and other documents attached hereto or incorporated herein by reference.

"***API***" means application programming interfaces including any interfaces necessary to achieve interoperability between the Deliverables and any Third Party systems.

"***Bankruptcy Code***" means the U.S. Bankruptcy Code, as amended.

"***Benefit***" is defined in **Section 2.6**.

"***Budget***" is defined in **Section 7.3.4**.

"***Change of Control***" means: (a) any transaction or combination of transactions as a result of which either a person, an entity, or a group of persons and/or entities that customarily has acted in concert and that presently is in control of Service Provider ceases to be in control of Service Provider; or (b) the sale, exchange, or other disposition (including disposition in full or partial dissolution) of the stock of Service Provider or the assets of Service Provider that constitute a substantial or material business segment of Service Provider; or (c) the divestiture, in whole or in part, of the business unit or division of Service Provider that has provided the Services and/or Deliverables to Customer. A Change of Control shall not include any public stock offering.

"***Change Order***," "***Change Request***," and "***Change Response***" are all defined in **Section 2.3**.

"***Confidential Information***" is defined in **Section 9.3.1**.

"***Confidentiality Agreement***" is defined in **Section 9.3.4**.

"***Critical Path Milestones***" is defined in **Section 2.1.2**.

"***Defect***" means any failure of the applicable Services and/or Deliverables, or components thereof, to operate in accordance with or otherwise conform to the applicable Documentation, Specifications, Service Levels, Interoperability Requirements, and Performance Standards.

"***Deliverables***" is defined in **Section 9.2.1**.

"***Disabling Code***" is defined in **Section 6.5**.

"***Disclosing Party***" is defined in **Section 9.3.4**.

"***Divested Unit***" is defined in **Section 2.6**.

"***Divested Date***" is defined in **Section 2.6**.

"***Documentation***" means, collectively all user, operator, system administration, technical, support and other manuals, and all other written, printed, electronic, or other format materials published or otherwise made available by Service Provider that describe or otherwise relate to the functional, operational, and/or performance capabilities of the Services, Deliverables and/or any APIs.

"***Effective Date***" is defined in the introductory paragraph of this Agreement.

"***Events of Default***" is defined in **Section 8.4**.

"***Force Majeure Events***" is defined in **Section 12.3.2**.

"***Incurred Cost Percentage***" means the aggregate incurred costs on the SOW to date, including Service Provider expenses, whether or not invoiced to Customer, divided by the aggregate amount of the currently effective Budget, multiplied by 100.

"***Incurred Fixed Fee Percentage***" means the percentage of the fixed fee accrued to date for billing purposes by Service Provider for purposes of monthly progress payments if permitted under the applicable SOW.

"***Indemnified Party***" is defined in **Section 10.3**.

"***Indemnifying Party***" is defined in **Section 10.3**.

"***Intellectual Property Rights***" means all inventions, patents, copyrights, trade secrets, trade names, know-how, intellectual property, software, shop rights, moral rights, licenses, developments, research data, designs, processes, formulas, and other intangible proprietary or property rights, whether or not patentable (or otherwise subject to legally enforceable restrictions or protections against unauthorized Third Party usage), and any and all applications for, and extensions, divisions, and reissuances of, any of the foregoing, and rights therein, and whether arising by statute or common law.

"***Interoperability Requirements***" is defined in **Section 3.3**.

"***Key Personnel***" are Service Provider Personnel set forth in the applicable Statement of Work as being "critical" for the performance of such Statement of Work.

"***Know-How***" is defined in **Section 3.5.3**.

"***Law***" or "***Laws***" means all national, intergovernmental, common law, federal, state, provincial, regional, territorial and local laws, statutes, ordinances, regulations, rules, executive orders, orders of a court or governmental agency, supervisory requirements, directives, circulars, opinions, interpretive letters, and other official releases of or by any government, or any authority, department or agency thereof.

"***Licensed Service Provider Materials***" is defined in **Section 9.1.2**.

"***Live Testing***" is defined in **Section 5.3**.

"***Live Testing Period***" is defined in **Section 5.3**.

"***Losses***" means all settlements, judgments, awards, fines, penalties, interest, liabilities, losses, costs, damages, and expenses (including reasonable attorneys' fees and disbursements and court costs).

"***Customer***" is defined in the introductory paragraph to this Agreement.

"***Customer Auditors***" is defined in **Section 9.5.1**.

"***Customer Indemnified Parties***" is defined in **Section 10.1.1**.

"***Customer Materials***" is defined in **Section 9.1.3**.

"***Customer Policies***" is defined in **Section 4.6**.

"***Customer SOW Manager***" is defined in **Section 4.9**.

"***Not to Exceed Amount***" is defined in **Section 7.3.3**.

"***Object Code***" shall mean computer programming code, substantially or entirely in binary form, which is intended to be directly executable by a computer after suitable processing but without the intervening steps of compilation or assembly.

"***Open Source***" is defined in **Section 6.6**.

"***Percentage of Completion***" means, with respect to any SOW, the aggregate percentage of work that has been completed on the Deliverables for such SOW, as reported in a SOW status report.

"***Performance Standards***" means, collectively: (a) the representations and warranties and performance standards set forth in **Article 6**; and (b) any other performance standards and criteria set forth in this Agreement and/or a Statement of Work.

"***Personal Information***" is defined in **Section 9.3.3**.

"***Pre-Live Testing***" is defined in **Section 5.2**.

"***Receiving Party***" is defined in **Section 9.3.4.**

"***SAS 70***" is defined in **Section 9.5.3.**

"***Service Levels***" is defined in **Section 2.1.2.**

"***Service Level Credit***" is defined in **Section 3.6.2.**

"***Service Provider***" is defined in the introductory paragraph to this Agreement.

"***Service Provider Audits***" and "***Service Provider Audit Reports***" are defined in **Section 9.5.3.**

"***Service Provider Indemnified Parties***" is defined in **Section 10.2.**

"***Service Provider Materials***" is defined in **Section 9.1.1.**

"***Service Provider Personnel***" shall mean those employees, representatives, contractors, subcontractors, and agents of Service Provider, Service Provider Affiliates, and subcontractors who perform any Services and/or provide any Deliverables under this Agreement.

"***Service Provider SOW Manager***" is defined in **Section 4.2.**

"***Service Provider Proposal***" is defined in the Recitals.

"***Service Taxes***" means any and all sales, use, excise, value added (including without limitation VAT), service, lease, personal property, consumption, and other similar taxes and duties that are assessed against either Party on the provision or receipt of the Services as a whole, or on any particular Service received by Customer Service Provider, excluding income taxes.

"***Services***" is defined in **Section 3.1.**

"***Services Procedures Guide***" is defined in **Section 3.8.**

"***Source Code***" shall mean computer programming code, other than Object Code, and related source code level system documentation, comments, and procedural code, such as job control language, which may be printed out or displayed in human readable form.

"***Source Code Materials***" means (a) available sub-programs, routines, program files, data files, file and data defined terms and relationships, data definition specifications, data models, program and system logic, interfaces, algorithms, program architecture, design concepts, system designs, program structure, sequence and organization, screen displays and report layouts related to interacting with or a part of the applicable software, whether in human-readable, electronic or machine-readable form; (b) Service Provider-developed maintenance and support tools, utilities, diagnostic programs, and supporting programs used or utilized by Service Provider internally in the support or maintenance of the applicable software, or externally in connection with supporting other customer locations, whether or not such items are made available to licensees generally or at an additional fee, whether in human-readable, electronic, or machine-readable form; and (c) available reference manuals, user and operating guides and manuals, design specifications, functional specifications, flow charts, internal use listings or manuals relating to error corrections, fixes and work-arounds, file and program cross-reference information (whether in manual, guide or other format), whether in human-readable, electronic, or machine-readable form.

"***Specifications***" means any written functional, technical, design, or other specifications applicable to the Deliverables and/or APIs, as the case may be, which are furnished or approved by Customer.

"***Statement of Work***" means a document that sets forth the specific terms and conditions pursuant to which Service Provider shall perform certain Services. Each Statement of Work will be in a form substantially similar to the Statement(s) of Work attached hereto as **Exhibit 1**.

"***System***" means any inter-connected grouping or aggregation of the services, equipment, networks, hardware, software, resources and materials, including those provided or utilized by Service Provider, in use by Customer or required to be used as of the Effective Date, and including all additions, modifications, substitutions, upgrades, and/or enhancements to such services, equipment, networks, hardware, software, resources, and materials.

"***Term***" is defined in **Section 8.1.1**.

"***Termination Assistance Period***" is defined in **Section 8.11**.

"***Test Plan***" is defined in **Section 5.1**.

"***Third Party***" means persons, corporations, and entities other than Service Provider, Customer or any of their Affiliates.

"***Transition***" is defined in **Section 3.4.1**.

"***Transition Milestones***" means Critical Path Milestones related to the Transition.

"***Transition Plan***" is defined in **Section 3.4.2**.

"***Warranty Period***" is defined in **Section 6.1**.

SCHEDULE 2.5

SOW STATUS REPORT

Each SOW status report shall be developed in accordance with **Section 2.5** and include the following items:

1. ***Accomplishments.*** A written summary of all of the accomplishments and difficulties encountered during the prior reporting period.

2. ***Current Status.*** A written summary of the current status of the SOW and the status of milestones that are due during the reporting period and of any milestones that were due during the previous reporting period but were not completed.

3. ***Jeopardy Items.*** A written summary of all concerns or issues for the current reporting period, along with the plan and projected date for resolution.

4. ***Scheduling and Staffing Items.*** A written summary of any special staffing or scheduling issues for the upcoming period.

5. ***Open Issues.*** A comprehensive and consolidated list of all outstanding SOW-related problems identified by Customer and Service Provider that remain to be resolved.

6. ***Resolved Issues.*** A written summary of the concerns or issues that were reported in the previous reporting periods that have been resolved and a description of the resolution.

7. ***Delays.*** Identification of any Customer or Third Party delays affecting Service Provider's ability to perform.

8. ***Suggestions.*** Suggestions and proposed actions for dealing with and resolving any identified difficulties and the anticipated results during the next reporting period.

9. ***Miscellaneous.*** Any other concern or information that will or may affect the SOW.

SCHEDULE 3.4.2

TRANSITION PLAN

SCHEDULE 7.1

GLOBAL PRICE LIST

[Document consisting of ____ ( ) pages attached hereto]

SCHEDULE 7.5

EXPENSE POLICY

[Document consisting of ____ ( ) pages attached hereto]

SCHEDULE 10.4

INSURANCE REQUIREMENTS

A. General Provisions Applicable to All Required Insurance.

1. All policies hereunder shall be endorsed to provide that their coverage will be primary and that any insurance carried or self insurance maintained by Customer and/or its Affiliates shall be excess and non-contributory.

2. Service Provider shall be liable for all deductibles, co-payments, and other liabilities relating to insurance coverages.

B. Workers' Compensation.

1. Limits

Coverage A	Statutory
Coverage B	
Bodily Injury by Accident	$100,000 each accident
Bodily Injury by Disease	$100,000 policy limit
Bodily Injury by Disease	$100,000 each employee

2. The policy shall be written to meet the statutory requirements for the state in which the work is to be performed, including Occupational Disease. Service Provider provides workers' compensation insurance through either qualified self-insurance or Third Party insurance.

The policy shall include a waiver of subrogation in favor of Customer and its Affiliates.

C. Commercial General Liability.

1. Limits

General Aggregate: $5,000,000
Products/Completed Operations Aggregate: $5,000,000
Personal/Advertising Injury: $2,500,000 any one person
Bodily Injury/Property Damage: $2,500,000 per occurrence

2. The policy shall be written on an occurrence basis using ISO Form CG 0001 or equivalent. The policy shall provide Premises/Operations, Products/Completed Operations, Independent Contractors, Personal Injury, Explosion, Collapse and Underground Property Damage, Broad Form Property Damage and Contractual Liability coverage.

The policy shall include Customer and its Affiliates as additional insureds.

The policy shall include a waiver of subrogation in favor of Customer and its Affiliates.

D. Commercial Automobile Liability.

1. Limits

Bodily Injury/Property Damage: $ 2,500,000 Combined Single Limit each accident.

2. The policy shall be written to cover all Owned, Non-owned, and Hired vehicles.

3. The policy shall include Customer and its Affiliates as additional insureds.

E. Errors and Omissions/Professional Liability.

1. Limits

Not less than $3,000,000 per claim.

2. The policy shall include Customer and its Affiliates as additional insureds. The "insured versus insured" exclusion must be deleted with respect to the work being done for Customer and its Affiliates.

EXHIBIT 1

STATEMENTS OF WORK

[DOCUMENTS PREPARED PURSUANT TO SECTION 2.1
AND ATTACHED HERETO]

EXHIBIT 2

CONFIDENTIALITY AND NONDISCLOSURE AGREEMENT FORM

[TO BE PROVIDED]

EXHIBIT 3

SERVICE PROVIDER PROPOSAL

[TO BE ATTACHED]

Bilateral Proprietary Information Agreement (Annotated)

THIS PROPRIETARY INFORMATION AGREEMENT is made this ___________ day of _____________, 20___ by and between _____________, a _____________ corporation, with its principal place of business at ___________ "Company"), and _____________, [a ___________ corporation][individually], with [its][his][her] principal place of business at _______________________ ("Covenantor").

- ***The parties should consider whether their subsidiaries and affiliates should be parties to this agreement. The answer will depend on whether the confidential information of any affiliate will be disclosed and whether any affiliate will receive any confidential information disclosed under this agreement. From the Furnishing Party's perspective, the prudent approach is to limit the number of entities receiving its confidential information and thus it should prohibit disclosure to the receiving party's affiliates unless there is a compelling business reason to do otherwise. If information will be disclosed to a party's affiliates, the receiving party should be contractually obligated to keep written records of which of its affiliates received what information.***

BACKGROUND

1. Company has extensive expertise in the creation and development of technical information, ideas, and concepts relating to the _________ industry including consulting, pricing, marketing, and implementation and system designs for such software, including without limitation, copyrights, trade secrets, plans, source codes, object codes, prototypes, working models, and production models (the "Confidential Information").

2. Covenantor has extensive expertise in ___________________________ ___ (collectively referred to with Company's expertise as the "Confidential Information").

- The parties should ensure that the definition of "Confidential Information" is broad enough to encompass all information that will be disclosed. The definition should be drafted in such a manner to include all reports, analysis and derivative works encompassing the confidential information. The definition should be modified in each agreement to reflect the actual information that will be disclosed in that transaction. The parties should be careful to make sure the definition is not so broad and amorphous that it is unenforceable.

3. The parties desire to exchange the Confidential Information in conjunction with ______________________________ **[give detailed description as to why the parties are exchanging information]**.

- The parties should narrowly define the purpose for exchanging information as the description establishes the limitations as to who may access such information and what purposes the information may be used for. See e.g., Section 2(d) below.

4. The "Furnishing Party" will be furnishing the other party, the "Recipient," with information and or other materials, in writing, orally, and in other tangible form, regarding the Furnishing Party. **Such information, in whole or in part, together with any analyses, compilations, studies, or other documents prepared by the Recipient, the Recipient's agents or employees, which contain or otherwise reflect such information and Recipient's review or interest in the Furnishing Party, shall be considered Confidential Information.**

- ***The Furnishing Party should ensure that the definition of "Confidential Information" includes "derivative" works to avoid later disputes over what constitutes confidential information and whether all such information has been returned or destroyed by the Recipient.***

5. The Confidential Information of Company and Covenantor is proprietary, secret, and confidential and is only being disclosed to the other party in conjunction with Company's business relationship or potential business relationship with Covenantor and for no other reason.

NOW THEREFORE, in consideration of the mutual covenants herein contained, the parties intending to be legally bound, agree as follows:

1. Company and Covenantor shall disclose to the other such Confidential Information as such party deems appropriate.

2. Company and Covenantor shall review and maintain the Confidential Information in accordance with the following terms and conditions:

(a) Company and Covenantor agree to treat all Confidential Information as defined above as confidential **and not to disclose the same to any third party. The documents containing such information should be designated "Confidential" or "Proprietary" and shall be so marked by the Furnishing Party provided, however, that all software provided to Covenantor hereunder shall be deemed to be proprietary and confidential regardless of whether it is marked "Confidential" or "Proprietary."**

- ***Nondisclosure agreements usually provide for one of two standards for the disclosure of confidential information. This agreement creates a strict liability standard by providing that the Recipient will not disclose the Furnishing Party's confidential information to a third party. Other agreements provide that the Recipient will use the same standards to protect the Furnishing Party's confidential information as it does to protect its own but no less than a reason-***

able standard of care. This "reasonable" standard provides a much lower level of protection to the Furnishing party and thus should be avoided if possible.

- ***The Furnishing Party should ensure that the Recipient may not disclose its Confidential Information to third parties without the Furnishing Party's consent. The Recipient is likely to argue that it needs to disclose the Furnishing Party's Confidential Information to its third party contractors and consultants but the Furnishing Party needs to ensure that these third parties are not competitors of the Furnishing Party.***

(b) No copies of the Confidential Information shall be made, unless agreed to in writing by the Furnishing Party.

(c) All of the Confidential Information shall be kept and maintained in a safe and secure place with adequate safeguards to ensure that unauthorized persons do not have access to the Confidential Information. Company and Covenantor shall, at all times, keep the other informed in writing of the location of the Confidential Information.

(d) Only r**epresentatives of Company and Covenantor whose review of the Confidential Information is necessary and appropriate for the purpose set forth in Paragraph 3 of the Background above shall have access to the Confidential Information. The Confidential Information shall be used by the Receiving Party solely for the purpose stated in Paragraph 3 of the Background above.**

- ***The Furnishing Party should ensure the agreement limits who may have access to its Confidential Information. Some parties seek to include language to the effect that the receiving party's employees must execute non-disclosure agreements equally restrictive to the overarching proprietary information agreement prior to accessing the confidential information. Under no circumstances should the receiving party agree to have its employees execute a proprietary information agreement directly with the disclosing party as such action potentially exposes its employees to personal liability.***

(e) Any oral discussions between Company and Covenantor that relate to the Confidential Information shall be kept secret and confidential and are deemed to be Confidential Information.

- ***Some nondisclosure agreements require the Furnishing Party to reduce to writing all oral disclosures and to provide such writing to the Recipient within 30 days of the disclosure in order for the disclosure to be considered Confidential Information. The likelihood of the Furnishing Party's employees remembering to do so after each disclosure is small. Thus, the language set forth above protects the Furnishing Party. The Recipient will argue, however, that unless the Confidential Information is reduced to writing and provided to the Recipient, the Recipient will have no way of knowing which disclosures are confidential.***

(f) Upon the request of the Furnishing Party or after the termination of this Agreement, the Recipient shall promptly return all of the Confidential

Information to the Furnishing Party **or destroy all such Confidential Information including all work products of the Recipient containing Confidential Information. The returning party shall certify that all Confidential Information and copies or extracts thereof have been returned or destroyed.**

- ***Some parties request the right to retain one copy of the Confidential Information for their records on the belief that if a dispute arises in the future, the Recipient will have no means to show what Confidential Information it received from the Furnishing Party. If the Furnishing Party allows the Recipient to keep a copy, the Recipient should be required to keep such information in a locked file in the General Counsel's office.***

(g) The Recipient agrees to immediately notify the Furnishing Party in writing of any misuse or misappropriation of the Confidential Information or violation of this Agreement that may come to its attention.

3. **Neither party, its agents, employees, representatives, subsidiaries, affiliates, or parent companies shall, for themselves or for the benefit of any person or entity other than the Furnishing Party**, use or disclose the Confidential Information of the other whether written or oral, software technology or otherwise for any purpose, at any time or in any place, without the express prior written approval of the Furnishing Party.

- ***The Furnishing Party should ensure that the Confidential Information should be used only for the purposes contemplated under the Agreement and that any restrictions bind not only to Recipient but also its agents, employees, representatives, subsidiaries, affiliates, or parent companies.***

4. Notwithstanding anything to the contrary herein, the Recipient shall have no obligation to preserve the confidentiality of any information that:

(a) Was previously known to the Recipient free of any obligation to keep it confidential as shown by the Recipient's written records, so long as the Recipient did not receive such information directly or indirectly from the Furnishing Party; or

(b) Is or becomes publicly available, by other than unauthorized disclosure; or

(c) Other than for patents, is independently developed by Recipient without knowledge of the Confidential Information as shown by the Recipient's written records; or

(d) Is disclosed to third parties by the Furnishing Party without restriction; or

(e) Is lawfully received from a third party whose disclosure would not violate any confidentiality or other legal obligation.

5. No liability shall arise under this Agreement due to the Recipient's disclosure of Confidential Information made pursuant to judicial or governmental order, provided the Recipient notifies the Furnishing Party as soon as possible and in any

event prior to such disclosure and cooperates with the Furnishing Party in the event the Furnishing Party elects to legally contest and avoid such disclosure.

6. Company and Covenantor agree that neither party acquires any title, ownership, or other intellectual property right or license under this Agreement.

7. **The obligations of this Agreement with respect to the disclosure of Confidential Information shall survive for a period of seven (7) years from the date of last disclosure or for as long as Company or Covenantor is commercially marketing the Confidential Information, whichever is longer.**

- ***The Furnishing Party should not agree on an artificial period of time for the Recipient's Confidential Information to survive. Often the parties agree on a period of two to three years but yet at the end of such period, the Confidential Information is still considered to be a trade secret of the Furnishing Party. To that end, the Furnishing Party should insist on the inclusion of language to the effect that the Recipient's obligations of confidentiality shall continue so long as the Furnishing Party considers the Confidential Information to be a trade secret.***

8. **Company and Covenantor recognize and agree that their obligations under Sections 2, 3, and 7 of this Agreement shall survive the termination of this Agreement and Company and Covenantor shall be bound by such obligations after termination hereof.**

- ***It is important that the parties state that their obligations of confidentiality survive any earlier termination of the non-disclosure agreement.***

9. This Agreement may be terminated by either party upon thirty (30) days prior written notice provided, however, that this Agreement may be terminated immediately and the return of all Confidential Information may be demanded upon written notice in the event that the other party breaches any material term of this Agreement, is declared bankrupt, creates, or permits an assignment for the benefit of its creditors, is dissolved, or ownership and control of said party is transferred to a third party.

- ***If the amount of information disclosed is voluminous, some parties agree that the receiving party may destroy the information instead of physically returning it to the disclosing party. In such event, an officer of the receiving party should certify in writing that the information has been destroyed.***

10. Company and Covenantor acknowledge their obligations to control access to technical data under the U.S. Export Laws and Regulations and agree to adhere to such laws and regulations with regard to any technical data received under this Agreement.

11. In the event either party breaches, or threatens to breach any of the covenants expressed herein, the **damages to the non-threatening or non-breaching party** will **be great and irreparable and difficult to quantify**; therefore, the non-threatening or non-breaching party may apply to a court of competent jurisdiction for injunctive or

other equitable relief to restrain such breach or threat of breach, without disentitling such party from any other relief in either law or equity.

- ***Both parties should be hesitant to acknowledge in advance that any damages "will" be great. Instead, prudent parties should provide that the damages "may" be great. Further, the party seeking an injunction should not be required to post a bond to do so.***

12. Covenantor and Company agree they will **indemnify and hold harmless the other party from all losses, damages, causes of action, and attorneys' fees** incurred by the other party arising from the breach of this Agreement by Covenantor or Company as the case may be.

- ***The parties should consider whether they want to indemnify each other as they already have a breach of contract claim. An indemnity claim will allow the aggrieved party to recover a greater level of damages that would otherwise be allowed under a contract claim.***

13. This Agreement merges and supersedes all prior Agreements between the parties hereto ***as to the subject matter hereof,*** and shall be governed by and construed in accordance with the domestic laws of the state of ____________________, of the United States of America, excluding its principles of conflicts of laws. The parties hereto agree that any action related to this Agreement shall solely be venued in the Federal District Court for the Eastern District of __________________ and the parties hereby irrevocably submit to the jurisdiction and venue of said court.

- ***To the extent the proprietary information agreement is executed in conjunction with another agreement such as a master services agreement, the parties should clearly provide that the agreements are separate and distinct and that the proprietary information agreement will survive the termination of the other agreement.***

14. This Agreement shall not be assigned by any party hereto without the express prior written consent of the other party. Any attempted assignment in contravention of this Section 14 shall be void.

- ***The parties need to state that any attempted assignment is void; otherwise, a court will allow the assignment to occur but award the non-consenting party monetary damages. See Chapter 4.A.7 for a more in-depth discussion.***

15. In the event that the Confidential Information is or becomes the subject of a patent application, patent, copyright application, or copyright, the Recipient agrees and understands that the Furnishing Party will have all the rights and remedies available to it under the law as a result of said patent applications, patents, copyright applications, or copyrights, and that disclosure of such Confidential Information to the Recipient does not in any way effect those rights and remedies.

16. It is understood by the Recipient that the Confidential Information disclosed hereunder may relate to products that are under development or planned for devel-

opment. THE FURNISHING PARTY DISCLAIMS ANY IMPLIED WARRANTY OF MERCHANTABILITY, ANY IMPLIED WARRANTY OF FITNESS FOR A PARTICULAR PURPOSE, ANY IMPLIED WARRANTY OF NON-INFRINGEMENT, AND ANY EXPRESS WARRANTY WITH RESPECT TO ANY OF THE CONFIDENTIAL INFORMATION AND DOCUMENTATION DISCLOSED HEREUNDER. The Furnishing Party accepts no responsibility as a result of any expenses, losses, damages, or actions incurred or undertaken by the Recipient as a result of the Furnishing Party's receipt or use of any Confidential Information or Documentation.

17. The waiver by either party hereto of any breach of the terms and conditions hereof will not be considered a modification of any provision, nor shall such a waiver act to bar the enforcement of any subsequent breach.

OPTIONAL

18. Covenantor acknowledges and agrees that Company has outstanding publicly traded shares, and that the Confidential Information disclosed hereunder may constitute material non-public information. Covenantor agrees to treat any such Confidential Information in accordance with the requirements of the United States securities laws, including Rule 10b-5 under the Securities Exchange Act of 1934, as amended.

- ***If one of the disclosing parties is a publically traded company, it may want to include the above language to protect itself from any claim that the information provided under the Agreement violated any applicable securities laws, including but not limited to Regulation FD.***

IN WITNESS WHEREOF, the parties have executed this Proprietary Information Agreement under seal effective the date first written above.

ATTEST:	**COMPANY**
______________________________	**By:** ________________________ **(SEAL)**
WITNESS/ATTEST:	**COVENANTOR**
______________________________	**By:** ________________________ **(SEAL)**

- ***If the party executing the agreement is signing in his/her corporate capacity, they should always use the designation "By:" prior to their signature. Further, the witness should always sign under the title "ATTEST." If the person signing is signing in their individual capacity, then the term "WITNESS" should be used.***

Non-Competition, Confidentiality, and Inventions Agreement

In consideration of employment of the Employee by Employer and payment to the Employee of salary or wages, this Non-Competition, Confidentiality and Inventions Agreement (the "Agreement") is made between ________________ ("Employer"), a ________________ corporation with its principal office at ______________________, and ____________________ ("Employee") whose principal address is ____________ ________________________.

1. **Loyalty and Best Efforts.** During the Employee's term of employment with Employer, the Employee will devote his or her full time and best efforts to the business of Employer and will not engage in any business activity which competes with the products or services being developed, marketed or sold by Employer.

2. **Non-competition. THIS SECTION MAY AFFECT YOUR RIGHT TO ACCEPT EMPLOYMENT WITH OTHER COMPANIES SUBSEQUENT TO YOUR EMPLOYMENT BY Employer.** The Employee agrees that during the term of Employee's employment with Employer and for a period of one (1) year after the termination of Employee's employment with Employer for any reason, whether with or without cause, the Employee will not render professional services of the type provided by Employee during Employee's employment with Employer, directly or indirectly, whether as an employee, employee of a third party, consultant, or otherwise, (a) to any person, firm, or organization that is a client of Employer or was a client of Employer at any time during the period of Employee's employment with Employer, with which Employee had any contact as a result of Employee's employment by Employer, or (b) to any prospective client of Employer if the Employee participated in the solicitation of the prospective client while employed by Employer.

3. **Non-solicitation.** The Employee agrees that, during the term of Employee's employment with Employer and for a period of one (1) year after the termination of such employment for any reason, whether with or without cause, the Employee will not, on the behalf of Employee or any other person, corporation or entity, (a) directly or indirectly, solicit business from or call upon entities or individuals that are current clients or active prospects of Employer at the time of the termination of Employee's employment with Employer and with which Employee had any contact as a result of Employee's employment by Employer, for the purpose of soliciting, serving, or selling services or products similar to those being developed, licensed, or marketed by Employer, or (b) recruit employees of Employer, or otherwise seek to induce such employees to terminate employment with Employer or violate any agreement with Employer.

4. **Proprietary Information.** The Employee will not disclose to anyone outside Employer, and will not use except in the business of Employer, any confidential, proprietary, or secret information or material relating to the products, services, customers or business operations, personnel or activities of Employer, its licensers, or its clients (collectively, "Proprietary Information"), either during or after employment by Employer, except with the written permission of Employer. The Employee agrees that all Proprietary Information (whether or not learned, obtained or developed solely by Employee or jointly with others) shall remain the property of Employer, and that upon termination of employment or at any earlier time as requested by Employer, the Employee will immediately deliver all Proprietary Information in Employee's possession or control to Employer. Proprietary Information includes, but is not limited to: source code, object code, operational and functional features, and limitations of Employer's software; Employer's research and development plans and activities; the prices, terms, and conditions of Employer's contracts with its customers; the identities, needs, and requirements of Employer's customers; Employer's pricing policies and price lists; Employer's business plans and strategies; Employer's marketing plans and strategies; personnel information (such as employee lists, telephone numbers, addresses); and financial information regarding Employer. The Employee's undertakings and obligations under this Paragraph shall not apply, however, to any information that: (i) is or becomes in the public domain through no action or failure to act on the Employee's part; (ii) is generally disclosed to third parties by Employer without restrictions on such third parties; or (iii) is approved for release by written authorization of the President of Employer.

5. **Inventions.** As used herein, "Invention" means any concept, design, plan, product, equipment, idea, method, computer program, software, system design, hardware, manual, manuscript, or other documentation, or other thing, tangible or intangible, which is: (i) made, developed or conceived solely by the Employee or jointly with others during or in the course of the Employee's employment by Employer; (ii) made, developed, or conceived wholly or partially as the result of any task assigned to the Employee or any work performed by the Employee for or on behalf of Employer; and/or (iii) made or developed with the use of Employer facilities or equipment. Any such Invention shall be considered a work made for hire. Employee hereby grants, assigns, and conveys to Employer all right, title, and interest in and to all Inventions, and irrevocably waives all moral rights in any Invention. The Employee further agrees that, during and at any time after Employee's employment by Employer, the Employee shall execute any and all documents necessary or advisable to effectuate such assignment solely to Employer or its nominees, and shall cooperate in every lawful fashion to effectuate such assignment.

6. **Conflicting Agreements.** The Employee represents that employment by Employer will not conflict with any agreement to which the Employee is subject, and that the Employee will not disclose to Employer, and will not induce Employer to use, any confidential information or material belonging to others.

7. **Return of Employer Property.** Employer may provide the Employee with a portable personal computer for Employee's use in the course of employment by Employer. The Employee acknowledges that any such personal computer, and all

other Employer property that comes to be in the Employee's custody, will remain the exclusive property of Employer. Upon termination of the Employee's employment with Employer, whether voluntary or involuntary, or at any other time as requested by Employer, the Employee agrees to deliver to Employer: (i) any such personal computer; (ii) all other Employer property in the Employee's control; and (iii) any and all records, notebooks, software, disks, tapes and other storage media, documentation, and other items relating to any research, experiment, or invention that could result in an Invention assignable to Employer pursuant to Paragraph 5.

8. Reasonableness. The Employee hereby agrees that the restrictions set forth in this Agreement are fair and reasonable and are reasonably required for the protection of the interests of Employer. However, if, in any judicial proceeding, any provision of this Agreement is found to be so broad as to be unenforceable, it is hereby agreed that such provision shall be interpreted to be only so broad as to be enforceable.

9. Survival. The Employee's obligations under this Agreement shall survive the termination of Employee's employment with Employer regardless of the manner of such termination, and shall be binding upon the Employee and the Employee's heirs, executors, and administrators.

10. **Employment at Will.** The Employee agrees that the Employee is an at-will employee of Employer and that both the Employee and Employer may terminate the Employee's employment at any time. The Employee understands that this Agreement does not create an obligation on the part of Employer or any other party to continue the employment of Employee.

11. **Assignability.** Employer shall have the unrestricted right to assign this Agreement to its parent company, its affiliates, and any and all successors in interest and this Agreement inures to the benefit of Employer, its subsidiaries, affiliated corporations, successors, and assigns. This Agreement, being personal, is not assignable by Employee.

12. **Remedies.** The Employee acknowledges that any breach of this Agreement by the Employee may cause irreparable injury to Employer, and in the event of such a breach, Employer shall have, in addition to any remedies at law, the right to an injunction to prevent or restrain a breach of the Employee's obligations hereunder.

13. **Governing Law.** This Agreement shall be governed and construed in accordance with the laws of the State of ___________, excluding, however, such laws as pertain to conflicts of law. Any action arising out of the Agreement or the termination of this Agreement, or the performance of services under this agreement, or the relationship between the parties established herein, shall be brought only in the ___________County Superior Court of _____________, or U.S. District Court for the District of ______________, and Employee hereby consents to and submits to the jurisdiction of either of such courts for such purpose.

14. **Waivers.** The waiver by Employer or the Employee of any action, right, or condition in this Agreement, or of any breach of a provision of this Agreement, shall not constitute a waiver of any other occurrences of the same event.

15. **Headings.** The section headings in this Agreement are for reference purposes only and shall not be deemed to be a part of this Agreement or to affect the meaning or interpretation of this Agreement.

16. **Entire Agreement; Amendments.** This Agreement constitutes the entire understanding of the parties with respect to its subject matter, supersedes any prior communication or understanding with respect thereto, and no modification or waiver of any provision hereof shall be valid unless made in writing and signed by the parties.

17. **Understanding of Agreement.** ***The Employee states that the Employee has had a reasonable period sufficient to study, understand, and consider this Agreement, that the Employee has had the opportunity to consult with counsel of the Employee's choice, that the Employee has read this Agreement and understands all of its terms, that the Employee is entering into and signing this Agreement knowingly and voluntarily, and that in doing so the Employee is not relying upon any statement or representations by Employer and its agents.***

IN WITNESS WHEREOF, the undersigned parties have executed this Agreement as a sealed instrument as of this ______ day of ______________ , 20 ___.

EMPLOYER	**Insert Name Here**
	THE EMPLOYEE
______________________	______________________
(Management Signature)	**(Employee Signature)**
	______________________
	Employee Start Date

Business Associate Agreement (Annotated)

This Business Associate Agreement ("Agreement") is effective as described below by and between ____________ ("Business Associate" or "BA") and any of the affiliated company(ies) of Customer[1] for which Business Associate is to provide services or functions and which are regulated by Subtitle F of Title II of the Health Insurance Portability and Accountability Act of 1996 ("HIPAA") and its implementing regulations (45 CFR Parts 160, 162 and 164) ("the Privacy Rules" and "the Security Rules" or "the HIPAA Rules"), and/or the "nonaffiliated third party" requirements of Title V of the Gramm-Leach-Bliley Act (15 U.S.C. § 6801 *et seq.*) ("GLBA") and, as applicable, state statutes and regulations implementing same, including its implementing regulations issued by the Insurance Commissioner of the State of New York - Regulation 169; the information collection and disclosure requirements set forth at N.J.S.A. 17:23A-1 et seq. - the New Jersey Information Practices Act, and its implementing bulletins, Bulletin Nos.: 00-15 and 01-10, issued by the Commissioner of the New Jersey Department of Banking and Insurance; and its implementing regulations issued by the Department of Insurance of the Commonwealth of Pennsylvania (collectively, "the GLBA Rules"), either because Customer is a Covered Entity under the HIPAA Rules or is itself a business associate of a Covered Entity under those Rules.

Customer and Business Associate mutually agree to the terms of this Agreement in order to comply with the business associate contracting requirements of the HIPAA Rules and the "nonaffiliated third party" requirements of the GLBA Rules.

This Agreement is effective on the last date written below ("the Effective Date").

A. Safeguarding Private Information.

1. **"Private Information" defined.** "Private Information" consists of the following information created or received on behalf of, or received from, Customer: Protected Health Information ("PHI") as defined by the HIPAA Rules, Personal or Privileged Information as defined by the New Jersey Information Practices Act, and Nonpublic Personal Financial and, as applicable, Health Information as defined by GLBA and the GLBA Rules.

---

1. The Customer affiliated companies are currently: [list affiliated companies] ____________. Affiliates identified with ** above are not Covered Entities subject to the HIPAA Rules. The designation of Customer affiliated companies as part of Customer's affiliated covered entity group is subject to change; affiliation is not intended to create joint liability for a violation of the HIPAA Rules or Customer's policies and procedures by one affiliate, nor any right of action by a covered member of one affiliate against other affiliates.

2. **Permitted Uses and Disclosures.** Business Associate will not Use, Disclose or make requests for Private Information except the minimum information that is necessary to accomplish its purposes as Required by Law and as permitted or required by this Agreement, as follows:

(a) Functions and Activities on Customer's Behalf. In addition to providing data aggregation services to Customer if and as Customer may request in accordance with the definitive Business Agreement to be entered into by Business Associate and Customer (the "Business Agreement"), Business Associate is permitted to Use, Disclose or make requests for Private Information only in connection with the services to be performed under the Business Agreement, as follows (and as the same may be amended form time to time): services in connection with the ______________ project.

(b) Data Aggregation. Upon request by Customer in order to fulfill Business Associate's duties to Customer under its Business Agreement with Customer ("Services"), Business Associate may conduct Data Aggregation services to the extent permitted by the HIPAA Rules and not otherwise prohibited by this Agreement.

(c) Disclosure to Subcontractors and Agents. Business Associate may Disclose Private Information to its agents and subcontractors to perform Services on its behalf pursuant to the Business Agreement to the extent permitted under this Agreement. Prior to such Disclosure, Business Associate will comply with Section B.3 of this Agreement.

3. **Prohibition on Unauthorized Use or Disclosure of Consumer Lists.** Business Associate will not develop any list, description or other grouping of individuals using, or use or disclose any such list derived from, Nonpublic Personal Financial Information received from, or created or received on behalf of, Customer, except as expressly permitted by this Agreement or in writing by Customer.

B. Compliance with the HIPAA Rules and Customer's Privacy and Security Policies and Procedures.

1. Business Associate will Use, Disclose and request Private Information only:

(a) consistent with the manner in which Customer is permitted by the HIPAA Rules (as amended from time to time) to Use, Disclose and request same;

(b) consistent with the manner in which Customer is permitted by applicable state law not preempted pursuant to 45 CFR Part 160, Subpart B of the HIPAA Rules to Use, Disclose and request same; and

(c) consistent with Customer's information privacy and security policies and procedures, as provided to Business Associate by Customer. Business Associate is not responsible for complying with a Customer policy or procedure or, as applicable, a change to same unless and until Customer gives notice and a copy of such policy, procedure or change; unless such policy, procedure or change reflects a requirement of state and/or federal laws and/or regulations and then only to the extent separately applicable to Business Associate or otherwise agreed to by Business Associate in accordance with Section F.3 hereof.

2. **Information Safeguards.** Business Associate will develop, implement, maintain and use appropriate administrative, technical and physical safeguards, in compliance with Social Security Act § 1173(d) (42 U.S.C. § 1320d-2(d)), 45 CFR § 164.530(c), any other implementing regulations issued in support of the HIPAA Rules and, as well, the GLBA Rules, to preserve the security, integrity and privacy of and to prevent non-permitted or violating Use, Disclosure or request of Private Information. Business Associate will document and keep these safeguards current.

Such safeguards shall include, by the later of the Effective Date or compliance date of the regulations set forth at 45 C.F.R. §§ 164.302 to 164.318 (the "Security Rules"), administrative, technical and physical safeguards appropriately protecting the confidentiality, integrity, and availability of Private Information in the manner set forth in the Security Rules (or in any amendment thereof), including but not limited to the documentation of such safeguards, to the extent that such Private Information is considered electronic PHI under those Rules.

Business Associate shall report to Customer as soon as practicable but in all events within 30 calendar days all Security Incidents known to Business Associate that occur within the control of Business Associate or its agents or subcontractors.

3. **Subcontractors and Agents.** Business Associate will require, in writing, each of its subcontractors and agents to which Business Associate is permitted by this Agreement to Disclose Private Information to provide reasonable assurance that said subcontractor or agent will comply with the same restrictions and conditions, including any privacy and security obligations, to which Business Associate is subject with respect to such Private Information.

C. Private Information Access, Amendment, Disclosure Accounting and Other Rights.

1. **Access.** In the event that Business Associate directly receives a request for access to Private Information from an Individual or an Individual's personal representative, Business Associate will notify Customer promptly—at which time Customer will, in its sole discretion, itself satisfy any such Individual request directly. Business Associate will submit to Customer, within 10 business days (or such shorter time frame as described below) of Customer's notice, all Private Information in its custody and control such that Customer may directly meet its access obligation under the Privacy Rules, at 45 CFR § 164.524 and the New Jersey Information Practices Act, if applicable. If a Customer customer requires Customer to respond more quickly than required by the HIPAA Rules, Customer will notify Business Associate of the shorter time frame for response; and Business Associate will use its reasonable best efforts

to respond to Customer in the time designated by Customer such that Customer can meet its customer's requirements.

In the event that Customer receives a request for access to Private Information from an Individual or an Individual's personal representative, Customer will, in its sole discretion, satisfy any such Individual request directly. Business Associate will submit to Customer, within 10 business days (or such shorter time frame as described below) of Customer's notice of its receipt of request, all Private Information in its custody and control such that Customer may directly meet its access obligation under the Privacy Rules, at 45 CFR § 164.524 and the New Jersey Information Practices Act, if applicable. If a Customer customer requires Customer to respond more quickly than required by the HIPAA Rules, Customer will notify Business Associate of the shorter time frame for response; and Business Associate will use its reasonable best efforts to respond to Customer in the time designated by Customer such that Customer can meet its customer's requirements.

2. **Amendment.** In the event that Business Associate directly receives a request for amendment from an Individual or an Individual's personal representative, Business Associate will notify Customer promptly—at which time Customer will, in its sole discretion, itself make a determination on any such request directly. Business Associate will amend, upon Customer's direction, within 3 business days (or such shorter time frame as described below) all Private Information in its custody and control which is related to the subject of the request, in order that Customer may directly meet its amendment obligation under the Privacy Rules, at 45 CFR § 164.526 and the New Jersey Information Practices Act, if applicable. Business Associate will assist Customer in meeting its amendment obligation, as needed and throughout any administrative hearings that may arise from any such request at Customer's expense. If a Customer customer requires Customer to respond more quickly than required by the HIPAA Rules, Customer will notify Business Associate of the shorter time frame for response and Business Associate will use its reasonable best efforts to respond to Customer in the time designated by Customer such that Customer can meet its customer's requirements.

In the event that Customer receives a request for amendment from an Individual or an Individual's personal representative, Customer will, in its sole discretion, make a determination on the Individual's request. Business Associate will amend, within 3 business days (or such shorter time frame as described below) all Private Information in its custody and control which is related to the subject of the request, in order that Customer may directly meet its amendment obligation under the Privacy Rules, at 45 CFR § 164.526 and the New Jersey Information Practices Act, if applicable. Business Associate will assist Customer in meeting its amendment obligation, as needed and throughout any administrative hearings that may arise from any such request, at Customer's expense. If a Customer customer requires Customer to respond more quickly than required by the HIPAA Rules, Customer will notify Business Associate of the shorter time frame for response and Business Associate will use its reasonable best efforts to respond to Customer in the time designated by Customer such that Customer can meet its customer's requirements.

3. **Disclosure Accounting.** In the event that Business Associate directly receives a request for an accounting of Disclosures from an Individual or an Individual's personal representative, Business Associate will notify Customer promptly—at which time Customer will, its sole discretion, itself make a determination on any such Individual request directly. Business Associate will submit to Customer, within 5 business days (or such shorter time frame as described below) of Customer's notice to Business Associate, an accounting of all such Disclosures, in order that Customer may meet its Disclosure accounting obligations under the Privacy Rules, at 45 CFR § 164.528. If a Customer customer requires Customer to respond more quickly than required by the HIPAA Rules, Customer will notify Business Associate of the shorter time frame for response; and Business Associate will use its reasonable best efforts respond to Customer in the time designated by Customer such that Customer can meet its customer's requirements.

In the event that Customer receives a request for an accounting of Disclosures from an Individual or an Individual's personal representative, Customer will, in its sole discretion, respond to the Individual's request directly. Business Associate will submit to Customer, within 5 business days (or such shorter time frame as described below) an accounting of all such Disclosures, in order that Customer may meet its Disclosure accounting obligations under the Privacy Rules, at 45 CFR § 164.528. If a Customer customer requires Customer to respond more quickly than required by the HIPAA Rules, Customer will notify Business Associate of the shorter time frame for response; and Business Associate will use its reasonable best efforts to respond to Customer in the time designated by Customer such that Customer can meet its customer's requirements.

In all events, Business Associate will document, and will require its agents and subcontractors to document, each Disclosure for which an accounting is required in accordance with the Privacy Rules, 45 CFR § 164.528, and Customer's privacy policies and procedures that is made by it or them of Private Information; and will notify Customer promptly of any such Disclosure.

4. **Prohibition on Unauthorized Use or Disclosure.** Business Associate will not Use, Disclose, or make requests for Private Information received from another business associate of Customer, except as permitted or required by this Agreement, as Required by Law, or as otherwise permitted in writing by Customer.

5. **Personal Representatives.** In the event Business Associate receives a request from an Individual to treat another person as the Individual's personal representative, Business Associate promptly will notify Customer of such request promptly—at which time Customer will, in its sole discretion, itself make a determination on the request. Business Associate will treat as a personal representative any person so designated by the member and accepted by Customer.

In the event Customer receives a request from an Individual to treat another person as the Individual's personal representative, Customer will, in its sole discretion, make a determination on the request directly. Business Associate will treat as a personal representative any person so designated by the member and accepted by Customer.

6. **Confidential Communication.** In the event Business Associate receives a request from an Individual or an Individual's personal representative for communications by alternative means or at alternative locations, due to the Individual's assertion that he/she will be endangered if communications occur through the normal means or to the normal location ("confidential communications" under the Privacy Rules), Business Associate promptly will notify Customer of such request – at which time Customer will, in its sole discretion, itself make a determination on the request. Business Associate will communicate with the Individual in the alternative means or location, as agreed to by Customer, at Customer's expense, if any.

In the event Customer receives a request from an Individual or an Individual's personal representative for confidential communications under the HIPAA Rules, Customer will, in its sole discretion, make a determination on the request directly. Business Associate will communicate with the Individual in the alternative means or location, as agreed to by Customer, at Customer's expense, if any.

7. **Restrictions of Use and Disclosure of Private Information.** In the event Business Associate receives a request from an Individual or an Individual's personal representative for restrictions on the Use and Disclosure of Private Information for Treatment, Payment and Health Care Operations purposes as permitted by the Privacy Rules, Business Associate promptly will notify Customer of such request – at which time Customer will, in its sole discretion, itself make a determination on the request. Business Associate will follow the restrictions on Use and Disclosure of Private Information, as agreed to by Customer, at Customer's expense, if any.

In the event Customer receives a request from an Individual or an Individual's personal representative for restrictions on the Use and Disclosure of Private Information for Treatment, Payment and Health Care Operations purposes as permitted by the Privacy Rules, Customer will, in its sole discretion, make a determination on the request. Business Associate will follow the restrictions on Use and Disclosure of Private Information, as agreed to by Customer, at Customer's expense, if any.

8. **Audit and Inspection of Books and Records.** Upon no less than 5 business days' notice, Business Associate will make its internal practices, books, records, and other documents, including proof of the performance of any of its obligations under this Agreement relating to its Use, Disclosure and request, as well as its safeguarding, of Private Information, available to Customer for audit and compliance purposes during regular business hours at its place of business; and to the U.S. Department of Health and Human Services to determine compliance with the HIPAA Rules, 45 CFR Parts 160, 162 and 164 of this Agreement, subject to Business Associate's reasonable confidentiality and security requirements.

D. Notification to Customer by Business Associate Relative to Privacy and Security.

Unless otherwise provided for herein or directed otherwise, Business Associate will provide Customer's Privacy Official with oral notice of all of the following, if and as any should occur:

(a) Complaints received about Customer's or Business Associate's privacy or security policies or practices, including those of its agents and subcontractors;
(b) Requests by Individuals for access and/or amendment to Private Information, as described above;
(c) Requests by Individuals for accountings of Disclosures as described above, as well as Disclosures of Private Information made by Business Associate or its subcontractors and agents that are considered subject to the need for accounting in accordance with 45 CFR § 164.512 of the Privacy Rules and Customer's privacy policies and procedures;
(d) Inquiries regarding Customer's or Business Associate's privacy or security policies or practices, including inquiries about and requests for Customer's Notice of Information Privacy Practices;
(e) Need for an authorization and requests for designation of personal representatives;
(f) Requests for confidential communications, as described above;
(g) Requests for other restrictions on Use or Disclosure of Private Information, as described above;
(h) Any request that exercises a member's rights relative to his or her Private Information;
(i) The occurrence of any Security Incidents, whether or not any such attempts are successful, with respect to Private Information;
(j) Business Associate becomes aware of any criminal action; and
(k) An external investigation or inquiry is made, including a compliance investigation or audit contemplated by paragraph D.8 of this Agreement or otherwise.

E. Breach of Privacy or Security Obligations.

1. **Reporting.** Business Associate will provide written notice to Customer of any Use or Disclosure of, or request for, Private Information not permitted either by this Agreement or otherwise in writing by Customer, or which is otherwise in violation of the HIPAA Rules, the New Jersey Information Practices Act, if applicable, or GLBA and the GLBA Rules; as well as of any Security Incidents as defined in the Security Rules. Business Associate shall provide such notification without regard for whether the violation arose from the conduct of the Business Associate, one of its employees, agents or subcontractors. Business Associate will notify Customer's Legal Department and its Privacy Official not more than 2 business days after Business Associate learns of such non-permitted or violating Use, Disclosure or request; or of any Security Incident. Business Associate's notice will at least, based on knowledge known at that time:

(a) identify the nature of the non-permitted or violating Use, Disclosure or request, or Security Incident;

(b) identify the Private Information Used, Disclosed or requested, or involved in the Security Incident;

(c) identify who made the non-permitted or violating Use, request, or Disclosure, or was responsible for the Security Incident, and who received the Private Information as a result of the non-permitted or violating Disclosure or Security Incident, if known;

(d) identify what corrective action Business Associate took or will take to prevent further non-permitted or violating Use, Disclosure or request, or reoccurrence of the Security Incident;

(e) identify what Business Associate did or will do to mitigate any deleterious effect of the non-permitted or violating Use or Disclosure, or Security Incident; and

(f) provide such other information, including a written report, as Customer may reasonably request.

2. **Termination of Agreement.**

(a) Right to Terminate for Breach. If Customer determines that Business Associate has breached any material provision of this Agreement Customer may notify Business Associate of such breach. If Customer notifies Business Associate of the breach, Business Associate shall cure the breach or end the violation as soon as possible, but in no event later than 30 days after receiving notice of such breach. If Business Associate fails to take reasonable steps to affect such a cure within such time period, Customer may report the problem to the Secretary of Health and Human Services or, if feasible, terminate this Agreement with Business Associate.

Customer may, following any cure period, exercise the right to terminate this Agreement by providing Business Associate written notice of termination, stating the breach that provides the basis for the termination. Any such termination will be effective immediately upon receipt by Business Associate or at such other date specified in Customer's notice of termination.

(b) Immediate Termination Relating to Judicial or Administrative Proceedings. Notwithstanding clause (a) above, Customer may terminate this Agreement, effective immediately, if: (i) Business Associate is named as a defendant in a criminal proceeding for a violation of the HIPAA Rules or other privacy or security laws; or (ii) a finding or stipulation that Business Associate has violated any standard or requirement of the HIPAA Rules or other privacy or security laws is made or entered in any administrative or civil proceeding in which Business Associate has been joined.

(c) Obligations upon Termination.

(i) Return or Destruction. Upon termination, cancellation, expiration or other conclusion of this Agreement or the business relationship between Business Associate and Customer, Business Associate will, in Customer's sole discretion, return to Customer or destroy all Private Information in whatever form or medium (including in any electronic medium under Business Associate's custody or control), including all copies of and any data or compilations derived from and allowing identification of any Individual who is a subject of the Private Information. Business Associate will complete such return or destruction as promptly as possible, but in no event later than 30 days after the effective date of the termination, cancellation, expiration or other conclusion of this Agreement or the business relationship. Business Associate will identify any Private Information that cannot feasibly be returned to Customer or destroyed, and will extend all the protections afforded Private Information under this Agreement to any such information, as well as limit its further Use or Disclosure of that Private Information to those purposes that made return or destruction of that Private Information infeasible.

Within such 30 days, Business Associate will certify in writing to Customer that such return or destruction has been completed; and will deliver to Customer the identification of any Private Information for which return or destruction is infeasible and, for that Private Information, will certify that it will only Use or Disclose such Private Information for those purposes that make return or destruction infeasible.

(ii) Continuing Privacy and Security Obligations. Business Associate's obligation to protect the privacy and security of Private Information not returned or destroyed will be continuous and survive termination, cancellation, expiration or other conclusion of this Agreement or its Services for Customer.

3. **Indemnification.**

(a) Indemnification by Business Associate. Business Associate will indemnify and hold harmless Customer and any Customer affiliate, officer, director, employee or agent from and against any third party claim, cause of action, liability, damage, cost or expense, including attorneys' fees and court or proceeding costs, arising out of or in connection with any non-permitted or violating Use or Disclosure of Private Information or other breach of this Agreement by Business Associate or any subcontractor, agent, person or entity under Business Associate's control.

(b) Right to Undertake Defense. If Customer is named a party in any judicial, administrative or other proceeding arising out of or in connection with any non-permitted or violating Use or Disclosure of Private Information or other breach of this Agreement by Business Associate or any subcontractor, agent, person or entity under Business Associate's control, Customer will tender its defense to Business Associate, in which case Business Associate will provide qualified attorneys to represent Customer's interests at Business Associate's expense, subject to Customer's right to reasonably approve of any final settlement, compromise or other resolution proposed by Business Associate in the context of any such proceeding, and to participate in its own defense with counsel of its own choosing at its own expense.

(c) Injunctive Relief. Business Associate expressly agrees that a breach or threatened breach of any provision of this Agreement by Business Associate, any agent of Business Associate or employee of Business Associate may cause irreparable harm to Customer and that Customer shall be entitled to seek temporary, preliminary and/or permanent injunctive relief to protect its interests and the interests of affected individuals; provided, however, that no specification of a particular legal or equitable remedy is to be construed as a waiver, prohibition, or limitation of any legal or equitable remedies in the event of a breach hereof.

F. General Provisions.

1. **Definitions.** Capitalized terms not defined in this Agreement shall have the meaning set forth in the HIPAA Rules or the GLBA Rules, as applicable.

2. **Data Ownership.** Business Associate acknowledges and agrees that, during the term of this Agreement and after the termination thereof, it has no ownership rights whatsoever with respect to the Private Information; and that all such Private Information is owned by Customer.

3. **Amendment to Agreement.** Upon the effective date of any final regulation or amendment to final regulations promulgated by the U.S. Department of Health and Human Services with respect to the privacy and security of Private Information or Standard Transactions, or by the Insurance Commissioners of the states in which Customer is licensed to conduct business with respect to Nonpublic Personal Financial and Health Information or Personal or Privileged Information, as applicable, Customer shall timely propose an amendment to this Agreement such that the obligations they impose on Business Associate remain in compliance with these laws and regulations. Pending discussion and final approval of the amendment (including, any attendant changes needed under the Business Agreement to reflect any change in cost structures imposed on Business Associate as a result of such amendment), Business Associate will use its reasonable best efforts to act in a manner consistent with such changes in law.

4. **Conflicts.** The terms and conditions of this Agreement will override and control any conflicting term or condition of the Business Agreement between Customer and Business Associate. All nonconflicting terms and conditions of this Agreement remain in full force and effect.

5. **No Third-Party Beneficiaries.** No third-party beneficiaries are intended to benefit from this Agreement and no third-party beneficiary rights will be implied from anything contained in this Agreement.

6. **Interpretation.** Any ambiguity in this Agreement will be resolved in favor of a meaning that permits the applicable Covered Entity to comply with the HIPAA Rules.

7. **Survival.** Sections F.1. and F.3. (Breach of Privacy or Security Obligations Reporting and Indemnification), and G.2. (Data Ownership) of this Agreement shall survive the expiration or any termination of this Agreement. Otherwise, the provisions of this Agreement shall survive the expiration or any termination of this Agreement to the extent that the Business Associate continues to maintain Private Information.

8. **Governing Law.** All disputes arising under this Agreement shall by governed by ________________ law unless otherwise provided in the underlying Services agreement.

9. **Notices.** Unless otherwise provided herein, notices will be deemed given when properly addressed to Customer's Privacy Official of record, for Customer, and to the Business Associate contact person of record, for Business Associate, upon the date of receipt if hand-delivered, or 4 business days after deposit in the U.S. mail if mailed by registered or certified mail, postage prepaid, or 1 business day after deposit with a national overnight courier for next business day delivery, or upon the date of electronic confirmation of receipt of a facsimile transmission.

IN WITNESS WHEREOF, Customer and Business Associate execute this Agreement in multiple originals to be effective on the earlier of the date on which Business Associate began providing Services to Customer or the last date written below.

BUSINESS ASSOCIATE	CUSTOMER or its affiliate(s)
By: ____________________ Name	By: ____________________ Name
Title: ____________________	Title: ____________________
Date: ____________________	Date: ____________________

Third Party Access Agreement

This **THIRD PARTY ACCESS AGREEMENT** ("TPAA") is entered into this ____ day of ____________, 20___, by between and among ____________, a ________________ corporation ("Licensor") and ____________________ ("Company") and is related to the Master Agreement dated ____________, 20___ (the "Licensor-Customer Agreement") between Licensor and ____________________________, a ______________ nonprofit corporation ("Customer"). Licensor or Company may be referred to herein as a "Party", and collectively as the "Parties". For purposes of this TPAA, Licensor, Company and Customer include any parent, subsidiary, affiliate of, or entity that is wholly owned or controlled by any entity constituting Licensor, Company or Customer.

RECITALS

WHEREAS, pursuant to the Licensor-Customer Agreement, Licensor has licensed to Customer certain software (the "Licensor Software"), and

WHEREAS, Company has been selected by Customer as an Authorized Contractor under the Licensor-Customer Agreement to perform services ("Services") on behalf of Customer involving access to, and use of, Customer's authorized licensed copies of the Licensor Software pursuant to the Licensor-Customer Agreement, and subject to the limitations therein, as well as documentation and other Licensor Confidential Information (as defined below) (the "Purpose"), and

WHEREAS, the Licensor-Customer Agreement requires that, prior to Customer providing Access (as hereinafter defined) to the Licensor Software and Licensor Confidential Information to Company, that Company and Licensor enter into a "Third Party Access Agreement", and

WHEREAS, Licensor and Customer intend that this TPAA shall satisfy such TPAA requirement.

NOW, THEREFORE, for and in consideration of the mutual obligations contained herein, and other good and valuable consideration, the receipt and adequacy of which is hereby acknowledged, the Parties hereto agree as follows:

1. **Access to Licensor Software and Confidential Information.** Licensor hereby acknowledges that pursuant to a written agreement between them, Customer has named Company an Authorized Contractor under the Licensor-Customer Agreement, and that as a result, Company has been granted by Customer the right to have its employees Access the Licensor Software and Licensor Confidential Information solely to permit Authorized Employees (as defined below) of Company to provide Services to Customer, subject to execution of this TPAA by Company and compli-

ance by Company with its terms. For purposes of this TPAA, "Access" shall mean the right to access, use, display, load, utilize, view, store, display, and configure the Licensor Software and make works that interoperate with the Licensor Software, and access Licensor Confidential Information, limited solely to the Purpose. Company agrees that it has no right to Access the source code for any Licensor Software, and it shall not permit any of its personnel to have such Access.

2. **Confidential Information.** "Confidential Information" means a Party's non-public, proprietary information relating to the Party's products and business operations, whether oral or written, furnished by Licensor, the Company or Customer or their respective directors, officers, or employees, to the other party or parties, including:

(a) unpublished patent applications,
(b) trade secrets,
(c) ideas, concepts, samples, techniques, sketches, drawings, works of authorship, data models, inventions, know-how, finances, facilities, development plans, processes, apparatuses, equipment, algorithms, software programs (including Licensor Software), software source documents, schema, documentation, meta data, data relating to performance, scalability, functionality and capabilities related to the current, future, and proposed products and services of each of the Parties, and their respective information concerning research, experimental work, development, design details and specifications, engineering, financial information, pricing, costs, purchasing, manufacturing, customer lists, investors, employees, business and contractual relationships, business forecasts,
(d) sales and merchandising, marketing plans and information the disclosing Party provides regarding third parties, (including each Party's customers, partners and vendors, and individuals using the services or any of those parties or information maintained by Licensor or Company on behalf of a third party),
(e) and Protected Health Information ("PHI") as defined under the Health Insurance Portability and Accountability Act of 1996, Public Law 104-191 and regulations promulgated thereunder by the U.S. Department of Health and Human Services ("HIPAA").

The term Confidential Information will not, however, include information (except PHI) which (i) is or becomes generally publicly available other than as a result of a disclosure by the receiving Party, (ii) is or becomes available to the receiving Party on a non-confidential basis from a source (other than the disclosing Party) rightfully in possession of such information and that is not prohibited from disclosing such information to the receiving Party by a legal, contractual, fiduciary or other obligation, (iii) is independently developed by the receiving Party; or (iv) was rightfully known by the receiving Party prior to disclosure to the receiving Party by the disclosing Party and such receiving Party is not prohibited from disclosing such information by a legal, contractual, fiduciary or other obligation, any and all of the above exceptions as demonstrated by written or documented evidence. Any combination of Confidential Information with information that is not deemed Confidential Information pursuant to the preceding sentence shall be deemed to be Confidential Information to the extent of the Confidential Information contained in such combination.

3. **Obligations of the Parties.** Each of Licensor and the Company: (i) will keep the Confidential Information of the other Party confidential and will not (except as required by applicable law, regulation or legal process, and only after compliance with the provisions below), without the prior written consent of the disclosing Party, disclose any such Confidential Information in any manner whatsoever, and (ii) will not use any Confidential Information for any purpose other than the Purpose and subject at all times to paragraph 7, "Access and Use Restrictions" and to Exhibit A; provided, however, that each Party may reveal the Confidential Information to its employees: (a) who need to know the Confidential Information for the purpose of performing Services within the Purpose, and (b) who are informed of the confidential nature of the Confidential Information, and (c) who have agreed in writing with Company to protect the confidentiality of information, such as the Confidential Information (each an "Authorized Employee"). Each Party will use commercially reasonable efforts to cause the Authorized Employees to observe the terms of this TPAA, but in any event efforts no less than it would use to protect its own Confidential Information, and each Party will be responsible for any breach of this TPAA by any of its employees. If the receiving Party believes that the disclosing Party's Confidential Information has been used, disseminated or published in violation of this TPAA, it will promptly (a) notify the disclosing Party, (b) take all reasonable action to minimize the impact of such use, dissemination or publication, and (c) use commercially reasonable efforts to address the source of the breach in order to prevent a further breach of this TPAA. Each Party will not (except as permitted under this TPAA and except as required by applicable law, regulation or legal process, and only after compliance with paragraph 5 below), without the prior written consent of the disclosing Party, disclose to any person or entity the fact that the Confidential Information exists or has been made available to the other Party.

4. **Required Disclosure.** If a Party is requested pursuant to, or required by, applicable law, regulation or legal process to disclose any of the Confidential Information, such Party will notify the disclosing Party promptly in writing of such request or requirement and the documents or Confidential Information requested, so that the other Party may seek a protective order or other appropriate remedy or, in its or their sole discretion, waive compliance with the terms of this TPAA. If no such protective order or other remedy is obtained, or the other Party does not waive compliance with the terms of this TPAA, such Party will furnish only that portion of the Confidential Information which it is advised by its counsel is legally required. In any event, each Party agrees that it will not oppose an action by the other Party to obtain a protective order, other remedy or reliable assurance that confidential treatment will be accorded the Confidential Information.

5. **Return of Confidential Information.** Upon termination of access rights under this TPAA under Section 16, the receiving Party will either (i) promptly destroy all copies of the written Confidential Information of the disclosing Party in its posses-

sion and confirm such destruction to the disclosing Party in writing, or (ii) promptly deliver to the disclosing Party all copies of the written Confidential Information of the disclosing Party in its possession. The receiving Party will not retain any copies, exhibits, notes, memoranda or other writings containing or based on the Confidential Information of the disclosing Party; provided, however, that the receiving Party may retain one copy of such Confidential Information for archival and associated purposes only, which copy will remain subject to the terms of this TPAA.

6. **No Other Liability.** Except as expressly set forth herein, the Company and Licensor will have no liability to each other with respect to any Services performed by Company for Customer related to the Purpose (other than liability for breach of this TPAA).

7. **Remedies, Injunction.** Each Party acknowledges that remedies at law may be inadequate to protect the other Party against any actual or threatened breach of this TPAA by such Party, and, without prejudice to any other rights and remedies otherwise available to the other Party, each Party will be entitled to seek temporary, preliminary and permanent injunctive relief and specific performance without the posting of any bond or other security, or if required, then the minimum bond or security required.

8. **Waiver.** Failure or delay by a Party in exercising any right, power or privilege hereunder will not operate as a waiver thereof, nor will any single or partial exercise thereof preclude any other or further exercise thereof or the exercise of any right, power or privilege hereunder.

9. **Governing Law.** This TPAA will be governed by and construed in accordance with the laws of the State of _______________ applicable to contracts between residents of that State and executed in and to be performed in that State. The receiving Party will comply with all applicable laws, rules and regulations relating to the export or re-export of the disclosing Party's Confidential Information, and will not export or re-export such Confidential Information, or the product thereof, in violation of applicable laws, rules or regulations.

10. **Entire Agreement.** As between Licensor and the Company, this TPAA supersedes and cancels all prior communications, understandings and agreements and contains the entire agreement between Licensor and the Company concerning the use and confidentiality of the Confidential Information on behalf of Customer, and no modifications of this TPAA or waiver of the terms and conditions hereof will be binding upon Licensor or the Company, unless approved in writing by each of Licensor and the Company. The term "including" means by way of example and not limitation. Nothing herein shall relieve Licensor and the Customer from their respective obligations as set forth in agreements previously entered into between them.

11. **No Creation of Ownership Interests.** Except as expressly stated herein, nothing in this TPAA will be construed to convey to either Party any right, title, license or other interest in the Confidential Information of the other Party, or to Company,

in the Licensor Software. No license is hereby granted or implied under any patent, copyright or trademark, any application for any of the foregoing, or any trade name, trade secret or other proprietary information, in which the disclosing Party has any right, title or interest, except as expressly granted herein for the limited use of Confidential Information.

12. **Successors and Assigns.** This TPAA will inure to the benefit of and be binding on the Parties hereto and their respective successors and assigns.

13. **Warranty Exclusion.** Each Party agrees that it has the right to make the disclosure of the Confidential Information contemplated by this TPAA. Except as set forth in the preceding sentence, the Confidential Information is provided **"AS IS," without any warranty of any nature, express or implied**.

14. **Term of Agreement.** The obligations of this TPAA will continue to apply to all trade secrets disclosed hereunder for so long as they remain trade secrets or are otherwise protected by applicable law, regulation or legal process, and to all other Confidential Information for five years after the date of the last disclosure of Confidential Information hereunder, at which time this TPAA will terminate. The Access rights granted to Company under this Agreement shall terminate on the earliest of termination of the agreement pertaining to the Purpose executed between Customer and the Company, termination of the Licensor-Customer Agreement, and termination of this TPAA due to material breach of this TPAA by Company.

15. **Counterparts.** This TPAA may be executed in one or more counterparts, each of which when executed will be deemed to be an original but all of which taken together will constitute one and the same agreement. This TPAA will become effective when counterparts have been signed by each of the Parties and delivered by facsimile or other means to the other Party.

16. **Severability.** If any provision or portion of this TPAA is held invalid, illegal, void or unenforceable by reason of any rule of law, administrative or judicial provision or public policy, it will be deemed to be modified to the minimum extent necessary to be valid, legal and enforceable, or if it cannot so modified, then it will be deleted,

and in either case, all other provisions of this TPAA will nevertheless be construed so as to remain in full force and effect.

IN WITNESS WHEREOF, the Parties hereto have executed this TPAA by their duly authorized officers or representatives as of the date first above written.

ATTEST:	**COMPANY**
______________________________	**By:** ________________________ **(SEAL)**
ATTEST:	**CUSTOMER**
______________________________	**By:** ________________________ **(SEAL)**
ATTEST:	**LICENSOR**
______________________________	**By:** ________________________ **(SEAL)**

EXHIBIT A

Access and Use Restrictions

Company shall not make any copies of Licensor Software without the prior written consent of Licensor or otherwise attempt to extract operational or performance information about Licensor Software that is not specifically performed as part of the Services.

EXHIBIT B

Services

1. **Access.** Company may access Licensor Confidential Information as permitted in this TPAA to the extent necessary to enable Company to provide the following Services:

[Insert description of Services to be provided by Company to Licensor]

Settlement Agreement and Mutual Release

THIS SETTLEMENT AGREEMENT AND MUTUAL RELEASE is dated as of ________, 20___, by and between ____________________ a ___________________ corporation with its principal offices at ______________________________________ ("Customer"), and ___________________________, a __________ corporation with its principal offices at ____________________________________ ("Licensor").

WITNESSETH:

WHEREAS, Customer and Licensor entered into that certain ______________________ agreement (the "Agreement") pursuant to which Licensor agreed to [license, develop and install for Customer Licensor's proprietary ________________________® Version __________________ software]; and

WHEREAS, certain disputes have arisen between Customer and Licensor relating to Licensor's performance under the Agreement and subsequent understandings between Customer and Licensor; and

WHEREAS, Customer and Licensor wish to compromise and resolve the outstanding disputes relating to the Agreement and terminate the Agreement.

NOW, THEREFORE, in consideration of the premises and the mutual covenants, conditions, representations and agreements contained herein, the parties hereto hereby agree as follows:

1. **Termination of Agreement.** Subject to the terms and conditions of this Settlement Agreement and Mutual Release, the parties hereto hereby agree that the Agreement is hereby terminated and shall have no further force and effect, [provided, however, that the terms of Section ______ relating to the grant of the license to use the Software shall survive such termination.] **[IS THERE ANY OTHER SECTION SUCH AS PAYMENTS, AUDIT RIGHTS THAT NEEDS TO SURVIVE?]**

2. **Licensor Payment to Customer.** Licensor hereby agrees to pay Customer U.S. $ __________________ by [DATE].

3. **Return of Licensor Equipment.** Customer hereby agrees that, within ____ days of the execution of this Settlement Agreement, it shall return and deliver to Licensor's _____________________ office, at its sole cost and expense, the following Licensor equipment, hardware and software consigned by Licensor to Customer:

[LIST EQUIPMENT AND SOFTWARE]

4. **Mutual Releases.**

(a) Customer for itself, and its affiliates, predecessors, successors, assigns, trustees, officers, directors, partners, employees, representatives and agents, and their heirs, executors and administrators, does hereby remise, release and forever discharge Licensor, its predecessors, successors, assigns, trustees, officers, directors, shareholders, affiliates, parent, partners, employees, representatives and agents, and its heirs, executors and administrators both individually and in their representative corporate capacity, from all claims, demands, actions, damages, costs, expenses, dividends, covenants, contracts, agreements, and compensation whatsoever, whether now known or unknown, foreseen or unforeseen, patent or latent, which it can claim or assert against Licensor, or its predecessors, successors, assigns, trustees, officers, directors, shareholders, affiliates, parent, partners, employees, representatives or agents that may be made in or in connection with the Agreement from the beginning of the world to date of this Release and for all time thereafter.

(b) Licensor for itself, and its predecessors, successors, assigns, trustees, partners, employees, representatives and agents, and their heirs, executors and administrators, does hereby remise, release and forever discharge Customer, its predecessors, successors, assigns, trustees, officers, directors, shareholders, affiliates, parent, partners, employees, representatives and agents, and its heirs, executors and administrators both individually and in their representative corporate capacity, from all claims, demands, actions, damages, costs, expenses, dividends, covenants, contracts, agreements, and compensation whatsoever [**BUT EXCLUDING INVOICES** __________], whether now known or unknown, foreseen or unforeseen, patent or latent, which it can claim or assert against Customer, or its predecessors, successors, assigns, trustees, officers, directors, shareholders, affiliates, parent, partners, employees, representatives or agents that may be made in or in connection with the Agreement from the beginning of the world to date of this Release and for all time thereafter. [**ARE THERE OTHER AGREEMENTS THAT NEED TO BE EXCLUDED?**]

5. **Representations and Warranties; Further Assurances; Confidentiality; Certain Covenants.**

(a) Each of Customer and Licensor hereby represents and warrants that the execution, delivery and performance of this Settlement Agreement and Mutual Release has been duly authorized and approved by all necessary action on its part. Each of the parties hereto hereby represents and warrants that, upon its execution and delivery of this Settlement Agreement and Mutual Release (assuming the execution and delivery of this Settlement Agreement and Mutual Release by the other party hereto), this Settlement Agreement and Mutual Release will constitute the valid and binding obligation of such party, enforceable against it in accordance with its terms. Each of Customer and Licensor hereby further represents and warrants that it has not assigned or transferred, in whole or in part any claim such party now has or may have against the other, or any portion thereof or interest therein to any person or entity and that all right, title and interest to such claims is held by the releasing party.

(b) Each of the parties hereto agrees to take any and all further actions necessary on its part to carry out the terms of this Settlement Agreement and Mutual Release.

(c) Each of the parties hereto agrees to treat the terms of this Settlement Agreement and Mutual Release, and agrees to cause its directors, officers, employees, representatives and agents to treat the terms of this Settlement Agreement and Mutual Release, as non-public, sensitive and confidential information.

(d) Notwithstanding anything to the contrary contained in this agreement, each of the parties hereto hereby agrees that any confidentiality and non-disclosure covenants set forth in any agreement entered into between the parties, including without limitation that certain Proprietary Information Agreement dated ______________________, shall remain in full force and effect in accordance with the terms thereof. In addition, each of the parties hereto hereby agrees to return promptly to the other party any proprietary or confidential information of such other party in its possession.

6. **Miscellaneous Provisions.**

(a) This Settlement Agreement and Mutual Release constitutes the entire and only agreement and understanding between Customer and Licensor with respect to the subject matter hereof and may not be altered, enlarged or abridged except by an agreement in writing executed by both of the parties hereto. **[ARE THERE ANY COLLATERAL AGREEMENTS THAT SHOULD BE INCLUDED OR EXCLUDED?]** No waiver of any one or several of the terms, conditions or obligations of this Settlement Agreement and Mutual Release, and no partial waiver thereof, shall be construed as a waiver of any of the other terms, conditions or obligations of this Settlement Agreement and Mutual Release. No failure or delay by any party at any time to enforce one or more of the terms, conditions or obligations of this Settlement Agreement and Mutual Release shall constitute a waiver of such terms, conditions or obligations or shall preclude such party from requiring performance by the other party at any time.

(b) All the provisions of this Settlement Agreement and Mutual Release shall be considered as separate terms and conditions. In the event any of the provisions hereof is determined to be invalid, prohibited or unenforceable by a court or other body of competent jurisdiction, this agreement shall be construed as if such invalid, prohibited or unenforceable provision has been more narrowly drawn so as not to be invalid, prohibited or unenforceable. Notwithstanding the foregoing two sentences, in the event that any of the provisions of this Settlement Agreement and Mutual Release should be determined to be invalid, prohibited or unenforceable, the validity, legality and enforceability of the remaining provisions contained in this Settlement Agreement and Mutual Release shall not in any way be affected or impaired thereby; provided, however, that in the event Section 4 of this Settlement Agreement and Mutual Release should be determined to be invalid, prohibited or unenforceable, this Settlement Agreement and Mutual Release shall be null and void.

(c) The provisions of this Settlement Agreement and Mutual Release shall inure to the benefit of, and be binding upon, the parties hereto and their respective successors and assigns.

(d) This Settlement Agreement and Mutual Release shall be governed by and construed in accordance with the laws of the [**Commonwealth/State**] of ___________ [**THE GOVERNING LAW SHOULD MIRROR THE GOVERNING LAW OF THE AGREEMENT AND NDA**] applicable to contracts executed and performed entirely therein.

(e) This Settlement Agreement and Mutual Release may be executed in more than one counterpart, each of which shall be deemed an original, but all of which together shall constitute one and the same instrument.

(f) Notwithstanding anything to the contrary, nothing in this Agreement is intended to or constitutes a waiver of any rights any party has under this Agreement, including, but not limited to, the parties' right to enforce the obligations set forth on Paragraphs 2, 3 and 5(a).

IN WITNESS WHEREOF, the parties hereto have signed this Agreement as of the date first above written.

ATTEST:	CUSTOMER
______________________________	By: ______________________________
	Name:
	Title:______________________________
ATTEST:	LICENSOR
______________________________	By: ______________________________
	Name:
	Title:______________________________

Settlement Agreement

(Releasing Party Contemplating Bankruptcy)

WHEREAS, _______________ ("Licensor") has filed a lawsuit against _______________ ("Customer") in the United States District Court for the District of _________________ captioned _________________________________ ("the Lawsuit");

WHEREAS, Licensor and Customer desire to resolve their differences;

NOW, THEREFORE, in consideration of the payments and promises contained herein, and other good and valuable consideration, the receipt and sufficiency of which is hereby acknowledged, the parties agree as follows:

1. Immediately upon execution of this Agreement, Customer will pay Licensor _____________________________DOLLARS ($_________________) via wire transfer to: ______________________________; ABA #________________; DDA #_____________.

2. Licensor shall file the stipulation of dismissal attached hereto as Exhibit A upon execution of the agreement and receipt of the amount set forth in paragraph one.

3. Customer hereby acknowledges that the total amount due to Licensor under the contract(s) is $_____________ plus interest and further acknowledges that the litigation would have resulted in a judgment against Customer in the amount of $_____________ plus interest on or about _________, 20__.

4. The Parties jointly acknowledge that Customer has ceased doing business and begun a consensual liquidation and distribution to its creditors. The Parties further acknowledge that the Settlement Payment is an amount less than the value of Licensor's pro-rata share of Customer's assets, that Customer has offered and Licensor has accepted the Settlement Payment in exchange for dismissing this litigation with prejudice because Customer has limited funds and pursuing the litigation to judgment is unlikely to benefit either party.

5. The Parties recognize that in the event the Settlement Payment is recovered in any subsequent proceeding including but not limited to proceedings under state insolvency law or the United States Bankruptcy Code that Licensor's liquidated claim against Customer will be $________________, plus pre-judgment interest through __________________, 20__ and post-judgment interest thereafter and that this settlement is void and any and all claims of Licensor against Customer will be reinstated.

6. Customer represents and warrants that it has no intention of filing for bankruptcy within the next 90 days and that it has no knowledge, information or

belief that any other entity intends to file an involuntary petition for bankruptcy of Customer.

7. Licensor knowingly and voluntarily releases, acquits and forever discharges Customer its officers, directors, employees, board members, affiliates, parents, subsidiaries, successors, and assigns (collectively referred to as "Customer Releasees") from any and all claims or causes of action which Licensor has or may have, known or unknown, legal or equitable, asserted or unasserted, against Customer Releasees from the beginning of time until the date of this agreement, including but not limited to, any and all claims asserted in the Lawsuit.

8. Customer knowingly and voluntarily releases, acquits and forever discharges Licensor, its officers, directors, employees, board members, affiliates, parents, subsidiaries, successors and assigns (collectively referred to as "Licensor Releasees") from any and all claims or causes of action which Customer has or may have, known or unknown, legal or equitable, asserted or unasserted, against Licensor Releasees from the beginning of time until the date of this agreement, including but not limited to, any and all claims asserted in the Lawsuit.

9. Licensor and Customer agree that neither they nor their attorneys nor their representatives shall reveal to the parties, any of the terms of this Agreement or any of the amounts, numbers or terms, conditions or substance of any sums payable hereunder. Nothing contained herein shall be construed to restrict or limit Licensor or Customer from: (i) responding to a request for information or documents in any legal proceeding; or (ii) responding to inquiries made pursuant to an order of a court of competent jurisdiction provided, however, that if Licensor or Customer receive any such oral or written request for information or documents regarding this Agreement, then such party shall promptly notify the other party (as provided below) and inform it regarding both the request and the documents or information provided (or being provided). Notice shall be made by contacting the other party's counsel at the telephone numbers and addresses set forth below:

Licensor Counsel Address *Customer Counsel Address*

Furthermore, this paragraph does not prohibit either party from disclosing necessary information to their respective tax advisors or accountants for tax and accounting purposes.

10. Licensor agrees not to oppose any motion to seal the Lawsuit which Customer may file.

11. This Agreement may be executed in any number of counterparts, each of which shall be deemed an original, but all of which together shall be deemed one and the same instrument.

12. This Settlement Agreement and attachments hereto constitute the entire agreement between the parties.

13. The parties hereby agree that they have not transferred or assigned any claims released in this agreement.

14. If any term, covenant, condition, or provision of this Agreement, or the application of them to any circumstances is, at any time or to any extent, determined by a court of competent jurisdiction to be invalid or unenforceable, the remainder of

this Agreement or its application to circumstances other than those to which it is held invalid or unenforceable shall not be affected, and each term, covenant, condition, and provision of this Agreement shall be valid and enforceable to the fullest extent permitted by law.

15. This Agreement shall be governed by and construed in accordance with the law of the State of ________________.

16. The signatories below each represent and warrant that they have the power and authority to sign for and bind the party for which they have signed this agreement.

CUSTOMER

Date: ________________________ ________________________________

Name:

Title:

LICENSOR

Date: ________________________ ________________________________

Name:

Title:

Definitions Library

7 x 24 x 365
Acceptance
Acceptance Criteria
Adaptation
Affiliate(s)
Agreement
Applications Software or **Applications**
Approve or **Approval**
Approved Subcontractors
Arising
Attorneys' Fees
Authorized User
Best Efforts
Best Practices
Business Day
Certification
Change of Control
Change of Control
Claims
Commercially Reasonable Efforts
Concurrent Devices/Concurrent Accesses
Confidential Information
Control
Coordinate
Corporate License
CPI
CPI Adjustment
CPU License
Critical Defect
Custom Programming
Custom Programming Materials
Customer Data
Data Center
Data Network
Data Security Breach
Defect
Defect Analysis
Derivative Work
Disabling Code

Documentation
ECI
Effective Date
Electronic Data Interchanges or EDI
Embedded Third Party Software
Enhancements
Fix
Fixed Price Basis
Final Resolution
Full-Time
GAAP
Go Live
Including
Indemnified Parties
Identified User
Information Technology Support and Maintenance Services
Intellectual Property Rights
Interface(s)
Interim Resolution
Internal Purposes
Interoperate or **Interoperability**
Know How
Knowledge
Law or Laws
Licensed
Losses
Low Defect
Maintenance or **Maintain**
Material Defect
Medium Defect
New Features
Non-Permissive Open Source Code
Non-production Use
Named User
Object Code
Out-of-Pocket Expenses
Performance Standards
Permissive Open Source Code
Permitted Auditors
Personal Data
Personal Information
Personally Identifiable Information
Previous Sequential Release
Privacy Laws
Privileged Information

Procedures Manual
Productive Use
Professional Named User
Programmer
Project Acceptance
Quality Assurance
Query User
Reasonable Efforts
Regulatory Requirements
Release
Required Consents
Residuals
Root Cause Analysis
Services
Site License
Software
Source Code
Source Code Specifications
Source Materials
Specifications
Statement of Work
System
Systems Software
Termination Assistance Period
Third Parties
Third Party
Third Party Software
Time and Materials Basis
Tools
Trainees
Underlying Works
Update(s)
Upgrades
Use
User
User Limit
Vendor
Vendor Underlying Works
Version
WAN
Workaround
Work Product
Written Deliverables

"7 x 24 x 365" shall mean 24 hours, 7 days per week, and 365 days per year, including Vendor holidays.

"Acceptance" shall mean the date on which Vendor issues a certificate of completion pursuant to Section ____ ("Certification of Completion") hereof.

"Acceptance Criteria" shall mean the specifications set forth in the applicable Statement of Work. If relevant objective specifications are not included in the Statement of Work, acceptance shall be based upon the parties' reasonable determination that the Deliverables are satisfactory in all material respects.

"Adaptation" shall mean a non-programming alteration of Licensed Software, capable of being modified utilizing software tools provided with the Licensed Software by a Third Party Vendor or Vendor and other user controlled features (e.g., the creation, deletion, and alteration of screens, pathways, reports, profiles, documents, and data dictionary elements).

"Affiliate(s)" means any person, firm, corporation (including, without limitation, service corporation and professional corporation), partnership (including, without limitation, general partnership, limited partnership, and limited liability partnership), limited liability company, joint venture, business trust, association, or other entity **that now or in the future, directly or indirectly:** (a) controls, is controlled with or by or is under common control with a party; or (b) with respect to Customer, is acquired, **managed**, operated **governed, or supervised by** Customer, whether by membership, stock ownership, joint operating agreement or other substantial relationship, including without limitation, any physician-hospital organizations, medical service organizations, and independent practice organizations in which Customer or any Affiliate of Customer has a membership or stock interest. For purposes of the foregoing, "control" shall mean the direct or indirect control of fifty percent (50%) or more of the voting power to elect directors thereof, or for any other entity, the power to direct the management of such entity.

> * ***This definition benefits the customer through the use of nebulous wording including "managed," "governed," and "supervised," making it difficult for the vendor to limit use of the software. Further, the definition also includes entities that may be acquired in the future. See Chapter 12.A for a definition that protects the licensor's interests by definitively listing the licensee's Affiliates.***

Alternatively:

"Affiliate(s)" means all entities which control, are controlled by or are under common control of the named party, whether directly or through one (1) or more intermediaries, with "control" and "controlled" defined as ownership of more than fifty percent (50%) of the voting capital stock or other interest having voting rights with respect to the election of the board of directors or similar governing authority.

Potential Additional Language
Should Licensee divest a Licensee Affiliate or should a Licensee Affiliate cease to satisfy this definition, all existing Statements of Work with such divested Licensee Affiliate shall remain in effect; however, the divested Licensee Affiliate will no longer be authorized to initiate new Statements of Work under this Agreement.

"Agreement" means this Services Agreement by and between Customer and Vendor, inclusive of all Schedules, Exhibits, Attachments, Addenda, and other documents incorporated herein by reference.

"Applications Software" or ***"Applications"*** shall mean those programs and programming (including the supporting documentation, media, on-line help facilities, and tutorials) that perform specific user related data processing and telecommunications tasks in connection with the Services. Applications Software includes compilers, database managers, and development tools. Applications Software in use as of the Effective Date is identified in Schedule __, as amended and updated in accordance with the process set forth in the Procedures Manual by the Parties as necessary to reflect evolution of and changes in the Services.

"Approve" or ***"Approval"*** shall mean (1) the written authorization by Customer's Chief Information Officer (or his or her designee) or the Customer Applications Partnership Executive (or his or her designee) for any consent, authorization, amendment, and/or other approval required from Customer under this Agreement, and (2) with respect to any consent, authorization, amendment, and/or approval requiring the authorization of payment, or imposing an obligation on Customer for any fees, costs, or other expenses, the written authorization of the applicable Customer Applications Partnership Executive.

"Approved Subcontractors" shall mean those subcontractors of Vendor approved by Customer prior to the Effective Date and identified in Schedule __ or whose approval is not required under the provisions of Section _____, and any other subcontractor(s) approved by Customer in accordance with Section ____, unless and until approval of such subcontractor is rescinded by Customer in accordance with Section ____.

"Arising" References to matters "arising" (or which "arise" or "arises") "out of this Contract" include matters which arise in connection with this Contract or have a causal connection with or which flow from this Contract or which would not have arisen or occurred but for the entering into this Contract or the performance of or failure to perform obligations under this Contract.

"Attorneys' Fees" shall mean the reasonable fees and expenses of counsel to the parties hereto and fees billed for law clerks, paralegals, librarians and others not admitted to the bar but performing services under the supervision of an attorney. The term "Attorneys' Fees" shall include, without limitation, all such fees and expenses incurred with respect to appeals, mediations, arbitrations and bankruptcy proceeding.

"Authorized User" means: (a) **Company and its employees and authorized agents;** (b) Company's Affiliates and its employees and authorized agents; (c) **third party consultants and other independent contractors performing services for Company;** (d) any governmental bodies lawfully requesting or requiring access to the Applications; and (e) any Company-authorized facility managers or service bureaus, provided such use shall be solely for the benefit and use of Company.

Alternatively:

"Authorized User" means, with respect to any Software identified in a Statement of Work (i) **any employee or representative of Customer [and its affiliates]**; (ii) any physician with patient admitting privileges at a Facility for which the Software is licensed; (iii) any employee or representative of such physician; and (iv) any medical professional who is authorized to perform services for Customer, its affiliates, or at a Facility.

Alternatively:

"Authorized User" means: (a) Customer and its Affiliates; (b) employees, **consultants, authorized agents,** students (medical, nursing, and other students), **volunteers,** nurses, physicians; medical staff members, and all technicians and other personnel or agents on staff or otherwise associated with Customer or its Affiliates; (c) nurses, technicians, and other clinicians associated with such physicians and assistants of staff physicians, and agents of Customer and its Affiliates; (d) **Third Party consultants, auditors, and other independent contractors performing services for Customer or any Customer Affiliate**; (e) any governmental, accrediting or regulatory bodies lawfully requesting or requiring access to any of Customer's data; and (f) such other parties as Customer and Vendor may mutually agree.

> * ***These definitions benefit the customer as they allow the customer's third party consultants to access/use the vendor's proprietary software, creating a risk of misappropriation and potentially limiting the vendor's income from consulting and maintenance services.***

"Bankruptcy Code" means the U.S. Bankruptcy Code, as amended.

"Best Efforts" means that the obligated party is required to make a diligent and good faith effort to accomplish the applicable objective. Some obligation, however, does not require a material expenditure of funds or the incurrence of a material liability on the part of the obligated party, nor does it require that the obligated party act in a manner that would be contrary to normal commercial practices in order to accomplish the objective. The failure to accomplish a given objective is no indication and shall not be admitted as evidence in any proceeding to establish that the obligated party did not in fact utilize its Best Efforts in attempting to accomplish the objective.

"Best Practices" shall mean (whether or not capitalized) established procedures or processes developed or used by Vendor, utilizing its accumulated knowledge as a world class technology service provider, to deliver Services in a high quality, effective, and efficient manner.

"Business Day" means any weekday other than a day designated as a holiday under the then applicable Customer holiday schedule. Any reference herein to "day" that is not specifically referenced as "Business Day" means calendar day.

"Certification" shall occur for each Service, Licensed Product, and Custom Program when Customer notifies Vendor in writing that the applicable testing has been completed successfully for such Service, Licensed Product, or Custom Program and that all Deliverables related to such Service, Licensed Product, or Custom Program have been provided to Customer.

"Change of Control" means: (a) any transaction or combination of transactions as a result of which either a person, an entity, or a group of persons and/or entities that customarily has acted in concert and that presently is in control of Vendor ceases to be in control of Vendor; or (b) the sale, exchange, or other disposition (including disposition in full or partial dissolution) of the stock of Vendor or the assets of Vendor that constitute a substantial or material business segment of Vendor; or (c) the divestiture, in whole or in part, of the business unit or division of Vendor that has provided the Services, the Software, and/or Deliverables to Customer. A Change of Control shall not include any public stock offering.

Alternatively:

"Change of Control" means each of (a) the sale of all or substantially all of the stock or assets of Licensee (or its ultimate parent company) other than any distribution of Licensee's stock (or similar transaction) to the shareholders of Licensee's ultimate parent company, (b) any merger, reorganization, combination, consolidation or amalgamation of Licensee (or its ultimate parent company) with any other entity, and (c) the acquisition, directly or indirectly, by any person or entity, or by any group of persons or entities acting together, the power to direct or cause the direction of the management and policies of Licensee (or its ultimate parent company), whether through the ownership of voting securities, by contract or otherwise, including, without limitation, the direct or indirect acquisition of 50% or more of the outstanding equity interests in Licensee (or its ultimate parent company).

"Claims" For avoidance of doubt, the Parties agree that the term "Claims" includes without limitation: (i) any claims against any Indemnitee alleging that as a result of any action and/or failure to act by Licensor or any of Licensor's officers, employees or agents, there has been a violation of any rule, regulation, order, statute or ordinance of any governmental authority having jurisdiction; and (ii) any civil penalties, fines, assessments or damages arising from, out of, or related to any such violations.

"Commercially Reasonable Efforts" means taking such steps and performing in such a manner as a well managed business would undertake where such business was acting in a determined, prudent, and reasonable manner to achieve a particular desired result for its own benefit.

Alternatively:

"Commercially Reasonable Efforts" means spending $______ in a single instance or $________ in the aggregate for all costs (including without limitation reasonable attorney's, engineers, scientists, consultants and accountants fees and expenses) associated with a specific action or all actions, respectively, which are required to be taken under this Agreement.

"Concurrent Devices/Concurrent Accesses" means the maximum number of input devices accessing the Programs at any given point in time. If multiplexing software or hardware (e.g., a TP monitor) is used, this number must be measured at the multiplexing front end.

"Confidential Information" means any material, data, or information in whatever form or media of a party to this Agreement that is provided or disclosed to the other, except for any information that is: (a) publicly available or later becomes available other than through a breach of this Agreement; (b) known to the Receiving Party or its employees, agents, or representatives prior to such disclosure or is independently developed by the Receiving Party or its employees, agents, or representatives subsequent to such disclosure; or (c) subsequently lawfully obtained by the Receiving Party or its employees, agents, or representatives from a Third Party without obligations of confidentiality. Confidential Information shall include the following categories of information whether disclosed orally or not marked as confidential: Written Deliverables, network configurations, network architecture, Services rendered by Vendor to Customer, financial and operational information, and other matters relating to the operation of the parties' business, including information relating to actual or potential customers and customer lists, customer usage or requirements, business and customer usage forecasts and projections, accounting, finance or tax information, pricing information, and any information relating to the corporate and/or operational structure of Customer and its Affiliates, Software, Equipment, Deliverables or Services rendered under the Agreement and any amendments thereto, any information exchanged between the parties pursuant to the Nondisclosure Agreement, and all information and materials relating to Third Party vendors, systems integrators, or consultants of Customer that have provided or that may provide in the future any part of Customer's information or communications infrastructure to Customer.

"Control" and its derivatives mean with regard to any entity the legal, beneficial, or equitable ownership, directly or indirectly, of: (i) fifty percent (50%) or more of the capital stock (or other ownership interest, if not a stock corporation) of such entity ordinarily having voting rights; (ii) (A) twenty percent (20%) or more of the capital stock (or other ownership interest, if not a stock corporation), and (B) either (1) a greater percentage than any other juridical person, or (2) management control by agreement; or (iii) (with respect to an entity not domiciled in the United States) the greater of twenty percent (20%) of the capital stock (or other ownership interest, if not a stock corporation) and the maximum percentage allowed by local law for a U.S. corporation to directly or indirectly own.

"Coordinate" means that Vendor will, while providing the Services, communicate, cooperate, and collaborate with Customer and Third Party Vendors whose products and services impact the Services. Coordination includes communicating, cooperating, and collaborating with Customer and the applicable Third Party Vendor to organize the scheduling and performance of the Services, and Customer's and the Third Party Vendor's tasks. Supplier will inform Customer in writing of occurrences in which Customer and/or the identified Third Party Vendor fails to communicate, cooperate, or collaborate with Vendor relating to the performance of the Services and the identified Third Party Vendor's tasks.

"Corporate License" means a license which grants to Customer the right to use and duplicate Licensed Software for use at as many Customer sites and on as many Customer owned, leased or operated Central Processing Units (CPU) as Customer desires for a single license fee.

"CPI" means the official Consumer Price Index, All Urban Consumers, U.S. City Average, All Items, published by the Bureau of Labor Statistics, U.S. Department of Labor.

"CPI Adjustment" shall mean a percentage adjustment to a price, fee, or payment specified in this Agreement in an amount equal to the percentage change in the Consumer Price Index for All Urban Consumers, for the United States, "All Items" (1982–1984=100), published by the U.S. Department of Labor, Bureau of Statistics ("Index"), based on the percentage difference between the Index published immediately preceding the Reference Date and the Index published immediately preceding the date on which the adjustment is to be effective. All adjustments shall be made retroactively to the appropriate date as necessary to account for delays in reporting of the Index. If the Index is changed so that the base year of the Index differs from that specified above, the Index shall be converted in accordance with the conversion factor published by the U.S. Department of Labor, Bureau of Labor Statistics. If the Index is discontinued or revised during the term, such other governmental index or computation with which it is replaced shall be used in order to obtain substantially the same result as would be obtained if the Index had not been discontinued or revised.

> * ***The parties should carefully consider the best index to which any cost increases are tied. While many parties utilize the CPI, the CPI may not be representative of the services and products provided by the vendor. The CPI is a broad basket of costs including energy, real estate, and food, which often have no bearing on technology costs. A better approach is to adopt an index that closely reflects the costs of the services and products to be provided by the vendor. The Department of Labor has many specialized indexes which may be more applicable to the products and services being provided. See Chapter 23. Form B.1 § 8.4.***

"CPU License" means a license which grants the Customer the right to use Licensed Software on a singled designated CPU. Any CPU license may be temporarily transferred to a back up CPU which may be at the same Customer site, another Customer site or at a site owned by a third party.

"Critical Defect" means any Defect that severely impacts Customer's ability to receive or Vendor's ability to provide Services, or any Defect that has a significant financial impact on Customer or a direct impact on Customer's managed care services, or the failure of any network element, such as a printer, to be operable.

Alternatively:

"Critical Defect" means any Defect that exposes Company to adverse or significant financial liability or severely impacts Company's ability to use an Application(s), because of operational, functional, or informational deficiencies that arise from or are related to the Application's failure to operate in accordance with the applicable Release Specifications.

"Custom Programming" means any Software programming developed, authored, written, and/or created by Vendor or its agents or subcontractors for or on behalf of Customer as provided in Section ___.

"Custom Programming Materials" means any Custom Programming, including all source code and materials developed by Vendor, all intermediate and partial versions thereof, as well as all specifications, program materials, flow charts, notes, outlines, and the like created in connection therewith.

"Customer Data" means all data and information (i) submitted to Vendor by or on behalf of Customer and its affiliates, successors or agents, or (ii) obtained, developed or produced by Vendor in connection with an Statement of Work to the extent such data or information is based on, summarizes or includes data and information of Customer or its affiliates or Customer agents submitted to or obtained by Vendor under an Statement of Work.

"Data Center" means Vendor's facility located in ___________.

Alternatively:

"Data Center" means the physical premises, computer hardware, and equipment operated by Vendor on which the Applications run, including all communications equipment and links necessary to connect such hardware and equipment to each Site.

"Data Network" shall mean the Equipment, Software, lines, interconnect devices, and cabling used to connect and transmit data among the Data Center, End User Locations, Customer external locations, and disaster recovery centers providing recovery services to Customer, including between one End User Location and another End User Location.

"Data Security Breach" means: (a) the loss or misuse (by any means) of Personal Data; (b) the inadvertent, unauthorized, and/or unlawful Processing, disclosure, access, alteration, corruption, transfer, or sale or rental, destruction, or use of Personal Data; or (c) any other act or omission that compromises the security, confidentiality, or integrity of Personal Data.

"Defect" means: (1) any failure of the Software to operate in accordance with the Specifications or the Performance Standards; and/or (2) any failure of Vendor to perform the Services in accordance with the Service Level Standards.

"Defect Analysis" means a fax, email, or telephone call from Vendor acknowledging that an Incident Report has been received, details on what Vendor has learned about the Defect as of the time of communication, that appropriate technical personnel have been assigned to work on the Defect, and Vendor's initial analysis of and action plan for resolving the reported Defect.

"Derivative Work" means a work that is based upon one or more preexisting works, such as a revision, modification, translation, abridgment, condensation, expansion, or any other form in which such preexisting works may be recast, transformed, or adapted (including by linking a preexisting work into the Derivative Work so that a web browser would display the preexisting work within the Derivative Work), and that, if prepared without authorization of the owner of the copyright in such preexisting work, would constitute a copyright infringement. For purposes hereof, a Derivative Work shall also include any compilation that incorporates such a preexisting work.

"Disabling Code" is defined as any virus, worm, trap door, back door, timer, clock, counter, or other limiting routine, instruction, or design that would erase data or programming or otherwise cause any Customer system to become inoperable or incapable of being used in the full manner for which it was designed and created.

"Documentation" means, collectively: (a) all available manuals, including operations, reference user, and support and maintenance guides and manuals relating to the Applications; (b) the interface specifications, if applicable; (c) any Application Specifications and other mutually agreed specifications, including design and functionality specifications, or other written materials prepared or developed by Vendor in connection with its performance under this Agreement; (d) written materials describing installation of the Applications; (e) flow charts; (f) internal use listings or manuals relating to error corrections, fixes, and workarounds; (g) file and program cross reference information; and (h) any and all mutually agreed revisions to the above documents.

Alternatively:

"Documentation" means all user and administrator manuals, operating instructions, installation guides, help files, and other printed, electronic, and online material generally made available to Licensor's customers with respect to Licensed Products, and all other printed, electronic, or online materials provided or made available to Customer, that describe the features, functions, or operation of Licensed Products.

** The first definition of "Documentation" set forth above expands the traditional definition to include many ancillary "documents" that may be useful to the licensee in its use of the software. A prudent licensee should seek the broadest possible definition as the more information it receives, the more flexibility it will have in operating the software.*

Alternatively:

"Documentation" means applicable documentation with respect to Deliverables or Services, including but not limited to descriptions of all functions provided thereby, all documentation required to use, operate and, if applicable, modify such Deliverables or Services, and all user related documentation.

"ECI" means Employment Cost Index, Compensation, Private Industry, White Collar Occupations, Not seasonally adjusted, (June 1989 = 100), as published by the U.S. Department of Labor, Bureau of Labor Statistics.

"Effective Date" is defined in the introductory paragraph of this Agreement.

"Electronic Data Interchanges or EDI" is defined as all Federal and State standards and regulations regarding electronic data interchanges transactions (including 45 CFR Part 142).

"Embedded Third Party Software" means that certain Third Party Software provided by Vendor to Customer that constitutes an integral part of the System and/or Services provided to Customer by Vendor pursuant to this Agreement.

"Enhancements" means any new Software releases, versions, improvements, modifications, upgrades, updates, fixes, New Features, and additions to the Software that the applicable vendor markets or makes available to its customers who are eligible to receive maintenance support services from time-to-time to correct deficiencies and/or to improve or extend the capabilities of the Software. Enhancements shall include Regulatory Requirements modifications and any replatformed software, whether on different operating systems or equipment; provided, however, that Enhancements shall not include new, separate product offerings.

** Licensees should carefully review the definition of "Enhancements" to ensure that they receive all "improvements" made to the software by the licensor while under maintenance or warranty. The licensee wants to avoid having the licensor define "Enhancement" so narrowly that an improvement made by the licensor is considered a new version and must be purchased from the licensor.*

"Fix" means the repair or replacement of object or executable code of the Software to remedy an Error such that the repair or replacement renders the Software to perform and comply with the Documentation, including Licensor's published performance specifications.

"Fixed Price Basis" shall mean a compensation arrangement in which Vendor assumes full responsibility for the performance of the Services and delivery of any Deliverables.

"Final Resolution" means a Vendor provided correction or modification of the System that corrects the Defect.

"Full-Time" shall mean a forty-hour (40 hour) work week providing services solely and exclusively for Customer.

"GAAP" is defined as Generally Accepted Accounting Principles.

"Go Live" means the successful completion by Vendor of the implementation, testing, and other services necessary to make the Applications available for use by Customer and its Authorized Users, all as set forth herein.

"Including," whether or not capitalized, means "including, but not limited to."

"Including," and its derivatives (such as "include" and "includes"), shall mean "including without limitation." This term is as defined, whether or not capitalized in the Agreement.

"Indemnified Parties" means the other party and its Affiliates, members, directors, officers, shareholders, employees, representatives, agents, attorneys, successors, and assigns.

> * ***Representatives, agents, contractors, attorneys, etc. should never be indemnified.***

"Identified User" means a unique active user ID issued by Customer for a particular active Permitted User, all of whom are permitted to access the Software simultaneously.

"Information Technology Support and Maintenance Services" means the support and maintenance services provided by Vendor to Customer in order to maintain the System.

> * ***This definition is so broad that it is essentially meaningless. The parties should specifically set forth in detail the specific services to be provided and the time in which they will be provided.***

"Intellectual Property Rights" means copyrights (including the right to use, reproduce, modify, distribute, publicly display, and publicly perform the copyrighted work), trademarks (including trademark, trade names, service marks, and trade dress), patents (including the exclusive right to make, use, and sell), trade secrets, rights of publicity, rights of privacy, moral rights, goodwill, and all other intellectual property rights as may exist now and/or hereafter come into existence and all renewals and extensions thereof, regardless of whether such rights arise under the laws of the United States or any other state, country or other jurisdiction.

"Interface(s)" when used as a noun, shall mean either a computer program developed by, or licensed to, Customer or Vendor (i) to translate or convert data from Customer or Vendor format into another format used by Vendor at Customer as a standard format, or (ii) to translate or convert data in a format used by Vendor or Third Party Vendor to a format supported by Vendor at Customer or vice versa. "Interface" when used as a verb, shall mean to operate as described above.

"Interim Resolution" means Vendor: (a) reinitiates or restarts, as applicable, the System, or affected part thereof, if the reported Defect caused the System to be inoperative; (b) enables Customer to access the System, if the reported Defect caused Customer to be unable to access the System; or (c) provides Customer with an acceptable workaround that solves or mitigates a reported Defect, which workaround can be provided with minimal Customer inconvenience.

"Internal Purposes" means **all internal purposes** including processing on multiple workstations and at multiple sites, **and the engagement of Authorized Users (and the disclosure of source code, documentation, and other confidential information thereto) to prepare system modifications and provide other services. Internal Purposes also includes engaging an Authorized User on an outsourcing or similar basis to provide services for the internal purposes of the Party engaging the outsourcer. Internal Purposes of Customer also includes the provision of data and claims processing services to current and future Customer Affiliates and to entities that hereafter become former Customer Affiliates, provided that processing for such former Customer Affiliates shall be deemed "Internal Purposes" for a period of two years after such entity ceases to be a Customer Affiliate.**

> * ***This definition benefits the customer as it allows the customer to outsource the system/software to a third party and allow a third party access to the software/system to monitor and support. Further, the customer's ex-affiliates the right to utilize the software for up to two years after they are divested, thereby limiting the vendor's ability to charge additional fees for a now unrelated entity and significantly increasing the vendor's costs of providing support.***

"Interoperate" or ***"Interoperability"*** means architectural functions and structural integration between and among the Applications such that the Applications have the capability to communicate, execute programs or transfer data seamlessly.

"Know How" means the accumulation of skills, processes, information, experience and documents related to the Software and needed to enable Licensee, itself or third-party sublicensees, to utilize the Software to manufacture, service and sell the XXXX Product, including, but not limited to, any and all materials, technical information, blueprints, process documents, drawings, CAD-CAM and other electronic files, supplier lists, specifications, trade secrets, techniques, discoveries, processes, procedures, methods, protocols, designs, diagrams, test results, studies, raw material sources, data, formulation, production technology and other such materials.

"Knowledge" means all ideas, concepts, techniques, information, reports, programs, designs, materials, source code, Documentation, diagrams, discoveries, notes, outlines, flow charts, user interfaces, techniques, technology, formulas, processes, algorithms, inventions and the like, that vendor develops during the course of implementing the Project.

"Law" or ***"Laws"*** means all federal, state, provincial, regional, territorial and local laws, statutes, ordinances, regulations, rules, executive orders, supervisory requirements, directives, circulars, opinions, interpretive letters, and other official releases of or by any government, or any authority, department or agency thereof or self regulatory organization (**SRO**). Laws shall include (i) the Health Insurance Portability and Accountability Act of 1996, as amended, and the regulations promulgated thereunder (**HIPAA**); (ii) the Social Security Act, regulations and pronouncements thereunder, including but not limited to, the provisions related to hospitals and conditions of participation, 42 U.S.C. 1395 et. Seq., policies of Centers for Medicare and Medicaid Services and the Medicare fiscal intermediaries, state hospital licensure and related laws and regulations; (iii) federal and state false claims statutes and regulations, federal and state health fraud laws and regulations, federal and state public contract anti-kickback laws and regulations, including the anti-kickback provisions of the Social Security Act, 42 U.S.C. §§ 1320a-7b(b), the attendant safe harbors and the relevant regulations including 42 C.F.R. Part 1001.952; (iv) the federal Physician Ownership and Referral Law, 42 U.S.C. § 1395nn, and the regulations promulgated thereunder; (v) state and federal health care provider and hospital laws and regulations; (vi) the Standards for Privacy of Individually Identifiable Health Information, 45 C.F.R. Parts 160 and 164; (vii) the Security Standards, 45 C.F.R. Parts 160, 162, and 164; (viii) the Standards for Electronic Transactions, 45 C.F.R. Parts 160 and 162); (ix) FDA (Food and Drug Administration) GLP (Good Laboratory Practices), GCP (Good Clinical Practices), and GMP (Good Manufacturing Practices) (collectively, **GxP**) regulations and FDA regulations Part 607 (Establishment Registration and Product Listing for Manufacturers of Human Blood and Blood Products); (x) laws and regulations governing the Department of Defense health programs (CHAMPUS/TRICARE); (xi) federal and state laws and regulations pertaining to state health care programs, including state Medicaid programs and the Medicare Conditions of Participation; (xii) certification or accreditation requirements of JCAHO; (xiii) all generally accepted accounting principles (**GAAP**); and **(xiv) any other laws in force in any jurisdiction in which the Services are being provided or received. Laws include modifications to any Laws by applicable authorities.**

> * ***This definition benefits the customer as not only is it broadly written, subsection (xiv) has the effect of subjecting the vendor to any subsequently enacted laws and any liability or costs arising therefrom.***

Alternatively:

"Law" or ***"Laws"*** means all national, intergovernmental, common law, federal, state, provincial, regional, territorial and local laws, statutes, ordinances, regulations, rules, executive orders, orders of a court or governmental agency, supervisory requirements, directives, circulars, opinions, interpretive letters and other official releases of or by any government, or any authority, department or agency thereof.

"Licensed Software" shall mean individually each, and collectively all, of the computer programs, **including Interfaces**, licensed by Customer or Vendor from a Third Party Vendor, or otherwise provided by Vendor to Customer under this Agreement (exclusive of Application Development, if any), **including any embedded and/or remarketed Third Party Vendor software, including as to each program, the processes and routines used in the processing of data, the object code, source code** (as to Third Party Vendors' source code, when rights to the source code may be obtained), tapes, disks, **Enhancements to such programs as may generally be made available by the applicable Third Party Vendor or Vendor, and any and all programs provided by a Third Party Vendor or Vendor in the future under this Agreement.** Licensed Software shall include New Software, Developed Software, Customer Proprietary Software, Customer Third Party Software, Vendor Proprietary Software, and Vendor Third Party Software.

> * ***From the licensee's perspective, this definition is all encompassing. The licensor should ensure that this definition does not include third party software, obligating the licensor to maintain third party software unless the licensor is being paid to do so.***

Alternatively:

"Licensed Software" means the computer programs, databases, and related products listed on Schedule A together with all files required for proper operation thereof and all associated tools, utilities, programs, and files that Licensor provides to Licensee pursuant to the Agreement, all the foregoing as furnished and as installed.

> * ***By definitively listing the licensed software, the licensor is able definitively quantify its risk.***

"Live Date" means the earlier of: (i) the date upon which the Software is first available for Productive Use; or (ii) the date specified in the applicable implementation plan upon which the Software is intended to be available for Productive Use, provided, however, that the date determined in accordance with this subsection (ii) will be extended by one day for each day that the Software is not available for Productive Use to the extent caused by Licensee's acts or omissions.

"Losses" means all settlements, judgments, awards, fines, penalties, interest, liabilities, losses, costs, damages and expenses (including reasonable attorneys' fees and disbursements and court costs).

"Low Defect" means any Defect that is of de minimis nature.

"Maintenance" or ***"Maintain"*** shall mean: (A) with respect to Equipment—supporting and maintaining all Equipment in good operating condition, subject to normal wear and tear, undertaking and performing repairs and maintenance on Equipment in accordance with the applicable manufacturer's recommendations and specifications, and such other services and repairs required to maintain the Equipment so that it operates properly and in accordance with the applicable specifications; and (B) with respect to Software—supporting and correcting (or causing to be corrected) any failure of the Software to perform in accordance with the applicable specifications, and providing such services and repairs required to maintain the Software so that it operates properly and in accordance with the applicable Specifications (including fixes, patches, upgrades, defect repairs, programming corrections, and/or remedial programming).

"Material Defect" means Critical Defects and/or Medium Defects.

"Medium Defect" means any Defect that adversely affects Customer's ability to receive or Vendor's ability to provide the Services but for which an alternative temporary solution or workaround acceptable to Customer may be accomplished.

"New Features" shall mean Enhancements (including, if applicable, Regulatory Requirements modifications) to the System and/or Software that provide significant new functionality or new modules.

"Non-Permissive Open Source Code" means any software program, or portion thereof, that is licensed under a license that requires as a condition of use, modification, and/or distribution of the software subject to the license, that such software or other software combined and/or distributed with such software be (i) disclosed or distributed in source code form; (ii) licensed for the purpose of making derivative works; or (iii) redistributable at no charge.

"Non-production Use" shall mean, Licensee may only use Licensed Program internally for testing and training purposes; not in a production environment. Licensee shall not resell the Licensed Programs nor shall Licensee have ownership rights of the Licensed Program.

"Named User" means an individual authorized by Licensee to use the Licensed Programs which are installed on a single server or multiple servers, regardless of whether the individual is actively using the programs at any given time. A non-human operated device will be counted as a Professional User in addition to all individuals authorized to use the programs, if such devices access the Licensed Programs. If multiplexing hardware or software (e.g., a TP monitor or a web server product) is used, this number must be measured at the multiplexing front end. Each Named User will have varying access to the Licensed Program depending upon the type of Named User access purchased above.

"Object Code" shall mean computer software code, instructions, and data definitions in a machine-readable form output by an assembler, compiler, pre-processor, or other translator. Object Code includes, but is not limited to, object files, precompiled modules, library modules, and executable programs containing native, emulated, intermediate, pseudo-code, or virtual machine instructions substantially or entirely in binary, tokenised or script form and is intended to be directly or indirectly executed, emulated, interpreted, or processed by a computer.

> ** **Licensees and Licensors need to ensure the definition of "object code" reflects the contemplated use of the software and any changes in technology. The definition of "object code" set forth in Chapter 23.B.1 § 1.14 is insufficient in today's technology environment.***

"Out-of-Pocket Expenses" shall mean the reasonable and actual out-of-pocket expenses incurred by Vendor for equipment, materials, supplies, or other Services provided to Customer under this Agreement, but excluding Vendor's overhead costs (or allocations thereof), administrative expenses or other mark-ups.

> ** **From a licensee's perspective it is important to exclude any licensor markups for administrative expenses and to make sure that the expenses paid by the licensee reflect to benefit of any rebates or discounts paid by any third party such as airlines, hotels, or travel agents.***

"Performance Standards" shall mean, individually and collectively, the quantitative and qualitative performance standards and commitments for the Services contained in this Agreement, including Service Levels.

"Permissive Open Source Code" means any software program, or portion thereof, that is licensed under a license that (a) grants the user the right to freely use, copy, modify, distribute and display the source code for a software program and (b) does not require as a condition of use, modification, and/or distribution of the software subject to the license, that such software or other software combined and/or distributed with such software be (i) disclosed or distributed in source code form; (ii) licensed for the purpose of making derivative works; or (iii) redistributable at no charge. For purposes of clarity, software subject to the Berkeley Style Database license, available on the Open Source Initiative website (www.opensource.org), would be considered Permissive Open Source Code while software licensed under the General Public License (also available on the Open Source Initiative website) would not.

"Permitted Auditors" shall have the meaning as specified in Section 34.2 (Audits Authorized by Customer) of the Agreement.

"Personal Data" means any information that can be used to identify, locate, or contact an individual, including, but not limited to: (a) first and last name; (b) home or other physical address; (c) telephone number; (d) email address or online identifier associated with an individual; (e) social security number or similar identifier; (f) employment, financial, or health information; or (g) any other information relating to an individual that is combined with any of the above.

"Personal Information" means an individual's first name or first initial and his or her last name in combination with any one or more of the following data elements, when either the name of the data elements are not encrypted or redacted: (1) social security number, (2) driver's license number or California identification card number, (3) account number, credit, or debit card number, in combination with any required security code, access code, or password that would permit access to an individual's financial account, (4) "Medical Information," meaning any individually identifiable information in electronic or physical form, regarding the individual's medical history or medical treatment or diagnosis by a health care professional; or (5) personally identifiable information as such term is used in Section 631 of the Cable Communications Policy Act of 1984, as amended (47 U.S.C. § 551). Personal Information does not include publicly available information that is lawfully made available to the general public from federal, state or local government records.

"Personally Identifiable Information" shall mean any information which, alone or in combination with other information, relates to a specific, identifiable individual. Personally Identifiable Information includes individual names, social security numbers, telephone numbers, home address, driver's license number, account number, email address, and vehicle registration number. Any information that can be associated with Personally Identifiable Information shall also be Personally Identifiable Information. For example, an individual's age by itself is not Personally Identifiable Information, but if such age is capable of being associated with one or more specific identifiable individuals then such age would be deemed Personally Identifiable Information.

"Previous Sequential Release" means a Release of the Software which has been replaced by a subsequent Release of the same software. Notwithstanding anything else to the contrary herein, (i) each Previous Sequential Release will be supported by Licensor for a period of no less than eighteen (18) months after release of the subsequent release. In addition, Licensor agrees that it shall provide Licensee with written notice no less than twelve (12) months prior to support services for each Previous Sequential Release expiring in accordance with the foregoing.

"Privacy Laws" **means all Laws (including implementing legislation and regulations) relating to privacy, patient consent, insurance or medical records, trans-border data flow, or data protection.** Privacy Laws include the implementing legislation and regulations of the European Union member states under the European Union Directives 95/46/EC and 2002/58/EC and the Gramm-Leach Bliley Act, HIPAA, California security-breach-notification law (or California SB 1 and SB 1386), the Standards for Privacy of Individual Information, 45 C.F.R. Parts 160 and 164, and the Security Standards, 45 C.F.R. Parts 160, 162, and 164.

> * ***This definition is broadly written to benefit the customer as there is no limitation as to which laws the licensor must comply. Under this language, the licensor is obligated to comply with the laws of the European Union (EU) even though the licensor may not be licensing its software for use in the EU.***

"Privileged Information" means: (a) any patient data, histories, and other patient information, memoranda, flow sheets, and similar patient reports; (b) physician information or data and information relating to Customer's employees; (c) other information of a similar nature and identified by Customer as privileged; and (d) such other information that the parties mutually agree should be privileged.

"Procedures Manual" shall describe how Vendor shall perform and deliver the Services under this Agreement, the Equipment and Software being used, and the documentation (e.g., operations manuals, user guides, specifications) that provide further details of such activities. The Procedures Manual shall describe the activities Vendor proposes to undertake in order to provide the Services, including those direction, supervision, monitoring, staffing, reporting, planning, and oversight activities normally undertaken to provide services of the type Vendor is to provide under this Agreement. The Procedures Manual also shall include the descriptions of the acceptance testing and quality assurance procedures approved by Customer and other standards and procedures of Vendor pertinent to Customer's interaction with Vendor in obtaining the Services. The Procedures Manual shall be suitable for use by Customer to understand the Services.

"Productive Use" means use of Software to process live data for purposes other than Software testing or evaluation (including parallel processing).

"Professional Named User" is a Named User who is permitted to access the Licensed Programs and is able to access all functionality of such Licensed Programs.

"Programmer" means a Full-Time, on-site software programmer provided by Vendor to perform Custom Programming and any other Services at the request of Customer.

"Project Acceptance" for each Project shall occur only when: (a) Vendor has provided to Customer all Deliverables required to be provided to Customer pursuant to the applicable Implementation Work plan; (b) if applicable, Vendor has achieved Certification; and (c) (i) Customer notifies Vendor in writing that all Services related to the Project have been successfully completed in accordance with the terms of this Agreement; or (ii) Vendor provides to the Customer Project Manager a written notice of completion stating that Vendor believes all such Deliverables and Services have been successfully provided, unless Customer provides Vendor with notice of objection within fifteen (15) calendar days following the date of receipt of the applicable Customer Project Manager of Vendor's written notice of completion.

"Quality Assurance" means the actions, planned and performed, to provide confidence that all processes, Systems, Equipment, Software, and components that influence the quality of the Services are working as expected individually and collectively.

"Query User" is a Named User with read only access rights to the applicable Licensed Program so that such Query Named User may run queries or generate reports from the applicable Licensed Program.

"Reasonable Efforts" shall mean activity reasonably calculated to obtain the approval by action or expenditure not disproportionate in the circumstances.

* ***Although definitions of this type are subjective, a subjective definition is often better than no definition at all. For a discussion of "reasonable efforts"***, see, **Stabile v. McCarthy, *145 N.E.2d 821 (Mass. 1957).***

"Regulatory Requirements" shall mean those federal and state governmental and quasi-governmental regulatory requirements, statutes, ordinances, policies, edicts, rules, guidelines, or standards related to Customer's use of the Services or the functions of the System including, without limitation, all standards or guidelines established by committees, agencies or other standard-setting organizations implementing regulatory requirements, policies, or operating standards adopted by the healthcare industry and any other such modifications or changes that may be required to meet the then-current, industry-accepted specifications or standards for Third Party Software with which the System interfaces and all federal, state, and regulatory requirements that relate to Customer's provision of Medicaid managed care services Without limiting the generality of the foregoing, Regulatory Requirements shall mean those requirements as set forth in the Prime Contract and shall include, without limitation, all federal and state standards and regulations regarding electronic data interchange transactions (including, without limitation, 45 CFR Part 142 and any other standards or regulations addressing the mandates of Section 262 (Administrative Simplification) of the Health Insurance Portability and Accountability Act of 1996).

* ***This definition benefits the customer as the vendor assumes the risk of any subsequently enacted law.***

"Release" shall mean a redistribution of Software that contains new features, new functionality, and/or performance improvements.

"Required Consents" shall mean such consents as may be required for the assignment to Vendor, or the grant to Vendor of rights of use, of resources otherwise provided for in this Agreement.

"Residuals" means Vendor's general knowledge, skills, and experience, and any ideas, concepts, know-how, methodologies, and techniques that are not protected or susceptible of protection under U.S. patent or copyright laws but are used by Vendor within the scope of Vendor's business practice and may be used by it in the course of providing the Services; except, however, that Residuals shall not include any Work Product, Customer Data, or Customer Confidential Information.

"Root Cause Analysis" means the formal process, specified in the Policy and Procedures Manual, to be used by Vendor to diagnose the underlying cause of problems at the lowest reasonable level so that corrective action can be taken that will eliminate repeat failures. Vendor shall implement a Root Cause Analysis as specified in Section __ or as requested by Customer.

"Services" means, individually or collectively, all installation, implementation, integration, testing, development, conversion, training, consulting, Information Technology

Support, and Maintenance Services and any other professional or other services that may be provided by Vendor to Customer.

"Site License" means a license which grants to Customer the right to use the Licensed Software on any and all computer systems owned, leased, or operated by Customer at a single location or installation known or identified by a single street or mailing address.

"Software" means all software that is utilized by Vendor in connection with the System and the provision of Services to Customer including, without limitation, all interfaces, Vendor Software, Licensed Products, Third Party Software, Embedded Third Party Software and Custom Programming, and all Enhancements thereto.

Alternatively:

"Software" means computer programs and program objects of any kind (including source code and object code), program set-up and customization parameters, tools, and data and the tangible media on which any of the foregoing are recorded. Software includes all software that is utilized by Vendor in connection with the Vendor System and the provision of Services to Customer, including all interfaces, Vendor Software, Third Party Software, and Custom Programming, and all Enhancements to the foregoing.

> * ***Licensors should avoid broad, far reaching definitions and instead seek to definitely list the "Software" on a schedule.***

"Software Maintenance Services" in relation to a Software product, means corrections of Software or Documentation due to defects in the Software or Documentation, as applicable, **and improvements to existing functionality provided by Vendor after the Software delivery date but not otherwise separately priced or marketed by Vendor and Software Maintenance Services then currently available as described in a Contract Supplement.** Vendor and Customer shall comply with Vendor's written Software Maintenance Services procedures as contained in the Vendor Support Manual incorporated herein by reference, as may be reasonably modified from time to time.

> * ***Licensee should ensure the definition of "maintenance" protects its ability to receive all "improvements" to the software made by the licensor.***

"Source Code" shall mean the software in human-readable form, which when compiled, assembled, interpreted, pre-processed, post-processed, or translated becomes the Object Code of a software program, the Source Code for another compiler, assembler, interpreter, pre-processor, postprocessor, or translator, or results in the execution of the commands, statements, expressions, procedures, functions, or instructions to the software program. Source Code also includes all logic diagrams, flow charts, developer comments, source files, header files, hypertext mark-up, graphics, resource files, and web pages concerning the relevant software.

* ***It is important to realize that as the nature of software and its uses change, the corresponding definitions need to be "updated" to recognize and incorporate such changes. The first definition of source code set forth above is an example of the "traditional" definition that has been utilized for the past 20 years. The second definition reflects subsequent changes in the industry, especially the influence of the Internet. A prudent practitioner needs to recognize that changes will occur and craft their definitions accordingly.***

"Source Code Specifications" means: (a) available sub-programs, routines, program files, data files, file and data defined terms and relationships, data definition specifications, data models, program and system logic, interfaces, algorithms, program architecture, design concepts, system designs, program structure, sequence and organization, screen displays and report layouts related to interacting with or a part of the Software (excluding Third Party Software), whether in human-readable, electronic, or machine-readable form; (b) Vendor-developed maintenance and support tools, utilities, diagnostic programs, and supporting programs used or utilized by Vendor internally in the support or maintenance of the Software, or externally in connection with supporting other Customer locations, whether or not such items are made available to licensees generally or at an additional fee, whether in human-readable, electronic, or machine-readable form; (c) available reference manuals, user and operating guides and manuals, design specifications, functional specifications, flow charts, internal use listings or manuals relating to error corrections, fixes and workarounds, file and program cross-reference information (whether in manual, guide, or other format), whether in human-readable, electronic or machine-readable form; and (d) a list of all the names and business addresses and telephone numbers of each key programmer or author, currently employed by Vendor, of any portion of the Software.

"Source Materials" shall mean all materials necessary for a reasonably experienced programmer to maintain and enhance the Software, including, but not limited to, (i) a copy of source code, in machine readable form and all source code documentation, (ii) all proprietary or special tools and an identification of other software reasonably necessary to create object code and executable code from the source code and to modify the source code and related documentation, and (iii) a description of the development system, hardware, software, compilers, third party software and similar materials sufficient for Customer (or its agents or subcontractors) to continue development, enhancement, and support for the Software.

* ***From the licensee's perspective, this definition should be as broad as possible as the "source materials" will likely only be released in the event of the licensor's breach or bankruptcy.***

"Specifications" means the functional and operational characteristics of the Software as described in Vendor's Documentation or as otherwise described in Exhibit __.

Alternatively:

"Specifications" means, with respect to processes, Software, Equipment, Systems, or other contract deliverables to be designed, developed, delivered, integrated, installed, and/or tested by Vendor, the technical, design, and/or functional specifications set forth in this Agreement in third party vendor documentation, in a Services or Project description requested and/or approved by Customer, or otherwise agreed upon in writing by the Parties.

Alternatively:

"Specifications" means all Software functional and performance characteristics and capabilities mutually agreed upon by Customer and Licensor under the applicable Service Schedule. In addition, without limiting the foregoing, all functional and performance characteristics and capabilities demonstrated to Customer as part of any site visit or product demonstration shall be deemed included within the definition of Specifications unless expressly communicated to Customer at the time of demonstration that particular characteristics or capabilities are inapplicable to Customer. In the event of a conflict between Specifications and Documentation, the Specifications will prevail.

"Statement of Work" means an attachment to this Agreement and a series of detailed project plans consistent therewith that specify in as much detail as possible the Project and Services to be performed under the Statement of Work including a clear, unambiguous and comprehensive definition of the Project scope, the tasks to be performed by Vendor, the tasks to be performed by Customer, the Deliverables to be delivered by Vendor, acceptance criteria to be applied to each Deliverable, personnel to be provided by Vendor, assumptions, the respective obligations of the parties, a schedule according to which the tasks specified in the Statement of Work will be completed, and the professional services fees, payment schedule, and anticipated expenses associated with the Statement of Work attached hereto as Schedule __.

Alternatively:

"Statement of Work" shall mean an attachment to this Agreement that defines, with respect to a specific Project, one or more of the following elements: the scope of the Project, Deliverables, responsibilities of Customer, responsibilities of Vendor, the acceptance criteria applicable to Deliverables, the fees and payment schedule pertinent to the Project, and any modifications of the terms of this Agreement as they apply to the Project.

"System" means an interconnected grouping of manual or electronic processes, including Equipment, Software and associated attachments, features, accessories, peripherals and cabling, and all additions, modifications, substitutions, Upgrades or enhancements to such System, to the extent a Party has financial or operational responsibility for such System or System components under Schedule ___. System shall include all Systems in use or required to be used as of the Commencement Date, all additions, modifications, substitutions, Upgrades, or enhancements to such Systems and all Systems installed or developed by or for Customer or Vendor following the Commencement Date.

"Systems Software" shall mean those programs and programming (including the supporting documentation, media, on-line help facilities and tutorials) that perform (i) tasks basic to the functioning of the Equipment and which are required to operate the Applications Software; or (ii) tasks, other than as performed by Applications Software, otherwise supporting the provision of the Services by Vendor. Systems Software includes operating systems, utilities, telecommunication protocols, and network operating systems (including measuring and monitoring tools), data security software, middleware, and telecommunications monitors.

Alternatively:

"Systems Software" means all software programs and programming (and all modifications, replacements, Upgrades, enhancements, documentation, materials and media related thereto) that perform tasks basic to the functioning of the Equipment and are required to operate the Applications Software or otherwise support the provision of Services by Vendor, to the extent a Party has financial or operational responsibility for such programs or programming under Schedule ___. Systems Software shall include all such programs or programming in use or required to be used as of the Commencement Date, including those set forth in Schedule ___, and those as to which Vendor received reasonable notice and/or access prior to the Commencement Date. Systems Software also shall include all such programs or programming developed and/or introduced by or for Customer or Vendor after the Commencement Date to the extent a Party has financial or operational responsibility for such programs or programming under Schedule ___. System Software will not include Software that is Application Software, but includes *[Antivirus Software, Asset Management Software, Compilers, Database Software, Engineering Software, LAN Software, Imaging Software, Monitoring Software, Operating System Software, Remote Management Software, WAN Software, and other applicable Software].*

"Termination Assistance Period" means **a period of time designated by Customer,** commencing on the date upon which this Agreement expires or terminates for any reason, **including a default on the part of Customer**, and continuing until the date (the "End Date") specified by Customer. The End Date will be a date at the end of the number of months as set forth in Exhibit __ after the expiration or termination of this Agreement.

> * ***This definition benefits the licensee as it requires the licensor to provide transition service for a time period determined by the customer. Further, the licensor is required to provide transition services in the event of licensee's breach.***

"Third Parties" shall mean all non-Affiliate third parties using the System or on behalf of whom Licensee uses the System in accordance the terms and conditions of this Agreement. Licensor shall not have any obligation, responsibility or liability (including, without limitation, warranty maintenance, and performance obligations hereunder) to Third Parties under this Agreement, including, without limitation, with respect to Third Parties' use of the System. The Third Parties' use of the System shall end simultaneously with the expiration or earlier termination of Company's use of the System under this Agreement.

"Third Party" means persons, corporations, and entities other than Vendor, Customer or any of their Affiliates.

"Third Party Software" shall mean the Applications Software and Systems Software used to provide the Services that are provided under license to Vendor or Customer by a third party, and shall include any ongoing services (e.g., maintenance and support services, upgrades, subscription services) provided by third parties (e.g., Vendor, manufacturer, lessor) in the same license covering such Software.

"Time and Materials Basis" shall mean a compensation arrangement in which Vendor estimates the number of hours and cost of materials required to perform the Services and, if applicable, complete and deliver any Deliverable(s), and bills Customer for the hours actually worked and material actually expended.

"Tools" mean any software maintenance and support tools, methodologies, processes, technologies, or algorithms used by Vendor in providing the Services and authorized by Customer.

Alternatively:

"Tools" shall mean any and all of Vendor's proprietary materials, information, and know-how, used by Vendor in the conduct of its business, including, by way of illustration but not limitation, technical information, plans, designs, templates, processes, methodologies, procedures, reusable software (such as source code, object code, routines, and libraries that are commonly used in connection with, and are generic to the development of, a typical computer program), and generic software features (such as text, graphics, menus, icons, and other commonly-used elements that are generic to computer programs), together with improvements and modifications thereof.

"Trainees" means any vendor personnel who are assigned or designated to perform such tasks who have less than the required twelve (12) months of experience.

"Underlying Works" means tangible and intangible information and developments that: (i) had already been conceived, invented, created, or acquired by Vendor or third parties prior to the Effective Date and were not conceived or created for Customer's use or benefit in connection with this Agreement; or (ii) were conceived, invented, created, or acquired by Vendor or third parties after the Effective Date but do not constitute Work Product hereunder. An Underlying Work includes all intermediate and partial versions thereof, including all source code and object code with respect thereto, and all designs, specifications, inventions, discoveries, improvements, materials, program materials, software, flow charts, notes, outlines, lists, compilations, manuscripts, writings, pictorial materials, schematics, other creations, and the like, whether or not patented or patentable or otherwise protectable by law.

"Update(s)" shall mean a redistribution of Software that corrects an error as well as addressing common functional and performance issues.

Alternatively:

"Update(s)" will mean the release of error corrections, intermediate releases to maintain conformity with industry standards, and software deliveries not containing increases in functionality. In a numbering scheme consisting of x.y.z., the "z" represents an Update.

Alternatively:

"Update(s)" shall mean patches and other Error corrections or minor enhancements issued from time to time to Licensor customers who have purchased Software Maintenance and Support from Licensor. An Update typically is identified by a change in a number to the right of the first decimal point in the Software's version number (e.g., 6.0 to 6.1 or 6.1.1).

"Upgrades" will mean both Major and Minor Releases. **"Major Release"** means the introduction of the first release of the Software as well as releases with the addition of significant new functionality, adaptations for new hardware configurations, and/or the incorporation of new major third party software. **"Minor Release"** means releases of error corrections, additions of minor functionality, minor adaptations for new hardware configurations, and adaptations for new releases of third party software. In a numbering scheme consisting of x.y.z, the "x" represents a Major Release, and the "y" represents a Minor Release.

Alternatively:

"Upgrades" shall mean a new release or version of the Software provided to Licensor's customers who have purchased Software Maintenance and Support from Licensor. An Upgrade typically is identified by a change in a number to the left of the first decimal point in the Software's version number (e.g., 6.0 to 7.0). Notwithstanding the foregoing, if any new release or version of a Licensor software product contains the same core functionality as the Software, then such release or version shall be considered and deemed to be an Upgrade. For the sake of clarity, Updates and Upgrades shall be considered and deemed to be the Software under this License Agreement.

Alternatively, a more generalized definition is as follows:

"Upgrade" and its derivatives mean the updates, renovations, enhancements, additions, and/or new versions or releases of Software or Equipment by Supplier. Unless otherwise agreed, financial responsibility for the costs, fees, and expenses associated with an Upgrade of Software or Equipment shall be allocated between the Parties in accordance with Sections ___ and Schedule ___.

"Use" shall mean, in the context of Software, to use (in both source and object code if source code is otherwise to be provided hereunder), copy, execute, reproduce, display, maintain, modify, enhance, distribute, or create Derivative Works.

Alternatively:

"Use" is the right of Customer: (i) to copy, including without limitation, to transmit, any portion of the Software onto CPUs, Networks, desktops, servers, processors, storage units or media; (ii) to transfer any portion of any Software for use on a Network between desktops, CPUs, servers, and other units in the Network; and (iii) to use the Digital System in accordance with the Documentation and this Agreement.

> * ***The definition of "use" is one of the most important in any agreement as it sets the parameters on the licensee's use of the licensed software. The licensee needs to ensure that the definition not only satisfies it present needs but those needs that can be reasonably contemplated for the foreseeable future.***

"User" shall mean a Qualified Employee who uses the Licensed Program for Approved Use under the terms hereof.

"User Limit" shall mean, as applicable, either the maximum number of Qualified Employees permitted to make an Approved Use of the Licensed Program under the terms and conditions of this Schedule ____, or the total number of employees employed by the Licensee, in either case, such User Limit is set forth on Order Form.

"Vendor" means ____________________and any permitted successors and assigns.

"Vendor Underlying Works" are those conceived, invented, created, or acquired by Vendor, rather than by a third party.

"Version" shall mean any delivery of Software that is a Release and/or a collection of Updates.

"WAN" means wide area network.

"Workaround" means a change in the procedures followed or data supplied by Licensee to avoid an Error without substantially impairing Licensee's use of the Software.

"Work Product" means information, documentation, computer programs (and all configurations and set-ups of any such program and all templates reflecting same), and developments and all intermediate and partial versions thereof, including all source code and object code with respect thereto, and all designs, specifications, inventions, discoveries, improvements, materials, program materials, software, flow charts, notes, outlines, lists, compilations, manuscripts, writings, pictorial materials, schematics, templates of configurations and set-up elections regarding the Vendor System, other creations, and the like, whether or not patented or patentable or subject to copyright, or otherwise protectable by law, created, invented, or conceived for the use or benefit of Customer in connection with this Agreement, by Customer, by Vendor, or by any other Person engaged by Customer or Vendor, including work product created pursuant to the Implementation Services Statement of Work, pursuant to the Ongoing Services Statement of Work, or as Custom Programming. Work Product shall not include Residuals or Underlying Works.

"Written Deliverables" means all written reports, requirements documents (including newly created technical and non-technical data embodied therein), specifications, program materials, flow charts, notes, outlines and the like that are developed, conceived, originated, prepared, or generated by Vendor in connection with Vendor's performance under this Agreement including, without limitation, all copyright, trademark, trade secret, and all other proprietary rights therein and derivative works created there from.

Clause Library

(Cross referenced to the text; Unless otherwise noted, Section references correspond to Sections in Chapter 23.B.1)

Index

A. Acceptance (Chapter 4.B.4; § 7)

1. *Acceptance – Deliverables*

Licensee shall have thirty (30) days after delivery of a Deliverable to perform acceptance tests to confirm that the Deliverable conforms to the Acceptance Criteria. If the period or procedures for acceptance testing are not set forth in Exhibit __ Licensee shall provide written notice to Licensor before the end of the thirty (30) day evaluation period if the Deliverables do not conform to the Acceptance Criteria. If Licensee does not provide such notice, the Deliverables shall not be deemed accepted until and upon the date of payment-infill or first productive use, whichever comes later; after which, the Deliverables shall be deemed accepted. Such notice shall describe the nature of the nonconformance. If Licensee gives timely notice that the Deliverable or Licensee's performance is nonconforming, Licensee shall, at no additional cost to Licensee, make and submit to Licensee changes that may reasonably be required to correct the deficiencies described in the notice within fifteen (15) days following receipt of each notice. Unless a different period or procedure is specified in the Statement of Work, Licensee shall have thirty (30) days from receipt of the corrected Deliverable to determine if the Deliverable conforms to the Acceptance Criteria, and the corrected Deliverable shall be deemed accepted by Licensee, unless it provides written notice to Licensor before the end of the thirty (30) day re-evaluation period that the Deliverable still does not conform to the Acceptance Criteria. In the event the corrected Deliverable is still nonconforming, at the sole option of Licensee, Licensee may then terminate the Statement of Work by written notice to Licensor, or elect that the foregoing process continue for one or more additional thirty (30) day intervals until it either terminates the Statement of Work or the Deliverable is accepted as provided herein. Upon acceptance of a Deliverable, Licensee shall promptly pay the designated balance due, if any, under the applicable Statement of Work. The time periods specified herein for the performance of acceptance tests and correction of deficiencies may be modified in the applicable Statement of Work.

2. *Acceptance of Services and Deliverables for Multi-Phase Projects*

1.1 **Acceptance of Services.** To the extent a Statement of Work provides for Services:

(a) **Preliminary Acceptance.** Unless otherwise specified in a Statement of Work, Licensee shall have fifteen (15) business days from the completion of each phase or major milestone to test the Services relating thereto in order to determine whether such Services meet the standards and/or accomplish the objectives or other criteria for such Services as established in the applicable Statement of Work ("Services Preliminary Acceptance Period"). If Licensee does not give notice of Acceptance or non-Acceptance of the Service within the Services Preliminary Acceptance Period, the Service shall be deemed to have been accepted. If Licensee gives notice of non-

Acceptance: (i) Licensee shall describe the reasons for non-Acceptance to Licensor in reasonable detail; (ii) Licensor shall have five (5) business days (or such longer period of time as shall be reasonable under the circumstances) to re-perform the deficient Services until the applicable standards, objectives, and/or other criteria are met to Licensee's reasonable satisfaction; and (iii) a ten (10) calendar day re-testing preliminary acceptance period shall begin.

(b) **Final Acceptance; Multi-Phase Projects.** Upon completion of all related Services for a particular project (including upon completion of an intermediate phase of a project or entire project, as specified in a Statement of Work), and unless a different time frame is provided in the applicable Statement of Work, Licensee shall have fifteen (15) business days after completed performance of the final phase of Services to test whether they meet the specifications set forth in the Statement of Work ("Specifications"), in all material respects (the "Services Final Acceptance Period"), unless a different time frame is specified in a Statement of Work. The Statement of Work shall identify any applicable preliminary and final acceptance milestones, deadlines or other criteria for acceptance. The Services Final Acceptance Period shall not begin until any related Documentation, if any, has been delivered to Licensee. If Licensee does not give notice of Acceptance or non-Acceptance of the Services within the Services Final Acceptance Period, the Services shall be deemed to have been accepted as of the last date of the Services Final Acceptance Period. If Licensee gives notice of non-Acceptance: (i) Licensee shall describe the reasons for non-Acceptance to Licensor in reasonable detail; (ii) Licensor shall have fourteen (14) calendar days (or such longer period of time as shall be reasonable under the circumstances) to re-perform the deficient Services at no additional cost to Licensee until the deficiency is corrected; and (iii) the Services Final Acceptance Period shall begin again. In the event Licensor fails to re-perform a rejected Service to conform to the Specifications, as determined in Licensee's reasonable discretion, Licensee may terminate the applicable Statement of Work immediately and receive from Licensor a refund of the fees previously paid to Licensor for the rejected Services on a pro rata basis commensurate with the deficiency in functionality that is the basis for rejection. If Services are deemed unacceptable despite efforts to correct deficiencies pursuant to the foregoing procedures, and the Parties fail to resolve the matter to their reasonable satisfaction, then either party may submit the matter for dispute resolution pursuant to the procedures provided for in Article ___, (Dispute Resolution). If the Parties intend that all Services and/or Deliverables performed and provided in multiple phases under a Statement of Work are to be subject to final Acceptance testing under this paragraph, because such interim phases culminate in an integrated deployment or other solution, notwithstanding any preliminary acceptance that may have been determined during an intermediate phase of the project, then the Parties shall so explicitly provide in the Statement of Work. To the extent a project involves Deliverables integrated with Services, then the foregoing testing, rejection and refund procedures and remedies shall include all related Deliverables.

1.2 **Acceptance of Deliverables.** To the extent a Statement of Work provides for Deliverables, the Statement of Work shall identify whether the Deliverable will be subject to Licensee review (a "Review Deliverable") or will be subject to Licensee testing (a "Test Deliverable"). Any reference to a "Deliverable" herein shall include reference to a Test Deliverable or a Review Deliverable, as the context requires.

(a) **Preliminary Acceptance.** Unless otherwise specified in the applicable Statement of Work, Licensee shall have fifteen (15) calendar days after receipt to review each Review Deliverable or thirty (30) calendar days to test each Test Deliverable (or portions thereof if such Deliverable is to be delivered in portions as set forth in the applicable Statement of Work) to determine whether it meets the Specifications (the "Preliminary Acceptance Period"). This Preliminary Acceptance Period shall not begin until the Documentation has been delivered to Licensee and the Deliverables are fully installed and operational as determined by the Parties. If Licensee does not give notice of Acceptance or non-Acceptance of the Deliverable within the Preliminary Acceptance Period, the Deliverable shall be deemed to have been accepted. If Licensee gives notice of non-Acceptance, (i) Licensee shall describe the reasons for non-Acceptance to Licensor in reasonable detail; (ii) Licensor shall have five (5) business days (or such longer period of time as shall be reasonable under the circumstances) to correct the Deliverable; and (iii) the Preliminary Acceptance Period shall begin again.

(b) **Final Acceptance; Multi-Phase Projects.** Upon final delivery of all related Deliverables, (including upon completion of an intermediate phase of a project or entire project, as specified in a Statement of Work), Licensee shall have ten (10) calendar days after receipt to review the Review Deliverables or thirty (30) calendar days to test the Test Deliverables to determine whether they meet the Specifications (the "Deliverables Final Acceptance Period"), unless a different time frame is specified in a Statement of Work. This Deliverables Final Acceptance Period shall not begin until the Documentation has been delivered to Licensee and the Deliverables are fully installed and operational as determined by the Parties. If Licensee does not give notice of Acceptance or non-Acceptance of the Deliverables within the Deliverables Final Acceptance Period, the Deliverables shall be deemed to have been accepted as of the last date of the Deliverables Final Acceptance Period. If Licensee gives notice of non-Acceptance, (i) Licensee shall describe the reasons for non-Acceptance to Licensor in reasonable detail; (ii) Licensor shall have fourteen (14) calendar days (or such longer period of time as shall be reasonable under the circumstances) to correct the Deliverables; and (iii) the Deliverables Final Acceptance Period shall begin again. In the event Licensor fails to modify a rejected Deliverable to conform to the Specifications contained in the applicable Statement of Work, as determined in Licensee's reasonable discretion, Licensee may terminate the applicable Statement of Work immediately and receive from Licensor a refund of the fees previously paid to Licensor for the rejected Deliverable on a pro rata basis commensurate with the deficiency in functionality that is the basis for rejection, or if the Deliverable as a whole does not meet Licensee's requirements, then a refund of all fees paid to Licensor for such deliverable. Except as otherwise agreed in advance in writing by Licensor or following any refund under this Section ____, any continuing use by Licensee of the Deliverables for the purposes intended shall constitute deemed acceptance by Client. If Deliverables are deemed unacceptable and the Parties fail to resolve the matter to their reasonable satisfaction, then either party may submit the matter for dispute resolution pursuant to the procedures provided for in Article ___, (Dispute Resolution). If the Parties intend that all Services and/or Deliverables performed and provided in multiple phases under a Statement of Work are to be subject to final Acceptance testing under this paragraph, because such interim phases culminate in an integrated deployment or other solution, notwithstanding any preliminary acceptance that may have been determined during an intermediate phase of the project, then the Parties shall so explicitly provide in the Statement of Work. To the extent a project involves Deliverables integrated with Services, then the foregoing testing, rejection and refund procedures and remedies shall include all related Services.

B. Access to Computer Network

1. Access to Licensee's Network – Neutral

Should it be necessary for Licensor to access and/or use Licensee's computer or network, either by remote means or in-person, it may do so provided that: (i) such need is specifically stated in the applicable SOW, (ii) access is only by Licensor's employees, and (iii) each of such personnel will be issued and always use a unique User ID and password. Access to the Licensee Network by Licensor shall only be upon the express written permission of Licensee's Chief Privacy and Data Security Administrator. Furthermore, Licensor agrees to (i) cause each such personnel to first sign Licensee's Network Usage Policy, (ii) ensure their compliance with appropriate policies and procedures of Licensee, and (iii) promptly report to Licensee any privacy or security incidents.

2. Access to Licensee's Network – Licensee Oriented

Licensor will not access or attempt to access any part of Licensee's computer system, database or information technology service without the prior written consent of the applicable Party (which may be provided via e-mail). Where access is required for performance of Services, Licensor will seek the minimum access required to complete the Services. Licensor will comply with all Licensee computer system access requirements, whether such access is on-site or off-site. Licensor will ensure that each of its personnel having such access: (a) will be assigned a separate log-in ID by Licensee and will use only that ID when logging onto Licensee's computer system; (b) will log-off Licensee's computer system immediately upon completion of each session of service; (c) will not knowingly allow other individuals to log-in and access Licensee's computer system using the individual ID; and (d) will treat the ID and all other information that enables such access as Confidential Information. Licensor will immediately notify Licensee, as applicable, upon termination or reassignment of personnel with access to Licensee computer system so that Licensee may change access codes for such personnel and take other necessary preventive measures to prevent unauthorized access. If Licensee revises the requirements for access to its computer system, Licensee will notify Licensor in writing of the change or additional requirements and Licensor will comply with such new requirements as a prerequisite to further access. Licensor will notify all of its personnel who have access to Licensee's computer system of Licensee's policies regarding computer access. Licensor will be responsible for compliance with such policies by all Licensor personnel performing Services, wherever situated. All Licensor laptop computers and other equipment or devices will have current operating system patches, current virus definitions and weekly updates and scans. Licensor will take commercially reasonable measures to ensure its personnel, computers, equipment and devices do not introduce a virus, harmful code or disabling devices that may damage, interfere with or otherwise adversely affect Licensee's computer, database or system.

C. Arbitration (Chapter 16; § 30)

1. Singapore Arbitration Language

Dispute Resolution

Any dispute arising in connection with this Agreement and which cannot be settled by good faith negotiations between the parties or their nominated representatives shall be submitted to binding arbitration in accordance with the Rules for the Conduct of International Arbitrations for the time being of the Singapore International Arbitration Centre and governed by the International Arbitration Act. During such arbitration, both parties may be legally represented. Three Arbitrators will be nominated, one each by Licensor and the Licensee, with the third, to be the President of the arbitration tribunal, to be nominated by the Singapore International Arbitration Centre or as otherwise mutually agreed. The arbitration shall be conducted in Singapore in the English language.

2. Singapore Arbitration Language – Alternative Language

1.1 En the event of any dispute arising in connection with this Agreement, the parties shall comply with the following dispute resolution process:

(a) The party claiming that a dispute has arisen shall give written notice ("Dispute Notice") to the other party stating details of the matter in dispute and requiring that the meeting be resolved by a meeting between the parties;

(b) The parties shall within fourteen (14) days from the serving of the Dispute Notice, use reasonable efforts and seek in good faith to resolve the dispute, including but not limited to, having a meeting between the senior management of each party.

(c) If the parties cannot resolve the dispute in accordance with Clause 1.1(b) within fourteen (14) days from the serving of the Dispute Notice, the parties may, by mutual agreement:

(i) extend the period for parties to privately negotiate a resolution of the dispute; or

(ii) refer the dispute to mediation by the Singapore Mediation Centre.

1.2 In the absence of agreement under clause 1.1(c) or in the event mediation by the Singapore Mediation Centre is unsuccessful, the dispute shall be forthwith submitted to and finally settled by arbitration in Singapore in accordance with the arbitration rules of the Singapore International Arbitration Centre for the time being in force. The parties may be represented by lawyers in the arbitration. Unless otherwise agreed between parties, the tribunal shall consists of one (1) arbitrator to be mutually agreed and appointed by parties and failing such agreement, to be appointed by the Chairman of the Singapore International Arbitration Centre. Arbitration proceedings shall be conducted wholly in the English language.

1.3 Except where clearly prevented by the area in dispute, both parties agree to continue performing their respective obligations under this Agreement (including the payment of all fees) while the dispute is being resolved unless and until such obligations are terminated or expire in accordance with the provisions of this Agreement.

1.4.1 Nothing in this Agreement prevents either party at any time seeking injunctive or other equitable relief in order to protect its rights.

COMMENT: Singapore is a leading global financial and commercial center. The Singapore International Arbitration Centre is well respected and the location of choice for dispute resolution throughout the Asia region. Singapore has also adopted the UNCITRAL Model Law as the basis for regulating international arbitration.

3. Vietnamese Arbitration Language

1.1 In the event of any dispute arising in connection with this Agreement, the parties shall comply with the following dispute resolution process:

(a) The party claiming that a dispute has arisen shall give written notice ("Dispute Notice") to the other party stating details of the matter in dispute and requiring that the meeting be resolved by a meeting between the parties;

(b) The parties shall within sixty (60) days from the serving of the Dispute Notice, use reasonable efforts and seek in good faith to resolve the dispute, including but not limited to, having a meeting between the senior management of each party.

(c) If the parties cannot resolve the dispute in accordance with Clause 1.1(b) within sixty (60) days from the serving of the Dispute Notice, the parties may, by mutual agreement, extend the period for parties to privately negotiate a resolution of the dispute.

1.2 In the absence of agreement under clause 1.1(c), the dispute shall be forthwith submitted to and finally settled by arbitration in Ho Chi Minh City, Vietnam in accordance with the arbitration rules of the Vietnam International Arbitration Centre for the time being in force. The parties may be represented by lawyers in the arbitration. Unless otherwise agreed between parties, the tribunal shall consist of one (1) arbitrator to be nominated by each party, with the third arbitrator, if not agreed by the parties, to be appointed by the Chairman of the Vietnam International Arbitration Centre. Arbitration proceedings shall be conducted wholly in the English language.

1.3 Except where clearly prevented by the area in dispute, both parties agree to continue performing their respective obligations under this Agreement (including the payment of all fees) while the dispute is being resolved unless and until such obligations are terminated or expire in accordance with the provisions of this Agreement.

1.4 Nothing in this Agreement prevents either party at any time seeking injunctive or other equitable relief in order to protect its rights.

COMMENT: Choice of law is not always a simple decision. Many licensors do not take the time to identify which provisions of the licensor's contract may be unenforceable under the laws of a particular country, in this case Vietnam. A party cannot assume that a clearly written provision will be interpreted in a logical way by a local court as local law may override such provision.

A party should not assume a country's arbitration system will be applied fairly to a foreign entity. Vietnam has chosen not to adopt the UNCITRAL Model Law governing arbitration and the enforcement of arbitral decisions. As such, negotiating arbitration and governing law provisions will likely involve an element of "forum shopping." The licensee may insist on selecting local laws to obtain a "home court" advantage in addition to making it more costly and inconvenient for the licensor to bring an action in Vietnam.

D. Assignment (Chapter 4.A.7; § 22)

1. Divestiture/Assignment (§ 42)

Where permitted by law, the rights of this Agreement may be assigned or not assigned, at the election of Licensee, in whole or in part, to a successor of Licensee's business and/or to any affiliates of Licensee, including any divested entity providing service to Licensee and its affiliates and any entity, that is acquired by Licensee during the term of this Agreement and including, for a period of 12 months after any divestiture, any entity that is divested by Licensee during the term of this Agreement.

Should Licensee, from time to time, sell or otherwise transfer the assets or equity ownership of any Licensee division, affiliate or business unit (all jointly referred to as "Business Unit"), and as part of such transfer **Buyer agrees to provide transitional services to the Business Unit in connection with the transfer of such Business Unit, including the use of the Products and/or Services by Licensor for such Business Unit, then Buyer shall have the right to do so for a period of 12 months after the completion of any such transfer with no additional payment to Licensor.** If Buyer, as part of any agreement with such Business Unit, is required to provide such services for a period beyond 12 months, then Buyer shall have the right to provide such services for up to an additional six months period subject to a mutually agreed upon payment to Licensor.

Licensee shall provide Licensor with thirty (30) days written notice of its intent to assign this Agreement. Licensor shall seek the written consent of Buyer prior to any assignment of this Agreement.

> ***COMMENT:* *The licensor should carefully consider whether to accept this language as it may significantly increase the cost to the licensor. From the licensor's perspective, the licensor should agree to provide such services at a fixed hourly rate.***

2. *Assignments Void*

Any attempted assignment in contravention of this Section ___ shall be void *ab initio*. A Change of Control with respect to a party shall constitute an assignment requiring prior written consent.

E. Audit (Chapter 5.E; §§ 38.J, 9.13(i))

1. *SAS 70 Audit – Neutral (§ 9.13(i))*

Licensor will provide Licensee and its representatives with this information and assistance as reasonably requested to perform the audits but the parties will arrange any assistance so it does not interfere with Licensor's performance. Any third parties performing an audit under this subsection must execute a nondisclosure agreement reasonably satisfactory to Licensor.

1.1 **Optional Statement of Auditing Standards No. 70 (SAS 70) Report.** In addition to granting Licensee access in a fiscal period to conduct an operational audit regarding internal controls on financial reporting, Licensor will provide Licensee, upon request, an auditor's report concerning the Licensor's activities issued under SAS 70. The SAS 70 must be: (i) a "Type II" report; (ii) prepared by a certified public accountant registered with the Public Licensor Accounting Oversight Board; (iii) cover a time period and scope; (iv) the results must be sufficient to evidence a favorable assessment by Licensee of Licensor's internal controls over financial reporting and Licensor auditors' attestation; and (v) reasonably acceptable to Licensee. The SAS 70 report will be provided solely at the expense of Licensor.

1.2 **Results of Operational Audit or Security Assessment.** If any operational audit or security assessment reveals an inadequacy or insufficiency of Licensor's security, confidentiality, privacy practices and standards, disaster recovery capabilities, or fail-over planning or ineffectiveness of internal controls, Licensor will promptly develop and implement a corrective action plan reasonably satisfactory to Licensee. The cost of developing and implementing this plan will be Licensor's sole responsibility. Licensee may perform one or more additional follow up operational audits or security assessments to verify performance under the corrective action plan without regard to the once-per-year limitation.

2. *SAS 70 Audit – Licensee Oriented (§ 9.13(i))*

In addition to its other obligations under this Section ____, Licensor shall cause a Type II Statement of Auditing Standards (**SAS**) 70 audit (or equivalent audit) to be conducted on an annual or more frequent basis for each Licensor shared services facility at or from which the Services are provided to Licensee and/or the Eligible Recipients. Licensor shall permit Licensee to participate in the planning of each such audit, confer with Licensee as to the scope and timing of each such audit and accommodate Licensee's requirements and concerns to the extent practicable. Unless otherwise agreed by the Parties, each SAS 70 audit shall be designed and conducted to facilitate periodic compliance reporting by Licensee and the Eligible Recipients under the Sarbanes-Oxley Act of 2002 (and implementing regulations promulgated by the United States Securities and Exchange Commission and Public Licensor Accounting Oversight Board) and comparable Laws in other jurisdictions. To the extent the resulting audit report is relevant to Licensee and/or the Eligible Recipients, Licensor shall provide a copy of such report to Licensee and its independent auditors for review and comment as soon as reasonably practicable and in all events within thirty (30) days of completion. Licensor shall respond to such report in accordance with Section _____.

To the extent Licensee provides reasonable notice and requests that, in addition to the Type II SAS 70 audit described above, Licensor conduct a Licensee-specific Type II SAS 70 audit, Licensor shall do so and Licensee will be financially responsible for the third party auditors fees and expense for such audit (provided Licensor notifies Licensee of such fee and expense, obtains Licensee's approval, and uses commercially reasonable efforts to minimize such fees and expense). If, however, Licensor undertakes additional or different Type II SAS 70 audits (or equivalent audits) of Licensor Facilities at, from or through which Services are provided to Licensee and/or the Eligible Recipients (other than customer-specific audits requested and paid for by other Licensor customers), Licensor shall accord Licensee the rights described in the preceding paragraph with respect to such audits.

3. *Right of Audit – Limiting Right of Licensee to Audit Licensor's Fees – Licensor Oriented*

Only to the extent necessary to verify the accuracy and completeness of fees and out-of-pocket expenses **or to** enable Licensor and Licensee to meet applicable legal, regulatory and contractual requirements (in each case to the extent applicable to the Services and/or the fees for such Service)

> ***COMMENT: While this language appears to benefit the licensor by qualifying the licensee's right to audit, the licensor should insist on inserting greater detail to limit the licensee's ability to conduct a broad based audit instead of a narrowly focused audit. This language gives the licensee carte blanche to conduct the audit.***

4. Right of Audit – Prohibition on Licensor Auditing Number of Licensee Users – Licensee Oriented (§ 8.J)

Based on the enterprise scope of license, there is no need for and Licensor shall not request an audit of Licensee. If Licensor believes that Licensee is in violation of [**the license grant provisions**], **Licensor can request a written compliance certificate provided that such certificate shall not create a separate cause of action.**

> ***COMMENT: Licensors should reject language similar to that set forth above. Further, this language prevents the licensor from bringing an action against the licensee in the event the licensee provides the licensor a fraudulent certificate.***

5. Right of Audit – Allows Licensee to Audit Licensor Books to Confirm Proper Billing by Licensor for Services

Licensee and its authorized representatives shall have the right at all reasonable times during the term of this Agreement and for a period of two (2) years thereafter to inspect and audit Licensor's books, payrolls, and other records relating to matters under this Agreement for which payment by Licensee is to be or has been made on the basis of (a) Licensor's actual costs or reimbursement of actual costs incurred and paid by Licensor and (b) unit prices for materials and fixed unit rates for the period worked by Licensor's personnel and equipment; provided, however, that such inspection and audit of charges based on fixed unit rates and unit prices shall be limited to Licensor's personnel schedules for periods paid by Licensor, time sheets, payroll classification data, equipment schedules and material issue and delivery records.

6. Right of Audit – Allows Licensee to Ensure Licensor is Complying with Applicable Laws and Licensee Policies – Licensee Oriented

1. Licensor shall maintain appropriate documentation necessary to demonstrate Licensor's compliance with applicable law, regulation and Licensee policy and as otherwise necessary to comply with applicable law and the terms of the License Agreement between Licensee and Licensor (the "Agreement").

2. Licensee reserves its right to confirm and validate Licensor's compliance with the terms of the Agreement through periodic audits of Licensor's documents and systems. Licensee' representatives, designees, auditors and regulators as Licensee may from time to time designate ("Licensee' Auditors") shall, upon reasonable notice, have the right to audit Licensor's documents, systems and operations, and conduct

interviews with Licensor employees, permitted subcontractors and agents. Licensor shall provide access at all reasonable times and after reasonable notice to Licensee' Auditors to any facility or part of a facility at which Licensor is providing the Services and to any and all data and records relating to the Services provided to Licensee. The foregoing audit rights shall include when applicable, audits (a) of practices and procedures, (b) of systems, (c) of security practices and procedures, (d) of disaster recovery and backup procedures, and (e) necessary to enable Licensee to meet applicable law and/or regulations.

3. The expense of an audit or examination shall be borne by Licensee unless an audit reveals that Licensor or permitted subcontractor or agent is not in compliance with the terms of the Agreement or there has been an overcharge. If, as a result of an audit, it is determined that Licensor has overcharged Licensee or has charged Licensee for any time involving the management of employees of the Licensor with regard to administrative tasks performed for the benefit of Licensor and not directed to the management or conduct of a Licensee project, Licensee shall notify Licensor of the amount of such overcharge and Licensor shall promptly pay to Licensee the amount of the overcharge, plus interest at the rate of 1.5% per month calculated from the date of receipt by Licensor of the overcharged amount until the date of payment to Licensee. The expenses associated with correcting deficiencies (including payment of any government-levied penalties) that may be identified as a result of the audit or government inspection/enforcement action shall be the responsibility of Licensor unless otherwise agreed upon, in writing, by both parties.

4. Licensor shall fully cooperate with Licensee's auditors and/or governmental authorities in connection with audit conducted under terms of the Agreement. Further, Licensor shall notify Licensee, within 24 hours, promptly by telephone or by email if any governmental or regulatory authority requests an inspection or makes written or oral inquiries of Licensor regarding any aspect of Licensee' activities pursuant to the Agreement. Unless otherwise required by applicable law or regulation, Licensor shall not allow access to any governmental or regulatory authority relating to such activities without giving Licensee the right to have a representative present. Licensor and Licensee shall cooperate in resolving any concerns of any governmental or regulatory authority. Licensor shall promptly notify Licensee by telephone or by email if Licensor believes that the actions or inactions of any governmental or regulatory authority, including the issuance or failure to issue any report, permit, or license, may cause a negative impact on Licensor's ability to perform the Services.

5. Licensor shall retain all records, documents and other information required to meet Licensee' audit requirements under the Agreement for the longer of (a) five years from the termination or expiration of the Agreement, (b) until final resolution of any dispute concerning the Agreement or (c) as long as required by law, regulation or Licensee Policy.

6. Licensor shall promptly make available the results of a review or audit conducted by Licensor, its affiliates, permitted subcontractors or agents (including internal and external auditors), relating to Licensor's operating practices and procedures to the extent relevant to the Services or Licensee (including, e.g., any SAS-70 reports) to the Licensee Senior Director, Corporate Compliance Audit or other individual

identified by Licensee. Licensor shall, and shall cause permitted subcontractors and agents to provide all audit-related materials to Licensee at Licensor's expense.

7. Without limiting the generality of this Agreement, upon ten (10) days' prior notice from Licensee to Licensor that Licensee wishes an information security audit to be performed, Licensor shall conduct or allow Licensee to conduct, as specified in Licensee' notice, such information security audit to test the compliance with generally accepted industry standards or such other security standards and procedures as determined by Licensee and as established by Licensee policy. To the extent that Licensor is conducting an information security audit, this information security audit shall be conducted either by Licensor or a third party designated by Licensor which is acceptable to Licensee, in accordance with standards acceptable to Licensee, and at no expense to Licensee. To the extent that Licensee elects to conduct an information security audit pursuant to this Section 7, Licensor acknowledges and agrees that Licensee Auditors may conduct an information security audit of the environment used to provide the Services, including security, policies, and operational matters. Regardless as to who is conducting the audit, Licensor shall, at no expense to Licensee: (a) provide any Licensee or Licensor designated auditor with all assistance and resources reasonably required to conduct any information security audit authorized pursuant to this Section 7, and (b) remedy any deficiencies identified during any such information security audit as directed by Licensee. Licensee may only provide Licensor with a notice requiring an audit pursuant to this Section 7 once per calendar year unless Licensee in good faith believes that there is a potential or actual information security risk or breach.

7. Source Code Audit - Allows licensor to audit Escrow Agent to confirm compliance with Source Code release terms

Escrow Agent shall maintain, for two (2) years from the calendar year in question, adequate records concerning its treatment of the Source Code so that Licensor may determine that Escrow Agent has taken adequate precautions to prevent unauthorized use or disclosure of the Source Code. Escrow Agent agrees that Licensor may, directly or through its advisors, inspect, review and obtain copies of such records from Escrow Agent upon reasonable notice and subject to confidentiality agreements reasonably satisfactory to Escrow Agent for the purposes of confirming Escrow Agent's treatment of the Source Code. Such audits shall occur not more often than once per year (unless the previous audit disclosed material deficiencies that made an inadvertent release highly probable). ***The parties agree that the failure by Escrow Agent to strictly adhere to Section _____ (Release of Source Code) shall not be deemed to be a material breach of this Agreement unless such failure causes a release of the Source Code that cannot be remedied.***

> **COMMENT: Licensors should be hesitant to agree to the last sentence as it potentially releases the escrow agent from any liability for its wrong-**

ful actions. The escrow agent should bear responsibility for its failure to comply with its contractual obligations.

F. Bankruptcy (Chapter 17)

1. Termination in the Event of Bankruptcy

In the event of Licensor's bankruptcy, Licensee may by giving written notice to Licensor, terminate this Agreement in whole or in part and without charge, as of the date specified in such notice of termination. Any licenses granted under this Agreement or which are provided pursuant to this Agreement are intended to be licenses of rights in intellectual property as contemplated by Section 365(n) of the United States Bankruptcy Code, 11 U.S.C. § 365(n). In the event that Licensor becomes a debtor under the United States Bankruptcy Code, it is the intent of the Parties that Licensee shall have all benefits granted to licensees under the provisions of the United States Bankruptcy Code including, without limitation, Section 365(n) of Title 11 of the U.S.Code (11 U.S. 365(n)).

2. Affirmation of Rights Under Section 365(n) of the Bankruptcy Code (Chapter 23.C.4 § 13)

All rights and licenses granted under or pursuant to this Agreement by Licensor to Licensee (including the license) are, and shall otherwise be deemed to be, for the purposes of Section 365(n) of the United States Bankruptcy Code (the "**Bankruptcy Code**"), licenses to rights in "intellectual property" as defined under Section 101 (35A) of the Bankruptcy Code. As licensee of such rights under this Agreement, Licensee shall retain and may fully exercise all of its rights and elections under the Bankruptcy Code. Upon the event of the commencement of bankruptcy proceedings by or against Licensor under the Bankruptcy Code, Licensee shall be entitled to retain all of its rights under this Agreement (including the license rights).

3. Affirmation of Rights Under Section 365(n) of the Bankruptcy Code – Licensee Oriented (Chapter 23.C.4 § 13)

In the event Licensor voluntarily or involuntarily becomes subject to the protection of the Bankruptcy Code and Licensor or the trustee in bankruptcy rejects this Agreement under Section 365 of the Bankruptcy Code, Licensee shall have the right to: (a) treat this Agreement as terminated; or (b) retain Licensee's rights under this Agreement, specifically including the right to exercise its rights granted herein to the Licensed Software (and to all work-in-progress relating thereto). Failure by Licensee to assert its right to retain its benefits to the intellectual property embodied in the Licensed Software pursuant to Section 365(n)(1)(B) of the Bankruptcy Code with respect to an executory contract rejected by Licensor or the trustee in bankruptcy shall not be construed by the courts as a termination of such contract by Licensee under Section 365(n)(1)(A) of the Bankruptcy Code.

4. Termination Due To Adverse Changes in Licensor's Financial Circumstances

If Licensor (i) files a petition in bankruptcy; (ii) has an involuntary petition in bankruptcy filed against it which is not challenged within twenty (20) days and dismissed within sixty (60) days; (iii) becomes insolvent, (iv) makes a general assignment for the benefit of creditors; (v) admits in writing its inability to pay its debts as they mature; (vi) has a receiver appointed for its assets; (vii) has any significant portion of its assets attached; or (viii) experiences a material negative change in its net assets (i.e., total assets minus total liabilities); then Customer may by giving written notice to Licensor, terminate this Agreement in whole or in part and without charge, as of the date specified in such notice of termination. Any licenses granted under this Agreement or which are provided pursuant to this Agreement are intended to be licenses of rights in intellectual property as contemplated by Section 365(n) of the United States Bankruptcy Code, 11 U.S.C. § 365(n). In the event that Licensor becomes a debtor under the United States Bankruptcy Code, it is the intent of the Parties that Customer shall have all benefits granted to licensees under the provisions of the United States Bankruptcy Code including, without limitation, Section 365(n) of Title 11 of the U.S. Code (11 U.S. 365(n)).

G. Benchmarking (Chapter 5.K)

1. Use of Benchmarking Data – Licensor Oriented (§ 8.B)

With respect to any benchmark reports, Licensee acknowledges that the contents of each benchmark report are based upon information contained in Licensor's database. Licensee acknowledges Licensor's claim that the contents of such database belong solely to Licensor and may be used by Licensor in future engagements for other customers. Licensee also acknowledges that the information contained in each benchmark report and other deliverables may become a part of Licensor's database and may be used in future engagements for other customers. Licensor cannot use any Confidential Information in Licensor's database unless such data are coded to preserve Licensee's anonymity and the security of its information. Under no circumstances may Licensor include any Personal Information that Licensee has identified as Personal Information in the database.

H. Boilerplate (Chapter 6)

1. *Code of Business Conduct*

Licensee has adopted a Code of Business Conduct ("Code"), which governs the conduct of every employee of Licensee and establishes ethical standards for its employees. Certain significant provisions of the Code include conflicts of interest, gifts or gratuities, kickbacks, entertainment, improper payments, and protecting information. A copy of the Code is available at http://www.customercodeofconduct.com. Licensor agrees to support this Code by avoiding action that could place a Licensee employee in violation of this Code. Licensor shall promptly notify Licensee if it becomes aware of a violation of this Code.

> ***COMMENT: At a minimum, the party modifying the URL site should have the obligation to notify the other party of any changes to the contructual terms set forth in the URL as a condition precedent to the other party being bound by such changes. Otherwise, the other party will have to continually monitor the URL to identify potential changes. A party should be hesitant to agree to be bound by a policy set forth in a URL as the policy will likely change binding the party without regard to cost or effort.*** See, Margae, Inc. v. Clear Link Technologies, LLC., ***2008 WL 2465450 (June 16, 2008 D. Utah 2008) (amendment of contract between two sophisticated parties by one party posting modifications online not unconscionable).***

2. *Joinder – Addition of Additional Licensee Related Parties to License (§§ 1.2, 1.2.A)*

Additional participants may become Parties to this Agreement by executing a joinder counterpart signature page hereto which is acknowledged in writing by Parent and may contain attachments thereto relating to such Affiliate to the extent agreed to by Parent. Thereafter, Exhibit A (List of Participating Affiliates) will be amended to include such new participant.

3. *Use of English Language*

Multiple languages are spoken throughout the Licensee's workplace and facilities; as such, there is no rule that English must be spoken at all times at Licensee workplaces. Licensee is guided by common sense and mutual respect in the workplace. The most important principle is that all participants understand the business conversations that take place; *therefore*, Licensee expects that when multilingual personnel, including Licensor's Representatives, are involved in a business discussion with others, one or more of whom only speak English or the dominant local language spoken at the Licensee's facility where the Services are being performed, the discussion will naturally shift to English or such local language, not only out of respect and courtesy but to ensure that business is conducted efficiently, safely and in compliance with laws and regulations. Individuals should otherwise feel free to speak their native language or whatever language they choose.

4. Covenant of Licensor's Future Performance – Licensee Oriented

Licensee shall have the right to require Licensor to provide Licensee with adequate assurance that Licensor will perform its obligations in a timely fashion in accordance with the License. Should Licensee request Licensor to provide adequate assurance, or a statement by Licensor that Licensor cannot or will not perform in a timely fashion in accordance with the License, or any act of omission of Licensor which makes it, in Licensee's judgment, improbable at the time that Licensor will perform in accordance with the License shall permit Licensee to terminate the License for default under Paragraph ___ (Termination).

> ***COMMENT: The Licensor should not agree to the inclusion of this language as it creates a right of anticipatory breach that may not otherwise exist. Further, it may create additional liability on the licensor's behalf if the licensor provides such adequate assurance and later breaches. This language is overreaching and overbearing, providing the licensee with a remedy but not a right it already has. If the licensee is concerned about the licensor's ability to meet certain delivery obligations, the licensee can protect itself through the inclusion of milestones in the license agreement.***

5. Covenant of Further Assurances – Mutual

Licensee and Licensor covenant and agree that, subsequent to the execution and delivery of this Agreement and without any additional consideration, each of Licensee and Licensor shall execute and deliver any further legal instruments and perform any acts which are or may become necessary to effectuate the purposes of this Agreement.

6. Electronic/Facsimile Signatures

This Agreement may be validly executed via facsimile transmission or through other electronic means showing the signatures of the parties and each such reproduced copy of this Agreement shall constitute an original Agreement for all purposes.

7. Counterparts/Facsimile Signatures

This Agreement may be executed in one or more duplicate originals, all of which together shall be deemed one and the same instrument. This Agreement shall be binding on the Parties through facsimile signatures, with originals to follow by regular mail or overnight courier.

8. Exclusivity – Agreement Does not Grant Licensor Exclusive Right to Licensee's Business

This Agreement with Licensor is not exclusive, and Licensee may, at its sole discretion, elect to utilize the services of additional vendors to perform services such as the Services performed by Licensor hereunder.

9. Notice Provision for International Contracts

All notices, demands and other communications to be given or delivered under or by reason of the provisions of this Agreement will be in writing, in the English language, and will be deemed to have been given (a) when delivered if personally delivered by hand, (b) when received if sent by a nationally or internationally recognized overnight courier service (receipt requested), (c) seven (7) Business Days after being mailed, if sent by first class mail, return receipt requested, or (d) when receipt is acknowledged by an affirmative act of the party receiving notice, if sent by facsimile, e-mail, telecopy or other electronic transmission device (provided that such an acknowledgement does not include an acknowledgment generated automatically by a facsimile, e-mail, telecopy machine or other electronic transmission device). Notices, demands and communications to Licensor and Licensee will, unless another address is specified in writing, be sent to the address indicated below:

If to Licensee:
Name
Company
Street
City, State Zip Code

With a copy of legal notices to (which shall not constitute notice):

If to Licensor:
Name
Company
Street
City, State Zip Code

With a copy of legal notices to (which shall not constitute notice):

COMMENT: Neither party should agree that a notice is effective within a set number of days after mailing. Both U.S. and international mail are notoriously unreliable. As such, notice should only be effective upon receipt. Notices should not be sent via email or fax as the chance for mis-delivery or non-delivery is significant. For example, if the intended beneficiary moves, the sending party may still receive confirmation of receipt from the receiving fax even though the intended beneficiary never received the notice. Similarly, a recipient may receive an email while on an extended absence from the office and have no knowledge of an email's content, but yet the period for any required action has begun.

10. Prior Review and Counsel

Each party agrees that (a) it was provided a fair and reasonable time to evaluate this Agreement and to negotiate the terms and conditions of this Agreement, (b) it has had a fair and reasonable opportunity to consult with an attorney at law of its choice licensed to practice law in such party's country or state of residence (which attorney is not and was not the other party's attorney), and (c) it has read and fully understands this Agreement and its terms and conditions. Each party agrees that it is not acting under undue influence or based on unwritten promises in executing this Agreement and that execution of this Agreement is done freely, knowingly and voluntarily.

11. Pronouns

All personal pronouns used in this Agreement shall include the other gender, whether used in the masculine or feminine or neuter gender; and the singular shall include the plural whenever and as often as may be appropriate.

12. Relationship of Parties

The Parties acknowledge that they are independent contractors, and nothing set forth in this Agreement shall be deemed or construed to render the Parties as joint venturers, partners or employer and employee. Under no circumstances shall Licensee be considered the employer of any Licensor personnel, nor shall Licensor have any right with respect to any employee of Licensee.

13. Right to Provide Services to Other Parties (§ 9.12)

Licensee recognizes that Licensor's employees performing the Services under this Agreement and the Statements of Work issued hereunder may perform similar services for others, and this Agreement shall not prevent Licensor from providing services or developing materials that are competitive with those developed or provided hereunder regardless of any similarity to such services or materials, provided, however, that Licensor shall not use or infringe upon any Confidential Information of Licensee, any Deliverable or any of Licensee's other proprietary and intellectual property rights in the performance of such services for others.

> ***COMMENT:** The licensor should seek to include an affirmative statement in the license agreement that the licensor can provide similar services to other potential customers regardless of whether the potential customer is a competitor of the customer. By addressing this issue in the contract, the licensor can avoid any subsequent problems that may arise if the customer later seeks to limit the licensor's ability to provide services to the third parties.*

14. Reference to Dates and Days

All references to dates and days shall be according to the Gregorian calendar. Days shall mean consecutive calendar days.

15. Specific Performance (§ 5.3.4)

Notwithstanding the procedures set forth in Article __ (Dispute Resolution), in the event of any actual or threatened default in, or breach of, any of the terms, conditions and provisions of this Agreement or any Ancillary Agreement, the party or parties who are to be hereby or thereby aggrieved shall have the right to specific performance and injunctive or other equitable relief of its rights under this Agreement or such Ancillary Agreement, in addition to any and all other rights and remedies at law or in equity, and all such rights and remedies shall be cumulative. The other party or parties shall not oppose the granting of such relief. The parties to this Agreement and any Ancillary Agreement agree that the remedies at law for any breach or threatened breach hereof or thereof, including monetary damages, are inadequate compensation for any loss and that any defense in any action for specific performance that a remedy at law would be adequate is waived. Any requirements for the securing or posting of any bond with such remedy are waived.

16. Specific Performance – Alternate Language (§ 5.3.4)

The parties hereto agree that irreparable damage would occur in the event any provision of this Agreement were not performed by a party in accordance with the terms hereof and that, prior to the termination of this Agreement pursuant to Section __ (Termination), the parties shall be entitled to specific performance of the terms hereof, in addition to any other remedy at law or equity. The parties acknowledge that each party shall be entitled to an injunction or injunctions to prevent breaches of this Agreement by the other party or to enforce specifically the terms and provisions of this Agreement, in addition to any other remedies available at law or in equity.

COMMENT: A Licensor should never agree to accept the remedy of specific performance. Although this language is mutual, in practicality, it has limited application to the licensee as usually the licensee's only obligation is payment. If the licensee breaches the terms of the license agreement or its confidentiality obligations, the licensor will likely be able to obtain injunctive relief.

17. Structural Change in Licensor's Business

Licensor shall promptly notify Licensee of any material changes in its structure or operations occurring during the term of this Agreement, including, without limitation: material changes in Licensor's composition, ownership, management, financial condition, information systems, insurance coverages or other matters materially affecting Licensor's operations.

18. Trading in Securities

Each party hereto shall refrain from trading in securities of the other party while in possession of material non-public information pertaining to the other party.

19. Waivers of Default

Waiver by any party hereto or to this or any Ancillary Agreement of any default by any other party hereto or thereto of any provision of this Agreement or such Ancillary Agreement shall not be deemed a waiver by the waiving party of any subsequent or other default.

20. Sublicense Agreements

Licensee agrees to forward to Licensor a copy of any and all sublicense agreements promptly upon execution by the parties.

21. Remedies Not Exclusive

Subject to Section ___ (Arbitration and Disputes), no remedy conferred by any of the specific provisions of this Agreement is intended to be exclusive of any other remedy, and each and every remedy will be cumulative and will be in addition to every other remedy given hereunder or now or hereafter existing at law or in equity or by statute or otherwise. The election of any one or more remedies will not constitute a waiver of the right to pursue other available remedies.

22. Order of Precedence

In the event of any conflict or inconsistency between the terms and conditions of this Agreement and the terms and conditions of any Statement of Work, the terms and conditions of this Agreement shall control.

23. Equitable Relief

Such equitable relief shall be in addition, and without prejudice, to any other remedies available to the non-breaching Party at law or under this Agreement for any such breach or threatened breach. If either Party seeks injunctive relief, such action shall not constitute a waiver of the provisions of this Agreement to arbitrate, which shall continue to govern any and every dispute between the Parties including, without limitation, the right of damages, permanent injunctive relief, and any other remedy at law or in equity. For the avoidance of doubt, and consistent with Section 3 of the Arbitration Schedule (See Form 23.I.10), the Parties agree that such equitable relief may be sought from any court of competent jurisdiction.

24. Time of Performance – Alternate Language to Time is of the Essence

Licensor and Licensee will use commercially reasonable efforts to fulfill their respective obligations in a timely manner in order to achieve the agreed milestones and dates set forth in the Statement of Work.

25. Certification of Compliance with Terms of Agreement

Upon request by Licensee, Licensor shall provide Licensee with reasonable assurances of Licensor's compliance with the terms of this Agreement and any Exhibit(s). Reasonable assurances may include, but are not limited to, Licensor's signed certification of such compliance, as it applies to certain requirements, and/or the Agreement or Exhibit(s) generally.

26. Governing Law and Jurisdiction – Providing for English Law

This Agreement shall be governed by and construed in accordance with the laws of England, to the exclusion of the Rules on the Conflict of Laws ("Private International Law") that lead to the application of the laws of any other jurisdiction. All disputes arising out of or in connection with this Agreement shall be finally and exclusively settled through arbitration in accordance with the rules of the London Court of International Arbitration. The arbitral tribunal shall be composed of three (3) arbitrators and the place of arbitration shall be London, England. The language to be used in the arbitral proceedings, as well as of the award, shall be English.

The award rendered in any arbitration commenced hereunder shall be final and conclusive, and enforcement thereof may be entered in any court or authority having jurisdiction for its enforcement.

I. Breach (Chapter 4.B.5; § 5)

1. Problem Management

The Licensor shall be responsible for tracking, managing, and resolving any unscheduled event that adversely affects the Services (each a "Problem") arising from or relating to the Services ("Problem Management"). The Licensor's general responsibilities with respect to Problem Management shall include the following steps:

1.1 Licensor will log reported Problems with respect to the Services upon receipt of notice from Licensee, automated alarm, or other source. Licensor shall identify and log Problems arising in the performance of the Services with the appropriate Licensee level-1 help desk support. For each Problem, Licensee shall assign a severity level and the Licensor will prioritize resolution of Problems in accordance with the Services Agreement.

1.2 Licensor will monitor, control, and manage each Problem arising from or relating to the Services until it is corrected or resolved, including reporting on charge related outages. The Subcontractors will provide any assistance that Licensor may reasonably request in monitoring, controlling, and managing Problems. To the extent a Problem does not arise from or relate to the Services, Licensor shall refer such Problem to the appropriate entity, as identified by Licensee, for resolution.

1.3 Licensor will correct or resolve Problems within the scope of the Licensor's responsibilities. Resolution of a Problem will be subject to the Licensee level-1 help desk's verification that the Problem has been resolved.

1.4 Licensor will adhere to the procedures for Problem escalation, review and reporting specified by Licensee in writing, and also take appropriate measures to avoid reoccurrence of Problems.

1.5 Licensor will perform Problem analysis, including identification of the source of the Problem.

1.6 Licensor will monitor, measure, and provide reports on Problems including statistics on the types of Problems, total number of Problems, outstanding Problems, resolution times (including the average time to resolve Problems), and as otherwise required to report the Licensor's compliance with the requirements of each of the related agreements. Licensor shall undertake best efforts to improve the average time to resolve Problems.

1.7 Licensor shall maintain communications with the appropriate Licensee level-1 help desk support on Problems through resolution. Licensor shall, for each Problem, provide prompt notification to Licensee of system outages on critical systems and otherwise provide the appropriate level 1 help desk support with regular and timely progress updates (at least hourly with respect to Level-1 Problems) that clearly indicate the nature of the Problem, the estimated time to completion, and potential short-term alternatives. Licensor shall make known to the appropriate Licensee level-1 help desk support information regarding the status of Severity 1 Problems and Severity 2 Problems on at least a daily basis or more frequently as appropriate. Licensor shall track and report any backlog of unresolved Problems.

1.8 Licensor shall maintain a Problem tracking and management tool. Such tool shall include a mechanism to capture, store, and retrieve solutions for reuse by Licensor Personnel and Licensee. Licensor shall grant Licensee access to monitor and view the Problem management database on an ongoing basis upon the request of Licensee authorized personnel. In addition, Licensor shall have access to, and leverage, for reuse any Licensor-wide cross-customer solutions from central problem resolution databases maintained by the Licensor.

1.9 Licensor shall provide or dispatch support specialists to provide on-site troubleshooting and maintenance response as necessary to identify and resolve Problems.

1.10 Licensor shall engage and manage third party suppliers and vendors as necessary to localize and resolve Problems that arise from or relate to the Services as received from the Licensee level-1 help desk support, automated alarm or other source.

2. *Walk in Rights – Licensee's rights to assume licensor's subcontracts in event of licensor's breach (§ 5.3.7)*

If, (i) there is a dispute between Licensor and any Subcontractor; (ii) Licensor is in breach of this Agreement; and (iii) the applicable Subcontractor elects to exercise its rights to terminate the applicable Subcontract, then Licensee will have the right to assume the rights and responsibilities of Licensor ("Step In") under the Subcontract as such rights and responsibilities would have existed under the Subcontract on the date that Licensee exercises its Step In rights (the "Step In Date") had Licensor not been in breach. If Licensee exercises its rights to Step In under a Subcontract, (a) Licensee will not be liable for any breaches of Licensor under the Subcontract and will not be obligated to cure any such breaches; (b) Licensee will have the rights and responsibilities of Licensor arising on or after the Step In Date, including the obligation to pay the Subcontractor for any services performed for Licensee under the Subcontract on or after the Step In Date; and (c) the Subcontractor will not be entitled to terminate the Subcontract for any grounds accruing prior to the Step In Date or based upon any action or inaction by Licensor.

> ***COMMENT:** To protect its interests, the Licensee should insist on the right to assume the vendor's contract with the Licensor's subcontractors. By doing so, the Licensee can hopefully avoid any disruptions in the project and also have a better understanding of the role each subcontractor plays in the project.*

3. *Electronic Self-Help*

Licensor agrees that in the event of any dispute with Licensee regarding an alleged breach of this Agreement or for any other reason, Licensor will not use any type of electronic means to prevent or interfere with Licensee's use of any system or Deliverable created for Licensee under this Agreement or any SOW without first obtaining a valid court order authorizing same. Licensee shall be given proper notice and an opportunity to be heard in connection with any request for such a court order. Licensor understands that a breach of this provision could foreseeably cause substantial harm to Licensee and to numerous third parties having business relationships with Licensee. No limitation of liability shall apply to a breach of this paragraph.

J. Change Management (Chapter 5.D; § 9.8)

1. *Change Management (§ 9.8)*

Change Management

1.1 **"Change"** means any material addition to, modification or removal of any aspect of the Software or the Services or the IT Infrastructure. ***"Change Request"*** means a written request for a change submitted by a Party. ***"Change Management Process"*** means a written procedure for considering, analyzing, approving, and carrying out Changes designed to ensure that only desirable Changes are made and that Changes are carried out in a controlled manner with minimal disruption to the Services or the Software and Licensee's and its Affiliates' business operations. Notwithstanding any implication to the contrary in the provisions below, the Licensor will coordinate all Changes with Licensee.

1.2 Working in consultation with Licensee, Licensor will develop a Change Management Process. The Change Management Process will provide, at a minimum, that:

1.2.1 Any Equipment and Software provided by or on behalf of Licensor that connects to Licensee's IT environment will comply with Licensee's enterprise and application architecture, IT standards (including security standards), and strategic direction and will only be introduced into the IT Infrastructure in accordance with the Change Management Process.

1.2.2 No Change will be implemented without Licensee's approval except as may be necessary on a temporary basis to maintain the continuity of the Services. Licensor will document and report emergency changes to Licensee no later than the next business day after the Change is made.

1.2.3 Licensor will schedule all Changes (other than emergency Changes) so as not to unreasonably affect Licensee's (or its Affiliates') business operations or degrade the Services or the Software. The Licensor will coordinate closely with Licensee on all Changes so as to prevent any disruption from occurring as a result of conflicting or inconsistent Changes being undertaken.

1.2.4 On a monthly basis, the Licensor will prepare a rolling quarterly "look-ahead" schedule for ongoing and planned Changes for the next three (3) months. The Licensor will monitor and report the status of Changes against the applicable schedule and without jeopardizing the Master Schedule.

1.2.5 Licensor will not make any Change that may require Licensee to install a new version, release or upgrade of, or replacement for, any Software or equipment or to modify any Software or equipment without first obtaining Licensee's approval, which Licensee may withhold in its discretion.

1.2.6 Upon Licensee's request, the Licensor will perform a comparison at a reasonable and mutually agreed level of detail, between the amount of resources required by the affected Software and Equipment to perform a representative sample of the processing being performed for Licensee immediately prior to the Change and immediately after the Change. Licensee will not be required to pay for increased resource usage resulting from a Change except to the extent Licensee approved the Change after notice from Licensor of the increased resource usage.

1.2.7 Licensor will not make any Change except in accordance with the Change Management Process and with Licensee's approval. Licensee will not be obliged to approve Changes requested by Licensor and, conversely, Licensor will not be obliged to carry out any proposed Change that Licensee does not approve.

1.3 If Licensee submits a Change Request to a Licensor, Licensor (working with any Subcontractor(s), as applicable) will prepare and submit to Licensee without undue delay (and in any event within thirty (30) days) a proposal for carrying out the Change. The proposal will contain a proposed plan for carrying out the Change, an assessment of the effect of carrying out the Change on the charges under the Services Agreement, and an assessment of the impact of the Change on the Services and the Software, including an assessment as to whether the Change would adversely affect the specifications, functionality, operability, performance, accuracy, speed, responsiveness, quality, or resource efficiency of any systems or Services or the Software or require any material changes to Licensee's (or its Affiliates') facilities, systems, equipment or Software.

1.4 Except as otherwise approved by Licensee in writing, Licensor will bear all costs and expenses associated with making a Change or resulting from implementation of a Change.

1.5 By giving written notice within a reasonable time, Licensee may accept a proposal for Change or reject it. Should the Parties agree on carrying out a Change, a written document will be prepared describing the Change and its effects on the Services and the Software, the charges, and any affected components of the Services Agreement (a ***"Change Order")***. Licensor will not begin performing any proposed Change until it has been authorized by a Change Order signed by a duly authorized representative of Licensee. If Licensor does so, it will be deemed to have provided such performance gratuitously.

1.6 If an approved Change would result in New Services or a change in any of the related agreements, the Change must be authorized via a contract amendment or modification made pursuant to Section _____ (Contract Amendments and Modifications) of the Services Agreement.

COMMENT: Change Management is very important as large projects inevitably change over time. To avoid disputes and delays, the parties should set forth in detail Change Management procedures in their agreement.

K. Compliance with Laws (Chapter 5.Q; § 25)

1. Licensor Responsible for Compliance with Laws – Change in Law Justifies Change in Rates – Licensor Oriented

The Licensor shall comply with all federal, state, and local laws applicable to is Services, including, but not limited to, all statutes, regulations and rules that are in effect as of the Effective Date of the Agreement and shall procure at its expense all licenses and all permits necessary for the fulfillment of its obligation.

If any existing laws, regulation or policy is changed or if any new law, regulation or policy is enacted that affects the services provided under this Agreement, the parties to the Agreement shall modify this Agreement to the extent reasonably necessary to (i) ensure that such services will be in full compliance with such laws, regulations and/or policies; (ii) modify the rates applicable to such services and (iii) address any schedule impacts.

COMMENT: The wording of this clause is favorable to the licensor as the licensor does not bear the financial risk of a change in the law. Under this wording the licensor is able to pass any additional costs on to the licensee.

2. Licensor Responsible for Identification and Compliance with Applicable Laws

Licensor is responsible for the identification of, interpretation of, and compliance with, any applicable laws, regulations and statutes that affect it or the Licensee's applications or business.

COMMENT: A party should never agree to blindly comply with all applicable laws. Rather, an agreement to comply with laws should be limited to those laws in existence at the time of contract signature or those laws related to the licensor's software. To do otherwise shifts the burden of risk (and any resulting costs) associated with a change in the law from the licensee to the licensor.

L. Confidentiality (Chapter 14; § 12)

1. Licensor Information – Licensee oriented as licensor prohibited from providing confidential information to licensee

Licensor shall not, whether in connection with the performance of Licensor's obligations under this Agreement or otherwise, transfer, submit, or otherwise disclose to Licensee in any manner any information of a confidential or proprietary nature. In the event Licensor desires to disclose any information of a proprietary or confidential nature to Licensee, Licensor shall first provide written notice to Licensee identifying the nature of such information without disclosing any proprietary or confidential aspects of such information. If Licensee determines, in its sole discretion, to receive such information, the Parties shall enter into a separate confidentiality and non-disclosure agreement with respect to such information, under which Licensor shall provide such information to Licensee; provided, however, that such agreement shall only apply to the disclosure of such information previously identified in writing by Licensor in accordance with the first sentence of this Section ___. In the event Licensor transfers, submits, or otherwise discloses to Licensee any information of a proprietary or confidential nature without first entering into such a confidentiality and nondisclosure agreement, Licensor hereby grants Licensee a royalty-free, perpetual, irrevocable, worldwide license and right (with the right to sublicense) to make, have made, use, reproduce, distribute, modify, enhance, and create derivative works of such information and all associated Intellectual Property Rights.

> ***COMMENT: Under no circumstances should a licensor agree to this or similar language even if the contract in question only pertains to services or maintenance. A licensor may have many types of confidential information including employee lists, prices, methodologies, vendors and subcontractors as well as tools.***

2. Survival of Confidentiality Obligations – Trade Secrets (§ 12)

Recipient's obligations under this Agreement shall expire on the fifth (5th) anniversary of the effective date, except with respect to those items of confidential information which constitute trade secrets of the discloser, which obligations of nondisclosure will remain in effect until such time as such item no longer is a trade secret.

> ***COMMENT: Both parties should insist on the insertion of language that recognizes each party's obligations to maintain the confidentiality of the disclosing party's trade secrets after the expiration of the non-disclosure agreement or any artificial time period. The parties should always include language that maintains the confidentiality of any trade secrets so long***

as the information remains a trade secret. Often the parties enter into a confidentiality agreement obligating the parties to keep the information received confidential for an artificially agreed time period such as five or seven years. These agreements fail to recognize that a trade secret may continue well beyond any such agreed upon time period.

3. Disclosure of Confidential Information to Third Parties – Licensor Oriented (§ 12)

Licensee promises and agrees not to disclose or otherwise make the System, including but not limited to any additions, supplements, Customizations, or Modifications to the System, available to any person other than employees of Licensee required to have such knowledge for normal use of the System. In the event Licensee desires to disclose the System to a third party consultant, Licensee must obtain Licensor's prior written consent, not to be unreasonably withheld, and Licensee, Licensor, and such third party consultant must execute a Licensor nondisclosure agreement. For the purposes of this Agreement, it will be reasonable for Licensor to withhold its approval if (i) such consultant is a software vendor which markets, services, and/or develops computer software programs similar to System; (ii) Licensor has reason to believe that such consultant will not abide by the confidentiality provisions herein, or (iii) that consultant is not financially secure to guarantee its obligations hereunder.

COMMENT: This language is equally important for the licensor and the licensee. The licensee wants to ensure that it has the right to disclose the licensor's confidential information to its consultants and contractors so that they may support the system avoiding the necessity of using the licensor and its likely higher rates. The licensor wants to limit third party access to protect its trade secrets and to potentially protect its revenue. The licensee needs to ensure that the right granted under this paragraph will meet the licensee's needs not only in the present but also in the future.

4. Business Associate Agreement (Form 23.G.7)

If the parties enter into a Business Associate Agreement setting forth the terms and conditions applicable to Personal Health Information (as such term is defined in 45 C.F.R. § 160.103), the terms of such Business Associate Agreement shall be deemed incorporated herein and made a part hereof, but shall supersede the provisions of this Section ___.

5. *No Restriction on Marketing Independently Developed Information*

Nothing in this Agreement will be construed as a representation or agreement that the Recipient will not market, distribute, develop, or have developed for it, products, concepts, systems or techniques that are similar to or compete with the products, concepts, systems or techniques contemplated by or embodied in the Confidential Information of the other party, provided that the Recipient does not violate any of its obligations under this Agreement or the intellectual property rights of the other party in connection with such development. Nothing herein shall obligate either party to enter into or continue to pursue any business relationship or transaction with the other party. Without limiting the foregoing, no obligation to buy or sell products, negotiate or conclude any transaction or enter into or negotiate any agreement shall result unless and until the parties, at each party's sole discretion, execute a written agreement, and only in accordance with its terms.

6. *Presentations and Publications*

Licensor shall not present or publish, nor submit for publication, any work resulting from Licensor's services without Licensee's prior written approval.

7. *Residuals – Short Form (§ 12.7)*

Nothing in this Agreement shall prohibit or restrict either party's right to develop, make, use, market, license or distribute products or services similar to or competitive with those of the other party disclosed in the Confidential Information as long as it shall not thereby breach this Agreement. Each party acknowledges that the other may already possess or have developed products or services similar to or competitive with those of the other party disclosed in the Confidential Information. Further, either party shall be free to use for any purpose the residuals (defined below) resulting from access to or work with Confidential Information disclosed hereunder. The term "**residuals**" means information in non-tangible form which may be retained in the unaided memory by persons who have had access to the Confidential Information so long as such persons have not studied the information for the purpose of replicating the same from memory. Neither party shall have any obligation to limit or restrict the assignment of such persons or to pay royalties for any work resulting from the use of residuals.

8. *Residuals – Unilateral – Feedback (§ 12.7)*

During the course of this Agreement, Licensor may provide or Licensee may solicit Licensor's input regarding Licensee's Software, products, services, business or technology plans, including, without limitation, comments or suggestions regarding the possible creation, modification, correction, improvement or enhancement of Licensee Software, products and/or services, or input as to whether Licensor believes Licensee's development direction is consistent with their own business and IT needs, the technology marketplace in general, and the like (collectively "**Feedback**"). Licensor acknowledges and agrees that any information disclosed by Licensee during discussions related to Feedback shall be considered Licensee Confidential Information and shall be protected from disclosure in accordance with the terms of this Agreement. In order for Licensee to utilize such Feedback, Licensor grants to Licensee a non-exclusive, perpetual, irrevocable, worldwide, royalty-free license, with the right to sublicense to Licensee's licensees and customers, under all relevant Licensor intellectual property rights, to use, publish, and disclose such Feedback in any manner Licensee chooses and to display, perform, copy, make, have made, use, sell, and otherwise dispose of Licensee's and its sublicensee's products or services embodying Feedback in any manner and via any media Licensee chooses, without reference to the source. Licensee shall be entitled to use Feedback for any purpose without restriction or remuneration of any kind with respect to Licensor and/or its representatives. Licensor acknowledges that the information related to Licensee's Software, products, services, business or technology plans, disclosed to it under this Agreement, is only intended as possible strategies, developments, and functionalities of the Licensee products or services and is not intended to be binding upon Licensee to any particular course of business, product strategy, and/or development.

9. Residuals – Expanded (§ 12.7)

Nothing in this Agreement shall restrict any employee or representative of a Party from using general ideas, concepts, practices, learning, or know-how relating to the Services that are retained in the unaided memory of such employee or representative after performing the obligations of such Party under this Agreement, except to the extent that such use infringes upon any patent, copyright, or other intellectual property right of a Party or its Affiliates (or, in the case of Licensor, any Eligible Recipient); provided, however, that this Section ___ shall not (i) be deemed to limit either Party's obligations under this Agreement with respect to the disclosure or use of Proprietary Information, or (ii) operate or be construed as permitting an employee or representative of Licensor to disclose, publish, disseminate, or use (a) the source of any Proprietary Information of Licensee or an Eligible Recipient, (b) any financial, statistical, or personnel information of Licensee or an Eligible Recipient, or (c) the business plans of Licensee or the Eligible Recipients. An individual's memory is unaided if the individual has not intentionally memorized the Proprietary Information for the purpose of retaining and subsequently using or disclosing it and does not identify the information as Proprietary Information upon recollection. For avoidance of doubt, the foregoing would not permit Licensor Personnel to use Proprietary Information of Licensee or an Eligible Recipient (other than ideas, concepts, practices, learning, and know-how relating generally to application management, selection and design,

IT Infrastructure services, enterprise resource planning, and clinical application and revenue cycle services and systems) for any purpose other than the provision of Services under this Agreement.

10. SEC Disclosures

As necessary to perform its obligations under this Agreement, the Receiving Party may disclose Confidential Information of the Furnishing Party to any employee, officer, director, contractor, agent or representative of the Receiving Party who has a legitimate "need to know" the information in question and who is bound to the Receiving Party to protect the confidentiality of the information in a manner substantially equivalent to that required of the Receiving Party under this Agreement. Licensee may provide Confidential Information of Licensor to contractors (including outsourcing suppliers that may replace Licensor under this Agreement) (i) who have a legitimate "need to know" the Confidential Information in question in order to provide services to Licensee, and (ii) who are bound to Licensee and Licensor to protect the confidentiality of the information in a manner substantially equivalent to that required of Licensee under this Agreement. The Receiving Party may also disclose Confidential Information of the Furnishing Party to the Receiving Party's Auditors provided they are made aware of the Receiving Party's obligations of confidentiality with respect to the Furnishing Party's Confidential Information, and with respect to non-regulatory Auditors, agree to be bound to protect the information in a manner substantially equivalent to that required hereunder. Licensee and its Affiliates may also disclose Licensor Confidential Information, including this Agreement and the transactions contemplated by this Agreement, in any periodic reports filed or required to be filed with the Securities and Exchange Commission (*"SEC"*) pursuant to the rules and regulations promulgated by the SEC, as well as to the New York Stock Exchange and any other regulatory agency or body charged with the administration, oversight or enforcement of regulations applicable to any business conducted by Licensee or any of its Affiliates, to the extent Licensee determines in its sole discretion that such information is required to be disclosed. Licensee shall solicit Licensor's views as to any confidential information that Licensor would like to redact from any such filing in advance of such filing, and shall grant any such redaction requests of Licensor as it reasonably can while still being responsive to the disclosure requirements of the SEC, and acting in a manner consistent with Licensee's ordinary practices for disclosures of a similar nature, Licensee will give particular consideration to Licensor requests for the redaction of any pricing, and other terms with financial impact (e.g. service level credit amounts), provided, however, final decision shall be made by Licensee on the content of all such disclosures.

11. Insider Trading – Tipping (Chapter 23.I.3)

Each party is expressly prohibited from buying or selling the others' shares or other securities on the basis of the Confidential Information, a practice commonly known as "insider trading," and is also prohibited from providing other people with such information or recommending that they buy or sell securities, a practice commonly known as "tipping." Licensor agrees to be bound by customer's Insider Trading Policy attached here to as Exhibit __. (Chapter 23.I.3)

12. Injunctive Relief for Breach of Confidentiality Obligations (§§ 5.5.3, 12)

Each party recognizes that the disclosing party and its affiliates may suffer irreparable harm as the result of the unauthorized disclosure, reproduction, or use of any Confidential Information and that monetary damages may be inadequate to compensate the disclosing party for such breach. Therefore, the receiving party agrees that in the event of any failure to comply with the provisions of this Section, the disclosing party will be entitled to a preliminary injunction, and an order of seizure and impoundment under Section 503 of the Copyright Act upon an ex parte application by the disclosing party to protect and recover the Confidential Information, and neither the receiving party nor any of its Agents object to the entry of an injunction or other equitable relief against the receiving party or any of its Agents on the basis of an adequate remedy at law or any other reason.

13. Damages – For Breach of Confidentiality Obligations

Notwithstanding anything contained in this Agreement to the contrary, including, but not limited to, Section 2.2.2 of the Arbitration Schedule (Form 23.I.10), in the event the receiving party breaches the confidentiality obligations contained in this Confidentiality Schedule with regard to Confidential Information, the disclosing party shall be entitled to indirect, consequential, special, incidental or damages and any such finder of fact shall be entitled to award such indirect damages.

14. Non-Disclosure Language – Incorporates Trade Secret Language

(a) Except with the prior written consent of the disclosing party, the receiving party agrees that it will not disclose or use for the receiving party's own benefit any Trade Secret, Proprietary Property or Confidential Information acquired from the disclosing party, the disclosing party's customers, suppliers, consultants, affiliates or third parties under contract with the disclosing party.

(b) For the purposes of this Agreement, a "Trade Secret" is information that is not generally known to the public, and that gives or may give the disclosing party an advantage over its competitors. Trade Secrets include, but are not limited to (i) research being planned and developed, (ii) research methods and processes, (iii) sources of supplies and materials of any type, (iv) materials used in research or manufacturing, (v) equipment and methods used in research or manufacturing, (vi) marketing plans, (vii) information concerning the filing or pendency of patent applications, and (viii) pricing, methodologies, approaches, etc.

(c) For the purposes of this Agreement, "Confidential Information" includes, but is not limited to:

(i) any information concerning data, documentation, procedures, inventions, nucleic acid and amino acid sequences, formulae, methods, processes and other intellectual property or the business plans, customers, finances, property and related business information belonging to or created by the disclosing party or any client, customer or third party contracting with the disclosing party; and

(ii) any advice or information that the receiving party provides to the disclosing party in accordance with this Agreement.

Notwithstanding the above, however, "Confidential Information" does not include any information which is demonstrated in writing:

(i) to be public knowledge at the time this Agreement commences, or which thereafter becomes public knowledge through no fault or involvement of the receiving party;

(ii) to have been properly provided to the receiving party without restriction by an independent third party; or

(iii) was already known to the receiving party at the time of disclosure by the disclosing party.

(d) the receiving party shall treat all Trade Secrets, Proprietary Property and Confidential Information in strict confidence, and shall take all reasonable steps necessary to preserve the confidentiality and secrecy of such information, including, without limitation, executing and complying with the terms of any additional confidentiality agreement(s) or security procedure(s) required or reasonably requested by the disclosing party or any client or customer of the disclosing party, and to return to the disclosing party any and all original and reproduced materials embodying such information immediately upon expiration or termination of this Agreement.

(e) The non-disclosure obligations with regards to:

(i) Trade Secrets shall be perpetual and shall survive the termination or expiration of this Agreement; and

(ii) Confidential Information and Proprietary Property shall be in effect for the term of this Agreement and shall survive for a period of seven (7) years after termination or expiration of this Agreement.

(f) In the event receiving party is required or compelled to disclose any Trade Secret, Proprietary Property or Confidential Information by any law or governmental authority, receiving party shall notify disclosing party of such requirement or compulsion as soon as possible to allow disclosing party to seek a protective order or similar measure.

15. Media Releases and Public Disclosures Related to Agreement

Without the prior written consent of the other party, neither party shall issue or release any statement, article, advertisement, public or private announcement, media release or other similar publicity relating in any manner to: (a) any aspect of this Agreement; (b) any aspect of the Licensed Software; or (c) the fact that the parties have engaged in any discussions or negotiations regarding any of the foregoing. Neither party shall use the name or any business name, trade name, trademark, service mark or logo of the other party without the prior written consent of the other party.

> ***COMMENT: A party bound by this or similar language should notify its marketing department not to use the other party's name or logo on its website or on any list of clients.***

16. Retention of Confidential Information

Upon completion of Licensor's assignment for Licensee, Licensee shall return or destroy, as Licensor may direct, all documentation in any medium that contains, refers to, or relates to Confidential Information within thirty (30) days; provided that auditors performing audit functions may retain their work papers. Licensee shall deliver to Licensor written certification of its compliance with the preceding sentence signed by an officer of Licensee. **Notwithstanding the foregoing, Licensee shall be permitted to retain (subject to the terms herein) such Confidential Information as may be required to comply with applicable professional obligations and standards and internal policies. For the avoidance of doubt, anything that is stored on routine back-up media for the purpose of disaster recovery will be subject to destruction in due course. Notwithstanding the foregoing, latent data such as deleted files and other non-logical data types, such as memory dumps, swap files, temporary files, printer spool files and metadata that can customarily only be retrieved by computer forensics experts and are generally considered inaccessible without the use of specialized tools and techniques will not be within the requirement for return or destruction of Confidential Information as set forth by this paragraph.**

> ***COMMENT: Some parties seek to return one copy of the confidential information for its records after the termination of the confidentiality obligations. They do so in the belief that if they were ever accused of violating the non-disclosure provisions, they would be unable to protect themselves because they lack a record of the confidential information they received from the disclosing party. If the disclosing party is willing to allow the receiving party to retain a copy for its records, the receiving party should be required to keep such information in the locked files of its legal department.***

M. Data Privacy/Security (Chapter 10; § 12)

1. Data Security and Protection (§ 12)

1.1 **"Licensee Data" Defined.** "Licensee Data" means all data in any form, whether or not Confidential Information, collected by any Licensor Personnel in performing the Services or furnished, disclosed, or otherwise made available to Licensor Personnel, directly or indirectly, by or on behalf of Licensee or a Service Recipient, including data of or pertaining to Licensee's or its Affiliates' customers and any Derivative Works of such data.

1.2 **Licensee Data, Generally.** As between the Parties, Licensee Data will be and remain the property of Licensee. No Licensor may use Licensee Data for any purpose other than to render the Services. No Licensee Data may be sold, assigned, leased, or otherwise disposed of to third parties or commercially exploited by or on behalf of any Licensor. No Licensor may possess or assert any lien or other right against or to Licensee Data. Without limiting the generality of the foregoing, each Licensor may only use personal identifying information as strictly necessary to render the Services and must restrict access to such information to Licensor Personnel on a strict need-to-know basis.

1.3 **Data Security.**

1.3.1 The parties' respective responsibilities for data and systems security are as set forth in Schedule A to the Services Agreement. Each Licensor agrees to abide by and is responsible for its performance of the responsibilities for data and systems security are as set forth in Schedule A to the Services Agreement.

1.3.2 When present at Licensee Facilities or accessing Licensee Data or Licensee systems, each Licensor will observe and comply with Licensee's security procedures that have been communicated to such Licensor.

1.3.3 Each Licensor will establish and maintain safeguards against the destruction, loss, or alteration of Licensee Data in its possession or control that are no less rigorous than those maintained by Licensee as of the Effective Date and are no less rigorous than those maintained by such Licensor for its own data of a similar nature. Licensee may keep backup Licensee Data in its possession if it chooses and establish backup security for Licensee Data.

1.3.4 Without limiting the generality of the foregoing, each Licensor will use Commercially Reasonable Efforts, including through systems security measures, to guard against the unauthorized access, alteration, or destruction of Software and Licensee Data. Such measures will include the installation of Software that: (A) requires all users to enter a user identification and password prior to gaining access to the information systems; (B) controls and tracks the addition and deletion of users; and (C) controls and tracks user access to areas and features of the information systems.

1.3.5 Licensor Personnel will not attempt to access, or allow access to, any Licensee Data that they are not permitted to access under any of the Various Agreement. If such access is attained, the applicable Licensor will immediately report such incident to Licensee, describing in detail the accessed Licensee Data, and take all necessary measures to stop the access, prevent recurrences, and return to Licensee any copied or removed Licensee Data.

1.4 **Compliance with Data Privacy and Data Protection Laws, Regulations, and Policies.** In carrying out their activities under each of the Various Agreement, each Party will observe and comply with all applicable data privacy and data protection laws and regulations. In addition, when accessing or handling any Licensee Data that contains personal identifying information, each Licensor will comply with all policies of Licensee that have been disclosed to the Licensor relating to the use and disclosure of such information, specifically including Licensee's cardholder information security program (CISP) and PCI Data Security Standard.

1.5 **Protection of LPNI.** Notwithstanding any other provision herein: (a) each Licensor shall not disclose without Licensee's prior written approval any Licensee Proprietary Network Information (**LPNI**) or personally identifiable information of any End User (past or present), including without limitation mobile directory numbers (**MDNs**) (collectively, **PII**) to any person, except that a Licensor may disclose LPNI and PII without prior Licensee approval to its employees, agents and employees who have a need to know to perform the Licensor's obligations under any of the Various Agreements or to the extent the Licensor is required to do so by force of law; (b) each Licensor shall require any person or entity to whom the Licensor discloses LPNI or PII to be bound by a nondisclosure obligation that prohibits the disclosure or use of the LPNI or PII; (c) without limiting the Licensor's liability or obligations with respect to LPNI and PII, each Licensor shall disclose to Licensee in writing any disclosure or use of LPNI or PII that is in violation of any of the Various Agreements by persons or entities to whom the Licensor disclosed LPNI or PII, promptly upon obtaining knowledge of such violative disclosure or use; and (e) each Licensor shall comply with all applicable federal and state privacy laws and Licensee policies governing access to, disclosure of, and use of, LPNI or PII of which Licensor is informed in writing by Licensee.

1.6 **Personal Information.** Each Party shall implement and maintain reasonable security procedures and practices appropriate to the nature of the information, to protect any "Personal Information" obtained hereunder from unauthorized access, destruction, use, modification, or disclosure. For purposes of this section: "Personal Information" means an individual's first name or first initial and his or her last name in combination with any one or more of the following data elements, when either the name of the data elements are not encrypted or redacted: (1) social security number, (2) driver's license number or California identification card number, (3) account number, credit, or debit card number, in combination with any required security code, access code, or password that would permit access to an individual's financial account, (4) "Medical Information," meaning any individually identifiable information in electronic or physical form, regarding the individual's medical history or medical treatment or diagnosis by a health care professional; or (5) personally identifiable information as such term is used in Section 631 of the Cable Communications Policy Act of 1984, as amended (47 U.S.C. § 551). Personal Information does not include publicly available information that is lawfully made available to the general public from federal, state or local government records.

2. Data Security – Alternate Language (§ 12)

To the extent that Licensor or any of its personnel is provided access to any of the automated information systems, data or voice networks or telecommunications facilities or computer systems or related equipment of Licensee located at any Licensee facility or used by or for Licensee, or any part thereof, along with any data the foregoing contain (collectively, the "Licensee Network"), the following provisions shall apply to Licensee and its personnel (and Licensee shall be responsible for its personnel's compliance therewith): (i) such access will be provided by Licensee solely to allow Licensor to provide the services to and for Licensee; (ii) Licensor shall not access or modify the Licensee Network or any data on the Licensee Network without express written authorization from Licensee; (iii) Licensor shall not break, bypass, or circumvent, or attempt to break, bypass, or circumvent, any security system or measure of Licensee; (iv) Licensor shall not obtain, or attempt to obtain, access to any hardware, program or data other than that which Licensor owns, is maintaining pursuant to this Agreement, or to which Licensor has been given access intentionally by Licensee; (v) Licensor shall observe and comply with all security, conduct and safety measures, procedures and regulations including encryption of data as Licensee may establish or provide to Licensor from time to time; and (vi) in the event that Licensor learns that it or any of its personnel have breached any of the foregoing restrictions, Licensor shall (A) promptly notify Licensee of the details for the same of which it is aware, and (B) cooperate as requested by Licensee in any investigation thereof.

> ***COMMENT: Data security is assuming increasing importance with the adoption of both federal data protection and privacy laws such as HIPAA, Gramm-Leach-Bliley, and state data protection and privacy laws. A party wrongfully disclosing protective information must ensure the necessary protective measures have been taken to avoid liability.***

3. Publishing of Web Content

Should Licensor be granted access to Licensee's network, it shall use such access solely to meet its obligations under this Agreement, including the applicable SOW. Notwithstanding the foregoing, however, Licensor shall have neither the right nor the obligation to make the final decision as to whether a particular content or date shall be posted on a Licensee website that is available on the Internet or an Extranet; only a Licensee employee shall be deemed a website Publisher, as such term is defined in Licensee's Website Policy. A copy of the policy will be made available to Licensor, as necessary, upon request. Finally, should a SOW require Licensor to create or modify software, data or content to be used on or to support Licensee's website, Licensor shall make every reasonable effort to comply with Licensee's applicable policies, procedures and standards; and, if it cannot do so, it shall promptly notify Licensee.

4. Attorney-Client Privileged Documents

Licensor recognizes that it may obtain access to client documents, data and databases created by and for Licensee and associated communications related thereto and which may be marked as "Attorney Work Product" or "Attorney-Client Privilege" (collectively, "Privileged Document Deliverables") which are confidential attorney work product or subject to the attorney-client privilege. Licensor shall not intentionally reveal Privileged Document Deliverables to third parties and Licensor shall institute reasonable safeguards to prevent the unintentional disclosure of Privileged Document Deliverables to third parties. The only project staff who may have access to Privileged Document Deliverables shall be those for whom such access is necessary for the purpose of providing services to Licensee as provided in this Agreement. Licensor recognizes that Privileged Document Deliverables have been prepared in anticipation of litigation and that Licensor is performing the Services in respect of Privileged Document Deliverables as an agent of Licensee, and that all matter related thereto is protected from disclosure by Rule 26 of the United States Federal Rules of Civil Procedure (or any similar Law in other local jurisdictions). Should Licensor ever be notified of any judicial or other proceeding seeking to obtain access to Privileged Document Deliverables, Licensor shall (1) promptly notify Licensee and (2) at Licensee's expense, take such reasonable actions as may be specified by Licensee to resist providing such access. Licensee shall have the right and duty to represent Licensor in such resistance or to select and compensate counsel to so represent Licensor or to reimburse Licensor for reasonable attorneys' fees and expenses incurred in resisting such access.

(a) Licensor represents that it is not a citizen of an embargoed country or a prohibited entity under applicable United States anti-terrorism laws, regulations or lists.

(b) Licensor warrants that no representative sent on site to work at Licensee has been convicted of a felony under state or federal law.

5. Ownership of Customer Data

All Customer Data (defined below) is, will be and will remain the property of Customer or its designees and will be deemed Confidential Information of such parties. Customer or such designees shall have all right, title and interest in and to, including worldwide ownership of trade secret rights, copyrights, patents and other proprietary rights in the Customer Data and all copies thereof. At Vendor's expense, Vendor will promptly notify Customer and correct any errors or inaccuracies in the Customer Data and the reports delivered to Customer under an applicable Statement of Work, to the extent caused by Vendor. At the request of Customer, Vendor will promptly correct any other errors or inaccuracies in the Customer Data or such reports in accordance with applicable Customer policies and procedures. "Customer Data" means all data and information (i) submitted to Vendor by or on behalf of Customer and its affiliates, successors or agents, or (ii) obtained, developed or produced by Vendor in connection with an Statement of Work to the extent such data or information is based on, summarizes or includes data and information of Customer or its affiliates or Customer agents submitted to or obtained by Vendor under an Statement of Work.

6. *Errors in Data Conversion – Licensor Oriented*

Licensee acknowledges that data conversion is subject to the likelihood of human and machine errors, omissions, delays, and losses, including inadvertent loss of data or damage to media, that may give rise to loss or damage. Licensor shall not be liable for any such errors, omissions, delays, or losses of either Licensee or Licensee's licensees. Licensee and Licensee's licensees are responsible for adopting measures to limit the impact of such problems, including backing up of data, and adopting procedures to ensure the accuracy of input data; examining and confirming results prior to use, and adopting procedures to identify and correct errors and omissions, replace lost or damaged media, and reconstruct data.

N. Delay in Performance

1. *Timing – Neutral Bilateral*

Subject to Section __ (Force Majeure), the Approval Process with respect to each Deliverable shall be performed within the times prescribed therefore in the Statement of Work; provided, that, (i) dates for performance by a party as set forth in the Statement of Work shall be adjusted for delays caused by the other party hereto (the **Delaying Party**), but only to the extent required by such Delaying Party's delay (i.e., only dependent tasks shall be re-scheduled and then only for a day-for-day period, or if the parties mutually agree, for the period of time reasonably necessary to afford the party the period for performance that it would have had absent the delay); (ii) in the case of any Deliverable for which no time period is prescribed in the Statement of Work, Evaluation of any Deliverable (whether initially delivered or fixed and re-delivered) shall be ten (10) business days from the date of delivery or re-delivery; (iii) the fix/re-delivery period shall be ten (10) business days from the date of receipt of notice of Nonconformities or such longer period as mutually agreed by the parties; and (iv) if at the end of any Evaluation period or re-Evaluation Period, Client shall not have issued either an Approval or a notice of Nonconformities, Vendor may so notify Client in writing and Client shall, within five (5) business days thereafter, notify Vendor of all Nonconformities or the Deliverable will be deemed Approved. Unless the parties otherwise agree in writing, a failure by Vendor to timely make any delivery or submission for the Approval Process shall count as a failed delivery and shall have the same effect as if the Deliverable had been delivered with Nonconformities.

2. Timing – Delay by Licensee – Neutral

If Licensee fails to timely complete scheduled work which delays Licensor, Licensee agrees that the entire schedule set forth in Subsection ____ shall be extended by a number of days equal to the number of days which Licensee delays Licensor.

If either party anticipates that it cannot meet the completion dates for assigned tasks or responsibilities and it is probable that a completion date for a Phase may be delayed, such party shall immediately notify the other party in writing of the reason for such delay and the estimated impact on the Phase's schedule. At a minimum, the completion dates for the Phase and any interrelated tasks shall be extended by the period of any such delay.

3. Timing – Licensor Oriented

If Licensee's failure to timely perform any of its responsibilities set forth in the Implementation Plan directly and adversely affects Licensor's ability to perform Licensor's obligations under the Implementation Plan, Licensee shall (a) extend the performance due date for the implementation of any milestone in the Implementation Plan affected thereby by the same number of days such failure continues (i.e., a "day-for-day" basis), and (b) reimburse Licensor for any additional incremental costs actually and reasonably incurred by Licensor as a direct result of such failure (but only to the extent Licensor uses commercially reasonable efforts to minimize such costs). Performance shall be extended as provided under (a) above, provided, however that any resulting extension of the implementation of a milestone in the Implementation Plan that is identified as being in the critical path of any other milestone in the Implementation Plan or the overall completion date of the Implementation Plan will extend the date of such other milestone or such overall completion date, as applicable, by the same number of days.

4. Timing – Licensee Oriented

Licensor's nonperformance of its obligations under this Agreement shall be excused if and to the extent (i) such Licensor nonperformance results from Licensee's (including its Affiliates' or its subcontractors') failure to perform its responsibilities; and (ii) Licensor provides Licensee with reasonable notice of such nonperformance and (if requested by Licensee) uses Commercially Reasonable Efforts to perform notwithstanding Licensee's failure to perform (with Licensee being responsible to reimburse Licensor for its additional Out-of-Pocket Expenses for such efforts).

O. Disaster Recovery (Chapter 5.G; § 35)

1. Movement of Licensor Personnel

Licensee may, for any reasonable reason whatsoever, request that Licensor move all or some of the Licensor Personnel engaged on efforts listed in Task Order __ attached hereto to a location reasonably selected by Licensee (the "Contingency Location") including, without limitation, a Licensee Location in the United States or off-shore, a Licensor Service Location in the United States or the country in which Licensor is performing the Services or a third party location reasonably equipped to facilitate performance of the Services. In the event of such a request, Licensor agrees that it shall (a) continue to provide the Services without any disruption, (b) promptly commence arrangements to move such personnel to the Contingency Location and (c) use commercially good faith efforts to have such resources or a significant portion thereof relocated in no more than ninety-six (96) hours from the time of the request. The parties acknowledge and agree that the Licensor Personnel may change from time to time upon mutual agreement of the Parties. A current list of the agreed upon Licensor Personnel shall at all times remain with the Licensee Task Order Manager and the project manager, if any. In the event that any Licensor Personnel are relocated pursuant to the foregoing to a location outside of the country in which such Licensor Personnel was performing services, Licensee shall pay Licensor the then applicable onsite rate for the applicable location. Licensor agrees that at all times during the Task Order Term all Licensor Personnel shall (a) be authorized to work in the United States (b) maintain valid visas or such other similar work permits as may be required by the relevant jurisdiction in the United States to permit such personnel to travel upon notice to such locations. A Force Majeure Event shall only excuse Licensor's obligations to relocate personnel as described herein as set forth in Section ____ (Force Majeure) including that Licensor use reasonable precautions to prevent such events and that Licensor agree to use commercially good faith efforts to take such reasonable precautions.

P. Employee Related Terms (Chapter 18)

1. Hiring Employees of Other Party – Exclusive Remedy

This Section ___ sets forth the exclusive remedy of Licensor and Licensee in each instance in which a party hires a present or former employee of the other, provided, however, that the parties shall not waive the additional right to pursue appropriate legal action and/or equitable relief (i) if a former employee uses or discloses confidential or proprietary information or trade secrets in breach of any employment agreement or the common law, or (ii) any claim against the other party for tortious interference with such contractual relations arising out of such breach. The parties expressly agree that a fee calculated in accordance with this Article is reasonable and adequate.

2. *Hiring Employees of Other Party- Liquidated Damages Calculation*

Licensee may offer employment and employ, from time to time, any of Licensor's contractors performing Services for Licensee pursuant to this Agreement. In the event Licensee employs any of such Licensor's contractors, Licensee shall pay to Licensor a finder's fee calculated by taking the applicable percentage set forth below of such individual's new full-time annual salary, to be paid by Licensee to said individual pursuant to said offer of employment ("Finder's Fee"), and such Finder's Fee will be payable within thirty (30) days after such individual officially commences employment with Licensee. The Finder's Fee percentage payment will be based on the time period from start of contractor's services at Licensee until the individual's official employment start date.

Effective date of employment with Licensee, calculated from 1st day of employee's assignment	Percentage of individual's annual salary paid by Licensee
1–30 calendar days	25.0%
31–60 calendar days	20.0%
61–90 calendar days	15.0%
91–120 calendar days	10.0%
121–150 calendar days	5.0%
151–180 calendar days	2.5%

Licensee will give Licensor prior notice of Licensee's intent to make a formal, written offer of employment to Licensor's then-current contractor(s).

Notwithstanding the foregoing, Licensee may employ any of Licensor's contractors who respond directly to public employment offers from Licensee and who are subsequently hired by Licensee through its standard hiring processes, without any percentage payments of such contractor's new employee salary at Licensee.

3. *Violent Crime Control and Law Enforcement Acts – Insurance Industry*

Licensor acknowledges that under 18 U.S.C.A. § 1033, it may be a federal criminal offense for Licensee to willfully permit an individual who has been convicted of a felony involving dishonesty or breach of trust to perform any act for it which is incidental to the writing of insurance. Licensor will not assign any officers, directors, agents, or employees that it knows have ever been convicted of any felony involving dishonesty or breach of trust to perform the Services hereunder. Licensor shall notify Licensee in writing promptly if at any time Licensor becomes aware that any such officers, directors, agents or employees is convicted of a felony involving dishonesty or breach of trust, by any court in any state or country, or subsequently learns that any such officers, directors, agents, or employees have ever been convicted of such.

This obligation shall be continuing and shall be binding on Licensor's assignees and successors in interest.

4. *Workplace Violence*

Vendor shall (1) advise its employees and those of its subcontractors that it is the policy of Customer to provide a safe workplace for all people on its site and avoid violence in the workplace; (2) discourage its employees and those of its subcontractors from confronting or engaging in physical and/or verbal confrontations with violent or potentially violent individuals; and (3) address any reports of such behavior on the part of its employees or those of its subcontractors immediately in a reasonable and confidential manner. If a Customer employee is involved, Vendor shall notify the appropriate Customer supervisor immediately. Joint action will be taken to ensure fair and timely treatment of all involved.

5. *Pre-Approval of Licensor's Personnel*

Licensee shall have the right, but not the obligation, to pre-approve all employees and personnel to be used by Licensor to perform the Services. If Licensee is at any time dissatisfied for any reason with Licensor's personnel providing any of the Services (including the Licensor Account Executive), Licensee will notify Licensor of such dissatisfaction. Upon receipt of Licensee' notice, Licensor will promptly discontinue using such objectionable person to perform any Services hereunder and promptly replace such person with someone of suitable skill and experience. In addition, Licensor shall not at any time remove from any Licensee project or reassign any Licensor employees then currently providing Services without the prior written consent of Licensee, not to be unreasonably withheld. If personnel who have been providing the Services are replaced with other personnel, hourly fees for the Services provided by the replacement personnel, if applicable, shall be at the rates for the Services provided by the replaced personnel or at such other rates as the Parties may agree; provided, that Licensee shall not be obligated to pay for any time that replacement personnel spend performing Services until such time as the replacement personnel have reached the level of proficiency required to effectively perform their required roles.

6. *Pre-Approval of Licensor's Contractors*

Licensor may not subcontract any portion of the Services to any Contractors, including Affiliates of Licensor, without Licensee's express prior written consent. All such approved Contractors shall be required to execute a binding written agreement to (i) protect the Confidential Information and Proprietary Information of Licensee to at least the same extent as Licensor is required to protect such information pursuant to the terms of this Agreement, (ii) assign all Results to Licensee to the fullest extent required by Section ___ (Ownership of Intellectual Property) below and (iii) comply with all other obligations, duties and responsibilities required of Licensor under this Agreement and in any applicable Statement of Work with respect to the Services to be performed or delivered by such Contractor. Licensor will not disclose any Confidential or Proprietary Information of Licensee to any Contractor or permit any Contractor to perform any Services unless and until such Contractor has executed such binding written agreement. Notwithstanding the foregoing, Licensor will remain responsible for the obligations performed by any of its Contractors to the same extent as if such obligations were performed by Licensor's personnel.

7. Required Employee Screens – Not Reimbursable (§ 9)

Costs associated with completing, as appropriate, medical (except drug screens, which shall be performed by Licensee's approved medical facility, invoiced direct to Licensor and reimbursed by Licensee at actual cost), and background investigation requirements under Licensor's program, shall not be directly reimbursable under the Contract and shall be included in Licensor's overhead costs. For any screening activity which Licensor has not approved, reimbursement shall be as set forth in Paragraph (i) above, as applicable. All self-screening must be pre-approved by Licensee's Security Department.

Fingerprinting and General Employee Training (GET) will be provided by Licensee to all Licensor personnel at no cost to Licensor. Time associated with access screening/training time for all Licensor personnel shall be compensated as set forth in the Contract compensation provisions. Licensor will not be reimbursed any cost or expense of any kind to replace individuals who terminate their assignment for any reason prior to the scheduled assignment completion date (including termination for cause by Licensee), for personnel used to accommodate vacations and other absences, except for actual hours worked, or for personnel who fail to satisfy Licensee's site access requirements.

Q. Export (Chapter 5.M)

1. Compliance with Export Controls

Each party shall be responsible for ensuring that its actions with respect to the Licensed Software are in compliance with the export control Laws of the United States ("**Export Control Laws**"). Licensor immediately shall notify Licensee in writing if the Licensed Software is or becomes subject to export control restrictions under any Export Control Laws, and shall provide Licensee with reasonable cooperation and information, at no additional cost or expense to Licensee, to assist Licensee in complying with any licensing or similar requirements that may be imposed under such Export Control Laws, including promptly furnishing to Licensee upon request any export control classification numbers applicable to the Software. Licensor covenants to Licensee that, as of the Effective Date, the License Software is not subject to export control restrictions under any Export Control Laws.

R. Foreign Labor

1. Waiver of Moral Rights (Chapter 5.A.2)

LICENSOR HEREBY WAIVES IN FAVOR OF LICENSEE ANY AND ALL ARTIST'S OR MORAL RIGHTS (INCLUDING WITHOUT LIMITATION, ALL RIGHTS OF INTEGRITY AND ATTRIBUTION) IT MAY HAVE PURSUANT TO ANY STATE OR FEDERAL LAWS OF THE UNITED STATES IN RESPECT OF ANY DELIVERABLES AND ALL SIMILAR RIGHTS UNDER THE LAWS OF ALL OTHER APPLICABLE JURISDICTIONS.

> ***COMMENT:** Under the Berne Convention, moral rights may not be assigned, only waived. As such, the licensee should obtain a waiver of all moral rights by the licensor and the licensor's employees and subcontractors if any deliverable which the licensee will own is created outside of the United States. The United States does not recognize and enforce all of the provisions of the Berne Convention and thus a waiver is not necessary if the work is performed within the United States. Nonetheless, a prudent licensee will include the above language in the relevant agreement to provide comprehensive protection.*

2. No Use of Offshore Labor – Warranty

Licensor warrants and represents that any and all Services and Deliverables hereunder shall only be provided by its employees residing within the United States of America. Licensor will ensure that any information learned by it as a result of entering into this Agreement shall never leave the jurisdiction of the United States of America and shall never be accessed by anyone from outside the United States of America or by anyone who is not an employee of Licensor. Any modification to the foregoing limitation shall require the express written consent signed in ink by Licensee's President, Chief Operating Officer or Executive Vice President. Any breach of the foregoing shall constitute a material breach of this Agreement.

3. No Use of Offshore Labor

Licensor shall not be permitted to utilize services of non-United States staffing or contracted labor without the express written permission of Licensee. In the event Licensor has secured Licensee's permission to perform some of the tasks in connection with the provision of the Services to Licensee at an offshore location, Licensor will comply with Licensee's requirements respecting offshore performance, including the requirements set out in Exhibit __ ("Security").

4. Assignment of Foreign Nationals to Project (§§ 9, 43)

Licensor agrees that it will not supply nationals of those countries for which the U.S. government or any agency thereof requires an export license or other government approval, who are not permanent residents or citizens of the United States unless Licensor first notifies Licensee and Licensee specifically agrees that said national may provide services without requiring an export license (or unless Licensor first obtains such a license and provides a copy to Licensee). Licensor shall be solely responsible for determining the nationality of its employees and contractors.

5. Prohibition on Working From Home by Offshore Employees

Licensor agrees that it will not permit its Offshore employees and Project Managers delivering Services under Statements of Work to work from home without Licensee's prior written approval. Licensee may impose such reasonable conditions and restrictions with respect to any Licensee-approved Onshore work-from-home arrangements as it deems appropriate, in its sole discretion with a thirty (30) days prior written notice to Licensor.

6. Proof of Right to Work in United States

Licensee reserves the right to ask for and Licensor shall agree to provide such proof of all Licensor Personnel's right to work lawfully in the United States. If such right is not proven, Licensor will cure the breach or immediately find a replacement or reimburse Licensee, and Licensor shall indemnify, hold harmless and pay any and all fees and costs, for any loss and damage, directly or indirectly, caused by the breach (including but not limited to the cost of replacement and training of replacement as well as any legal cost).

7. Onsite and Onshore Labor – Certification by Licensor that it can Supply Required Foreign Labor

It is contemplated by the Parties that the services to be provided pursuant to each Statement of Work will include resources to be provided by Licensor Onsite at Licensee Service Locations designated by Licensee, as well as resources to be provided by Licensor Onshore at Licensor Service Locations designated by Licensee. Licensor, upon acceptance of a SOW, represents and warrants that it has the capability to provide such Onsite and Onshore resources in the number and of the qualifications required to provide Services under such SOW. Licensor shall have administrative and financial responsibility for all visa, approval and other activities necessary to provide all Onsite and Onshore resources.

8. Secondary Displacement

Licensee acknowledges and understands that Licensor may from time to time assign its employees Onsite throughout the United States on H-1B non-immigrant status to perform Services. Licensee is therefore subject to the provisions of U.S. Immigration laws and labor laws pertaining to such non-immigrant visas, including the American Competitiveness and Workforce Improvement Act (ACWIA). Licensor confirms that it has not displaced, and does not intend to displace, any U.S. worker in an "essentially equivalent" position during the 90 days prior to placement of Licensor's personnel in H-1B status at Licensee's facilities in the same geographic region. Furthermore, as of the date of this Agreement, Licensor does not intend to displace any such U.S. workers during the 90 days subsequent to such placement.

> ***COMMENT: The ACWIA prohibits certain employers from displacing full time employees with H-1 B visa holders. The intent of the law is to protect U.S. workers by preventing the Licensor from displacing any of the Licensee's U.S. workers through the use of H-1 B visa holders.***

9. Assignment of Copyright Interests – Indian Employees (Chapter 5.A)

All worldwide right, title and interest in and to all Licensee Intellectual Property and New Intellectual Property, together with any and all intellectual property rights inherent in any of the Licensee Intellectual Property and New Intellectual Property and appurtenant thereto including all patent rights, copyrights, trademarks, know-how and trade secrets, shall belong exclusively to Licensee perpetually. Licensor hereby assigns, transfers and conveys irrevocably and perpetually to Licensee all of its worldwide right, title and interest in and to any and all Licensee Intellectual Property and New Intellectual Property. Licensor hereby waives any and all of its rights under (i) Section 57 of the Indian Copyright Act, 1957, as amended, relating to certain "moral rights" that Licensor may have in any Licensee Intellectual Property or New Intellectual Property, and (ii) Section 53A of the Indian Copyright Act, 1957, as amended, relating to rights that Licensor may have in certain resale proceeds of certain of any Licensee Intellectual Property and New Intellectual Property that may be deemed to be literary works for purposes of such Section 53A.

10. Transition of Foreign Employees in Event of Termination

(a) In addition to any other rights set forth in Section ___ (Transition Services) or otherwise herein, from the date hereof and through the final expiration of this Agreement, Licensor shall, and shall cause their officers, directors, employees and attorneys and other personnel, to assist and cooperate with Licensee and its Affiliates, and its and their employees, agents and legal representatives, with any immigration process, registration, filing, continuation, extension or other procedure necessary or desirable to comply with any Legal requirements so that each Rehired Employee who is a foreign national (including those employees listed in Schedule _____ (collectively, the "Foreign Employees") is either in valid non-immigrant status entitling such employee to work for Licensor, or the Licensor' successor-in-interest for immigration purposes, (whether in the H1-B, L-1A or L-1B status), or has a valid Employment Authorization Document (EAD) entitling such Foreign Employee to work for Licensor or for a subsequent employer as a new hire by virtue of a filed application for adjustment of status pending for more than 180 days, and that all of their dependents can remain legally in the United States on the Closing Date in accordance with any and all Legal Requirements.

(b) As soon as possible on or after _______, 20__, Licensor shall, and shall cause its officers, directors, employees and attorneys and other personnel, to file an H1-B petitions and change of status applications for the individuals listed on Schedule _____ (the "L-1 Employees"). Licensor hereby agrees that from the Termination Date through the date that amended H1-B petitions can be and have been filed by Licensee for the L-1 Employees (no sooner than ___________, 20___ and no later than ___________, 20___), such L-1 Employees shall remain in the Licensor's employ, and under the supervision of the Licensor to provide transitional services to Licensee. Provision of such services shall not be an arrangement to provide labor for hire, but rather shall be a placement in connection with the provision of a service for which specialized knowledge specific to the Licensor employer is necessary to complete the sale of the Business. Throughout this transitional period, the L-1 employees shall be paid from the Licensor's payroll and shall continue to be eligible to participate prior to the consummation of the transactions contemplated in this Agreement. Licensee agrees to reimburse Licensor for all out-of-pocket filing fees required in connection with the change of status of all L-1 Employees to H-1B and any filing fees associated with filing for their dependents.

(c) Licensor hereby acknowledges and agrees that it has filed or is in the process of filing any necessary extensions with respect to any Foreign employee and his or her dependents whose non-immigration status or employment authorization documents will expire between the date hereof and ninety (90) days after the Closing Date, except in the case of all L-1 Employees, which must have their L-1 status extended until at least ____________, 20___.

(d) As soon as possible after the day hereof, Licensor shall advise all Foreign Employees of the prospective Closing and provide specific information to all Foreign Employees regarding the implications of travel outside the U.S. to prevent inadvertent delays overseas in the case of visa expiration or Advance parole expiration prior to the Closing and/or prior to direct employment with Licensee in the case of the L-1 Employees.

(e) Immediately after the date hereof, and, in the case of the L-1 Employees, until such employees begin employment directly with Licensee, Licensor will take all steps necessary to protect to the fullest extent possible, the priority date and all processes associated with permanent residency applications (in whichever stage) filed on behalf of all Foreign Employees and their dependents. Without limiting the generality of the foregoing, Licensor shall, and shall cause their officers, directors, employees and attorneys and other personnel, to: (i) provide copies of all immigration files of the Foreign Employees and their dependents retained by the Licensor or its Affiliates; (ii) assist in obtaining all documentation from each such Foreign Employee (and their dependents) necessary to make any filing on behalf of such Foreign Employee (and their dependents); (iii) provide financial documentation of the Licensor's ability to pay the wage offered in the labor certification application of such Foreign Employees at the time the labor certification was filed; (iv) abstain from revoking or withdrawing any pending or approved labor certification application or I-140 petitions obtained by the Licensor or its Affiliates on behalf of any of the Foreign Employees (and their dependents); (v) protect the permanent immigration cases and non-immigrant cases of each Foreign Employee (and their dependents), including, without limitation, any labor certification application, any I-140 petitions and any applications for adjustment of status; (vi) in the case of any pending labor certification, Licensor shall provide affirmative responses on the 45-day letter; (vii) provide copies to Licensee of all correspondence pertaining to all Foreign Employees both to and from Licensor; (viii) provide original approvals received after Closing of labor certifications or other approvals pertaining to such Foreign Employees and L-1 Employees (and their dependents); and (ix) take any and all other steps to preserve permanent residence processing and enable Licensee to file documentation as a successor-in-interest for immigration purposes. Any out-of-pocket third party expenses incurred by Licensor in order to satisfy their obligations under this Section _____ shall be reimbursed by Licensee.

S. Indemnity (Chapter 4.B.2 and 3; §§ 15 and 16)

1. General and Intellectual Property Indemnity – Neutral

1.1 **General Indemnifications.** Licensor shall indemnify, defend and hold Licensee, its Affiliates and their respective directors, officers, shareholders, members, employees, successors and assigns (collectively, "**Licensee Indemnified Parties**") harmless from and against, and shall pay any and all Losses sustained or incurred by any of the Licensee Indemnified Parties, based upon, relating to or arising from, any and all third party claims, actions, suits, proceedings or investigations in connection with or pertaining to any of the following: (a) any actual or alleged bodily injury or death, or damage to tangible personal or real property, notwithstanding the form in which any such action is brought (e.g., contract, tort or otherwise), to the extent such injuries or damages arise directly or indirectly from acts, errors or omissions that constitute negligence, willful misconduct or violations of Law by Licensor; (b) any actual or alleged breach of the following Licensor warranties – **Sections ____________ (Warranties)**; (c) Licensor's breach or failure to perform any of the obligations set forth in **Section ___** (Confidential Information); (d) any breach or failure by Licensor to comply with its obligations under **Section ___**, and any fines, penalties, sanctions, underpayments and/or other remedies to the extent such fines, penalties, sanctions, underpayments and/or other remedies relate to any breach of any Laws by Licensor or any Licensor Personnel; and (e) any failure by Licensor to pay applicable taxes, together with any interest and penalties, assessed or imposed against Licensee for which Licensor has responsibility pursuant to **Section ___** (Taxes) or applicable Laws.

1.2 **Indemnification Against Liability for Infringement.** Licensor shall indemnify, defend and hold the Licensee Indemnified Parties harmless from and against, and shall pay, any and all Losses sustained or incurred by any of the Licensee Indemnified Parties, based upon, relating to or arising from, any and all third party claims, actions, suits, proceedings or investigations alleging that the Licensed Software infringes, misappropriates and/or violates and/or Licensee's use of the Licensed Software in accordance with the terms of this Agreement constitutes a misappropriation, infringement and/or violation of any Intellectual Property Right of any third party.

2. Intellectual Property Indemnity – Licensee Oriented (§ 14)

Licensor shall promptly and fully defend, indemnify and hold harmless Licensee and its affiliates and their respective officers, directors, agents and employees (the "**Indemnified Parties**") against all claims, demands and judgments made or recovered against them for damages to or loss of real or tangible personal property, ***including Licensee's Confidential Information, data files, web content, software applications*** or for bodily injury or death to any person arising out of, or in connection with this Agreement, to the extent that such damage, injury or death was caused by an action or omission of Licensor, its subcontractor or its employees or agents, or on the issue of infringement of any patent, copyright, trade secret, trademark, or trade dress related to a Deliverable or the Services. Licensee shall notify Licensor of any such written claim or demand received by Licensee, and give Licensor reasonable control of the defense of any action or such claim or demand provided that any settlement or compromise which requires contribution from the Indemnified Parties must be approved by the Indemnified Parties and the Indemnified Parties shall, at Licensor's expense, cooperate with the indemnifying party in a reasonable way to facilitate the settlement or defense of such claim or demand. The Indemnified Parties may, at their expense and option, use counsel of their choosing to observe the defense of any such claim, and will have reasonable access to all defense documents during the defense.

3. Intellectual Property Indemnity – Long Form (§ 14)

Licensor represents and warrants to Licensee the following:

1.1 Licensor is the developer and owner of the Software or Licensor has the authority to grant the licenses to be granted hereunder, free and clear of any liens, claims and encumbrances, (a) there is no claim or proceeding pending or threatened with respect to the Software or any component thereof and (b) **the Software does not infringe or violate any patents, copyrights, trademarks, trade secrets, or other**

proprietary rights of any third party. There are no open source components included in the Software.

1.2 Licensor will indemnify and hold harmless Licensee, Affiliates and its and their officers, employees, directors, shareholders, representatives, attorneys, successors, and assigns from all damages, costs, losses, expenses **(including refunds of license fees,** settlement awards and attorneys' fees) and **other liabilities arising** from or in connection with (i) any breach of the warranty set forth in Section _____ (Warranties) above, (ii) any claim that Licensor does not have sufficient right or interest in the Software to enter into or perform this Agreement, or (iii) any claim that the Software or any component thereof infringes or violates any patent, copyright, trademark, trade secret, or other proprietary right of a third party.

1.3 **Licensor will, with counsel selected by Licensor and approved by Licensee, which approval shall not be unreasonably withheld,** defend, at its own expense, any suit or proceeding brought against Licensee or any Affiliate based on any breach of the warranty set forth in Section 1.1 above, any claim that Licensor does not have sufficient right or interest in the Software to enter into or perform this Agreement or any claim that the Software or any component thereof infringes any patent, copyright, mask work right, trademark, trade secret, or other proprietary right of a third party. **Licensee will give Licensor prompt written notice of any such claim and shall give Licensor reasonable cooperation and assistance (at no cost to Licensee)** with respect to such defense. Licensor will pay all damages and costs awarded against Licensee with respect to any such suit, proceeding or claim. Such indemnification will include all actions brought alleging an infringement or violation by Licensor of any patents, copyrights, trademarks, trade secrets, or other proprietary rights of any third party.

> ***COMMENT: This language benefits the licensee as it provides that any support given to vendor shall be "at no cost to Licensee." It is unclear whether the Licensor must reimburse the Licensee for its out-of-pocket costs as well as its internal/overhead costs. Further, is the Licensee relieved from its obligation of cooperation if such cooperation will incur a cost for the Licensee?***

1.4 Licensor shall have the full responsibility for the defense of any such suit or proceeding; provided, however, that (i) such defense shall be conducted at Licensor's sole cost and expense, (ii) Licensor shall keep Licensee informed of, and consult with Licensee in connection with, the progress of such litigation; and (iii) Licensor shall not have the right to settle any such claim if such settlement arises from or is part of any criminal action, suit or proceeding or contains a stipulation to, or admission or acknowledgment of, any wrongdoing (whether in tort or otherwise) on the part of Licensee or any Affiliate.

1.5 **Written notice of Licensor's intention to defend, accompanied by an acknowledgment, in writing, reasonably satisfactory to counsel for Licensee, that such claim is, subject to the provisions of Section 1, covered in its entirety by this indemnity** (the "Acknowledgment"), shall be delivered to Licensee within 10 days from the date of Licensor's notice of the institution of the claim. **Until Licensee receives the Acknowledgment, Licensee shall be entitled to defend such claim at**

Licensor's cost and expense, and Licensor shall be bound in the manner set forth in Section 1.6, below, *except* that Licensee shall not be entitled to settle such claim without the written consent of Licensor (which consent will not be unreasonably delayed or withheld).

1.6 If Licensor fails to deliver the Acknowledgment within the specified period or otherwise provide the defense or follow the procedures required by this Section 1, **or if Licensee reasonably concludes that Licensor will be unable to indemnify or defend them as required hereby or Licensor gives its written consent**, then Licensor shall not thereafter be entitled to control such defense, and Licensee shall be entitled, upon written notice to Licensor specifically referencing this Section 1.6, to **assume and control the defense, at Licensor's expense, with counsel of Licensee's own choosing.** In such event, Licensee may contest or settle the claim as it may choose, and Licensor shall be bound by and shall be liable for the results obtained by Licensee, including, without limitation, the amount of any judgment or good faith, out-of-court settlement or compromise, and all costs and fees of counsel. Licensor, at its own expense, shall be entitled to be present at such litigation, and Licensee shall keep Licensor informed of, and consult with Licensor in connection with, the progress of such litigation and settlement, and shall exercise reasonable efforts to minimize costs and fees incurred in connection with such defense and settlement.

1.7 Licensor shall have no liability for any claim of infringement based on: (i) modifications of the Software by Licensee if such infringement would have been avoided by the use of the Software without such modifications; or (ii) the combination, operation, or use of the Software with non-Licensor provided programs, data, or documentation if such infringement would have been avoided by the use of the Software without combination with such programs, data or documentation, unless such combination was contemplated by the Design Specifications.

1.8 Licensor shall either procure, at its own expense, the right for Licensee to continue using the Software or shall replace or modify the Software with functionally equivalent software so that it becomes non-infringing. If neither of the foregoing alternatives is feasible without undue expense, Licensor will accept the return of the Software and grant Licensee a refund based on the payments made by Licensee for the Software, as depreciated over a 60-month period.

4. Intellectual Property Indemnity – Licensor Oriented

1.1 **Third Party Infringement Claims.** Licensor will defend at its own expense any action against Licensee brought by a third party to the extent that the action is based upon a claim that the Licensed Software directly infringes any U.S. copyright or misappropriates any trade secret recognized as such under the Uniform Trade Secret Law, and Licensor will pay those costs and damages finally awarded against Licensee in any such action that are specifically attributable to such claim or those costs and damages agreed to in a monetary settlement of such action.

1.2 **Conditions.** Licensor's obligations under the preceding paragraph with respect to an action are conditioned on (a) Licensee notifying Licensor promptly in writing of such action, (b) Licensee giving Licensor sole control of the defense thereof and any related settlement negotiations, and (c) Licensee cooperating with Licensor in such defense (including, without limitation, by making available to Licensor all documents and information in Licensee's possession or control that are relevant to the infringement or misappropriation claims, and by making Licensee's personnel available to testify or consult with Licensor or its attorneys in connection with such defense).

1.3 **Licensor's Options.** If the Licensed Software becomes, or in Licensor's opinion is likely to become, the subject of an infringement or misappropriation claim, Licensor may, at its option and expense, either (a) procure for Licensee the right to continue using [distributing] the Licensed Software, (b) replace or modify the Licensed Software so that it becomes non-infringing, or (c) terminate Licensee's right to use [distribute] the Licensed Software **and give Licensee a refund or credit for the license fees actually paid by Licensee or Licensor for the infringing components of the Licensed Software less a reasonable allowance for the period of time Licensee has used the Licensed Software.**

> ***COMMENT: See Clause 6 below for language providing for a pre-rated refund.***

1.4 **Exclusions.** Not withstanding the foregoing, Licensor will have no obligation or otherwise with respect to any infringement or misappropriation claim based upon (a) any use [or distribution] of the Licensed Software not in accordance with the Agreement or for purposes not intended by Licensor, (b) any use of the Licensed Software in combination with other products, equipment, software or data not supplied by Licensor, (c) any use [or distribution] of any release of the Licensed Software other than the most current release made available to Licensee, or (d) any modification of the Licensed Software made by any person other than Licensor.

1.5 **THIS SECTION STATES LICENSOR'S ENTIRE LIABILTY AND LICENSEE'S SOLE AND EXCLUSIVE REMEDY FOR INFRINGEMENT AND MISAPPROPRIATION CLAIMS AND ACTIONS.**

5. Intellectual Property Indemnity – Licensee Oriented

1.1 **Indemnification.** Licensor will indemnify and hold Licensee [and its distributors, subdistributors, and customers] harmless from and against any and all claims, losses, liability, damages, costs, and expenses (including attorney's fees, expert witness fees, and court costs) directly or indirectly arising from or related to any actual or alleged infringement (including contributory infringement), misappropriation, or violation of any third party's patents, copyrights, trade secret rights, trademarks, or other intellectual property or proprietary rights of any nature in any jurisdiction in the world, resulting from the use [or distribution] of the Licensed Software by Licensee [or any of its distributors, subdistributors, and customers]. If Licensee's continued use [or distribution] of the Licensed Software is restricted or prohibited as a result of any such infringement, misappropriation, or violation of third party rights, Licensor shall, at Licensee's option and at no charge to Licensee, and in addition to Licensee's other rights and remedies, (a) secure for Licensee the right to continue using [and distributing] the Licensed Software as allowed under this Agreement, (b) modify or replace the infringing components of the Licensed Software so that they are non-infringing with no loss or degradation of features, functionality, or performance, or (c) refund to Licensee all amounts paid by Licensee [or its customers] for the Licensed Software.

1.2 [**Exclusions.** Notwithstanding the foregoing, Licensor will not be obligated to indemnify Licensee to the extent that an infringement or misappropriation claim is based upon (i) use [or distribution] of the Licensed Software in breach of this Agreement, if such infringement or misappropriation would not have occurred but for such breach; (ii) use of the Licensed Software in combination with other products not supplied or recommended by Licensor or specified by Licensor as being compatible with the Licensed Software, if such infringement or misappropriation would not have occurred but for such combined use; (iii) use [or distribution] of any release of the Licensed Software other than the most current release made available to Licensee, if the most current release was furnished to Licensee specifically to avoid such infringement or misappropriation and if such infringement or misappropriation would have been avoided by use [or distribution] of the most current release; or (iv) any modification of the Licensed Software made by Licensee (other than at Licensor's direction), if such infringement or misappropriation would not have occurred but for such modification.]

1.3 **Defense of Third Party Suits.** Licensee will use reasonable efforts to notify Licensor promptly of any third party claim, suit, or action (a "Claim") for which Licensee believes it is entitled to indemnification under this Section __ and which Licensee desires Licensor to defend. However, Licensee's failure to provide such notice or delay in providing such notice will relieve Licensor of its obligations under this Section __ only if and to the extent that such delay or failure materially prejudices Licensor's ability to defend such Claim. If Licensee tenders the defense of a Claim to Licensor, Licensor will have the right and the obligation to defend such Claim with counsel of its choice; however, Licensee may participate in the defense of the Claim with its own counsel and at its own expense. Once Licensor assumes defense of a Claim, it will be conclusively presumed that Licensor is obligated to indemnify Licensee for such Claim, and Licensee will cooperate with Licensor, at Licensor's reasonable request and at Licensor's expense, in the defense of the Claim. No settlement of a Claim will be binding on Licensee without Licensee's prior written consent.

6. Intellectual Property Indemnity – Prorated Refund of License Fee

. . . refund the License Fees paid to Licensee in respect of the Software to which the claim pertains, depreciated from the time of payment on a three-year, straight-line basis, to the extent that Licensor is obligated to issue corresponding refunds to End Users in respect of the software.

7. Intellectual Property Indemnity Exclusions

Licensor's foregoing indemnification obligations shall not apply to the extent the claim is based on: (a) modification of the Deliverables by the Licensee that did not receive prior express written authorization from the Licensor, (b) use of the Deliverables by the Licensee that is not compliant with the written usage recommendations provided by the Licensor or which violates the provisions of this Agreement, (c) specifications supplied by the Licensee and on the basis of which the disputed Deliverables were developed, (d) use of the disputed Deliverables in association with products or services not previously recommended or supplied by the Licensor, or (e) Licensee's failure to take the necessary actions to protect its rights in the Deliverables (e.g., filing patent applications).

8. General Indemnification – Balanced

Each party (the "Indemnifying Party") shall indemnify and hold harmless the other party and all of its officers, directors, partners, principals, employees, representatives and agents (collectively, the "Indemnified Party") from and against any and all demands, claims and actions by third parties, and all liabilities, judgments, damages, costs and expenses (including reasonable attorneys' fees) incurred in connection therewith, arising or resulting from personal injury or death, or damage to tangible personal or real property, caused by the Indemnifying Party. Neither party's indemnification obligation shall extend to Claims to the extent resulting from the fault of the Indemnified Party. The Indemnified Party shall provide prompt written notice of a Claim to the Indemnifying Party. The Indemnifying Party shall have sole control of the defense and settlement of such Claim, provided that the Indemnifying Party shall not settle any such Claim without the prior written consent of the Indemnified Party, which shall not be unreasonably withheld, delayed or conditioned. The Indemnified Party shall reasonably cooperate with the Indemnifying Party in the defense and settlement of such Claim.

T. Insurance (Chapter 6.C; § 38)

1. Licensor's Insurance Coverage

A. **General Requirements.** Within ten days of the Effective Date and upon request, Licensor shall provide to Licensee evidence of all insurance required hereunder. The insurance companies providing such insurance shall have an A.M. Best rating of A-X or better and be licensed or authorized to conduct business in all states in which Licensee or its affiliates does business. Licensee shall have the right to require Licensor to obtain the insurance required under this section from another insurance carrier in the event Licensee determines that Licensor's then current insurance carrier does not have an A.M. Best rating of A-X or better or is not licensed or authorized to conduct business in all states in which Licensee and its affiliates do. All policies and certificates of insurance shall be written as primary policies with Services performed and deliverable items produced by Licensor and its subcontractors and not written as policies contributing to, or to be used in excess of Licensee's insurance policies or any self-insurance program in which Licensee may participate with respect to such Services and Deliverable. The insurance requirements under this section are mandatory; failure of Licensee to request certificates of insurance shall not constitute a waiver of Licensor's obligations and requirements to maintain the minimal coverages specified.

B. **Types and Amounts.** During the term of this Agreement, and at its own cost and expense, Licensor shall obtain and maintain the following insurance coverages or self-insurance:

i. Commercial General liability insurance with a combined single annual aggregate limit of not less than Five Million Dollars ($5,000,000).

ii. Errors and Omissions insurance in amounts not less than Two Million Dollars ($2,000,000) per claim and not less than Five Million Dollars ($5,000,000) in the aggregate.

iii. Workers' compensation insurance and other insurance as required by statutes in the states in which the work will be performed. Coverage shall include Employers Liability with a limit not less that $1,000,000 for each occurrence.

iv. Business Automobile Liability Insurance covering owned and unowned vehicles with a combined single limit of not less than One Million Dollars ($1,000,000).

v. If Licensor purchases "claims made" insurance, all acts and omissions of Licensor and its representatives and agents, shall be, during the term of this Agreement, "continually covered" notwithstanding the termination of this Agreement or the provisions of this Agreement allowing Licensor to purchase "claims made" insurance coverage. In order for the acts and omissions of Licensor and its representatives and agents to be "continually covered" there must be insurance coverage for the entire period commencing on the Effective Date of this Agreement and ending on the date that is at a minimum of three (3) years after the final date that this Agreement is effective, including any extensions or renewals hereof, and such insurance must satisfy the liability coverage requirements provided for in this Agreement. Licensor acknowledges and agrees that the provisions of this Paragraph B may require Licensor to purchase "tail insurance" if its coverage lapses or "nose insurance" and/or "tail insurance" if Licensor changes insurance carriers, even after this Agreement is terminated.

C. **Subcontractors.** Licensor agrees to require any subcontractors it uses to perform work at Licensee's premises, if any, to carry, or Licensor will carry on behalf of said subcontractors, at a minimum, the following limits of insurance:

i. Workers' Compensation and other insurance in the amount required by statute in the state in which the work will be performed.

ii. Commercial General Liability Insurance, including independent contractors coverage, written on a broad form basis in a combined single limit of One Million Dollars ($1,000,000) per occurrence with an aggregate of not less than Two Million Dollars ($2,000,000).

iii. Business Automobile Liability Insurance covering any auto with a combined single limit of not less than One Million Dollars ($1,000,000).

D. **Policy Requirements.** Licensee shall be listed on all such insurance policies obtained by Licensor (except worker's compensation) as "**Additional Insureds**" up to the amount required of Licensor in this Exhibit __ of this Agreement. Licensor shall similarly require certain subcontractors to list Licensee as "Additional Insureds" if Licensor does not carry on behalf of such subcontractors the insurance required in Paragraph C of this Exhibit __. The provisions of this Exhibit __ shall not be deemed to limit the liability of Licensor hereunder, or limit any rights that Licensee, or its affiliates may have including, without limitation, rights of indemnity or contribution. Notwithstanding any other provisions of this Agreement, the provisions of this Exhibit __ shall survive termination of this Agreement.

2. *Licensor's Insurance Coverage – Alternate Language*

1.1 **Insurance.** Licensor shall, throughout the Master Term, maintain in full force and effect from a third party that is rated "A-" or better in Best's Insurance Guide, or otherwise reasonably acceptable to Licensee, the following insurance coverage for its operations worldwide:

1.1.1 Workers' Compensation complying with all statutory requirements of the state(s) in which work is to be performed and Employer's Liability insurance. The Employer's Liability shall be provided in amounts of $500,000.00 per occurrence.

1.1.2 Automobile liability covering all vehicles owned, non-owned, hired and leased in an amount of $1,000,000.00 per claim (combined single limit for bodily injury and property damage).

1.1.3 Commercial general liability insuring and the Umbrella policy against bodily injury, property damage, contractors' completed operations and contractual liability (covering Licensor's indemnification obligations contained herein) with a combined single limit of $5,000,000.00 per claim. This constitutes commercial general liability with a basic cover of U.S. $1,000,000 per occurrence and U.S. $ 2,000,000 as general aggregate.

1.1.4 Professional liability and errors and omissions insurance in an amount of $5,000,000.00 per claim.

In addition, Licensor, at Licensor's expense, shall forthwith procure and thereafter keep in full force and effect a fidelity bond or insurance policy reasonably satisfactory in form to Licensee, payable to Licensee, and issued by a bonding, insurance, or casualty company satisfactory to Licensee, pursuant to which Licensee will be held harmless by the surety or insurer in an amount of at least Five Million Dollars ($5,000,000.00) from any loss of money or other personal property belonging to Licensee or for which Licensor is legally liable, caused by larceny, embezzlement, forgery, misappropriation, wrongful abstraction, or any dishonest or fraudulent acts committed on or after the date hereof, by Licensor, its officers, directors, shareholders, or Employees.

1.2 **Inspection.** Licensor shall allow Licensee and Licensee or their representatives or property insurance company representatives, at any time with reasonable advance notice, to inspect, test or examine fire protection and security equipment, systems and procedures at the Licensor Service Location.

1.3 **Certificates.** Licensor shall within 15 Business Days following the Master Effective Date provide to Licensee certificates of insurance evidencing the above coverage, including a written acknowledgement from the insurance providers that Licensor's operations are covered worldwide (including India). Licensee and Licensee shall be listed as an additional insured on the policies noted in 1.1.2 and 1.1.3, above. Certificates furnished by Licensor shall provide that the policies shall not be materially changed or cancelled without providing 30 days written notice to Licensee.

1.4 **Use of Proceeds.** Proceeds received by Licensor from any claims under the insurance policies referenced in this Section shall be used to rapidly effect necessary repairs or replacement or to reimburse the affected Licensee Entities.

U. Intellectual Property (Chapter 3)

1. Copyright Notices

Licensor will affix the following Copyright Notice to the Developed Works developed under this Section and all accompanying documentation: "Copyright © [year] by the Licensee. All Rights Reserved." This notice shall appear on all tangible versions of the Developed Works delivered under this Agreement and any associated documentation. It shall also be programmed into any all Developed Works delivered hereunder so that it appears at the beginning of all visual displays of such Developed Works.

2. Trademark Protection

(a) **Limited License.** The parties acknowledge that Licensor may be required to reproduce and otherwise use certain trademarks and service marks of Licensee, including, without limitation, [Name of Mark] and [Name of Mark] (collectively, the "Trademarks") in the course of performing the Services. Licensee hereby grants Licensor a nonexclusive license to reproduce and display the Trademarks in such manner as Licensee may specifically direct from time to time. Licensor acknowledges the limitations on the scope of the foregoing license and shall make no use of any of the Trademarks beyond the scope of such limited license or otherwise not expressly approved by Licensee pursuant to the provisions of this Agreement.

(b) **Rights in Trademarks.** Licensor acknowledges that, as between Licensor and Licensee, all right, title, and interest in the Trademarks and the goodwill that they symbolize shall belong exclusively to Licensee and that all uses of the Trademark shall inure to the benefit of Licensee for all purposes. Licensor shall take no actions inconsistent with Licensee's ownership of and rights in the Trademarks. Licensor shall not file any application for registration of the Trademarks (or challenge any existing registrations or applications to register any of the Trademarks). Rather, Licensor shall, at Licensee's expense, fully cooperate with Licensee in maintaining and defending the validity and ownership of, and prosecuting any applications to register any of the Trademarks.

(c) **Specifications and Requirements.** Licensor will use the Trademarks strictly in accordance with such reasonable specifications and requirements as Licensee may from time to time prescribe. Any proposed use of the Trademarks by Licensor that is essentially the same as, and does not materially differ from, a prior approved use thereof shall be deemed acceptable to Licensee; provided, however, that Licensor shall provide Licensee with samples of such use sufficiently in advance of mass production thereof that Licensee may effectively object in the event it deems the use not to be essentially the same as one previously approved.

(d) **Quality Control.** In order to ensure that the use of the Trademarks is in compliance with the specifications and requirements prescribed by Licensee, Licensor shall send Licensee such samples of Licensor's use thereof as Licensee may reasonably require for the purpose of allowing Licensee to verify that such samples conform to such specifications and requirements. If any such samples do not conform to such specifications and requirements, Licensee shall so notify Licensor in a writing which describes the nonconformance, and Licensor shall promptly take appropriate steps to cause such its use of the Trademarks to so conform. In addition, Licensor shall permit duly authorized representatives or agents of Licensee at reasonable times during normal business hours and on reasonable written notice to visit Licensor's premises, review records relevant to the use of the Trademarks and meet with Licensor's personnel to oversee the use of the Trademarks.

3. *Jointly Owned Software – Use and Copyright Notice*

Upon acceptance by Customer, ownership of any Custom Software which consists partially of Vendor's Standard Software ("Vendor Portion") and partially of Customer Software specifically written by Vendor for Customer ("Customer Portion"), shall be as follows:

(a) The Customer Portion shall become the exclusive property of Customer, including title to copyrights and right to register the copyright in all copyrightable material in the Customer Portion. The ownership of all rights to the Customer Portion, including but not limited to copyrights, is hereby assigned to Customer.

(b) The Vendor Portion shall be specifically identified as being Vendor's Standard Software in Exhibit B and shall remain the exclusive property of Vendor; provided, however, that Customer shall have an unrestricted nontransferable, nonexclusive, royalty free, perpetual license to reproduce, use, modify, and sublicense the Vendor Portion, including any software provided to Vendor under the license from another supplier.

(c) If the Vendor Portion contains Software provided to Vendor under license from another supplier, such software shall be deemed Standard Software and shall remain the property of such other supplier. Any such Standard Software is identified in Exhibit B.

Vendor shall place the following notice on all disks or other media containing a copy of the Custom Software, which includes Vendor's Standard Software, and on all program material and shall embed it in the Customer Software so that it appears when the Custom Software is run or printed out:

> ***"This contains material which is the confidential, unpublished property licensed to Customer. Receipt or possession of it does not convey any rights to divulge, reproduce, use or allow others to use it without the specific written authorization of Customer, and use must conform strictly to the license agreement between user and Customer.***
>
> ***Copyright © 20__ [Vendor Legal Name]. All rights reserved***
>
> ***Copyright © 20__ [Customer Legal Name]. All rights reserved"***

Any portion of Custom Software which is not designated as being Vendor Portion shall be deemed to be Customer Portion.

V. Limitation of Liability (Chapter 4.B.7)

1. Tolling of Statute of Limitations for Matters Submitted to Arbitration

The statute of limitations with respect to any claim or matter submitted to arbitration shall be suspended as of the date of a demand for arbitration hereunder (or, if not determinable, as of the date of Receipt of such request), and shall be tolled until the date of any formal settlement agreement entered into by the Parties or the date of any final determination issued by an arbitrator, as the case may be, but in any event not longer than six (6) months from the date such statute of limitations was suspended, unless the Parties specifically agree in writing to a different tolling period.

W. Maintenance (Chapter 5.H)

1. Reinstatement of Maintenance (Chapter 5.H; § 3.14)

Licensor's obligation to offer support for the full Committed Support Period is conditional on continuous services; any request by Licensee to reestablish services after a period of time in which such services were not provided (regardless of whether within the Committed Support Period or otherwise) shall only be accepted in Licensor's sole discretion, and shall be subject to payment of a fee specified by Licensor at the time.

Licensee may reinstate Maintenance Services for any Application hereunder by paying a reinstatement charge consisting of an amount equivalent to the *pro rata* portion of the Annual Maintenance Fee that would have been due hereunder for the period elapsed since termination; provided, however, that such reinstatement charge shall not exceed twenty-five percent (25%) of the license fee for such Application in effect at the time of reinstatement.

Licensee may reinstate any terminated Maintenance Services by giving the Licensor at least thirty (30) days' written prior notice. Upon such reinstatement, the Licensor shall provide Licensee with the most current Upgrades at no additional cost. There will be no reinstatement penalty or fee. Upon reinstatement, the fees for Maintenance Services shall not exceed the fees in effect at the time of termination plus any increases permitted hereunder.

> ***COMMENT: Reinstatement addresses the situation where a customer ceased purchasing maintenance and later seeks to resume maintenance. Stopping and starting maintenance is problematic for the licensor as the licensee most likely is no longer operating the most current version of the software because it did not receive the updates and enhancements that were implemented during the period it did not purchase maintenance. In general, most licensors support only the two most recent versions of the supported product. Licensors want to prevent a customer from "gaming" the system (i.e., not paying maintenance in the hopes that nothing breaks, or is substantially upgraded), and then resuming maintenance once there is a new version or some other reason to resume maintenance of the software.***

2. *Reinstatement of Maintenance – Alternate Language (Chapter 5.H; § 23.B.2)*

In the event that Licensee terminates Maintenance, Licensee may later reinstate Maintenance provided the Software licensed by Licensee is upgraded to the then-current Software Release. The fee charged for such Maintenance reinstatement shall be equal to the cumulative standard Maintenance charges applicable for the Maintenance Terms during which Maintenance lapsed, plus an amount equal to 1.5 multiplied by the Maintenance charges for the then-current Maintenance Term.

3. *Commitment to Offer Support on Listed Operating Environments*

Licensor shall provide support for the Software on Licensee's hardware and in Licensee's current and *future operating environments provided those operating environments are listed by Licensor* as supported operating environments for the software.

COMMENT: Licensors should carefully consider making any commitment to maintain "future operating environments" as the licensor may lack the ability to do so or it may not be cost efficient to do so. The language above provides an element of protection to the licensor as the operating environment is limited to the operating environments listed in the attached exhibit.

4. Maintenance Fee Credit – Arising from Failure of Software to Achieve Acceptance in a Timely Manner

Licensor and Licensee will work together diligently and in good faith to achieve acceptance of the Software not later than [**date**], time being of the essence. In the event that Licensee provides timely cooperation to Licensor and the Software is not accepted by [**date**], then the Maintenance Fees set forth in Exhibit A of this Agreement shall be reduced by one percent (1%) [**for the initial Maintenance Term**]. In the event that Licensee provides timely cooperation to Licensor and the Software is not accepted by [**insert a later date than the previously inserted date**], then the Maintenance Fees sets forth in Exhibit A of this Agreement shall be reduced by two percent (2%) [**for the initial Maintenance Term**].

COMMENT: This paragraph provides for liquidated damages if the software is not accepted within the contractually required time frame. This language has been carefully drafted to require the licensee's "timely cooperation" as a condition precedent to the imposition of liquated damages.

5. Rejection of Update (Chapter 5.H; § 23.B.2)

Licensee must install patches and any new version of the Software within a reasonable time following commercial release of such new version by Licensor. Licensor shall not be responsible for maintenance services with respect to the Software if the Licensee refuses to permit updating of the Software by all applicable maintenance releases or if Licensee has not ensured that the hardware and network services are correctly configured and operating according to specifications, and operating system software and other third party software is current, and has all manufacturer/supplier-recommended updates and patches.

X. Miscellaneous

1. Health Crisis Preparations – Pandemics

1.1 In connection with Customer's health crisis preparedness and business continuation efforts and to maintain a safe working environment, Vendor agrees to the following:

(a) Vendor must immediately report to Customer's Chief Medical Officer or his/her designee all cases of communicable or infectious diseases that are required to be reported to any applicable state or federal authorities and that are contracted by any Employees who have been on-site at Customer and the location where the Employees provided Services to Customer. Vendor's reporting requirement with respect to any individual will continue for ninety (90) days following the date the individual in question was at Customer's site. Vendor should not disclose the name of the applicable Employee to Customer. Vendor will cooperate with the Chief Medical Officer or his/her designee in investigating the risk to Customer's personnel from possible exposure to Employees.

(b) In the event of a health crisis, only Employees who have been approved for access to a Customer site by using Customer's on-line screening tool found at http://www.XXXXX.com or, alternatively, by completing a phone or in-person screening of a similar nature will be provided access. If such Employee(s) or personnel is not approved to access a Customer site or is advised that Customer's pandemic or health crisis policies will prohibit entry onto Customer's site, Customer shall not be responsible for making payment to Vendor for such time that the Employee(s) or personnel was not permitted to enter the Customer site(s).

1.2 Vendor also acknowledges and agrees that Customer may (a) disclose information regarding its facilities and/or personnel to public health authorities as required by law and/or as the situation requires, and (b) update its pandemic preparedness and business continuation requirements from time to time and/or as the situation requires. In furtherance of the foregoing, Vendor at its own cost will take whatever reasonable remedial action is requested by Customer and in accordance with industry standards and applicable laws.

COMMENT: With significant media focus on the Swine flu, H1N1 virus and other health pandemics, many customers are seeking to impose certain health reporting standards. These issues have raised the question of whether a health pandemic would qualify as an event of force majeure given such pandemics they are widely discussed in the media and by government agencies and are thus foreseeable. Prudent parties will implement their own policies and implement backup plans to ensure they can meet their contractual obligations in the event of a health pandemic.

2. *Electronic Purchase Orders*

A material inducement for Customer to enter into this Agreement with the Vendor is Vendor's commitment to work with Customer to create an OCI[1] compliant Product and Services catalogue from which Customer can (i) send electronic Purchase Orders for the Vendor's Products and Services, (ii) receive an electronic Product shipment confirmation (also known as advanced shipping notice), (iii) receive an electronic proof of delivery and (iv) receive an electronic invoice. The Vendor's failure to implement this end-to-end E-business process in a timely manner shall be considered sufficient cause for Customer to terminate the Agreement in accordance with the terms of the Agreement.

Y. Open Source Software (Chapter 8; § 16.AA)

1. *Restrictions on Open Source Software*

The parties contemplate the use of certain open source software, and agree as follows:

1.1 **"Non-Permissive Open Source Code"** means any software program, or portion thereof, that is licensed under a license that requires as a condition of use, modification, and/or distribution of the software subject to the license, that such software or other software combined and/or distributed with such software be (i) disclosed or distributed in source code form; (ii) licensed for the purpose of making derivative works; or (iii) redistributable at no charge.

1.2 **"Permissive Open Source Code"** means any software program, or portion thereof, that is licensed under a license that (a) grants the user the right to freely use, copy, modify, distribute and display the source code for a software program and (b) does not require as a condition of use, modification, and/or distribution of the software subject to the license, that such software or other software combined and/or distributed with such software be (i) disclosed or distributed in source code form; (ii) licensed for the purpose of making derivative works; or (iii) redistributable at no charge. For purposes of clarity, software subject to the Berkeley Style Database license available on the Open Source Initiative website (www.opensource.org) would be considered Permissive Open Source Code while software licensed under the General Public License (also available on the Open Source Initiative website) would not.

2.1 The parties acknowledge that a portion of the software to be delivered under this Agreement may be Permissive Open Source Code. Licensor represents and warrants that Licensor shall not take any action for the Term of this Agreement that would alter such software's status as Permissive Open Source Code as defined above.

1 OCI refers to Open Catalogue Interface, a type of punch-out technology developed by SAP, Inc.

2.2 Licensor represents and warrants that any and all software to be delivered under this Agreement does not, and will not, contain or require to function properly, any Non-Permissive Open Source Code except as identified on Exhibit __.

Z. Performance Standards (Chapter 5.F; § 3.10.3.B)

1. *Service Levels*

(a) Licensor shall provide the Services in compliance with the Service Responsibility Matrix, Service Levels and Credits attached hereto as Exhibit __, as amended from time to time, for each individual Service. Licensor also agrees to provide the Services in compliance with the aggregate Service Levels set forth in Exhibit __.

(b) In the event that a Service Level has not been met, Licensor shall (1) perform a root-cause analysis to identify the cause of such failure, (2) promptly correct such failure within the timeframe set forth in Exhibit __, (3) provide Licensee with a written report detailing the cause of, and procedure for correcting, such failure and (4) provide Licensee with reasonable evidence that such failure will not reoccur. Licensor shall promptly provide to Licensee the report described in (3) and the evidence described in (4), within fourteen (14) days after such Service Level failure has occurred.

(c) In the event that the Services have not been provided in accordance with the applicable Service Levels, Licensee shall receive the credits and payments from Licensor as identified in Exhibit __.

2. *In Absence of Service Levels*

All Services without expressly defined Service Levels must be performed at least to the same degree of accuracy, completeness, efficiency, quality and timeliness as is provided by well-managed suppliers providing services similar to the Services, so long as such performance is commercially and operationally reasonable. For where there are expressly defined Service Levels, or where performance can be commercially reasonably reported, Licensor will measure and report its performance against these standards on at least a monthly basis, except as many otherwise be agreed between the Parties in respect of Services performed less frequently than monthly.

3. *Performance Standards For Delivery of Services – General Language*

Licensor will devote commercially reasonable efforts to perform the Services ethically, promptly and diligently and commensurate with professional standards associated with Licensor's profession.

AA. Policies (Chapter 23.J)

1. Customer Policies – General

Vendor agrees to comply with, and cause its Employees to comply, with any and all Customer policies, procedures and standards, including without limitation, Customer's travel and expense policies, privacy and information security policies, Customer's security procedures applicable to persons performing Services at Customer's premises, and Customer's policies for vendors at http://www.xxxxxx.com, all of which Customer may update or revise from time to time.

> ***COMMENT: Licensors should be hesitant to agree to be bound by policies set forth on a URL, as they may change causing the licensor to be in breach of the agreement or incur additional costs. At a minimum, the licensor should require the licensee to notify the licensor in advance of any changes to the policies and compensate the licensor for any increased costs it incurs in complying with the policy.***

2. Use of Internet Access by Licensor Employees Working at Licensee Site

Licensee acknowledges that Licensor's workers may have business reasons to access the Internet on site at Licensee's during billable work time. Licensee requires that this Internet access be limited to business use only. Licensee will monitor Internet usage for compliance with this section. In the event a Licensor worker accesses the Internet for non Licensee business reasons, Licensor will be notified of the time spent in non-business related activity. Licensor shall reimburse Licensee for all non-Licensee Internet usage in half hour increments at the current billing rates for non-Licensee usage during billable work time, within thirty (30) days of the reported violation.

Accessing or attempting to access unauthorized sites such as those containing adult content and/or any material that would be considered offensive or disrespectful to others is cause for immediate dismissal of the Licensor worker from Licensee's premises and without any required advance notice to Licensor. This type of Internet usage is considered cause for cancellation of all Licensor contractual obligations by Licensee with advance notice and opportunity to cure. Licensor will be notified by Licensee in writing of the immediate dismissal and the objectionable access by its worker. Licensor shall replace the individual with another equally qualified representative within forty-eight (48) hours.

3. Policy and Procedures Manual

(a) **Delivery and Contents.** As part of the Services, and at no additional charge to Licensee, Licensor shall deliver to Licensee for its review, comment and approval (i) an outline of the topics to be addressed in the Policy and Procedures Manual within thirty (30) days after the Commencement Date; (ii) a final draft of the sections of the Policy and Procedures Manual relating to each Functional Service Area within forty-five (45) days after the initiation of Services in such Functional Service Area; and (iii) an integrated Policy and Procedures Manual for all Services within ninety (90) days after the initiation of Services in the last of the Functional Service Areas to be initiated (the "**Policy and Procedures Manual**"). At a minimum, the Policy and Procedures Manual shall include the following:

(i) a detailed description of the Services and the manner in which each will be performed by Licensor, including (A) the Equipment, Software, and Systems to be procured, operated, supported, or used; (B) documentation (including operations manuals, user guides, specifications, policies/procedures, and disaster recovery plans) providing further details regarding such Services; (C) the specific activities to be undertaken by Licensor in connection with each Service, including, where appropriate, the direction, supervision, monitoring, staffing, reporting, planning, and oversight activities to be performed by Licensor under this Agreement; (D) the checkpoint reviews, testing, acceptance, controls, and other procedures to be implemented and used to assure service quality; and (E) the processes, methodologies, and controls to be implemented and used by Licensor to ensure compliance with applicable Laws;

(ii) the procedures for Licensee/Licensor interaction and communication, including (A) call lists; (B) procedures for and limits on direct communication by Licensor with Licensee personnel; (C) problem management and escalation procedures; (D) Change Control Procedures; (E) priority and project procedures; (F) Acceptance related procedures (subject to Section _____); (G) quality assurance procedures and checkpoint reviews; (H) the project formation process and implementation methodology; and (I) annual and quarterly financial objectives, budgets, and performance goals; and

(iii) practices and procedures addressing such other issues and matters as Licensee shall require.

Licensor shall incorporate Licensee's then-current policies and procedures in the Policy and Procedures Manual to the extent it is directed to do so by Licensee.

(b) **Revision and Maintenance.** Licensor shall incorporate any comments or suggestions of Licensee into the Policy and Procedures Manual and shall deliver a final revised version to Licensee within fifteen (15) days of its receipt of such comments and suggestions for Licensee's approval. The Policy and Procedures Manual will be delivered and maintained by Licensor in hard copy and electronic formats and will be accessible electronically to Licensee management and Authorized Users in a manner consistent with Licensee's security policies.

(c) **Compliance.** Licensor shall perform the Services in accordance with applicable Laws and Licensee's then-current policies and procedures until the Policy and Procedures Manual is finalized and agreed upon by the Parties. Thereafter, Licensor shall perform the Services in accordance with the Policy and Procedures Manual. In the event of a conflict between the provisions of this Agreement and the Policy and

Procedures Manual, the provisions of this Agreement shall control unless the Parties expressly agree otherwise and such agreement is set forth in the relevant portion of the Policy and Procedures Manual.

(d) **Modification and Updating.** Licensor shall promptly modify and update the Policy and Procedures Manual quarterly to reflect changes in the operations or procedures described therein and to comply with Licensee Standards, the Technology Plan, and Strategic Plans as described in Section ___. Licensor shall provide the proposed changes in the manual to Licensee for review, comment and approval. To the extent such change could (i) increase Licensee's total costs of receiving the Services; (ii) have adverse impact or require changes as described in Section ___ (Change Orders), or (iii) violate or be inconsistent with the Licensee Standards, the Technology Plan, or Strategic Plans, Licensor shall not implement such change without first obtaining Licensee's approval, which Licensee may withhold in its sole discretion.

(e) **Annual Review.** The Parties shall meet to perform a formal annual review of the Policy and Procedures Manual on each anniversary of the Effective Date.

4. *Policy and Procedures Manual – Alternate Language*

1.1 The "Procedures Manual" shall describe how Licensor shall perform and deliver the Services under this Agreement, the Equipment and Software being used, and the documentation (e.g., operations manuals, user guides, specifications) that provides further details of such activities. The Procedures Manual shall describe the activities Licensor proposes to undertake in order to provide the Services, including those direction, supervision, monitoring, staffing, reporting, planning, and oversight activities normally undertaken to provide services of the type Licensor is to provide under this Agreement. The Procedures Manual also shall include the items described in Section ____of Schedule ____, descriptions of the acceptance testing and quality assurance procedures approved by Licensee, and other standards and procedures of Licensor pertinent to Licensee's interaction with Licensor in obtaining the Services. The Procedures Manual shall be suitable for use by Licensee to understand the Services.

1.2 Within ninety (90) days after the Effective Date, Licensor shall deliver a draft Procedures Manual to Licensee, for Licensee's comments and review. Licensor shall incorporate reasonable comments or suggestions of Licensee and shall finalize the Procedures Manual thirty (30) days after receiving Licensee's comments. The final Procedures Manual shall be subject to the approval of Licensee. Licensor shall periodically update the Procedures Manual to reflect changes in the operations or procedures described therein. Updates of the Procedures Manual shall be provided to Licensee for review, comment, and approval. Licensor shall perform the Services in accordance with the Procedures Manual. The Procedures Manual shall not be used to amend this Agreement. In the event of a conflict between the provisions of this Agreement and the Procedures Manual, the provisions of this Agreement shall control.

BB. Price/Payment (Chapter 4.B.8; § 8)

1. Currency Conversion

License fees shall be paid in United States dollars in [City, State] or at such other place as Licensor may reasonably designate consistent with the laws and regulations controlling in any foreign country. If any currency conversion shall be required in connection with the payment of license fees hereunder, such conversion shall be made by using the exchange rate prevailing at ______________ Bank on the last business day of the calendar month of the quarterly reporting period to which such royalty payments relate.

2. Currency Exchange Control

If at any time legal restrictions prevent the prompt remittance of part or all of any license fees with respect to any country in the Territory where any Software is licensed, payment shall be made through such lawful means or methods as the parties reasonably shall determine, the parties agreeing to fully cooperate in effecting such remittance.

> ***COMMENT: Some countries prohibit the export of "hard" currencies without the approval of the country's central bank. These approvals can be quite lengthy and cumbersome. As such, the licensor should carefully consider this risk prior to entering into a licensing agreement in a third world country and seek alternate payment mechanisms that do not require central bank approval.***

3. Annual Adjustment to Charges

A. **Adjustment to Charges.** Unless otherwise expressly provided in an Authorization Letter with respect to the charges to be paid thereunder, the Parties acknowledge and agree to use the Employment Cost Index for Total Compensation (not seasonally adjusted), Private Industry Workers, White-collar occupations excluding sales, June 1989 = 100 (the "ECI"), as the basis for annual adjustments to [all] charges to be paid by Licensee to Licensor under each Authorization Letter for those Services listed in Section E of this Schedule ____ (the "ECI Adjustable Charges").

The ECI is published by the Bureau of Labor Statistics (the "BLS") of the U.S. Department of Labor. For purposes of this Schedule ___, the most recently published ECI as of any anniversary of the Effective Date is the "ECI Current Index", and the "ECI Base Index" is the ECI Current Index from the prior anniversary of the Effective Date (or, for the first anniversary, the ECI most recently published as of the Effective Date). If, on any anniversary of the Effective Date, the ECI Current Index is higher than the ECI Base Index, then, effective as of such anniversary, an adjustment to the ECI Adjustable Charges will be made by increasing the ECI Adjustable Charges by the percentage that the ECI Current Index increased from the ECI Base Index. In calculating the percentage increase, the Parties agree to round to one decimal place. If, on any anniversary of the Effective Date, the ECI Current Index is lower than the ECI Base Index, no adjustment to the ECI Adjustable Charges will be made. If the period from the ECI Base Index to the ECI Current Index is other than 12 months, an adjustment to a full year will be made in the manner indicated in the example set forth in Section C of this Schedule ___. The ECI is published quarterly at the end of the month following the quarter measured, and the most recently published ECI as of the Effective Date was the ECI published on or around ____________ **[insert month, day and year]** for the quarter ending ______________ **[insert month and year]**. The Parties acknowledge and agree the Licensor will adjust the ECI Adjustable Charges and will advise Licensee of such adjustment in writing so that the new charges will amend this Agreement and become effective on the applicable anniversary of the Effective Date. If no adjustment is made on an anniversary date for any reason, Licensor will advise Licensee in writing of such fact.

B. **Adjustment to Charges Example.** The following is an example of the adjustments described in Section A of this Schedule ___. The specific numbers used in the example are for illustration purposes only and are not necessarily reflective of an actual calculation hereunder or the actual ECI.

Annual Adjustment on First Anniversary Date:

Example Charge under this Agreement	$1,500.00
ECI Current Index	136.0
ECI Base Index (as of Effective Date)	129.0
Percentage Change	(136.0 – 129.9) / 129.9 – 4.7%
Charge Increased by (1+ Percentage Change)	$1,500.00* (1 + 4.7%)
Equals Adjusted Charge	$1,570.50

Annual Adjustment on Second Anniversary Date:

Adjusted Charge as of First Anniversary Date	$1,570.50
ECI Current Index	143.2
ECI Base Index (as of First Anniversary Date)	136.0
Percentage Change	(143.2 – 136.0) / 136.0 = 5.3%
Charge Increased by (1+ Percentage Change)	$1,570.50* (1 + 5.3%)
Equal Adjusted Charge	$1,653.74

Annual Adjustment on Third Anniversary Date:

Adjusted Charge as of Second Anniversary Date	$1,653.74
ECI Current Index	140.9
ECI Base Index (as of Second Anniversary Date)	143.2
Percentage Change	No adjustment is made
Charge Increased by (1+ Percentage Change)	$1,653.74* (1 + 0.0%)
Equals Adjusted Charge*	$1,653.74

* The ECI Base Index for the fourth anniversary date would be 143.2.

C. **Changes to Index.** In the event that the BLS should stop publishing the ECI or should substantially change the content, format or calculation methodology of the ECI, the Parties will substitute another comparable measure published by a mutually agreeable source, except as noted below. If the change is to redefine the base period for the ECI from one period to some other period, the Parties will continue to use the index but will use the new base period figures for all future adjustments. If the change is to the name of the ECI, the new name will be used instead of the old name so long as the numbers previously published for the index have not changed. If the change is to the publication schedule, the Parties may agree in writing to use a different publication schedule and to adjust any partial year to a full year, if needed. The adjustment to convert a partial year to a full year is shown below.

ECI Current Index as of July 20XX	151.0
ECI Base Index as of June 20XX-1	145.2
Percentage Change (rounded to 3 decimals)	(151.0-145.2)/145.2=3.994%
Percent Times 12 Divided # of Months in Period	3.994% * 12 / 13
Equals Percentage Change (rounded to 1 decimal)* 3.7%	

* This calculation method will be used instead of the Percentage Change calculation shown in Section B of this Schedule ___ if the period between the ECI Base Index and the ECI Current Index is other than 12 months.

D. **Adjustments Using Davis Index.** The Parties acknowledge and agree to use the percent change in "Total Cash Compensation" for Systems Integrators (the "Percent Change") as the basis for annual adjustments to [all] charges to be paid by Licensee to Licensor under each Authorization Letter for those Services listed in Section 5 of this Schedule ___ as being subject to this Section D (the "Davis Index Adjustable Charges"), as the Percent Change is either reported in the Davis and Neusch Index for Total Cash Compensation (the "Index") or as such Systems Integrators job information is otherwise made available by the consulting firm of Davis & Neusch, Inc. no longer make comparable Systems Integrators job information available). If, on any September 1 during the term of this Agreement, the most recently published or available Percent Change is positive, an adjustment to the Davis Index Adjustable charges will be made by increasing the Davis Index Adjustable Charges by such Percent Change. If an adjustment is not made on a September 1 for any reason, then the basis for measuring the Percent Change for the following September 1 will be same as the basis for measuring the Percent Change for the September 1 on which no adjustment was made. The Parties acknowledge and agree that Licensor will adjust the David Index Adjustable Charges and will advise Licensee of such adjustment in writing so that the new charges will amend this Agreement and become effective on the applicable September 1. If no adjustment is made on a September 1 for any reason, Licensor will advise Licensee in writing of such fact.

E. **Service Categories.** The Parties acknowledge and agree that the following Services will be subject to adjustment in accordance with Section A of this Schedule ____: ________________. **[NOTE – THESE SERVICES SHOULD BE THOSE THAT ARE NOT PRIMARILY SYSTEMS ENGINEERING OR SYSTEMS ADMINISTRATOR RELATED AND ARE TO BE ADJUSTED PURSUANT TO THE ECI**

PERCENTAGE CHANGES.] The Parties acknowledge and agree that the following Services will be subject to adjustment in accordance with Section D above of this Schedule ___ **[NOTE - THESE SERVICES SHOULD BE THOSE THAT ARE PRIMARILY SYSTEMS ENGINEERING OR SYSTEMS ADMINISTRATOR RELATED AND ARE TO BE ADJUSTED PURSUANT TO THE DAVIS INDEX.]**

4. *Fee Increases Tied to United States CPI*

Fee increases tied to United States CPI: Notwithstanding the foregoing, in no event shall the fees for Services in any year increase over the prior year's fees by more than the lesser of (a) the Consumer Price Index (All Items) published for the United States for the prior year; or (b) 3%.

> ***COMMENT: The licensor should clearly state that in the*** **event the CPI is negative, the licensor's prices will not be reduced. Further, the licensor may want to provide for a minimum annual increase.**

5. *Fee Increases Tied to Indian CPI*

In addition, the fees, if any, for off-shore resources will not increase by greater than 6% per year or the percentage change in the UNME (as defined below) and the percentage change in the exchange ratios between the U.S. Dollar and the Indian Rupee, as described below, whichever is less, and if Licensor increases its rates for all of its customers. The calculation for the hourly rates relating to Licensor's employees providing Services in India shall be determined in two steps by utilizing the Indian Consumer Price Index for Urban Non-Manual Employees (the "UNME") and determining the increase or decrease in the exchange ratio between the U.S. Dollar and the Indian Rupee. The following calculation shall be done first, the product of (i) the applicable the applicable hourly rate and (ii) the sum of (x) one (1) and (y) the quotient of (a) the UNME for January of the current calendar year less the UNME for January of the prior calendar year (the "Prior Year UNME") over (b) the Prior Year UNME. The amount calculated in accordance with the previous sentence shall be adjusted upward or downward by the percentage increase or decrease in the exchange rate between the U.S. Dollar and the Indian Rupee from the previous January 1 to the then current January 1.

6. *Disputed Amounts*

If an invoiced amount is disputed in good faith by Licensee then, until resolution of the dispute, Licensee may suspend disputed payments and toll the running of time for default by: (a) paying the undisputed amount, if any; and (b) sending a written statement of exceptions to Licensor. All of Licensor's obligations shall continue unabated during the duration of the dispute resolution.

COMMENT: The licensor should seek to limit the amount the licensee can withhold and provide for interest in the event the licensor prevails in the dispute.

7. Pass-Through Charges

Licensee shall not be responsible for any pass-through charges or license fees to be paid by Licensor directly to a third party for any Third Party Products or otherwise unless Licensee has expressly agreed to such charges in **Appendix __**.

COMMENT: To avoid any financial surprises, the licensee should avoid agreeing to pay for any third party charges. The licensee should require the licensor to list any third party fees or products which the licensee is responsible for purchasing or paying for as an exhibit to the underlying agreement. The licensor should be responsible for any fees or products not listed on the exhibit on the time of contract signature.

8. Letter of Credit

The Letter of Credit shall secure the performance of Licensor, including without limitation performance of the Services in accordance with the Work Plan and providing Deliverables in accordance with the Specifications, and shall secure any damages, cost, or expenses resulting from Licensor's default in performance hereunder or liability caused by Licensor. In the event of default, the Letter of Credit shall become payable to Licensee for any outstanding damage assessments made by Licensee against Licensor. An amount up to the full amounts of the Letter of Credit may also be applied to Licensor's liability for any administrative costs and/or excess costs incurred by Licensee in obtaining similar Software, Deliverables, other products, and Services to replace those terminated as a result of Licensor's default. Licensee may seek other remedies in addition to this stated liability.

9. Liens/Security Interests

Licensor shall not file, or by its action or inaction permit, any liens to be filed on or against property or realty of Licensee. In the event that any such liens arise as a result of Licensor's action or inaction, Licensor shall obtain a bond to fully satisfy such liens or otherwise remove such liens at its sole cost and expense within ten (10) business days. If Licensor fails to do so, Licensee may, in its sole discretion, pay the amount of such lien, and/or deduct such amounts from payments due to the Licensor.

Licensor has not granted to any third party any security interests over any Intellectual Property Rights (i) used by Licensor in connection with the provision of the Services to Licensee or (ii) licensed to Licensee under this Agreement.

10. Liens – Alternative Language

Licensor will keep the premises, facilities, improvements, machinery, and equipment of Licensee and its affiliates free and clear from any and all liens arising out of the Services performed or materials furnished hereunder. Licensor will obtain properly executed waivers and releases from all subcontractors or other persons entitled to liens for Services or materials furnished in accordance with this Agreement. Licensor hereby indemnifies, defends and holds harmless Licensee and its affiliates against any and all costs, expenses, losses and all damages resulting from the filing of any such liens against Licensee or its affiliates. As a condition to payment hereunder, Licensor will from time to time, upon request by Licensee, furnish waivers or releases of such liens or receipts in full for all claims for such Services or materials and an affidavit that all such claims have been fully satisfied.

11. Pricing Based on Number of CPU Cores

The number of required licenses shall be determined by multiplying the total number of cores of the Processor by a core Processor licensing factor specified on the Company Processor Core Factor Table, which can be accessed at http://xxxxx.com/contracts. All cores on all multi-core chips for each licensed program are to be aggregated before multiplying by the appropriate core processor licensing factor and all fractions of a number are to be rounded up to the next whole number. When licensing the Software, a Processor is counted equivalent to an occupied socket; however, in the case of multi-chip modules, each chip in the multi-chip module is counted as one occupied socket.

12. Change in Credit Rating

In the event Customer's credit rating falls to the following ratings as published by the respective rating agencies (i) payment terms shall change to thirty (30) days in advance of services at an amount equal to the average monthly billing from the previous twelve (12) months and (ii) any deferred amounts shall immediately become due.

AGENCY	RATING
S & P	BBB-
Moody's	Baa3
Fitch	BBB-
AM Best	B+
Demotech	<A

13. Prospective Cost Reduction

Licensor and Licensee will work together diligently and in good faith to achieve acceptance of the Software not later than [**date**], time being of the essence. In the event that Licensee provides timely cooperation to Licensor and the Software is not accepted by [**date**], then all fees accruing thereafter shall be reduced by five percent (5%). In the event that Licensee provides timely cooperation to Licensor and the Software is not accepted by [**insert a later date than the previously inserted date**], then all fees accruing thereafter shall be reduced by seven percent (7%).

CC. Purchase Orders/Work Orders (Chapter 5.C)

1. Manner of Executing Work Orders

Customer may from time to time request Licensor to prepare and submit a proposed Statement of Work signed by Licensor. Should it choose to comply, Licensor bears the expense of preparing and submitting the proposal. A proposed Statement of Work becomes part of the Agreement only if Customer accepts it by:

(i) Signing the proposed Statement of Work (or an identical counterpart). Customer may then issue a purchase order solely for administrative purposes. If so, neither the terms and conditions of the purchase order nor anything else about it affects the agreed Statement of Work.

(ii) Issuing its standard form of purchase order solely for the purpose of accepting the proposed Statement of Work without revision. Neither the terms and conditions of the purchase order nor anything else about it affects the proposed Statement of Work.

> ***COMMENT: If a substantial amount of time and effort will be expended in creating the statement of work, the licensor should consider charging the customer for preparing the requested statement of work on a time and materials basis. Otherwise, the licensor bears the financial risk that the customer does not enter into the statement of work that the licensor prepared and thus cannot recoup its costs. The licensor should clearly state that the terms of any purchase order issued by the customer shall not apply to avoid unknowingly accepting potentially disadvantageous terms.***

2. Unauthorized Work; Pre-Contract Work Authorization

Licensee will not be required to compensate Licensor for any work not described in a Statement of Work, order form, or other appropriate writing signed by an authorized representative of Licensee, either as originally agreed to or as changed pursuant to the change control procedures set forth in Section ___ (Change Control) herein. An exception to the requirement of an executed Statement of Work may be made if Licensee determines there is an urgent requirement to commence work and authorizes commencement of work before the finalization of a written Statement of Work by way of a Pre-Contract Work Authorization ("PCWA") duly signed by Licensee; provided, however, that Licensee can terminate the PCWA at anytime if not satisfied with the progress being made toward finalization of a written Statement of Work.

DD. Quality Assurance (Chapter 5.E; § 9.13)

1. Quality Assurance and Internal Controls (§ 9.13(i))

(a) General. Licensor shall develop and implement Quality Assurance and internal control (e.g., financial and accounting controls, organizational controls, input/output controls, system modification controls, processing controls, system design controls, and access controls) processes and procedures, including implementing tools and methodologies, to ensure that the Services are performed in an accurate and timely manner, in accordance with (i) the Service Levels and other requirements of this Agreement; (ii) generally accepted accounting principles (applied in accordance with SAS-69 and generally accepted auditing standards); (iii) the best practices of leading providers of services that are the same as or similar to the Services; (iv) the Laws applicable to Licensee and the Eligible Recipients (including the Privacy Laws), and (v) industry standards (i.e., QS 9000, ISO 9001/2000, ISO 14000, ISO 17799, and BS 7799) applicable to Licensee and the Eligible Recipients and the performance of the Services, including applicable requirements for certification or accreditation of the Joint Commission on Accreditation of Healthcare Organizations (JCAHO). Such processes, procedures, and controls shall include verification, checkpoint reviews, testing, acceptance, and other procedures for Licensee to assure the quality and timeliness of Licensor's performance. Without limiting the generality of the foregoing, Licensor shall:

(i) Maintain a strong control environment in day-to-day operations, to assure that the following fundamental control objectives are met: (1) financial and operational information is valid, complete, and accurate; (2) operations are performed efficiently and achieve effective results, consistent with the requirements of this Agreement; (3) assets are safeguarded; and (4) actions and decisions of the organization are in compliance with Laws;

(ii) Build the following basic control activities into work processes: (1) accountability clearly defined and understood; (2) access properly controlled; (3) adequate supervision; (4) transactions properly authorized; (5) transactions properly recorded; (6) transactions recorded in proper accounting period; (7) policies, procedures; and responsibilities documented; (8) adequate training and education; (9) adequate separation of duties; and (10) recorded assets compared with existing assets;

(iii) Develop and execute a process to ensure periodic control self-assessments are performed with respect to all Services (such self-assessments to be performed at least annually unless and until Licensee approves less frequent self-assessments);

(iv) Maintain an internal audit function to sufficiently monitor the processes and Systems used to provide the Services (i.e., perform audits, track control measures, communicate status to management, drive corrective action, etc.). As part of such internal audit function, Licensor shall:

(1) Develop and execute an annual risk assessment process to evaluate risk in the Services. This assessment shall become the basis to create an annual risk-based audit plan of Services. The plan shall be provided to Licensee for its review and approval in sufficient time to permit Licensee to comply with its obligations and requirements;

(2) Promptly provide audit reports resulting from subsequent audit activity to Licensee, and make related work papers available to Licensee upon request;

(3) Adopt a qualitative methodology (i.e., high, medium, low effectiveness) of reporting the level of controls and internal audit results; and

(4) Provide to Licensee a summary of planned audit activity, audit activity performed, associated significant findings, and status of follow-up activity, and a summary of control incidents (i.e., frauds, conflict of interest situations, etc.) and related corrective action, at least quarterly; and

(v) Conduct investigations of suspected fraudulent activities within Licensor's organization that impact or could impact Licensee or the Eligible Recipients. Licensor shall promptly notify Licensee of any such suspected fraudulent activity and the results of any such investigation as they relate to Licensee or the Eligible Recipients. At Licensor's request, Licensee shall provide reasonable assistance to Licensor in connection with any such investigation;

(vi) Comply with the Licensee Code of Conduct set forth in Schedule __;

(vii) Comply with all applicable requirements and guidelines established by Licensee in order to assist Licensee to meet the requirements of the Sarbanes-Oxley Act of 2002 and implementing regulations promulgated by the Licensee Securities and Exchange Commission and Public Licensor Accounting Oversight Board; and

(viii) Recommend and, with Licensee's prior approval, implement compliance measures to satisfy Sarbanes-Oxley requirements, including, certification as to internal controls as requested by Licensee.

(b) **Approval by Licensee.** Licensor shall submit such processes, procedures, and controls to Licensee for its review, comment, and approval within thirty (30) days after the Effective Date and shall use commercially reasonable efforts to finalize such processes, procedures, and controls and obtain Licensee's final approval on or before the Commencement Date. Upon Licensee's approval, such processes and procedures shall be included in the Policy and Procedures Manual. Prior to the approval of such processes and procedures by Licensee, Licensor shall adhere strictly to Licensee's then-current policies procedures and controls. No failure or inability of the quality assurance procedures to disclose any errors or problems with the Services shall excuse Licensor's failure to comply with the Service Levels and other terms of this Agreement.

EE. Remedies (Chapter 4.B.6; § 5.3)

1. Express Remedies

In the event the Licensed Program fails to meet the limited express warranty set forth in Section ___ (Warranty), Licensor may at its sole discretion choose to (a) use commercially reasonable efforts to repair or replace (at Licensor's option) the Licensed Program with computer software that meets such warranty or (b) refund a pro rated portion of the applicable License Fee calculated across the ninety (90) day period, or in the case of errors in the Documentation, Licensor may in its sole discretion either (x) correct the Documentation so that it correctly represents the performance of the Licensed Program or (y) publish errata addressing such errors. Notwithstanding anything in this Schedule ___ to the contrary, if and to the extent that any part of the Licensed Program is owned by a third party and licensed to Licensor for distribution, Licensee agrees (i) to be bound by any terms and conditions of use required by such third party and (ii) to look solely to such third party for any warranty concerning such software. With regards to any such third party licensed program, Licensor agrees to provide notice of each such third party software and if, more restrictive than the terms contained herein, provide the terms and conditions of such license to Licensee. THIS SECTION ___ SETS FORTH LICENSOR'S SOLE REMEDIES FOR A BREACH OF SECTION ___ (WARRANTY) REGARDING THE LICENSED PROGRAM.

2. Limitation on Damages – Broken Out by Type Including Personally Identifiable Information ("PII") and Failure to Comply with Laws

1.1 **Consequential Damages.** Neither Customer nor Licensor shall be liable for any indirect, incidental, special, or consequential damages, arising out of or relating to its performance or failure to perform under this Agreement, even if advised of the possibility of such damages.

1.2 **Direct Damages**

(a) **Definition of Direct Damages.** Notwithstanding the provisions of Section 1.1 **(Consequential Damages)**, each Party shall be liable to the other Party for any direct damages arising out of or relating to such Party's performance or failure to perform under this Agreement, which damages include: (i) costs of reconstructing or reloading data; (ii) costs of implementing and performing work-arounds regarding a service failure; (iii) costs of replacing lost, stolen or damaged goods or materials; (iv) costs to procure replacement services from an alternate source as a result of a failure to perform, to the extent in excess of the applicable Fees; (v) overtime, straight time and related expenses and allocated overhead (including travel, lodging, wages) as a result of a failure to perform; and (vi) payments or penalties imposed by a governmental or regulatory body as a result of a failure to comply.

(b) **Cap on Direct Damages.** Notwithstanding Section 1.2(a) **(Definition of Direct Damages)** and subject to Section 1.2(c) **(Cap for PII Claims and Claims for Failure to Comply With Laws)**, the liability of Customer and Licensor, whether based on an action or claim in contract, equity, negligence, tort or otherwise, for any event, act or omission shall not exceed an amount equal to the sum of the aggregate of: (i) Fees paid for the 12 consecutive month period immediately preceding the date of the first occurrence of the applicable event, act, or omission giving rise to such damages (or if less than 12 months have elapsed since the Effective Date, then 12 times the average monthly Fees paid during the elapsed time since the Effective Date); and (ii) the Service Level Credits incurred to date by Licensor on the date such damages are awarded; and

(c) **Cap for PII Claims and Claims for Failure to Comply With Laws.** Notwithstanding Sections 1.2(a) **(Definition of Direct Damages)** and 1.2(b) **(Cap on Direct Damages)**, the liability of Licensor, whether based on an action or claim in contract, equity, negligence, tort or otherwise, for (i) PII Claims; (ii) any other claims arising out of a breach of Licensor's obligations under Sections [**cross-reference to sections addressing compliance with laws, change in laws, representation regarding compliance with law, covenant regarding compliance with laws (i.e., obtaining permits)**], or; and (iii) the indemnity obligations set forth in: (A) Section [**cross-reference to indemnity related to representation regarding compliance with law**], (B) Section [**cross-reference to indemnity for violation of laws for employment claims (e.g., protected classes)**], to the extent such claims arises out of a failure of Licensor to comply with applicable Laws as set forth therein; and (C) Section [**cross-reference to indemnity related breach of Licensor's obligations with respect to Customer Data**], to the extent such Customer Data constitutes PII; collectively, shall not exceed the greater of: (1) an amount equal to the sum of the aggregate of the amount determined in accordance with Section 1.2(b) **(Cap on Direct Damages)** <u>plus</u> an additional amount equal to the Fees paid by Customer to Licensor for the 18-month period immediately preceding the date of first occurrence of the applicable event, act or omission giving rise to such damages (or if less than 18 months have elapsed since the Effective Date, then 18 times the average monthly Fees paid during the elapsed time since the Effective Date); or (2) $______________. Notwithstanding the foregoing, the amount specified in clause (2) above shall be reduced by the amount of any damages paid by Licensor that are subject to the damages caps set forth in Section 1.2 (b) **(Cap on Direct Damages)** and in clause (1) of this Section 1.2 (c).

1.3 **Exclusions.** The limitations or exculpations of liability set forth in Section 1.1 **(Consequential Damages)** and Section 1.2 **(Direct Damages)** shall not apply to: (a) the failure of: (i) Customer to make payments of undisputed Fees; or (ii) Licensor to issue credits (including Reduced Resource Credits and Service

Level Credits) or otherwise make payments due under this Agreement; (b) a Party's indemnification obligations, as set forth in Sections [**cross-reference to specified indemnities**] (other than the indemnity obligations which are subject to the cap in Section 1.2(c) **(Cap for PII Claims and Claims for Failure to Comply With Laws)** as described therein); (c) breaches of Article [**cross-reference to intellectual property article**], Article [**cross-reference to confidentiality article**] (other than with respect to a PII Claim, which shall be subject to the cap set forth in Section 1.2(c) **(Cap for PII Claims and Claims for Failure to Comply With Laws)**; (d) Licensor obligations with respect to Customer Data (other than PII Claims); (e) liability resulting from the fraud, gross negligence, recklessness, or intentional or willful misconduct of a Party; (f) damages occasioned by Licensor's wrongful termination of the Agreement, abandonment of work performed or to be performed, or willful refusal to provide the Services; (g) any amounts, including taxes, interest and penalties, assessed against a Party that are the obligation of the other Party pursuant to Article [**cross-reference to taxes article**]; (h) relating to personal injury (including death) or real or tangible personal (excluding data) property loss or damage resulting from the acts or omissions of a Party or its Affiliates or, in the case of Customer, the Customer Agents and in the case of Licensor, the Licensor Agents; (i) fines, sanctions, damages, judgments or other penalties imposed on a Party by a Governmental Authority or arbitrator as a result of a breach of such Party's obligations under this Agreement; and (j) otherwise to the extent that such limitation is not permitted by applicable Law.

"**PII**" means any information which identifies or is capable of identifying an individual, or is otherwise defined as "personal data" by applicable Laws (including the European Union Data Protection Directive (Directive 95/46/EC)) that is disclosed to or accessed by Licensor by or on behalf of, or collected by Licensor from, Customer, Customer's Affiliates or any Customer Agents, including: (a) an individual's name, address, phone number, e-mail address, initials, social security number, ID number or credit card information; and (b) information, data and materials, including demographic, medical and financial information, that relate to the past, present, or future physical or mental health or condition of an individual or the provision of health care to an individual.

"**PII Claim**" means any claim by Customer or a third party that arises out of or in connection with a breach by Licensor of its data privacy and data security obligations under the Agreement, including Licensors' obligations under Section ___ **(Confidentiality)** and ____ **(Data Privacy and Security)** of the Agreement that relates to or involves PII.

FF. Representations, Warranties and Covenants (Chapter 4.B.1; § 16)

1. Survival of Covenants

Except as expressly set forth in this Agreement, (a) the covenants in this Agreement and the liabilities for the breach of any obligations in this Agreement and (b) any covenants, representations or warranties contained in this or any Ancillary Agreement and any liabilities for the breach of any obligations contained in any Ancillary Agreement, in each case, shall survive the termination of this Agreement and shall remain in full force and effect.

2. *Child Labor Warranty (§ 16)*

Licensor warrants that it does not employ children, prison labor, indentured labor, bonded labor, or use corporal punishment or other forms of mental and physical coercion as a form of discipline. Moreover, Licensor agrees that it will not conduct business with vendors employing children, prison labor, indentured labor, bonded labor or who use corporal punishment or other forms of mental and physical coercion as a form of discipline. In the absence of any national or local law, Licensee and Licensor agree to define "child" as less than 15 years of age. If local minimum age law is set below 15 years of age, but is in accordance with exceptions under International Labor Organization (ILO) Convention 138, the lower age will apply. Licensee has the right to audit Licensor's premises to ensure compliance with this paragraph.

3. *Documentation*

Any Documentation provided by Licensor will be sufficient to allow a reasonably knowledgeable professional to understand, use, maintain, support and modify, as applicable, the Deliverables or Services to which the Documentation pertains, provided that, in the event that a Deliverable consists solely of object code and may not be modified absent the source code, Documentation required for modification of such code may be included together with any agreed source code escrow.

4. *International Warranty/Alliance Partner Warranty*

Licensor represents and warrants that it is knowledgeable of the laws of the Country of **(insert country or countries here)** as it pertains to the operation and use of Software, and further that it is knowledgeable as to the copyright laws and other intellectual property laws governing the use of Software in the Country of **(insert country or countries here)** and other countries where the Software may be installed and operating. Licensor hereby agrees to comply with all applicable copyright and intellectual property laws in **(insert country or countries here)** and other countries where the Software may be installed or in operation. Licensor's failure to comply with this provision shall constitute a material breach for which Licensee may immediately terminate this Agreement in accordance with Section ___ (Termination) and seek other remedies that may be available to it in law or equity, whether domestically or internationally.

5. Licensed Software Functionality and Performance

Licensor represents and warrants to Licensee that the Licensed Software provided under this Agreement shall: (a) contain the functionality specified in **Appendix __** (Documentation); and (b) for the period of time of sixty (60) days from the effective date (the "**Warranty Period**") operate without material defect in accordance with **Appendix __** (Documentation), and the service level and performance requirements. Licensor shall correct, at no additional cost or expense to Licensee, any failure of the Licensed Software to operate in accordance with the warranties set forth above. If additional software, equipment and/or services are required to remedy Licensor's breach of the warranty, Licensor shall provide to Licensee, at no additional cost or expense to Licensee, the additional software, equipment and/or services required for the Licensed Software to operate in accordance with the warranties set forth above. In the event Licensor is unable to correct such failure within thirty (30) days after receiving notice thereof, Licensee shall have the right to terminate in accordance with **Section __ (Termination)**. This warranty shall survive the expiration or termination of this Agreement for the applicable Warranty Period.

6. Intellectual Property Infringement – Knowledge Limitation

Licensor represents and warrants to Licensee that to the best of Licensor's knowledge after due investigation and inquiry, the Licensed Software and Licensee's use of the Licensed Software does not and shall not infringe upon any Intellectual Property Rights of any third party, and Licensor further represents and warrants to Licensee there is currently no actual or, to the best of Licensor's knowledge after due investigation and inquiry, threatened suit against Licensor by any third party based on an alleged violation of such Intellectual Property Rights.

> ***COMMENT: Representations and warranties related to intellectual property infringement are the subject of significant negotiation between the parties. Many licensors believe that they are unneeded as the licensor is also indemnifying the licensee in the event of a claim of intellectual property infringement. Many licensees, however, insist on a "belt and suspenders" approach to provide the greatest possible protection in the event a problem arises. To the extent it is able to do so, a licensor should seek to limit its risk by providing a "knowledge" representation and warranty. A knowledge limitation is not appropriate for infringement for a United States patent, copyright or other United States intellectual property right. If the licensor is asked to make a representation and warranty related to the infringement of intellectual property rights registered in countries that are not signatories to the Berne Convention, the licensor should insist on a knowledge qualifier.***

7. Compliance with Laws

Licensor represents and warrants to Licensee that Licensor is not, and covenants that it shall not be, in violation of any Laws to which it is subject, and has not failed, and shall not fail, to obtain any licenses, permits, franchises or other governmental authorizations necessary for the provision of the Licensed Software, ownership of its properties or the conduct of its business, which violation or failure, either individually or in the aggregate, might adversely affect its business, properties or financial condition, the consummation of the transactions contemplated by this Agreement, or the performance of its obligations hereunder.

8. Open Source Software

Licensor represents and warrants to Licensee that Licensor has not and will not incorporate any Software (whether in source code or object code format) into the Work Product, Deliverables, Developed Software, Licensee Software, Licensor Software, Licensor Proprietary Materials or any other Software used in connection with providing the Services (collectively, "Affected Products"), and none of the Affected Products or any portion thereof is or will be subject to or distributed under any license, other agreement or understanding, that (i) would require the distribution of source code with the Affected Products or require source code to be made available when such is distributed to any Third Party; (ii) would impact, restrict or impair in any way Licensee's ability to license the Affected Products (to the extent owned or licensable by Licensee) pursuant to terms of Licensee's choosing; or (iii) would impact or limit Licensee's ability to enforce Licensee's patent or other Intellectual Property Rights against any Third Party in any manner.

9. Open Source Software – Alternate Language

Unless otherwise agreed by the parties in writing, Licensor warrants to Licensee that the Licensed Software provided pursuant to this Agreement shall not contain any "**Open Source.**" For purposes of this Agreement, "Open Source" means any software code that: (a) contains, or is derived in any manner (in whole or in part) from, any software that is distributed as free software, open source software, shareware (e.g., Linux), or similar licensing or distribution models; and (b) is subject to any agreement with terms requiring that such software code be (i) disclosed or distributed in Source Code or Object Code form, (ii) licensed for the purpose of making derivative works, and/or (iii) redistributable. Open Source includes, but is not limited to, software licensed or distributed under any of the following licenses or distribution models, or licenses or distribution models similar to any of the following: (A) GNU's General Public License (GPL) or Lesser/Library GPL (LGPL); (B) the Artistic License (e.g., PERL); (C) the Mozilla Public License(s); (D) the Netscape Public License; (E) the Berkeley software design (BSD) license including Free BSD or BSD-style license; (F) the Sun Community Source License (SCSL); (G) an Open Source Foundation License (e.g., CDE and Motif UNIX user interfaces); (H) the Apache Server license; and (I) any licenses listed at www.opensource.org/licenses.

10. Services – General Warranty

Licensor further warrants that the Services will be rendered by qualified personnel in accordance with generally-accepted, sound practices in the software services business, and Licensor will correct any Services not in conformance with the foregoing provided that (a) Licensee notifies Licensor in writing within thirty (30) days of such performance, (b) there is no material change in the relevant system configuration and/or operating system, and (c) the Deliverable is not modified, after delivery, by any party other than Licensor.

11. Services Warranty

The Licensor shall perform the Services required hereunder with care, skill and diligence, in accordance with the applicable professional standards currently recognized by such profession, and shall be responsible for the professional quality, technical accuracy, completeness and coordination of all reports, designs, drawings, plans, information, specifications and other items and Services furnished hereunder. If Licensor fails to meet applicable professional standards, the Licensor shall, without additional compensation, re-perform the Services and/or correct or revise any errors or deficiencies in the Supplier's reports, drawings, specifications, designs, deliverables and other items constituting the Services.

12. Software/Services

Vendor warrants that the products, Software and services sold hereunder will conform to the requirements of this Agreement and any SOW, are new, of good quality, free from material defects in materials, workmanship and design (to the extent not manufactured pursuant to Customer's custom drawings), are free from all liens and encumbrances, and in the case of services, are performed by technically competent personnel in a professional manner. Vendor warrants that Software will correctly recognize, process, and otherwise support the calendar year 2000 and beyond, and that any services performed by Vendor under the Agreement will be provided in a manner that maintains correct future date processing. Vendor agrees that for sixty (60) days after completion, Vendor shall re-perform any defective or non-conforming services, reports, and/or deliverables provided hereunder at no additional charge to Customer within thirty (30) days (or as otherwise defined in the SOW) of Customer supplying written proof of non-compliance with the original specifications. Vendor warrants that it is the owner of, or otherwise has a right to license the Software and services. All representations, warranties and conditions shall survive any inspection, test, acceptance or use of the products or services, and run to Customer, its successors and assigns. THE FOREGOING WARRANTIES AND THOSE IN ANY STATEMENT OF WORK ATTACHED HERETO ARE IN LIEU OF ALL OTHER IMPLIED WARRANTIES, INCLUDING BUT NOT LIMITED TO ANY WARRANTIES OF MERCHANTABILITY OR FITNESS FOR A PARTICULAR PURPOSE.

13. Third Party Product Warranties and Indemnities

For any Third Party Products provided by Licensor to Licensee, Licensor hereby assigns to Licensee all end-user warranties and indemnities relating to such Third Party Products. To the extent that Licensor is not permitted to assign any of such end-user warranties and indemnities through to Licensee, Licensor shall enforce such warranties and indemnities on behalf of Licensee to the extent Licensor is permitted to do so under the terms of the applicable third party agreements. The Licensor obligations set forth in this **Section** ___ are in addition to and not in lieu of Licensor's warranty and indemnification obligations, responsibilities and liabilities with regard to such Third Party Products under this Agreement. This warranty shall survive the expiration or termination of this Agreement.

14. No Conflict of Interest by Licensor

Licensor represents that it has not paid and will not pay any fees or made any payments or rebates to any employee, officer, representative or designee of Licensee.

15. Third Party Products – Licensor Oriented

In the event that Vendor provides to Customer third-party hardware or software products on a pass through basis and only to the extent that such hardware or software is not Software Products as defined in this Agreement the following shall apply: Vendor makes no representations or warranties as to any third-party hardware or software provided to Customer, all of which is transferred to Customer on an "AS IS" basis and subject to any third party terms and conditions. With respect to such third party hardware or software that is warranted by a third party, Vendor shall (i) obtain written approval from Customer for the use of such third party hardware or software, and (ii) use commercially reasonable efforts to pass through any such warranties and intellectual property rights to Customer. Customer shall look solely to the warranties and remedies provided by the equipment manufacturer and third-party software licensor, if any.

16. Operating Systems Compatibility – Future modifications must be compatible with the releases of operating system, databases, etc. (§ 10.H)

Licensor shall provide to Licensee any and all modifications to each Application that may be required to enable such Application to operate in conjunction with any new generally available releases and versions of the operating system, database, and other computer programs with which the installed version of the Applications is designed to operate as soon as Licensor has installed and operated said modification for its own internal use or for the use of any one of Licensor's other commercial customers.

> ***COMMENT: The licensor should carefully consider whether to accept this language. The cost of ensuring the compatibility of the licensor's application with the licensee's third party applications could be significant especially since the licensor has no control over subsequent enhancements or changes made by such third party vendors.***

17. Performance in Hosted Environment

When installed on Licensee's servers by Licensor pursuant to the terms of this Agreement, the Software, including Third Party Software that is then part of Licensor's application, will operate in substantially the same way as such software operates in Licensor's hosted environment as of such installation date.

18. Consultant Personnel and Performance of Services

Consultant represents and warrants that: (i) it shall complete all tasks identified in a Statement of Work unless this Agreement or the Statement of Work is terminated as permitted by this Agreement; (ii) all services provided by Consultant to Licensee (including without limitation any installation, support and training) will be performed in a timely, competent, professional, and workmanlike manner, using qualified employees in conformity with standards generally accepted in the software industry; (iii) it has a sufficient number of competent, professional and qualified employees to provide the services specified in a Statement of Work in a timely manner; and (iv) each of its employees providing services to Licensee have had full-time working experience in the computer industry and have had experience in the specific technology required for the duties to be performed.

19. Unauthorized Code

Unauthorized Code means computer instructions that alter, destroy or inhibit Licensee's processing environment, including, but not limited to, data storage and computer libraries. Unauthorized Code includes, but is not limited to, instructions programmed to activate at a predetermined time or upon a specified event such as time bombs, and programs that self-replicate without manual intervention and/or that purport to do a meaningful function but are designed for a destructive function, such as viruses. During the term of this Agreement, Licensor represents and warrants that: (a) Licensed Software will not contain any Unauthorized Code; (b) Licensor shall take reasonable steps to test all Licensed Software for the presence of Unauthorized Code; and (c) Licensor shall not intentionally insert any Unauthorized Code into Licensee's environment and/or systems or intentionally invoke any Unauthorized Code that may be part of Third Party Products provided by Licensor and installed on Licensee's environment and/or systems.

20. Viruses – Neutral – Bilateral (§ 16.L)

Each Party will use commercially reasonable efforts to prevent viruses from being coded or introduced into the computer systems used to provide the Services in compliance with Licensor's policies regarding virus protection as documented in the SOW. In the event a virus is found to have been coded or introduced into the computer systems utilized in connection with the Services delivered by Licensor, Licensor will use commercially reasonable efforts to eliminate the effects of the virus. If Licensee is found to have introduced a virus into the computer systems utilized in connection with the Services, the Licensee will pay Licensor its standard hourly rates to eliminate the effects of the virus. Licensor will be excused from any SLRs that are negatively impacted by any virus introduced by Licensee until it is removed, provided that Licensor uses good faith efforts to remove such virus as soon as possible.

"**Virus**" means an extraneous piece of computer code knowingly and maliciously inserted by any person for the purpose of causing undisclosed disruption or other harm to the operation of a computer program. Nothing in this Section __ will serve to reduce Licensor's disaster recovery obligations pursuant to Section __ (Disaster Recovery).

21. Viruses – Licensor Oriented (§ 16.L)

Notwithstanding any other provision in this Agreement to the contrary, if the Licensor or any of its employees, subcontractors or consultants introduces a virus or malicious, mischievous or destructive programming onto the Licensee's software or computer networks and has failed to comply with the Licensee software security standards, and provided further that the Licensee can demonstrate that the virus or malicious, mischievous or destructive programming was introduced by the Licensor or any of its employees, subcontractors or consultants, the Licensor shall be liable for any damage to any data and/or software owned or licensed by the Licensee. The Licensor shall be liable for any damages incurred by the Licensee including, but not limited to, the expenditure of Licensee funds to eliminate or remove a computer virus or malicious, mischievous or destructive programming that result from the Licensor's failure to take proactive measures to keep virus or malicious, mischievous or destructive programming from originating from the Licensor, its servants, agents or employees through appropriate firewalls and maintenance of anti-virus software and software security updates (such as operating systems security patches, etc.). In the event of destruction or modification of software, the Licensor shall eliminate the virus, malicious, mischievous or destructive programming, restore the Licensee's software, and be liable to the Licensee for any resulting damages. The Licensor shall be responsible for reviewing Licensee's software security standards in effect at the commencement of the Agreement and complying with those standards. The Licensor's liability shall cease if the Licensee has not fully complied with its own software security standards.

22. Warranty Disclaimer

The Parties hereby agree that, in respect of information and computer programs provided by one Party to the other Party under this Agreement, and except to the extent there are express warranties stated in this Agreement, if any: THERE ARE NO WARRANTIES (A) AGAINST INTERFERENCE WITH ENJOYMENT OF INFORMATION, (B) AGAINST INFRINGEMENT, (C) THAT INFORMATON, EITHER PARTY'S EFFORTS, OR SYSTEMS, AS EACH MAY BE PROVIDED UNDER THIS AGREEMENT, WILL FULFILL ANY OF EITHER PARTY'S PARTICULAR PURPOSES OR NEEDS, AND (D) WITH RESPECT TO DEFECTS IN THE INFORMATION OR SOFTWARE WHICH AN EXAMINATION SHOULD HAVE REASONABLY REVEALED. THE PARTIES HEREBY EACH DISCLAIM IMPLIED WARRANTIES OF MERCHANTIBILITY, QUALITY, AND ACCURACY. THE INFORMATION AND COMPUTER PROGRAMS PROVIDED UNDER THIS AGREEMENT ARE PROVIDED WITH ALL FAULTS, AND THE ENTIRE RISK AS TO SATISFACTORY QUALITY, PERFORMANCE, ACCURACY, AND EFFORT IS WITH THE USER OF SUCH INFORMATION AND COMPUTER PROGRAMS.

23. Warranty Disclaimer – Alternate Language

Disclaimer of Warranties. EXCEPT AS PROVIDED IN SECTIONS ___ (LIMITED WARRANTY) AND ___ (INTELLECTUAL PROPERTY WARRANTY), THE LICENSED PROGRAM AND THE MEDIA UPON WHICH IT IS SUPPLIED ARE PROVIDED "AS IS". LICENSOR EXPRESSLY DISCLAIMS ALL OTHER WARRANTIES, EXPRESS OR IMPLIED, INCLUDING, BUT NOT LIMITED TO, THE IMPLIED WARRANTIES OF MERCHANTABILITY, FITNESS FOR A PARTICULAR PURPOSE, COURSE OF CONDUCT, AND USAGE OF TRADE. LICENSEE UNDERSTANDS THAT LICENSOR OBTAINS DATA INCLUDED IN THE LICENSED PROGRAM FROM THIRD PARTIES, INCLUDING GOVERNMENT AGENCIES, AND THAT LICENSOR IS UNDER NO OBLIGATION TO CONTINUE THE DEVELOPMENT

OF THE LICENSED PROGRAM OR TO CORRECT ANY ERROR, OMISSION OR MALFUNCTION THEREIN. NEITHER LICENSOR NOR ANY OF ITS SALES REPRESENTATIVES SHALL BE OBLIGATED TO UPDATE OR SUPPORT THE LICENSED PROGRAM. LICENSEE EXPRESSLY AGREES THAT LICENSOR DOES NOT REPRESENT OR WARRANT THAT (i) THE OPERATION OF THE SOFTWARE OR ANY SUBSEQUENT RELEASES SHALL BE UNINTERRUPTED OR ERROR-FREE, (ii) FUNCTIONS CONTAINED IN THE SOFTWARE SHALL OPERATE IN COMBINATIONS THAT MAY BE SELECTED BY LICENSEE, (iii) THE SOFTWARE OR THE SOFTWARE RELEASES SHALL MEET LICENSEE'S REQUIREMENTS, OR (iv) THE SOFTWARE OR THE SOFTWARE RELEASES SHALL OPERATE ON COMPUTER HARDWARE OR OPERATING SYSTEMS OTHER THAN THE PLATFORM, IF ANY, SPECIFIED IN THE APPLICABLE DOCUMENTATION. THE PARTIES ACKNOWLEDGE THAT EACH OF THE PROVISIONS OF THIS SCHEDULE __, INCLUDING WITHOUT LIMITATION THE PAYMENT PROVISIONS HEREOF, WERE BASED, IN PART, ON THE PROVISIONS OF SECTIONS ___ (LIMITED WARRANTY), ___ (EXPRESS WARRANTY), ___ (INTELLECTUAL PROPERTY WARRANTY) AND THIS SECTION ___, AND THAT EACH PARTY FULLY UNDERSTANDS AND ACCEPTS THE OBLIGATIONS AND LIMITATIONS DESCRIBED IN SECTIONS ___ (LIMITED WARRANTY), ___ (EXPRESS WARRANTY), ___ (INTELLECTUAL PROPERTY WARRANTY) AND THIS SECTION ___, WHICH SHALL SURVIVE THE TERMINATION, FOR ANY REASON, OF THIS AGREEMENT.

24. Express Negligence

THE INDEMNIFICATION, RELEASE AND ASSUMPTION PROVISIONS PROVIDED FOR IN THIS AGREEMENT SHALL BE APPLICABLE WHETHER OR NOT THE LOSSES, COSTS, EXPENSES AND DAMAGES IN QUESTION AROSE SOLELY OR IN PART FROM THE ACTIVE, PASSIVE OR CONCURRENT NEGLIGENCE, STRICT LIABILITY OR OTHER FAULT OF ANY INDEMNIFIED PARTY. PARTNER AND LICENSOR ACKNOWLEDGE THAT THIS STATEMENT COMPLIES WITH THE EXPRESS NEGLIGENCE RULE AND IS CONSPICUOUS.

25. Use of Licensee as Alpha/Beta Site

Licensor shall not use Licensee as an alpha or beta site for any Software or Services to be provided, if any, without the prior written consent of Licensee.

26. Obligation to Notify Other Party of Material Action

Each party warrants that it has disclosed, and agrees it is under a continuing obligation to disclose promptly to the other party, claims or actions against such party that may adversely affect performance under this Agreement, including claims or actions alleging intellectual property infringement.

27. Intellectual Property

Each party warrants that all information and materials furnished by such party hereunder and products licensed pursuant to this Agreement will not infringe any third party's intellectual property rights issued, honored or enforceable under U.S. laws or international convention(s) (including but not limited to the Berne Convention, Paris Convention, Universal Copyright Convention, Patent Cooperation Treaty) including but not limited to patents, copyrights, trademarks, trade names and trade secrets.

28. Corporate Authority

Licensor represents and warrants to Licensee that: (a) Licensor is a **[STATE OF INCORPORATION]** corporation, and is qualified and registered to transact business in all locations where the performance of its obligations hereunder would require such qualification; (b) Licensor has all necessary rights, powers, authority, consents, licenses, approvals and permissions to enter into and perform this Agreement, and the execution, delivery and performance of this Agreement by Licensor have been duly authorized by all necessary corporate action; (c) the execution and performance of this Agreement by Licensor shall not breach any agreement, covenant, court order, judgment or decree to which Licensor is a party or by which it is bound; and (d) Licensor has, and promises that it shall maintain in effect, all governmental licenses and permits necessary for it to provide the Services and/or contemplated by this Agreement.

GG. RFP Related (Chapter 2)

1. Vendor Disclaimer Related to RFP Submission

Vendor has reviewed the Master Services Agreement (MSA) attached to this RFP and believes that at such time as more business details are agreed upon, including the information to be contained in the various schedules, that the parties will be able to readily come to satisfactory closure on all of the terms contained in the MSA. For example, and not by way of limitation, Vendor seeks to discuss with Customer: (i) the scope and application of the indemnifications and the language regarding same, (ii) the need for deliverable specific changes to the warranty contained in Section ___ (Warranties) and a disclaimer of implied and non-express warranties; (iii) the need for some more specific detail with regard to Customer's ownership right in reports generated by Vendor, including a reservation of right in Vendor's pre-existing IP, and industry standard limitations on the party's liability for any claims arising in connection with the MSA. Vendor reserves the right to comment in greater detail on these and other issues in the MSA at such time as is appropriate based on the availability of known business details and any down selection of Vendor as may occur.

HH. Subcontractor Issues (Chapter 5.A; 14.A)

1. Appropriate Employee and Subcontractor Agreements

Vendor has enforceable written agreements with all of its employees and subcontractors involved in the performance of the Services under this Agreement: (i) assigning to Vendor ownership of all Intellectual Property Rights created in the course of their employment or engagement; and (ii) obligating such employees and subcontractors, as the case may be, upon terms and conditions equivalent to the confidentiality obligations of Article __ (Confidential Information) of the Master Agreement, not to use or disclose any Customer Company Information.

2. Subcontractor Flow downs

The requirements of this Article __ and the requirements in Articles __ (Expenses), __ (Warranties), __ (Termination without Cause), __ (Termination for Cause), __ (Meetings), __ (Access and Security Requirements), __ (Proprietary Rights), __ (Confidentiality), __ (General Provisions), __ (Independent Contractor), __ (Compliance with Laws), __ (Regulatory Compliance), __ (Right to Inspect), __ (Licensee Policies), __ (Publicity), Exhibit __ (Licensee Travel and Expense Policy) and the Licensor Code of Conduct (Exhibit __) of the Agreement will apply to any subcontractors retained by Licensor to perform Services, as permitted by this Agreement, and will be included in any subcontracts (including any independent contractor agreements) entered into by Licensor for such Services.

3. Cooperation with and Access by Third Parties

Licensee may from time to time hire outsourcers, subcontractors, consultants, or other third Parties ("Licensee Third-Party Contractors") to perform services or provide products relating to Licensee's business, and which may be integrated with the Services or Products provided by Licensor hereunder (an "Integrated Project"). Licensor shall cooperate with and work in good faith with any Licensee Third-Party Contractor(s) as requested by Licensee. Such cooperation may include knowledge sharing of standards, policies, quality assurance and testing processes, as applicable, to ensure smooth deployment of Integrated Projects and/or the smooth and efficient transition of any Services (or component of Services) to, from, or among Licensee, Licensor and any Third Party Contractor. Moreover, nothing in the Agreement shall restrict access by such persons to the Services, Products, and/or Deliverables, as applicable, as reasonably required for such Third Party Contractors to perform functions for and on behalf of Licensee; and provided that such Third Party Contractors shall use or access the Products and/or Services solely for Licensee's benefit and shall have agreed to confidentiality provisions no less restrictive than those contained in this Agreement, and Licensee shall remain responsible for such Third Party Contractor's use or access to the Products and/or Services in accordance with the terms of this Agreement.

COMMENT: A licensor should carefully consider granting third parties access to the licensor's proprietary software, information and technology. In some situations, such as a systems integration project with many sub-contractors, it may be justified. In outsourcing transactions providing such access may not be prudent. The success of a licensor's business depends on maintaining the confidentiality and proprietary nature of the licensor's product. As such, the licensor should not provide third parties access to its intellectual property.

The outsourcer may be a competitor or seek to obtain experience in maintaining the licensor's product in order to create a new service offering. Perhaps the only reason a customer seeks to allow a third party access to a licensor's intellectual property is to reduce the customer's costs. At a minimum the licensor should demand financially compensation. In the event of an outsourcing transaction, a savvy licensor should enforce the terms of the license, which likely prohibits third party access to its intellectual property, and require the outsourcer to enter into a subcontract with the licensor for the licensor to continue providing the software and services pursuant to its contract with the customer. This structure allows the customer to continue to use the licensor's product while denying the outsourcer access to the licensor's intellectual property.

II. TAXES (Chapter 4.B.A; § 8.6)

1. Taxes – Indefinite Work Assignment – Tax Gross Up (§ 8.6)

If Licensee requires that any person render Services at Licensee's site for more than 12 consecutive months: (a) Internal Revenue Code (IRC) § 162 will classify all of that person's Services as an Indefinite Work Assignment (IWA), (b) beginning with the thirteenth consecutive month of work at the Licensee's site, all of that person's reimbursed business expenses, including travel, lodging, meals and car rental, must be treated as taxable personal income to that person under IRC § 162, (c) Licensee will include these reimbursed expenses in the person's taxable compensation, and will increase that person's compensation to cover those taxes and the personal income and withholding taxes on that increase, and (d) Licensee shall reimburse Licensee for the entire amount of that increase. Invoices shall provide such detail as may be reasonably required by Licensee. Upon request of Licensee, Licensee shall make available to Licensee in timely manner documentation for expenses reimbursement by Licensee. Licensee's itemized invoices shall be substantially in the form mutually agreed to by the Parties.

2. *Taxes – Indefinite Work Assignment – Alternative Language*

Licensor shall separately state the amount of tax or other charges in its invoice to Licensee. Licensee is not responsible for payment of any employment, self-employment, or withholding taxes imposed as a result of the performance of Services under this Agreement, whether by Licensor, its employees, or assistants. Licensor shall maintain records of the employee benefits provided to any employee of Licensor performing Services to Licensee on a substantially full time basis for a period of one year or longer and such other information needed by Licensee to demonstrate compliance with the requirements of Internal Revenue Code Section 414(n) and related sub-sections, as amended from time to time, pertaining to "leased employees". For this purpose "on a substantially full time basis" shall mean 1,500 hours in a twelve (12) month period or such amount specified by U.S. tax regulation or notice in effect during the term of this Agreement. Licensor shall maintain such records for at least six (6) years and furnish such data, and such other information as is reasonably related to this Agreement, including but not limited to Forms W-9 or SBA documentation, to Licensee at its request.

3. *Sales Tax Exclusion*

North Carolina Permit Number ______ and Pennsylvania Permit Number ______ authorize Licensee to accrue and pay its sales tax liability directly to the NC and PA Departments of Revenue. Accordingly, Licensor agrees that it will not invoice Licensee for North Carolina or Pennsylvania sales tax, nor will it invoice Licensee for other sales or use tax without prior notice, and to the extent any such other sales tax is invoiced it will be separately itemized. Licensor shall bear all responsibility and liability for all sales, use, excise, services, consumption, and other taxes and duties payable by Licensor on any goods or services used or consumed by Licensor in providing the Services hereunder where the tax is imposed on Licensor's acquisition or use of such goods or services. Licensor shall also bear all responsibility and liability for the payment of all income taxes due on money received from Licensee hereunder and filing all appropriate tax returns and other forms with respect thereto.

4. *Taxes – Licensee not responsible for foreign taxes*

Prices are exclusive of, and Licensee shall pay all applicable sales, use, excise and other taxes or duties imposed by any U.S. federal, state and/or local Governmental Authority on the Services, **except for taxes based on Licensor's net income or resulting from Licensor performing or delivering Services or Deliverables from outside the United States.** Notwithstanding the foregoing, Licensee shall be responsible for any taxes or duties disclosed in an SOW to the extent resulting from Licensee specifying in writing that Deliverables be delivered, or Services be used, at a Site outside of the United States. Licensee shall promptly provide Licensor with any documentation required for exemption from applicable sales, use or other taxes or duties. The parties shall cooperate with one another in any contest, legal or administrative proceeding related to the validity, payment or amount of any such taxes or duties.

> ***COMMENT: Occasionally licensees balk at paying non-U.S. taxes a vendor may incur in the delivery of the services through offshore employees. Many licensors attempt to have the licensee agree that if the licensor performs services offshore at the licensee's request (i.e., use an India based affiliate or subcontract or to gain the advantage of lower labor rates), the licensee will pay any taxes levied by the foreign jurisdiction to the same extent they would for services rendered in the United States (i.e., the licensee would pay services based taxes such as VAT, but not the licensor's foreign income taxes). Many licensees reject this position arguing that they are contracting with a United States entity and will pay U.S. taxes only. Although it may be impractical to do so, a licensor can control its exposure by simply not utilizing offshore resources for any work to be performed under the contract.***

5. Taxes – Licensor Oriented

1.1 **Generally.**

Except for income taxes levied on Licensor's net income, Licensee shall pay or reimburse Licensor for all national, federal, provincial, state, local or other taxes and assessments of any jurisdiction, including sales or use taxes, data processing taxes, royalty taxes, property taxes, international withholding taxes (including those in lieu of income taxes), customs or other import or export taxes, value added taxes and amounts levied in lieu thereof based on charges set, services performed or to be performed, or payments made or to be made hereunder. Licensee shall not be entitled to deduct the amount of any such taxes, duties or assessments from payments made to Licensor under this Agreement. This provision shall survive the termination of this Agreement and shall be applicable regardless of the time frame in which the requirement of the payment of such taxes or assessments is asserted (e.g., a deficiency assessment by a taxing authority as a result of an audit after the termination of this Agreement). Licensor will cooperate with Licensee to attempt to minimize the amount of taxes and assessments payable by the Licensee in accordance with applicable statutes, rules and regulations.

1.2 **Indemnification.**
In the event that a taxing authority or other entity asserts that Licensor is responsible for the payment of any taxes, interest or penalties for which Licensee is responsible pursuant to this Section, Licensee shall defend, indemnify and hold harmless Licensor from any and all liability for the payment of such taxes, interest or penalties and any expenses and fees (including reasonable attorneys' fees) incurred by Licensor as a result of such assertion. Licensee shall take all reasonable steps, including the posting of a bond, to remove any lien from Licensor property, which arises from such assertion.

1.3 Tax Exempt Entities.
If Licensee is a tax exempt entity or if any transaction covered by this Agreement is a tax exempt transaction, Licensee will provide a copy of such tax exemption certificate to Licensor immediately after the execution of this Agreement. If Licensee has a direct pay certificate that allows the direct payment to the proper taxing authority of Licensee's obligations under this Section, Licensee shall provide a copy of such direct pay certificate to Licensor immediately upon the execution of this Agreement.

1.4 Tax Status.
Licensee represents and warrants that it has or will provide the following to Licensor:

[ ] Tax exempt certificate
[ ] Direct Pay permit
[ ] Resale Certificate
[ ] Not Applicable (taxes may apply)

JJ. Termination (Chapter 4.B.5; § 5)

1. Termination in the Event of Change in Licensor's Financial Status

Notwithstanding any other provision of this Agreement to the contrary, Licensee may terminate a Statement of Work immediately for cause in the following circumstances:

Upon the Financial Instability of Licensor. For purposes of this Section ___ only, "Financial Instability" shall exist if: (i) Licensor does not meet its undisputed obligations, including judgments, to third parties as those obligations become due, (ii) Licensor's stock is removed or delisted from a trading exchange, (iii) Licensor's long term debt goes on a watch or warning list, or (iv) Licensor's long term debt rating is downgraded more than two levels from its debt rating as of the Effective Date.

COMMENT: A licensor should never agree to this or similar language as it is unrelated to the licensor's performance. Sub-section (iv) is especially overbroad as a licensor's long term debt maybe placed on a watch list for reasons totally unrelated to the licensor's financial solvency. Further,

the bankruptcy laws protect the licensee in the event the licensor declares bankruptcy.

2. Termination Following a Change of Control of Licensor

"Change of Control of Licensor" means an announcement by Licensor (i) that any other entity, person or "group" (as such term is used in Section 13(d) of the Securities Exchange Act of 1934, as amended) will acquire Control, of all or substantially all of the assets, of Licensor (or any parent company of Licensor), whether directly or indirectly, in a single transaction or series of related transactions, or (ii) that Licensor (or any parent company of Licensor) will consolidate with, or be merged with or into, another entity, or will sell, assign, convey, transfer, lease or otherwise dispose of all or substantially all of its assets to another person(s) or entity(ies). After Licensor notifies Licensee of a Change of Control of Licensor, Licensee shall make a good faith evaluation of the ability of the surviving entity to perform under this Agreement, and any risks associated with such new arrangement. If after conducting such evaluation that Licensee determines is appropriate and after consulting with Licensor, Licensee concludes that such proposed new arrangement creates a risk that Licensee is not willing to assume, then at any time within six (6) months after the effective date of the consummation of the events described in (i) or (ii) above, Licensee may terminate this Agreement, in whole or in part by giving Licensor at least ninety (90) days prior written notice specifying the terminated Services and designating the termination date. Such termination shall be without charge, except that Licensee shall pay any outstanding charges for all Services completed through to the effective date of termination (including for work in progress).

3. Orderly Transfer Upon Termination

Upon the termination of a Statement of Work for any reason whatsoever (including a default by either party), (i) Licensor will provide such information, cooperation and assistance to Licensee, as Licensee may reasonably request, to assure an orderly return or transfer to Licensee or Licensee' designee of all proprietary data (and related records and files) and materials of Licensee, and all work product and Deliverables for which payment has been or is made, in their then current condition, and (ii), Licensee may notify Licensor that Licensee desires a transition period of up to three (3) months from the effective date of the termination ("Transition Period"). During the Transition Period, the parties will continue to be bound by and perform in accordance with the Statement of Work, and Licensor will assist Licensee in the orderly and efficient transition of the Software and Software Support to Licensee or a third party designated by Licensee. If Licensee initially designates a Transition Period of less than three (3) months, it may extend the Transition Period prior to its expiration upon five (5) days' advance notice to Licensor, so long as the total Transition Period does not exceed three (3) months.

4. Improper Termination – Conversion of Termination for Breach to Termination for Convenience

If it is later determined that the Licensee erred in terminating this Agreement for default, then the Agreement shall be deemed to have been terminated for convenience under Subsection (a) above (Termination for Convenience).

> ***COMMENT: This provision protects the licensee in the event it wrongfully terminates the licensor for breach as it automatically "converts" the termination to a termination for convenience which under most agreements limits the licensor's recovery to the services rendered as of the termination date. Licensors should not accept this language as licensees should be fully responsible for their actions if they wrongfully terminate the agreement. Otherwise, there is no downside to claiming a termination for breach even when it may not be justified.***

5. Licensor Continued Performance

So long as Licensee shall in good faith pursue and fulfill its obligations under (a) and (b) below in the event of such breach, Licensor shall not, except as specifically provided under this Agreement, terminate this Agreement or applicable SOW hereunder, or withhold or refuse to perform Services or intentionally fail to meet any applicable deadline, requirement, Service Level as defined in any SOW, or other provision hereof or seek relief through arbitration or by way of equitable relief or otherwise that has the effect of permitting any of the foregoing; provided that in the event of a material breach by Licensee hereunder, Licensee shall (a) in good faith participate in the dispute resolution process set forth in Section ___ (Dispute Resolution) and (b) comply with the disposition of the dispute established pursuant to that procedure. Upon any termination of this Agreement or the applicable SOW, Licensee shall be entitled to receive the termination services pursuant to Section ____ (Transition Services). The foregoing notwithstanding, Licensor shall not be obligated to continue to provide those Services if (i) Licensee fails to pay undisputed amounts by the due date in this Agreement, and (ii) Licensor provides Licensee sixty (60) days' prior written notice that such undisputed amounts have not been paid and Licensor intends to cease providing Services, and (iii) Licensee fails to pay such undisputed amounts due during such sixty (60) day period.

6. Suspension of Work for Licensee's Convenience

Licensee may, by written or telephone notice to Licensor, suspend, delay, or interrupt all or any part of the Work of the Contract for the period of time that Licensee determines appropriate for Licensee's convenience. Upon receipt of notification of suspension Licensor shall, unless notified otherwise, immediately discontinue all services affected, including delivery or order of equipment and material upon terms satisfactory to Licensee; provided, however, that Licensor shall continue to perform any part of the work not otherwise suspended, as well as such services as necessary in the sole judgment of Licensee to preserve and protect Work in progress, including equipment, material, and plan constructed or in progress. If the performance of all or any part of the Work is (for an unreasonable period of time) suspended, delayed, or interrupted, an equitable adjustment shall be made and the Contract modified in writing accordingly. However, no adjustment shall be made under this provision for any suspension, delay, or interruption to the extent that performance would have been so suspended, delayed, or interrupted by any other cause, including the fault or negligence of the Licensor, or for which an equitable adjustment is provided for or excluded under any other provision of this Contract.

> ***COMMENT: While in theory this language may not seem objectionable, the licensor should avoid being placed in a situation where its development/ installation team is placed on hold and becomes unbillable. If the licensor cannot reassign these individuals to a new project because the licensee has not given a start date, the licensor could incur a significant loss. As such, this language should be modified to allow the licensor to recoup its cost and provide a reasonable time period in which to reassemble a team to complete the work.***

KK. Third Party Software

1. Third Party Content

If Licensor intends to develop a Deliverable in a manner that incorporates or requires Licensee to use any software or other intellectual property of a third party (including any open source software) (the "Third Party Content") in order to use such Deliverable, then Licensor will (i) provide Licensee with prior notice, specifying in reasonable detail the nature of the Deliverable's dependency on or use of the Third Party Content, and (ii) provide Licensee with (for no additional cost or on such terms as may be acceptable to Licensee) a perpetual, irrevocable, royalty-free, non-exclusive right and license for Licensee and the Licensee Affiliates to use the Supplier provided Third Party Content in connection with the use of the Deliverable.

2. Licensee Provided Software

Licensee shall obtain all consents required to secure any rights of use of, or access to, or rights to modify, any third party software provided by Licensee, required by the Licensor in providing the Software and Services. Licensee will indemnify and defend Licensor from any and all claims against Licensor or Licensee regarding Licensor's use or modification of such third party software provided by Licensee.

3. Clearance for Certain Licensee Provided Software

If Licensee will provide any software or access to software to Licensor, then before commencement of Licensor's Services (if specified on the applicable Statement of Work) or before such software is accessed or used by Licensor (if the software is not specified on the applicable Statement of Work), Licensee shall have the opportunity to ascertain whether it has the license rights to permit Licensor to access and use the third-party software needed for such Project. Licensee may cancel or postpone any specific work with Licensor (without any financial penalty and without such cancellation constituting a breach of contract by Licensee) if Licensee determines that it does not possess the needed license for Licensor to perform the Services for which such third-party software is needed. Unless explicitly provided for in a Statement of Work, Licensor is responsible for any software, equipment, supplies, materials or other provisions it may need in performing Services or providing Deliverables.

LL. Uniform Computer Information Transactions Act ("UCITA") (Chapter 11; §16.1.4.A)

1. Opt Out of UCITA

The Parties hereby agree to waive and opt-out of any application of the Uniform Computer Information Transactions Act (UCITA), or any version thereof, adopted by any State in any form.

2. Opt Out of UCITA – Alternate Language

TO THE MAXIMUM EXTENT PERMITTED UNDER APPLICABLE LAW, THE PARTIES DISCLAIM AND NONE OF THIS AGREEMENT SHALL BE SUBJECT TO THE UNIFORM COMPUTER INFORMATION TRANSACTIONS ACT ("UCITA") (PREPARED BY THE NATIONAL CONFERENCE OF COMMISSIONERS ON UNIFORM STATE LAWS) AS CURRENTLY ENACTED OR AS MAY BE ENACTED, CODIFIED OR AMENDED FROM TIME TO TIME BY ANY JURISDICTION. TO THE EXTANT THAT ANY ASPECT OF THIS AGREEMENT OR ANY LICENSE GRANTED UNDER THIS AGREEMENT IS UNCLEAR OR DISPUTED BY THE PARTIES AND UCITA, IF APPLIED, WOULD CLARIFY SUCH LICENSE OR RESOLVE SUCH DISPUTE, THE PARTIES AGREE TO CLARIFY SUCH LICENSE OR RESOLVE SUCH DISPUTE INDEPENDENTLY OF UCITA BY APPLYING THE INTENT OF THE PARTIES AT THE TIME THAT THEY ENTERED THIS AGREEMENT.

3. Adoption of UCITA subsequent to Execution of Agreement

If any version of the Uniform Computer Information Transactions Act ("UCITA") is enacted as a part of the law of the aforementioned state, said statute shall not govern any aspect of this Agreement or any license granted hereunder, and instead the laws that existed prior to such enactment shall govern.

MM. Use (Chapter 3)

1. Third Party Software (§ 16.P)

Third Party Software is provided on a pass through or sublicense basis and may be subject to separate license agreements or registration requirements and limitations on copying and use and Licensee agrees to be bound by the terms of any such third party license agreements. Third Party Software shall be warranted on a pass through basis in the same manner and for the same period and extent provided by the original software manufacturer.

> ***COMMENT: The licensor should insist on the insertion of this language to ensure it is not obligated to provide a more comprehensive warranty than the warranty it is receiving from the original manufacturer.***

2. Ordinary Course of Business

Each of the licenses granted by Licensor hereunder has been granted in the ordinary course of Licensor's business.

3. Ownership of Software Modifications (§§ 3.5, 6.4)

In the event Licensee desires Licensor to develop a Modification to the System for Licensee's sole use, Licensee must advise Licensor of this restriction prior to development. Upon receipt of such notice, the Modification shall be designated as a "Licensee-Specific Modification" and identified as such in the associated Work Order. The parties agree that the Licensee-Specific Modification shall remain the sole property of Licensor; however, Licensee shall retain a license to use such Licensee-Specific Modification for so long as Licensee retains a license to use the System to which such Licensee-Specific Modification is made. Licensor agrees that it shall not make a Licensee-Specific Modification available or disclose a Licensee-Specific Modification to a third party without Licensee's prior written consent. At Licensee's election, Licensee may retain the only copy/copies of a Licensee-Specific Modification and upon termination or expiration of the license for such Licensee-Specific Modification, Licensee may elect to either return such Modification to Licensor or destroy such Modification and all copies thereof and provide Licensor with an affidavit of such destruction. **Notwithstanding the foregoing, Licensee acknowledges that Licensor is in the business of providing computer software and services to the insurance industry and nothing contained herein shall prevent Licensor from independently developing computer software that performs the same or similar function(s) as the Licensee-Specific Modification(s).**

> ***COMMENT: Licensors who are marketing a product should insist on including language to this effect to maintain the sanctity of their product. Licensors cannot effectively license and market their product if individual components are owned by many different clients. Licensees should not be overly concerned about owning a module of the product, as their goals (i.e., exclusivity, royalties, rebates, etc.) can usually be achieved by other means.***

4. Changing Business Practices – Limits on Licensor's Ability to Restrict Future Uses of Software (§ 3.1)

If Licensor develops future limitations, qualifications, and/or restrictions in how it licenses the Software to its customers, such future limitations, qualifications, and/or restrictions shall have no effect on the scope of the license granted herein to Licensee and Licensor expressly disclaims the right to claim otherwise.

5. Construction of License Grant – Ambiguity Interpreted Against Licensor (§ 45)

Licensor acknowledges that the intent of the scope of the license is to make Licensee's rights to the Software as broad as possible and, accordingly, the grant language shall not be interpreted strictly or narrowly in favor of Licensor, but rather broadly in favor of Licensee.

6. Third Party Access – Licensee Oriented

Licensee shall have the right to permit its third party vendors and service providers to use the Software and Documentation in the performance of their duties, responsibilities and obligations on behalf of and/or for the benefit of Licensee and its Affiliates, all at no additional cost to Licensee.

7. Use for Subsequently Acquired Companies – Licensor Oriented

Licensee shall use {single copy licenses: [a single logical production copy of]} the Software only to process data related to the internal operations or the financial services offerings of itself, *excluding businesses, blocks of business, or lines of business acquired thereby from a third party after the effective date of this Agreement.*

> ***COMMENT: Licensors should include language to this effect to avoid losing revenue from the expansion of the licensee's business. Similarly, the licensee should reject this language to avoid paying additional license fees as its business expands.***

8. Copyright License – Marketing Materials

Promptly after the Effective Date and from time to time during the Term upon reasonable written request from Licensee, Licensor shall furnish Licensee with electronic data files of artwork and information to create materials for use in connection with the marketing, distribution and sale of the XXXX Product ("**Product Marketing Materials**"). Licensor hereby grants to Licensee (including its present and future affiliates), and Licensee accepts, under Licensor's copyrights and other Intellectual Property Rights relating to the Product Marketing Materials, a non-exclusive, sublicensable and transferable (subject to the provisions hereof) right to use, reproduce, prepare derivative works (including translations) of, display and distribute the Product Marketing Materials in the Territory during the Term in connection with the XXXX Product. If Licensor objects in writing to any versions of the Product Marketing Materials prepared or used by Licensee, the parties shall cooperate in good faith to resolve Licensor's concerns. Licensee agrees to place such notices on Product Marketing Materials and translated versions thereof as are reasonably requested by Licensor to protect its copyrights in such materials and in the Licensed Trademarks used therein. Nothing in this Section __ shall prevent or restrict Licensee from freely creating, distributing or using any marketing materials for XXXX Products that do not incorporate the Licensed Trademarks and that do not infringe on Licensor's copyrights or other Intellectual Property Rights.

9. Source Code Restrictions

In addition to the obligations under Section ___ (Use), Licensee agrees that it will disclose the Source Code only to those employees and Qualified Developers who have a need to know such information and who have signed a written confidentiality agreement prior to receiving access to the Source Code, which is consistent with the protections required under this Agreement. Licensee shall ensure that all its employees and Qualified Developers who have access to the Source Code are adequately instructed as to the Source Code handling requirements hereunder and shall take adequate precautions to prevent unauthorized use or disclosure of the Source Code. Without limiting the foregoing provisions, Licensee and its employees and Qualified Developers shall protect the Source Code during the Term by:

(a) keeping all copies of Source Code in secure, locked facilities when such copies are not in actual use;

(b) marking storage media, printouts, machine-readable files, and other copies or extracts of the Source Code with a restrictive legend stating that such materials are proprietary and confidential to Licensor and that their handling is subject to the terms of this Agreement;

(c) maintaining current records that show: (i) each employee or Qualified Developer authorized to access the Source Code, and (ii) each physical storage media containing the Source Code and its location (other than such media under the control of a Qualified Developer); and

(d) implementing appropriate systems security for Source Code which is stored in soft copy or electronically in information processing systems, including password protection and completely overwriting any physical storage media containing Source Code before it is released for reuse.

10. Third Party Access – Licensor Oriented

Licensee shall not use the Software to process the data of anyone else, such as by providing service bureau or outsourcing services. Licensee shall not make the Software available for use by anyone else, whether for the benefit of Licensee or anyone else. Licensee may make additional copies of Documentation for the Software as reasonably necessary for use of the Software within the scope of Licensee's license.

11. Third Party Access – Administrative Services

Licensee agrees that Licensor may use third party suppliers (the "Administrative Services Licensors") to perform certain contract administration services and other Licensor back office functions (the "Administrative Services"). For purposes of the Administrative Services, Licensor is hereby authorized to disclose and provide [this Agreement - amend as appropriate for document] to the Administrative Services Licensors subject that all commercially sensitive information including pricing tables and information subject to data privacy considerations will be removed and not be made available to the Administrative Services Licensors. The Administrative Services would be managed by Licensor and would have no effect upon Licensee's receipt of the Services. The costs for the Administrative Services are borne by Licensor. This Administrative Services Licensors shall be required to satisfy the same obligations as Licensor with respect to [Confidential and Proprietary Information and Materials - amend as appropriate to document] and other provisions of [this Agreement - amend and appropriate to document] applicable to third parties as required herein.

***COMMENT:** This language allows a licensor to use a third party for administrative back office services without violating the terms of the parties' non-disclosure agreement. A prudent licensor will incorporate language into its agreement providing that it is not required to obtain the licensee's approval to provide access to the agreement to its administrative suppliers after the agreement is signed.*

12. Conversion of Exclusive License to Non-Exclusive Licence

At the end of the exclusive period, the license granted hereunder shall become nonexclusive and shall extend to the end of the term or terms for which any Patent Rights are issued, unless sooner terminated as hereinafter provided. The period of exclusivity may be extended with the written consent of Licensor, on a field of use basis, which consent shall not unreasonably be withheld, conditioned or delayed, provided that Licensee is a licensee in good standing, owing no fees, royalties or any other monies to Licensor, and having met all the diligence milestones pertaining to the particular field of use in which an extension of the period of exclusivity is under consideration.

13. Grant of Limited License – Seat License

Licensor grants Customer the right to use the Software for its own business use and benefit by the number of authorized Users licensed herein. The Software is in use on a computer when it is loaded or installed into temporary or permanent memory. Customer may use the Software on file server(s) on a compatible local area network provided the total number of Users in the system at any time does not exceed the number of Users of the Software. Except for disaster recovery, in no event may Customer loan, rent, lease, sublicense or otherwise transfer this license to a non-Customer entity without the prior written consent of Licensor which consent may be withheld at its sole discretion.

"**User**" means the persons using the Product on behalf of Customer and to conduct Customer's business, including internal and external resources (i.e. staff, agents, contractors, brokers or service agencies, etc.).

14. Grant of Limited License – Non-Production Use License

Licensor, as of the License Date and for the duration of the Term, grants to Licensee a nonexclusive and nontransferable license for the sole purpose of using the Licensed Program for Non-production Use and, to the extent Licensee has received Software Releases pursuant to Schedule 3, those shall be deemed to be included in the definition of Licensed Program on this Schedule 1.1 for the Approved Use by Qualified

Employees under the conditions set forth in this Schedule 1.1. In no event shall Licensee use the Licensed Program in a service bureau capacity or provide services to any third party.

15. Grant of Software License with Right of Sublicense

(a) Licensor hereby grants to Licensee (including its present and future affiliates), and Licensee accepts, a non-exclusive, world-wide, sublicensable and transferable (subject to the provisions hereof) license to access, distribute, display, host, translate into local languages in the Territory and otherwise commercially exploit the Software in connection with the manufacture, marketing, distribution and sale of XXXX Products in the Territory. For clarity, monitoring services may be based outside of the Territory provided such services are directed at XXXX Products in the Territory.

(b) Licensor grants to Licensee a non-exclusive, non-sublicensable (except as provided herein) right to use the Source Code to correct, localize, adapt, revise and update the Source Code, and to compile and distribute object and executable code versions of the Software based upon such modified Source Code, provided that (i) Licensee may not disclose any Source Code to any third party other than a Qualified Developer, and (ii) other than changes to the Software to localize it to other languages for use in the Territory and to comply with local requirements, safety listings or other laws or regulations, Licensee shall obtain Licensor's consent prior to distributing XXXX Products including such modifications to any third parties. Licensee must strictly protect the Source Code as confidential pursuant to the terms of Section 10. Licensee may engage reputable third-party software developers located inside or outside the Territory who (iii) are subject to written confidentiality and non-use agreements consistent with this Agreement and (iv) meet the qualification requirements to be mutually agreed upon or attached hereto as Exhibit __ (each, a "Qualified Developer") to make permitted modifications of the Source Code. Licensor retains the rights to the master copy of the Source Code.

16. Title

1.1 Title and sole and exclusive ownership of any invention, device, design or idea developed by Licensor while performing services hereunder, whether patentable or otherwise, shall vest in Customer and Licensor agrees to take all necessary steps, and execute all documents reasonably required by Customer to effectuate the vesting of such title and ownership; **provided, however, that in no event shall Licensor appoint Customer its attorney-in-fact.** Any development, modification or translation by Licensor of copyrightable material shall be considered a "work for hire" under the U.S. copyright laws and the copyright in and to such material shall belong to Customer. To the extent the development, modification or translation may not be deemed a "work for hire"; Licensor shall be deemed to have assigned all copyright rights therein to effect such assignment. Licensor shall promptly provide Customer with copies of all developments, modifications or translations made by or for Licensor. This ownership shall not prevent Licensor and its agents from using technology or techniques of general applicability to develop similar products for others.

> ***COMMENT: Licensors should never agree to language appointing the customer as its attorney in fact as the Licensor has no control over the customer's actions. A more prudent approach is to state that the failure to cooperate shall constitute a material breach of the agreement.***

1.2 Licensor shall not, without the written consent of Customer incorporate any Publicly Available Software (defined below) into any part of the product or the end result of the services that are delivered to Customer, except to the extent already incorporated by Customer in the underlying product or services. As used herein, the term "Publicly Available Software" means any software that requires as a condition of use, modification or distribution that such software or other software incorporated into, derived from or distributed with such software: (a) be disclosed or distributed in source code form, (b) be licensed for the purpose of making derivative works, or (c) be redistributable at no charge. If Licensor incorporates Publicly Available Software except as described in this paragraph without Customer's written consent, then any such Publicly Available Software will be deemed to be considered "Software Product" with regard to the terms and conditions of Sections ___ (Authorized Agents of Customer), ___ (Intellectual Property Indemnification), ___ (Usage and Distribution) and ___ (Warranty) below.

1.3 Licensor shall not, without the written consent of Customer, incorporate any third party product into any part of the product or the end result of the services that are delivered to Customer, except to the extent already incorporated by Customer in the underlying product or services. If Licensor incorporates any third party product except as described in this paragraph without Customer's written consent, then any such third party product shall be deemed to be considered "Software Product" with regard to the terms and conditions of Sections ___ (Authorized Agents of Customer), ___ (Intellectual Property Indemnification), ___ (Usage and Distribution) and ___ (Warranty) below.

1.4 Licensor and its agents shall own all right, title and interest, including all worldwide intellectual property rights, in and to any pre-existing software, documents, coding, processes, template tools and methodology, and any enhancements or improvements thereto not conceived of or developed under this Agreement ("Intellectual Capital"). With respect to any Intellectual Capital, Licensor hereby grants to Customer and to any Customer Affiliate a non-exclusive, non-transferable, limited, perpetual, royalty-free license to use such Intellectual Capital in the normal course of Customer's business. Intellectual Capital shall not include Licensor's commercial software products, which shall be licensed in accordance with Licensor's commercial license terms as may be separately agreed between the parties.

NN. Waiver of Jury Trial (Chapter 6.F; § 32)

1. Waiver of Jury Trial

THE PARTIES HEREBY UNCONDITIONALLY WAIVE THEIR RESPECTIVE RIGHTS TO A JURY TRIAL OF ANY CLAIM OR CAUSE OF ACTION ARISING DIRECTLY OR INDIRECTLY OUT OF, RELATED TO, OR IN ANY WAY CONNECTED WITH, THE PERFORMANCE OR BREACH OF THIS AGREEMENT, OR THE RELATIONSHIP THAT IS BEING ESTABLISHED BETWEEN THEM. The scope of this waiver is intended to be all encompassing of any and all disputes that may be filed in any court or other tribunal (including, without limitation, contract claims, tort claims, breach of duty claims, and all other common law and statutory claims). THIS WAIVER IS IRREVOCABLE, MEANING THAT IT MAY NOT BE MODIFIED EITHER ORALLY OR IN WRITING, AND THE WAIVER SHALL APPLY TO ANY SUBSEQUENT AMENDMENTS, RENEWALS, SUPPLEMENTS OR MODIFICATIONS TO THIS AGREEMENT, AND RELATED DOCUMENTS, OR TO ANY OTHER DOCUMENTS OR AGREEMENTS RELATING TO THIS TRANSACTION OR ANY RELATED TRANSACTION. In the event of litigation, this Agreement may be filed as a consent to a trial by the court.

Data Privacy/Security Checklist

THIS CHECKLIST IS TO BE USED ONLY AS A GUIDE WHEN ASSESSING THE ACCEPTABILITY OF CLIENT PROPOSED DATA PRIVACY AND SECURITY RELATED REQUIREMENTS AND RELATED CONTRACTUAL PROVISIONS. IT IS NOT INTENDED TO BE A COMPREHENSIVE LIST OF THE DATA PRIVACY AND SECURITY ISSUES/RISKS ASSOCIATED WITH A PARTICULAR TRANSACTION. IT DOES NOT PROVIDE SUGGESTED LANGUAGE AROUND ALL PRIVACY AND SECURITY ISSUES IN DIFFERENT TYPES OF TRANSACTIONS. EACH CLIENT'S PRIVACY/SECURITY REQUIREMENTS SHOULD BE REVIEWED IN THE CONTEXT OF THE UNDERLYING TRANSACTION, CLIENT'S PARTICULAR INDUSTRY AND ANY CONTROLLING POLICIES/ AGREEMENTS.

THIS CHECKLIST APPLIES TO U.S. COMMERCIAL DOMESTIC AGREEMENTS UNDER WHICH THE DATA IS U.S. DATA ONLY. IF DATA OF CITIZENS OF OTHER COUNTRIES IS BEING PROCESSED OR IF SERVICES ARE BEING PROVIDED INTERNATIONALLY, INTERNATIONAL COUNSEL NEEDS TO BE CONSULTED.

CLIENT: ______________________________

CONTRACT: ______________________________

I. Client Policies

1. Nature of the Policies

Are Client's policies static or fluid (i.e., set forth on a web-portal and subject to change)?

If static, attach, or reference, if appropriate, the negotiated policy to the underlying agreement as an exhibit.

NOTE: For purposes of this checklist, specific contractual security/confidentiality/data privacy obligations in a contract should be considered in the same manner as policies.

If fluid, how is Licensor protected in the event of a change to the policy? Who on the Licensor project team is responsible for identifying ongoing changes made to the policy and ensuring compliance with such changes? Is Client obligated to notify Licensor of any changes to its policies after execution of the agreement? Who bears the additional cost, if any, of complying with the change in policies? What if the requirements are unreasonable or cost prohibitive?

> *NOTE: If at all possible, Licensor should not agree to comply with a policy posted to a Client's web-portal due to the risk of Licensor failing to identify subsequent changes to the policy and the inability of Licensor to protect against the financial risk arising from future changes. If Licensor agrees to be bound by polices posted on Client's web-portal, Client should have the obligation to notify Licensor when a change is made. Financial or other impacts of a policy change should ideally be addressed through the change order process. Licensor cannot bear the risk of future changes unless its pricing has contemplated such changes. If Client is unwilling to utilize a change order process, Licensor should have the right to reject any material change to Client's policies that impacts Licensor's cost or ability to comply, in which case Client may as its sole remedy terminate the Agreement (or applicable Statement of Work) upon reasonable advance notice to Licensor. Termination should be a "convenience" type of termination and be fee-burdened if a termination for convenience would otherwise be fee bearing.*

For transactions with a total contract value of US$500,000 or more or a high level of risk, has Licensor's project management team assigned a lead information risk manager (LIRM) or issued a comprehensive information security policy, operating procedures, and associated responsibility statements based on Licensor's contractual obligations and Client's policies? Who will fill the role of LIRM if the project cannot support a FTE in this role? These policies and procedures should be drafted upon execution of the Agreement by the project team and distributed internally to all members of the team. It should be noted that the process of generating these items may be billable internally and would have to be priced into the project at commencement to avoid dilution of anticipated margin.

2. Disclosure of Information

Will Licensor (as opposed to Client using Licensor's systems) share, transfer, or release any information to third parties?

- With whom, if anyone, is the information being shared, transferred, or released? This includes subsidiaries, partners, contractors, VARs, government investigatory agencies/bodies, etc.
- Will Client expect to be notified before any transfer? Will it be only under certain conditions? Will Licensor be required to document all such disclosures and produce such documentation to Client?
- What specific information, if any, is being shared, transferred, or released?
- What is the geographic location of these individuals and entities? What state specific or country specific laws apply, in particular, what state specific data breach notification requirements may there be?

As to subpoenas from governmental entities or third parties in disputes with Client:

- What are Licensor's contractual responsibilities once it receives a subpoena? Who bears the cost of complying with the subpoena should it be determined that information must be generated and turned over to an opposing party or investigating agency or other body?

Are the limitations on disclosure of information broad enough to allow Licensor to disclose the information to those employees, contractors, auditors and subcontractors who need access to support the contract? Do those limitations on disclosure require that we have any particular contractual or other restrictions with those to whom access is provided? If so, who on the account team is responsible for ensuring that the restrictions have been complied with prior to disclosure?

Is Licensor going to use employees and contractors outside of the United States on the project? If so, are there additional/special limits on Licensor disclosing information to Licensor employees and contractors working outside of the United States? What about non-U.S. citizens working in the U.S.; do they need to be identified?

Client imposed limitations on Licensor's ability to disclose confidential information to employees/contractors outside of the U.S. may prevent Licensor from efficiently performing the services, and may result in increased costs of the services. Has project management considered the export implications of moving such information offshore or the costs of being restricted from doing so?

NOTE: In most cases, Licensor cannot be limited as to how it allocates the work among different countries and it must retain the ability to allocate work in the most effective and cost-efficient manner possible. Licensor prefers not to condition its right to perform work outside the United States on Client's prior consent, but can agree to notify Client in the event any work will be performed outside of the United States. In some transactions, Client may be in a bargaining position to impose limitations. If so, consent to a broad list of locations should be obtained as part of the initial contract.

---

3. Use of Information

May Licensor use information and data derived from Client's confidential information for Licensor's own purposes, if Licensor removes all personally identifiable information?

NOTE: The right to use de-identified Client information may be very important for future data warehouse projects where Licensor seeks to create a "product." It can also be very helpful for use as a "test bed of data" for future software development projects.

Model language:

> **Notwithstanding any other provision of this Agreement, Licensor may utilize data capture and analysis tools, and other similar tools, to extract, compile, synthesize, analyze, and use any Blind Data. "Blind Data" means non-individually identifiable and non-client identifiable data or information created from Client's data submitted for data processing. Blind Data excludes: 1) any specific Client identifiable information such as individual names and physical addresses; and 2) any specific Client information related to a report, or any party to a report, such as name, gender, race, ethnicity, human resources identification number, social security or international identification number, E-Mail address, home address, and home phone number. To the extent that any Client Blind Data is collected or compiled by Licensor, such Blind Data shall be solely owned by Licensor without any restrictions whatsoever. Client acknowledges that Licensor's ability to use and dispose of Blind Data is part of the consideration Client is paying to Licensor for the services and no fee or other consideration will be paid or owing to Client by Licensor for Licensor's use and /or disposal of the Blind Data.**

ALTERNATIVE LANGUAGE: Below is language Licensor uses in contracts for systems financial services organizations host on Licensor servers.

> **7. DATA REPORTS**
>
> **7.1 Composition of Data Reports. During the term of this Work Assignment, Client authorizes Licensor to collect data reports from Client relating to Client's use of the Licensed System ("Data Reports"). The Data Reports shall not include information which would identify Client as the source of the Data Reports and shall not include any of the following data fields with respect to any individual claimant or insured, which data fields shall be overwritten or omitted in the Data Reports: Comments, Claim/Claimant Number and Format, Non-Medical Information, Claimant Name (or other details), Insured Name (or other details), Adjuster Name, History Log Data, Consultation History Data, or any other basic or customized claim information (except that Date of Loss, Date of Assessment, Age/Date of Birth, and Gender will be collected).**
>
> **7.2 Title to Data Reports. Licensor shall be the sole owner of all rights and title in and to the Data Reports described herein and the Data Reports shall be considered to be Licensor Confidential Information pursuant to the terms of the Agreement.**
>
> **8. Data Privacy Warranty, Representation, and Indemnity**
>
> **8.1 Warranty and Representation. Client warrants and represents that provision of data to Licensor and Licensor's use of the data to exercise its rights and perform its obligations under this Work Assignment and**

the Agreement (including but not limited to the provision by Licensor to Client of the Services described in this Work Assignment and creation of the Data Reports) will be in compliance with all applicable laws, including but not limited to, any application of the Health Insurance Portability and Accountability Act of 1996 and associated regulations, the Gramm-Leach-Bliley Act and associated regulations, the Federal Trade Commission Act, other consumer protection laws, and other laws governing the collection, use, maintenance and disclosure of personal information, and any applicable court order or Client contractual commitment.

8.2 Indemnity. Client agrees to defend, indemnify, and hold Licensor (and its affiliates) harmless from and against any claims, demands, and actions, and any liabilities, damages, or expenses resulting there from, including court costs and reasonable attorney fees, arising out of or relating to a breach or alleged breach of the warranty and representation in Section 8.1 of this Work Assignment. Client's obligations under this Section shall survive the termination of this Work Assignment for any reason. Licensor agrees to give Client prompt notice of any such claim, demand, or action of which Licensor receives notice and shall, to the extent Licensor is not adversely affected, cooperate fully with Client in the defense and settlement thereof.

8.3 Exception to Indemnity. Client shall have no duty under Section 8.2 of this Work Assignment to indemnify Licensor against any claims arising out of or relating to Licensor's material breach of Section _____ (Composition of Data Reports) of this Work Assignment.

4. Client Information

Does Licensor have a plan to minimize the collection of Client data in order to comply with any contractual obligation to restrict access and use of the data solely for the purposes contemplated by the Agreement?

Who is responsible for ensuring Licensor complies with Licensor's contractual data related obligations? (e.g., the Project Manager or someone else?) Have these obligations been effectively communicated by Legal during the negotiation process to all members of the delivery and project management team and have limitations to access been built into the business process to ensure no inappropriate disclosure happens? Who is responsible for tracking all Client data throughout the lifecycle of the engagement so it can all be returned or destroyed at the end of the engagement? If Licensor is instructed by Client to destroy the data and also provide certification as to such destruction, who within Licensor will undertake the secure destruction and provide the actual Certificates of Destruction and who will pay for that service?

5. Stated Standards

Why does Licensor need to comply with the stated standards? Is Licensor's compliance required by law or simply desired by Client? If Licensor stores (on behalf of Client) certain data types, and there is a breach, government agencies may hold Licensor directly liable, so how does Licensor mitigate that risk?

Does Licensor's proposed approach to the performance of services meet/comply with the stated standard?

If the standards are stated by reference to particular statutes are the requirements understood by the account team? Is there a procedure in place to monitor changes in the referenced standards?

Are the stated standards static or fluid (e.g., set forth on a web site and subject to change)?

If static, attach (or reference) the stated standard as an exhibit.

If fluid, how is Licensor protected in the event of a change to the standard? Who bears the additional cost, if any, of complying with the change in the standard?

Will Licensor supplement the information received directly from Client with additional information received from third parties, or information received by mechanisms other than those to which Client has explicitly consented? If so, are there additional standards that need to be complied with relative to amendment of data, commingling of data, and storage of data?

NOTE: Responsibility for compliance resides with the project group, not Legal. Please make sure the project group understands this.

NOTE: Do not assume that Licensor or a particular division within Licensor complies with a particular standard. You must confirm that the Licensor Division in question actually complies. If multiple Licensor Divisions will be providing services, you must confirm that EVERY Division complies. Contact NAME to determine which divisions of Licensor are compliant with a particular standard. Avoid agreeing to broad based statements of compliance that apply to all of Licensor. For example, some divisions of Licensor may be ISO 9000/1 compliant, while others may not be.

Standards to Which Licensor is Not Compliant

Licensor is not a signatory to the "Safe Harbor" privacy principles associated with the European Data Protection Directive (95/46/EC), although it is willing to state that it adheres to the Eight Principles of Data Protection (the "Principles") as set forth in the Directive, but there must be an individual accountable to ensure such adherence.

NOTE: If required to comply with a particular standard, negotiated responses may include: (i) limiting the compliance obligation to a particular division within Licensor or to the individual transaction;(ii) challenging such obligation on the grounds that Licensor's compliance is not legally required; or (iii) agreeing that Licensor will seek compliance provided Licensor's costs are covered. The actual response will depend on the standard in question.

For example, Licensor does not state that its products/services/systems are "HIPAA Compliant" but rather "HIPAA- Ready" under the belief that Licensor would be giving a legal opinion to state they are "HIPAA Compliant." Either term is acceptable provided the stated definition of the term is appropriate. In complex service agreements, Licensor's obligations may be limited to complying with specific requirements specified by Client as meeting its view on HIPAA compliance.

For any questions regarding compliance speak to NAME.

---

6. Project Management

Who within Licensor is responsible for the following aspects of compliance for the project or contract as a whole?

Project Manager: ______________________________

Administrative Safeguards: ______________________________

Physical Safeguards: ______________________________

Technical Safeguards: ______________________________

Point of Contact for Security Issues: ______________________________

Point of Contact for Human Resource Issues: ______________________________

Point of Contact for Incident Notification & Escalation: ______________________________

Point of Contact for Issue Resolution and Communication: ______________________________

7. Employee/Contractor Issues

If applicable, who is responsible for developing an Acceptable Use Policy (AUP) for Licensor employees and contractors outlining the contractual obligations, as well as the consequences of misuse of Client data? If the project manager is not going to prepare an AUP, have they been apprised of the risk of not doing so? Who is responsible for ensuring no potential conflicts of interest exist?

If required, have all employees and contractors executed written acknowledgements of their understanding and acceptance of Client's information/security policies? If so, who is responsible for maintaining those records?

Has the execution of properly signed confidentiality agreements been verified before proprietary and/or sensitive information is disclosed, in any form, to employees and non-Licensor individuals? (Most employees will have satisfied this requirement through the execution of a standard non-disclosure agreement that was part of their on-boarding process with Licensor.) Do employee/contractors understand their obligation to encrypt sensitive and confidential data? Whose obligations is it to ensure that employee/contractor is provided equipment that enables encryption of such data (whether on a desktop, laptop, USB drive, PDA, Blackberry, etc.)?

Is the Licensor project manager and/or service delivery manager aware of any ongoing training requirements? Has he/she established ongoing training during the term of the Agreement to meet the contractual requirements? Has a process to document completion of such training been established and who is responsible for maintaining those records?

8. Licensor Obligations upon Termination of Agreement

Do Client policies require that Licensor dispose Client data in a particular manner? Are these requirements consistent with Licensor policies? Is Licensor protected in the event of a dispute where Licensor might need the data to defend a claim with Client that may, or may not, be subject to a Litigation Hold/Preservation Order?

> *NOTE: Data conversion and storage can be very expensive. Licensor should ensure that it has no obligation to store or convert Client data after the termination of the Agreement unless Licensor is compensated for doing so. If Licensor is obligated to return Client's data and the data is expected to be voluminous, has Licensor included the cost to do so in its pricing? If not, Client should pay all costs associated with the return of such data. In the alternative, Licensor should have the contractual right to simply destroy such data, in which case Client should also be obligated to pay such destruction costs.*

Model language:

> **Upon termination of this Agreement for any reason, Licensor shall return or destroy all Confidential Information received from Client, or created or received by Licensor on behalf of Client. In the event that Licensor determines in its reasonable discretion that returning or destroying the Confidential Information is not feasible, Licensor shall notify Client of the conditions that make return or destruction infeasible and shall extend the protections of this Agreement to such Confidential Information and limit further uses and disclosures of such Confidential Information to those purposes that make the return or destruction infeasible, for so long as Licensor maintains such Confidential Information.**

II. Related Contractual Provisions

1. Contractors/Subcontractors/Vendors (collectively subcontractors)

Is Licensor required to flow down any standards, policies, or contractual terms to its subcontractors?

Who is responsible for ensuring their compliance? Have all applicable provisions been flowed down to Licensor's subcontractors?

How is Licensor protected in the event its contractors/subcontractors fail to comply? Has Licensor obtained an indemnity from its contractors/subcontractors for their failure to comply?

2. Changes in the Law

Who bears the risk of changes in the law? Who is responsible for tracking changes in the law?

Has Licensor priced the financial risk of complying with any changes into its pricing?

What ability does Licensor have to protect itself in the event of increased costs due to changes in the law?

NOTE: Licensor should only agree to comply with all laws in existence at the time the contract is executed. Licensor should not agree to comply with all laws as they exist throughout the duration of the contract. Changes in the law should be addressed through the change order process. Client should not be able to transfer the risk of a change in the law to Licensor as this risk originally resided with Client and there is no reason it should flow to Licensor solely because Licensor is providing services to Client.

ALTERNATIVE POSITION: If the change in law impacts Licensor in its capacity generally as an IT services vendor (e.g., proposed changes to HIPAA to apply directly to Business Associates), then Licensor should bear the risk of its compliance. However, if the change in law impacts Licensor because of a particular service it is providing on behalf of Client and the change is specific to that service (e.g., Medicare Part D claims processing), then Client should bear the risk.

Licensor can agree to comply with all laws brought to its attention by Client provided Licensor is compensated for any additional cost associated with Licensor's compliance and the change is implemented through the contract's change control provisions. Licensor lacks the ability to track all potentially applicable laws throughout the United States and the world. Client is in a better position to do so through its knowledge of its industry and its mem-

bership in industry organizations. (While this position may not be valid in an outsourcing transaction, it is more tenable in systems integration/services agreements.)

Model language:

Licensor will comply with the following state privacy laws [OPTION: as directed by Client] but only to the extent such laws are applicable to the Services and to the extent Client was in compliance with such laws at the time Licensor commenced providing services: [SPECIFY STATE STATUTES].

Client shall monitor and promptly identify and notify Licensor of all changes in Applicable Laws occurring on or after the Effective Date and all non-compliance existing as of the date Licensor commences services (collectively "Legal Changes"). Client and Licensor will work together to identify the effects of Legal Changes on the provision or receipt of the Services. With respect to Legal Changes, the parties will discuss, in a timely manner, what modifications to the Services, if any, are necessary to comply with such Legal Changes. Licensor shall promptly thereafter propose any amendments or change orders to the Agreement associated with such Legal Changes. Upon Client's consent, Licensor shall implement the changes to the Services in a timely manner.

3. Indemnification

In general, indemnification for breach of laws should be confined to laws (including data privacy laws) that are actual laws or regulations, which have the force of law. This often involves revisiting the definition of laws in the Agreement.

Indemnification should be only for those losses asserted by third parties who are not affiliates (with "affiliates" or "unaffiliated" being a defined term). Indemnities for breach of confidentiality/security should be addressed to Licensor's obligations under the Agreement, which should consist of a set of discrete known tasks and policies. Attorney's fees and costs of litigation should be covered only in the event of a wrongful refusal to accept a tender of indemnity. Cross-indemnities for breach of laws should be obtained. The extent to which indemnities are excluded from any limitation of liability needs to be addressed on a case-by-case basis.

NOTE: *Licensor's contracting guidelines provide that Licensor may indemnify against claims related to breaches of confidentiality or security obligations, use of client supplied materials in a noncompliant way, claims (including fines and penalties) related to failure to comply with its obligations related to laws, and claims related to breach of its obligations with respect to client data subject to security and confidentiality obligations.*

Licensor should attempt to reject any demand by Client for indemnification on the premise that Client's remedy lies in a claim for breach of contract (damages). No statute requires a vendor to indemnify a client. Many clients will argue that an indemnity is industry standard. If Licensor must give an indemnity, the indemnity should be narrowly drawn to limit Licensor's risk and apply only to unaffiliated third party claims. Licensor should not indemnify Client for breach of a policy or breach of the Agreement. The indemnity set forth below requires that the indemnified claim be both a violation of the applicable law and a material breach of the Agreement. In addition, it excludes third party claims arising from instructions received from Client. Licensor should seek to make any indemnity mutual.

Model language:

Licensor agrees to indemnify, defend and hold harmless Client against all actual direct losses suffered by Client as a result of unaffiliated third party claims arising directly from the use or disclosure of Confidential Information by Licensor or its agents which is both in violation of the [Applicable Laws] and in material breach of this Agreement. Said responsibility adheres only to violations solely attributable to the actions/inactions of Licensor and/or its agents and not to actions/inactions taken or not taken at the request of Client or to actions/inactions of Licensor that are permitted under the [Applicable Laws] and/or this Agreement.

Client agrees to indemnify, defend and hold harmless Licensor against all actual direct losses suffered by Licensor as a result of unaffiliated third party claims arising from any action or inaction of Licensor taken or not taken by Licensor at the request of Client or to actions/inactions of Licensor that are permitted under the [Applicable Laws] and/or this Agreement.

NOTE: "unaffiliated" needs to be a defined term.

---

4. *Representations and Warranties*

NOTE: Licensor should not represent or warrant compliance with any particular law, standard or policy. Instead, Licensor should agree (covenant) that it will comply with the applicable policy or <u>law in existence at the time of the Agreement's execution</u>. Licensor cannot commit to comply with future policies or law without financial and operational protections.

> As a matter of course, Licensor will sign up to a warranty/covenant that it is in and will remain in compliance in all material respects with all applicable laws that apply to Licensor as a provider of IT services. Licensor is responsible for complying with existing laws and future changes to laws applicable to it as a provider of IT services. Client is responsible for all other existing laws and future changes to laws.

---

5. Limitation of Liability

If Client's policies are contained in a freestanding document, does that document contain a limitation of liability? Confirm that the over-arching Agreement's limitations of liability limit Licensor's liability for breach of the policy or that the policy contains its own limitation of liability.

If Client's policies are an attachment to the underlying Agreement, is the Agreement clear that breaches of those policies are subject to the Agreement's limitations of liability?

In general, Licensor seeks to limit its responsibility to breach of specific policies and contractually specified tasks as well as its contractual obligation to comply with laws (which may be narrower than laws generally). This is different than a "reasonable standard of care" which may be acceptable for confidential information that is not client data submitted for processing. Licensor also seeks to have the limitation of liability apply to these obligations, at least as to those matters that are operational in nature; e.g., a firewall server down should be treated as any other server down. Deviations from current Licensor norms around risk allocation should be escalated to NAME if he is available.

An exception to a limitation of liability for failure to comply with laws should be addressed through the approval process. It is preferable to limit this exception to discrete activities such as the giving of any required legal notice, the payment of fines or penalties, and the like.

> *NOTE: Any carve-out from the Agreement's limitation of liability should be narrowly drafted such that the exclusion applies only to breach of Licensor's confidentiality obligations and not to a breach of the applicable policy. This carve-out should be mutual so that Client also has unlimited liability for any breach by it of its confidentiality obligations relative to Licensor Confidential Information.*

---

6. Right to Cure

Does the policy provide Licensor with the right to cure or may Client immediately terminate the underlying Agreement in the event of an alleged breach by Licensor? Does the policy set forth a notice and escalation process?

NOTE: Licensor must have a specified way to cure any alleged breach. Client should provide Licensor written notice describing the breach in detail. Occasionally, Client will point out that it is not possible to cure a security breach if the data is not fully recovered and knowledge of it has not spread outside Licensor and Client. Thus, it may not be practical in all instances for Licensor have a cure period.

The government's own Business Associate Agreement ("BAA") template recognizes a Business Associate's right of cure:

> **Termination for Cause. Upon Covered Entity's knowledge of a material breach by Business Associate, Covered Entity shall either:**
>
> **1. Provide an opportunity for Business Associate to cure the breach or end the violation and terminate this Agreement [and the _________ Agreement/ sections ____ of the ______________ Agreement] if Business Associate does not cure the breach or end the violation within the time specified by Covered Entity;**
>
> **2. Immediately terminate this Agreement [and the _________ Agreement/ sections ____ of the ______________ Agreement] if Business Associate has breached a material term of this Agreement and cure is not possible; or**
>
> **3. If neither termination nor cure is feasible, Covered Entity shall report the violation to the Secretary.**

See http://www.hhs.gov/ocr/privacy/hipaa/understanding/coveredentities/contractprov.html. *See also* 45 CFR 314(a)(1)(i)(B).

From the OCR Privacy Guidance:

"Where a covered entity knows of a material breach or violation by the business associate of the contract or agreement, the covered entity is required to take reasonable steps to cure the breach or end the violation, and if such steps are unsuccessful, to terminate the contract or arrangement. If termination of the contract or agreement is not feasible, a covered entity is required to report the problem to the Department of Health and Human Services (HHS) Office for Civil Rights (OCR)."
45 C.F.R. §§ 164.502(e), 164.504(e), 164.532(d) and (e).

7. Mitigation

Is Licensor obligated to mitigate any breach of a policy? What is the extent of Licensor's obligation to mitigate its breach?

Licensor should not assume a broad obligation to mitigate any breach to Client's satisfaction. Licensor should do only what is reasonable and leave it to Client to pursue damages if Client believes more is warranted.

NOTE: Clients increasingly seek to impose a mitigation obligation on Licensor to mitigate any deleterious effects from improper disclosure of confidential information. The scope of the mitigation obligation is often undefined, but could include detailed notices to a very large pool, call-in hotlines and, in the case of Gramm-Leach-Bliley data obligations, credit watch services. Mitigation of the harmful effects is a requirement under HIPAA, but the rules do not define what actions must be taken or the scope of mitigation. The issue is one of conceding contractual language that could obligate Licensor to incur expenses in excess of what would otherwise be required to comply with law, based on the demands of Client. The language below obligates Licensor to use "reasonable efforts" to limit "additional losses" but expressly disclaims any obligations that would result in Licensor incurring a material financial expense.

Model language:

Licensor agrees to mitigate, to the extent practicable, any harmful effect that is actually known to Licensor of a Security Incident, caused by Licensor or its subcontractor(s) arising from its provision of the Services. Licensor's obligation to mitigate shall consist of reasonable efforts to limit additional losses after a Security Incident has occurred. Licensor shall not be required to undertake any actions which cause Licensor to incur a material financial expense.

[OPTIONAL: For purposes of this Agreement, a material financial expense shall mean an expense which will cost in total an amount which is equal to or exceeds five percent (5%) of the fees under the Agreement associated with the provision of Covered Services in the immediately preceding three (3) months.]

8. Viruses

Is Licensor representing, warranting or covenanting that it will not introduce any viruses into Client's systems?

NOTE: Licensor should only agree to apply commercially reasonable virus detection software to any software delivered to Client and to use its good faith efforts to remediate any problems caused by a virus introduced by Licensor. To avoid a dispute as to what is "reasonable," you should identify the particular software Licensor will use. Licensor should insist that the negotiated Agreement contain a reciprocal provision from Client. Outside of blocking downloads from certain web sites, Licensor cannot guarantee that a virus will not be introduced into Client's system. Virus detection software is only reactive, not proactive. Alternatively, Licensor should seek to limit its obligations to a covenant that Licensor will not "knowingly and intentionally" introduce a virus.

9. Third Party Beneficiaries

The Agreement/policies should specifically exclude any third party beneficiaries to limit any potential third party claims against Licensor. HIPAA, for example, does not provide a private cause of action to the owner of Protected Health Information ("PHI") against a Business Associate who violates the terms of HIPAA or a Business Associate Agreement.

Model language:

> **Nothing express or implied in this Agreement is intended to confer, nor shall anything herein confer, upon any person other than the parties and the respective successors and assigns of the parties, any rights, remedies, obligations or liabilities whatsoever. There are no third party beneficiaries. [OPTIONAL – Licensor might want to state that there are no third party beneficiaries other than as specified in the indemnification provisions.]**

10. Notices

Due to the inability to confirm actual receipt by the intended recipient, Licensor should not agree to the provision of formal notices via E-Mail or facsimile. The preferred means of delivery is certified mail, return receipt requested or overnight courier. Notices should be sent to legal counsel for the group/entity entering into the Agreement, with a copy to a business team member or the applicable member of the contracts department. All notices should be effective upon receipt.

11. Unilateral Amendment of Underlying Agreement by Client

Is Client allowed to unilaterally amend the Agreement for changes in the law or in the event Client believes a change is necessary to clarify an ambiguity or ensure compliance with an applicable law?

How is Licensor protected from increased costs or other obligations? Will any negative impact be addressed through the change order process?

NOTE: Licensor should not agree to allow unilateral change, except when absolutely insisted upon by Client and then only if subject to reasonable advance notice and Client's binding commitment to financially compensate Licensor for any negative impact, and the other terms, such as timing of implementation, are satisfactory to Licensor. In the alternative, Licensor should be allowed to reject any unilaterally proposed amendment, whereupon Client may terminate the Agreement.

III. Audits, Etc.

1. Security Audits

What types of security audits are required by Client (i.e., SAS 70 Type I, SAS 70 Type II)?

Is Licensor already performing this type of audit for the data center in question?

NOTE: If not, the requirements for any such audit will have to be separately coordinated in advance with Licensor's Corporate Internal Audit Department, and Client should be made to pay for the audit. Additionally, the results of that audit should be restricted to an executive summary specific to Client, if possible.

Who is entitled to review the results?

NOTE: Any disclosure of the audit results should be limited and treated as confidential information. Client should not be permitted to disclose the results to any third party outside of its auditors and possibly its "advisors." Licensor should specifically require any third party to execute a Non-Disclosure Agreement with Licensor prior to receiving a copy of the results and exclude Licensor competitors from receiving a copy.

Does a security breach trigger a right to audit with respect to security protocols? If the breach occurred because of an employee act, is Client entitled to access the employee's laptop or records to investigate without Licensor's consent?

2. Books and Records

Are the audit provisions overly broad (e.g., potentially extending to information regarding other clients, internal memos, or privileged/personal information)?

Do they extend beyond books and records to include facility audits, and audits of practices and procedures?

Is the audit triggered by a Licensor breach or at the demand of Client? How will "breach" be defined? How often may Client demand an audit and who should pay?

Is the audit subject to appropriate controls?

NOTE: Client should be required to provide at least seven (7) days' prior written notice of its desire to audit Licensor's books and records to allow Licensor the time necessary to collect and make available for review the relevant records. Client's audit rights should be clearly stated and limited. Further, the audit should occur at the Licensor office where the books and records are stored during normal business hours, and subject to all applicable confidentiality and Licensor security controls. The length of the audit should be limited to a set period of time to limit disruption to Licensor's business operations. Licensor should be concerned as to the possibility that an audit of a facility or systems could expose other client data, personal data of employees and/or deficiencies in Licensor's compliance.

Model language:

Licensor agrees to make those internal practices, books, and records specifically relating to the use and disclosure of Confidential Information received from, or created or received by Licensor on behalf of Client available to Client, or at the request of Client to [third party auditor], in a reasonable time and manner agreed to by Client and Licensor, for the purpose of [Insert limited purpose]. Such books and records shall exclude any legally privileged information, as well as non-relevant personal data or Confidential Information of other Licensor clients.

IV. Miscellaneous

1. Background Checks/Drug Tests

Is the obligation to conduct background checks and drug tests limited to those employees who enter Client sites and/or access Client systems or does it apply to any Licensor employee, subcontractor or vendor who comes in contact with Client confidential information? Are there any specific requirements for conducting background checks and drug tests on Licensor employees, subcontractors or vendors?

Has Licensor's Human Resources Department been notified to determine if these requirements go beyond the tests already conducted by Licensor?

Do the background checks and drug tests apply to subcontractor personnel, and if so, have parallel requirements been incorporated in the subcontractor agreement?

How often must the drug test be given, and who is responsible for paying for them and maintaining records about them?

Who is responsible for ensuring Licensor's compliance including ensuring all subcontractors and vendors have all applicable requirements flowed down and audited?

NOTE: You need to determine the scope of checks and tests undertaken by Licensor at the time of the employee's hiring, and if those results will satisfy the requirements of the contract. Who is the contact person for ensuring compliance?

NOTE: All background checks for Licensor employees should be discussed with the applicable HR manager assigned to that group. The contract should be very clear about which Licensor employees this requirement will apply to – for example, if Licensor hosts Client data on its own servers – will Client require anyone with access to those servers to have a background check and drug test? If so, this may be a broader spectrum of Licensor employees than merely those going to Client site. The costs associated with such checks and tests should be considered when pricing the deal.

---

2. Project Budget

Does the pricing model include the cost of specific security requirements required by Client and offered by Licensor as separately chargeable services?

Does the project budget contain a set-aside for the potential cost of complying with ongoing data related requirements, including potential incident response?

3. Training Requirements

Does the Agreement require any continuous training (e.g., HIPAA, Gramm Leach Bliley, etc.) during the term of the Agreement? Has the project manager established ongoing training during the term of the Agreement to meet contractual requirements, and who will maintain records regarding such training?

4. Internal Licensor Resources

If you require additional information, the following Licensor resources may be helpful:

Business Associate Agreement/HIPAA Checklist

THIS CHECKLIST IS TO BE USED ONLY AS A GUIDE WHEN ASSESSING THE ACCEPTABILITY OF CLIENT PROPOSED HIPAA/BAA RELATED REQUIREMENTS AND RELATED CONTRACTUAL PROVISIONS. IT IS NOT INTENDED TO BE A COMPREHENSIVE LIST OF THE HIPAA/BAA ISSUES/RISKS ASSOCIATED WITH A PARTICULAR TRANSACTION. EACH CLIENT'S HIPAA/BAA REQUIREMENTS SHOULD BE REVIEWED IN THE CONTEXT OF THE UNDERLYING TRANSACTION AND ANY CONTROLLING POLICIES/AGREEMENTS.

THIS CHECKLIST APPLIES TO U.S. COMMERCIAL DOMESTIC AGREEMENTS UNDER WHICH THE PHI IS U.S. PHI ONLY. IF DATA OF CITIZENS OF OTHER COUNTRIES IS BEING PROCESSED OR IF SERVICES ARE BEING PROVIDED INTERNATIONALLY, INTERNATIONAL COUNSEL NEEDS TO BE CONSULTED.

CLIENT: ______________________________

CONTRACT: ______________________________

I. Client Policies

1. Nature of the Policies

Are Client's policies static or fluid (i.e., set forth on a web site and subject to change)? If static, attach the negotiated policy to the underlying Agreement as an exhibit.

NOTE: For purposes of this Checklist, specific contractual HIPAA-related obligations in an Agreement should be considered in the same manner as Client policies.

If fluid, how is Licensor protected in the event of a change to policy? Who on the Licensor project team is responsible for identifying ongoing changes made to policy and ensuring compliance with such changes? Is Client obligated to notify Licensor of any changes to its policies after execution of the Agreement? Who bears the additional cost, if any, of complying with the change in policies?

NOTE: If at all possible, Licensor should not agree to comply with a policy posted to a Client's web-portal due to the risk of Licensor failing to identify subsequent changes to the policy and the inability of Licensor to protect against the financial risk arising from future changes. If Licensor agrees to be bound by polices posted on Client's web-portal, Client should have the obligation to notify Licensor in advance when a change is made. Financial or other impacts of a policy change should ideally be addressed through the change order process. Licensor cannot bear the risk of future changes unless its pricing has contemplated such changes. Changes that will result in a material change in processes or operations or result in an increased financial burden or legal exposure should be negotiated by Client and Licensor as part of the change order process. If Client is unwilling to utilize a change order process, Licensor should have the right to terminate the Agreement in the event of a material change.

Any obligations imposed on Licensor based on client policy versus the law should be closely scrutinized and approved by the appropriate Licensor security personnel to determine whether Licensor can comply.

For transactions with a TCV of US$500,000 or with a high level of risk, has Licensor's project management team issued a comprehensive information security policy, operating procedures, and associated responsibility statements based on Client's policies?

2. *Disclosure of PHI*

Will Licensor share, transfer, or release any PHI to third parties?

- With whom, if anyone, is the PHI being shared, transferred, or released? This includes subsidiaries, partners, contractors, etc.
- What specific PHI, if any, is being shared, transferred, or released and under what authority?
- What is the geographic location of these individuals and entities? What state specific law may apply, in particular, what state specific data breach notification requirements may there be?

Are the limitations on disclosure of PHI broad enough to allow Licensor to disclose the PHI to those employees, contractors, auditors and subcontractors who need access to support the contract? Do those limitations on disclosure require that we have any particular contractual or other restrictions with those to whom access is provided? If so, who on the account team is responsible for ensuring that the restrictions have been complied with prior to disclosure?

Is Licensor going to use employees and contractors outside of the United States on the project? If so, are there limits on Licensor disclosing PHI to Licensor employees and contractors working outside of the United States?

Client imposed limitations on Licensor's ability to disclose confidential information to employees/contractors outside of the US may prevent Licensor from efficiently performing the Services, and may result in increased costs of the Services. Has project management considered the export implications of moving such information offshore or the costs of being restricted from doing so?

NOTE: In most cases, Licensor cannot agree to limit how it allocates the work among different countries and must retain the ability to allocate work in the most efficient manner possible. Licensor prefers not to condition its right to perform work outside the United States on Client's prior consent, but can agree to notify Client in the event any work will be performed outside of the United States. In some transactions, Client may be in a bargaining position to impose limitations. If so, consent to the broadest range of Licensor locations around the world which is practical should be obtained as part of the initial contract.

---

3. Use of Information

May Licensor use information and data derived from the PHI for Licensor's own purposes, if Licensor removes all personally identifiable information?

NOTE: The right to use de-identified PHI may be very important for healthcare projects and data warehouse projects where Licensor seeks to create a "product." The ability to use this data in any fashion will usually not be granted in a major outsourcing transaction.

Model language:

Notwithstanding any other provision of this Agreement. Licensor may utilize data capture and analysis tools, and other similar tools, to extract, compile, synthesize, analyze, and use any Blind Data. "Blind Data" means non-individually identifiable and non-client identifiable data or information created from Client's data submitted for data processing. Blind Data excludes: 1) any specific Client identifiable information such as individual names and physical addresses; and 2) any specific Client information related to a report, or any party to a report, such as name, gender, race, ethnicity, human resources identification number, social security or international identification number, E-Mail address, home address, and home phone number. To the extent that any Client Blind Data is collected or compiled by Licensor, such Blind Data shall be solely owned by Licensor without any restrictions whatsoever. Client acknowledges that Licensor's ability to use and dispose of Blind Data is part of the consideration Client is paying to Licensor for the services and no fee or other consideration will be paid or owing to Client by Licensor for Licensor's use and/or disposal of the Blind Data.

4. Protected Health Information ("PHI")

Does Licensor have a plan to minimize the collection of PHI in order to comply with any obligation to restrict access and use of PHI solely for the purposes contemplated by the Agreement and thereby eliminate any unnecessary risk of exposure/liability? Who is responsible for tracking all PHI throughout the lifecycle of the engagement so it can all be returned or destroyed at the end of the engagement? If Licensor is instructed by Client to destroy the PHI and also provide certification as to such destruction, who within Licensor will undertake the secure destruction and provide the actual Certificates of Destruction and who will pay for that service?

Who is responsible for ensuring Licensor complies with Licensor's contractual data related obligations, e.g., the Project Manager or someone else? Have these obligations been effectively communicated by Legal during the negotiation process to all members of the delivery and project management team and have limitations to access been built into the business process to ensure no inappropriate disclosure happens?

5. Stated Standards

Why does Licensor need to comply with the stated standards? Is Licensor's compliance required by law or simply desired by Client? If Licensor stores (on behalf of Client) PHI, and there is a breach, government agencies may hold Licensor directly liable, so how does Licensor mitigate that risk?

Does Licensor meet/comply with the stated standard?

Does the relevant division meet/comply with the stated standard?

If the standards are stated by reference to particular statutes, are the requirements fully understood and communicated? Is there a procedure in place to monitor changes in the referenced laws and who is responsible for such monitoring?

Are the stated standards static or fluid (e.g., set forth on a website and subject to change)?

If static, attach (or reference) the stated standard as an exhibit.

If fluid, how is Licensor protected in the event of a change to the standard? Who bears the additional cost, if any, of complying with the change in the standard?

NOTE: Responsibility for compliance resides with the project group, not Legal. Please make sure the project group understands this.

NOTE: Do not assume that Licensor or a particular Division within Licensor complies with a particular standard. You must confirm that the Division in question actually complies. If multiple Licensor Divisions will be providing services, you must confirm that EVERY Division complies. Avoid agreeing to broad based statements of compliance that apply to all of Licensor. For example, some Divisions of Licensor may be ISO 9000/1 compliant while others may not be.

NOTE: Licensor should not represent or warrant compliance with HIPAA or a Client policy. Instead, Licensor should agree (covenant) that it will comply with the applicable policy or HIPAA in existence at the time of the Agreement's execution. Licensor cannot commit to comply with future policies or law without financial protection.

Will Licensor supplement the information received directly from Client with additional PHI received from third parties, or information received by mechanisms other than those to which Client has explicitly consented? If so, are there additional standards that need to be complied with relative to amendment of data, commingling of data, and/or storage of data?

6. *Project Management*

Who within Licensor is responsible for the following aspects of compliance for the project?

Project Manager: ______________________________

Administrative Safeguards: ______________________________

Physical Safeguards: ______________________________

Technical Safeguards: ______________________________

Point of Contact for Security Issues: ______________________________

Point of Contact for Human Resource Issues: ______________________________

Point of Contact for Incident Notification & Escalation: ______________________________

Point of Contact for Issue Resolution and Communication: ______________________________

7. *Employee/Contractor Issues*

If applicable, who is responsible for developing an Acceptable Use Policy (AUP) for Licensor employees and contractors outlining the contractual obligations, as well as the consequences of misuse of PHI? If the Project Manager is not going to prepare an AUP, have they been apprised of the risk of not doing so? Who is responsible for ensuring no potential conflicts of interest exist?

Have all employees and contractors executed written acknowledgements of their understanding and acceptance of Client's Business Associate Agreement ("BAA") or information/security policies?

Has the execution of properly signed confidentiality agreements been verified before PHI is disclosed, in any form, to employees and non-Licensor individuals? (Most employees will have satisfied this requirement through the execution of a standard non-disclosure agreement that was part of their on-boarding process with Licensor.) Do employee/contractors understand their obligation to encrypt PHI? Whose obligations is it to ensure that employee/contractor is provided equipment that enables encryption of PHI (whether on a desktop, laptop, USB drive, PDA, Blackberry, etc.)?

Is the Licensor project manager aware of any ongoing training requirements? Has he/she established ongoing training during the term of the Agreement to meet the contractual requirements? Has a process to document completion of such training been established and who is responsible for maintaining those records?

Have all Licensor employees received HIPAA compliance training prior to receiving PHI? Has a process to document completion of such training been established and who is responsible for maintaining those records?

8. Licensor Obligations upon Termination of Agreement

Do Client policies require that Licensor dispose of PHI in a particular manner? Are these requirements consistent with Licensor policies and if not, who will pay for the added costs of secure destruction?

NOTE: Data conversion and storage can be very expensive. Licensor should ensure that it has no obligation to store or convert Client data/PHI after the termination of the Agreement unless Licensor is compensated to do so. If Licensor is obligated to return Client's PHI and that PHI is expected to be voluminous, Client should pay all costs associated with the return of such PHI. In the alternative, Licensor should have the contractual right to simply destroy such PHI in which case Client should also be obligated to pay such destruction costs.

Model language:

Upon termination of this Agreement for any reason, Licensor shall return or destroy all Confidential Information/PHI received from Client, or created or received by Licensor on behalf of Client. In the event that Licensor determines in its reasonable discretion that returning or destroying the Confidential Information/PHI is not feasible, Licensor shall notify Client of the conditions that make return or destruction infeasible and shall extend the protections of this Agreement to such Confidential Information/PHI and limit further uses and disclosures of such Confidential Information/PHI to those purposes that make the return or destruction infeasible, for so long as Licensor maintains such Confidential Information/PHI.

II. Related Contractual Provisions

1. Contractors/Subcontractors/Vendors

Is Licensor required to flow down all standards, policies, or contractual terms to its contractors, subcontractors and vendors?

Who is responsible for ensuring their compliance? Have all applicable provisions been flowed down to Licensor's contractors, subcontractors and vendors?

How is Licensor protected in the event its contractors/subcontractors/vendors fail to comply? Has Licensor obtained an indemnity from its contractors/subcontractors/vendors for their failure to comply?

2. Changes in the Law

Who bears the risk of changes in the law/HIPAA? Who is responsible for tracking changes in the law/HIPAA?

Has Licensor priced the financial risk of complying with any changes into its pricing?

What ability does Licensor have to protect itself in the event of increased costs due to changes in the law?

NOTE: Licensor should only agree to comply with all laws in existence at the time the contract is executed. Licensor should agree to comply with all laws as they exist throughout the duration of the contract. Changes in the law should be addressed through the change order process. Client should not be able to transfer the risk of a change in the law to Licensor as this risk originally resided with Client and there is no reason it should flow to Licensor solely because Licensor is providing services to Client.

ALTERNATIVE POSITION: If the change in law impacts Licensor in its capacity generally as an IT services vendor (e.g., changes to apply HIPAA provisions directly to BAs), then Licensor should bear the risk of its compliance. However, if the change in law impacts Licensor because of a particular service it is providing on behalf of Client and the change is specific to that service (e.g., Medicare Part D claims processing), then Client should bear the risk.

Licensor can agree to comply with all laws brought to its attention by Client provided Licensor is compensated for any additional cost associated with Licensor's compliance. Licensor lacks the ability to track all potentially applicable laws throughout the United States and the world. Client is in a better position to do so through its knowledge of its industry and its membership in industry organizations.

Model language:

> **Licensor will comply with the following state privacy laws [OPTION: as directed by Client] but only to the extent such laws are applicable to the Services and to the extent Client was in compliance with such laws at the time Licensor commenced providing services: [SPECIFY STATE STATUTES].**
>
> **Client shall monitor and promptly identify and notify Licensor of all changes in Applicable Laws occurring on or after the Effective Date and all noncompliance existing as of the date Licensor commences services (collectively "Legal Changes"). Client and Licensor will work together to identify the effects of Legal Changes on the provision or receipt of the Services. With respect to Legal Changes, the parties will discuss, in a timely manner, what modifications to the Services, if any, are necessary to comply with such Legal Changes. Licensor shall promptly thereafter propose any amendments or change orders to the Agreement associated with such Legal Changes including applicable charges necessary to implement such Legal Changes. Upon the parties' agreement to the relevant amendment or change order, Licensor shall implement the changes to the Services in a timely manner.**

3. *Indemnification*

Is the indemnification narrowly tailored to those liabilities arising directly from Licensor's breach of a limited aspect of the policy versus a broadly worded indemnity related to the breach of the policy or the Agreement? Is Licensor indemnified by Client for liabilities claimed by third parties arising from Client's breach of the law or Client's policies?

> *NOTE: Licensor should attempt to reject any demand by Client for indemnification on the premise that Client's remedy lies in a claim for breach of contract (damages). HIPAA does not require a vendor to indemnify a Client. Many Clients will argue that an indemnity is industry standard. If Licensor must give an indemnity, the indemnity should be narrowly drawn to cover third party claims arising from violations of the Agreement and the law. Licensor should not indemnify Client for breach of a policy or breach of the Agreement alone. The indemnity set forth below requires that the indemnified claim be both a violation of the Applicable Law and a material breach of the Agreement. In addition, it excludes third party claims arising from instructions received from Client. Licensor should seek to make any indemnity mutual.*
>
> *Indemnification should be only for those losses asserted by third parties who are not affiliates (with "affiliates" or "unaffiliated" being a defined term. Attorney's fees and costs of litigation should be covered only in the event of a*

wrongful refusal to accept a tender of indemnity. Cross-indemnities for breach of laws should be obtained. The extent to which indemnities are excluded from any limitation of liability needs to be addressed on a case-by-case basis.

Model language:

Licensor agrees to indemnify, defend and hold harmless Client against all actual direct losses claimed by unaffiliated third parties arising directly from the use or disclosure of PHI by Licensor or its agents which is both an express violation of the [Applicable Laws] and a material breach of this Agreement ("Licensor Indemnified Claim"). Said responsibility adheres only to violations solely attributable to the actions/inactions of Licensor and/or its agents. The foregoing indemnity will not cover any third party claims arising from any action or inaction of Licensor taken or not taken by Licensor at the request of Client or to action or inactions of Licensor that are permitted under [Applicable Laws] and/or this Agreement. For the avoidance of doubt, a Licensor Indemnified Claim may not be asserted under any other indemnity provided by Licensor to Client.

Client agrees to indemnify, defend and hold harmless Licensor against all actual direct losses claimed by an unaffiliated third party arising from any action or inaction of Licensor taken or not taken by Licensor at the request of Client or to actions/inactions of Licensor that are permitted under the [Applicable Laws] and/or this Agreement.

NOTE: "Unaffiliated" needs to be a defined term.

4. Reliance on Instructions

To the extent not otherwise addressed, Licensor should attempt to include a provision specifying Licensor is entitled to rely on Client's instructions.

Model language:

In performing its obligations under this BAA, Licensor will be entitled to rely upon any instructions, authorizations, approvals, or other information provided to Licensor by Client. Licensor will incur no liability or responsibility of any kind in relying on or complying with any such instructions or information.

5. Representations and Warranties

NOTE: Licensor should not represent or warrant compliance with HIPAA or a Client policy. Instead, Licensor should agree (covenant) that it will comply with the applicable policy or HIPAA in existence at the time of the Agreement's execution. Licensor cannot commit to comply with future policies or law without financial protection.

6. Limitation of Liability

If Client's policies are contained in a free-standing document, does that document contain a limitation of liability? Confirm that the over-arching Agreement's limitation of liability limits Licensor's liability for breach of the policy or that the policy contains its own limitation of liability.

If Client's policies are an attachment to the underlying Agreement, does the Agreement/policies clearly state that the policies are subject to the Agreement's limitation of liability?

Is a breach of Client's policies carved out from the Agreement's limitation of liability? An exception to a limitation of liability for failure to comply with laws should be addressed through the approval process. It is preferable to limit this exception to discrete activities such as the giving of any required legal notice, the payment of fines or penalties, etc.

NOTE: Any carve-out from the Agreement's limitation of liability should be narrowly drafted such that the exclusion applies only to breach of Licensor's confidentiality obligations and not to a breach of the applicable policy. This carve-out should be mutual so that Client also has unlimited liability for any breach by it of its confidentiality obligations relative to Licensor's Confidential Information.

7. Right to Cure

Does the policy provide Licensor with the right to cure or may Client immediately terminate the underlying Agreement in the event of an alleged breach by Licensor? Does the policy set forth a notice and escalation process?

NOTE: Licensor must have a thirty (30) day period to cure any alleged breach. Client should provide Licensor written notice describing the breach in detail. Even the government's own Business Associate Agreement ("BAA") template recognizes a Business Associate's right of cure. Occasionally, Client will point out that it is not possible to cure a breach if the data is not fully recovered and knowledge of it has not spread outside Licensor and Client. Thus, it may not be practical in all instances for Licensor have a cure period.

Model language:

> **Termination for Cause. Upon Client's knowledge of a material breach by Licensor, Client shall provide Licensor written notice of the existence of the alleged material breach and provide Licensor 30 days from the delivery of such notice within which to cure the breach or end the violation. Client may terminate this Agreement [and the ________ Agreement/ sections ____ of the ______________ Agreement] if Licensor does not cure the breach or end the violation within such 30-day time period by Client. If neither termination nor cure are feasible as reasonably determined by Licensor and Client, Client shall report the violation to the Secretary. Client's report to the Secretary shall be limited to the specific information giving rise to the breach.**

See http://www.hhs.gov/ocr/privacy/hipaa/understanding/coveredentities/contractprov.html. *See also* 45 C.F.R. § 314(a)(1)(i)(B).

From the OCR Privacy Guidance:

"Where a covered entity knows of a material breach or violation by the business associate of the contract or agreement, the covered entity is required to take reasonable steps to cure the breach or end the violation, and if such steps are unsuccessful, to terminate the contract or arrangement. If termination of the contract or agreement is not feasible, a covered entity is required to report the problem to the Department of Health and Human Services (HHS) Office for Civil Rights (OCR)."

45 C.F.R. §§ 164.502(e), 164.504(e), 164.532(d) and (e).

8. Mitigation

Is Licensor obligated to mitigate any breach? What is the extent of Licensor's obligation to mitigate Licensor's breach of the BAA?

Licensor should not assume a broad obligation to mitigate any breach to Client's satisfaction. Licensor should do only what is reasonable and leave it to Client to pursue damages if Client believes more is warranted.

> *NOTE: Clients increasingly seek to impose a mitigation obligation on Licensor to mitigate any deleterious effects from improper disclosure of PHI. The scope of the mitigation obligation is often undefined, but could include detailed notices to a very large pool, and call-in hotlines. Mitigation of the harmful effects is a requirement under HIPAA, but the rules do not define what specific actions must be taken or the scope of mitigation. The issue is one of conceding contractual language that could obligate Licensor to incur expenses in excess of what would otherwise be required to comply with law, based on the demands of Client. The language below obligates Licensor to use "reasonable efforts" to limit "additional losses" but expressly disclaims any obligations that would result in Licensor incurring a material financial expense.*

The new HIPAA HITECH rules will statutorily require Licensor as a Business Associate to mitigate any damages. Licensor will also need to implement new obligations concerning patient notification.

Model language:

Licensor agrees to mitigate, to the extent practicable, any harmful effect that is actually known to Licensor of a Security Incident, caused by Licensor or its subcontractor(s) arising from its provision of the Services. Licensor's obligation to mitigate shall consist of reasonable efforts to limit additional losses after a Security Incident has occurred. Licensor shall not be required to undertake any actions which would be unduly burdensome in terms of time or resources or cause Licensor to incur a material financial expense. [For purposes of this BAA, a material financial expense shall mean an expense which will cost in total an amount which is equal to or exceeds five percent (5%) of the fees under the Agreement associated with the provision of Covered Services in the immediately preceding three (3) months.]

9. Third Party Beneficiaries

The Agreement/policies should specifically exclude any third party beneficiaries to limit any potential claims against Licensor by individuals whose PHI is breached. HIPAA, for example, presently does not provide a private cause of action to the owner of PHI against a Business Associate who violates the terms of HIPAA or a BAA.

Model language:

Nothing express or implied in this Agreement is intended to confer, nor shall anything herein confer, upon any person other than the parties who sign this Agreement any rights, remedies, obligations or liabilities whatsoever. There are no intended third party beneficiaries. [OPTIONAL – Licensor might want to state that there are no third party beneficiaries other than as specified in the indemnification provisions.]

10. Notices

Due to the inability to confirm actual receipt by the intended recipient, Licensor should not agree to the provision of formal notices via E-Mail or facsimile. The preferred means of delivery is certified mail, return receipt requested or overnight courier. Notices should be sent to the General Counsel in LOCATION or to counsel for the group/entity entering into the Agreement, with a copy to a business team member. All notices should be effective upon receipt.

11. Unilateral Amendment of Underlying Agreement by Client

Is Client allowed to unilaterally amend the Agreement for changes in the law or in the event Client believes a change is necessary to clarify an ambiguity or ensure compliance with an Applicable Law?

How is Licensor protected from increased costs or other obligations? Will any negative impact be addressed through the change order process?

NOTE: Licensor cannot agree to the automatic amendment of the BAA or other agreement to comply with law. Licensor must have a consent and approval right. Licensor should only allow unilateral change if Licensor is financially compensated for any negative/cost impact and the other terms, such as timing of implementation are satisfactory to Licensor. In the alternative, Licensor should be allowed to reject any unilaterally proposed amendment, where upon Client may terminate the Agreement.

---

12. Records Retention

How long is Licensor required to retain the PHI or other records?

NOTE: Medicare has a ten (10) year requirement to retain records. If Licensor is an ASP for Client, the Agreement must clearly spell out what happens to the records and who is going to pay for it.

III. Audits, Etc.

1. Compliance Audits

What type of compliance audits are required by Client?

Is Licensor already performing this type of audit for the data center in question?

NOTE: If not, the requirements for any such audit will have to be separately coordinated in advance with Licensor's Corporate Internal Audit Department, and Client should be made to pay for the audit. Additionally, the results of that audit should be restricted to an executive summary specific to Client, is possible.

Who is entitled to review the results?

NOTE: Any disclosure of the audit results should be limited and treated as Confidential Information. Client should not be permitted to disclose the results to any third party outside of its auditors and possibly its "advisors." Licensor should specifically require any third party execute a Non-Disclosure Agreement with Licensor prior to receiving a copy of the results and exclude Licensor competitors from receiving a copy.

Does a security breach trigger a right to audit with respect to HIPAA compliance? If the breach occurred because of an employee act, is Client entitled to access the employee's laptop or records to investigate such breach without Licensor's consent?

2. Books and Records

Are the audit provisions overly broad?

NOTE: Attorney-client privileged materials and materials not related to Client should be excluded.

Do they extend beyond books and records to include facility audits, and audits of practices and procedures?

NOTE: Except for very rare situations, Licensor should never agree to facility audits.

Is the audit triggered by a Licensor breach or at the demand of Client? How is "breach" defined? How often may Client demand an audit and who should pay for each?

Is the audit subject to appropriate controls?

NOTE: Client should be required to provide at least seven (7) days prior written notice of its desire to audit Licensor's books and records to allow Licensor the time necessary to collect and make available for review the relevant records. Client's audit rights should be clearly stated and limited. Further, the audit should occur at the Licensor office where the books and records are stored during normal business hours, and be subject to all applicable confidentiality and Licensor security controls. The length of the audit should be limited to a set period of time to limit disruption to Licensor's business operations. Licensor should be concerned as to the possibility that an audit of a facility or systems could expose other client PHI and/or deficiencies in Licensor's compliance.

Model language:

> **Licensor agrees to make those internal practices, books, and records specifically relating to the use and disclosure of Confidential Information received from, or created or received by Licensor on behalf of Client available to Client, or at the request of Client to [third party auditor], in a reasonable time and manner agreed to by Client and Licensor, for the purpose of [Insert limited purpose]. Such books and records shall exclude any legally privileged information, as well as non-relevant personal data or Confidential Information of other Licensor clients.**

IV. Miscellaneous

1. Project Budget

Does the pricing model include the cost of specific security requirements required by Client and offered by Licensor as separately chargeable services?

Does the project budget contain a set-aside for the potential cost of complying with ongoing data related requirements, including potential incident response?

2. Training Requirements

Does the Agreement require any training requirements during the term of the Agreement? Has the project manager established ongoing training during the term of the Agreement to meet the contractual requirements and who will maintain records regarding such training?

3. Internal Licensor Resources

If you require additional information, the following Licensor resources may be helpful:

Table of Cases

Index

B

C

About the Author

Mr. Classen is Deputy General Counsel of Computer Sciences Corporation with responsibility for CSC's North American business solutions, world sourcing, healthcare, and financial services business units.

A graduate of Trinity College (Connecticut), Mr. Classen received a Juris Doctor from Catholic University and a Master of Business Administration from the Wharton School of the University of Pennsylvania. While in law school, Mr. Classen was a member of the *Catholic University Law Review* and Editor in Chief and Founder of *The Journal of Contemporary Health Law and Policy.*

Mr. Classen serves on a number of business, professional, and civic boards, including The Walters Art Museum, the Board of Advisors of The Intellectual Property Counselor, as well as The Commercial Law Advisor. He is the author of the three volume set *Classen's Commercial Forms* as well as *Classen's Merger and Acquisition Forms.* Mr. Classen has been widely published in legal journals and spoken extensively before professional groups both domestically and internationally. His recent articles address technology licensing, export controls, law department management, and managing inside/outside counsel relationships. Mr. Classen welcomes any thoughts on this book or suggestions on how it may be improved. He may be contacted at hclassen@csc.com.

CD-ROM Contents: *A Practical Guide to Software Licensing for Licensees and Licensors*

Chapter 23: Model Forms

A. RFI/RFP Related Documents
Form 23.A.1: Request for Information (RFI)
Form 23.A.2: Request for Information—Alternate Form
Form 23.A.3: Request for Proposal (RFP)
Form 23.A.4: RFP Response Matrix
Form 23.A.5: RFP Nondisclosure Agreement
Form 23.A.6: Request for Proposal: Legal Terms and Conditions (Customer Oriented)
Form 23.A.7: RFP Nondisclosure Agreement
Form 23.A.8: Model RFP Responses
Form 23.A.9: Declaration of Conflict of Interest (if Vendor Employee involved in Selection process)
Form 23.A.10: RFP Representations and Warranties
Form 23.A.11: Memorandum of Understanding
Form 23.A.12: RFP Terms and Conditions

B. Principal Agreements
Form 23.B.1: Software License and Services Agreement (Annotated)
Form 23.B.2: Software License, Maintenance, and Subscriber Billing Services Agreement
Form 23.B.3: Systems Integration Agreement (Customer Oriented)
Form 23.B.4: Business Process Outsourcing Services Agreement (Customer Oriented)
Form 20.B.5: Source Code License Agreement
Form 23.B.6: ABA Model Software License Provisions
Form 23.B.7: Non-Production Use License (Software used by Licensor Partners)
Form 23.B.8: Demonstration License
Form 23.B.9: Software License and Support Agreement - Seat license (Informal Tone)
Form 23.B.10: Software License – Seat License for Mainframe and Client Server (Formal Tone)
Form 23.B.11: Sublicense

C. Secondary Agreements
Form 23.C.1: Transition and Continuing Services Agreement
Form 23.C.2: Software Maintenance and Services Agreement
Form 23.C.3: Source Code Escrow Agreement (Annotated)
Form 23.C.4: Source Code Escrow Agreement—Alternate Form
Form 23.C.5: Certificate of Acceptance - Software
Form 23.C.6: Certificate of Acceptance - Services
Form 23.C.7: Benchmarking
Form 23.C.8: Affiliate Agreement
Form 23.C.9: Transfer and Novation Agreement
Form 23.C.10: Statement of Work ("SOW")
Form 23.C.11: Statement of Work – Alternate Form
Form 23.C.12: Change Order
Form 23.C.13: Service Levels
Form 23.C.14: Certificate of Electronic Delivery

D. Alternative Licensing Agreements
Form 23.D.1: Application Service Provider (ASP) Services Agreement (Customer Oriented)
Form 23.D.2: Hosting Agreement (Long Form—Negotiated)
Form 23.D.3: Hosting Agreement (Short Form—Vendor Oriented)
Form 23.D.4: Systems Integration and Hosting Agreement (Customer Oriented)
Form 23.D.5: Software as a Service ("SaaS") Subscription Agreement

E. Open Source Licenses and Related Documents
Form 23.E.1: MIT License
Form 23.E.2: GNUv3 License
Form 23.E.3: Licensor Oriented Open Source Software Warranty
Form 23.E.4: Customer Oriented Open Source Software Warranty
Form 23.E.5 - Open Source and Third Party Software Request for Software Approval (RFSA)
Form 23.E.5 – Open Source Software Request for Participation Approval (RFPA)

F. Consulting Agreements and Related Documents
Form 23.F.1: Consulting Agreement
Form 23.F.2: Master Services Agreement (Customer Oriented)
Form 23.F.3: Assignment (of Intellectual Property Rights) Agreement (Contractor to Employer)
Form 23.F.4: Vendor Employee Statement of Acknowledgment and Assignment (Licensor Employee/Contractor to Licensee)
Form 23.F.5: Employee Deed Of Assignment (For Indian Employees Outside U.S.)
Form 23.F.6: Step-In Agreement
Form 23.F.7: Acknowledgment Agreement (For Licensor Employees who Executed Defective Assignment Agreement)

G. Confidentiality/Data Privacy Related Agreements
Form 23.G.1: Proprietary Information Request Form
Form 23.G.2: Unilateral Proprietary Information Agreement
Form 23.G.3: Bilateral Proprietary Information Agreement (Annotated)
Form 23.G.4: Three Party Confidentiality Agreement (between Customer and multiple Licensors/Vendors)
Form 23.G.5: Non-Competition, Confidentiality, and Inventions Agreement
Form 23.G.6: Proprietary Information Certification
Form 23.G.7: Business Associate Agreement (Annotated)
Form 23.G.8: Licensor Certification – Return of Confidential Information
Form 23.G.9: Reminder of Customer's Non-Disclosure Obligations
Form 23.G.10: Worker Responsibility and Confidentiality Agreement
Form 23.G.11: Third Party Access Agreement
Form 23.G.12: Employee Reaffirmation of Confidentialty Obligations

H. Litigation/Dispute Related Agreements
Form 23.H.1: Tolling Agreement
Form 23.H.2: Settlement Agreement and Mutual Release
Form 23.H.3: Settlement Agreement (Releasing Party Contemplating Bankruptcy)
Form 23.H.4: Attorney-Client Privilege Request for Internal Information
Form 23.H.5: Document Preservation Memo
Form 23.H.6: Arbiter Qualifications
Form 23.H.7: Alternative Dispute Resolution Terms
Form 23.H.8: Vendor Ability to Perform Letter
Form 23.H.9: Early Warning Report

I Miscellaneous Agreements
Form 23.I.1: Network Access Agreement
Form 23.I.2: Corporate Guaranty
Form 23.I.3: Insider Trading and Blackout Restrictions Applicable to Vendors
Form 23.I.4: Tax Matrix
Form 23.I.5: Foreign Corrupt Practices Act Questionnaire
Form 23.I.6: Contract Transmittal/Approval Form
Form 23.I.7: Authority Matrix
Form 23.I.8: Consent for Independent Service Organization ("ISO") to Access Licensor Software
Form 23.I.9: Risk Analysis Sheet
Form 23.I.10: Arbitration Terms
Form 23.I.11: Employee Acknowledgment of Prior Employment Terms

J. Model Policies
Form 23.J.1: IT Security Standards
Form 23.J.2: Travel Policy
Form 23.J.3: Privacy-Data Security Policy
Form 23.J.4: Vendor Code of Conduct
Form 23.J.5 Compliance with Gramm-Leach-Bliley Act and Non-U.S. Data Protection
Form 23.J.6: Screening and Background Checks – Short Form
Form 23.J.7: Background Investigations
Form 24.J.8: Use of Personal Data
Form 24.J.9: Vulnerability Assessment Agreement
Form 24.J.10: Licensee Obligations
Form 24.J.11: Credit Risk Policy

K. Libraries
Form 23.K.1: Definitions Library
Form 23.K.2: Clause Library

L Checklists
Form 23.L.1: Data Privacy/Security Checklist
Form 23.L.2: HIPAA Checklist